Rajeev Alur Thomas A. Henzinger
Eduardo D. Sontag (Eds.)

Hybrid Systems III

Verification and Control

Volume Editors

Rajeev Alur
AT&T Bell Laboratories
600 Mountain Avenue, Murray Hill, NJ 07974, USA

Thomas A. Henzinger
Department of Electrical Engineering and Computer Science
University of California at Berkeley
Berkeley, CA 94720, USA

Eduardo D. Sontag
Department of Mathematics
Rutgers University
New Brunswick, NJ 08903, USA

Cataloging-in-Publication data applied for

Die Deutsche Bibliothek - CIP-Einheitsaufnahme

Hybrid systems. - Berlin ; Heidelberg ; New York ; Barcelona ; Budapest ; Hong Kong ; London ; Milan ; Paris ; Santa Clara ; Singapore ; Tokyo : Springer.
Literaturangaben
3. Verification and control / Rajeev Alur ... (ed.). - 1996
(Lecture notes in computer science ; 1066)
ISBN 3-540-61155-X
NE: Alur, Rajeev [Hrsg.]; GT

CR Subject Classification (1991): C.1.m, C.3, D.2.1,F.3.1, F.1-2

ISBN 3-540-61155-X Springer-Verlag Berlin Heidelberg New York

Printed in Germany

Typesetting: Camera-ready by author
SPIN 10512821 06/3142 – 5 4 3 2 1 0 Printed on acid-free paper

Lecture Notes in Computer Science 1066

Edited by G. Goos, J. Hartmanis and J. van Leeuwen

Springer
Berlin
Heidelberg
New York
Barcelona
Budapest
Hong Kong
London
Milan
Paris
Santa Clara
Singapore
Tokyo

Preface

This volume contains the proceedings of the DIMACS/SYCON *Workshop on Verification and Control of Hybrid Systems*, organized October 22–25, 1995, at Rutgers University in New Brunswick, New Jersey. The workshop was part of the DIMACS 1995–96 Special Year on Logic and Algorithms. DIMACS is a Science and Technology Center, funded by the National Science Foundation, whose participating institutions are Rutgers University, Princeton University, AT&T Bell Laboratories, and Bellcore. SYCON is a Rutgers University Center dedicated to research in control theory and closely associated topics.

The workshop was the fifth in an annual series of workshops on hybrid systems. The previous workshops of the series were organized in 1991 and 1994 in Ithaca, New York, in 1992 in Lyngby, Denmark, and in 1993 in Boston, Massachusetts. The proceedings of these workshops were published in the Springer-Verlag Lecture Notes in Computer Science series, volumes 736 and 999.

The focus of the workshop was on mathematical methods for the rigorous and systematic design and analysis of hybrid systems. A hybrid system consists of digital devices that interact with analog environments. Driven by rapid advances in digital controller technology, hybrid systems are objects of investigation of increasing relevance and importance. The emerging area of hybrid systems research lies at the crossroads of computer science and control theory: computer science contributes expertise on the digital aspects of a hybrid system, and control theory contributes expertise on the analog aspects. Since both research communities speak largely different languages, and employ largely different methods, it was the purpose of the workshop to bring together researchers from both computer science and control theory. The workshop succeeded in this goal by attracting a registered audience of 125 researchers from both communities.

The four-day workshop featured 4 invited keynote speakers, 6 invited panelists, 32 talks by invited participants, and 24 talks that were selected by the program committee from 47 submissions. The keynote talks were "A game-theoretic approach to hybrid system design" by Shankar Sastry (University of California at Berkeley), "Hybrid systems: the computer science view" by Amir Pnueli (Weizmann Institute of Science), "Stabilization of device networks using hybrid commands" by Roger Brockett (Harvard University), and "Modeling and verification of automated transit systems, using timed automata, invariants, and simulations" by Nancy Lynch (MIT). The panelists Robert Kurshan (AT&T Bell Laboratories), Anil Nerode (Cornell University), Mike Reed (Oxford University), Joseph Sifakis (VERIMAG Grenoble), Jan van Schuppen (CWI), and Pravin Varaiya (University of California at Berkeley) discussed the topic "Hybrid systems research: achievements, problems, and goals."

We are grateful to all invitees and contributors for making the workshop a success. In addition, we wish to thank the DIMACS staff, especially Pat Toci and Barbara Kaplan, for administrating the workshop organization; the DIMACS management, Andràs Hajnal and Stephen Mahaney, and the organizing committee for the DIMACS Special Year on Logic and Algorithms, Eric Allender, Robert Kurshan, and Moshe Vardi, for their generous sponsorship; Anil Nerode for organizational advice; and the program committee members Albert Benveniste (INRIA-IRISA Rennes), John Guckenheimer (Cornell University), Bruce Krogh (Carnegie Mellon University), Amir Pnueli (Weizmann Institute of Science), Peter Ramadge (Princeton University), Shankar Sastry (University of California at Berkeley), Fred Schneider (Cornell University), Hector Sussmann (Rutgers University), and Joseph Sifakis (VERIMAG Grenoble) for assisting in the selection process.

Murray Hill, New Jersey
Berkeley, California
New Brunswick, New Jersey

Rajeev Alur
Thomas A. Henzinger
Eduardo D. Sontag

January 1996

Table of Contents

A Game-Theoretic Approach to Hybrid System Design *

John Lygeros, Datta N. Godbole and Shankar Sastry
Intelligent Machines and Robotics Laboratory
University of California, Berkeley
Berkeley, CA 94720
lygeros, godbole, sastry@robotics.eecs.berkeley.edu

Abstract. We present a design and verification methodology for hybrid dynamical systems. Our approach is based on optimal control and game theory. The hybrid design is seen as a game between two players. One is the disturbances that enter the dynamics. The disturbances can encode the actions of other agents (in a multi-agent setting), the actions of high level controllers or unmodeled environmental disturbances. The second player is the control, which is to be chosen by the designer. The two players compete over cost functions that encode the properties that the closed loop hybrid system needs to satisfy (e.g. safety). The control "wins" the game if it can keep the system "safe" for any allowable disturbance. The solution to the game theory problem provides the designer with continuous controllers as well as sets of safe states where the control "wins" the game. These safe sets can be used to construct an interface that guarantees the safe operation of the combined hybrid system. Extensions of this approach can also be used for verification of hybrid systems as well as the generation of abstractions of the lower layer behavior (e.g. timed abstractions).

1 Introduction

The Need for Hybrid Control. The demand for increased levels of automation and system integration have forced control engineers to deal with increasingly large and complicated systems. Recent technological advances, such as faster computers, cheaper and more reliable sensors and the integration of control considerations in the product design and manufacturing process, have made it possible to extend the practical applications of control to systems that were impossible to deal with in the past.

To deal with large, complex systems engineers are usually inclined to use a combination of continuous and discrete controllers. Continuous controllers have some obvious selling points: the interaction with the physical plant is essentially analog (i.e. continuous) from the engineering point of view, continuous models

* Research supported by the Army Research Office under grant DAAH 04-95-1-0588 and the California PATH program, Institute of Transportation Studies, University of California, Berkeley, under MOU-135.

have been used and validated extensively in the past and powerful techniques have already been developed to control them. An equally compelling case can be made in favor of discrete controllers, however: discrete abstractions make it easier to manage the complexity of the system, are easier to compute with, and facilitate the introduction of linguistic and qualitative information in the controller design. We will use the term "hybrid systems" to describe systems that incorporate both continuous and discrete dynamics.

A very interesting class of systems that are naturally suited for hybrid control are multiagent, scarce resource systems such as highway systems, air traffic management systems and power generation and distribution systems. Their common characteristic is that many agents are trying to make optimum use of a congested, common resource. For example, in highway systems, the vehicles can be viewed as agents competing for the highway (which plays the role of the resource) while in air traffic management systems the aircraft compete for air space and runway space. Typically in systems like these the optimum policy for each agent does not coincide with the "common good". Therefore, compromises need to be made. To achieve the common optimum we should ideally have a centralized control scheme that computes the global optimum and commands the agents accordingly. A solution like this may be undesirable, however, as it is likely to be very computationally intensive, it may be less reliable[2], information exchange may require excessive communication bandwidth and the number of agents may be large and/or dynamically changing.

If a completely decentralized solution is unacceptable and a completely centralized solution is prohibitively complex or expensive, a compromise needs to be found. Such a compromise features semi-autonomous agent operation: each agent tries to optimize its own usage of the resource and coordinates with neighboring agents in case there is a conflict of objectives. It should be noted that semiautonomous agent control is naturally suited for hybrid designs. *At the continuous level each agent chooses its own optimal strategy, while discrete coordination is used to resolve conflicts.* This is the class of hybrid systems that we will be most interested in.

Hybrid Control Methodologies. A common approach to the design of hybrid controllers involves independently coming up with a reasonable design for both the discrete and continuous parts. The combined hybrid controller is then put together by means of interfaces and verification is carried out to ensure that it satisfies certain properties. This approach has been motivated by the success of automatic verification techniques for finite state machines and the fact that many hybrid designs already operating in practice need to be verified, without having to redesign them from scratch. Verification algorithms for finite state machines, timed automata [1] and linear hybrid systems [2] have been developed and efficient programs exist to implement them (COSPAN [3], HSIS [4], STATEMATE [5], KRONOS [6], HyTech [7] etc.). They have proved very successful in verification problems for communication protocols, software algorithms, digital

[2] The consequences could be catastrophic if the centralized controller is disabled

circuit design and real-time software. Progress in the direction of automatic verification has been impeded, however, by **undecidability** and **computational complexity**. To guarantee that an automatic verification algorithm will terminate in a finite number of steps with a conclusive answer, the system needs to satisfy very stringent technical requirements [8]. Moreover, even relatively simple hybrid systems lead to very large numbers of discrete states when looked at from the point of view of automatic verification. Even though efficient algorithms exist, the problem may still be prohibitively large for current computers [9].

A different approach has been to design the hybrid controller so that performance is a-priori guaranteed [10, 11, 12]. This eases the requirements on verification somewhat since a large part of the complexity can be absorbed by careful design. The techniques presented in this paper fit in with this way of thinking. The plan is to start by modeling the system dynamics at the continuous level. Two factors affect the system evolution at this level. The first is the **control**, which the designer has to determine. The second is the **disturbances** that enter the system, over which we assume no control. We will distinguish two classes of disturbances:

- **Class 1:** Exogenous signals such as unmodeled forces, sensor noise, etc. and unmodeled dynamics.
- **Class 2:** The actions of other agents, in a multiagent setting.

Disturbances of Class 1 are standard in classical control theory. Class 2 will be the most interesting one from the point of view of hybrid control. Recall that, at this stage, we are merely modeling the plant; therefore, we assume no cooperation between the agents. As a result, each agent views the actions of its neighbors as uncontrollable disturbances.

In the continuous domain specifications about the closed loop system can be encoded in terms of cost functions. Acceptable performance can be encoded by means of thresholds on the final cost. Our objective is to derive a continuous design for the control inputs that guarantees performance despite the disturbances. If it turns out that the disturbance is such that the specifications can not be met for any controller, the design fails. For disturbances of Class 2 it may be possible to salvage the situation by means of coordination between the agents. In this case, the objective is to come up with a discrete design that limits the disturbance in a way that a continuous design is feasible.

In this paper we will limit our attention to the design of continuous control laws and interfaces between these laws and the discrete world. The design of the continuous laws will be optimal with respect to the closed loop system requirements. An ideal tool for this kind of set up is game theory. In the game theoretic framework the control and the disturbances are viewed as adversaries in a game. The control seeks to improve system performance and the disturbance seeks to make it worse. If we set a threshold on the cost function to distinguish between acceptable and unacceptable performance we can say that the control wins the game if the requirement is satisfied for any allowable disturbance, while the disturbance wins otherwise. Game theoretic ideas have already been applied in this context to problems with disturbances of Class 1 and quadratic cost functions.

The resulting controllers are the so called H_∞ or L_2 optimal controllers [13]. We will try to extend these ideas to the multiagent, hybrid setting.

Extensions: Verification and Abstraction. Optimal control and gaming ideas may prove useful in other hybrid settings. Here we touch upon two of them, verification and abstraction. Standard automatic verification techniques involve some form of exhaustive search, to verify that all possible runs of the systems satisfy a certain property. As discussed above this leads to undecidability and complexity problems. An optimal control approach to verification could be to obtain the worst possible run by solving an optimal control problem, and verifying that the property holds for this run; then it will also hold for all other runs.

Verification of closed loop hybrid systems is better suited for optimal control, rather than game theory, as one of the two players (the controller) has its strategy fixed a-priori. An interesting class of disturbances that need to be considered in this context is:

- **Class 3:** Commands from the discrete controller.

From the point of view of the continuous system (where the optimal control problem is to be solved) these commands can be viewed as signals that make the continuous system switch between control laws, fixed points etc. Optimal control can be used to determine the discrete command sequences that force the continuous system to violate the performance specifications. If the discrete design is such that these command sequences are excluded then the hybrid design is verified. Examples of this approach can be found in [14] and [15].

The main advantage of the optimal control point of view to verification is that, by removing the requirement for an exhaustive search, the limitations of complexity and undecidability disappear. On the down side, verification using optimal control requires a lot of input from the user. Moreover, optimal control problems will, in general, be very hard to solve analytically. It is therefore unlikely that this approach can be applied, at least by hand, to systems with more than a few discrete states.

Optimal control ideas can also be used to generate abstractions of continuous system behavior in terms of discrete languages. For example, optimal control can be used to obtain the minimum and maximum times that a hybrid system spends in each discrete state. These bounds can then be used as a rudimentary timed abstraction of the hybrid system. Again the requirement for designer input limits the complexity of the problems that can be handled analytically.

2 Game Theoretic Framework

As our starting point we will use a rather general state space model for the continuous plant. Let $x(t) \in \mathbb{R}^n$ represent the state, $u(t) \in \mathbb{R}^m$ represent the input and $d(t) \in \mathbb{R}^p$ represent any disturbance that affects the dynamics, at time

t. The plant dynamics will be described by a differential equation and the value of the state at a given time, say t_0:

$$\dot{x}(t) = f(x(t), u(t), d(t), t) \tag{1}$$
$$x(t_0) = x^0 \tag{2}$$

The behavior of the system at time t is assumed to be monitored through a set of outputs $y(t) \in \mathbb{R}^q$. Their value depends on a map:

$$y(t) = h(x(t), u(t), d(t), t) \tag{3}$$

Physical considerations (such as actuator saturation, etc.) impose certain restrictions on the system evolution. We assume that these restrictions are encoded in terms of constraints on the state, inputs and disturbances.[3]

$$x() \in \mathcal{X} \subset PC^1(\mathbb{R}, \mathbb{R}^n) \tag{4}$$
$$u() \in \mathcal{U} \subset PC(\mathbb{R}, \mathbb{R}^m) \tag{5}$$
$$d() \in \mathcal{D} \subset PC(\mathbb{R}, \mathbb{R}^p) \tag{6}$$

We assume that the differential equation 1 has a unique solution.

Both inputs and disturbances are exogenous functions of time. The difference is that the disturbances are assumed to be beyond the control of the designer and can take arbitrary values within the constraint set $\mathcal{D}$. The designer's objective is to use the inputs to regulate the outputs, despite the actions of the disturbances. We will assume that the whole state is available for feedback. Extensions to the case of output feedback should also be possible.

In this paper we will not deal at all with the design of the discrete layer. In terms of the continuous layer the outcome of the discrete design will be represented by a sequence of way points x_i^d, $i \in \mathbb{N}$ that should be tracked, a set of cost functions

$$J_i : \mathbb{R}^n \times PC \times PC \longrightarrow \mathbb{R} \tag{7}$$

$i = 1, \ldots, N$, that encode desired properties and a set of thresholds $C_i, i = 1, \ldots, N$ that specify acceptable limits on the cost functions. An acceptable trajectory must be such that $J_i(x^0, u, d) \leq C_i$ for all $i = 1, \ldots, N$. We assume that the cost functions are ordered in the order of decreasing importance. Qualitatively, the most important cost functions encode things such as safety while the least important ones encode performance aspects such as resource utilization. The design should be such that the most important constraints are not violated in favor of the less important ones.

[3] $PC(\cdot, \cdot)$ denotes the set of piecewise continuous functions whereas $PC^1(\cdot, \cdot)$ represents the set of piecewise differentiable functions.

2.1 Continuous Design

At the first stage we treat the design process as a two player, zero sum dynamic game with cost J_1. One player, the control u, is trying to minimize the cost, while the other, the disturbance d, is trying to maximize it. Assume that the game has a saddle point solution, i.e. there exist input and disturbance trajectories, u_1^* and d_1^* such that:

$$J_1^*(x^0) = \max_{d\in\mathcal{D}} \min_{u\in\mathcal{U}} J_1(x^0, u, d) = \min_{u\in\mathcal{U}} \max_{d\in\mathcal{D}} J_1(x^0, u, d) = J_1(x^0, u_1^*, d_1^*)$$

Consider the set:

$$V_1 = \{x \in \mathbb{R}^n | J_1^*(x) \leq C_1\}$$

This is the set of all initial conditions for which there exists a control such that the objective on J_1 is satisfied for the worst possible allowable disturbance.

u_1^* can now be used as a control law. It will guarantee that J_1 is minimized for the worst possible disturbance. Moreover if the initial state is in V_1 it will also guarantee that the performance requirement on J_1 is satisfied. u_1^* however does not take into account the requirements on the remaining J_i's. To include them in the design let:

$$\mathcal{U}_1(x^0) = \{u \in \mathcal{U} | J_1(x^0, u, d_1^*) \leq C_1\} \tag{8}$$

The set $\mathcal{U}_1(x^0)$ is the subset of admissible controls which guarantees that the requirements on J_1 are satisfied, whenever possible. Within this class of controls we would like to select the one that minimizes the remaining cost functions J_i, $i = 2, \cdots, n$. To do this, we solve a sequence of games one for each J_i.

At the $i + 1^{\text{st}}$ step we are given a set of admissible controls $\mathcal{U}_i(x^0)$ and a set of initial conditions V_i such that: for all $x^0 \in V_i$ there exists $u_i^* \in \mathcal{U}_i(x^0)$ such that for all $d \in \mathcal{D}$, $J_j(x^0, u_i^*, d) \leq C_j$, where $j = 1, \ldots, i$. Assume the two player, zero sum dynamic game for J_{i+1} has a saddle solution, u_{i+1}^*, d_{i+1}^*:

$$J_{i+1}^*(x^0) = J_{i+1}(x^0, u_{i+1}^*, d_{i+1}^*)$$

Define:

$$V_{i+1} = \{x \in V_i | J_{i+1}^*(x) \leq C_{i+1}\} \tag{9}$$

$$\mathcal{U}_{i+1}(x^0) = \{u \in \mathcal{U}_i(x^0) | J_{i+1}(x^0, u, d_{i+1}^*) \leq C_{i+1}\} \tag{10}$$

The process can be repeated until the last cost function. The result is a control law u_N^* and a set of initial conditions $V_N = V$ such that for all $x^0 \in V_N$ and for all $d \in \mathcal{D}$, $J_j(x^0, u_N^*, d) \leq C_j$, where $j = 1, \ldots, N$. The controller can be extended to values of the state in the complement of V using a switching scheme:

$$u^*(x) = \begin{cases} u_N^*(x) & x \in V \\ u_{N-1}^*(x) & x \in V_{N-1} \setminus V \\ \cdots & \cdots \\ u_1^*(x) & x \in \mathbb{R}^n \setminus V_2 \end{cases} \tag{11}$$

The algorithm presented above is sound in theory but can run into technical difficulties when applied in practice. For example, there is no guarantee that the dynamic games will have a saddle solution. Moreover, there is no straightforward way of computing $\mathcal{U}_i(x^0)$ and there is no guarantee that the sets V_i (and consequently $\mathcal{U}_i(x^0)$) will be non-empty.

2.2 Interface

The sets V impose conditions that the discrete switching scheme needs to satisfy. The discrete layer should not issue a new command (way point) if the current state does not lie in the set V for the associated controller. Essentially these sets offer a way of consistently abstracting performance properties of the continuous layer.

It should be noted that, by construction, the sets V_i are nested. Therefore there is a possibility that an initial condition lies in some V_i but not in V. This implies that certain requirements on the system performance (e.g. safety) can be satisfied, while others (e.g. efficient resource utilization) can not. This allows the discrete design some more freedom. It may, for example, choose to issue a new command if it is dictated by safety, even though it violates the requirements of efficiency. This construction provides a convenient way of modeling gradual performance degradation, where lower priority performance requirements are violated in favor of higher priority ones.

3 Train-Gate Controller Example

In this section we investigate how the approach developed in Section 2 can be useful in applications. We consider a classic example from the timed automata verification literature, the "train gate controller". For a more complicated example from highway automation the reader is refered to [14]. To simplify the notation, time dependency of the states inputs and outputs will be suppressed unless explicitly stated.

Problem Statement. The train gate problem set up is shown in Figure 1. We will work on the problem formulation of [16]. For simplicity we assume that the train is going around on a circular track of length L, where L is large enough to ensure adequate separation between consecutive train appearances. We also assume that the train can be approximated by a point.

The train moves clockwise around the track. Let $x_2 \in \left[-\frac{L}{2}, \frac{L}{2}\right)$ denote the position of the train, with the implicit assumption that x_2 wraps around at $L/2$. The details of the train dynamics are abstracted away by assuming that the train velocity is bounded, i.e. $\dot{x}_2 \in [v_1, v_2]$. In order to guarantee that the problem is well defined assume that $0 < v_1 \leq v_2 < \infty$.

The crossing is located at position $x_2 = 0$ on the train track. It is guarded by a gate that, when lowered, prevents the cars from crossing the tracks. Let

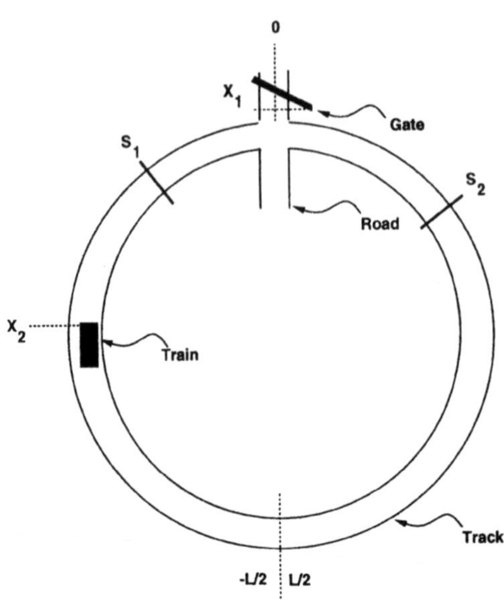

Fig. 1. The train-gate set up

$x_1 \in [0°, 90°]$ denote the angle of the gate in degrees. Assume that the gate dynamics are described by a first order differential equation:

$$\dot{x}_1 = -\frac{1}{2}x_1 + u$$

where u is the input to be chosen by the designer of the gate controller.

We will assume that there are two sensors located at distances S_1 and S_2 respectively on the track. The sensor at S_1 detects when the train is approaching the crossing, while the one at S_2 detects when it has moved away. In order for the control problem to have a solution we need to assume that:

$$-\frac{L}{2} < S_1 < 0 < S_2 < \frac{L}{2}$$

Two requirements are imposed on the design: *safety* and *throughput*. For *safety* it is required that the gate must be lowered below a certain threshold whenever the train reaches the crossing. For *throughput* it is required that the gate should be opened whenever it is safe to do so. This is done to maximize the number of cars that get to cross the tracks.

Game Theoretic Formulation. The problem can immediately be cast in the game theoretic framework. The two players (agents) are the gate controller, u and the train speed (disturbance), d. The dynamics are linear in the state and affine in the two inputs. Let $x = [x_1 \; x_2]^T \in \mathbb{R}^2$ denote the state:

$$\dot{x} = \begin{pmatrix} -1/2 & 0 \\ 0 & 0 \end{pmatrix} x + \begin{pmatrix} 1 \\ 0 \end{pmatrix} u + \begin{pmatrix} 0 \\ 1 \end{pmatrix} d \tag{12}$$

The state is constrained to lie in the set X:

$$x \in X = \{(x_1, x_2) \in \mathbb{R}^2 | x_1 \in [0°, 90°]; x_2 \in \left[-\frac{L}{2}, \frac{L}{2}\right)\} \subset \mathbb{R}^2$$

The input is constrained to lie in the set $U = [0, 45]$ while the disturbance lies in the set $D = [v_1, v_2]$.

The two players compete over two cost functions J_1 and J_2. J_1 encodes the requirement for safety. Given initial conditions $x^0 \in X$ let $T(x^0) = \min\{t \geq 0 | x_2(t) = 0\}$ be the first time that the train reaches the crossing. Then the requirement for safety can be encoded by the cost function:

$$J_1(x^0, u, d) = x_1(T(x^0)) \leq C_1 \tag{13}$$

The requirement for throughput can be encoded by a number of cost functions. A simple one is:

$$J_2(x^0, u, d) = \int_0^\infty (90° - x_1(t))^2 dt$$

Minimizing J_2 implies that the gate is open for as long as possible.

The system dynamics given in equation (12) are simple enough to allow us to write an analytic expression for the value of the state at time t:

$$x_1(t) = e^{-t/2} x_1^0 + \int_0^t e^{-(t-\tau)/2} u(\tau) d\tau \tag{14}$$

$$x_2(t) = x_2^0 + \int_0^t d(\tau) d\tau \tag{15}$$

It is easy to show that [14]:

Lemma 1 *If $x^0 \in X$ and the input constraints are satisfied, $x(t) \in X \; \forall t \geq 0$.*

Our first goal is to find the safe set of initial conditions and the control that makes them safe. In other words we are looking for $x^0 \in X$ and u^* with $u^*(t) \in U$ such that for all d satisfying $d(t) \in D$, $J(x^0, u^*, d) \leq C_1$. Fortunately the dynamics are simple enough to allow us to guess a candidate saddle solution:

$$u^*(t) \equiv 0 \tag{16}$$

$$d^*(t) \equiv v_2 \tag{17}$$

The state trajectories for the candidate saddle strategy are:

$$x_1(t) = e^{-t/2} x_1^0$$
$$x_2(t) = x_2^0 + v_2 t$$

From (13):

$$J_1^*(x^0) = J_1(x^0, u^*, d^*) = e^{x_2^0/(2v_2)} x_1^0$$

Lemma 2 *(u^*, d^*) is globally a saddle solution.*

Proof: The proof consists of verifying that for any admissible (u, d):

$$J_1(x^0, u^*, d) \leq J_1^*(x^0) \leq J_1(x^0, u, d^*) \tag{18}$$

Then, by definition, (u^*, d^*) is a global saddle solution. The details of the calculation are given in [14]. □

Lemma 3 *The set of safe initial conditions is:*

$$V = \left\{ x^0 \in X | x_2^0 > 0 \text{ or } x_2^0 \leq 2v_2 \ln(\frac{C_1}{x_1^0}) \right\} \tag{19}$$

Proof: For sufficiently large values of L, all initial conditions with $x_2^0 > 0$ are safe (the train has already passed the crossing). For $x_2^0 \leq 0$ safety is equivalent to:

$$J_1^*(x^0) = e^{x_2^0/(2v_2)} x_1^0 \leq C_1$$

The conclusion follows as v_2 and x_1^0 are positive and the exponential is monotone. □

"Optimal" Controller. As $x_1(t) \leq 90°$, maximizing throughput (minimizing J_2) is equivalent to maximizing $x_1(t)$. It is easy to show that this is equivalent to setting:

$$u(t) \equiv 45 \tag{20}$$

The optimal controller can now be obtained by combining the designs for safe and efficient operation. Let S = interior(V). As safety takes precedence over efficiency the resulting controller will be:

$$u = \begin{cases} 0 & x \in S^c \\ 45 & x \in S \end{cases} \tag{21}$$

It should be noted that, by design, the controller of (21) will be safe. Moreover any controller which uses $\hat{S} \subset S$ in the place of S will also be safe, but not as efficient in terms of throughput. These observations are summarized below:

Theorem 1 *A switching controller of the form of (21) with switching taking place at $\hat{S}$ will be safe if $\hat{S} \subset S$ and $x^0 \in V$.*

Proof: The result follows from Lemmas 1, 2, 3 and the fact that $\hat{S} \subset S \subset V$. □

Discrete Controller. Due to its bang-bang nature, the optimal controller can easily be implemented by a discrete scheme, using the discrete sensor and an appropriate actuator as an interface.

Theorem 2 *The discrete control scheme will be safe if:*

$$S_1 \leq 2v_2 \ln(\frac{C_1}{90°})$$
$$S_2 > 0$$

Proof: When viewed as an input-output system in the continuous domain, the combination of the discrete controller and the interface looks like:

$$u = \begin{cases} 0 & S_1 \leq x_2 < S_2 \\ 45 & \text{otherwise} \end{cases} \tag{22}$$

Here we assume that all discrete transitions take place instantaneously. Let $\hat{S} = \{x \in X | S_1 \leq x_2 < S_2\}$. By Theorem 1 the controller will be safe if $\hat{S} \subset S$, i.e. $S_2 > 0$ and $S_1 \leq 2v_2 \ln(\frac{C_1}{x_1^0})$ for all $x_1^0 \in [0°, 90°]$. As the logarithm function is monotone, the above conditions are the same as the ones in the theorem statement. □

The Possible Role of Coordination. If the sensors were placed improperly, for example $S_1 > 2v_2 \ln(\frac{C_1}{90°})$, the above analysis can not guarantee a safe controller. One solution would be to obtain a promise from the train that it will slow down once it enters the sensor range, i.e. promise that $\dot{y} \in [v_1, v_2']$ with $v_2' < v_2$. For appropriate choices of v_2' (in particular $v_2' \leq \frac{S_1}{\ln(C_1/90°)}$) safe operation with a discrete controller will still be possible. This example indicates how inter-agent communication (which can be used to provide such promises) can bias the game in the controllers' favor and help the designer produce an acceptable design.

4 Concluding Remarks

We presented an approach to the design of hybrid controllers for complex systems. The starting point was game theory in the continuous domain. In addition to optimal continuous controllers the solution to the game also provided requirements on the discrete switching policy. A hybrid controller is guaranteed to meet certain performance specifications if the discrete part obeys these requirements. The application of similar ideas to verification and generation of discrete abstractions was also discussed.

The missing link in this framework is a technique for designing the higher (discrete) levels. The approach presented here only gives continuous designs and switching guidelines. The designer still has to come up with a discrete design that follows the guidelines. An interesting issue that needs to be addressed in the discrete setting is what happens if the abstractions indicate that conflicting objectives (e.g. safety and efficiency) can not be met. As discussed in the introduction, the problem may still be solvable in this case by using inter-agent coordination. The questions of how are the higher levels to be designed to achieve sufficient coordination and where is the line between feasible and infeasible performance requirements are very interesting and still require a great deal of work to be answered.

References

1. R. Alur, C. Courcoubetis, and D. Dill, "Model checking for real-time systems," *Logic in Computer Science*, pp. 414–425, 1990.
2. A. Puri and P. Varaiya, "Decidebility of hybrid systems with rectangular differential inclusions," in *Computer Aided Verification*, pp. 95–104, 1994.
3. Z. Har'El and R. Kurshan, *Cospan User's Guide*. AT&T Bell Laboratories, 1987.
4. Adnan Aziz, et al., "HSIS: a BDD-based environment for formal verification," in *ACM/IEEE International Conference on CAD*, 1994.
5. M. Heymann, "Hierarchical decomposition of hybrid systems." (preprint), 1994.
6. C. Daws and S. Yovine, "Two examples of verification of multirate timed automata with KRONOS," in *Proc. 1995 IEEE Real-Time Systems Symposium, RTSS'95*, (Pisa, Italy), IEEE Computer Society Press, Dec. 1995.
7. R. Alur, C. Courcoubetis, T. A. Henzinger, and P. H. Ho, "Hybrid automaton: An algorithmic approach to the specification and verification of hybrid systems," in *Hybrid System* (R. L. Grossman, A. Nerode, A. P. Ravn, and H. Rischel, eds.), pp. 209–229, New York: Springer Verlag, 1993.
8. T. Henzinger, P. Kopke, A. Puri, and P. Varaiya, "What's decidable about hybrid automata," in *STOCS*, 1995.
9. F. Balarin, K. Petty, and A. L. Sangiovanni-Vincentelli, "Formal verification of the PATHO real-time operating system," in *IEEE Control and Decision Conference*, pp. 2459–2465, 1994.
10. A. Deshpande, *Control of Hybrid Systems*. PhD thesis, Department of Electrical Engineering, University of California, Berkeley, California, 1994.
11. M. S. Branicky, V. S. Borkar, and S. K. Mitter, "A unified framework for hybrid control: Background, model and theory," Tech. Rep. LIDS-P-2239, Laboratory for Information and Decision Systems, Massachusetts Institute of Technology, 1994.
12. A. Nerode and W. Kohn, "Multiple agent hybrid control architecture," in *Hybrid System* (R. L. Grossman, A. Nerode, A. P. Ravn, and H. Rischel, eds.), pp. 297–316, New York: Springer Verlag, 1993.
13. T. Basar and P. Bernhard, *H^∞-Optimal Control and Related Minimax Design Problems*. Birkhauser, 1991.
14. J. Lygeros, D. N. Godbole, and S. Sastry, "A game theoretic approach to hybrid system design," Tech. Rep. UCB/ERL-M95/77, Electronic Research Laboratory, University of California Berkeley, 1995.
15. A. Puri and P. Varaiya, "Driving safely in smart cars," in *American Control Conference*, pp. 3597–3599, 1995.
16. A. Puri and P. Varaiya, "Verification of hybrid systems using abstractions," in *Hybrid Systems II, LNCS 999*, Springer Verlag, 1995.

Verifying Clocked Transition Systems*

Yonit Kesten† Zohar Manna‡ Amir Pnueli†

Abstract. This paper presents a new computational model for real-time systems, called the *clocked transition system* (CTS) model. The CTS model is a development of our previous *timed transition* model, where some of the changes are inspired by the model of *timed automata*. The new model leads to a simpler style of temporal specification and verification, requiring no extension of the temporal language. We present verification rules for proving safety properties (including waiting-for and time-bounded response properties) of clocked transition systems, and separate rules for proving (time-unbounded) response properties. All rules are associated with verification diagrams. The verification of *response* properties requires adjustments of the proof rules developed for untimed systems, reflecting the fact that progress in the real time systems is ensured by the progress of time and not by fairness. The style of the verification rules is very close to the verification style of untimed systems which allows the (re)use of verification methods and tools, developed for untimed reactive systems, for proving properties of real-time systems.

1 Introduction

In this paper we present a new computational model for real-time systems: *clocked transition system* (CTS). This model represents time by a set of clocks (timers) which increase uniformly whenever time progresses, but can be set to arbitrary values by system (program) transitions. The CTS model can be viewed as a natural first-order extension of the timed automata model [AD94].

It is easy and natural to stipulate that one of the clocks T is never reset. In this case, T represents the *master clock* measuring real time from the beginning of the computation. This immediately yields the possibility of specifying timing properties of systems by unextended temporal logic, which may refer to any of the system variables, including the master clock T.

Consider, for example, the following two important timed properties:

* This research was supported in part by the National Science Foundation under grant CCR-92-23226, by the Advanced Research Projects Agency under NASA grant NAG2-892, by the United States Air Force Office of Scientific Research under grant F49620-93-1-0139, and by Department of the Army under grant DAAH04-95-1-0317, by a basic research grant from the Israeli Academy of Sciences, and by the European Community ESPRIT Basic Research Action Project 6021 (REACT).

† Department of Computer Science, Weizmann Institute, Rehovot, Israel, e-mail: yonit@wisdom.weizmann.ac.il

‡ Department of Computer Science, Stanford University, Stanford, CA 94305, e-mail: manna@cs.stanford.edu

- *Bounded response*: Every p should be followed by an occurrence of a q, not later than d time units.
- *Minimal separation*: No q can occur earlier than d time units after an occurrence of p.

Within the CTS computational model, these two yardstick properties can be specified by the following (unextended) temporal formulas:

- Bounded response: $p \wedge (T = t_0) \Rightarrow \Diamond(q \wedge T \leq t_0 + d)$.
- Minimal separation: $p \wedge (T = t_0) \Rightarrow \Box(T < t_0 + d \rightarrow \neg q)$.

The new computational model has several advantages over previous models such as the model of *timed transition systems* (TTS, see [HMP94]) in which time itself is not explicitly represented but is reflected in a time stamp affixed to each state in a computation of a TTS.

The first advantage of the new model, as shown above, is that it leads to a more natural style of specification, explicitly referring to clocks, which are just another kind of system variables, instead of introducing special new constructs, such as the *bounded temporal operators* proposed in *metric temporal logic* (MTL) (see [KVdR83], [KdR85], and [Koy90]) or the *age function* proposed in [MP93].

A second advantage of the CTS model is that we can reuse many of the methods and tools developed for verifying untimed reactive systems (e.g. [MP95]) for verifying real-time systems under the CTS model. The move from TTS to CTS brings us closer to the approach proposed in [AL94], which also recommends handling real time with a minimal extension of the reactive-systems formalism.

A model similar to the CTS model presented here was introduced in [AH94], and proof rules for establishing response properties for that model were presented in [HK94]. However, the response verification rules presented there for the general case were based on consideration of the region graph associated with timed automata which, in many cases, becomes very big. Our approach to response verification, while considering the general case, does not refer to the region graph and can be viewed as a natural modification of the response rules for untimed fair transition systems, except that the notion of fairness is replaced by the guaranteed progress of time.

We refer the reader to [AH89], [Ost90], [AL94], and the survey in [AH92], for additional logics, models, and approaches to the verification of real-time systems. In the process algebra school, some of the representative approaches to real time are [NSY92], [MT90], and many others are listed in [Sif91].

The paper is organized as follows. In Section 2, we present the real-time computational model of *clocked transition systems* (CTS). In Section 3, we show how a program augmented with timing bounds for the execution of statements can be represented as a CTS. In Section 4, we present rules and verification diagrams for verifying safety properties of CTS's. In Section 5, we present rules and verification diagrams for establishing response properties of CTS's.

A fuller version of this paper is available as the technical report [KMP95].

2 Clocked Transition System

Real-time systems are modeled as *clocked transition systems* (CTS). A clocked transition system $\Phi = \langle V, \Theta, \mathcal{T}, \Pi \rangle$ consists of:

- V : A finite set of *system variables*. The set $V = D \cup C$ is partitioned into $D = \{u_1, \ldots, u_m\}$ the set of *discrete variables* and $C = \{c_1, \ldots, c_k\}$ the set of *clocks*. Clocks always have the type *real*. The discrete variables can be of any type. We introduce a special clock $T \in C$, representing the *master clock*, as one of the system variables.
- Θ : The *initial condition*. A satisfiable assertion characterizing the initial states. It is required that

$$\Theta \quad \rightarrow \quad T = 0,$$

  i.e., $T = 0$ at all initial states.
- $\mathcal{T}$: A finite set of *transitions*. Each transition $\tau \in \mathcal{T}$ is a function

$$\tau : \Sigma \mapsto 2^{\Sigma},$$

  mapping each state $s \in \Sigma$ into a (possibly empty) set of τ-*successor* states $\tau(s) \subseteq \Sigma$.
  The function associated with a transition τ is represented by an assertion $\rho_\tau(V, V')$, called the *transition relation*, which relates a state $s \in \Sigma$ to its τ-successor $s' \in \tau(s)$ by referring to both unprimed and primed versions of the system variables. An unprimed version of a system variable refers to its value in s, while a primed version of the same variable refers to its value in s'. For example, the assertion $x' = x + 1$ states that the value of x in s' is greater by 1 than its value in s.
  For every $\tau \in \mathcal{T}$, it is required that

$$\rho_\tau \quad \rightarrow \quad T' = T,$$

  i.e., the master clock is modified by no transition.
- Π : The *time-progress condition*. An assertion over V. The assertion is used to specify a global restriction over the progress of time.

Extended Transitions

Let $\Phi : \langle V, \Theta, \mathcal{T}, \Pi \rangle$ be a clocked transition system. We define the set of *extended transitions* $\mathcal{T}_T$ associated with Φ as follows:

$$\mathcal{T}_T = \mathcal{T} \cup \{tick\}.$$

Transition *tick* is a special transition intended to represent the passage of time. Its transition relation is given by:

$$\rho_{tick}: \quad \exists \Delta. \, \Omega(\Delta) \ \wedge \ D' = D \ \wedge \ C' = C + \Delta,$$

where $\Omega(\Delta)$ is given by

$$\Omega(\Delta): \quad \Delta > 0 \ \wedge \ \forall t \in [0, \Delta).\, \Pi(D, C + t).$$

Let $D = \{u_1, \ldots, u_m\}$ be the set of discrete variables of Φ and $C = \{c_1, \ldots, c_k\}$ be the set of its clocks. Then, the expression $C' = C + \Delta$ is an abbreviation for

$$c_1' = c_1 + \Delta \ \wedge \ \cdots \ \wedge \ c_k' = c_k + \Delta,$$

and $\Pi(D, C + t)$ is an abbreviation for $\Pi(u_1, \ldots, u_m, c_1 + t, \ldots, c_k + t)$.

Runs and Computations

Let $\Phi : \langle V, \Theta, \mathcal{T}, \Pi \rangle$ be a clocked transition system. A *run* of Φ is a finite or infinite sequence of states $\sigma : s_0, s_1, \ldots$ satisfying:

- *Initiation:* $s_0 \models \Theta$
- *Consecution:* For each $j \in [0, |\sigma|)$, $s_{j+1} \in \tau(s_j)$ for some $\tau \in \mathcal{T}_T$.

A state is called (Φ-)*accessible* if it appears in a run of Φ.

A *computation* of Φ is an infinite run satisfying:

- *Time Divergence:* The sequence $s_0[T], s_1[T], \ldots$ grows beyond any bound. That is, as i increases, the value of T at state s_i increases beyond any bound.

A Frequently Occurring Case

In many cases, the time-progress condition Π has the following special form

$$\Pi: \quad \bigwedge_{i \in I} (p_i \rightarrow c^i < E_i),$$

where I is some finite index set and, for each $i \in I$, the assertion p_i and the real-valued expression E_i do not depend on the clocks, and $c^i \in C$ is some clock. This is, for example, the form of the time-progress condition for any CTS representing a real-time program. For such cases, the time-increment limiting formula $\Omega(\Delta)$ can be significantly simplified and assumes the following form:

$$\Omega(\Delta): \quad \Delta > 0 \ \wedge \ \bigwedge_{i \in I} (p_i \rightarrow c^i + \Delta \leq E_i)$$

Note, in particular, that this simpler form does not use quantifications over t.

Non-Zeno Systems

A CTS is defined to be *non-zeno* if every finite run can be extended into a computation (see [AL94], [Hen92]). An equivalent formulation is that Φ is non-zeno if it satisfies

> A finite sequence σ is a run of Φ iff σ is a prefix of some computation of Φ.

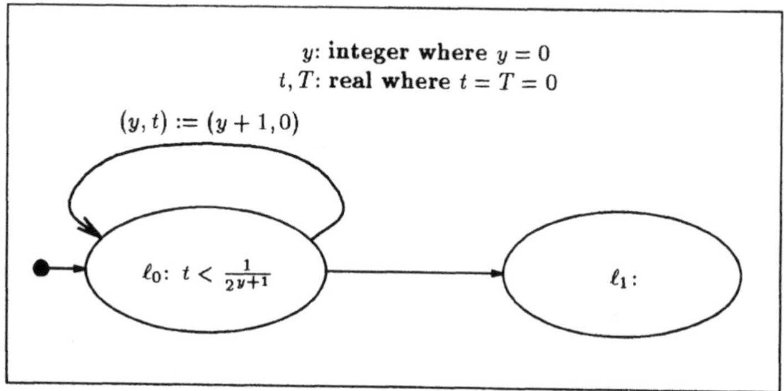

Fig. 1. CTS Φ_1.

A consequence of Φ being non-zeno is that a state s is Φ-accessible iff it appears in some computation of Φ.

Example 1. Consider CTS Φ_1 presented in Fig 1. In Fig 2, we present this CTS in textual form. The system variables include the control variable π, which assumes the values 0 or 1 to indicate that the system is currently at location ℓ_0 or ℓ_1, respectively. The predicate $pres(y,t,T)$ is an abbreviation for the assertion

$$pres(y,t,T):\quad y' = y \ \wedge\ t' = t \ \wedge\ T' = T,$$

stating that y, t, and T, are preserved by the transition.

$$V\colon \underbrace{\{\pi\colon \{0,1\};\, y\colon \textbf{integer}\}}_{D} \cup \underbrace{\{t, T\colon \textbf{real}\}}_{C}$$

$\Theta\colon \pi = y = t = T = 0$

$\mathcal{T}\colon \{\tau_0, \tau_1\}$with transition relations

$\tau_0\colon \pi = \pi' = t' = 0 \ \wedge\ y' = y + 1 \ \wedge\ pres(T)$

$\tau_1\colon \pi = 0 \ \wedge\ \pi' = 1 \ \wedge\ pres(y,t,T)$

$\Pi\colon \pi = 0 \rightarrow t < \frac{1}{2^y+1}$

Fig. 2. CTS Φ_1 in textual form.

It is not difficult to establish that Φ_1 is a non-zeno CTS. This is becaues, from any accessible state, we can always move to state ℓ_1 from which we can continue to take infinitely many time steps with increment 1.

The *tick* transition for CTS Φ_1 is given by

$$\rho^1_{tick}\colon\quad \exists\Delta > 0.\, pres(\pi, y) \wedge (t', T') = (t+\Delta, T+\Delta) \wedge (\pi = 0 \rightarrow t+\Delta \leq \frac{1}{2^y+1}).$$ ∎

3 Programs as Clocked Transition Systems

In this section we show how to represent real-time programs as clocked transition systems.

In [MP91b], we introduced a simple programming language SPL. Here we consider a subset of the language, restricting our attention to the following statements:

> *skip, assignment, await, noncritical, critical, conditional, concatenation, selection, while,* and *block*.

Not including the *cooperation* statement has the effect that parallelism is allowed only at the top level of the program. That is, a program is a parallel composition of processes, each of which is sequential.

We refer the reader to Chapter 0 of [MP95] for the construction of a *fair transition system* (FTS) Φ_P corresponding to an SPL program P. This construction introduces an explicit control variable π which ranges over sets of locations. System Φ_P associates a single transition with each *executable* statement, which includes all statements except *concatenation*, *selection*, and *block*. Here, we deviate from the construction of [MP95] in the transition associated with the *await* statement. Instead, we associate with each statement of the form

ℓ: **await** c; $\quad \widehat{\ell}$:

a transition τ_ℓ, whose transition relation ρ_ℓ is given by

$$\rho_\ell: \quad \ell \in \pi \wedge \begin{pmatrix} c \wedge \pi' = \pi - \{\ell\} \cup \{\widehat{\ell}\} \\ \vee \\ \neg c \wedge \pi' = \pi \end{pmatrix} \wedge \mathit{pres}(V - \{\pi\}).$$

This revised version ensures that the transition is always enabled when control is at ℓ, regardless of the value of condition c.

Another difference from [MP95] is that we only associate transitions with the executable statements and do not add the idling transition τ_I.

Let P be an SPL program. To obtain a real-time program, we associate with each S, an executable statement of P, a pair of values $[l_S, u_S]$, called the *lower* and *upper* bounds of S. These values, satisfying $0 \leq l_S \leq u_S \leq \infty$, are intended to provide a lower and upper bound on the length of time the statement can be enabled without being taken. We refer to a program with an assignment of time bounds as an SPL$_T$ program, and view it as a real-time program.

For locations ℓ_i, ℓ_j, and ℓ_k, we denote:

$$\begin{array}{ll} at\_\ell_i & : \ell_i \in \pi \\ at\_\ell_{j,k} & : at\_\ell_j \vee at\_\ell_k \end{array}$$

3.1 The CTS corresponding to an SPL$_T$ program

Let P be an SPL$_T$ program. That is, an SPL program with time bounds $[l_\tau, u_\tau]$ associated with each transition $\tau \in \mathcal{T}_P - \{\tau_I\}$. We will show how to construct a CTS Φ_P corresponding to the SPL$_T$ program P.

As a first step, we construct the FTS Φ_P: $\langle V, \Theta, \mathcal{T}, \mathcal{J}, \mathcal{C} \rangle$ corresponding to program P. Note that if program P uses only the statements in the previously presented subset, then $\mathcal{J} = \mathcal{T}-\{\tau_I\}$ and $\mathcal{C} = \emptyset$. Assume that program P is a parallel composition of m processes. That is, P has the form

$$\text{declarations}; \quad P_1 \parallel \cdots \parallel P_m,$$

where each P_i is a (sequential) statement.

The CTS corresponding to P is given by $\Phi_P\colon \langle \widetilde{V}, \widetilde{\Theta}, \widetilde{\mathcal{T}}, \Pi \rangle$, where

- *System Variables:* $\widetilde{V} = V \cup \{t_1, \ldots, t_m, T\}$.
  Thus, $\widetilde{V}$ consists of the system variables of Φ_P, to which we add $m+1$ clocks, one clock t_i for each process P_i, $i = 1, \ldots, m$, plus the master clock T.
- *Initial Condition:* $\widetilde{\Theta}$: $\Theta \wedge t_1 = \cdots = t_m = T = 0$.
- *Transitions:* $\widetilde{\mathcal{T}}\colon \{\widetilde{\tau} \mid \tau \in \mathcal{T}-\{\tau_I\}\}$.
  Let $\tau \in \mathcal{T} - \{\tau_I\}$ be a transition corresponding to an executable statement in process P_i. The transition relation for transition $\widetilde{\tau}$ is given by:

  $$\widetilde{\rho_\tau}\colon \quad \rho_\tau \wedge t_i \geq l_\tau \wedge t_i' = 0 \wedge pres(t_1, \ldots, t_{i-1}, t_{i+1}, \ldots, t_m, T).$$

  Thus, the transition can be taken only when t_i, the clock corresponding to process P_i, is not below l_τ, the lower bound associated with τ. When taken, the transition resets clock t_i to 0.
- *Time-progress condition Π:* For each executable statement $\ell\colon S$ in process P_i, Π includes the conjunct

  $$\ell \in \pi \quad \rightarrow \quad t_i < u_S,$$

  where u_S is the upper bound associated with statement S. This ensures that control cannot wait at location ℓ for more than u_S without the transition associated with S (or another transition causing control to move away from ℓ) being taken.

Note that the lower bounds of statements are added as constraints to transitions, while the upper bounds are added as constraints to the time-progress condition Π.

Example 2. Figure 3 presents a simple program consisting of two processes communicating by the shared variable x.

$$x, y\text{: integer where } x = y = 0$$

$$\left[\begin{array}{l} \ell_0 : \textbf{while } x = 0 \textbf{ do} \\ \quad \ell_1 : y := y + 1 \\ \ell_2 : \end{array}\right] \quad \Bigg\| \quad \left[\begin{array}{l} m_0 : x := 1 \\ m_1 : \end{array}\right]$$

$$- \; P_1 \; - \qquad\qquad - \; P_2 \; -$$

Fig. 3. Program ANY-Y.

To make it an SPL$_T$ program, we uniformly associate each of its executable statements with the time bounds $[3, 5]$. The CTS $\Phi_{\text{ANY-Y}[3,5]}$ associated with ANY-Y$[3,5]$ is defined as follows:

- *System Variables:* $V = \{\pi, x, y, t_1, t_2, T\}$. In addition to the control variable π and data variables x and y, the system variables also include clock t_1, measuring delays in process P_1, clock t_2, measuring delays in process P_2, and the master clock T, measuring time from the beginning of the computation.
- *Initial Condition:*

$$\Theta: \quad \pi = \{\ell_0, m_0\} \wedge x = y = 0 \wedge t_1 = t_2 = T = 0.$$

- *Transitions:* $\mathcal{T}: \{\ell_0, \ell_1, m_0\}$ with transition relations:

$$\rho_{\ell_0}: \ell_0 \in \pi \wedge \begin{pmatrix} x = 0 \wedge \pi' = \pi - \{\ell_0\} \cup \{\ell_1\} \\ \vee \\ x \neq 0 \wedge \pi' = \pi - \{\ell_0\} \cup \{\ell_2\} \end{pmatrix} \wedge t_1 \geq 3 \wedge t_1' = 0 \\ \wedge\, pres(\{x, y, t_2, T\})$$

$$\rho_{\ell_1}: \ell_1 \in \pi \wedge \pi' = \pi - \{\ell_1\} \cup \{\ell_0\} \wedge y' = y + 1 \wedge t_1 \geq 3 \wedge t_1' = 0 \\ \wedge\ pres(\{x, t_2, T\})$$

$$\rho_{m_0}: m_0 \in \pi \wedge \pi' = \pi - \{m_0\} \cup \{m_1\} \wedge x' = 1 \wedge t_2 \geq 3 \wedge t_2' = 0 \\ \wedge\ pres(\{y, t_1, T\}).$$

- *Time-progress condition:*

$$\Pi: \quad (at\_\ell_{0,1} \rightarrow t_1 < 5) \wedge (at\_m_0 \rightarrow t_2 < 5)$$

The *tick* transition for this system is given by

$$tick: \ \exists \Delta > 0.\ pres(\pi, x, y) \ \wedge\ (t_1', t_2', T') = (t_1 + \Delta, t_2 + \Delta, T + \Delta) \wedge \\ (at\_\ell_{0,1} \rightarrow t_1 + \Delta \leq 5) \wedge (at\_m_0 \rightarrow t_2 + \Delta \leq 5)$$ ▪

3.2 Specification Language

To specify properties of reactive systems, we use the language of temporal logic, as presented in [MP91b]. We use only the following:

- *State formulas (assertions)* - any first-order formula, possibly including at_ℓ expressions.
- $\Box p$ — Always p, where p is an assertion. We refer to such a formula as an *invariance formula*.
- $p \Rightarrow (q\, \mathcal{W}\, r)$ — p entails q waiting for r, where p, q, and r are assertions. We refer to such a formula as a *waiting-for formula*.
- $p \Rightarrow \Diamond r$ — p entails eventually r, where p and r are assertions. We refer to such a formula as a *response formula*.

For a state s and assertion p, we write $s \models p$ to indicate that p holds (is true) over s. Let $\sigma: s_0, s_1 \ldots$ be an infinite sequence of states, to which we refer as a *model*. For an assertion p, we say that $j \geq 0$, is a *p-position* if $s_j \models p$. Satisfaction of (the three considered) temporal formulas over a model σ is defined as follows:

- A model σ satisfies the invariance formula $\Box p$, written $\sigma \models \Box p$, if all positions within σ are p-positions.

- A model σ satisfies the waiting-for formula $p \Rightarrow (q \mathcal{W} r)$, written $\sigma \models p \Rightarrow (q \mathcal{W} r)$, if every p-position i within σ initiates an interval of positions, all of which satisfy q. This interval of contiguous q-positions, called a q-interval, can either extend to infinity or terminate in an r-position which is not in the interval. That is,

$$\sigma[i] \Vdash p \text{ implies } \sigma[j] \Vdash q \text{ for all } j \geq i, \text{ or}$$
$$\sigma[k] \Vdash r \text{ for some } k \geq i \text{ and } \sigma[j] \Vdash q \text{ for all } j,\ i \leq j < k.$$

- A model σ satisfies the response formula $p \Rightarrow \Diamond r$, written $\sigma \models p \Rightarrow \Diamond r$, if every p-position i within σ is followed by an r-position $j \geq i$.

A temporal formula φ is said to be *valid over* CTS Φ (or Φ*-valid*), denoted $\Phi \models \varphi$ if $\sigma \models \varphi$ for every computation σ of Φ. An assertion p is called Φ*-state valid*, denoted $\Phi \Vdash p$ if it holds at every Φ-accessible state.

In the case that CTS Φ is derived from an SPL_T program P, we use the terms P-valid, P-state valid, and P-accessible as synonymous to Φ_P-valid, Φ_P-state valid, and Φ_P-accessible. We also write $P \models \varphi$ and $P \Vdash p$ to denote $\Phi_P \models \varphi$ and $\Phi_P \Vdash p$, respectively.

4 Verifying Safety Properties of Clocked Transition Systems

As explained in [MP91b], the properties expressible by temporal logic can be arranged in a hierarchy that identifies different classes of properties according to the form of formulas expressing them.

In this section, we present methods for verifying safety properties of clocked transitions systems. As representative of the safety class, we consider the properties that can be specified by a *waiting-for* formula of the form

$$p \quad \Rightarrow \quad q \mathcal{W} r.$$

We refer to such properties as *precedence properties*.

Rule WAIT, presented in Fig. 4, is the main tool for verifying precedence properties of a CTS Φ.

For assertions p, q, φ, and r,

$$\begin{array}{ll}
\text{U1.} & \varphi \rightarrow q \\
\text{U2.} & p \rightarrow r \vee \varphi \\
\text{U3.} & \rho_\tau \wedge \varphi \rightarrow r' \vee \varphi' \quad \text{for every } \tau \in \mathcal{T}_T \\
\hline
 & P \models p \Rightarrow q \mathcal{W} r
\end{array}$$

Fig. 4. Rule WAIT (waiting-for) applied to CTS P.

The rule uses an auxiliary assertion φ. Premise U1 of rule WAIT requires that the auxiliary assertion φ implies assertion q. Premise U2 requires that every p-state must satisfy r or φ. Premise U3 requires that every τ-successor of a φ-state satisfies r or φ, where τ is any transition in $\mathcal{T}_T^{\Phi}$ (the extended transitions of Φ). It follows that every p-state in a computation of Φ initiates a (possibly empty) φ-interval, which can be terminated only by an r-state. Due to implication U1, every φ-state is also a q-state and, therefore, formula $p \Rightarrow (q \mathcal{W} r)$ is Φ-valid.

Example 3. We use rule WAIT to establish the precedence property

$$\underbrace{\Theta}_{p} \quad \Rightarrow \quad \underbrace{at\_\ell_{0,1}}_{q} \, \mathcal{W} \, \underbrace{at\_m_1}_{r}$$

over program ANY-Y (Fig. 3). This formula claims that process P_1 cannot terminate before process P_2. That is, process P_1 cannot reach ℓ_2 before P_1 reaches location m_1.

We apply rule WAIT to this choice of p, q, and r, taking

$$\varphi: \quad x = 0 \land at\_\ell_{0,1}$$

as the auxiliary assertion. It is not difficult to see that all premises of rule WAIT are state valid for this choice of p, q, r, and φ.

This establishes that the considered waiting-for formula is valid over program ANY-Y, i.e.,

$$\text{ANY-Y} \quad \models \quad \Theta \Rightarrow (at\_\ell_{0,1} \, \mathcal{W} \, at\_m_1). \quad ▟$$

For assertions p and q and transition τ, we introduce the abbreviation

$$\{p\}\tau\{q\} \qquad \text{standing for} \qquad \rho_\tau \land p \rightarrow q'.$$

Verification Diagrams

An effective way of presenting the verification of a precedence property by rule WAIT is provided by the graphical formalism of *verification diagrams* [MP94]. A *waiting (verification) diagram* is a directed labeled graph, constructed as follows:

- *Nodes* in the graph are labeled by assertions $\varphi_0, \varphi_1, \ldots, \varphi_m$. We will often refer to a node by the assertion labeling it.
  Node φ_0 is considered a *terminal* node and is graphically identified by being drawn with bold-face boundaries.
- *Edges* in the graph represent transitions between assertions. Each edge is labeled by the name of a transition in the program. We refer to an edge labeled by τ as a *τ-edge*. No edges depart form the terminal node.
- Some of the nodes are designated as *initial nodes*. They are annotated by an entry arrow ↴.

For example, in Fig. 5 we present a verification diagram for program ANY-Y.

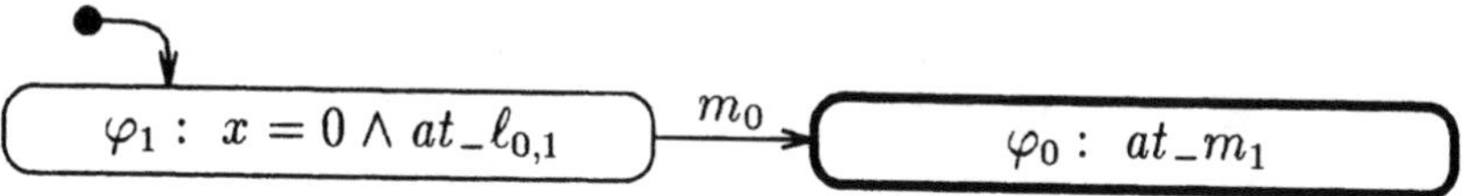

Fig. 5. A Waiting Verification Diagram.

Verification Conditions Implied by a Waiting Diagram

Consider a nonterminal node labeled by assertion φ. Let $\tau \in \mathcal{T}_T$ be a transition and let $\varphi_1, \ldots, \varphi_k$, $k \geq 0$, be the successors of φ by edges labeled with τ (possibly including φ itself). With each such node and transition, we associate the following verification condition:

$$\rho_\tau \wedge \varphi \quad\rightarrow\quad \varphi' \vee \varphi_1' \ \vee\ \cdots\ \vee\ \varphi_k'.$$

In particular, if $k = 0$ (i.e., φ has no τ-successors), the associated verification condition is

$$\rho_\tau \wedge \varphi \quad\rightarrow\quad \varphi'.$$

Valid Waiting Diagrams

A waiting diagram is said to be *valid over* CTS Φ (Φ*-valid* for short) if all the verification conditions associated with the diagram are Φ-state valid.

The consequences of having a valid waiting diagram are stated in the following claim:

Claim 1 *A Φ-valid waiting diagram with nodes $\varphi_0, \ldots, \varphi_m$ establishes*

$$\Phi \models (\bigvee_{j=0}^{m} \varphi_j) \Rightarrow (\bigvee_{j=1}^{m} \varphi_j)\,\mathcal{W}\,\varphi_0.$$

If, in addition, $\varphi_0 = r$,

$$\text{D1:}\quad \Phi \Vdash (\bigvee_{j=1}^{m} \varphi_j) \rightarrow q, \qquad \textit{and} \qquad \text{D2:}\quad \Phi \Vdash p \rightarrow \bigvee_{j=0}^{m} \varphi_j,$$

then we can conclude:

$$\Phi \models p \Rightarrow q\,\mathcal{W}\,r.$$

Justification We observe first that the verification conditions associated with a waiting diagram imply premise U3 of rule WAIT, when we take φ to be $\varphi_1 \vee \cdots \vee \varphi_m$ and r to be φ_0.

If we further take $p = \varphi_0 \vee \cdots \vee \varphi_m$ and $q = \varphi_1 \vee \cdots \vee \varphi_m$, we find that premises U1 and U2 of the rule hold trivially. This yields the first part of the claim.

The second part of the claim considers different p and q but explicitly requires, using D1 and D2, that premises U1 and U2 are Φ-state valid. The conclusion follows by rule WAIT. ┛

For example, all the verification conditions associated with the diagram of Fig. 5 are valid over program ANY-Y and so are $\varphi_0 = r$, and conditions D1, D2 for the choice of $p: \Theta$, $q: at\_\ell_{0,1}$, and $r: at\_m_1$. Consequently. the verification diagram establishes

$$\text{ANY-Y} \quad \models \quad \Theta \Rightarrow (at\_\ell_{0,1} \mathcal{W} \, at\_m_1).$$

Encapsulation Conventions

There are several encapsulation conventions that improve the presentation and readability of verification diagrams. We extend the notion of a directed graph into a structured directed graph by allowing *compound nodes* that may encapsulate other nodes, and edges that may depart or arrive at compound nodes. A node that does not encapsulate other nodes is called a *basic node*. We use the following conventions:

- *Labels of compound nodes*: A diagram containing a compound node n, labeled by an assertion φ and encapsulating nodes $n_1, \ldots, n_k$ with assertions $\varphi_1, \ldots, \varphi_k$, is equivalent to a diagram in which n is unlabeled and nodes $n_1, \ldots, n_k$ are labeled by $\varphi_1 \wedge \varphi, \ldots, \varphi_k \wedge \varphi$, respectively.
- *Edges entering and exiting compound nodes*: A diagram containing an edge e connecting node A to a compound node n encapsulating nodes $n_1, \ldots, n_k$ is equivalent to a diagram in which there is an edge connecting A to each n_i, $i = 1, \ldots, k$, with the same label as e. Similarly, an edge e connecting the compound node n to node B is the same as having a separate edge connecting each n_i, $i = 1, \ldots, k$, to B with the same label as e.

These encapsulation conventions are illustrated in the following example.

Example 4. We use rule WAIT to prove that program ANY-Y$_{[3,5]}$ terminates within 15 time units, as specified by the following precedence formula:

$$\Theta \quad \Rightarrow \quad (T \leq 15) \, \mathcal{W} \, (at\_\ell_2 \wedge at\_m_1)$$

This formula claims that, as long as the program has not terminated, T is bounded by 15. Since in all computations, time must eventually exceed 15, this guarantees terminations within 15 time units.

The proof is presented by the waiting diagram of Fig. 6. Note that no edge in the diagram is labeled by the *tick* transition. This implies that all verification conditions involving the *tick* transition are of the form $\{\varphi_i\}$ *tick* $\{\varphi_i\}$ claiming that the *tick* transition preserves each of the assertions in the diagram. ▪

Completeness of Rule WAIT

Rule WAIT is complete for verifying precedence properties of non-zeno clocked transition systems. This is stated by the following claim.

Claim 2 *If formula* $p \Rightarrow (q \, \mathcal{W} \, r)$ *is valid over non-zeno* CTS Φ, *then there exists an assertion* φ *such that premises* U1-U3 *of rule* WAIT *are* Φ*-state valid.*

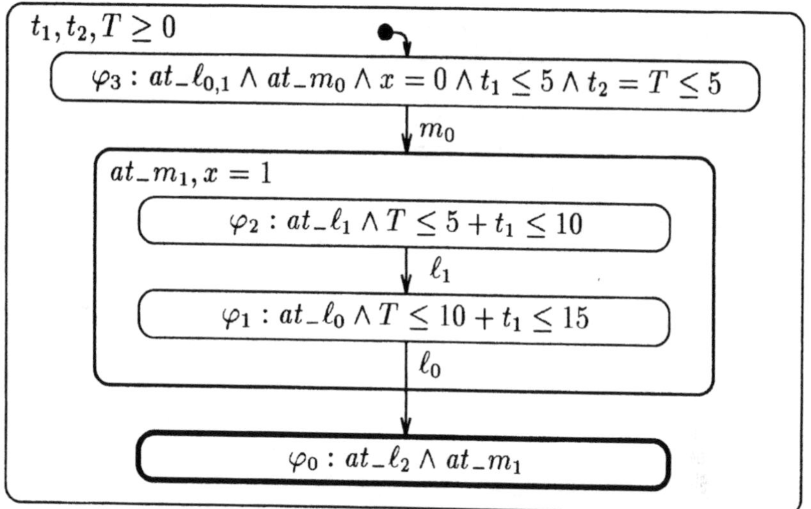

Fig. 6. Termination of ANY-$Y_{[3,5]}$ within 15 time units.

Justification Consider a non-zeno CTS Φ and assertions p, q, and r, such that $p \Rightarrow (q \mathcal{W} r)$ is Φ-valid.

We define an (*execution*) *segment* (of Φ) to be a sequence $\sigma : s_1, \ldots, s_k$, $k > 0$, such that, for every $i \in \{1, \ldots, k-1\}$, $s_{i+1} \in \tau(s_i)$ for some $\tau \in \mathcal{T}_T$. We say that the segment σ *departs from* s_1. For a segment $\sigma : s_1, \ldots, s_k$ and assertion ψ, we define $earliest_\sigma(\psi)$ to be the smallest $j \in \{1, \ldots, k\}$ such that s_j satisfies ψ, or $k+1$ if there exists no such j (i.e., no state in σ satisfies ψ). A segment σ is called a $(q \mathcal{W} r)$-*segment* if

$$earliest_\sigma(r) \leq earliest_\sigma(\neg q).$$

Otherwise, σ is called a $\neg(q \mathcal{W} r)$-*segment*. It is not difficult to see that all models extending a given $\neg(q \mathcal{W} r)$-segment σ satisfy $\neg(q \mathcal{W} r)$. A state s is defined to be a $(q \mathcal{W} r)$-*state* if all execution segments departing from s are $(q \mathcal{W} r)$-segments.

Following are some properties of $(q \mathcal{W} r)$-states:

P1. Every r-state is a $(q \mathcal{W} r)$-state.
P2. If s is a $(q \mathcal{W} r)$-state which does not satisfy r, then s satisfies q and every τ-successor of s is also a $(q \mathcal{W} r)$-state.
P3. Under the assumption that $p \Rightarrow (q \mathcal{W} r)$ is Φ-valid, every accessible p-state is a $(q \mathcal{W} r)$-state.

To establish property P3, assume to the contrary that there exists an accessible p-state $\widehat{s}$ which is not a $(q \mathcal{W} r)$-state. This implies that there exists a finite run $\sigma: s_0 \ldots, s_a, \ldots, s_b$, such that $s_a = \widehat{s}$, and $s_a, \ldots, s_b$ is a $\neg(q \mathcal{W} r)$-segment. Since Φ is non-zeno, the run σ can be extended into a computation σ^*. However, position a of σ^* satisfies p (since $s_a = \widehat{s}$ is a p-state) but does not satisfy $q \mathcal{W} r$, since no extension of $s_a \ldots, s_b$ can satisfy $q \mathcal{W} r$. This contradicts the assumption that $p \Rightarrow (q \mathcal{W} r)$ is Φ-valid.

Using the techniques of [MP91a] or Chapter 2 of [MP95], we can construct a (first-order) assertion *waiting* which precisely characterizes the set of $(q \mathcal{W} r)$-states, i.e., a state satisfies the assertion *waiting* iff it is a $(q \mathcal{W} r)$-state. We take φ to be $waiting \wedge \neg r$ and show that all premises of rule WAIT are Φ-state valid. Since we are only proving *relative* completeness, it is enough to show Φ-state validity of the premises, assuming an oracle that provides proofs or otherwise verifies all generally Φ-state valid assertions.

U1. $\varphi \rightarrow q$
This is a direct consequence of property P2, since a state satisfying the assertion φ: $waiting \wedge \neg r$, is a $(q \mathcal{W} r)$-state which does not satisfy r.

U2. $p \rightarrow r \vee \varphi$
By the definition of φ and property P1, $r \vee \varphi$ is equivalent to *waiting*. The premise then follows from property P3.

U3. $\rho_\tau \wedge \varphi \quad \rightarrow \quad r' \vee \varphi'$, for each $\tau \in \mathcal{T}$.
Observing that $r' \vee \varphi'$ is equivalent to *waiting'*, this premise follows again from property P2.

This concludes the proof of completeness of rule INV. ■

The following example demonstrates that the assumption that Φ is non-zeno is essential to the completeness of the rule.

Example 5. Consider the CTS Φ_3 which is presented in Fig. 7. Clearly, CTS Φ_3

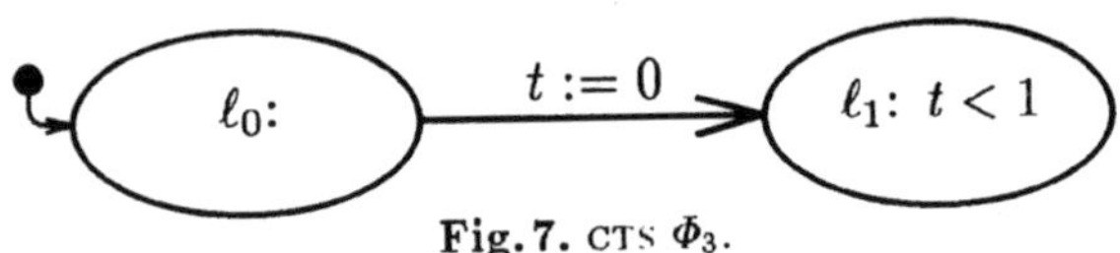

Fig. 7. CTS Φ_3.

is a possibly-zeno system because, once a run enters location ℓ_1, time is bounded and cannot diverge. Thus, a run entering location ℓ_1 cannot be extended into a computation of Φ_3. A result of the fact that no computation of Φ_3 ever enters location ℓ_1 is that the waiting-for formula $\Theta \Rightarrow (at\_\ell_0 \mathcal{W} \text{F})$ is Φ_3-valid. Note, however, that this formula is not valid over all *runs* of Φ_3. In particular, any run that enters state ℓ_1 falsifies $\Theta \Rightarrow (at\_\ell_0 \mathcal{W} \text{F})$.

Examination of the arguments for the soundness of rule WAIT shows that, in fact, the rule establishes the validity of $p \Rightarrow (q \mathcal{W} r)$ over all runs of Φ. Consequently, rule WAIT cannot be used to verify $\Theta \Rightarrow (at\_\ell_0 \mathcal{W} \text{F})$ which is valid over all computations of Φ_3 but not over all runs of Φ_3. ■

The invariance formula $\Box p$ can be viewed (and verified) as the waiting-for formula $\Theta \Rightarrow (p \mathcal{W} \text{F})$. We refer readers to [MP95] for detailed discussions of methods for verifying invariance formulas.

5 Verifying Response Properties of Clocked Transition Systems

In this section, we present methods for verifying response properties of clocked transitions systems.

5.1 Clock-Bounded Chain Rule

The basic rule for proving response properties of clocked transition systems is the (*clock-bounded*) *chain rule* (rule CB-CHAIN) presented in Fig. 8. The rule uses auxiliary assertions $\varphi_1, \ldots, \varphi_m$ and refers to assertion q also as φ_0. With each assertion φ_i we associate one of the clocks $c_i \in C$, to which we refer as the ***helpful clock***, and a real-valued upper bound b_i. The intention is that while remaining in states satisfying φ_i, the clock c_i is bounded by b_i. Since time in a computation grows beyond any bound, this will imply that we cannot continually stay at φ_i-state for too long.

For assertions p, q, and $\varphi_0 = q, \varphi_1, \ldots, \varphi_m$,
clocks $c_1, \ldots, c_m \in C$, and
real constants $b_1, \ldots, b_m \in \mathbb{R}$,

C1. $p \rightarrow \bigvee_{j=0}^{m} \varphi_j$

The following two premises hold for $i = 1, \ldots, m$

C2. $\rho_\tau \wedge \varphi_i \rightarrow (\varphi_i' \wedge c_i' \geq c_i) \vee \bigvee_{j<i} \varphi_j'$ for every $\tau \in \mathcal{T}_T$

C3. $\varphi_i \rightarrow c_i \leq b_i$

$p \Rightarrow \Diamond q$

Fig. 8. Rule CB-CHAIN (clock-bounded chain rule for response).

Premise C1 requires that every p-position satisfies one of $\varphi_0 = q, \varphi_1, \ldots, \varphi_m$.

Premise C2 requires that every τ-successor (for any $\tau \in \mathcal{T}_T$) of a φ_i-state s is a φ_j-state for some $j \leq i$. In the case that the successor state satisfies φ_i, it is required that the transition does not decrease the value of c_i.

Premise C3 requires that assertion φ_i implies that c_i is bounded by the constant b_i.

The following claim states the soundness of the rule:

Claim 3 *Rule* CB-CHAIN *is sound for proving that a response formula is Φ-valid.*

Justification: Assume that the premises of the rule are Φ-state valid, and let σ be a computation of Φ. We will show that σ satisfies the rule's consequence

$$p \Rightarrow \diamondsuit q,$$

i.e., every p-position in σ is followed by a q-position.

Assume that p holds at position k and no later position $i \geq k$ satisfies q. By C1 some φ_j must hold at position k. Let j_k denote the minimal index such that φ_{j_k} holds at k. Obviously $j_k > 0$ by our assumption that q never occurs beyond position k.

By C2, state s_{k+1} must satisfy φ_j for some j, $0 < j \leq j_k$. Let j_{k+1} denote the minimal such index. Continuing in this manner we obtain that every position i beyond k satisfies some φ_{j_i}, where $j_i > 0$ and

$$j_k \geq j_{k+1} \geq j_{k+2} \geq \cdots .$$

Since we cannot have an infinite non-increasing sequence of natural numbers which decreases infinitely many times, there must exist a position $r \geq k$ such that

$$j_r = j_{r+1} = j_{r+2} = \cdots .$$

Denote the value of this eventually-stable assertion index by $u = j_r$.

Consider the value of the clock c_u at states s_i, $i \geq r$. By C2, the value of c_u never decreases. Also, whenever a *tick* transition with increment Δ is taken, c_u increases (as do all clocks) by Δ. It follows that the master clock T cannot increase by more than $b_u - s_r[c_u]$ from its value at state s_r. This contradicts the fact that σ is a computation in which the master clock increases beyond all bounds.

We conclude that our assumption of the existence of a p-position not followed by any q-position is false. Consequently, if the premises of the rule hold then every p-position must be followed by a q-position, establishing the consequence of the rule. ▟

Example 6. We illustrate the use of rule CB-CHAIN to prove the termination of program ANY-Y$_{[3,5]}$, which can be stated by the response formula

$$\underbrace{(\,at\_\ell_0 \wedge at\_m_0 \wedge x = t_1 = t_2 = T = 0\,)}_{p} \quad \Rightarrow \quad \diamondsuit\underbrace{(\,at\_\ell_2 \wedge at\_m_1\,)}_{q}.$$

To apply rule CB-CHAIN, we use the following auxiliary assertions, helpful clocks, and bounds:

φ_0: $at\_\ell_2 \wedge at\_m_1$	–	–
φ_1: $at\_\ell_0 \wedge at\_m_1 \wedge x = 1 \wedge t_1 \leq 5$	c_1: t_1	b_1: 5
φ_2: $at\_\ell_1 \wedge at\_m_1 \wedge x = 1 \wedge t_1 \leq 5$	c_2: t_1	b_1: 5
φ_3: $at\_\ell_{0,1} \wedge at\_m_0 \wedge x = 0 \wedge t_1 \leq 5 \wedge t_2 \leq 5$	c_3: t_2	b_1: 5

We can check that all premises of rule CB-CHAIN are state valid. It follows that the response formula

$$(at\_\ell_0 \wedge at\_m_0 \wedge x = t_1 = t_2 = T = 0) \quad \Rightarrow \quad \diamondsuit(at\_\ell_2 \wedge at\_m_1)$$

is valid over program ANY-Y$_{[3,5]}$. ▟

5.2 Clock-Bounded Chain Diagrams

The main ingredients of a proof by rule CB-CHAIN can be conveniently and effectively presented by a special type of verification diagrams that summarize the auxiliary assertions with their helpful clocks and bounds, and display the possible transitions between the assertions. We define a (*clock-bounded*) *chain diagram* to be a directed labeled graph constructed as follows:

- *Nodes* in the graph are labeled by assertions. Each node is labeled by a pair of assertions: ϕ_i and β_i, for $i = 0, \ldots, m$. The assertion β_i has the form $c_i \leq b_i$, where $c_i \in C$ is a clock and b_i is a real constant. We refer to the conjunction $\phi_i \wedge \beta_i$ as φ_i, and say that the node is labeled by the (combined) assertion φ_i. We often refer to nodes by the assertion φ_i labeling them. The node labeled by φ_0 is called the *terminal node* and is graphically identified by being drawn with bold-face boundaries.
- *Edges* in the graph represent transitions between assertions. Each edge connects one assertion to another and is labeled by one or more transitions. An edge can connect node φ_i to node φ_j only if $i \geq j$. This imposes the restriction that the graph of a chain diagram is weakly acyclic, i.e., the only cycles in the graph consist of a node connected to itself.

Verification Conditions Implied by a Chain Diagram

Consider a nonterminal node labeled by assertion φ: $\phi \wedge \beta$ where the clock-bound assertion is β: $c \leq b$. Let $\tau \in \mathcal{T}_T$ be a transition and let $\varphi_1, \ldots, \varphi_k$, $k \geq 0$, be the successors of φ by edges labeled with τ (possibly including φ itself). With each such node and transition, we associate the following verification condition:

$$\rho_\tau \wedge \varphi \quad \rightarrow \quad (\varphi' \wedge c' \geq c) \vee \varphi'_1 \vee \cdots \vee \varphi'_k.$$

In particular, if $k = 0$ (i.e., φ has no τ-successors), the associated verification condition is

$$\rho_\tau \wedge \varphi \quad \rightarrow \quad \varphi' \wedge c' \geq c.$$

Valid Chain Diagrams

A chain diagram is said to be *valid over* CTS Φ (Φ-*valid* for short) if all the verification conditions associated with the diagram are Φ-state valid.

The consequences of having a valid chain diagram are stated in the following claim:

Claim 4 *A Φ-valid chain diagram with nodes $\varphi_0, \ldots, \varphi_m$ establishes*

$$\Phi \models (\bigvee_{j=0}^{m} \varphi_j) \Rightarrow \Diamond \varphi_0.$$

If, in addition, $\varphi_0 = q$ *and*

$$\text{C1:}\quad \Phi \quad \models \quad p \ \rightarrow \ \bigvee_{j=0}^{m} \varphi_j,$$

then we can conclude:

$$\Phi \quad \models \quad p \Rightarrow \Diamond q.$$

The claim follows from the observation that the verification conditions associated with a chain diagram precisely correspond to premise C2 of rule CB-CHAIN. Premise C1 is trivially satisfied for the first part of the claim, where we take p to be $\bigvee_{j=0}^{m} \varphi_j$. It is explicitly provided in the second part of the claim. Premise C3 is trivially satisfied by having β_i: $c_i \leq b_i$ as an explicit conjunct of $\varphi_i = \phi_i \wedge \beta_i$.

Example 7. In Fig. 9, we present a chain diagram for proving that

$$(at\_\ell_0 \wedge at\_m_0 \wedge x = t_1 = t_2 = T = 0) \quad \Rightarrow \quad \Diamond(at\_\ell_2 \wedge at\_m_1)$$

is valid over program ANY-Y$_{[3,5]}$.

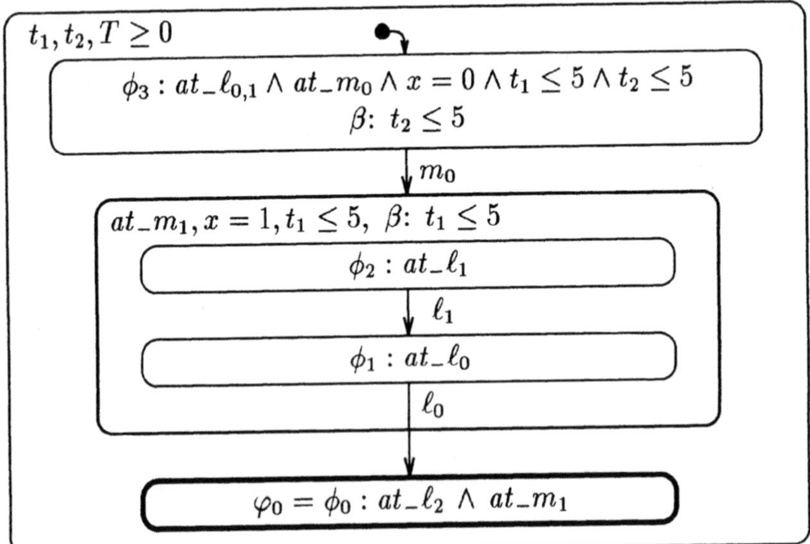

Fig. 9. Verifying termination of program ANY-Y$_{[3,5]}$.

Note the use of encapsulation in labeling the compound node by the common clock bound $t_1 \leq 5$, which is factored out of nodes φ_1 and φ_2. We also remove the index from the β assertion labeling a node and write β instead of β_i. ┘

5.3 Clock-Bounded Well-Founded Rule

Rule CB-CHAIN is adequate for proving response properties in which a q-state is achieved in a number of helpful steps which is a priori bounded. For example, in verifying termination of program ANY-Y$_{[3,5]}$, there were 3 helpful step leading to termination. These are represented in the chain diagram of Fig. 9 by the edges entering nodes ϕ_2–ϕ_0.

In many cases, the number of helpful steps needed to reach the goal q cannot be bounded a priori. For these cases we need a stronger rule, based on well-founded domains.

Well-founded Domains

We define a *well-founded domain* $(\mathcal{A}, \succ)$ to consist of a set $\mathcal{A}$ and a *well-founded* binary relation $\succ$ on $\mathcal{A}$. The binary relation $\succ$ is called *well-founded* if there does not exist an infinitely descending sequence $a_0, a_1, \ldots$ of elements of $\mathcal{A}$ such that

$$a_0 \succ a_1 \succ \cdots .$$

For $\succ$, an arbitrary binary relation on $\mathcal{A}$, we define its *reflexive extension* $\succeq$ to hold between a, $a' \in \mathcal{A}$ if either $a \succ a'$ or $a = a'$.

A frequently used well-founded domain is the domain of *lexicographic tuples* $(\mathbb{N}^k, \succ)$, where $\mathbb{N}^k$ is the set of k-tuples of natural numbers, and the lexicographic order $\succ$ is defined by

$$(n_1, \ldots, n_k) \succ (m_1, \ldots, m_k) \quad \text{iff} \quad \begin{array}{l} n_1 = m_1, \ \ldots, \ n_{i-1} = m_{i-1}, \ n_i > m_i \\ \text{for some } i, \ 1 \le i \le k. \end{array}$$

For example, for $k = 3$, $(7,\ 2,\ 1) \succ (7,\ 0,\ 45)$. It is easy to show that the domain $(\mathbb{N}^k, \succ)$ is well-founded.

It is possible to make lexicographic comparisons between tuples of integers of different lengths. The convention is that the relation holding between $(a_1, \ldots, a_i)$ and $(b_1, \ldots, b_k)$ for $i < k$ is determined by lexicographically comparing $(a_1, \ldots, a_i, 0, \ldots, 0)$ to $(b_1, \ldots, b_i, b_{i+1}, \ldots, b_k)$. That is, we pad the shorter tuple by zeros on the right until it assumes the length of the longer tuple. According to this definition, $(0,\ 2) \succ 0$, since $(0,\ 2) \succ (0,\ 0)$. In a similar way, $1 \succ (0,\ 2)$.

Rule CB-WELL

In Fig. 10, we present the *clock-bounded well-founded response rule* (rule CB-WELL) for proving response properties of clocked transition systems. The rule uses auxiliary assertions $\varphi_1, \ldots, \varphi_m$ and refers to assertion q also as φ_0. With each assertion φ_i, $i > 0$, we associate one of the clocks $c_i \in C$, to which we refer as the *helpful clock*, and an upper bound B_i, which is a real-valued expression. Also required are a well-founded domain $(\mathcal{A}, \succ)$, and ranking functions $\delta_i\colon\ \Sigma \mapsto$

For assertions p, q, and $\varphi_0 = q, \varphi_1, \ldots, \varphi_m$,
clocks $c_1, \ldots, c_m \in C$,
real expressions $B_1, \ldots, B_m \in \mathrm{R}$,
a well-founded domain $(\mathcal{A}, \succ)$, and
ranking functions $\delta_1, \ldots, \delta_m \colon \Sigma \mapsto \mathcal{A}$,

$$\text{W1.} \quad p \rightarrow \bigvee_{j=0}^{m} \varphi_j$$

The following two premises hold for $i = 1, \ldots, m$

$$\text{W2.} \quad \rho_\tau \wedge \varphi_i \rightarrow \bigvee_{j=0}^{m} (\varphi_j' \wedge \delta_i \succ \delta_j') \vee (\varphi_i' \wedge \delta_i' = \delta_i \wedge c_i \leq c_i' \wedge B_i' \leq B_i) \quad \text{for every } \tau \in \mathcal{T}_T$$

$$\text{W3.} \quad \varphi_i \rightarrow c_i \leq B_i$$

$$p \Rightarrow \Diamond q$$

Fig. 10. Rule CB-WELL (clock-bounded well-founded rule for response).

$\mathcal{A}$, $i = 1, \ldots, m$, mapping states of the system to elements of $\mathcal{A}$. The ranking functions measure progress of the computation towards the goal q.

Premise W1 requires that every p-position satisfies one of $\varphi_0 = q, \varphi_1, \ldots, \varphi_m$.

Premise W2 requires that every τ-successor (for any $\tau \in \mathcal{T}_T$) of a φ_i-state s is a φ_j-state for some j, with a rank δ_j' not exceeding δ_i. In the case that the successor state satisfies φ_i, it is allowed that $\delta_i' = \delta_i$ but is required that the transition does not decrease the value of c_i or increase the value of B_i. In all other cases it is required that $\delta_j' \prec \delta_i$, i.e., that the rank strictly decreases.

Premise W3 requires that assertion φ_i implies that c_i is bounded by the expression B_i.

The following claim states the soundness of the rule:

Claim 5 *Rule* CB-WELL *is sound for proving that a response formula is Φ-valid.*

Justification: Assume that the premises of the rule are Φ-valid, and let σ be a computation of Φ. We will show that σ satisfies the rule's consequence

$$p \Rightarrow \Diamond q.$$

Assume that p holds at position k and no later position $i \geq k$ satisfies q. By W1 some φ_j must hold at position k. Let $u_k \in \mathcal{A}$ be the minimal rank of state s_k, i.e. the minimal value of $\delta_j(s_k)$ among all φ_j which hold at s_k. Thus, $u_k = \delta_{j_k}(s_k)$, which implies that φ_{j_k} holds at s_k.

By W2, state s_{k+1} must satisfy φ_j for some $j > 0$, implying that s_{k+1} has a defined rank u_{k+1}. Premise W2 requires that $u_{k+1} \preceq u_k$.

proceeding in this manner we obtain that every position i beyond k has a rank u_i, such that

$$u_k \succeq u_{k+1} \succeq u_{k+2} \succeq \cdots .$$

Since $\mathcal{A}$ is well-founded, there must exist a position $r \geq k$ such that

$$u_r = u_{r+1} = u_{r+2} = \cdots .$$

Denote the value of this eventually-stable rank by $u = u_r$, and let $j_r > 0$ be the index of the assertion such that $\delta_{j_r}(s_r) = u$. Since the rank never decreases beyond r, all states beyond this position satisfy φ_{j_r}, and the value of c_{j_r} never decreases.

Consider the value of the expression $B_{j_r} - c_{j_r}$ at states s_i, $i \geq r$. By W3, this expression is always non-negative. By W2, its value never increases. Also, whenever a *tick* transition with increment Δ is taken, c_{j_r} increases (as do all clocks) by Δ. Since B_{j_r} does not increase (by W2 and the assumption that the rank remains the same), the value of $B_{j_r} - c_{j_r}$ decreases by Δ in such a *tick* transition. It follows that the master clock T cannot increase by more than $s_r[B_{j_r} - c_{j_r}]$[4] from its value at state s_r. This contradicts the fact that σ is a computation in which the master clock increases beyond all bounds.

We conclude that our assumption of the existence of a p-position not followed by any q-position is false. Consequently, if the premises of the rule hold then every p-position must be followed by a q-position, establishing the consequence of the rule. ■

Claim 6 *Rule* CB-WELL *is complete for proving that a response formula is valid over a non-zeno system Φ.*

Justification (A sketch): The meaning of this claim is that if the response formula $p \Rightarrow \Diamond q$ is valid over the non-zeno system Φ, then there exist constructs as required by rule CB-WELL, such that all premises of the rule are Φ-state valid.

An execution segment σ is called *q-free* if no state in σ satisfies q. A state s' is said to be a *¬q-follower* of state s if there is a q-free Φ-execution segment leading from s to s'. We follow the techniques of [MP91a] and take for (a single) φ the assertion $pending_q$, constructed in such a way that

$s \models pending_q$ iff s is a $\neg q$-follower of a Φ-accessible p-state.

We define a binary relation $\sqsupset$ such that $s \sqsupset s'$ if s satisfies $pending_q$, s' is a $\neg q$-follower of s, and $s'[T] \geq s[T] + 1$. Obviously, $\sqsupset$ is well-founded, because an infinite sequence $s_0 \sqsupset s_1 \sqsupset s_2 \sqsupset \cdots$ would lead to a computation violating $p \Rightarrow \Diamond q$.

Based on a transcendentally inductive construction, we can define a ranking function $\delta: \Sigma \mapsto \mathcal{O}rd$, mapping states into the ordinals, such that

O1. If s' is a $\neg q$-follower of the $pending_q$-state s, then $\delta(s) \geq \delta(s')$.
O2. If $s \sqsupset s'$, where s is a $pending_q$-state, then $\delta(s) > \delta(s')$.

[4] The value of $B_{j_r} - c_{j_r}$ at state s_r

x, y: **integer where** $x = y = 0$

$$\left[\begin{array}{l} \ell_0 : \textbf{while } x = 0 \textbf{ do} \\ \quad \ell_1 : \; y := y + 1 \\ \ell_2 : \textbf{while } y > 0 \textbf{ do} \\ \quad \ell_3 : \; y := y - 1 \\ \ell_4 : \end{array}\right] \;\Big\|\; \left[\begin{array}{l} m_0 : x := 1 \\ m_1 : \end{array}\right]$$

$- \; P_1 \; -$ $\qquad$ $- \; P_2 \; -$

Fig. 11. Program UP-DOWN.

Given a pending state s, let $B(s)$ denote the supremum of all values $s'[T]$ where s' is a $\neg q$-follower of s and $\delta(s') = \delta(s)$. Due to property O2, this supremum exists and is bounded by $s[T] + 1$. It can now be shown that all premises of rule CB-WELL hold for the choice of $m = 1$, $\varphi_1 = pending_q$, $c_1 = T$, $B_1 = B(s)$, $(\mathcal{A}, \succ) = (\mathcal{O}rd, >)$, and $\delta_1 = \delta$ as defined above.

A fuller version of this proof is presented in [KMP95]. ▲

The following example illustrates an application of rule CB-WELL.

Example 8. Consider program UP-DOWN presented in Fig. 11.

This program can be viewed as a generalization of program ANY-Y in which, after terminating the while loop at ℓ_0, ℓ_1, process P_1 proceeds to perform a second while loop at ℓ_2, ℓ_3, decrementing y until it reaches 0.

Assume, we assign the uniform time bounds $[L, U]$ to all executable statements of program UP-DOWN, where our only information about L and U is given by

$0 \leq L < U < \infty$.

We use rule CB-WELL to verify that program UP-DOWN terminates. This property can be expressed by the response formula

$$\underbrace{(at\_\ell_0 \wedge at\_m_0 \wedge x = y = t_1 = t_2 = T = 0)}_{p} \quad \Rightarrow \quad \Diamond\underbrace{(at\_\ell_4 \wedge at\_m_1)}_{q}.$$

As the well-founded domain, we take $(\mathbb{N}^2, \succ)$, i.e., the domain of lexicographic pairs. As time bounds, we use B_i: U for all $i = 1, \ldots, 5$. The auxiliary assertions, helpful clocks, and ranking functions are given by the following table:

φ_0: $at\_\ell_4 \wedge at\_m_1$ $\qquad$ δ_0: 0

φ_1: $at\_\ell_3 \wedge at\_m_1 \wedge x = 1 \wedge y > 0 \wedge t_1 \leq U$ $\qquad$ c_1: t_1 $\qquad$ δ_1: $(1, 2y)$

φ_2: $at\_\ell_2 \wedge at\_m_1 \wedge x = 1 \wedge y \geq 0 \wedge t_1 \leq U$ $\qquad$ c_2: t_1 $\qquad$ δ_2: $(1, 2y + 1)$

φ_3: $at\_\ell_0 \wedge at\_m_1 \wedge x = 1 \wedge y \geq 0 \wedge t_1 \leq U$ $\qquad$ c_3: t_1 $\qquad$ δ_3: 2

φ_4: $at\_\ell_1 \wedge at\_m_1 \wedge x = 1 \wedge y \geq 0 \wedge t_1 \leq U$ $\qquad$ c_4: t_1 $\qquad$ δ_4: 3

φ_5: $at\_\ell_{0,1} \wedge at\_m_0 \wedge x = 0 \wedge y \geq 0 \wedge t_1 \leq U \wedge t_2 \leq U$
$\qquad$ c_5: t_2 $\qquad$ δ_5: 4

It can be shown that all premises of rule CB-WELL are state valid. This establishes that the response property

$$(at\_\ell_0 \wedge at\_m_0 \wedge x = y = t_1 = t_2 = T = 0) \quad \Rightarrow \quad \Diamond(at\_\ell_4 \wedge at\_m_1).$$

is valid over program UP-DOWN. ▲

5.4 Ranked Diagrams

The main ingredients of a proof by rule CB-WELL can be conveniently and effectively presented by a special type of verification diagrams that summarizes the auxiliary assertions, their helpful clocks and bounds, and their ranking functions, and display the possible transitions between the assertions.

We define a *ranked diagram* to be a directed labeled graph constructed as follows:

- *Nodes* in the graph are labeled by assertions. Each node is labeled by a pair of assertions: ϕ_i and β_i, for $i = 0, \ldots, m$, and a ranking function δ_i. The assertion β_i has the form $c_i \leq B_i$, where $c_i \in C$ is a clock and B_i is a real-valued expression. We refer to the conjunction $\phi_i \wedge \beta_i$ as φ_i, and say that the node is labeled by the (combined) assertion φ_i. We often refer to nodes by the assertion φ_i labeling them.
  The node labeled by φ_0 is called the *terminal node* and is graphically identified by being drawn with bold-face boundaries.
- *Edges* in the graph represent transitions between assertions. Each edge is labeled by one or more transitions.

Verification Conditions Implied by a Ranked Diagram

Consider a nonterminal node labeled by assertion φ: $\phi \wedge \beta$ where the clock-bound assertion is β: $c \leq B$ and the ranking function is δ. Let $\tau \in \mathcal{T}_T$ be a transition and let $\varphi_1, \ldots, \varphi_k$, $k \geq 0$, be the successors of φ by edges labeled with τ (possibly including φ itself). With each such node and transition, we associate the following verification condition:

$$\begin{aligned}\rho_\tau \wedge \varphi \quad \rightarrow \quad & (\varphi' \wedge \delta' = \delta \wedge c \leq c' \leq B' \leq B) \vee (\varphi' \wedge \delta \succ \delta') \vee \\ & (\varphi_1' \wedge \delta \succ \delta_1') \vee \cdots \vee (\varphi_k' \wedge \delta \succ \delta_k').\end{aligned}$$

In particular, if $k = 0$ (i.e., φ has no τ-successors), the associated verification condition is

$$\rho_\tau \wedge \varphi \quad \rightarrow \quad (\varphi' \wedge \delta' = \delta \wedge c \leq c' \leq B' \leq B) \vee (\varphi' \wedge \delta \succ \delta').$$

Valid Ranked Diagrams

A ranked diagram is said to be *valid over* CTS Φ (Φ*-valid* for short) if all the verification conditions associated with the diagram are Φ-state valid.

The consequences of having a valid ranked diagram are stated in the following claim:

Claim 7 *A Φ-valid ranked diagram with nodes $\varphi_0, \ldots, \varphi_m$, establishes*

$$\Phi \quad \models \quad \bigvee_{j=0}^{m} \varphi_j \quad \Rightarrow \quad \Diamond \varphi_0.$$

If, in addition, $\varphi_0 = q$ *and*

$$\text{W1:} \quad \Phi \quad \Vdash \quad p \quad \rightarrow \quad \bigvee_{j=0}^{m} \varphi_j,$$

then we can conclude:

$$\Phi \quad \models \quad p \quad \Rightarrow \quad \Diamond q.$$

Example 9. In Fig. 12, we present a ranked diagram which establishes that the response property

$$(at\_\ell_0 \wedge at\_m_0 \wedge x = y = t_1 = t_2 = T = 0) \quad \Rightarrow \quad \Diamond(at\_\ell_4 \wedge at\_m_1).$$

is valid over program UP-DOWN. ▟

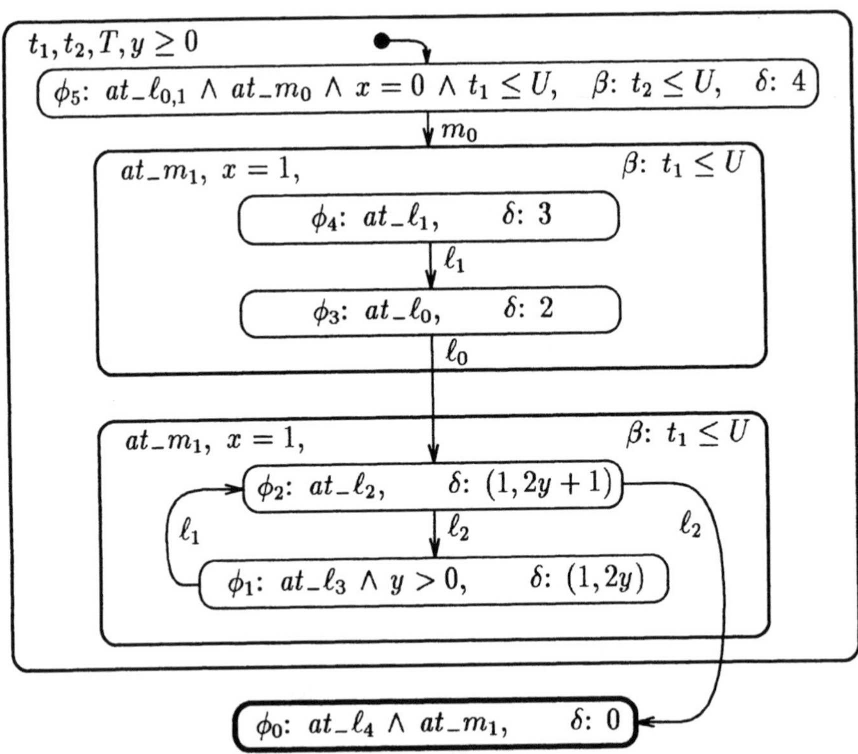

Fig. 12. A ranked diagram, establishing the formula $(at\_\ell_0 \wedge at\_m_0 \wedge x = y = t_1 = t_2 = T = 0) \quad \Rightarrow \quad \Diamond(at\_\ell_4 \wedge at\_m_1)$

5.5 From Waiting-for to Response Properties

In many useful cases, we can infer response formulas from a waiting-for formula of a particular form.

Rule W→R, presented in Fig. 13, infers a response formula from a waiting-for formula of a special form.

For assertions p, q, and r, and rigid expression B,
$p \;\Rightarrow\; (q \land T \leq B)\,\mathcal{W}\,r$
$p \;\Rightarrow\; \Diamond r$

Fig. 13. Rule W→R (from waiting-for to response formulas).

Justification: Assume that the waiting-for premise is Φ-valid. Consider a Φ-computation σ, and a p-position $j \geq 0$ in σ. By the waiting-for formula, j initiates an interval, all of whose positions satisfy $q \land T \leq B$, which either extends to infinity or is terminated by an r-position. Since σ is a computation, T must grow beyond all values and cannot remain bounded by $a + b$ ($T \leq B$ is equivalent to $T \leq a + b$) at all positions. It follows that j must be followed by an r-position. ▪

Example 10. Consider the SPL$_T$ program UP-DOWN$_{[1,5]}$, which is program UP-DOWN with time bounds [1,5] uniformly assigned to all executable statements.

We use rule W→R to verify that the response formula

$$(at\_\ell_0 \land at\_m_0 \land x = y = T = 0) \quad\Rightarrow\quad \Diamond(at\_\ell_4 \land at\_m_1 \land T \leq 50)$$

is valid over program UP-DOWN$_{[1,5]}$.

In Fig. 14, we present a waiting diagram which establishes the UP-DOWN$_{[1,5]}$-validity of the waiting-for formula

$$(at\_\ell_0 \land at\_m_0 \land x = y = T = 0) \quad\Rightarrow\quad (T \leq 50)\,\mathcal{W}\,(at\_\ell_4 \land at\_m_1 \land T \leq 50)$$

Note that the assertion describing the initial state does not specify initial values for either t_1 or t_2. To show that the waiting diagram is valid, we rely on the following invariant:

$$\Box((at\_\ell_0 \;\rightarrow\; 0 \leq t_1 \leq 5) \land (at\_m_0 \;\rightarrow\; 0 \leq t_2 \leq 5)).$$

This invariant can be separately established, using the methods of Section 4. ▪

5.6 Are Rules CB-CHAIN and CB-WELL Really Necessary?

Rule W→R enables the derivation of a response property from a timed waiting-for property, which can be established using rule WAIT. Rule WAIT (and its equivalent formulation in terms of waiting diagrams) is, in principle, simpler than either rule CB-CHAIN or rule CB-WELL, because it does not require the identification of explicit time bounds or ranking functions as auxiliary constructs.

In view of this, a naturally rising question is why do we need the response-specific rules CB-CHAIN and CB-WELL. Isn't rule W→R adequate for establishing all response properties of interest?

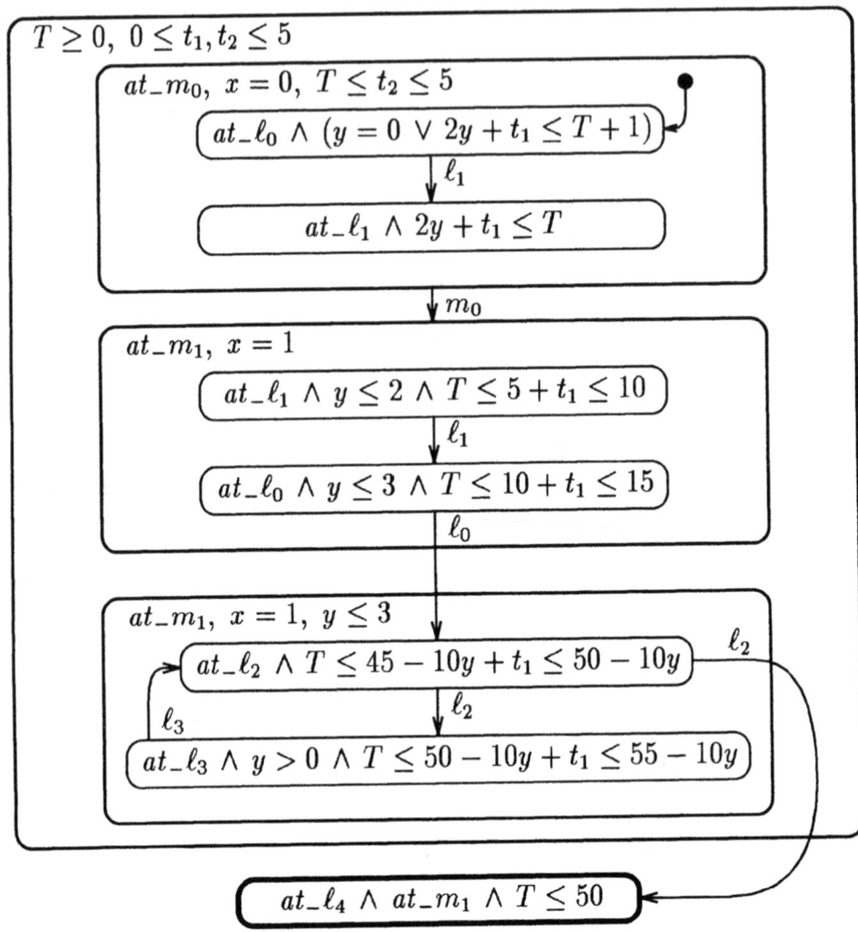

Fig. 14. A waiting diagram, establishing the formula
$(at\_\ell_0 \wedge at\_m_0 \wedge x = y = T = 0) \quad \Rightarrow \quad (T \leq 50)\, \mathcal{W}\, (at\_\ell_4 \wedge at\_m_1 \wedge T \leq 50)$

We provide two answers to this question. The first answer is that there are some response properties that cannot be established through timed waiting-for properties.

To support this point, consider again program UP-DOWN but with general (uniform) time bounds, $[L, U]$, such that $0 \leq L \leq U < \infty$. For all cases that $L > 0$, we can essentially repeat the analysis done in Example 10, and establish the waiting-for formula

$$(at\_\ell_0 \wedge at\_m_0 \wedge x = y = T = 0) \quad \Rightarrow \quad (T \leq B)\, \mathcal{W}\, (at\_\ell_4 \wedge at\_m_1 \wedge T \leq B),$$

where

$$B = (6 + 2 \left\lfloor \frac{U}{2L} \right\rfloor) U.$$

Applying rule W→R to this formula, one can infer the response formula

$$(at\_\ell_0 \wedge at\_m_0 \wedge x = y = T = 0) \quad \Rightarrow \quad \Diamond(at\_\ell_4 \wedge at\_m_1 \wedge T \leq B),$$

guaranteeing termination within B time units.

One can see that as L gets closer to 0, the bound on termination time gets larger. It is therefore not surprising that when $L = 0$, there is no bound on the time it takes the program to terminate. Yet, all computations of this program eventually lead to the termination state at_ℓ_4. Thus, termination of program UP-DOWN in the case of $L = 0$ is a response property that cannot be verified using rule W→R. On the other hand, in Example 8, we established termination of UP-DOWN, using rule CB-WELL, in a proof that is valid for all $L \geq 0$. This illustrates the case of a response property that cannot be proven by rule W→R, but is provable by rule CB-WELL.

As the second answer justifying the introduction of rule CB-WELL, we propose to compare the verification diagram of Fig. 12 with that of Fig. 14, both establishing termination of UP-DOWN for the time bounds $[1, 5]$ (Fig. 12 actually established it for general $[L, U]$). It is obvious that diagram 14 require a much more detailed analysis of the precise time interval which we can spend at each of the diagram nodes. In comparison, the diagram of Fig. 12 said very little about these time intervals: the only timing information included in this diagram was that the time spent at each of the nodes is bounded by U. Thus, when we need or are ready to conduct a very precise analysis of the time intervals spent at each node, it makes sense to use waiting diagrams and rule W→R. If, on the other hand, we are content with less quantitative analysis, and are only interested in the qualitative fact that *eventually* q will occur (which is the essence of the $\Diamond$ temporal operator), we may use rule CB-WELL or rule CB-CHAIN. These rules may be conceptually more complicated than rule WAIT, but their application calls for a simpler analysis of the program.

Acknowledgment

We gratefully acknowledge the careful reading and critical comments of Oded Maler, Henny Sipma, and Tomás Uribe.

References

[AD94] R. Alur and D.L. Dill. A theory of timed automata. *Theor. Comp. Sci.*, 126:183–235, 1994.

[AH89] R. Alur and T.A. Henzinger. A really temporal logic. In *Proc. 30th IEEE Symp. Found. of Comp. Sci.*, pages 164–169, 1989.

[AH92] R. Alur and T. Henzinger. Logics and models of real time: A survey. In J.W. de Bakker, C. Huizing, W.P. de Roever, and G. Rozenberg, editors, *Proceedings of the REX Workshop "Real-Time: Theory in Practice"*, volume 600 of *Lect. Notes in Comp. Sci.*, pages 74–106. Springer-Verlag, 1992.

[AH94] R. Alur and T.A. Henzinger. Real-time system = discrete system + clock variables. In T. Rus and C. Rattray, editors, *Theories and Experiences for*

Real-time System Development, AMAST Series in Computing 2, pages 1–29. World Scientific, 1994.

[AL94] M. Abadi and L. Lamport. An old-fashioned recipe for real time. *ACM Trans. Prog. Lang. Sys.*, 16(5):1543–1571, 1994.

[Hen92] T.A. Henzinger. Sooner is safer than later. *Info. Proc. Lett.*, 43(3):135–142, 1992.

[HK94] T.A. Henzinger and P.W. Kopke. Verification methods for the divergent runs of clock systems. In H. Langmaack, W.-P. de Roever, and J. Vytopil, editors, *FTRTFT 94: Formal Techniques in Real-time and Fault-tolerant Systems*, Lecture Notes in Computer Science 863, pages 351–372. Springer-Verlag, 1994.

[HMP94] T. Henzinger, Z. Manna, and A. Pnueli. Temporal proof methodologies for timed transition systems. *Inf. and Comp.*, 112(2):273–337, 1994.

[KdR85] R. Koymans and W.-P. de Roever. Examples of a real-time temporal logic specifications. In B.D. Denvir, W.T. Harwood, M.I. Jackson, and M.J. Wray, editors, *The Analysis of Concurrent Systems*, volume 207 of *Lect. Notes in Comp. Sci.*, pages 231–252. Springer-Verlag, 1985.

[KMP95] Y. Kesten, Z. Manna, and A. Pnueli. Clocked transition systems. Technical report, Dept. of Comp. Sci., Stanford University, 1995.

[Koy90] R. Koymans. Specifying real-time properties with metric temporal logic. *Real-time Systems*, 2(4):255–299, 1990.

[KVdR83] R. Koymans, J. Vytopyl, and W.-P. de Roever. Real-time programming and asynchronous message passing. In *Proc. 2nd ACM Symp. Princ. of Dist. Comp.*, pages 187–197, 1983.

[MP91a] Z. Manna and A. Pnueli. Completing the temporal picture. *Theor. Comp. Sci.*, 83(1):97–130, 1991.

[MP91b] Z. Manna and A. Pnueli. *The Temporal Logic of Reactive and Concurrent Systems: Specification.* Springer-Verlag, New York, 1991.

[MP93] Z. Manna and A. Pnueli. Models for reactivity. *Acta Informatica*, 30:609–678, 1993.

[MP94] Z. Manna and A. Pnueli. Temporal verification diagrams. In T. Ito and A. R. Meyer, editors, *Theoretical Aspects of Computer Software*, volume 789 of *Lect. Notes in Comp. Sci.*, pages 726–765. Springer-Verlag, 1994.

[MP95] Z. Manna and A. Pnueli. *Temporal Verification of Reactive Systems: Safety.* Springer-Verlag, New York, 1995.

[MT90] F. Moller and C. Tofts. A temporal calculus of communicating systems. In J.C.M. Baeten and J.W. Klop, editors, *Proceedings of Concur'90*, volume 458 of *Lect. Notes in Comp. Sci.*, pages 401–415. Springer-Verlag, 1990.

[NSY92] X. Nicollin, J. Sifakis, and S. Yovine. From ATP to timed graphs and hybrid systems. In J.W. de Bakker, C. Huizing, W.P. de Roever, and G. Rozenberg, editors, *Proceedings of the REX Workshop "Real-Time: Theory in Practice"*, volume 600 of *Lect. Notes in Comp. Sci.*, pages 549–572. Springer-Verlag, 1992.

[Ost90] J.S. Ostroff. *Temporal Logic of Real-Time Systems.* Advanced Software Development Series. Research Studies Press (John Wiley & Sons), Taunton, England, 1990.

[Sif91] J. Sifakis. An overview and synthesis on timed process algebra. In K.G. Larsen and A. Skou, editors, *3rd Computer Aided Verification Workshop*, volume 575 of *Lect. Notes in Comp. Sci.*, pages 376–398. Springer-Verlag, 1991.

Compositional and Uniform Modelling of Hybrid Systems *

Albert Benveniste[1]

IRISA-INRIA, Campus de Beaulieu, 35042 Rennes cedex, France; benveniste@irisa.fr

1 Motivation and Introduction

Hybrid Systems have been a topic of growing interest and activity in the recent years. It is our opinion that relevant real-life applications of hybrid systems paradigm mainly consist of very large, complex, distributed, systems. A good example might be air traffic control, or, more generally, transportation systems. For such systems, *modularity* in modelling, simulation, control design, and verification, is mandatory. Object oriented approaches are often considered today as suitable for this purpose, but they are not supported by a clean mathematical semantics of the behaviours of systems and programs. Another case is that of modelling complex physical systems governed by some balance equations (electricity, flow, thermodynamics,...). For such systems, bond graphs [3, 5] have become popular, hybrid extensions in the form of "switch" bond graphs have been proposed [4]. The key point to notice here is that modelling is naturally performed via subsystems interacting in continuous time. Our final example is that of the VHDLA language, an extension of VHDL originally designed for hybrid hardware, and also experimented on hybrid systems modelling in areas such as electromechanics, etc...

This short overview reveals the following requirements for a hybrid systems paradigm: discrete and continuous features closely interplay, both should be handled in a uniform way, in particular as for compositionality is concerned.

As a starting point, let us discuss the issue of modularity for continuous time systems. Ordinary Differential Equations (ODE) of the form " $\dot{x} = f(x,u)$ ", in which inputs and outputs are considered, do not compose. For instance, the composition of $\dot{x} = f(x,u)$ and $\dot{x} = g(x,u)$ degenerates to the single algebraic constraint $f(x,u) = g(x,u)$, which is not an ODE any more. It is wellknown today in numerical analysis that the right framework toward compositionality is that of Differential Algebraic Equations (DAE) of the form " $F(z,\dot{z}) = 0$ ", in which z collects all variables. Thus DAE model "balance equations" such as frequently inherited from physics (electricity, mechanics, thermodynamics,...). Clearly, DAE compose.

Let us discuss next the most commonly accepted model today of a hybrid system [1]. According to this model, a hybrid system is a continuous time dynamical system having persistent phases and instantaneous transitions occurring

* This work has been supported in part by NSF/ESPRIT grant Nr. EC-US-043.

at a divergent sequence of instants. Such a triple

$$\boxed{\text{phase}} \xrightarrow[\text{transition}]{} \boxed{\text{new phase}} \tag{1}$$

is shown below ($\dot{x}$ denotes the time derivative of function $x(t)$, and u, a function of time, is the exogeneous control) :

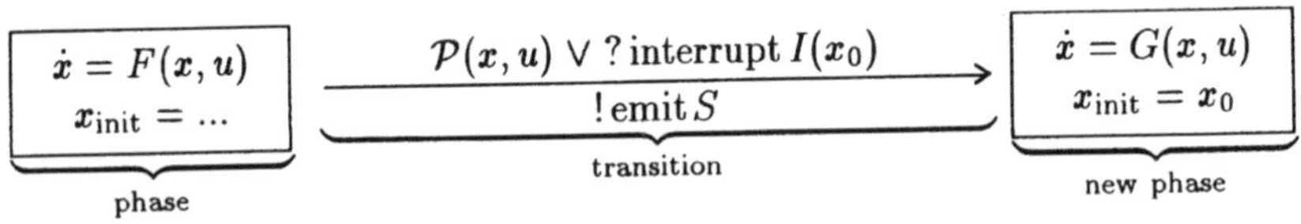

Thus, phases are characterized by constraints on continuous trajectories — expressed here in the form of differential equations. Transitions are triggered either by *guards,* i.e., predicates on state variables ($\mathcal{P}(x, u)$), or by external interrupts possibly carrying reset values for the new phase (? interrupt $I(x_0)$). Transitions can output signals of any type (bool, integer, real,... : ! emit S). Here follow some features of this model:

- it is a continuous time systems model, its time index is global and unique, and is $\mathbf{R}_+ = [0, +\infty)$,
- discrete time "timers" occur in the form of the various sequences of "interrupts" or "emit" events,
- events trigger transitions, hence they are the vehicle for switching from one continuous behaviour to another one,
- continuous behaviours in turn can create events (by testing guards over continuous time state variables), this is the mechanism for creating discrete time from continuous time,

!! such systems can be composed only via their discrete parts [2] : discrete signals and events are the only vehicle for systems interaction ; in contrast, continuous state variables are local. At least, ODE specifying phases cannot be freely combined.

It is a major objective of this paper to provide a framework for hybrid systems in which continuous and discrete parts are handled in a uniform way including system composition and hierarchy.

2 A General Hybrid Systems Model

2.1 Motivations

Recall we want a framework for hybrid systems in which continuous and discrete parts are handled in a uniform way including system composition. In addition,

[2] There is one exception I know, namely the work [8] in which continuous time boolean automata with latency constraints are considered. Interaction can hold in continuous time, but the approach uses the fact that data types are finite.

we would like to provide multiform time, let me discuss this. For discrete time, it has been argued in [2] that counting seconds, or meters, or events of any kind, should be handled in a uniform way : this is the motivation for considering time as a *multiform, logical* notion, not as a physical and rigid one. Similarly, for continuous time mechanical systems such as robot arms, it is convenient to play with different "time variables" : physical time (of course), but also so-called generalized coordinates (e.g., angular position in robots, etc...). Thus, multiform time and change of variable in differential equations is also useful in continuous time.

Thus we shall provide a new concept of *multiform* and *logical* time for hybrid systems, which can be both discrete or continuous. We shall provide means to express constraints relating different times (e.g., distance = physical time × velocity), or inequalities (e.g., a given time is "less frequent", or "slower" than another one). All such relations we want to express will not depend on the particular "physical unit" used to measure time: it can be seconds, hours, meters, it can even be a time-varying unit provided by a jittering watch, all above listed relations will remain unchanged.

Another problem related to time is that of modularity and compositionality of our model. If we want full compositionality, time must be bound to each particular module, not to a global program, since the notion of a global program does not fit compositionality — any "global" program can be further combined with another one, thus becoming a component. This raises an issue similar to what happens for discrete time in synchronous languages [7]. In particular, presence/absence cannot be encoded via boolean signals since these are not symmetric notions: presence can be directly observed, but absence is observed relatively to some given environment.

The above remarks motivate our hybrid systems model we describe now.

2.2 Primitives

Time Our time index set is $\mathbf{R} = (-\infty, +\infty)$ viewed as a totally ordered dense and continuous set, we also write $\overline{\mathbf{R}} = [-\infty, +\infty]$. This choice only specifies that we work with a continuous, totally ordered, and one-dimensional time. It does not imply, however, that we are bound to a single time t, as we shall see later.

Presences Time will be used as index set for signals, or for "task activation" (we do not define formally what we mean by a task here). Time index sets can be assigned to each signal. Time index sets will be referred to in the sequel as "*presences*". We want to handle both discrete and continuous time in a uniform way. There are two most typical and useful kinds of presence for systems :

- Discrete presences (i.e., presences that are finite or divergent sequences), they model discrete time [3].

[3] For those who know, this is equivalent to the notion of *clock* as used in SIGNAL [7].

- Phases, are used in hybrid automata, or to activate continuous time tasks, they consist of sequences of disjoint nonempty intervals, say for instance, left closed and right open : $[s_1, t_1) \cup [s_2, t_2) \cup \ldots$, in which $t_n < s_{n+1}$.

A point to notice is that we do not consider presences starting from $-\infty$, this means that signals or tasks do not exist since ever in the past. Thus, if $\mathcal{T}$ is a presence, the complement of $\mathcal{T}$ in $\mathbf{R}$ cannot be a presence, so we cannot encode presences as $\mathbf{R}$-indexed booleans signals. On the other hand, the following operations on presences will be useful : union, intersection, and set difference.

From the above discussion the following definition emerges : a *presence* is any Borel subset $\mathcal{T}$ of $\mathbf{R}$ such that $\mathcal{T} \cap (-\infty, x) = \emptyset$ for some finite x [4]. The family of presences are equipped with the following set theoretic operations, namely : union, intersection, and set difference.

As an example of use of such relations, pick a phase $\mathcal{T}$ and a discrete presence (i.e., a "clock") H. The constraint $H \subset \mathcal{T}$ expresses that instants of clock H must occur during phase $\mathcal{T}$, but can do so any time during $\mathcal{T}$.

Signals A *signal* is a map

$$X \quad : \mathcal{T}_X \mapsto D_X, \text{ written } t \mapsto X_t \tag{2}$$

where $\mathcal{T}_X$ is a presence (the presence of X), D_X is some topological space, the *type* of X, and map $t \mapsto X_t$ is *piecewise continuous*. Thus signals are partial functions of time, whose domain we call a "presence". Signals will be used to model trajectories, both discrete or continuous time.

Delaying signals If X is a signal with presence $\mathcal{T}_X$, we define its delayed version : $Y = \mathbf{pre}(X)$ **init** x_0, by setting :

$$\mathcal{T}_Y = \mathcal{T}_X = \mathcal{T}, \quad \forall t \in \mathcal{T} \; : \; Y_t = \begin{cases} X_{t_-} \text{ if } \mathcal{T} \cap (-\infty, t) \neq \emptyset \\ x_0 \text{ if otherwise,} \end{cases} \tag{3}$$

where X_{t_-} is the left limit of X at t, defined as follows. Let t_- denote the upper boundary of the set $\mathcal{T} \cap (-\infty, t)$. Thus if there are $s \in \mathcal{T}, s < t$ that are arbitrarily close to t, then simply $t_- = t$. In the other hand, if the distance from t to $\mathcal{T} \cap (-\infty, t)$ is strictly positive, then t_- equals the largest instant of $\mathcal{T} \cap (-\infty, t)$. Then we define

$$X_{t_-} = \lim_{s \in \mathcal{T}, s < t, s \nearrow t_-} X_s \; .$$

Also, x_0 is an initial condition required when t is the initial instant of $\mathcal{T}$. See Figure 1 for an illustration of our notion of a delay.

[4] The reader not willing to bother with technicalities can discard the "Borel" assumption. Note however that we cannot restrict ourselves to open sets (we would not get discrete time), or alternatively to closed sets (we would not get phases), and we require that the family of presences is invariant under union, intersection, and set difference.

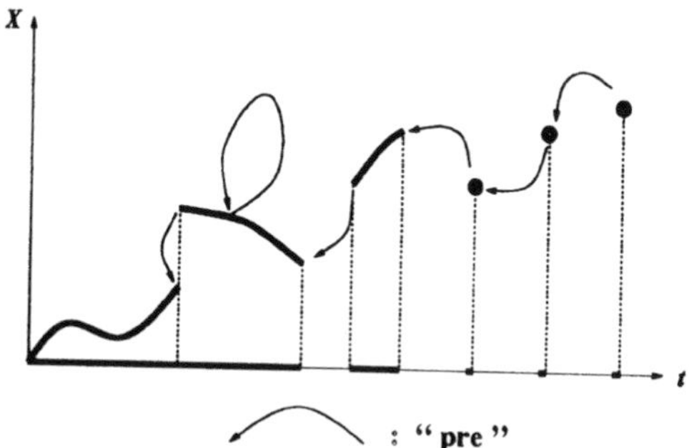

Fig. 1. *The delay operator.* For selected instants t, the backward arrow indicates which value is taken as a definition of $\mathbf{pre}(X)$ **init** x_0. For isolated t points, the previous value is taken and our delay operator behaves like a shift register. For points t in the interior of the presence of X, our delay delivers the value of X "just prior" to t.

In particular, if t lies in the interior of $\mathcal{T}$ and signal X has continuous trajectories in the interior of $\mathcal{T}$, then $X_{t_-} = X_t$ thus our delay operator is just the identity and is not very useful. Otherwise, if t lies in the interior of $\mathcal{T}$ but signal X has discontinuities [5] then $\mathbf{pre}(X)$ **init** x_0 delivers the left limits of X.

Finally, and this is the most likely use of this delay operator, if X has discrete and divergent presence $\mathcal{T}_X = \{s_1, s_2, ...\}$, then its delayed version $Y = \mathbf{pre}(X)$ **init** x_0 is equal to

$$\mathcal{T}_Y = \mathcal{T}_X, \quad Y_{s_k} = \begin{cases} X_{s_{k-1}} \text{ if } k > 1 \\ x_0 \text{ if } k = 1 \end{cases} \tag{4}$$

thus "$\mathbf{pre}(X)$ **init** x_0" is a shift register, and coincides with the SIGNAL delay operator denoted "$".

NOTA : We do not provide continuous time delays. Delaying in continuous time cannot be regular (in the sense of regular vs. nonregular languages). For instance, the delay-differential equation $\dot{x}_t = f(x_{t-\delta})$ where δ is a real delay, requires unbounded dimension for its simulation when accuracy is increased. Similarly, equation $y_t = f(x_{t-\delta})$ requires unbounded memory, unless x has finite domain. Also, for "continuous time" signals, our delay operator is the limit of the discretized delay operator when the discretization step converges to zero.

Pointwise constraints on signals Pick two signals X, Y with presences $\mathcal{T}_X$ and $\mathcal{T}_Y$ respectively. Let $\mathcal{T}$ be a presence. Let $C \subset D_X \times D_Y$ be a constraint defined on the types of X, Y. We shall say that signals (X, Y) satisfy the constraint

$$\text{on } \mathcal{T} : C(X, Y) \tag{5}$$

[5] Recall we only require signals to be piecewise continuous.

if

$$C(X_t, Y_t) \ \text{holds} \ \forall t \in \mathcal{T} , \tag{6}$$

this requires in particular that the involved signals are present at each instant of $\mathcal{T}$:

$$\mathcal{T} \subseteq \mathcal{T}_X \cap \mathcal{T}_Y . \tag{7}$$

An interesting particular case is

$$\text{on } \mathcal{T} : Y = f(X) \tag{8}$$

where f is a function.

Differential equations (ODE,DAE) In this subsection, we shall consider signals X of type real, with presence $\mathcal{T}_X$ which we assume to be an open set, such that $t \in \mathcal{T}_X, t \mapsto X_t$ is *differentiable*, we denote by $\dot{X}$ this derivative. Pick two such signals X, Y with presences $\mathcal{T}_X$ and $\mathcal{T}_Y$ respectively. Let $\mathcal{T}$ be an open presence. We shall say that X is a solution of the differential equation

$$\text{on } \mathcal{T} : \frac{dX}{dY} = g(X, Y) \tag{9}$$

if

$$\frac{\dot{X}_t}{\dot{Y}_t} = g(X_t, Y_t) \quad \text{holds} \ \forall t \in \mathcal{T} , \tag{10}$$

and again, (7) is required. Definitions (9,10), referred to as Ordinary Differential Equations (ODE), extend to implicit differential equations (also called DAE, where A stands for "Algebraic")

$$\text{on } \mathcal{T} : C\left(\frac{dX}{dY}, X, Y\right) \tag{11}$$

if

$$C\left(\frac{\dot{X}_t}{\dot{Y}_t}, X_t, Y_t\right) \quad \text{holds} \ \forall t \in \mathcal{T} ,$$

and (7) is required.

EXAMPLES :

- Take $Y_t = t$ and $\mathcal{T}_Y = [0, +\infty) = \mathcal{T}$. We get as a particular case the usual ODE $dx/dt = g(x,t)$ on $[0, +\infty)$.
- For $\mathcal{T}$ of the form $\{t \in \mathbf{R} \ : \ Y_t \geq 0\}$, DE (10) specifies the differential equation $dx/dy = g(x,y)$, i.e., y is now taken as a "time variable", and the "time domain" in which this DE is defined is $[0, +\infty)$ since the presence of signal Y was specified through the predicate $\{Y_t \geq 0\}$. This gives an illustration of our mechanism of multiform time for differential equations.
- The standard chain rule for successive differentiations yields the usual chain rule for change of variables in differential equations:

$$\frac{dX}{dZ} = \frac{dX}{dY}\frac{dY}{dZ}$$

In formulae (8) and (9), we could interpret signal X as a time variable, we just need that X_t be nondecreasing. Thus we would view (8) as a way to define a function of this new time, and (9) as a differential equation with respect to this new time variable. Since several different such X's can be used, we have a mechanism which allows us to handle *multiform continuous time*, exactly as in synchronous languages SIGNAL [7] and ESTEREL [2]. For instance, time can be a distance run by a mobile, a rotated angle in a robot joint, or just time. Such different time bases can be either continuous, or discrete. Using our operations, such different times can be, but do not need to be related to each other. For instance, the speed of a mobile relates usual time to distance trough a differential equation.

2.3 Hybrid Systems and their Composition

Our model makes use of "real time". However, only *relative* timing is relevant, not absolute time. Thus what is important is to know that two time variables are equal, or that two discrete clocks are related by inclusion of their sets of instants, etc. Thus, prior to defining what is a hybrid system, we need to consider objects and operations "up to time change". This is what we formalize first[6].

Time changes A *time change* is a map $\sigma \ : \ \overline{\mathbf{R}} \mapsto \overline{\mathbf{R}}$, which is bijective, increasing, and continuous with continuous inverse [7]. Time changes change signals in the following way:

$$Y =_{\text{def}} \sigma(X) \text{ defined by } Y_t = X_{\sigma(t)}$$

[6] For completely different purposes, the importance of invariance via time change has been recognized and utilized in [6].

[7] In fact, the statement "continuous with continuous inverse" is a consequence of σ being bijective and increasing.

Lemma 1 invariance. *The following properties establish invariance under time change of all operations we have defined so far:*

$$\text{on } S \ : \ C(X,Y) \Leftrightarrow \text{on } \sigma(S) \ : \ C\left(\sigma(X), \sigma(Y)\right)$$

$$\text{on } S \ : \ C\left(\frac{dX}{dY}, X, Y\right) \Leftrightarrow \text{on } \sigma(S) \ : \ C\left(\frac{d\sigma(X)}{d\sigma(Y)}, \sigma(X), \sigma(Y)\right)$$

As a consequence, all operations on signals we have defined so far are invariant under time changes.

Hybrid Systems Consider a set $\{\mathtt{X}_1, \ldots, \mathtt{X}_k\}$ of signal names, and associated types $\{D_1, \ldots, D_k\}$.

A *hybrid system* P, of sort $\{\mathtt{X}_1, \ldots, \mathtt{X}_k\}$, is a set of k-tuples $(X_1, \ldots, X_k)$ of signals of respective types $\{D_1, \ldots, D_k\}$, which is *invariant under time change*. This means that, if $(X_1, \ldots, X_k) \in P$ and σ is a time change, then $(\sigma(X_1), \ldots, \sigma(X_k)) \in P$. Note that, in this definition, both the value and presence of signals are variable.

By this definition, only relative timing is relevant in our definition of hybrid systems. No hybrid system P can have signals bound to some given fixed presence : if X is a signal in P with presence $\mathcal{T}_X$, then we must also have in P all presences of the form $\sigma(\mathcal{T}_X)$, where σ ranges over the time changes. As an example, it is not possible to specify that a signal has $[0, +\infty)$ as index set. To specify presences, we just pick a signal (it can be input, local, or output) and refer to its presence, this is fairly consistent with the technique of constructing multiform discrete time in both SIGNAL and ESTEREL, where different discrete times can be built simply by counting events. This point of view is convenient to express relations between presences, e.g., two signals have the same presence, or they are mutually exclusive, etc.

Thanks to the previous subsection, all relations on signals we have introduced specify hybrid systems: union/intersection/difference of presences, pointwise constraints on signals (5), differential equations (11).

Hybrid Systems Composition If P and Q have the same sort, then

$$P \parallel Q \ =_{\text{def}} \ P \cap Q$$

otherwise, if P has sort $\mathbf{X}$ and Q has sort $\mathbf{Y}$, then

$$P \parallel Q \ =_{\text{def}} \ \mathbf{proj}^{-1}_{\mathbf{X} \cup \mathbf{Y} \mapsto \mathbf{X}}(P) \bigcap \mathbf{proj}^{-1}_{\mathbf{X} \cup \mathbf{Y} \mapsto \mathbf{Y}}(Q)$$

where $\mathbf{proj}_{\mathbf{X} \cup \mathbf{Y} \mapsto \mathbf{X}}$ denotes the canonical projection of the set of all signals of sort $\mathbf{X} \cup \mathbf{Y}$ onto that of all signals of sort $\mathbf{X}$. Note that, since intersection preserves invariance via time change, the composition of hybrid systems is a hybrid system.

2.4 Some useful constructions

To be able to describe some examples, we need some "macros". These are listed now.

For B a boolean signal with presence $\mathcal{T}$, we define the presence

$$\mathbf{true}(B) \ =_{\text{def}} \ \{t \in \mathcal{T} \ : \ B_t = \mathit{true}\}$$

to be the instants t at which B_t is true, and similarly for **false**(B). For a presence $\mathcal{T}$, we define

$$\mathbf{start}(\mathcal{T}) \ =_{\text{def}} \ \overleftarrow{\mathcal{T}} \cap \left(\overrightarrow{\mathcal{T}}\right)^c \ , \mathbf{stop}(\mathcal{T}) \ =_{\text{def}} \ \overrightarrow{\mathcal{T}} \cap \left(\overleftarrow{\mathcal{T}}\right)^c$$

In these formulae, A^c denotes the complement of set A, and $\overleftarrow{A}$ and $\overrightarrow{A}$ respectively denote the left and right closure of set A [8]. For example, if $\mathcal{T}$ is a "gentle" sequence of phases $\mathcal{T} = [s_1, t_1) \cup [s_2, t_2) \cup \ldots$, in which $t_n < s_{n+1}$, then $\mathbf{start}(\mathcal{T}) = \{s_1, s_2, \ldots\}$, and $\mathbf{stop}(\mathcal{T}) = \{t_1, t_2, \ldots\}$.

For $\mathcal{S}, \mathcal{T}$ two presences, we define the new presence

$$[\,\mathcal{S}\,,\mathcal{T}\,[\ =_{\text{def}} \bigcup_{s \in \mathcal{S}} [s, t_s[\quad , \quad \text{where}$$

$$t_s \ = \ \inf\{t \in \mathbf{R}, t > s \ : \ t \in \mathcal{T}\}$$

Note that, since in fact union can be taken over a denumerable set of points $s \in \mathcal{S}$, $[\,\mathcal{S}\,,\mathcal{T}\,[$ is Borel, and is thus a presence. Next, we define

$$\begin{aligned}]\,\mathcal{S}\,,\mathcal{T}\,[\ &=_{\text{def}} [\,\mathcal{S}\,,\mathcal{T}\,[\ \setminus \ \mathbf{start}(\mathcal{S}) \\ [\,\mathcal{S}\,,\mathcal{T}\,] \ &=_{\text{def}} [\,\mathcal{S}\,,\mathcal{T}\,[\ \cup \ \mathbf{start}(\mathcal{T}) \end{aligned}$$

etc. The resulting formalism will be called HYBRID.

2.5 A nasty example

This example is illustrated in Figure 2. The corresponding HYBRID model is given in Figure 3.

3 Short discussion and perspectives

We have proposed a framework for hybrid systems in which continuous and discrete parts are handled in a uniform way including system composition. Our model seems quite general. It is a behavioural model, today I do not see how to build a state oriented version of it — extensions of the hybrid automaton

[8] thus $\overleftarrow{A} = \{x \ : \ x = \lim_n y_n\}$ for some decreasing sequence of elements of A, and $\overrightarrow{A} = \{x \ : \ x = \lim_n y_n\}$ for some increasing sequence of elements of A.

Fig. 2. *The car example.* The car has a crazy driver, and an intelligent brake. The driver does not see the wall. The brake has collision avoidance system, which results in a feedback whose dynamics is governed by the distance to wall. Will the car hit the wall?

$$
\begin{array}{l}
(\ \textbf{on}\ \text{Start} \ : \ (\ D = D_0 \ \| \ F_{\text{brake}} = 0 \ ) \\
\| \ \textbf{on}\ ]\ \text{Start}\ ,\ \text{Scratch}\ [\ : \\
\qquad (\ d^2D/dt^2 = (F_{\text{driver}} - F_{\text{brake}}) \,/\, \text{Mass} \quad \%\ \textit{the physics} \\
\qquad \| \ dF_{\text{brake}}/dD = g\,(F_{\text{brake}}, D) \qquad \%\ \textit{intelligent feedback} \\
\qquad) \\
\| \ \text{Scratch} = \textbf{stop}(D > 0) \\
)
\end{array}
$$

Fig. 3. *The car example: hybrid system model.* Symbols t, D denote time and distance to wall respectively. Then, $F_{\text{driver}}, F_{\text{brake}}$ denote the forces applied by the driver and brake respectively. In the first ODE, derivative is taken with respect to time, as usual. In the second ODE, derivative is taken with respect to distance to wall. This is unusual, but it reflects the fact that the dynamics of the brake is based on the distance to wall, which is the ultimate constraint.

idea would not do. Clearly, issues related to differential geometry or discretization schemes of differential equations have not been considered. These are longer term issues. A feature of our model is its relational nature. This makes compositionality much easier, which facilitates specification. In turn, this makes program execution nontrivial, and timing and causality calculi are needed. Finally, one can suspect that the techniques of separate compilation and desynchronization developed in particular for SIGNAL could be extended to provide distributed hybrid systems simulation, in which different DAE solvers cooperate for the simulation of a hybrid systems, and interact at discrete events.

ACKNOWLEDGEMENT : *Oded Maler is gratefully acknowledged for his highly stimulating, inspiring, and nearly theological remarks, which I did not fully exploit yet. Also, thanks are due to Paul Caspi and Eric Rutten for improving early versions of this manuscript.*

References

1. R. ALUR, C. COURCOUBETIS, T. HENZINGER, AND P. HO, *Hybrid automata: an algorithmic approach to the specification and verification of hybrid systems*, in Hybrid systems, Lecture Notes in Computer Science, vol 736, Springer Verlag, 1993, pp. 209–229.
2. F. BOUSSINOT AND R. DE SIMONE, *The* ESTEREL *language*, Proceedings of the IEEE, 79 (1991), pp. 1293–1304.
3. P. BREEDVELD, R. ROSENBERG, AND T. ZHOU, *Bibliography of bond graph theory and applications*, Journal of the Franklin Institute, 328 (1991), pp. 1067–1109.
4. J. BROENINK AND K. WIJBRANS, *Describing discontinuities in bond graphs*, in Proc. of the 1st Int. Conf. on bond graph modeling, SCS Simulation Series, 25 No 2, 1993.
5. F. CELLIER AND J. G. EDS., *See the technical sessions on hybrid systems*, in Proc. of the 2nd Int. Conf. on bond graph modeling, SCS Simulation Series, 27 No 2, 1995.
6. T. HENZINGER, *Hybrid Automata with Finite Bisimulations*, preprint, Cornell University, 1995.
7. P. L. GUERNIC, T. GAUTIER, M. L. BORGNE, AND C. L. MAIRE, *Programming real-time applications with* SIGNAL, Proceedings of the IEEE, 79 (1991), pp. 1321–1336.
8. O. MALER AND A. PNUELI, *Timing analysis of asynchronous circuits using timed automata*, Tech. Rep., Laboratoire Verimag, Imag, 1995.

Hybrid cc, Hybrid Automata and Program Verification

(Extended Abstract)

Vineet Gupta * Radha Jagadeesan ** Vijay Saraswat *

1 Introduction

Synchronous programming. Discrete event driven systems [HP85,Ber89,Hal93] are systems that react with their environment at a rate controlled by the environment. Such systems can be quite complex, so for modular development and re-use considerations, a model of a composite system should be built up from models of the components compositionally. From a programming language standpoint, this modularity concern is addressed by the analysis underlying synchronous languages [BB91,Hal93,BG92,HCP91,GBGM91,Har87,CLM91,SJG95], (adapted to dense discrete domains in [BBG93]):

- Logical concurrency/parallelism plays a role in determinate reactive system programming analogous to the role of procedural abstraction in sequential programming — the role of matching program structure to the structure of the solution to the problem at hand.
- Preemption — the ability to stop a process in its tracks — is a fundamental programming tool for such systems [Ber93]. Examples of preemption include process suspension ("cntrl-Z") and process abortion("cntrl-C").
- The language should allow the expression of multiple notions of *logical time*, *i.e.* any signal can serve as a notion of time.

The design of synchronous programming languages has two distinct pieces: 1) A notion of defaults analyzed at the level of the basic (untimed) concurrent language. 2) The discrete timed synchronous language obtained by extending the untimed language uniformly over discrete time. Defaults allow the expression of the preemption constructs that rely on instantaneous detection of negative information. Furthermore, there are expressiveness advantages to be gained from building the programming language on top of a logic that allows expression of defaults — recent results [GKPS95] suggest that such programs can be exponentially more succinct than programs that do not admit expression of defaults.

* Xerox PARC, 3333 Coyote Hill Road, Palo Alto Ca 94304; `{vgupta,saraswat}@parc.xerox.com`

** Dept. of Mathematical Sciences,Loyola University-Lake Shore Campus, Chicago, Il 60626; `radha@math.luc.edu`

Hybrid cc. In earlier work[GJSB,GJSB95], we extended the analysis underlying synchronous programming to build an executable modeling and programming language for hybrid systems, Hybrid cc. Hybrid cc integrates conceptual frameworks for continuous and discrete change, as exemplified by the theory of differential equations and real analysis on the one hand, and the theory of programming languages on the other. As before, the language is built on top of a notion of defaults analyzed at the level of the basic (untimed) concurrent logic language. The hybrid programming synchronous language is obtained by extending the untimed language uniformly over continuous (real) time.

As in synchronous programming languages, various patterns of temporal activity can be defined in Hybrid cc — for example, the instantaneous preemption combinators of synchronous programming. In [GJSB], we provided precise operational semantics and described an interpreter that implements the operational semantics. In [GJSB95], we showed how to build and execute compositional models for various problems described in the literature. We also demonstrated that the process of building models was facilitated by a denotational semantics that allowed a more abstract view of programs as (temporal) constraints.

This paper. In this paper, we demonstrate the relationship of Hybrid cc to the methodology and tools developed in the research on verification of hybrid systems — for example, see earlier proceedings of this conference for a variety of approaches and tools [GNRR93,hyb95].

We aim to establish Hybrid cc as a high-level programming notation for hybrid automata — much as synchronous programming languages are high level notation for discrete automata. Concretely, we establish the expressiveness of Hybrid cc in two ways:

- For any given hybrid automaton, we describe a Hybrid cc program whose only traces are valid runs of the system.
- For any given safety property expressed in (real-time) temporal logic, we show how to write a Hybrid cc program that "detects" if the property is violated.

Furthermore, we aim to make programs written in Hybrid cc amenable to the tools developed for the verification of hybrid systems. For any Hybrid cc program, we build an automaton whose valid runs are precisely execution traces of the program.

2 Hybrid cc— The underlying computational intuition.

Hybrid cc is a language in the concurrent constraint programming framework, augmented with a notion of continuous time and defaults. In this section, we present an intuitive sketch of Hybrid cc — for a detailed formal development, we refer readers to [GJSB].

The (concurrent) constraint (cc) programming paradigm [Sar89] replaces the traditional notion of a store as a valuation of variables with the notion of a store as a constraint on the possible values of variables. Computation progresses by accumulating constraints in the store, and by checking whether the store entails constraints.

A salient aspect of the cc computation model is that programs may be thought of as imposing constraints on the evolution of the system. Default cc [SJG95] provides five basic constructs: (tell) a (for a a primitive constraint), parallel composition (A, B), positive ask (**if** a **then** A), negative ask (**if** a **else** A), and hiding (**new** X **in** A). The program a imposes the constraint a. The program (A, B) imposes the constraints of both A and B — logically, this is the conjunction of A and B. **new** X **in** A imposes the constraints of A, but hides the variable X from the other programs — logically, this can be thought of as a form of existential quantification. The program **if** a **then** A imposes the constraints of A provided that the rest of the system imposes the constraint a — logically, this can be thought of as intuitionist implication. The program **if** a **else** A imposes the constraints of A unless the rest of the system imposes the constraint a — logically, this can be thought of as a form of *defaults* [Rei80].

This declarative way of looking at programs is complemented by an operational view. The basic idea in the operational view is that of a network of programs interacting with a shared store of primitive constraints. The program a is viewed as adding a to the store instantaneously. The program (A, B) behaves like the simultaneous execution of both A and B. **new** X **in** A starts A but creates a new local variable X, so no information can be communicated on it outside. The program **if** a **then** A behaves like A if the current store entails a. The program **if** a **else** A behaves like A if the current store on quiescence does *not* entail a.

Continuous evolution over time. Hybrid cc is obtained by uniformly extending Default cc across real (continuous) time. This is accomplished by two technical developments.

First, we enrich the underlying notion of a constraint system to make it possible to describe the continuous evolution of state. Intuitively, we allow constraints expressing initial value (integration) problem, using tokens of the form **hence** d or d, where d is of the form $dot(X, m) = r$, for X a variable, m a non-negative integer and r a real number. The token $dot(X, m) = r$ states that the mth derivative of X is r and **hence** $dot(X, m) = r$ states that for all time $t > 0$ the mth derivative of X is r. From $X = 0,$ **hence** $dot(X, 0) = 1$, we can infer at time t that $X = t$. *Integration* operators $\int^r$, for every $r \in \mathbb{R}$ are generated by the entailment relation: intuitively, $\int^r c$ is the constraint entailed by c after evolving for r units of time. In this example, $\int^r c$ does correspond with to the usual integral. The technical innovation here is the presentation of a *generic* notion of continuous constraint system (ccs), which builds into the very general notion of constraint sytems just the extra structure needed to enable the definition of continuous control constructs (without committing to a *particular* choice of vocabulary for constraints involving continuous time). As a result subsequent development is *parametric* on the underlying constraint language: for each choice of a ccs we get a hybrid programming language.

Secondly, we add to the untimed **Default** cc a single temporal control construct: **hence** A. Logically, **hence** A imposes the constraints of A at every time instant after the current one. Operationally, if **hence** A is invoked at time t, a new copy of A is invoked at each instant in (t, ∞).

Agents	Propositions
a	a holds now
if a **then** A	if a holds now, then A holds now
if a **else** A	if a will not hold now, then A holds now
new X **in** A	exists an instance $A[t/X]$ that holds now
A, B	both A and B hold now
hence A	A holds at every instant after now

Intuitively, **hence** might appear to be a very specialized construct, since it requires repetition of the *same* program at every subsequent time instant. However, **hence** can combine in very powerful ways with positive and negative ask operations to yield rich patterns of temporal evolution. The key idea is that negative asks allow the instantaneous preemption of a program — hence, a program **hence if** a **else** A will in fact not execute A at all those time instants at which a is true.

Let us consider some concrete examples. First, clearly, one can program **always** A (which executes A at every time instant) by (A, **hence** A). Now suppose that we require that a program A be executed at every time instant beyond the current one until the first time at which a is true. This can be expressed as **new** X **in** (**hence** (**if** X **else** A, **if** a **then always** X)). Intuitively, at every instant beyond the current one, the condition X is checked. Unless it holds, A is executed. X is local — the only way it can be generated is by the other program (**if** a **then always** X), which, in fact generates X continuously upon detecting a. Thus, a copy of A is executed at each time point beyond the current one upto (and excluding) the first time point at which a is detected. Similarly, to execute A precisely at the first time instant (assuming there is one) at which a holds, execute: **new** X **in hence** (**if** X **else if** a **then** A, **if** a **then hence** X). Analogously, one can define the following combinators that are characteristic of synchronous programming:

- Process abortion — **do** A **watching** a — execute the process A until the event a happens.
- Multiform time — **time** A **on** a — the process A runs only during the times a holds.

While conceptually simple to understand, **hence** A requires the execution of A at every subsequent real time instant. Such a powerful combinator may seem impossible to implement computationally. For example, it may be possible to express programs of the form **new** T **in** ($T = 0$, **hence** $dot(T) = 1$, **hence if** $rational(T)$ **then** A) which require the execution of A at every rational $q > 0$. Such programs are not implementable — because rationals and irrationals are everywhere dense as a subset of the reals. We show that in fact

Hybrid cc is computationally realizable. The basic intuition we exploit is that, in general, physical systems change "slowly", with points of discontinuous change, followed by periods of continuous evolution. Technically, we introduce a *stability* condition for continuous constraint system that guarantees that for every constraint a and b there is a neighborhood around 0 in which a either entails or disentails b at every point. This rules out constraints such as `rational(T)` as inadmissible.

With this restriction, computation in Hybrid cc may be thought of as progressing in alternating phases of computation at a time point, and in an open interval. Computation at the time point establishes the constraint in effect at that instant, and sets up the program to execute subsequently. Computation in the succeeding open interval determines the length of the interval r and the constraint whose continuous evolution over $(0, r)$ describes the state of the system over $(0, r)$. At time r the program set up in the interval is executed to determine the point constraint, and so on.

3 Compiling Hybrid cc to Hybrid automata

We now present an algorithm to compile Hybrid cc programs into Hybrid cc automata. The Hybrid cc automata we compile to are variations of the hybrid automata presented in [ACH+95]. An automaton accepts traces from the environment, and determines if the traces are in the denotation of the Hybrid cc program that the automaton was constructed from.

Given a constraint system $\mathcal{C} = (D, \vdash)$, define **cont** $\mathcal{C} = (\{\texttt{cont}\ d \mid d \in D\}, \vdash')$ — a copy of $\mathcal{C}$ with all tokens prefixed by a *cont* to distinguish them from the tokens of $\mathcal{C}$. The inference relation on **cont** $\mathcal{C}$ is induced by $\vdash$; an integration relation on **cont** $\mathcal{C}$ is induced by the integration relation of the continuous constraint system built on $\mathcal{C}$. Now, define the constraint system $\mathcal{C}'$ as the cartesian product $\mathcal{C} \times$ **cont** $\mathcal{C}$ in the category of constraint systems.

A Hybrid cc automaton consists of:

- A set of states St. States are of two kinds, point states and interval states. Each state is labeled with a Default cc program on the constraint system $\mathcal{C}$, and each interval state is labeled with a constraint in $\mathcal{C}$. One of the point states is designated a start state.
- A set of transitions between states. Each transition is labeled by a constraint in $\mathcal{C}'$. Transitions can go from point states to interval states and vice versa, and also from an interval state to itself. The set of labels on the outgoing transitions from any state is closed under least upper bounds.

The input trace supplied to the automaton is a pair of functions (Q, C), where $Q : \mathbb{R}^{\geq 0} \rightarrow St, C : \mathbb{R}^{\geq 0} \rightarrow \mathcal{C}$ satisfying:

- Q, C are partial functions with the same domain; the domain is a prefix of the real line.

- Q is finitely variable — Q changes only finitely many times in any bounded interval. Thus for all t in the domain of Q, Q is constant over some succeeding open interval — we refer to this value of Q as $Q(t+)$. Also for all $t > 0$ in the domain of Q, Q is constant over some preceding open interval — we refer to this value of Q as $Q(t-)$. Both $Q(t-)$ and $Q(t+)$ are required to be interval states. Finally, if $Q(t-) \neq Q(t)$, we demand that $Q(t)$ be a point state.
- For each $t \geq 0.\exists\epsilon_t > 0$, C is smooth over $(t, t+\epsilon_t)$, *i.e.* there is a constraint $c \in C'$ such that for all $t' \in (t, t+\epsilon_t).C(t') = \int^{t'-t} c$. The constraint c that establishes the smoothness of C beyond t is always of the form $(a_t, \mathbf{cont}\ b_t)$, and we define $C(t+) = \mathbf{cont}\ b_t$.

Let (C, Q) be a trace. The automaton accepts this trace if:

- $Q(0)$ is the start state of the automaton.
- For all t, $C(t)$ is a fixed point of the program in state $Q(t)$.
- For all t, the automaton takes the transition determined by $C(t), C(t+)$ — the transition with the greatest label below $C(t), C(t+)$ — to the interval state $Q(t+)$ (which may be the same as $Q(t)$, in which case nothing is done).
- For all $t > 0$, if $Q(t-) \neq Q(t)$, the automaton takes the transition out of $Q(t-)$ determined by $C(t), C(t+)$ — the transition with the greatest label below $C(t), C(t+)$ — from $Q(t-)$ to the point state $Q(t)$.

Examples of Hybrid cc automata are given below. In the third automaton, for example, the trace $C(0) = b, Q(0) = 1, C((0,3)) = (a,b,c), Q((0,3)) = 4$ is accepted, while the trace $C([0,3)) = (a,b), Q(0) = 1, Q((0-3)) = 4$ is not accepted, as (a,b) is not a fixed point of the program (b,c). (Note that no other values for Q would have worked either — Q is essentially unique for any C.)

Compilation algorithm. We now show how to compile a program P into an automaton which accepts only those traces which satisfy the constraints imposed by P. In order to compile a program P, we first put it in a normal form, and then compile the normal form.

Normal form for Hybrid cc *programs.* A Hybrid cc program is in normal form if it can be written as the parallel composition of fragments generated as follows:

$$N ::= \mathbf{if}\ a\ \mathbf{then}\ \mathbf{if}\ b_1\ \mathbf{else}\ \ldots \mathbf{if}\ b_n\ \mathbf{else}\ b,\ n \geq 0$$
$$\mid \mathbf{if}\ a\ \mathbf{then}\ \mathbf{if}\ b_1\ \mathbf{else}\ \ldots \mathbf{if}\ b_n\ \mathbf{else}\ \mathbf{hence}\ N,\ n \geq 0$$

The number of **hence** 's in a fragment is called the depth of the fragment. The program may be converted into such a normal form by repeated application of the following rewrite rules:

$$\mathbf{hence}\ \mathbf{hence}\ A \rightarrow \mathbf{hence}\ A$$
$$\mathbf{if}\ a\ \mathbf{else}\ \mathbf{if}\ b\ \mathbf{then}\ A \rightarrow \mathbf{if}\ b\ \mathbf{then}\ \mathbf{if}\ a\ \mathbf{else}\ A$$
$$\mathbf{if}\ a\ \mathbf{then}\ \mathbf{if}\ b\ \mathbf{then}\ A \rightarrow \mathbf{if}\ (a \sqcup b)\ \mathbf{then}\ A$$
$$\mathbf{if}\ \mathit{true}\ \mathbf{then}\ A \leftrightarrow A$$
$$\mathbf{hence}\ (A,B) \rightarrow \mathbf{hence}\ A, \mathbf{hence}\ B$$
$$\mathbf{if}\ a\ \mathbf{then}\ (A,B) \rightarrow \mathbf{if}\ a\ \mathbf{then}\ A, \mathbf{if}\ a\ \mathbf{then}\ B$$
$$\mathbf{if}\ a\ \mathbf{else}\ (A,B) \rightarrow \mathbf{if}\ a\ \mathbf{else}\ A, \mathbf{if}\ a\ \mathbf{else}\ B$$

Compilation of the Normal form. We first show how to compile each of the fragments, and a product construction will provide the final automaton. Compiling a fragment F is done inductively, based on the depth of the fragment. A dead state is defined as an interval state with the program `true` and a single transition labeled `true` going back to it. Examples of automata for programs of depth less than or equal to 1 are shown here — the general case follows immediately.

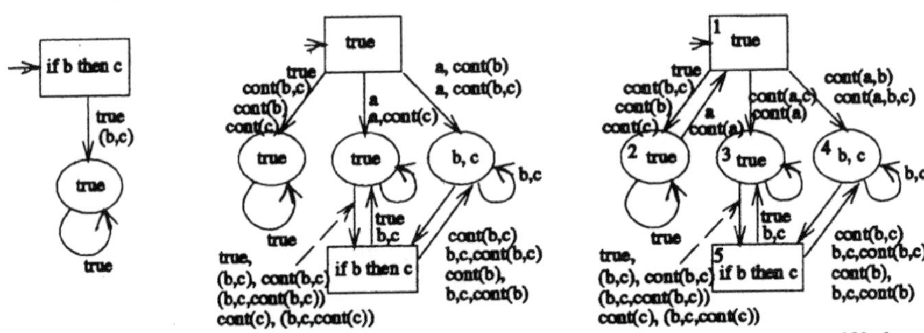

Program: if b then c   Program : if a then hence if b then c   Program : hence if a then hence if b then c

Some labels have been omitted to avoid cluttering. In the third automaton, the start state has been merged with the original start state.

If the depth is greater than one, then $F =$ **if** a **then if** b_1 **else** ... **if** b_n **else hence** F'. Let $F' =$ **if** a' **then if** b'_1 **else** ... **if** b'_m **else hence** .... We first construct the automaton for F' inductively. Now we convert this into the automaton for F as follows.

- Add arcs from the start state of F' with labels consisting of subsets of $\{$`cont` a', `cont` $b'_1, \ldots$ `cont` $b'_m\}$ (and their conjunctions with the other labels) — each going to the same state where the corresponding arc without `cont` went.
- If q is the dead state reached from the start state (on the transition say `true`), add from it arcs with labels from subsets of $\{a', b'_1, \ldots b'_m,$ `cont` a', `cont` $b'_1, \ldots,$ `cont` $b'_m\}$. The arcs a', `cont` a' and $(a',$ `cont` $a')$ go to the start state, the others back to q.
- Add a new start state labeled `true`. The arcs from it are all the arcs from the (modified) start state of F', with their labels conjoined with a. All other arcs go to a new dead state.

We now combine the fragments to get the automaton for the entire program by performing a standard product construction. States are pairs of states in the automata for A and B, and are labeled by programs which are parallel compositions of the programs in the component states. A state is an interval state if an only if both its components are interval states, otherwise it is a point state. The start state is the joint start state of the component automata. Transitions are induced by pairs of transitions from the individual automata.

Hiding. Consider the program **wait** 5 **do** $A =$ **new** X **in** ($X = 0$, **hence** ($dX/dt = 1$, **if** $X = 5$ **then** A))). This program starts A exactly 5 seconds after being started. This program has uncountably many "control points" (more precisely derivatives in the parlance of synchronous programming), one for each real in the interval $[0, 5]$. This makes a general compilation of the hiding combinator impossible. However, the above compilation algorithm can be extended to hiding of variables whose values do not evolve autonomously. The hidden variables used in the definition of the defined combinators and the hidden variables in the programs in this paper are of this kind. A more systematic semantic study remains to be undertaken.

Correctness of Automata. The correctness of our compilation is proved via the denotational semantics. Details are omitted for lack of space.

4 Testers for Hybrid Automata

In this section, we illustrate the expressive power of Hybrid cc relative to hybrid automata — we show that given a hybrid automaton, we can construct a Hybrid cc program accepting exactly the same traces as the automaton. For concreteness, we consider the hybrid automata presented in [ACH+95].

We recall the definition of hybrid automata from [ACH+95] for reference. A hybrid automaton is described by a 6-tuple:

- A finite set of locations, Loc.
- A finite set of real-valued variables Var. A valuation v is an assignment of real values to all variables in Var.
- A set of labels Lab.
- A finite set of transitions. Each transition consists of (l, a, μ, l'), where l, l' are the source and target locations, a is a label, and μ relates source valuations to target valuations.
- A function which labels each location with a set of *activities* — an activity is a function from $\mathbb{R}^{\geq 0}$ to valuations.
- A function assigning each location l_i with an invariant $Inv(l_i)$, which is a set of valuations.

Now a run of the automaton is defined as a finite or infinite sequence of 4-tuples: $\langle(l_0, v_0, f_0, t_0), (l_1, v_1, f_1, t_1), \ldots\rangle$ is a run if for all $i \geq 0$, f_i is an activity in l_i, $f_i(0) = v_i$, $\forall t, 0 \leq t < t_i \rightarrow f_i(t) \in Inv(l_i)$ and $(l_i, \_, \mu_i, l_{i+1})$ is a transition with $(f_i(t_i), v_{i+1}) \in \mu_i$.

Translation. Given a hybrid automaton, we show how to build an "equivalent" Hybrid cc program — more precisely, we build a Hybrid cc program whose observations are exactly the runs of the given hybrid system. It is helpful to view the Hybrid cc program that we build as an acceptor of the valid runs of the given hybrid automaton.

In order for us to be able to write the Hybrid cc program, we will need to be able to express as constraints various aspects of the given hybrid automaton. This will mean that our constraint system should be expressive enough. Also, if we desire a finite program, these aspects will have to be finitely representable. We summarize these representability conditions below:

- For each location l_i, the constraint $v \in Inv(l_i)$ must be expressible as a constraint in our constraint system.
- The set of activities in any location must be representable by the evolution of a set of constraints. For example, we could have the constraint $dx/dt \geq 3$ representing the set of all activities with the derivative of x greater than 3. What we require is a set of such constraints such that they exactly capture the activities at a location.
- In each transition, the relation μ must be representable as a constraint.

These conditions are not too strict — the examples of hybrid systems given in [ACH+95], these requirements are met by the simple constraint system described in [GJSB].

The program will be given as a set of Hybrid cc agents, each of which represents a location l_i. When the system enters a location l_i, the agent st_i is activated. The agent examines the initial valuations, and starts up a number of testers to check the run. Each tester keeps reporting **ok** as long as the run is in the allowed set of activities of that tester. Since it is initially not known which activity in the set is being taken, several testers are started in parallel, and as long as any one of them says **ok**, the run is allowed. Simultaneously, another tester keeps checking that the run does not violate the invariant of the location. The construct *abort* accepts nothing — if no tester reports **ok**, *abort* rejects the run.

The testers are written using the construct **while** a **do** A, which keeps on executing A while the constraint a is true. Thus for example, if we wanted to test for the set of all activities in which $dx/dt \geq 3$, then we would write **while** $(dx/dt \geq 3)$ **do always** *ok*, this would keep generating an **ok** while the constraint holds. If it stopped holding at some time, then no further **ok**'s would be generated.

These testers are kept running while the program counter **pc** indicates that the location is still l_i. As soon as it changes, the testers are killed. Now the second part of the agent is activated — **first** a **do** A starts A at the first instant (if any) that a holds. This part consists of one tester for each transition whose source is l_i. These check that the last valuation of the current location and the first valuation of the next location are in the relation μ for some transition, which also has the right target and the right label. (Labels may be omitted if desired.) If any check succeeds, then an **ok** is generated, and the agent for the next location is activated. The current location agent does nothing more.

```
st_i ::
new ok in [
while (pc = l_i) do [
```

```
      if (v in v_1) then while c_1 do always ok,
      if (v in v_2) then while c_2 do always ok,
      ...,
      always if ok else abort,
      always if (v in Inv(l_i)) else abort],
first (pc =/= l_i) do
      [if ((prev(v), v) in mu_1 and pc = l_k and label = a_1)
            then (ok, st_k),
       if ((prev(v), v) in mu_2 and pc = l_k' and label = a_2)
            then (ok, st_k'),
       ...,
       if ok else abort]].
```

The program for the system is now as follows. It just starts the appropriate location agent at the beginning of the run.

```
system::
    if pc = l_1 then st_1,
    if pc = l_2 then st_2,
       ... .
```

An important property of this translation is that the parallel composition of two hybrid automata is recognized by the parallel composition of the two testers for these automata — in particular, the synchronization of transitions is done as expected.

Now the various cases of hybrid automata can be described by testers over specific constraint systems. For example, a hybrid automaton is *linear* iff it can be tested by a tester over the constraint system in which for any variable dx/dt is a constant, and linear terms are allowed.

5 Testers for safety properties

We will now show how to write testers for real-time safety properties in Hybrid cc. The basic idea is that a tester for a safety property raises a flag whenever the safety property is violated. This section shows that Hybrid cc can serve as a language for description of properties in addition to serving as a language for the description of systems.

The particular logic that we consider to write safety properties is (the past properties of) integrator computation tree logic(ICTL) [AHH93]. The encoding itself is essentially a real-time extension of extant encodings of safety properties of discrete linear time temporal logics [MP91] in synchronous languages [JPVO95]. We will exploit the structuring facilities of the programming language to achieve modularity in the encoding; thus, the following translation is *compositional*.

The tester for a basic constraint c just checks if c is true now, and raises a flag if it is not. Note that the flag is not cumulative — so if c was false at some time in the past, it does not mean that the flag will remain raised now. However, also note that the tester for c detects violation of the safety property c at all points of time — it actually functions as a tester for $\Box c$.

To test $\neg A$, we build a tester for A. If A raises a flag in the current state, then we do nothing, otherwise a flag is raised. $A \vee B$ is tested by making sure that either one of A or B holds, if both raise flags, then the tester for $A \vee B$ raises a flag. The tester for A since B makes sure that whenever B becomes true (determined by a flag raised by the tester for $\neg B$), a process is started to check for A, and as soon as A becomes false, A since B becomes false and remains false forever. Finally $(z : p)A$ is tested by testing A, we simply use the **time** A **on** c construct of Hybrid cc to yield a compositional translation of the integrator variables of ICTL.

Property ϕ	Tester $T(\phi)$
c	**always if** c **else** $err(c)$
$\neg A$	$T(A)$, **always if** $err(A)$ **else** $err(\neg A)$
$A \vee B$	$T(A), T(B)$, **always if** $(err(A) \wedge err(B))$ **then** $err(A \vee B)$
A since B	$T(\neg B), T(A)$, **first** $err(\neg B)$ **do** **always if** $err(A)$ **then always** $err(A \text{ since } B)$
$(z : p)A$	$T(A), z = 0$, **time** (**always** $dz/dt = 1$) **on** p, **time** (**always** $dz/dt = 0$) **on** $not(p)$, **always if** $err(A)$ **then** $err((z : p)A)$.

Acknowledgements. Work on this paper has been supported in part by ONR through grants to Vijay Saraswat and to Radha Jagadeesan, and by NASA. Radha Jagadeesan has also been supported by a grant from NSF.

References

[ACH+95] R. Alur, C. Courcoubetis, N. Halbwachs, T.A. Henzinger, P.-H. Ho, X. Nicollin, A. Olivero, J. Sifakis, and S. Yovine. The algorithmic analysis of hybrid systems. *Theoretical Computer Science*, 138:3–34, 1995.

[AHH93] Rajeev Alur, T.A. Henzinger, and P.-H. Ho. Automatic symbolic verification of embedded systems. In *Proceedings of the 14th Annual IEEE Real-time Systems Symposium*. IEEE, 1993.

[BB91] A. Benveniste and G. Berry. The synchronous approach to reactive and real-time systems. In *Special issue on Another Look at Real-time Systems*, Proceedings of the IEEE, September 1991.

[BBG93] A. Benveniste, M. Le Borgne, and Paul Le Guernic. *Hybrid Systems: The SIGNAL approach*. Number 736 in LNCS. Springer Verlag, 1993.

[Ber89] G. Berry. Real-time programming: General purpose or special-purpose languages. In G. Ritter, editor, *Information Processing 89*, pages 11 – 17. Elsevier Science Publishers B.V. (North Holland), 1989.

[Ber93] G. Berry. Preemption in concurrent systems. In *Proc. of FSTTCS*. Springer-Verlag, 1993. LNCS 781.

[BG92] G. Berry and G. Gonthier. The ESTEREL programming language: Design, semantics and implementation. *Science of Computer Programming*, 19(2):87 – 152, November 1992.

[CLM91] E. M. Clarke, D. E. Long, and K. L. McMillan. A language for compositional specification and verification of finite state hardware controllers. *Proceedings of the IEEE*, 79(9), September 1991.

[GBGM91] P. Le Guernic, M. Le Borgne, T. Gauthier, and C. Le Maire. Programming real time applications with SIGNAL. In *Special issue on Another Look at Real-time Systems*, Proceedings of the IEEE, September 1991.

[GJSB] Vineet Gupta, Radha Jagadeesan, Vijay Saraswat, and Daniel Bobrow. Computing with continuous change. Submitted to *Science of Computer Programming*.

[GJSB95] Vineet Gupta, Radha Jagadeesan, Vijay Saraswat, and Daniel Bobrow. Programming in hybrid constraint languages. In *Hybrid Systems II*, volume 999 of *Lecture notes in computer science*. Springer Verlag, November 1995.

[GKPS95] G. Gogic, H. Kautz, C. Papadimitriou, and B. Selman. The comparitive linguistics of knowledge representations. In *14th International joint conference on Artificial intelligence*, 1995.

[GNRR93] Robert Grossman, Anil Nerode, Anders Ravn, and Hans Rischel, editors. *Hybrid Systems*. Springer Verlag, 1993. LNCS 736.

[Hal93] N. Halbwachs. *Synchronous programming of reactive systems*. The Kluwer international series in Engineering and Computer Science. Kluwer Academic publishers, 1993.

[Har87] D. Harel. Statecharts: A visual approach to complex systems. *Science of Computer Programming*, 8:231 – 274, 1987.

[HCP91] N. Halbwachs, P. Caspi, and D. Pilaud. The synchronous programming language LUSTRE. In *Special issue on Another Look at Real-time Systems*, Proceedings of the IEEE, September 1991.

[HP85] David Harel and Amir Pnueli. *Logics and Models of Concurrent Systems*, volume 13, chapter On the development of reactive systems, pages 471–498. NATO Advanced Study Institute, 1985.

[hyb95] *Hybrid Systems II*. Springer Verlag, 1995. LNCS 999.

[JPVO95] L.J. Jagadeesan, C. Puchol, and J.E. Von Olnhausen. Safety property verification of ESTEREL programs and applications to telecommunications software. In *Proceedings of CAV*, LNCS 939, 1995.

[MP91] Z. Manna and A. Pnueli. *The Temporal Logic of Reactive and Concurrent Systems*. Springer-Verlag, 1991. 427 pp.

[Rei80] Ray Reiter. A logic for default reasoning. *Artificial Intelligence*, 13:81 – 132, 1980.

[Sar89] Vijay A. Saraswat. *Concurrent Constraint Programming Languages*. PhD thesis, Carnegie-Mellon University, January 1989. To appear, Doctoral Dissertation Award and Logic Programming Series, MIT Press, 1992.

[SJG95] V. A. Saraswat, R. Jagadeesan, and V. Gupta. Default Timed Concurrent Constraint Programming. In *Proceedings of Twenty Second ACM Symposium on Principles of Programming Languages, San Francisco*, January 1995.

Controlled Switching Diffusions as Hybrid Processes

Mrinal K. Ghosh[1], Steven I. Marcus[2] and Aristotle Arapostathis[3]

1 Introduction

A switching diffusion is a typical example of a stochastic hybrid process, where the state $(X(t), S(t))$ of the system has a continuous component $X(t)$ taking values in $\mathbb{R}^d$ and a discrete component $S(t)$ taking values in a finite set $S := \{1, 2, \cdots, M\}$. It arises in numerous applications of systems with multiple modes [16] such as in the hierarchical control of flexible manufacturing systems or large scale interconnected power networks [10]. See [1], [3], [6]-[16], [19] for relevant problems and applications. In this paper we discuss controlled switching diffusions as a particular class of hybrid control systems. This class of systems is also of interest in the study of deterministic hybrid systems, since deterministic hybrid systems can exhibit random behavior [9]. This work can be compared with the work of Branicky, et. al. for deterministic hybrid systems [7], [8]; our work allows less general jump rules and does not treat impulse control, but we are able to obtain very complete results for the class of systems considered.

In particular, we consider infinite horizon stochastic control problems with both discounted and average cost criteria [9], [10]. In order to solve these problems, we must deal with a number of issues of interest for the study of hybrid systems in general, including well-posedness of hybrid stochastic differential equations, transforming the problem into a linear programming problem on a space of measures, derivation of dynamic programming equations, and examination of stability issues for hybrid systems.

Our paper is organized as follows. We describe the abstract formulation of the problem in Section 2. Section 3 describes a convex analytic approach to the problem. Dynamic programming equations are treated in Section 4. Section 5 presents an application to a simplified manufacturing problem [12], [13] (motivated by [1], [2], [8]). Section 6 deals with some generalizations and other relevant remarks.

[1] Department of Mathematics, Indian Institute of Science, Bangalore 560012, India, mkg@math.iisc.ernet.in

[2] Electrical Engineering Department and Institute for Systems Research, University of Maryland, College Park, Maryland 20742, marcus@isr.umd.edu

[3] Electrical and Computer Engineering Department, University of Texas, Austin, Texas 78712, ari@mail.utexas.edu

2 Problem Formulation

Let U be a compact metric space and $V = \mathcal{P}(U)$, the space of probability measures on U endowed with the topology of weak convergence. Let $S = \{1, 2, \cdots, N\}$. Let

$$b : \mathbb{R}^d \times S \times V \to \mathbb{R}^d, b(\cdot,\cdot,\cdot) = [b_1(\cdot,\cdot,\cdot), \cdots, b_d(\cdot,\cdot,\cdot)]'$$

$$\sigma : \mathbb{R}^d \times S \to \mathbb{R}^{d\times d}, \sigma(\cdot,\cdot)[\sigma_{ij}(\cdot,\cdot)], 1 \leq i,j \leq d.$$

$$\lambda_{ij} :^d \times U \to \mathbb{R}, 1 \leq i,j \leq N, \lambda_{ij}(\cdot,\cdot) \geq 0, i \neq j, \quad \sum_{j=1}^N \lambda_{ij}(\cdot,\cdot) = 0.$$

We make the following assumption on b, σ, λ (for weaker assumptions see [12], [13]).

(A1) (i) For each $i \in S, b(\cdot, i, \cdot)$ is bounded, continuous and Lipschitz in its first argument uniformly with respect to the third.
(ii) For each $i \in S, \sigma(\cdot, i)$ is bounded and Lipschitz with the least eigenvalue of $\sigma\sigma'(\cdot, i)$ uniformly bounded away from zero.
(iii) For $i, j \in S, \lambda_{ij}(\cdot,\cdot)$ is bounded, continuous and Lipschitz in its first argument uniformly with respect to the second. Also, there exists a $\lambda_0 > 0$ such that $\lambda_{ij}(x, u) \geq \lambda_0$ for all $x \in \mathbb{R}^d, u \in U$.

For $x \in \mathbb{R}^d, i, j, \in S$ $v \in V$, define

$$\bar{b}_j(x, i, v) = \int_U b_j(x, i, u) v(du), j = 1, \cdots, d$$

$$\bar{b}(x, i, v) = [\bar{b}(x, i, v), \cdots, \bar{b}(x, i, v)]'$$

$$\bar{\lambda}_{ij}(x, v) = \int_U \lambda_{ij}(x, u) v(du).$$

Let $(X(\cdot), S(\cdot))$ be an $\mathbb{R}^d \times S$-valued process given by

$$dX(t) = \bar{b}(X(t), S(t), v(t))dt + \sigma(X(t), S(t))dW(t), \tag{2.1a}$$

$$P(S(t + \delta t) = j |\, S(t) = i, X(s), S(s), s \leq t) = \bar{\lambda}_{ij}(X(t), v(t))\delta t + 0(\delta t), i \neq j, \tag{2.1b}$$

$$X(0) = x \in \mathbb{R}^d, S(0) = i \in S. \tag{2.1c}$$

Here, $W(\cdot,\cdot) = [W_1(\cdot), \cdots, W_d(\cdot)]'$ is a standard Wiener process and $v(\cdot)$ is a V-valued "nonanticipative" process. Indeed, one can show that [12] there exists a measurable function $h : \mathbb{R}^d \times S \times V \times \mathbb{R} \to \mathbb{R}$ such that

$$dS(t) = \int_{\mathbb{R}} h(X(t), S(t-), v(t), z)\, p(dt, dz) \tag{2.1d}$$

where $p(dt, dz)$ is a Poisson random measure independent of $W(\cdot)$ with intensity $dt \times m(dz)$, where m is the Lebesgue measure on $\mathbb{R}$. Thus $(X(\cdot), S(\cdot))$ is driven by the Wiener process $W(\cdot)$ and the Poisson random measure $p(\cdot, \cdot)$ and nonanticipativity of $v(\cdot)$ is with respect to $W(\cdot)$ and $p(\cdot, \cdot)$. See [12] for more information on this issue. Such a process $v(\cdot)$ will be called an *admissible (control) policy*. If $v(\cdot)$ is a Dirac measure, i.e., $v(\cdot) = \delta_{u(\cdot)}$, where $u(\cdot)$ is a U-valued process, then it is called an it admissible nonrandomized policy. An admissible policy is called *feedback* if $v(\cdot)$ is progressively measurable with respect to the naturål filtration of $(X(\cdot), S(\cdot))$. A particular subclass of feedback policies is of special interest. A feedback policy is called a *(homogeneous) Markov policy* if $v(t) = \tilde{v}(X(t), S(t))$ for a measurable map $\tilde{v} : \mathbb{R}^d \times S \to V$. With an abuse of notation, the map $\tilde{v}$ itself is called a Markov policy. If $(W(\cdot), p(\cdot, \cdot), v(\cdot))$ satisfying the above are given on a prescribed probability space $(\Omega, \mathcal{F}, P)$, then under (A1), (2.1) will admit an almost surely unique solution. If $v(\cdot)$ is a Markov policy then the process $(X(\cdot), S(\cdot))$ will be a strong Feller process [12]. We now introduce some notation that will be used throughout. Define for $p \geq 1$,

$$L^p(\mathbb{R}^d \times S) = \{f \;:\; \mathbb{R}^d \times S \to \mathbb{R} \;:\; \text{for each } i \in S, f(\cdot, i) \in L^p(\mathbb{R}^d)\}.$$

$L^p(\mathbb{R}^d \times S)$ is endowed with the product topology of $(L^1(\mathbb{R}^d))^N$. Similarly we define $C_0^\infty(\mathbb{R}^d \times S), W^{2,p}_{loc}(\mathbb{R}^d \times S)$, etc. For $f \in W^{2,p}_{loc}(\mathbb{R}^d \times S)$ and $u \in U$, we write

$$L^u f(x,i) \;=\; L^u_i f(x,i) + \sum_{j=1}^{N} \lambda_{ij}(x,u) f(x,j) \tag{2.2}$$

where

$$L^u_i f(x,i) = \frac{1}{2} \sum_{j,k=1}^{d} a_{jk}(x,i) \frac{\partial^2 f(x,i)}{\partial x_j \partial x_k} + \sum_{j=1}^{d} b_j(x,i,u) \frac{\partial f(x,i)}{\partial x_j}$$

$$a_{jk}(x,i) \;=\; \sum_{\ell=1}^{d} \sigma_{j\ell}(x,i)\, \sigma_{k\ell}(x,i) \tag{2.3}$$

and more generally for $v \in V$

$$L^v f(x,i) \;=\; \int_U L^u f(x,i) v(du). \tag{2.4}$$

Let $c : \;\mathbb{R}^d \times S \times U \to \mathbb{R}_+$ be the cost function.

(A2) Assume that for each $i \in S, c(\cdot, i, \cdot)$ is bounded, continuous and Lipschitz in its first argument uniformly with respect to the third.

Let $\bar{c} : \;\mathbb{R}^d \times S \times V \to \mathbb{R}$ be defined as

$$\bar{c}(\cdot, \cdot, v) \;=\; \int_U c(\cdot, \cdot, u) v(du). \tag{2.5}$$

We consider two cost evaluation criteria, *viz.* discounted cost and average cost.

Discounted Cost (DC). Let $\alpha > 0$ be the discount factor. For an admissible policy $v(\cdot)$ the total α-discounted cost under $v(\cdot)$ is defined as

$$J_\alpha^v(x,i) \;:=\; E_{x,i}^v\,[\int_0^\infty e^{-\alpha t}\,\bar{c}(X(t),S(t),v(t))dt]. \tag{2.6}$$

Let

$$V_\alpha(x,i) \;:=\; \inf_{v(\cdot)} J_\alpha^v(x,i). \tag{2.7}$$

The function $V_\alpha(x,i)$ is called the α-discounted value function. An admissible policy v is called α-DC optimal for the initial condition (x,i) if

$$V(x,i) \;=\; J_\alpha^v(x,i).$$

If a Markov policy v (the map) is α-DC optimal for any initial condition (x,i), it is called α-DC optimal.

Average Cost (AC). For an admissible policy $v(\cdot)$ the average cost is defined as

$$J^v(x,i) \;:=\; \limsup_{T\to\infty} \frac{1}{T}\, E_{x,i}^v \int_0^T \bar{c}(X(t),S(t),v(t))dt. \tag{2.8}$$

AC-optimality is defined analogously. One can also consider pathwise average optimality (see [13] for details). A Markov policy $v(\cdot)$ is called *stable* if the corresponding process $(X(\cdot),S(\cdot))$ has a unique invariant probability measure denoted by $\eta_v \in \mathcal{P}(\mathbb{R}^d \times S)$. Under such a policy, for any $(x,i) \in \mathbb{R}^d \times S$

$$J^v(x,i) \;=\; \sum_{i=1}^N \int_{\mathbb{R}^d} \bar{c}(x,i,v(x,i))\;\eta_v(dx,\{i\}) \;:=\; \rho_v. \tag{2.9}$$

For the AC-case we want to establish the existence of a stable Markov policy which is AC-optimal.

Remark 2.1. The boundness condition in (A2) can be replaced by an appropriate growth condition.

3 Existence Results

We first consider the DC-criterion. Following [12] we will use a convex analytic approach to establish the existence of a DC-optimal policy. To this end we define α-discounted occupation measures. Let $v(\cdot)$ be an admissible policy and $(X(\cdot),S(\cdot))$ the corresponding process with fixed initial condition (x,i). Define the α-discounted occupation measure $\nu_\alpha[v] \in \mathcal{P}(\mathcal{R}^d \times S \times U)$ by

$$\sum_{i=1}^N \int_{\mathbb{R}^d \times U} f(x,i,u)\nu_\alpha[v]\,(dx,\{i\},du)$$

$$= \alpha\, E^v_{x,i}\Big[\int_0^\infty e^{-\alpha t}\int_U f(X(t),S(t),u)v(t)(du)dt\Big], \tag{3.1}$$

for $f \in C_b(\mathbb{R}^d \times S \times U)$. In fact $\nu_\alpha[v]$ will depend on the initial condition (x,i), but we suppress this dependence for notational convenience. In terms of $\nu_\alpha[v]$, (2.6) becomes

$$J^v_\alpha(x,i) \;=\; \alpha^{-1}\sum_{i=1}^N \int_{\mathbb{R}^d\times U} c(x,i,u)\nu_\alpha[v](dx,\{i\},du). \tag{3.2}$$

Let

$$M_1 = \{\nu^v_\alpha[v] \;\in \mathcal{P}(\mathbb{R}^d \times S \times U) \mid v(\cdot) \text{ is an admissible policy}\} \tag{3.3}$$

$$M_2 = \{\nu^v_\alpha[v] \;\in \mathcal{P}(\mathbb{R}^d \times S \times U) \mid v(\cdot) \text{ is a Markov policy}\} \tag{3.4}$$

$$M_3 \;=\; \{\nu^v_\alpha[v] \;\in \mathcal{P}(\mathbb{R}^d \times S \times U) \mid v(\cdot) \text{ is a Markov nonrandomized policy}\} \tag{3.5}$$

In view of (3.2), the DC-optimal control problem becomes a linear programming problem on the space of discounted occupation measures M_1. Using some techniques from probability and analysis the following result is proved in [12].

Theorem 3.1. $M_1 = M_2$, and M_2 is compact and convex. Also, $M_2^e \subset M_3$, where M_2^e denotes the set of extreme points of M_2.

Theorem 3.2. Under (A1), (A2) there exists a Markov nonrandomized policy which is α-DC optimal.

Proof (Sketch). Clearly the map

$$M_2 \ni \nu \longmapsto \sum_i \int_{\mathbb{R}^d\times U} c\; d\nu$$

is continuous. Thus for a fixed initial condition (x,i) there exists a Markov policy v^* such that

$$J^{v^*}_\alpha(x,i) \;=\; V_\alpha(x,i). \tag{3.6}$$

Using the strong Feller property of the corresponding process $(X(\cdot),S(\cdot))$, one can show that (3.6) holds for any initial condition (x,i). Since M_2 is compact, by Choquet's theorem [17] $\nu_\alpha[v^*]$ is the barycenter of a probability measure ℓ supported on M_2^e. Therefore

$$\sum_{i=1}^{N} \int_{\mathbb{R}^d \times U} c(x,i,u)\nu_\alpha[v^*](dx,\{i\},du) = \int_{M_2^e} (\sum_{i=1}^{N} \int_{\mathbb{R}^d \times U} c(x,i,u)\, \mu(dx,\{i\},du))\, \ell(d\mu). \tag{3.7}$$

Since v^* is optimal, it follows from (3.7) that there exists a $\nu_\alpha[\bar{v}] \in M_2^e$ such that

$$\sum_{i=1}^{N} \int_{\mathbb{R}^d \times U} c(x,i,u)\, \nu_\alpha[v^*]\,(dx,\{i\},du) = \sum_{i=1}^{N} \int_{\mathbb{R}^d \times U} c(x,i,u)\, \nu_\alpha[\bar{v}]\,(dx,\{i\},du).$$

Thus $\bar{v}$ is also optimal. By Theorem 3.1, $\bar{v}$ is nonrandomized. ■

Remark 3.1. It is interesting to note the similarities between ordinary linear programming in a Euclidean space and our treatment of establishing the existence of a Markov nonrandomized policy which is α-DC optimal. In the usual LP, the objective function is linear and the feasible domain is a compact, convex polygon in a Euclidean space. By compactness and continuity there is a point in the polygon where the objective function attains its minimum. By the Minkowski theorem [18, p. 50], any point in the polygon can be expressed as a convex combination of its vertices (extreme points). By linearity of the objective function, there is a vertex where the minimum is also attained. We have extended this idea to our problem. Technical details, though, are vastly different.

We next consider the AC-criterion. Let v be a stable Markov policy. Recall the definition of η_v and ρ_v from (2.9). Since we seek an AC-optimal policy which is stable, Markov and nonrandomized, it is natural to assume that one such policy exists. Our goal is, in general, not achievable as the following simple counterexample shows [4, Chapter 6]. Let $c(x,i,u) = exp(-\,|x|^2)$. Then for every stable policy the average cost is positive, while one can find an unstable Markov policy for which the average cost is zero, making it an optimal policy. We want to rule out this possibility, as stability is a very desirable property. We carry out our study under two alternate sets of hypotheses: (a) a condition on the cost which penalizes unstable behavior, (b) a blanket stability condition which implies that all Markov policies are stable.

Let

$$\rho^* := \inf_{v \text{ stable Markov}} \rho_v . \tag{3.8}$$

(A3) Assume that for each $i \in S$

$$\liminf_{|x| \to \infty} \inf_{u \in U} c(x,i,u) > \rho^* . \tag{3.9}$$

Intuitively, (3.9) penalizes the drift of the process away from some compact set, requiring the optimal policy to exert some kind of "centripetal force" pushing the process back towards this compact set. Thus, the optimal policy gains the desired stability property. If $c(x,i,u) = K(|x|)$ for some increasing function $K : \mathbb{R}_+ \to \mathbb{R}_+$ then (3.9) is satisfied. Such cost functions arise quite often in practice. The condition of the type (A3) is referred to as near-monotonicity condition [4, Chapter 6].

(A4) There exists a $w \in C^2(\mathbb{R}^d \times S), w \geq 0$ such that
(i) $w(x,i) \to \infty$ as $|x| \to \infty$ uniformly in $|x|$ for each i,
(ii) For each Markov policy v, $E^v_{x,i} w(X(t), S(t))$ and $E^v_{x,i} \mid L^v w(X(t), S(t)) \mid$ are locally bounded.
(iii) There exist $p > 0, q > 0$ such that

$$L^u w(x,i) \leq p - qw(x,i) \text{ for each } u \in U.$$

Remark 3.2. Note that (A4) is a Liapunov type stability condition. Under (A1) and (A4) all Markov policies are stable. For more information on Liapunov functions for switching diffusions, we refer to [2].

For a stable Markov policy v we define the ergodic occupation measure $\mu[v] \in \mathcal{P}(\mathbb{R}^d \times S \times U)$ as

$$\mu[v](dx, \{i\}, du) \ = \ \eta_v(dx, \{i\}) v(x,i)(du). \tag{3.10}$$

Let

$$I_1 \ = \ \{\mu[v] : \ v \text{ is a stable Markov policy}\}$$

$$\mathrm{I}_2 \ = \ \{\mu[v] : \ v \text{ is a stable Markov nonrandomized policy}\}$$

Lemma 3.1. Under (A1), the sets I_1, I_2 are closed, I_1 is convex and the set of extreme points of I_1 lie in I_2. Under (A1) and (A4), I_1, I_2 are compact.

Note for a stable Markov policy v

$$J_v(x,i) \ = \ \rho_v \ = \sum_{i=1}^{N} \int_{\mathbb{R}^d \times U} c(x,i,u) \ \mu[v](dx, \{i\}, du).$$

Hence the AC-optimality on the set of Markov policies becomes a linear programming problem on I_1. We can then develop a linear programming approach to this case to conclude the following result. For details see [12].

Theorem 3.3. Under (A1), (A2), (A3) or (A1), (A2), (A4) there exists a stable Markov nonrandomized policy which is AC-optimal.

4 Hamilton-Jacobi-Bellman (HJB) Equations

Using the existence results of the previous section, we can drive the dynamic programming or HJB equations for both DC and AC criteria. These equations are weakly coupled systems of quasilinear uniformly elliptic equations. We can then characterize the optimal policy as a minimizing selector of an appropriate "Hamiltonian". Here we present only the results; for proofs and other details see [12], [13]. We first consider the DC-case.

Theorem 4.1. Under (A1), (A2) the α-discounted value function $V_\alpha(x,i)$ is the unique solution in $C^2(\mathbb{R}^d \times S) \cap C_b(\mathcal{R}^d \times S)$ of

$$\alpha\psi(x,i) = \inf_{u\in U} [L^u\psi(x,i) + c(x,i,u)]. \tag{4.1}$$

A Markov nonrandomized policy v is α-DC optimal if and only if

$$\sum_{m=1}^{d} b_j(x,i,v(x,i)) \frac{\partial V_\alpha(x,i)}{\partial x_j} + \sum_{k=1}^{N} \lambda_{ik}(x,v(x,i))\, V_\alpha(x,k) + c(x,i,v,(x,i))$$

$$= \inf_{u\in U} [\sum_{j=1}^{N} b_j(x,i,u) \frac{\partial V_\alpha(x,i)}{\partial x_j} + \sum_{k=1}^{N} \lambda_{ik}(x,u)\, V_\alpha(x,k)$$

$$+ c(x,i,u)], a.e. x \in \mathbb{R}^d, i \in S. \tag{4.2}$$

The AC-case is much more involved. The HJB equations for this case are given by

$$\inf_{u\in U} [L^u\psi(x,i) + c(x,i,u)] = \rho \tag{4.3}$$

where $\psi : \mathbb{R}^d \times S \to \mathbb{R}$ and ρ is a scalar. Solving (4.3) means finding an appropriate pair (ψ,ρ) satisfying (4.3). To establish the existence of a solution to (4.3) we follow the vanishing discount approach, *i.e.*, we derive the HJB equations for the AC-case as a vanishing limit of the HJB equations for α-DC criterion as $\alpha \to 0$. Under (A1), (A2), (A3) or (A1), (A2), (A4) one first shows that for some $\alpha_0 > 0$, $| V_\alpha(x,i) - V_\alpha(y,j) |, \alpha \in (0,\alpha_0)$ is uniformly bounded in α, for x,y belonging to compact subsets of $\mathbb{R}^d$ and any $i,j \in S$. Then setting $\alpha \to 0$ and using various results from the theory of uniformly elliptic *p.d.e.* one derives a solution of (4.3).

Theorem 4.2. Under (A1), (A2) and (A3), there exists a unique pair $(V,\rho^*) \in C^2(\mathbb{R}^d \times S) \times \mathbb{R}$ satisfying (4.3) and

$$V(0,i_0) = 0, \inf_x V(x,i) > -\infty \text{ and } \rho \le \rho^*. \tag{4.4}$$

Under (A1), (A2) and (A4), (4.3) admits a unique solution (V,ρ^*) in the class $C^2(\mathbb{R}^d \times S) \cap 0(w(\cdot))$, satisfying $V(0,i_0) = 0$ for a fixed $i_0 \in S$. Also, under (A1), (A2), (A3) or (A1), (A2), (A4), a stable Markov nonrandomized policy v is AC-optimal if and only if

$$\inf_u [\sum_{j=1}^{d} b_j(x,i,u) \frac{\partial V(x,i)}{\partial x_j} + \sum_{j=1}^{N} \lambda_{ij}(x,u)\, V(x,j) + c(x,i,u)]$$

$$= [\sum_{j=1}^{d} b_j(x,i,v(x,i)) \frac{\partial V(x,i)}{\partial x_j} + \sum_{j=1}^{N} \lambda_{ij}(x,v(x,i))\, V(x,j)$$

$$+ c(x,i,v(x,i))] \text{ a.e. } x \in \mathbb{R}^d, i \in S. \tag{4.5}$$

5 An Application to a Simplified Manufacturing Model

We consider a modified version of [1]. Suppose there is one machine producing a single commodity. We assume that the demand rate $d > 0$. Let the machine state $S(t)$ take values in $\{0,1\}, S(t) = 0$ or 1, according to whether the machine is down or functional. Let $S(t)$ be a continuous time Markov chain with generator

$$\begin{bmatrix} -\lambda_0 & \lambda_0 \\ \lambda_1 & -\lambda_1 \end{bmatrix}.$$

The inventory $X(t)$ is governed by the equation

$$dX(t) \; = \; (u(t) - d)dt \; + \; \sigma \, dW(t) \tag{5.1}$$

where $\sigma > 0$. The production rate is constrained by

$$u(t) \; = \; \begin{cases} 0 \text{ if} & S(t) = 0 \\ \in [0, R] \text{ if } S(t) = 1. \end{cases}$$

Let $c : \mathbb{R} \to \mathbb{R}_+$ be the cost function which is assumed to be convex and Lipschitz continuous. The α-discounted value function $V_\alpha(x, i)$ is the minimal nonnegative C^2 solution of the HJB equation given by

$$\begin{bmatrix} \frac{\sigma^2}{2} \, V_\alpha''(x,0) \; - \; dV_\alpha'(x,0) \\ \frac{\sigma^2}{2} \, V_\alpha''(x,1) \; + \; \min_{u \in [0,R]} \{(u-d)V'(x,i)\} \end{bmatrix} = \begin{bmatrix} \lambda_0 + \alpha & -\lambda_0 \\ -\lambda_1 & \lambda_1 + \alpha \end{bmatrix} \begin{bmatrix} V_\alpha(x,0) \\ V_\alpha(x,1) \end{bmatrix}$$
$$- \begin{bmatrix} 1 \\ 1 \end{bmatrix} c(x). \tag{5.2}$$

Using the convexity of $c(\cdot)$, it can be shown that $V_\alpha(\cdot, i)$ is convex for each i. Hence there exists x^* such that

$$V_\alpha'(x,1) \begin{array}{l} \leq 0 \text{ for } x \leq x^* \\ \geq 0 \text{ for } x \geq x^*. \end{array} \tag{5.3}$$

From (5.2) it follows that the value of u which minimizes $(u - d)V'(x, 1)$ is

$$u = \begin{cases} R \text{ if } x \leq x^* \\ 0 \text{ if } x \geq x^* \end{cases}$$

At $x = x^*, V_\alpha'(x, 1) = 0$ and therefore any $u \in [0, R]$ minimizes $(u - d)V_\alpha'(x, 1)$. Thus, in view of Theorem 4.1, we can choose any $u \in [0, R]$ at $x = x^*$. To be specific, we choose $u = d$ at $x = x^*$. It follows that the following Markov nonrandomized policy is α-DC optimal:

$$v(x,0) = 0, v(x,1) \; = \; \begin{cases} R \text{ if } x < x^* \\ d \text{ if } x = x^* \\ 0 \text{ if } x > x^*. \end{cases} \tag{5.4}$$

We note at this point that the corresponding piecewise deterministic model, in general, would lead to a singular control problem when $V'(x, 1) = 0$ [1], [14].

In the switching diffusion case the additive noise in (5.1) induces a smoothing effect to remove the singular situation.

We now discuss briefly the more complex multiple machine manufacturing model described in [12] and [14]. The machine state is again a prescribed continuous time Markov chain taking values in $\{1, \cdots, M\}$. For each $i \in S$, the product rate $u = (u_1, \cdots, u_N)$ takes values in U_i, a convex polyhedron in $\mathbb{R}^N$. The demand rate is $d = [d_1, \cdots, d_N]'$. In this case if the cost function $c : \mathbb{R}^N \to \mathbb{R}_+$ is Lipschitz continuous and convex, then it can be shown that for each $i \in S$, the α-discounted value function $V_\alpha(x, i)$ is convex. From this fact alone optimal policies of the type (5.4) cannot be obtained. However, since an α-DC optimal Markov nonrandomized policy is determined by minimizing

$$\sum_{i=1}^{N} (u_j - d_j) \frac{\partial V_\alpha(x, i)}{\partial x_j}$$

over $U_i, v(x, i)$ takes values at extreme points of U_i. Thus, for each machine state i, an optimal policy divides the buffer state space into a set of regions in which the production rate is constant. If the gradient $\nabla V_\alpha(x, i)$ is zero or orthogonal to a face of U_i, a unique minimizing value does not exist. But again, in view of Theorem 4.1, we may prescribe arbitrary production rates at those points where $\nabla V_\alpha(x, i) = 0$, and if $\nabla V_\alpha(x, i)$ is orthogonal to a face of U_i, we can choose any corner of that face. Hence, once again, we can circumvent the singular situation.

We next consider the AC-case for the single machine problem. Let the cost function $c(x) = \bar{c}(|x|)$ for some $\bar{c} : \mathbb{R}_+ \to \mathbb{R}_+$ which is increasing. Thus $c(\cdot)$ satisfies (A3). The HJB equations in this case are

$$\begin{bmatrix} \frac{\sigma^2}{2} V''(x, 0) - dV'(x, 0) \\ \frac{\sigma^2}{2} V''(x, 1) + \min_{u \in [0, R]} \{(u - d)V'(x, 1)\} \end{bmatrix} + \begin{bmatrix} -\lambda_0 & \lambda_0 \\ \lambda_1 & -\lambda_1 \end{bmatrix} \begin{bmatrix} V(x, 0) \\ V(x, 1) \end{bmatrix}$$

$$= \begin{bmatrix} 1 \\ 1 \end{bmatrix} \rho - \begin{bmatrix} 1 \\ 1 \end{bmatrix} c(x). \tag{5.5}$$

As before, $V(x, 1)$ is convex and there exists an $\bar{x}$ such that $V'(\bar{x}, 1) = 0$. Thus the following policy $\bar{v}$ is AC-optimal.

$$\bar{v}(x, 0) = 0, \bar{v}(x, 1) = \begin{cases} R \text{ if } x < \bar{x} \\ d \text{ if } x = \bar{x} \\ 0 \text{ if } x > \bar{x}. \end{cases} \tag{5.6}$$

The stability of the policy (5.6) is ensured if

$$\frac{R - d}{\lambda_1} > \frac{d}{\lambda_0}. \tag{5.7}$$

The condition (5.6) is very appealing from an intuitive point of view. Note that λ_0^{-1} and λ_1^{-1} are mean sojourn times of the chain in states 0 and 1, respectively. In state 0 the mean inventory depletes at a rate d while in state 1 it builds up at a rate $(R-d)$. Thus, if (5.6) is satisfied, one would expect the zero-inventory policy v given by

$$v(x,0)=0, v(x,1)=\begin{cases} R \text{ if } x\leq 0 \\ 0 \text{ if } x>0 \end{cases} \tag{5.8}$$

to stabilize the system. The analysis carried out in [13] confirms this intuition. In [3], Bielecki and Kumar have studied the mean square stability of the piecewise deterministic system, *i.e.*, (5.1) with $\sigma = 0$. They have shown that for

$$\frac{R-d}{\lambda_1} \leq \frac{d}{\lambda_0} \tag{5.9}$$

the policy (5.8) is mean square stable. Our analysis in [13] shows that additive noise in (5.1) retains the stability of the zero-inventory policy as long as strict inequality holds in (5.8). Note that if the zero-inventory policy is stable then the policy given in (5.6) is also stable. For more details see [13].

6 Concluding Remarks

We have studied controlled switching diffusions as a particular class of hybrid control systems. The defining characteristics of hybrid control systems are the involvement of and interaction between the continuous and discrete components and an input (control) process altering the course of either or both the components. The discrete behavior arises due to several factors such as autonomous/controlled jumps, etc. Branicky *et al.* [8] have studied deterministic hybrid control systems in a very general framework. Their model incorporates autonomous/controlled switchings, autonomous/controlled jumps, impulses as well as switching and impulse delays, etc. Their model subsumes all the existing deterministic hybrid models in the literature. In their model the dynamics between the switchings and jumps is purely deterministic. One can incorporate various uncertainties and develop a stochastic hybrid model where the evolution between the switchings and jumps is governed by stochastic differential equations [5]. The controlled switching diffusion model studied here incorporates controlled switchings but not controlled jumps. The drift of the continuous component changes discontinuously as the discrete component jumps, but there is no discontinuity in the sample path of the continuous component. One advantage of this model lies in the study of the stability of the system. Under a Markov policy the process $(X(t), S(t))$ is a strong Feller process. Due to nondegeneracy it is irreducible. Hence for this system the stability is equivalent to the existence of a unique invariant probability measure of the process $(X(t), S(t))$. This plays a crucial role in the ergodic control problem as we have observed in this paper.

7 References

[1] R. Akella and P. R. Kumar, Optimal control of production rate in a failure prone manufacturing system, IEEE Trans. Aut. Cont., 31 (1986), 116-126.

[2] G. K. Basak, A. Bisi and M. K. Ghosh, Controlled random degenerate diffusions under long-run average cost, Preprint.

[3] T. Bielecki and P. R. Kumar, Optimality of zero-inventory policies for unreliable manufacturing systems, Opers. Res. 36 (1988), 532-546.

[4] V. B. Borkar, Optimal Control of Diffusion Processes, Pitman Research Notes in Math. Ser. No. 203, Longman, Harlow, UK, 1989.

[5] V. S. Borkar, M. K. Ghosh and P. Sahay, Stochastic hybrid systems, in preparation.

[6] E. K. Boukas and A. Haurie, Manufacturing flow control and preventive maintenance: a stochastic control approach, IEEE Trans. Automat. Control, AC-35 (199), 1024-1031.

[7] M. S. Branicky, Studies in hybrid systems: modeling, analysis, and control, Technical Report LIDS-TH-2304, Laboratory for Information and Decision Systems, Massachusetts Institute of Technology, June 1995.

[8] M. S. Branicky, V. S. Borkar and S. K. Mitter, A unified framework for hybrid control: background, model and theory, Preprint.

[9] C. Chase, J. Serrano, and P. J. Ramadge, Periodicity and chaos from switched flow systems: contrasting examples of discretely controlled continuous systems, IEEE Trans. Automat. Control, 38 (1993), 70-83.

[10] D. A. Castanon, M. Coderch, B. C. Levy and A. S. Willsky, Asymptotic analysis, approximation, and aggregation methods for stochastic hybrid systems, Proc. 1980 Joint Aut. Cont. Conference, San Francisco, CA, 1980.

11] M. K. Ghosh, A. Arapostathis and S. I. Marcus, A note on an LQG regulator with Markovian switching and pathwise average cost, Technical Report TR92-81rl, Institute for Systems Research, University of Maryland at College Park; to appear in IEEE Trans. Automat. Control.

[12] M. K. Ghosh, A. Arapostathis and S. I. Marcus, Optimal control of switching diffusions with application to flexible manufacturing systems, SIAM J. Control Optim. 31 (1993), 1183-1204.

[13] M. K. Ghosh, A. Arapostathis and S. I. Marcus, Ergodic control of switching diffusions, Technical Research Report, Systems Research Center, University of Maryland at College Park, TR92-80rl.

[14] J. Kimenia and S. B. Gershwin, An algorithm for the computer control of a flexible manufacturing system, IIE Trans., 15 (1983), 343-362.

[15] M. Lehoczky, S. Sethi, H. M. Soner and M. Taksar, An asymptotic analysis of hierarchical control of manufacturing systems under uncertainty, Math. Oper. Res., 16 (1991), 596-608.

[16] M. Mariton, Jump Linear Systems in Automatic Control, Marcel Dekker, New York, 1990.

[17] R. Phelps, Lectures on Choquet's Theorem, Van Nostrand, New York, 1966.

[18] J. Van Tiel, Convex Analysis, John Wiley, New York, 1984.

[19] W. M. Wonham, Random differential equations in control theory, Probabilistic Methods in Applied Mathematics, A. T. Bharucha-Reid, ed., vol. 2, Academic Press, New York, 1970, 131-212.

Hybrid Systems: Chattering Approximation to Relaxed Controls

Xiaolin Ge*[1] and Wolf Kohn**[2] and Anil Nerode***[3] and Jeffrey B. Remmel†[4]

[1] Mathematical Sciences Institute, Cornell University, Ithaca, New York 14853
e-mail:xge@math.cornell.edu

[2] Sagent Corporation, 11201 SE 8th Street #J140, Bellevue, Washington 98004
e-mail: Wolf_Kohn@sagent.com

[3] Mathematical Sciences Institute, Cornell University, Ithaca, New York 14853
e-mail: anil@math.cornell.edu

[4] Department of Mathematics, University of California at San Diego, La Jolla, California 92093
e-mail: jremmel@ucsd.edu

Abstract. We explain a main connection between relaxed control and hybrid systems. We summarize the non-multiple agent aspects of our research. We describe new algorithms for approximating relaxed optimal controls based on a generalized form of linear programming using convex analysis. Finally we use chattering to derive an analogue of the Hamilton-Jacobi-Bellman equation and dynamic programming in our hybrid systems model.

1 Introduction

Our view is that hybrid systems arise whenever we need to augment a physical system with a feedback control and no physically realizable continuous real valued feedback control law exists which can enforce the desired behavior. Suppose we are given a continuous plant with state x and an actuator to change plant state, and we would like a feedback control law $c = F(x)$ for actuator control values which produces a plant state trajectory $x(t)$ minimizing the integral (cost) of a non-negative cost function (Lagrangian) $L(x, \dot{x})$ along the trajectory, subject to constraints and goals. The calculus of variations which underlies optimal control often cannot guarantee that there exists a real valued optimal control function $F(x)$. But if we allow relaxed control functions $F(x)$ whose values are

* Research supported by U.S. Army Research Office contract DAAL03-91-C-0027.

** Research supported by SDIO contract DAA H-04-93-C-0113, Dept. of Commerce Agreement 70-NANB5H1164.

*** Research supported by U.S. Army Research Office contract DAAL03-91-C-0027, SDIO contract DAA H-04-93-C-0113, Dept. of Commerce Agreement 70-NANB5H1164.

† Research supported by U.S. Army Research Office contract DAAL03-91-C-0027, Dept. of Commerce Agreement 70-NANB5H1164, NSF grant DMS-9306427.

probability measures on the space of real control values, very often a relaxed solution exists when no real valued solution exists ([W72], [Y80]). The lack of real valued optimal solutions is usually due to the lack of convexity of the manifold on which trajectories evolve or the lack of convexity of $g(u) = L(x, u)$ with respect to u. Such relaxed, but not real valued, solutions are not physically meaningful or implementable, but exist as a result of Hilbert's direct method for proving the existence of solutions to variational problems by Ascoli's lemma.

Chattering Controls.

The Kohn-Nerode MAHCA multiple agent hybrid control architecture ([KN93c], [KN93a]) for extraction of digital control programs to enforce behavior is based on the following principle in the single agent case.

a) First, ease the optimality criterion to ϵ-optimality, that is, produce a trajectory that esnusre that the integral of the Lagrangian over the trajectory is within a prescribed ϵ of the absolute minimum. Here ϵ determined by the end user and the cost of achieving that optimality.

b) Second, construct a finite state digital program (digital control automaton) and a time control interval Δ. Presented with a digital observation of plant state as evaluated through sensors, at times $n\Delta$ the automaton issues a "chattering approximation" to the measure valued non-implementable optimal control and uses this chattering control up to time $(n+1)\Delta$ in such a way that an ϵ-optimal trajectory is obtained. What is a chattering control? We confine ourselves to the case when the description of the plant is by an ordinary autonomous differential equation $\dot{x} = f(x, c, \ldots)$ with control parameters $c, \ldots$. Then a chattering control is a finite sequence $c = c_i$ of control values, each used successively in the equation as a value of c for a specific percent $100\alpha_i$ of the control time interval of length Δ. The α_i's have to be non-negative and add up to 1. These α_i's are the chattering coefficients of the corresponding control values c_i.

Carrier Manifolds.

We have called the manifold on which the plant state trajectory evolves the "carrier manifold" of the problem. The local coordinates of the carrier manifold contain the plant state coordinates but also coordinates for control values and whatever else is involved in determining the total Lagrangian cost of the trajectory. We abuse notation by using x here for the local coordinates of a carrier manifold point. When there are also digital constraints, such as logic constraints, we "continualize" the discrete constraints so that all constraints are jointly represented by the carrier manifold ([KNRG95]).

Control Derivations.

Differentiating f with respect to any control parameter c defines a "control vector field" on the carrier manifold. Each such control vector field has an infinitesimal generator which is a derivation of the algebra of scalar functions on the manifold, the vector field being the Lie exponential of the derivation. The derivations arising from the finite number of control parameters generate a Lie algebra, which may or may not be finite dimensional vector space. If finite dimensional, there are powerful algebraic methods available. If not, approximations by iterated Lie brackets using Lie-Taylor expansions of exponentials and Trotter's formula are needed.

Chattering Controls as Lie Words.

In practice, there are only a finite number of control parameters, and each parameter is employed for a time which is an integer multiple of a fixed minimal δ. So $\Delta = k\delta$ for a fixed integer k. In this case we can omit explicit mention of the chattering coefficients and time δ and code each chattering control of duration Δ as a "Lie word" $d_{i_1} \cdots d_{i_k}$ in the finite alphabet consisting of the derivations obtained by differentiating f with respect to each of its control parameters. The value of the feedback function $F(x)$ may as well be such a word $d_1 \cdots d_k$ of length k. To repeat, this value is a sequence of k derivations $d_1, \ldots, d_k$ used jointly as a chattering control over a time interval $[n\Delta, (n+1)\Delta]$ when the initial state at time $n\Delta$ was x_0. That is, the trajectory evolves from $x_0 = x$ for time δ according to the vector field generated by exponentiating d_1, ending at x_1, which is then evolved according to the vector field generated by exponentiating d_2, getting x_2, etc., finally getting x_n at time $(n+1)\Delta$.

Such words are Lie descriptions of possible digital outputs for the finite state control automata. They have to be converted by a digital to analog converter into control settings for actuators so that the evolution can take place in applications to physical systems.

The Resulting Hybrid System.

In the situation above, sensor readings have to be converted to digital form before being input to the control automaton, the control automaton digital output has to be converted by a digital to analog converter to a continuous signal to input to the actuator. We thus obtain a hybrid system consisting of the original continuous plant, sensor, actuator, and analog to digital and digital to analog converter. The feedback loop is completed by the digital control automaton.

Remarks.

1) Chattering can also be useful for problems in which a real valued optimal control exists.

2) Chattering controls can sometimes achieve lower values than any real valued control.

3) Chattering controls can be easier to implement than optimal real valued controls.

Small Topologies on Plant States.

We view the input alphabet of the control automaton as coding observations of plant state. We have argued elsewhere that arbitrarily small fluctuations in plant state should not change which one of the finitely many input letters is fired, hence that each input letter should be fired by an open set of states. We have shown that the minimal non-empty open sets of the finite topology generated by the open sets firing the input alphabet can be taken as the set of states of the finite control automaton achieving the ϵ-optimal system behavior. We call this finite topology the associated small topology on the plant state space.

Finsler Manifolds and Optimal Control.

In [KNR95], we transform optimal control problems to parametric variational problems by introducing time as explicit variable (following Weierstrass). The basic hypotheses about the new $L(x,\dot{x})$ so obtained are:

L is homogeneous of degree 1 in $\dot{x}$.

$$L(x,\lambda\dot{x}) = \lambda L(x,\dot{x}) \text{ for } \lambda \geq 0, \tag{1}$$

and

$L(x,\dot{x})$ is positive definite in $\dot{x}$.

$$(g_{ij}(x,\dot{x})) = \left(\frac{1}{2}\frac{\partial^2(L^2(x,\dot{x}))}{\partial\dot{x}_i\partial\dot{x}_j}\right) \tag{2}$$

is a positive definite matrix for each fixed x.

Finsler discovered that, with suitable smoothness assumptions, the Hessian g_{ij} of a regular parametric calculus of variations problem on a manifold induces a corresponding element of arclength or metric ground form, ds^2. The infinitesimal arclength for the Finsler manifold is defined by

$$ds^2 = \sum_{ij} g_{ij}(x,dx)dx_i dx_j. \tag{3}$$

The homogeneity of degree 2 in $\dot{x}$ of $L^2(x,\dot{x})$ implies that

$$L^2(x,\dot{x}) = \sum_{ij} g_{ij}(x,\dot{x})\dot{x}_i\dot{x}_j. \tag{4}$$

Thus another expression for the same thing is

$$ds^2 = L^2(x,dx). \tag{5}$$

This leads to defining $\dot{x}$ to be of *Finsler* length 1 if $L(x,\dot{x}) = 1$. This unit sphere defines a norm on the tangent space to the manifold at x. This unit sphere is called the tangent indicatrix ([B90], [M86], [R59], [R66]). (We confine ourselves in this discussion to real valued optimal control laws.) The geodesics under the metric ground form are the extremals of the corresponding parametric variational problem, that is, they are solutions to the Euler-Lagrange equations.

$$\frac{d}{ds}\frac{\partial L(x,\dot{x}_i)}{\partial\dot{x}_i} - \frac{\partial L(x,\dot{x})}{\partial x_i} = 0. \tag{6}$$

Control Policies From Connections.

We illustrate here the simple case when for a point x_0 on the Finsler manifold and a non-zero tangent vector y_1 at any other point x_1, x_1 can be reached by exactly one geodesic so that the tangent vector at x_1 is y_1. Since geodesics are extremals for the parametric variational problem, to achieve the goal of reaching x_1 with tangent vector y_1, we should follow an appropriate geodesic from initial point x_0. To continue along the appropriate geodesic, at any intermediate point x, we always have to head along the tangent y to that geodesic at the point x. So when at point x, the problem is to compute the tangent vector y of the required geodesic which leads to goal (x_1, y_1). Fixing the goal, we can write $y = P(x)$ as the desired control policy. Now embed the carrier manifold of dimension n in $n(n+1)/2$ dimensional Euclidean space. Following Cartan ([C34]) and Levi-Civita, introduce an orthogonal basis, or moving frame, with origin at x on a geodesic and with the principal normal to the geodesic as first member of the basis, so the rest is an orthogonal basis for the tangent space to the manifold. Consider a pair of infinitely close tangent planes, one at x, one at $x + dx$, along the geodesic, intersecting on a line, and form the equations of the infinitesimal rotation over that line as axis of the tangent plane at x into the tangent plane at $x + dx$. Integrating this one point boundary value problem we get the "equations of parallel transport" which compute how the moving frame moves down the geodesic starting at x_1 to get an image frame at x. The image of tangent vector y_1 in the tangent plane at x_1 under parallel transport is a tangent vector y at x. The desired control policy is $y = P(x)$. The equations of parallel transport define an affine connnection and involve the Christoffel ceofficients. Other connections, affine or otherwise, could be used instead. It is not yet clear which is best computationally.

The Hamilton-Jacobi Equation on Manifolds.

In a sequel in preparation ([KNR96]), we go to the dual analytical mechanics formulation based on plant state x and generalized momentum p as coordinates. The so-called figuratrix is the unit sphere on the tangent space.

The derivation outlined above of the Levi-Civita-Cartan connection, writing the equations of an infinitesimal rotation between nearby tangent planes along a geodesic and integrating, is very similar to the derivation of the integral Bellman equation from the principle of optimality by integrating the equations of the infinitesimal equation obtained by taking x and $x + \delta x$ on an optimal trajectory, subtracting the "cost to go" function at point x from the corresponding "cost to go" at $x + \delta x$, dividing that difference by δx, and letting δx approach zero.

This analogy is no accident. It makes sense in Finsler manifolds provided the points are on the same geodesic. Thus one is led to using the Hamilton-Jacobi equations in Finsler space as Bellman equations. We do this and are interested in solving the Bellman-Hamilton-Jacobi equations for optimal control policies. Because Finsler manifolds arising from variational problems generally have nonzero curvature, the symbolic solutions to the Bellman equations on the manifold will contain the Christoffel coefficients. This leads to consideration of Carathèodory's "complete figure" and geodesic fields.

An ϵ-optimal policy implemented by a finite state control automaton should, as we have said above, issue as control commands Lie words which chatter vector fields and produce a plant state trajectory approximately following a Finsler geodesic to the goal. If we take a Taylor series with indeterminate coefficients around x and substitute it into both sides of the Bellman-Hamilton-Jacobi equation, we get an infinite set of recurrence equations by equating coefficients of like terms. This infinite set of recursion equations can, for the purpose of achieving ϵ–optimality, be reduced to a finite set of equations. This is because states in the same minimal open set in the small topology on plant state space are indistinguishable and the number of minimal open sets in the small topology is finite. Since solving the Bellman-Hamilton-Jacobi equations gives an optimal control policy which tells what direction $\dot{x}$ to steer in terms of control values, that is, gives a control derivation, we can write the finite set of equations as equations whose solutions are non-commutative power series in derivations. The finite state character of the solutions arising from the non-empty minimal open set structure on plant states means that we are looking for rational non-commutative Schutzenberger power series solutions. These represent finite automata that assure ϵ-optimality.

The Eilenberg [E74] elimination algorithm for solving such equations could be used to compute the transition diagram of a non-deterministic finite control automaton meeting the requirements and solving the finite set of equations. But this is computationally infeasible. Instead we solve only for the chattering control which is currently required for carrying out the control policy when we are in current state x on the carrier manifold. Thus the total finite control automaton state transition table is never computed.

Agents.

There is another reason for not bothering to have the transition diagram in table form. This is because we are likely to change it online to adapt to changing circumstances. In real time applications there are always partially unknown dynamics. There is a need to change the old automaton for a new one whenever we observe that a conservation law is violated which would hold if the model used were a correct representation of the world. This leads to our concept of agent, a software program to deal with the online redefinition of both the carrier manifold and the Lagrangian, and the online recomputation of the automata equations and the desired control automaton output law when the system is in state x. (For multiple agents the situation is similar but more complicated ([KNRG95], [GNRR93]).)

Where do we get the conservation laws which serve as warnings that we need to change the model and the control automaton? The conservation laws used to observe a deviation from desired behavior can be obtained by the application of the Noether algorithm for deriving conservation laws for variational problems by symbolic manipulations. However, computing conservation laws derived by the Noether algorithms requires having the higher derivatives of the Christoffel symbols. Thus it requires substantial smoothness assumptions on the Lagrangian $L(x, \dot{x})$

In this paper we do not attempt to treat relaxed (measure valued) control on Finsler manifolds. We will publish an account in the future, since there is no literature on this topic.

Non-Parametric Calculus of Variations.

This program can also be carried out without reduction to a parametric problem and without the Finsler manifold language. But the geometric Finsler language has been very helpful in suggesting symbolic algorithms to replace numerical algorithms.

2 An Overview of the Convexity Method

The main results of this paper will be devoted to giving a direct account of a foundation for optimal chattering control based on convex analysis in Euclidean space of the convexification $g^{**}(u) = L^{**}(x,u)$ of $g(u) = L(x,u)$ with respect to u , which have the same absolute minimum value. The algorithms implement Carathèodory's theorem on extreme points spanning convex sets in Euclidean n-space where n the dimension of vector u. For fixed x, the chattering coefficents needed for exercising optimal control are convex combination coefficients sufficient to represent some absolute extremum of $g^{**}(u) = L^{**}(x,u)$ as a convex combination of a collection of relative extrema of g. These extrema are the controls that we chatter between. We make no assumption of uniqueness for either the relative extrema or absolute extrema; there may be many. Further, we only develop algorithms for computing ϵ-optimal solutions for each fixed ϵ. This necessary for the following reason.

Non-Constructivity of Optimal Solutions.

These algorithms compute an ϵ-optimal solution for a prescribed ϵ and are continuous in small changes in parameters. However these algorithms cannot be refined to give an *algorithm* converging to an optimal solution. This is because, given a list of $1/2^n$-optimal solutions for $n = 1, 2, \ldots$, to get an optimal solution one has to apply something like the proof of Ascoli's Lemma to produce a uniformly convergent subsequence from a uniformly bounded equicontinuous family. But all proofs of Ascoli's lemma are non-constructive unless additional smoothness assumptions are added. For a proof of the non-recursiveness of the existence principles of the direct method of the calculus of variations without additional assumptions, see [NG95].

A Generalized Form of Linear Programming.

The very general algorithms we outline below cannot be expected to be very efficient because they assume as little smoothness as possible. The practical algorithms mentioned earlier are based on differential geometry, using affine connections and Lie-Taylor series expansions. They rest on more smoothness assumptions and the availability of calculus tests in n dimensions for locating extrema. The general algorithms introduced below give a different insight. They reduce the problem to a generalized form of linear programming in which one has to determine the space in which the linear program is being solved while simultaneously solving the linear program. Here is how this happens.

Convex Sets Spanned by Extreme Points.

As we have said, at point x, an absolute extremum in u for the convexified problem for L^{**} is a convex combination of local extrema of the original problem for L. The local extrema used must span a certain convex set. This reduces the problem of computing a near to optimal chattering control for the original non-convexified problem to the problem of finding an algorithm for computing close approximations to *both* enough extrema *and* their coefficients in the convex combination representing an optimal control for the convexified problem. This is an algorithmic question about convex sets. It requires in full generality a "divide and conquer" algorithm. Our universal algorithm uses a tree of tube decompositions of the domain, computes a local extremum for each such tube, and uses a real linear program to solve for the required convex combination coefficients.

These algorithms can be viewed from a constructive mathematics point of view as providing a constructive replacement for Ekeland's existence proof for optimal solutions ([E83], 157–161). His proof as it stands is not in the least constructive. Our constructive proof shows that a theorem of Ekeland and Temam is a simple consequence of the simplex algorithm. We believe that the non-constructive way in which all previous existence proofs were expressed discouraged many control specialists from investigating applications of relaxed control since they did not see how to compute or implement them. Kohn's early papers were the first to identify good algorithms for this purpose.

3 Example: Non-convex Minimization with Chattering

In [Y80], L.C. Young introduced the following problem as a problem with no real valued solution which can be solved vie his theory of relaxed control.

Problem P

Find an $x(t)$ minimizing

$$\int_0^1 (1+x^2)(1+[\dot{x}^2-1]^2)dt,$$

with $x(0)=0$ and $x(1)=0$ ([Y80], p.159).

An even number of smaller and smaller zigzags of alternate slopes 1, -1 running from 0 to 1 do better and better. The optimal path is intuitively a "dense zig-zag" from 0 to 1.

We can learn a lot from this example. The ideal would be to find a solution $x(t)$ such that for all $t \in [0,1]$, $x(t)=0$, and $\dot{x}(t)^2=1$. But this is not possible for real valued functions.

An ϵ-optimal solution $x(t)$ is one that comes within ϵ of the minimum of the possible values of the integral. In this case that minimum value is 1.

It is easy to verify that we can get ϵ-optimal solutions $x(t)$ if we divide $[0,1]$ into a sufficiently large even number of left closed right open subintervals of the same length and put $\dot{x}(t)$ alternately and consecutively equal to 1 and -1 in successive intervals, a finite zigzag. The optimal solution should, by analogy, be some sort of "infinitely dense" zigzag. There are several possible mathematical formalizations of this notion.

1) This can be accomplished quite literally if we appeal to non-standard analysis. . Simply divide the unit interval into a non-standard even number of parts to construct an actual infinite zigzag in a non-standard model of the reals such that $x(0)=x(1)=0$, while $\dot{x}(t)$ is alternatively +1 and -1 on successive intervals. The standard part of the resulting integral is 0, the infinite zigzag is

a non-standard function on a non-standard model of analysis. See [T94] for the non-standard version of relaxed control.

2) We can also define an optimal solution as a measure valued function. This is the route Warga([W72]) and Young ([Y80]) took.

3) There is a third route, convexification. First we determine $u = \dot{x}$, then we integrate to get $x(t)$. So we replace the derivative $\dot{x}$ in the integrand by a variable u, and want to minimize the quantity

$$\int_0^1 (1+x^2) + (1+x^2)(u^2-1)^2 dt.$$

Let $g(x,u)$ be the second term of the integrand

$$g(x,u) = (1+x^2)(u^2-1)^2.$$

Let $g^{**}(x,u)$ be the convex upper envelope of $g(x,u)$ with respect to u, that is,

$$g^{**}(x,u) = \begin{cases} 0, & \text{if } |u| \le 1 \\ g(x,u) & \text{otherwise} \end{cases}$$

The convex problem P^{**} corresponding to a possibly non-convex problem P is to minimize

$$\int_0^1 (1+x^2) + g^{**}(x,\dot{x})dt \tag{7}$$

subject to the endpoint conditions.

This g has two local minima, one at $g(x,1)$, the other at $g(x,-1)$. The convex closure of the graph of g contains the line segment joining these two local minima. The graph of g^{**} can be constructed from the graph of g by taking out the part between the two local minima of g and putting in the straight line connecting the two local minima.The optimal solution to P^{**} is obviously $\bar{x} = 0$, while the minimum value for P^{**} is 1. To construct an ϵ-optimal solution for P^{**}, divide $[0,1]$ into subintervals

$$[t_0,t_1],[t_1,t_2],\ldots,[t_{n-1},t_n],$$

where $t_0 = 0$ and $t_n = 1$, and the intervals have a common length Δ smaller than ϵ. Since g^{**} convexifies g, we should expect to express values of g^{**} as convex combinations of values of g. We try to determine coefficients for the following "magic" convex combination. At the end of the first interval $[0,\Delta]$

$$\alpha_1 + \alpha_2 = 1 \tag{8}$$

$$\alpha_1 w_1 + \alpha_2 w_2 = \dot{\bar{x}}(t_0) = 0 \tag{9}$$

$$\alpha_1 g(\bar{x}(t_0), w_1) + \alpha_2 g(\bar{x}(t_0), w_2) = g^{**}(\bar{x}(t_0), \dot{\bar{x}}(t_0)) \tag{10}$$

$$\alpha_1 \geq 0, \alpha_2 \geq 0 \tag{11}$$

Of course,

$$g^{**}(\bar{x}(t_0), \dot{\bar{x}}(t_0)) = g^{**}(0,0)$$

has zero as its minimum value. If suitable w_1 and w_2 can be determined, then we can solve for the α's by linear algebra. We compute the local minima w_i by freshman calculus to be $w_1 = 1$ and $w_2 = -1$. We then solve the linear equations (8 - 11) to get the values of α, $\alpha_1 = 0.5$, $\alpha_2 = 0.5$. In this case, (10) vanishes. We construct $\dot{x}(t)$ for all $t \in [0, \Delta]$ by $\dot{x}(t) = w_1 = 1$ if $t \in [0, \alpha_1 \Delta]$, $\dot{x}(t) = w_2 = -1$ if t is in $[\alpha_1 \Delta, (\alpha_1 + \alpha_2)\Delta]$, and $x(t) = \int_0^t \dot{x}(s)ds$. If we substitute for both $x(t)$and $\dot{x}(t)$ in the integrand of problem P^{**} , we get

$$\begin{aligned}
&\int_0^{\Delta} (1 + x^2)(1 + (\dot{x}^2 - 1)^2)dt \\
&\leq \Delta(1 + \Delta^2/2)((1 + (1^2 - 1)^2)\alpha_1 + (1 + ((-1)^2 - 1)^2)\alpha_2) \\
&= \Delta(1 + \Delta^2/4)
\end{aligned}$$

We apply this algorithm repeatedly on successive intervals $[\Delta, 2\Delta]$, $[2\Delta, 3\Delta]$, ...to construct a solution over the whole interval [0,1]. This is an ϵ-optimal solution because

$$\int_0^1 (1 + x^2)(1 + (\dot{x}^2 - 1)^2)dt \leq (1 + \Delta^2/4) = 1 + \epsilon^2/4. \tag{12}$$

4 Magic Combinations

In this section we discuss how to solve for the α's in the magic combinations by linear programming. Suppose we are given a Lagrangian

$$L : [0, T] \times [-1, 1]^n \times [-1, 1]^n \to [-M, M].$$

We want to solve P:

$$\text{minimize} \int_0^T L(t, x, \dot{x})dt$$

subject to endpoint condition $x(0) = x_0$.

Assumptions on L.

We assume the hypotheses of Ekeland's existence theorems of ([E83], pp. 86–90) to assure the convergence of the algorithms of this section. That is, we assume that the following two conditions on

$$L : [0, T] \times [-1, 1]^n \times [-1, 1]^n \to [-M, M].$$

are satisfied.

(i) $L(\cdot, \cdot, u)$ is continuous for each u.

(ii) $(t, x, \cdot)$ is lower semicontinuous for all t and x.

Assuming that L is C^2 will guarantee robustness of our algorithms. We start by replacing $\dot{x}$ by u in L to get $L(t,x,u)$. We intend, in the end, to recover x from $u = \dot{x}(t)$ by integration. We define $L^{**}(t,x,u)$ to be the convexification of L with respect to u .

Let P^{**} be the problem

$$\text{minimize} \int_0^T L^{**}(t,x,\dot{x})dt$$

with $x(0) = 0$

Using the convexification L^{**}, we get a solution $\bar{x}(t)$ for P^{**}. Of course, our major concern is to find an ϵ-optimal solution for problem P. The relation between the convexified optimal solution and the original problem is that $epiL^{**}(t,x,\cdot)$ is the convex hull of $epiL(t,x,\cdot)$ for all x and t where $epiL(t,x,\cdot)$ denotes the epigraph of $L(t,x,\cdot)$. If we denote $inf(P)$ as the infimum of $\int_0^T L(t, x(t), \dot{x}(t))dt$ over all possible trajectories, then one can show that $inf(P^{**}) \leq inf(P)$. Ekland's existence theorem guarantee's that an optimal solution of P^{**} exists whose integral achieves $inf(P^{**})$.

Lemma (Ekeland and Temam [ET76], pp 280–283) Fix t and x. Then for any u there exist $w_1, ..., w_{n+1}$ and $\alpha_1, ...\alpha_{n+1}$ such that:

$$\Sigma_1^{n+1} \alpha_i = 1 \tag{13}$$

$$\Sigma_1^{n+1} \alpha_i w_i = u \tag{14}$$

$$\Sigma_1^{n+1} \alpha_i L(t,x,w_i) = L^{**}(t,x,u) \tag{15}$$

$\alpha_i \geq 0,\ for\ 1 \leq i \leq n+1$.

Remark. Carathèodory ([Rud91], p.73) proved that there exist $n+2$ points w_i, which are extreme points of a certain convex set which perform this function. Ekeland and Temam reduced the number needed to $n+1$, as asserted in the lemma above. Later we show that this Ekeland–Temam result is a simple consequence of linear programming.

The problem of finding the α_i at first may look like pure linear programming. But the problem is that, not only are the α_i unknown, but also the w_i are initially unknown extrema of a convex closure. So we need to compute all the w_i as well. There is an additional algorithmic problem. There is no guarantee that u, the needed time derivative $\dot{x}(t)$ of $x(t)$, lies in the convex hull of the selected w_i's. To adjust for this, we use a domain decomposition into tubes, which gives an algorithm which is universally correct.

A *domain decomposition centered at point* u is a subdivision of the tube $[-1,1]^n$ into 2^n tubes all of which have u as common center vertex. We use a superscript j to denote the j-th coordinate of a such point w_i. For fixed t we write

$$\dot{\bar{x}} = \frac{d\bar{x}}{dt} = (\frac{d\bar{x}}{dt}^1, \ldots, \frac{d\bar{x}}{dt}^n).$$

Let $\frac{d\bar{x}}{dt}$ be the solution u satisfying P^{**}. Choose a domain decomposition centered at point $\frac{d\bar{x}}{dt}$. For $i = 1, ..., 2^n$, let w_i be a point in the i-th tube at which the minimum of $L(t, \bar{x}, u)$ over that i-th tube is achieved. We wish to solve the following system for the α's by linear programming:

$$\Sigma_1^{2^n} \alpha_i = 1, \tag{16}$$

$$\Sigma_1^{2^n} \alpha_i w_i^{(j)} = \frac{d\bar{x}^{(j)}}{dt}, \; j = 1...n \tag{17}$$

$$\Sigma_1^{2^n} \alpha_i L(t, x, w_i) = L^{**}(t, x, \frac{d\bar{x}}{dt}), \tag{18}$$

$$\alpha_i \geq 0, \; for \; 1 \leq i \leq 2^n. \tag{19}$$

This linear program has $n + 2$ equations, 2^n variables, and the constraints

$$\alpha_i \geq 0, : \text{for } 1 \leq i \leq 2^n.$$

In this problem there is no cost function to minimize. Any basic feasible solution will do. With this formulation we need only the "feasibility half" of a linear programming algorithm.

A New Proof of an Ekeland-Temam Lemma.

Suppose that we add to the system above the constraint:

$$\text{minimize } \Sigma_1^{2^n} \alpha_i L(t, x, w_i).$$

The quantity being minimized is the left-hand side of (18). The Carathèodory theorem guarantees the existence of an optimal solution, thus forcing equality (18). But there are at most $n+1$ nonzero α's for a basic feasible optimal solution because there are only $n + 1$ equations. This proves the Ekeland-Temam lemma. Special classes of problems can have more efficient algorithms. We used the domain decomposition above to get a universally applicable algorithm. We can often reduce the number of variables involved by a "generate and test" procedure. Since there exists a solution with only $n + 1$ nonzero α's, we should initially generate at most $n + 1$ of the w_i's and then test for the existence of the α 's. If they exist, the algorithm terminates. If not, generate another w_i and test. The technique of adding new variables β's is standard in linear programming. The additional point here is to generate as little as possible of equations (16), (17) and (18). There are other ways to increase algorithmic efficiency.

Here is an algorithm. Fix t_0.

The α-Finder Algorithm.

Introduce new variables $\beta_1, ..., \beta_{n+2}$. Choose $n + 2$ tubes of the domain decomposition to generate $w_1, ..., w_{n+2}$. Use the simplex method to solve

SYSTEM A

$$\begin{aligned}
\text{minimize } \Sigma_1^{n+2}\beta_i &= z, \text{ subject to} \\
(\Sigma\,\alpha_i) + \beta_1 &= 1 \\
(\Sigma\,\alpha_i w_i^{(j)}) + \beta_{j+1} &= \frac{d\bar{x}(t_0)^{(j)}}{dt},\ j = 1, \dots, n \\
(\Sigma\,\alpha_i L(t_0, \bar{x}(t_0), w_i)) + \beta_{n+2} &= L^{**}(t_0, \bar{x}(t_0), \frac{d\bar{x}(t_0)}{dt}) \\
\alpha_i &\geq 0, \text{ for } 1 \leq i \leq n+1. \\
\beta_j &\geq 0, \text{ for } 1 \leq j \leq n+2.
\end{aligned}$$

Make the right-hand side non-negative at the start. At stage 1, let α be 0 and put β equal to be the right-hand side. Use the simplex method and get an optimal solution. If $z = 0$, terminate with the current candidates for the α's and w 's. Otherwise, pick a new tube not used at any previous stage and compute anew w to be added to **A** and continue the simplex method with the current solution as the initial basic feasible solution. If $\alpha_1, \dots, \alpha_{n+2}$ is a solution to the system, construct the desired $\dot{x}(t)$ on the interval $[t_0, t_0 + \Delta]$ as follows. Divide the underlying interval of length Δ into successive subintervals,

$$[t_0, t_0 + \alpha_1\Delta], [t_0 + \alpha_1\Delta, t_0 + (\alpha_1 + \alpha_2)\Delta], \dots$$

Define

$$\dot{x}(t) = w_i \tag{20}$$

for t in the i-th subinterval. Starting with $x(t_0) = x_0$, define $x(t)$ over the first subinterval of length Δt. Then starting with initial condition $x(t_0 + \Delta t)$ at the end of that interval, as in the Euler method, repeat the procedure and define $\dot{x}(t)$ on the next subinterval. Continue and extend $x(t), \dot{x}(t)$ to the whole interval.

Error Estimate.

Compute

$$\begin{aligned}
\Delta\bar{x}(t_0) - \Delta x(t_0) &= \int_{t_0}^{t_0+\Delta} \dot{\bar{x}}(t_0)dt - \int_{t_0}^{t_0+\Delta} \dot{x}(t_0)dt \\
&= \int_{t_0}^{t_0+\Delta} \dot{\bar{x}}(t_0)dt - \dot{\bar{x}}(t_0)\Delta \\
&= O(\Delta^2).
\end{aligned}$$

Since both $\bar{x}$ and x start with the same initial value, the difference of the two is roughly $O(\Delta)$, where Δ is the length of the interval. Our major concern is how close we have come to a minimum for problem P . The relative error can be checked by computing

$$|\int_{t_0}^{t_0+\Delta} L^{**}(t, \bar{x}, \dot{\bar{x}}) - L(t, x, \dot{x})dt|. \tag{21}$$

We can employ this formula to develop adaptive methods for selecting new Δ's to increase efficiency.

5 Example: Chattering to a Relaxed Control

We compute ϵ-optimal chattering controls approximating to a solution to a very simple relaxed problem.

Let problem C be:

$$\text{minimize} \quad \int_0^T L(t, x(t), u(t))dt \tag{22}$$

$$\dot{x}(t) = f(t, x(t), u(t)) \tag{23}$$

$$u(t) \in U \tag{24}$$

$$x(0) = x_0 \tag{25}$$

Assumptions.

1. $L : [0, T] \times [-1, 1]^{2\times n} \to R^+$ is C^2.
2. $f(t, x, v)$ is **affine** with respect to v.
3. Equation
$$\dot{x}(t) = f(t, x(t), v(t))$$
has a unique solution for given initial conditions and any continuous $v(t)$.

One can get by with much weaker assumptions than being affine with respect to v, but this gives a short example.

Problem C^{**}

(V is the set of all measurable functions v as admissible controls.)

$$\text{minimize} \quad \int_0^T L^{**}(t, x(t), v(t))dt \tag{26}$$

$$\dot{x}(t) = f(t, x(t), v(t)) \tag{27}$$

$$v(t) \in V \tag{28}$$

$$x(0) = x_0. \tag{29}$$

Since L^{**} is convex and the set V consists of all measurable functions, a solution to problem C^{**} always exists ([ET76], p.260), and can be computed numerically.

Assumption for Chattering.

Assume as given a solution $(\bar{x}, v)$ of C^{**}. We wish to solve the system below for the α's by linear programming. Let $\bar{x}, v$ be a solution to C**. Choose a domain decomposition centered at point $v(t)$. For $i = 1, ..., 2^n$, let w_i be a point in the i-th tube at which the minimum of $L(t, \bar{x}, .)$ over the i-th tube is achieved. The formal system we are going to solve is as follows:

$$\Sigma_1^{2^n} \alpha_i = 1, \tag{30}$$

$$\Sigma_1^{2^n} \alpha_i w_i^{(j)} = v^{(j)}(t_0), \; j = 1...n \tag{31}$$

$$\Sigma_1^{2^n} \alpha_i L(t_0, x, w_i) = L^{**}(t_0, x, v(t_0)), \tag{32}$$

$$\alpha_i \geq 0, \; for \; 1 \leq i \leq 2^n \tag{33}$$

Algorithm.

Fix Δ. Divide $[0, T]$ into subintervals of length Δ, written $[t_0, t_0 + \Delta]$. For each such subinterval, call "α-finder" to solve the above system of equations. Suppose $(\alpha_1, ..., \alpha_{n+2})$ is a solution of the system. Construct the $u(t)$ desired on interval $[t_0, : t_0 + \Delta]$ as follows. Divide the underlying interval of length Δ into successive subintervals,

$$[t_0, t_0 + \alpha_1 \Delta], [t_0 + \alpha_1 \Delta, t_0 + (\alpha_1 + \alpha_2)\Delta], \ldots.$$

Define

$$u(t) = w_i \tag{34}$$

for t in the i-th subinterval.

End of Algorithm.

This $u(t)$ is a piecewise constant function on $[t_0, t_0 + \Delta]$. Suppose that f is affine with respect to u. Then we get the error estimate

$$\begin{aligned} &\int_{t_0}^{t_0+\Delta} f(t_0, \bar{x}(t_0), u(t))dt \\ &= \Sigma_1^{n+2} \alpha_i f(t_0, \bar{x}(t_0), w_i)\Delta \\ &= f(t_0, \bar{x}(t_0), \Sigma \alpha_i w_i)\Delta \\ &= f(t_0, \bar{x}(t_0), v)\Delta \\ &\simeq \int_{t_0}^{t_0+\Delta} f(t, \bar{x}(t), v(t))dt. \end{aligned}$$

So the difference between the integral on the optimal trajectory of problem C^{**} and the integral on the trajectory of the approximate solution constructed for problem C is $O(\Delta)$. The piecewise constant control $u(t)$ so constructed uses w_i's solving the system

$$\Sigma_1^{2^n} \alpha_i = 1,$$
$$\Sigma_1^{2^n} \alpha_i w_i^{(j)} = v^{(j)}(t_0),\ j = 1...n$$
$$\Sigma_1^{2^n} \alpha_i L(t_0, x, w_i) = L^{**}(t_0, x, v(t_0)),$$
$$\alpha_i \geq 0,\ for\ 1 \leq i \leq 2^n.$$

Remark. The w_i's are points which achieve local extrema. A digital control program operating in real time can output only a finite number of distinct control actions u altogether. Call these control actions $u_1, ..., u_M$. So in practice the best we can do is to compute α 's which come close to achieving a control which minimizes

$$\Sigma_{i=1}^M \alpha_i L(t_0, x, u_k),$$

subject to constraints. The α_i's constitute the local time schedule for use of the available control actions.

6 Magic Combinations are Relaxed Controls

The above solutions to convexified problems induce measure-valued solutions to the original non-convex problem. The local extema of the convexified Lagrangian and the chattering coefficents of the "magic" combination will be seen below to provide the measure-value $\mu(t) = \mu_t$ for each t of the measure-valued solution. This is reflected computationally in being able to derive ϵ -optimal measure valued solutions, concentrated on the finite set of local extrema used in the chattering "magic combination" and the values the chattering coefficients.

Problem C

$$\text{Minimize} \quad \int_0^T \int_R L(t, x(t), s) d\mu_t(s) dt \tag{35}$$

$$\dot{x}(t) = \int f(t, x(t), s) d\mu_t(s) \tag{36}$$

$$\mu_t \in \{\text{Probability Measures on R}\} \tag{37}$$

$$x(0) = x_0, \tag{38}$$

where L and f satisfy the conditions of the previous sections. Here $\mu(t)$ is a function on $[0, T]$ with probability measures as values.

Compare with

Problem C^{**}

$$\text{Minimize} \quad \int_0^T \int_R L^{**}(t, x(t), u(t))dt \tag{39}$$

$$\dot{x}(t) = f(t, x(t), u(t)) \tag{40}$$

$$x(0) = x_0 \tag{41}$$

Let x, u be a solution to C^{**}

For each t choose a domain decomposition centered at point $u(t)$. Let w_i be a point in the i-th tube, $i = 1, ..., 2^n$, which is an extreme point of the epigraph of $L(t, \bar{x}(t), \cdot)$. The system we are going to solve is the following.

$$\Sigma_1^{2^n} \alpha_i = 1, \tag{42}$$

$$\Sigma_1^{2^n} \alpha_i w_i^{(j)} = u^{(j)}(t), \; j = 1...n \tag{43}$$

$$\Sigma_1^{2^n} \alpha_i L(t, x, w_i) = L^{**}(t, x, u(t)), \tag{44}$$

$$\alpha_i \geq 0, \text{ for } 1 \leq i \leq 2^n. \tag{45}$$

For each choice of $t, x(t), u(t)$, there exist w_i's and α_i's. Applying the selection theorem as stated in (Ekeland–Temam, [ET76] (Proposition X.3.1., p. 283), the w_i's and α_i's can be chosen as measurable functions of t. Earlier algorithms enable us to compute, for each fixed t, the $w_i(t)$ and the $\alpha_i(t)$ as follows. We define a function $\mu(t)$ from $[0, T]$ to the set of probabilty measures on R as follows.

(i) $\mu(t)$ is a probability measure on R;

(ii) The measure $\mu(t)$ is concentrated entirely on the $w_i(t)$;

(iii) The measure of $\{w_i(t)\}$ is $\alpha_i(t)$.

Then for all t,

$$\int_{-\infty}^{+\infty} f(t, x(t), s) d\mu_t(s)$$

$$= f(t, x(t) \Sigma_1^{n+1} \alpha_i(t) w_i(t))$$

$$= \Sigma_1^{n+1} \alpha_i f(t, x(t), w_i)$$

$$= \dot{x}(t).$$

and

$$\int_0^T \int_R L(t, x(t), s) d\mu_t(s) dt$$

$$= \int_0^T L^{**}(t, x(t), u(t)) dt$$

This achieves the infimum of problem C^{**} and hence the infimum of problem C.

7 The Hybrid Bellman Equation and Dynamic Programming

We shall end this paper with one final application of chattering. Namely, we shall briefly outline how we can use chattering to derive a hybrid Bellman equation. Each agent wants to minimize the intergral of a Lagrangian over trajectories on the carrier manifold M. More precisely, fix a goal x_1 and an element y_1 in the tangent space T_{x_1} Then for any given initial condition $x(0) = x_0$, each agent wants to force the plant to follow a trajectory $x(\cdot)$ such that $\int_0^T L(x(t), \dot{x}(t), t)dt$ is with ϵ of

$$min_{x(\cdot)\in M} \int_0^T L(x(t), \dot{x}(t), t)dt. \tag{46}$$

How does one compute with the connection along an integral curve or geodesic $\alpha : [0,T] \to M$ such that $x_0 = \alpha(0)$ and $x_1 = \alpha(T)$? Suppose that the curve lies entirely within some chart (U, ψ) on the manifold where U is an open set of the manifold and ψ is a homeomorphism of U to a region of Euclidean space. Assume that the manifold is n-dimensional and that in the local coordinates of the chart, the curve α is given by $\psi(\alpha(t)) = (\alpha_1(t), \ldots, \alpha_n(t))$. Let TM_x denote the tangent space of M at the point x. Now suppose that we are given a tangent vector $y_1 \in TM_{x_1}$.

We want to do a parrallel transport of the tangent vector $y_1 \in TM_{x_1}$ along the geodesic α to get a tangent vector y_0. In such a case, we will write that $x_1 = \mathbf{x_0}(T)$ and that $y_1 = \mathbf{y_0}(T)$. This requires transporting y_1 to a vector $g(t) = \mathbf{y_0}(t)$ tangent to the surface at the point $\alpha(t) = \mathbf{x_0}(t)$ for all intermediate t. Now $g(t)$ is in the tangent space of the manifold at $\alpha(t)$ and hence in local coordiantes will be of the form

$$g(t) = \sum g_i(t)\frac{\partial}{\partial x_i}. \tag{47}$$

The condition that $g(t)$ is parallel along $\alpha(t)$ is that the covariant derivative be zero along that path. Omitting the reference to α, this says that $g(t)$ satisfies

$$0 = \nabla g = \sum_i \left[\frac{dg_i}{dt}\frac{\partial}{\partial x_i} + g_i \nabla \frac{\partial}{\partial x_i}\right] = \sum_{ijk}\left[\frac{dg_k}{dt} + g_i \frac{d\alpha_j}{dt}\Gamma_{ij}^k\right]\frac{\partial}{\partial x_k}. \tag{48}$$

Hence $g(t)$ is parallel along $\alpha(t)$ if and only if the coordinates functions $g_i(t)$ satisfy the follwing system of ordinary differential equations

$$\frac{dg_k}{dt} + \sum_{ik} g_i \frac{d\alpha_j}{dt}\Gamma_{ij}^k = 0, \; k = 1, \ldots, n. \tag{49}$$

Here the Γ_{ij}^k are the Christoffel symbols. These are computed by formulas form the chart for the manifold and, for Finsler metrics arising from parametric variational problems of the type we are considering, there are explicit formulas for the Γ_{ij}^k's in terms of the Hessian of the Lagrangian L, $\left(\frac{1}{2}\frac{\partial^2(L^2(x,\dot{x}))}{\partial \dot{x}_j \dot{x}_i}\right)$.

When we impose the boundary condition that $g(T) = y_1$, the solution to the system of differential equations gives the desired y_0, namely $g(0)$. If we assume a global Lipschitz condition for the sytem of differential equations on the manifold, we can apply the Picard method of successive approximations to compute g_i on the chart (U, ψ) from the boundary condition $g(T) = y_1$. Thus we get a formula for $g(t)$ in general. If the curve extends over several charts, the uniqueness of solutions for Lipschitz condition ordinary differential equations plus the smoothness of the transition overlaps between charts implies that we can compute a formula for $g(t)$ from chart to chart and hence compute $y_0 = g(0)$.

Now suppose $(N+1)\Delta = T$. Then we can rewrite (46) as

$$min_{x(\cdot)\in M} \sum_{n=0}^{N} \int_{n\Delta}^{(n+1)\Delta} L(x(t), \dot{x}(t), t)dt. \tag{50}$$

Next define a counting variable Z_i by

$$Z_i = \sum_{n=0}^{i} \int_{n\Delta}^{(n+1)\Delta} L(x(t), \dot{x}(t), t)dt \tag{51}$$

so that

$$Z_{i+1} = Z_i + \int_{(i+1)\Delta}^{(i+2)\Delta} L(x(t), \dot{x}(t), t)dt. \tag{52}$$

If we replace the integral on the righthand side of (52) by a chattering approximation, we can define a new sequence of counting variables $\tilde{Z}_i$ by

$$\tilde{Z}_{i+1} = \tilde{Z}_i + \sum_{k=0}^{s} L(x((i+1)\Delta), v_{i+1}^k, (i+1)\Delta)\alpha_{i+1}^k \Delta. \tag{53}$$

where for each i

(a) v_i^k for $k = 0, \ldots, s$ is in the field of extremals of the original problem (46) at $x(i\Delta)$ and

(b) α_i^k are nonnegative real numbers such that

$$\sum_{k=0}^{s} \alpha_i^k = 1.$$

Note the desired minumum of the original problem 46 is a geodesic on the carrier manifold M so that we can obtain $x((i+1)\Delta)$ and v_{i+1}^k for $k = 0, \ldots, s$ by parallel transport from $x(i\Delta)$ and v_i^k for $k = 0, \ldots, s$. Thus in (53), we have that $x((i+1)\Delta) = \mathbf{x(i\Delta)}(\Delta)$ and $v_{i+1}^k = \mathbf{v_i^k}(\Delta)$ for $k = 0, \ldots, s$. The original problem 46, which is to find $min_{x(\cdot)\in M}\ Z_{N+1}$, is replaced by a relaxed problem, which is to find

$$inf_{\alpha_i^j}\ \tilde{Z}_{N+1} \tag{54}$$

where

$$min_{x(\cdot)\in M}\ Z_{N+1} + O(\Delta^2) \geq inf_{\alpha_i^j}\ \tilde{Z}_{N+1}. \tag{55}$$

We can easily derive a dynamic programming equation for this relaxed problem. Define

$$V(\tilde{Z}_i, x, i\Delta) = inf_{\alpha_j^k} \tilde{Z}_i + \sum_{t=i+1}^{N} \sum_{k=0}^{s} L(x(t\Delta), v_t^k, t\Delta)\alpha_t^k \Delta. \tag{56}$$

where $x = x(i\Delta)$ and for each $t > i$
(i) $x(t\Delta) = \mathbf{x}((\mathbf{t}-\mathbf{1})\boldsymbol{\Delta})(\Delta)$ and $v_t^k = \mathbf{v}_{\mathbf{t-1}}^{\mathbf{k}}(\Delta)$ for $k = 0, \ldots, s$,
(ii)) v_t^k for $k = 0, \ldots, s$ is in the field of extremals of the original problem 46 at $x(t\Delta)$, and
(iii) α_t^k are nonnegative real numbers such that

$$\sum_{k=0}^{s} \alpha_t^k = 1.$$

Assuming, as Bellman always does, his Principle of Optimality,

$$V(\tilde{Z}, x, i\Delta) = \tag{57}$$
$$inf_{\alpha_i^k} \ V(\tilde{Z} + \sum_{k=0}^{s} L(\mathbf{x}(\Delta), \mathbf{v}_{\mathbf{x}}^{\mathbf{k}}(\Delta), (i+1)\Delta)\alpha_{i+1}^k \Delta, x((i+1)\Delta), (i+1)\Delta)$$

with boundary condition that

$$V(\tilde{Z}, x, N+1) = \tilde{Z}.$$

It then follows that

$$V(\tilde{Z}, x, i\Delta) = \tag{58}$$
$$inf_{\alpha_i^k} \begin{bmatrix} V(\tilde{Z}, x, i\Delta) + \\ \frac{\partial_c V}{\partial_c \tilde{Z}}(\tilde{Z}, x, i\Delta) \cdot (\sum_{k=0}^{s} L(\mathbf{x}(\Delta), \mathbf{v}_{\mathbf{x}}^{\mathbf{k}}(\Delta), (i+1)\Delta)\alpha_{i+1}^k \Delta + \\ \frac{\partial_c V}{\partial_c x}(\tilde{Z}, x, i\Delta) \cdot (\mathbf{x}(\Delta) - x) + \\ \frac{\partial_c V}{\partial_c t}(\tilde{Z}, x, i\Delta) \cdot \Delta + \\ O(\Delta^2) \end{bmatrix}.$$

Here the notation $\frac{c\partial}{c\partial u}$ stands for the covariant partial derivative with respect to u. Simplifying (58) and dividing both sides by Δ, we obtain that

$$0 = inf_{\alpha_i^k} \begin{bmatrix} \frac{\partial_c V}{\partial_c \tilde{Z}}(\tilde{Z}, x, i\Delta) \cdot (\sum_{k=0}^{s} L(\mathbf{x}(\Delta), \mathbf{v}_{\mathbf{x}}^{\mathbf{k}}(\Delta), (i+1)\Delta)\alpha_{i+1}^k + \\ \frac{\partial_c V}{\partial_c x}(\tilde{Z}, x, i\Delta) \cdot \frac{(\mathbf{x}(\Delta) - x)}{\Delta} + \\ \frac{\partial_c V}{\partial_c t}(\tilde{Z}, x, i\Delta) + \\ \frac{O(\Delta^2)}{\Delta} \end{bmatrix}. \tag{59}$$

Note that in (59), the term $\frac{\partial_c V}{\partial_c t}(\tilde{Z}, x, i\Delta)$ does not depend on the α_i^k's so that we have that

$$-\frac{\partial_c V}{\partial_c t}(\tilde{Z}, x, i\Delta) = \tag{60}$$

$$inf_{\alpha_i^k} \begin{bmatrix} \frac{\partial_c V}{\partial_c \tilde{Z}}(\tilde{Z}, x, i\Delta) \cdot (\sum_{k=0}^{s} L(\mathbf{x}(\Delta), \mathbf{v}_{\mathbf{x}}^{\mathbf{k}}(\Delta), (i+1)\Delta)\alpha_{i+1}^k + \\ \frac{\partial_c V}{\partial_c x}(\tilde{Z}, x, i\Delta) \cdot \frac{(\mathbf{x}(\Delta)-x)}{\Delta} + \\ \frac{O(\Delta^2)}{\Delta} \end{bmatrix}.$$

We can compute the terms $\mathbf{x}(\Delta)$ and $\mathbf{v}_{\mathbf{x}}^{\mathbf{k}}(\Delta)$ which appear on the righthand side of (60) by the following procedure. We can embed the manifold M into a Euclidean space E^n for sufficiently large n. In E^n, the geodesics are straight lines and the the second derivatives along the geodesics are 0. Thus we can take the explicit equations of the geodesics and transfer them back to the carrier manifold. In local coordinates, we then get the following equations for the geodesics.

$$\frac{d_c^2 x^j}{d_c t^2} = -\sum_{h=1}^{n}\sum_{k=1}^{n} \Gamma_{h,k}^j \frac{d_c x^h}{d_c t}\frac{d_c x^k}{d_c t} \tag{61}$$

where the $\Gamma_{k,l}^j$ are the Christoffel coefficients for our affine connection on M and $\frac{d_c}{d_c u}$ denotes the total covariant derivative with respect to u. Thus if we write

$$y^j = \frac{d_c x^j}{d_c t}, \tag{62}$$

then we end up with the equations

$$\begin{aligned} d_c x^j &= y^j \Delta + x^j \\ d_c y^j &= -(\sum_{h=1}^{n}\sum_{k=1}^{n} \Gamma_{h,k}^j y^h y^k)\Delta + y^j \end{aligned} \tag{63}$$

from which we can recover $\mathbf{x}(\boldsymbol{\Delta}) - x$ via integration. Similary we can show that the j-th coordinate of the k-th element of the field of extremals at x, $v_x^{k,j}$ satisfies the equation

$$v_{\mathbf{x}(\Delta)}^{k,j} = -(\sum_{s=1}^{n}\sum_{l=1}^{n} \Gamma_{s,l}^j v_x^{k,s}(y^l + x^l))\Delta. \tag{64}$$

It follows that we can use these equations to give an explict expression for $\frac{\partial_c V}{\partial_c t}$ and thus derive an explicit generalization of the Hamilton-Jacobi-Bellman equation.

8 Further Information

See [KNR95] for the Finsler approach. See [NG95] for a more extensive treatment of the topics in this paper, including approximate solutions to the Bellman equation and approximating to optimal controls using finitely many control actions. For our multiple agent control architecture (MAHCA), and extraction of distributed control programs for systems of cooperating agents controlling distributed hybrid systems, see ([KN92b], [NY92], [NY93b], [NY93a], [KN93b], [KN93a], [NRY93b], [KNRY95], [GKNR95], and [KNRG95].)

References

[AKNS95] P. Antsaklis,W. Kohn, A. Nerode, S. Sastry, eds.: *Hybrid Systems II*, Lecture Notes in Computer Science vol. 999, Springer-Verlag. (1995)

[AE84] J. P. Aubin and I. Ekeland: *Applied Non-Linear Analysis* Wiley. (1984)

[B90] A. Bejancu: *Finsler geometry and applications*, Harwood. (1990)

[Bel57] R. Belleman, *Dynamic Programming*, Princeton University Press, Princeton, NJ, (1957).

[BK65] R.E. Bellman and R. Kalaba, Dynamic Programming and Modern Control Theory, Academic Press, New York (1965).

[C34] E. Cartan: Les Espaces de Finsler, Actualities scientifiques et industrielle 79, Exposes de geometrie II. (1934)

[Cl89] F. H. Clarke: *Methods of Dynamics and Nonsmooth Optimization*, SIAM, Philadelphia. (1989)

[Cl90] F. H. Clarke: *Optimization and Nonsmooth Analysis*, SIAM, Philadelphia. (1990)

[CRSS] J. N. Crossley, J. B. Remmel, R. A. Shore, and Moss E. Sweedler: *Logical Methods* Birkhauser. (1993)

[E74] S. Eilenberg: *Automata, Languages, and Machines* (vol. A), Academic Press, New York. (1974)

[ET76] I. Ekeland and R. Temam: *Convex analysis and variational problems* North-Holland. (1976)

[E83] I. Ekeland: *Infinite Dimensional Optimization and Convexity*, University of Chicago Lecture Notes in Mathematics, University of Chicago Press. (1983)

[E90] I. Ekeland: *Convexity methods in Hamiltonian mechanics*, Springer-Verlag. (1990)

[F18] P. Finsler: *Über Kurven und Flächen in allegmeinen Räumen*. Diss. Göttingen (1918) (republished by Verlag Birkhäuser Basel (1951))

[GKNR95] X. Ge, W. Kohn, A. Nerode, and J. B. Remmel: Algorithms for Chattering Approximations to Relaxed Optimal Control. MSI Tech. Report 95-1, Cornell University. (1995)

[GNRR93] R. L. Grossman, A. Nerode, A. Ravn, and H.Rischel, eds., *Hybrid Systems*, Lecture Notes in Computer Science 736, Springer-Verlag. (1993)

[K88a] W. Kohn: A Declarative Theory for Rational Controllers, Proc. 27th IEEE CDC. (1988) 130-136.

[K88b] W. Kohn and T. Skillman: Hierarchical Control Systems for Autonomous Space Robots, Proc. AIAA. (1988) 382-390.

[K88c] W. Kohn: Application of Declarative Hierarchical Methodology for the Flight Telerobotic Servicer, Boeing Document G- 6630-061, Final Report of NASA-Ames Research Service Request 2072, Job Order T1988. Jan 15 (1988)

[KS88] W. Kohn: Autonomous Space Robots, Proc. AIAA Conf. on Guidance, Navigation, and Control, v. 1. (1988), 382-390.

[K89] W. Kohn: The Rational Tree Machine: Technical Description and Mathematical Foundations, IR and D BE-499, Technical Document 905-10107-1, Boeing Computer Services. July 7 (1989)

[K89b] W. Kohn: Rational Algebras: A Constructive Approach, IR andD BE-499, Boeing Computer Service Technical Document D-905- 10107-2. July 7 (1989)

[K89c] W. Kohn: Cruise Missile Mission Planning: A Declarative Control Approach, Boeing Computer Services Technical Report. (1989)

[K90] W. Kohn: Declarative Multiplexed Rational Controllers, Proc. 5th IEEE Int. Symp. Intelligent Cont. (1990) 794-803.

[K90b] W. Kohn and C. Johnson: An Algebraic Approach to Formal Verification of Embedded Systems, IRD Tech. Rpt. D-180-31989-1, Boeing Computer Services. (1990)

[K91] W. Kohn: A Knowledge-Based Planning and Declarative Control, Boeing Computer Services, Technical Document IRD BCS-021,in ISMIS 91. (1990)

[KC89] W. Kohn and K. Carlsen: Symbolic Design and Analysis in Control, Proc. 1988 Grainger Lecture Series, U. of Illinois. (1989) 40-52.

[KM91] W. Kohn and A. Murphy: Multiple Agent Reactive Shop Control, ISMIS91.

[KN92a] W. Kohn and A. Nerode: Multiple Agent Autonomous Control Systems, Proc. 31st IEEE CDC (Tucson). (1992) 2956-2966.

[KN92b] W. Kohn and A. Nerode: An autonomous control theory: an overview. IEEE Symposium on Computer Aided Control System Design (March 17–19, 1992, Napa Valley, Ca. (1992) 204–210.

[KN93a] W. Kohn and A. Nerode: A Multiple agent Hybrid Control Arcitecture. In *Logical Methods* (J. Crossley, J. B. Remmel, R. Shore, M. Sweedler, eds.), Birkhauser. (1993) 593-623

[KN93b] W. Kohn and A. Nerode: Models for hybrid systems: automata, topologies, controllability and observability. In [GNRR93]. (1993) 317-356.

[KN93c] W. Kohn and A. Nerode: Multiple Agent Hybrid Control Architecture. In [GNRR93]. (1993) 297-316.

[KNR95] W. Kohn, A. Nerode, and J. B. Remmel, Hybrid Systems as Finsler Manifolds: Finite State Control as Approximation to Connections. In [AKNS95]. (1995)

[KNR96] W. Kohn, A. Nerode, and J. B. Remmel, Hybrid Systems as Finsler Manifolds II: The Bellman–Hamilton–Jacobi equations and Automata, in prep.

[KNRG95] W. Kohn, A. Nerode, J. B. Remmel, and X. Ge: Multiple agent hybrid control: carrier manifolds and chattering approximations to optimal control. CDC94 (1994)

[KNRY95] W. Kohn, A. Nerode, and J. B. Remmel, A. Yakhnis: Viability in hybrid systems. J. Theoretical Computer Science. **138** (1995) 141-168.

[Lo93] P. D. Loewen, *Optimal Control via Nonsmooth Analysis*: AMS, Providence. (1993)

[LGKNC94] J. Lu, X. Ge, W. Kohn, A. Nerode, and N. Coleman: A semi-autonomous multiagent decision model for a battlefield environment. MSI Technical Report, Oct. 1994, Cornell University. (1994)

[Ma92] M. M. Makela: *Nonsmooth Optimization: Analysis of Algorithms with Applications to Optimal Control*, World Scientific, Singapore. (1993)

[M86] Matsumoto, M.: *Foundations of Finsler geometry and special Finsler spaces.* Kaiseisha Press, Shigkan. (1986)

[NG95] A. Nerode and X. Ge: Effective Content of the Calculus of Variations, MSI Tech. Report, Feb. 1995, Cornell University. (1995)

[NJK92] A. Nerode, J. James, and W. Kohn: Multiple agent declarative control architecture: A knowledge based system for reactive planning, scheduling and control in manufacturing systems. Intermetrics Report, Intermetrics, Bellevue, Wash. Nov. (1992)

[NJK94] A. Nerode, J. James, and W. Kohn: Multiple Agent Hybrid Control Architecture: A generic open architecture for incremental construction of reactive planning and scheduling. Intermetrics Report, Intermetrics, Bellevue, Wash. June (1994)

[NJK94a] A. Nerode, J. James, and W. Kohn: Multiple agent reactive control of distributed interactive simulations. Proc. Army Workshop on Hybrid Systems and Distributed Simulation, Feb. 28-March 1. (1994)

[NJK94b] A. Nerode, J. James, and W. Kohn: Multiple agent reactive control of wireless distributed multimedia communications networks for the digital battlefield. Intermetrics Report, Intermetrics, Bellevue, Wash. June (1994)

[NJKD94] A. Nerode, J. James, W. Kohn, and N. DeClaris: Intelligent integration of medical models. Proc. IEEE Conference on Systems, Man, and Cybernetics, San Antonio. 1-6 Oct. (1994)

[NJKD94b] A. Nerode, J. James,W. Kohn, and N. DeClaris: Medical information systems via high performance computing and communications. Proc. IEEE Biomedical Engineering Symposium, Baltimore, MD. Nov. (1994)

[NJKHA94] A. Nerode, J. James, W. Kohn, K. Harbison, and A. Agrawala: A hybrid systems approach to computer aided control system design. Proc. Joint Symposium on Computer Aided Control System Design. Tucson AZ 7-9 March (1994)

[NRY93a] A. Nerode, J. B. Remmel, and A. Yakhnis: Hybrid system games: Extraction of control automata and small topologies, MSI Technical Report 93-102, Cornell University. (1993)

[NRY93b] A. Nerode, J. B. Remmel, and A. Yakhnis: Hybrid systems and continuous Sensing Games. 9th IEEE Conference on Intelligent Control, August 25-27. (1993)

[NRY95] A. Nerode, J. B. Remmel, and A. Yakhnis: Controllers as Fixed Points of Set-Valued Operators, in [AKNS95]. (1995)

[NY92] A. Nerode and A. Yakhnis: Modelling hybrid systems as games, CDC92. (1992) 2947-2952.

[NY93a] A. Nerode and A. Yakhnis: Hybrid games and hybrid systems, MSI Technical Report 93-77, Cornell University. (1993)

[NY93b] A. Nerode and A. Yakhnis: An example of extraction of a finite control automaton and A. Nerode's AD-converter for a discrete sensing hybrid system, MSI Technical Report 93-104, Cornell University (1993)

[Rud91] W. Rudin: Functional Analysis, McGraw Hill (1991)

[R59] H. Rund: *The Differential Geometry of Finsler Spaces*, Springer. (1959)

[R66] H. Rund: *The Hamilton Jacobi Theory*, Van Nostrand. (1966)

[T94] C. Tuckey: *Non-Standard Methods in the Calculus of Variations*, Wiley. (1993)

[W72] J. Warga: *Optimal Control of Differential and Functional Equations*, Academic Press, New York and London. (1972)

[Y80] L. C. Young: *Lectures on the Calculus Of Variations and Optimal Control Theory*, Chelsea Pub. Company, New York, NY. (1980)

Verification of Automated Vehicle Protection Systems

(extended abstract)

H.B. Weinberg [*] Nancy Lynch [†] Norman Delisle [‡]

Abstract. We apply specification and verification techniques based on the *timed I/O automaton* model of Lynch and Vaandrager to a case study in the area of *automated transit*. The case study models and verifies selected safety properties for automated Personal Rapid Transit (PRT) systems such as PRT 2000™, a system currently being developed at Raytheon. Due to their safety critical nature, PRT 2000™ and many other automated transit systems divide the control architecture into *operation* and *protection* subsystems. The operation system handles the normal control of vehicles. The protection system maintains safety by monitoring and possibly taking infrequent but decisive action. In this work, we present both a high-level treatment of a generic protection system and more detailed examinations of protection systems that enforce speed limits and vehicle separation.

1 Introduction

This paper presents a case study in the application of formal methods from computer science to the modeling and verification of hybrid systems. Our group's work is based on the Lynch-Vaandrager *timed I/O automaton* model [1] and uses a combination of several representation and verification methods. This is the second in a series of case studies undertaken by our group that focus on automated transit systems. An overview of our methods, the series of case studies, and our group's long term goals appears in this volume [2]. In the process of conducting these case studies, we extended the timed I/O automaton model to allow the precise description of continuous behavior. We call these extensions the *hybrid I/O automaton* model; a complete formal definition of this model appears in this volume [3].

Raytheon engineers are currently working on the design and development of a new PRT system called PRT 2000™. This system uses 4-passenger vehicles that

*hbw@theory.lcs.mit.edu. MIT Laboratory for Computer Science, Cambridge, MA 02139.
Research supported an NSF Graduate Fellowship and the grants and contracts below.

†lynch@theory.lcs.mit.edu. Research supported by NSF Grant 9225124-CCR, U.S. Department of Transportation Contract DTRS95G-0001-YR.8, AFOSR-ONR Contract F49620-94-1-0199, and ARPA Contracts N00014-92-J-4033 and F19628-95-C-0118.

‡Norman_M_Delisle@ccmail.ed.ray.com. Raytheon Company, 1001 Boston Post Road, Marlborough, MA 01752.

travel on an elevated guideway with Y-shaped diverges and merges. Passengers on this system board at stations and travel directly to their desired destination stations without intermediate stops. Compared to conventional transit systems, a PRT system can provide shorter average trip times and shorter average waiting times with equivalent passenger throughput. These performance improvements are achieved because the vehicles are separated on the guideway by only a few seconds, instead of the minutes typical of a conventional transit system. The vehicles are controlled by a distributed network of computers, which receive data from sensors on the vehicles and in the tracks. An important feature of the design is its absolute safety requirements: for example, vehicles must never collide and they must never exceed designated maximum speed limits, regardless of the behavior of the control software and hardware. These stringent design criteria have led to the complete separation of system functionality into two parallel components: Automated Vehicle Operation (AVO) and Automated Vehicle Protection (AVP). AVO is responsible for the normal control of the vehicles and can be composed of complex software and hardware. AVP is responsible for emergency control of vehicles and is designed to be simple and reliable. In ordinary operation, AVP is not supposed to take any action – it merely monitors the behavior of the vehicles, awaiting some potentially dangerous situation. However, AVP must monitor and react strongly enough to guarantee that, *regardless* of the behavior of AVO, basic safety is maintained. Note that this requirement includes the possibility that AVO contains errors.

The separation of operation and protection functions is a generally recognized engineering paradigm for the design of safety critical systems. In the transportation area, this structure was initially used in the design of railroad systems. Automatic safety systems were added to human-controlled railroad systems to protect against human error and mechanical malfunctions. As railroad and mass transit systems have evolved to become more automated, this division of labor has been retained, in the form of Automatic Train Operation and Automatic Train Protection systems. This paradigm occurs in most existing automated train systems, including the Washington Metro, the Miami People Mover, the O'Hare People Mover, the Detroit People Mover, and systems in Toronto, Vancouver, and Jacksonville. The use of this split migrated to automated vehicle systems with the pioneering Morgantown PRT system in the late sixties; this system has been in continuous active use for over 20 years with no serious accidents.

Our goal in this paper is to formalize the desired safety properties of an AVP system such as the one being developed by Raytheon. Specifically, we have examined overspeed protection and collision protection on straight tracks and during merges. These are by no means the only safety rules that the Raytheon AVP system enforces, but they are among the most complex. In each case, AVP receives frequent sensor data and takes some actions when parameters are getting too close to "bad values". Too close, in each case, means that it is possible that it will actually (eventually) reach a bad value if no action is taken at the present time. We view the relationship between AVP and the rest of the system as adversarial — the AVP system must maintain safety despite Byzantine faults in the rest of the system. Interesting modeling questions arise in deciding what powers the adversary has (it is certainly limited by the basic physics of motion, but what other limits are there?) and what control AVP can exert.

In this paper, we present a preliminary treatment of these AVP functions using hybrid I/O automata. First, in Section 2, we give an informal problem statement. Next, in Section 3, we present a high-level model of the adversarial relationship between physical system and AVP. In Section 4, we derive a generic theorem about the correctness of a class of AVP systems. In the remaining sections, we specialize this general model to two examples of particular AVP functions: overspeed protection and safe separation enforcement. The correctness of each of the specializations is a corollary of the general correctness theorem of Section 3. The proof methods we employ are predominantly assertional, with operational reasoning used in certain individual cases within inductive proofs, usually for describing the physics of the system. The inductive structure provides a convenient framework for the proofs, while allowing the use of standard types of reasoning about continuous functions where it is convenient. In this extended abstract we state only the final results and omit the intermediate lemmas and proofs.

2 Informal Problem Statement

A protection system is a subsystem that monitors the physical state for hazards and averts mishaps. The problem can be viewed as a "game" between AVP and an *adversary* that controls the physical system. The game proceeds by turns — on each turn AVP receives sensor information, takes some action, and the adversary chooses some evolution for the physical system. The game can be made more complex by introducing delays and uncertainty into the turn sequence; however, in this paper we will consider only the simple turn sequence that results from reliable, periodic, and timely communication. AVP cannot rely on the correct functioning of other computer systems, such as the AVO system. For this reason, AVO will not even figure in our models; rather, we will assume that AVP can be sure only that the system will not exceed its inherent physical limitations and those specifically imposed by AVP itself. In the interest of making protection systems robust, designers keep them simple; instead of having complex control abilities, protection systems depend only on the correct functioning of a few decisive emergency commands. We formalize this notion of limited, simple emergency controls by defining the powers of AVP to be *monotonically constraining.*

By "monotonic", we mean that the action AVP takes is irreversible. A typical action available to AVP is to activate an emergency brake; our monotonicity assumption means that, once engaged, the brake cannot be disengaged. Of course, in a real system some method to reverse the action is necessary, but typically this requires manual intervention and we do not model it in this paper.

By "constraining", we mean that AVP commands do not enable some behavior that was previously unavailable, but rather simply limit the possible behaviors of the system. For example, if a vehicle can exert a certain braking force in response to a command to brake, then it is reasonable to believe that it can achieve that force *without* the command. In terms of the game, the adversary cannot gain new abilities as the result of actions taken by AVP — in fact it usually loses them.

3 Generic Physical System

In this section, we present an abstract model of a generic physical system. The model is abstract because it does not specify any particular properties for the physical system, not even that there are vehicles or tracks. We also define what it means for an AVP subsystem (AVPS) responsible for averting a given mishap to be correct. This section is organized as follows: we introduce some notation, present a formal hybrid I/O automaton (HIOA) description of the physical system, and define correctness for an AVPS.

3.1 Notation

Let $\mathcal{P}(S)$ denote the set of all subsets of an arbitrary set S. Given an automaton, we write $s \xrightarrow{a} s'$ to mean that discrete action a in state s can lead to state s' in the automaton. Similarly, we say "s' is reachable from s " and write $s \leadsto s'$ to mean that there exists an execution fragment of the automaton which begins in s and ends in s'. If R is a predicate on states of an automaton, then we say "s' is R-reachable from s" and write $s \leadsto_R s'$ to mean that s' is reachable from s and R holds on all states in the execution fragment. For any $f : A \rightarrow B$, we define extensions of f mapping $\mathcal{P}(A) \rightarrow B$, and overload the symbol f so that it refers to both functions. If $f : A \rightarrow B$ and we write $f \equiv b$ for $b \in B$, then f is the constant function whose value is b everywhere. If R is a predicate on the valuations of some subset Q of the variables of an automaton, then we extend it to states s of the automaton via projection: $f(s)$ if and only if $f(s\lceil Q)$. If s is a state of an automaton and x is a variable of that automaton, then $s.x$ is the value of the variable in state s. If f is a function to states of an automaton, then $f.x$ is the projection of f onto the variable x. When defining the trajectory set of an automaton we use the symbol w to quantify over all the possible trajectories and the symbol I for the domain of w. The trajectories of an automaton are all the w what satisfy the conditions given in the trajectory set definition.

3.2 Physical System Automata

The physical system is modeled as three automata: GP (generic plant), SENSOR, and ACTUATOR.

The GP **Automaton:** We do not define GP explicitly but rather give a set of properties that it must satisfy. The restrictions on GP are of two types: we specify GP's signature and give an axiom that GP must satisfy. Our specification of the signature describes the relationship between GP and other components; the axiom formalizes the notion of constraint.

The signature of an HIOA consists of its state variables and actions and a partition of them into three groups: input, output, and internal. GP has exactly one input variable *con* (discussed below); it has no internal variables; and it may have arbitrary output variables, except that they must include the usual current time variable *now*. GP may have arbitrary input, output, and internal actions. We denote a single state of GP by p. Furthermore, P denotes a set of states; $\mathbf{P}$ denotes the set of all states. We use $p\lceil L$ to denote the projection of a state of GP to its local state — in other words, the state minus the *con* variable.

The input variable *con* models the current constraint set imposed on the physical system by the protection system's actuators. The powers of the protection system are modeled as a set of constraints, $\mathcal{C}$. The variable *con* takes values over $\mathcal{P}(\mathcal{C})$.

The GP must also satisfy the following axiom:

> **Constraint Axiom** For all $p, q \in \mathbf{P}$, if $p\lceil L = q\lceil L$ and $p.con \supseteq q.con$ then:
>
> 1. For all $p' \in \mathbf{P}$ and for all discrete actions a, if $p \xrightarrow{a} p'$ and $p.con = p'.con$, then there exists $q' \in \mathbf{P}$ such that $q \xrightarrow{a} q'$, $p'\lceil L = q'\lceil L$ and $q.con = q'.con$.
> 2. For all closed trajectories $w : [0,t] \to \mathbf{P}$, if $w(0) = p$ and $w.con \equiv p.con$ then there exists a trajectory $y : [0,t] \to \mathbf{P}$ such that $y(0) = q$, $y\lceil L = w\lceil L$, and $y.con \equiv q.con$.

The axiom says that if a local state is reachable in one step or trajectory under a certain constraint, then the same local state is reachable under any weaker constraint. A consequence of this axiom is a similar condition involving multi-step executions instead of just single steps.

The SENSOR **and** ACTUATOR **automata:** Due to space considerations we do not present these simple automata, but merely describe them informally. The SENSOR automaton has all of GP's state variables as inputs. Fix a constant δ. At time zero and every δ time units thereafter, the SENSOR outputs this entire state p through the discrete action `snapshot`(p).

The ACTUATOR automaton has input actions `constrain`(C) for $C \subseteq \mathcal{C}$ and output variable *con*. The input actions model the sequence of constraints added by the AVPS; these constraints accumulate in *con* via set union. This captures the "monotonic" part of monotonically constraining, i.e. the set of active constraints never shrinks. Note that to compose multiple automata with `constrain` output actions, we will require a separate `constrain`$(C)_i$ action for each source where i varies over some index set of the sources. We omit the subscripts when convenient.

3.3 Definition of AVPS

We define an AVPS to be an automaton with no input or output variables and exactly the following input and output actions: the set of input actions is $\{\texttt{snapshot}(p) \mid p \in \mathbf{P}\}$ and the set of output actions is $\{\texttt{constrain}(C)_i \mid C \subseteq \mathcal{C} \text{ and } i \in N\}$ where N is a finite subset of $\mathbb{N}$. The set N allows for an AVPS to be composed of multiple automata that output the **constrain** action. An AVPS may have arbitrary internal variables and internal actions. The composition of two compatible AVPSs yields an AVPS. We will usually ignore the subscripting of the **constrain** actions and assume that subscripts are assigned in a way that makes the AVPSs we wish to compose compatible.

We define a notion of correctness for an AVPS. We characterize certain states as "bad": these are the states that the AVPS is supposed to protect against. We also qualify (i.e. weaken) the claim of correctness of an AVPS by saying that the AVPS only protects against bad states when GP starts out in a certain set of local states and remains in a certain (possibly different) set of local states.

Let A be an AVPS; let bad, S, and R be predicates on the local state of GP; let ALL be the composition of GP, SENSOR, ACTUATOR, and A. We define that *A averts* bad *in* GP *starting from S under invariant R*, when no execution of ALL that begins in an S state and contains only R states leads to a bad state. If R or S is just "true" then we omit it.

This definition of correctness leads to two useful theorems about the composition of AVPSs. The first addresses independent AVPSs; the second, a one-way dependence among AVPSs.

Theorem 3.1 *If AVPSs A_1 and A_2 are compatible, A_1 averts* bad_1 *in* GP *starting from S_1 under invariant R_1, and A_2 averts* bad_2 *in* GP *starting from S_2 under invariant R_2, then $A_1||A_2$ averts* $\text{bad}_1 \vee \text{bad}_2$ *in* GP *starting from $S_1 \wedge S_2$ under invariant $R_1 \wedge R_2$.*

Theorem 3.2 *If AVPSs A_1 and A_2 are compatible, A_1 averts* bad_1 *in* GP *starting from S_1 under invariant R_1, and A_2 averts* bad_2 *in* GP *starting from S_2 under invariant* $\neg\text{bad}_1 \wedge R_2$, *then $A_1||A_2$ averts* $\text{bad}_1 \vee \text{bad}_2$ *in* GP *starting from $S_1 \wedge S_2$ under invariant $R_1 \wedge R_2$.*

4 A Generic Protection System: PROTECTOR

Fix predicates bad and R on the local state of GP. In Figure 1, we give an example AVPS called PROTECTOR and below a predicate **safe**, such that PROTECTOR averts bad in GP starting from **safe** under the invariant R. The PROTECTOR automaton receives each **snapshot** and immediately responds with an appropriate constraint. The heart of PROTECTOR is the pair of functions $\bar{C}$ and **future** and the predicate **next-safe**. These are defined as follows:

$\bar{C} : \mathbf{P} \to \mathbf{P}$, where $C \subseteq \mathcal{C}$, defined by

$\bar{C}(p) = p'$ where $p' \lceil L = p \lceil L$ and $p'.con = p.con \cup C$.

This function mimics the effect on GP of a $\texttt{constrain}(C)$ action. We extend it to sets of states as follows: $\bar{C}(P) = \{p' | p \in P \text{ and } p' = \bar{C}(p)\}$

`future` : $(\mathbb{R}^{\geq 0} + \infty) \times \mathbf{P} \rightarrow \Pi$, defined by

$\texttt{future}(t, p) \equiv \{p' | (p \rightsquigarrow_R p' \text{ with } con \text{ constant}) \wedge (p'.now - p.now \leq t)\}$

This function returns the set of states R-reachable from state p in t time with the *con* input variable held constant. We extend the function to sets of states as follows: $\texttt{future}(t, P) = \bigcup_{p \in P} \texttt{future}(t, p)$

The definition of **`next-safe`** requires some auxiliary functions:

`tick` : $\mathbf{P} \rightarrow \Pi$, defined by $\texttt{tick}(p) \equiv \texttt{future}(\delta, p)$

This function returns the set of states R-reachable from p in δ time or less. If p is a state reported in a `snapshot` action, then this function returns the set of states R-reachable from state p up to and including the time of the next snapshot. We extend it to sets of states: $\texttt{tick}(P) = \bigcup_{p \in P} \texttt{tick}(p)$

`panic` : $\mathbf{P} \rightarrow \Pi$, defined by $\texttt{panic}(P) \equiv \texttt{future}(\infty, \vec{\mathcal{C}}(\texttt{future}(0, P)))$

This functions returns the set of all states R-reachable from state p if all constraints are applied before any time passes. Note that the inner use of `future` allows some discrete actions to occur before the full constraint set is applied. We extend `panic` to sets of states: $\texttt{panic}(P) = \bigcup_{p \in P} \texttt{panic}(p)$

Given these auxiliary functions we define the **`safe`** predicate which is necessary both for the definition of **`next-safe`** and as the restriction on the initial states of GP. A safe state is one where if the protection system can act before any more time passes, it can avoid R-reachable bad states. Because of the Constraint Axiom, this is equivalent to saying that applying all the constraints before any more time passes would avoid all R-reachable bad states for the rest of the evolution of the system.

`safe` : $\mathbf{P} \rightarrow bool$, defined by $\texttt{safe}(p) \equiv \neg\texttt{bad}(\texttt{panic}(p))$

We extend `safe` to sets of states as follows: $\texttt{safe}(P) \equiv \bigwedge_{p \in P} \texttt{safe}(p)$

Finally, we define the **`next-safe`** predicate. A next-safe state is one where, if the protection system takes no action for δ time, then the system will be safe from now up to and including that time. Usually we are examining the states that are reported in a **`snapshot`** action, in which case a next-safe state is one where if the protection system takes no action until the time of the next snapshot, then the system will be safe from now up to and including that time. Every next-safe state is itself a safe state. A state which is safe but not next-safe is hazardous.

`next-safe` : $\mathbf{P} \rightarrow bool$, defined by $\texttt{next-safe}(p) \equiv \texttt{safe}(\texttt{tick}(p))$

We extend `next-safe` to sets of states as follows:

$\texttt{next-safe}(P) \equiv \bigwedge_{p \in P} \texttt{next-safe}(p)$

This completes the definition of PROTECTOR.

One can imagine a "trivial" AVPS that immediately applies the entire constraint set. Such a controller would correctly avert bad states if the system starts in a safe state. However, we are interested in less restrictive controllers, i.e. controllers that send weaker constraint sets than the complete set when possible. An AVPS may find weaker constraint sets by testing whether a candidate set is sufficient to guarantee the safety of the system *until the next snapshot*. This idea is captured by the next-safe states: our PROTECTOR AVPS identifies hazardous states and imposes any constraint that converts them to next-safe states. An "optimal" version would choose the weakest possible constraint.

Due to space considerations we give only the final result:

Figure 1 PROTECTOR automaton description

Actions:	Input:	`snapshot`(p), where $p \in \mathbf{P}$
	Output:	`constrain`(C), where $C \subseteq \mathcal{C}$
Variables:	Internal:	$send \in \mathcal{P}(\mathcal{C}) \cup \{$ none $\}$, initially none

Transitions:

`snapshot`(p)
Eff: $send := C$, where $C \subseteq \mathcal{C}$ such that `next-safe`$(\bar{C}($`future`$(0,p)))$ holds, if any exists; otherwise $C = \mathcal{C}$.

`constrain`(C)
Pre: $send = C$
Eff: $send :=$ none

Trajectories:
$w.send \equiv$ none

Theorem 4.1 *AVPS* PROTECTOR *averts* bad *in* GP *starting from* safe *under invariant R.*

5 Example 1: Overspeed

In this section, we present a model of n vehicles on a single infinite track and an AVPS that stops vehicles from exceeding a speed limit provided that they do not collide. In an actual system, speed limits may vary from one region to another; in this section, we assume a single global speed limit. The model of the physical system, called VEHICLES, conforms to the restrictions on the GP automaton of Section 3. We define an AVPS, called OS-PROT, which enforces the speed limit on all vehicles. This AVPS is the composition of n separate copies of another AVPS called OS-PROT-SOLO, one copy for each vehicle. Each OS-PROT-SOLO$_i$ for $1 \leq i \leq n$ implements the abstract PROTECTOR automaton of Section 3 and enforces the speed limit for one vehicle.

We describe in detail those aspects of the model which were only abstract in Section 3. These include: the bad states; the constraint set C; the unspecified variables, trajectories, and discrete actions of GP. The constraints model AVP's ability to order a vehicle or set of vehicles to "emergency brake"; the unspecified variables model (among other things) the position, velocity, and acceleration of each vehicle; the trajectories model the motion of the vehicles, within physical constraints; there are internal discrete actions of the physical system that model the possibility that vehicles stop suddenly.

To give an implementation of the AVPS, we will introduce closed form redefinitions of the predicates of Section 3. The predicates of Section 3 were defined in terms of the possible future states of GP; the analogous predicates in this section will instead be defined in terms of the current state. The proof of correctness relies on the fact that the new versions are conservative approximations of the abstract versions.

5.1 Plant: VEHICLES

There are n vehicles modeled in a single automaton called VEHICLES described in Figure 2. Each vehicle is modeled with three variables, x_i, $\dot{x}_i$, and $\ddot{x}_i$, for i where $1 \leq i \leq n$. These are the position, velocity, and acceleration of each vehicle. The acceleration of a vehicle is bounded above and below: $\ddot{x}_i \in [\ddot{c}_{min}, \ddot{c}_{max}]$, where $\ddot{c}_{min} < 0 < \ddot{c}_{max}$. Furthermore, when braking the vehicles have exactly $\ddot{x}_i = \ddot{c}_{brake}$, where $\ddot{c}_{min} < \ddot{c}_{brake} < 0$. The difference between the minimum acceleration and the braking acceleration reflects a conservative estimate of the effectiveness of the vehicles' braking systems. The velocity is also restricted to be non-negative. The constraint set is $\mathcal{C} = \{1, \ldots, n\}$. When $i \in con$, this means that vehicle i is emergency braking. An internal action called **brick-wall** models the instantaneous stopping of a vehicle — as if it hit a brick wall.

We must specify the bad states for the overspeed protector: these are the states in which a vehicle exceeds the maximum velocity $\dot{c}_{max}$. More formally, the overspeed "bad" predicate is:

overspeed : $\mathbf{P} \rightarrow bool$, defined by **overspeed**$(p) \equiv \exists i \;\; p.\dot{x}_i > \dot{c}_{max}$

This predicate is the instantiation of the **bad** predicate from the generic case. It is extended to sets of states in a similar way to **bad**; a set of states is **overspeed** if any element of the set is **overspeed**.

5.2 Protection System: OS-PROT-SOLO$_i$

We can build an AVPS for overspeed protection from a single AVPS for each vehicle. We define the vehicle-wise "bad" predicate **overspeed-solo**$_i$ to be $\dot{x}_i > \dot{c}_{max}$. To construct the corresponding single vehicle protection system, we define "safe" and "next-safe" predicates that only test each vehicle separately.

Figure 3 shows OS-PROT-SOLO$_i$, an example protection system which maintains $\neg$**overspeed-solo**$_i$. It is a special case of PROTECTOR of Section 4. For the automaton definition to be complete we must give definitions for **os-safe-solo**$_i$ and **os-next-safe-solo**$_i$ which are analogous to **safe** and **next-safe**. They are extended to sets of states in the same manner as **safe** and **next-safe**.

os-safe-solo$_i$: $\mathbf{P} \rightarrow bool$, defined by **os-safe-solo**$_i(p) \equiv \neg$**overspeed-solo**$_i(p)$

os-next-safe-solo$_i$: $\mathbf{P} \rightarrow bool$, defined by **os-next-safe-solo**$_i(p) \equiv$
$(\dot{x}_i \leq \dot{c}_{max} - \delta\ddot{c}_{max})$

This completes the definition of OS-PROT-SOLO$_i$. Let **os-safe** be the conjunction of **os-next-safe-solo**$_i$ for all i. Let OS-PROT be the composition of OS-PROT-SOLO$_i$ for all i.

Corollary 5.1 *AVPS* OS-PROT-SOLO$_i$ *averts* **overspeed-solo**$_i$ *in* VEHICLES *starting from* **os-safe-solo**$_i$.

This result can be proved by showing that the automata of this section are a specialization of those of Section 3 and applying Theorem 4.1.

Corollary 5.2 *AVPS* OS-PROT *averts* **overspeed** *in* VEHICLES *starting from* **os-safe**.

This result follows from Corollary 5.2 and Theorem 3.1.

Figure 2 VEHICLES automaton description

Actions: Internal: `brick-wall`(i) for all $i \in \{1, \ldots, n\}$

Variables: Output: $x_i, \dot{x}_i, \ddot{x}_i \in \mathbb{R}$ for all $i \in \{1, \ldots, n\}$
$stopped_i$, boolean, for all $i \in \{1, \ldots, n\}$, all initially `false`

Input: $con \subseteq \{1, \ldots, n\}$, the dynamic-type is constant functions

Transitions:

`brick-wall`(i)
  Eff: $stopped_i :=$ **true**
  $\ddot{x}_i := \dot{x}_i := 0$

Trajectories:
  for all $i \in \{1, \ldots, n\}$
    the function $w.\ddot{x}_i$ is integrable
    for all $t \in I$ where $t \neq 0$
      $w(t).stopped_i = w(0).stopped_i$
      $0 \leq w(t).\dot{x}_i$
      $w(t).\dot{x}_i = w(0).\dot{x}_i + \int_0^t w(s).\ddot{x}_i \, ds$
      $w(t).x_i = w(0).x_i + \int_0^t w(s).\dot{x}_i \, ds$
      if $w(t).stopped_i$ then $w(t).\ddot{x}_i = 0$
      else if $i \notin con$ then $w(t).\ddot{x}_i \in [\ddot{c}_{min}, \ddot{c}_{max}]$
        else if $w(t).\dot{x}_i = 0$ then $w(t).\ddot{x}_i = 0$
          else $w(t).\ddot{x}_i = \ddot{c}_{brake}$

Figure 3 OS-PROT-SOLO$_i$ automaton description (subscript i omitted)

Actions: Input: `snapshot`(p), where p ranges over the states of VEHICLES
Output: `constrain`(C) for $C \subseteq \mathcal{C}$

Variables: Internal: boolean $send \in \mathcal{P}(C) \cup \{$ none $\}$, initially none

Transitions:

`snapshot`(p)
  Eff: if `os-next-safe-solo`(p) then
      $send := \emptyset$
    else
      $send := \{i\}$

`constrain`(c)
  Pre: $send = c$
  Eff: $send :=$ none

Trajectories:
  $w.send \equiv$ none

6 Example 2: Safe Separation on a Single Track

This section is similar to Section 5; instead of an overspeed protection system, here we model a collision protection system for the same physical system, VEHICLES. This AVPS can apply the same constraints and receives the same snapshot information as that section's OS-PROT. However, the collision protection system relies on the overspeed protection system. As in Section 5 the protector of this section, called CL-PROT, is an instantiation of the generic PROTECTOR from Section 3.

The mishap we wish to avoid is that two vehicles collide. Each vehicle occupies some distance on the track given by the **extent** function:

extent : $\mathbb{R} \to \mathcal{P}(\mathbb{R})$, defined by $\texttt{extent}(x) = [x, x + c_{len}]$

It takes as an argument the current position of a vehicle and maps it to the section of track occupied by the vehicle. The positive constant c_{len} captures the minimum allowable separation between vehicles; this includes the length of the vehicle plus any desired extra margin specified by the system designer. Now we define the predicate **collide** which tests if the extents of two vehicles overlap.

collide : $\mathbf{P} \to bool$, defined by $\texttt{collide}(P) \equiv$
$$\exists i\, \exists j \;\; (i \neq j) \wedge (\texttt{extent}(p.x_i) \cap \texttt{extent}(p.x_j) \neq \emptyset)$$

Due to space considerations we do not present CL-PROT, the collision protector. The main ideas are captured in the definitions of the **cl-safe** and **cl-next-safe** predicates. To define them we first introduce some useful notation and five auxiliary functions. A *configuration* X of a vehicle is a 4-tuple of type $\mathbb{R} \times \mathbb{R} \times bool \times bool$ which represent respectively: position, velocity, whether the vehicle is stopped and whether the vehicle is braking. If X is a configuration then $X.x$, $X.\dot{x}$, $X.stopped$, and $X.brake$ refer respectively to the elements of the configuration. If p is a state of VEHICLES, we use $p.X_i$ to denote the configuration of vehicle i.

cl-stop-dist($\dot{x}$) is the distance required to stop a vehicle with speed $\dot{x}$ assuming $\ddot{c}_{brake}$ deceleration.

cl-fast-dist(X) is the maximum distance a vehicle with configuration X can travel in δ time units, assuming maximum acceleration and correct overspeed protection.

cl-fast-vel(X) is the maximum velocity achievable in δ time (as in cl-fast-dist).

cl-safe-dist(X) is the distance in front of a vehicle that the vehicle "owns"; that is, the length of the vehicle plus the distance that it might travel even if braked immediately. If the ownerships of two vehicles overlap then the state is not safe.

cl-next-safe-dist(X) is the distance in front of a vehicle that the vehicle "claims"; that is, the length of the vehicles plus the distance that it might travel if left unbraked for δ time units and then braked. If the claims of two vehicles overlap then the state is not next-safe.

Formal definitions of these functions and of the **cl-safe** and **cl-next-safe** predicates appears in Table 1. A state is safe if there is no ownership overlap; a state is next-safe if there is no claim overlap. The strategy of CL-PROT is to brake the trailing vehicle when two vehicles have a claim overlap.

We give only the final results:

Table 1 Functions used in the definition of CL-PROT.

$$\texttt{cl-stop-dist}(\dot{x}) = -\frac{\dot{x}^2}{2\ddot{c}_{brake}}$$

$$\texttt{cl-fast-dist}(X) = \begin{cases} 0 & \text{if } stopped \\ \dot{x}t + \frac{1}{2}\ddot{c}_{brake}t^2, & \\ \quad \text{where } t = \min(\delta, \frac{-\dot{x}}{\ddot{c}_{brake}}) & \text{if } \neg stopped \text{ and } brake \\ \dot{x}t + \frac{1}{2}\ddot{c}_{max}t^2 + \dot{c}_{max}(\delta - t), & \\ \quad \text{where } t = \min(\delta, \frac{\dot{c}_{max} - \dot{x}}{\ddot{c}_{max}}) & \text{otherwise} \end{cases}$$

$$\texttt{cl-fast-vel}(X) = \begin{cases} 0 & \text{if } stopped \\ \max(0, \dot{x} + \delta(\ddot{c}_{brake})) & \text{if } \neg stopped \text{ and } brake \\ \min(\dot{c}_{max}, \dot{x} + \delta(\ddot{c}_{max})) & \text{otherwise} \end{cases}$$

$$\texttt{cl-safe-dist}(X) = c_{len} + \texttt{cl-stop-dist}(\dot{x})$$

$$\texttt{cl-next-safe-dist}(X) = c_{len} + \texttt{cl-fast-dist}(X) + \texttt{cl-stop-dist}(\texttt{cl-fast-vel}(X))$$

$$\texttt{cl-safe}(p) \equiv \forall i\, \forall j \;\; i \neq j \text{ implies } [x_i, x_i + \texttt{cl-safe-dist}(X_i)] \text{ and } [x_j, x_j + \texttt{cl-safe-dist}(X_j)] \text{ are disjoint}$$

$$\texttt{cl-next-safe}(p) \equiv \forall i\, \forall j \;\; i \neq j \text{ implies } [x_i, x_i + \texttt{cl-next-safe-dist}(X_i)] \text{ and } [x_j, x_j + \texttt{cl-next-safe-dist}(X_j)] \text{ are disjoint}$$

Corollary 6.1 *AVPS* CL-PROT *averts* `collide` *in* VEHICLES *starting from* `cl-safe` *under invariant* ¬`overspeed`.

This follows from Theorem 4.1.

Corollary 6.2 *The composition of* OS-PROT *and* CL-PROT *averts* (`overspeed` ∨ `collide`) *in* VEHICLES *starting from* `os-safe` *and* `cl-safe`.

This follows from Theorem 3.2 and Corollaries 5.2 and 6.1.

7 Conclusions and Future Work

In this work we have demonstrated how hybrid I/O automaton techniques can be applied to the specification and verification of a very general automated transit problem. The specification technique involves refinement of an abstract model. The proof structure permits extensive reuse of reasoning. Compositional properties are exploited to yield a hierarchical decomposition of the protection system that reflects the dependencies among critical components.

This treatment of protection systems is a preliminary case study. We would like to examine less idealized cases, including cases where the communication is unreliable and/or delayed and where vehicle sensor information is reported asynchronously.

The formalization presented in this paper has already had an influence on the PRT system under development at Raytheon. In particular, the formalization of `next-safe` exposed important safety criteria that led to practical methods to handle latencies and uncertainties due to discrete sampling and scheduling of the protection system. For example, the formalization of the overspeed protector revealed that the maximum speed attainable by a vehicle is strictly greater than the minimum speed which the protection system considers a hazard. This precise characterization of the overspeed protector is critical to the safe operation of the system, especially because other components of the system such as the collision protection system rely on guarantees made by the overspeed protection system.

We believe the techniques developed in this paper complement more traditional safety analysis. For example, safety engineers typically perform a fault-tree analysis to identify possible causes of each system hazard and related dependencies among system components. In our work, we use composition of automata to formalize these dependencies: to yield a speed limited system, we compose the physical system with a set of overspeed protectors, one for each vehicle — this formalizes the independence of overspeed protection for separate vehicles; conversely, the collision protection system controls the speed limited system — this formalizes the dependence of collision protection on overspeed protection. We believe a more comprehensive treatment in this style of all the protection subsystems would as a by-product yield a significant subtree of the fault-tree.

This treatment of transit systems overall is a work in progress. Our goal is to develop a general theoretical framework for specifying, verifying, and analyzing transit systems.

Acknowledgments: We thank Steve Spielman and Victor Luchangco for helpful discussions and Ekaterina Dolginov for a careful reading of the manuscript.

References

[1] Nancy Lynch and Frits Vaandrager. Forward and backward simulations – Part II: Timing-based systems. Technical Memo MIT/LCS/TM-487.c, Laboratory for Computer Science, Massachusetts Institute of Technology, Cambridge, MA 02139, April 1995. To appear in Information and Computation.

[2] Nancy Lynch. Modelling and verification of automated transit systems, using timed automata, invariants and simulations. This volume.

[3] Nancy Lynch, Roberto Segala, Frits Vaandrager, and H.B. Weinberg. Hybrid I/O automata. This volume.

Extended RTL in the Specification and Verification of an Industrial Press

Rogério de Lemos[1] and Jon G. Hall[2]

[1]Centre for Software Reliability
Department of Computing Science
University of Newcastle upon Tyne, NE1 7RU, UK
r.delemos@newcastle.ac.uk

[2]High Integrity Systems Engineering Group
Department of Computer Science
University of York, YO1 5DD, UK
jon.hall@minster.york.ac.uk

Abstract. Extended Real Time Logic (ERTL) is proposed for the modelling and analysis of hybrid systems, taking as a basis Real Time Logic (RTL). RTL is a first order logic with uninterpreted predicates which relate events of a system to the time of their occurrence, thereby providing the means for reasoning about absolute timing properties of real-time systems. The extensions provided by ERTL allow reasoning about system behaviour in both value and time domains through predicates defined in terms of system variables. We illustrate the use of ERTL through the modelling and analysis of an industrial press.

1 Introduction

The use of the event-action model, proposed by Jahanian and Mok (including concepts introduced in [7, 8] for specifying the software requirements of the operational flight program for the A-7 aircraft) allows the specifier to capture the temporal ordering of computational actions of computing system. The model is based on the basic notions of event and action related through timing constraints. It is also possible to express the derived notion of a 'state predicate', i.e., a predicate on the discrete system state. These concepts have shown themselves to be adequate for the modelling and analysis of computer based systems for which software has to be developed.

The language in which the event-action model is represented is Real Time Logic (RTL), [9, 10]. RTL is a first order logic in which events, actions, state predicates and timing constraints may all be expressed. The essential motivation for extending RTL as a formal notation for the specification and verification of hybrid systems is that the basic concepts of the event-action model continue to be applicable in the wider setting. With the proper extensions, it can be used to model system behaviour ranging from the activities of the physical entities which form the part of the environment of a computing system, to the temporal ordering of the computational tasks of the computing system itself [1,2,3].

However, with the problems characteristic of hybrid systems introduced through the continuous time model and continuous valued variables, to fully exploit the event-action model we have found it necessary to extend the event-action model with another basic concept, that of a *formula*, which complements the concept of event. Whereas an event is a temporal marker, a formula will typically have duration and so, in particular, can be used to model properties of a system which are dependent on the continuous nature of time. That the introduction of formulae increases the expressive power of RTL is given by the observation that it is possible to specify that a system variable should be continuous. Notationally, it is the extensions to RTL which allows it to refer to formulae which define the subject of this paper: Extended Real Time Logic or ERTL.

The rest of the paper is organised as follows. Section 2 gives a brief introduction to the syntax and semantics of ERTL. Section 3 presents the case study based on an industrial press. Finally, in Section 4 some concluding remarks are presented.

2 Extended Real Time Logic

ERTL is a specialisation of first order set theory. Due to limitations of space, in the following we give only a brief exposition ofits semantics ([5]). The interpretation of the logic is given with respect to points and intervals of the time line $\mathcal{T} = \mathcal{R}_+ \cup \{0\}$. An *event* e is a countable[1] set $[\![e]\!] = \{e_1, \ldots\} \subseteq \mathcal{T}$ of time points (those times at which the event occurs). The interpretation of a *formula* f is a countable set of intervals $[\![f]\!] = \{f_1, \ldots\} \subseteq \mathcal{PT}$ (the coarsest contiguous covering of the times at which the formula holds). Interpretations of logical connectives formulae are defined point-wise; universal and existential quantifications are written using the usual convention for ranges of variables, e.g., $\forall t' : (t, \infty) \bullet P$ is equivalent to $\forall t' : t < t' < \infty \Rightarrow P$, and $\exists t' : (t, \infty) \bullet P$ is equivalent to $\exists t' : t < t' < \infty \wedge P$. When the range is omitted it is assumed to be $\mathcal{T}$. In addition, i will range over $\mathcal{N}^+$.

A system in terms of ERTL is characterised by an *occurrence relation* $\Theta \subseteq \mathcal{PT} \times \mathcal{T}$, from RTL, which defines events, and a *holding relation* $\Phi \subseteq \mathcal{PPT} \times \mathcal{T}$, introduced into ERTL, which defines formulae.

The relationship between formulae and events is given through *transition events*; the transition events associated with a formula f, $\nearrow f$ and $\searrow f$, mark, respectively, the transition of f from *false* to *true*, and from *true* to *false*. They are defined by:

$$\begin{aligned} \forall t \bullet \Theta(\nearrow f, t) \Leftrightarrow & \Phi(f, t) \wedge (t = 0 \vee \exists t_1 : [0, t) \bullet \forall t_2 : (t_1, t) \bullet \neg\Phi(f, t_2)) \\ & \vee \neg\Phi(f, t) \wedge \exists t_1 : (t, \infty) \bullet \forall t_2 : (t, t_1) \bullet \Phi(f, t_2) \qquad (1) \\ \forall t \bullet \Theta(\searrow f, t) \Leftrightarrow & \neg\Phi(f, t) \wedge (t = 0 \vee \exists t_1 : [0, t) \bullet \forall t_2 : (t_1, t) \bullet \Phi(f, t_2)) \\ & \vee \Phi(f, t) \wedge \exists t_1 : (t, \infty) \wedge \forall t_2 : (t, t_1) \bullet \neg\Phi(f, t_2) \qquad (2) \end{aligned}$$

[1] Neither uncountable events nor formulae are considered here.

For convenience, we will assume that a $\nearrow f$ event occurs at time 0 if f is initially true; and that a $\searrow f$ event occurs at time 0 if f is initially false. (This is the source of the $t = 0$ conjunct in the above definition.)

Motivated by their use in RTL, the number of times an event has occurred, or a formula has held contiguously, is useful in ERTL. We therefore derive indexed relations $\dot{\Theta} \subseteq \mathcal{PT} \times \mathcal{N}^+ \times \mathcal{T}$ and $\dot{\Phi} \subseteq \mathcal{PPT} \times \mathcal{N}^+ \times \mathcal{T}$:

$$\forall t \bullet \dot{\Theta}(e, 1, t) \Leftrightarrow \Theta(e, t) \wedge \forall t_1 : [0, t) \bullet \neg\Theta(e, t_1) \quad (3)$$

$$\forall t \bullet \dot{\Theta}(e, i+1, t) \Leftrightarrow \Theta(e, t) \wedge \exists t_1 : [0, t) \bullet \dot{\Theta}(e, i, t_1) \wedge \forall t_2 : (t_1, t) \bullet \neg\Theta(e, t_2) \quad (4)$$

and

$$\forall t \bullet \dot{\Phi}(f, i, t) \Leftrightarrow$$
$$\Phi(f, t) \wedge \exists t_1 : [0, t] \bullet \hat{\Theta}(\nearrow f, i, t_1) \wedge \forall t_2 : [0, t) \bullet \neg\hat{\Theta}(\searrow f, i + \delta_f, t_2) \quad (5)$$

where $\delta_f = \begin{cases} 0 & \Phi(f, 0) \\ 1 & \neg\Phi(f, 0) \end{cases}$ provides for the initial conditions. For convenience, we will write the undecorated predicate symbols for both indexed and unindexed versions.

3 Case Study: An Industrial Press

The case study involves establishing design parameters for the safe operation of an industrial press. The press comprises a plunger, an operator and a programmable logic controller (PLC). At its maximum height the plunger is held by a latch. Once the latch is removed the plunger moves downwards. Its upward motion is controlled by a motor. The operator controls the movement of the plunger via two buttons placed 1 meter apart. The states of the buttons are interpreted by the PLC which controls the latch and motor.

The informal requirements for the design of the press are intended to ensure its safe operation:

1. the press will start to close if the operator presses both buttons within 0.5 seconds;
2. if the operator releases either button while the press is closing, the press will start to open.

As the plunger is a very heavy object, closing the press is dangerous. Indeed, it should be prevented from closing fully if the operator can be injured. However, there will be positions in the plunger downward motion at which the motor will not be able to prevent the plunger from closing fully. At these positions, any danger will prolonged if we attempt to prevent the press from closing as such an action can only slow the plunger without stopping it.

In the formal modelling and analysis of the plunger, we identify a particular position in its motion before which the motor is able to stop the plunger, but after which the plunger should be allowed to close. We call such a point *the point of no return*. This point provides the basis for a control strategy which distinguishes two basic modes of operation associated with the press.

1. *normal mode*, the press closes without interruption until it is closed, and it then opens without interruption;
2. *exceptional mode*, if the press is closing and the operator releases either one of the two buttons while the plunger has not yet passed the physical point of no return, then closing is interrupted. In this mode the plunger should return to its open position without first moving to its closed position.

The approach adopted for the modelling and analysis of the industrial press broadly matches that of [3] in which a formal model of the environment of the controller is obtained, and from which is established the requirements specification of the controller to be designed.

Although the modelling of the behaviour of the whole operation cycle of the press has been completed (see [6]), for the sake of brevity in this presentation we do not provide a full analysis and will concentrate on the behavioural issues which are directly concerned with the safety requirement. We also make certain assumptions in the behaviour of the press to simplify its modelling and analysis. These assumptions are clearly stated in the text.

3.1 Modelling of the Press

In the approach to be followed, the initial step would be to identify and model the behaviour of the components of the environment of the controller, i.e., the plunger, motor, sensors, buttons, operator, *etc.*, relevant for the specification of the control strategy. We would then compose and consider the plant and the interface (between the plant and the controller) as a single component which behaves like a discrete event system (DES plant) [2, 11]. For reasons of space, however, we will assume that this individual characterisation has been completed, together with their composition, so that we may begin immediately with the description of the DES plant (the plunger/motor assembly).

Plunger/Motor Assembly. The behaviour of the plunger/motor assembly can be characterised by a single continuous variable, the vertical position y of the plunger, together with its velocity y', and acceleration y''. Table 1 lists the constants and variables for the modelling of the plunger/motor assembly. There are various static invariants [2] stated by the table. For illustration, the first static invariant, $\forall t \bullet \Phi(0 \leq y \leq y_{max}, t)$, states that at all times the height of the plunger should be bounded below by 0 and above by y_{max} (inclusive). The other formulae may be interpreted similarly.

We next give the first invariant of the behaviour of the plunger motion, which states the (uniform) continuity of the position of the plunger:

$$\begin{aligned} &\forall t \bullet \forall \epsilon \bullet \exists \delta \bullet \forall t' : [t, t+\delta) \bullet \\ &\quad \forall u_1, u_2 \bullet \Phi(y = u_1, t) \wedge \Phi(y = u_2, t') \Rightarrow |u_1 - u_2| < \epsilon \end{aligned} \tag{6}$$

[2] I.e., defining the envelope of the behaviour of the plunger.

Plunger Constants

Constants	Range	Comments	Units
y_{max}	R_+	The maximum vertical position of the plunger.	m
M	R_+	The mass of the plunger.	Kg
B	R_+	The viscous frictional coefficient between plunger and its supporting structure.	$N/m/s$
F_g	R	The gravitational force.	N
F_h	R	The force that keeps the plunger moving down at a constant velocity.	N
F_H	R	The force applied to stop the plunger moving down.	N
v_{min}	R	The minimum velocity of the plunger.	m/s
v_{max}	R	The maximum velocity of the plunger.	m/s
v_c	R_-	The steady state velocity of the plunger when closing.	m/s
v_o	R_+	The velocity of the plunger when opening.	m/s
a_{min}	R	The minimum acceleration of the plunger.	m/s^2
a_{max}	R	The maximum acceleration of the plunger.	m/s^2

Plunger Variables

Variables	Range	Comments	Units
y	R	The vertical position of the plunger, $\forall t \bullet (0 \leq y \leq y_{max}, t)$.	m
y'	R	The velocity of the plunger, $\forall t \bullet \Phi(v_{min} \leq y' \leq v_{max}, t)$.	m/s
y''	R	The acceleration of the plunger, $\forall t \bullet \Phi(a_{min} \leq y'' \leq a_{max}, t)$.	m/s^2

Table 1. Constants and variables associated with the plunger

Physical Laws. The physical law that is relevant for our subsequent analysis is Newton's law of motion relating incident forces and acceleration. Its specialisation to the plunger is:

$$\forall t \bullet \Phi(\sum Forces = My'', t) \tag{7}$$

of which there are two instances:

1. when the plunger moves down (plunger closing):

$$\Phi(My'' = F_h - F_g - By', t) \tag{8}$$

2. when the plunger moves under the influence of the motor (plunger stopping):

$$\Phi(My'' = F_H - F_g - By', t) \tag{9}$$

Together with the requirement of continuity of motion, the conjunction of these equation give a behavioural invariant for the plunger/motor assembly:

$$\forall t \bullet \Phi(My'' = F_h - F_g - By', t) \vee \Phi(My'' = F_H - F_g - By', t) \tag{10}$$

which should be conjoined with the static invariants, established in Table 1, to give the full invariant of the plunger/motor assembly.

For brevity in the modelling of the press, we will assume that the plunger moves with its 'steady-state' velocity when closing. Equation 8 is then:

$$\Phi(0 = F_h - F_g - By', t) \tag{11}$$

Solving the equation gives $v_c = \frac{F_h - F_g}{B}$.

Modes of Operation. The *modes of operation* of a system partition the state space of that system. To structure the formulae which describe the system we use *mode abbreviations*, a simple structuring mechanism akin to Schemas in the Z notation, which are assertions defining a timed propositional variable[3], which characterises the mode it abbreviates. The ERTL definitions of the mode abbreviations for the plunger/motor assembly are:

$$\forall t \bullet \Phi(Opened, t) \Leftrightarrow \Phi(y{=}y_{max} \wedge y'{=}0 \wedge y''{=}0, t) \tag{12}$$

$$\forall t \bullet \Phi(Closing, t) \Leftrightarrow \Phi(0{<}y{<}y_{max} \wedge y'{<}0, t) \tag{13}$$

$$\forall t \bullet \Phi(Closing\_Off, t) \Leftrightarrow \Phi(Closing, t) \wedge \Phi(y'{=}-v_c \wedge y''{=}0, t) \tag{14}$$

$$\forall t \bullet \Phi(Closing\_On, t) \Leftrightarrow \Phi(Closing, t) \wedge \Phi(-v_c{<}y'{<}0 \wedge y''{=}(F_H - F_g - By')/M, t) \tag{15}$$

$$\forall t \bullet \Phi(Stopped, t) \Leftrightarrow \Phi(0{<}y{<}y_{max} \wedge y'{=}0 \wedge y''{=}0, t) \tag{16}$$

$$\forall t \bullet \Phi(Closed, t) \Leftrightarrow \Phi(y{=}0 \wedge y'{=}0 \wedge y''{=}0, t) \tag{17}$$

The relationship between modes (i.e., the interrelationship of transition events) is, in general, derivable from the invariant of the plunger/motor assembly. For instance, the continuity of y forces a $\searrow Opening$ event to be followed by $\nearrow Closing$

[3] Which behaves as a propositional variable at each point in time.

and not, for instance, $\nearrow Stopping$. Their explicit statement, however, often facilitates the analysis, and so would be provided in a less brief account. What is not given by the invariant is the control of the transition events between the identified modes, and signal generation therein. We must state these explicitly:

$$\forall t \bullet \Phi(Opened, t) \Leftrightarrow \Phi(Top^T, t) \tag{18}$$

$$\forall t \bullet \Phi(Closed, t) \Leftrightarrow \Phi(Bottom^T, t) \tag{19}$$

$$\forall t \bullet \Theta(\searrow Opening, t) \Leftrightarrow \Theta(Start^R, t) \tag{20}$$

$$\forall t \bullet \Theta(\nearrow Closing\_On, t) \Leftrightarrow \Theta(Abort^R, t) \tag{21}$$

i.e., the *Top* signal is transmitted (indicated by the T decoration) while in the *Opened* mode, the *Bottom* signal is transmitted while in the *Closed* mode, the *Opening* mode may only be left if accompanied by the reception of a *Start* signal (indicated by the R decoration), and the *Closing_On* mode may only be entered if accompanied by the reception of an *Abort* signal.

Initial Conditions. As initial condition we assume that the industrial press at time 0 is open:

$$\Phi(Opened, 0) \tag{22}$$

Press Buttons. The buttons form the interface between operator and controller. The relevant component of their behaviour for this case study is that the release of a button when both are depressed is accompanied by the transmission of a *One Button Release* (*OBR*) event:

$$\forall t \bullet \Theta(\searrow Two, t) \Leftrightarrow \Theta(OBR^T, t) \tag{23}$$

Signal Latency. By *signal latency* we refer to the delays that are associated with the transmission of signals between the DES plant and controller. We will use the notational convention that the signal S, transmitted by a component is denoted S^T and the delayed signal received by the other component is denoted S^R:

$$\forall t \bullet \Phi(S^T, t) \Leftrightarrow t < \Delta_{IO} \vee \Phi(S^R, t + \Delta_{IO}) \tag{24}$$

3.2 Analysis of the Press

Safety Requirement. A *safety requirement* is a condition imposed on the system which, if violated, might breach the safe behaviour of the system. In the case of the industrial press the plunger should not close fully when the press is incorrectly operated, so that an operator is not injured. (Recall that 'incorrectly operated' means release of one of the two depressed buttons while the plunger is *Closing*.)

A naive transliteration of the above natural language requirement into ERTL is relatively straight forward:

$$\begin{aligned}&\forall t \bullet \forall i \bullet \Theta(OBR^T, t) \wedge \Phi(Closing, i, t) \Rightarrow \\ &\quad [\forall t' \bullet \Theta(\searrow Closing, i+1, t') \Rightarrow \Theta(\nearrow Stopped, t')]\end{aligned} \tag{25}$$

One advantage of a naive transliteration into ERTL is that it is demonstrably close to the natural language original. Its disadvantage, as the reader will readily see, is that it is not a physically realisable as a control strategy for the controller for (at least) two reasons:

1. an OBR event may occur arbitrarily close to the ending of a *Closing* mode. The naive requirement assumes that the motor is able to provide an arbitrarily large force to prevent the plunger closing;
2. it ignores the latency of signal propagation between the components of the press.

As we are not, therefore, able to implement a control strategy which ensures the customer's safety requirement we must look for implementable safety strategies which are *optimal* given a particular system architecture (where, by optimal, we mean that any other control strategy would be demonstrably worse). The necessary formulation of the notion of optimality is not possible in this brief account, we refer the reader to the full version of this paper [6].

Unsafe States and Transitions. We will define the plunger/motor assembly to be unsafe at time t if an attempt to stop the press is doomed to fail. Using plunger/motor assembly initial condition 21 and ERTL axiom 5 this gives:

$$\begin{aligned}&\forall t \bullet \Phi(Unsafe, t) \Leftrightarrow [\exists i : \Phi(Closing\_On, i, t) \\ &\quad \wedge \forall t' \bullet \Theta(\searrow Closing\_On, i+1, t') \Rightarrow \Theta(\nearrow Closed, t')]\end{aligned} \tag{26}$$

Unsafe states and transitions can be further characterised through the relationship between consecutive $\nearrow Closing\_On$ and $\searrow Closing\_On$ events. Suppose that the plunger/motor assembly enters the *Closing_On* state at time t_{on} and at height u, say:

$$\Theta(\nearrow Closing\_On, i, t_{on}) \wedge \Phi(y = u, t_{on}) \tag{27}$$

The plunger will certainly close[4] when:

$$\begin{aligned}&[\Theta(\searrow Closing\_On, i+1, t') \Rightarrow \Theta(\nearrow y = 0, t')] \\ &\Rightarrow u \leq \frac{(F_H - F_g)M}{B^2}[1 + \log[\frac{F_H - F_h}{F_H - F_g}]]\end{aligned} \tag{28}$$

[4] That this approach is sufficient follows from the fact that the position of the plunger decreases monotonically in the *Closing* mode. A formal treatment would be possible in a longer exposition.

We will name the constant identified above y_{ponr}, the *point of no return.* So as to be able to communicate the point of no return to the controller, a sensor will be provided at position y_{oponr} to be determined. The signal generated by the sensor, *Ponr*, will occur in the *Closing* mode:

$$\forall t \bullet \Theta(Ponr^T, t) \Rightarrow \Phi(Closing, t) \quad (29)$$

The point of no return partitions *Closing_Off* into two: before, from which entering mode *Closing_On* will succeed in preventing the press from *Closing* completely, and after, from which it will fail:

$$\forall t \bullet \Phi(Closing\_Off\_Above, t) \Leftrightarrow \Phi(Closing\_Off, t) \wedge \Phi(y \geq y_{ponr}, t) \quad (30)$$
$$\forall t \bullet \Phi(Closing\_Off\_Below, t) \Leftrightarrow \Phi(Closing\_Off, t) \wedge \Phi(y < y_{ponr}, t) \quad (31)$$

Indirectly, the point of no return also partitions mode *Closing_On* into two:

$$\forall t \bullet \Phi(Closing\_On, t) \Leftrightarrow \Phi(Closing\_On\_Safe, t) \vee \Phi(Closing\_On\_Unsafe, t) \quad (32)$$

defined by the transitions:

$$\forall t \bullet \Theta(\searrow Closing\_Off\_Above, t) \Leftrightarrow \Theta(\nearrow Closing\_Off\_Below, t) \vee \Theta(\nearrow Closing\_On\_Safe, t) \quad (33)$$
$$\forall t \bullet \Theta(\searrow Closing\_Off\_Below, t) \Leftrightarrow \Theta(\nearrow Closed, t) \vee \Theta(\nearrow Closing\_On\_Unsafe, t) \quad (34)$$

and such that

$$\forall t \bullet \Theta(\searrow Closing\_On\_Safe, t) \Leftrightarrow \Theta(\nearrow Stopped, t) \quad (35)$$
$$\forall t \bullet \Theta(\searrow Closing\_On\_Unsafe, t) \Leftrightarrow \Theta(\nearrow Closed, t) \quad (36)$$

Mission Requirement. The mission requirement we impose on the system is that the exceptional mode of behaviour should only be entered when a button release is detected, guaranteeing that the press is functional. Again, using the plunger/motor assembly initial condition 21 and ERTL axiom 5, we may transliterate the mission requirement into an ERTL formula:

$$\forall t \bullet \forall i \bullet \Theta(\searrow Closing\_Off, i+1, t) \wedge \Theta(\nearrow Closing\_On, t) \Rightarrow [\exists t' : (t', \infty) \bullet \Phi(Closing\_Off, i, t') \wedge \Theta(obr, t')] \quad (37)$$

Controller Variables

Variables	Range	Comments	Units
top	**B**	A flag which indicates that the plunger is at $y = y_{max}$.	
bottom	**B**	A flag which indicates that the plunger is at $y = 0$.	
ponr	**B**	A flag which indicates whether the plunger has passed the point of no return sensor.	
two	**B**	A flag which indicates that both buttons are pressed.	
abort	**B**	A flag which indicates that an *Abort* signal has been transmitted.	

Table 2. Variables of the controller for the industrial press

3.3 Controller Design

The development of the controller begins from the description of the modes, identified in the analysis of the plunger/motor assembly, as interpreted by the controller. We introduce variables—in an implementation, hardware flags accessible to the program and controlled by I/O—described in Table 2, from which the controller modes[5] are derived. To distinguish the mode abbreviations of the controller we will prefix them with '*C_*'.

The ERTL definition of the controller mode abbreviations is:

$$\forall t \bullet \Phi(C\_Opened, t) \Leftrightarrow \Phi(top \wedge \neg bottom, t) \tag{38}$$

$$\forall t \bullet \Phi(C\_Closing, t) \Leftrightarrow \Phi(\neg top \wedge \neg bottom, t) \tag{39}$$

$$\forall t \bullet \Phi(C\_Closing\_Off, t) \Leftrightarrow \Phi(C\_Closing, t) \wedge \Phi(\neg abort, t) \tag{40}$$

$$\forall t \bullet \Phi(C\_Closing\_On, t) \Leftrightarrow \Phi(C\_Closing, t) \wedge \Phi(abort, t) \tag{41}$$

$$\forall t \bullet \Phi(C\_Closed, t) \Leftrightarrow \Phi(\neg top \wedge bottom, t) \tag{42}$$

$$\forall t \bullet \Phi(C\_Closing\_Off\_Above, t) \Leftrightarrow \Phi(C\_Closing\_Off, t) \wedge \Phi(\neg ponr, t) \tag{43}$$

$$\forall t \bullet \Phi(C\_Closing\_Off\_Below, t) \Leftrightarrow \Phi(C\_Closing\_Off, t) \wedge \Phi(ponr, t) \tag{44}$$

The invariant of the plunger motion was sufficiently powerful to imply the relationship between modes. This invariant also imposes a similar relationship

[5] The usual term for modes of a discrete device is state. However, we will continue using mode for consistency.

between the modes of the controller, for instance:

$$\forall t \bullet \Theta(\searrow C\_Opened, t) \Leftrightarrow \Theta(\nearrow C\_Closing, t) \tag{45}$$

However, we must again explicitly note the controlled transitions:

$$\forall t \bullet \Theta(\nearrow C\_Closing\_On, t) \Leftrightarrow \Theta(Abort^T, t) \tag{46}$$

The *Abort* signal which is related to this *abort* flag will make the plunger enter mode *Closing_On*.

Initial Conditions. We assume that the initial state of the controller matches that of the plunger/motor assembly:

$$\Phi(C\_Opened, 0) \tag{47}$$

Control Strategy. A *control strategy* is a way of maintaining safe behaviour by manipulating the controllable factors of a system. In the case of the industrial press, from the model of the controller and the initial conditions[6], we infer the following control strategy for maintaining the safety requirement:

$$\begin{aligned}\forall t \bullet \forall i{:}\, &\Phi(C\_Closing\_Off\_Above, i, t) \wedge \Theta(obr, t) \\ &\Leftrightarrow [\forall t' \bullet \Theta(\searrow C\_Closing\_Off\_Above, i+1, t') \\ &\quad \Rightarrow \Theta(\nearrow C\_Closing\_On, t')]\end{aligned} \tag{48}$$

implemented by

$$\forall t \bullet \Phi(C\_Closing\_Off\_Above, t) \wedge \Theta(obr, t) \Leftrightarrow \Theta(Abort^T, t + \Delta_{Alg}) \tag{49}$$

where Δ_{Alg} is the time required for the controller to generate the *Abort* signal.

In determining the control strategy for the controller, we must possible solutions to the control problem, and produced an implementation. The final stage of the design is to show that they satisfy the safety and mission requirements. For the details of this stage of the analysis we refer the reader to the full version of this paper.

4 Conclusions

Instead of proposing a novel formal technique for the modelling and analysis of hybrid systems, in this paper we have presented an approach based on the well established basis of RTL. The proposed extensions are relatively straight forward, allowing ERTL to be used in the modelling and analysis of hybrid systems, particularly for the stage of requirements analysis, in the process of software development.

Although much of the analysis of the industrial press which appears in this paper is elementary and *ad hoc*, we see many points at which broad principles are being addressed, and this provides hope that ERTL will form a notational basis suitable for extension to a formal method for hybrid systems, fully supported by tools. However, very much work remains to be done on this.

[6] Which determines the relationship between indices.

Acknowledgments

The authors would like to acknowledge the financial support of EPSRC (UK) SCHEMA Project.

References

1. T. Anderson, R. de Lemos, J. Fitzgerald and A. Saeed. "On Formal Support for Industrial-Scale Requirements Analysis". *Hybrid Systems.* Eds. R. L. Grossman et al. Lectures Notes in Computer Science 736. Springer-Verlag. 1993. pp. 426-451.
2. P. J. Antsaklis, J. A. Stiver, M. Lemmon. "Hybrid System Modelling and Autonomous Control Systems". *Hybrid Systems.* Eds. R. L. Grossman et al. Lectures Notes in Computer Science 736. Springer-Verlag. 1993. pp. 367-392.
3. R. de Lemos, A. Saeed, T. Anderson. *" Analysing Safety Requirements for Process-Control Systems". IEEE Software 12.* 1995. pp. 42-53.
4. R. de Lemos, A. Saeed, T. Anderson. "Formal Techniques for Requirements Analysis for Safety-Critical Systems". *Mathematics of Dependable Systems.* C. Mitchell and V. Stavridou (Eds.). Oxford University Press. 1995. pp. 63-95.
5. R. de Lemos, J. Hall. *"ERTL: An Extension to RTL for Requirements Analysis for Hybrid Systems"*. Department of Computing Science Technical Report Series. University of Newcastle upon Tyne, UK. (also presented at the 2nd European Workshop on Real-Time and Hybrid Systems. May/June 1995. Grenoble, France.)
6. R. de Lemos, J. Hall. *"Extended RTL in the Specification and Verification of an Industrial Press"*. Department of Computer Science Technical Report Series. University of York, UK.
7. K. L. Heninger, J. Kallander, D. L. Parnas and J. E. Shore. *"Software Requirements for the A-7E Aircraft"*. NRL Memorandum Report 3876. November 1978.
8. K. L. Heninger. "Specifying Software Requirements for Complex Systems: New Techniques and their Applications". *IEEE Transactions on Software Engineering Vol. SE-6 (1).* January 1980. pp 2-13.
9. F. Jahanian, A. K. Mok. "Safety Analysis of Timing Properties in Real-Time Systems". *IEEE Transactions on Software Engineering Vol. SE-12 (9).* September 1986. pp 890-904.
10. F. Jahanian, A. K. Mok, D. A. Stuart. *"Formal Specifications of Real-Time Systems"*. Department of Computer Science TR-88-25. University of Texas at Austin, TX. June 1988.
11. J. Raisch, S. O'Young. "A DES Approach to Control of Hybrid Dynamical Systems". Proceedings of the Workshop on Verification and Control of Hybrid Systems. New Brunswick, NJ. 1995. (In this volume.)

Abstract Verification of Structured Dynamical Systems

Michel Sintzoff

Université Catholique de Louvain
Department of Computing Science and Engineering
Place Sainte Barbe 2
B-1348 Louvain-la-Neuve, Belgium
(ms@info.ucl.ac.be)

Abstract. Dynamical systems combining different kinds of time are analyzed with the help of homomorphisms which allow time abstraction besides the usual state abstraction and which do preserve fundamental temporal properties. Dynamical systems are composed by restriction, union, synchronization, concatenation and iteration. Thanks to abstraction and structure, the qualitative analysis of systems which are hard to understand can be reduced to that of simpler, homomorphic systems.

1 Introduction

Abstraction proves fruitful in the qualitative study of dynamical systems, including programs. An instructive example is the abstraction of point-based functions by set functions, viz. predicate transformers [Dij76]. This abstraction helps to characterize certain control modes [RW87, KG93], to understand programs as relational dynamical systems [Si92], and to analyze rich dynamics obtained by composition [SG95].

In the present work, we use the abstraction principle to study dynamical systems with both discrete and continuous times. Systems with either discrete or continuous time are classical, e.g. [Wi90]. The challenge is to integrate both modes in the same systems. Results in this direction have been reported, e.g. [AM95, MW95, ZM95]. In [Si95], it is observed that the verification of invariance and termination properties is structurally identical in the discrete- and continuous-time cases; moreover, discrete-time systems can be linearly interpolated into continous-time ones without loosing invariance or termination. This provides a common ground for the composition of subsystems using different types of time.

Here, we do not anymore map discrete-time systems on particular continuous-time ones by a standard interpolation. We rather abstract classes of continuous-time systems by discrete-time ones. Namely, we introduce abstraction homomorphims which allow time abstraction besides state abstraction and which preserve essential qualitative properties. Well-chosen time- and state-abstractions may thus reduce the verification of difficult systems to that of simpler counterparts. Moreover, we use a model of dynamics which welcomes different kinds of time, and we integrate synchronized parallelism.

Hybrid systems, e.g. [MP92], also support the composition of continuous state-transitions and discrete ones, but the latter ones are assumed to be instantaneous. Since we view discrete state-changes as abstractions of continuous ones, discrete transitions are assumed to take non-zero time; we can treat zero-time steps as small-time ones by shrinking the time scale as much as needed.

The paper is organized as follows. Section 2 shows how to analyze dynamical systems by using abstraction homomorphisms. Section 3 extends the approach to the case of structured dynamical systems. A discussion in Section 4 serves as conclusion.

Conventions Unless stated otherwise, we use the concepts and terminology given in [Ak93, MW95, Wi90] for dynamical systems, and those in [Dij76] for programs.

A function application $f(u)$ may be written fu when no ambiguity arises. Function application is extended to sets by $fU = \{fu \mid u \in U\}$ and $f^{-1}V = \{u \mid fu \in V\}$. The composition of two functions f and g is expressed by $(f \circ g)u = f(gu)$. The restriction of a function f on a set U is denoted $f|_U$.

The set of the nonnegative real numbers completed with the infinity element ∞ is denoted $\mathbb{R}^+$, and $\mathbb{N}$ is the set of nonnegative integers also completed with ∞. We write $min(I)$ for the lower bound of a left-closed subset I of $\mathbb{R}^+$, and $max(J)$ for the upper bound of a right-closed subset J of $\mathbb{R}^+$.

2 Abstract Verification

2.1 Motions

Let S be a set of states, and let the time set T be a closed subset of $\mathbb{R}^+$ containing 0. A *time domain* I is a closed subset of T containing 0.

Definition 2.1 (Motion) *A motion is a pair (I, p) where I is a time domain and p a total function $I \to S$.*

In a motion, parts can be continuous-time flows as well as discrete-time cascades. As in [MW95], no semigroup properties are assumed: in general, time domains are not semigroups.

The range $ran(I, p)$ of a motion (I, p) is pI. The *initial* and *final states* of p are $p0$ and $p(max(I))$. A *null motion* is a motion $(\{0\}, p)$, which yields only the initial and final state $p0$.

A motion (I, p) is *infinite*, viz. non terminating, if $max(I) = \infty$; otherwise, it is *finite*. We assume S contains a distinguished undefined state ω such that, for any motion p, $pt = \omega$ iff $t = \infty$.

Definition 2.2 (Dynamical system) *A dynamical system is a set of motions.*

A dynamical system may well contain different motions having the same initial state: non determinism is allowed.

2.2 Abstraction Homomorphism

The principle of abstraction is classical, viz. the representation theory for groups. In the context of dynamical systems, examples of abstract systems are symbolic systems, e.g. [He69], semiconjugate systems, e.g. [Ak93], and comparison systems [MW95]; symbolic dynamics has already been considered in 1898 by Hadamard [Wi90, p.95]. As to automata and programs, abstraction is introduced in various ways, e.g. as homomorphic simulation [Gi68], as system reduction, as abstract interpretation, or as the dual concepts of refinement and reification. The only difference is our use of time abstraction in addition to state abstraction; this amounts to consider time as another state-component. Existing definitions of abstraction are based for instance on homeomorphisms, homomorphisms, or adjunctions (e.g. [Ak93]). In the present context, homomorphisms provide a sufficient degree of freedom without loosing qualitative precision: times and states can been smoothed out as desired, without weakening essential properties.

Let T_i and S_i $(i = 1, 2)$ be time- and state-spaces. An *abstraction mapping* h is a pair of a time-function $h_T : T_1 \rightarrow T_2$ and of a state-function $h_S : S_1 \rightarrow S_2$; both h_T and h_S are total and surjective, and h_T preserves the extremal times $0, \infty$, and the time ordering: $h_T 0 = 0, h_T \infty = \infty$, and $\forall t, t' \in T_1 \,.\, t \leq t' \Rightarrow h_T t \leq h_T t'$.

Definition 2.3 (Abstraction homomorphism) *The motion $\pi_1 = (I_1, p_1)$ is abstracted into the motion $\pi_2 = (I_2, p_2)$ iff there exists an abstraction mapping $h = (h_T, h_S)$ such that $h_T I_1 = I_2$ and $h_S \circ p_1 = p_2 \circ h_T$.*

A system D_1 is abstracted into D_2 iff there exists an abstraction map h such that $hD_1 = D_2$.

The abstraction ordering is transitive. It is written $\pi_1 \sqsubseteq \pi_2$, $h\pi_1 = \pi_2$, or $D_1 \sqsubseteq D_2$; we also read $\sqsubseteq$ as *refines*. Since $\{h\pi_1 | \pi_1 \in D_1\} = \{\pi_2 | \pi_2 \in D_2\}$, the abstraction homomorphism $h = (h_T, h_S)$ maps each motion $(I_1, p_1) \in D_1$ into some motion $(I_2, p_2) \in D_2$ such that $h_T I_1 = I_2$ and $h_S \circ p_1 = p_2 \circ h_T$, and each motion in D_2 is such an image by h.

2.3 Homomorphic Verification

The qualitative analysis of given systems can be reduced to that of systems related to the first ones by an abstraction homomorphism. The reduction can go upwards as well as downwards, viz. from concrete to abstract or conversely. The usefulness of time abstraction, or time refinement in the dual viewpoint, for the analysis of timed systems has been stressed in previous works. Stuttering has been the first form of time refinement to be proposed [La83]; stuttering-invariance of temporal properties is akin to homomorphic verification as introduced here. Related concepts are compression-, dilation-, and sample-invariance [BL93, AM95].

We focus our attention on two basic temporal properties, namely to reach a given set of states always or to reach it sometimes. They correspond to the fundamental qualitative aspects of dynamical systems (viz. invariance and attraction, e.g. [Ak93, MW95]) and of programs (viz. safety and liveness, e.g. [La83]). As to attraction, we restrict our attention to finite-time attraction; this means motions do reach a given set in finite time, and is an essential property we are interested in. The general case of attraction after infinite time should be tackled in a similar way.

Definition 2.4 (Reachability at all times) *A set P is always reached by a motion π iff $ran(\pi) \subseteq P$. A set P is always reached by a dynamical system D iff P is always reached by every motion in P.*

This can be detailed as $\forall (I,p) \in D. \forall t \in I. pt \in P$. The notation is $All(\pi, P)$ and $All(D, P)$.

A set P is invariant under D iff $All(D|_P, P)$, where $D|_P = \{(I,p) \mid (I,p) \in D, p0 \in P\}$. Only the motions starting in P must remain in P. This is written $Invar(D, P)$.

Definition 2.5 (Reachability after some time) *A set P is reached after some time by a motion π iff $ran(\pi) \cap P \neq \emptyset$. A set P is reached after some time by a dynamical system D iff P is reached after some time by every motion in D.*

This can be detailed as $\forall (I,p) \in D. \exists t \in I. pt \in P$. The notation is $Some(\pi, P)$ and $Some(D, P)$.

Theorem 2.6 (Homomorphic verification) *Let D_1, D_2 be two dynamical systems and let P_1, P_2 be two sets. If $h = (h_T, h_S)$ is an abstraction homomorphism from D_1 to D_2 such that $h_S P_1 = P_2$, then*
$All(D_1, P_1) \equiv All(D_2, P_2)$, and $Some(D_1, P_1) \equiv Some(D_2, P_2)$.

Proof Assume $\forall (I,p) \in D_1.\ pI \subseteq P_1$ and consider an arbitrary $(I_2, p_2) \in D_2$. Since $D_2 \subseteq hD_1$, there is $(I_1, p_1) \in D_1$ such that $(I_2, p_2) = h(I_1, p_1)$. By assumption, $p_1 I_1 \subseteq P_1$, hence $h_S p_1 I_1 \subseteq h_S P_1$, hence $p_2 h_T I_1 \subseteq h_S P_1$, hence $p_2 I_2 \subseteq P_2$. This proves $All(D_1, P_1) \Rightarrow All(D_2, P_2)$. The proof of $All(D_2, P_2) \Rightarrow All(D_1, P_1)$ is obtained by symmetry, using $hD_1 \subseteq D_2$.

Assume $\forall (I,p) \in D_1.\ pI \cap P_1 \neq \emptyset$ and consider an arbitrary $(I_2, p_2) \in D_2$. Since $D_2 \subseteq hD_1$, there is $(I_1, p_1) \in D_1$ such that $(I_2, p_2) = h(I_1, p_1)$. By assumption, $p_1 I_1 \cap P_1 \neq \emptyset$, hence $h_S p_1 I_1 \cap h_S P_1 \neq \emptyset$, hence $p_2 h_T I_1 \cap h_S P_1 \neq \emptyset$, hence $p_2 I_2 \cap P_2 \neq \emptyset$. This proves $Some(D_1, P_1) \Rightarrow Some(D_2, P_2)$. The proof of $Some(D_2, P_2) \Rightarrow Some(D_1, P_1)$ is obtained by symmetry, using $hD_1 \subseteq D_2$. □

We also have $Invar(D_1, P_1) \equiv Invar(D_2, P_2)$ because $h(D_1|_{P_1}) = (hD_1)|_{h_S P_1} = (D_2)|_{P_2}$. This preservation of qualitative properties under abstraction is akin to the preservation of topology under conjugacy, e.g. [Ak93]. See [AS85, Kw91] for relationships between topological and dynamical properties.

In Definition 2.3 of abstraction homomorphism, we could require $hD_1 \subseteq D_2$ only. We would then be able only to prove $All(D_2, P_2) \Rightarrow All(D_1, P_1)$, and $Some(D_2, P_2) \Rightarrow Some(D_1, P_1)$. We could still shift the qualitative analysis of D_1 at the level of D_2, although not conversely. Yet, the analysis of a discrete-time system may be simpler in terms of a continuous-time one, for instance by using geometry or calculus: it is sometimes useful to hide secondary, discrete irregularities in a smooth, continuous view. Thus $D_1 \sqsubseteq D_2$ should sometimes be understood as an abstraction of D_2 by D_1.

Example Lyapunov functions constitute a paradigmatic example of abstraction homomorphisms serving to prove reachability after some time: in this case, $T_1 = T_2 = S_2 = \mathbb{R}^+$, h_T is the identity, h_S is a Lyapunov function, and D_2 is a set of motions obeying the differential inequation $\dot{v} \leq -1$ for $v(t) \in S_2$. This illuminating view of Lyapunov functions is promoted in [MW95]. Floyd functions, used for proving program termination (e.g. [Dij76]), must also be seen in the same light: in this case, $T_1 = T_2 = S_2 = \mathbb{N}$, h_T is the identity, h_S is a Floyd function, and D_2 is a set of motions verifying the difference inequation $v(n+1) \leq v(n) - 1$ for $v(n) \in S_2$. We can go one step further, and view Floyd functions as abstractions of Lyapunov functions: take $T_1 = S_1 = \mathbb{R}^+, T_2 = S_2 = \mathbb{N}$, and $h_T r = h_S r = \lfloor r \rfloor$. This illustrates the transitivity of abstraction, viz. the vertical composability of successive time- and state-homomorphisms.

3 Structured Verification

Abstract qualitative analysis, as any verification, greatly benefits from a compositional structure of dynamical systems.

3.1 Composition operators

We use the following operations for composing dynamical systems: state-based restriction, union, parallel synchronization, concatenation, and iteration. These operations are akin to classical ones in program composition.

Definition 3.1 (Restriction) *Let $\pi = (I, p)$ be a motion, and let Q be a subset of the state space such that the subset $J = I \backslash p^{-1}Q$ of I is empty or left closed. The restriction of π by Q is the motion $(Q \rightarrow \pi)$ defined as follows:*

If $J = \emptyset$, *then* $(Q \to \pi) = \pi$.
If $J \neq \emptyset$, *then* $(Q \to \pi) = \pi \cap [0, min(J)]$,
where $(I, p) \cap [0, m] = (I \cap [0, m],\ p|_{[0,m]})$.

Let D *be a dynamical system, and let* Q *be a set such that, for each motion* $(I, p) \in D$, *the subset* $I \backslash p^{-1}Q$ *is empty or left closed. The restriction of* D *by* Q *is the dynamical system* $(Q \to D) = \{Q \to \pi \mid \pi \in D\}$.

Note $I \backslash p^{-1}Q = \{t \mid t \in I, pt \notin Q\}$. Consider for instance $T = S = \mathbb{R}^+$, $Q = \mathbb{R}^+ \cap [0, 18)$, and $pt = 2t$. The subset $\mathbb{R}^+ \backslash p^{-1}Q = \mathbb{R}^+ \backslash [0, 9) = \mathbb{R}^+ \cap [9, \infty]$ is left closed. Hence, the restriction $(Q \to (\mathbb{R}^+, p)) = \{([0, 9], p) \mid \forall t \in [0, 9].pt = 2t\}$ is well defined. The restriction operation keeps all the times t such that $pt \in Q$, plus the first time $m \in I$, if any, for which $pm \notin Q$. This final state pm serves in the concatenation of a restriction and another motion, see below.

Motion restriction is related to restriction in [NK93] and is a case of partial motion in [MW95].

Definition 3.2 (Union) *The union of two dynamical systems* D_1, D_2 *is the dynamical system* $D_1 \cup D_2$.

Stronger definitions of union generate richer dynamics [SG95].

Definition 3.3 (Synchronization) *Let* $\pi_i = (I_i, p_i)$ *be two motions such that* $p_1|_{I_1 \cap I_2} = p_2|_{I_1 \cap I_2}$. *Their synchronization* $(\pi_1 || \pi_2)$ *is the motion* $(I_1 \cup I_2, p)$ *such that* $p|_{I_i} = p_i$ *for* $i = 1, 2$.

The synchronization $(D_1 || D_2)$ *of two dynamical systems* D_i *is the dynamical system* $\{(I_1, p_1) || (I_2, p_2) \mid (I_i, p_i) \in D_i,\ p_1|_{I_1 \cap I_2} = p_2|_{I_1 \cap I_2}\}$.

This synchronization of dynamical systems is akin to the synchronization of languages in [Ma95]. Two motions can be synchronized whenever they agree on their common times, viz. by coincidence. Dynamical systems here are in general non deterministic: the matching pairs of motions are selected among the set of all possible pairs.

Definition 3.4 (Concatenation) *Let* $\pi_i = (I_i, p_i)$ *for* $i = 1, 2$ *be two motions such that* $p_1 m_1 = p_2 0$, *where* $m_1 = max(I_1)$; *their concatenation* $(\pi_1; \pi_2)$ *is the dynamical system* $((I_1 \cup m_1 + I_2), p)$ *such that* $\forall t_1 \in I_1.\ pt_1 = p_1 t_1$ *and* $\forall t_2 \in I_2.\ p(m_1 + t_2) = p_2 t_2$. *The concatenation* $(D_1; D_2)$ *of the dynamical systems* D_1 *and* D_2 *is the dynamical system*

$$\{(p_1; p_2) \mid p_i \in D_i,\ p_1 m_1 = p_2 0\} \cup \{p_1 \mid p_1 \in D_1,\ \forall p_2 \in D_2.\ p_1 m_1 \neq p_2 0\}.$$

The notation $m_1 + I_2$ stands for $\{m_1 + t_2 \mid t_2 \in I_2\}$.

Motion concatenation is akin to concatenation in [NK93] and to motion composition in [MW95]. It is an elementary case of synchronization: the final state of the first one coincides with the initial state of the second one. The concatenation of two systems is progressive in the sense that each motion from D_1 is extended by motions from D_2 whenever possible; if no such extension is possible, e.g. for an infinite motion in D_1, the D_1-motion is kept as is. Recall $pt = \omega$ iff $t = \infty$ (§2.1); hence, $p\infty \neq p'0$ for any p, p'.

Definition 3.5 (Iteration) *The iteration of a dynamical system D is the dynamical system D^∞ defined by*
$$D^\infty = lim_{n\to\infty} D^n, \quad D^0 = \{(\{0\}, p) \mid p0 \in S\}, \quad D^{n+1} = D^n; D.$$

All possible null motions are included in D^0; thus, for each $s \in S$, D^∞ contains a motion with initial state s. The motions in D^∞ are obtained by concatenating the motions in D as long as possible. A motion in D^∞ is infinite if its tail is an infinite motion of D or if it is an infinite concatenation of finite motions of D. If the motions in D are gentle, e.g. linear or smooth, then the iteration of D consists of piecewise gentle motions; this allows to organize the dynamics in terms of sequences of regular phases, e.g. [AP95, Gu95].

Induction principles can be used for the verification of iterated systems. The system D^∞ can be seen as a solution of the fixpoint equation $X = (X; D)$. Iteration is similar to infinite concatenation in [NK93].

3.2 Compositional Verification

Given the above composition operations, we can suggest a compositional style of qualitative analysis; this is well known in program verification and is also useful for dynamical systems [Ge95]. The principle is to deduce a property A of a composed system $D = D_1 \otimes D_2$ by deducing properties A_i of D_i $(i = 1, 2)$ such that $A \equiv A_1 \oplus A_2$; this amounts to another kind of homomorphism. Clearly, the analysis of the subproperties A_i could well be carried out on abstract versions D'_i of D_i. Then, A should hold for $D' = D'_1 \otimes D'_2$ too. Here, we just give a few immediate applications of this principle.

Property 3.6 (Compositional verification) *Let P, Q be two sets and let D_1, D_2 be two dynamical systems.*

If $All(D_1, P)$ and $All(D_2, P)$, then $All(Q \to D_1, P)$, $All(D_1 + D_2, P)$, $All(D_1 || D_2, P)$, $All(D_1; D_2, P)$, and $All(D_1^\infty, P)$.

If $Some(D_1, P)$ and $P \subseteq Q$, then $Some(Q \to D_1, P)$. If $Some(D_1, P)$ and $Some(D_2, P)$, then $Some(D_1 + D_2, P)$.

As well known, the compositional verification of $Some(D_1 || D_2, P)$ is harder. The problem is to ensure D_1 and D_2 are sufficiently compatible so that enough acceptable motions are kept in $D_1 || D_2$, e.g. [Co94]. In the case of concatenation and iteration, reachability after some time is better verified by induction or by abstraction, using for instance iterative deductions, gradient functions, symbolic systems, or finite-state automata.

3.3 Examples

We first introduce auxiliary notions used in examples. Note the characterization of realizable dynamical systems is not tackled in this paper.

Cylindrification Consider $(D_1||D_2)$. If D_i is defined on S_i $(i = 1, 2)$, we can first extend each D_i to D'_i defined on $S_1 \times S_2$, where $D'_1 = \{(I, p') \mid (I, p) \in D_1, \forall t \in I. \exists s_2 \in S_2.\, p't = (pt, s_2)\}$, and similarly for D'_2. In the same vein, a motion (I, p) with $m = max(I)$ can be viewed as representing the set $\{([0, m], q) \mid (q|_I) = p\}$ of the motions obtained by choosing at will the states in $q([0, m]\backslash I)$.

Presentation of Dynamical Systems If the function f can be integrated, the expression $\dot{x} = f(x)$ denotes the dynamical system $\{(I\!R^+, p^x) \mid x \in S, \forall t \in I\!R^+.\ p^x t = x + \int_0^t f dt\}$. If the function f is computable, the expression $x := f(x)$ denotes the dynamical system $\{(I\!N, p^x) \mid x \in S, p^x 0 = x,\ \forall t \in I\!N.\, p^x(t+1) = f(p^x t)\}$. The pause-symbol "$\cdots$" stands for the dynamical system $\{([0, r], p^x) \mid r \in I\!R^+, r \neq \infty, x \in S, \forall t \in [0, r]. p^x t = x\}$.

If E is an expression of the dynamical system D and B is a boolean characteristic predicate of the set Q, then the expression $(B \rightarrow E)$ denotes the system $(Q \rightarrow D)$ which remains in Q, and $[B]E$ denotes the system $D|_Q$ which starts in Q (§2.3).

If E_i denotes D_i $(i = 1, 2)$, then $(E_1|E_2)$ denotes $(D_1 \cup D_2)$, $(E_1||E_2)$ denotes $(D_1||D_2)$, $(E_1; E_2)$ denotes $(D_1; D_2)$, **do** E_1 **od** denotes D_1^∞, and $E_1 \sqsubseteq E_2$ denotes $D_1 \sqsubseteq D_2$.

Assume two sets P_i $(i = 1, 2)$ can be defined by characteristic predicates C_i in first-order logic, viz. $P_i = \{s \mid C_i(s)\}$. Then, $h_s P_1 = P_2$ iff $\forall s \in S_1.\ C_1(s) \equiv C_2(h_S s)$. This gives a syntactical expression for the homomorphic abstraction of sets in Thm 2.6.

The state and time sets of a dynamical system denoted by some expression may be left implicit, and then should be determined using common sense.

From fine to coarse grains Consider $T_1 = S_1 = I\!R^+$, $D_1 = \{(I\!R^+, p_1) \mid \forall t \in I\!R^+. p_1 t = \frac{1}{2}t\}$, and $T_2 = S_2 = I\!N$, $D_2 = \{(I\!N, p_2) \mid \forall t \in I\!N. p_2 t = t\}$. Consider $h_T t_1 = t_1 \div 2, h_S x_1 = \lfloor x_1 \rfloor$. Then $h_S p_1 t_1 = h_S(\frac{1}{2}t_1) = \lfloor \frac{1}{2}t_1 \rfloor = t_1 \div 2$ and $p_2 h_T t_1 = p_2(t_1 \div 2) = t_1 \div 2$. Hence $D_1 \sqsubseteq D_2$ by (h_T, h_S), viz. $[x_1 = 0](\dot{x}_1 = 0.5) \sqsubseteq [x_2 = 0](x_2 := x_2 + 1)$.

From infinitely to finitely many grains Let E_1 be $[x_1 = 0]$ **do** $x_1 < 10 \rightarrow \dot{x}_1 = 2$ **od** and E_2 be $[x_2 = 0](x_2 := 10)$. Thus, $T_1 = S_1 = I\!R^+, D_1 = \{([0, 5], p_1) \mid \forall t \in [0, 5]. p_1 t = 2t\}$ and $T_2 = S_2 = I\!N, D_2 = \{(\{0, 1\}, p_2) \mid p_2 0 = 0, p_2 1 = 10\}$. We prove $D_1 \sqsubseteq D_2$ by using $h = (h_T, h_S)$ such that $h_T 0 = 0$, $h_T((0, 5]) = 1$, $h_S 0 = 0$, $h_S((0, 10]) = 10$. Indeed, $\forall t_1 \in [0, 5]. h_S p_1 t_1 = p_2 h_T t_1$.

Consider then the predicates $C_1(x_1) \equiv 0 \leq x_1 \leq 10$ for D_1, and $C_2(x_2) \equiv (x_2 = 0) \vee (x_2 = 10)$ for D_2. We observe $C_1(x_1) \equiv C_2(h_S x_1)$ since $(h_S x_1 = 0) \equiv (x_1 = 0)$ and $(h_S x_1 = 10) \equiv (0 < x_1 \leq 10)$. The invariance of C_2 by D_2 is obvious, and the invariance of C_1 by D_1 follows. This kind of drastic reduction of the verification space is characteristic of finite-state proofs for hybrid systems, e.g. [Al95].

Abstract Synchronicity This example is inspired by a railroad-crossing system: read x_i as train distance on the track, y_i as gate level, and z_i as control state. For illustrative purposes, the gate is modelled by a discrete-time system. The first exercise is to verify the following abstraction relation:

$$\begin{array}{ll}
& \mathbf{do}\ z_1 := 1; x_1 := 0;\ \mathbf{do}\ x_1 < 500 \rightarrow \dot{x_1} = 5\ \mathbf{od}\ ; z_1 := 0; \\
& \qquad\qquad\qquad\qquad\qquad \mathbf{do}\ x_1 < 750 \rightarrow \dot{x_1} = 5\ \mathbf{od} \quad \mathbf{od} \\
& \|\ \mathbf{do}\ z_1 := 1; y_1 := 2;\ \mathbf{do}\ y_1 > 0 \rightarrow y_1 := y_1 - 1\ \mathbf{od}\ ; \cdots ; z_1 := 0; \cdots\ \mathbf{od} \\
\sqsubseteq & \quad \mathbf{do}\ z_2 := 1; x_2 := 0; x_2 := 500; z_2 := 0; x_2 := 750\ \mathbf{od} \\
& \|\ \mathbf{do}\ z_2 := 1; y_2 := 2; y_2 := 0; z_2 := 0; y_2 := y_2 \quad \mathbf{od} \\
= & \mathbf{do}\ z_2 := 1; (x_2, y_2) := (0, 2); (x_2, y_2) := (500, 0); \\
& \quad z_2 := 0; (x_2, y_2) := (750, y_2) \qquad\qquad \mathbf{od}
\end{array}$$

At the concrete level, we have $T_1 = \mathbb{R}^+, S_1 = [0, 750] \times \{2, 1, 0\} \times \{0, 1\}$. At the abstract level, we have $T_2 = \mathbb{N}, S_2 = \{0, 500, 750\} \times \{2, 0\} \times \{0, 1\}$. The elements of S_i are (x_i, y_i, z_i). See the previous example for details of the corresponding motions. The time abstraction h_T is defined, for $k \in \mathbb{N}$, by $h_T(153k + [0, 1)) = 5k$, $h_T(153k + [1, 2)) = 5k + 1$, $h_T(153k + [2, 102)) = 5k + 2$, $h_T(153k + [102, 103)) = 5k + 3$, $h_T(153k + [103, 153)) = 5k + 4$. The state abstraction $h_S = (h_x, h_y, h_z)$ is defined as follows: $h_x 0 = 0$, $h_x((0, 500]) = 500$, $h_x((500, 750]) = 750$, $h_y 2 = 2$, $h_y(\{1, 0\}) = \{0\}$, and h_z is the identity function.

Our second exercise is to check the invariance of the concrete predicate $500 < x_1 \leq 750 \Rightarrow y_1 = 0$: while the train is crossing the road, the gate is closed. The corresponding abstract predicate is $x_2 = 750 \Rightarrow y_2 = 0$: if the train is there, the gate is closed. By the given abstraction homomorphism, the verification of concrete invariance reduces to that of abstract invariance, which is a simple proof.

4 Discussion

To conclude, we summarize the approach presented above, compare it with other ones, discuss open issues, and suggest future work.

We have introduced a framework for the time- and state-abstraction of dynamical systems. It is based on a classical use of homomorphisms and allows to improve the level of reasoning as desired, going up or down. The generalization of homomorphic functions to homomorphic relations could add useful flexibility. Basic temporal properties are preserved under abstraction homomorphims. A similar result for more general temporal predicates can be hoped for. Properties such as absorption, viz. self-stabilization, deserve more attention too.

In principle, a well-chosen abstraction homomorphism reduces a difficult verification task to a manageable one. The problem then becomes the discovery of the right abstraction. We may think of characterizing significant classes of concrete systems for which adequate abstraction schemes would be identified once for all.

We use composition operations for dynamical systems. This supports approaches based on piecewise smooth phases. The operations we consider are restriction, union, synchronization, concatenation and iteration. Synchronization allows the parallel coordination of dynamical systems; a geometric view of such parallel dynamics would foster a better qualitative analysis. Moreover, to scale up system design, hierarchical and recursive composition is mandatory: fixpoints and higher-order dynamics should be integrated. As to compositional abstract verification, we just gave a few simple results; we should ensure in general the monotonicity of abstraction and verification wrt. composition operations.

In hybrid systems, the continuous view and the discrete one are both supported but they are usually tackled by different techniques. The continuous-time phases are driven by differential equations, whereas the discrete-time transitions are defined by automata; the two corresponding time spaces are kept independent. The continuous-time flows and the discrete-time cascades are thus combined by juxtaposition, not by abstraction or refinement; indeed, hybrid systems mainly serve to compose discrete-time controllers with continuous-time plants. Here, we aim at a harmonious synergy between continuous- and discrete-time systems; in any context, one can play the role of the other.

The difference between linear and nonlinear dynamics is sometimes identified with the difference between linear and nonlinear functions. It seems appropriate to characterize that difference by the structural properties of the composition of gentle functions: nonlinear dynamics corresponds to piecewise gentle phases with a nontrivial global organization. This is why the composition of simple local transitions (continuous-time constant derivatives or discrete-time elementary assignments) may yield rich global dynamics.

The freedom of choosing between data types in programs should be extended to the freedom of choosing between types of time. Thanks to the uniform framework introduced, the structure of reasoning remains stable when time types are changed. As a consequence, the analysis and design methods known for continuous-time systems can be applied to the case of discrete-time systems, and conversely. The time spaces we use here are flat: the structuration of time should be investigated on a par with time abstraction, as it is classical for states.

Acknowledgements It is a pleasure to acknowledge valuable discussions with E. Asarin and F. Geurts, and thoughtful comments by members of IFIP Working Group 2.3 on Programming Methodology and by participants at the 1995 Workshop on the Verification and Control of Hybrid Systems at DIMACS, Rutgers University.

References

Ak93 Akin, E., *The General Topology of Dynamical Systems*, American Math. Soc., Providence, 1993.

Al95 Alur, R., et al., The algorithmic analysis of hybrid systems, *Theor. Computer Sci.* 138(1995) 3-34.

AM95 Alfaro, L. de, and Z. Manna, Verification in continuous time by discrete time reasoning, in: V.S. Alagar and M. Nivat (eds.), *Algebraic Methodology and Software Technology,* LNCS 936, Springer, Berlin, 1995, pp. 292-306.

AP95 Asarin, E., O. Maler and A. Pnueli, Reachability analysis of dynamical systems having piecewise-constant derivatives, *Theor. Comput. Sci.* 138(1995) 35-65.

AS85 Alpern, B., and F.B. Schneider, Defining liveness, *Information Proc. Letters* 21(1985) 181-186.

BL93 Benveniste, A., M. Le Borgne and P. Le Guernic, Hybrid systems: the SIGNAL approach, in: R.L. Grossman et al. (eds.), *Hybrid Systems*, LNCS 736, Springer, Berlin, 1992, pp. 230-254.

Co94 Collette, P., *Design of Compositional Proof Systems - Application to Unity*, Ph.D. thesis, U. Louvain, 1994.

Dij76 Dijkstra, E.W., *A Discipline of Programming*, Prentice-Hall, Englewood Cliffs, 1976.

Ge95 Geurts, F., Compositional complexity in dynamical systems, RR95-14, Dept Computing Sci. and Eng., U. Louvain. Also in: *Proc. 1995 Intl Symp. on Nonlinear Theory and its Applications*, IEICE, Tokyo, 1995.

Gi68 Ginzburg, A., *Algebraic Theory of Automata*, Academic Press, New York, 1968.

Gu95 Guckenheimer, J., A robust hybrid stabilization strategy for equilibria, *IEEE Trans. Automatic Control* 40(1995) 321-326.

He69 Hedlung, G.A., Endomorphisms and automorphisms of the shift dynamical system, *Math. Systems Theory* 3(1969) 320-375.

KG93 Kumar, R., V. Garg and S.I. Marcus, Predicates and predicate transformers for supervisory control of discrete event dynamical systems, *IEEE Trans. Automatic Control* 38(1993) 232-247.

Kw91 Kwiatkowska, M.Z., On topological characterization of behavioural properties, in: G.M. Reed et al. (eds), *Topology and Category Theory in Computer Science*, Oxford Sci. Publ., 1991, 153-177.

La83 Lamport, L., What good is temporal logic?, in: R. Mason (ed.), *Information Processing 83*, North-Holland, Amsterdam, 1983, pp. 657-668.

Ma95 Mazurkiewicz, A., Introduction to trace theory, in: V. Diekert and G. Rozenberg (eds.), *The Book of Traces*, World Scientific, Singapore, 1995.

MP92 Maler, O., Z. Manna and A. Pnueli, From timed to hybrid systems, in: J.W. de Bakker et al. (eds.), *Real Time: Theory and Practice*, LNCS 600, Springer, Berlin, 1992, pp. 447-484.

MW95 Michel, A.N., and K. Wang, *Qualitative Theory of Dynamical Systems*, Marcel Dekker, New-York, 1995.

NK93 Nerode, A., and W. Kohn, Models of hybrid systems: Automata, topologies, controllability, observability, in: R.L. Grossman et al. (eds.), *Hybrid Systems*, LNCS 736, Springer, Berlin, 1992, pp. 317-356.

RW87 Ramadge, P.J., and W.M. Wonham, Modular feedback logic for discrete-event systems, *SIAM J. Control and Optimization* 25(1987) 1202-1218.

Si92 Sintzoff, M., Invariance and contraction by infinite iterations of relations, in: J.P. Banâtre and D. Le Métayer (eds.), *Research Directions in High-Level Parallel Programming Languages*, LNCS 574, Springer, Berlin, 1992, pp. 349-373.

Si95 Sintzoff, M., Invariance and termination in structured dynamical systems, RR95-13, Dept Computing Sci. and Eng., U. Louvain. Also in: *Proc. 1995 Intl Symp. on Nonlinear Theory and its Applications*, IEICE, Tokyo, 1995.

SG95 Sintzoff, M., and F. Geurts, Analysis of dynamical systems using predicate transformers - Attraction and composition, in: S.I. Andersson (ed.), *Analysis of Dynamical and Cognitive Systems*, LNCS 888, Springer, Berlin, 1995, pp. 227-260.

Wi90 Wiggins, S., *Introduction to Applied Nonlinear Dynamical Systems and Chaos*, TAM2, Springer, Berlin, 1990.

ZM95 Zhang, Y., and A.K. Mackworth, Constraint nets: a semantic model for hybrid dynamic systems, *Theor. Computer Sci.* 138(1995) 211-239.

Design and Evaluation Tools for Automated Highway Systems [1]

Akash Deshpande, Datta Godbole, Aleks Göllü, Pravin Varaiya
{akash,godbole,gollu,varaiya}@eecs.berkeley.edu
Department of Electrical Engineering and Computer Sciences
University of California at Berkeley
Berkeley, CA 94720

1 Introduction

The Automated Highway Systems (AHS) project at UC-Berkeley is part of a comprehensive program initiated by the U.S. government under the Intermodal Surface Transportation Efficiency Act of 1991 to improve safety and reduce congestion in the surface transportation system. UC-Berkeley's PATH program is a partner in a nine-member consortium along with General Motors, Bechtel, Parsons Brinckerhoff, Martin Marietta, Delco, Hughes, Caltrans, and Carnegie Mellon University. The consortium is funded in part by the U.S. Department of Transportation and it is responsible for designing, evaluating, and demonstrating a prototype AHS.

There is also substantial related activity in Europe under the PROMETHEUS[2] and the DRIVE[3] projects, and in Japan under the RACS[4], AMTICS[5] and VICS[6] projects.

In the rest of this section we present a brief description of the PATH hierarchical control architecture for AHS. In section 2 we present the framework for AHS design and evaluation and give a summary of simulation and analysis tool needs. In section 3 we describe some of these tools being developed by us based on the hybrid systems approach.

1.1 The PATH AHS Architecture

The PATH Program at UC-Berkeley has proposed a hierarchical control architecture that yields up to four-fold increase in transportation capacity while enhancing safety [4, 3]. The architecture proposes a strategy of platooning several vehicles as they travel along the highway. The separation of vehicles within a platoon is small (2m) while separation of platoons from each other is large (60m). The movement of vehicles is realized through simple maneuvers—join, split, lane change, entry, and exit—that are coordinated.

The automation strategy of the PATH AHS architecture is organized in a control hierarchy with the following layers:

---

1 This research is supported by California PATH, Institute of Transportation Studies, University of California at Berkeley

2 Program for European Traffic with Highest Efficiency and Unprecedented Safety

3 Dedicated Road Infrastructure for Vehicle Safety in Europe

4 Road/Automobile Communication System

5 Advanced Mobile Traffic Information and Communication System

6 Vehicle Information and Communication System

Physical Layer—

the automated vehicles. The vehicle dynamical models are given in terms of nonlinear ordinary differential equations.

Regulation Layer—

control and observation subsystems responsible for safe execution of simple maneuvers such as join, split, lane change, entry, and exit. Control laws are given as vehicle state or observation feedback policies for controlling the vehicle dynamics.

Coordination Layer—

communication protocols that vehicles and highway segments follow to coordinate their maneuvers for achieving high capacity in a safe manner. The protocols are given in terms of finite state transition systems.

Link Layer—

control strategies that the highway segments follow in order to maximize throughput. Control laws are given as traffic state and observation feedback policies for controlling the highway traffic using activity flow models. And,

Network Layer—

end-to-end routing so that vehicles reach their destinations without causing congestion. Control laws are given in terms of queuing models.

The physical, regulation, and coordination layers reside on each vehicle and the link and network layers reside on the roadside.

To avoid single-point failures and to provide maximum flexibility, the design proposes distributed multi-agent control strategies. Each vehicle and each highway segment is responsible for its own control. However, these agents must coordinate with each other to produce the desired behavior of high throughput and safety.

The PATH architecture demonstrates hybrid system characteristics in three significant ways.

- Interaction between the coordination and regulation layers. The coordination layer acts as a planning and supervisory controller that selects maneuvers to be executed by the vehicle based on safety and throughput considerations. It then directs the regulation layer to activate the appropriate feedback control laws for controlling the vehicle dynamics.

  This illustrates the usual hybrid control configuration treated in literature wherein a discrete event controller supervises a continuous parameter plant.
- Interaction between the link and coordination layers. The link layer acts as an optimizing controller that selects vehicle activity profiles on highway segments based on throughput optimization considerations. It then directs the vehicles' coordination layer controllers to select maneuvers consistent with the desired activity profiles.

  This illustrates a novel hybrid control configuration wherein a continuous parameter controller directs the behavior of a discrete event plant.
- Switched modes of operation. The system's operating modes are switched when available system capability changes due to failure events and weather conditions.

2 Framework for AHS Design and Evaluation

The PATH AHS architecture is one amongst several possible AHS design concepts. For example, it is possible to envision AHS employing one or more of the following approaches: fully centralized control of all vehicles on the AHS, fully automated but uncoordinated vehicles, semiautomated vehicles requiring active driver participation, mixed automated and manual vehicles on the AHS, and different entry and exit configurations, amongst others.

The AHS consortium is responsible for identifying several AHS design concepts, evaluating and selecting six of these for detailed study, specifying, evaluating and selecting three AHS designs from these six concepts, and finally synthesizing a single AHS design from the three.

Different categories of tools are required to accomplish these tasks. Significant amongst these are simulation tools for system-level AHS simulation, technical analysis tools for safety, highway productivity, comfort, environmental impact, and cost, and design tools for vehicle, highway, communication, driver interface, and other technologies. We present a framework in which these tool needs can be discussed (see [1]).

An AHS *design* consists of four specifications: vehicle design, infrastructure design, AHS operating rules, and failure events. An AHS is designed for deployment in an *environment* specified in terms of *benchmark scenarios*. The benchmark scenarios are given in terms of highway configuration, travel demand, weather conditions, and abnormal events. The performance of an AHS design under the specified benchmark scenarios is judged by a set of *performance metrics*. The performance metrics are employed to rank viable designs.

The design tools aid the design of AHS-related modifications of existing technologies and components and AHS-specific development of new technologies. The evaluation tools provide the following:

1. A uniform language or templates for describing the AHS designs, the benchmark scenarios, and the performance metrics.
2. A set of analytical and simulation approaches for evaluating the performance of a specified AHS design, under a specified scenario, with respect to a specified metric. The results of these exercises are used by evaluators to compare different designs. The results are also used by AHS system designers to refine their designs.

The three succeeding subsections describe the components of AHS designs, benchmark scenarios, and performance metrics.

2.1 AHS Design

Every AHS design or concept comprises four elements: vehicle design, infrastructure design, AHS operating rules, and failure events.

Vehicle Design The *vehicle* design consists of conventional vehicle design and AHS-specific design. The conventional design includes the engine, transmission, steering, braking, weight, size and other parameters that determine the capabilities of each vehicle type. More detailed specifications include the variations in these parameters, their changes over time, the likelihood of defects and faults, and so on. The AHS-specific design includes on-board sensors, communication devices, control algorithms and actuators.

Possible on-board sensors include those measuring the vehicle's own state (self-state sensors), those sensing the infrastructure (roadway geometry sensors), those gathering information about its surroundings (traffic sensors and stationary object sensors) and driver state sensors. The self-state sensors can be used to measure parameters such as engine speed, vehicle speed, intake manifold temperature, acceleration, yaw, roll, and weight. (Vehicle's weight may also be measured by the infrastructure and communicated to the vehicle.) Roadway geometry sensors are needed to recognize relevant roadway geometric parameters, e.g. lane markings, lane merge, lane division, and curve. Traffic and stationary object sensors are needed to ensure safe vehicle movement and maneuvers. Driver state sensors may also be needed for safe transition from automated driving mode back to manual driving mode. Communication devices include those equipped for vehicle-infrastructure and vehicle-vehicle communication. Given the sensed and communicated information, the control algorithms command the vehicle's actuators for automated steering, propulsion and braking.

Infrastructure Design The *infrastructure* design comprises the highway configuration such as the number and size of automated and manual lanes and how they are separated (whether by a physical or symbolic barrier), and the manner in which vehicles move between manual and automated lanes (whether via a transition lane or dedicated access ramps); the roadway facilities for check-in and check-out; arrangements for emergency vehicles; arrangement for non-compliant vehicles or drivers; the interfaces with urban arterials and other non-AHS roadway facilities; the distance between entrances and between exits; toll collection facilities. Whether the AHS is for urban or rural use is also indicated by the highway configuration.

Infrastructure design also includes the sensors located in the roadway for assisting vehicle maneuvers and monitoring traffic, such as magnetic or other markers, beacons, vision surveillance, loop detectors, and weigh-in-motion scales.

Lastly, the infrastructure design includes the communication system for roadway-vehicle, roadway-roadway, and roadway-Traffic Management Center communication.

Operating Rules The *operating rules* specify the ways in which vehicles are controlled individually, how they interact, and how their collective behavior is managed. An example of such a specification is the PATH AHS architecture.

An operating *mode* or *regime* is a collection of compatible operating rules. The system's operating modes are switched when available system capability changes due to events or weather conditions. There are at least two modes: normal mode and degraded mode. Normal mode assumes that the AHS is operating within normal conditions. Under fault conditions, or in adverse environments, the system is operated in a degraded mode. In an extreme form of a degraded mode, for example, vehicles in the automated lane are brought to a standstill, waiting for emergency assistance. Of course, different sections of the AHS may (indeed, will) operate under different modes at the same time.

Failure Events Failure events specify vehicle and infrastructure component failures and the resultant loss of system capabilities that are possible in the design. Associated to the failure events are their rates and distributions.

2.2 Benchmark Scenarios

The benchmark scenario, or operating environment, is specified by highway configuration, travel demand, weather, and fault events. Collectively, the environment stresses the AHS.

Highway Configuration The *highway configuration* specifies the physical configuration of the highway including such attributes as number and arrangement of manual and automated lanes, exclusive rights of way, types of barriers (symbolic, physical) used to separate them, the interfaces between manual and automated lanes and non-AHS arterials, amongst others.

Demand The *demand* specifies the AHS trips, either as a trace or statistically, differentiated by vehicle type, entry, exit, time of day, and location. The demand acts as "inputs" to the AHS, just as vehicles leaving the AHS act as "inputs" to the non-AHS system.

Weather The *weather* specifies the conditions of the roadway that can affect the capabilities of the vehicles, sensors, and operating rules. For example, a slippery road surface reduces the vehicles' maximum acceleration and braking, and fog or rain may reduce the capabilities of vision or other sensors.

Abnormal Events *Abnormal events* specify instances of faults and malfunctions, collisions and other rare events. Events, too, are specified statistically or as a time trace. Events may cause the AHS operation to switch between operating modes.

2.3 Performance Metrics

The different AHS designs will be evaluated by five stakeholders: the government, auto industry, insurance industry, public interest groups, and the users. Users include operators of automobiles, transit vehicles, and trucks, amongst others. Each of the five stake holders will examine the AHS performance metrics of its interest and evaluate the AHS concepts and design. For convenience of discussion, related metrics are grouped into classes.

For the purpose of identifying tool needs we consider the following performance metric classes and subcategories.

Safety

1. Collision rates: the expected number of collisions per vehicle kilometer traveled
2. Injury rates: the expected number of injuries of different severity types per vehicle kilometer traveled
3. Total property damage and medical expenses per vehicle kilometer traveled
4. Collision-free guarantees under fault-free conditions: A guarantee that the design does not lead to a collision when no failure events or abnormal events occur
5. Fault tolerance: the number and types of faults and fault combinations despite which the design does not lead to collisions

Productivity

1. Throughput: source-destination flows in vehicles per hour and passengers per hour for each type of vehicle
2. Delays: expected travel time between source-destination pairs
3. Travel time predictability: variance of the above delays
4. Entry and exit productivity: traffic flows through entries and exits, delays at entries and exits, queue lengths, and exit success rates.
5. Non-AHS impact: locally, the buffer and throughput requirements imposed on non-AHS arterials by the AHS; globally, the network level abstraction of the AHS leading to changes in traffic patterns and driver behavior

Comfort

1. Maximum longitudinal and lateral acceleration
2. Maximum longitudinal and lateral deceleration
3. Maximum speed
4. Separation and closing rates: separation between vehicles and the relative velocity and acceleration during maneuvers such as join or lane change.
5. User interface: driver interface within the vehicle to access AHS features, and feedback information provided to driver from the AHS.
6. Complexity of AHS driving tasks

Environmental Impact

1. Air pollution: emissions of carbon monoxide, hydrocarbons, and nitrous oxides by vehicle type and per vehicle kilometer traveled.
2. Fuel consumption: consumption of fuel per vehicle kilometer traveled for each vehicle type.
3. Noise pollution: effect of traffic speed, volume, acceleration profiles, tire designs, sound walls and elevated structures on noise pollution.
4. Land use: local issues such as land used in construction of the AHS highways and global issues such as impact on regional traffic patterns.

Cost

1. Infrastructure modification cost: cost of building the AHS infrastructure.
2. Vehicle modification cost: cost of building the AHS vehicles.
3. Operating cost: cost of operating the AHS.
4. Macroeconomic impact: overall economic benefits of the AHS such as job creation, technological advantages, and economies of scale.

An important characteristic of a design not measured by the above metrics is its flexibility to satisfy the demands of different operating constraints. For example, different local administrations may choose to impose different constraints on the operation of the AHS within their domain of control. Similarly, different constraints may be imposed based on the time of day, allowing, for example, exclusive use of the AHS by heavy vehicles between midnight and 6:00 AM.

The flexibility of the design can be judged partially by variations in the performance metrics for different benchmark scenarios. To judge completely the flexibility of a design, further qualitative investigations may be required.

2.4 Evaluation Methodology

Evaluating a single design or comparing alternative designs requires a methodology of using analysis and simulation tools. These tools provide formal or standardized languages or templates for specifying AHS designs, benchmark scenarios or the environment, and performance metrics. Standardization facilitates the objective comparison of different alternatives and promotes meaningful communication among different groups. The formal structure may be in the language of mathematics or in a programming language, assisted by aids such as block diagrams and other user-friendly interfaces.

The relationship between the AHS design, benchmark scenarios, performance metrics and evaluation tools is shown in Figure 1. Once an AHS design, environment and performance metric are specified, one or several tools may be used to evaluate the performance of the design. Symbolically, if D stands for design, E for environment, and P for performance metric, all formally specified, then an appropriate tool evaluates the functional relationship,

$$P = f(D, E)$$

For two reasons, a suite of tools rather than a single tool will be needed. First, different performance metrics may require different formalizations, and, second, the design, environment and performance metric may be modeled with different levels of emphasis or abstraction. It is expected that differentiating among initial designs may be carried out by tools that require relatively abstract models. Designs that survive this initial screening can only be compared using more detailed specifications. Objective comparisons will now require a unified framework that is capable of representing faithfully greater levels of detail.

Three roles are involved in the tool use for evaluation of AHS designs: the evaluator, the AHS designer, and the tool designer. The evaluator chooses the performance

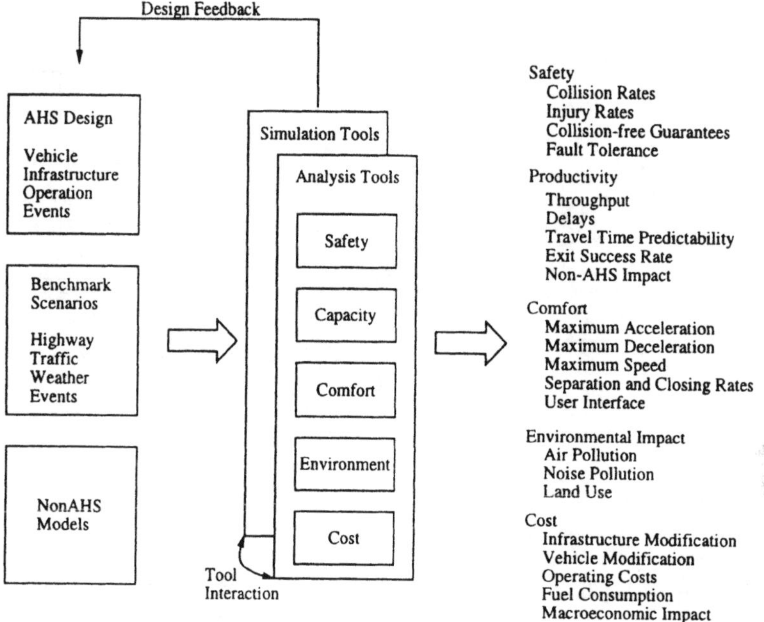

Fig. 1. Evaluation Tools

metric to be analyzed, and picks a suite of evaluation tools to be used for this purpose. The AHS designers and the tool designers collaborate to model the design in terms of the input parameters of the tools. This may entail the use of additional tools as prefilters to process the design. Similarly, the tool designers and the evaluator collaborate to model the chosen benchmark scenario in terms of the input parameters of the tool. After using the tools to generate the performance metrics, all three collaborate to interpret them. At this stage, decision support tools may be required to collate the large arrays of design performance metrics for utility-directed aggregation.

The design and evaluation tools also play an important role in the design process (see Figure 2). The design tools are used in proposing the initial design, and the design and evaluation tools are used in successively refining the design until it meets performance requirements.

3 Design and Evaluation Tools

Design tools are required for developing sensors, actuators, controllers, communications, fault management, and driver interfaces. Sensors comprise vehicle and roadside sensor models, sensor performance, and sensor fusion. Actuators comprise vehicle actuator models and performance, vehicle dynamical models and parameter databases. Controllers comprise regulation layer emulators and performance, coordination layer

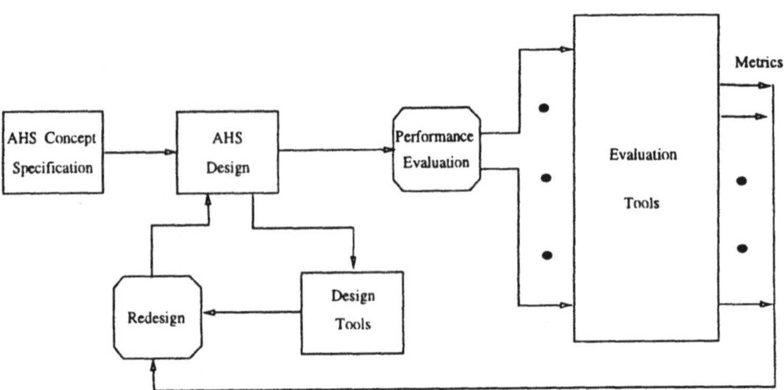

Fig. 2. AHS Design Process

protocol simulators and verifiers, and link and network layer controllers. Communications comprise vehicle-vehicle, vehicle-roadside, and roadside-TMC communications using infrared, radio, satellite, fiber and other channels. Fault management comprises fault prediction or detection, diagnosis, tolerance, and recovery. Driver interface comprises interface design and driver fitness testing.

Evaluation tools are required for system- and component-level simulation and technical analysis to yield performance metrics for a given design and benchmark scenario. In the following sections we discuss the system-level microsimulation tool and safety and productivity analysis tools.

3.1 AHS Simulation

SmartAHS is a microsimulator for AHS designs and scenarios. It models the AHS as a dynamic network of interacting hybrid systems. This model can be used to describe control architectures with several granularities of time- and event-driven simulation requirements. It can be used to specify distributed agent control laws.

SmartAHS can be used to describe several modes of system operation in terms of different dynamical models and control policies. For example, under abnormal weather conditions such as rain or ice, the system can activate different sensor, actuator, and vehicle models and control laws.

SmartAHS provides full access to system state and state trajectories. Consequently, SmartAHS can be used to specify various state monitors that inspect components of the system state to generate different performance metrics both on-line and off-line. For example, occurrence of collisions can be checked on-line, while fuel efficiency and air pollution can be checked off-line.

Simulation runs can be stopped, changed, and continued for full control over the simulation scenarios. Consequently, traffic events and weather conditions specified in the benchmark scenarios can be introduced during runs using the simulation control mechanism.

SmartAHS provides graphical user interfaces for specifying the inputs, controlling the simulation runs, and visualizing the outputs. For example, highway configurations in a benchmark scenario can be specified graphically using a highway editor. Similarly, the vehicle traces can be visualized graphically.

SmartAHS can interface to non-AHS traffic simulators such as Integration, FreeSim, and NetSim using link or network layer interfaces, and it can interface to vehicle simulators using regulation layer interfaces.

A prototype version of SmartAHS has been developed and a full-functionality version is under development.

SmartPath is a fully-developed microsimulator for the PATH AHS architecture. Its performance depends on the time-granularity of the simulation. If the integration routines used to calculate vehicle displacement are set to 5–50ms step size, and vehicle position on the highway is updated every 100ms, 50 vehicles can be simulated in real-time on a Sun Sparc 10 workstation ([5, 6]). (The integration step-size is dynamically adjusted based on vehicle displacement.) Simulation profiles indicate that 80% of the simulation time is spent on time-driven simulation of the differential equations that model vehicle dynamics.

A multiprocessor version of SmartPath has also been implemented. In this implementation, the overall communication load due to distributed processing is 10% and the performance scales linearly with the number of processors employed.

3.2 Safety Analysis

The safety analysis tools check for collision-free behavior in the absence of design failures and collision rates in presence of failures. The challenging problem is to guarantee that an AHS design does not result in an inter-vehicle collision. In the PATH architecture, individual vehicle dynamics are governed by the hybrid control system formed by the interacting coordination and regulation layer controllers. Thus, collision analysis is equivalent to hybrid system verification. Although verification problems for general hybrid dynamical systems are undecidable, we are using optimal control techniques (see [8]) to get conservative guarantees and estimates of inter-vehicle collisions.

3.3 Productivity Analysis

SmartCap is a link layer macro-simulator that performs numerical computation of the analytical activity flow model [9], an extension of traditional traffic flow models. It permits differentiation of discrete activities such as entry, exit, merge, join, lane change, and cruise, performed by vehicles and it captures the impact of these activities on highway productivity. Activities are characterized by the amount of highway space and time that they use. For example, a lane change activity might take 100m of longitudinal distance and be 15s in duration. These two parameters are used in the model to determine the aggregate delay or capacity loss incurred due to that activity. Users specify an activity flow profile as input to SmartCap, and SmartCap deduces the highway productivity under the profile. Specifying the maneuvers in terms of their activity flow profiles is not a trivial task. We envision that the users will specify detailed dynamical models in the SmartAHS format and then SmartAHS simulations will be used to obtain activity flow profiles for individual maneuvers.

The activity flow model consists of conservation of vehicles, evolution of average velocities on highway sections, and physical constraints on the vehicles and the highway. The conservation law extends standard traffic flow models by keeping track of activity flows as well. The average velocity dynamics accounts for anticipation due to follower behavior, relaxation due to reference velocity-tracking control laws, and vehicle interactions due to speed variations between activities. Constraints capture vehicle limitations on velocity and acceleration, permitted sequence of activities, and highway space-time limitations.

4 Conclusions

We have presented a brief description of the Automated Highway Systems project and have discussed the PATH design for AHS. The design proposes a hierarchical control architecture that can be modeled and analyzed using the hybrid systems approach. We have presented the framework for AHS design and evaluation and have given the tool needs for these tasks.

The AHS design and evaluation program poses several challenging tool development and research problems. We are developing tools for modeling, controller synthesis, formal verification, simulation and automated testing of hybrid systems targeted for the AHS application domain.

References

1. NAHSC Consortium. *Task No. B4A: Tool Needs for AHS Design and Evaluation—Draft.* April 1995.
2. OSI/Network Management Forum. "OSI Basic Reference Model." ISO 7498-1. 1992.
3. Steve Shladover *et al.* "Automated Vehicle Control Developments in the PATH program." *IEEE Trans. Vehicular Tech.* Vol. 40. pp. 114-130. Feb. 1991.
4. P. Varaiya. "Smart Cars on Smart Roads: Problems of Control." *IEEE Trans. Automatic Control.* Vol. 38, No 2. Feb. 1993.
5. A. Göllü, A. Deshpande, P. Hingorani, P. Varaiya. "SmartDb: An Object Oriented Simulation Framework for Highway Systems." *Fifth Annual Conference on AI, Simulation and Planning in High Autonomy Systems.* Gainesville, Florida. 1994.
6. F. Eskafi, Delnaz Khorramabadi, and P. Varaiya, "An Automatic Highway System Simulator." *Transpn. Res.-C* Vol. 3, No. 1, pp. 1-17, 1995.
7. A. Göllü. "Object Management Systems." *Ph.D. Thesis*, University of California at Berkeley. 1995.
8. A. Puri and P. Varaiya, "Driving safely in smart cars," in *American Control Conference*, pp. 3597–3599, 1995.
9. M. E. Broucke and P. Varaiya, "A theory of traffic flow in automated highway systems." (preprint), 1995.

Hybrid Control in Sea Traffic Management Systems

John-Morten Godhavn, Trygve Lauvdal and Olav Egeland

The Norwegian Institute of Technology
N-7034 Trondheim, Norway
John.Morten.Godhavn, Trygve.Lauvdal, Olav.Egeland@itk.unit.no

Abstract. Increasing traffic on highways and in the air has in the recent years motivated the design of hierarchical hybrid control systems. In this paper we will propose a hierarchical hybrid control system for the control of traffic on sea, a Sea Traffic Management System (STMS). The motivation is to reduce delays and improve the efficiency and safety in increasingly overcrowded harbors, busy straits and narrow areas on sea. A controller unit on land plans the whole traffic scenario, and interacts with advanced (hybrid) autopilots placed on each ship. A system as described above should take advantage of the new available technology, such as satellite based navigation (GPS-systems), digital sea maps, faster and more powerful computers, and more and better actuators.

Keywords: Hierarchical Hybrid Control, Sea Traffic Management, Autopilot.

1 Introduction

In some busy harbors of today there exists systems for traffic control and surveillance. Most ships of today are at the same time equipped with some kind of autopilot. In this paper we will propose a way to combine these two kinds of systems into one control system. Every aspect of the motion of every ship in a limited area on sea will then be controlled by this system. To do this, the land based unit must be modified, the autopilots on board each ship must be made more advanced and hybrid, and we need a fast communication link between the ships and the landbased unit. We will propose a solution with a hierarchical structure, define what should be taken care of on each level in this structure, and how the different levels interact.

A system with no human interaction as described in this paper is not realistic to be implemented within many years from now. The captain of the ship must at least be able to control the ship manually when something fails. Laws and regulations on sea must also be changed significantly in order to make an all automatic solution legal. An important issue for safety is redundancy, i.e. if some component fails, then there should exist a backup component to take over. The captain of the ship is the backup for the overall control of the ship.

The present set of tools for analysis of hierarchical hybrid systems is not satisfactory. The discrete part alone can be analyzed by existing methods in computer science. Likewise is it possible to analyze the continuous subsystems by well-established tools of control engineering. Simulations of hybrid systems can be used to identify problems, but simulations can of course not be used to verification or to prove stability.

Technical advances that can make an STMS a reality include the availability of todays fast and relative inexpensive real time computers on board ships and in the land based Sea Traffic Controller (STC). Knowledge of local conditions and regulations can be programmed into computers so that the need of pilots (people) with this knowledge can be relaxed. Improved navigation equipment as GPS measuring systems allows more exact tracking and detailed digital sea maps allows safer and more flexible route planning. Ships built in the latest years are also often equipped with more actuators than the standard propeller-rudder combination. This gives a larger feasible set of trajectories, which should be utilized by the STC in narrow areas on sea. Todays system involve the use of sea lanes, i.e. dedication of broad routes on sea for the ships. These sea lanes are not very efficient and not optimal. The result is both planned and unplanned delays in sea travel. The potential improvement of both the safety and the performance is great if the STC and the autopilots on board cooperate continuously.

2 Proposed Architecture

A hierarchical structure has to be utilized due to the high complexity with both a great number of control decisions (Discrete events) and a multiple set of low-level control laws (Continuous systems). A possible hierarchical control architecture for an STMS is shown in Fig.1.

2.1 Sea Traffic Controller

The STC is a discrete event control unit responsible for monitoring, coordination, and scheduling. This controller is the only part which is not placed on board the ships. Overall safety and performance is taken care of on this level. The STC monitors the motion of the ships with its own position sensors, which typically is a set of radars.

The actual commands from the STC are packages with a sequence of via-points to each ship. A via-point is a set of coordinates (x_i, y_i) and a time interval $[t_{i,\min}, t_{i,\max}]$. The ships should then reach the given via-points within the given time intervals. These sequences of via-points ensure safety, i.e. if all ships cross their via-points, then collision should be avoided. This implies that an increasing number of ships will demand an increasing number of via-points per ship (see Fig. 2). If it is impossible for the ship to follow the required path, then the autopilot renegotiates with the STC.

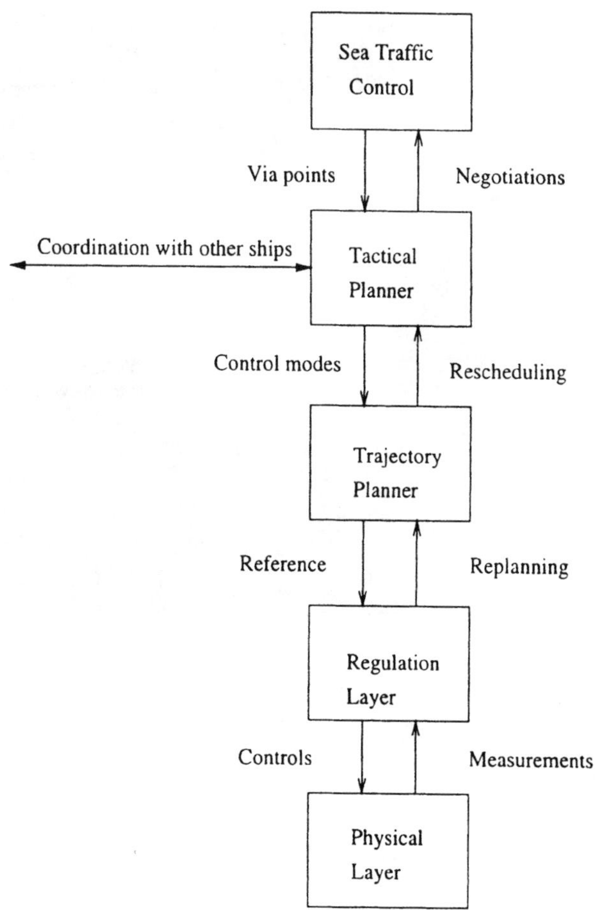

Fig. 1. Architecture of the STMS control system.

2.2 Tactical Planner

A detailed tactical plan is generated from the information given by the STC. A tactical plan takes the via-points and partitions the route into segments with different control modes. Typical control modes are:

- Conventional mode: constant speed along straight lines or parts of circles (or more advanced motion).
- Speed mode: Change speed, most often during straight line motion.
- Stop-on-track mode: Stop ship and hold position. This is called Dynamic Positioning (DP) in the ship control literature.

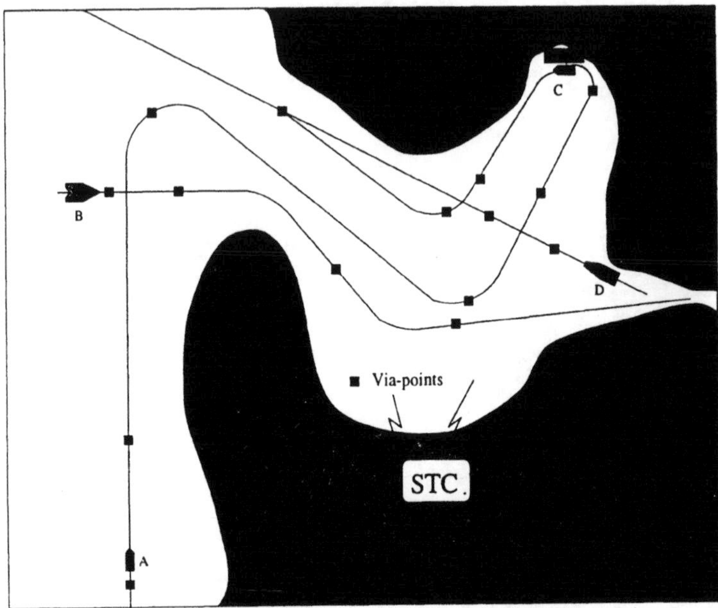

Fig. 2. Scenario for STMS: The figure shows ship A on its way to the quay, ship B wants to go through the strait, ship C is leaving the quay, and ship D wants to go from the strait and out to open sea. The STC has given several via-points to each ship in order to make this possible.

- Come alongside quay (CAQ) mode: Special trajectories for approaching the dock, could be a nonholonomic problem.

An automaton for the Tactical Planner is shown in Fig. 3.

Simplified mathematical models, such as kinematical models with bounds on velocities and turning radius, will be used in the construction of the tactical plan. Water current might be considered here by considering relative motion, i.e. compensate for the constant part of the water current in planning on this level.

The via-points generated by the STC have to be very dense to guarantee safety. To reduce the workload and to increase the flexibility of the system, it is desired that only a limited number of via-points are considered for regular traffic. Some protocols (rules) for collision avoidance are hence necessary for the Tactical Planner. The autopilots on board should be able to detect and solve possible conflicts without involving the STC. This feature is critical if e.g. the STC has a power failure.

When maneuvers are aborted, the Tactical Planner renegotiates via-points with the STC. The Tactical Planner is a discrete event system (DES).

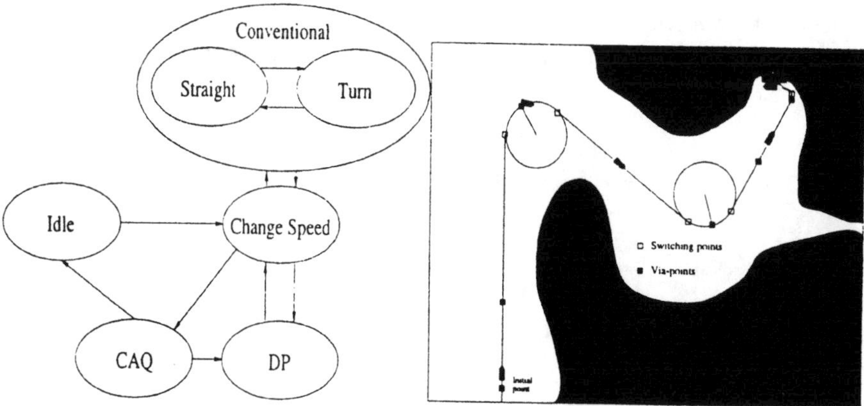

Fig. 3. Tactical Planner Automaton: The figure shows how the Tactical Planner assigns straight lines and circles so that the ship passes through the given via-points, and where the autopilot switches control mode along the trajectory.

2.3 Trajectory Planner

Trajectory planning is done on this level. A smooth reference trajectory is generated, where performance limitations of the ship and other aspects such as passenger comfort and fuel consumption are considered. If a trajectory satisfying some ship dependent conditions is impossible to obtain, rescheduling is requested from the Tactical Planner. This is repeated until a feasible trajectory is found. A detailed dynamical model of the ship with disturbances and input saturation limits is considered. The Trajectory Planner is a hybrid system, since it deals with both discrete (control modes) and continuous time (smooth trajectories) signals.

2.4 Regulation Layer

The trajectory generated on the previous level is fed to the Regulation Layer. Individual robust linear or nonlinear controllers are then applied for the different control modes. Each of these controllers has its own set of active and inactive actuators and measurements.

One possible solution of stabilizing the system around a feasible trajectory is described in [9], where a time varying linear control law exponentially stabilizes the system locally. If the error grows outside the stable part of the statespace, then a new trajectory should be requested from the Trajectory Planner.

Controllers are switched when entering a new control mode. These switches are difficult to analyze, but in this case most of the switches are predictable (time-dependent), and there is a limited number of them. If the controller is unable to stabilize the ship along the trajectory, due to e.g. rudder saturation, a new trajectory is requested from the Trajectory Planner.

3 Similarities to and Differences from ATMS

The architecture here is motivated by the one proposed by prof. Sastry and his group at the UC Berkeley Robotics Lab for Air Traffic Management Systems (ATMS) [8]. This makes sense since the control of an airport and a harbor has several similarities. Both systems have to serve a large number of customers who want access a limited set of resources. The objectives are efficiency and safety. Typically there is a higher number of agents on an airport for some period of time, but on the sea each object stays for a longer period of time and thus have to be supervised longer.

The geometry is simpler in a sea area since we then operate in only three degrees of freedom (DOF) instead of six. However, with only three DOF a severe limitation of space is the result. In the air planes can be "put on top of" each other and several trajectories can "cross" in (x, y)-coordinates without any danger. In addition they have a greater speed and thus their trajectory is released quicker. This is not the case in an area on sea, e.g. if a ship has been allocated to a trajectory and runs at a very low speed, other ships has to be allowed to cross this trajectory before the ship reaches the via-point. Thus time is an important parameter for the STC when approval is given to a ships via-points. Otherwise optimality is unreachable.

Also ships can wait, while airplanes can not stand still in the air, they need space to do circles in the air while waiting. Due to the simple geometry, interagent coordination (i.e. identifying neighbor ships) is much simpler in an STMS architecture than in an ATMS architecture. Other related work is done on Intelligent Vehicle Highway Systems (IVHS), see e.g. [5] and the references therein.

4 Planning and Controller Design

The way to an implemented system of the type mentioned above is very long and challenges appear at several levels. Some of these challenges are described below.

4.1 Collision Avoidance

We propose that this problem should be shared between the STC and the ships. The STC should be responsible for keeping the total number of ships in the crowded area small enough and the ships distributed around so that collision avoidance is achievable, while the autopilot on board each ship should have procedures for collision avoidance on a lower level. The help from the STC makes it necessary to consider only a limited number of different potential conflict scenarios. In most systems of today ships take care of this problem by themselves in a decentralized matter. Smaller, faster, and ships coming from the left must yield, is the main rule. In most cases this is sufficient, since most ships are moving with low speed. However, with the new high speed vessels, the need for more advanced controllers arises to maintain an acceptable level of safety on sea.

4.2 Tactical Planning

Based on the via-points received from the STC the automatic Trajectory Planner should make an optimal trajectory in order to interpolate them. There are several possibilities, e.g. shortest distance through the points. The work of L. E. Dubins [3] applies directly to generating paths of minimal length in the plane for vehicles moving only in the forward direction with a constraint on average curvature. The theorem says that the planar curve of minimal length consists of an arc of an circle, a straight line and an arc of an circle. This result can be used by the Tactical Planner. A more general approach for the planning of a trajectory seems to be a minimization of an optimal criterion:

$$J = \int_0^T L(\boldsymbol{x}(\tau), \boldsymbol{u}(\tau), \tau) d\tau \tag{1}$$

where $L(\cdot)$ is some criterion for optimality, $\boldsymbol{x}(\tau)$ is the state vector and $\boldsymbol{u}(\tau)$ is the actuator vector. The weighting coefficients will vary from ship to ship based on priorities, e.g. a tanker will prefer a fuel optimization criterion while a high-speed passenger vessel will prefer a comfort criterion.

Optimization with respect to a fuel consumption criterion seems to be of limited interest done within a small area, but significant when a trajectory is planned over a long distance. Thus an STMS covering a large area has a great potential for fuel reduction just by including via-points with a time specification. This is due to the fact that the water resistance of the ship does not increase linearly with respect to speed, and that the fuel consumption on a distance L with optimal speed, is smaller than if the same distance is covered with a larger speed. Thus the autopilot can plan the speed necessary to arrive at the quay in time to get the desired resources and does not have to speed up in order to try to reach the destination within a specified time if the resource is available at a more suitable (later) time.

Environmental disturbances which are predictable, e.g. slowly varying water current, should be compensated for on this level. This can be done by considering the notion of relative motion. This can be explained by looking at the kinematical model of a ship under the influence of constant water current:

$$\begin{aligned} \dot{x} &= u\cos\psi - v\sin\psi + W_x \\ \dot{y} &= u\sin\psi + v\cos\psi + W_y \\ \dot{\psi} &= r \end{aligned} \tag{2}$$

where (x, y) are position coordinates in an earth-fixed coordinate system, u is surge velocity (forward speed), v is sway velocity (sideways speed), ψ is yaw angle (course angle) and r is angular velocity in yaw. W_x and W_y represent the water current velocities along the inertial x- and y-axes. The velocities u and v are relative to the water and not to the inertial frame. Then only variations of the water current have to be considered as a disturbance by the Regulation Layer.

4.3 Trajectory Planning

The somewhat coarse trajectory proposed by the Tactical Planner is modified on this level by considering a more detailed dynamical model of the ship including disturbances and actuator saturation limits. The dynamical model can be written on the form

$$\frac{d}{dt}\begin{bmatrix} u \\ v \\ r \end{bmatrix} = \boldsymbol{f}(u, v, r, \delta, X, \boldsymbol{d}) \tag{3}$$

where the control inputs for this ship are the rudder δ and the propeller X, and the external disturbances are represented by $\boldsymbol{d}$.

4.4 Regulation

The classical ship autopilot has only one objective and that is to make the ship track a desired yaw angle. The disadvantage of this approach is the following; if the ship is traveling a large distance from (x_1, y_1) to (x_2, y_2), the course has to be changed several times because a small deviation from the correct angle result in a large error. The actual trajectory is then intuitively not optimal with respect to any criterion and thus unsatisfactory for an STMS. However, some ships have an additional controller with position feedback and can track a straight line between the two points.

The traditional task of trajectory tracking is simple because it only consists of a straight line until a new line is defined (in addition the ship speed is approximated constant). Thus switching between the two control modes are only done on a limited number of occasions. The traditional trajectory cannot be compared with the trajectory in an STMS. The trajectories in this system are more complex due to the possibility that it may include maneuvers as *stop on track*, *change speed* and *come alongside quay*. As a consequence switching between the control modes becomes an important issue and must be considered further.

4.5 Description of Control Modes

The different control modes introduced are described. Implemented solutions and unsolved problems are discussed.

Course Keeping and Course Changing In a ship autopilot designed for trajectory following, these two control objectives belongs naturally together and will be considered as one control mode in the STMS. However, in conventional autopilots they are divided into two separate modes due to the complexity of the controller under course changing. This control strategy is called ***cross-tracking.***

Another trajectory following principle (see [6] for details) is called *Line of Sight* (LOS) and is based on way points which, like the via-points, are sets of coordinates given in an earth-fixed frame. The problem with the LOS algorithm is that only the yaw-angle is controlled (not the position). Some timing must also be included to be a good solution of the tracking problem in an STMS.

Course Keeping Standard course-keeping autopilots are easily implemented on ships and there are several approaches to solve this task. In the literature course keeping autopilots range from simple PID-controllers, to more sophisticated non-linear controllers, e.g. feedback linearization. However these autopilots can only maintain the desired course angle, and in trajectory tracking one has to guarantee that the ship does not run in parallel with the trajectory. Thus an outer control loop is necessary to ensure that the ship follows a given path. This is not implemented on all ships.

A conventional tracking system today is usually designed by rotating the earth-fixed coordinate system, neglecting the sway mode, and assuming constant ship speed, to obtain the simplified kinematics:

$$\dot{y} = U\psi + d_y \tag{4}$$

where d_y is a slow-varying parameter describing errors due to linearization and environmental disturbances and U is a constant cruise speed. Thus the control objective is to ensure $y = 0$, and a simple PI-controller will guarantee tracking, i.e.

$$\psi_d = K_p y(t) + K_i \int_{t_0}^{t} y(\tau) d\tau \tag{5}$$

will make the ship track a straight line between to points, (x_1, y_1) and (x_2, y_2) even with the presence of disturbances. However, with a speed controller in parallel the ship speed U is not necessary constant and correction to changes in speed has to be made to ensure acceptable tracking under speed changes. This is usually done by gain scheduling with respect to ship speed.

Course Changing When a ship track a circular trajectory the kinematics introduce a control problem due to its nonlinear nature. The solution to this problem is an additional controller rotating the earth-fixed coordinate system the desired angle at *every sample*. Thus the arguments in the previous section can be transfered and an extra controller rotating the earth-fixed coordinate system is introduced. Thus the course keeping controllers guarantee asymptotic tracking also of the circular trajectory. Further research is necessary to develop nonlinear control laws.

Speed Control Due to the time specification related to position (x, y) ship speed control with acceptable accuracy is an important issue in an STMS. The ship speed equations of motion are highly nonlinear differential equation. To obtain maximum accuracy a nonlinear control law should be implemented. For details see [4].

Nonlinear speed controllers are commercially available, and no research is necessary. However far from all ships have this kind of controller installed and speed regulation is often based on radio communication from the bridge to the engine room.

Dynamic Positioning In order to control a ship in three DOF, extra thrusters are required in addition to the rudder and a propeller in the main direction. Two controls and three DOF gives what we call an *underactuated* control system. This problem is similar to the well known parking problem for a wheeled vehicle. It can be shown that no continuous static state feedback can stabilize such systems. Either discontinuous or time varying feedback have to be applied, as it is done in control of nonholonomic systems (see e.g. [7]). If a ship with this equipment is required to maintain its position (DP), an advanced controller is required. The dynamic positioning of an under-actuated ship does not have the same accuracy due to the fact that motion in surge is required to stabilize the ship.

Systems for dynamic positioning (DP) are commercially available and present no problem in the STMS if only ships with extra thrusters are allowed to enter the area. See e.g. [4] and [1] for details on two different approaches to the problem of DP systems. A dynamic positioning system is based on controlling the forces in x- and y-direction and moment round the z-axis. Since most ships have more thrusters than degrees of freedom there are several ways of allocating the thrusters, and an optimal thruster allocation algorithm is not available.

Come Alongside Quay The task of automatic control the ship to quay is not very challenging if the ship is equipped with the necessary thrusters, i.e. the same equipment needed for dynamic positioning. The autopilot needs an extra set of sensors with very good accuracy and there has to be equipment on land which indicates where the ship is going to be secured. Except from the extra equipment a DP control system can easily be extended to an automatic CAQ system. This kind of control system is however not commercially available, but is expected to be so within few years.

4.6 Requirements

It is required that all ships which enter the controlled area on sea has an advanced hybrid autopilot on board, which can be controlled remotely from a land based unit. The autopilot must include all the modes described above. Especially all ships need a speed controller, something which is not the case today, where speed control often is done by radio communication between the bridge and the engine room.

4.7 Hybrid Control Issues

From the continuous point of view the different discrete events present interrupts of the continuous control. One example of this is when two ships come to close, where "to close" is modeled by a safety area dependent on distance in x- and y-direction and the relative speed and acceleration of the ships in these directions. Then an alarm procedure is initiated in the Tactical Planner. If via-points have to be changed, then the changes must also be approved by the STC.

From the discrete point of view the dynamics and kinematics of the ships present disturbances which partially are unpredictable. The DES does not know what will happen at what time. E.g. failure in the engine of one ship may cause a total replanning.

4.8 Stability and Performance

The individual autopilots are assumed to give sufficient local stability and performance properties while working in continuous mode, i.e. between the switches. Stability problems may however appear when control modes are switched. But on sea the time between each switch is typically very long compared to the time of (practical) convergence of each autopilot, i.e. we assume the control deviation is small in every switch. Then old control modes will in most cases not interact with new, and each control mode may be analyzed individually. Stability of the continuous part seems therefore to be achievable, although the switching problem has to be considered in more detail.

Stability and performance of the total STMS is hard to analyze, and the present tools are not satisfactory. While waiting for appropriate tools to be developed, simulations are used. Some work has been done on stability analysis of switched systems by e.g. [2].

5 Final Remarks

The goal with an STMS is to reduce the time spent by each ship inside the crowded area on sea. More cost-efficient, reliable and predictable traffic is what we are looking for. Solutions to many of the control problems exist, e.g. autopilots for different operations on sea in [4], and many are available commercially today. Similarly there exists manual systems for sea traffic control in some busy areas on sea (e.g. Brevikstrømmen in Norway), and there exists several systems for anti collision on sea (e.g. in The Oslo Fjord). The hybrid challenge is to combine these two kinds of systems together into one hierarchical control system that takes care of both safety and performance.

References

[1] Balchen, J. G., Jenssen, N. A., Sælid, S.: Dynamic Positioning of Floating Vessels Based on Kalman Filtering and Optimal Control. Proceedings of the 19th IEEE Conference on Decision and Control (1980) 852–864.

[2] Branicky, M. S.: Stability of Switched and Hybrid Systems. Proc. of the IEEE Conf. Decision and Control (1994) 3498-3503.

[3] Dubins, L.E.: On curves of Minimal Length with a Constraint on Average Curvature, and with Prescribed Initial and Terminal Positions and Tangents. American Journal of Mathematics, 79:497–516 (1957).

[4] Fossen, T. I.: Guidance and Control of Ocean Vehicles. John Wiley and Sons Ltd. (1994).

[5] Godbole, D. N., Lygeros, J.: Longitudinal Control of the Lead Car of a Platoon. IEEE Trans. Vehicular Techn. vol 43 nr 4 (1994) 1125-1135.

[6] Healey, A. J., Lienard, D.: Multivariable Sliding Mode Control for Autonomous Diving and Steering of Unmanned Underwater Vehicles. IEEE Journal of Ocean Engineering vol OE-18 nr 3 (1993) 327–339.

[7] Murray, R. M., M'Closkey, R. T.: Exponential Stabilization of Driftless Nonlinear Control Systems using Homogeneous Feedback. CDS, Tech. Report nr 95–012, Caltech (1995).

[8] Sastry, S., Meyer, G., Tomlin, C., Lygeros, J., Godbole, D., Pappas, G.: Hybrid Control in Air Traffic Management Systems. UC Berkeley Memo UCB/ERL M95/82 October 1995.

[9] Walsh, G., Tilbury, D., Sastry, S., Murray, R., and Laumond, J.-P.: Stabilization of Trajectories for Systems with Nonholonomic Constraints. IEEE Transactions on Automatic Control, January, 1994.

Verification of Hybrid Systems: Monotonicity in the AHS Control System *

John A. Haddon**, Datta N. Godbole, Akash Deshpande, John Lygeros
Department of Electrical Engineering and Computer Sciences
University of California at Berkeley
Berkeley, California 94720
haddon,godbole,akash,lygeros@eecs.berkeley.edu

Abstract. Numerous approaches to verifying the safety of vehicles in the AHS architecture of PATH have been proposed (see [1] and [2]). One approach involves finding a boundary between safe and unsafe initial conditions. This task is significantly easier if we can guarantee that the severity of an accident is monotonic in the initial conditions. Simulation results are presented in which it is shown that this condition does not hold for the design of [1], and a hybrid automaton model explaining this situation is presented. Finally, some attempts to modify the control laws to obtain monotonicity are presented.

1 Introduction

The California PATH program, an Automated Highway Systems (AHS) project, is aimed at improving the safety and efficiency of road transportation systems. Each vehicle on the proposed AHS is controlled automatically, allowing higher speeds and closer spacing than would be safe with human drivers. Vehicles travel in platoons—groups of vehicles which move together as one unit, with very little spacing (*e.g.* 2m) between cars in a platoon, and large spacing (*e.g.* 60m) between platoons. The close spacing within a platoon is designed to ensure that any collision between vehicles in a platoon is a low relative velocity collision, while the large spacing between platoons is designed to ensure that platoons are isolated—small disturbances in the velocity of one platoon do not propagate to following platoons. An in-depth discussion of the PATH design is given in [3].

Safety is an important consideration in the design of such systems, *i.e.* the proposed communication and control mechanisms themselves should not cause accidents. In this paper, we consider a lane change scenario and its effect on the adaptive cruise control law used by the leader of every platoon as a default longitudinal law.

The longitudinal control law presented in [1] applies linearizing feedback to the nonlinear dynamics of the car, so that the engine jerk (*i.e.* the rate of change

* Research supported by the California PATH program, Institute of Transportation Studies, University of California, Berkeley under grant MOU-135

** Research supported by a University of California Regents Fellowship and by ARO under grant DAAH04-94-G-0026

of acceleration) of the vehicle can be directly controlled by the input u. We assume that at time t the controller can observe the entire state $(x_i(t), \dot{x}_i(t), \ddot{x}_i(t))$ of car i as well as the relative distance and relative velocity of the preceding car.

The objective of the cruise control law described in [1] is to follow the preceding car, car $i-1$, at a safe distance, given by an affine function of the velocity. This is achieved by using a switched mode controller that switches between different feedback control policies depending on which region of the state space the system is in. The switching is necessary to ensure passenger comfort and stability of the system. The system can be modeled as a hybrid automaton—a continuous time, continuous variable system with phased operation. This hybrid automaton model has been introduced in [4] and [5].

In our lane change scenario, a vehicle from an adjacent lane cuts into the given car's safety distance, throwing it out of normal operation. Such a lane change can be dangerous if the vehicle cuts in too close ahead moving at a slower speed. If we know the set of initial conditions for which the cruise controller does not result in a collision, then all the lane changes that might lead to a collision can be blocked by using communication.

Of particular relevance to the task of proving safety of the longitudinal control law is the concept of monotonicity. Recall that a function $f : \mathbb{R} \to \mathbb{R}$ is defined to be monotone increasing if $f(x) \geq f(y)$ whenever $x > y$. Monotone decreasing is similarly defined. In this paper, we consider the monotonicity of minimum spacing between two vehicles as a function of the initial conditions of the two cars.

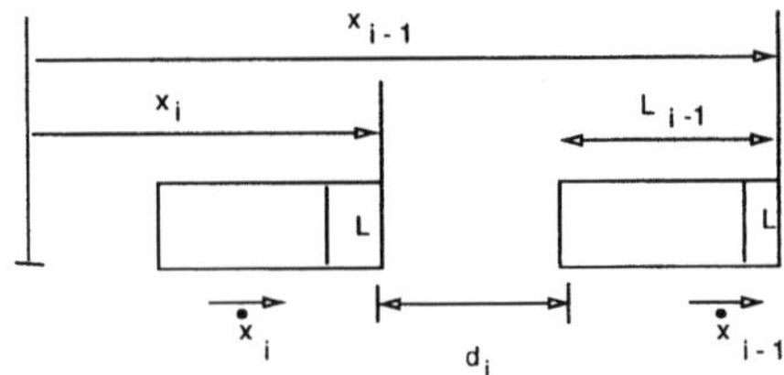

Fig. 1. State Variables

Define the state variables as follows (see Figure 1):

$$
\begin{aligned}
z_1 &= \dot{x}_i \\
z_2 &= \ddot{x}_i \\
z_3 &= x_{i-1} - x_i - L_{i-1} \\
z_4 &= \dot{x}_{i-1} - \dot{x}_i
\end{aligned}
$$

Thus, z_1 is the velocity of the car of interest, z_2 is its acceleration, z_3 is the spacing between it and the car in front, and z_4 is the relative velocity. The dynamics are described by:

$$\frac{\mathrm{d}}{\mathrm{d}t}\begin{bmatrix} z_1 \\ z_2 \\ z_3 \\ z_4 \end{bmatrix} = \begin{bmatrix} 0 & 1 & 0 & 0 \\ 0 & 0 & 0 & 0 \\ 0 & 0 & 0 & 1 \\ 0 & -1 & 0 & 0 \end{bmatrix} \begin{bmatrix} z_1 \\ z_2 \\ z_3 \\ z_4 \end{bmatrix} + \begin{bmatrix} 0 \\ 1 \\ 0 \\ 0 \end{bmatrix} u(z) + \begin{bmatrix} 0 \\ 0 \\ 0 \\ 1 \end{bmatrix} \ddot{x}_{i-1} \tag{1}$$

u specifies the switched cruise control law of [1]. Note that the system has some constraints, due to the actuator saturation limits. In particular, the car cannot move backwards ($\dot{x}_i \geq 0$), it cannot brake faster than 5m/s^2 ($\ddot{x}_i \geq -5$) and it cannot accelerate faster than 3m/s^2 ($\ddot{x}_i \leq 3$).

We will consider the situation in which the vehicle $i-1$ that moves into the lane of vehicle i maintains constant velocity after cutting in. Thus $\ddot{x}_{i-1} = 0$ in Equation 1. We examine how the minimum spacing between the two vehicles over a whole trajectory varies with the initial conditions—the conditions immediately after the car has cut in. In particular, we are interested in monotonicity, because of the statements we can make about safety if minimum spacing is monotonic. If we know, for example, that minimum spacing is monotonically increasing in initial spacing, then if some initial condition $z_3^*(0)$ is safe, then any initial condition $z_3(0)$ which is greater than $z_3^*(0)$ will also be safe. Thus, if we find initial conditions which *just* cause an accident (*i.e.* minimum spacing is zero), then the set of these points is a boundary between "safe" initial conditions (those that do not lead to an accident) and "unsafe" initial conditions (those that do lead to an accident). We do not actually need to check any initial conditions individually then. Instead, we merely need to determine on which side of the boundary they lie.

It is reasonable to expect the minimum spacing between the two vehicles, *i.e.* $\hat{z}_3 = \min_t z_3(t)$, to be monotone in $z_1(0)$, $z_3(0)$ and $z_4(0)$. (We take $z_2(0) \equiv 0$.) If the initial spacing is less, the accident should be more severe[3]. Similarly, a more negative relative velocity should result in a more severe impact.

Regarding the dependence of $\hat{z}_3$ on $z_1(0)$, we might expect this to be constant. Consider a set of initial conditions which do not cause an accident. From the point of view of a passenger in car i, changing $z_1(0)$ has no effect on the relative motion of the two cars[4]. However, the system control does depend on absolute speed, so one might expect $\hat{z}_3$ to be monotone decreasing as a function of $z_1(0)$.

The rest of the paper is organized as follows: Section 2 describes observations from simulations of the system; Section 3 proposes a partial explanation of the observations using a hybrid automaton and suggests a method of analysis that can be used to determine whether monotonicity holds; Section 4 discusses some results obtained from modification of the control laws, in an attempt to obtain monotonicity; and Section 5 discusses directions of future work.

---

[3] For the purposes of this paper, we allow the unrealistic assumption that minimum spacing can be negative, and consider it as a measure of the seriousness of the impact.

[4] Here we are ignoring the constraint that vehicle velocities must be nonnegative.

2 Preliminary Simulation Study

Although simulation of a continuous system does not constitute proof of its performance, it can be used to provide counterexamples to propositions. By plotting a graph of minimum spacing against one component of the initial state, we can see whether or not the relationship is monotone.

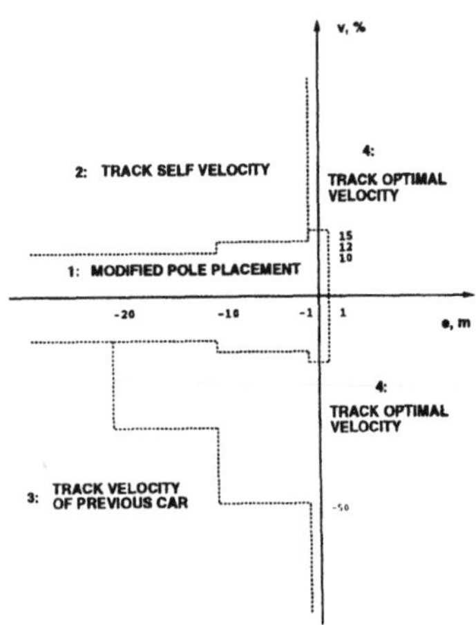

Fig. 2. The e-v plane.

The switched mode controller is described as follows: define e as $z_3 - \lambda_v z_1 - \lambda_p$, and v as $100\frac{z_4}{z_1}$. The e-v plane is divided into four regions, and a different controller is used in each region (Figure 2). We will not consider Region 2 in this paper for reasons which will become clear later. Regions 3 and 4 use affine feedback. Region 1 uses a nonlinear time-varying feedback. Controllers in Regions 1 and 4 are designed for passenger comfort, whereas the controller in Region 3 employs severe braking to avoid colliding with the preceding vehicle. Refer to [1] for more details.

For a large number of initial conditions, the dependence of $\hat{z}_3$ (the minimum spacing) on the initial conditions appears to be monotone. For example, the graph of minimum spacing is a monotone increasing function of initial spacing. However, this is not always the case. Figure 3 shows the graph of $\hat{z}_3$ *vs.* $z_1(0)$ with three local extrema, separating four separate monotone segments. One might conjecture that these extrema correspond to trajectories with initial conditions on the boundary between two switching regions. To test this hypothesis, we plot the trajectories in the e-v plane (Figure 4). For an initial velocity of 18m/s (the first minimum in Figure 3), we notice that the trajectory starts on the boundary between two regions. For the next extremum (23.3m/s initial velocity), the trajectory passes through a corner in the boundary between Regions 3 and 4.

The third extremum is more difficult to explain. Figure 4 shows that for

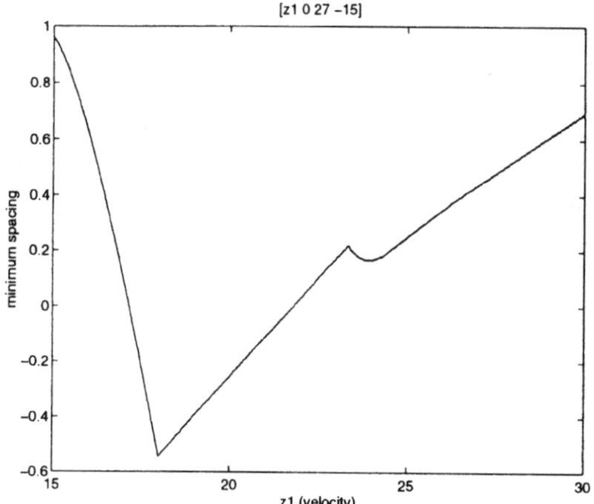

Fig. 3. Nonsmooth transitions between regions

an initial velocity of 23.8m/s (the minimum), the trajectory neither begins on a boundary nor passes through a corner. The next greatest $z_1(0)$ for which the trajectory does pass through a corner is 24.2m/s. (Beyond this value, trajectories no longer enter Region 4 at all.) Thus the segment between 23.8m/s and 24.2m/s is not monotone.

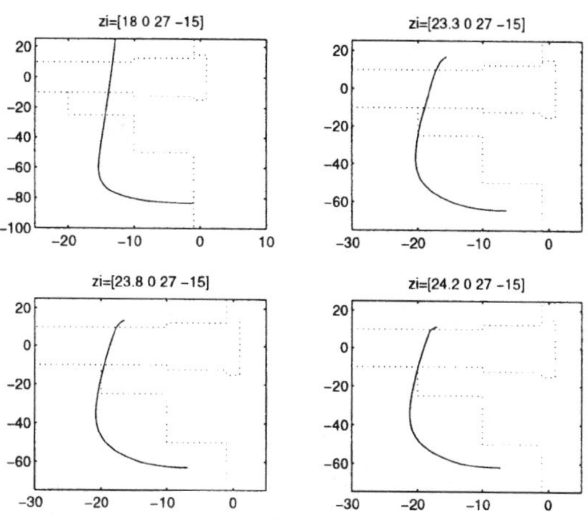

Fig. 4. Trajectories in the e-v plane

3 Extended Hybrid Automaton

The switched mode controller presented in [1] has four discrete states corresponding to different modes of operation, with complicated boundaries and dynamics. By extending the number of states, we can describe a new hybrid automaton with simple dynamics in each state. A portion of such an automaton sufficient to describe the trajectories discussed in Section 2 is proposed in Figure 5.

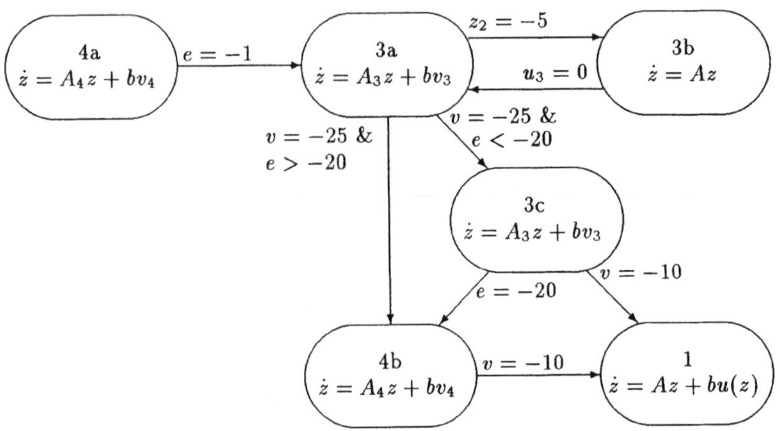

Fig. 5. The extended automaton

Region 3 is split into 3 regions. Region 3c corresponds to $v > -25$. Since there is a lower bound of 5m/s^2 on the acceleration (z_2), we split the rest of Region 3 into two more regions: Region 3a for $v < -25$ and $z_2 > -5$ and Region 3b for $v < -25$ and $z_2 = -5$. When the acceleration reaches -5m/s^2, the car cannot decelerate any faster. So as long as the *desired* control (the engine jerk) is negative, the actual control will be zero (Region 3b). Once the desired control becomes positive, the regular Region 3 dynamics apply once again (Region 3a).

Region 4 has been split into 2 regions, to avoid possible apparent looping—once Region 3 has been entered, the trajectory will not come back to Region 4a. Although this is quite sufficient for the small range of initial conditions being considered here, if we are to expand this automaton to explain a wider range of initial conditions, it will be necessary to examine the conditions under which the trajectory will pass from Region 3 into the lower portion of Region 4. The transitions between regions are all deterministic—"as soon as" one transition for a particular state is enabled, the automaton will take that transition.

It may seem strange that we chose to end the automaton in Region 1, since most trajectories will continue through Region 1 into Region 2, before returning to the equilibrium in Region 1. Note that we are interested in the minimum spacing. Since spacing (z_3) is differentiable, it must have a zero derivative at its minimum. The derivative of spacing is relative velocity (z_4). If $z_4 = 0$, then it follows that $v = 100\frac{z_4}{z_1} = 0$, which occurs in Region 1 (for $e < 0$). Thus, we know that the minimum spacing occurs in Region 1, and we need only examine the value of z_3 when $z_4 = 0$ to determine the value of minimum spacing.

With this hybrid automaton model, we can now examine the different portions of Figure 3. Each segment of Figure 3 corresponds to a different sequence of automaton states. Since each region (with the exception of Region 1) has linear dynamics, we can further investigate the dependence of minimum spacing on initial conditions, considering each region separately. We can see that the hybrid automaton adequately describes the behavior of the actual system by plotting the simulation results with the model results. There is very close agreement between the two graphs.

3.1 Monotonicity in Switched Linear Systems

It is very tempting to argue that, since the system is linear in each region, the set of initial conditions corresponding to one run will vary monotonically; since $z(t) = e^{At}z(0)$, clearly, changing the initial conditions can only have a monotone effect on each component of $z(t)$. This argument would hold as long as t is held constant, but we leave a region of the hybrid automaton not at a particular time, but rather at a particular value of the state variable. Thus, the exit time will vary depending on the initial conditions, and the matrix e^{At} will not be constant (an example is found in [6]).

However, if we consider only flows evolving on one side of the line, it is true that for a planar linear system, the monotonicity condition will be satisfied. If we do not have monotonicity, then there must be some point at which two trajectories cross. But this contradicts uniqueness of solutions for linear systems[5].

Unfortunately, this does not hold for higher dimensions. Consider the linear system given by

$$\dot{x} = \begin{bmatrix} -1 & 0 & 0 \\ 0 & 0 & -1 \\ 0 & 1 & 0 \end{bmatrix} x$$

Expressing x explicitly as a function of time,

$$x(t) = \begin{bmatrix} e^{-t} & 0 & 0 \\ 0 & \cos t & -\sin t \\ 0 & \sin t & \cos t \end{bmatrix} x(0)$$

so the flows are helix-like.

[5] Guckenheimer and Johnson describe conditions for extremal points in planar hybrid systems in [7].

Let us consider initial conditions along the line $x = \begin{bmatrix} \alpha \\ 0 \\ 1 \end{bmatrix}$, with switching surface [6] $x_1 = 1$. Starting with α equal to $e^{2\pi-\epsilon}, e^{2\pi}$ and $e^{2\pi+\epsilon}$, the trajectories cross the switching surface at the points $\begin{bmatrix} 1 \\ \epsilon \\ 1-\epsilon^2 \end{bmatrix}$, $\begin{bmatrix} 1 \\ 0 \\ 1 \end{bmatrix}$ and $\begin{bmatrix} 1 \\ -\epsilon \\ 1-\epsilon^2 \end{bmatrix}$ respectively. The final points are not monotone in the initial conditions.

By analogy with the previous case, we can suggest a necessary condition for monotonicity: a line of initial conditions must map to a line on the final switching surface[7]. If this condition is not satisfied, there will be three collinear points A, B and C which map to A', B' and C', which describe a nondegenerate triangle. Depending on the choice of basis, this can be projected onto a line such that any one of A', B' or C' are in between the other two points. Thus, the order of the points will not be preserved in all bases, so the mapping is not monotone.

3.2 Analytic Differentiation

Another characterization of monotonicity uses derivatives: a monotone increasing function will have a nonnegative derivative everywhere. Using this fact, we can check monotonicity by examining the derivative $\frac{dz^f}{dz^i}$. (For ease of notation, we define $z^i = z(0)$ and $z^f = z(t^f)$, where t^f is the time at which the trajectory leaves the region of interest.)

For the linear regions, we can determine the derivative fairly easily. We first note that

$$\frac{dz^f}{dz^i} = \left.\frac{\partial z}{\partial t}\right|_{t^f} \frac{\partial t^f}{\partial z^i} + \frac{\partial z^f}{\partial z^i} \tag{2}$$

Again, note that t^f *does* depend on z^i.

In all of the regions with linear control, the control law given by equation 1 can be reduced to the form

$$\dot{z} = A_k z + bv \tag{3}$$

where v is a constant. This gives us $\left.\frac{\partial z}{\partial t}\right|_{t^f}$ directly as a function of $z(t^f)$. Given a time t, we can write

$$z(t) = e^{A_k t} z^i + \int_0^t e^{A_k \tau} d\tau \, bv \tag{4}$$

from which we can see that

$$\frac{\partial z^f}{\partial z^i} = e^{A_k t}$$

[6] We may consider the initial switching surface to be the plane $x_3 = 1$, and the region of interest to be $x_3 \leq 1$.

[7] Note that in dimensions higher than two, the final switching surface will be more than just a line. For example, in $\mathbb{R}^3$, a linear condition will give a plane, so a line of initial conditions may map to a planar curve.

To find the derivative $\frac{\partial t^f}{\partial z^i}$, we express the exit condition from the region of interest as

$$cz^f = k$$

where c is a row vector, and k is a scalar. Multiplying equation (2) by c, we have

$$c \left. \frac{\partial z}{\partial t} \right|_{t^f} \frac{\partial t^f}{\partial z^i} + c \frac{\partial z^f}{\partial z^i} = 0$$

Since $c \left. \frac{\partial z}{\partial t} \right|_{t^f}$ is a scalar, we can solve for $\frac{\partial t^f}{\partial z^i}$:

$$\frac{\partial t^f}{\partial z^i} = - \frac{c \frac{\partial z^f}{\partial z^i}}{c \left. \frac{\partial z}{\partial t} \right|_{t^f}}$$

Thus, given t^f, we can find the derivative $\frac{dz^f}{dz^i}$. Unfortunately, there is no closed-form solution for t^f. However, it is possible to find this numerically using Newton's method, which converges rather quickly.

We can carry out this procedure for any of the states of the automaton with linear dynamics. However, this method does require a prior hypothesis of the run of the automaton, since one needs to know which exit conditions to check for.

Unfortunately, the way in which one might extend this method to the nonlinear control law in Region 1 is by no means clear. One approach is to make a conservative estimate of how much spacing might be lost while in Region 1. One could then check to see if the system has at least that much spacing on entry into Region 1. Another possibility would be to approximate the nonlinear control by a linear control. Since the trajectory does not spend very much time in Region 1 before it reaches minimum spacing, one would not expect such approximations to yield large errors.

The whole discussion on monotonicity is merely a means towards the ultimate goal of finding a boundary between collisions ($\hat{z}_3 < 0$) and no collisions ($\hat{z}_3 > 0$). Even if we cannot guarantee monotonicity, finding the derivative gives us another important piece of information. If we have some z^i which gives us $\hat{z}_3 = 0$, then the change in z_3^f if we change z^i by dz^i will be $\frac{dz_3^f}{dz^i} dz^i$. Since all points on the boundary have the same z_3^f, we want this to be zero. In other words, $\frac{dz_3^f}{dz^i}$ gives us the normal to the boundary surface. Knowing the surface normal, we do not need to search randomly for points on the boundary—given one point on the boundary, the surface normal gives a good idea of where the rest of the boundary is.

All of this is valid only within the set of states described by one run of the hybrid automaton. We then need to ask, what is this set of states? One way of approaching this problem involves taking exit conditions from one automaton state, and integrating backwards until the exit conditions for the previous state are reached. This should be very similar to the above procedure. Unfortunately, it is not always completely clear which state preceded a given state. By making use of invariance conditions (*e.g.* in Region 3b, we always have $u_3 < 0$ and $z_2 = -5$) we should be able to determine the preceding state uniquely.

4 Control Law Modifications

It is clear that with the current control laws, the minimum spacing does not vary monotonically with the initial velocity. We therefore experimented with some modifications to the switching surfaces to see if it might be possible to remove some or all of these monotonicities. This problem may be considered to be a specific example of a problem for switched linear systems: If linear controllers have been designed for different regions of state space, where exactly should the boundaries between these regions be placed in order to satisfy certain conditions?

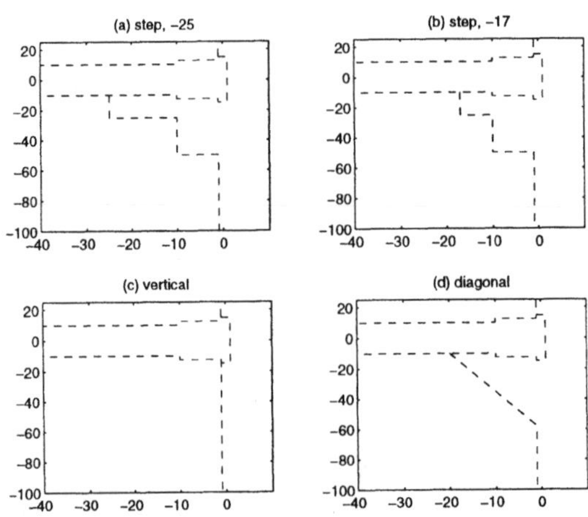

Fig. 6. Switching region modifications

Five possible boundary modifications were suggested. The first two involve moving the position of the boundary between Regions 3 and 4 for $-25 < v < -10$ from $e = -20$ to either $e = -25$ or $e = -17$ (Figure 6a,b). The next modification involved making this boundary a vertical line at $e = -1$ (Figure 6c). The fourth modification was to make the boundary a diagonal line in approximately the same place as the steps were (Figure 6d). The final modification was to make the boundary parallel to the flow lines in one region.

For the modified step with boundary at $e = -25$, we get a curve which is qualitatively the same as the original curve. (See [6] for the graph.) The cusps still correspond to trajectories starting on a boundary or passing through a corner of a boundary. However, now the middle segment is monotone decreasing, while in the original case, it was not monotone at all. Similarly, the curve for the boundary at $e = -17$ is qualitatively the same. However, this time, the middle segment is monotone increasing, which means that the whole function is monotone increasing for $z_1(0) > 18$. However, there is no guarantee that this solves the problem: we have monotonicity for this set of initial conditions, but what about other initial conditions? In fact, even with a slightly different set of initial conditions (the car cutting in traveling 1.3m/s faster), minimum spacing is no longer monotone.

Since monotonicity tends to be lost around corners in the boundary, it seemed that a vertical line boundary might solve the problem. Unfortunately, for the vertical line case, we found that monotonicity is now lost at points where the trajectory is tangent to the boundary.

The diagonal line boundary was presented as a compromise between the step boundary and the vertical line. Unfortunately, this is worse than any other case. There are trajectories starting on the boundary, passing through a corner, and passing tangent to a boundary, all of which result in cusps in the graph of minimum spacing *vs.* initial velocity.

The flow line boundary was not attempted, due to the difficulty of implementation. In theory, this would avoid any cusps since, in one region, one would be traveling parallel to the boundary, while, in the other region, one would either go towards the boundary and remain on it, or diverge from it. However, flow lines are difficult to describe analytically. This problem is made even more complex when we consider that not all trajectories starting from the same point in the e-v plane are identical in the e-v plane—there are two more dimensions which are not taken into account for switching. The boundary between regions is a 3-dimensional hyperplane, which, if we try to make the boundary follow the flow lines, will not have a simple projection onto any plane. The problem of finding this 3-dimensional boundary is no less complicated than the original problem of finding a boundary between safe and unsafe regions.

5 Further Work

It would be most desirable to be able to find a derivative map for Region 1, analogous to those discussed above for the other regions. It might be possible to do this numerically. Another option is merely to approximate $\frac{\partial z^f}{\partial z^i}$ by e^{At^f}. Tests indicate that this is fairly accurate. If it were possible to place a bound on the error obtained by such an approximation, this method might be feasible.

Obviously, this paper has only discussed a very small region of the state space. The formalism presented in Section 4 needs to be extended to other runs of the hybrid automaton. The six states presented here are sufficient to describe only this one line of initial conditions—other initial conditions will likely require other states. One also needs to address the question of the finiteness of the language—is there a finite set of sequences of states that the automaton may follow?

Having attained our goal of determining safe and unsafe regions, we could use this knowledge to modify the control laws. In some cases where the current control law does result in a collision, the collision could be avoided simply by maintaining an acceleration of -5m/s^2. If we can determine safety critical regions, we can apply this extreme control in order to avoid a collision.

Finally, all of this analysis has assumed that the car cutting in maintains constant velocity. We need to check that the safe regions are in fact safe for all possible acceleration profiles. It is suggested in [2] that the worst case scenario is most likely the situation where the car in front cuts in and then applies maximum braking. If we can find the safe conditions for the worst case, we can be guaranteed that these conditions will be safe for all other cases.

6 Conclusions

We have seen that the dependence of minimum spacing on the initial conditions is certainly not monotonic in the components of the initial state. However, even with sudden switching between control regions, it is piecewise smooth. Even though we have not been able to show monotonicity in minimum spacing, we have developed a technique that gives us the normal to the surface between collision conditions and safe conditions. This enables us to find this surface much more easily than by searching 4-space for it. Changing the switching surfaces of the control law did not yield monotonicity.

We would like to extend this analysis to a general framework for analysis of switched linear systems and gain scheduling. In particular, we would like to be able to prove certain invariant conditions of such systems, *e.g.* safety.

Acknowledgements

We thank Professor Shankar Sastry and Professor Pravin Varaiya for their constant encouragement and support.

References

1. Datta Godbole and John Lygeros. Longitudinal control of the lead car of a platoon. *IEEE Transactions on Vehicular Technology*, 43(4):1125–1135, 1994.
2. Anuj Puri and Pravin Varaiya. Driving safely in smart cars. In *Proceedings of American Control Conference*, pages 3597–3599, 1995.
3. Pravin Varaiya. Smart cars on smart roads: Problems of control. *IEEE Transactions on Automatic Control*, AC-38(2):195–207, 1993.
4. R. Alur, C. Courcoubetis, T. Henzinger, and P. Ho. Hybrid automata: An algorithmic approach to the specification and verification of hybrid systems. In *Hybrid Systems, Lecture Notes in Computer Science 736*. Springer-Verlag, 1993.
5. A. Deshpande and P. Varaiya. Viable control of hybrid systems. In *Hybrid Systems II, Lecture Notes in Computer Science*. Springer-Verlag, 1995.
6. John A. Haddon, Datta N. Godbole, Akash Deshpande, and John Lygeros. Verification of hybrid systems: Monotonicity in the AHS control system. Memorandum, California PATH Program, 1996.
7. John Guckenheimer and Stewart Johnson. Planar hybrid systems. In *Hybrid Systems II, Lecture Notes in Computer Science*. Springer-Verlag, 1995.

Examples of Stabilization with Hybrid Feedback

Zvi Artstein[1]

Department of Theoretical Mathematics, The Weizmann Institute of Science, Rehovot 76100, Israel

Abstract. Via examples, this paper examines the possibility of stabilizing a continuous control plant, through an interaction with a discrete time controller. Such a hybrid feedback complements the output feedback within the plant when the latter fails to stabilize the system or fails to produce smooth stabilization. The displayed examples point to both the mathematical and the design challenges that the method poses.

1 Introduction

The hybrid feedback paradigm models an autonomous interaction of a discrete controller and a continuous time feedback. This paper considers applications of the model to the stabilization of continuous dynamical systems. The framework we use follows the recent developments in hybrid systems, as displayed in Nerode and Kohn [9], although the present paper emphasizes the autonomous nature of the system, namely the structure of the automaton employed in the stabilization. To this end the formalism of hybrid automata, as described in Alur et al. [1], or in Henzinger and Ho [6], is of value. We employ it along with the traditional control theory paradigm. The stability and stabilization notions that we address are the classical ones, as given in Sontag [12], though at some points the notions are modified to suit the hybrid dynamics. Results on stabilization using a hybrid systems approach are available in the literature. A partial list is Antsaklis et al. [2], Branicky [4], Guckenheimer [5], Sontag [11]. We shall not make here a detailed comparison between these contributions and the present paper.

The point of view in this paper is that the underlying continuous plant is given, and the challenge is to stabilize it efficiently with a hybrid device. The efficiency may be reflected mathematically as a minimal number of automaton states, or by simple connections that use a minimum of information exchange between the continuous and the discrete parts. In particular, we do not just attempt to attach to the continuous plant a discrete one which will approximate or mimic continuous dynamics (see the note in Kompass [7]). Although we do not provide here a definition of efficiency, various facets of the problem are addressed.

The paper is organized as follows. In Sect. 2 we display the control setting, and describe the stabilization problem. In Sect. 3 a concrete example, namely the harmonic oscillator with position feedback, is recalled. This system cannot

[1] Incumbent of the Hettie H. Heineman Professorial Chair in Mathematics

be stabilized with output feedback. For further reference and comparison, we show how it can be stabilized with dynamic feedback. In Sect. 4 the notions of an elementary hybrid system, hybrid feedback and the stabilization by such a feedback are described and discussed. In Sect. 5 we show how to stabilize the harmonic oscillator. Several strategies are displayed and the tradeoff is examined. In Sect. 6 a modification to the stabilization notion is given, namely practical stability, along with the relevant applications and examples. Some concluding remarks close the paper.

2 The control setting

This section displays the general control system referred to throughout, and then identifies the stabilization problem.

System 2.1. We consider the system

$$\begin{aligned} \frac{dx}{dt} &= f(x, u) \\ y &= c(x) \, , \end{aligned} \tag{2.1}$$

with $x \in R^n$ describing the physical or the plant state, $y \in R^m$ is the output, namely the quantity that can be measured, and the control u is an element of a fixed set U in a metric space, say $U \subset R^\ell$. It is assumed throughout that $f : R^n \times U \to R^n$ and $c : R^n \to R^m$ are continuous functions.

The stabilization problem is to choose a control strategy $u(\cdot)$ such that a prescribed state, say $x = 0$, becomes stable (a definition follows). Only the quantity that can be measured, namely the output y, can be used by the control. In the classical output feedback paradigm (which becomes the state feedback in the case $c(x) = x$), one tries to find a feedback $u(y) = u(c(x))$ that results in 0 being asymptotically stable. If the feedback $u(y)$ is continuous, solutions to the resulting differential equation are well defined. Here is the formal definition of a stabilizer under the continuity assumption.

Definition 2.2. The continuous mapping $u(y) : R^m \to U$ is an output feedback stabilizer of the system (2.1) if $x = 0$ is an asymptotically stable point of the resulting differential equation

$$\frac{dx}{dt} = f(x, u(c(x))) \, . \tag{2.2}$$

Namely:

(i) For every $\epsilon > 0$ there exists a $\delta > 0$ such that if $x(t)$ is a solution of (2.2), and $|x(0)| \leq \delta$, then $|x(t)| \leq \epsilon$ for $t \geq 0$, and
(ii) All solutions $x(t)$ of (2.2) satisfy $x(t) \to 0$ as $t \to \infty$.

Remark 2.3. The continuity assumption on $u(y)$ (and on $c(x)$) is there to assure that solutions of (2.2) are well defined. At times it is necessary to employ discontinuous feedback control, e.g. when U is discrete. The definition applies as long as the dynamics of $x(t)$ is determined.

Remark 2.4. Notice the autonomous nature of the equation resulting from the feedback, namely (2.2). A perturbation from the equilibrium $x = 0$ is depicted as a state $x_0 \neq 0$. If a perturbation occurs, it becomes the initial condition $x(0) = x_0$ of a solution of (2.2), and the solution converges to 0.

The need to modify the output feedback paradigm arises since the output feedback may fail to stabilize even simple systems. The next section displays a concrete example.

3 The harmonic oscillator

Example 3.1. Consider a particular case of (2.1) with $x = (\xi, \eta)$ being two-dimensional, and y a scalar, as follows:

$$\begin{aligned} \frac{d\xi}{dt} &= \eta \\ \frac{d\eta}{dt} &= -\xi + u \\ y &= \xi , \end{aligned} \tag{3.1}$$

and with $U = R$ the real line. This is the harmonic oscillator, with the control being the external force, and the only measured quantity, namely the output, is the position variable.

Although the system (3.1) is both controllable and observable, it cannot be stabilized by (even discontinuous) output feedback. See e.g. Sontag [12, Example 6.2.1]; an argument is that the function $V(\xi, \eta) = \eta^2 + 2\int_0^\xi (-\rho + u(\rho))d\rho$ is an invariant of the dynamics generated by (3.1), if $u = u(\xi)$. Thus, a modification of the output feedback paradigm is needed. In the next section we display the hybrid paradigm, and apply it to Example 3.1 in Sect. 5. For comparison we show here how another approach, namely dynamic feedback, operates.

Example 3.2. We use dynamic feedback to stabilize (3.1). To this end we follow the recipe laid out in Sontag [12, page 253] for general linear systems (employing here an appropriate change of variables). First rewrite the differential equations in a system form (a dot above a variable signifies differentiation) as follows.

$$\begin{pmatrix} \dot{\xi} \\ \dot{\eta} \end{pmatrix} = \begin{pmatrix} 0 & 1 \\ -1 & 0 \end{pmatrix} \begin{pmatrix} \xi \\ \eta \end{pmatrix} + \begin{pmatrix} 0 \\ 1 \end{pmatrix} u \, . \tag{3.2}$$

Along with (3.2), consider the control system

$$\begin{pmatrix} \dot{\zeta} \\ \dot{\theta} \end{pmatrix} = \begin{pmatrix} 0 & 1 \\ -2 & -2 \end{pmatrix} \begin{pmatrix} \zeta \\ \theta \end{pmatrix} + \begin{pmatrix} 0 \\ 1 \end{pmatrix} v . \tag{3.3}$$

Now let the output ξ of (3.2) serve (with a negative sign) as a control input to (3.3). Arrange for $-\zeta$ to be the output of (3.3) and use it as the control input to (3.2). Namely, define

$$u = -\zeta , \quad v = -\xi . \tag{3.4}$$

The relation (3.4) interconnects (3.2) and (3.3). In fact (as the underlying theory assures, see Sontag [12, Sect. 6.2]), we now have two harmonic oscillators coupled via position output. The four dimensional linear differential equation in the $(\xi, \eta, \zeta, \theta)$ space has a coefficients matrix whose eigenvalues all have negative real parts. This follows from the general argument in Sontag [12, page 253], or by direct checking, say with *Mathematica*, which reveals that the eigenvalues are $-\frac{1}{2} \pm i\frac{\sqrt{3}}{2}$. Hence the origin in the four dimensional space is asymptotically stable with respect to (3.2)–(3.3) with (3.4). In particular, any perturbation in the (ξ, η) space is driven to 0 by the dynamic feedback.

Notice that the system described in Example 3.2 is autonomous (compare with Remark 2.4). It requires the attaching of a predesigned continuous system to the harmonic oscillator (3.1). In Sect. 5 we show how to reach the stabilization by attaching a discrete automaton to (3.1).

4 Elementary hybrid feedback and stabilization

This section starts with a description of the ingredients of what we call an elementary hybrid system. It is a simple version of a hybrid system, yet suffices for the stabilization of the harmonic oscillator (as shown in the next section) and many other systems. More involved variations of hybrid systems are mentioned in the closing section. Following the definition we describe the induced hybrid dynamics, define what stabilization is, and conclude with some remarks. The construction mimics the developments in Nerode and Kohn [9], Alur et al. [1], and Henzinger and Ho [6].

Hybrid System 4.1. The elementary hybrid system consists of (a) a continuous plant, (b) a timed automaton, and (c) a hybrid feedback. Here are the specifications of each of the components.

(a) The continuous plant is the one given in System 2.1.

(b) The timed automaton is a triplet

$$\mathcal{A} = (Q, I, M) \tag{4.1}$$

composed as follows. The set Q is finite,

$$Q = \{q_1, \ldots, q_k\} , \tag{4.2}$$

and contains the automaton states, also called locations. With each $q \in Q$, a number $T(q) > 0$ is associated; it determines the period at which the automaton stays at q between transition times. The set I is finite,

$$I = \{\iota_1, \ldots, \iota_p\} , \tag{4.3}$$

and contains the input alphabet. The transition map

$$M(q, \iota) : Q \times I \to Q \tag{4.4}$$

indicates the location after a transition time, based on the previous location q and the input ι at the time of transition; it is allowed that $M(q, \iota) = q$.

(c) The hybrid feedback consists of k feedback maps

$$u(y, q) : R^m \to U \quad (q \in Q) , \tag{4.5}$$

each one associated with a location $q \in Q$, and assumed continuous in the y variable (see though Remark 2.3). In addition, a feedback map

$$\iota(y) : R^m \to I , \tag{4.6}$$

is designed; it provides the input letter ι to the transition map (4.4) at a transition time. Recall that y is the output of the system (2.1), namely $\iota = \iota(c(x))$ is a mapping of the physical state. The feedback $\iota(y)$ is applied only at a transition instance.

The hybrid dynamics. An important component in the definition of the hybrid dynamics is the identification of the state space of the hybrid system; we call it the hybrid state. It is given by a triplet

$$(x, q, \Delta) \tag{4.7}$$

which is an element of $R^n \times Q \times (0, \infty)$, satisfying $0 < \Delta \leq T(q)$. The interpretation is that x and q are the plant and the automaton states, and Δ is the time remaining till the next transition instance. Hence $\Delta \leq T(q)$. We think of Δ as a variable that satisfies $\dot{\Delta} = -1$ on $(\tau_j, \tau_j + T(q))$, where τ_j is the time at which the transition to q occurred. Note the inequality $\Delta > 0$, namely, the transition instance is associated with the next location.

The hybrid trajectories reflect the evolution in the space of hybrid states. A hybrid trajectory is a mapping

$$(x(t), q(t), \Delta(t)) , \tag{4.8}$$

defined on a time interval, with the following qualifications: The time domain of the function (4.8) can be partitioned by

$$\cdots < \tau_i < \tau_{i+1} < \tau_{i+2} < \cdots \tag{4.9}$$

(it could start at a finite time τ_0 or at $-\infty$), such that $q(t)$ is constant on each half closed interval, say $q(t) = q_i$ on $[\tau_i, \tau_{i+1})$. At the instances τ_i, which are the transition times, the relation $q_{i+1} = M(q_i, \iota(c(x(\tau_i))))$ holds. On each interval $\frac{d\Delta}{dt} = -1$ and the equalities $\Delta(\tau_i) = \tau_{i+1} - \tau_i$ and $\Delta(\tau_i) = T(q_i)$ hold, except possibly for, respectively, the last interval (where a blow-up may occur), and the first interval (which may start with a perturbation). The physical trajectory $x(t)$ is continuous, and on each $[\tau_i, \tau_{i+1}]$ it is a solution of (2.1) with $u = u(y, q_i)$.

It is clear that one can give a recursive description of a hybrid trajectory, starting with an initial condition

$$(x(0), q(0), \Delta(0)) . \tag{4.10}$$

Then $q(t) = q(0)$ and $\dot{\Delta} = -1$ on $[0, \Delta_0)$ with $\Delta_0 = \Delta(0)$, and $x(t)$ solves (2.1) with $u = u(y, q(0))$. If the solution $x(t)$ does not blow up before Δ_0, namely, $x(\Delta_0)$ is defined, then the data $q(\Delta_0)$ is given by $M(q(0), \iota(c(x(\Delta_0))))$, and $\Delta_1 = \Delta(\Delta_0)$ is equal to $T(q(\Delta_0))$. Now $(x(\Delta_0), q(\Delta_0), \Delta(\Delta_0))$ serves as an initial condition for the next recursive step, and so on. Notice that the existence of the hybrid trajectory and its uniqueness for a given initial condition, depend on the corresponding properties of the continuous plant (2.1) with the designed feedback. Starting with initial time $t = 0$ is arbitrary as the hybrid dynamics is autonomous (compare with Remark 2.4).

We now give the definition of stability with the hybrid system; it refers to the Hybrid System 4.1 and its hybrid trajectories.

Definition 4.2. The hybrid feedback stabilizes the continuous system if the following two conditions hold.

(i) For every $\epsilon > 0$ a $\delta > 0$ exists, such that if $(x(t), q(t), \Delta(t))$ is a hybrid trajectory, and $|x(0)| \le \delta$, then $|x(t)| \le \epsilon$ for $t \ge 0$, and
(ii) All hybrid trajectories $(x(t), q(t), \Delta(t))$ satisfy $x(t) \to 0$ as $t \to \infty$, and the convergence is uniform for initial physical states $x(0)$ in compact sets.

Remark 4.3. The idea underlying Definition 4.2 is the same as the Liapunov stability of Definition 2.2, namely that small perturbations do not blow up, and all perturbations will die out by the dynamics. A perturbation here, however, is in the hybrid state space, namely an initial condition of the form $(x(0), q(0), \Delta(0))$ (the condition $\Delta(0) \le T(q(0))$ reflects compatibility, otherwise the automaton is inconsistent, namely broken; allowing $\Delta(0) \in R$ may not lead to the uniform convergence of $x(t)$). Only the stability of the physical state is of interest to us, therefore no requirements are placed on the dynamics of the $(q(t), \Delta(t))$ components of the hybrid system. (Thus, in terms of the full state we face partial stabilization; see Rouche et al. [10] for this notion.) In dynamic stabilization however, it is customary to demand that the auxiliary variable be asymptotically stable as well, see Sontag [12, Definition 6.2.5] or Bacciotti [3, Sect. 1], as indeed is the case in Example 3.2.

Remark 4.4. Definition 4.2 requires that the plant trajectories $x(t)$ converge uniformly with respect to $x(0)$ in compact sets, while Definition 2.2 does not explicitly require the uniformity. In fact, this uniformity in the case of the ordinary differential equation (2.2) can be easily deduced from (i) and (ii) of Definition 2.2. This is not the case for hybrid systems, even when the system is elementary, namely both Q and I are finite, as the following example shows.

Example 4.5. We use the hybrid automaton description in Fig. 1. The explanation is that q_1, q_2 are the locations, and $T(q) = 1$ for both locations. Thus the initial time for Δ after a transition is 1, and then $\Delta(t)$ satisfies $\dot{\Delta} = -1$ until $\Delta = 0$, where a new transition occurs. The input to the automaton is then based on the information whether at the transition time $|x| < 1$ or $|x| \geq 1$, namely a two-letter alphabet. We write $x(tr.)$ for x at transition time. The control feedback at each location results in the indicated differential equation. Note that in this example neither one of the locations separately stabilizes the system. It is clear however that in this example each solution $x(t)$ of the hybrid system tends to 0, but the convergence is not uniform for $x(0) \in [-1, 1]$. In Example 4.6 we display the same phenomenon with linear plant equations.

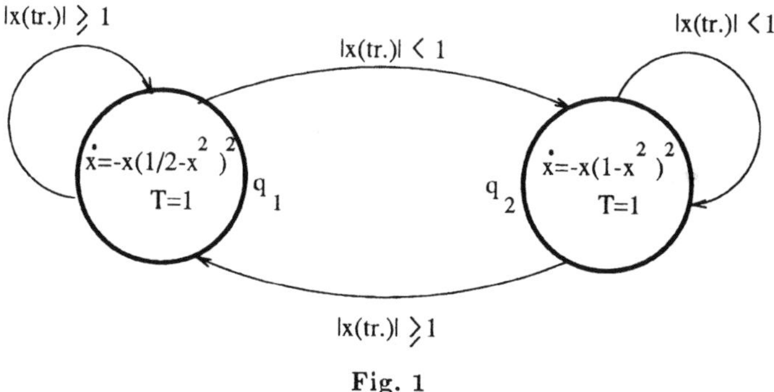

Fig. 1

Example 4.6. In the previous example the cause of the nonuniform convergence is the nonlinearity of the plant equation (or rather, the respective equilibria). But the same phenomenon can be achieved with linear plant equations as follows. Consider the harmonic oscillator $\dot{\xi} = \eta$, $\dot{\eta} = -\xi + u$ with output $y = (\xi, \eta)$ to be the full physical state. Let the automaton connections be as in Fig. 1, with the following data: $T(q_1) = 1$, $T(q_2) = \frac{\pi}{4}$, $u(y, q_1) = 0$, $u(y, q_2) = -\xi$, and the transition condition is such that $|x(tr.)| < 1$ and $|x(tr.)| \geq 1$ in Fig. 1 are replaced by $y(tr.) \notin D$ and $y(tr.) \in D$, where

$$D = \{y : \eta \geq 100|\xi| \text{ and either } \xi^2 + \eta^2 \geq 1 \text{ or } \eta \leq 1 - 100|\xi|\} .$$

The reasoning is that, starting at D in the location q_2 after a transition, results in a proportional decrease of the norm $|y|^2 = \frac{1}{2}(\xi^2 + \eta^2)$, and each trajectory passes through q_2 infinitely often. This implies that each trajectory converges to

0, but nonuniformly, as it may take arbitrarily long to reach an initial condition in D on a level set close to but smaller than $|y| = 1$.

5 Stabilizing the harmonic oscillator

In this section the harmonic oscillator with position output is stabilized by an elementary hybrid system. Three versions are offered. The first one uses only two automaton states, but the control $u(\xi)$ is nonlinear. In the other two examples the plant feedback functions are linear, and the automata have three and two locations, the tradeoff being the rate of convergence. We make the comparisons following the formulation of the examples.

Example 5.1. We display a hybrid feedback for the system (3.1). The connections are depicted in Fig. 2. In each location we write the corresponding continuous feedback function, where

$$u_+(\xi) = \begin{cases} 0 & \text{for } \xi \geq 0 \\ -3\xi & \text{for } \xi < 0 \end{cases}$$

and

$$u_-(\xi) = \begin{cases} -3\xi & \text{for } \xi \geq 0 \\ 0 & \text{for } \xi < 0 \, . \end{cases}$$

Notice that the information needed by the automaton at transition time is whether $\xi \geq 0$ or $\xi < 0$, namely a two-letter alphabet.

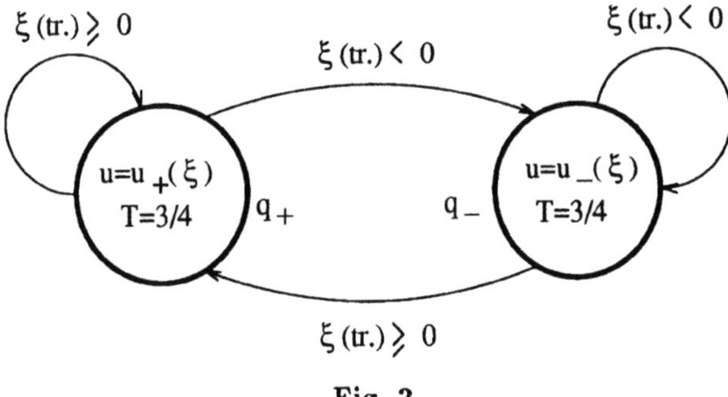

Fig. 2

To verify that such a hybrid feedback stabilizes (3.1), consider the energy function $V(\xi, \eta) = \frac{1}{2}(\xi^2 + \eta^2)$. In the region where $u = 0$ there is no change in energy. When $u(\xi) = -3\xi$, the time derivative of the energy along the solution is

$$\frac{d}{dt}\left(\frac{1}{2}(\xi^2(t) + \eta^2(t))\right) = -3\xi(t)\eta(t) \, ,$$

namely it decreases if $\xi \cdot \eta > 0$. As the connection in Fig. 2 reveals, after a transition, the control $u = -3\xi$ is in operation only when the sign of $\xi(t) \cdot \eta(t)$ changes from negative to positive, and then for at most $\frac{3}{4}$ time units, in which $\xi(t) \cdot \eta(t)$ stays positive. This can be violated only when a perturbation occurs with an arbitrary initial condition. But then a transition will occur within $\frac{3}{4}$ time units. Since $\frac{3}{4}$ and π are rationally independent, it follows that every physical solution converges to zero, and the uniformity holds as well.

The stabilization with linear plant feedback and three locations is as follows.

Example 5.2. Consider the continuous plant (3.1). Design an automaton as depicted in Fig. 3, with $\delta > 0$ small. (In each location we write the corresponding control, rather than the resulting differential equation.) Note that the input alphabet is with two letters, one corresponding to $\xi \geq 0$ and the second to $\xi < 0$.

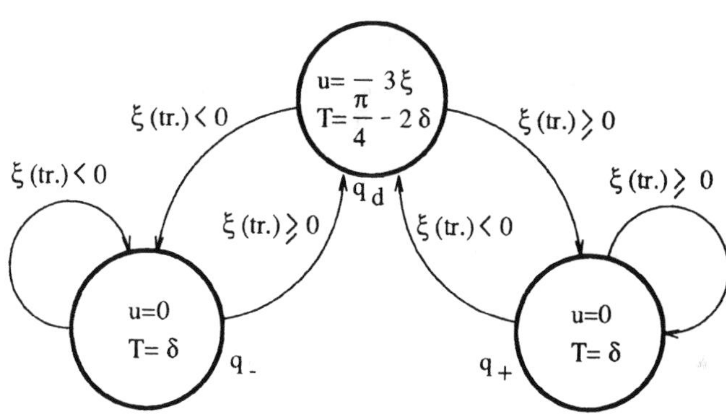

Fig. 3

In order to verify that the designed hybrid system stabilizes the oscillator (3.1), consider again the energy function

$$V(\xi, \eta) = \frac{1}{2}(\xi^2 + \eta^2) \; .$$

At the locations q_+ and q_- there is no change in the energy. The two locations serve to detect a shift of ξ from positive to negative in the case of q_+, and from negative to positive in the case of q_-. In both cases the change in sign will occur within a bounded number ($\leq \frac{\pi+1}{\delta}$) of transition periods. Then the location is shifted to q_d, which serves as a dissipation period (hence the subscript d). Furthermore, since during both q_+ and q_- the trajectory goes clockwise, when q_d is switched on, the initial condition starts at either the first or the third orthant (i.e. $\xi \cdot \eta \geq 0$), and since $T(q_d) = \frac{\pi}{4} - 2\delta$, the solution stays at that orthant as long as q_d is on. Furthermore, when the location q_d is reached after a transition, there is a loss of order (up to δ) of three quarters of the euclidean energy before one of the locations q_+ or q_- is switched on (depending whether $\xi \geq 0$ or $\xi < 0$), and the search for the change of sign starts again.

All in all, once q_+ is on with $\xi \geq 0$, or q_- is on with $\xi < 0$, the hybrid trajectory passes through q_d indefinitely often, with bounded gaps ($\leq \pi$) between occurrences, and each time there is a proportional loss of energy of order close to $\frac{3}{4}$. The conclusion is that $\xi^2(t) + \eta^2(t)$ tends to 0, uniformly for $(\xi(0), \eta(0))$ in a compact set. This proves the stabilization, provided the initial condition $((\xi, \eta), q, \Delta)$ satisfies $\xi \geq 0$ and $q = q_+$, or $\xi < 0$ and $q = q_-$. It is straightforward to see that starting from an arbitrary initial condition, the hybrid trajectory reaches the qualified condition within an interval of length $\frac{\pi}{2}$. This completes the verification.

The following construction of stabilization of (3.1) with linear feedback and only two locations was shown to me by Felipe Pait.

Example 5.3. Consider the hybrid feedback portrayed in Fig. 4. It is a twist of the previous example, in that the dissipation period goes on for $\frac{3}{4}\pi$, rather than $\frac{1}{4}\pi$. The loss of energy in this period is therefore identical to the loss guaranteed in Example 5.2 (although now the euclidean energy is not monotonic during the dissipation period). However, waiting $\frac{3}{4}\pi$ drives the oscillator to the location q_- each time. In all other respects the verification arguments are identical to those of the previous example.

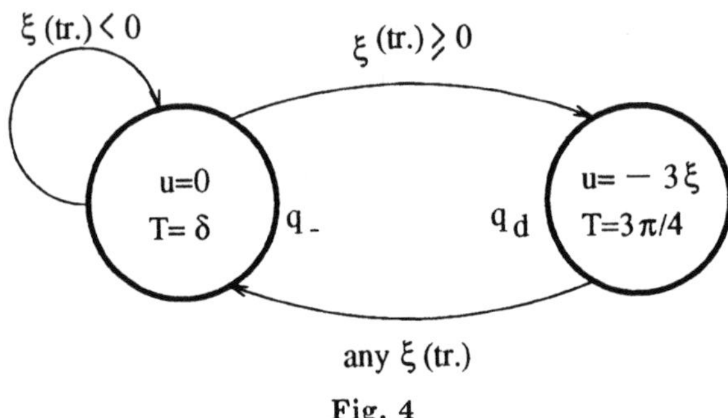

Fig. 4

Remark 5.4. The tradeoffs: Notice that in the three examples of the stabilization of (3.1), the same feedback elements (namely $u = 0$ and $u = -3\xi$) are used. This enables to pinpoint the tradeoff between the complexity of the automaton and the stability performance. The elimination of one location when Example 5.2 is modified to Example 5.3 costs in terms of speed of convergence to the equilibrium. Indeed (up to an approximation of order δ), the oscillator in Fig. 3 completes a full turn in $\frac{3}{2}\pi$ time units, at the end of which its euclidean norm is $\frac{1}{4}$ of what it was. The oscillator in Fig. 4 completes a full turn in $\frac{5}{4}\pi$ time units, but its energy is reduced only by half. The latter is therefore considerably slower.

Another tradeoff is in the frequency of transitions. The quantity $T = \delta$ in both Examples 5.2 and 5.3 must not be too large in order for the stabilization to be executed. The smaller the δ, the faster the convergence to the origin. A large δ, say $\delta = \frac{3}{4}$ time units, would not work. The nonlinear feedback of Example 5.1 allows low frequency of transitions, with a reasonable convergence rate (about $\frac{1}{\sqrt{2}}$ reduction of euclidean energy in every round).

6 Practical stability

There are natural systems that cannot be stabilized with an elementary hybrid feedback. Then we can try either to employ more sophisticated automata, or to settle for a weaker notion of stabilization. We examine here the latter possibility by modifying the notion of practical stability, as introduced by J.P. LaSalle [8], to the hybrid framework.

Definition 6.1. The hybrid feedback ϵ-practically stabilizes the continuous system if:

(i) There exists a $\delta > 0$ such that any hybrid trajectory $(x(t), p(t), \Delta(t))$ with $|x(0)| \leq \delta$ satisfies $|x(t)| \leq \epsilon$ for $t \geq 0$, and
(ii) Every hybrid trajectory satisfies $|x(t)| \leq \epsilon$ for t large enough, this uniformly for initial conditions $x(0)$ in compact sets.

It is clear that a hybrid feedback stabilizes a plant if and only if it practically stabilizes it for each $\epsilon > 0$.

Example 6.2. The Mathematical Thermostat: Consider the equation $\frac{dx}{dt} = u$, with $u \in \{-1, 1\}$. An interpretation is that u can assume an off/on position for a furnace, with x the temperature. Stabilization by setting $u(x) = -\text{sgn}\ x$ is mathematically acceptable, but may cause chattering near the equilibrium. It is natural to seek ϵ-practical stabilization for small enough ϵ. It can be achieved with a hybrid feedback (consult the analysis in Antsaklis et al. [2]) in a straightforward way, if δ in the automaton of Fig. 5 is small enough. Notice that the associated automaton has two locations and three letter input alphabet.

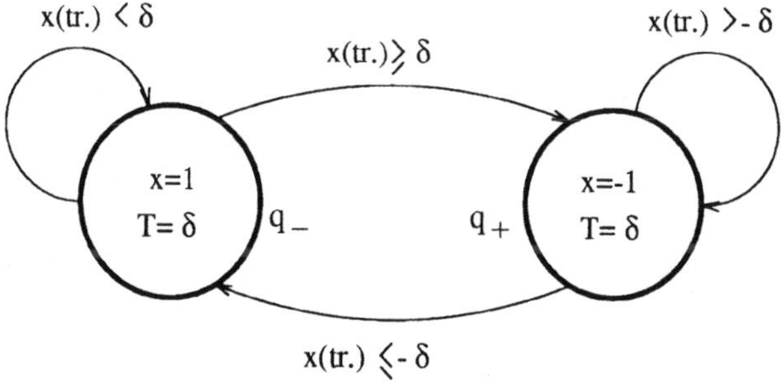

Fig. 5

Example 6.3. We consider the harmonic oscillator $\dot{\xi} = \eta$, $\dot{\eta} = -\xi + u$. We restrict the output to be revealed only at transition times, namely, we force u to be constant in any location. Also, suppose that the output shows only whether $\xi \geq 0$ or $\xi < 0$. Even with this very restrictive output information, the system can be ϵ-practically stabilized by an elementary hybrid feedback, if one employs the hybrid automaton of Fig. 6 with δ small enough.

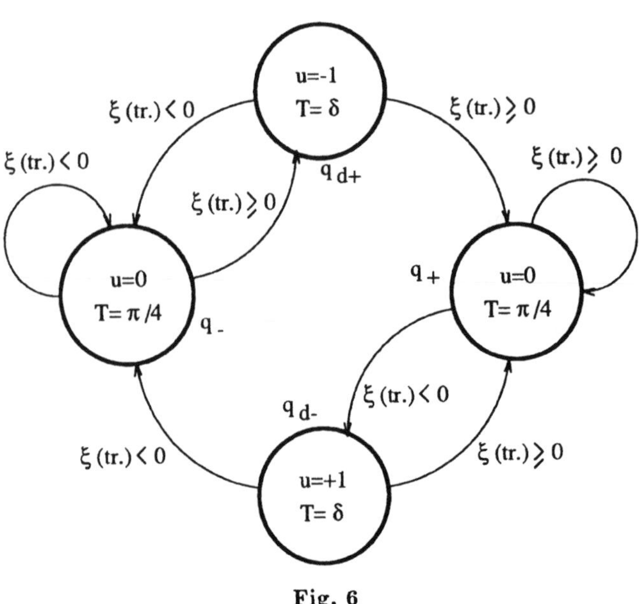

Fig. 6

7 Concluding remarks

Several very important issues and possibilities were left out of the present paper. Some are dealt with, to some extent, in the literature, and will also be touched upon in a forthcoming paper by the author.

One possibility is to employ more sophisticated automata. For instance, the time T associated with each location could be a function of the output $y(tr.)$ at transition time. This amounts to adding automata states, even a continuum of them if the output is a continuum. In turn we may require that the feedback $T = T(y)$ be continuous. It is easy to see how the mathematical thermostat of Example 6.2 can then be ϵ-practically stabilized using continuous feedback only. A more sophisticated automaton would set a parameter in each location, serving as a memory. In this paper we confined ourselves to examples of stabilization, and practical stabilization, using elementary hybrid systems. It is not entirely clear to me at this point to what extent elementary hybrid systems are applicable in stabilization, and in general how elementary the resulting schemes could be.

Another issue is the robustness. We wish to maintain the stability under errors in measurements. See Nerode and Kohn [9], and Guckenheimer [5]. We do not give here a rigorous definition of robustness, but note that all the procedures displayed in this paper are indeed robust.

Acknowledgement. I am indebted to Oded Maler and Amir Pnueli for illuminating discussions and references on the basis of hybrid systems, and to Eduardo Sontag for detailed discussions and references on hybrid systems and stability. My special thanks are given to Felipe Pait for coming up with Example 5.3.

References

1. Alur, R., Courcoubetis, C., Henzinger, T.A., Ho, P.-H.: Hybrid automata: an algorithmic approach to the specification and verification of hybrid systems. In: Hybrid Systems, Grossman, R.L. et al. (eds.) (Lecture Notes in Computer Science, vol. 736) Springer-Verlag, Berlin, 1993, pp. 209-229.
2. Antsaklis, R.J., Stiver, J.A., Lemmon, M.: Hybrid system modeling and autonomous control systems. In: Hybrid Systems, Grossman, R.L. et al. (eds.) (Lecture Notes in Computer Science, vol. 736) Springer-Verlag, Berlin, 1993, pp. 366-392.
3. Bacciotti, A.: Local Stabilizability of Nonlinear Control Systems. World Scientific, Singapore, 1992.
4. Branicky, M.S.: Studies in Hybrid Systems: Modelling, Analysis, and Control. Ph.D. Thesis, Massachusetts Institute of Technology, Cambridge, Massachusetts, June 1995.
5. Guckenheimer, J.: A robust hybrid stabilization strategy for equilibria. IEEE Trans. on Automatic Control **40** (1995) 321-326.
6. Henzinger, T.H., Ho, P.-H.: Algorithmic analysis of nonlinear hybrid systems. In: Computer Aided Verification, Wolper, P. (ed.) (Lecture Notes in Computer Science, vol. 939) Springer-Verlag, Berlin, 1995, pp. 225-238.
7. Kompass, E.J.: Open the loop for stable controls. Control Engineering **42**, Jan. 1995, p. 126.
8. LaSalle, J.P.: Asymptotic stability criteria. In: Proc. Symp. Appl. Math. Hydrodynamic Instability, vol. 13, Amer. Math. Soc., Providence, 1962, pp. 299-307.
9. Nerode, A., Kohn, W.: Models for hybrid systems: Automata, topologies, controllability, observability. In: Hybrid Systems, Grossman, R.L. et al. (eds.) (Lecture Notes in Computer Science, vol. 736) Springer-Verlag, Berlin, 1993, pp. 317-356.
10. Rouche, N., Habets, P., Laloy, M.: Stability Theory by Liapunov's Direct Method. Springer-Verlag, Berlin, 1977.
11. Sontag, E.: Nonlinear regulation: The piecewise linear approach. IEEE Trans. on Automatic Control **26** (1981) 346-358.
12. Sontag, E.: Mathematical Control Theory, Springer-Verlag, New York, 1989.

General Hybrid Dynamical Systems: Modeling, Analysis, and Control

Michael S. Branicky

Laboratory for Information and Decision Systems
Massachusetts Institute of Technology

Abstract. Complex systems typically possess a hierarchical structure, characterized by continuous-variable dynamics at the lowest level and logical decision-making at the highest. Virtually all control systems today perform computer-coded checks and issue logical as well as continuous-variable control commands. Such are "hybrid" systems. In this paper, we introduce a formal notion of such systems: "general hybrid dynamical systems"; they are interacting collections of dynamical systems, evolving on continuous-variable state spaces, and subject to continuous controls and discrete phenomena. We discuss modeling issues, giving definitions and conditions for hybrid trajectories and providing a taxonomy for hybrid systems models. We review our hybrid systems analysis results, including topological issues, complexity and computation, stability tools, and analyzed examples. We summarize our hybrid control results, including optimal control theory, control algorithms, and solved examples.

1 Introduction

Hybrid systems involve both continuous-valued and discrete variables. Their evolution is given by equations of motion that generally depend on all variables. In turn these equations contain mixtures of logic, discrete-valued or **digital** dynamics, and continuous-variable or **analog** dynamics. The continuous dynamics of such systems may be continuous-time, discrete-time, or mixed (sampled-data), but is generally given by differential equations. The discrete-variable dynamics of hybrid systems is generally governed by a **digital automaton**, or input-output transition system with a countable number of states. The continuous and discrete dynamics interact at "event" or "trigger" times when the continuous state hits certain prescribed sets in the continuous state space. See Fig. 1(a).

Hybrid control systems are control systems that involve both continuous and discrete dynamics and continuous and discrete controls. The continuous dynamics of such a system is usually modeled by a controlled vector field or difference equation. Its hybrid nature is expressed by a dependence on some discrete phenomena, corresponding to discrete states, dynamics, and controls. The result is a system as in Fig. 1(b).

Real-World Examples. The prototypical hybrid systems are digital controllers, computers, and subsystems modeled as finite automata coupled with controllers and plants modeled by partial or ordinary differential equations or difference equations. Thus, such systems arise whenever one mixes logical decision-making with the generation of continuous control laws. More specifically, real-world examples of hybrid systems include systems with relays, switches, and hysteresis, computer disk drives, transmissions, stepper motors, and other motion controllers, constrained robotic systems, intelligent vehicle/highway systems (IVHS), modern flexible manufacturing and flight control systems. Each of these, plus other examples, are discussed in some detail in [15]. Other important application areas for hybrid systems theory include embedded systems and analog/digital circuit co-design and verification.

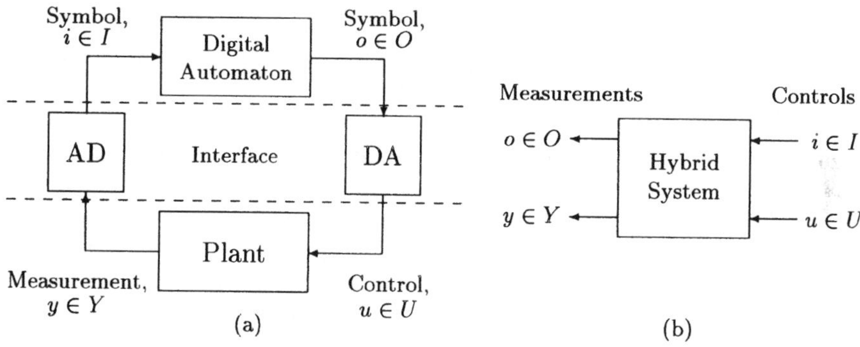

Fig. 1. (a) Hybrid System. (b) Hybrid Control System

Paradigms. We see four basic paradigms for the study of hybrid systems (summarizing from [15]):

1. **Aggregation**: suppress the continuous dynamics so that the hybrid system is a finite automaton or discrete-event dynamical system [1, 3, 26].
2. **Continuation**: suppress the discrete dynamics so that the hybrid system becomes a differential equation. This original idea of Prof. Sanjoy Mitter and the author is to convert hybrid models into purely continuous ones (modeled by ODEs) using differential equations that simulate automata [16, 20].
3. **Automatization** or **automata approach**. Treat the constituent systems as a network of interacting automata. The focus is on the input-output or language behavior. Automatization was pioneered in full generality by Nerode and Kohn [33].
4. **Systemization** or **systems approach**. Treat the constituent systems as interacting dynamical systems. The focus is on the state-space. Systemization was developed in full generality by the author [15], summarized here.

Research Areas. Research into hybrid systems may be broken down into four broad categories:

- **Modeling**: formulating precise models that capture the rich behavior of hybrid systems. i.e., *How do we "fill in the boxes" in Fig.* 1*? What is their* *dynamics? How can we classify their rich structure and behavior—and sort through the myriad hybrid systems models appearing?*

- **Analysis**: developing tools for the simulation, analysis, and verification of hybrid systems. i.e., *How do we analyze systems as in Fig.* 1(a)*? What does continuity mean? What is their complexity? How do they differ from continuous dynamical systems? How do we test their stability? or analyze examples?*
- **Control**: synthesizing hybrid controllers —which issue continuous controls and make discrete decisions—that achieve certain prescribed safety and performance goals for hybrid systems. i.e., *How do we control a plant as in Fig.* 1(b) *with a controller as in Fig.* 1(b)*? How can we synthesize such hybrid controllers?*
- **Design**: conceiving new schemes and structures leading to easier modeling, verification, and control.

Outline of Paper. In the next two sections, we concentrate on modeling and its related questions above. In particular, we introduce **general hybrid dynamical systems** as interacting collections of dynamical systems, each evolving on continuous state spaces, and subject to continuous and discrete controls, and some other discrete phenomena. We give explicit instructions for computing the orbits and trajectories of general hybrid dynamical systems, including sufficient conditions for existence and uniqueness. We introduce a hierarchy of such systems and provide a taxonomy of them based on their structure and the discrete phenomena they exhibit. In Sections 4 and 5, we quickly summarize our work on analysis and control, answering the questions above. In all cases, the reader is referred to [15] for more details and complete references.

2 Hybrid Dynamical Systems

The notion of dynamical system has a long history as an important conceptual tool in science and engineering. It is the foundation of our formulation of hybrid dynamical systems. Briefly, a **dynamical system** [36] is a system $\Sigma = [X, \Gamma, \phi]$, where X is an arbitrary topological space, the **state space** of Σ. The **transition semigroup** Γ is a topological semigroup with identity. The (**extended**) **transition map** $\phi : X \times \Gamma \to X$ is a continuous function satisfying the identity and semigroup properties [37]. A **transition system** is a dynamical system as above, except that ϕ need not be continuous.

Examples of dynamical systems abound, including autonomous ODEs, autonomous difference equations, finite automata, pushdown automata, Turing machines, Petri nets, etc. As seen from these examples, both digital and analog systems can be viewed in this formalism. The utility of this has been noted since the earliest days of control theory [34].

We also denote by "dynamical system" the system $\Sigma = [X, \Gamma, f]$, where X and Γ are as above, but the **transition function** f is the **generator** of the extended transition function ϕ.[1] We may also refine the above concept by

[1] In the case of $\Gamma = \mathbf{Z}$, $f : X \to X$ is given by $f \equiv \phi(\cdot, 1)$. In the case of $\Gamma = \mathbf{R}$,

introducing dynamical systems with initial and final states, input and output, and timing maps.[2]

Briefly, a hybrid dynamical system is an indexed collection of dynamical systems along with some map for "jumping" among them (switching dynamical system and/or resetting the state). This jumping occurs whenever the state satisfies certain conditions, given by its membership in a specified subset of the state space. Hence, the entire system can be thought of as a sequential patching together of dynamical systems with initial and final states, the jumps performing a reset to a (generally different) initial state of a (generally different) dynamical system whenever a final state is reached.

More formally, a **general hybrid dynamical system (GHDS)** is a system $H = [Q, \Sigma, \mathbf{A}, \mathbf{G}]$, with its constituent parts defined as follows.

- Q is the set of **index states**, also referred to as **discrete states**.
- $\Sigma = \{\Sigma_q\}_{q\in Q}$ is the collection of **constituent** dynamical systems, where each $\Sigma_q = [X_q, \Gamma_q, \phi_q]$ (or $\Sigma_q = [X_q, \Gamma_q, f_q]$) is a dynamical system as above. Here, the X_q are the **continuous state spaces** and ϕ_q (or f_q) are called the **continuous dynamics**.
- $\mathbf{A} = \{A_q\}_{q\in Q}$, $A_q \subset X_q$ for each $q \in Q$, is the collection of **autonomous jump sets**.
- $\mathbf{G} = \{G_q\}_{q\in Q}$, $G_q : A_q \to \bigcup_{q\in Q} X_q \times \{q\}$, is the collection of (**autonomous**) **jump transition maps**.

  These are also said to represent the **discrete dynamics** of the HDS.

Thus, $S = \bigcup_{q\in Q} X_q \times \{q\}$ is the **hybrid state space** of H. For convenience, we use the following shorthand. $S_q = X_q \times \{q\}$ and $A = \bigcup_{q\in Q} A_q \times \{q\}$ is *the* autonomous jump set. $G : A \to S$ is *the* autonomous jump transition map, constructed componentwise in the obvious way. The **jump destination sets** $\mathbf{D} = \{D_q\}_{q\in Q}$ are given by $D_q = \pi_1[G(A) \cap S_q]$, where π_i is projection onto the ith coordinate. The **switching** or **transition manifolds**, $M_{q,p} \subset A_q$ are given by $M_{q,p} = G_q^{-1}(p, D_p)$, i.e., the set of states from which transitions from index q to index p can occur.

A GHDS can be pictured as an automaton. Here, each node is a constituent dynamical system, with the index the name of the node. Each edge represents a possible transition between constituent systems, labeled by the appropriate condition for the transition's being "enabled" and the update of the continuous state.

Roughly,[3] the dynamics of the GHDS H are as follows. The system is assumed to start in some hybrid state in $S\backslash A$, say $s_0 = (x_0, q_0)$. It evolves according to $\phi_{q_0}(x_0, \cdot)$ until the state enters—if ever—A_{q_0} at the point $s_1^- = (x_1^-, q_0)$. At

$f : X \to TX$ is given by the vector fields $f(x) = d\,\phi(x,t)/dt|_{t=0}$.

[2] *Timing maps* provide the aforementioned mechanism for reconciling different "time scales," by giving a uniform meaning to different transition semigroups in a hybrid system. See below.

[3] We make more precise statements later.

this time it is instantly transferred according to transition map to $G_{q_0}(x_1^-) = (x_1, q_1) \equiv s_1$, from which the process continues.

Dynamical Systems. $|Q| = 1$ and $A = \emptyset$ *recovers all dynamical systems.*

Hybrid Systems. The case $|Q|$ finite, each X_q a subset of $\mathbf{R}^n$, and each $\Gamma_q = \mathbf{R}$ largely corresponds to the *usual* notion of a hybrid system, viz. a coupling of finite automata and differential equations [16, 17, 27]. Herein, a **hybrid system** is a GHDS with Q countable, and with $\Gamma_q \equiv \mathbf{R}$ (or $\mathbf{R}_+$) and $X_q \subset \mathbf{R}^{d_q}$, $d_q \in \mathbf{Z}_+$, for all $q \in Q$: $[Q, [\{X_q\}_{q\in Q}, \mathbf{R}_+, \{f_q\}_{q\in Q}], \mathbf{A}, \mathbf{G}]$, where f_q is a vector field on $X_q \subset \mathbf{R}^{d_q}$.[4]

Changing State Space. The state space may change. This is useful in modeling component failures or changes in dynamical description based on autonomous—and later, controlled—events which change it. Examples include the collision of two inelastic particles or an aircraft mode transition that changes variables to be controlled [32]. We also allow the X_q to overlap and the inclusion of multiple copies of the same space. This may be used, for example, to take into account overlapping local coordinate systems on a manifold [4].

Refinements. We may refine the concept of GHDS H by adding:

- inputs, including control inputs, disturbances, or parameters (see *controlled* HDS below).
- outputs, including **state-output** for each constituent system as for dynamical systems [15, 37] and **edge-output**: $H = [Q, \Sigma, \mathbf{A}, \mathbf{G}, \mathbf{O}, \eta]$, where $\eta : A \to O$ produces an output at each jump time.
- $\Delta : A \to \mathbf{R}_+$, the **jump delay map**, which can be used to account for the time which abstracted-away, lower-level transition dynamics actually take.[5]
- Marked states (including initial or final states), timing, or input and output for any constituent system.

Example 1 — Reconciling Time Scales. Suppose that each constituent dynamical system Σ_q of H is equipped with a timing map. That is $\tau = \{\tau_q\}_{q\in Q}$ where $\tau_q : X_q \times \Gamma_q \to \mathbf{R}_+$. Then, we may construct **trajectories** for H, i.e., a *function from "real-time" to state.* This is discussed below.

A **controlled general hybrid dynamical system (GCHDS)** is a system $H_c = [Q, \Sigma, \mathbf{A}, \mathbf{G}, \mathbf{V}, \mathbf{C}, \mathbf{F}]$, with its constituent parts defined as follows.

- Q, $\mathbf{A}$, and S are defined as above.
- $\Sigma = \{\Sigma_q\}_{q\in Q}$ is the collection of controlled dynamical systems, where each $\Sigma_q = [X_q, \Gamma_q, f_q, U_q]$ (or $\Sigma_q = [X_q, \Gamma_q, \phi_q, U_q]$) is a controlled dynamical

[4] Here, we may take the view that the system evolves on the state space $\mathbf{R}^* \times Q$, where $\mathbf{R}^*$ denotes the set of finite, but variable-length real-valued vectors. For example, Q may be the set of labels of a computer program and $x \in \mathbf{R}^*$ the values of all currently-allocated variables. This then includes Smale's tame machines [8].

[5] Think of modeling the closure time of a discretely-controlled hydraulic valve or trade mechanism imperfections in economic markets.

system as above with (extended) transition map parameterized by **control set** U_q.
- $\mathbf{G} = \{G_q\}_{q\in Q}$, where $G_q : A_q \times V_q \to S$ is the **autonomous jump transition map**, parameterized by the **transition control set** V_q, a subset of the collection $\mathbf{V} = \{V_q\}_{q\in Q}$.
- $\mathbf{C} = \{C_q\}_{q\in Q}$, $C_q \subset X_q$, is the collection of **controlled jump sets.**
- $\mathbf{F} = \{F_q\}_{q\in Q}$, where $F_q : C_q \to 2^S$, is the collection of **controlled jump destination maps.**

As shorthand, G, C, F, V may be defined as above. Likewise, jump destination sets D_a and D_c may be defined. In this case, $D \equiv D_a \cup D_c$.

Again, a GCHDS has an automaton representation. See Fig. 2. The notation ![condition] denotes that the transition *must* be taken when enabled. The notation ?[condition] denotes an enabled transition that *may be taken* on command; ":∈" means reassignment to some value in the given set.

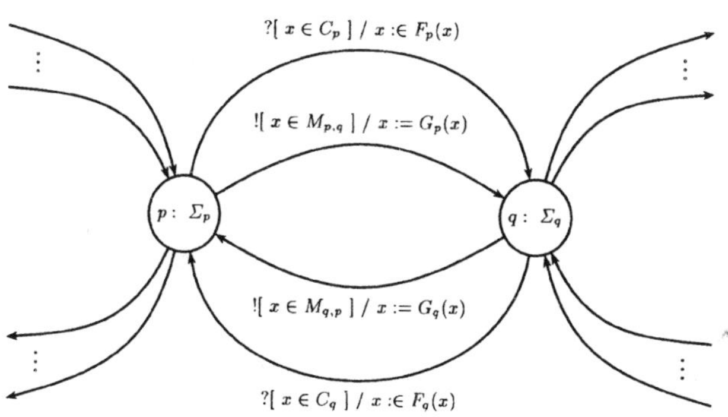

Fig. 2. Automaton Associated with GCHDS.

Roughly, the dynamics of H_c are as follows. The system is assumed to start in some hybrid state in $S\backslash A$, say $s_0 = (x_0, q_0)$. It evolves according to $\phi_{q_0}(\cdot,\cdot,u)$ until the state enters—if ever—either A_{q_0} or C_{q_0} at the point $s_1^- = (x_1^-, q_0)$. If it enters A_{q_0}, then it *must* be transferred according to transition map $G_{q_0}(x_1^-, v)$ for some chosen $v \in V_{q_0}$. If it enters C_{q_0}, then we *may* choose to jump and, if so, we may choose the destination to be any point in $F_{q_0}(x_1^-)$. In either case, we arrive at a point $s_1 = (x_1, q_1)$ from which the process continues. See Fig. 3.

Notes. (1) **Nondeterminism** in transitions may be taken care of by partitioning ?[condition] into those which are controlled and uncontrolled (cf. [28]). **Disturbances** (and other nondeterminism) may be modeled by partitioning U, V, and C into portions that are under the influence of the controller or nature respectively. Systems with state-output, edge-output, and autonomous and controlled jump delay maps (Δ_a and Δ_c, respectively) may be added as above. (2) The model includes the "unified" model posed by Branicky, Borkar, and Mitter

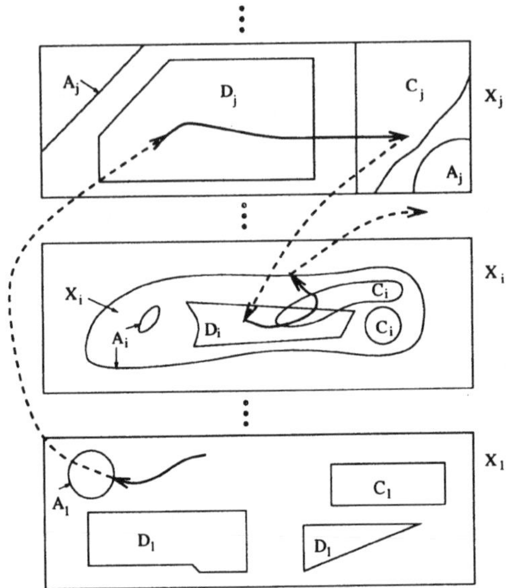

Fig. 3. Example dynamics of GCHDS.

(**BBM**; [17]) and thus several other previously posed hybrid systems models [3, 4, 21, 33, 39, 41]. It also includes systems with impulse effect [5] and hybrid automata [25]. (3) In particular, our unified BBM model is, briefly, a **controlled hybrid system**, with the form $\left[\mathbf{Z}_+, \left[\{\mathbf{R}^{d_i}\}_{i=0}^{\infty}, \mathbf{R}_+, \{f_i\}_{i=0}^{\infty}, \mathbf{U}\right], \mathbf{A}, \mathbf{V}, \mathbf{G}, \mathbf{C}, \mathbf{F}\right]$. Control results for this model are summarized in Section 5.

Definition 1. The **admissible control actions** available are the **continous controls** $u \in U_q$, exercised in each constituent regime; the **discrete controls** $v \in V_q$, exercised at autonomous jump times (i.e., on hitting set A); and the **intervention times** and **destinations** of controlled jumps (when the state is in C).

Now, we place some restrictions on GHDS in order to prove some behavioral properties. We assume that Γ is an ordered set with the least upper bound property, equipped with the order topology. Note that this implies Γ is a lattice [30]. We also assume addition to be order-preserving in the sense that if $a > 0$, then $a + b > b$. This last assumption ensures, among other things, that $\Gamma^+ = \{a \in \Gamma \mid a \geq 0\}$ is a semigroup; likewise for Γ^-, defined symmetrically. For brevity, we call such a group (semigroup) **time-like.**[6]

We now consider several initial value problems for GHDS. First, in the time-like case, given dynamical system $[X, \Gamma, \phi]$, we may define the **positive orbit**

[6] The most widely used time-like groups are **R**, **Z**, and $\rho\mathbf{Z}$, $\rho \in \mathbf{R}$, each under addition and in the usual order. Example semigroups are $\mathbf{R}_+$, $\rho\mathbf{Z}_+$, and the free monoid generated by a finite, ordered alphabet (in the dictionary order).

of the point x as $P(x) \equiv \phi(x, \Gamma^{+})$.[7]

Problem 2 — Reachability Problem. Compute the positive orbit for GHDS H.

Solution 3. The positive orbit is the *set* defined as follows. We consider only initial points in $I \equiv X \backslash A$. We restrict ourselves to the case where A_q is closed and $D_q \cap A_q = \emptyset$. Suppose $s_0 = (x_0, q_0) \in I$. If $P_{q_0}(x_0) = \phi_{q_0}(x_0, \Gamma^{+})$ does not intersect A_{q_0} we are done: the positive orbit is just $P_{q_0}(x_0)$. Else, let $g_1 = \inf\{g \in \Gamma_{q_0}^{+} \mid \phi_{q_0}(x_0, g) \in A_{q_0}\}$. Since A_{q_0} closed, Γ^{+} is time-like, and ϕ is continuous, the set in the inf equation is closed, g_1 exists, and $x_1^{-} = \phi_{q_0}(x_0, g_1) \in A_{q_0}$. Define $s_1 = G_{q_0}(x_1^{-}) \in I$ and continue.

When a GHDS is time-uniform with time-like group Γ, it induces a Γ^{+}-transition system $[I, \Gamma^{+}, \Phi]$. In this case, we may define its (forward) **trajectory** as a *function* from Γ^{+} into I.

Problem 4 — Trajectory Problem. Compute the trajectories for GHDS H.

Solution 5. A modification of the above. See [15] for details.

The above constructions allow us to formulate stability and *finite-time reachability* problems. Note that trajectories *may not be extendible to all of* Γ^{+}, i.e., we have not precluded the **accumulation** of an infinite number of jumps in finite time; this can be removed in the case of hybrid systems by, for example, assuming uniform Lipschitz continuity of the vector fields and uniform separation of the jump and destination set A and D [17]. **Note**: From above, if $D_q \cap A_q = \emptyset$ and A_q closed then (positive) orbits and trajectories exist (up to a possible accumulation time of finite jumps) and are unique. Similar to reachability, we have the following.

Problem 6 — Accessiblity Problem. Compute the set of points accessible under all admissible control actions from initial set I for GCHDS system H_c.

The solution is largely the same as above except that we must vary over all admissible control actions.

3 Classification of Hybrid Dynamical Systems

A Taxonomy for GHDS. The scope of hybrid dynamical systems presents a myriad of modeling choices. In this section, we classify them according to their structure and the discrete phenomena they possess. Below, the prefixes "c-," "d-," and "t-" are used as abbreviations for "continuous-," "discrete-," and "time-" respectively. If no prefix is given, either can be used.

Our *structural classification* is roughly captured by the following list.

[7] The negative orbit $B(x)$ may be defined even in the non-reversible case by $y \in B(x)$ if and only if $x \in P(y)$ [7].

- **Time-uniform**. The semigroups may be all be the same for each q.
- **Continuous-time, discrete-time, sampled-data**. Each constituent dynamical system may be of a special type that evolves in continuous-time ($\Gamma = \mathbf{R}$), discrete-time ($\Gamma = \mathbf{Z}$), or a mixture. However, if the GHDS is time-uniform, we refer to it by the appropriate label, e.g., continuous-time-uniform.
- **C-uniform**. The ambient state space may be the same for each q.
- **C-Euclidean, c-manifold**. Each ambient state space may be Euclidean[8] or a smooth manifold.
- **D-compact, d-countable, d-finite**. Special cases arise when the index space is compact, finite, or countably infinite.
- **Dynamically-uniform**. The dynamics may be the same for each q. Strictly, such a case would also require that the system be c-uniform and time-uniform. In these systems, the interesting dynamics arises from the transition map G_q [1, 26].
- **D-concurrent** versus **d-serial**. We may or may not allow more than one discrete jump to occur at a given moment of time.
- **Deterministic** versus **nondeterministic**.
- **Nonautonomous** versus **autonomous**. The continuous (or discrete)

Finally, a hybrid dynamical system may also be classified according to the discrete dynamic phenomena that it exhibits as follows (cf. [17]).

- **Autonomous-switching**. The autonomous jump map $G \equiv \nu$ is the identity in its continuous component, i.e., $\nu : A \to S$ has $\nu(x, q) = (x, q')$.
- **Autonomous-impulse**. $G \equiv J$ is the identity in its discrete component.
- **Controlled-switching**. The controlled jump map F is the identity in its continuous component, i.e., $F(x, q) \subset \{x\} \times Q$.
- **Controlled-impulse**. F is the identity in its discrete component.

With this notation, our GHDS model admits some special cases:

- H autonomous-impulse with $|Q| = 1$ and $\Gamma = \mathbf{R}$ is an **autonomous system with impulse effect** [5].
- H c-uniform, time-uniform, and autonomous-switching is an **autonomous switched system** [14].
- H continuous-time-uniform, c-Euclidean-uniform, d-countable, is what we called a **hybrid system**.

Classifying Hybrid Systems. In this section, we give explicit representations of the different classes of hybrid systems arising from the definitions above. We concentrate on the c-continuous-time, c-uniform, d-finite, time-invariant, autonomous case. Extensions to other cases above are straightforward.

---

[8] A subset of $\mathbf{R}^n$ in the usual topology

A (continuous-time) **autonomous-switching hybrid system** may be defined as follows:[9]

$$\dot{x}(t) = f(x(t), q(t)), \qquad q^+(t) = \nu(x(t), q(t)), \tag{1}$$

where $x(t) \in \mathbf{R}^n$, $q(t) \in Q \simeq \{1, \ldots, N\}$. Here, $f(\cdot, q) : \mathbf{R}^n \to \mathbf{R}^n$, $q \in Q$, each globally Lipschitz continuous, is the **continuous dynamics** of Eq. (1); and $\nu : \mathbf{R}^n \times Q \to Q$ is the **finite dynamics** of Eq. (1). An example is the Tavernini model. Adding a continuous control yields Witsenhausen's model.

An **autonomous-impulse hybrid system** is a system

$$\dot{x}(t) = f(x(t)), \;\; x(t) \notin M; \qquad x^+(t) = J(x(t)), \;\; x(t) \in M; \tag{2}$$

where $x(t) \in \mathbf{R}^n$, and $J : \mathbf{R}^n \to \mathbf{R}^n$. Examples include autonomous systems with impulse effect. Finally, a hybrid system with autonomous switching and autonomous impulses (i.e., the full power of autonomous jumps) is just a combination of those discussed above. where $x(t) \in \mathbf{R}^n$ and $q(t) \in Q \subset \mathbf{Z}$. Examples include the BGM model and hence autonomous versions of of the models in [3, 4, 21, 33] (see [16, 17]).

4 Hybrid Systems Analysis

Topological Results. In traditional feedback control systems—continuous-time, discrete-time, sampled-data—the maps from output measurements to control inputs are continuous (in the usual metric-based topologies). Continuity of state evolution and controls with respect to the states also plays a role. With these considerations in mind, we want to examine continuity for systems as in Fig. 1(a), where the set of symbols, automaton states, and outputs, are finite sets and the plant and controls belong to a continuum. Yet, in general, hybrid systems are not even continuous in the initial condition:

Example 2. Consider the following hybrid system on $X_1 = X_2 = \mathbf{R}^2$. The continuous dynamics is given by $f_1 \equiv (1,\ 0)^T$ and $f_2 \equiv (0,\ 1)^T$. The discrete dynamics is given by $A_1 = [0,\ 1]^2$ and $G(x, 1) = (x, 2)$. Now consider the initial conditions $x(0) = (-\epsilon, -\epsilon)^T$ and $y(0) = (-\epsilon, 0)^T$. Note that $x(1) = (1-\epsilon, -\epsilon)$ but $y(1) = (0, 1-\epsilon)$. Clearly, no matter how small ϵ, hence $\|x(0) - y(0)\|_\infty$, is chosen, $\|x(1) - y(1)\|_\infty = 1$.

Further, we note that the only continuous maps from a connected set to a disconnected one are the constant ones. Hence, the usual discrete topologies on a set of symbols do not lead to nontrivial continuous AD maps.

[9] Automata may be thought of as operating in "continuous time" by the convention that the state, input, and output symbols are piecewise right- or left- continuous functions. The notation t^- (resp. t^+) may used to indicate that the finite state is piecewise continuous from the right (resp. left), e.g., $q(t) = \nu(x(t), q(t^-))$ Here we have used Sontag's more evocative discrete-time transition notation [37] $q^+(t)$ to denote the "successor" of $q(t)$.

We have examined topologies that lead to continuity of each member of topologies for which the AD maps from measurements to symbols *are* continuous in [10]. In dynamics terms, we examined topologies that lead to continuity of each member of the family of maps $G \circ \phi_q$. One topology in particular, proposed by Nerode and Kohn [33], is studied in depth.

We also looked at what happens if we attempt to "complete the loop" in Fig. 1(a), by also considering the DA maps. We exhibited a topology making the whole loop continuous [10]. We further examined a different view of hybrid systems as a set of continuous controllers, with switching among them governed by the discrete state. A popular example is fuzzy control systems, consisting of a continuous plant controlled by a finite set of so-called fuzzy rules. On the surface, they are hybrid systems. Yet, we showed fuzzy control leads to continuous maps (from measurements to controls), and all such continuous maps may be implemented via fuzzy control [10].

Complexity Results. Computational equivalence (or simulation of computational capabilities) may be shown by comparing accepted languages [29], or simulating step-by-step behavior [9]. In order to examine the computational capabilities of hybrid and continuous systems we first must introduce notions of a continuous-time system simulating a discrete-time one [16]:

Definition 7. A continuous-time transition system $[X, \mathbf{R}_+, f]$ **simulates via section** or **S-simulates** a discrete-time transition system $[Y, \mathbf{Z}_+, F]$ if there exist a continuous surjective partial function $\psi : X \to Y$ and $t_0 \in \mathbf{R}_+$ such that for all $x \in \psi^{-1}(Y)$ and all $k \in \mathbf{Z}_+$, $\psi(f(x, kt_0)) = F(\psi(x), k)$.

Definition 8. A continuous-time transition system $[X, \mathbf{R}_+, f]$ **simulates via intervals** or **I-simulates** a discrete-time transition system $[Y, \mathbf{Z}_+, F]$ if there exist a continuous surjective partial function $\psi : X \to Y$ and $\epsilon > 0$ such that $V \equiv \psi^{-1}(Y)$ is open and for all $x \in V$ the set $T = \{t \in \mathbf{R}_+ \mid f(x,t) \in V\}$ is a union of intervals (τ_k, τ_k'), $0 = \tau_0 < \tau_0' < \tau_1 < \tau_1' < \cdots$, $|\tau_k' - \tau_k| \geq \epsilon$, with $\psi(f(x, t_k)) = F(\psi(x), k)$, for all $t_k \in (\tau_k, \tau_k')$.

When the continuous-time transition system is a HDS, the maps ψ above can be viewed as an edge-output and state-output map, respectively. In this case, S-simulation can be viewed as equivalent behavior at equally-spaced edges and I-simulation as equivalent behavior in designated nodes. S- and I-simulation are distinct; SI-simulation denotes both holding. In [16] we show

- Every dynamical system $[\mathbf{R}^n, \mathbf{Z}, F]$ can be S-simulated by an autonomous-switching, two-discrete-state hybrid system on $\mathbf{R}^{2n}$.
- Every dynamical system $[\mathbf{R}^n, \mathbf{Z}_+, F]$ can be S-simulated by an autonomous-jump, two-discrete-state hybrid system on $\mathbf{R}^n$.
- Every dynamical system $[Y, \mathbf{Z}, F]$, $Y \subset \mathbf{Z}^n$, can be SI-simulated by a (continuous) dynamical system of the form $[\mathbf{R}^{2n+1}, \mathbf{R}_+, f]$. Furthermore, if Y is bounded f can be taken Lipschitz continuous.

As corollaries to the last, we have (via demonstrated isomorphisms with dynamical systems on $\mathbf{Z}$)

- Every Turing machine, pushdown automata, and finite automaton can be SI-simulated by a (continuous) dynamical system of the form $[\mathbf{R}^3, \mathbf{R}_+, f]$.
- Using SI-simulation, there is continuous ODE in $\mathbf{R}^3$ with the power of universal computation.

Noting that even ordinary dynamical systems are so computationally powerful, we have used the famous asynchronous arbiter[10] problem [11, 31, 40] to distinguish between dynamical and hybrid systems [16]. In particular, we settled the problem in an ODE framework by showing that no system of the form $[\mathbf{R}^n, \mathbf{R}_+, B, f, W, h]$, with f Lipschitz and h continuous, can implement an arbiter [11, 16]. On the other hand, we exhibited a hybrid system of the form $[\{1,2\}, [\mathbf{R}^n, \mathbf{R}_+, B, \{f_1, f_2\}, W, h], \mathbf{A}, \mathbf{G}]$, with each f_q Lipschitz, h continuous, and $\mathbf{G}$ autonomous-switching, that satisfies the arbiter specifications.

Analysis Tools. We have developed general tools for analyzing continuous switched systems (where the vector fields agree at switching times) [12]. For instance, we prove an extension of Bendixson's Theorem to the case of Lipschitz continuous vector fields. This gives us a tool for analyzing the existence of limit cycles of continuous switched systems. We also proved a lemma dealing with the continuity of differential equations with respect to perturbations that preserve a linear part. Colloquially, this lemma demonstrates the robustness of ODEs with a linear part (**Linear Robustness Lemma**; [13]). This lemma is useful in easily deriving some of the common robustness results of nonlinear ODE theory [6]. It also becomes useful in studying singular perturbations if the fast dynamics are such that they maintain the corresponding algebraic equation to within a small deviation. Some simple propositions that allow this appear in [12].

In [14], we examined stability of switched and hybrid systems. We introduced **multiple Lyapunov functions** as a tool for analyzing Lyapunov stability of such systems. The idea here is to impose conditions on switching that guarantee stability when we have Lyapunov functions for each system f_i individually. Iterative function systems were presented as a tool for proving Lagrange stability and positive invariance. We also addressed the case where the finite switching set is replaced by an arbitrary compact set.

Analyzing Examples. We have analyzed example systems arising from a realistic aircraft controller problem (called the **max system**) which logically switches between two controllers—one for tracking and one for regulation about a fixed angle of attack—in order to achieve reasonable performance and safety [12]. While stability of such hybrid systems has previously only been examined using simulation [38], we were able to prove global asymptotic stability for a meaningful class of cases [12]. Using our linear robustness lemma to compare ODE solutions, we extended the result to a class of *continuations* of these systems, in which an ODE dynamically smooths the logical nonlinearity.

[10] An **arbiter** is a device that can be used to decide the winner of two-person races (within some tolerances). It has two input buttons, B_1 and B_2, and two output lines, W_1 and W_2, that can each be either 0 or 1.

5 Hybrid Control

Theoretical Results. We consider the following optimal control problem for controlled hybrid systems. Let $a > 0$ be a **discount factor**. We add to our model the following known maps:

- **Running cost**, $k : S \times U \to \mathbf{R}_+$.
- **Autonomous jump cost** and **delay**, $c_a : A \times V \to \mathbf{R}_+$ and $\Delta_a : A \times V \to \mathbf{R}_+$.
- **Controlled jump** (or **impulse**) **cost** and **delay**, $c_c : C \times D_c \to \mathbf{R}_+$ and $\Delta_c : C \times D_c \to \mathbf{R}_+$.

The total discounted cost is defined as

$$\int_{\mathbf{T}} e^{-at} k(x(t), u(t))\, dt + \sum_i e^{-a\sigma_i} c_a(x(\sigma_i), v_i) + \sum_i e^{-a\zeta_i} c_c(x(\zeta_i), x(\zeta_i')) \quad (3)$$

where $\mathbf{T} = \mathbf{R}_+ \backslash (\bigcup_i [\tau_i, \Gamma_i))$, $\{\sigma_i\}$ (resp. $\{\zeta_i\}$) are the successive pre-jump times for autonomous (resp. impulsive) jumps and ζ_j' is the post-jump time (after the delay) for the jth impulsive jump. The **decision** or **control** variables over which Eq. (3) is to be minimized are the *admissible controls* of our controlled hybrid system (see Def. 1). Under some assumptions (the necessity of which are shown via examples) we have the following results [17]:

- A finite optimal cost exists for any initial condition. Furthermore, there are only finitely many autonomous jumps in finite time.
- Using the relaxed control framework, an optimal trajectory exists for any initial condition.
- For every $\epsilon > 0$ an ϵ-optimal control policy exists wherein $u(\cdot)$ is precise, i.e., a Dirac measure.
- The value function, V, associated with the optimal control problem is continuous on $S \backslash (\partial A \cup \partial C)$ and satisfies the following **generalized quasi-variational inequalities (GQVIs)**.
  (1) $x \in S \backslash A$: $\min_u \langle \nabla_x V(x), f_i(x, u) \rangle - aV(x) + k(x, u) \le 0$.
  (2) On C: $V(x) \le \min_{z \in D} \left\{ c_c(x, z) + e^{-a\Delta_c(x,z)} V(z) \right\}$
  (3) On A: $V(x) \le \min_v \left\{ c_a(x, v) + e^{-a\Delta_a(x,v)} V(G(x, v)) \right\}$
  (4) On C: $(1) \cdot (2) = 0$

Algorithms and Examples. We have outlined four approaches to solving the generalized quasi-variational inequalities (GQVIs) associated with optimal hybrid control problems [15]. Our algorithmic basis for solving these GQVIs is the generalized Bellman Equation: $V^*(x) = \min_{p \in \Pi} \{ g(x, p) + V^*(x'(x, p)) \}$, where Π is a generalized set of actions. The three classes of actions available in our hybrid systems framework at each x are the admissible control actions from Def. 1. From this viewpoint, generalized policy and value iteration become solution tools [15].

The key to *efficient* algorithms for solving optimal control problems for hybrid systems lies in noticing their strong connection to the models of impulse control and piecewise-deterministic processes. Making this explicit, we have developed algorithms similar to those for impulse control [24] and one based on linear programming [23, 35] (see [15]).

Three illustrative examples are solved in [15]. First, we consider a hysteresis system that exhibits autonomous switching and has a continuous control. Then, we discuss a satellite station-keeping problem, where the on-off nature of the satellite's reaction jets creates a system involving controlled switching. We end with a transmission control problem, where the goal is to find the *hybrid* strategy of continuous accelerator input and discrete gear-shift position to achieve maximum acceleration. In each example, the synthesized optimal controllers verify engineering intuition.

References

1. R. Alur, C. Couroubetis, T.A. Henzinger, and P.-H. Ho. Hybrid automata: An algorithmic approach to the specification and verification of hybrid systems. In [27], pp. 209–229.
2. P. Anstaklis, W. Kohn, A. Nerode, and S. Sastry, editors. *Hybrid Systems II*. Lecture Notes in Computer Science. Springer-Verlag, New York, 1995.
3. P.J. Antsaklis, J.A. Stiver, and M.D. Lemmon. Hybrid system modeling and autonomous control systems. In [27], pp. 366–392.
4. A. Back, J. Guckenheimer, and M. Myers. A dynamical simulation facility for hybrid systems. In [27], pp. 255–267.
5. D.D. Bainov and P.S. Simeonov. *Systems with Impulse Effect*. Ellis Horwood, Chichester, England, 1989.
6. E.A. Barbashin. *Introduction to the Theory of Stability*. Wolters-Noordhoff, Groningen, The Netherlands, 1970.
7. N.P. Bhatia and G.P. Szegö. *Dynamical Systems: Stability Theory and Applications*, vol. 35 of *Lecture Notes in Mathematics*. Springer-Verlag, Berlin, 1967.
8. L. Blum, M. Shub, and S. Smale. On a theory of computation and complexity over the real numbers: NP-completeness, recursive functions and universal machines. *Bulletin of the American Mathematical Society*, 21(1):1–46, July 1989.
9. L. Bobrow and M. Arbib. *Discrete Mathematics*. W.B. Saunders, Phila., 1974.
10. M.S. Branicky. Topology of hybrid systems. In *Proc. IEEE Conf. Decision and Control*, pp. 2309–2314, San Antonio, December 1993.
11. M.S. Branicky. Why you can't build an arbiter. Tech. Rep. LIDS-P-2217, Lab. for Information and Decision Systems, Massachusetts Institute of Tech., Dec. 1993.
12. M.S. Branicky. Analyzing continuous switching systems: Theory and examples. In *Proc. American Control Conf.*, pp. 3110–3114, Baltimore, June 1994.
13. M.S. Branicky. Continuity of ODE solutions. *Applied Mathematics Letters*, 7(5):57–60, 1994.
14. M.S. Branicky. Stability of switched and hybrid systems. In *Proc. IEEE Conf. Decision and Control*, pp. 3498–3503, Lake Buena Vista, FL, December 1994.
15. M.S. Branicky. *Studies in Hybrid Systems: Modeling, Analysis, and Control*. PhD thesis, Massachusetts Institute of Technology, Dept. of Electrical Engineering and Computer Science, June 1995.
16. M.S. Branicky. Universal computation and other capabilities of hybrid and continuous dynamical systems. *Theoretical Computer Science*, 138(1):67–100, 1995.
17. M.S. Branicky, V. Borkar, and S.K. Mitter. A unified framework for hybrid control. Tech. Rep. LIDS-P-2239, Lab. for Information and Decision Systems, Massachusetts Institute of Technology, April 1994. Also: [18, 19].

18. M.S. Branicky, V.S. Borkar, and S.K. Mitter. A unified framework for hybrid control. In Cohen and Quadrat [22], pp. 352–358. Extended Abstract.
19. M.S. Branicky, V.S. Borkar, and S.K. Mitter. A unified framework for hybrid control. In *Proc. IEEE Conf. Decision and Control*, pp. 4228–4234, Lake Buena Vista, FL, December 1994.
20. R.W. Brockett. Smooth dynamical systems which realize arithmetical and logical operations. In H. Nijmeijer and J.M. Schumacher, editors, *Lecture Notes in Control and Information Sciences. Three Decades of Mathematical Systems Theory*, pp. 19–30. Springer-Verlag, Berlin, 1989.
21. R.W. Brockett. Hybrid models for motion control systems. In H.L. Trentelman and J.C. Willems, editors, *Essays in Control: Perspectives in the Theory and its Applications*, pp. 29–53. Birkhäuser, Boston, 1993.
22. G. Cohen and J.-P. Quadrat, editors. *Proceedings 11th INRIA International Conference on the Analysis and Optimization of Systems*, vol. 199 of *Lecture Notes in Control and Information Sciences*. Springer-Verlag, New York, 1994.
23. O.L.V. Costa. Impulse control of piecewise-deterministic processes via linear programming. *IEEE Trans. Automatic Control*, 36(3):371–375, 1991.
24. O.L.V. Costa and M.H.A. Davis. Impulse control of piecewise deterministic processes. *Math. Control Signals Syst.*, 2:187–206, 1989.
25. A. Deshpande and P. Varaiya. Viable control of hybrid systems. In [2].
26. S.D. Gennaro, C. Horn, S.R. Kulkarni, and P.J. Ramadge. Reduction of timed hybrid systems. In *Proc. IEEE Conf. Decision and Control*, pp. 4215–4220, Lake Buena Vista, FL, December 1994.
27. R.L. Grossman, A. Nerode, A.P. Ravn, and H. Rischel, editors. *Hybrid Systems*, vol. 736 of *Lecture Notes in Computer Science*. Springer-Verlag, New York, 1993.
28. Y.-C. Ho, editor. *Discrete Event Dynamic Systems: Analyzing Complexity and Performance in the Modern World*. IEEE Press, Piscataway, NJ, 1992.
29. J.E. Hopcroft and J.D. Ullman. *Introduction to Automata Theory, Languages, and Computation*. Addison-Wesley, Reading, 1979.
30. A.N. Kolmogorov and S.V. Fomin. *Introductory Real Analysis*. Prentice-Hall, Englewood Cliffs, NJ, 1970.
31. L.R. Marino. General theory of metastable operation. *IEEE Trans. on Computers*, 30(2):107–115, 1981.
32. G. Meyer. Design of flight vehicle management systems. In *Proc. IEEE Conf. Decision and Control*, Lake Buena Vista, FL, December 1994. Plenary Lecture.
33. A. Nerode and W. Kohn. Models for hybrid systems: Automata, topologies, stability. In [27], pp. 317–356.
34. L. Padulo and M.A. Arbib. *System Theory; A Unified State-Space Approach to Continuous and Discrete Systems*. W. B. Saunders, Philadelphia, 1974.
35. S.M. Ross. *Applied Probability Models with Optimization Applications*. Dover, New York, 1992.
36. K.S. Sibirsky. *Introduction to Topological Dynamics*. Noordhoff International Publishing, Leyden, The Netherlands, 1975. Translated by Leo F. Boron.
37. E.D. Sontag. *Mathematical Control Theory: Deterministic Finite Dimensional Systems*, vol. 6 of *Texts in Applied Mathematics*. Springer-Verlag, New York, 1990.
38. G. Stein. Personal communication. March 1992.
39. L. Tavernini. Differential automata and their discrete simulators. *Nonlinear Analysis, Theory, Methods, and Applications*, 11(6):665–683, 1987.
40. S. Ward and R. Halstead. *Computation Structures*. MIT Press, Cambridge, 1989.
41. H.S. Witsenhausen. A class of hybrid-state continuous-time dynamic systems. *IEEE Trans. Automatic Control*, 11(2):161–167, 1966.

The Residue of Model Reduction

Thomas I. Seidman

Department of Mathematics and Statistics, University of Maryland Baltimore County, Baltimore, MD 21228, USA e-mail: ⟨seidman@math.umbc.edu⟩.

1. Our intention is to explore some possibly overlooked consequences of the classical observation *"Natura in operationibus non facit saltus,"* — which we take to mean that

- *Any apparent discontinuity occurring in the real world is actually a continuous process having 'fine structure' on a more rapid time scale*

(perhaps omitting quantum mechanics). The significance of this observation for hybrid systems is that the nominal description involving discontinuity is merely a convenient approximation at the relevant time scale which involves the (unmodelled?) neglect of dynamics on any faster time scales — whose details are then necessarily lost in the process of model reduction. We will argue that some residue of these details must be retained to understand, in certain contexts, what will actually occur when these hybrid strategies are to be implemented in the real world.

For example, at a familiar level we think of the thermostat in an electric heater as simply switching the element on or off discontinuously, but it is certainly possible to 'open the box' and consider in more detail, if desirable, the moderately complicated internal operation of the thermostatic switch itself — or, for that matter, similarly to ask about the 'switching transient' involved in current flow to the heater element, rise time for its heating, etc.

From this point of view, the nominal description of the situation is a 'reduced order model', very much in the sense of the 'outer solution' of singular perturbation theory. Since the transitions between discrete values of logical variables are essential to the nature of hybrid systems, we might expect some likelihood that these considerations could become relevant for hybrid systems in appropriate contexts. In particular, we concentrate our attention in this note to the setting of 'chattering modes', for which switching is intentionally frequent so it is plausible to anticipate significant cumulative effects of the individually negligible switching transients, etc. As we shall see, there is then some possibility of (perhaps unpleasant) surprises if these are ignored.

The key to our analysis is the consideration of *time scales*. Suppose we are faced with a situation in which, on the 'natural' time scale, we have frequent switching between several available elementary modes

$$\dot{\xi} = F_1 \qquad \text{or} \qquad \dot{\xi} = F_2 \qquad \text{or} \qquad \ldots \tag{1}$$

(These are, of course, vector ODEs in some relevant state space $\mathcal{X}$.) We will refer to the composite zig-zag dynamics as a *chattering mode* and we seek a simplified (averaged) description, called the *sliding mode*, which provides an acceptable approximation for the chattering mode. It is even more likely that the simplified sliding mode represents the 'intention' under consideration at the level of control design and it is the chattering mode which is to be considered as an (implementable) acceptable approximation (cf., e.g., [9] or [5]) at the natural (design) time scale.

2. An easy analysis shows that in the case of rapid switching, solutions of (1) can be well approximated by considering

$$\dot{\xi} = \hat{F} := \Sigma_j \alpha_j F_j \tag{2}$$

where the coefficients α_j of this convex combination are the (local) *fractions of time spent* in each of the modes of (1) — provided there is some intermediate time scale for which these fractions are suitably definable yet short enough to take each F_j as approximately constant. Our point is that this relation of (2) to (1) necessarily comes from some specific *implementation.* If — e.g., as in [5] — the chattering mode would be explicitly constructed to provide explicitly specified time fractions α_j, then this relation is clear. In realistic cases such an (open loop) explicit construction may well be a burden and the control design may provide for an *implicit* determination (closed loop) of the switching times and so of the coefficients. All the usual arguments for the preference of closed loop over open loop control design applies to this point.

It is specifically in these situations that there are possible traps for the unwary in the determination of the correct sliding mode (2) to provide an acceptable approximation of reality — or, conversely, how one might design an implicit control structure providing an appropriate chattering mode.

The simplest analysis corresponds to a bimodal control specification:

$$(\mathbf{C0}) \qquad \begin{cases} \text{IF } x > 0, & \text{THEN: } \dot{\xi} = [u_1, v_1] \\ \text{ELSE (IF } x > 0\text{), THEN: } & \dot{\xi} = [u_2, v_2] \end{cases}$$

where we assume $u_1 < 0 < u_2$ and have written $\xi = [x, z] \in \mathcal{X}$ so x is one 'coordinate' (with z complementary in $\mathcal{X}$) or, more generally, is a sensor value. The surface $x = 0$ is the switching surface and we alternate between these modes — giving (1) with $F_j = [u_j, v_j]$. The 'inwardness condition' $u_1 < 0 < u_2$ ensures that we must zigzag across $x = 0$ so, as averaged in (2), we must have $x \equiv 0$ so $\dot{x} = 0$, requiring $\alpha_1 u_1 + \alpha_2 u_2 = 0$: in this situation the sliding mode is uniquely determined from **(C0)** with no further analysis needed.

At this point we note, as a warning, anecdotal evidence [6] that possible 'traps' may arise: a real apparatus was constructed corresponding to a 'control law' of the form **(C0)** with scalar z (2-dimensional dynamics) in which v_1, v_2 had the same sign yet the physically observed motion along $x = 0$ went paradoxically in the opposite direction.

To see how such an apparent paradox might occur and might be explained by details of the implementation which were neglected in the apparently complete description above, we consider a more complicated situation involving four (constant) fields in $\mathcal{X} = \mathbb{R}^3$:

$$F_1 \equiv \begin{bmatrix} -2 \\ -1 \\ 5 \end{bmatrix}, \qquad F_2 \equiv \begin{bmatrix} 1 \\ -2 \\ -4 \end{bmatrix}, qquad F_3 \equiv \begin{bmatrix} 2 \\ 1 \\ 5 \end{bmatrix}, \qquad F_4 \equiv \begin{bmatrix} -1 \\ 2 \\ -4 \end{bmatrix}.$$

Our control intention is to move along the z-axis ($x = y = 0$) in the positive direction. To this end we employ the control specification:

$$\textbf{(C1)} \quad \begin{cases} \text{IF } x > 0, \text{ THEN:} & \textbf{(C2)} \begin{cases} \text{IF } y > 0, \text{ THEN:} & \dot{\xi} = F_1 \\ \text{IF } y < 0, \text{ THEN:} & \dot{\xi} = F_4 \end{cases} \\ \text{ELSE } (x < 0): & \textbf{(C3)} \begin{cases} \text{IF } y > 0, \text{ THEN:} & \dot{\xi} = F_2 \\ \text{IF } y < 0, \text{ THEN:} & \dot{\xi} = F_3 \end{cases} \end{cases}$$

We can apply the same analysis as for **(C0)** to simplify **(C2)** and **(C3)** to obtain sliding modes in the plane $y = 0$, noting that we arrive at this plane for each of the alternatives ($x > 0$, $x < 0$). For $x > 0$, the condition that the y-component of the sliding mode must vanish implies coefficients $\alpha_1 = 2/3$, $\alpha_4 = 1/3$ for the convex combination of F_1, F_4 and we obtain similarly the coefficients $\alpha_2 = 1/3$, $\alpha_3 = 2/3$ for the convex combination of F_2, F_3 when $x < 0$. Thus we have the sliding modes

$$\hat{F}_2 = \begin{bmatrix} -5/3 \\ 0 \\ 2 \end{bmatrix}, \qquad \hat{F}_3 = \begin{bmatrix} 5/3 \\ 0 \\ 2 \end{bmatrix},$$

respectively, for these alternatives. Inserting these sliding modes in **(C1)** , we obtain the simplified control specification in the plane $y = 0$:

$$\textbf{(C1')} \quad \begin{cases} \text{IF } x > 0, \text{ THEN:} & \textbf{(C2')} \ \dot{\xi} \approx \hat{F}_2 \\ \text{ELSE } (x < 0): & \textbf{(C3')} \ \dot{\xi} \approx \hat{F}_3 \end{cases}$$

In this case a repetition of the same analysis now requires that the x-component of the convex combination of $\hat{F}_2$, $\hat{F}_3$ should vanish, giving coefficients $\hat{a}_2 = \hat{a}_3 = 1/2$. The resulting sliding mode gives the desired motion along the z-axis with velocity $+2$. So far, so good.

At this point we note that the control specification:

$$\textbf{(C4)} \quad \begin{cases} \text{IF } y > 0, \text{ THEN:} & \textbf{(C5)} \ \dot{\xi} = \{F_1 \text{ IF } x > 0; \text{ELSE } F_2\} \\ \text{ELSE } (y < 0): & \textbf{(C6)} \ \dot{\xi} = \{F_4 \text{ IF } x > 0; \text{ELSE } F_3\} \end{cases}$$

is logically equivalent to **(C1)** — each says, in a slightly different way, that one is to use F_j when in the jth quadrant of the x, y-plane. Now. however, applying the same method of analysis[1] to **(C4)** as was previously applied to **(C1)** now gives the sliding modes

$$\hat{F}_6 = \begin{bmatrix} 0 \\ -5/3 \\ -1 \end{bmatrix}, \qquad \hat{F}_6 = \begin{bmatrix} 0 \\ 5/3 \\ -1 \end{bmatrix},$$

in the plane $x = 0$ for $y > 0$ and $y < 0$, respectively, to give the simplified control specification in the plane $x = 0$:

$$(\mathbf{C4'}) \quad \begin{cases} \text{IF } y > 0, \text{ THEN}: & (\mathbf{C5'}) \ \dot{\xi} \approx \hat{F}_5 \\ \text{ELSE } (y < 0): & (\mathbf{C6'}) \ \dot{\xi} \approx \hat{F}_6 \end{cases}$$

and so to imply a resulting motion along the z-axis with velocity -1, i.e., in the direction opposite to what had been obtained earlier. If the sliding mode computed as for **(C1)** were in fact correct (so the motion actually occurring had $v = 2$ along the z-axis), then **(C4')** would present a paradoxical behavior within the plane $y = 0$, much as for the 'experimental' situation of [6].

3. Our principal concern in this section will be the resolution of the different results associated with **(C1)** and **(C4)** despite the apparent logical equivalence. The real understanding of **(C0)** — and so of **(C1)** and **(C4)** — comes from a somewhat more detailed consideration of the actual implementation which, for such a control specification as: "IF $x > 0$, THEN $\dot{\xi} = F_1$," would involve both a *sensor* X, tracking x and an *actuator* A producing F_1.

At this point we re-emphasize the intended significance of the sliding mode as providing a more easily computable formulation which is expected to provide a realistic approximation of satisfactory accuracy to 'what would, in fact, occur' when the control program is implemented in the real world or, conversely if one begins with an sliding mode at the design stage, the responsibility to ensure that the implementation will (approximately) produce what is intended when the ambiguities inherent in the discussion above show that this may not be 'automatic'.

Even apart from consideration of possible time sampling and/or quantization effects for X, the simplest version of the switching process, as implemented, will still have some delay δ_1' in the actual sensing of the state condition: if $x = 0$ at time t_0, then the controller will actually have the established state $(x > 0)$ at a time $t_1 = t_0 + \delta_1'$ (with $x = \varepsilon_1' > 0$) at which the actuator A is nominally set to F_1. One will then have some switching transient for the actuator corresponding to an evolution $(t = t_1 + \tau)$

$$\dot{\xi} = F_{21}^{*}(\tau) \qquad (0 < \tau < \delta_1'') \tag{3}$$

[1] It is also interesting to note that the plane $x = 2y$ is invariant if one uses only F_1 and F_3 and, again switching at $x = y = 0$, the analysis then gives motion along the z-axis with velocity $+5$.

with $F^*_{21} = F_2$ at $\tau = 0$ and $F^*_{21} \approx F_1$ after the further delay δ''_1; in a multimodal setting the switching transient and δ''_1 will obviously depend on the mode from which one is switching. Thus, $\delta_{21} = \delta'_1 + \delta''_1$ represents the time scale for switching from F_2 to F_1, etc.

Provided[2] δ'_1, δ'_2 are taken so $\delta''_j \ll \delta'_j$ (making (1) a plausible approximation), we see that the total period Δ_{21} for which the control state is $(x > 0)$ — i.e., the interval from t_1 when this becomes the state to t^*_0 when again $x = 0$ to $t^*_1 = t^*_0 + \delta'_2$ when the state has been switched to $(x < 0)$ — and the corresponding period Δ_{12} will each be of the same order of magnitude as δ_{21}; in this case we get (2) with coefficients $[\alpha_1, \alpha_2] = [\Delta_{21}/\Delta, \Delta_{12}/\Delta]$ (here $\Delta = \Delta_{21} + \Delta_{12}$ is the total 'cycle time') as well as the approximate relation $u_1\Delta_{21} + u_2\Delta_{12} \approx 0$ — leading to the same results as for the original (less detailed) analysis but with a more refined understanding of the justifying assumptions.

For the analysis of **(C1)** we observe from our most recent discussion that the approximate reduction to **(C1')** is justifiable only if the time scales for the separate consideration of **(C2)** and **(C3)** are each quite rapid compared to the alternation between them, i.e., if $\delta_{14}, \delta_{23} \ll \hat{\delta}_{23}$ where it is not difficult to see that $\hat{\delta}_{23}$ is comparable to δ_{12}, δ_{34}. Effectively, this analysis is justifiable provided the sensor Y were extremely fast compared to the sensor X and, conversely, the analysis given for **(C4)** would be justifiable provided the sensor X were extremely fast compared to the sensor Y. These are *implementation assumptions* and it is the distinction between them which resolves the paradox; compare the discussion in [7].

In this context we may understand the title of this paper as suggesting that the actual result of implementing such a control fragment as **(C1)** is impossible without taking into account some features of the implementation, some residue of reality which must be retained in the model reduction process as providing a 'selection principle'. The nature of this 'residue' is clear when, as just indicated, there might be a 'time scale separation' for the effects of the two switching surfaces. When this simplifying assumption is inapplicable — say, if X, Y are of comparable speed then the determination of a suitable sliding mode becomes much more problematic. Some partial analysis is presented in [7], but this very much remains work-in-progress.

We also note that another type of implementation may be plausible for this nominal context of four fields used in the quadrants defined by two intersecting switching surfaces. In some applications one might plausibly have a 'blending' of the fields F_j — corresponding to a 'fuzzy logic' interpretation of the state conjunctions. This is analyzed in [1], where it is shown that there is a computable sliding mode without any restriction, as above, that there be a time scale sep-

---

[2] With no such assumption it would be perfectly possible that by $t_2 = t_1 + \delta''_1$ one would already have $x < 0$ so one would abide in eternal transiency without the nominal description (1) ever becoming even approximately true. For simplicity we assume that — as is often done in practice for related reasons — δ'_1 is artificially increased, as necessary.

aration for the sensors. We note also the analyses of **(C1)** noted in [2] for a stochastic and for a delay interpretation.

4. We conclude with an observation that, apart from the correctness of the sliding mode approximation to the hybrid dynamics, there is a cumulative effect of the switching transients (3) — more precisely, of the distinction between these and the nominal (1) — to be taken into account for, e.g., consideration of total costs for optimization. E.g., for a thermostatically controlled gas furnace these 'switching costs' include both the control effect of 'rise time' delay and the 'waste' of gas at ignition of the gas flame. Note that these are ignored in the nominal (reduced) description which treats the situation as jumping instantly to the new mode as if in steady operation. The switching costs are individually small, but one must question the justification for their total neglect in a context of frequent switching.

Let us consider, for example, a control optimization problem with a cost functional of the form

$$\mathcal{J}_0 = \int_0^\infty e^{-\lambda t}\varphi(x,u)\,dt \tag{4}$$

so φ represents running costs as a function of (continuous) state x and control u. We are thinking of a setting in which this is minimized by some x_* corresponding to a 'relaxed control' u_*, expressible in the form $\Sigma_j \alpha_j u_j$ in terms of 'accessible' modes u_j so

$$\mathcal{J}_0^* = \int_0^\infty e^{-\lambda t}\Sigma_j \alpha_j \varphi(x_*, u_j)\,dt \tag{5}$$

and, following [5], one would approximate by a chattering mode in which (with suitable proportions) one cycles through the modes $\{u_j\}$ with cycle time Δ. Note that this gives the controlled trajectory $\hat{x}$ with, approximately, $\hat{x} \approx x_* + \Delta \cdot \xi$ for an appropriate (highly oscillatory) 'perturbation function' ξ. It is not too difficult to see that the resulting perturbation of $\mathcal{J}_0$ will be quadratic: one expects this to be 0 to first order here — even if, due to the control constraints, one would not have vanishing of the first order variation of $\mathcal{J}_0$. Thus, a control specification of this nature would give

$$\mathcal{J}_0 = \mathcal{J}_0^* + a\Delta^2 \tag{6}$$

with a computable coefficient a so long as we continue to ignore the switching costs $\mathcal{J}_1$. Clearly we can minimize (6) by taking Δ to be as small as possible, consistent with feasibility.

We now consider the total cost $\mathcal{J} = \mathcal{J}_0 + \mathcal{J}_1$ — i.e., including consideration of the switching cost — with, say,

$$\mathcal{J}_1 = \sum\nolimits_\nu e^{-\lambda t_\nu}\varepsilon\psi\left(x(t_\nu); j_\nu \leftarrow j_{\nu-1}\right) \tag{7}$$

where the sum is taken over all the switching times t_ν and $\varepsilon\psi$ is the associated cost of a single mode transition. Keeping ψ as 'order of 1', we have introduced $\varepsilon \ll 1$ here to indicate that this switching cost must be small or we could not reasonably be using the kind of control strategy we are describing here. Now suppose, for convenience, we chatter with round robin rotation of J modes $(1, \ldots, J$, in cyclic order) and cycle time Δ. Taking the leading term with respect to Δ, we would then have

$$\mathcal{J}_1 \approx (\varepsilon/\Delta) \int_0^\infty e^{-\lambda t} \left[\Sigma_r \psi_r(x)\right] dt \tag{8}$$

where we have set $\psi_r(x) := \psi(x; r \leftrightarrow r-1)$. Combining this with what we obtained just above in (6), one sees that the optimal choice of the cycle time can be simply computed. The total cost now takes the form

$$\mathcal{J} = \mathcal{J}_0^* + a\Delta^2 + b\varepsilon/\Delta \tag{9}$$

and this can be minimized with respect to Δ by elementary Calculus to obtain

$$\Delta_{opt} = [C\varepsilon]^{1/3} \quad \text{with } C = \frac{1}{2a} \int_0^\infty e^{-\lambda t} \left[\Sigma_r \psi_r(x)\right] dt. \tag{10}$$

[Thus, the optimal cycling frequency is $\mathcal{O}([\text{unit switching cost}]^{-1/3})$.] Note that in [5] the parameter Δ may itself be viewed as a control variable and we have here shown how its optimization is related to the switching cost when that is to be taken into account.

References

1. J.C. Alexander and T.I. Seidman, *Sliding modes in intersecting switching surfaces*, to appear.
2. E.A. Asarin and R.N. Izmailov, *Determining the sliding speed on a discontinuity surface*, Avtomatika i Telemekhanika no. 9 (1989), pp. 43–48. (transl., Automation and Remote Control **50** (1989), pp. 1181–1185.)
3. A.F. Filippov, *Differential equations with the right-hand discontinuous on intersecting surfaces* (in Russian), Dif. Uravn. **15** (1979), pp. 1814–1823.
4. A.F. Filippov, *Differential Equations with Discontinuous Righthand Sides*, Nauka, Moscow, 1985 [*transl.* Kluwer, Dordrecht, 1988].
5. X. Ge, A. Nerode, W. Kohn, and J.B. Remmel, *Algorithms for chattering approximations to relaxed optimal controls*, preprint, 1995.
6. M.A. Krasnosel'skiĭ, personal communication, 1990.
7. T.I. Seidman, *Some limit problems for relays* in *Proc. 1st Int'l. Congress of Nonlinear Analysts*, (Tampa, 1992), to appear.
8. T.I. Seidman, *Equations with hysteretically discontinuous right hand sides*, pp. 158–162 in *Models of Hysteresis*, (A. Visintin, ed.), Longman, Harlow (1993).
9. V.I. Utkin, *Sliding Modes and their Application in Variable Structure Systems*, Mir, Moscow, 1978.

The Tool KRONOS

C. Daws * A. Olivero ** S. Tripakis * S. Yovine *

VERIMAG***
Miniparc-Zirst, Rue Lavoisier,
38330 Montbonnot St. Martin, France.

1 Introduction

KRONOS [6, 8] is a tool developed with the aim to assist the user to validate complex real-time systems. The tool checks whether a real-time system modeled by a timed automaton [4] satisfies a timing property specified by a formula of the temporal logic TCTL [3]. KRONOS implements the symbolic model-checking algorithm presented in [11], where set of states are symbolically represented by linear constraints over the clocks of the timed automaton.

In this work we present two other verification approaches we have recently implemented in KRONOS, namely forward analysis and minimization, that rely on the same symbolic representation of the state space. The emphasis is given in illustrating the interest of the two approaches rather than thoroughly presenting their technical details which can be found in [15, 7].

Forward analysis is based on the symbolic simulation of a timed automaton. By computing the set of all possible runs, starting from some given set of initial states, we can verify some interesting temporal properties on the behavior of the system, such as *reachability*, *invariance* and *bounded response*. This method turns to be in many cases more efficient than model-checking and it has the advantage that it allows error diagnosis.

Minimization consists in constructing the smallest finite quotient of the timed model with respect to a bisimulation equivalence. This method allows using timed automata not only for describing the behavior of the system but also for specifying the requirements. We can then check whether the minimal model of the system simulates or is equivalent to the one of the specification.

The paper is organized as follows. In section 2 we review timed automata. In section 3 we present the basis of symbolic forward analysis and the algorithms implemented in KRONOS, and in section 4 we apply this method for verifying the FDDI protocol [12]. In section 5 we present the minimization algorithm and in section 6 we analyze the Fischer's mutual exclusion protocol [1].

* E-mail: {Conrado.Daws,Stavros.Tripakis,Sergio.Yovine}@imag.fr. Tel: +33 76 90 96 30. Fax: +33 76 41 36 20.

** E-mail: alfredo@fing.edu.uy

*** VERIMAG is a joint laboratory of CNRS, INPG, Université Joseph Fourier, and Verilog SA, associated with IMAG.

2 Timed automata

2.1 Definition

A timed automaton is an automaton extended with a finite set of real-valued variables, called *clocks*, whose values increase uniformly with time. The timing constraints related to the system are expressed by the association of an *enabling* condition to each transition. A clock can be reset to 0 or take the value of another clock at each transition[4].

Formally, a timed automaton $\mathcal{A}$ is a tuple $\langle \mathcal{S}, \mathcal{X}, \mathcal{L}, \mathcal{E}, I \rangle$ where:

1. $\mathcal{S}$ is a finite set of *locations*.
2. $\mathcal{X}$ is a finite set of *clocks*. A *valuation* $v \in \mathcal{V}$ is a function that assigns a non-negative real-value $v(x) \in \mathsf{R}^+$ to each clock $x \in \mathcal{X}$. Let $\Psi_{\mathcal{X}}$ be the set of predicates over $\mathcal{X}$ defined as a boolean combination of atoms of the form $x \# c$ or $x - y \# c$, where $x, y \in \mathcal{X}$, $\# \in \{<, \leq, =, \geq, >\}$ and c is an integer.
3. $\mathcal{L}$ is a finite set of *labels*.
4. $\mathcal{E}$ is a finite set of *edges*. Each edge e is a tuple (s, L, ψ, ρ, s') where $s \in \mathcal{S}$ is the *source*, $s' \in \mathcal{S}$ is the *target*, $L \subseteq \mathcal{L}$ are the *labels*, $\psi \in \Psi_{\mathcal{X}}$ is the *enabling* condition, and $\rho : \mathcal{X} \to \mathcal{X} \cup \{0\}$ is an assignment. We write $v[\rho]$ for the valuation v' such that for each $x \in \mathcal{X}$, if $\rho(x) = 0$ then $v'(x) = 0$, otherwise $v'(x) = v(\rho(x))$.
5. Let $\Phi_{\mathcal{X}}$ be the set of functions $\phi : \mathcal{S} \to \Psi_{\mathcal{X}}$ mapping each location s of the automaton to a predicate ψ. The invariant of $\mathcal{A}$ is a function $I \in \Phi_{\mathcal{X}}$. We write I_s for the invariant associated with s.

2.2 Semantics

A *state* of $\mathcal{A}$ is a location and a valuation of clocks satisfying the invariant associated with the location. Let $\mathcal{Q} \subseteq \mathcal{S} \times \mathcal{V}$ be the set of states of $\mathcal{A}$, that is, all pairs (s, v) such that v satisfies I_s. When $\mathcal{A}$ is in a state $(s, v) \in \mathcal{Q}$, it can evolve either by moving through an edge that changes the location and the value of some of the clocks (*discrete transition*), or by letting time pass without changing the location (*time transition*).

Discrete transitions. Let $e = (s, L, \psi, \rho, s')$. The state (s, v) has a discrete transition to (s', v'), denoted $(s, v) \xrightarrow{L}_0 (s', v')$, if $v \in \psi$ and $v' = v[\rho]$

Time transitions. Let $t \in \mathsf{R}^+$, we define $v + t$ to be the valuation v' such that $v'(x)$ is equal to $v(x) + t$ for all $x \in \mathcal{X}$. The state $(s, v) \in \mathcal{Q}$ has a time transition to $(s, v + t)$, denoted $(s, v) \xrightarrow{\emptyset}_t (s, v + t)$, if for all $t' \leq t$, $v + t' \in I_s$.

---

[4] The usual definition of timed automata only allows resetting clocks to 0. It has been shown in [14] that assignments of clock values does not affect decidability.

3 The forward analysis

The forward analysis verification technique is based on the computation of the symbolic runs from a given set of symbolic states. We give to the runs the structure of an oriented graph, called the *simulation graph*. Every symbolic state that appears in one or more of the runs corresponds to a single node of the graph and the simulation steps correspond to its arcs.

3.1 Symbolic runs

A *symbolic state* of the timed automaton $\mathcal{A}$ is a pair $\langle s, \psi \rangle$ where $s \in \mathcal{S}$ and $\psi \in \Psi_{\mathcal{X}}$ is a constraint such that $\emptyset \subset \psi \subseteq I_s$. The symbolic state $\langle s, \psi \rangle$ represents the set of states $(s, v) \in \mathcal{Q}$ such that $v \in \psi$. We denote $\Sigma_{\mathcal{A}}$ the set of symbolic states of $\mathcal{A}$. Let us expand the notions of discrete transition and time transition to symbolic states:

Symbolic discrete step. The discrete successor of $\langle s, \psi \rangle \in \Sigma_{\mathcal{A}}$ through the edge $e = (s, L, \psi_e, \rho, s')$ is the symbolic state $\langle s', \mathbf{post}_e(\psi) \rangle$ where $v \in \mathbf{post}_e(\psi)$ iff $\exists v' \in \psi \wedge \psi_e . v = v'[\rho]$. That is, the symbolic state representing the states that can be reached from some state of $\langle s, \psi \rangle$ by taking e.

Symbolic time step. The time successor of $\langle s, \psi \rangle \in \Sigma_{\mathcal{A}}$ constrained by $\psi' \in \Psi_{\mathcal{X}}$ is the symbolic state $\langle s, \mathbf{post}_t^s[\psi'](\psi) \rangle$ such that $v \in \mathbf{post}_t^s[\psi'](\psi)$ iff $\exists t \geq 0, v' \in \psi$ such that $v = v' + t$ and $\forall t'. 0 \leq t' \leq t, v' + t' \in I_s \wedge \psi'$. That is, the symbolic state representing the states that can be reached by letting time pass from a state of $\langle s, \psi \rangle$ ensuring that ψ' continuously holds.

A *symbolic run* π of $\mathcal{A}$ starting from $\langle s, \psi \rangle \in \Sigma_{\mathcal{A}}$ and constrained by $\phi \in \Phi_{\mathcal{X}}$ is a sequence of symbolic states $\pi = \langle s_0, \psi_0 \rangle e_1 \langle s_1, \psi_1 \rangle e_2 \ldots e_i \langle s_i, \psi_i \rangle \ldots$ such that $\langle s_0, \psi_0 \rangle = \langle s, \mathbf{post}_t^s[\phi_s](\psi) \rangle$ and $\forall i \geq 1, \langle s_i, \psi_i \rangle = \langle s_i, \mathbf{post}_t^{s_i}[\phi_{s_i}](\mathbf{post}_{e_i}(\psi_{i-1})) \rangle$.

3.2 Simulation graph

The simulation graph corresponding to $\mathcal{A} = \langle \mathcal{S}, \mathcal{X}, \mathcal{L}, \mathcal{E}, I \rangle$ computed from $\mathcal{S}_I \subseteq \Sigma_{\mathcal{A}}$ and constrained by $\phi \in \Phi_{\mathcal{X}}$, is the graph $\mathcal{SG}_{\mathcal{A}}(\mathcal{S}_I, \phi) = \langle \mathcal{S}_I, \mathcal{S}_S, \mathcal{E}_S \rangle$ where the set of nodes $\mathcal{S}_S \subseteq \Sigma_{\mathcal{A}}$ and the set of edges $\mathcal{E}_S \subseteq \mathcal{S}_S \times \mathcal{E} \times \mathcal{S}_S$ are the smallest sets such that:

1. **init:** $\mathcal{S}_I \subseteq \mathcal{S}_S$ is the set of initial states.
2. **iter:** For every $\langle s, \psi \rangle \in \mathcal{S}_S$ and $e \in \mathcal{E}$ an edge with source in s and target in s', if $\psi' = \mathbf{post}_t^{s'}[\phi_{s'}](\mathbf{post}_e(\psi))$ is not empty, then $\langle s', \psi' \rangle \in \mathcal{S}_S$ and $\langle \langle s, \psi \rangle, e, \langle s', \psi' \rangle \rangle \in \mathcal{E}_S$.

3.3 Verification

Given a timed automaton $\mathcal{A}$ we consider three verification problems that can be solved by applying the forward analysis: the *reachability*, the *invariance* and the *bounded response* problems.

Reachability: The reachability problem consists in finding if there is a run of the system, starting from a state $q \in \mathcal{Q}$ satisfying I, such that Q can be reached in a time $t \# c$, and for which P holds continuously before Q is reached (where $\mathsf{I}, \mathsf{P}, \mathsf{Q} \in \Phi_{\mathcal{X}}$). This problem corresponds to checking the non-emptyness of the characteristic set of the TCTL formula $\mathsf{I} \wedge \mathsf{P} \exists \mathcal{U}_{\# c} \mathsf{Q}$.

Algorithmically, this is done by computing $\mathcal{SG}_{\mathcal{A}}(\mathsf{I} \wedge (\mathsf{z} = 0), \mathsf{P} \vee \mathsf{Q}')$ where $z \notin \mathcal{X}$ is an extra clock, and $\mathsf{Q}' = \mathsf{Q} \wedge (\mathsf{z} \# \mathsf{c})$. Each time a new symbolic state $\langle s, \psi \rangle$ is computed, if $\psi \cap \mathsf{Q}' \neq \emptyset$, the algorithm gives a symbolic run that validates the property.

Invariance: The invariance problem consists in finding if for all the runs starting from all states $q \in \mathcal{Q}$ satisfying I, the property Q holds for every state of the runs. This problem corresponds to checking the emptyness of the characteristic set of the TCTL formula $\neg(\mathsf{I} \Rightarrow \forall \Box \mathsf{Q})$ which is equivalent to $\mathsf{I} \wedge \mathtt{true} \exists \mathcal{U} \neg \mathsf{Q}$, that is, finding if $\neg\mathsf{Q}$ is not reachable from I.

If during the construction of $\mathcal{SG}_{\mathcal{A}}(\mathsf{I}, \mathtt{true})$ the algorithm finds a symbolic state $\langle s, \psi \rangle$ such that $\psi \cap \neg \mathsf{Q} \neq \emptyset$ then the algorithm exhibits a symbolic run that invalidates the invariance property.

Bounded response: The bounded response problem consists in finding if for every run starting from all states $q \in \mathcal{Q}$ satisfying I, there is a state of the run that satisfies Q in a time $t \leq c$ for a given $c \in \mathbb{N}$. This problem corresponds to checking the emptyness of the characteristic set of the TCTL formula $\neg(\mathsf{I} \Rightarrow \forall \Diamond_{\leq \mathsf{c}} \mathsf{Q})$ which is equivalent to $\mathsf{I} \wedge \neg \mathsf{Q} \exists \mathcal{U}_{> \mathsf{c}} \mathtt{true}$, that is, finding if there is no run where Q holds during more than c time units.

This is done by computing $\mathcal{SG}_{\mathcal{A}}(\mathsf{I} \wedge (\mathsf{z} = 0), \neg \mathsf{Q} \vee \mathsf{z} > \mathsf{c})$ where $z \notin \mathcal{X}$ is an extra clock. If a symbolic state $\langle s, \psi \rangle$ such that $\psi \cap (z > c) \neq \emptyset$ is found, then the property is not satisfied and a counter-example is provided.

4 The FDDI communication protocol

FDDI (Fiber Distributed Data Interface) [12] is a high performance fiber optic token ring Local Area Network. In this section we show the verification of the temporal mechanism that limits the possession time of the token by each station.

4.1 Protocol Description

We consider a network composed by N identical stations $S_1, \ldots, S_N$ and a ring, where the stations can communicate by *synchronous* messages with high priority and *asynchronous* messages with low priority.

Station. Each station S_i can be either waiting for the token ($\mathtt{Idle}_i$), in possession of the token and executing the synchronous transmission ($\mathtt{T}_i$, $\mathtt{ST}_i$) or in possession of the token and executing the asynchronous transmission ($\mathtt{T}_i$, $\mathtt{AT}_i$).

The two clocks a station uses to control the possession time of the token are called TRT_i (Token Rotation Timer) and THT_i (Token Holding Timer).

- TRT_i counts the time since the last reception of the token by the station. This clock is reset to zero each time the station S_i takes the token.
- THT_i counts the time since the last reception of the token, added to the time elapsed since the precedent one, given by the value of the clock TRT_i just before it is re-initialized.

When the station S_i receives the token (action $\texttt{TT}_i$), the clock THT_i takes the value of the clock TRT_i. TRT_i is reset to zero, and the station S_i starts sending synchronous messages ($\texttt{BS}_i$). The duration of the synchronous transmission ($\texttt{ST}_i$) is given, for each station S_i, by a constant SA_i (Synchronous Allocation).

When the synchronous transmission ends (action $\texttt{ES}_i$), the station has the possibility of starting the transmission of asynchronous messages (action $\texttt{BA}_i$) if the current value of THT_i minus the time of synchronous transmission SA_i is greater than a global constant of the system called $TTRT$ (Target Token Rotation Timer). Before $THT_i - SA_i$ reaches the value $TTRT$, the station must release the token ($\texttt{RT}_i$), ending the asynchronous transmission ($\texttt{EA}_i$) if this one has began. The behavior of the station S_i is described by the timed automaton **Station**$_i$ of the Figure 1(a).

Ring. The ring controls the transmission of the token between two consecutive stations S_i and S_{i+1}. There is a delay of td (Token Delay) time units, measured by the clock T, in this transmission. The Figure 1(b) shows the timed automaton **Ring** that models the ring for two stations.

System. The timed automaton that models the protocol is obtained as the parallel composition $\mathbf{FDDI}_N = \mathbf{Ring} \parallel \mathbf{Station}_1 \parallel \ldots \parallel \mathbf{Station}_N$ where the automata synchronize through the actions $\texttt{TT}_i$ and $\texttt{RT}_i$.

4.2 Properties verification

We verify here two properties of the FDDI protocol.

Bounded time for accessing the ring. The time elapsed within two consecutives receptions of the token by any station is bounded by a constant c_1. We can express this property in TCTL with the following formula:

$$(\texttt{ST}_i \wedge T = 0) \Rightarrow \forall\Diamond_{\leq c_1}\texttt{enable}(\texttt{TT}_i) \tag{1}$$

where c_1 is equal to $TTRT + 2N.SA_i$, and $\texttt{enable}(\texttt{TT}_i)$ characterizes the symbolic states where the edge labeled $\texttt{TT}_i$ is enabled.

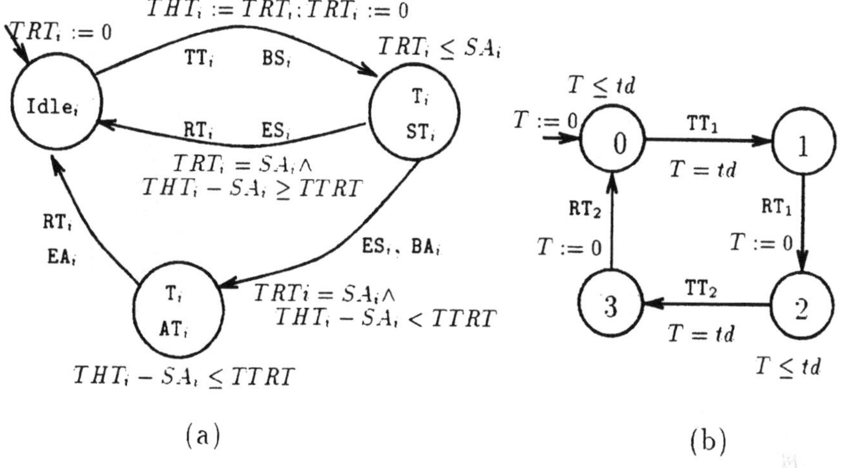

Fig. 1. Station$_i$ (a) : Ring (b)

Bounded time for sending asynchronous messages. Each idle station will send asynchronous messages before a time c_2. The formula of TCTL that describe this property is:

$$\texttt{Idle}_i \Rightarrow \forall\Diamond_{\leq c_2}\texttt{AT}_i \tag{2}$$

where c_2 is equal to $(N-1).TTRT + 2N.SA_i$.

Table 1 shows the results of the verification of properties (1) and (2), for different numbers of stations, applying symbolic model-checking (*backward* analysis) and symbolic simulation (*forward* analysis). We show the size of the timed automaton, the running times in seconds (*time*), the number of iterations for model-checking (*iter*) and the number of symbolic states generated for simulation (*symb*).

5 Minimization

We briefly present in this section the main ideas of the algorithm developed in [15] which is an adaptation of the minimal model generation algorithm given in [5]. In the next section we show that testing our algorithm on the Fischer's mutual exclusion protocol reveals more efficient than the minimization algorithm developed in [2].

automaton				*formula*	*backward*		*forward*		*eval*
#*sta*	#*loc*	#*arcs*	#*clocks*		*time*	*iter*	*time*	*symb*	
3	19	25	7	(1)	0.50	9	0.15	20	true
				(2)	25	29	6	1018	true
4	25	33	9	(1)	2.50	12	0.30	44	true
				(2)	3680	47	66	5522	true
5	31	41	11	(1)	10	15	1.20	92	true
				(2)	⊥	⊥	507	25532	true
6	37	49	13	(1)	61	18	3.50	188	true
7	43	57	15	(1)	435	21	10	380	true
8	49	65	17	(1)	3670	24	28	764	true
9	55	73	19	(1)	32917	27	73	1532	true
10	61	81	21	(1)	⊥	⊥	187	3068	true
11	67	89	23	(1)	⊥	⊥	483	6140	true
12	73	97	25	(1)	⊥	⊥	1123	12284	true

Table 1. Running times for different numbers of stations of the protocol FDDI with $TRTT = 50.N$, $SA_i = 20$ and $td = 0$.

5.1 Symbolic predecessors

Given a timed automaton $\mathcal{A}$, we define the notions of both discrete and time predecessors of a symbolic state as follows.

Symbolic discrete predecessor. The discrete predecessor of $\langle s', \psi' \rangle \in \Sigma_{\mathcal{A}}$ through the edge $e = (s, L, \psi_e, \rho, s')$ is the symbolic state $\langle s, \mathtt{pre}_e(\psi') \rangle$ where $v \in \mathtt{pre}_e(\psi')$ iff $v \in \psi_e$ and $v[\rho] \in \psi'$.

Symbolic time predecessor. The time predecessor of $\langle s, \psi \rangle \in \Sigma_{\mathcal{A}}$ constrained by $\psi' \in \Psi_X$ is the symbolic state $\langle s, \mathtt{pre}_t^s[\psi'](\psi) \rangle$ such that: $v \in \mathtt{pre}_t^s[\psi'](\psi)$ iff $\exists t \geq 0.\ v + t \in \psi$ and $\forall t'.0 \leq t' \leq t.\ v + t' \in I_s \wedge \psi'$.

5.2 Partitions and bisimulations

Let Π be a partition of Q such that all classes of Π are symbolic states in $\Sigma_{\mathcal{A}}$. For $\sigma, \sigma' \in \Pi$, let $\mathtt{pre}[\sigma](\sigma')$ stand for either $\sigma \cap \mathtt{pre}_e(\sigma')$ or $\mathtt{pre}_t[\sigma](\sigma')$. We define $Succs_\Pi(\sigma) = \{\sigma' \mid \mathtt{pre}[\sigma](\sigma') \neq \emptyset\}$ and $Preds_\Pi(\sigma) = \{\sigma' \mid \mathtt{pre}[\sigma'](\sigma) \neq \emptyset\}$.

A class $\sigma \in \Pi$ is *stable* if for all $\sigma' \in \Pi$, $\mathtt{pre}[\sigma](\sigma') \in \{\sigma, \emptyset\}$, that is, either no state in σ has a discrete (resp. time) transition to a state in σ', or for all states in σ there exists a discrete (resp. time) successor in σ'. The partition Π is a *bisimulation* if every symbolic state $\sigma \in \Pi$ is stable.

5.3 Minimization algorithm

Given an initial partition Π_{init}, and a set I of initial symbolic states, our goal is to compute the coarsest bisimulation Π which is finer than Π_{init} containing only those classes which are reachable from I. Π is computed by the following algorithm.

```
Π := Π_init ; Γ := {B ∈ Π_init | B ∩ I ≠ ∅} ; Δ := ∅ ;
while (∃B ∈ Γ \ Δ) do {
  C_B := Split(B, Π) ;                                              (1)
  if (C_B = {B}) then {                                             (2)
    Δ := Δ ∪ {B} ; Γ := Γ ∪ Succs^l_Π(B) ;                          (3)
  } else {                                                          (4)
    Γ := Γ \ {B} ; Π := (Π \ {B}) ∪ C_B ; Δ := Δ \ Preds^l_Π(B) ;   (5)
    if B ∩ I ≠ ∅ then   Γ := Γ ∪ {C ∈ C_B, | C ∩ I ≠ ∅} ;
} }
```

where Γ is the set of classes accessible from I and $\Delta \subseteq \Gamma$ is the set of stable accessible classes.

The function $Split(B, \Pi)$ refines the class B with respect to the current partition (1), by choosing a class $C \in \Pi$. If B is found to be stable with respect to Π, that is, $Split(B, \Pi) = \{B\}$ (2), the all successors of B are inserted to the set of accessible classes (3), since B is accessible. If B is not stable (4), $Split(B, \Pi) = \{B_1, B_2\}$, where $B_1 = \mathtt{pre}[B](C)$, $B_2 = B \cap \overline{B_1}$, and all its predecessors become unstable (5).

6 Fischer's mutual–exclusion protocol

We describe and verify here the Fischer's mutual exclusion protocol [1]. The system is made up of n timed automata $P_1, \ldots, P_n$, where P_i models the behavior of process i, along with automaton X, modeling the global variable which regulates access to the critical section (see figure 2). Δ is an upper bound on the time necessary for P_i to set X to i, after verifying that X equals 0 ; δ is a lower bound on the time that P_i has to wait before re-testing X and entering its critical section, if the value of X has not changed in the meanwhile.

Observing the behavior of the system. One expects that a correct mutual–exclusion protocol should behave as the abstract graph shown in figure 3(a). We would like to check whether this ideal model is indeed equivalent to the minimal one. Since the latter also contains irrelevant actions, such as "try_i", "setXi", as well as timed transitions, we proceed as follows : (1) we compute the minimal model of $(||P_i)||X$ using the adapted minimization algorithm described in the previous section ; (2) we then replace all labels different from "enter_i" and "setX0i" by

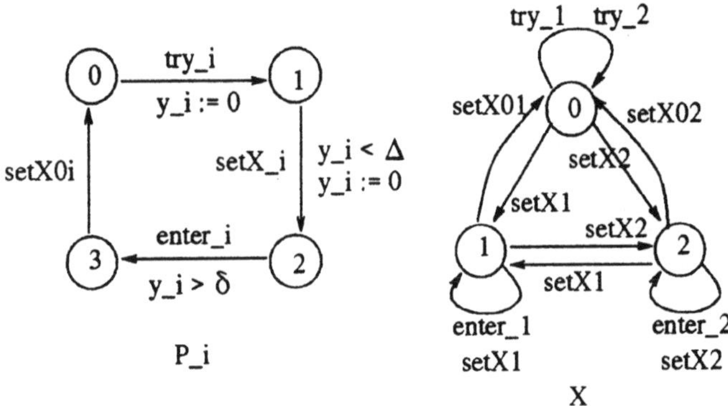

Fig. 2. Fischer's mutual-exclusion protocol specification with TA

the label τ; and (3) we further reduce the resulting graph with respect to the τ^*a bisimulation ($\approx_{\tau^*a}$), using the tool Aldebaran [9].

Performance results [5] are shown in table 2. G_{min} denotes the minimal model, and G_{τ^*a} its reduction with respect to $\approx_{\tau^*a}$. For each n, two versions of the protocol are tested : a correct one, for $\Delta = 5, \delta = 12$ (first line in the table), and an erroneous, for $\Delta = 5, \delta = 4$ (second line, marked with (*)). Figure 3(b) depicts G_{τ^*a} for $n = 2$, in the correct case [6]. It is easy to see that this graph is not equivalent to the ideal one in fig. 3(a). The reason is that the version of Fischer's protocol we have used so far permits the *starvation* of a process at control-state 2, if another process manages to get first into its critical section.

Avoiding starvation. To remedy the problem of starvation, we add an arc from state 2 to state 1, in the TA of P_i, as shown in figure 4(a). Then, we proceed as in steps (1),(2),(3) above and we find that the minimal model, for the correct case, is indeed equivalent to the ideal one in fig. 3(a). Results appear in table 3.

Comparison. The same example has been treated in [2] by minimizing a smaller TA, namely $(||P_i)||X||$Monitor, where the automaton Monitor (figure 4(b)) captures the violation of mutual exclusion, by entering an error state. Verification consists in ensuring that the minimal model contains no error state. Performance results of the two algorithms [7] are shown in table 4.

[5] We use a Sparc 10 with 128 Mbytes of main memory. $\perp$ denotes non-termination. We show only the time taken for minimization. The reduction with respect to $\approx_{\tau^*a}$ takes negligible time, except in the case marked †, where aldebaran needs 23 secs.

[6] This figure has been produced by bcg_draw [10], a tool for displaying graphs, included in the Aldebaran package.

[7] [2] have used a DEC-5100 with 40 Mbytes of main memory.

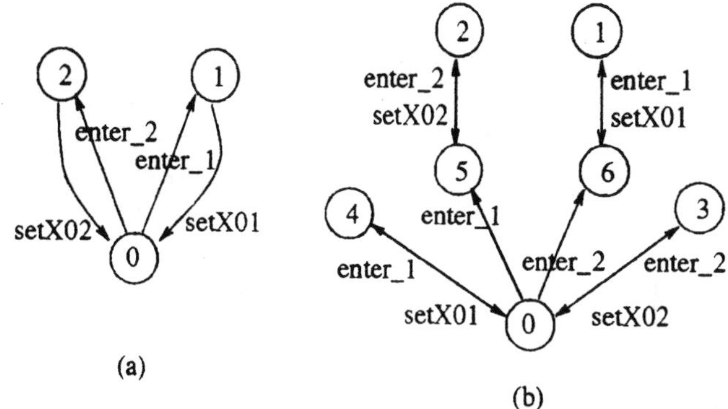

Fig. 3. Ideal mutual-exclusion (a) : Model allowing starvation (b)

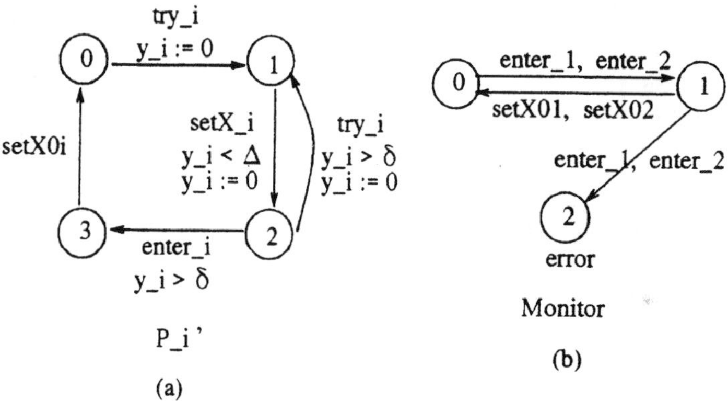

Fig. 4. Process avoiding starvation (a) ; Monitor(b)

n	composite TA		G_{min}		G_{τ^*a}		time
	states	arcs	states	trans.	states	trans.	(secs)
2	28	44	22	26	7	10	0
(*)			57	113	16	48	0
3	152	324	77	108	19	39	0.3
(*)			651	2.002	104	804	2.9
4	752	2.016	252	420	47	140	2.9
(*)			10.163	43.392	724	15,036	322 †
5	3,552	11.440	807	1.590	111	485	31.3
(*)			⊥	⊥			⊥

Table 2. Fischer's protocol : minimization of $(\|P_i)\|X$

n	composite TA		G_{min}		$G_{\tau^* a}$		time
	states	arcs	states	trans.	states	trans.	(secs)
2	28	48	22	30	3	4	0
3	152	360	77	132	4	6	0
4	752	2.240	252	524	5	8	2
5	3.552	12.640	807	1.990	6	10	24

Table 3. Fischer's protocol : minimization of $(\|P_i')\|X$ (no starvation)

n	composite TA		G_{min}		$G_{\tau^* a}$		time (secs)	
	states	arcs	states	trans.	states	trans.		[2]
2	24	34	22	26	7	10	0	1
(*)			47	85	12	27	0	3
3	119	213	77	108	19	39	0.2	8
(*)			402	1.117	47	205	1.5	887
4	548	1.164	252	420	47	140	2.1	192
(*)			4.437	17.902	174	1.333	40.4	$\perp$
5	2.402	5.850	807	1.590	111	485	16.3	not tested
(*)			$\perp$	$\perp$			$\perp$	not tested

Table 4. Fischer's protocol : minimization of $(\|P_i)\|X\|$Monitor

7 Conclusion

Both approaches presented in this paper considerably improve KRONOS performance and functionalities [8].

Forward analysis permits handling examples with a large number of clocks, as the example of the FDDI protocol shows : up to 25 clocks, which, to our knowledge, exceeds the clock–space dimension of similar examples treated in the literature. Moreover, this method is capable of providing a counter–example sequence, as a diagnosis in the case a system fails to verify an invariance or bounded response property.

Minimization considerably reduces the number of states and transitions of large systems, as the example of Fischer's protocol illustrates. It also allows for further analysis, using standard techniques for untimed systems, such as comparison and reduction with respect to behavioral equivalences. The combination of timed and untimed minimization allowed us to discover the problem of starvation in the first version of the mutual–exclusion protocol.

[8] For information on how to obtain the tool, please contact the authors.

We stress the fact that Fischer's protocol has been analyzed many times, using other real–time verification tools, in particular in [2, 13]. None of these two analyses, however, deals with starvation, while the versions of the protocol used are simpler.

Finally, both forward analysis and minimization prove helpful not only for verification but also for revealing intrinsic problems of modelization, thus giving better insight to the system analyzed.

References

1. M. Abadi and L. Lamport. An old-fashioned recipe for real-time. In *Proc. REX Workshop "Real-Time: Theory in Practice"*. LNCS 600, Springer-Verlag.
2. A. Alur, C. Courcoubetis, D. Dill, N. Halbwachs, and H. Wong-Toi. An implementation of three algorithms for timing verification based on automata emptiness. In *Proc. 13th IEEE RTSS*. IEEE Computer Society Press, 1992.
3. R. Alur, C. Courcoubetis, and D.L. Dill. Model checking in dense real time. *Information and Computation*, 104(1):2–34, 1993.
4. R. Alur and D.L. Dill. A theory of timed automata. *Theoretical Computer Science*, 126:183–235, 1994.
5. A. Bouajjani, J.C. Fernandez, N. Halbwachs, P. Raymond, and C. Ratel. Minimal state graph generation. *Science of Computer Programming*, 18:247–269, 1992.
6. C. Daws, A. Olivero, and S. Yovine. Verifying ET-LOTOS programs with KRONOS. In *Proc. FORTE'94*, pages 227–242, Bern, Switzerland, October 1994.
7. C. Daws and S. Yovine. Symbolic forward analysis of timed automata. Tech. Report Spectre 95-16, Verimag, Grenoble, November 1995.
8. C. Daws and S. Yovine. Two examples of verification of multirate timed automata with KRONOS. In *Proc. 1995 IEEE RTSS'95*, Pisa, Italy, December 1995. IEEE Computer Society Press.
9. J.Cl. Fernandez and L. Mounier. A tool set for deciding behavioural equivalences. In *CONCUR'91. Concurrency theory*. LNCS 527, Springer Verlag, August 1991.
10. H. Garavel, R. Mateescu, R. Ruffiot, and L.-P. Tock. Binary coded graphs — reference manuals of the bcg tools. Tech. Report Spectre 95-13, Verimag, Grenoble, October 1995.
11. T.A. Henzinger, X. Nicollin, J. Sifakis, and S. Yovine. Symbolic model checking for real-time systems. *Information and Computation*, 111(2):193–244, 1994.
12. R. Jain. *FDDI handbook: high-speed networking using fiber and other media*. Addison-Wesley, 1994.
13. K. G. Larsen, P. Petterson, and Y. Wang. Compositional and symbolic model-checking of real-time systems. In *Proc. 1995 IEEE RTSS'95*, Pisa, Italy, December 1995. IEEE Computer Society Press.
14. A. Olivero. Modélisation et analyse de systèmes temporisés et hybrides. Thèse, Institut National Polytechnique de Grenoble, Grenoble, France, September 1994.
15. S. Tripakis and S. Yovine. Analysis of timed systems based on time–abstracting bisimulations. Tech. Report Spectre 95-15, Verimag, Grenoble, November 1995.

Timing Analysis in COSPAN

Rajeev Alur and Robert P. Kurshan

AT&T Bell Laboratories, Murray Hill

Abstract. We describe how to model and verify real-time systems using the formal verification tool COSPAN. The verifier supports automata-theoretic verification of coordinating processes with timing constraints. We discuss different heuristics, and our experiences with the tool for certain benchmark problems appearing in the verification literature.

1 Introduction

Model checking is a method of automatically verifying concurrent systems in which a finite-state model of a system is compared with a correctness requirement. This method has been shown to be very effective in detecting errors in high-level designs, and has been implemented in various tools. We consider the tool COSPAN that is based on the theory of ω-automata (ω-automata are finite automata accepting infinite sequences, see [Tho90] for a survey, and [VW86, Kur94] for applications to verification). The system to be verified is modeled as a collection of coordinating processes described in the language S/R [Kur94]. The semantics of such a model M is the ω-language $L(M)$ corresponding to the infinite executions of the model. The property to be checked is described as another process T whose acceptance conditions classify the executions of M in "good" and "bad," and all the good behaviors are removed from the language. The model M satisfies the property T if the language of the product of M and T is empty. The language-emptiness test can be performed algorithmically. The verifier supports a variety of alternatives for performing this test including on-the-fly enumerative search and symbolic search using binary decision diagrams (BDDs) (see [McM93] for applications of BDDs to verification). In this paper, we describe the extension of COSPAN to model and verify real-time systems.

In recent years, model-checking methods based on finite-state machines have been extended to real-time and hybrid systems [AD94, ACD93, HNSY94, ACH+95]. In S/R, real-time constraints are expressed by associating lower and upper bounds on the time spent by a process in a local state. An execution is timing-consistent if its steps can be assigned real-valued time-stamps that satisfy all the specified bounds. The semantics of a timed S/R model M with a table B of bounds is, then, the set $L(M, B)$ of its timing-consistent executions. The timing verification problem corresponds to checking emptiness of the language $L(M \otimes T, B)$ for a suitably chosen process T. A variety of correctness requirements such as invariants, absense of deadlocks, liveness, and bounded response, can be modeled in this way. The expressiveness of timed S/R is the same as that of timed automata [AD94]. While we do not support a direct modeling of hybrid systems, verification of hybrid systems can sometimes be reduced to, or approximated by, verification of timed automata (see, for instance, [PV95]).

For checking emptiness of the language $L(M, B)$, the verifier automatically constructs another automaton A_B, also as a S/R process, which when composed with the original model, rules out behaviors that do not satisfy the timing constraints: $L(M \otimes A_B)$ equals $L(M, B)$. The existence of such a finite-state constraining automaton A_B follows from the so-called region construction for timed automata [AD94]. Our implementation augments the region construction with a variety of heuristics. The states of the constraining automaton correspond to sets of values for timers, and may be either regions or convex unions of regions called zones. Zones can be defined by difference-bound-matrices [BD91, Dil89], and are used in many other tools for timing verification such as KRONOS [DOY94], VERITI [Won94], ORBITS [Rok93], and UPPAAL [LPY95]. Once the definition of the constraining automaton has been generated, the original COSPAN verifier can be used as a black-box, and the actual search can be done either enumeratively or symbolically using BDDs. All these choices are coupled with an iterative solution which involves generating successive approximations to the constraining automaton (the theory underlying this approximation method is described in an earlier paper [AIKY95], which also reports an earlier implementation of timing verification in COSPAN. The current implementation with its combination of heuristics is typically one or two orders of magnitude faster than the one reported in [AIKY95]). Furthermore, the underlying continuous semantics of time can be approximated, in a conservative way, by the integers, and this also provides a heuristic simplification of the timing analysis (approximation of the dense semantics by the fictitious-clock semantics has been studied earlier, for instance, in [Bur89, HMP92]).

We describe our experiences with the tool for certain benchmark problems appearing in the verification literature. These include timing-based distributed protocols, embedded controllers, and timed circuits. The iterative option is sometimes effective in synthesizing requirements on the parameter values for a timed system to satisfy its specification. The search using zones is less sensitive to the constants in the bounds, and can analyze complex timing constraints. On the other hand, symbolic search using BDDs and regions can sometimes handle state-spaces that are a few orders of magnitudes larger.

2 Modeling

We give a brief and informal introduction to the relevant features of the S/R modeling language (see [Kur94] for a detailed and formal description).

2.1 Selection-Resolution Model

An S/R model M consists of a collection of coordinating components called *processes*. Each process has two variables: a *state* variable and a *selection* (or output) variable. We use $P.\$$ to denote the state variable of P and $P.\#$ to denote the selection variable of P. A state of P is a value of its state variable, and a selection of P is a value of its selection variable. A *global state* consists of states of all the processes and a *global selection* consists of selections of all the processes.

The declaration of a process P contains the type declaration of $P.\$$ and $P.\#$, a set of possible initial values for $P.\$$, and update commands for $P.\$$ and $P.\#$ specifying the transition relation. The update command for $P.\#$ specifies the set of possible selections as a function of the state of P and selections of some other processes. The update command for $P.\$$ specifies the set of possible next states as a function of the current state of P and the current global selection.

The execution of an S/R model proceeds in rounds. In the round 0, initial values of all the state variables are chosen. This is followed by an alternation of *selection* and *resolution* phases. Consider a round i such that the global state for the round i is determined. The selection of each process for round i is chosen in the selection phase. The selection of P in round i may depend on, apart from its state, selections of other processes in round i. The dependencies among the selection variables are required to be acyclic, and the S/R compiler determines a total order for the update of selection variables. In the following resolution phase, the global state for round $i+1$ is determined. The state of P in round $i+1$ depends upon its state in round i and the global selection for round i. We assume that the model is *complete*, that is, there is at least one choice for the new global state, and the execution can continue forever.

Thus, an execution of the model M produces an infinite *chain* r of the form $s_0 \xrightarrow{\sigma_0} s_1 \xrightarrow{\sigma_1} s_2 \xrightarrow{\sigma_2} \cdots$ of global states s_i and global selections σ_i. The acceptance conditions are used to rule out uninteresting runs. The S/R model allows two types of acceptance conditions, namely, *cycle-sets* and *recur-edges* [1]. If a set C of states of P is declared to be a cyset, then the chain r is removed (or excepted) if the state of P eventually always stays inside C. A local transition of P is a pair of its states. If a set E of local transitions of P is declared to be a *recur-condition*, then the chain r is removed if some transition in E repeats infinitely often. With the model M, we associate the set $L(M)$ consisting of all the chains that are not excepted by any of the cyset or recur declarations.

As an example, consider Figure 1 that describes a simple model of a train communicating with a gate. Each state is labeled with the set of selections possible from that state, and edges are labeled with predicates over selections. Observe that when ST selects *enter*, its state is updated to *near*, and simultaneously, the state of SG is updated to *closed*. The cyset specifies that any infinite chain in which ST stays forever in the state *inside* or *near* is excepted.

2.2 Asynchrony

While the S/R model is synchronous, asynchrony can be modeled using nondeterminism. Intuitively, whenever an asynchronous process changes its state, it waits a nondeterministic number of rounds before proceeding. Every asynchronous process P has an additional state variable called *the pause-bit*, denoted

[1] Processes with these two types of acceptance conditions are called L-processes, and are studied in [Kur94].

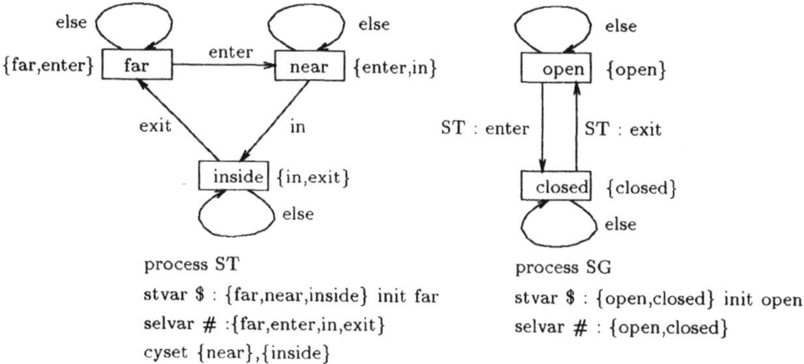

Fig. 1. Synchronous train-gate

P.pbit. The state of *P* is described by the value of both *P*.$ and *P.pbit*. The process *P* is said to be *pausing* when its *pbit* is set to true. For a value *v* of *P*.$, a reference to *v*@ indicates that the value of *P*.$ is *v* and *P.pbit* is true. The selection of *P* depends only on its state. For every value *v* of *P*.$, a unique selection is specified corresponding to the case when the *pbit* is true, and a set of selections is specified corresponding to the case when the *pbit* is false. Whenever the value of *P*.$ changes, the *pbit* is set to true. Every pausing state *v*@ is required to have a self-loop corresponding to the intuition that the pausing states capture delays. There is an implicit nondeterministic transition that changes the *pbit* to false.

The asynchronous mode of S/R is best understood by an example. Figure 2 shows the modified model of the train and the gate. The asynchronous process AG has 4 states: *AG*.$ can be *closed* or *open*, and *AG.pbit* may be true or false. When *AG*.$ is *open* its selection is *up* if the *pbit* is set, and *open* otherwise. The selection *wait* models the delay in opening the gate. Initially, *AG*.$ is *open* with its *pbit* false. When the selection of AT is *enter*, *AG*.$ changes to *closed*, and the *pbit* is set to true. The state of AG stays *closed*@ for a nondeterministic number of rounds, and then the *pbit* changes to false nondeterministically. Now the selection is *closed*, and the process awaits AT to select *exit*. The cyset *closed*@ models the assumption that the *pbit* is unset after a finite number of rounds. The asynchronous process AT is interpreted similarly.

A global state *s* of an asynchronous model *M* is said to be *stable* if it is possible that every asynchronous process does not change its state in the next resolution phase. For instance, a global state with the *pbit*s of all the asynchronous processes set to true, is stable. In Figure 2, if the *pbit* of AT is false, then the state is unstable. In the S/R semantics for asynchronous processes, time is spent only in stable states, and unstable states are assumed to be instantaneous. Along a chain in $L(M)$, it is required that every instantaneous state is followed by a stable state. If the transition structure forces two instantaneous states to follow each other, a stability failure is reported.

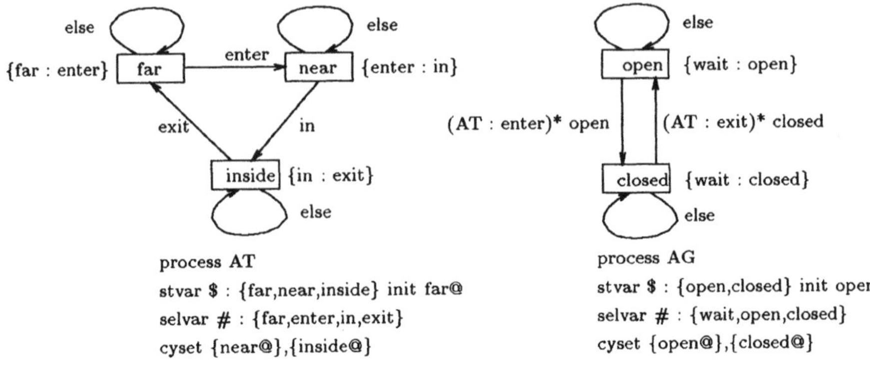

Fig. 2. Asynchronous train-gate

2.3 Timing

Timing is added to an asynchronous model M by specifying bounds on the time spent in the pausing states of individual processes. A *bounds-table* B for M consists of two functions *lb* and *ub*: the function *lb* maps each value v of $P.\$$, for an asynchronous process P, to a nonnegative integer, and the function *ub* maps each value v of $P.\$$ to a nonnegative integer or to ∞. The two functions *lb* and *ub* specify the lower and the upper bounds, respectively, on the time spent in each pausing state. A sample bounds-table for the asynchronous model of Figure 2 is shown in Figure 3. A *timed* S/R model consists of an asynchronous S/R model together with a bounds-table.

Consider a chain r consisting of global states s_i and global selections σ_i. Consider an asynchronous process P. If $P.pbit$ is set in state s_0, then P begins a pause at step 0. Consider $i > 0$.

- The process P *begins* a pause at step i if (1) the state of P in s_i is a pausing state $v@$, and (2) the state of P in s_{i-1} is not $v@$.
- The process P *ends* a pause at step i if (1) $P.\$$ is the same in both s_{i-1} and s_i, (2) $P.pbit$ is true in s_{i-1}, and (3) $P.pbit$ is false in s_i.
- The process P aborts a pause at step i if (1) the state of P in s_{i-1} is a pausing state $v@$, and (2) $P.\$$ is not v in state s_i.

The step i of the chain r is instantaneous iff some process ends a pause at step i and some process begins a pause at step $i+1$. The asynchronous semantics of S/R ensures that if the step i is instantaneous, then the step $i+1$ is not instantaneous. A *timing assignment* for the chain r is a sequence $t_0, t_1, \ldots$ of real-valued time-stamps such that for every step i, if the step i is instantaneous then $t_{i+1} = t_i$ else $t_{i+1} > t_i$.

The timing assignment $t_0, t_1, \ldots$ for the chain r of an asynchronous model M is said to be *consistent* with the bounds-table B if it satisfies the constraints imposed by B:

State Variable	Value	Lower bound	Upper Bound
AT.$	*far*	10	∞
AT.$	*near*	5	6
AT.$	*inside*	1	1
AG.$	*open*	1	2
AG.$	*closed*	1	2

Fig. 3. A sample bounds-table

- The duration of each pause does not exceed its upper bound: Suppose a process P begins a pause at step i with state $v@$. Then for every index $j > i$ such that P has not ended or aborted the pause at all steps $i < k < j$, the difference $t_j - t_i$ is at most $ub(v)$.
- Each pause can end only after the lower bound has elapsed: Suppose a process P begins a pause at step i with state $v@$, and ends the pause at step j without an end or abort at all steps $i < k < j$. Then the difference $t_j - t_i$ is at least $lb(v)$.

The chain r of an asynchronous model M is said to be *timing consistent* with the bounds-table B if it has a timing assignment consistent with B. The set of all chains of M that are timing consistent with B is the language of the timed model, and is denoted $L(M, B)$. Observe that $L(M, B)$ is a subset of $L(M)$.

Timed automata [AD94] offer an alternative way of introducing time in finite-state machines. It is straightforward to show that a timed S/R model can be translated to a timed automaton that uses one clock variable for every asynchronous process of the S/R model. Conversely, every timed automaton with k clocks can be translated to an S/R model with one process synchronously communicating with k asynchronous timed processes. Thus, timed automata and timed S/R are expressively equivalent formalisms to model real-time systems.

3 Verification

The verifier COSPAN checks whether the language of an S/R model is empty. Given a model M, if the language $L(M)$ is nonempty, COSPAN outputs a chain in $L(M)$, called the *error-track*. The error-track is a periodic chain that consists of a prefix followed by a cycle – called the *post-martem track*:

$$s_0 \xrightarrow{\sigma_0} s_1 \xrightarrow{\sigma_1} s_2 \xrightarrow{\sigma_2} \cdots s_m \xrightarrow{\sigma_m} (u_0 \xrightarrow{\nu_0} u_1 \xrightarrow{\nu_1} u_2 \xrightarrow{\nu_2} \cdots u_k \xrightarrow{\nu_k} u_0)^\omega$$

Since all processes are finite-state, the language $L(M)$ is ω-regular, and whenever the language $L(M)$ is nonempty, an error-track of the above form exists.

The test for emptiness is performed by searching through the reachable state-space of the model. COSPAN allows two types of search: an on-the-fly enumerative search, and a symbolic BDD-based search.

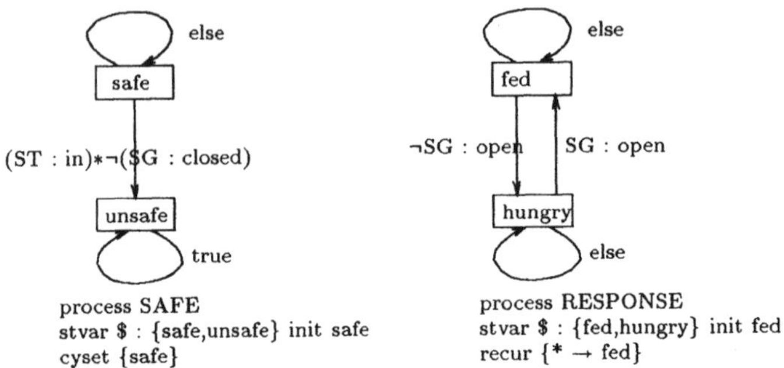

Fig. 4. Properties of train-gate

3.1 Checking Correctness

To check a property of an S/R model M, we add another process T, called *task*, to the model. The update of $T.\$$ depends upon the global selection of M. The behavior of the processes in the model M does not depend upon the task process, but the transition relation of the task process depends upon the behavior of M. The acceptance conditions of T specify which chains should be removed from the language. Formally, adding the task process T to the model M corresponds to the product operation (i.e. language intersection), and the restricted model is denoted $M \otimes T$. We have the language inclusion property: $L(M \otimes T) \subseteq L(M)$. The task is written so that the chains in $L(M \otimes T)$ correspond to undesirable behaviors. The model M satisfies the task T if the language $L(M \otimes T)$ is empty.

As an example, consider the tasks of Figure 4. The process SAFE specifies the requirement that the gate should be closed when the train is inside the gate. If the gate is not selecting *closed* when the train selects *in*, the state of SAFE is updated to *unsafe*. In the chains where this condition never holds, SAFE.$ is always *safe*, and is removed from the language. Given the model $ST \otimes SG$ and the task SAFE, the verifier correctly concludes that the resulting language is empty. The process SAFE can be used as a specification for the asynchronous train-gate model also (in Figure 4, the references to ST and SG need to replaced with AT and AG, respectively).

The task RESPONSE specifies the progress property that requires that the selection of the gate is *open* infinitely often (this implies that a closed gate eventually opens). The acceptance condition is specified using *recur* declaration; every chain that contains infinitely many transitions to the state *fed* is removed from the language.

3.2 Timing Verification

Recall that a timed model consisting of an asynchronous model M and a bounds-table B, specifies the language $L(M, B)$. As before, the correctness can

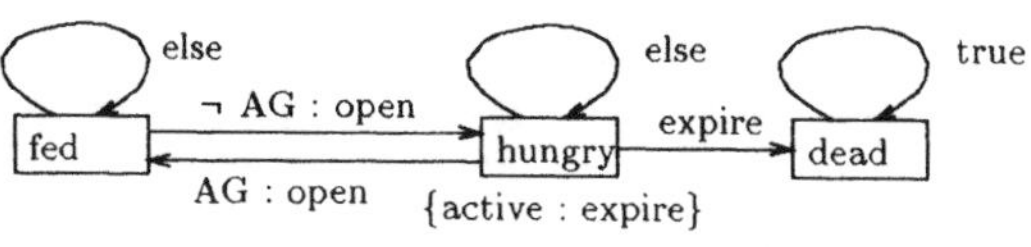


```
process TIMEDRESPONSE
stvar $ : {fed,hungry,dead} init fed
selvar # : {active, expire}
recur {* → fed}
```

Fig. 5. Real-Time Property

be specified by adding a task process T such that the chains in $L(M \otimes T, B)$ specify the undesirable behaviors. In particular, if we use the asynchronous train-gate model of Figure 2, the bounds-table of Figure 3, and the task SAFE of Figure 4, the resulting language is empty.

The task itself can be an asynchronous process, and lower and upper bounds on the states of the task can be used to check timing properties of the model. For instance, to verify that the gate always selects *open* within 10 units, use the task TIMEDRESPONSE (Figure 5) with the entry

TIMEDRESPONSE.$ hungry 10 10

added to the bounds-table of Figure 3. This is a typical real-time property requiring response within a bounded period.

Thus, the timing verification problem corresponds to checking emptiness of the timing-consistent language: given a model M and a bounds-table B, we need to check whether $L(M, B)$ is empty. Our solution is to construct another S/R process A_B, called the *constraint automaton*, such that $L(M \otimes A_B)$ equals $L(M, B)$. The S/R process A_B monitors the model M, and removes all the chains that are not timing consistent with B.

Let us consider the construction of the process A_B. The process A_B needs to ensure that the order in which the processes begin, end, and abort pauses is timing consistent. For a start, let us assume that A_B has, for every asynchronous process P, a real-valued state variable $P.timer$. Initially, $P.timer$ is 0. In every resolution phase, the process A_B chooses a real-valued increment δ denoting the time spent in the current global state. The value δ needs to satisfy the following constraints: (1) δ equals 0 if the current global state is instantaneous, and (2) for every asynchronous process P in a pausing state $v@$, adding δ to the value of $P.timer$ does not exceed the upper bound $ub(v)$. After choosing δ, the value of $P.timer$ is incremented by δ for every pausing process P. If P is ending a pause at state v, then the updated value of $P.timer$ should be at least $lb(v)$, if not, the resulting chain is removed from the language. Whenever P aborts its pause, or ends its pause, $P.timer$ is reset to 0.

This scheme involves real-valued state variables. If there are n asynchronous processes, then the state of A_B is a point in the n-dimensional space. Let c be the largest constant appearing in the bounds-table. Then, it suffices to consider only those points all of whose coordinates lie within $[0, c]$, this gives a bounded

n-dimensional cube. To obtain a finite-state process, such points need to be clustered together. The current implementation in COSPAN supports the following two clustering constructions:

- *Region Automaton* R_B: Two points in the cube belong to the same *region* iff they agree on the ordering of the fractional parts of the timer values and the integer parts of the timer values. The number of regions is finite, and the partitioning of the space in regions gives the so-called *time-abstract bisimulation*. Details about the theory of regions can be found in [AD94]. The states of the region automaton R_B correspond to these regions. Each region is described by n variables ranging over $0..c$ representing the integer parts of the timer values and n variables ranging over $0..n$ that represent ordering of the fractional parts.
- *Zone Automaton* Z_B: The states of the zone automaton correspond to convex unions of regions. Each such zone is described by a set of linear inequalities; each inequality gives a bound on a timer value or a bound on the difference between values of two timers. Such a set of linear inequalities is best represented by the so-called *difference-bounds-matrix* [Dil89]. The zone automaton Z_B has $n(n+1)$ integer variables ranging over $-c..c$ representing the differences, and has $n(n+1)$ boolean variables that represent whether the corresponding bound gives a strict or a nonstrict inequality.

Both Z_B and R_B are constraint automata, that is, $L(M, B) = L(M \otimes R_B) = L(M \otimes Z_B)$. It should be noted that, while the number of states of a constraint automaton grows exponentially with the bounds-table, the size of its definition is polynomial in the size of B. The actual states of the constraint automaton are constructed only on-the-fly, in conjunction with the exploration of M.

3.3 Approximations

Since checking emptiness of $L(M, B)$ is computationally expensive —PSPACE-complete—, we support the following two approximations.

Successive Approximations
The state-spaces of R_B or Z_B depend on the number of timed asynchronous processes and the constants in the bounds-table. Furthermore, not all the constraints in B may be relevant to proving the property. This suggests that the constraints should be added to B in an incremental fashion. In the successive approximation scheme, we wish to construct a sequence of approximations $B_0, B_1 \ldots$ such that

approximation: for each i, $L(M, B_i)$ is a superset of $L(M, B)$,
monotonicity: For each i, $L(M, B_{i+1})$ is a subset of $L(M, B_i)$, and
convergence: $L(M, B_i)$ converges to $L(M, B)$ as i increases.

The scheme is useful only if the constraint automata for the approximations B_i are simpler than the constraint automaton for B. To construct these approximations, observe that for two bounds-tables B and B', (1) if there exists a constant c such that each bound in B is c times the corresponding bound in B', then $L(M, B)$ and $L(M, B')$ are identical, and (2) if each lower bound in B is at least the corresponding lower bound in B', and each upper bound in B is at most the corresponding upper bound in B', then $L(M, B')$ is a superset of $L(M, B)$. This suggests that we can simplify a bounds-table by decreasing lower bounds, increasing upper bounds, and dividing by common factors.

As a first approximation B_0, our algorithm sets all lower bounds to 0 and all upper bounds to ∞. Thus, $L(M, B_0)$ equals $L(M)$. If $L(M, B_0)$ is empty then so is $L(M, B)$. If not, an error-track r is reported. If r is in $L(M, B)$ then it is reported as an error-track, else the next approximation B_1 is constructed so that r is inconsistent with B_1 (this ensures that B_1 is more restrictive than B_0). To construct B_1, the original B is simplified as much as possible preserving the inconsistency of r. This is done in a heuristic manner as described in [AIKY95]. Alternative schemes of approximations for timing verification are studied in [Won94] and [BS92].

Fictitious-Clock Approximation

The semantics of asynchronous S/R models requires that nonzero amount of time is spent in stable states. Let us relax this assumption: a *fictitious-clock timing assignment* for a chain r of an asynchronous model M is a sequence $t_0, t_1, \ldots$ of real-valued time-stamps such that $t_i \leq t_{i+1}$. Note that every timing assignment for r is also a fictitious-clock timing assignment. The chain r is said to be *fictitious-clock-timing-consistent* with the bounds-table B if it has a fictitious-clock timing assignment consistent with B, and let $L^f(M, B)$ denote the set of all such chains. The following two facts hold:

1. the set $L^f(M, B)$ is a superset of $L(M, B)$ and a subset of $L(M)$, and
2. if a chain r is fictitious-clock-timing-consistent then there is a fictitious-clock timing assignment $t_0, t_1, \ldots$ consistent with B such that all t_i's are integers.

The first fact says that proving emptiness of $L^f(M, B)$ implies emptiness of $L(M, B)$, and the second fact says that to check fictitious-clock-timing-consistency, it suffices to consider only integer valued time-stamps. The integer-valued time-stamps can be viewed as readings of a fictitious global discrete clock that is incremented at regular intervals; all events between successive increments of this clock get the same time-stamp (such models are studied in [AH94, HMP92]).

This gives the following scheme to check emptiness of $L(M, B)$. The first step is to check if $L^f(M, B)$ is empty. If so then so is $L(M, B)$, else let r be a periodic error-track in $L^f(M, B)$. If r is in $L(M, B)$ then r can be reported as an error-track, else check if $L(M, B)$ is empty by generating R_B or Z_B. Let us consider checking emptiness of $L^f(M, B)$. We construct an S/R process A^f_B such that $L(M \otimes A^f_B)$ equals $L^f(M, B)$. Since we can assume all time-stamps are integer valued, the region automaton R_B can be simplified to R^f_B. A state of R^f_B is a lattice point, and the variables encoding the ordering of fractional parts are not needed. Similarly, the zone automaton Z^f_B is simpler than Z_B since all inequalities can be assumed to be nonstrict.

The above scheme also requires checking whether a periodic error track is in $L(M, B)$. An algorithm for this purpose is described in [AIKY95], and its complexity is strongly polynomial.

4 Examples

We have used COSPAN on various benchmark examples for timing verification appearing in the literature. The performance of different heuristics varies depending on the choice of the example. Following observations hold in most cases.

1. There is no clear choice between region and zone automata. Typically, zone automaton leads to a smaller number of states, and is less sensitive to the actual magnitudes of constants. The BDD representation of the region automaton is smaller than that of the zone automaton. We use zone automata with enumerative search, or region automata with BDD-based search.
2. In most benchmark examples, fictitious-clock model suffices to prove or disprove language emptiness.
3. Iterative option is useful in understanding the behavior of the system being verified by identifying the bounds that are relevant in proving the property.

Space does not permit us a detailed description of the examples, a few are listed below.

Timed mutual exclusion: Many papers on timing verification have used Fischer's protocol for mutual exclusion to illustrate their approach. As the number of processes grows, the number of reachable states grows exponentially, and effectiveness of BDDs becomes apparent. For verifying the mutual exclusion property for 10 processes using the fictitious-clock region automaton, the number of reachable states is 6×10^{10}, and BDD-based search with regions requires 12 cpu minutes and 24 MB memory (other combinations run out of memory). For the timing-based protocol for fast mutual exclusion (see [AIKY95]), the given model has 3 timed processes, each with 11 pausing states, and the untimed S/R model has 125000 reachable states. When we run our iterative scheme, termination is obtained after 13 iterations of the fictitious-clock model with zone automata (the last iteration is the slowest, and takes about a minute). Out of the original 33 pausing states, the final bounds-table specifies simplified bounds only on 15 state; indeed the simplified bounds correspond to the tightest bounds required to prove the property.

Timed Circuits: A simple application of the tool is to analyze timing diagrams, and this is potentially useful as an industrial application. An interesting example for timing verification is the Seitz timed queue element (see [Bur89] or [Rok93] for details of this example).

Robot Controller: In [PV95], a model of a simple manufacturing plant is considered, and the authors show how to construct a timed automaton from the original description involving differential inclusions. In the COSPAN-model, both enumerative search wih zones or BDD-based search using regions work effectively.

References

[ACD93] R. Alur, C. Courcoubetis, and D.L. Dill. Model-checking in dense real-time. *Information and Computation*, 104(1):2–34, 1993.

[ACH+95] R. Alur, C. Courcoubetis, T. Henzinger, P. Ho, X. Nicollin, A. Olivero, J. Sifakis, and S. Yovine. The algorithmic analysis of hybrid systems. *Theoretical Computer Science*, 138:3–34, 1995.

[AD94] R. Alur and D.L. Dill. A theory of timed automata. *Theoretical Computer Science*, 126:183–235, 1994.

[AH94] R. Alur and T.A. Henzinger. A really temporal logic. *Journal of the ACM*, 41(1):181–204, 1994.

[AIKY95] R. Alur, A. Itai, R.P. Kurshan, and M. Yannakakis. Timing verification by successive approximation. *Information and Computation*, 118(1):142–157, 1995.

[BD91] B. Berthomieu and M. Diaz. Modeling and verification of time-dependent systems using time Petri nets. *IEEE Transactions on Software Engineering*, SE-17(3):259–273, 1991.

[BS92] F. Balarin and A. Sangiovanni-Vincentelli. A verification strategy for timing-constrained systems. In *Proceedings of the Fourth Workshop on Computer-Aided Verification*, LNCS 663, pages 151–163. Springer-Verlag, 1992.

[Bur89] J.R. Burch. Combining CTL, trace theory and timing models. In *Automatic Verification Methods for Finite State Systems: Proceedings of the First CAV*, LNCS 407, pages 197–212. Springer-Verlag, 1989.

[Dil89] D.L. Dill. Timing assumptions and verification of finite-state concurrent systems. In J. Sifakis, editor, *Automatic Verification Methods for Finite State Systems*, LNCS 407, pages 197–212. Springer–Verlag, 1989.

[DOY94] C. Daws, A. Olivero, and S. Yovine. Verifying ET-LOTOS programs with KRONOS. In *Formal Description Techniques VII, Proceedings of FORTE'94*, pages 227–242, 1994.

[HMP92] T.A. Henzinger, Z. Manna, and A. Pnueli. What good are digital clocks? In *ICALP 92: Automata, Languages, and Programming*, LNCS 623, pages 545–558. Springer-Verlag, 1992.

[HNSY94] T.A. Henzinger, X. Nicollin, J. Sifakis, and S. Yovine. Symbolic model-checking for real-time systems. *Information and Computation*, 111(2):193–244, 1994.

[Kur94] R.P. Kurshan. *Computer-aided Verification of Coordinating Processes: the automata-theoretic approach.* Princeton University Press, 1994.

[LPY95] K. Larsen, P. Pettersson, and W. Yi. Compositional and symbolic model-checking of real-time systems. In *Proceedings of the 16th IEEE Real-Time Systems Symposium*, 1995.

[McM93] K. McMillan. *Symbolic model checking: an approach to the state explosion problem.* Kluwer Academic Publishers, 1993.

[PV95] A. Puri and P. Varaiya. Verification of hybrid systems using abstractions. In *Hybrid Systems II*, LNCS 999. Springer-Verlag, 1995.

[Rok93] T. Rokicki. *Representing and modeling digital circuits.* PhD thesis, Stanford University, 1993.

[Tho90] W. Thomas. Automata on infinite objects. In J. van Leeuwen, editor, *Handbook of Theoretical Computer Science*, volume B, pages 133–191. Elsevier Science Publishers, 1990.

[VW86] M.Y. Vardi and P. Wolper. An automata-theoretic approach to automatic program verification. In *Proceedings of the First IEEE Symposium on Logic in Computer Science*, pages 332–344, 1986.

[Won94] H. Wong-Toi. *Symbolic approximations for verifying real-time systems.* PhD thesis, Stanford University, 1994.

UPPAAL — a Tool Suite for Automatic Verification of Real–Time Systems *

Johan Bengtsson[2] *Kim Larsen*[1]
Fredrik Larsson[2] *Paul Pettersson*[2] *Wang Yi*[**2]

[1] BRICS*** , Aalborg University, DENMARK
[2] Department of Computer Systems, Uppsala University, SWEDEN

Abstract. UPPAAL is a tool suite for automatic verification of safety and bounded liveness properties of real-time systems modeled as networks of timed automata. It includes: a *graphical interface* that supports graphical and textual representations of networks of timed automata, and automatic transformation from graphical representations to textual format, a *compiler* that transforms a certain class of linear hybrid systems to networks of timed automata, and a *model–checker* which is implemented based on constraint–solving techniques. UPPAAL also supports diagnostic model-checking providing diagnostic information in case verification of a particular real-time systems fails.
The current version of UPPAAL is available on the World Wide Web via the UPPAAL home page `http://www.docs.uu.se/docs/rtmv/uppaal`.

1 Introduction

UPPAAL is a new tool suite for automatic verification of safety and bounded liveness properties of networks of timed automata [13, 8, 6]. The tool was developed during the spring of 1995 as the result of intense research collaboration between BRICS at Aalborg University and Department of Computing Systems at Uppsala University. The two main design critea for UPPAAL has been *efficiency* and *ease of usage*.

The current version of UPPAAL, as well as its future extensions, is implemented in C++. Model–checking is often hampered by various state–explosion problems. In UPPAAL thes problems are dealt with by a combination of on–the–fly verification together with a new and coarser symbolic technique reducing the verification problem to that of solving simple linear constraint systems. The features and tools of UPPAAL includes:

* This work has been supported by the European Communieties (under CONCUR2 and REACT), NUTEK (Swedish Board for Technical Development) and TFR (Swedish Technical Research Council)

** This author would also like to thank the Chinese NSF and the Hong Kong Wang's Foundation for supporting a visit to the Institute of Software, Chinese Academy of Sciences, in 1995.

*** Basic Research in Computer Science, Centre of the Danish National Research Foundation.

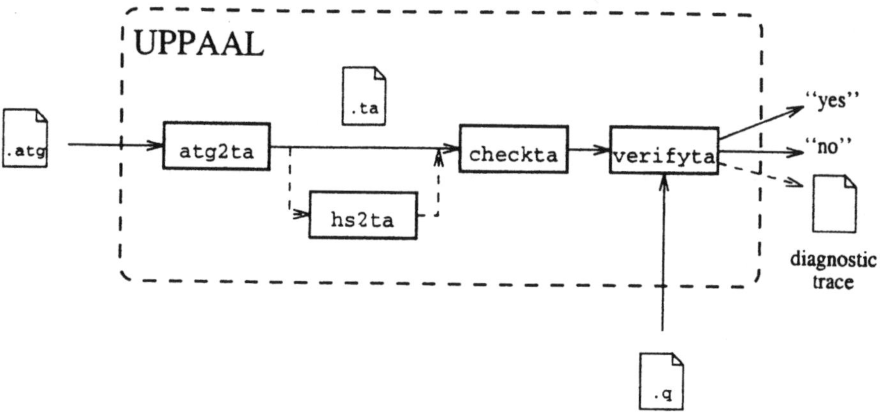

Fig. 1. Overview of UPPAAL

- A graphical interface based on Autograph.
- An automatic compilation of the graphical definition into a textual format.
- Analysis of certain types of hybrid automata by compilation into ordinary timed automata. In particular UPPAAL allows automata with varying and drifting time–speed of clocks.
- A number of simple, but in practice extremely useful syntactical checks are made before verification can commence.
- Generation of diagnostic traces in case verification of a particular real–time system fails.

In this paper we present the various features of UPPAAL, review and provide pointers to the theoretical foundation as well as applications to various case–studies.

2 An Overview of UPPAAL

UPPAAL consists of a suite of tools for verifying safety properties of real-time system. An overview of the system is shown in Figure 1. In this section we briefly describe the main features of UPPAAL.

2.1 Graphical Description of Networks of Timed Automata

It is possible to draw networks of timed automata using Autograph, given that certain syntactical rules are followed, e.g. the different automata in the network must be enclosed in boxes with the name of the process in the structural label, there must be a textual box describing the system configuration, i.e. declaration of clocks, channels and auxiliary integer variables. To be able

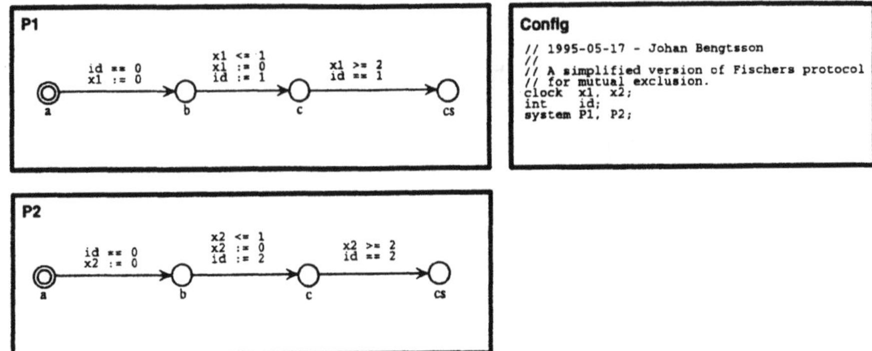

Fig. 2. Graphical Description of Fischers Mutual Exclusion Protocol

to import system descriptions, drawn with help of Autograph, into UPPAAL the system must be saved in the Autograph `.atg`-format. In Figure 2 the Autograph version of Fischers Protocol [1, 10] is shown.

2.2 Textual Description of Networks of Timed Automata

In addition, UPPAAL allows networks of timed automata to be described using a textual format (called `.ta`) providing a basic *programming language for timed automata*. In certain cases we found this textual format more convenient (and faster) to work with than the graphical interface. The compiler `atg2ta` automatically transforms system description in the graphical `.atg`–format into the textual `.ta`–format, thus supporting the important principle WYSIWYV[4]. Figure 3 shows the resulting `.ta`–format for Fischers Protocol from Figure 2.

2.3 Linear Hybrid Systems

Under certain conditions, the model of timed automata may be generalized to allow clocks with rates varying between a lower and an upper bound, and to allow clock rates to change between different control-nodes (vertices) [9]. This extension of timed automata is useful for modelling of hybrid systems where the behaviour of the system variables can be described or approximated using lower and upper bounds on their rates. Using abstraction techniques, this class of linear hybrid system can be transformed into timed automata and thus be verified using the techniques available for timed automata, implemented in UPPAAL. UPPAAL allows linear hybrid automata where the speed of clocks is given by an interval. Hybrid automata of this form may be transformed into ordinary timed automata using the translator `hs2ta`. Philips Audio-Control Protocol of [3] is one such linear hybrid system and for its Autograph version is shown in Figure 5.

[4] What You See Is What You Verify.

```
//
// Declarations
//
clock x1, x2;
int   id;

//
// Processes
//
process P1 {
   state a, b, c, cs;
   init  a;
   trans a -> b {
            guard  id == 0;
            assign x1 := 0;
         },
         b -> c {
            guard  x1 <= 1;
            assign x1 := 0, id := 1;
         },
         c -> cs {
            guard  x1 >= 2, id == 1;
         };
}
```

```
process P2 {
   state cs,c,b,a;
   init  a;
   trans c -> cs {
            guard  x2 >= 2, id == 2;
         },
         b -> c {
            guard  x2 <= 1;
            assign x2 := 0, id := 2;
         },
         a -> b {
            guard  id == 0;
            assign x2 := 0;
         };
}
```

```
//
// System Configuration
//
system P1,P2;
```

Fig. 3. Textual Description of Fischers Mutual Exclusion Protocol

2.4 Syntactical Checks

Given a textual description of a timed automata in the `.ta`-format the program `checkta` performs a number of syntactical checks. In particular the use of clocks, auxiliary integer variables and channels must be in accordance with their declaration, e.g. attempted synchronization on an undeclared channel will be captured by `checkta`.

2.5 Model–Checking

In the current version UPPAAL is able to check for reachability properties, in particular whether certain combinations of control-nodes and constraints on clocks and integer variables are reachable from an initial configuration. The desired mutual exclusion property of Fischers protocol (Figure 2 and Figure 3) falls into this class. Bounded liveness properties can be obtained by reasoning about the system in the context of testing automata. The model-checking is performed by the module `verifyta` which takes as input a network of timed automata in the `.ta`-format and a formula. `verifyta` can also be used interactively. In case verification of a particular real-time system fails (which happens more often than not), a *diagnostic trace* is automatically reported by `verifyta` [7]. Such a trace may be considered as diagnostic information of the error, useful during the subsequent debugging of the system. This principle could be called WYDVYAE[5].

3 The UPPAAL Model

In this section, we present the syntax and semantics of the model used in UPPAAL to model real–time systems. The emphasis will be put on the precise semantics of the model. For convenience, we shall use a slightly different syntax compared with UPPAAL's user interface.

We assume that a typical real–time system is a network of non–deterministic sequential processes communicating with each other over channels. In UPPAAL, we use finite–state automata extended with clock and data variables to describe processes and networks of such automata to describe real–time systems.

3.1 Syntax

Alur and Dill developed the theory of timed automata [2], as an extension of classical finite–state automata with clock variables. To have a more expressive model and to ease the modelling task, we further extend timed automata with more general types of data variables such as boolean and integer variables. Our final goal is to develop a modelling (or design) language which is as close as possible to a high–level real–time programming language. Clearly this will create problems for decidability. However, we can always require that the value domains of the data variables should be finite in order to guarantee the termination of a verification procedure. The current implementation of UPPAAL allows integer variables in addition to clock variables.

In a finite–state automaton, a transition takes the form $l \xrightarrow{\alpha} l'$ meaning that the process modelled by the automaton will perform an α–transition in state l and reach state l' in doing so. Note that there is no condition on the transition. Alur and Dill [2] extend the untimed transition to the timed version: $l \xrightarrow{g,a,\phi} l'$ where g is a simple linear constraint over the clock variables and ϕ is a set of clocks to be reset to zero. Intuitively, $l \xrightarrow{g,a,\phi} l'$ means that a process in control node l may perform the α-transition instantaneously when g is true of the current clock values and then reach control node l' with the clocks in ϕ being reset. The constraint g is called a *guard*. In UPPAAL, we allow a more general form of guard that can also be a constraint over data variables, and extend the reset–operation on clocks in timed automata to data variables.

Now assume a finite set of clock variables C ranged over by x, y, z etc and a finite set of data variables V ranged over by i, j, k etc.

Guard over Clock and Data Variables We use $G(C, V)$ to stand for the set of formulas ranged over by g, generated by the following syntax: $g ::= \; a \mid g \wedge g$,

[5] What You Don't Verify You Are Explained.

where a is a constraint in the form: $x \sim n$ or $i \sim n$ for $x \in C, i \in V, \sim \in \{\leq, \geq, =\}$ and n being a natural number. We shall call $G(C, V)$ *guards*. Note that a guard can be divided into two parts: a conjunction of constraints g_c's in the form $x \sim n$ over clock variables and a conjunction of constraints g_v's in the form $i \sim n$ over data variables. We shall use tt to stand for a guard like $x \geq 0$ which is always true, for a clock variable x as clocks can only have non-negative values. In UPPAAL's representation of automata, the guard tt is often omitted.

Reset–Operations To manipulate clock and data variables, we use reset–set in the form: $\overline{w} := \overline{e}$ which is a set of assignment–operations in the form $w := e$ where w is a clock or data variable and e is an expression. We use R to denote the set of all possible reset–operations.

The current version of UPPAAL distinguishes clock variables and data variables: a reset–operation on a clock variable should be in the form $x := n$ where n is a natural number and a reset–operation on an integer variable should be in the form: $i := c * i + c'$ where c, c' are integer constants. Note that c, c' can be negative.

Channel, Urgent Channel and Syncronization We assume that processes synchronize with each other via channels. Let A be a set of channel names and out of A, there is a subset U of urgent channels on which processes should synchronize that whenever possible. We use $\mathcal{A} = \{\alpha? | \alpha \in A\} \cup \{\alpha! | \alpha \in A\}$ to denote the set of actions that processes can perform to synchronize with each other. We use name(a) to denote the channel name of a, defined by name($\alpha?$) = name($\alpha!$) = α.

Automata with clock and data variables Now we present an extended version of timed automata with data variables and reset–operations.

DEFINITION 1. *An automaton A over actions $\mathcal{A}$, clock variables C and data variables V is a tuple $\langle N, l_0, E\rangle$ where N is a finite set of nodes (control-nodes), l_0 is the initial node, and $E \subseteq N \times G(C, V) \times \mathcal{A} \times 2^R \times N$ corresponds to the set of edges. To model urgency, we require that the guard of an edge with an urgent action should always be tt, i.e. if name(a) $\in U$ and $\langle l, g, a, r, l'\rangle \in E$ then $g \equiv$ tt. In the case, $\langle l, g, a, r, l'\rangle \in E$ we shall write, $l \xrightarrow{g,a,r} l'$ which represents a transition from the node l to the node l' with guard g (also called the enabling condition of the edge), action a to be performed and a set of reset–operations r to update the variables.* □

Concurrency and Synchronization To model networks of processes, we introduce a CCS–like parallel composition operator for automata. Assume that $A_1 ... A_n$ are automata with clocks and data variables. We use $\overline{A}$ to denote their parallel composition. The intuitive meaning of $\overline{A}$ is similar to the CCS parallel composition of $A_1 ... A_n$ with *all* actions being restricted, that is,

$$(A_1 | ... | A_n) \backslash A$$

Thus only synchronization between the components A_i is possible. We shall call $\overline{A}$ a network of automata. We simply view $\overline{A}$ as a vector and use A_i to denote its ith component.

3.2 Semantics

Informally, a process modelled by an automaton starts at node l_0 with all its clocks initialized to 0. The values of the clocks increase synchronously with time at node l. At any time, the process can change node by following an edge $l \xrightarrow{g,a,r} l'$ provided the current values of the clocks satisfy the enabling condition g. With this transition, the variables are updated by r.

Variable Assignment Now, we introduce the notion of a *variable assignment*. A variable assignment is a mapping which maps clock variables C to the non-negative reals and data variables V to integers. For a variable assignment v and a delay d, $v \oplus d$ denotes the variable assignement such that $(v \oplus d)(x) = v(x) + d$ for any clock variable x and $(v \oplus d)(i) = v(i)$ for any integer variable i. This definition of $\oplus$ reflects that all clocks operate with the same speed and that data variables are time–insensitive. For a reset-operation r (a set of assignment–operations), we use $r(v)$ to denote the variable assignment v' with $v'(w) = \text{val}(e, v)$ whenever $w := e \in r$ and $v'(w') = v(w')$ otherwise, where $\text{val}(e, v)$ denotes the value of e in v. Given a guard $g \in G(C, V)$ and a variable assignment v, $g(v)$ is a boolean value describing whether g is satisfied by v or not.

Control Vector and Configuration A *control vector* $\overline{l}$ of a network $\overline{A}$ is a vector of nodes where l_i is a node of A_i. We shall write $\overline{l}[l_i'/l_i]$ to denote the vector where the ith element l_i of $\overline{l}$ is replaced by l_i'.

A *state* of a network $\overline{A}$ is a configuration $\langle \overline{l}, v \rangle$ where $\overline{l}$ is a control vector of $\overline{A}$ and v is a variable assignment. The initial state of $\overline{A}$ is $\langle \overline{l}_0, v_0 \rangle$ where $\overline{l}_0$ is the initial control vector whose elements are the initial nodes of A_i's and v_0 is the initial variables assignment that maps all variables to 0.

Maximal Delay To model progress properties, we need a notion of maximal delay. Let $\langle l, v \rangle$ be a configuration of an automaton A. Note that A in location l may have a number of outgoing transitions with guards. The process modelled by A in state $\langle l, v \rangle$ may have to wait for the guards to become true, which enables the transitions. However, we do not want the process to stay forever in the same control–node, i.e. l; in other words, some discrete transition must be taken within a certain time bound. We require that the bound should be the maximal delay before all the guards are completely closed, that is, they will never become true again. This is formalized as follows:

DEFINITION 2. *(Maximal Delay for Automata)*

$$MD(l, v) = \max\{d \mid l \xrightarrow{g,a,r} l' \text{ and } g(v \oplus d)\} \qquad \Box$$

Note that $\max\{\} = 0$. This will be the case when all the guards for outgoing transitions in l have already been closed in state $\langle l, v\rangle$ or in other words, the process reaches a time-stop process, which means that A is physically unrealizable. Now we extend the notion of maximal delay to networks of automata, which insures that synchronization on urgent channels happens immediately.

DEFINITION 3. *(Maximal Delay for Networks of Automata)*

$$MD(\bar{l}, v) = \begin{cases} 0 & \text{if } \exists \alpha \in U, l_i, l_j \in \bar{l} : l_i \xrightarrow{\alpha?, r_i} \ \& \ l_j \xrightarrow{\alpha!, r_j} \\ \min\{MD(l, v) \mid l \in \bar{l}\} & \text{otherwise} \end{cases}$$

□

Transition Rules The semantics of a network of automata $\overline{A}$ is given in terms of a transition system with the set of states being the set of configurations and the transition relation defined as follows:

DEFINITION 4. *(Transition Rules for Networks of Automata)*

- $\langle \bar{l}, v\rangle \rightsquigarrow \langle \bar{l}[l_i'/l_i, l_j'/l_j], (r_i \cup r_j)(v)\rangle$ *if there exist* $l_i, l_j \in \bar{l}, g_i, g_j, \alpha, r_i$ *and* r_j *such that* $l_i \xrightarrow{g_i, \alpha!, r_i} l_i'$, $l_j \xrightarrow{g_j, \alpha?, r_j} l_j'$, $g_i(v)$ *and* $g_j(v)$.
- $\langle \bar{l}, v\rangle \rightsquigarrow \langle \bar{l}, v \oplus d\rangle$ *if* $d \leq MD(\bar{l}, v)$ □

4 The UPPAAL Model–Checker

In the current version, UPPAAL is able to check for reachability properties, in particular whether certain combinations of control–nodes and constraints on clock and data variables are reachable from an initial configuration.

Logic The properties that can be analysed are of the forms:

$$\varphi ::= \forall \Box \beta \mid \exists \Diamond \beta \qquad\qquad \beta ::= a \mid \beta_1 \wedge \beta_2 \mid \neg \beta$$

Where a is an atomic formula being either an atomic clock (or data) constraint (c) or a component location ($A_i$at l). Atomic clock (data) constraints are either integer bounds on individual clock (data) variables (e.g. $1 \leq x \leq 5$) or integer bounds on differences of two clock (data) variables (e.g. $3 \leq x - y \leq 7$).

Intuitively, for $\forall \Box \beta$ to be satisfied all reachable states must satisfy β. Dually, for $\exists \Diamond \beta$ to be satisfied some reachable state must satisfy β. Formally let $\rightsquigarrow$ denote the transitive closure of the delay– and action–transition relations between network configurations. Then the satisfaction relation $\models$ between network configurations and formulas are defined as follows:

$$\langle \bar{l}, v\rangle \models \exists \Diamond \beta \iff \exists \langle \bar{l}', v'\rangle . \langle \bar{l}, v\rangle \rightsquigarrow \langle \bar{l}', v'\rangle \wedge \langle \bar{l}', v'\rangle \models \beta$$
$$\langle \bar{l}, v\rangle \models \forall \Box \beta \iff \forall \langle \bar{l}', v'\rangle . \langle \bar{l}, v\rangle \rightsquigarrow \langle \bar{l}', v'\rangle \Rightarrow \langle \bar{l}', v'\rangle \models \beta$$

Satisfaction with respect to a boolean combination β of atomic formulas is defined inductively on the structure of β (behaving as usual with respect to the boolean connectives). Satisfaction with respect to an atomic formula is given by the following definitions:

$$\langle \bar{l}, v\rangle \models c \Leftrightarrow v \in c$$
$$\langle \bar{l}, v\rangle \models A_i \mathsf{at}\ l \Leftrightarrow l_i = l$$

Our (simple and efficient) model–checking technique extends to the logic presented in [7], which also allows for bounded liveness properties to be specified. Currently, bounded liveness properties are obtained by reachability analysis of the system in the context of testing (and time–sensitive) automata. We conjecture that all bounded liveness properties of the logic in [7] can be translated into reachability problems in this manner.

Model Checking The model–checking procedure implemented in UPPAAL is based on an interpretation using a finite–state symbolic semantics of networks. More precisely, we interpret the logic with respect to symbolic network configurations of the form $[\bar{l}, D]$, where D a constraint system (i.e. a conjunction of atomic clock and data constraints) and $\bar{l}$ a control–vector. Some of the rules defining this symbolic interpretation is given in Table 1.

$$\frac{D \subseteq c}{\vdash [\bar{l}, D] : c} \qquad \frac{l_i = l}{\vdash [\bar{l}, D] : A_i \mathsf{at}\ l} \qquad \frac{\vdash [\bar{l}, D] : \beta}{\vdash [\bar{l}, D] : \exists\Diamond\beta}$$

$$\frac{\vdash\ \left[\bar{l}[m_i/l_i, m_j/l_j], (r_i \cup r_j)(D \wedge g_i \wedge g_j)\right] : \exists\Diamond\beta}{\vdash [\bar{l}, D] : \exists\Diamond\beta} \begin{bmatrix} l_i \stackrel{g_i, \alpha?, r_i}{\longrightarrow} m_i \\ l_j \stackrel{g_j, \alpha!, r_j}{\longrightarrow} m_j \end{bmatrix}$$

$$\frac{\vdash [\bar{l}, D^{\uparrow}] : \exists\Diamond\beta}{\vdash [\bar{l}, D] : \exists\Diamond\beta}$$

Table 1. Symbolic Interpretation of Reachability Logic

To read the rules of Table 1 some notation needs to be explained. For D a constraint system and r a set of variables (to be reset) $r(D)$ denotes the set of variable assignments $\{r(v) \mid v \in D\}$. Now $D^{\uparrow}$ denotes the following set of variable assignments

$$D^{\uparrow} = \{w \mid \exists v \in D \exists d \leq \mathrm{MD}(\bar{l}, v).w = v \oplus d\}$$

An important observation is that, whenever D is a constraint system (i.e. a conjunction of atomic clock and data constraints), then so are both $r(D)$ and $D^{\uparrow}$.

Moreover, due to Richard-Bellman representing constraint systems as weighted directed graphs (with clock and data variables as nodes), these operations as well as testing for inclusion between constraint systems may be effectively implemented in $O(n^2)$ and $O(n^3)$ using shortest path algorithms [11, 12, 6].

Now, by applying the proof rules of Table 1 in a goal directed manner we obtain an algorithm (see also [13]) for deciding whether a given symbolic network configuration $[\bar{l}, D]$ satisfies a property $\exists\Diamond\beta$. To ensure termination (and efficiency), we maintain a (past–) list $\mathcal{L}$ of the symbolic network configurations encountered. If, during the goal directed application of the proof rules of Table 1 a symbolic network configuration $[\bar{l}, D']$ is generated which is already "covered" by a configuration $[\bar{l}, D]$ in $\mathcal{L}$ (i.e. $D' \subseteq D$) then the the goal directed search fails at $[\bar{l}, D']$ and backtracking is needed. If $[\bar{l}, D']$ "covers" some configuration $[\bar{l}, D]$ in $\mathcal{L}$ (i.e. $D \subseteq D'$) then $[\bar{l}, D']$ replaces $[\bar{l}, D]$ in $\mathcal{L}$.

5 Applications and Performance

UPPAAL has been used to verify various benchmark examples and applications including: several versions of Fischer's protocol, Philips Audio-Control Protocol, the Train Gate Controller, the Manufacturing Plant, the Steam Generator, the Mine-Pump Controller and the Water Tank.

In [8] an experiment was performed using four existing real-time verification tools: UPPAAL, HYTECH (Cornell), Kronos (Grenoble) and Epsilon (Aalborg). In the experiment it was verified that the so-called Fischer's mutual exclusion protocol [10, 1], shown in Figure 2, satisfies the mutual exclusion property $\forall\Box\neg((P_1 \texttt{ at } cs) \wedge (P_2 \texttt{ at } cs))$. With all the tools installed on the same machine[6] the standard Unix command `time` was used to measure execution time. The resulting time-performance diagram, shown in Figure 4, indicate that UPPAAL performs time- and space-wise favorably compared to the other tools in the experiment.

In [7], in this volume, the Philips Audio-Control Protocol [3, 4] was verified using UPPAAL. A version of the protocol is shown in Figure 5. In the verification of this protocol, we found the diagnostic model-checking feature of UPPAAL useful for detecting and correcting several errors in the description of the protocol. UPPAAL verifies that the received bit stream is guaranteed to be identical to the sent bit stream in 3.8 seconds[7].

6 Conclusion and Future Work

In this paper we have presented the main features of UPPAAL together with a review of and pointers to its theoretical foundation and application on case–studies.

---

[6] The tools were installed on a Sparc Station 10 running SunOS 4.1.3 with 64MB of primary memory and 64 MB of swap memory.

[7] UPPAAL version 0.95 was installed on a Sparc Station 10 running SunOS 4.1.3, with 64 MB of primary memory and 64 MB of swap memory.

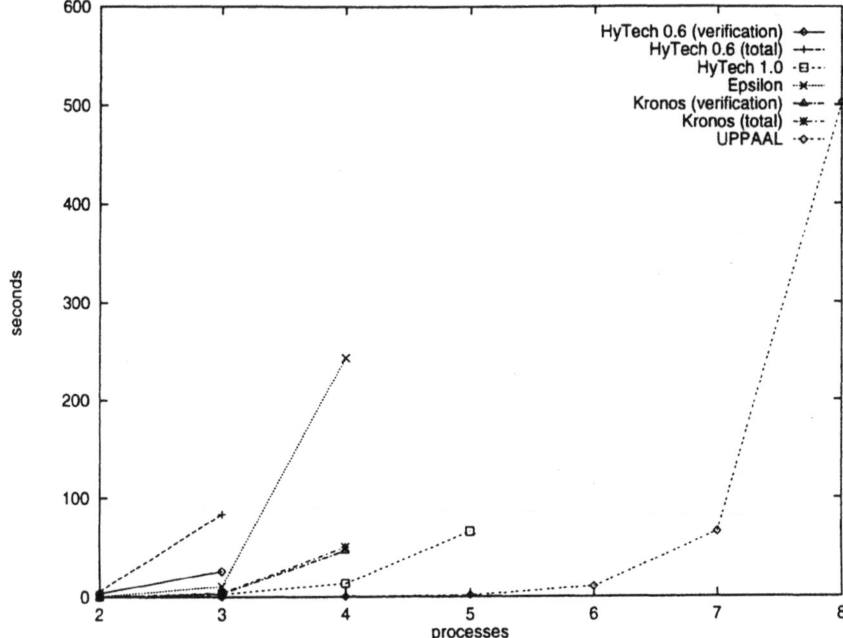

Fig. 4. Execution Times for Fischer's Protocol.

Future versions of UPPAAL will extend the current model–checker to the safety and bounded liveness logic of [7]. Also future versions of UPPAAL will integrate the newly developed compositional model–checking technique of [6], which, judged from experimental results using a CAML prototype implementation [5], seems to be a powerful technique in the on–going fight against explosion problems.

References

1. Martin Abadi and Leslie Lamport. An Old-Fashioned Recipe for Real Time. *Lecture Notes in Computer Science*, 600, 1993.
2. R. Alur and D. Dill. Automata for Modelling Real-Time Systems. In *Proc. of ICALP'90*, volume 443, 1990.
3. D. Bosscher, I. Polak, and F. Vaandrager. Verification of an Audio-Control Protocol. In *Proc. of FTRTFT'94*, volume 863 of *Lecture Notes in Computer Science*, 1993.
4. Pei-Hsin Ho and Howard Wong-Toi. Automated Analysis of an Audio Control Protocol. In *Proc. of CAV'95*, volume 939 of *Lecture Notes in Computer Science*. Springer Verlag, 1995.
5. F. Laroussinie and K.G. Larsen. Compositional Model Checking of Real Time Systems. In *Proc. of CONCUR'95*, Lecture Notes in Computer Science. Springer Verlag, 1995.

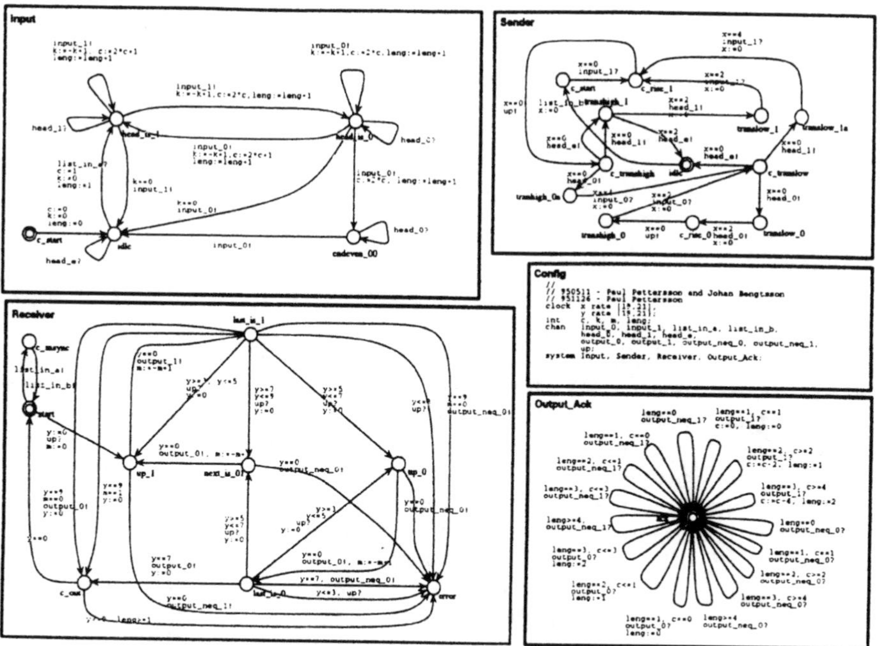

Fig. 5. Philips Audio-Control Protocol.

6. K.G. Larsen, P. Pettersson, and W. Yi. Compositional and Symbolic Model-Checking of Real-Time Systems. To appear in *Proc. of the 16*th *IEEE Real-Time Systems Symposium*, December 1995.
7. Kim G. Larsen, Paul Pettersson, and Wang Yi. Diagnostic Model-Checking for Real-Time Systems. In *Proc. of the 4*th *DIMACS Workshop on Verification and Control of Hybrid Systems*, Lecture Notes in Computer Science, October 1995.
8. Kim G. Larsen, Paul Pettersson, and Wang Yi. Model-Checking for Real-Time Systems. In *Proc. of Fundamentals of Computation Theory*, 1995.
9. A. Olivero, J. Sifakis, and S. Yovine. Using Abstractions for the Verification of Linear Hybrids Systems. In *Proc. of CAV'94*, volume 818 of *Lecture Notes in Computer Science*, 1994.
10. N. Shankar. Verification of Real-Time Systems Using PVS. In *Proc. of CAV'93.*, volume 697, 1993.
11. C.E. Leiserson T.H. Cormen and R.L. Rives. *Introduction to ALGORITHMS.* MIT Press, McGraw-Hil, 1990.
12. Mihalis Yannakakis and David Lee. An efficient algorithm for minimizing real–time transition systems. In *Proceedings of CAV'93*, volume 697 of *Lecture Notes in Computer Science*, pages 210–224, 1993.
13. Wang Yi, Paul Pettersson, and Mats Daniels. Autfomatic Verification of Real-Time Communicating Systems By Constraint-Solving. In *Proc. of the* 7th International Conference on Formal Description Techniques, 1994.

Optimal Design of Hybrid Controllers for Hybrid Process Systems

V.D. Dimitriadis, N.Shah and C.C. Pantelides

Centre for Process Systems Engineering
Imperial College of Science, Technology and Medicine
London SW7 2BY
United Kingdom

Abstract. The design of controllers for processing systems has mostly concentrated on the purely continuous and purely discrete cases. However, most chemical processes exhibit hybrid characteristics. This work presents a model-based approach to the controller synthesis problem for hybrid processing systems. A parameterised representation for hybrid controllers is presented that generalises the purely discrete and purely continuous cases. A discrete/continuous mathematical model of the process and the control system is constructed. Then, the mathematical formulations of the control system design and performance verification problems are introduced. The former can be used to design a controller that behaves optimally with respect to a given finite set of disturbance scenarios. The latter, given a controller, determines worst-case disturbance inputs that render the system infeasible or suboptimal. The two problems are finally combined into a two-stage, iterative design algorithm. A simple example is used to illustrate the potential of the proposed approach.

1 Introduction

This work considers the model-based design of hybrid feedback control schemes for general hybrid processes. Previous work on controller synthesis has focussed mostly on purely continuous and purely discrete processes. Reviews of the former area can be found in Nishida *et al.* (1981) and Stephanopoulos (1983). An extensive review of recent work in the area of controller design for purely discrete systems was given by Sanchez (1994).

However, the operation of most processing systems of practical interest is hybrid in nature, exhibiting both continuous and significant discrete characteristics. Continuous mathematical descriptions of transient behaviour – in terms of systems of algebraic, ordinary and partial differential equations and/or combinations of the above – are usually valid within narrow operating regions where no discontinuities are present. Outside these regions, discrete changes in their physical behaviour (*e.g.* phase transitions, flow regime transitions, *etc.*) and/or external actions imposed on them (*e.g.* digital control, batch operations, equipment failures, *etc.*) give rise to significant discontinuities (Pantelides, 1995). This fact has to be taken into account in the design and analysis of such systems and their corresponding control structures.

We begin by briefly describing the modelling framework used to construct models of hybrid systems of arbitrary complexity in a consistent way. Then, a general representation for controllers of such systems is introduced, resulting in a parameterised superstructure of control alternatives to be considered. Finally, the controller design problem is posed as an iterative two-stage procedure – consisting of a multiperiod design stage and a verification stage – that converges to a control system with performance guarantees for *all* possible disturbances within a given space.

2 Modelling of Hybrid Systems

In order to describe mathematically the behaviour of hybrid systems and construct mathematical models to represent it, we use the modelling framework introduced by Dimitriadis *et al.* (1995). According to this, a hybrid dynamic system operating in a *discrete* time domain $t = 0..\mathcal{H}$, may, at any time, exist in one of a finite number of distinct states $s \in \mathcal{S}$. Each of these states, s, is characterised by

- A set of continuous differential variables $\mathbf{x}_t^s \in \mathcal{X}^{(s)}$ and algebraic variables $\mathbf{y}_t^s \in \mathcal{Y}^{(s)}$.
- A set of equations, $\mathbf{f}^{(s)}(\mathbf{x}_{t+1}^s, \mathbf{x}_t^s, \mathbf{y}_t^s, \mathbf{u}_t) = 0$, that describe the behaviour of the system in that state.
- A (possibly empty) set of transitions, $\{(s, s')\}$, to other states s'.

Associated with each transition, $s \to s'$, is a logical condition that must be satisfied for the transition to take place, as well as a set of initialisation relationships which allow the condition of the system in state s' at time $t+1$ to be determined from the condition of the system in state s at time t. At any given time, t, the system is subject to external inputs $\mathbf{u}_t \in \mathcal{U}$ while a set of output variables $\mathbf{z}_t$ conveys information about the system to its environment. Both $\mathbf{u}_t$ and $\mathbf{z}_t$ may be either continuous or discrete valued or a combination thereof.

The above representation can be transformed into a discrete/continuous mathematical model that expresses the behaviour of the system in terms of algebraic equality and inequality constraints. Binary variables X_{st} are used to indicate if the system is in state s at time t or not. Moreover, binary variables $L_{ss't}$ and $\tilde{L}_{ss't}$ are used to determine if the logical condition corresponding to the transition from state s to state s' is true at time t, and if the transition actually takes place respectively. These two are not necessarily the same: the logical condition for the transition $s \to s'$ may well be true, but no transition will take place if the system is not currently in state s.

The exact form of the model can be found in Dimitriadis *et al.* (1995); for the purposes of this paper it suffices to say that it is of the general form:

$$\mathbf{G}(X_{st}, L_{ss't}, \tilde{L}_{ss't}, \mathbf{x}_t^s, \mathbf{y}_t^s, \mathbf{u}_t, \mathbf{z}_t) \leq 0$$
$$\mathbf{H}(X_{st}, L_{ss't}, \tilde{L}_{ss't}, \mathbf{x}_t^s, \mathbf{y}_t^s, \mathbf{u}_t, \mathbf{z}_t) = 0 \tag{1}$$

The initial condition of such a system is specified in terms of

- the values of the binary variables X_{s0} indicating the state s_0 of the system at time $t = 0$ ($X_{s_0 0} = 1; X_{s0} = 0\ ,\ \forall\, s \neq s_0$);
- the initial values of the differential variables, $\mathbf{x}_0^{s_0}$, in this state.

We assume that, given these initial conditions and a sequence of inputs $\{\mathbf{u}_t, t = 0..\mathcal{H}\}$, the model constraints (1) determine a unique sequence $\{X_{st}, \mathbf{x}_t^s, \mathbf{y}_t^s, \mathbf{z}_t;\ t = 1..\mathcal{H}\}$.

This representation is general enough to describe most hybrid processing systems and encapsulates the special cases of purely continuous and purely discrete systems. In the former case, there is only one possible system state with continuous variables $\mathbf{x}_t^s$, $\mathbf{y}_t^s$. In the latter case, no variables $\mathbf{x}_t^s$, $\mathbf{y}_t^s$ are necessary because the X_{st} variables are sufficient to describe the current state of the system which is now equivalent to a finite state automaton.

The introduction of the output variables, z_t, allows the construction of models for complex systems by simply connecting models of lower-level subsystems through their corresponding input and output variables.

Consider for example the simple hybrid dynamic system shown in Figure 1. A buffer tank is used to stabilise a time-varying upstream flowrate, F_i, so that a piecewise constant flowrate, F, can be maintained downstream. For this purpose, a positive displacement pump, P, is installed delivering a constant flowrate, F, when operating. Furthermore, a control stream of maximum flowrate F_c is available as a means of compensating for possible variations in F_i. Factors that may affect the behaviour of the system include the initial volume of liquid in the tank, $V(0)$, and disturbances such as the input flowrate, $F_i(t)$, and possible failures of the control valve, CV. Our objective is to design a control system that can, despite these disturbances, maintain system feasibility (*i.e.* avoid drainage and overflow of the tank) while optimising a performance-related objective function (*e.g.* maximising the amount of liquid delivered downstream).

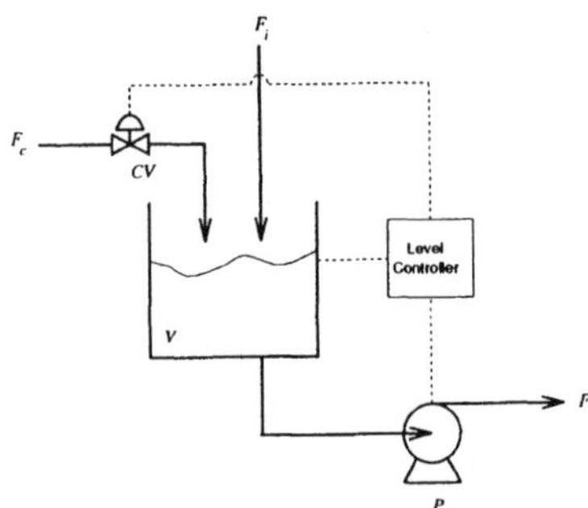

Fig. 1. Controlled buffer tank system

The models of the different system components are shown in Figures 2, 3 and 4 for the tank, pump and valve respectively. It is interesting to note that even such a simple system exhibits significant hybrid characteristics. Thus, the tank model comprises three different states corresponding to the "Normal", "Empty" and "Full" operating conditions with the dynamic mass balance equation taking a different form in each of them. The pump model has two states corresponding to the operational and non-operational modes. The transitions between these two states depend on the control signal sent to the pump. Finally, the valve model comprises one state that corresponds to normal operation and a number of states to represent the possibility of the valve malfunctioning. For example, if the valve fails open, it moves to the first of a series of "StuckOpen" states. The transition from a certain state in this series to the next one is "intrinsic", *i.e.* the logical condition associated with it is identically TRUE (see Dimitriadis *et al.* (1995)). Therefore, the valve has to pass through the whole series of "StuckOpen" states before it returns to the state corresponding to normal operation. The number of "StuckOpen" states must be equal to the number of time steps required to detect and repair the failure, and bring the valve back to functional status.

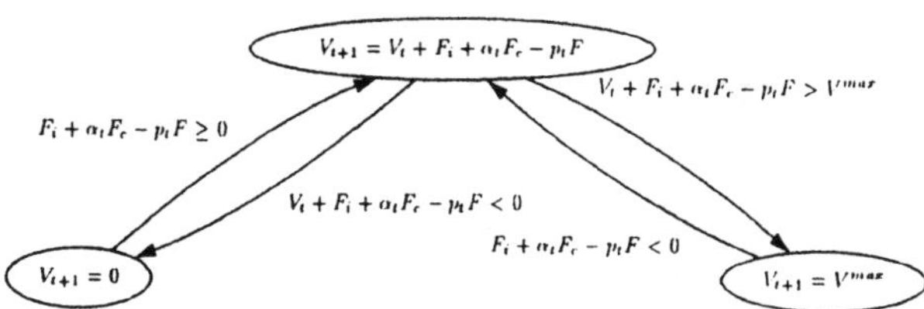

Fig. 2. Tank model

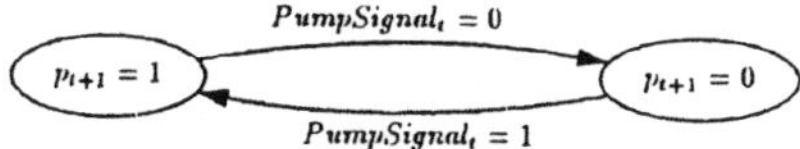

Fig. 3. Pump model

3 Modelling of Hybrid Controllers

Purely continuous feedback controllers monitor the values of continuous process measurements and use control laws to calculate the values of the process manipulated variables. On the other hand, purely discrete controllers either measure discrete-valued quantities or employ a quantiser that divides the space of continuous measurements into hyperectangular areas and supplies the controller with the resulting quantised or symbolic version of the plant output (*e.g.* a temperature is classified as "too high", "ok" or "too low"). The output of a discrete controller is also symbolic, typically a piecewise constant, discrete-valued signal (*e.g.* valve "open" or "closed").

Here, we consider a hybrid feedback control scheme that incorporates the characteristics of both of the above limiting cases (Figure 5). The space of the continuous system measurements is still divided into hyperectangular areas of arbitrary granularity. However, unlike the purely discrete case, the controller also has access to the continuous process measurements, and the control law within each of these areas can be arbitrarily

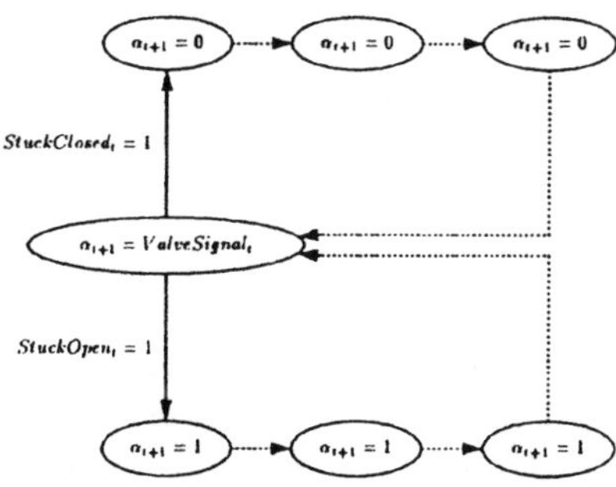

Fig. 4. Valve model

complex. This representation encapsulates the purely discrete and the purely continuous controllers as special cases, and incorporates a wealth of other possible control system alternatives for a given system.

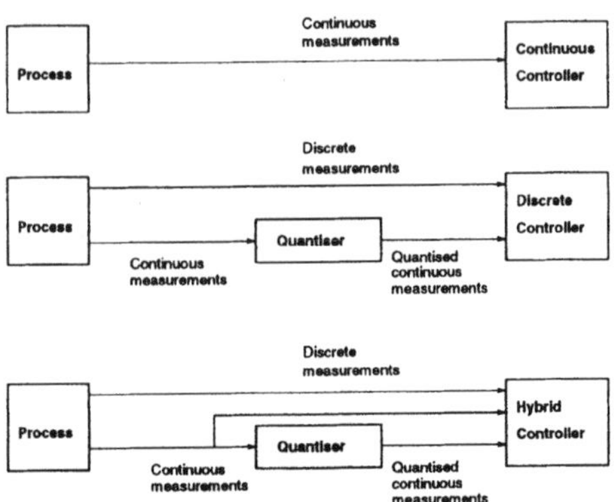

Fig. 5. Different types of controllers

It is straightforward to model this hybrid controller scheme (including the quantiser) within the modelling framework described in section 2. Each hyperectangular area in the space of the process measurements corresponds to a different state for the controller, and the corresponding control law provides the describing equations for this state. Transitions between the different states are triggered when the values of one or more measurements cross the boundaries between different areas.

For the purposes of controller design, it is important to express all possible controllers under consideration in terms of a *finite* vector of parameters. In particular, for a given number of quantisation intervals, the controller model can be parameterised with respect to the actual partitioning of the continuous measurement space to be employed, *i.e.* the positions of the boundaries between successive intervals. The values of the parameters defining the control law in each state (*e.g.* PID controller constants) may also be added to the vector of parameters to be determined by the design procedure.

Consider again the buffer tank example of the previous paragraph. Assuming that only level measurements are available and postulating a maximum of three quantisation intervals for the corresponding variable (*i.e.* level is "Low", "OK", "High"), results in a controller model with three states. Within each state, the control law is assumed to be a simple assignment of constant values to the two manipulated variables, namely the continuous valve signal and the discrete pump signal. This is equivalent to having a purely discrete controller.

The model of such a controller is shown in Figure 6. It is defined in terms of the following eight parameters:

i) the parameters V^{Low}, V^{High}, that determine the partitioning of the space of the continuous level measurement;
ii) the parameters $a^s, p^s, s \in \{Low, OK, High\}$, that determine the control law for each controller state.

The model for the entire system can now be constructed by connecting the models of its components through their input and output variables (Figure 7). Using the procedure

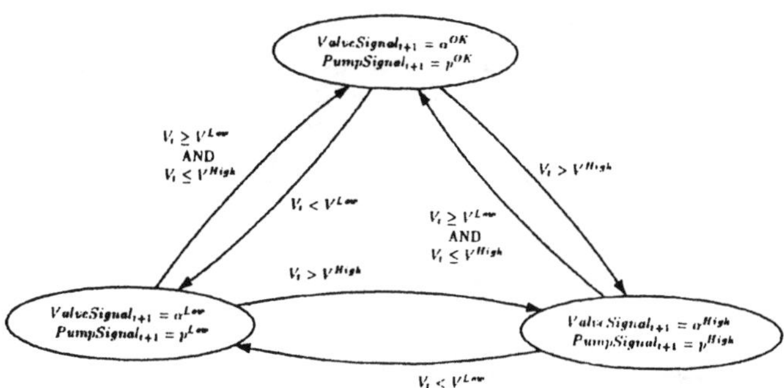

Fig. 6. Hybrid Controller model

described in Dimitriadis *et al.* (1995), this can be transformed into a discrete time, mixed discrete/continuous mathematical model. This model is used for the purposes of the design algorithm described in the next paragraph.

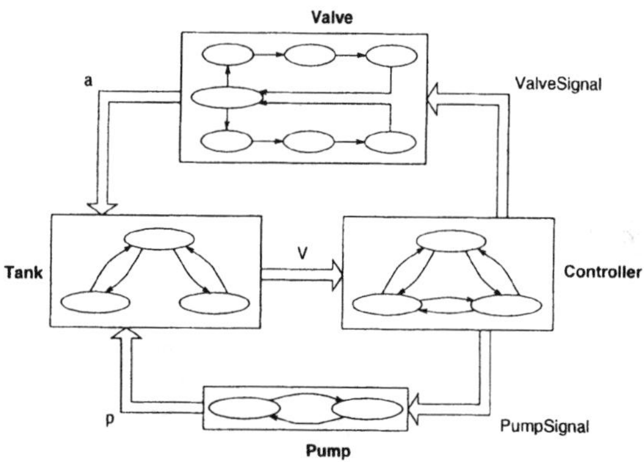

Fig. 7. Buffer tank system model

4 Multiperiod Controller Design

The parameterised mathematical model of the overall system will, in general, be of the form (1) where $\mathbf{u}_t$ represent a set of external inputs. Without loss of generality, we can assume that all of these are disturbances over which we have no influence. If this is not the case for one or more of these, we can simply treat them in the same manner as the system variables $\mathbf{y}_t^s$. The controller design problem can be posed as an optimisation problem to determine the values of the control system parameters that give a system response which is optimal with respect to a given criterion. The design is based on a *finite* set of scenarios ("periods"), each characterised by a given disturbance

sequence $\{\mathbf{u}_t, t = 1..\mathcal{H}\}$ and a given initial condition $\{X_{s0}, \mathbf{x}_0^{s0}\}$. The control system to be determined must be able to cope with any member of this set.
The design specifications imposed in this problem can normally be classified as either hard (feasibility) constraints or optimality specifications. The violation of hard constraints may pose significant operability and/or safety problems; they therefore must be strictly satisfied throughout the operation of the process. On the other hand, optimality specifications correspond to desirable characteristics that the process must exhibit; these are ultimately related to economic performance expressed as a function of the system variables and the controller design parameters, of the general form $\Phi(X_{st}, \tilde{L}_{ss't}, \mathbf{x}_t^s, \mathbf{y}_t^s, \mathbf{u}_t, \mathbf{z}_t, \mathbf{d}_c)$. For instance, in the buffer tank system, avoiding drainage and overflow of the tank are considered to be feasibility characteristics that any control system must exhibit, whereas the maximisation of the amount of product delivered downstream could be viewed as an economic optimality specification.
Feasibility specifications are naturally posed as constraints in the multiperiod design problem, whereas optimality specifications form part of the objective function. We can therefore express the multiperiod controller design problem in more detail as follows:
Problem [P1]:

$$\max_{\mathbf{d}_c} \phi$$

subject to:

$$\phi \leq \Phi(X_{stk}, \tilde{L}_{ss'tk}, \mathbf{x}_{tk}^s, \mathbf{y}_{tk}^s, \mathbf{u}_{tk}, \mathbf{z}_{tk}, \mathbf{d}_c) \quad , \quad k = 1..K \tag{2}$$

$$\mathbf{G}(X_{stk}, L_{ss'tk}, \tilde{L}_{ss'tk}, \mathbf{x}_{tk}^s, \mathbf{y}_{tk}^s, \mathbf{u}_{tk}, \mathbf{z}_{tk}, \mathbf{d}_c) \leq 0 \quad , \quad k = 1..K \tag{3}$$

$$\mathbf{H}(X_{stk}, L_{ss'tk}, \tilde{L}_{ss'tk}, \mathbf{x}_{tk}^s, \mathbf{y}_{tk}^s, \mathbf{u}_{tk}, \mathbf{z}_{tk}, \mathbf{d}_c) = 0 \quad , \quad k = 1..K \tag{4}$$

$$\mathbf{F}(X_{stk}, L_{ss'tk}, \tilde{L}_{ss'tk}, \mathbf{x}_{tk}^s, \mathbf{y}_{tk}^s, \mathbf{u}_{tk}, \mathbf{z}_{tk}, \mathbf{d}_c) \leq 0 \quad , \quad k = 1..K \tag{5}$$

where $\mathbf{F}(.)$ represents various controller feasibility specifications expressed in terms of inequality constraints, and $\mathbf{u}_{tk}$ are a *given* set of disturbance scenarios $k = 1..K$ being taken under consideration. The vector of parameters that define the hybrid control system is denoted by $\mathbf{d}_c$. The controller has to satisfy the performance specifications $\mathbf{F}$ for the entire set of disturbance inputs using a single set of parameters $\mathbf{d}_c$. Also the objective function ϕ is bounded from above by the economic performance measure for each scenario. Thus problem **[P1]** aims to optimise the worst-case performance of the system over all the scenarios currently under consideration.
The resulting controller is guaranteed to operate feasibly and optimally *only* for the set of disturbance inputs considered. For a disturbance input that is *not* included in this set, the control system selected may result in a suboptimal or even infeasible system response. Therefore, in addition to the controller design procedure described above, we need a way of testing the resulting controllers against the entire space of possible disturbances. This is the motivation behind the performance verification procedure that is described below.

5 Controller Performance Verification

Once the values of the controller parameters, $\mathbf{d}_c$, are fixed, the mathematical model of the system is completely determined for any given realisation of the disturbances. Therefore, it is possible to assess the controller performance by attempting to identify one or more critical disturbance inputs $\mathbf{u}_{tk}$ from within a given space of admissible disturbances, that render the design either infeasible (*i.e.* not satisfying the specification constraints) or uneconomical (*i.e.* giving the worst possible value for the economic objective function).

The critical disturbance inputs are obtained by solving one or more verification problems. The mathematical formulation of these problems is similar to the "safety verification" formulation described in Dimitriadis *et al.* (1995). Given a set of possible initial conditions, $\mathcal{I}$, a set of "unsafe" or otherwise undesirable conditions, $\mathcal{F}$, and a space of admissible disturbances, $\mathcal{U}$, the optimisation problem determines if there is a sequence of disturbances $\mathbf{u}_t \in \mathcal{U}$ which may lead the system from any initial condition in $\mathcal{I}$ to any potentially unsafe condition in $\mathcal{F}$ within the time horizon, $\mathcal{H}$, considered.

Note that the initial condition of the system need not be specified exactly. Instead, initially the system may be allowed to be in one and only one of a subset S_0 of its possible states $\{s\}$. We therefore have

$$\sum_{s \in S_0} X_{s0} = 1 \tag{6}$$

Furthermore, *if* the system is initially in a state $s \in S_0$, its differential variables $\mathbf{x}_0^s$ may lie anywhere within a given range $[\mathbf{x}_0^{sL}, \mathbf{x}_0^{sU}]$. This can be written as:

$$X_{s0}\mathbf{x}_0^{sL} \leq \mathbf{x}_0^s \leq X_{s0}\mathbf{x}_0^{sU} \tag{7}$$

Note that the above reduces to $\mathbf{x}_0^{sL} \leq \mathbf{x}_0^s \leq \mathbf{x}_0^{sU}$ if the system is indeed in state s (*i.e.* $X_{s0} = 1$). On the other hand, if the system is *not* in state s (*i.e.* $X_{s0} = 0$), it simply forces $\mathbf{x}_0^s$ to an (arbitrary) value of zero.

In any case, this initial condition is a potential source of uncertainty and must be handled as an additional degree of freedom in the performance verification problem so that any proposed control system can be checked against all its possible realisations.

The undesirable operating regions correspond to the feasibility and optimality constraints considered. For instance, consider the verification problem corresponding to the optimality specification. The objective of the optimisation is to find a disturbance sequence and initial condition that result in the worst possible value for the economic objective function:

Problem [P2]:

$$\min_{\mathbf{u}_t} \Phi(X_{st}, \tilde{L}_{ss't}, \mathbf{x}_t^s, \mathbf{y}_t^s, \mathbf{u}_t, \mathbf{z}_t, \mathbf{d}_c^\star)$$

subject to

$$\mathbf{G}(X_{st}, L_{ss't}, \tilde{L}_{ss't}, \mathbf{x}_t^s, \mathbf{y}_t^s, \mathbf{u}_t, \mathbf{z}_t, \mathbf{d}_c^\star) \leq 0 \tag{8}$$

$$\mathbf{H}(X_{st}, L_{ss't}, \tilde{L}_{ss't}, \mathbf{x}_t^s, \mathbf{y}_t^s, \mathbf{u}_t, \mathbf{z}_t, \mathbf{d}_c^\star) = 0 \tag{9}$$

$$\sum_{s \in S_0} X_{s0} = 1 \; ; \; X_{s0}\mathbf{x}_0^{sL} \leq \mathbf{x}_0^s \leq X_{s0}\mathbf{x}_0^{sU} \; \forall s \in S_0 \tag{10}$$

$$\mathbf{u}_t \in \mathcal{U} \tag{11}$$

where $\mathbf{d}_c^\star$ is the *given* vector of parameters that defines the controller currently under examination.

Consider, on the other hand, the problem of verifying the feasibility of the controller design with respect to a *scalar* design specification $\mathbf{F}(X_{st}, L_{ss't}, \tilde{L}_{ss't}, \mathbf{x}_t^s, \mathbf{y}_t^s, \mathbf{u}_t, \mathbf{z}_t, \mathbf{d}_c^\star) \leq 0 \; , \quad t = 1..\mathcal{H}$, by attempting to find a sequence of disturbances $\mathbf{u}_t$ and an initial condition that cause the constraint to be violated at one or more times t over the time

horizon $\mathcal{H}$. We can do this by solving the problem:
Problem [P3]:

$$\min_{\mathbf{u}_t} \sum_{t=1}^{\mathcal{H}} \sigma_t$$

subject to

$$\mathbf{G}(X_{st}, L_{ss't}, \tilde{L}_{ss't}, \mathbf{x}_t^s, \mathbf{y}_t^s, \mathbf{u}_t, \mathbf{z}_t, \mathbf{d}_c^\star) \leq 0 \quad (12)$$

$$\mathbf{H}(X_{st}, L_{ss't}, \tilde{L}_{ss't}, \mathbf{x}_t^s, \mathbf{y}_t^s, \mathbf{u}_t, \mathbf{z}_t, \mathbf{d}_c^\star) = 0 \quad (13)$$

$$\mathbf{F}(X_{st}, L_{ss't}, \tilde{L}_{ss't}, \mathbf{x}_t^s, \mathbf{y}_t^s, \mathbf{u}_t, \mathbf{z}_t, \mathbf{d}_c^\star) \geq \epsilon(1 - \sigma_t) - M\sigma_t \quad , \quad (14)$$

$$\sum_{s \in S_0} X_{s0} = 1 \; ; \; X_{s0}\mathbf{x}_0^{sL} \leq \mathbf{x}_0^s \leq X_{s0}\mathbf{x}_0^{sU} \; \forall s \in S_0 \quad (15)$$

$$\mathbf{u}_t \in \mathcal{U} \; , \; \sigma_t \in \{0, 1\} \quad (16)$$

where ϵ and M represent small and large positive constants respectively. Here, σ_t is a binary variable which is 1 if the specification $\mathbf{F}(.) \leq 0$ is satisfied at time t, and 0 otherwise. We note that, if $\sigma_t = 0$, the constraint (14) reduces to $\mathbf{F}(.) \geq \epsilon$, which implies a constraint violation. By minimising the summation $\sum_{t=1}^{\mathcal{H}} \sigma_t$, we are effectively trying to determine the $\mathbf{u}_t$ that makes the system as infeasible with respect to this specification as possible. Of course, if the optimal value of the objective function is $\mathcal{H}$, then no such $\mathbf{u}_t$ exists.

If we have a *vector* of specifications $\mathbf{F}(.) \leq 0$, then we can apply the above procedure to each of these in turn, potentially identifying different critical disturbance sequences $\mathbf{u}_t$ for each one of them.

In the buffer tank example, the potential problems that the final design must face are drainage and overflow of the tank. Thus, two verification problems must be solved at each iteration, aiming to find a worst-case set of disturbance inputs that leads the tank to a drained/overflowing state over as many time steps as possible. Obviously, if no such set can be found, the current controller design is guaranteed to be able to cope with the *entire* space of disturbances under consideration. Finally, the optimality-of-operation requirement gives rise to another verification problem that aims to find a set of disturbances that gives the *worst* possible value for the economic objective function.

6 Robust Controller Design over Finite Time Horizons

The multiperiod controller design problem can be used to design a hybrid controller that is able to deal with a *given* finite set of scenarios in an optimal way. On the other hand, the performance verification problem is a means of evaluating the performance of a *given* controller operating under the effect of all admissible disturbances. Although both formulations are useful in their own right, what is really needed is a procedure that results in the "best possible" controller, *i.e.* one that is able to keep the system feasible and with a minimum guaranteed economic performance for *any* admissable realisation of the disturbance inputs and initial conditions.

In order to achieve this objective, the multiperiod design and the performance verification formulations are combined in a two-stage, iterative design algorithm (Figure 8). Here, the performance of an initial design is first tested against the entire range of possible disturbances. In this way, one or more critical disturbance inputs (periods), that correspond to operation bottlenecks, are identified. Then, a multiperiod design problem is formulated taking account of *all* critical points identified so far. This results in a new design that satisfies the specifications for these points and at the same time optimises the economic objective function. Alternatively, one could initially specify an initial set of disturbance inputs, on which the first design attempt is based, and then proceed in the same fashion.

The algorithm converges when the verification part fails to identify new critical disturbance inputs, thus indicating that the final design is feasible for any possible disturbance input and its performance can never be worse than that achieved by the solution of the last design optimisation.

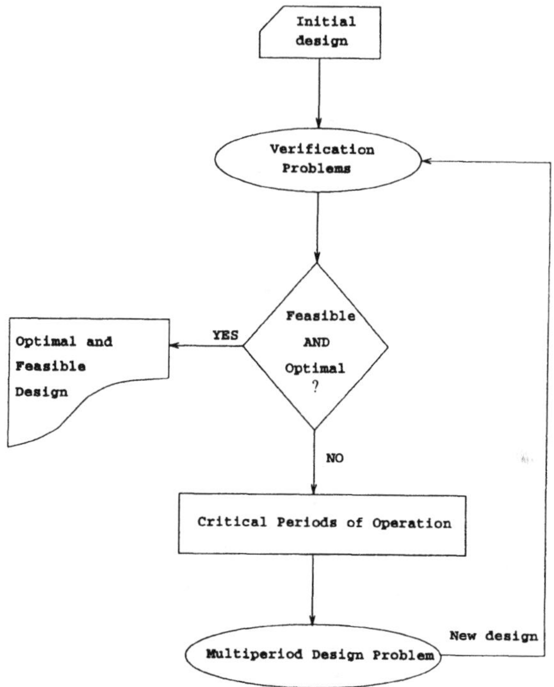

Fig. 8. Iterative multiperiod design algorithm

Provided that the verification problem(s) are solved to global optimality, Gustafson (1983) has shown that, for this type of optimisation problem, a sequence of accumulated points is generated that, in the limit, converges to a design that is feasible with respect to the imposed specifications. If, in addition, the multiperiod design problem is solved to global optimality, economic optimality, in the sense described above, will also be achieved.

7 Robust Controller Design over Infinite Time Horizons

Both the multiperiod design and the performance verification problems are solved for a time horizon of finite length $\mathcal{H}$. However, a guarantee is often required that the control system is able to satisfy the strict feasibility specifications for *any* time horizon. This can be achieved through the following additional design specification:

Specification F^{∞}:

"The controller must bring the system back into the space of initial conditions, $\mathcal{I}$, at (at least) one time $t > 0$ within the time horizon."

To understand how the above specification achieves the required aim of permanent feasibility, recall that the design procedure of section 6 effectively guarantees that:

Specification $F^{\mathcal{H}}$:

"If the system is in the initial condition space $\mathcal{I}$ at a given time t^*, then it remains feasible for (at least) the next $\mathcal{H}$ time intervals."

i.e.

$$\{X_{st^*}, \mathbf{x}^s_{t^*}\} \in \mathcal{I} \;\rightarrow\; \mathbf{F}(.) \leq 0,\; \forall t = t^* + 1..t^* + \mathcal{H} \tag{17}$$

Now, if as dictated by specification F^{∞}, the controller brings the system back into $\mathcal{I}$ at some time $t^* + \delta$, where $\delta \in [1, \mathcal{H}]$, then, by virtue of $F^{\mathcal{H}}$, we also have

$$\{X_{s,t^*+\delta}, \mathbf{x}^s_{t^*+\delta}\} \in \mathcal{I} \;\rightarrow\; \mathbf{F}(.) \leq 0,\; \forall t = t^* + \delta + 1..t^* + \delta + \mathcal{H}$$

This reasoning applied recursively shows that

$$\mathbf{F}(.) \leq 0,\; \forall t = t^* + n\delta + 1..t^* + n\delta + \mathcal{H}\;,\; \forall n = 0, 1, 2...$$

As a consequence of this, and since $\delta \geq 0$, we can deduce that $\mathbf{F}(.) \leq 0$ is satisfied for *all* $t \geq t^*$.

All that remains is to express F^{∞} in a manner that can be incorporated within the multiperiod design and verification formulations of sections 4 and 5 respectively. For the design problem, this can be done through the constraints:

$$X_{st}\mathbf{x}_0^{sL} - M(1-\eta_{tk}) \leq \mathbf{x}^s_{tk} \leq X_{st}\mathbf{x}_0^{sU} + M(1-\eta_{tk})\;,\; \forall\, s \in S_0,\; t = 1..\mathcal{H},\; k = 1..K \tag{18}$$

$$\sum_{t=1}^{\mathcal{H}} \eta_{tk} \geq 1\;,\; \forall\, k = 1..K \tag{19}$$

Here $\eta_{tk} \in \{0, 1\}$ is a binary variable that, for a given scenario k, takes a value of 1 if the system finds itself again within the space of initial conditions $\mathcal{I}$ at time $t \geq 0$, and 0 otherwise. Constraint (19) demands that at least one η_{tk} for each scenario k is one during the time horizon $t \in [1, \mathcal{H}]$. On the other hand, constraint (18) reduces to

$$\mathbf{x}_0^{sL} \leq \mathbf{x}^s_{tk} \leq \mathbf{x}_0^{sU} \tag{20}$$

if *both* $X_{st} = 1$ *and* $\eta_{tk} = 1$, *i.e.* the system is in state s and within the space of initial conditions. Otherwise, (18) is non-constraining.

The constraints to be included in the verification procedure can be derived from the above in a manner similar to that in which constraints (14) were derived from the design specification $\mathbf{F}(.) \leq 0$. The objective in this case is essentially to minimise the number of time steps that the system spends in the space of the initial conditions over the time horizon of interest, $\mathcal{H}$.

8 Application of Controller Design Procedure

The design algorithm outlined above is now applied to the buffer tank process. The relevant data are shown in Table 1. The requirements set for the control system are:

i) Drainage and overflow of the tank must be avoided.
ii) The controller must return the system to the space of initial conditions at least once during the time horizon.
iii) The amount of material dispensed downstream must be maximised. At the same time, however, the amount of material from the control stream that is used for this purpose must be minimised.

It can be seen that the first two requirements correspond to feasibility constraints for the multiperiod design problem whereas the last one defines the objective function of the problem. The verification step involves a total of four separate problems (two for drainage and overflow verification, one for controller robustness verification and one to verify the optimality of operation).

Tank	Volume	1.00
	Initial liquid holdup range	0.30 - 0.90
	Input flowrate, F_i, per time step	0.10 - 0.25
	Control flowrate, F_c, per time step	0.05
Pump	Operating modes	On/Off
	Throughput per time step when on	0.30
Valve	Operating modes	Functional/Under repair
	Position when functional	0.00 - 1.00
	Time needed to repair a failure	3 time steps

Table 1. Data for buffer tank system

The time horizon considered comprises five time steps, with the disturbances (*i.e.* the input flowrate F_i and the valve mode) assumed to be piecewise constant functions of time. The algorithm was initialised with the set of disturbance inputs shown in Table 2.

Initial holdup 0.30					
Time	0	1	2	3	4
F_i	0.10	0.10	0.10	0.10	0.10
Valve	StuckClosed	UnderRepair	UnderRepair	StuckClosed	UnderRepair

Table 2. Initial disturbance inputs for buffer tank

The design algorithm converges after seven iterations, with a total of seven periods of disturbances being considered in the final design problem. The resulting control system is described in Table 3. It is able to anticipate the entire space of disturbances considered and, since requirement (ii) is satisfied, this is guaranteed not only for the time horizon of five time steps considered here, but for *any* time horizon. Furthemore, the controller can guarantee that at least 0.60 volume units will be delivered during any six consecutive time steps, corresponding to a minimum overall delivery of approximately 0.10 units per time step.

Note that the parameterised control system superstructure that was initially assumed is, in fact, simplified in the solution: the "Low" controller state is effectively deleted by setting $V^{Low} = 0$.

Parameters governing controller state transitions	$V^{Low} = 0.00$
	$V^{High} = 0.29$
Parameters governing control law within states	$\alpha^{OK} = 1.00 \quad p^{OK} = 0$
	$\alpha^{High} = 1.00 \quad p^{High} = 1$

Table 3. Proposed control system for buffer tank

The performance of the resulting control system was tested by performing stochastic simulation runs. The initial level of liquid in the tank and the value of the input flowrate at each time step were selected randomly, assuming uniform probability distributions over their respective ranges of possible values. Random valve failures were created by assuming a 10 % probability that the valve fails open/closed at each time step where the valve is functional. A sample run for a total of 200 time steps is shown in Figure 9. It can be seen that the controller successfully acts against the randomly selected disturbances, keeping the system within the specified limits.

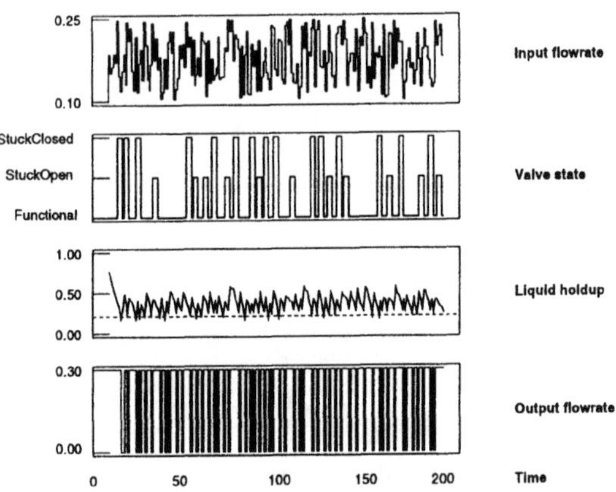

Fig. 9. Stochastic simulation of controlled buffer tank

The use of more time steps in the robust controller design procedure will obviously have no effect on the quality of the control system with respect to feasibility or robustness as these were constraints for the problem. However, it is possible that it has a great impact on the quality of the control system with respect to the economic objective function as the additional information provided from the extra time steps will probably result in less degenerate and more economical designs.

9 Concluding Remarks

The problem of designing control systems for dynamic processes with discrete/continuous operating characteristics has been considered in this paper. The discrete time, hybrid modelling framework introduced by Dimitriadis *et al.* (1995) was used to construct process models that explicitly account for the discrete operating characteristics as well as to construct a general, parameterised representation for the corresponding control scheme. A robust controller design algorithm was then introduced that involves iterating between a multiperiod design and a verification step until a control system with satisfactory performance for *all* possible disturbance inputs has been identified.
Despite its generality, the procedure presented is not without its limitations. First, we must ensure that all problems are solved to global optimality; our experience to date has been with linear systems only. Secondly, in common with other applications involving mixed integer programming, there remain several issues of computational complexity to be resolved.

References

Dimitriadis, V.D., N. Shah and C.C. Pantelides (1995). Modelling and Safety Verification of Discrete/Continuous Processing Systems Using Discrete Time Domain Models. Presented at the "*Workshop on Analysis and Design of Event-Driven Operations in Process Systems*", London.

Gustafson, S.A. (1983). A Three-Phase Algorithm for Semi-Infinite Programs. In *Semi-Infinite Programming and Applications* (Springer Verlag, Ed.). New York.

Nishida, N., G. Stephanopoulos and A.W. Westerberg (1981). A Review of Process Synthesis. *AIChE J.* **27**, 321.

Pantelides, C.C. (1995). Modelling, Simulation and Optimisation of Hybrid Processes. Presented at the "*Workshop on Analysis and Design of Event-Driven Operations in Process Systems*", London.

Sanchez, A. (1994). Formal Specification and Synthesis of Sequential/Logic Controllers for Process Systems. PhD thesis. University of London.

Stephanopoulos, G. (1983). Synthesis of Control Systems for Chemical Plants - A Challenge for Creativity. *Comp. Chem. Eng.* **7**, 331.

On-line Fault Monitoring of a Class of Hybrid Systems Using Templates with Dynamic Time Scaling

Lawrence E. Holloway*
Center for Manufacturing Systems and
Department of Electrical Engineering
University of Kentucky
Lexington, KY 40506-0108
email: holloway@engr.uky.edu

Abstract. Fault monitoring is the online analysis of process observations to determine if they correspond to correct process operation. In automated manufacturing systems, the observed input and output signals can commonly be characterized as observed time functions of discrete events, and fault monitoring can only rely on the analysis of the timing and sequencing of these events. In many situations, these timing and sequencing relationships are not fixed, but rather depend upon underlying continuous state dynamics of the system.
In this paper, we examine the issue of on-line fault monitoring of a class of hybrid dynamical systems in which the evolution of a continuous state is observed through and influenced by discrete events. Specifically, we consider a process for which the correct behavior is defined by the concurrent operation of any number of instances of a given hybrid automaton, where the hybrid automaton has a special structure formed from the composition of the discrete state structure of the actuators with the continuous state variable. We develop a distributed method for examining the discrete event observations from the process and determining on-line whether they are consistent with the model of correct behavior. The method presented, *dynamically scaled templates*, is an extension of the template monitoring method developed for monitoring of automated manufacturing systems.

1 Introduction

Fault monitoring is the online analysis of process observations to determine if they correspond to correct process operation. In automated manufacturing systems, the observed input and output signals can commonly be characterized as observed time functions of discrete events, and fault monitoring can only rely on the analysis of the timing and sequencing of these events. However, in

* L. E. Holloway has been supported in part by Rockwell International, NSF grant ECS-9308737, NASA grant NGT-40049, and the Center for Robotics and Manufacturing Systems at the University of Kentucky.

many situations, these timing and sequencing relationships are not fixed, but rather depend upon underlying continuous state dynamics of the system which are influenced by these events. The system being monitored is thus a hybrid dynamical system.

An example of the problem we consider is shown in the following figure [1]. Consider a portion of a conveyor system. As packages enter the conveyor system, a proximity sensor PS1 generates an event, and as packages leave the conveyor, a proximity sensor PS2 generates an event. We are interested in monitoring the system to confirm that no packages are dropped or jammed on the conveyor, and that the conveyor speed is consistent with the speed designated by the input control. The conveyor can operate at three speeds: stopped, slow, and fast. The speeds are changed by controller commands (events) *stop*, *slow*, and *fast.* The monitoring system is only able to observe the occurrence of these conveyor events and the events PS1 and PS2, but must determine if the system is operating correctly. Moreover, if there are multiple boxes on the conveyor, the observations will correspond to multiple concurrent event pairs of matching PS1 and PS2 events. Clearly, the time between the generation of event PS1 by a package and the generation of event PS2 by the same package depends on conveyor speed changes that occurred in the intervening period. The observations of the system are entirely discrete, but their timings depend upon the continuous-valued positions of the boxes, which evolve depending upon the discrete event inputs of the conveyor.

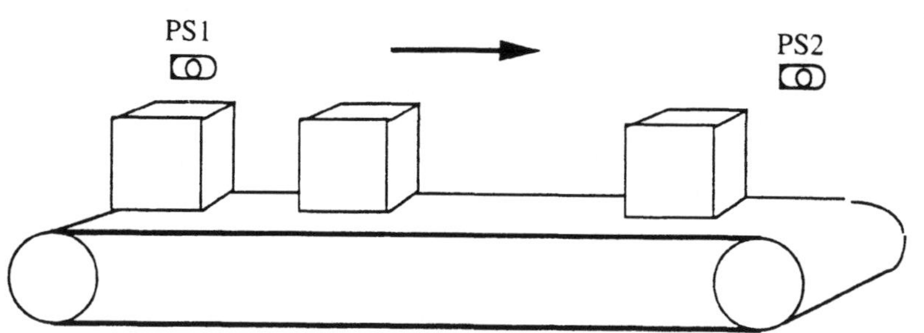

Fig. 1. A simple conveyor system.

In this paper, we examine the issue of on-line fault monitoring of hybrid dynamical systems in which the evolution of a continuous state is observed through and influenced by discrete events. Specifically, we consider a process for which the correct behavior is defined by the concurrent operation of any number of instances of a given hybrid automaton. We develop a distributed method for examining the discrete event observations from the process and determining on-line whether they are consistent with the model of correct behavior. The method presented, ***scaled template monitoring***, is an extension of the template monitoring method developed for monitoring of automated manufacturing systems [2, 3]. The template monitoring method has several characteristics desirable for application to manufacturing systems, including low processor requirements, functionality under unknown startup conditions and improper observations, and suitability for highly concurrent observations [4]. Furthermore, the distributed nature of the monitoring method reduces communication bottlenecks associated with centralized methods, and can also be used to provide robustness under processor failures.

It is important to note that the fault monitoring problem is closely related to the verification problem. In verification, we are given a system, and must confirm that it satisfies specifications of correct operation. Verification may be done by model analysis, or by probing the system with various inputs which may be chosen. In fault detection, we also must confirm that a system satisfies specifications of correct operation, typically represented as a process model. However, due to failures in the system, past satisfaction of specifications does not imply present or future satisfaction of specifications. It is the task of fault monitoring to determine *when* rather than if specifications have been violated. This means that fault detection must be done on-line, using available process observations. The closely related task of diagnosis, which we do not consider in this paper, then attempts to identify the source of the fault within the system.

Event based fault monitoring and diagnosis has been considered by several authors. Dersin and Florine use a describe a commercial method for on-line monitoring of event traces by stepping through a timed automaton model as events are received [5]. Process diagnosis using discrete event observations has been investigated by Sampath et al. [6]. Bavishi and Chong consider testability of systems modeled as a nondeterministic automaton [7]. Holloway and Chand consider distributed monitoring for systems representable as timed automata [2]. Holloway and Krogh considered fault monitoring for uncertain hybrid dynamical systems using behavioral models [8, 1].

This paper will be structured as follows. In section 2, we describe a class of hybrid automata to be used to specify the correct operation of the system. In particular, a correct timed event sequence will correspond to the concurrent operation of some unspecified number of these automata. In the example presented above, this would correspond to the existence of multiple boxes on the conveyor between the two proximity sensors. In section 3, we introduce dynamically-scaled templates and describe their use in monitoring. An algorithm is presented to automatically generate families of templates from a class of hybrid automata. In section 4, we present analytical results showing that under certain conditions, the timed event language accepted by the dynamically-scaled template monitoring procedure is equal to the timed event language corresponding to the concurrent operation of multiple instances of the hybrid automaton.

2 Hybrid system model

The hybrid systems we consider in this paper are related to the hybrid automata of [9]. A *hybrid automata* is a defined as $H = (Q, \Re, \Sigma, A, Rate)$, where Q is a finite set of discrete states, $\Re$ is the set of possible continuous states, Σ is a finite set of event labels, $A \subset Q \times \Im \times \Sigma \times \{\Re \longrightarrow \Re\} \times Q$ is a finite set of arcs (edges), where $\Im$ is the set of all intervals of the real line. An arc $(q_a, X_a, e_a, r_a, q'_a)$ extends from q_a to q'_a, and can only occur when the continuous state is in the interval X_a. When the system crosses the arc, the event e_a is generated. The continuous state then is reset to a value based on the function r_a (to be described more below). $Rate : Q \longrightarrow \Im$ is a function describing the evolution of the continuous state for a given deterministic state, where $\Im$ is a set of intervals of the real line.

A trace is a triplet $s = (x_d, x_c, a)$, where $x_d : T \longrightarrow Q$ is a timed trajectory of discrete states, $x_c : T \longrightarrow \Re$ is a timed trajectory of continuous state values, and $a : T \longrightarrow A \cup \{null\}$ is an arc-transition trajectory, where $\{null\}$ indicates no edge was traversed at time t. Let S denote the set of all traces.

Definition 1. A trace $s \in S$ is a *run* of hybrid automaton H if the following are satisfied:

1. for all $t \in T$ with $a(t) = null$,
   (a) $\dot{x}_c(t) \in Rate(x_d(t))$.
   (b) $x_d(t) = x_d(t^-)$
2. if $a(t) \neq null$, then
   (a) $x_d(t^-) = q_{a(t)}$, $x_d(t) = q'_{a(t)}$,
   (b) $x_c(t^-) \in X_{a(t)}$,
   (c) $x_c(t) = r_{a(t)}(x_c(t^-))$
3. for all $a \in A$ with $q_a = x_d(t)$,
   (a) $x_c(t) \leq \max(X_a)$ if $Rate(x_d(t)) \subset \Re^+$,
   (b) $x_c(t) \geq \min(X_a)$ if $Rate(x_d(t)) \subset \Re^-$.

The set of all runs for the hybrid automaton H is denoted $S_H \subseteq S$.

The first item in the above definition states that if no arc-transition occurred at time t, then the continuous state evolved within the rate parameter *Rate* defined by the discrete state, and the discrete state does not change. We use the notation $x_d(t^-)$ to indicate the discrete state immediately before time t, i.e. the limit of $x_d(t')$ as t' approaches time t from the left. We define $x_c(t^-)$ in a similar manner. Item 2 above states that when an arc crossing $a(t) \neq null$ occurs at time t, the discrete state changes from $q_{a(t)}$ to $q'_{a(t)}$. The continuous state variable immediately prior to t was in the enabling region $X_a(t)$, but is reset to the value given by $r_{a(t)}(x_c(t^-))$. Finally item 3 above describes when an arc crossing must occur. In words, a continuous state variable which is increasing cannot pass through the maximum enabling value for an arc from that discrete state without the arc transition occurring. Similarly, a decreasing continuous state variable cannot cross through the minimum enabling value without an arc transition occurring. Note that this implies that for any run, for any state q and any incoming arc a_{in} and outgoing arc a_{out}, if *Rate*(q) is positive, then $r_{a_{in}}(x) < \max(X_{a_{out}})$ for any state x that could occur into state q. In other words, a run will never have a reset produce a continuous state that is beyond any enabling for the given discrete state.

The class of systems we consider represent the interaction of an internal state (such as the state of the package) with an externally determined state of actuators. The actuator states influence the timing and evolution of the internal continuous and discrete state. However, the actuator states are determined independent of the internal state. Since the hybrid automata we consider is a form of product between the internal (hybrid) state automata and the external actuator (discrete) state automata, the hybrid automata has a very useful structure. Let G_{act} be a state machine representation of the actuator state. G_{act} will be replicated for every internal discrete state, such that the actuator state only determines the *Rate* value within the states associated with an internal discrete state. An example of the resulting structure is best illustrated with a simple example, as shown in figure 2. In the figure, q_1, q_2, and q_3 represent the states where the package is before sensor PS1, and the conveyor has speed fast, and slow, and stop, respectively. Together these states comprise the macrostate Q_1. The macrostates Q_2 and Q_3 also consist of three states each, for fast, slow, and stop states of the actuator, but where the package is between sensors PS1 and PS2 for Q_2, and past PS2 for Q_3.

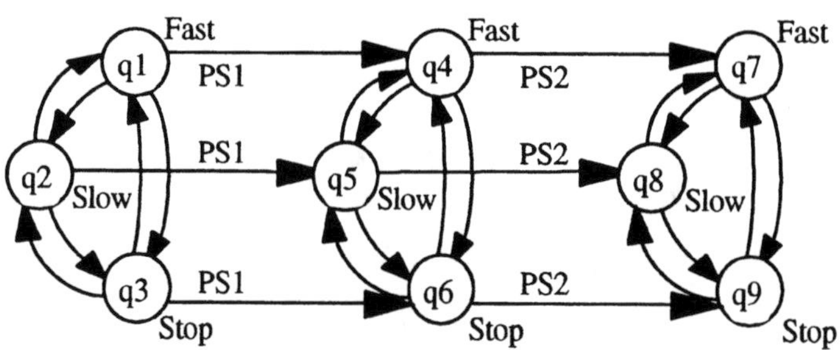

Fig. 2. The state structure of the hybrid automaton of the package/conveyor system.

The above considerations lead to a class of systems with the following properties:

1. The set Σ of event labels are partitioned into the sets Σ_c which indicate continuous state information, and Σ_d which are events which do not indicate any continuous state information.

   (a) for each $e \in \Sigma_d$, $X_a = \Re$, and $r_a(x) = x$ for all x.
   (b) for each $e \in \Sigma_c, \exists \alpha_e \in \Re$ such that for every arc a with $e_a = e, r_a(x) = \alpha_e$ for all x.
2. A *macrostate* is a (maximal) set of states connected by arcs with labels in Σ_d. Macrostates will be denoted by sets Q_i for some index i. Each macrostate is isomorphic to an untimed automaton G_{act}, referred to as the *actuator automaton*, with state set Q_{act}. For macrostate Q_i and state q in Q_{act}, let $\Upsilon_i(q) \in Q_i$ denote the state in Q_i corresponding to state q.
3. For any macrostates Q_i, Q_j, if there exists an arc (q, X, e, r, q') with $e \in \Sigma_c$, $q \in Q_i$, and $q' \in Q_j$, then for every $q_{act} \in Q_{act}$, there exists an arc $(\Upsilon_i(q_{act}), X, e, r, \Upsilon_j(q_{act})) \in A$.
4. For each $e \in \Sigma_d$, there exists some state q_e in the actuator automaton G_{act} such that all arcs with label e lead to q_e.

We refer to systems satisfying these as time-scalable hybrid automata. We assume that the systems we consider satisfy the above. Although this may seem like a rather limited class of hybrid automata, it is representative of systems where a component with continuous and discrete state interacts with actuator devices, which determine the rates of increase or decrease of the continuous state variable. Since these types of simple systems have come up repeatedly in our investigation of fault monitoring of manufacturing processes, it is important to be able to address them.

An *observation trajectory* is a timed sequence of event sets $v : \Re \longrightarrow 2^{\Sigma}$. The set of all observation trajectories is denoted $\mathcal{V}$. Given a run s of H, the corresponding observation trajectory is defined as the time function of events corresponding to the arc-transition trajectory, $v_s(t) = \{e_{a(t)}\}$.

In this paper, we are interested in the observations corresponding to the concurrent operation of some unspecified number of instances of a given hybrid automaton. Given a nonnegative integer n, the independent operation of n instances of a hybrid automaton is represented by the cross product of the automata traces, $(s_1, s_2, \cdots, s_n)$. For a time interval $\underline{\mathbf{t}}$, the set of timed observation sequences corresponding to the parallel operation of n hybrid automata is represented by

$$\begin{aligned} V_{H^n}(\underline{\mathbf{t}}) := \{ v \in \mathcal{V} \mid \exists s_1, s_2, \ldots, s_n \in S_H \text{ such that} \\ \text{for } t \in \underline{\mathbf{t}}, v(t) = \cup_{i=1}^{n} v_{s_i}(t) \} \end{aligned}$$

The set of all observation sequences corresponding to any number of parallel hybrid automata H over period $\underline{\mathbf{t}}$ is

$$V_{H^*}(\underline{\mathbf{t}}) := \{ v \in V_{H^n}(\underline{\mathbf{t}}) \mid n \geq 0 \}$$

We can now define precisely the problem we consider. Given a hybrid automaton H and an observation v_{obs} over a time period $\underline{\mathbf{t}}_{obs}$, we want to determine if $v_{obs} \in V_{H^*}(\underline{\mathbf{t}}_{obs})$. If it is not, then the observation v_{obs} does not correspond to any number of concurrent runs of H, so a fault must be declared.

3 Templates and Distributed Monitoring

The *template monitoring method* was introduced in [2] as a method of distributed monitoring of discrete event systems. Templates were defined to represent simple timing and sequencing relationships between events. The monitoring method was developed to be highly distributable, to be computationally simple, to be robust under unknown initial state conditions, and to be suitable for monitoring multiple concurrent processes. In this paper, we generalize the method to represent event relationships based on an underlying state variable, instead of time.

A *scalable template* $m = (e_m, C_m, scale_m)$ consists of a *trigger event* e_m, a set of *consequences* C_m, and a partial mapping $scale_m : \Sigma \longrightarrow \Re$. A consequence $c = (e_c, \underline{\mathbf{t_c}}) \in C_m$ is an event $e_c \in \mathcal{E}$ and an interval-valued clock delay $\underline{\mathbf{t_c}} \in \Im$. Define $\mathcal{C} := (\mathcal{E} \times \Im)$ as the universe of consequences, and $\mathcal{M} := (\mathcal{E} \times 2^{\mathcal{C}})$ as the universe of templates. As will be explained below, a template will be interpreted as follows: for any occurrence of the trigger event e_m, for at least one of the consequences $c \in C_m$, the event e_c should occur with clock delay within the interval $\underline{\mathbf{t_c}}$. The rate of the clock is dynamically scaled to the value $scale_m(e)$ with the occurrence of any event e for which $scale_m(e)$ is defined. Let Σ_m be the set of events over which $scale_m(e)$ is defined. Note that the clock rates may be negative, and the clock delay interval $\underline{\mathbf{t_c}}$ may indicate a negative delay, and thus represent a time in which a previous event should have occurred. There is no knowledge of the rate of the clock unless some event in Σ_m has occurred in the past. When Σ_m is the emptyset, then the rate is 1 always.

An expectation is a template associated with a *trigger time*, and is denoted by a pair $(t, m) \in \Re \times \mathcal{M}$. Given an observation trajectory $v \in \mathcal{V}$ over a time period $\underline{\mathbf{t}} \in \Im$ and given a set of templates $M \subset \mathcal{M}$, the expectations set for M is defined as

$$\Gamma_M(v, \underline{\mathbf{t}}) := \{(t, m) \mid t \in \underline{\mathbf{t}}, m \in M, e_m \in v(t)\}$$

Thus, for each event occurrence $e \in v(t)$ for any time $t \in \underline{\mathbf{t}}$, there is an expectation $(t', m) \in \Gamma(v, \underline{\mathbf{t}})$ for all $m \in M$ for which e is a trigger event. For any expectation (t, m), define $expire(t, m) = t + \max\{t' \in \underline{\mathbf{t_c}} \mid (e_c, \underline{\mathbf{t_c}}) \in C_m\}$.

A scalable template is best understood by initially considering the case where $\Sigma_m = \emptyset$. This is the class of templates considered in [2, 3]. In this situation, the scale of the template is always 1, so the continuous variable underlying the templates is simply time. The template then indicates that whenever the triggering event occurs, event e_c will occur within delay period τ_c, where $(e_c, \tau_c) \in C_m$ is one of the consequences for the template. Only one consequence needs to be satisfied.

For the case where $\Sigma_m \neq \emptyset$, the time scale for the consequence delays is modified by the occurrence of events in Σ_m. For the conveyor example presented earlier, suppose that it takes 2 seconds for a box to travel from PS1 to PS2 when the conveyor is at fast speed and 4 seconds when the conveyor is at slow speed. Let m be the template $(e_m, C_m, scale_m)$ with e_m as PS1 event and $C_m = \{(e_c, \tau_c)\}$ with e_c as PS2 event and $\tau_c = [4]$. Define $\Sigma_m = \{stop, slow, fast\}$

where $scale_m(stop) = 0$, $scale_m(slow) = 1$, and $scale_m(fast) = 2$. This scaled template is considered in a manner similar to the nonscaled template earlier. The template states that event PS2 should occur after a delay from the occurrence PS1, but the time scale of the clock of the delay is modified upon the occurrence of events in Σ_m. As figure 2 shows, on the scaled timeline t', the events PS1 and PS2 are always 4 time units apart, although they may not be 4 time units apart on the actual time line.

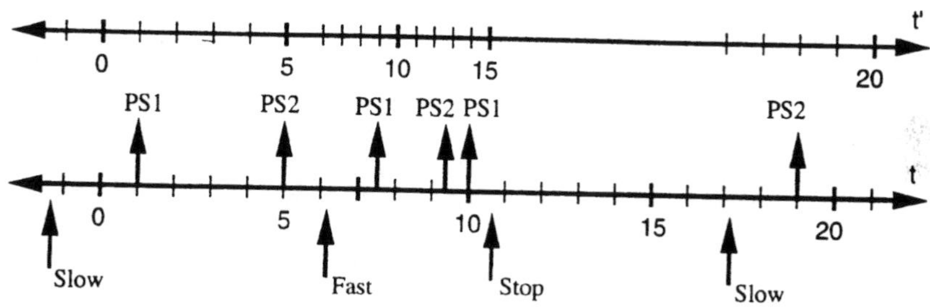

Fig. 3. Time scaling due to conveyor speed changes.

Let $\mathcal{P}$ be a partition over $\mathcal{M}$ such that for each $M \in \mathcal{P}$, all templates in M have the same time scale function, that is, there exists some function $scale_M$ such that $scale_m = scale_M$ for all $m \in M$. Let $time_M : \Re \rightarrow \Re$ be a *local time clock* for template set M such that for all time t,

$$\frac{d(time_M(t))}{dt} = scale_M(t)$$

The template sets in $\mathcal{P}$ can be distributed over any number n of processors, where $n \leq |\mathcal{P}|$. For each template set $M \in \mathcal{P}$, we have the following algorithm.

The set O_M in the algorithm is the set of expectations which have not yet reached their expiration time. In the first portion of the algorithm, any events received at time t are used to add a template with local time stamp $time_M(t_k)$ to the set of open templates, O_M. In the second portion of the algorithm, any template that expires at the current time (under the local time clock) is removed from O_M. If the expired template did not have any satisfied consequences, then a fault is declared.

The set of timed event strings accepted by the monitoring algorithm over templates M over time $\underline{\mathbf{t}}$ will be denoted by $V_M(\underline{\mathbf{t}})$. Any observation that does not lie in $V_M(\underline{\mathbf{t}})$ generates a fault alarm.

Fig. 4. Procedure DISTRIBUTED.TIMESCALED.MONITOR.UPDATE for template set $M \in \mathcal{P}$ for time t_k.

Procedure: DISTRIBUTED.TIMESCALED.MONITOR.UPDATE(t_k)

```
O_M(t_k) <= O_M(t_{k-1})
For each template m ∈ M with e_m ∈ v(t_k) {
   O_M(t_k) <= O_M(t_k) ∪ {(time_M(t_k), m)}
}
For each expectation (t', m') ∈ O_M(t_k) with expire(t', m') ≤ time_M(t_k) {
   O_M(t_k^i) <= O_M(t_k^i) − {(t', m')}
   If ∀(e_c, t_c) in C_{m'}, e_c ∉ v(t'') for any t'' s.t. time_M(t'') ∈ t_c {
      Declare Fault
   }
}
```

4 Generating Scaled Templates from Hybrid Automata

In [2], a method was developed to convert timed automata specifications into (unscaled) template models for monitoring. A similar approach can be used for converting hybrid automata specifications into scaled templates. The approach is modified, however, to recognize the distinction of events which indicate a value of an underlying continuous state variable. Arcs in the hybrid automata with a reset value r_a equal to a constant or otherwise restricted through the range of X_a will provide information about the underlying continuous state value, and will be used for template triggering events. Note that any arcs generated by an external controller and thus arising from the underlying actuator automaton G_{act} will have $X_a = \Re$, since the controller can have no knowledge of the underlying continuous state. As indicated in section 2, sets of states which are connected by actuator events (events in Σ_d) comprise a macrostate. The procedure we present develops templates over these states using only events (in Σ_c) which provide continuous state variable information. Events internal to the macrostate (events in Σ_d) are used to set the scale for the local time of the template monitors.

The generation of templates from the hybrid automaton is shown in the procedure in figure 5. The procedure of figure 5 builds *forward* templates from the hybrid automaton, i.e. templates that have consequence time intervals that are intervals of the positive reals, and thus look forward in time. This set is denoted $M_F(H)$. The procedure is then repeated but using the reverse graph, where the directions of the arcs are reversed. This provides us with a set of *backward templates*, where the delay times in the template consequences are subsets of the negative real numbers. Backward templates represent tests for the context in which a trigger event occurs, i.e. they confirm the prior occurrence of events before the trigger event occurs.

The procedure begins by considering event labels from Σ_c, since only they indicate continuous state information. The difference between the state value,

Fig. 5. Procedure FORWARD.TEMPLATE.GENERATION

Procedure: FORWARD.TEMPLATE.GENERATION
For each set Q_i in the partition of states {
  For each event $e \in \Sigma_c$ {
    For any arc a with label e and destination in Q_i {
      Let $r_0 \Leftarrow r_a$, $C \leftarrow \emptyset$
      For each arc a' departing Q_i {
        $C \Leftarrow C \cup \{(e_{a'}, X_{a'} - r_0)\}$
      }
      For each arc a' in Q_i with $e'_a \in \Sigma_d$ {
        $scale(e_{a'}) \Leftarrow Rate(q)$ for q destination of a'
      }
      Define $M_f = M_f \cup (e, C, scale)$
    }
  }
}

---

r_0, upon entering macrostate Q_i and the state value X'_a when exiting Q_i gives us a delay on the scaled time. This delay is used to define a template. The actuator events $e \in \Sigma_d$ are used to define the scaling of the local time of the template.

To simplify the presentation, we have made the assumption that all arcs with a given event in Σ_c are associated with only one macrostate source and destination. In [2], a procedure similar to the above but for timed automata considers the determination of templates without this assumption. Our assumption is formally stated as follows.

Definition 2. A time scalable hybrid automaton model H satisfies the *macrostate unique event labeling condition* (MUEC) if for any two arcs $a_1, a_2 \in \mathcal{A}$, $e(a_1) = e(a_2)$ if and only if there are macrostates Q_i and Q_j such that both arcs come from Q_i, and both terminate at Q_j.

Given the set of templates M generated from a hybrid automaton model H, we compare the languages $V_M(\underline{\mathbf{t}})$ and $V_{H^*}(\underline{\mathbf{t}})$ over any time period $\underline{\mathbf{t}}$. In [2], a procedure similar to the above was given for generating templates from timed automata models (not hybrid). The results of [2] can be extended in a straightforward way for our class of time-scaled hybrid automata by recognizing that the rate information in the model can be separated from the continuous state value information. This allows us in effect to convert the hybrid automaton to a timed automaton as in [2], but with a scaling of time. This leads to the following result, which shows that the automaton model and the templates $M_f(H) \cup M_b(H)$ are equivalent specifications.

Theorem 3. *Let H be a time scalable hybrid automaton satisfying the MUEC, and let $M = M_f(H) \cup M_b(H)$. Given an observation trajectory $v \in \mathcal{V}$ and finite time period $\underline{\mathbf{t}} \in \Im$, $v \in V_{H^*}(\underline{\mathbf{t}})$ if and only if $v \in V_M(\underline{\mathbf{t}})$.*

Theorem 3 then leads to the following result.

Corollary 4. *Let H be a time scalable hybrid automaton satisfying the MUEC such that $V_{H^*}(\underline{t})$ is the specification of acceptable system observations over any time period $\underline{t}$. Consider that there are n monitor processors executing the distributed monitor update procedure of figure 4, where each monitor i, $1 \leq i \leq n$ has its own template set M_i with $M_1 \cup M_2 \cup \cdots M_n = M_f(H) \cup M_b(H)$. A fault is declared by at least one monitor processor if and only if $v \notin V_{H^*}(\underline{t})$.*

The above corollary states that when the MUEC is true for a time scalable hybrid automaton H used for specifying the correct system operation, then the distributed fault monitoring system will correctly declare a fault if and only if the system observations do not satisfy the automaton specification of correct operation.

5 Summary

In this paper, we have presented a class of hybrid automata which are equivalent to timed automata with dynamically scaled times. Examples of systems which can be modeled by this class of automata arise commonly in modeling low-level manufacturing processes, such as conveyor systems, filling operations, and others. The structure of these time scalable hybrid automata allows the use of simple and distributed fault monitoring procedures based on time templates. The method is particularly attractive when monitoring multiple concurrent instances of a given automaton model. Rather than tracking the continuous state values of each automaton instance, only the local scalable time needs to be tracked. The inter-event timings to be monitored then are just fixed delays on the local scaled time.

References

1. Lawrence E. Holloway. *On-Line Fault Detection in Discrete Observation Systems Using Behavioral Models.* PhD thesis, Carnegie Mellon University, 1991.
2. Lawrence E. Holloway and Sujeet Chand. Time templates for discrete event fault monitoring in manufacturing systems. In *Proceedings of the 1994 American Control Conference*, pages 701–706, Baltimore, June 1994.
3. L.E. Holloway and S. Chand. Distributed fault monitoring in manufacturing systems using concurrent discrete-event observations. *Integrated Computer-Aided Engineering.* special issue on Detecting and Resolving Errors in Manufacturing Systems, to appear.
4. L. E. Holloway and S. Chand. Fault monitoring in manufacturing systems using concurrent discrete-event observations. In *Proceedings of AAAI 1994 Spring Symposium on Detecting and Resolving Errors in Manufacturing Systems*, Palo Alto, California, March 1994.
5. Pierre Dersin and Jean Florine. Firmware transitional logic for on-line monitoring and control. In *Proceedings of IEEE conference on decision and control*, Athens, Greece, December 1986.

6. M. Sampath, R. Sungupta, S. Lafortune, K. Sinnamohideen, and D. Teneketzis. Diagnosability of discrete event systems. In *Proceedings of 11th International Conference on Analysis and Optimization of Systems: Discrete Event Systems*, Sophia-Antipolis, France, June 1994.
7. Sanjiv Bavishi and Edwin K. P. Chong. Testability analysis using a discrete event systems framework. In *Proceedings of the 1995 ACC*, volume 4, pages 2621–2625, Seattle, June 1995.
8. Lawrence E. Holloway and Bruce H. Krogh. On-line fault detection via trajectory encoding. In *Proceedings of IFAC Symposium on Information Control Problems in Manufacturing Technology*, Toronto, May 1992.
9. Akash Deshpande and Pravin Varaiya. Information structures for control and verification of hybrid systems. In *Proceedings of 1995 American Control Conference*, volume 4, pages 2642–2647, Seattle, June 1995.

Hierarchical Design of a Chemical Concentration Control System

Xu Qiwen and He Weidong*

International Institute for Software Technology
The United Nations University
P.O.Box 3058, Macau

Abstract. We use a variant of the Duration Calculus to design a chemical concentration control system which has both nontrivial dynamics and control programs. The system is developed by refinement along the lines proposed in formal methods of software construction. Refinement rules for durational specification formulae are investigated for this purpose.

1 Introduction

The presence of both discrete and continuous components in hybrid systems has made the correctness of the system much harder to ensure. The difficulty is proportional to the complexity of discrete as well as continuous components. In this paper, using formal methods we design a chemical concentration control system which has both nontrivial dynamics and control programs. For a complex system like this one, formal methods offer a strong tool for achieving high assurance.

A formal development theory has two parts. First is a formal language for expressing requirements and design. Second is a set of rules which support the design, in particular, rules that facilitate the transformation of design from one level to another. Our formal tool is a variant of the Duration Calculus. Along the lines proposed in formal software construction, the system is developed by refinement.

Suppose that the system we are to construct is P (here P is merely a name without any structural contents), and it is expected to satisfy requirement R under assumption A. In a durational calculus framework, A and R are durational formulae, and the semantics of P is also defined by a durational formula, say $[\![P]\!]$. Then the correctness of the design is expressed by

$$A \wedge [\![P]\!] \Rightarrow R$$

Pair $\langle A, R \rangle$ constitutes the specification of P. In a hierarchical design, the system is developed by refinement. The correctness of the refinement is guaranteed by rules specially designed for this purpose. In this paper, a refinement rule is basically of the form

$$\frac{A_1 \wedge [\![P_1]\!] \Rightarrow R_1, \cdots, A_n \wedge [\![P_n]\!] \Rightarrow R_n}{A \wedge ([\![P_1]\!] \oplus_1 \cdots \oplus_n [\![P_n]\!]) \Rightarrow R}$$

* Email: {qxu,hwd}@iist.unu.edu

and it means that if the formulae above the line, namely, $A_i \wedge [\![P_i]\!] \Rightarrow R_i$ are valid, then the formula under the line, namely, $A \wedge ([\![P_1]\!] \oplus_1 \cdots \oplus_n [\![P_n]\!]) \Rightarrow R$ is also valid. When $n > 1$, we can apply this rule to verify the decomposition of $[\![P]\!]$ into

$$[\![P_1]\!] \oplus_1 \ldots \oplus_n [\![P_n]\!]$$

and the original proof obligation $A \wedge ([\![P_1]\!] \oplus_1 \ldots \oplus_n [\![P_n]\!]) \Rightarrow R$ is discharged into proof obligations about the components $A_i \wedge [\![P_i]\!] \Rightarrow R_i$. The design process continues with the new formulae $A_i \wedge [\![P_i]\!] \Rightarrow R_i$. When $n = 1$, the system structure is not changed, and only the specification is mapped into another one (the rule says that any implementation which satisfies the new specification also satisfies the original one). This happens typically when the new specification either gives more information towards implementation or is more suitable for further refinement.

In an ideal top-down design, the system is refined repeatedly until the components can be easily implemented. The advantage of such a constructive approach is that as soon as a design step is carried out one can check its correctness, so that the design and verification proceed at the same time. However, it is not always convenient to follow such a top-down paradigm strictly. For example, when refining P into $P_1 \oplus P_2$. In a strict top-down order, one would define the specifications of P_1 and P_2 before moving on to the design of these components. But sometimes it is difficult to know the exact logical connections of P_1 and P_2. For example, if P_1 passes a value to P_2, it is not always clear what property this value should have before the components are further developed. In this case, it may be easier to design P_2 bottom-up. Afterwards, one extracts a specification of P_2 based on which the specification of P_1 can then be constructed. Therefore, in practice, top-down and bottom-up designs are often used together.

Our method is illustrated by the design of a chemical concentration control system:

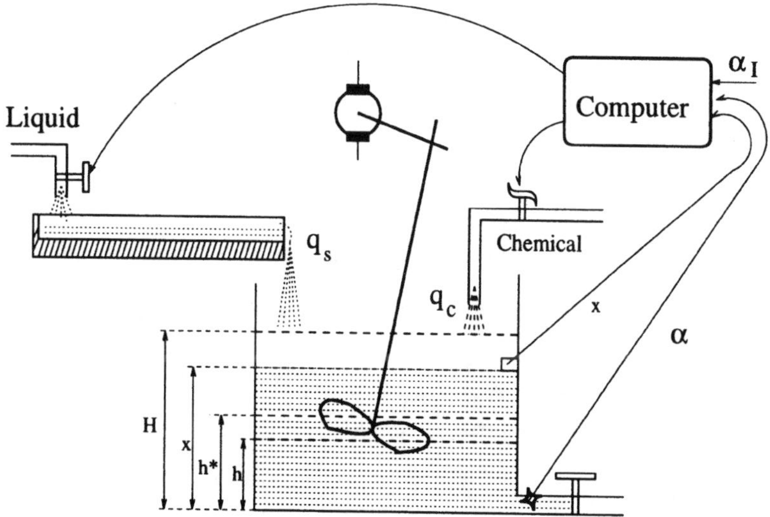

The main components of the system are a tank in which a chemical is dissolved in a liquid and a computer which controls the process. The principal requirement is that the output solution of the tank should be within a limited bound with the requested level and the the solution should be sufficiently uniform.

2 A variant of the Duration Calculus

2.1 Basics

The Duration Calculi is a family of real-time interval logics [4, 5] and have been used in a number of examples of hybrid systems. They are extensions of Moszkowski's Interval Temporal Logic [1]. We shall use a variant of the Duration Calculus as our formal language. In this section, we introduce some basic features of the calculus.

The real-time model of the Duration Calculus consists of a collection of state functions which map from non-negative reals (representing time) to values.

Definition 1. For an arbitrary state P and an arbitrary closed interval $[c, d]$ $(d \geq c)$ the accumulation of P, $\int P$, is defined by the value of integral of P over the interval $[c, d]$:

$$\int P\,[c, d] = \int_c^d P(t)dt$$

When P is a function from time to Booleans (represented by $\{0, 1\}$), $\int P$ gives the duration that P holds in the interval.

Following [5], we provide a way to refer to the state at the beginning and the end of the interval. We adopt the common notation in programming and use a unprimed variable to denote the state at beginning and a primed variable to denote the state at the end of the interval. Building on these primitives, we can write durational formulae. Formally speaking, durational formulae are functions from the set of all the intervals to Booleans. Durational formula B is satisfied over interval $[c, d]$ if

$$B\,[c, d] = \mathsf{true}$$

For example, for a state function x and a constant m

$$((x = m) \wedge (x' = m + 1)\,[c, d]) = (x(c) = m \wedge x(d) = m + 1)$$

For a state predicate r, let r' be the same predicate with all the state functions primed. By this convention, the above formula can also be written as $(x = m) \wedge (x = m + 1)'$. As another example,

$$x = x_0 \wedge \int \dot{x} \leq m \Rightarrow x' \leq x_0 + m$$

is a valid formula, because for any interval $[c, d]$,

$$\begin{aligned}&(x = x_0 \wedge \int \dot{x} \leq m \Rightarrow x' \leq x_0 + m)\,[c, d]\\ &= (x(c) = x_0 \wedge \int_c^d \dot{x} \leq m \Rightarrow x(d) \leq x_0 + m)\\ &= \mathsf{true}\end{aligned}$$

Definition 2. For a Boolean state P, $\lceil P \rceil$ is the everywhere operator,

$$\lceil P \rceil\,[c, d] = \forall c \leq t \leq d . P(t)$$

Definition 3. Let P and Q be two formulae. $P; Q$, in which ; is called *chop*, is satisfied in interval $[c, d]$ iff there exists h $(c \leq h \leq d)$ such that P is satisfied in $[c, h]$ and Q is satisfied in $[h, d]$. P^*, called *chop star*, is satisfied in interval $[c, d]$, iff there exists a partition $c = h_0 \leq h_1 \leq \ldots \leq h_{n-1} \leq h_n = d$ such that P is satisfied in all $[h_i, h_{i+1}]$ where $0 \leq i \leq n-1$.

There are some other operators in the Duration Calculus, but we do not introduce them here, since they are not needed for our case study. For the same reason, we do not introduce a full formal proof system of the Duration Calculus. Our design will be primarily supported at a higher level by a number of refinement rules. The soundness of these rules can be proved by the following axioms, where p is a state predicate and A, B are durational formulae.

(AX1)	$p \wedge (A; B) = (p \wedge A); B$
(AX2)	$(A \wedge p'); B = A; (p \wedge B)$
(AX3)	$\lceil p \rceil = \neg(\neg p'; \mathsf{true})$

2.2 Refinement rules

In this section, p, q and r are state predicates, and $[\![S]\!]$, $[\![S_1]\!]$, $[\![S_2]\!]$ and B are durational formulae. The main combinator that our example system uses is the chop operator. The following rule allows us to refine a system into two parts connected by the chop operator.

$$\frac{\begin{array}{l} p \wedge [\![S_1]\!] \Rightarrow r' \\ r \wedge [\![S_2]\!] \Rightarrow q' \end{array}}{p \wedge [\![S_1]\!]; [\![S_2]\!] \Rightarrow q'} \qquad \text{(Rule 1)}$$

The formulae are of the form $p \wedge [\![S]\!] \Rightarrow q'$. Its meaning is that for any interval if $[\![S]\!]$ holds and p holds at the beginning then q holds at the end of the interval. Following the terminology in program logic, we call p and q the pre- and post-conditions respectively. The above rule indicates that to ensure that q holds at the end of the interval, it is sufficient to find a predicate r such that it holds after the first phase, and that q holds after the second phase under r as the pre-condition. Notice that when r serves as the post-condition of the first phase, it is primed, and when it serves as the pre-condition of the second phase, it is unprimed. One can see the analogy between this rule and the one for sequential composition in Hoare logic. In a closer setting, a similar rule appeared in Interval Temporal Logic [2].

$$\frac{\begin{array}{l} p \wedge [\![S_1]\!] \Rightarrow \lceil q \rceil \wedge r' \\ r \wedge [\![S_2]\!] \Rightarrow \lceil q \rceil \end{array}}{p \wedge [\![S_1]\!] ; [\![S_2]\!] \Rightarrow \lceil q \rceil} \qquad \text{(Rule 2)}$$

The second rule is similar in spirit: to ensure that $\lceil q \rceil$ holds, we ensure that it holds in the first phase under the original pre-condition p and holds in the second phase under the new pre-condition r. By applying this rule repeatedly, we have the following rulę about chop star.

$$\frac{\begin{array}{l} p \Rightarrow r \\ r \wedge [\![S]\!] \Rightarrow \lceil q \rceil \wedge r' \end{array}}{p \wedge [\![S]\!]^* \Rightarrow \lceil q \rceil} \qquad \text{(Rule 3)}$$

The following rule gives a method for guaranteing $p \wedge [\![S]\!] \Rightarrow \lceil q \rceil$: find a formula B such that the two premises hold. The first premise says that if $p \wedge [\![S]\!]$ holds over an interval, then B holds over any sub-interval with the same beginning point. The second premise indicates that if $p \wedge B$ holds over an interval, then q holds at the end. Therefore, for any interval $[c, d]$ over which $p \wedge [\![S]\!]$ is satisfied, it follows that there exists a formula B such that B holds over $[c, t]$ for any $t \leq d$ and consequently q holds at t (end point of $[c, t]$).

$$\frac{\begin{array}{l} p \wedge [\![S]\!] \Rightarrow \neg((\neg B); \mathsf{true}\,) \\ p \wedge B \Rightarrow q' \end{array}}{p \wedge [\![S]\!] \Rightarrow \lceil q \rceil} \qquad \text{(Rule 4)}$$

Lastly, we need a rule concerning what are called freeze variables. In contrast to state variables, freeze variables do not occur in implementation but only in specifications. They are widely used in program logic, and we find them useful in the durational framework too. When the freeze variables do not occur freely in the conclusion, the following rule allows the condition concerning freeze variables to be removed from the assumption.

$$\frac{p \wedge (X = X_0) \wedge [\![S]\!] \Rightarrow B}{p \wedge [\![S]\!] \Rightarrow B} \qquad \text{(Rule 5)}$$

where X is a list of state functions, and X_0 is a list of same number of freeze variables which do not occur freely in B.

Having introduced the refinement rules, we now turn to specifying the chemical concentration control system.

3 Specification

Let the concerned physical state variables be as follows:

- m_c: mass of the chemical in the tank
- m_s: mass of the liquid in the tank
- m_{c1}: mass of dissolved chemical in the tank
- α: concentration level,
- α_*: concentration level if all chemical was dissolved,
- q_c: rate of supply of the chemical
- q_s: rate of supply of the liquid
- Q: rate of outflow
- x: solution depth

They are all functions from non-negative reals to non-negative reals. All except q_c, q_s and Q are continuous. The dynamics of the system are described by the following equations:

$$\begin{cases} \alpha = \frac{m_{c1}}{m_s + m_{c1}} \\ \alpha_* = \frac{m_c}{m_s + m_c} \\ \dot{\alpha} = 5(\alpha_* - \alpha) - \frac{\alpha(1-\alpha)}{m_s} q_s \\ \dot{m}_c = q_c - \alpha Q \\ \dot{m}_s = q_s - (1-\alpha)Q \\ x = k_1(m_c + 3m_s) \end{cases} \tag{DY}$$

The third equation characterises the change of α: $5(\alpha^* - \alpha)$ represents the effect from the dissolving process while $\frac{\alpha(1-\alpha)}{m_s} q_s$ represents the effect from adding the liquid. The last equation relates the depth of the solution to the quantities of the chemical and the liquid in the tank.

The execution of the system is divided into three phases. The first one is the waiting phase. At the end of it the user requests a desired concentration level α_I (α_I is then a discrete variable). Upon receiving such a request, the system enters the handling phase in which appropriate amounts of the chemical and the liquid are added to the tank. Afterwards, the outlet is opened and some solution is sent to the next workplace. This can be illustrated by the following diagram.

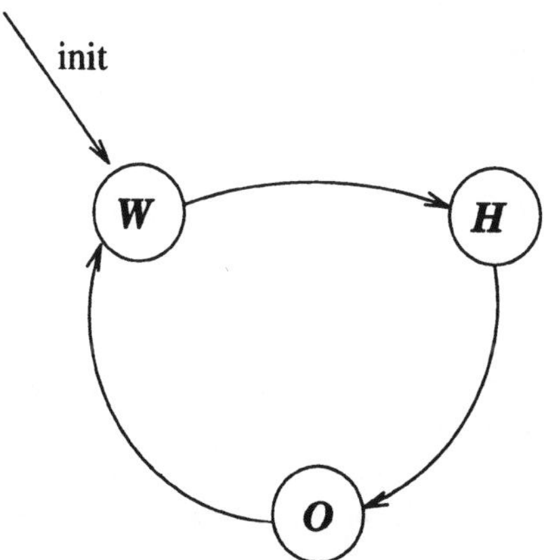

Formally, the system is defined by

$$sys = init \wedge ([\![\mathcal{W}]\!];[\![\mathcal{H}]\!];[\![\mathcal{O}]\!])^*$$

where *init* is the initial condition and $[\![\mathcal{W}]\!]$, $[\![\mathcal{H}]\!]$ and $[\![\mathcal{O}]\!]$ are durational formulae characterising the corresponding phases. Phases $[\![\mathcal{W}]\!]$ and $[\![\mathcal{O}]\!]$ involve mainly activities of the user. To achieve the control objectives, we can rely on some assumptions. In practice, the requested concentration level is within a limited range. In this case, α_I lies between 60% and 75%. The rate of outflow Q is limited, and in particular, we assume $Q \le 5(m_c + m_s)$. In every opening phase, the change in the solution depth is limited to between h and $\frac{4}{3}h$. In summary, the assumptions are as follows

$$\begin{aligned} ass = & \lceil 60\% \le \alpha_I \le 75\% \wedge Q \le 5(m_c + m_s)\rceil \\ & \wedge([\![\mathcal{O}]\!] \Rightarrow \lceil \mathsf{unchanged}(\alpha_I) \wedge q_s = q_c = 0\rceil \wedge h \le \textstyle\int \dot{x} \le \frac{4}{3}h) \\ & \wedge([\![\mathcal{W}]\!] \Rightarrow \lceil Q = q_s = q_c = 0\rceil) \end{aligned}$$

Formula $\lceil \mathsf{unchanged}(\alpha_I)\rceil$ holds if and only if α_I is not changed in the interval. It can be defined precisely, but such details are not important for the purpose of this paper.

We next examine the requirements. The main objective is that the concentration level of the solution flowing out of the tank should be close enough to the requested one. In particular, it is required that the difference between α and α_I should not be more than $0.1\%\alpha_I$. To ensure that the solution is sufficiently uniform, it is stipulated that $\alpha_* - \alpha$ should not be more than 2%. There are some other relatively easier to satisfy requirements: The chemical can only be put into the tank when $x \ge h^* = \frac{7}{6}h$, and the solution depth x should be restricted to a range between $H = 3h$ and h. Also, obviously, in the handling phase the value of α_I should not be changed.

To summarise, the requirements are listed below

$$\begin{aligned} req = & \lceil Q > 0 \Rightarrow |\alpha - \alpha_I| \le 0.1\%\alpha_I\rceil & req_1 \\ & \wedge\lceil \alpha_* - \alpha \le 2\%\rceil & req_2 \\ & \wedge\lceil q_c > 0 \Rightarrow x \ge \tfrac{7}{6}h\rceil \wedge \lceil h \le x \le H\rceil \wedge ([\![\mathcal{H}]\!] \Rightarrow \lceil \mathsf{unchanged}(\alpha_I)\rceil) \end{aligned}$$

Our design task is to refine $[\![\mathcal{H}]\!]$ into specifications which can be easily implemented and in the meantime ensure that the system satisfies the overall requirements. Correctness of the design amounts to proving

$$Th(DY) \vdash ass \wedge sys \Rightarrow req$$

Here Th(DY) before the $\vdash$ sign indicates the theory about the dynamics of the system can be used in the proof.

To avoid getting into too many details, we concentrate on req_1 and req_2. In a strictly top-down development, the next step would be to derive the specification of $[\![\mathcal{W}]\!];[\![\mathcal{H}]\!];[\![\mathcal{O}]\!]$. As it turns out, the specification of $[\![\mathcal{W}]\!];[\![\mathcal{H}]\!];[\![\mathcal{O}]\!]$ is quite simple and the correctness of the overall system can be easily proved with the help of Rule 3. However at this stage it is difficult to postulate the specification. Therefore, we switch to the bottom-up approach and proceed with the design of $[\![\mathcal{H}]\!]$ instead.

4 Design of $[\![\mathcal{H}]\!]$

As a natural and specific design decision, the handling phase is decomposed into four sub-phases: sampling, calculating, adding and resolving.

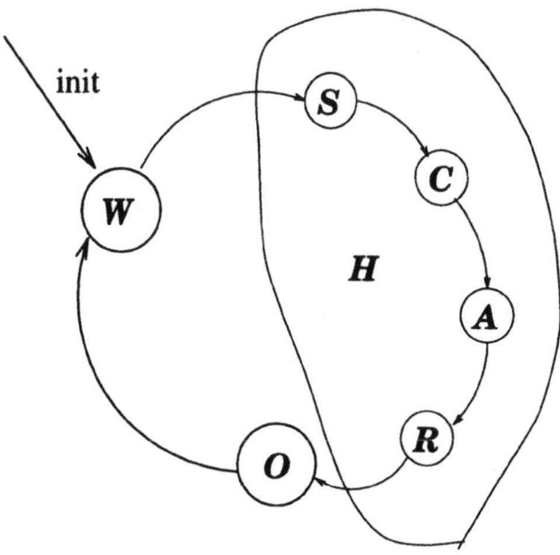

$$[\![\mathcal{H}]\!] = [\![\mathcal{S}]\!]; [\![\mathcal{C}]\!]; [\![\mathcal{A}]\!]; [\![\mathcal{R}]\!]$$

In the calculating phase, the control program computes the appropriate chemical and liquid increments to be added into the tank in the next phase. Clearly, the increments depend on the quantities of the chemical and the liquid in the tank. Therefore, the calculating phase is preceded by a sampling phase in which the related data are collected.

Theorem 1 *At any time point,*

$$\begin{cases} m_s = \frac{x(1-\alpha_*)}{k_1(3-2\alpha_*)} \\ \\ m_c = \frac{x\alpha_*}{k_1(3-2\alpha_*)} \end{cases}$$

The depth x can be measured, but α_* cannot. However, α_* and α are reasonably close when req_2 is satisfied. Therefore, concentration level α is sampled instead and its value is used together with the sampled value of x to calculate the approximated values of m_s and m_c. Let x^0 and α^0 be freeze variables denoting the sampled values. The approximated values are

$$\begin{cases} m_s^@ \stackrel{\text{def}}{=} \frac{x^0(1-\alpha^0)}{k_1(3-2\alpha^0)} \\ \\ m_c^@ \stackrel{\text{def}}{=} \frac{x^0\alpha^0}{k_1(3-2\alpha^0)} \end{cases} \qquad \text{(F0)}$$

Let the chemical increment and the liquid increment be denoted by program variables Δm_c and Δm_s. Recall that α_I denotes the next desired concentration. We choose Δm_c and Δm_s that satisfy

$$\alpha_I = \frac{m_c^@ + \Delta m_c}{m_c^@ + \Delta m_c + m_s^@ + \Delta m_s} \tag{F1}$$

Obviously, there exist many pairs of such Δm_c and Δm_s. A control program which chooses the exact values of Δm_c and Δm_s will be constructed later. But at this level, we do not consider the details of the control program. Instead, now we only postulate the specifications of the sub-phases and prove that if these specifications are satisfied by future implementations then the overall system will satisfy req_1 and req_2.

Recall the requirement that the chemical can only be added when the depth is above $\frac{7}{6}h$. Therefore, if the depth is lower than $\frac{7}{6}h$, only the liquid can be added, and in order for the chemical to be added, the depth after all the liquid is poured in must be at least $\frac{7}{6}h$. Let formula F2 be

$$k_1(m_c + 3(m_s + \Delta m_s)) \geq \frac{7}{6}h \tag{F2}$$

To ensure req_2,

$$\alpha_* - \alpha \leq 2\% \tag{F3}$$

must be satisfied at the beginning. To this end, we postulate the proof obligation for the first two sub-phases

Proof Obligation 1

$$\begin{aligned} & x = x^0 \wedge \alpha = \alpha^0 \wedge m_c = m_c^0 \wedge m_s = m_s^0 \wedge F3 \wedge [\![\mathcal{S}]\!];[\![\mathcal{C}]\!] \\ & \Rightarrow (\exists m_s^@, m_c^@ . F0 \wedge F1)' \wedge F2' \wedge m_c' = m_c^0 \wedge m_s' = m_s^0 \wedge req_2 \\ & \quad \wedge \lceil \mathsf{unchanged}(\alpha_I) \rceil \end{aligned}$$

where m_c^0 and m_s^0 are freeze variables. In the adding phase, the chemical and the liquid are added into the tank according to the values calculated in the last phase, and in such a way that req_2 is satisfied if $F3$ holds at the beginning. The outlet is closed in this period.

$$\begin{aligned} [\![\mathcal{A}]\!] \stackrel{\text{def}}{=} F2 \Rightarrow & \textstyle\int q_s = \Delta m_s \wedge \int q_c = \Delta m_c \\ & \wedge \lceil Q = 0 \wedge \mathsf{unchanged}(\alpha_I) \wedge (q_c > 0 \Rightarrow x \geq \tfrac{7}{6}h) \rceil \wedge (F3 \Rightarrow req_2) \end{aligned}$$

Condition $F2$ is assumed, for without it $[\![\mathcal{A}]\!]$ may not be possible to implement. The chemical is then left to dissolve for one time unit or more.

$$[\![\mathcal{R}]\!] = \lceil Q = q_s = q_c = 0 \wedge \mathsf{unchanged}(\alpha_I) \rceil \wedge l \geq 1$$

We have proved a number of lemmas which are primarily about each sub-phases. Basing on these lemmas and using the refinement rules, we obtain the following theorem about the composition of the whole handling phase with the opening phase. Details of the proofs can be found in [3].

Theorem 2

$$F3 \wedge (\frac{\alpha_* - \alpha}{\alpha_*} \leq 0.0002246) \wedge [\![\mathcal{H}]\!];[\![\mathcal{O}]\!] \Rightarrow req_1 \wedge req_2 \wedge (\frac{\alpha_* - \alpha}{\alpha_*} \leq 0.0002246)'$$

Let $init \stackrel{\text{def}}{=} F3 \wedge (\frac{\alpha_* - \alpha}{\alpha_*} \leq 0.0002246)$. Using Rule 1 and Rule 2, we can prove

Theorem 3 $\quad init \wedge [\![\mathcal{W}]\!];[\![\mathcal{H}]\!];[\![\mathcal{O}]\!] \Rightarrow req_1 \wedge req_2 \wedge (\frac{\alpha_* - \alpha}{\alpha_*} \leq 0.0002246)'$

Applying refinement Rule 3, we finally conclude that

Theorem 4 $\quad init \wedge ([\![\mathcal{W}]\!];[\![\mathcal{H}]\!];[\![\mathcal{O}]\!])^* \Rightarrow req_1 \wedge req_2$

5 Refinement of $[\![\mathcal{A}]\!]$

In the specification of $[\![\mathcal{A}]\!]$, it is stipulated that if $F3$ holds at the beginning then req_2 holds. However, being an appropriate specification statement at a high level, it does not give any information about how to achieve this. Clearly, adding the chemical increases the difference between α_* and α, and therefore the chemical should be added in a sufficiently gentle way. The addition of the liquid has a somewhat more complex impact: it follows from DY that $\alpha_* - \alpha$ increases if $m_c m_{c1} > m_s^2$ and decreases if $m_c m_{c1} < m_s^2$. The specification of $[\![\mathcal{A}]\!]$ can be refined into

$$\begin{aligned}F2 \Rightarrow & \int q_s = \Delta m_s \wedge \int q_c = \Delta m_c \\ & \wedge \lceil Q = 0 \wedge \mathsf{unchanged}(\alpha_I) \wedge (q_c > 0 \Rightarrow x \geq \tfrac{7}{6}h)\rceil \\ & \wedge (F3 \Rightarrow \lceil \exists k_c, k_s. k_c \geq \tfrac{m_s}{(m_c+m_s)^2} \wedge k_s \geq (\tfrac{m_{c1}}{(m_{c1}+m_s)^2} - \tfrac{m_c}{(m_c+m_s)^2}) \\ & \qquad \wedge k_c q_c + k_s q_s \leq 0.1\rceil)\end{aligned}$$

As a typical lower level specification, it contains a lot of details. Based on it, it is easy to design a control algorithm which ultimately decides the values of q_c and q_s.

6 Development of $[\![\mathcal{S}]\!];[\![\mathcal{C}]\!]$

Proof Obligation 1 specifies the behaviours of the composition of the sampling and the calculating phases. We now decompose the specification further. Let $\bar{x}$ and $\bar{\alpha}$ be two program variables for storing the sampled values of x and α. At the end of the sampling phase, $\bar{x}$ and $\bar{\alpha}$ are given the initial values of x and α. Hence, let

$$\begin{aligned}[\![\mathcal{S}]\!] \stackrel{\text{def}}{=} & \; x = x^0 \wedge \alpha = \alpha^0 \wedge m_c = m_c^0 \wedge m_s = m_s^0 \wedge F3 \\ & \Rightarrow (\bar{x} = x^0 \wedge \bar{\alpha} = \alpha^0 \wedge m_c = m_c^0 \wedge m_s = m_s^0)' \wedge req_2 \wedge \lceil \mathsf{unchanged}(\alpha_I)\rceil\end{aligned}$$

The calculating process then computes the amount of increments based on the sampled values.

$$\begin{aligned}[\![\mathcal{C}]\!] \stackrel{\text{def}}{=} & \; \bar{x} = x^0 \wedge \bar{\alpha} = \alpha^0 \wedge m_c = m_c^0 \wedge m_s = m_s^0 \wedge F3 \\ & \Rightarrow ((\exists m_s^{@}, m_c^{@}. F0 \wedge F1) \wedge F2)' \wedge m_c' = m_c^0 \wedge m_s' = m_s^0 \\ & \quad \wedge req_2 \wedge \lceil \mathsf{unchanged}(\alpha_I)\rceil\end{aligned}$$

Given the above definitions of $[\![\mathcal{S}]\!]$ and $[\![\mathcal{C}]\!]$, it is trivial to show that Proof Obligation 1 indeed holds.

We do not develop the sampling program any further whereas propose an algorithm for the calculating phase. The input-output behaviours of the algorithm will be proved using the traditional program logic for total correctness and the results are incorporated into the durational framework based on the following rule. Suppose P is a program and $[\![P]\!]$ is its durational semantics, then

$$\frac{p\ \{P\}\ q}{p \wedge [\![P]\!] \Rightarrow q'} \qquad \text{(Rule 6)}$$

Recall the assumption that in any opening phase the solution depth can only be lowered by $\frac{4}{3}h$, therefore the depth will not fall below h if after each adding phase, the depth is at least $\frac{7}{3}h$. Moreover, to limit the depth below H and leave more room for adjustment in the next round, the new depth should be as low as possible. The algorithm works as follows. First, calculate the amount of the chemical and the liquid if the solution depth is $\frac{7}{3}h$ with concentration level α_I. If the amount of the chemical (or the liquid) is less than the estimated amount of the chemical (or the liquid) already in the tank, then Δm_c (or Δm_s) is taken to be 0. If the amount of the liquid is more than that estimated in the tank, but the difference is not enough to raise the depth over $\frac{7}{6}h$ (recall that the chemical can only be added after that), then Δm_s will be chosen so that after the liquid is added, the depth is $\frac{7}{6}h$. Once one increment is decided, the other increment can be calculated from F1.

The algorithm is simple, but the reason why it works depends on some facts about the dynamics of the system and therefore its verification is not entirely trivial. The algorithm is presented below together with some predicates outlining its verification.

$\{\bar{x} = x^0 \wedge \bar{\alpha} = \alpha^0 \wedge x^0 = k_1(m_c^0 + 3m_s^0)\}$
procedure $\mathcal{C}$
var: $m_s^@, m_s', m_c^@, m_c'$;
$m_s' := \frac{7h(1-\alpha_I)}{3k_1(3-2\alpha_I)}; m_c' := \frac{7h\alpha_I}{3k_1(3-2\alpha_I)}$;
$m_s^@ := \frac{\bar{x}(1-\bar{\alpha})}{k_1(3-2\alpha_I)}; m_c^@ := \frac{\bar{x}\bar{\alpha}}{k_1(3-2\alpha_I)}$;
$\Delta m_s := m_s' - m_s^@; \Delta m_c := m_c' - m_c^@$;
$\{F0 \wedge \bar{x} = k_1(m_c^0 + 3m_s^0)\}$
if $\Delta m_s < 0 \rightarrow \{x^0 \geq \frac{7}{6}h\} \Delta m_s := 0; \Delta m_c := \frac{\alpha_I(m_s^@ + m_c^@) - m_c^@}{1-\alpha_I}$
$[\,]$ $\Delta m_c < 0 \rightarrow \{x^0 \geq \frac{7}{6}h\} \Delta m_c := 0; \Delta m_s := \frac{m_c^@ - \alpha_I(m_s^@ + m_c^@)}{\alpha_I}$
$[\,]$ $0 < \Delta m_s < \frac{\frac{7}{6}h - \bar{x}}{3k_1} \rightarrow \Delta m_s := \frac{\frac{7}{6}h - \bar{x}}{3k_1}; \Delta m_c := \frac{\alpha_I(m_s^@ + m_c^@)}{1-\alpha_I} - m_c^@$
$[\,]$ else $\rightarrow$ skip fi
$\{(\exists m_s^@, m_c^@ . F0 \wedge F1) \wedge k_1(m_c^0 + 3(m_s^0 + \Delta m_s)) \geq \frac{7}{6}h\}$

We can use $x^0 = k_1(m_c^0 + 3m_s^0)$ as part of the pre-condition, because it is a theorem following from the dynamics of the system. This program only achieves the input-output behaviour of the $[\![\mathcal{C}]\!]$. Having constructed the control algorithm, the implementation of phase $[\![\mathcal{C}]\!]$ is easy: just run the program while keeping all the valves closed. Formally, using Rule 6 we have the following theorem:

Theorem 5 $[\![\text{procedure } \mathcal{C}]\!] \wedge \lceil Q = q_s = q_c = 0 \rceil \Rightarrow [\![\mathcal{C}]\!]$

7 Discussion

We find the case study worthwhile. Firstly, the system has non-trivial dynamics and control structures, and consequently the reasoning needed in the design is involved. One of the authors of this paper is from control engineering and the system was first designed without using formal methods. There were serious questions about the correctness of the system. Without a formal notation, the informal arguments were unclear at many places, and without proper structures, many details cannot be covered at reasonable length. The formal design has greatly improved our confidence in the system, and has clarified many points. Secondly, this case study has helped us to identify a number of rules which are useful in the design. We believe these design rules are of general uses and more rules should be studied in order to facilitate the practical applications of the Duration Calculus.

In this case study, we proposed a design and showed that it is correct with respect to the requirements. There are many other interesting properties in control engineering such as stability[2] and robustness which we have not touched. As topics for future study, we shall examine which of these control engineering concepts can be formalised.

Acknowledgements We thank Zhou Chaochen, Chris George and Dines Bjørner for encouragement and helpful comments.

References

1. B. Moszkowski: A Temporal Logic for Multilevel Reasoning about Hardware. *IEEE Computer*, 18,2,pp.10-19,1985.
2. B. Moszkowski: Some Very Compositional Temporal Properties, In *Programming Concepts, Methods and Calculi (A-56)*, E.-R. Olderog (Editor), Elsevier Science B.V. (North-Holland), pp. 307-326, 1994.
3. Xu Qiwen and He Weidong: Hierarchical Design of a Chemical Concentration Control System. UNU/IIST Report No. 41, 1995.
4. Zhou Chaochen, C.A.R. Hoare and A.P. Ravn: A Calculus of Durations. In *Information Processing Letters*, Vol. 40, No. 5, pp. 269-276, 1991.
5. Zhou Chaochen, A.P. Ravn and M.R. Hansen: An Extended Duration Calculus for Hybrid Real-Time Systems. In *Hybrid Systems*, LNCS 736, R.L. Grossman, A. Nerode, A.P. Ravn and H. Rischel (Editors), pp. 36-59, 1993.

[2] Stability is not really a difficulty for our system.

Switched Bond Graphs as Front-End to Formal Verification of Hybrid Systems

Jan-Erik Strömberg[1], Simin Nadjm-Tehrani[2] and Jan L. Top[3]

[1] Div. of Automatic Control, Dept. of Electrical Engineering, Linköping University, S-581 83 Linköping, Sweden, e-mail: janerik@isy.liu.se

[2] Dept. of Computer & Information Science, Linköping University, S-581 83 Linköping, Sweden, e-mail: simin@ida.liu.se

[3] Agrotechnological Research Institute ATO-DLO, P.O. Box 17, NL-6700 AA Wageningen, The Netherlands, e-mail: j.l.top@ato.dlo.nl

Abstract. Formal verification of safety and timing properties of engineering systems is only meaningful if based on models which are systematically derived. In this paper we report on our experience using switched bond graphs for the modelling of hardware components in hybrid systems. We present the basic ideas underlying bond graphs in general and switched bond graphs in particular. Switched bond graphs are tailored for the modelling of physical systems undergoing abrupt structural changes. Such abrupt changes appear frequently in plants closed by discrete controllers. We illustrate our approach by means of an aircraft landing gear system and prove safety and timeliness properties using the proof system of extended duration calculus.

Keywords: hybrid system, physical modelling, bond graph, verification, duration calculus

1 Introduction

In this paper we report on our experience on using switched bond graphs as a front-end to hardware engineers in verifying complex hybrid systems involving both software and hardware components. We present the basic ideas underlying bond graphs in general and switched bond graphs in particular. We compare briefly the bond graph approach to physical systems modelling with the recently proposed 'object oriented' approach as represented by *e.g.* Omola and Dymola [8, 3]. Switched bond graphs were introduced in 1993 [16] as an extension to classical bond graphs in order to deal with hardware undergoing abrupt structural changes; so-called *mode-switching* physical systems. Such behaviour is common in general but are particularly common in physical plants closed by software implemented *discrete controllers.*

Building mathematical models of complex hybrid systems is a delicate process. The problem is that assumptions made are often difficult to express — if mentioned at all. For models of physical devices, the bond graph language helps in solving this problem.

The most important advantages of bond graphs are the following. First, since the language is based on ***physical*** rather than ***mathematical*** concepts, it forces the modeller to articulate important modelling assumptions. Mathematical models always need additional clarification in the form of explanatory illustrations or text. By using bond graphs, an important part of this explanation is structured and standardised, thus increasing the quality of the models created. This is not unlike the situation in software engineering, where high level programming languages have been developed for reasons of efficiency and quality assurance. Secondly, the energy concepts of bond graphs are general enough to enable efficient communication between electrical, mechanical hydraulic and thermal engineers - without even writing equations. This provides major leverage to design projects in which several disciplines are involved. Thirdly, the energy concepts also help maintaining a clear distinction between the behaviour of a physical object and the object *per se*. As will be shown later, it is not always possible to associate behaviour to an individual object.

In recent years, formal analysis of hybrid systems has become an active area of research [4]. Its objective is to provide means for proving that a particular device, interacting with a discrete controller, meets certain safety and timing requirements. So far, much of the work has focused on the development of efficient methods and tools for system analysis. However, hybrid verification efforts equally depend on the quality of the models employed; hence the relevance of bond graphs for this field.

The type of models we are concerned with will be examined in the next section. Later we discuss the problems associated with modelling physical systems in general and mode-switching systems in particular. We present the classical bond graph language and its recently proposed switched extension. Then we move on to the specific use of switched bond graphs in formal verification of embedded systems. To this end we present an aerospace application, namely the landing gear system of the Swedish multi-role combat aircraft JAS-39 Gripen. We exemplify the derivation of some simplified models and present the basic structure of the proof of a safety and a timliness property in Extended Duration Calculus (EDC) [2]. The proofs involve time-linear as well as non-timelinear mathematical models.

2 Apparatus Modelling

We let the term 'apparatus' refer to anything that is controlled by a discrete embedded controller and of which the behaviour is described by physical laws. Note that this excludes software components. Apparatus models cover electromechanical or electrohydraulic actuators, the systems governed by these actuators and the sensors used to measure the effect of the actuation. As an example, Fig. 1 depicts an apparatus model of a system involving three different physical domains: electric, hydraulic and mechanic. This particular diagram is a model of the landing gear subsystem of an aircraft.

Industrial documentation of the components constituting an apparatus, whether they are electric, hydraulic or mechanic, is typically informal. The icons used in Fig. 1 are fairly well standardized in as far as they refer to *functions* within the system, implemented by specific devices. However, they are ambiguous with respect to the underlying physics: it is not clear which physical effects must be taken into account.

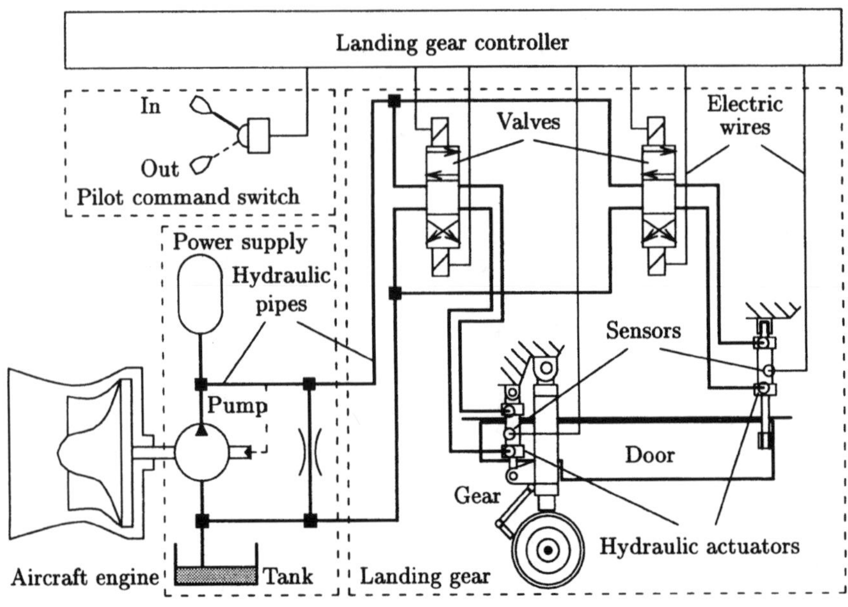

Fig. 1. The landing gear system as documented by a mechanical engineer.

As a matter of fact, it is not even possible to precisely define the underlying physics of a device component. The reason for this is that the behaviour of a component depends on the circumstances in which the device is used and its characteristics with respect to accuracy, timing, dynamic range *et c.* Hence, the type of 'models' typically used in industry are in themselves not informative enough for determining a unique mathematical behaviour model suitable for *e.g.* formal verification.

Nevertheless, it is possible to link, in an organized way, mathematical models to each of the icons (objects) used in schematic diagrams, provided we know the context in which the objects are being used. This is the approach adopted in so called 'object oriented modelling languages' such as Omola [8, 1] and Dymola [3]; see Fig. 2. Links between objects and mathematical relations describing the behaviour of each object are here made explicit. Once the behaviour of the individual objects has been specified, the composed overall model can be automatically generated. This compositional approach is of course necessary in order to allow for the modelling of real-sized systems.

Although the object oriented approach solves some problems, there are still some unresolved ones. For example, a major problem is how to describe the assumptions underlying the mathematical device models in a standardized way. Also, we have the more fundamental problem of having to link behaviour models to unique objects. This is not always possible since behaviour ever so often emerges from the interaction *between* two or more devices or objects. In 'object oriented' languages such as Omola/Dymola, this problem is typically circumvented by introducing abstract 'interaction objects'.

A clarifying example of an interaction effect is *friction*. Friction is the effect of two bodies moving relative to each other. In languages like Omola or Dymola a 'friction object' is to be inserted in between the objects representing the two moving bodies. Hence, in that case the clear relationship between the objects in the original schematic diagram and the Omola/Dymola type of representation cannot be maintained. Thus we get an intermingling of concrete devices with models of abstract interactions.

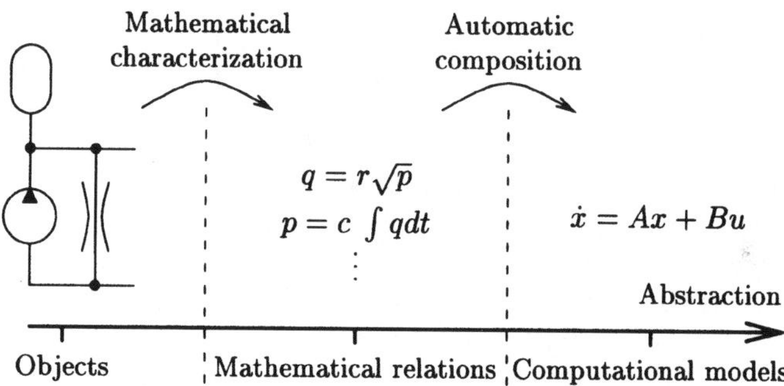

Fig. 2. The structure of 'object oriented' modelling languages such as Omola/Dymola.

Bond graphs [13, 6], however, provide a neater solution to these fundamental modelling problems. This is done by introducing an additional modelling formalism 'in between' the concrete device oriented *technical level* and the more abstract mathematical level; see Fig. 3.

3 Classical Bond Graphs

As opposed to the Dymola/Omola type of language, the bond graph language is *not* a programming language. Bond graphs represent the energetic interaction structure of an apparatus and nothing else. This also implies that bond graphs are restricted to systems which can be naturally represented using energy as the basic concept. The advantage of adopting energy concepts is that they are well

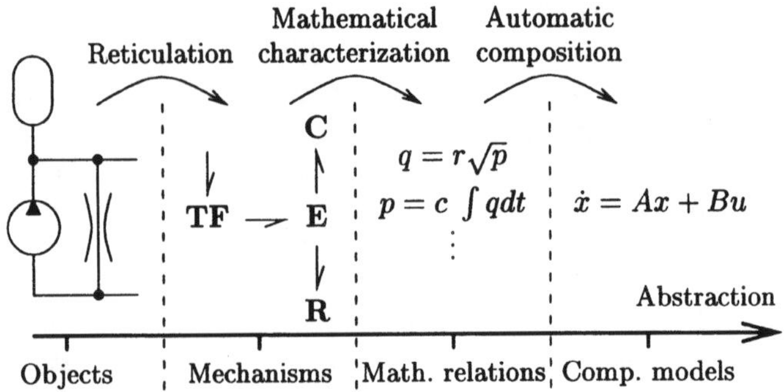

Fig. 3. The structure of the energy oriented bond graph language.

understood and have a common meaning to almost all hardware engineers; no matter the particular engineering domain.

The original bond graph language consists of only nine basic elements. These nine elements form the nodes of a graph connected by half-arrow shaped *bonds* representing exchange of energy. The elements represent energy processes. With each bond a pair of power variables *effort* and *flow* is associated, with $e \times f =$ *power*. Effort and flow are generalisations of force and velocity, voltage and current, temperature and entropy flow in different domains.

The nine energy processes defined by the language fall into one of the following five categories: (1) sources (**Se**, **Sf**), (2) storages (**C**, **I**), (3) dissipations (**R**), (4) distributions (**E**, **F**) and (5) conversions (**TF**, **GY**). Each of these processes corresponds to a well defined ideal physical mechanism. For example, a bond graph **C**-element represents an idealized model of a hydraulic accumulator, an electric capacitor or a mechanic mass-less spring (see Fig. 4). By selecting and combining these ideal elements, the modeller is forced to express every assumption in a standard and formal way.

Hydraulic
$p = e$ [Pa]
$q = f$ [m^3/s]
Electric
$i = f$ [A]
$u = e$ [V]
Mechanic
$v = f$ [m/s]
$F = e$ [N]
Bond graph
e
f
C

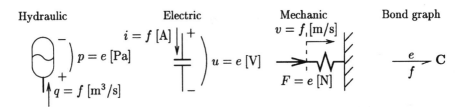

Fig. 4. The bond graph representation of three different storage mechanisms.

The first phase in the bond graph modelling procedure is referred to as *reticulation* [13]. As a matter of fact, this inherently difficult modelling phase is always present no matter the modelling approach employed. Based on the purpose of the model and the context in which the devices are used it is here decided which physical effects to consider. Bond graphs are unique in that they force the modeller to represent this phase and the decisions made explicitly. Moreover, bond graphs accommodate the modeller with the smallest possible set of primitive concepts sufficient for a wide class of apparatus. Of course bond graphs provide little or no support when systems outside this class are considered.

Once the system has been reticulated successfully, *i.e.* the bond graph has been drawn, the mathematical characterization of the nodes in the graph is in most cases straightforward. This is due to the fact that each node is associated with a well defined mathematical structure: the *constitutive relation*. Note that a constitutive relation is a relation in the original mathematical sense; *not* a computation. Therefore, a bond graph is *acausal*, *i.e.* a declarative description of a computational model. The composition of the individual relations into a complete computational whole is completely algorithmic. The result of automatic composition is a system of differential and algebraic equations (DAE). This provides a well-defined mathematical semantics for bond graphs [15].

4 Switched Bond Graphs

Classical bond graphs allow for finite flows of energy only and are thus restricted to modelling continuous changes. However, many practical devices undergo abrupt changes in their behaviour, mostly due to external or internal discrete control. Such devices will be referred to as *mode-switching* systems. An example of an internally controlled mode-switching system is shown in Fig. 5. The figure depicts a pump proposed already in 1697 by the Swedish engineer C. Polhem [5, 7]. This pump has lately been shown to work, but was unfortunately never built in those years due to lack of suitable analysis techniques. By means of an intricate mechanism controlling the shunt valve F, the air-pressure in the closed vessel I is brought to oscillate between the value of the overpressure and the underpressure source respectively. The internally controlled check-valves allow the water to flow upwards only. It is clear that the siphon pump is best characterized as a *hybrid system*, *i.e.* a computational system consisting of a set of continuous DAEs and a set of Boolean transition conditions.

In order to carry over the bond graph methodology to mode-switching systems, an extension referred to as the *switched bond graph* was introduced in 1993 [16, 17, 15, 14]. The idea is to allow for reticulation of hybrid systems without loosing any of the conceptual clarity of the traditional bond graph language.

The main ingredient in the extension is a new ideal element, *viz.* the *ideal generalized switch* (**Sw**) [16, 14]. As opposed to the other bond graph elements, the **Sw**-element is *not* associated with a constitutive mathematical relation over effort and flow. Instead, it is associated with a discrete mathematical structure determining the discrete state of the switch. Once all elements of a switched bond graph have been mathematically characterized – including the **Sw**-elements – it can be automatically converted into a computational hybrid system: a set of

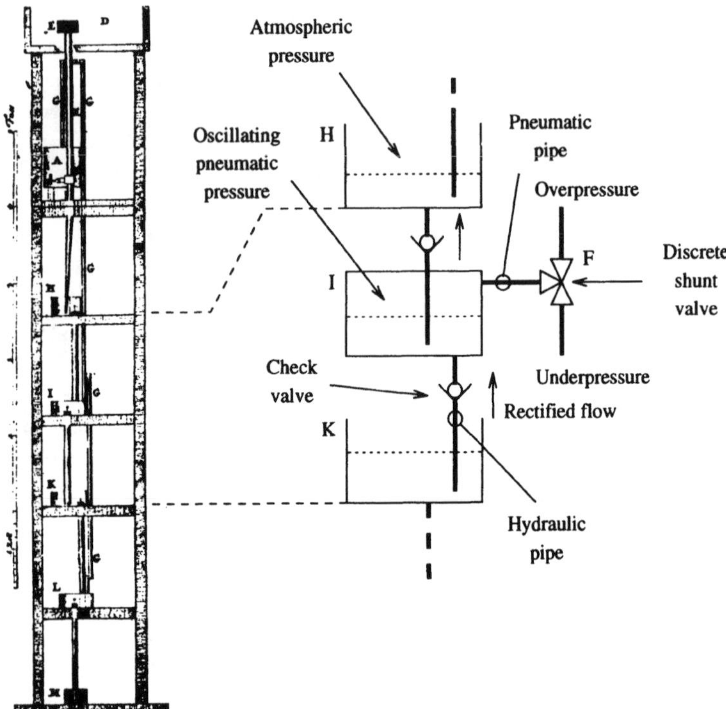

Fig. 5. The 1697 siphon pump machine. Left: original drawing. Right: modern schematic diagram. H and K are open tanks whereas I is a closed vessel.

DAEs and Boolean transition conditions. Further details on how to characterize individual **Sw**-elements and how to compose a switched bond graph to a computational whole, is provided in [15, 14].

5 The Landing Gear Model

The landing gear system has been chosen as one of the test cases in an ongoing multi-disciplinary research effort in cooperation with aerospace industries in Sweden. The project concerns evaluation and development of tools and methods for the modelling and formal analysis of complex hybrid systems.

The system involves hydro-mechanic, electro-hydraulic and electro-mechanic hardware components interacting with hardwired as well as software based modules performing diagnostic and controlling tasks. The system contains continuous control loops, implemented in hydro-mechanic hardware, and discrete control loops, implemented in hardware and software. Finally, the system interacts with a human operator, namely the pilot, who in turn critically depends on its proper operation.

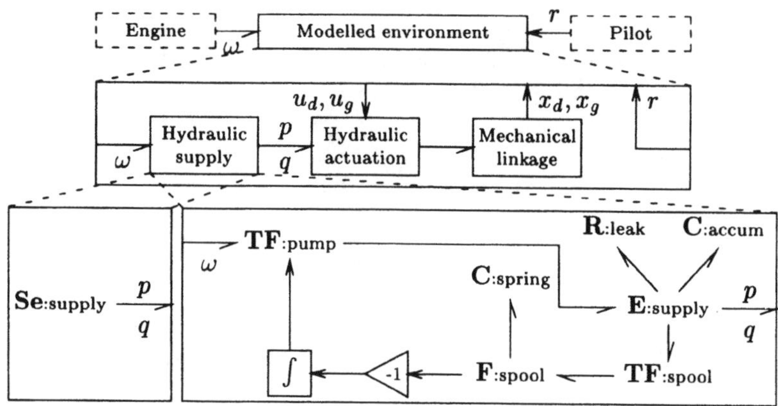

Fig. 6. The physical environment models. Left: the coarsest model of the hydraulic supply. Right: the model including a hydro-mechanically regulated pump.

The hardware components in the landing gear system consist of the landing gear itself, *i.e.* the wheel–and–suspension system, a pair of doors protecting the gear during flight and landing, and a pair of hydraulic actuators for the manouvering of the gear and the doors; see also Fig. 1. As part of the landing gear system, the hydraulic power supply system provides the hydro-mechanic energy needed to manoeuvre the gear and the doors under all operating conditions.

The software components implements a discrete controller for the door and gear actuators, as well as a diagnosis module which detects malfunctions in the hydraulic power supply system.

For the purpose of illustration, we present two different bond graph models of the hydraulic power supply subsystem and a single model of the door–and–gear subsystem. These models differ in the assumptions made about the subsystems, and therefore illustrate the capability of bond graphs to make such assumptions clear.

In the coarsest model of the hydraulic power supply we represent the assumption that the hydraulic power supply system behaves as an ideal constant pressure source; see the lowest left-most box in Fig. 6. Combining it with the model of the door–and–gear subsystem, the overall plant model converts to a simple time-linear dynamic system

$$\dot{x}_d = \alpha_d \, u_d, \quad x_d \in [0,1] \tag{1}$$

$$\dot{x}_g = \alpha_g \, u_g, \quad x_g \in [0,1] \tag{2}$$

where $\alpha_d, \alpha_g > 0$ are constants (time-invariants), x_d (x_g) the normalized door (gear) position and u_d (u_g) $\in \{-1, 0, +1\}$ is the three-valued door (gear) control signal.

In the more detailed model of the power supply system (lowest right-most box in Fig. 6), we no longer assume that the hydraulic pressure is ideal. Instead we make an explicit model of the hydro-mechanic regulator which in fact attempts to make the pressure 'as constant as possible'. This second coarsest model is depicted to the right in Fig. 6. In this case the overall bond graph converts to a non-timelinear dynamic system

$$\dot{x}_d = \alpha'_d \, p \, u_d, \quad x_d \in [0,1] \tag{3}$$

$$\dot{x}_g = \alpha'_g \, p \, u_g, \quad x_g \in [0,1] \tag{4}$$

$$\dot{p} = -(\gamma + \gamma_d \, |u_d| + \gamma_g \, |u_g|) \, p + \beta \tag{5}$$

where $\alpha'_d, \alpha'_g, \gamma_d, \gamma_g > 0$ are constants and p is the hydraulic supply pressure. The quotient β/γ is a monotonic function of the aircraft engine velocity ω.

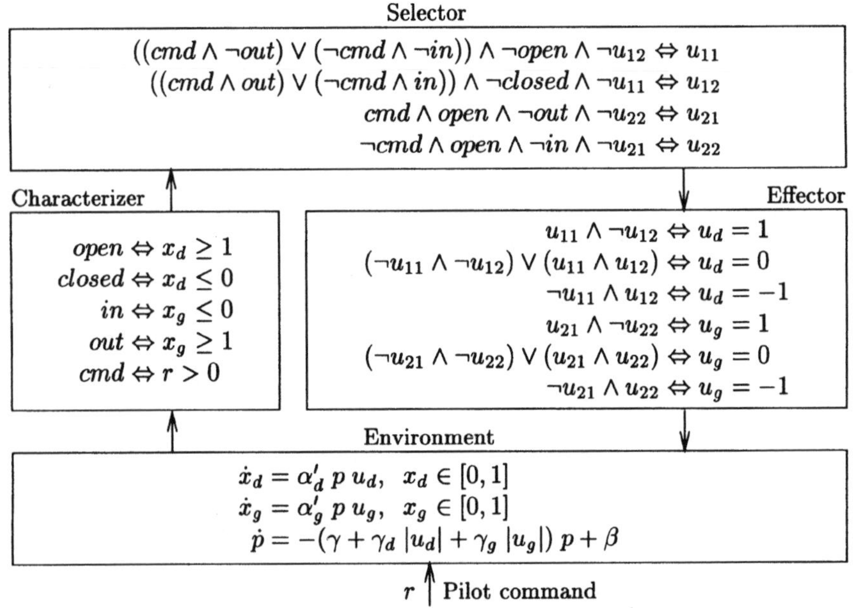

Fig. 7. The closed loop mathematical model.

The DAE models derived can now be plugged into the model of the closed loop system as required. To do this we use a hybrid modelling architecture proposed earlier [9, 10]; see Fig. 7. The full arrows in this notation denote the flow of information. As an example we have included the coarsest environment model (1), (2) in the *environment* box. The interaction with the pilot is modelled through the variable r which represents the landing command ($r = 1$ for landing). The *characterizer* model provides a mapping between continuous plant variables and the discrete events used by the selector. The *selector* is a model of the discrete controller, and the *effector* provides the mapping between control signals and actuators.

The mathematical model of the selector is based on the block diagram in Fig. 8, which is a static controller. This is a simplified version of the actual landing gear controller, *i.e.* its behaviour is identical with the actual controller implemented in Pascal, from which details concerning redundant plant sensors and some diagnostic functions have been excluded. The static selector model obviously ignores delays. A dynamic landing gear controller incorporating computation delays is studied in [11].

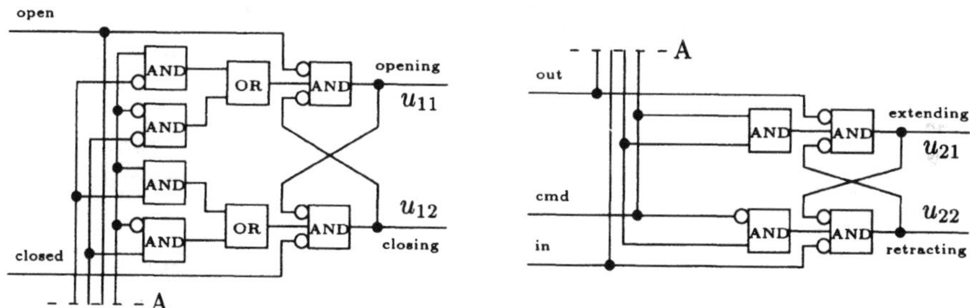

Fig. 8. Block diagram based selector model.

6 Verification of Closed-Loop Properties

We study two different properties of the closed-loop system. First we require that the door will never collide with the gear while in motion. Hence we require that the following condition must always be met:

$$(\dot{x}_g = 0) \vee (x_d \geq 1) \tag{6}$$

Secondly, we require that the gear must be fully extended (retracted) and the doors fully closed within T seconds after the appropriate pilot command has been issued. Hence we require that

$$(r > 0) \wedge \neg((x_g \geq 1) \wedge (x_d \leq 0)) \tag{7}$$

and

$$\neg(r > 0) \wedge \neg((x_g \leq 0) \wedge (x_d \leq 0)) \tag{8}$$

must never hold for longer intervals than T seconds. These properties can be expressed by the following EDC formulas:

$$R_1 \equiv \Box(\lceil(\dot{x}_g = 0) \vee (x_d \geq 1)\rceil \vee \lceil\,\rceil)$$
$$R_2 \equiv \lceil(r > 0) \wedge \neg((x_g \geq 1) \wedge (x_d \leq 0))\rceil \rightarrow \ell \leq T$$
$$R_3 \equiv \lceil\neg(r > 0) \wedge \neg((x_g \leq 0) \wedge (x_d \leq 0))\rceil \rightarrow \ell \leq T$$

where l denotes the length of the interval during which the respective formulas hold. Furthermore, $\Box$ corresponds to the temporal logic operator "always" in an interval setting, and $\lceil P \rceil$ denotes "P holds almost everywhere in the interval" [2].

The closed loop model of the system can be obtained using a conjuction of the formulas in Fig. 7, *i.e.*

$$S \equiv \text{Env} \land \text{Char} \land \text{Sel} \land \text{Eff}$$

Then the goal of the verification task is then to prove that

$$\lceil S \rceil \models R_1 \land R_2 \land R_3$$

Earlier we have provided the EDC proofs for a closed loop model which included the coarse (time-linear) environment component [11]. The proof of the non-linear case follows the same structure in presence of the following two additional lemmas.

Lemma 1. *For any combinations of values for u_d and u_g there exist values for the constants $\alpha'_d, \alpha'_g, \gamma_d, \gamma_g$ and the engine velocity ω such that $p \to p^+$ as $t \to \infty$ where $p^+ > 0$.*

Lemma 2. *For any interval in which u_d and u_g have fixed values, p is monotonic in t.*

For further details on the proof, the reader is referred to [12].

7 Summary

Formal verification of safety and timing properties of engineering systems is only meaningful if based on models which are systematically derived and refined. Building mathematical models of physical apparatus is a delicate process. The problem is that these models depend on assumptions which are often difficult to express — if mentioned at all. Bond graphs and their switched extension, however, provide the modeller with a small but sufficiently rich set of well defined concepts which allows the precise articulation of such assumptions. We have illustrated this important aspect of bond graphs, and the application of the same in verification, by means of an aerospace application studied together with aerospace industries in Sweden.

Acknowledgements

This research was funded by the Swedish National Board for Industrial and Technical Development (NUTEK). Also, the authors wish to thank Göran Backlund and his associates at Saab Military Aircraft, Linköping and Arne Jansson at the division of Fluid Power, dept. of Mechanical Engineering, Linköping University, for many valuable contributions and comments on the hydraulic and mechanical models. Finally, the authors wishes to thank Ulf Söderman at Modea Dynamics, Mjärdevi Science Park, Linköping for all inspiring discussions on conceptual modelling and bond graphs.

References

1. M. Andersson. *Object-Oriented Modeling and Simulation of Hybrid Systems.* PhD thesis, Lund Institute of Technology, Lund, 1994. Dissertation no. ISRN LUTFD2/TFRT-1043-SE.
2. Z. Chaochen, A.P. Ravn, and M.R. Hansen. An extended duration calculus for hybrid real-time systems. In *Hybrid Systems, Lecture Notes in Computer Science, No. 736*, pages 36–59, Berlin, 1993.
3. H. Elmqvist. *Dymola User's Manual.* Dynasim AB, Lund, 1994.
4. R.L. Grossman, A. Nerode, A.P. Ravn, and H. Rischel, editors. *Proc. of Workshop on Theory of Hybrid Systems*, LNCS 736, Lyngby, October 1992. Springer Verlag.
5. J.C. Hansen. Letters about a siphon machine installation at Harz: September 5, 1727 - August 4, 1729. In *Collection of the Royal Library*, volume I.p.23:I. Stockholm, 1727. Letters 138-140, 142, 143, 147, 151, 154, 160. In German.
6. D.C. Karnopp, R.C. Rosenberg, and D. Margolis. *System dynamics - A unified approach (2nd edition).* John Wiley & Sons, New York, 1990.
7. S. Lindroth. *Christoffer Polhem och Stora Kopparberget.* Stora Kopparbergs Bergslags AB, Uppsala, 1951. In Swedish with abstract in German.
8. S.E. Mattsson and M. Andersson. Omola - An object oriented modeling language. In Jamshidi and Herget, editors, *Recent advances in computer-aided control systems engineering*, volume 9, pages 291–310, 1993.
9. M. Morin, S. Nadjm-Tehrani, P. Österling, and E. Sandewall. Real-time hierarchical control. *IEEE software*, 9(5):51–57, 1992.
10. S. Nadjm-Tehrani. *Reactive Systems in Physical Environments: Compositional Modelling and Framework for Verification.* PhD thesis, Linköping University, Linköping, 1994. Dissertation no. 338.
11. S. Nadjm-Tehrani and J.E. Strömberg. Proving Dynamic Properties in an Aerospace Application. In *Proc. of the 16th International Symposium on Real-time Systems.* IEEE Computer Society Press, December 1995.
12. S. Nadjm-Tehrani, J.E. Strömberg, and A. Jansson. Modelling and verification of the JAS landing gear and hydraulic power supply system. Technical Report to appear, Dept. of Electrical Engineering, Linköping University, Sweden, 1995.
13. H.M. Paynter. *Analysis and design of engineering systems.* MIT Press, Cambridge, M.A., 1961.
14. U. Söderman. *Conceptual modelling of mode switching physical systems.* PhD thesis, Linköping University, Linköping, 1995. Dissertation no. 375.
15. J.E. Strömberg. *A mode switching modelling philosophy.* PhD thesis, Linköping University, Linköping, 1994. Dissertation no. 353.
16. J.E. Strömberg, J.L. Top, and U. Söderman. Variable causality in bond graphs caused by discrete effects. In *Proc. First Int. Conf. on Bond Graph Modeling (ICBGM '93)*, number 2 in SCS Simulation Series, volume 25, pages 115–119, San Diego, 1993.
17. J.L. Top. *Conceptual modelling of physical systems.* PhD thesis, University of Twente, Enschede, 1993.

Formal Specification of Stability in Hybrid Control Systems*

Wang Ji** and He Weidong***

International Institute for Software Technology
The United Nations University
P.O.Box 3058, Macau

Abstract. The *stability* of a control system is of primary interest and always appears as a critical property in the performance specification. In this paper, we formalize the criteria of stability in hybrid systems and present a formal approach to design of a hybrid dynamic system while the sufficient condition for stability is enforced. The formalism adopted is the Extended Duration Calculus with infinite intervals EDC^i.

1 Introduction

Hybrid control systems are systems involving continuous dynamic variables and discrete event variables, the last years have witnessed that hybrid control systems have become one of the most active areas in computer science and control theory. Hybrid systems seem to have the great potential in complex control systems where complexity is both in dynamics as well as in the discrete events. In order to analyze the interaction, *formal methods* seems to be helpful to the design and analysis of those systems. There are many approaches having been developed to specify the performance and behaviors of the hybrid control systems[ACH93, BGM93, HB92, KNR95, MP93, ZRH93], but most of them restrict themselves to some special hybrid systems, such as linear hybrid systems[ACH95, KNR95] in which change rates of all the dynamic variables are constants in a phase, and to present some techniques for dealing with such kinds of hybrid systems. The dynamic characteristics in linear hybrid systems are very simple, and people are always able to intuitively ascertain whether or not they are stable. Such kind of linear hybrid systems are difficult to be abstracted from engineering practice. In control theory, linear systems are systems which satisfy *Principle of Superposition*[D89], they involve much dynamics.

The *stability* of a control system is of primary interest and always appears as a critical property in the performance specification[K91], it is one of most important requirements which should first be satisfied. A *stable system* is defined as a system with a bounded system response. That is, if the system is subjected to a bounded input or disturbance and the response is bounded in magnitude, the system is said to be stable. However, in literature, only few authors have examined the *stability* in hybrid control systems, and so far there almost no formal approach to be developed to specify the stability (here referred to Lyapunov Stability) in hybrid control systems. Stability involves much dynamics, but most formal approaches have very weak capabilities to cope with dynamics, that is why some of them restrict themselves to linear hybrid system. Fortunately Duration Calculus (abbreviated *DC*)[ZHR91, Z93, ZL93] has been extended to that which has capability to analyze the real functions, integrals, derivatives and differential equations, called Extended Duration Calculus (abbreviated *EDC*)[ZRH93] ; Another extension of Duration Calculus, A Duration Calculus with Infinite Interval (abbreviated DC^i) [ZDL95], has also been developed to deal with fairness and liveness. In this paper, based on [H95], we show a duration calculus approach, which is the combination of *EDC* and DC^i abbreviated

* This paper is supported in part by 863 Hi-Tech programme of China.

** On leave from Department of Computer Science, Changsh a Institute of Technology, 410073, P.R. China.

*** On leave from Department of Automatic Control, Beijing University of Aero. & Astro., 100083, P.R. China.

EDC^i, to analyses and design of stability in general phase transition hybrid control systems. EDC can deal with the dynamics in the finite interval, and DC^i can deal with the properties in infinite interval, thus EDC^i is desired to handle the dynamics in finite interval or infinite interval. The novel features can be listed as below.

1. To present a theory about functions to reason about stability in EDC^i. A set of useful rules about limits, functions are introduced.
2. To show a formal proof of basic sufficient conditions for stability and asymptotic stability in hybrid systems.
3. To present a proved specification scheme of decision maker in style of refinement laws with respect to stable requirement.

As a result, for a hybrid dynamic system, our formal approach views the stability design as a transformation process hopefully.

The rest of the paper is organized as follows, Section 2 briefly introduces the combination (EDC^i)of EDC and DC^i; In section 3, formal specification of stability is discussed; A formal stability design approach is given in section 4; Finally some remarks are concluded in section 5.

2 Extended Duration Calculus with Infinite Intervals

The Duration Calculi is a family of real-time interval logics[Z93, ZHR91, ZL93, ZRH93, S94, ZDL95] and has been used in a number of examples of hybrid systems[YWZ94, W95]. In this section, we shape a practical version of Duration Calculus, EDC^i, for reasoning about stability in dynamic systems and hybrid systems. Compared to integral calculus[ZHR91] in Duration Calculi, EDC^i introduces piecewise continuity/differentiability of functions[ZRH93], and infinite intervals[ZDL95] in the calculus.

Definition 1. For an arbitrary Boolean state P and an arbitrary closed interval $[c,d]$, the duration of P, $\int P$, is defined by the value of integral of P over the interval $[c,d]$: $\int_c^d P(t)dt$, and denotes the length (ℓ) of the interval (i.e. $\ell = \int 1 = d - c$).

Definition 2. $\lceil P \rceil \widehat{=} (\int P = \ell) \wedge (\ell > 0)$, $\lceil P \rceil$ means that state P presents (almost) everywhere in a non-point interval. $\lceil\ \rceil (\widehat{=} \ell = 0)$ defines point intervals.

Definition 3. Let B and C be formulas. $B \frown C$ is a formula constructed from B and C by the *chop* operator, designated by $\frown$. $B \frown C$ is satisfied in interval $[c,d]$, iff there exists m ($c \leq m \leq d$), such that B is satisfied in $[c,m]$, and C is satisfied in $[m,d]$.
Let D be formula. D^* is a formula constructed from D by the *star* operator. D^* is satisfied in interval $[c,d]$, iff there exists a partition $m_1, \cdots, m_n$, ($c \leq m_1 \leq \cdots \leq m_n \leq d$), such that D is satisfied in $[c,m_1]$, $[m_n,d]$ and all $[m_j, m_{j+1}]$($j \in [1, n-1]$).

DC is an extension of Interval Temporal Logic (ITL). It therefore employs all axioms and rules of ITL, but also has a small set of additional axioms and rules, which constitute a relatively complete inference system. They are

$$\begin{array}{ll} 1.\ \int 0 = 0 & 2.\ \int P + \int Q = \int (P \vee Q) + \int (P \wedge Q) \\ 3.\ \int P \geq 0 & 4.\ (\int P = r + s) \Leftrightarrow (\int P = r) \frown (\int P = s) \end{array}$$

States are assumed to be *finitely variable*. That is, a state can have only finite alternations of its presence and absence in a (finite) interval. DC also establishes two induction rules which axiomatize finite variability(omitted here).

EDC is an extension of DC which can deal with functions of real value, where point properties of real-valued functions are taken to be states, and lifted to interval properties by the ceiling operator $\lceil \cdot \rceil$. In general, given a point property H of function f, $\lceil H(f) \rceil$ holds for interval $[c,d]$, iff $[c,d]$ is not a point interval, and $H(f(t))$ is true for all t, $c < t < d$. That is, $H(f)$ holds everywhere *within* the interval. For a non-point interval $[c,d]$, the values of $\mathbf{b}.f$ and $\mathbf{e}.f$ in the interval $[c,d]$ are defined as the *right limit* of f at point b and the *left limit* of f at point e respectively. That is,

$$\mathbf{b}.f = f(c^+) = \lim_{t \to c+0} f(t), \qquad \mathbf{e}.f = f(d^-) = \lim_{t \to d-0} f(t).$$

When f is *right continuous* at b, $\mathbf{b}.f$ is equal to the value of f at c. Similarly $\mathbf{e}.f = f(d)$, if f is *left continuous* at d.

Reasoning in the extended DC has the virtue of incorporating conventional mathematical theories of functions, such as theory of differential equations. A rule, called MT, is therefore established in the extended DC.

MT:
Let $R(\lceil H(f) \rceil, \mathbf{b}.f, \mathbf{e}.f, \ell)$ be a formula of the extended DC, which contains no occurrence of the chop ($\frown$) operator.
If

$$\forall c < d. R(\forall t \in (c,d). H(f(t)), f(c^+), f(d^-), d-c)$$

is true in a given mathematical theory of f, then

$$\lceil\,\rceil \vee R(\lceil H(f) \rceil, \mathbf{b}.f, \mathbf{e}.f, \ell)$$

is a theorem of EDC.

EDC^i is a first order logic of finite and infinite satisfactions of EDC. EDC^i designates finite satisfaction of EDC formula D by D^f, and infinite satisfaction of D by D^i. D^f holds for finite intervals only, and D^i for infinite intervals only. EDC^i shares models with EDC. A finite interval satisfies D^f under a model, iff the interval satisfies D in terms of the semantics of EDC. An infinite interval satisfies D^i under a model, iff all its *finite* prefixes satisfy D in terms of the semantics of EDC. Let $[a,b]$ stand for finite intervals and $[a,\infty)$ for infinite intervals henceforth. We define

1. $\Pi, [a,b] \models_i D^f$ iff $\Pi, [a,b] \models_{EDC} D$
   where $\models_i$ designates the satisfaction relation of EDC^i.
2. $\Pi, [a,\infty) \not\models_i D^f$
3. $\Pi, [a,b] \not\models_i D^i$
4. $\Pi, [a,\infty) \models_i D^i$ iff $\Pi, [a,b] \models_{EDC} D$ for all b ($> a$).

3 Analysis of Stability in Hybrid Systems

3.1 Some Rules about Real Functions over Time

Now, we give four rules into EDC^i to formulate a theory for reasoning about stability. Let X be a state function, a limit of X when t tends to $+\infty$ is defined as

$$\lim_{t \to +\infty} X = X_\infty \widehat{=} \forall \varepsilon > 0 \exists \delta (\ell > \delta \Rightarrow \ell = \delta \frown \lceil |X - X_\infty| \le \varepsilon \rceil)^i.$$

Rule 3.1 (Clip) *Let X and Y be state functions over $TIME$.*

$$\frac{\lceil f(X) \le g(Y) \le 0 \rceil^i \wedge \lim_{t \to +\infty} f(X) = 0}{\lim_{t \to +\infty} g(Y) = 0} \qquad \frac{\lceil 0 \le g(Y) \le f(X) \rceil^i \wedge \lim_{t \to +\infty} f(X) = 0}{\lim_{t \to +\infty} g(Y) = 0}$$

Proof: We just proof the first one.

$$\begin{array}{ll} & \lim_{t \to +\infty} f(X) = 0 \\ \Rightarrow & \forall \varepsilon > 0 \exists \delta (\ell > \delta \Rightarrow \ell = \delta \frown \lceil |f(X)| \le \varepsilon \rceil)^i \quad \text{definition} \\ \Rightarrow & \forall \varepsilon > 0 \exists \delta (\ell > \delta \Rightarrow \ell = \delta \frown \lceil |g(Y)| \le \varepsilon \rceil)^i \quad \text{premise} \\ \Rightarrow & \lim_{t \to +\infty} g(Y) = 0 \quad \text{definition} \end{array}$$

♣

Rule 3.2 (Press)

$$\frac{\lceil f(X) > a \wedge \dot{f}(X) < 0\rceil^i \vee \lceil f(X) < a \wedge \dot{f}(X) > 0\rceil^i}{\exists f_\infty \lim_{t\to+\infty} f(X) = f_\infty}$$

Rule 3.3 (Place)

$$\frac{\begin{array}{l}\lceil (X = 0 \Leftrightarrow f(X) = 0) \wedge X \geq 0 \wedge f(X) \leq 0\rceil^i \\ X_1 < X_2 \Leftrightarrow f(X_1) > f(X_2) \\ \lim_{t\to+\infty} f(X) = 0\end{array}}{\lim_{t\to+\infty} X = 0}$$

Rule 3.4 (Mean Value)

$$\frac{\begin{array}{ll}\lceil X \geq 0 \wedge f(X) \leq 0\rceil^i & (MV1) \\ ((\mathbf{b}.X \leq \mathbf{e}.X \Rightarrow \mathbf{b}.f(X) \geq \mathbf{e}.f(X)) \wedge (\mathbf{b}.X \geq \mathbf{e}.X \Rightarrow \mathbf{b}.f(X) \leq \mathbf{e}.f(X)))^i & (MV2)\end{array}}{\lceil 0 \geq \int_0^X f(\theta)d\theta \geq f(X) \times X\rceil^i}$$

All these rules can be found in the mathematical analysis books, here they are just for illustrating how to apply EDC^i to specify the real functions, limits and others, and these four rules will be used also to verify the stability theorems introduced in the following subsections.

3.2 Stability in Hybrid Systems

To characterize a bounded system response, a system is *stable* if the system is subjected to a bounded input or disturbance and the response is bounded in magnitude. Without loss of generality, by coordinate transformation, a dynamic system S can be specified by

$$\dot{\mathbf{x}} = F(\mathbf{x}, t) \qquad F(0, t) = 0 \qquad \text{(lya)}$$

where $\mathbf{x}$ is state vector of dimension n. It is assumed that F has solutions for all $t > 0$. The equilibrium point is assumed to be at the origin. A system (lya) is stable if

$$\forall \varepsilon > 0 \exists \delta \forall \mathbf{x}_I |\mathbf{x}_I| < \delta \Rightarrow |\mathbf{x}(t)| < \varepsilon$$

where $\mathbf{x}_I$ is initial condition. It is asymptotically stable if it is stable and $\lim_{t\to+\infty} |\mathbf{x}| = 0$.

We can formalize the stability concept in terms of EDC^i. Let $STABLE(S)$ mean that a system S is stable, by the definition above, we have

$$STABLE(S) \mathrel{\hat{=}} \forall \varepsilon > 0 \exists \delta (\mathbf{b}.|\mathbf{x}| < \delta \Rightarrow \lceil |\mathbf{x}| < \varepsilon\rceil)^i.$$

Similarly, asymptotic stability becomes

$$ASYM\_STA(S) \mathrel{\hat{=}} STABLE(S) \wedge (\forall \varepsilon > 0 \exists \delta (\ell > \delta \Rightarrow \ell = \delta ^\frown \lceil |\mathbf{x}| < \varepsilon\rceil)^i)$$

Lyapunov Sufficient Condition Lyapunov has shown a sufficient condition to analyze the stability of dynamic system[AW89]. For a system S specified in Equation (lya), consider a function $V: R^{n+1} \to R$ such that

1. $V(0, t) = 0$ for all $t \in R$. 2. V is differentiable in $\mathbf{x}$ and t.
3. V is positive definite, i.e. $V(\mathbf{x}, t) \geq g(|\mathbf{x}|) > 0$ when $|\mathbf{x}| > 0$,

where $g: R \to R$ is continuous and increasing with $\lim_{r\to+\infty} g(r) = +\infty$.

A sufficient condition for Equation(lya) to be stable is

$$\dot{V}(\mathbf{x}, t) = \frac{\partial V}{\partial t} + F^T(\mathbf{x}, t)\frac{\partial V}{\partial \mathbf{x}} \leq 0.$$

A sufficient condition for Equation(lya) to be *asymptotically stable* if

$$\dot{V}(\mathbf{x},t) = \frac{\partial V}{\partial t} + F^T(\mathbf{x},t)\frac{\partial V}{\partial \mathbf{x}} < 0 \quad \text{for } \mathbf{x} \neq 0.$$

is negative definite. $V(\mathbf{x},t)$ is called *Lyapunov function* of system S.

We would like to formalize Lyapunov's Method as an inference law in the application part of EDC^i. Let $DIFF_v^V$ mean that function V is differentiable over v. Therefore, the fact that $V(\mathbf{x},t)$ is differentiable in $\mathbf{x}$ and t can be specified as

$$DIFF(V) \mathrel{\widehat{=}} \bigwedge_{\mathbf{x}\in R^n \wedge t\in R} DIFF_{\mathbf{x}}^V \wedge DIFF_t^V.$$

Let $POSI(V)$ mean that function V is positive definite over $\mathbf{x}$ and t.

$$POSI(V) \mathrel{\widehat{=}} \exists g.(\forall \mathbf{x}\lceil |\mathbf{x}| > 0 \Rightarrow V(\mathbf{x}) \geq g(|\mathbf{x}|) > 0\rceil^i)$$

if $g(r)$ is increasing with $\lim_{r\to+\infty} g(r) = +\infty$. then

$$POSI^*(V) \mathrel{\widehat{=}} \exists g.((\forall r_0 \exists r_1 \forall r \geq r_1, g(r) > g(r_0)) \wedge \forall \mathbf{x}\lceil |\mathbf{x}| > 0 \Rightarrow V(\mathbf{x}) \geq g(|\mathbf{x}|) > 0\rceil^i)$$

And let $NEGA(V)$ mean that function V is negative definite over $\mathbf{x}$ and t.

$$NEGA(V) \mathrel{\widehat{=}} \exists g.(\forall \mathbf{x}\lceil |\mathbf{x}| > 0 \Rightarrow V(\mathbf{x}) \leq g(|\mathbf{x}|) < 0\rceil^i)$$

Definition 4 Candidate of Lyapunov Function. A function $V(\mathbf{x},t)$ is called a *candidate of Lyapunov function* for system in Equation (lya) iff

$$LYA\_CDD(V) \mathrel{\widehat{=}} \lceil V(\mathbf{0}) = 0\rceil^i \wedge DIFF(V) \wedge POSI^*(V)$$

By Lyapunov Theorem, we formulate the following rules: For stability, we have

Rule 3.5 (Lyapunov Stability) *Given a control system* $S :: \dot{\mathbf{x}} = F(\mathbf{x})$, *the following holds.*

$$\frac{\begin{array}{l}\lceil S\rceil^i \\ \lceil S\rceil^i \Rightarrow (\mathrm{b}.\mathbf{x} = \mathbf{0} \Rightarrow \lceil \mathbf{x} = \mathbf{0}\rceil)^i \\ LYA\_CDD(V) \\ \lceil \dot{V}(\mathbf{x}) \leq 0\rceil^i\end{array}}{STABLE(S)} \tag{2}$$

Rule 3.6 (Lyapunov Asymptotic Stability) *Given a control system* $S :: \dot{\mathbf{x}} = F(\mathbf{x})$, *the following holds.*

$$\frac{\begin{array}{l}\lceil S\rceil^i \\ \lceil S\rceil^i \Rightarrow (\mathrm{b}.\mathbf{x} = \mathbf{0} \Rightarrow \lceil \mathbf{x} = \mathbf{0}\rceil)^i \\ LYA\_CDD(V) \\ NEGA(\dot{V})\end{array}}{ASMP\_STA(S)} \tag{3}$$

Stability in Hybrid Systems In general, hybrid real-time systems require a mixture of continuity and discreteness so that they can switch between variety of feedback strategies. Basically, corresponding to the possible feedback loops, we decompose the state space into a finite subspace.

$$S = \bigcup_{j\in J} S_j$$

where J is a finite index set and S_j is a connected subset of R^n. S_j can be described in terms of certain constraints as PRE_j which is a boolean expression over $\mathbf{x}$, such as $S_1 : x > 0, S_2 : x \leq 0$. The closure of PRE_j denoted as $\overline{PRE_j}$ is defined as follows

$$\overline{PRE_j} \mathrel{\widehat{=}} \{\mathbf{x}' \mid \forall\delta\exists\mathbf{x} \in PRE_j |\mathbf{x}' - \mathbf{x}| < \delta\}$$

So, behavior of a hybrid system can specified as below.

- Completeness of phases. $\lceil \bigvee_{j\in J} PRE_j \rceil^i$
- Exclusiveness. $\bigwedge_{k\in J} \lceil PRE_k \Rightarrow \neg \bigvee_{j\in J, j\neq k} PRE_j \rceil^i$
- Evolutions. $\bigwedge_{j\in J} \lceil PRE_j \Rightarrow \dot{\mathbf{x}} = F_j(\mathbf{x}, u) \rceil^i$

Given a hybrid systems $S ::\begin{cases} \dot{\mathbf{x}} = F_1(\mathbf{x}, u)\ PRE_1 \\ \dot{\mathbf{x}} = F_2(\mathbf{x}, u)\ PRE_2 \\ \vdots \qquad \vdots \\ \dot{\mathbf{x}} = F_n(\mathbf{x}, u)\ PRE_n \end{cases}$ we have the theorem for stability of hybrid systems, which is a generalization of conventional Lyapunov theorems.

Theorem 5 Stability in Hybrid Systems.

$$\frac{\begin{array}{l} \lceil S \rceil^i \wedge \lceil S \Rightarrow \bigvee_{j\in J} PRE_j \rceil^i \\ \bigwedge_{k\in J} \lceil PRE_k \Rightarrow \neg \bigvee_{j\in J, j\neq k} PRE_j \rceil^i \\ \bigwedge_{j\in J} (\lceil 0 \in PRE_j \rceil \Rightarrow (\mathbf{b}.\mathbf{x} = 0 \Rightarrow \lceil \mathbf{x} = 0 \rceil))^i \\ LYA\_CDD(V) \\ \bigwedge_{j\in J} \lceil PRE_j \Rightarrow \dot{V}(\mathbf{x}) \leq 0 \rceil^i \end{array}}{STABLE(S)} \qquad (4)$$

Proof:

$$\begin{array}{ll} \quad \lceil S \rceil^i \wedge \lceil S \Rightarrow \bigvee_{j\in J} PRE_j \rceil^i \quad \wedge \quad \bigwedge_{j\in J} \lceil PRE_j \Rightarrow \dot{V}(\mathbf{x}) \leq 0 \rceil & \\ \Rightarrow \lceil \dot{V}(\mathbf{x}) \leq 0 \rceil^i & (*) \\ \quad \lceil S \rceil^i \wedge \lceil S \Rightarrow \bigvee_{j\in J} PRE_j \rceil^i \quad \wedge \quad \bigwedge_{j\in J} (0 \in PRE_j \Rightarrow (\mathbf{b}.\mathbf{x} = 0 \Rightarrow \lceil \mathbf{x} = 0 \rceil))^i & \\ \Rightarrow \lceil S \rceil^i \Rightarrow (\mathbf{b}.\mathbf{x} = 0 \Rightarrow \lceil \mathbf{x} = 0 \rceil)^i & (**) \\ \quad \lceil S \rceil^i \wedge (*) \wedge (**) \wedge LYA\_CDD(V) & \\ \Rightarrow STABLE(S) & \text{Rule 3.5} \end{array}$$

Theorem 6.

$$\frac{\begin{array}{l} \lceil S \rceil^i \wedge \lceil S \Rightarrow \bigvee_{j\in J} PRE_j \rceil^i \\ \bigwedge_{k\in J} \lceil PRE_k \Rightarrow \neg \bigvee_{j\in J, j\neq k} PRE_j \rceil^i \\ \bigwedge_{j\in J} \lceil PRE_j \Rightarrow \dot{\mathbf{x}} = F_j(\mathbf{x}, u) \rceil^i \\ \lceil \bigwedge_{j\in J} 0 \in PRE_j \Rightarrow F_j(0) = 0 \rceil^i \\ LYA\_CDD(V) \\ \bigwedge_{j\in J} \exists g_j \lceil (\overline{PRE_j} \wedge \mathbf{x} \neq 0) \Rightarrow \dot{V}(\mathbf{x}) \leq g_j(|\mathbf{x}|) < 0 \rceil^i \qquad (3.2.6) \end{array}}{ASYM\_STABLE(S)}$$

Proof: Similar to the proof of Theorem 5, $STABLE(S)$ holds, and therefore by definition, we have $\forall \varepsilon \exists \delta (\mathbf{b}.|\mathbf{x}| < \varepsilon \Rightarrow \lceil |\mathbf{x}| < \delta \rceil)^i$.
Let

$$\varphi(|\mathbf{x}|) \widehat{=} \begin{cases} \max_{j\in J} \sup_{|\mathbf{x}| \leq |\mathbf{x}'| \leq \delta \wedge \overline{PRE_j}} g_j(|\mathbf{x}'|) & |\mathbf{x}| \neq 0 \\ 0 & |\mathbf{x}| = 0 \end{cases} \qquad \psi(|\mathbf{x}|) \widehat{=} \frac{\int_0^{|\mathbf{x}|} \varphi(\theta) d\theta}{|\mathbf{x}| + 1}.$$

By using closure of PRE_j, φ is well defined.

$$
\begin{array}{ll}
\text{Definition of } \varphi \wedge (3.2.6) & \\
\Rightarrow \begin{array}{l} (\varphi(\|\mathbf{x}\|) \leq 0) \wedge \left(\wedge \begin{array}{l} \mathbf{b}.\|\mathbf{x}\| \leq \mathbf{e}.\|\mathbf{x}\| \Rightarrow \mathbf{b}.\varphi(\|\mathbf{x}\|) \geq \mathbf{e}.\varphi(\|\mathbf{x}\|) \\ \mathbf{b}.\|\mathbf{x}\| \geq \mathbf{e}.\|\mathbf{x}\| \Rightarrow \mathbf{b}.\varphi(\|\mathbf{x}\|) \leq \mathbf{e}.\varphi(\|\mathbf{x}\|) \end{array} \right)^{i} \\ \wedge \bigwedge_{j \in J} \lceil (\overline{PRE_j} \wedge \mathbf{x} \neq 0) \Rightarrow \dot{V}(\mathbf{x}) \leq g_j(\|\mathbf{x}\|) \leq \varphi(\|\mathbf{x}\|) < 0 \rceil^{i} \end{array} & \text{(Properties of } \varphi) \\
\Rightarrow \lceil \frac{\int_0^{\|\mathbf{x}\|} \varphi(\theta) d\theta}{\|\mathbf{x}\|} \geq \varphi(\|\mathbf{x}\|) \rceil^{i} & \text{(Mean Value)} \\
\Rightarrow \lceil \psi(\|\mathbf{x}\|) \geq \varphi(\|\mathbf{x}\|) \rceil^{i} & \text{(Definition of } \psi) \\
\Rightarrow \lceil \dot{V}(\mathbf{x}) \leq \psi(\|\mathbf{x}\|) \rceil^{i} & (3.2.6)
\end{array}
$$

$$
\begin{array}{ll}
\text{Definition of } \psi \wedge \text{(Properties of } \varphi) & \\
\Rightarrow \frac{d\psi}{d\|\mathbf{x}\|} < 0 & \text{(Arithmetic)} \\
\Rightarrow X_1 < X_2 \leq 0 \Leftrightarrow \psi(X_1) > \psi(X_2) & \text{(Properties of } \psi)
\end{array}
$$

Considering

$$
\begin{array}{ll}
\lceil V(\mathbf{x}) > 0 \wedge \dot{V}(\mathbf{x}) < 0 \rceil^{i} & (3.2.6), (\text{LYA\_CDD(V)}) \\
\Rightarrow \exists V_\infty \lim_{t \to \infty} V(\mathbf{x}) = V_\infty \wedge \lceil V(\mathbf{x}) \geq V_\infty \rceil^{i} & \text{(Press)}
\end{array}
$$

and $LYA\_CDD(V) \Rightarrow \exists k.\lceil \|\mathbf{x}\| \geq \frac{V_\infty}{k} \rceil^{i}$. we conclude,

$$
\begin{array}{ll}
(\mathbf{e}.V(\mathbf{x}) = \mathbf{b}.V(\mathbf{x}) + \int \dot{V}(\mathbf{x}))^{i} & \\
\Rightarrow (\mathbf{e}.V(\mathbf{x}) \leq \mathbf{b}.V(\mathbf{x}) + \int \psi(\|\mathbf{x}\|)^{i} & \\
\Rightarrow \exists k.(\mathbf{e}.V(\mathbf{x}) \leq \mathbf{b}.V(\mathbf{x}) + \int \psi(\frac{V_\infty}{k}))^{i} & \\
\Rightarrow \exists k.(\mathbf{e}.V(\mathbf{x}) \leq \mathbf{b}.V(\mathbf{x}) + \psi(\frac{V_\infty}{k}) \times \ell)^{i} & \\
\Rightarrow V_\infty = 0 & \\
\Rightarrow \lim_{t \to \infty} \|\mathbf{x}\| = 0 & (\text{LYA\_CDD(V), Place})
\end{array}
$$

♣

4 Stability Design in Hybrid Systems

In the previous sections, we formulate the sufficient conditions for stability, and we try to show refinement laws which envision them being enforced by design. The design of stability becomes a task to solve inequalities.

Let $W(\mathbf{x}, u) < 0$ be an inequality to be solved. $< C(\mathbf{x}), u = H(\mathbf{x}) >$ is said to be a *solution* of $W(\mathbf{x}, u) < 0$ if

$$\lceil C(\mathbf{x}) \wedge u = H(\mathbf{x}) \Rightarrow W(\mathbf{x}, u) < 0 \rceil^{i}.$$

Let κ be a finite index set. A set $\{< C_k(\mathbf{x}), u = H_k(\mathbf{x}) > | k \in \kappa\}$ is said to be *a complete solution set* of $W(\mathbf{x}, u) < 0$ if

$$
\begin{array}{l}
\bigwedge_{k \in \kappa} \lceil C_k(\mathbf{x}) \wedge u = H_k(\mathbf{x}) \Rightarrow W(\mathbf{x}, u) < 0 \rceil^{i} \wedge \\
\lceil \bigvee_{k \in \kappa} C_k(\mathbf{x}) \rceil^{i} \quad \wedge \quad \bigwedge_{k \in \kappa} \lceil C_k(\mathbf{x}) \Rightarrow \neg \bigvee_{k' \in \kappa, k' \neq k} C_{k'}(\mathbf{x}) \rceil^{i}
\end{array}
$$

There might be more than one complete solution sets for a same inequality. The state space of a system will be partitioned disjointly by $\{C_k(\mathbf{x}) | k \in \kappa\}$, where $C_k(\mathbf{x})$ is some inequalities. From this point, for a dynamic plant, the control part may be designed as either one controller if a singleton complete solution set of the inequality about derivative of its candidate of Lyapunov function can be found, or the combination of several controllers and some phase transition conditions which are also the solution of the inequality about derivative of its candidate of Lyapunov function.

Consider a system $\dot{\mathbf{x}} = F(\mathbf{x}, u) = \begin{cases} F_1(\mathbf{x}, u) & \text{if } PRE_1 \\ \cdots & \cdots \\ F_r(\mathbf{x}, u) & \text{if } PRE_r \end{cases}$ where $r > 0$. The stability design begins with considering a candidate of Lyaponov function $V(\mathbf{x}, t)$. Therefore,

$$\lceil V(0) = 0 \rceil^i \wedge DIFF(V) \wedge POSI^*(V)$$

holds. Computing the derivative of V, we get

$$\dot{V}(\mathbf{x}, t) = \frac{\partial V}{\partial t} + F^T(\mathbf{x}, t)\frac{\partial V}{\partial \mathbf{x}}$$

The stability design becomes to solving the following inequality group.

$$\bigwedge_{0<j\le r} PRE_j \wedge \frac{\partial V}{\partial t} + F_j^T(\mathbf{x}, t)\frac{\partial V}{\partial \mathbf{x}} \le 0 \qquad (IQ.1)$$

For the asymptotic stability design, the inequality group is as follows

$$\bigwedge_{0<j\le r} (\overline{PRE_j} \wedge \mathbf{x} \ne 0) \wedge \frac{\partial V}{\partial t} + F_j^T(\mathbf{x}, t)\frac{\partial V}{\partial \mathbf{x}} \le g_j(\|\mathbf{x}\|) < 0 \qquad (IQ.2)$$

where g_j may be a piecewise continuous real function.

Suppose $\{< C_k(\mathbf{x}), u = H_k(\mathbf{x}) > | k \in \kappa\}$ be *a complete solution set* of $IQ.1$ (or $(IQ.2)$). Then a decision maker may be designed to do the following steps iteratively:

Step 1: Select one and only one open guard $C_k(\mathbf{x})$. Obviously it will be guaranteed by completeness and mutually exclusiveness of $\{C_k(\mathbf{x}) | k \in \kappa\}$.

Step 2: Execute the corresponding controller specified by a nonterminating process $< u = H_k(\mathbf{x}) >$. However, this process will be interrupted by the event that the boolean value of $\neg C_k(\mathbf{x})$ becomes true from false, and followed by SKIP.

Step 1 and Step 2 can be captured by (Adding $*$ as the iterative operator)

$$C :: (\|_k (C_k(\mathbf{x}) \rightarrow < u = H_k(\mathbf{x}) > \ [\neg C_k(\mathbf{x})] \ \texttt{SKIP})^*$$

Note that for asymptotic stability design, it is demanded that

$$\bigwedge_{k\in\kappa} < \overline{C_k(\mathbf{x})} \wedge u = H_k(\mathbf{x}) \Rightarrow IQ.2 >$$

Design by Refinement 4.1 (Stability)

$$\frac{\begin{array}{c} LYA\_CDD(V) \\ \bigwedge_{k\in\kappa} \lceil C_k(\mathbf{x}) \wedge u = H_k(\mathbf{x}) \Rightarrow \bigwedge_{j\in J} (PRE_j \Rightarrow \dot{V}(\mathbf{x}) \le 0) \rceil^i \\ \lceil \bigvee_{k\in\kappa} C_k(\mathbf{x}) \rceil^i \wedge \bigwedge_{k\in\kappa} \lceil C_k(\mathbf{x}) \Rightarrow \neg \bigvee_{k'\in\kappa, k'\ne k} C_{k'}(\mathbf{x}) \rceil^i \end{array}}{STABLE(S :: (\|_k (C_k(\mathbf{x}) \rightarrow \left\langle \begin{array}{c} u = H_k(\mathbf{x}) \\ \dot{\mathbf{x}} = F_j(\mathbf{x}, u) \end{array} \right\rangle [\neg C_k(\mathbf{x})] \ \texttt{SKIP}))^*)}$$

Similarly, we can archive an asymptotically stable design by

Design by Refinement 4.2 (Asymptotic Stability)

$$\frac{\begin{array}{c} LYA\_CDD(V) \\ \bigwedge_{k\in\kappa} \lceil \overline{C_k(\mathbf{x})} \wedge u = H_k(\mathbf{x}) \Rightarrow \bigwedge_{j\in J} (\|\mathbf{x}\| \ne 0 \Rightarrow \overline{PRE_j} \wedge \exists g_j (\dot{V}(\mathbf{x}) \le g_j(\|\mathbf{x}\|) < 0) \rceil^i \\ \lceil \bigvee_{k\in\kappa} C_k(\mathbf{x}) \rceil^i \wedge \bigwedge_{k\in\kappa} \lceil C_k(\mathbf{x}) \Rightarrow \neg \bigvee_{k'\in\kappa, k'\ne k} C_{k'}(\mathbf{x}) \rceil^i \end{array}}{ASYM\_STABLE(S :: (\|_k (C_k(\mathbf{x}) \rightarrow \left\langle \begin{array}{c} u = H_k(\mathbf{x}) \\ \dot{\mathbf{x}} = F_j(\mathbf{x}, u) \end{array} \right\rangle [\neg C_k(\mathbf{x})] \ \texttt{SKIP}))^*)}$$

Example Consider a time-varying dynamic system

$$Plant :: \begin{bmatrix} \dot{x}_1 \\ \dot{x}_2 \end{bmatrix} = \begin{bmatrix} -6 & -\cos t \\ \sin t & 3 \end{bmatrix} \begin{bmatrix} x_1 \\ x_2 \end{bmatrix} + \begin{bmatrix} 1 \\ 1 \end{bmatrix} u$$

We choose $V(x, \dot{x}) = x_1^2 + x_2^2$ as a candidate of Lyapunov function, it satisfies $LYA\_CDD(V)$, and its differential can be calculated

$$\begin{aligned} \dot{V}(x, \dot{x}) &= 2x_1\dot{x}_1 + 2x_2\dot{x}_2 \\ &= 2(x_1(-6x_1 - x_2 \cos t + u) + x_2(x_1 \sin t + 3x_2 + u)) \\ &= 2(-6x_1^2 + (\sin t - \cos t)x_1x_2 + 3x_2^2 + (x_1 + x_2)u) \end{aligned}$$

By enforcing theorem 6, an inequality is obtained (for $(x_1 \neq 0 \vee x_2 \neq 0)$)

$$2(-6x_1^2 + (\sin t - \cos t)x_1x_2 + 3x_2^2 + (x_1 + x_2)u) \leq g(x_1, x_2) < 0$$

We have a solution listed as below.

κ	1	2
C	$x_1x_2 \geq 0$	$x_1x_2 < 0$
H	$-4x_2$	$5.5x_1 - 3.5x_2$
g	$2(-6x_1^2 - 2x_1x_2 - x_2^2)$	$2(-0.5x_1^2 - 0.5x_2^2)$

According to Design by Refinement 4.2, we have

$$\frac{\begin{array}{c} LYA\_CDD(V) \\ \left\lceil \begin{pmatrix} x_1x_2 \geq 0 \wedge u = -4x_2 \Rightarrow (x_1^2 + x_2^2 \neq 0 \Rightarrow \dot{V}(x,t) \leq -2(6x_1^2 + 2x_1x_2 + x_2^2) < 0) \\ \wedge\, x_1x_2 \leq 0 \wedge u = 5.5x_1 - 3.5x_2 \Rightarrow (x_1^2 + x_2^2 \neq 0 \Rightarrow \dot{V}(x,t) \leq -2(0.5x_1^2 + 0.5x_2^2) < 0) \end{pmatrix} \right\rceil^i \\ \lceil x_1x_2 \geq 0 \vee x_1x_2 < 0 \rceil^i \wedge \lceil x_1x_2 \geq 0 \Leftrightarrow \neg(x_1x_2 < 0) \rceil^i \end{array}}{(D_M) :: \begin{pmatrix} (x_1x_2 \geq 0 \rightarrow \left\langle \begin{array}{c} u = -4x_2 \\ Plant \end{array} \right\rangle [\neg x_1x_2 \geq 0]\ \text{SKIP}) \\ \| \\ (x_1x_2 < 0 \rightarrow \left\langle \begin{array}{c} u = 5.5x_1 - 3.5x_2 \\ Plant \end{array} \right\rangle [\neg x_1x_2 < 0]\ \text{SKIP}) \end{pmatrix}}$$

According to Asymptotic Stability Law, the above design is asymptotic stable. And D_M is the stable design program which can be used to control the plant.

5 Concluding Remarks

In this paper, with the combination EDC^i of the Extended Duration Calculus and Duration Calculus with Infinite Intervals, we apply EDC^i to specifying the stability in hybrid control systems. We also show a formal approach to analysis and design of stability in hybrid control systems. The sufficient conditions for stability and asymptotic stability in these systems are formulated and proved in EDC^i. The related refinement laws are presented based on solutions of inequalities in order to derive initial $\mathcal{HCSP}$ specifications from stability requirements directly.

Since the condition for stability is a sufficient condition, it is not guaranteed that a stable design would be derived even if there exists a control to make the plant stable. It depends on at least two factors in our approach: one is the selection of candidate of Lyapunov function; another is solution of inequalities. However, the idea of formulation is of a general sense. It can be applied to another sufficient condition for stability of hybrid systems as Mike Branicky's condition [B94]. And the specification of the stability is helpful for specifying other dynamic properties in a hybrid control systems, as the stability is a basic critical safety requirements in any dynamic hybrid control systems.

Acknowledgments: We thanks Prof. Zhuo Chaochen, Prof. Anders P. Ravn, Dr. Xu Qiwen, Prof. Lu Jian and Mr. Yang Zhengyu for their encouragement and comments.

References

[ACH93] R. Alur, C. Courcoubetis and T.A. Henzinger: Hybrid Automata: An Algorithm Approach to the Specification and Verification of Hybrid Systems. In *Hybrid Systems, LNCS 736. Edited by R.L.Grossman, A. Nerode, A.P.Ravn and H. Rischel*, pp. 209-229, Springer Verlag, 1993.

[ACH95] R. Alur,C. Courcoubetis, T.A. Henzinger and etc. : The Algorithmic Analysis of Hybrid Systems, In *Theoretical Computer Science*, Vol.138, pp 3-34, 1995.

[AW89] Karl Johan Åström and Björn Wittenmark: *Adaptive Contol*, Addison-Wesley Publishing Company, 1989.

[B94] M.S. Branicky: Stability of Switched and Hybrid Systems. In Proc. 33rd IEEE Conf. Decision Control, Lake Buena Vista, FL, Dec. 14–16, 1994.

[BGM93] A. Back, J. Guckenheimer and M. Myers: A Dynamical Simulation Facility for Hybrid Systems. In *Hybrid Systems, LNCS 736. Edited by R.L.Grossman, A. Nerode, A.P.Ravn and H. Rischel*, pp. 255-267, Springer Verlag, 1993.

[D89] Richard C. Dorf: *Modern Control Systems*, Fifth Edition, Addison-Wesley Publishing Company, 1989.

[HB92] He Jifeng and J. Bowen: Time Interval Semantics and Implementation of A Real-Time Programming Language. In *Proc. 4th Euromicro Workshop on Real Time Systems*, IEEE Press, June 1992.

[H95] He Weidong: Design of Stability in Hybrid Control Systems. *UNU/IIST Report No. 45*, March 1995. To appear in *IFAC 95 Workshop on Artificial Intelligence Real Time Control, 1995*

[K91] B.C. Kuo: *Automatic Control Systems* (sixth edition), Prentice-Hall International Inc., 1991.

[KNR95] W. Kohn, A.Nerode, J.B. Remmel and A. Yaknis: Viability in Hybrid Systems. In *Theoretical Computer Science* special issue on hybrid systems, edited by: A. Pnueli and J. Sifakis. Vol. 138, pp. 141-168. Feb. 1995.

[MP93] Z. Manna and A. Pnueli: Verifying Hybrid Systems. In *Hybrid Systems, LNCS 736. Edited by R.L.Grossman, A. Nerode, A.P.Ravn and H. Rischel*, pp. 4-35, Springer Verlag, 1993.

[S94] J.U. Skakkebæk: Liveness and Fairness in Duration Calculus. In *CONCUR'94: Concurrency Theory*, LNCS 836, B. Jonsson and J. Parrow(Editors), pp. 283–298, 1994.

[W95] B.H. Widjaja, Chen Zongji, He Weidong and Zhou Chaochen: A Cooperative Design for Hybrid Control System. *UNU/IIST Report No.36*, 1995.

[YWZ94] Yu Xinyao, Wang Ji, Zhou Chaochen and P.K. Pandya: Formal Design of Hybrid Systems. In *Formal Techniques in Real-Time and Fault-Tolerant Systems*, LNCS 863, H. Langmaack, W.-P. de Roever and J. Vytopil (Editors), pp. 738-755, Sept. 1994.

[Z93] Zhou Chaochen: Duration Calculi: An Overview. In *the Proceedings of Formal Methods in Programming and Their Applications*, LNCS 735, D. Bjørner, M. Broy and I.V. Pottosin (Editors), pp. 256-266, July 1993.

[ZDL95] Zhou Chaochen, Dang Van Hung and Li Xiaoshan: Duration Calculus with Infinite Intervals, *UNU/IIST Report No. 40*, 1994.

[ZHR91] Zhou Chaochen, C.A.R. Hoare and A.P. Ravn: A Calculus of Durations. In *Information Processing Letters*, Vol. 40, No. 5, pp. 269-276, 1991.

[ZL93] Zhou Chaochen and Li Xiaoshan: A Mean Value Calculus of Durations. In *A Classical Mind (Essays in Honour of C.A.R. Hoare)*, A.W.Roscoe (Editor), Prentice-Hall, pp. 431-451,1994.

[ZRH93] Zhou Chaochen, A.P. Ravn and M.R. Hansen: An Extended Duration Calculus for Hybrid Real-Time Systems. In *Hybrid Systems*, LNCS 736, R.L. Grossman, A. Nerode, A.P. Ravn and H. Rischel (Editors), pp. 36-59, 1993.

Requirements Specifications for Hybrid Systems

Constance Heitmeyer
Code 5546
Naval Research Laboratory
Washington, DC 20375

1 Introduction

The purpose of a computer system requirements specification is to describe the computer system's required external behavior. To avoid overspecification, the requirements specification should describe the system behavior as a mathematical relation between entities in the system's environment. When some of these entities are continuous and others are discrete, the system is referred to as a "hybrid" system.

Although computer science provides many techniques for representing and reasoning about the discrete quantities that affect system behavior, practical approaches for specifying and analyzing systems containing both discrete *and* continuous quantities are lacking. The purpose of this paper is to present a formal framework for representing and reasoning about the requirements of hybrid systems. As background, the paper briefly reviews an abstract model for specifying system and software requirements, called the Four Variable Model [12], and a related requirements method, called SCR (Software Cost Reduction) [10, 1]. The paper then introduces a special discrete version of the Four Variable Model, the SCR requirements model [8] and proposes an extension of the SCR model for specifying and reasoning about hybrid systems.

2 Background

2.1 The Four Variable Model

The Four Variable Model, which is illustrated in Figure 1, describes the required system behavior as a set of mathematical relations on four sets of variables—monitored and controlled variables and input and output data items. A *monitored variable* represents an environmental quantity that influences system behavior, a *controlled variable* an environmental quantity that the system controls. Input devices (e.g., sensors) measure the monitored quantities and output devices set the controlled quantities. The variables that the devices read and write are called *input* and *output data items.*

The four relations of the Four Variable Model are REQ, NAT, IN, and OUT. The relations REQ and NAT provide a black box specification of the required

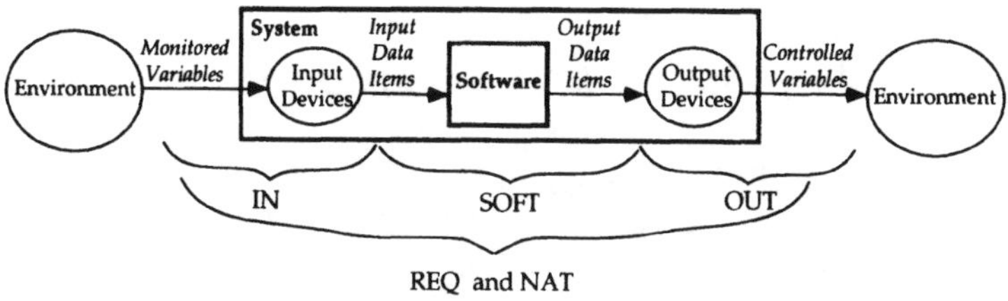

Fig. 1. Four Variable Model.

system behavior. NAT describes the natural constraints on system behavior—that is, the constraints imposed by physical laws and by the system environment. REQ defines the system requirements as a relation the system must maintain between the monitored and the controlled quantities.

One approach to describing the required system behavior, REQ, is to specify the *ideal* system behavior, which abstracts away timing delays and imprecision, and then to specify the *allowable* system behavior, which bounds the timing delays and imprecision. Typically, a function specifies ideal system behavior, whereas a relation specifies the allowable system behavior. The allowable system behavior is a relation rather than a function because it may associate a monitored variable with more than a single value of a controlled variable. For example, if the system is required to display the current water level, it may be acceptable for the displayed value of water level at time t to deviate from the actual value at time t by as much as 0.1 cm.

The system requirements are easier to specify and to reason about if the ideal behavior is defined first. Then, the required precision and timing can be specified separately. This is standard engineering practice. Moreover, this approach provides an appropriate separation of concerns, since the required system timing and accuracy can change independently of the ideal behavior [3].

The relation IN specifies the accuracy with which the input devices measure the monitored quantities and the relation OUT specifies the accuracy with which the output devices set the controlled quantities. To achieve the allowable system behavior, the input and output devices must measure the monitored quantities and set the controlled quantities with sufficient accuracy and sufficiently small timing delays. In the Four Variable Model, the software requirements specification, called SOFT, defines the required relation between the input and output data items. SOFT can be derived from REQ, NAT, IN, and OUT.

2.2 SCR Requirements Specifications

The SCR requirements method was introduced in 1978 with the publication of the requirements specification for the A-7 Operational Flight Program [10, 1]. Since its introduction, the method has been extended to specify system as well as software requirements and to include, in addition to functional behavior, the required system timing and accuracy [12, 13, 14]. Designed for use by engineers,

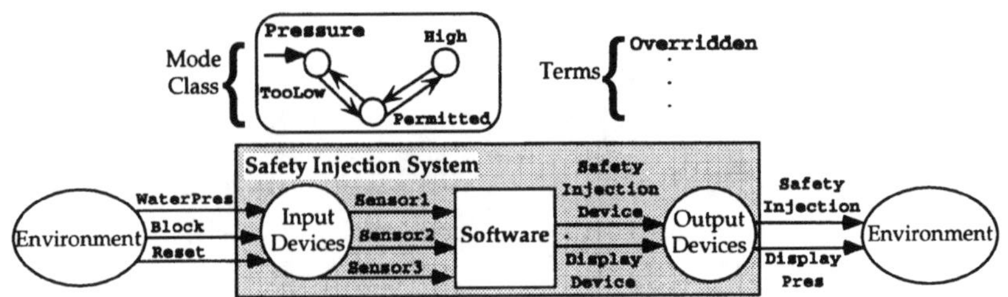

Fig. 2. Requirements Specification for Safety Injection.

the SCR method has been successfully applied to a variety of practical systems, including avionic systems; a submarine communications system [9]; and safety-critical components of a nuclear power plant [14]. More recently, a version of the SCR method called CoRE [4] was used to document requirements of Lockheed's C-130J Operational Flight Program (OFP) [5]. The OFP consists of more than 100K lines of Ada code, thus demonstrating the scalability of the SCR method.

To represent requirements both abstractly and concisely, SCR specifications use two special constructs, called mode classes and terms. A *mode class* is a state machine, defined on the monitored variables, whose states are called *system modes* (or simply *modes*) and whose transitions are triggered by changes in the monitored variables. Complex systems are defined by several mode classes operating in parallel. A *term* is an auxiliary function defined on monitored variables, mode classes, or other terms. In SCR specifications, conditions and events are used to describe the system states. A *condition* is a logical proposition defined on a single system state, whereas an event is a logical proposition defined on a pair of system states. An *event* occurs when a system entity (that is, a monitored or controlled variable, a mode class, or a term) changes value. A special event, called an *monitored event*, occurs when a monitored variable changes value. Another special event, called a *conditioned event*, occurs if an event occurs when a specified condition is true.

To illustrate the SCR method, we consider a simplified version of the control system for safety injection described in [2]. The system uses three sensors to monitor water pressure and turns on a safety injection system (which adds coolant to the reactor core) when the pressure falls below some threshold. The system also displays the current value of water pressure. The system operator blocks safety injection by turning on a "Block" switch and resets the system after blockage by turning on a "Reset" switch. Figure 2 shows how SCR constructs are used in specifying the requirements of the control system. Water pressure and the "Block" and "Reset" switches are represented as monitored variables, `WaterPres`, `Block`, and `Reset`; safety injection and the display as controlled variables, `SafetyInjection` and `DisplayPres`; each sensor value as an input data item; and the hardware interfaces between the control system software and the safety injection system and the display output as output data items.

The specification for the control system includes a mode class `Pressure`, a term `Overridden`, and several conditions and events. The mode class `Pressure`,

Old Mode	Event	New Mode
TooLow	@T(WaterPres ≥ Low)	Permitted
Permitted	@T(WaterPres ≥ Permit)	High
Permitted	@T(WaterPres < Low)	TooLow
High	@T(WaterPres < Permit)	Permitted

Table 1. Mode Transition Table for Pressure.

Mode	Events	
High	False	@T(Inmode)
TooLow, Permitted	@T(Block=On) WHEN Reset=Off	@T(Inmode) OR @T(Reset=On)
Overridden	True	False

Table 2. Event Table for Overridden.

an abstract model of the monitored variable WaterPres, contains three modes, TooLow, Permitted, and High. At any given time, the system must be in one of these modes. A drop in water pressure below a constant Low causes the system to enter mode TooLow; an increase in pressure above a larger constant Permit causes the system to enter mode High. The term Overridden denotes situations in which safety injection is blocked. An example of a condition in the specification is "WaterPres < Low". Events are denoted by the notation "@T". Two examples of events are the monitored event @T(Block=On) (the operator turns Block from Off to On) and the conditioned event @T(Block=On) WHEN WaterPres < Low (the operator turns Block to On when water pressure is below Low).

SCR requirements specifications use special tables, called condition tables, event tables, and mode transition tables, to represent the required system behavior precisely and concisely. Each table defines a mathematical function.[1] A condition table describes a controlled variable or a term as a function of a mode and a *condition*; an event table describes a controlled variable or term as a function of a mode and an *event*. A mode transition table describes a mode as a function of another mode and an event. While condition tables define total functions, event tables and mode transition tables may define partial functions, because some events cannot occur when certain conditions are true. For example, in the control system above, the event @T(Pressure=High) WHEN Pressure=TooLow cannot occur, because starting from TooLow, the system can only enter Permitted when a state transition occurs.

Tables 1–3 are part of REQ, the requirements specification for the control system. Table 1 is a mode transition table describing the mode class Pressure as

[1] Although SCR specifications can be nondeterministic, our initial model is restricted to deterministic systems.

Mode	Conditions	
`High, Permitted`	True	False
`TooLow`	`Overridden`	NOT `Overridden`
`Safety Injection`	`Off`	`On`

Table 3. Condition Table for `Safety Injection`.

a function of the current mode and the monitored variable `WaterPres`. Table 2 is an event table describing the term `Overridden` as a function of `Pressure`, `Block`, and `Reset`. Table 3 is a condition table describing the controlled variable `Safety Injection` as a function of `Pressure` and `Overridden`. Table 3 states, "If `Pressure` is `High` or `Permitted`, or if `Pressure` is `TooLow` and `Overridden` is *true*, then `Safety Injection` is `Off`; if `Pressure` is `TooLow` and `Overridden` is *false*, then `Safety Injection` is `On`."[2]

3 SCR Requirements Model

To provide a formal foundation for tools analyzing the specifications and simulating system execution [7, 6], we have developed a discrete version of the Four Variable Model, called the SCR requirements model [8]. The SCR model represents a system as a finite state machine and each monitored and controlled quantity as a discrete variable. Presented below are excerpts from the definition of the formal model [8] and a description of the interpretation of the REQ and NAT relations within the SCR model.

3.1 Summary of the SCR Model

Entities and Types. We require the following sets.

- *MS* is the union of *N* nonempty, pairwise disjoint sets, $M_1, M_2, \ldots, M_N$, called *mode classes*.
- *TS* is a union of data types, where each type is a nonempty set of values.[3]
- *VS* is a set of entity values with $VS = MS \cup TS$.
- *RF* is a set of entity names r, which is partitioned into the set of mode names MR, the set of monitored variable names IR, the set of term names GR, and the set of controlled variable names OR. For all $r \in RF$, $TY(r) \subseteq VS$ is the type (i.e., the set of possible values) of entity r.

System State and Conditions. A *system state* s is a function that maps each entity name r in *RF* to a value. That is, for all $r \in RF$: $s(r) = v$, where $v \in TY(r)$. Conditions are logical propositions defined on entities in *RF*.

---

[2] The notation "@T(Inmode)" in a row of an event table describes system entry into the group of modes in that row.

[3] For example, the type "nonnegative integers" is the set $\mathcal{N} = \{0, 1, 2, \ldots\}$, the type Boolean is the set $\mathcal{B} = \{true, false\}$, etc.

System and Events. A system is a state machine whose transition from one state to the next is triggered by special events, called monitored events. More precisely, a *system*, Σ, is a 4-tuple $\Sigma = (E^m, S, s_0, T)$, where

- E^m is a set of monitored events. A *primitive event* is denoted as @T$(r = v)$, where $r \in RF$ is an entity and $v \in \mathrm{TY}(r)$. A *monitored event* is a primitive event @T$(r = v)$, where $r \in IR$ is a monitored variable.
- S is the set of possible system states.
- s_0 is a special state called the initial state.
- T is the system transform, a function from $E^m \times S$ into S.

In addition to denoting primitive events, the "@T" notation also denotes conditioned events. A *simple conditioned event* is expressed as

$$@\mathrm{T}(c) \text{ WHEN } d,$$

where @T(c) is any event (i.e., a change in a state variable) and d is a simple condition or a conjunction of simple conditions. A *conditioned event* e is a logical proposition composed of simple conditioned events connected by the logical connectors $\wedge$ and $\vee$. The proposition represented by a simple conditioned event is defined by

$$@\mathrm{T}(c) \text{ WHEN } d \;=\; \text{NOT } c \wedge c' \wedge d,$$

where the unprimed version of c represents c in one state (the old state) and the primed version of c represents c in another state (the new state).

System History Associated with every monitored variable $r \in IR$ is a set of ordered pairs V_r,

$$V_r = \{(v, v') \mid v \neq v', v \in \mathrm{TY}(r), v' \in \mathrm{TY}(r)\},$$

that defines all possible transitions of r and that contains r's initial value. A monitored event @T$(r = v')$ is *enabled in* state s if $(s(r), v') \in V_r$. A history Π of a system is a function from the set of nonnegative integers $\mathcal{N}$ to $E^m \times S$ such that (1) the second element of $\Pi(0)$ is s_0, (2) for all $n \in \mathcal{N}$, if $\Pi(n) = (e, s)$, then e is enabled in s, and (3) for all $n \in \mathcal{N}$, if $\Pi(n) = (e, s)$ and $\Pi(n+1) = (e', s')$, then $T(e, s) = s'$.

Ordering the Entities. Given an input event e in E^m, states s and s' in S, and $T(e, s) = s'$, the value of each entity r in state s' may depend on any entity in the old state s but on only some entities in the new state s'. To describe the dependencies of any entity $r \in \mathrm{RF}$ on entities in the new state, we order the entities in RF as a sequence R,

$$R = \langle r_1, r_2, \ldots, r_I, r_{I+1}, \ldots, r_K, r_{K+1}, \ldots, r_P \rangle,$$

where $\langle r_1, r_2, \ldots, r_I \rangle$, $r_i \in IR$, is the subsequence of monitored variables, $\langle r_{I+1}, r_{I+2}, \ldots, r_K \rangle$, $r_i \in GR \cup MR$, is the subsequence containing terms and modes, and $\langle r_{K+1}, r_{K+2}, \ldots, r_P \rangle$, $r_i \in OR$ is the subsequence of controlled variables.

Modes	Conditions			
m_1	$c_{1,1}$	$c_{1,2}$	...	$c_{1,p}$
m_2	$c_{2,1}$	$c_{2,2}$	...	$c_{2,p}$
...	...	...	...	...
m_n	$c_{n,1}$	$c_{n,2}$	...	$c_{n,p}$
r_i	v_1	v_2	...	v_p

Table 4. Typical Format for a Condition Table.

The entities $r_i \in R$ are partially ordered so that for all $i, i', i > I, 1 \leq i' \leq K$, the value of entity r_i in any state s can only depend on the value of entity $r_{i'}$ in the same state s if $i' < i$. This definition reflects the fact that each monitored variable can only be changed by external events and cannot depend on the other entities in R. In contrast, each term in s can depend on the monitored variables, the modes, or other terms in s. Similarly, each mode in s can depend on the monitored variables, the terms, or other modes in s. Finally, each controlled variable in s can depend on any entity that precedes it in the sequence R.

Computing the Transform Function. Each controlled variable, term, and mode class $r_i \in RF \setminus IR$ is defined by a function F_i. The transform function T computes the new state by composing the F_i's. In an SCR requirements specification, most of the F_i's are described by tables.

Table 4 shows a typical format for one class of tables, condition tables. A condition table describes an output variable or term r_i as a relation ρ_i,

$$\rho_i = \{(m_j, c_{j,k}, v_k) \in M_{\mu(i)} \times C_i \times TY(r_i) \mid 1 \leq j \leq n, 1 \leq k \leq p\},$$

where C_i is a set of conditions defined on entities in RF and $M_{\mu(i)}$ is the mode class associated with r_i. The relation ρ_i must satisfy the following properties:

1. The m_j and the v_k are unique.
2. $\cup_{i=1}^{n} m_j = M_{\mu(i)}$ (All modes in the mode class are included).
3. For all j: $\vee_{k=1}^{p} c_{j,k} = \mathit{true}$ (**Coverage:** The disjunction of the conditions in each row of the table is *true*).
4. For all $j, k, l,\ k \neq l$: $c_{j,k} \wedge c_{j,l} = \mathit{false}$ (**Disjointness:** The pairwise conjunction of the conditions in each row of the table is always *false*).

Given these properties, we can show that ρ_i is a function, which can be expressed as: for all $j, k,\ 1 \leq j \leq n, 1 \leq k \leq p$, $\rho_i(m_j, c_{j,k}) = v_k$.

To make explicit entity r_i's dependencies on other entities, we consider an alternate form F_i of the function ρ_i. To define F_i, we require the *new state dependencies set*, $\{y_{i,1}, y_{i,2}, \ldots, y_{i,n_i}\}$, where $y_{i,1}$ is the entity name for the associated mode class and for all j, $2 \leq j \leq n_i$, $y_{i,j}$ appears in some condition c in C_i.

Based on this set and ρ_i, we define F_i as

$$F_i(y_{i,1}, y_{i,2}, \ldots, y_{i,n_i}) = \begin{cases} v_1 \text{ if } (y_{i,1} = m_1 \wedge c_{1,1}) \vee \ldots \vee (y_{i,1} = m_n \wedge c_{n,1}) \\ v_2 \text{ if } (y_{i,1} = m_1 \wedge c_{1,2}) \vee \ldots \vee (y_{i,1} = m_n \wedge c_{n,2}) \\ \vdots \\ v_p \text{ if } (y_{i,1} = m_1 \wedge c_{1,p}) \vee \ldots \vee (y_{i,1} = m_n \wedge c_{n,p}). \end{cases}$$

The four properties guarantee that F_i is a total function.

3.2 The SCR Model, REQ, and NAT

NAT. In the SCR model, NAT models the behavior of the monitored and controlled quantities. Consider the monitored variable **Block** in the example above and let m_1 = **Block**. The type definition of m_1 is TY(m_1) = {**Off, On**} and the possible changes of m_1 from one state to the next are defined by V_{m_1} = {(**Off, On**), (**On, Off**)}; that is, **Block** can change from **Off** to **On** or from **On** to **Off**. Similarly, for the monitored variable m_2 = **Reset** and the controlled variable c_1 = **SafetyInjection**, TY(m_2) =TY(c_1) = {**Off, On**} and $V_{m_2} = V_{c_1}$ = {(**Off, On**), (**On, Off**)}.

The current SCR model describes all monitored and controlled quantities, even those which are naturally continuous, as discrete variables. Doing so allows us to represent the system as a finite state machine. This representation facilitates formal analysis of the specifications and symbolic execution of the system via simulation. For example, to model **WaterPres** as a discrete variable, we assign m_3 = **WaterPres** the type definition $TY(m_3) = \{14, 15, \ldots, 2000\}$, that is, m_3 is any integer between 14 and 2000. We constrain changes in **WaterPres** by requiring that **WaterPres** can change from one state to the next by no more than 1 psi, that is,

$$|s'(m_3) - s(m_3)| \in \{0, 1\},$$

where s and s' are any two consecutive states. This assumption implies the statement in Section 2.2 that the mode class **Pressure** cannot transition directly from **TooLow** to **High** or from **High** to **TooLow**. Similarly, we can define the type of controlled variable c_2 = **DisplayPres** as $TY(c_2) = \{14, 15, \ldots, 2000\}$ and constrain changes in c_2 by requiring that, if s and s' are any two consecutive states, then $|s'(c_2) - s(c_2)| \in \{0, 1\}$.

Ideal Behavior. In the SCR model, the transform function T defines the ideal system behavior. As noted above, T computes the new state from an event and the current state by composing the functions F_i that define the values of terms, mode classes, and controlled variables. Clearly, reasoning about the ideal system behavior using T abstracts away timing delays and imprecision.

4 Extending the SCR Model to Hybrid Systems

To use the SCR model to specify and to reason about hybrid systems, we need to extend the model in two ways:

- Each monitored quantity and controlled quantity that is naturally continuous is represented by a continuous (rather than a discrete) variable.
- The allowable system behavior is defined by associating timing and accuracy requirements with each controlled variable.

4.1 Adding Continuous Variables

As an example, consider the monitored variable m_3 = `WaterPres` and the controlled variable c_2 = `DisplayPres`. We can define m_3 as a real number between 14.0 and 2000.0, that is, $\mathrm{TY}(m_3) = \{x \mid x \in R^+ \wedge 14.0 \leq x \leq 2000.0\}$. Physical laws (part of NAT) bound the rate at which m_3 can change. To express this bound, we may state in the specification that, in any time interval of length 0.1 seconds, the maximum change in the value of `WaterPres` is 0.03 psi; that is,

$$|m_3(t') - m_3(t)| \leq .03,$$

when $t' - t = 0.1$ sec. The constraints on c_2 may be defined in a similar way. Clearly, the bounds can be expressed by more complex functions, e.g., by continuously differentiable functions, by piecewise continuous functions, or by bounded derivatives.

We note that any reasoning that used the discrete models of `WaterPres` and `DisplayPres` to analyze system behavior should be reevaluated to make sure the reasoning is still valid when more accurate models of these two naturally continuous quantities are used. This is especially important when discrete approximations of continuous quantities are used in verifying critical system properties.

4.2 Adding Time

The SCR model introduced in Section 3.1 is untimed. Thus if an event occurs in state s that changes a controlled variable, we assume that the next state s' reflects the change in the controlled variable (as well as changes in the monitored variable that triggered the new state and any resulting changes in mode classes, terms, and other controlled variables). To add time to the SCR model, we adapt the approach developed by Lynch and Vaandrager [11] for timed automata. This approach associates each event in a state history with a time. More precisely, for each state history, $s_0, (e_1, s_1), (e_2, s_2), \ldots$, we define a sequence of the form $(e_1, t_1), (e_2, t_2), \ldots$, where each e_i is either a monitored event or an event changing the value of a controlled variable and each t_i is a non-negative real-valued time. We require that, for all i, $i+1$, $t_{i+1} \geq t_i$ and define a function TIME that maps each event e in a system history to a time t, that is, $\mathrm{TIME}(e) = t$.

4.3 Specifying the Actual System Behavior

To specify the allowable system behavior, we associate timing and accuracy requirements with each controlled variable. Consider, for example, the controlled variable **DisplayPres** in the example, and let c_2 = **DisplayPres**. To specify the constraints on c_2, we must state the degree of accuracy that is required in the displayed value of **WaterPres**. For example, we may require that the displayed value of **WaterPres** at any given t is within 0.1 psi of the actual value of **WaterPres** at time t, that is, $|c_2(t) - m_3(t)| \leq 0.1$ psi.

Consider a system design that uses a given input device to measure **WaterPres**, a given output device to write the value of **WaterPres** to the display, and specific hardware and software. Then, the maximum rate at which **WaterPres** can change in a given time interval (defined by NAT), the degree of accuracy and timing delays associated with the input and output devices (defined by IN and OUT), and the system delay in reading from and writing to the devices together determine whether the required accuracy can be achieved.

To specify the requirements for turning the safety injection system on and off, we must specify timing constraints on the controlled variable **SafetyInjection**. Let c_1 represent **SafetyInjection**. Suppose that the safety injection system must be turned on within, say, 0.2 seconds after the occurrence of the triggering event (e.g., **WaterPres** drops below **Low** when **Overridden**= *false*). Then, if the triggering event e_k occurs at time t, that is, $\mathrm{TIME}(e_k) = t$, the event e_{k+j} that turns on **SafetyInjection** must occur within the time interval $[t, t + 0.2]$, that is, $\mathrm{TIME}(e_{k+j}) \in [t, t + 0.2]$. By considering a particular system design—that is, the timing delays and degree of accuracy of the input and output devices and computer hardware and software that control safety injection—we can compute whether safety injection will always be activated within the required time interval.

5 Summary

We have presented several examples to show how the SCR requirements model can be extended to specify and to reason about hybrid systems. The next step is to extend the formal definition of the SCR model to include continuous variables, time, and accuracy. By adding such information to system and software requirements specifications, we can provide precise guidance to the developers of computer systems and a formal foundation for analyzing the behavior of these systems.

Acknowledgments

The perceptive and constructive comments of Stuart Faulk, Ralph Jeffords, Jim Kirby, and Bruce Labaw on an earlier draft are gratefully acknowledged.

References

1. Thomas A. Alspaugh, Stuart R. Faulk, Kathryn Heninger Britton, R. Alan Parker, David L. Parnas, and John E. Shore. Software requirements for the A-7E aircraft. Technical Report NRL-9194, Naval Research Lab., Wash., DC, 1992.
2. P.-J. Courtois and David L. Parnas. Documentation for safety critical software. In *Proc. 15th Int'l Conf. on Softw. Eng. (ICSE '93)*, pages 315–323, Baltimore, MD, 1993.
3. Stuart Faulk, Lisa Finneran, James Kirby, Jr., and Assad Moini. Consortium requirements engineering handbook. Technical Report SPC-92060-CMC, Software Productivity Consortium, Herndon, VA, December 1993.
4. Stuart R. Faulk, John Brackett, Paul Ward, and James Kirby, Jr. The CoRE method for real-time requirements. *IEEE Software*, 9(5):22–33, September 1992.
5. Stuart R. Faulk, Lisa Finneran, James Kirby, Jr., S. Shah, and J. Sutton. Experience applying the CoRE method to the Lockheed C-130J. In *Proc. 9th Annual Conf. on Computer Assurance (COMPASS '94)*, pages 3–8, Gaithersburg, MD, June 1994.
6. Constance Heitmeyer, Alan Bull, Carolyn Gasarch, and Bruce Labaw. SCR*: A toolset for specifying and analyzing requirements. In *Proc. 10th Annual Conf. on Computer Assurance (COMPASS '95)*, pages 109–122, Gaithersburg, MD, June 1995.
7. Constance Heitmeyer, Bruce Labaw, and Daniel Kiskis. Consistency checking of SCR-style requirements specifications. In *Proc., International Symposium on Requirements Engineering*, March 1995.
8. Constance L. Heitmeyer, Ralph D. Jeffords, and Bruce G. Labaw. Tools for analyzing SCR-style requirements specifications: A formal foundation. Technical Report NRL-7499, Naval Research Lab., Wash., DC, 1995. In preparation.
9. Constance L. Heitmeyer and John McLean. Abstract requirements specifications: A new approach and its application. *IEEE Trans. Softw. Eng.*, SE-9(5):580–589, September 1983.
10. Kathryn Heninger, David L. Parnas, John E. Shore, and John W. Kallander. Software requirements for the A-7E aircraft. Technical Report 3876, Naval Research Lab., Wash., DC, 1978.
11. Nancy Lynch and Frits Vaandrager. Forward and backward simulations for timing-based systems. In *Proceedings of REX Workshop "Real-Time: Theory in Practice"*, volume 600 of *Lecture Notes in Computer Science*, pages 397–446, Mook, The Netherlands, June 1991. Springer-Verlag.
12. David L. Parnas and Jan Madey. Functional documentation for computer systems. Technical Report CRL 309, McMaster Univ., Hamilton, ON, Canada, September 1995.
13. A. John van Schouwen. The A-7 requirements model: Re-examination for real-time systems and an application for monitoring systems. Technical Report TR 90-276, Queen's Univ., Kingston, ON, Canada, 1990.
14. A. John van Schouwen, David L. Parnas, and Jan Madey. Documentation of requirements for computer systems. In *Proc. RE'93 Requirements Symp.*, pages 198–207, San Diego, CA, January 1993.

Validation of Hybrid Systems by Co-simulation

D. Sinclair[1] *, E. Holz[2], D. Witaszek[2] and M. Wasowski[2]

[1] School of Computer Applications, Dublin City University, Glasnevin, Dublin 9,Ireland.
[2] Humboldt Universität zu Berlin, Lindenstrasse 54a, PSF 1297, D-10099 Berlin, Germany.

Abstract. This article describes the INSYDE[3] methodology for the design of hybrid systems. This methodology covers the development life-cycle from initial requirements capture, through design and implementation, to validation. The validation of a hybrid system is achieved by co-simulating a formal description of the hybrid system. This formal description is derived from the initial requirements capture by integrating an object-oriented analysis and modelling tool, OMT, with two domain-specific formal description languages, SDL and VHDL, for the description of the software and hardware subsystems respectively. The automatic translation of the system, described in a formal variant of OMT, to SDL and VHDL ensures that descriptions of the software and hardware subsystems together form a coherent description of the hybrid system. The article describes how this formal description forms the basis for co-simulation. The advantages of using heterogeneous co-simulation for validating hybrid systems are described, and the article shows how the methodology, and supporting tools, support the co-simulation by automatically generating the necessary code to connect and synchronise the individual SDL and VHDL simulators.

1 Introduction

This article describes the INSYDE methodology's approach to the validation of hybrid systems based on co-simulating the various hardware and software components of the hybrid system.

The INSYDE methodology is an integrated methodology that addresses the whole life-cycle of hybrid systems project, from requirements capture, through system level and detailed level design, to implementation and validation. This is accomplished by integrating an object-oriented analysis and modelling technique, OMT[1] , with two domain-specific design techniques, SDL[2] [3] [4] and VHDL[5]. The system is initially described using OMT and this description is automatically translated into the formal description languages SDL and VHDL, which describes the software and hardware subsystems respectively. The detailed software and hardware design is completed in SDL and VHDL respectively.

* Contact author. E-mail: David.Sinclair@compapp.dcu.ie

[3] INSYDE is a CEC ESPRIT III funded project (P8641). The members of the INSYDE consortium are Alcatel Bell Telephone, Dublin City University, Humboldt Universität zu Berlin, Intracom S.A., Verilog S.A. and Vrije Universiteit Brussel

1.1 Overview of the INSYDE Methodology

OMT is a rigorous, non-formal, method for modelling systems in an object-oriented manner. OMT provides three inter-related views of the system; a static object view, that describes the objects in the system and how they are inter-related; a dynamic view that describes the dynamic behaviour of each object; and a functional view that models how the data values contained in the objects are transformed. As such it provides an excellent tool for capturing the requirements of the system in a way that both designer and analyst/customer can understand. These three inter-related views of the system form the first model of the INSYDE methodology, the *conceptual model*. The *conceptual model* is the result of the *Analysis Phase* of the methodology and captures the requirements of the system.

The *conceptual model* is also the starting point for the next phase of the methodology, the *System Design Phase*. The goal of this phase is to partition the design into hardware and software objects, define how these objects interact and to define the interfaces between these objects. OMT is a non-formal rigorous methodology very suited to analysis and modelling. Therefore, while OMT is ideal for describing the *conceptual model* of the system, its lack of a precise semantics for its concepts makes it unsuitable for the design phase in which objects are given precise meanings and behaviours. *System Design* requires a language with precise semantics, and this is provided in the INSYDE methodology by a language OMT*[7]. OMT* is a subset of OMT concepts that have been given a precise semantics. Since the *system design model* in OMT* will be translated into an SDL description of the software subsystems and a VHDL description of the hardware subsystems, the semantics of an OMT* concept is defined by the semantics of the concept into which it will be translated. These *transformational semantics* enable the automatic translation to SDL and VHDL during the next phase of the methodology. The result of the *System Design Phase* is the *system design model* which defines the hardware and software objects in the system and the interactions.

The next phase in the INSYDE methodology, the *Detailed Design Phase* takes the *system design model* in OMT* and automatically translates this model into an SDL description of the software components of the hybrid system and a VHDL description of the hardware components of the hybrid system. The hybrid system specification can be refined and developed further, following the general guidelines for SDL and VHDL, to include detailed descriptions of the behaviour of the software and hardware objects within the hybrid system. The result of the *Detailed Design Phase* is the *architectural model*. This model is a formal specification of the architecture and functionality of the hybrid system in terms of the two formal description languages (FDTs). Since these two formal descriptions of the software and hardware subsystems were derived from a common *system design model* the SDL and VHDL descriptions together form a coherent description of the hybrid system.

Because the *architectural model* is a formal model of the hybrid system, it is from this model that code generation, hardware synthesis and co-simulation is possible.

Figure 1 summarises the various phases of the INSYDE methodology and the models produced by each phase.

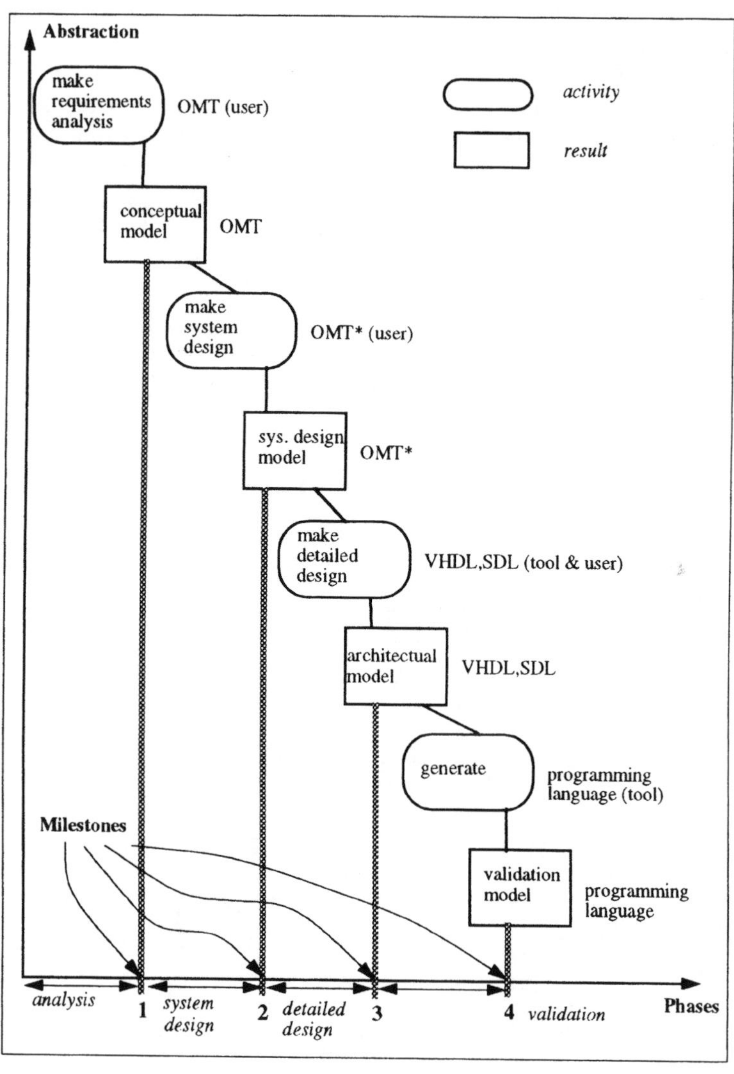

Fig. 1. INSYDE methodology: Phases and Models

2 Example

The following example gives a vision of the application of the INSYDE methodology and how the generation of a formal model of a hybrid systems can be part of the software/hardware development process. To keep the example small and to fit it within the size restrictions of this article many details had to be omitted. However, significant milestones within the development process are shown as diagrams and explained by accompanying text. The example selected is the development of a computerised car control system. It shall provide the typical features of a conventional automatic car (e.g. brake and accelerator pedals, automatic gear changing) but also include a cruise control unit. In contrast to conventional systems there will be no gear lever with a mechanic control of the gear unit. A push-button box controlling the gear box by electronic and electric means will be used instead. The Car Control System will automatically change the gears in response to the selected driving direction, upper gear limit, position of brake and accelerator pedals, current speed of the car and the rotational speed of the engine. If the Cruise controller is in use, a desired speed can be set. The cruise controller then takes over control of the engine speed. It will accelerate or brake in order to keep the desired speed. The driver can interrupt the cruise controller by pressing the brake or pushing the off-button of the cruise controller. In Figure 2 the class diagram at the *Analysis Phase* is given. The system consists of two main classes, Car Control System (CCS) and Engine.

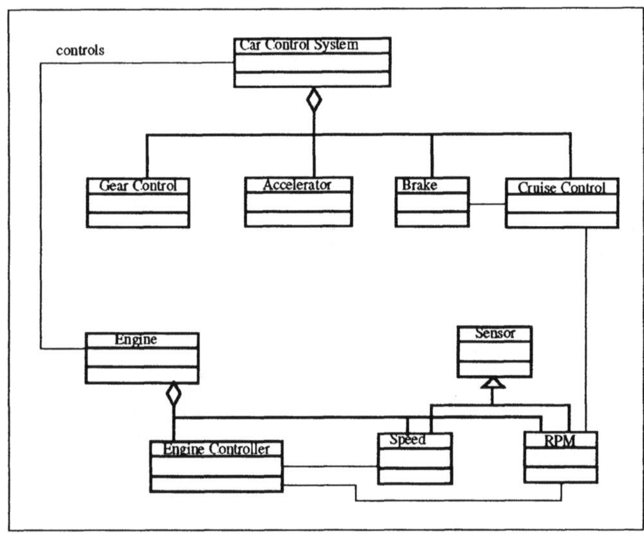

Fig. 2. Class Diagram (Analysis)

The association between classes expresses that the CCS controls the engine.

Both classes are aggregations of other classes. The CCS consist of the Gear Control (i.e. the push-button box), the Accelerator, the Brake and the Cruise Controller. The Engine has three components, the Engine Controller modelling the physical device for gear changing and the sensors for speed and RPM. Common features of both sensors are generalised in the class Sensor. Two additional associations between the Cruise Controller and both sensors, describe the exchange of information between these classes. The diagram is not yet the final *conceptual model* since operations and attributes are still missing, and dynamic models for the active components are also needed.

An initial *system design model* is given in Figure 3. It takes into account a series of design requirements:

- The system shall be implemented as an hybrid HW/SW system.
- The SW part shall comprise the control logic within the push-button box and the cruise controller.
- Due to the real-time requirements the engine controller shall be implemented as hardware. It switches the gears according to the speed, engine performance and pre-selected gear and driving direction.
- Sensors will be implemented using existing HW components.

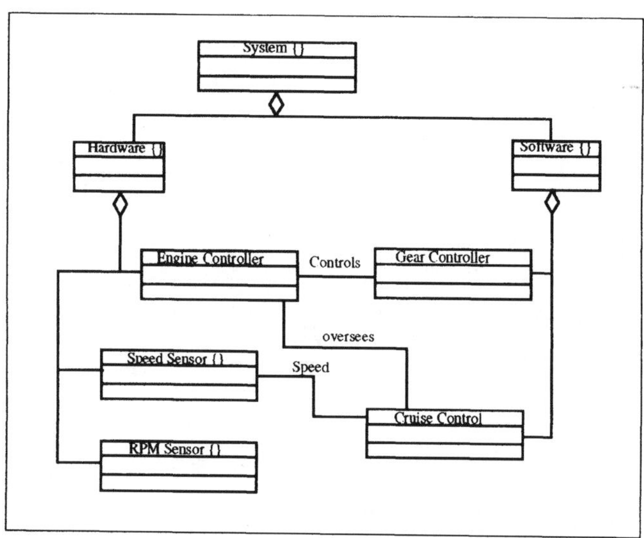

Fig. 3. Class Diagram (Design)

As it can be seen in the figure additional abstract classes (System, Hardware, Software) were introduced to structure the system according to the design requirements. The classes Accelerator and Brake do not appear in this diagram because they are moved to the environment module. The class Sensor has been removed completely and the classes Speed Sensor and RPM Sensor were marked as abstract to express the reuse of existing HW components. Three associations connect the HW part with the SW part. Their tasks can be grouped as follows:

Controls: A communication connection transmitting general control information from the Gear Controller to the Engine Controller (e.g. driving direction, selected gear)

Oversees: A communication connection transmitting information from the Cruise Controller to the Engine Controller. These information comprise accelerate, brake, select gear etc.

Speed: A communication connection between the Speed Sensor and the Cruise Controller transmitting information about the current speed to the Cruise Controller.

The following two figures describe the behaviour of the Gear Controller and of the Engine Controller.

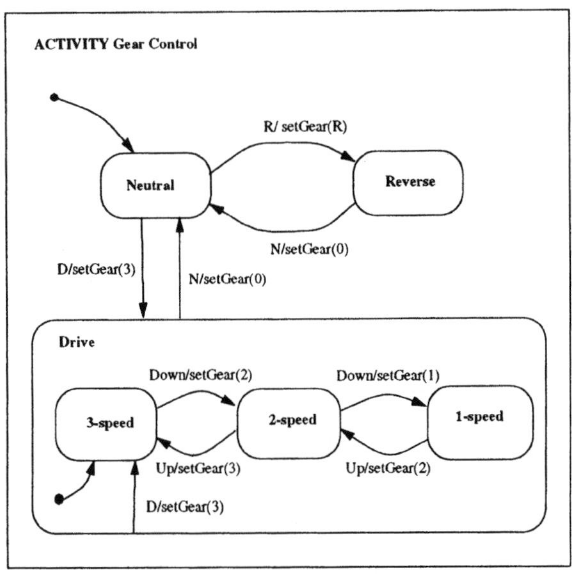

Fig. 4. State Diagram Gear Controller

The Gear Controller has a very simple behaviour. It consists of three main states: *Neutral*, *Reverse* and *Drive*. *Drive* is divided into three substates corresponding to the three different upper gear limits. Some important aspects of the control logic can be seen:

- A transition to *Reverse* is only possible from the *Neutral* state.

- 3-Speed is the default upper gear limit.
- From each position one can directly change to *Neutral*.

The action *SetGear* correspond to the sending of an event to the Engine Controller.

The behaviour of the Engine Controller is shown in Figure 5.

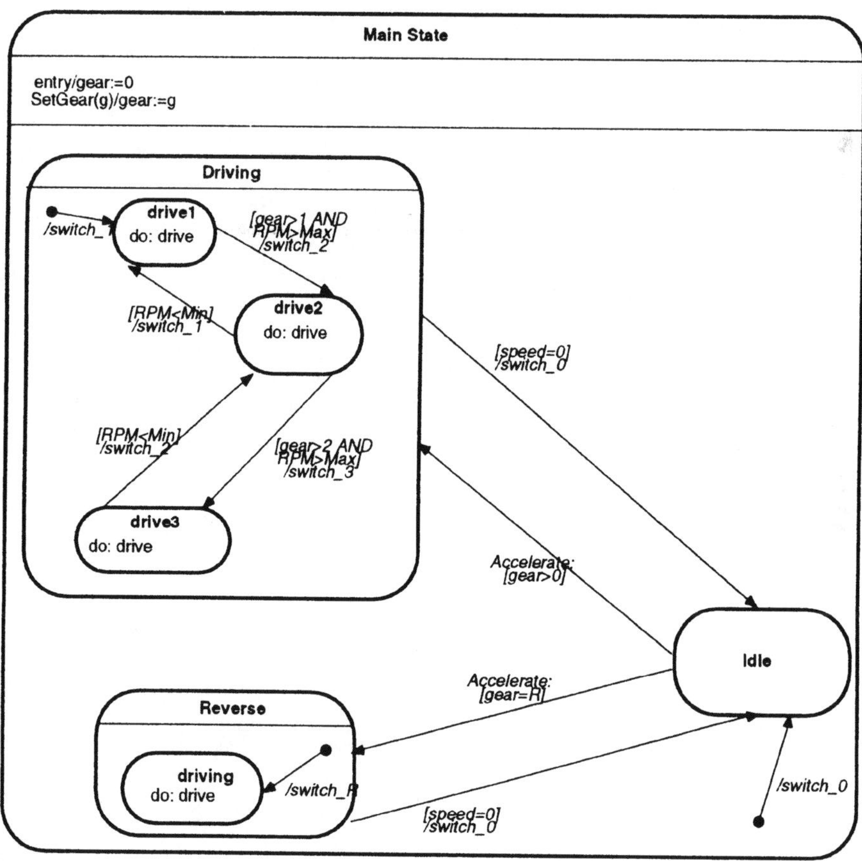

Fig. 5. State Diagram Engine Controller

Again three main states can be recognised: *Idle*, *Driving* and *Reverse*, however, the transitions are triggered by different events. An *Accelerate* triggers transitions to leave *Idle* under the precondition that a gear (1,2,3 or R) was selected. A speed of zero will trigger transitions to the *Idle* state. Also within the *Driving* state the transition are triggered by guarded events. Gears will be switched depending on the speed and the pre-selected upper gear limit. The activity *drive*, which is called in all substates, models the increasing or slowing down depending on the accelerator and the brake information. Its description has been omitted here.

The final step of the INSYDE methodology is the *Detailed Design Phase*. The software related classes will be translated into SDL, the hardware related into VHDL In Figure 6 the SDL Process Type GearControl can be seen.

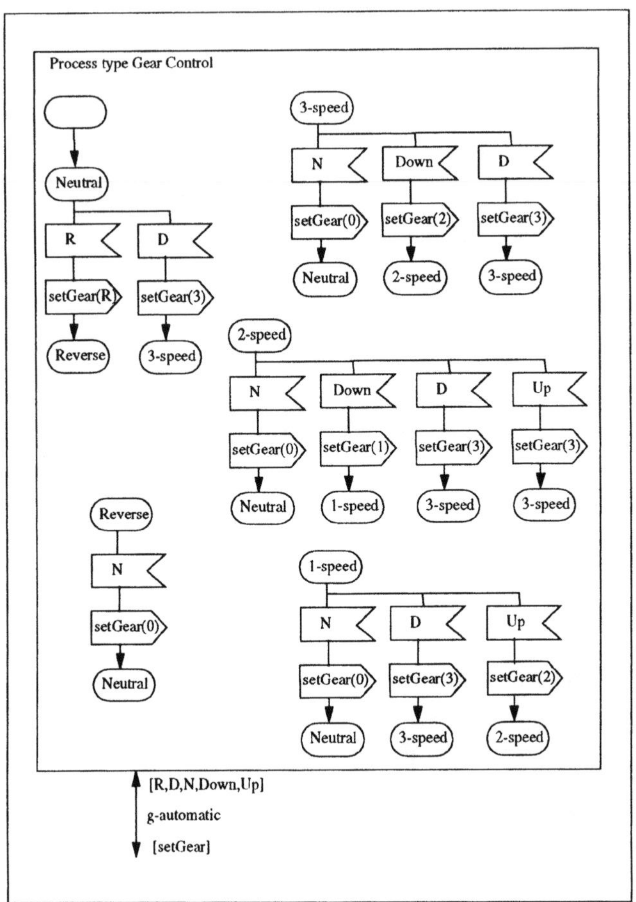

Fig. 6. SDL Diagram GearControl

The transformation to SDL has been rather straight forward due to the simple OMT* state diagram. Because SDL does not provide nested states, the state

Drive had to be flattened. A gate was introduced to the process type, describing the information flow from (SetGear) and to the process (R ,N, D, Up, Down). At the structural level two channels will be connected to that gate transmitting the information to the environment of the SDL specification, namely the hardware part. Because VHDL has no succinct graphical representation it is omitted. However the combined SDL/VHDL specification of the system, generated as part of the development process, provides the formal model of the system that can be validated by co-simulation.

3 Validation in INSYDE

Validation of a hybrid system specification (*architectural model*) in the INSYDE methodology is by co-simulating the SDL and VHDL specifications of the software and hardware subsystems respectively. A co-simulation of the software and hardware subsystems, as opposed to individual simulations of the subsystems, is necessary since the *emergent properties* of a system[6] are due to the interaction of the various subsystems and will not be apparent in the individual simulations.

The validation of the hybrid system has two goals within INSYDE:

1. to test for self-consistency of the specification (e.g. under certain conditions does the system deadlock? Are any processes starved? Is an error condition which affects both hardware and software handled correctly?); and
2. to test if the specification is consistent with the specifications contained in the *conceptual model* and the *system design models*.

Validation within INSYDE is used to determine the behaviour of the hybrid system under specified conditions. Hence the absence of deadlock, for example, under a specified sequence of interacting events from the environment can be tested; but the absence of deadlock under all possible conditions cannot. Such verification of the dynamic system properties is outside the scope of the current INSYDE project, but it is intended to add such verification in a follow-on project.

Simulation as a means of validating the behaviour of a system really only has value if there is an a priori description of the systems behaviour. If such an a priori description does not exist then the decisions that a designer makes about the simulation output could be considered suspect. The output may look right but is it what was expected? The INSYDE methodology provides three a priori behavioural descriptions of the hybrid system, the dynamic models from the *conceptual model*, the *system design model* and *architectural models*. An additional advantage is that these three behavioural descriptions are at different level of abstraction (analysis, system level design and detailed design). So as well as validating the behaviour of the hybrid system to the software and hardware designers, the system can be demonstrably validated to the customer/analyst and the system designer.

The co-simulation of a hybrid system can be viewed at two levels (Fig. 7):

1. the **language level** which consists of an SDL specification and a VHDL specification, and describes, in an abstract manner, the exchange of signals between them; and
2. the **simulator level** which describes the concepts used to implement the co-simulation.

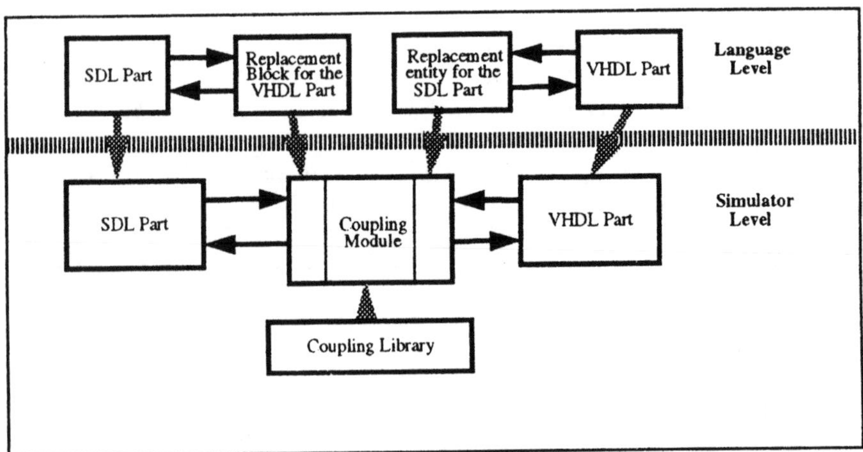

Fig. 7. The Architecture of a Hybrid VHDL/SDL Specification on the Language and Simulator Level

3.1 The Language Level

The language level addresses the language related issues of co-simulation. Specifically, how the VHDL specification is represented to the SDL simulator and how the SDL specification is represented to the VHDL simulator. This is done by adding a replacement unit to the SDL and VHDL specifications which model the interface to and from the VHDL and SDL specifications respectively. These replacement units are automatically generated as part of the OMT*→SDL and OMT*→VHDL translation tools.

VHDL Replacement Unit In the case of the SDL simulator the VHDL replacement is achieved by adding a block to the SDL specification that contains two concurrent processes:

- one process which models the reception of signals from the VHDL part of the hybrid system and the sending of signals to the SDL part; and

- another process which models the reception of signals from the SDL part of the hybrid system and the sending of signals to the VHDL part.

VHDL signals are represented as remote non-delay SDL variables within this replacement unit.

SDL Replacement Unit In the case of the VHDL simulator the SDL replacement is achieved by adding a VHDL entity with an architecture containing concurrent signal assignments (with delta delay). Each signal that can be sent to, or received from, the SDL specification is represented by a local signal in the architecture of the replacement entity, which are contained in the port of the replacement entity.

3.2 The Simulator Level

While the language level defines the signals that can be exchanged between the SDL and VHDL specifications, it is the simulator level that defines the semantics of the signal exchange. There are three possible approaches to the co-simulation of a hybrid system:

1. The **Single Base Approach** in which both the SDL and VHDL specifications are translated into a third language and a single language simulator for this language is used to simulate the hybrid system.
2. The **Translation Approach** in which either the SDL or VHDL is translated into VHDL or SDL respectively, and then an VHDL or SDL simulator is used to simulate the hybrid system.
3. The **Heterogeneous Approach** in which an SDL simulator is used to simulate the SDL specification and a VHDL simulator are used to simulate the VHDL specification. The two simulators are connected and synchronised via a coupling module.

The INSYDE methodology use the Heterogeneous Approach to co-simulate the hybrid system. The theoretical justification for this selection is the recognition that the software and hardware subsystems of a hybrid system may not necessarily use a common internal time base. Typically software is asynchronous in nature, the rate of progression though the code does not affect the semantics of the code and only has an effect on the system when it needs to synchronise with the hardware subsystems. The practical advantage of the Heterogeneous Approach is that multiple simulators can be used to increase the speed of the simulation.

The Coupling Module. The Coupling Module connects and synchronises the SDL and VHDL simulators. It contains the SDL and VHDL replacement units and is automatically generated as part of the the OMT*→SDL and OMT*→VHDL translation process. The Coupling module realises:

- the connection between the simulators as defined by the replacement units,
- the exchange of information between the SDL and VHDL simulators, including any data transformations that are necessary, and,
- the synchronisation of the SDL and VHDL simulators to a common time base.

4 Conclusions

The INSYDE methodology addresses the development cycle of hybrid systems from requirements capture, through design and implementation, to validation. By integrating OMT with two domain-specific FDTs, a formal coherent description of the hybrid system is obtained in terms of an SDL description of the software subsystem and a VHDL description of the hardware subsystem. This formal description of the hybrid system, the *architectural model*, forms the base from which the system can validated using heterogeneous co-simulation of the SDL and VHDL descriptions. Co-simulation of the hybrid system allows for the testing for certain dynamic properties when the hybrid system is excited by a specified sequence of input conditions. In addition the results of the co-simulation can be compared with three a priori behavioural descriptions of the hybrid system. Each behavioural description of the hybrid system (the dynamic models of the *conceptual* and *system design models*, and the *architectural model*) describe the same system, but at different levels of abstraction. Each level of abstraction is focussed at a different "end-user", the customer/analyst, the system designer and the software and hardware designers, enabling the validation of the system to be understood and accepted by each level of "end-user".

References

1. Rumbaugh J., Blaha M., Premerlani W., Eddy F., Lorensen W.: Object Oriented Modeling and Design. Prentice Hall, International Editions, 1991.
2. CCITT: CCITT Specification and Description Language SDL, Recommendation Z.100 (Blue Book). Geneva, 1988.
3. CCITT: CCITT Specification and Description Language SDL, Recommendation Z.100 (SDL'92). Geneva, 1992.
4. ITU: ITU Specification and Description Language SDL, Recommendation Z.100 Annex I (SDL'92 User Guidelines). 1993
5. IEEE: IEEE Standard VHDL Language Reference Manual. IEEE Standard 1076-1987. 1988
6. Checkland P.B., Scholes J.: Soft Systems Methodology in Action. John Wiley & Sons Ltd. 1990.
7. CEC: INSYDE-Deliverable 1.2: "Application Guidelines". ESPRIT-III Project P8641, Public Report. April 1995.

Proofs from Temporal Hypotheses by Symbolic Simulation

Sanjai Narain

Bellcore, 445 South Street, Morristown, NJ 07960, narain@bellcore.com

Abstract. DMOD is a system for modeling and simulating real-time, discrete-event systems. It formalizes the popular discrete-event simulation technique but retains its powerful intuitions such as events, state, causality, event preemption, and variable advance of simulation time. DMOD has been successfully applied to analysis of real systems in telecommunications. This paper describes a method of using DMOD to prove an important class of temporal properties of the form `property p holds infinitely often`. The method is illustrated by verifying a robotic arm controller, a hybrid system with both discrete and continuous state. An important aspect of this method is that considerable control can be exercised over how efficiently theorems are proved. System models, temporal properties, and theorem provers are all programs in the logic programming language CLP(R). Algorithmic knowledge about how to efficiently compute abstractions needed for proof, and how to control the shape and size of search spaces can be encoded in these programs. Proofs are constructed by executing these programs. As an example of the resulting efficiency, the robotic arm controller is verified in just a few seconds.

1 Introduction

DMOD [4] is a formalization of the popular discrete-event modeling and simulation technique. It has been successfully applied to the simulation and testing of fiber-optics networks e.g., [7] [5]. A system model consists of a definition of the causality relation between events. `causes(E,HE,F)` means event `E` causes event `F` where `HE` is the sequence of all events prior to `E`. Histories are computed by maintaining a global event queue. The effects of the last event in a partial history are computed and inserted into the queue. The next event is the temporally earliest event in the queue. The initial queue consists of just the initial event. A useful feature of DMOD is that event preemption is modeled in a simple, logical manner, instead of by deleting events from the queue or by resetting timers. Event preemption is inference from the *absence* of information over a period of time. A symbolic simulation procedure was also developed which allows input parameters to be variables, and computes symbolic histories parameterized by these variables. By reasoning about symbolic histories, one can reason about each of their infinite concrete instances. However, this reasoning strategy is restricted to systems whose histories are finite.

This paper presents a method of reasoning about systems with infinite histories, specifically, for proving theorems of the form `property p holds infinitely` `often`. The method is illustrated by verifying a linearized version of the robotic arm controller example proposed in [6].

Let `extend(H,Q,H1,Q1)` mean that `(H1,Q1)` is derived from `(H,Q)` in one or more steps by the simulation (history computation) procedure. Here `H` is a partial history and `Q` is the event queue associated with it, so that `(H,Q)` represents a simulation state. Let `prop(H,Q)` be a property of simulation states, and let `prop` and `extend` be defined in the constraint logic programming language CLP(R) [2]. Let `H,Q` be variables and suppose that executing:

```
prop(H,Q)
```

yields just a *single* answer constraint **AC**. By the semantics of constraint-logic programming, **AC** is a finite representation of all partial histories and event queues satisfying `prop`. Now, let `H,Q,H1,Q1` be variables and suppose that executing:

```
prop(H,Q), extend(H,Q,H1,Q1), prop(H1,Q1)
```

also yields the answer constraint **AC** (for `H,Q`). We can then conclude that every `(H,Q)` satisfying `prop` can be extended to `(H1,Q1)` satisfying `prop`. Hence, if `prop` holds once, it holds infinitely often. To show that `prop` holds at least once, let `Init` be the initial event. Then the initial queue is `[Init]`. Now simply show that the following query succeeds:

```
extend([Init], [Init], H, Q), prop(H, Q)
```

The main problem with this scheme is that in general, there will be an infinite number of `(H,Q)` such that `prop(H,Q)`. Thus, there will be an infinite number of answer constraints returned upon typing `prop(H,Q)`. This problem is solved using an alternate representation of partial histories. See Section 6 for details.

A slight variation of the above scheme allows us to prove properties of the form `whenever p holds eventually q holds`. After deriving the answer constraint for the query `p(H,Q)`, check that the query

```
p(H,Q),extend(H,Q,H1,Q1),q(H1,Q1)
```

also yields the same answer constraint.

Section 2 describes the verification problem for the robotic arm controller. Section 3 describes the verification using the above scheme. Section 4 contains a formal description of DMOD. Section 5 outlines the DMOD model of the robotic arm controller. Section 6 discusses how to finitely represent all histories satisfying `prop`.

2 Verification Problem

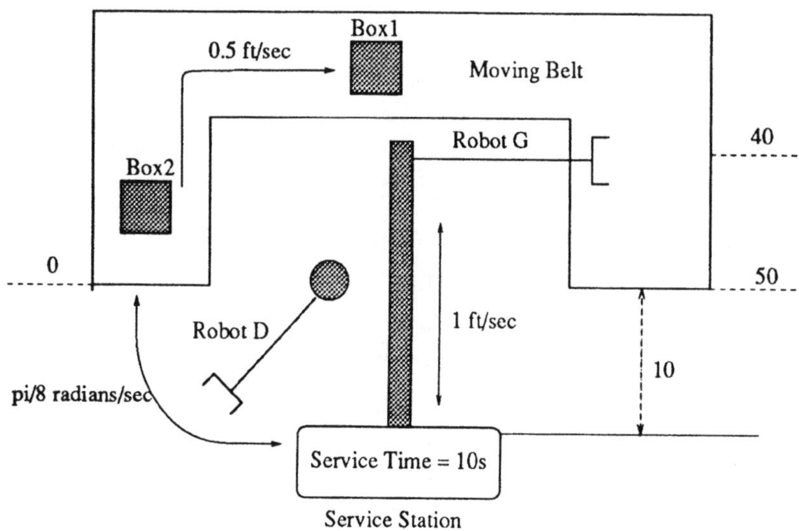

Figure 1

In the figure above, Box1 and Box2 are placed at position 0 on the moving belt. The belt transports the boxes from left to right. When a box reaches 40, Robot G picks it up and brings it down to the service station. When the box is serviced, Robot D picks it up and brings it back to 0. If G reaches its stay position after a box reaches 40, then G attempts to follow the box and grab it before it falls off at 50. G moves up and down a vertical track at 1ft/sec. Its arm takes 2 seconds to fully elongate from fully retracted position, and vice versa. Only one box at a time can be serviced at the service station. The problem is to show that under certain initial conditions Box1 and Box2 will never fall off. Note that if the initial delay between placement of the boxes at 0 is too small or too large then one box will fall off. The initial conditions are that Box1, Box2 are placed at position 0 at times, respectively, 0, 70, and that the status of service station, G, D is, respectively, idle, stay, wait. A simulation of the system produces the history in Figure 2.

Next Event	Event queue
Init	[Init]
begin_moving(box1, 0)	[begin_moving(box1, 0), begin_moving(box2, 70)]
begin_moving(box2, 70)	[begin_moving(box2, 70), reach(box1, 40, 80)]
■	
reach(box1, 40, 80)	[reach(box1, 40, 80), reach(box2, 40, 150)]
begin_follow(g, box1, 80)	[begin_follow(g, box1, 80), reach(box2, 40, 150)]
grab(g, box1, 80)	[grab(g, box1, 80), reach(box2, 40, 150)]
g_leave(grab_position, box1, 80)	[g_leave(grab_position, box1, 80), reach(box2, 40, 150)]
g_arrive(ss, box1, 102)	[g_arrive(ss, box1, 102), reach(box2, 40, 150)]
begin_service(box1, 102)	[begin_service(box1, 102), reach(box2, 40, 150)]
g_leave(ss, 102)	[g_leave(ss, 102), end_service(box1, 112), reach(box2, 40, 150)]
end_service(box1, 112)	[end_service(box1, 112), g_arrive(top, 124), reach(box2, 40, 150)]
d_leave(ss, box1, 112)	[d_leave(ss, box1, 112), g_arrive(top, 124), reach(box2, 40, 150)]
become_idle(112)	[become_idle(112), d_arrive(top, box1, 116), g_arrive(top, 124), reach(box2, 40, 150)]
d_arrive(top, box1, 116)	[d_arrive(top, box1, 116), g_arrive(top, 124), reach(box2, 40, 150)]
deposit(d, box1, 116)	[deposit(d, box1, 116), g_arrive(top, 124), reach(box2, 40, 150)]
begin_moving(box1, 116)	[begin_moving(box1, 116), d_arrive(ss, 120), g_arrive(top, 124), reach(box2, 40, 150)]
d_arrive(ss, 120)	[d_arrive(ss, 120), g_arrive(top, 124), reach(box2, 40, 150), reach(box1, 40, 196)]
g_arrive(top, 124)	[g_arrive(top, 124), reach(box2, 40, 150), reach(box1, 40, 196)]
reach(box2, 40, 150)	[reach(box2, 40, 150), reach(box1, 40, 196)]
begin_follow(g, box2, 150)	[begin_follow(g, box2, 150), reach(box1, 40, 196)]
grab(g, box2, 150)	[grab(g, box2, 150), reach(box1, 40, 196)]
g_leave(grab_position, box2, 150)	[g_leave(grab_position, box2, 150), reach(box1, 40, 196)]
g_arrive(ss, box2, 172)	[g_arrive(ss, box2, 172), reach(box1, 40, 196)]
begin_service(box2, 172)	[begin_service(box2, 172), reach(box1, 40, 196)]
g_leave(ss, 172)	[g_leave(ss, 172), end_service(box2, 182), reach(box1, 40, 196)]
end_service(box2, 182)	[end_service(box2, 182), g_arrive(top, 194), reach(box1, 40, 196)]
d_leave(ss, box2, 182)	[d_leave(ss, box2, 182), g_arrive(top, 194), reach(box1, 40, 196)]
become_idle(182)	[become_idle(182), d_arrive(top, box2, 186), g_arrive(top, 194), reach(box1, 40, 196)]
d_arrive(top, box2, 186)	[d_arrive(top, box2, 186), g_arrive(top, 194), reach(box1, 40, 196)]
deposit(d, box2, 186)	[deposit(d, box2, 186), g_arrive(top, 194), reach(box1, 40, 196)]
begin_moving(box2, 186)	[begin_moving(box2, 186), d_arrive(ss, 190), g_arrive(top, 194), reach(box1, 40, 196)]
d_arrive(ss, 190)	[d_arrive(ss, 190), g_arrive(top, 194), reach(box1, 40, 196), reach(box2, 40, 266)]
g_arrive(top, 194)	[g_arrive(top, 194), reach(box1, 40, 196), reach(box2, 40, 266)]
■	
reach(box1, 40, 196)	[reach(box1, 40, 196), reach(box2, 40, 266)]
begin_follow(g, box1, 196)	[begin_follow(g, box1, 196), reach(box2, 40, 266)]
grab(g, box1, 196)	[grab(g, box1, 196), reach(box2, 40, 266)]
g_leave(grab_position, box1, 196)	[g_leave(grab_position, box1, 196), reach(box2, 40, 266)]
g_arrive(ss, box1, 218)	[g_arrive(ss, box1, 218), reach(box2, 40, 266)]
begin_service(box1, 218)	[begin_service(box1, 218), reach(box2, 40, 266)]
g_leave(ss, 218)	[g_leave(ss, 218), end_service(box1, 228), reach(box2, 40, 266)]
end_service(box1, 228)	[end_service(box1, 228), g_arrive(top, 240), reach(box2, 40, 266)]
d_leave(ss, box1, 228)	[d_leave(ss, box1, 228), g_arrive(top, 240), reach(box2, 40, 266)]
become_idle(228)	[become_idle(228), d_arrive(top, box1, 232), g_arrive(top, 240), reach(box2, 40, 266)]
d_arrive(top, box1, 232)	[d_arrive(top, box1, 232), g_arrive(top, 240), reach(box2, 40, 266)]
deposit(d, box1, 232)	[deposit(d, box1, 232), g_arrive(top, 240), reach(box2, 40, 266)]
begin_moving(box1, 232)	[begin_moving(box1, 232), d_arrive(ss, 236), g_arrive(top, 240), reach(box2, 40, 266)]
⋮	⋮

Figure 2. Simulation of Robotic Arm Controller

The left column shows successive next events, while the right column shows the event queue prevailing immediately before the first event in the queue has occurred. We notice that the sequence of events and event queues between the blocks (■) appears to repeat infinitely often (with different timestamps). The events should be self-explanatory, however, they are defined in Section 5. The set of all simulation states (partial history, event queue) pairs derivable from a simulation state can be laid out in the form of a *simulation tree*. See Section 4 for a formal definition. In the present case, this tree for the initial simulation state has just a single branch.

3 Verification

To show that `box1` and `box2` never fall off, it is sufficient to show that events of `Box1` and `Box2` reaching position `40` occur infinitely often. This can be shown if in the simulation of the robotic arm controller, queues containing both these events arise infinitely often. The simulation procedure ensures that if a queue contains an event, that event occurs in the history. By CLP(R) convention, all identifiers beginning with capital letters are variables, otherwise they are constants. The definition of `prop` is:

```
prop(H, Q):-
     H = [reach(box1, 40, T1) | HT],
     Q = [reach(box1, 40, T1), reach(box2, 40, T2)],
     T1>0, T2-T1 > 50, T2-T1<72,
     status(ss, idle, H),
     status(g, stay, H),
     status(d, wait, H).
```

3.1 General Case

We first show that if `prop` holds once then it eventually holds again. If we type to CLP(R) the query:

```
H=[E | hs(DB)], prop(H,Q).
```

we obtain the *single* answer constraint `C`:

```
H = [reach(box1, 40, T1) | hs(DB)],
Q = [reach(box1, 40, T1), reach(box2, 40, T2)],
DB = [status(ss, idle),
      status(g, stay),
      status(d, wait) | RestDB]
T1>0, T2-T1 > 50, T2-T1<72.
```

By discussion in Section 6, this constraint represents the set of all `(H,Q)` such that `prop(H,Q)`. Intuitively, `DB` represents a system "state" and `hs(DB)` represents a generic partial history with state `DB`. This state only specifies the status of `ss`, `g` and `d`. As `RestDB` is a variable, values of other state parameters are left unspecified. If we now type to CLP(R):

```
H=[E | hs(DB)],
prop(H,Q),
extend(H, Q, H1,Q1),
prop(H1, Q1).
```

we again obtain `C` as before, extended with the following constraints on `(H1,Q1)` (partial histories are maintained in reverse temporal order):

```
Q1 = [reach(box1, 40, T1 + 116), reach(box2, 40, T2 + 116)]
H1 = [reach(box1, 40, T1 + 116),
      g_arrive(top, T2 + 44),
      d_arrive(ss,T2 + 40),
      begin_moving(box2, T2 + 36),
      deposit(d, box2, T2 + 36),
      d_arrive(top, box2, T2 + 36),
      become_idle(T2 + 32),
      d_leave(ss, box2, T2 + 32),
      end_service(box2, T2 + 32),
      g_leave(ss, T2 + 22),
      begin_service(box2, T2 + 22),
      g_arrive(ss, box2, T2 + 22),
      g_leave(grab_position, box2, T2),
      grab(g, box2, T2),
      begin_follow(g, box2, T2),
      reach(box2, 40, T2),
      g_arrive(top, T1 + 44),
      d_arrive(ss, T1 + 40),
      begin_moving(box1, T1 + 36),
      deposit(d, box1, T1 + 36),
      d_arrive(top, box1, T1 + 36),
      become_idle(T1 + 32),
      d_leave(ss, box1, T1 + 32),
      end_service(box1, T1 + 32),
      g_leave(ss, T1 + 22),
      begin_service(box1, T1 + 22),
      g_arrive(ss, box1, T1 + 22),
      g_leave(grab_position, box1, T1),
      grab(g, box1, T1),
      begin_follow(g, box1, T1),
      reach(box1, 40, T1) | hs(DB)]
```

This means that every (H,Q) such that (H=[E | hs(DB)], prop(H,Q)) can be extended to (H1,Q1) such that prop(H1,Q1). The sequence of events which when prepended to H yields H1 is also output in symbolic form. This sequence occurs infinitely often. We can now conclude that if prop holds once it holds infinitely often.

3.2 Base Case

We now show that starting from the initial simulation state, there is at least one (H,Q) such that prop(H,Q). To show this, let:

```
InitEvent = start(InitState, 0)
InitH = [InitEvent]
InitQ = [InitEvent]
InitState = [status(ss,idle),
             status(g, stay),
             status(d, wait),
             position(box1, -1),
             position(box2, -1),
             velocity(box1, 0),
             velocity(box2, 0),
             placement_delay(70)]
```

Then typing to CLP(R):

```
extend(InitH, InitQ, H1, Q1), prop(H1, Q1)
```

yields the constraint:

```
H1 = [reach(box1, 40, 80),
      begin_moving(box2, 70),
      begin_moving(box1, 0),
      InitEvent]
Q1 = [reach(box1, 40, 80), reach(box2, 40, 150)]
```

Thus prop holds at least once. Together with the conclusion derived for the base case, the theorem is established.

4 Overview of DMOD

DMOD is based upon the assumption that the behavior of a system can be modeled by its history, i.e. the sequence of the *discrete* events which occur in it. Thus, simulation of a system can be regarded as computing its history. A DMOD *structure* is a tuple (Events, time, causes) where:

- Events is an enumerably infinite set of objects called **events**
- time(E) is a function mapping an event E to a non-negative real number called the timestamp of E
- causes(E,HE,F) is a relation between events E and F, and a finite sequence HE of events in Events satisfying:

$$\forall E \forall HE.\{F|\mathtt{causes}(E, HE, F)\} \text{ is finite}$$
$$\forall E \forall HE \forall F.\ (\mathtt{causes}(E, HE, F) \Rightarrow \mathtt{time}(E) \leq \mathtt{time}(F))$$
$$\forall E \forall HE \forall F.\ (\mathtt{causes}(E, HE, F) \Rightarrow (F \neq E \wedge (F \notin HE))).$$

An event is assumed to be discrete and instantaneous. Note that an event consists of both an event "type" as well as a timestamp. causes(E,HE,F) means E causes F given that HE is the sequence of all the events which have occurred before E.

Let P be a DMOD structure and $S = E_0, E_1, ...$ be a finite, or enumerably infinite sequence of events. Then S is said to be *temporally ordered* if for each $i, i \geq 0 \Rightarrow \mathtt{time}(E_i) \leq \mathtt{time}(E_{i+1})$ whenever E_{i+1} exists.

Let P=(Events, time, causes) be a DMOD structure. Let $S = E_0, E_1, E_2, ...$ be a finite or enumerably infinite sequence of events. Then S is said to be *causally-sound* if every event in S has a cause in S, i.e.:

$$\forall j (j > 0 \Rightarrow \exists i (i < j \wedge \mathtt{causes}(E_i, [E_0, .., E_{i-1}], E_j))).$$

Note that the singleton sequence E_0 is trivially causally sound.

Let P=(Events, time, causes) be a DMOD structure and $S = E_0, E_1, E_2, ...$ be a finite or enumerably infinite sequence of events. Then S is said to be *causally-complete* iff it contains all caused events, i.e.

$$\forall G \forall i\ (\mathtt{causes}(E_i, [E_0, .., E_{i-1}], G) \Rightarrow \exists j (j > i \wedge E_j = G))$$

Let P be a DMOD structure and init be an event. A history H for P beginning with init is a finite or enumerably infinite sequence of events such that:

- H begins with init
- H is temporally ordered
- H is causally-sound
- H is causally-complete.

Event E is said to be *earlier* than event F if $\mathtt{time}(E) \leq \mathtt{time}(F)$. Let S be a set of events. Then $E \in S$ is said to be an *earliest event in* S if E is earlier than every event in S. Note that if S contains concurrent events (i.e. with the same timestamp), there can be more than one earliest event in S.

Let $Seq = E_0, E_1, ...$ be a temporally ordered sequence of events. Then Seq is said to be *strictly progressive* iff either Seq is finite, or for each real number t there is an i such that $t < \mathtt{time}(E_i)$. Note that a sequence of events is not strictly progressive if its timestamps converge.

Let $E_0, E_1, .., E_k$ be a sequence of events. The set of all effects of E_k w.r.t. E_0, .., E_{k-1} is the set $\{F|causes(E_k, [E_0, .., E_{k-1}], F)\}$. By the restriction on **causes**, this set is finite.

Procedure I. Let P=(Events, time, causes) be a DMOD structure and **init** be an event. The procedure computes histories for P beginning with **init**. Each such history is of the form $E_0, E_1, ...$ where $E_0 = init$. The procedure also computes an auxiliary sequence of "queues" of events $Q_0, Q_1, ...$ where for each i, Q_i denotes the set of events "waiting to occur" after E_{i-1} occurs. In particular, $Q_0 = \{init\}$. Suppose that for some $k \geq 0$ the sequences of events and queues have been computed, respectively, as $E_0, .., E_k$ and $Q_0, .., Q_k$. We show how to compute E_{k+1}. Let $Effects_k$ be the set of effects of E_k w.r.t. $E_0, .., E_{k-1}$. Let $Q_{k+1} = (Q_k - \{E_k\}) \cup Effects_k$. If Q_{k+1} is empty, print $E_0, .., E_k$ as a history. Otherwise, let E_{k+1} be an earliest event in Q_{k+1} ■

Note that Q_{k+1} can contain more than one earliest event (i.e. concurrent events) so the procedure is non-deterministic. A different history would be computed for each choice of E_{k+1}. Also note that all events in $Effects_k$ occur in Q_{k+1}.

Note also that the initial event provides a convenient device for parameterizing simulations. Values of input parameters can be specified in the initial event, and the corresponding histories computed starting at that event.

We can now prove the theorems below. For their proofs see [Narain & Chadha 1995].

Theorem 2.1. Procedure I always computes temporally ordered sequences. Let P = (Events, time, causes) be a DMOD structure and **init** be an event. Let Procedure I compute a sequence of events $E_0, E_1, ...$. Let $Q_0, Q_1, ...$ be the corresponding sequence of queues. Then $E_0, E_1, ...$ is temporally ordered.

Theorem 2.2. Soundness and Completeness of Procedure I. Let P = (**Events**, **time**, **causes**) be a DMOD structure. Let $E_0, E_1, ...$ be a strictly progressive sequence containing no duplicate events. Then Procedure I computes this sequence iff it is a history.

Let H be a finite sequence of temporally ordered events and Q be a finite event queue. A *simulation tree* rooted at (H,Q) is obtained as follows: if (H,Q) cannot be extended in one step by Procedure I, then the tree consists of (H,Q) itself. Otherwise, let $(H_1, Q_1) \cdots (H_k, Q_k)$, $k \geq 1$ be the set of (event-sequence, event queue) pairs derivable from (H,Q) in one step by Procedure I. Construct the derivation tree rooted at each (H_i, Q_i) and attach it as a subtree of (H,Q). Let $(H_0, Q_0) \cdots (H_k, Q_k)$ be a branch in a derivation tree rooted at (H_0, Q_0). Then, for all $i, H_{i+1} = [E|H_i]$, for some event E.

A DMOD structure, particularly the causality relation can be easily expressed in a logic programming language such as CLP(R). We have implemented the following relations:

extend(H, Q, H1, Q1): (H,Q) can be extended to (H1, Q1) in one or more steps via the simulation Procedure.

simulate(H, Q, H1, Q1): (H, Q) can be extended to (H1, Q1) but (H1, Q1) cannot be extended. **simulate** also prints out the intermediate events and queues as they are computed.

5 Robotic Arm Controller Model

5.1 Event Types

Every event is of one of the forms below. The last argument of every event is its timestamp.

`start(DB,0)`: The initial event with timestamp `0`. `DB` represents the initial state as described in Section 6.
`begin_moving(Box, T)`: `Box` is placed on the belt at position `0`.
`d_leave(ss, Box, T)`: `D` leaves the service station with `Box`.
`d_arrive(top, Box, T)`: `D` arrives at the beginning of the belt with `Box`.
`deposit(d, Box, T)`: `D` deposits `Box` at the beginning of the belt.
`reach(Box, P, T)`: `Box` reaches position `P` on belt.
`begin_follow(g, Box, T)`: `G` begins following `Box`.
`grab(g, Box, T)`: `G` grabs `Box`
`g_leave(grab_position, Box, T)`: `G` begins moving towards service station with `Box`.
`g_arrive(ss, Box, T)`: `G` arrives at the service station with `Box`.
`g_leave(ss, T)`: `G` leaves the service station with `Box`.
`g_arrive(top, T)`: `G` arrives at its waiting position.
`begin_service(Box, T)`: Service station begins servicing `Box`
`end_service(Box, T)`: Service station completes servicing `Box`
`become_idle(T)`: Service station has no box to service. `D` has picked it up.

5.2 Causality Rules

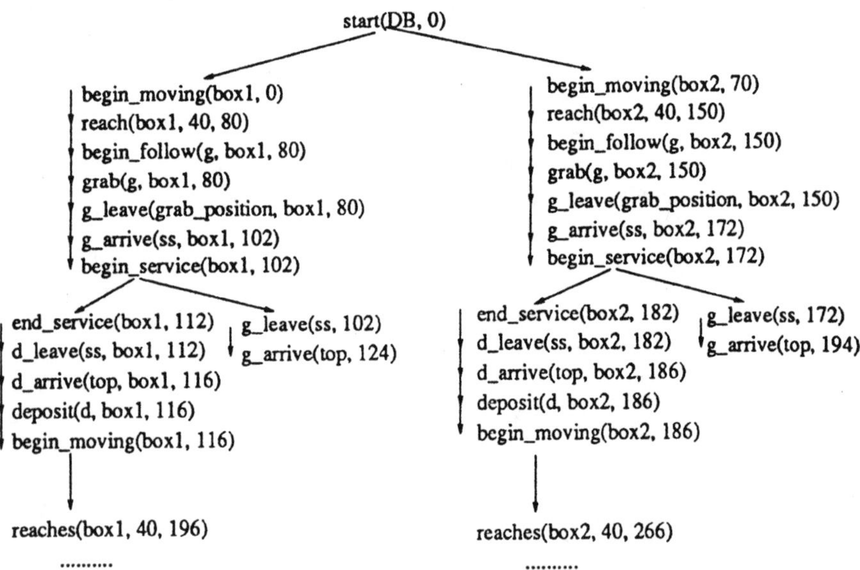

Figure 3. Causality Chains

A graphical display of the causality relation is as above. Examples of rules defining this relation are:

```
causes(E, HE, F):-
        E = begin_follow(g, Box, T),
        F = grab(g, Box, T+Delta),
        position(Box, PBox, [E|HE]),
        Delta = (PBox-40)/(1-0.5).

causes(E, HE, F):-
        E = grab(g, Box, T),
        F = g_leave(grab_position, Box, T).

causes(E, HE, F):-
        E = g_leave(grab_position, Box, T),
        F = g_arrive(ss, Box, T+(50-Pos)+D+2),
        position(Box, Pos, [E|HE]),
        dist_belt_end_ss(D, HE).
```

The definition of `position` is:

```
position(Box, 0, Hist) :-
        Hist = [begin_moving(Box, T) | _].
position(Object, NewPos, Hist) :-
        Hist=[E|HE],
        position(Object,OldPos,HE),
        velocity(Object,V,HE),
        time(E,TE),
        time_hist(HE,THE),
        NewPos = OldPos+V*(TE-THE).
```

6 Representing a Set of Partial Histories Satisfying prop

Let DB be a list of ground (variable-free) terms of the form $p(t_1, .., t_k), k \geq 0$ such that $\lambda H.p(t_1, .., t_k, H)$ represents a condition upon a partial history H. An *hs-term* is defined to be a term of the form: $[E_0, .., E_k | hs(DB)], k \geq 0$. hs(DB) represents the set of all partial histories satisfying each condition in DB.
$[E_0, .., E_k | hs(DB)], k \geq 0$. represents the set of all partial histories of the form $[E_0, .., E_k, F_0, .., F_m], m > 0$ such that $[F_0, .., F_m]$ is in the set represented by hs(DB). Our plan is to simulate with hs-terms, and to ensure that whatever can be concluded for an hs-term can also be concluded for each of the partial histories in the set represented by that hs-term. Formally, we ensure that for every hs-term $HS = [E_0, .., E_k | hs(DB)], k > 0$:

- prop(HS,Q) iff for every partial history HP represented by HS, prop(HP,Q).
- extend(HS, Q, H1, Q1) iff for every partial history HP represented by HS, extend(HP, Q, H1, Q1).

In other words, prop and extend do not "see" the difference between an hs-term and a partial history that hs-term represents. For the robotic arm controller, we can ensure these conditions by letting DB in hs(DB) represent the "state" of the system. This state contains enough information that during the computation of prop and extend it is not necessary to examine the individual events that hs(DB) represents. Specifically, DB is always of the form:

```
[position(box1, P1),
 position(box2, P2),
 velocity(box1, V1),
 velocity(box2, V2),
 status(g, S_g),
 status(d, S_d),
 status(ss, S_ss),
 placement_delay(Delay),
 time(T)]
```

time refers to the timestamp of the last event in a partial history. To extract the state information, we add the following rules to the DMOD program:

```
position(Box, P, hs(DB)) :- member(position(Box, P), DB).
velocity(Box, V, hs(DB)) :- member(velocity(Box, V), DB).
status(Entity, Stat, hs(DB)) :- member(status(Entity, Stat),DB).
placement_delay(D, hs(DB)) :- member(placement_delay(D), DB).
time(T, hs(DB)):- member(time(T), DB).
```

Due to the definition of prop, every partial history H such that prop(H,Q) will be contained in the set represented by an hs-term of the form [E | hs(DB)]. Thus, the answer constraint returned by the query:

```
H=[E | hs(DB)], prop(H,Q)
```

also represents the set of all (H,Q) such that prop(H,Q), as was required to be shown in Section 3.1.

References

1. Alur, R., Courcoubetis, C., Henzinger, T., Ho, P.-H., Nicollin, X., Olivero, A., Sifakis, J., Yovine, S. The algorithmic analysis of hybrid systems. *Proceedings of 11th International Conference on Analysis and Optimization of Systems,* Guy Cohen & Jean-Pierre Quadrat (eds.), Lecture Notes in Control and Information Sciences 199, Springer Verlag (1994)
2. Jaffar, J., Maher, M. Constraint Logic Programming: A Survey. *Journal of Logic Programming,* vols.19/20, May-July, 1994.
3. Kowalski, R. *Logic for problem solving.* Elsevier North-Holland, New York, 1979.

4. Narain, S., Chadha, R. Symbolic Discrete-Event Simulation. Invited paper, *Discrete-Event Systems, Manufacturing Systems and Communication Networks,* Editors: P.R. Kumar and P. Varaiya, IMA volume 73 in Mathematics and its Applications, Springer Verlag, 1995.
5. Narain, S., Chadha, R., Cockings, O. A Formal Model of SONET's Alarm-Surveillance Procedures and Their Simulation. *Proceedings of Formal Description Techniques Conference,* 1993.
6. Puri, A., Varaiya, P. Verification of Hybrid Systems using Abstractions. *Proceedings of Hybrid Systems Workshop,* Mathematical Sciences Institute, Cornell University, October, 1994.
7. Seda-Poulin, M., Narain, S. Linear Automatic Protection Switching Test Methodology. *Proceedings of National Fiber Optics Engineers Conference,* 1995.

On Controlling Timed Discrete Event Systems*

Darren D. Cofer[1] and Vijay K. Garg[2]

[1] Honeywell Technology Center, Minneapolis, MN 55418
[2] Dept. of Elec. & Comp. Eng., The University of Texas at Austin, Austin, TX 78712

Abstract. This paper is a survey of our work on controlling discrete event systems modelled by timed event graphs. Such systems are structurally related to finite state machines in that both can be described by linear equations over an appropriate algebra. Using this structural similarity, we have extended supervisory control techniques developed for untimed DES to the timed case. When behavioral constraints are given as a range of acceptable schedules, it is possible to compute an extremal controllable subset or superset of the desired behavior. When constraints are expressed in terms of minimum separation times between events, it is possible to determine whether there is a controllable schedule which realizes the desired behavior.

1 Introduction

Timed discrete event systems (DES) which are characterized by synchronization constraints can be modelled by automata known as *timed event graphs* (TEG). A TEG is a timed place Petri net in which forks and joins are permitted only at transitions. Places represent processes in the system and have an associated delay time while transitions represent events corresponding the the initiation of those processes. Since the underlying processes are normally continuous in nature, certain properties of hybrid systems can be modelled by a TEG.

TEGs and the finite state machines (FSM) used to model untimed DES can both be described by algebraic structures known as *semirings* or *dioids*. Work on the performance analysis of TEGs modelled in the "max–plus" semiring is described in [6] and [2]. Discussion of FSMs modelled with a semiring based on regular languages can be found in [7] and [1]. In section 2 we will briefly review these algebraic structures and elaborate on their similarities.

A well–developed theoretical framework has been established by Ramadge and Wonham for studying the control of untimed DES modelled by FSMs [10]. Certain events in the system are designated as being controllable and may be disabled by a *supervisor* which is separate from the system. The goal of the supervisor is to restrict the system to some specified desirable behavior. In section 3 we will show how the algebraic similarity between FSMs and TEGs can be used to define an analogous control framework for certain timed DES.

The timed DES behaviors we consider form a lattice structure. Consequently, fixed–point results for lattices which have been used to study the existence and

* This work was supported in part by NSF grants ECS-9414780 and CCR-9520540.

computation of optimal supervisors for logical DES [8] can also be applied to timed DES modelled by TEGs. This is the subject of section 4. These results are described in greater detail in [5].

In [9] control of untimed DES is studied via the *synchronous composition* of two FSMs, one representing the system and one representing the supervisor. In their synchronous composition an event which is common to both the system and the supervisor may only occur if it is enabled in both. In section 5, we use an analogous definition of synchronous composition for TEGs to study the controllability of behaviors specified in terms of minimum separation times between events. Additional details of this approach are discussed in [4].

2 Timed Event Graphs

In [2] and [6] the dynamic behavior of TEGs is studied using algebraic techniques based on idempotent semirings. Recall that a semiring differs from a ring most notably in that its elements form a monoid rather than a group under the sum operation (denoted $\oplus$).

Consider a TEG $G \equiv (T, A)$ where T is a set of N transitions and A is an $N \times N$ matrix of delay functions at places connecting the transitions. Let $x_i(k)$ denote the kth firing time of transition t_i. Then the sequence x_i of firing times satisfies

$$x_i = \max\{\max_{1 \leq j \leq n} \{A_{ij} x_j\}, v_i\} \tag{1}$$

where v_i specifies an earliest starting time for t_i. Let $\mathcal{S}$ be the set of sequences over $\mathcal{R} \cup \{\pm\infty\}$. Using the shorthand of max-algebra where $\oplus$ denotes pointwise maximization in $\mathcal{S}^N$, (1) can be written in matrix form as

$$x = Ax \oplus v. \tag{2}$$

The delay functions in A are required to be *lower-semicontinuous* functions, meaning that they distribute over the $\oplus$ operator in $\mathcal{S}$. The absence of a place connecting t_j to t_i is denoted by the function $A_{ij} = \varepsilon$, which represents a delay of $-\infty$ and hence no restriction. To model the effect of tokens in the initial marking of a TEG, we use the index backshift function γ defined by $\gamma x(k) = x(k-1)$. Each of the m tokens in the initial marking of a place causes a backshift since the $(k-m)$th token to enter the place will be the kth to depart and enable its successors. Therefore a place which adds a delay of five and contains two initial tokens is described by composing the unary addition function 5 with two γ functions, yielding $5\gamma^2$.

Assuming there are no other constraints and since transitions fire as soon as they are enabled, the actual behavior of the system is given by the least solution to (2) which is $x = A^*v$, where $A^* = \bigoplus_{i \geq 0} A^i$. We denote the behavior of G by $L(G)$.

Timed event graphs are structurally very similar to finite state machines. Both are directed graphs with labelled edges. While in a TEG the nodes correspond to events and the edges to process delays, the nodes in a FSM represent the system states and the edges correspond to events. This is illustrated by comparing the automata in Figure 1. Both TEGs and FSMs are classes of Petri nets. While a TEG has its forks and joins only at transitions, a FSM has forks and joins only at places. Because of the structural similarities between these

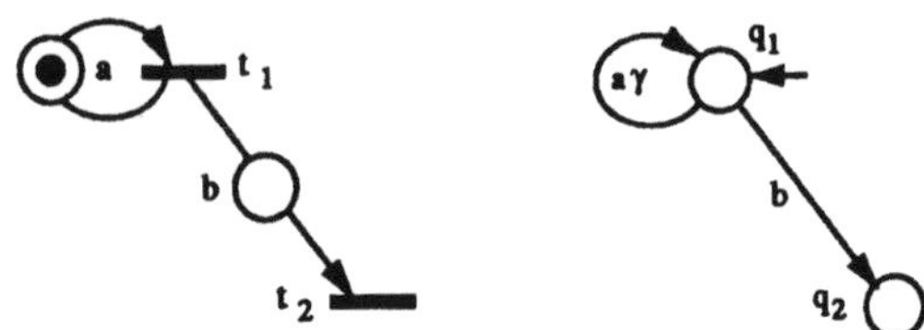

Fig. 1. (a) Timed event graph and (b) finite state machine with same structure.

automata there is an algebraic similarity as well. The event sequences generated by a FSM can be described in a semiring framework based on set union on concatenation. The system is therefore governed by an equation of the form $x = Ax \oplus v$ as for the TEG. It is this algebraic similarity which suggests that control of timed event graphs may be studied using techniques developed for untimed DES.

3 Supervisory Control

Suppose that some events $T_c \subseteq T$ are controllable, meaning that their transitions may be delayed from firing until some arbitrary later time. The delayed enabling times $u_i(k)$ are provided by a supervisor, with $u_i(k) = -\infty$ for t_i uncontrollable. Then the supervised system is described by $x = Ax \oplus v \oplus u$.

Now let Y be a set of desired behaviors (time sequences) to which we would like to restrict the system. We say that Y is controllable if enabling the controllable transitions at any times allowed by Y is sufficient to guarantee that the resulting behavior remains in Y. To compute the effect of uncontrollable events, let I_c denote the matrix having the identity function on diagonal elements i for which $t_i \in T_c$ and ε elsewhere. Then for any desired sequence $y \in Y$ the supervisor provides firing times $u = I_c y$. This results in actual behavior $x = A^*(I_c y \oplus v)$. Since the desired behavior must be invariant under uncontrollable actions, we formalize the definition of controllability as follows [3].

Definition 1. A set of sequences $Y \subseteq S^N$ is *controllable* with respect to A, v, and T_c if

$$A^*(I_c Y \oplus v) \subseteq Y. \tag{3}$$

Intuitively, this means that enabling controllable events at any time allowed by the specification set Y must result in behavior within Y for all events. Notice that, as in the untimed model, no new behavior is introduced by the supervisor. System operation can never be accelerated — events can only be delayed.

Example 1. For the system in Figure 1(a) with t_1 controllable with the specification the set $Y = \{x \in \mathcal{S}^N \mid x \leq y\}$ where

$$y = \left\{ \begin{bmatrix} 0 \\ 3 \end{bmatrix}, \begin{bmatrix} 3 \\ 5 \end{bmatrix}, \begin{bmatrix} 6 \\ 7 \end{bmatrix}, \dots \right\}.$$

To determine if Y is controllable, we compute

$$A^* I_c y \oplus A^* v = \begin{bmatrix} (2\gamma)^* & \varepsilon \\ 3(2\gamma)^* & 0 \end{bmatrix} \begin{bmatrix} y_1 \\ \varepsilon \end{bmatrix} \oplus A^* v = \left\{ \begin{bmatrix} 0 \\ 3 \end{bmatrix}, \begin{bmatrix} 3 \\ 6 \end{bmatrix}, \begin{bmatrix} 6 \\ 9 \end{bmatrix}, \dots \right\} > y$$

so Y is not controllable.

4 Control of Extremal Behaviors

When a specification is not controllable we would like to find an optimal set of controllable behaviors which meets the specification. Depending on the situation this may be the supremal controllable subset or the infimal controllable superset of the specified behavior. To find these extremal controllable behaviors we rely on the fact that the power set of $\mathcal{S}^N$ is a *complete lattice* with respect to the ordering of set containment, meaning that every arbitrary subset X has both a greatest lower bound ($\inf X$) and a least upper bound ($\sup X$).

A lattice *inequation* is an expression of the form $f(x) \leq g(x)$ over a lattice $(\mathcal{X}, \leq)$, where we wish to find $x \in \mathcal{X}$ to satisfy the given expression. In the previous section we saw that the controllability of certain timed DES is characterized by inequation (3).

The problem of finding optimal controllable behaviors is equivalent to finding extremal solutions to one or more inequations. It is shown in [8] that finding such extremal solutions can be reduced to extremal fixed–point computations for certain induced functions. The relevant results are summarized in the following definition and theorem.

Definition 2. Let $(\mathcal{X}, \leq)$ be a complete lattice. A function $f : \mathcal{X} \to \mathcal{X}$ is

- *monotone* if $\forall x, y \in \mathcal{X} : x \leq y \Rightarrow f(x) \leq f(y)$.
- *disjunctive* if $\forall X \subseteq \mathcal{X} : f(\sup X) = \sup_{x \in X}\{f(x)\}$.
  The *dual* of a disjunctive function is $f^{\perp}(y) = \sup\{x \in \mathcal{X} | f(x) \leq y\}$.
- *conjunctive* if $\forall X \subseteq \mathcal{X} : f(\inf X) = \inf_{x \in X}\{f(x)\}$.
  The *co-dual* of a conjunctive function is $f^{\top}(y) = \inf\{x \in \mathcal{X} | y \leq f(x)\}$.

Theorem 3. *Let Y be the set of all solutions of the system of inequations*

$$\{f_i(x) \leq g_i(x)\}_{i \leq n} \tag{4}$$

and define functions h_1 and h_2 by

$$h_1(y) = \inf\{f_i^{\perp}(g_i(y))\}, \quad h_2(y) = \sup\{g_i^{\top}(f_i(y))\}.$$

1. *If f_i is disjunctive and g_i is monotone $\forall i \leq n$, then* $\sup Y$ *equals the supremal fixed point of h_1. Furthermore, if the iterative computation*

$$y_0 := \sup \mathcal{X}, \quad y_{k+1} := h_1(y_k).$$

converges to y_m for some $m \in \mathcal{N}$ then $y_m = \sup Y$.

2. *If f_i is monotone and g_i is conjunctive $\forall i \leq n$, then* $\inf Y$ *equals the infimal fixed point of h_2. Furthermore, if the iterative computation*

$$y_0 := \inf \mathcal{X}, \quad y_{k+1} := h_2(y_k).$$

converges to y_m for some $m \in \mathcal{N}$ then $y_m = \inf Y$.

Suppose we are given a set $Y \subseteq \mathcal{S}^N$ of acceptable sequences. We wish to find the least subset or the greatest superset of Y such that enabling the controllable events at times given by a sequence in the extremal set results in an actual behavior which lies in the extremal set. That is, we seek extremal sets of sequences which are invariant under uncontrollable actions.

To find the supremal controllable subset of Y we must find the supremal solution to the pair of inequations

$$A^*(I_c X \oplus v) \subseteq X, \quad X \subseteq Y. \tag{5}$$

It is easy to show that $A^*(I_c(\cdot) \oplus v)$ and the identity function are disjunctive and that the constant function Y is monotone. Therefore, we meet the conditions of the first part of Theorem 3, with

$$h_1(X) = Y \cap (A^*(I_c X \oplus v))^{\perp}.$$

Similarly, to find the infimal solution greater than Y let the second inequation in (5) be $Y \subseteq X$. Since the constant function Y is monotone and the identity function is conjunctive we can use the second part of Theorem 3 with

$$h_2(X) = Y \cup A^*(I_c X \oplus v)$$

where we use the fact that the co-dual of the identity is itself.

Summarizing, we have the following result.

Theorem 4. *Given $G = (T, A)$ with controllable events T_c and a set of acceptable behaviors $Y \in \mathcal{S}^N$, the supremal controllable subset of Y and the infimal controllable superset of Y both exist.*

In computing the supremal controllable behavior it is possible to take a modular approach and consider constraint sets individually.

Theorem 5. *Let Z_1 and Z_2 be the supremal controllable subsets of Y_1 and Y_2, respectively. Then the supremal controllable subset of $Y_1 \cap Y_2$ is given by $Z_1 \cap Z_2$.*

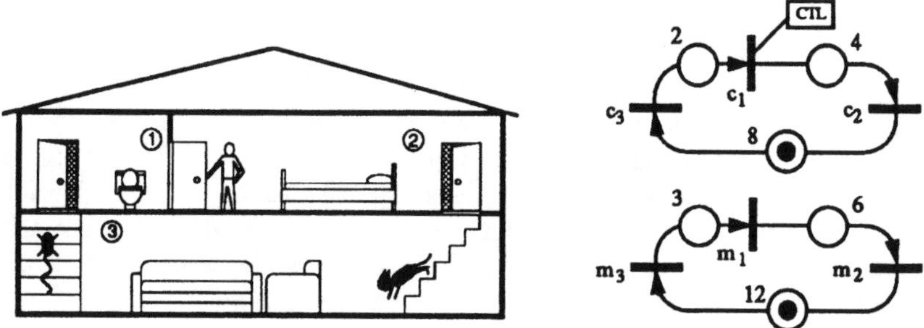

Fig. 2. The cat and mouse problem.

Example 2. Suppose a cat chases a mouse through the three-room house in Figure 2. Event m_i corresponds to the mouse leaving room i. One of the doors (c_1, the controllable event) can be held shut to prevent the cat from entering the next room. Initially the cat and mouse are at opposite ends of room 3, giving the mouse an 8 second headstart. The cat and mouse are governed by

$$x_m = \begin{bmatrix} \varepsilon & \varepsilon & 3 \\ 6 & \varepsilon & \varepsilon \\ \varepsilon & 12\gamma & \varepsilon \end{bmatrix} x_m \oplus \begin{bmatrix} \bar{0} \\ \bar{0} \\ \bar{0} \end{bmatrix}, \quad x_c = \begin{bmatrix} \varepsilon & \varepsilon & 2 \\ 4 & \varepsilon & \varepsilon \\ \varepsilon & 8\gamma & \varepsilon \end{bmatrix} x_c \oplus \begin{bmatrix} \bar{0} \\ \bar{0} \\ \bar{8} \end{bmatrix}$$

where the overbar denotes a constant sequence. Our (admittedly questionable) objective is to shut the controllable door at the proper times to keep the cat from catching the mouse.

1. The mouse must stay ahead of the cat for all time and therefore $x_c \geq x_m$.
2. The mouse must not enter a room until the cat has left and so

$$x_c \leq Sx_m = \begin{bmatrix} \varepsilon & \varepsilon & \gamma^{-1} \\ \gamma^{-1} & \varepsilon & \varepsilon \\ \varepsilon & 0 & \varepsilon \end{bmatrix} x_m .$$

Specification (1) can be met if $Y_1 = \{x \in \mathcal{S}^N \mid x \geq x_m\}$ is controllable with respect to the cat system. However, we find that $C^*(I_c x_m \oplus v_c) \notin Y_1$, showing that Y_1 is not controllable. Similarly, we find that for specification (2) $Y_2 = \{x \in \mathcal{S}^N \mid x \leq Sx_m\}$ is not controllable. Using Theorem 3, we compute the supremal controllable subsets of Y_1 and Y_2 which are $Z_1 = \{x \in \mathcal{S}^N \mid x \geq z_1\}$ and $Z_2 = \{x \in \mathcal{S}^N \mid x \leq z_2\}$, where

$$z_1 = \left\{ \begin{bmatrix} 10 \\ 14 \\ 8 \end{bmatrix}, \begin{bmatrix} 30 \\ 34 \\ 22 \end{bmatrix}, \begin{bmatrix} 51 \\ 55 \\ 42 \end{bmatrix}, \ldots \right\}, \quad z_2 = \left\{ \begin{bmatrix} 18 \\ 24 \\ 9 \end{bmatrix}, \begin{bmatrix} 39 \\ 45 \\ 30 \end{bmatrix}, \begin{bmatrix} 60 \\ 66 \\ 51 \end{bmatrix}, \ldots \right\}.$$

Finally, by Theorem 5 we know that the supremal controllable subset of the overall desired behavior is $Z_1 \cap Z_2 = \{x \in \mathcal{S}^N \mid z_1 \leq x \leq z_2\}$.

5 Control of Separation Times

In the previous section desired behavior was specified as a set or range of acceptable schedules (the sequences of event occurrence times). In this section we consider the situation where there are minimum separation times between certain event occurrences which must be enforced. For example, we may want to ensure that there is sufficient time between the successive outputs of a machine to perform an inspection or we may want to delay the departure of an airplane until all of its connecting flights have been on the ground for some minimum time. Such a specification will take the form

$$x_i \geq S_{ij} x_j$$

where S_{ij} is a function giving the required delay between events t_i and t_j. The set of acceptable behaviors is then

$$Y = \{x \in \mathcal{S}^N \mid x \geq Sx\}. \tag{6}$$

The problem now is to find the earliest controllable schedule (i.e., a single sequence y such that $A^*(I_c y \oplus v) = y$) which belongs to this set.

Note that the minimum required separation times S essentially form another TEG in the same way as the system delay times A. We must determine whether the system and supervisor automata can be combined in a way consistent with the controllable event set to yield an actual behavior that meets the specification in (6). Synchronous composition of timed event graphs can be defined in a manner similar to that for FSMs. Transitions which are common to both graphs fire only when they are enabled in both graphs. Transitions which appear in only one of the graphs fire when enabled by their own local predecessors, as before. The construction of the synchronous composition of two TEGs is straightforward. Given two TEGs with delay matrices A_1 and A_2, if the respective event sets T_1 and T_2 are identical then their synchronous composition, denoted $G_1||G_2$, is governed by

$$x = (A_1 \oplus A_2)x \oplus v$$

where $v \equiv v_1 \oplus v_2$. If the event sets are not identical, events are mapped into $T_1 \cup T_2$. For simplicity we assume hereafter that all TEGs are defined over a common event set unless stated otherwise.

An important observation is that synchronization may be used to realize a control policy for a TEG since some of its events may be delayed if they are synchronized to events in another TEG.

Theorem 6 [4]. $L(G_1||G_2) \geq L(G_1) \oplus L(G_2)$.

We must now account for the effect of the uncontrollable events. The specification is a legitimate supervisor for the plant if it does not *directly* delay the occurrence of uncontrollable events. That is, the specification may require uncontrollable event t_i to occur d seconds after some other event t_j, but this delay cannot be imposed directly; only through the action of controllable events and delays within the plant. This is analogous to the requirement that a FSM supervisor should not disable any uncontrollable events.

To verify this we must check if the synchronous composition of the plant and supervisor is changed by deleting from the supervisor all incoming edges to uncontrollable events. Let I_c be defined as before. Then $\hat{G}_s = (T, I_c S)$ removes from the supervisor graph all incoming edges to events which are uncontrollable in the plant. We may sum up this condition with the following definition.

Definition 7. A supervisor S is *complete* with respect to A and T_c if the synchronous operation of the supervisor and plant does not depend upon any delay of uncontrollable events imposed directly by the supervisor; that is,

$$L(G_p \| \hat{G}_s) = L(G_p \| G_s)$$
$$\text{or } (A \oplus I_c S)^* v = (A \oplus S)^* v.$$

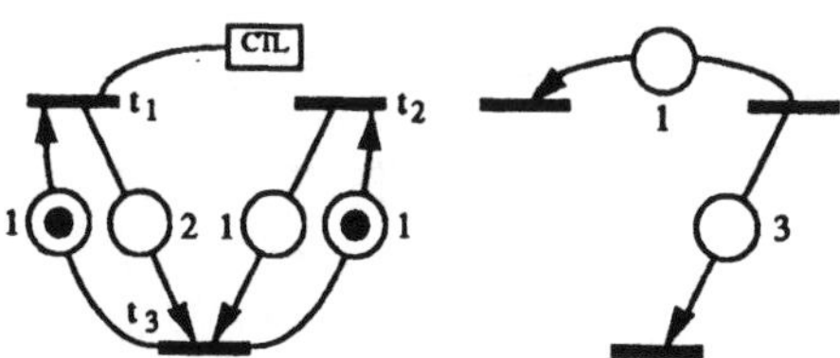

Fig. 3. Plant A and complete supervisor S.

Example 3. Consider the plant and supervisor in Figure 3. Here

$$A \oplus S = \begin{bmatrix} \varepsilon & 1 & 1\gamma \\ \varepsilon & \varepsilon & 1\gamma \\ 2 & 3 & \varepsilon \end{bmatrix}, \quad A \oplus I_c S = \begin{bmatrix} \varepsilon & 1 & 1\gamma \\ \varepsilon & \varepsilon & 1\gamma \\ 2 & 1 & \varepsilon \end{bmatrix}$$

and $(A \oplus S)^* = (A \oplus I_c S)^*$ so the supervisor is complete.

If the completeness condition holds, then the specification is implemented simply by means of the synchronous composition of the plant and the specification event graphs. The resulting behavior is controllable and meets the separation time requirements.

Theorem 8. *If supervisor S is complete with respect to A and T_c then $y \equiv L(G_p \| G_s)$ is a controllable sequence and $y \geq Sy$. Furthermore, y is the least sequence satisfying both of these properties.*

It turns out that the components of a specification may be evaluated individually to make a valid judgement regarding the completeness and, therefore, the controllability of the whole specification.

Theorem 9. *If each of the supervisors in the collection* $\{S_i\}$ *is complete then* $\bigoplus_i S_i$ *is complete.*

The next theorem gives us a check for completeness which is both necessary and sufficient.

Theorem 10. *A supervisor* S *is complete for any initial condition iff*

$$S \leq (A \oplus I_c S)^*. \tag{7}$$

Suppose that the given specification S is not complete. Assuming that it is important to achieve at least the event separation times given by S we would like to find the smallest $\hat{S} \geq S$ which is complete. Unfortunately, such a specification does not always exist [4]. Consider a transition t_i that fails the completeness test in (7). For the supervisor to influence the behavior of t_i so as to meet the specification, there must be a path from some controllable transition to t_i. We characterize the existence of such a path as follows.

Definition 11. A transition t_i is *structurally controllable* if it is reachable from some controllable transition; that is, there exists $n < N$ and $t_k \in T_c$ such that $[(A)^n]_{ik} > \varepsilon$. In this case, $[(A)^n]_{ik}$ may be decomposed as $\bigoplus_p f_p$ with $f_p = a_p \gamma^{m_p}$. Each f_p is called a *controllable path.*

Theorem 12. *Suppose* S *is not complete. Let* U *denote the set of transitions for which the completeness condition (7) fails to hold. Then a complete specification greater than* S *exists if the following two conditions are satisfied:*

1. *Every transition in* U *is structurally controllable.*
2. *For each* $t_i \in U$ *with* $[S]_{ij} \equiv g > \varepsilon$ *there exists a controllable path* f *containing fewer tokens in its initial marking than* g.

Consider a typical situation shown in Figure 4. If every event $t_i \in U$ which requires a delay g from some t_j is reachable from a controllable event t_c via controllable path f (condition 1) then the result follows by adding delay h from t_j to t_c such that $fh \geq g$. Condition 2 is necessary since we must have a non-negative initial marking for h.

Example 4. To illustrate, return to the cat and mouse example. This time we specify the desired behavior in terms of minimum separation times between the cat and the mouse (Figure 5).

1. The cat must leave each room at least one second after the mouse does. This is expressed in terms of the event occurrence times by $x_c \geq S_1 x_m$.
2. The mouse must not enter a room until the cat has left, so we must have $x_m \geq S_2 x_c$.

Using Theorem 12 we find that S_1 fails completeness with $U = \{c_2, c_3\}$. These transitions are found to be structurally controllable from c_1. Adding a delay of 1 from m_2 to c_1 achieves the desired delay for both transitions. This results in an $\hat{S}_1$ which is complete. Next, we can verify that S_2 is complete due to the initial condition. By Theorem 9, the resulting supervisor is complete.

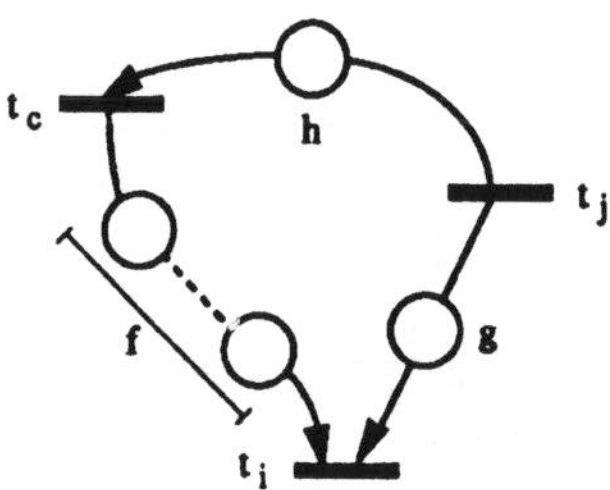

Fig. 4. Delay h added to achieve required separation g.

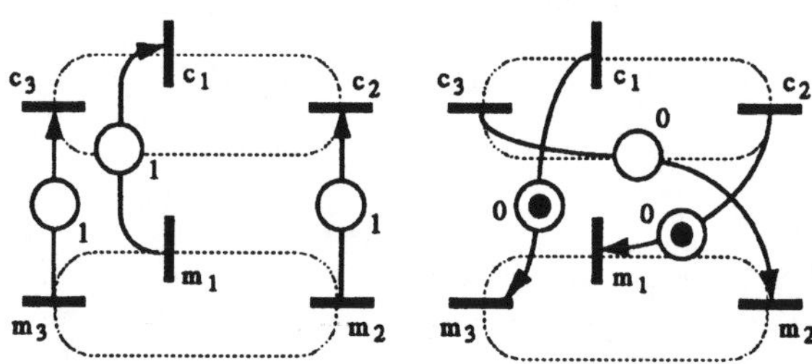

Fig. 5. TEGs for specifications S_1 and S_2.

References

1. A. V. Aho, J. E. Hopcroft, J. D. Ullman (1974), *The Design and Analysis of Computer Algorithms*, Addison–Wesley.
2. F. Baccelli, G. Cohen, G. J. Olsder, J. P. Quadrat (1992), *Synchronization and Linearity*, Wiley, New York.
3. D. D. Cofer (1995), *Control and Analysis of Real-time Discrete Event Systems*, Ph.D. Thesis, Dept. of Elec. & Comp. Eng., The University of Texas at Austin.
4. D. D. Cofer, V. K. Garg (1994), 'Supervisory control of timed event graphs,' in *Proc. 1994 IEEE Conf. on Sys, Man & Cyb.*, San Antonio, 994–999.
5. D. D. Cofer, V. K. Garg (1995), 'Supervisory control of real–time discrete event systems using lattice theory,' *Proc. 33rd IEEE Conf. Dec. & Ctl.*, Orlando, 978–983 (also to appear in *IEEE Trans. Auto. Ctl., Feb. 1996*).
6. G. Cohen, P. Moller, J. P. Quadrat, M. Viot (1989), 'Algebraic tools for the performance evaluation of DES,' *Proc. IEEE*, **77** 39–58.
7. M. Gondran, M. Minoux (1984), *Graphs and Algorithms*, Wiley, New York.
8. R. Kumar, V. K. Garg (1995), *Modeling and Control of Logical Discrete Event Systems*, Kluwer.
9. R. Kumar, V. K. Garg, S. I. Marcus (1991), 'On controllability and normality of discrete event dynamical systems,' *Sys. & Ctl. Ltrs*, **17** 157–168.
10. P. J. Ramadge, W. M. Wonham (1989), 'The control of discrete event systems,' *Proc. IEEE*, **77** 81–98.
11. E. Wagneur (1991), 'Moduloids and pseudomodules: 1. Dimension theory,' *Discrete Mathematics*, **98** 57–73.

Supervisory Control of Real-Time Systems Using Prioritized Synchronization

Ratnesh Kumar[1] and Mark A. Shayman[2]

[1] Department of Electrical Engineering
University of Kentucky
Lexington, KY 40506-0046
Email: kumar@engr.uky.edu
[2] Department of Electrical Engineering and ISR
University of Maryland
College Park, MD 20742
Email: shayman@src.umd.edu

Abstract. The theory of supervisory control of discrete event systems is extended to the real-time setting. The real-time behavior of a system is represented by the set of all possible timed traces of the system. This is alternatively specified using timed automata where each transition is associated with an event occurrence time set during which time the transition can occur. Our model for time is more general in that the time advances continuously as compared to a model where time advances discretely. We extend the notion of prioritized synchronous composition to the real-time setting to use it as the control mechanism. It is shown that a suitable extension of the controllability condition to the real-time setting yields a condition for the existence of a supervisor achieving a desired timed behavior. Although the real-time controllability is similar in form to its untimed counterpart, they are different in the sense that one does not imply the other and vice-versa.

Keywords: Discrete event systems, timed automata, real-time systems, prioritized synchronization, supervisory control, real-time controllability, real-time relative-closure

1 Introduction

Control of logical or untimed behavior of discrete event systems has extensively been studied since its initiation by Ramadge-Wonham [20]. Refer for example to the survey articles [21, 24] and the book [14]. The untimed behavior of a system retains the event ordering information but ignores the event timing

* This research was supported in part by the Center for Robotics and Manufacturing, University of Kentucky, in part by by the National Science Foundation under the Grants NSFD-CDR-8803012, NSF-ECS-9409712, NSF-ECS-9312587, the Minta Martin Fund for Aeronautical Research, and the General Research Board at the University of Maryland.

information. The event timing information must also be retained when the design objective involves real-time constraints such as in a communication system where a transmitted message should be received within a fixed time delay. This paper deals with an extension of the supervisory control theory to the real-time setting.

Sets of timed traces, i.e., finite sequences of pairs, each consisting of an event and its occurrence time, is used to describe the real-time behavior of a discrete event system. This is alternatively represented using timed automata where each transition is associated with an event occurrence time set. Each event has a timer (a stop-watch) which advances when the automaton is in an *activity state* where the event is enabled; the transition occurs when the event timer lies within the occurrence time set of the transition. Timed automaton model of the real-time behavior of a system is appealing since from the work of Alur-Dill [3, 2], its associated "region automaton" is finite so that the emptiness of the set of its accepted timed traces can be algorithmically verified.

There has been extensive prior work on verification of real-time systems. This includes the work of Ostroff-Wonham on real-time temporal logic [17], Alur-Dill on timed automata [3], Reed-Roscoe [22] on timed CSP, Coolahan-Roussopoulos [8] and Berthomieu-Diaz [4] on timed Petri-nets, Jahanian-Mok on safety analysis [12], etc.

The control and synthesis of supervisors for the real-time systems has received some attention recently. In the work of Brave-Heymann [7] and also in the work of Brandin-Wonham [5] a discretized model for time has been used: the time advances when a "tick" transition of the timer occurs. Such a model is not as general as the ones in which a dense model for time is used [1, Section 2.3.2]. Furthermore, the possibility of pre-empting a "tick" transition by a *forcible* event as in the work of Brandin-Wonham [5] is an artifact arising due to the discretized model of time, and is unrealistic. The work of Wong-Toi-Hoffman [25] uses a dense model of time, and we extend their work to consider control by way of prioritized synchronous composition (PSC) of plant and supervisor.

In this paper we represent real-time behavior using timed automaton which uses a dense model of time. The control is achieved by prioritized synchronous composition of a plant and a supervisor timed automaton. We have extended the notion of prioritized synchronization first given by Heymann [9] and later used by Shayman-Kumar [23] for the untimed systems to the real-time setting. We show that the prioritized synchronous composition is associative and under certain mild conditions which hold in the supervisory control setting can be reduced to the strict synchronous composition by using the technique of *augmentation*.

The conditions for the existence of a supervisor achieving a given closed-loop specification are the natural generalizations of the controllability and relative-closure conditions for the untimed case. So the earlier results such as the existence of a unique maximally permissive supervisor, etc., automatically follow. The algorithmic tests and computations however differ from the untimed case but are conceptually similar. In order to illustrate the differences and similarities we give an algorithmic test for the real-time controllability. This exploits the finiteness of the "region automaton" associated with a timed automaton. The real-time controllability condition is similar in form to its untimed counterpart, however, they are unrelated in the sense that neither of them imply the other.

The rest of the paper is organized as follows: In Section 2 we introduce our notation. Section 3 defines the timed automaton and the associated timed trace model. In Section 4 we define the prioritized synchronous composition of timed automaton and also of timed traces and establish their consistency and associativity, whereas in Section 5 we obtain its reduction to strict synchronous composition using the notion of augmentation. Section 6 deals with the supervisory control issues and introduces the notion of controllability and relative-closure for the real-time setting. Finally we conclude our work in Section 7.

2 Notation and Preliminaries

We use Σ to denote the set of events, and Σ^* to denote the set of all finite length event sequences, called traces. ϵ is used to denote the zero length trace. For a trace s, $|s|$ denotes its length; $pr(s) \subseteq \Sigma^*$ denotes the set of all prefixes of s; and for $k \leq |s|$, s^k denotes the prefix of length k of s. If a trace s_1 is a prefix of a trace s_2, then it is denoted as $s_1 \leq s_2$; if s_1 is a proper prefix of s_2, then it is written as $s_1 < s_2$.

A *timed trace* is an element of $(\Sigma \times \mathcal{R}_+)^*$. Thus given a timed trace e, it is of the form:

$$e = (\sigma_1(e), t_1(e))(\sigma_2(e), t_2(e)) \ldots (\sigma_{|e|}(e), t_{|e|}(e)),$$

where $\sigma_i(e) \in \Sigma$ and $t_i(e) \in \mathcal{R}_+$ are the ith event and its corresponding occurrence time, and $|e|$ denotes the length of e. By definition the sequence of event occurrence times $\{t_i(e)\}$ is monotonically increasing. The notation $tr(e) := \sigma_1(e)\sigma_2(e)\ldots\sigma_{|e|}(e)$ is used to denote the associated "untimed" trace of e. We use $pr(e)$ to denote the set of all prefixes of e; and for $k \leq |e|$, e^k denotes the prefix of length k of e. The notation $(\epsilon, 0)$ is used to denote the timed trace of length zero. Given two timed traces e and f, we use $e \leq f$ (respectively, $e < f$) to denote that e is a prefix (respectively, a proper prefix) of f.

3 Timed Automata and Timed Trace Model

We use a pair of timed trace sets to describe the real-time behavior of a discrete event system. The set of *generated* timed traces consists of all sequences of pairs consisting of an event and its occurrence time that are possible in the system; a subset of it is the set of *accepted* timed traces whose execution results in completion of certain tasks.

A timed automata is a six tuple:

$$\mathcal{P} := (X_\mathcal{P}, \Sigma, \delta_\mathcal{P}, \mathcal{T}_\mathcal{P}, x^0_\mathcal{P}, X^m_\mathcal{P}),$$

where $X_{\mathcal{P}}$ is the finite set of *activity states*, Σ is the finite set of events, $\delta_{\mathcal{P}} : X_{\mathcal{P}} \times \Sigma \rightarrow 2^{X_{\mathcal{P}}}$ is the *activity state transition function*, $\mathcal{T}_{\mathcal{P}} : X_{\mathcal{P}} \times \Sigma \times X_{\mathcal{P}} \rightarrow 2^{\mathcal{R}_+}$ is the *occurrence time set function*, $x^0_{\mathcal{P}} \in X_{\mathcal{P}}$ is the *initial activity state*, and $X^m_{\mathcal{P}} \subseteq X_{\mathcal{P}}$ is the set of *final activity states*. A triple $(x, \sigma, x') \in X_{\mathcal{P}} \times \Sigma \times X_{\mathcal{P}}$ is called an activity state transition if $x' \in \delta_{\mathcal{P}}(x, \sigma)$. For each activity state transition (x, σ, x'), we require that its occurrence time set $\mathcal{T}_{\mathcal{P}}(x, \sigma, x')$ be a finite union of intervals with rational end-points. If (x, σ, x') is not an activity state transition, then we assume that the associated occurrence time set is empty, i.e., $\mathcal{T}_{\mathcal{P}}(x, \sigma, x') = \emptyset$. For $x \in X_{\mathcal{P}}$, we define $\Sigma_{\mathcal{P}}(x) := \{\sigma \in \Sigma \mid \delta_{\mathcal{P}}(x, \sigma) \neq \emptyset\}$ to be the set of events defined at state x in $\mathcal{P}$.

In order to describe the evolution of the system as the time advances, a timer is associated with each event. We use $\tau \in \mathcal{R}^{|\Sigma|}_+$ to denote the *timer vector* and $\tau(\sigma) \in \mathcal{R}_+$ to denote the timer associated with event σ. When the system is in an activity state where a transition on a certain event is defined, then the timer for the associated event advances as the time elapses, and thus keeps track of the enablement time of the event. If the event enablement time lies within the occurrence time set of the associated transition, then the transition can occur resulting in a change of the activity state. The event timer is reset to zero whenever the transition occurs.

The state of the system is a pair $(x, \tau) \in \overline{X}_{\mathcal{P}} := X_{\mathcal{P}} \times \mathcal{R}^{|\Sigma|}_+$ consisting of an activity state x and a timer vector τ. An event σ can occur at state (x, τ) if there is an activity state transition on event σ defined at state x and the event timer value $\tau(\sigma)$ lies within the occurrence time set associated with that transition. Given $\hat{\Sigma} \subseteq \Sigma$, we use $\tau \downarrow_{\hat{\Sigma}}$ to denote the timer vector obtained by resetting each of the timers associated with events in $\hat{\Sigma}$ to zero; and given $t \in \mathcal{R}_+$, $\tau \oplus_{\hat{\Sigma}} t$ is used to denote the timer vector obtained by adding t to each of the timers associated with events in $\hat{\Sigma}$.

In this paper we only study systems that are deterministic, i.e., systems in which the next state is uniquely determined by the current state and the event that occurs in that state. It is not difficult to verify that for a timed automaton to represent a deterministic system the following should hold: Whenever there is a nondeterministic activity state transition on a certain event in the timed automaton, the occurrence time sets associated with those transitions are disjoint. Hence we have the following definition of a deterministic timed automaton:

Definition 1 A timed automaton $\mathcal{P}$ is said to be *deterministic* if

$$\forall x \in X_{\mathcal{P}}, \sigma \in \Sigma : \exists x_1, x_2 \in \delta_{\mathcal{P}}(x, \sigma), x_1 \neq x_2 \Rightarrow \mathcal{T}_{\mathcal{P}}(x, \sigma, x_1) \cap \mathcal{T}_{\mathcal{P}}(x, \sigma, x_2) = \emptyset.$$

The activity transition function of $\mathcal{P}$ can be extended to obtain the deterministic state transition function $\overline{\delta}_{\mathcal{P}} : \overline{X}_{\mathcal{P}} \times \Sigma \rightarrow \overline{X}_{\mathcal{P}}$ as follows ($(x, \tau) \in \overline{X}_{\mathcal{P}}$):

$$\overline{\delta}_{\mathcal{P}}((x, \tau), \sigma) := \begin{cases} (x', \tau \downarrow_{(\Sigma_{\mathcal{P}}(x) - \Sigma_{\mathcal{P}}(x')) \cup \{\sigma\}}) & \exists x' \in \delta_{\mathcal{P}}(x, \sigma) : \tau(\sigma) \in \mathcal{T}_{\mathcal{P}}(x, \sigma, x') \\ \text{undefined} & \text{otherwise} \end{cases}$$

Thus when activity state is x and the event timer $\tau(\sigma)$ lies within the interval $\mathcal{T}_{\mathcal{P}}(x, \sigma, x')$ for some $x' \in \delta_{\mathcal{P}}(x, \sigma)$ (note that by the requirement of determinism there exists at most one such x'), then the event σ can occur. This results in the new activity state x', and also in the resetting of the event timer for σ as well as of the event timers for all those events that are no more defined at the activity state x'.

The state transition function can be extended from events to timed traces inductively as follows (the extension is denoted by $\overline{\delta}^*_{\mathcal{P}}$):

$$\overline{\delta}^*_{\mathcal{P}}((x,\tau),(\epsilon,0)) := (x,\tau)$$
$$\overline{\delta}^*_{\mathcal{P}}((x,\tau),(\sigma,t)) := \delta_{\mathcal{P}}((x,\tau \oplus_{\Sigma_{\mathcal{P}}(x)} t),\sigma)$$
$$\overline{\delta}^*_{\mathcal{P}}((x,\tau),e(\sigma,t)) := \overline{\delta}^*_{\mathcal{P}}(\overline{\delta}^*_{\mathcal{P}}((x,\tau),e),(\sigma,t))$$

This extended transition function can be used to define the set of timed traces *generated* and *accepted* by $\mathcal{P}$, denoted $T(\mathcal{P})$ and $T^m(\mathcal{P})$, respectively:

$$T(\mathcal{P}) := \{e \mid \overline{\delta}^*_{\mathcal{P}}((x^0_{\mathcal{P}},0),e) \text{ defined}\}; T^m(\mathcal{P}) := \{e \in T(\mathcal{P}) \mid \overline{\delta}^*_{\mathcal{P}}((x^0_{\mathcal{P}},0),e) \in X^m_{\mathcal{P}}\}.$$

The pair $(T^m(\mathcal{P}), T(\mathcal{P}))$ is called the timed trace model of $\mathcal{P}$. It is clear that

$$pr(T^m(P)) \subseteq T(\mathcal{P}) = pr(T(\mathcal{P})) \neq \emptyset. \tag{1}$$

The system is said to be *non-blocking* if instead of the containment, the equality holds in (1).

Remark 1 It is clear from the definition of the timed trace model of $\mathcal{P}$ that a transition of $\mathcal{P}$ whose occurrence time set is a union of say i disjoint intervals can be replaced by i transitions, each with occurrence time set a unique interval, without altering the time trace model of $\mathcal{P}$. So the definition of the timed automaton given above is a special case of that given by Alur-Dill [3, 2], where more general timers (that are not necessarily associated with events) and more general timer constraints (that are not necessarily constraints on unique timers) are permitted. Hence using a result of Alur-Dill [3, 2], it follows that the "region automaton" associated with $\mathcal{P}$ is finite, and hence the emptiness of its generated or accepted timed traces can be algorithmically determined.

4 Prioritized Synchronous Composition

Prioritized synchronous composition (PSC) has been proposed by Heymann [9] and Heymann-Meyer [10] as a suitable mechanism of control, and it has been applied for the control of nondeterministic discrete event systems modeled using *trajectory* sets or *refusal trace* sets in [23, 15, 16]. Here we extend the definition of prioritized synchronization to the real-time setting.

For prioritized synchronous composition each system is assigned a priority set of events, and for an event to occur in the composed system each sub-system having priority over the event must participate. If an event belongs only to the priority set of one system, then the event occurs asynchronously (without the participation of the other system) if the other system cannot participate in its occurrence, otherwise it occurs synchronously. This kind of synchronization is called *broadcast synchronization*. Note that in the special case when the two priority sets are identical to the entire event set, prioritized synchronous composition reduces to strict synchronous composition (SSC) [11] where all events always occur synchronously.

In the context of supervisory control, the priority set of the plant includes the controllable and the uncontrollable events, whereas the priority set of the supervisor includes the controllable and the driven events. Since controllable events are common to the two priority sets, they occur synchronously in plant and supervisor, which is consistent with the fact that their occurrence in the closed-loop system is controlled by the supervisor. Uncontrollable events can occur asynchronously in the plant which is consistent with the fact that their occurrence cannot be prevented by the supervisor; however, the supervisor can track their occurrence by means of broadcast synchronization. Driven events are the duals of the uncontrollable events, and their occurrence requires the participation of the supervisor but not necessarily synchronization by the plant.

Next we formalize the notion of prioritized synchronization in the real-time setting by appropriately extending the definition given by Heymann.

Definition 2 Letting $A \subseteq \Sigma$ and $B \subseteq \Sigma$ denote the priority sets of timed automata $\mathcal{P}$ and $\mathcal{Q}$ respectively, their *prioritized synchronous composition* (PSC), denoted $\mathcal{P} \;{}_A\|_B\; \mathcal{Q}$, is the timed automaton $\mathcal{R}$, where $X_{\mathcal{R}} := X_{\mathcal{P}} \times X_{\mathcal{Q}}$; $x^0_{\mathcal{R}} := (x^0_{\mathcal{P}}, x^0_{\mathcal{Q}})$, and $X^m_{\mathcal{P}} := (X^m_{\mathcal{P}} \times X^m_{\mathcal{Q}})$. The activity transition function is defined as follows ($x_r = (x_p, x_q) \in X_{\mathcal{R}}, \sigma \in \Sigma$):

$$\delta_{\mathcal{R}}(x_r, \sigma) := \begin{cases} \delta_{\mathcal{P}}(x_p, \sigma) \times \delta_{\mathcal{Q}}(x_q, \sigma) & \text{if } \delta_{\mathcal{P}}(x_p, \sigma), \delta_{\mathcal{Q}}(x_q, \sigma) \neq \emptyset \\ \delta_{\mathcal{P}}(x_p, \sigma) \times \{x_q\} & \text{if } \delta_{\mathcal{P}}(x_p, \sigma) \neq \emptyset, \sigma \notin B \\ \{x_p\} \times \delta_{\mathcal{Q}}(x_q, \sigma) & \text{if } \delta_{\mathcal{Q}}(x_q, \sigma) \neq \emptyset, \sigma \notin A \\ \emptyset & \text{otherwise} \end{cases}$$

The occurrence time set function is defined as follows ($x_r = (x_p, x_q), x'_r = (x'_p, x'_q) \in X_{\mathcal{R}}$ and $\sigma \in \Sigma$):

$$\mathcal{T}_{\mathcal{R}}(x_r, \sigma, x'_r) := \begin{cases} \mathcal{T}_{\mathcal{P}}(x_p, \sigma, x'_p) \cap \mathcal{T}_{\mathcal{Q}}(x_q, \sigma, x'_q) & \text{if } x'_r \in \delta_{\mathcal{P}}(x_p, \sigma) \times \delta_{\mathcal{Q}}(x_q, \sigma) \\ \\ \mathcal{T}_{\mathcal{P}}(x_p, \sigma, x'_p) & \text{if } x'_r \in \delta_{\mathcal{P}}(x_p, \sigma) \times \{x_q\} \\ -\bigcup_{x'_q \in \delta_{\mathcal{Q}}(x_q, \sigma)} \mathcal{T}_{\mathcal{Q}}(x_q, \sigma, x'_q) & \quad -\delta_{\mathcal{P}}(x_p, \sigma) \times \delta_{\mathcal{Q}}(x_q, \sigma) \\ \\ \mathcal{T}_{\mathcal{Q}}(x_q, \sigma, x'_q) & \text{if } x'_r \in \{x_p\} \times \delta_{\mathcal{Q}}(x_q, \sigma) \\ -\bigcup_{x'_p \in \delta_{\mathcal{P}}(x_p, \sigma)} \mathcal{T}_{\mathcal{P}}(x_p, \sigma, x'_p) & \quad -\delta_{\mathcal{P}}(x_p, \sigma) \times \delta_{\mathcal{Q}}(x_q, \sigma) \end{cases}$$

Thus we have three different cases to consider: (i) A transition (x_r, σ, x'_r) in $\mathcal{R}$ is present whenever there is a transition (x_p, σ, x'_p) in $\mathcal{P}$ and a transition (x_q, σ, x'_q) in $\mathcal{Q}$. Since such a transition occurs synchronously, its occurrence time set in $\mathcal{R}$ is the intersection of the occurrence time sets of the corresponding transitions in $\mathcal{P}$ and $\mathcal{Q}$. (ii) If σ is not in the priority set of $\mathcal{Q}$ but there is a transition (x_p, σ, x'_p) in $\mathcal{P}$, then a transition $(x_r, \sigma, (x'_p, x_q))$ is present in $\mathcal{R}$. Thus if a transition (x_q, σ, x'_q) is present in $\mathcal{Q}$, then this transition in $\mathcal{R}$ of case (ii) is in addition to the transition at the same state and on same event in $\mathcal{R}$ of case (i). Since such a transition occurs asynchronously in $\mathcal{P}$ (when $\mathcal{Q}$ is unable to participate), the occurrence time set of this transition in $\mathcal{R}$ is the difference between the occurrence time set of the corresponding transition in $\mathcal{P}$ and the union over the occurrence time sets of all the transitions labeled σ at state x_q in $\mathcal{Q}$. (iii) The third case is the dual of the second case and can be understood analogously.

It can be verified from the above definition that the determinism of timed automata is preserved under prioritized synchronous composition, i.e., determinism of $\mathcal{P}$ and $\mathcal{Q}$ implies determinism of $\mathcal{P}\ {}_A\|_B\ \mathcal{Q}$ for any A and B. The following result establishes another desirable property of prioritized synchronous composition that it is associative.

Theorem 1 Given timed automata $\mathcal{P}, \mathcal{Q}, \mathcal{R}$ with priority sets A, B, C respectively.

$$\mathcal{P}\ {}_A\|_{B\cup C}\ (\mathcal{Q}\ {}_B\|_C\ \mathcal{R}) = (\mathcal{P}\ {}_A\|_B\ \mathcal{Q})\ {}_{A\cup B}\|_C\ \mathcal{R}.$$

Next in order to obtain a relationship between the timed trace model of the composed system and those of the component systems, we define the prioritized synchronous composition of timed traces.

Definition 3 Given priority sets A and B, the prioritized synchronous composition of timed traces e_p and e_q, denoted $e_p\ {}_A\|_B\ e_q$, is defined inductively on $|e_p| + |e_q|$ as follows:

$(\sigma, t)\ {}_A\|_B\ (\epsilon, 0) = (\epsilon, 0)\ {}_A\|_B\ (\sigma, t) := (\sigma, t)$
For $|e_p|+|e_q| \geq 1$, let $\sigma_p := \sigma_{|e_p|}(e_p), \sigma_q := \sigma_{|e_q|}(e_q), t_p := t_{|e_p|}(e_p), t_q := t_{|e_q|}(e_q)$, then $e_p\ {}_A\|_B\ e_q := T_1 \cup T_2 \cup T_3$, where

$$T_1 := \begin{cases} \{e(\sigma_p, t_p) \mid e \in e_p^{|e_p|-1}\ {}_A\|_B\ e_q\} & \text{if } |e_p| \geq 1, \sigma_p \notin B \\ \emptyset & \text{otherwise} \end{cases}$$

$$T_2 := \begin{cases} \{e(\sigma_q, t_q) \mid e \in e_p\ {}_A\|_B\ e_q^{|e_q|-1}\} & \text{if } |e_q| \geq 1, \sigma_q \notin A \\ \emptyset & \text{otherwise} \end{cases}$$

$$T_3 := \begin{cases} \{e(\sigma, t) \mid e \in e_p^{|e_p|-1}\ {}_A\|_B\ e_q^{|e_q|-1}\} & \text{if } |e_p|, |e_q| \geq 1; \sigma_p = \sigma_q := \sigma; t_p, t_q := t \\ \emptyset & \text{otherwise} \end{cases}$$

The following result states that the prioritized composition of timed event traces defined above is consistent with the definition of the composition of the timed automata.

Theorem 2 Given timed automata $\mathcal{P}$ and $\mathcal{Q}$ with priority sets A and B respectively, let $\mathcal{R} := \mathcal{P}\ {}_A\|_B\ \mathcal{Q}$. Then

$$T^m(\mathcal{R}) = \bigcup_{e_p \in T^m(\mathcal{P}), e_q \in T^m(\mathcal{Q})} e_p\ {}_A\|_B\ e_q; \quad T(\mathcal{R}) = \bigcup_{e_p \in T(\mathcal{P}), e_q \in T(\mathcal{Q})} e_p\ {}_A\|_B\ e_q.$$

Remark 2 The result of Theorem 2 can be used to extend the definition of composition of timed traces to timed trace models: Given timed trace models

(P^m, P) and (Q^m, Q) with priority sets A and B respectively, their composition is the timed trace model (R^m, R), where

$$R^m := \bigcup_{e_p \in P^m, e_q \in Q^m} e_p \;{}_A\|_B\; e_q; \quad R := \bigcup_{e_p \in P, e_q \in Q} e_p \;{}_A\|_B\; e_q.$$

It also follows from Theorem 1 that this composition is also associative.

5 Reduction of PSC to SSC by Augmentation

In this section we show that in the special case when the priority sets jointly exhaust the entire event set, prioritized synchronization can be expressed as strict synchronization of each system augmented with those events that belong to the priority set of the other system only.

Given a timed automaton $\mathcal{P}$ and an augmentation event set $D \subseteq \Sigma$, the augmentation of $\mathcal{P}$ with events in D, denoted $\mathcal{P}^D$, adds a self-loop transition at each activity state on every event in D and assigns an occurrence time set to it so that the union of the occurrence time sets associated with all D-labeled transitions at any activity state exhausts the set of positive reals. Thus the augmented system is always able to execute each event in D. So if we augment a given system with events in the sole priority set of another system, then in the composition such events will always occur synchronously since the second system must participate in their occurrence whereas the augmented system can always participate in their occurrence.

Using the definition of augmentation and the associativity of prioritized synchronous composition it can be shown that the PSC can be reduced to SSC of suitably augmented systems when the priority sets jointly exhaust the entire event set.

Theorem 3 Given timed automata $\mathcal{P}$ and $\mathcal{Q}$ with priority sets A and B, respectively, satisfying $A \cup B = \Sigma$, we have

$$\mathcal{P} \;{}_A\|_B\; \mathcal{Q} = \mathcal{P}^{\Sigma - A} \;{}_\Sigma\|_\Sigma\; \mathcal{Q}^{\Sigma - B}.$$

This result is particularly useful in the supervisory control setting since the requirement $A \cup B = \Sigma$ is naturally satisfied, as each event must belong to the priority set of either plant or supervisor.

Remark 3 It follows from Theorem 3 that when $A \cup B = \Sigma$, the timed trace model of the composed system can be obtained by intersecting the timed trace models of the augmented systems. Formally,

$$T^m(\mathcal{P} \;{}_A\|_B\; \mathcal{Q}) = T^m(\mathcal{P}^{\Sigma - A}) \cap T^m(\mathcal{Q}^{\Sigma - B}); T(\mathcal{P} \;{}_A\|_B\; \mathcal{Q}) = T(\mathcal{P}^{\Sigma - A}) \cap T(\mathcal{Q}^{\Sigma - B}).$$

6 Synthesis and Computation of Supervisor

For supervisory control of a discrete event plant, both plant and supervisor are modeled by timed automata. The priority set A of a plant $\mathcal{P}$ consists of the controllable and the uncontrollable events, whereas the priority set B of a supervisor $\mathcal{S}$ consists of the controllable and the driven events. Thus in this case $A \cup B = \Sigma$, and PSC can be reduced to SSC by using the techniques of augmentation. The control objective is to design a supervisor $\mathcal{S}$ such that the controlled plant or the closed-loop system $\mathcal{P}\ {}_A\|_B\ \mathcal{S}$ meets certain desired constraints specified as a target behavior $K \subseteq (\Sigma \times \mathcal{R}_+)^*$, i.e., it is required that $T^m(\mathcal{P}\ {}_A\|_B\ \mathcal{S}) = K$. Since the following holds for the target behavior: $K = T^m(\mathcal{P}\ {}_A\|_B\ \mathcal{S}) = T^m(\mathcal{P}^{\Sigma-A}) \cap T^m(\mathcal{Q}^{\Sigma-B}) \subseteq T^m(\mathcal{P}^{\Sigma-A})$, there is no loss of generality in assuming that $K \subseteq T^m(\mathcal{P}^{\Sigma-A})$. Furthermore, it is also desired that any generated timed trace of the controlled plant be a prefix of some timed trace that signifies completion of a task, i.e., a *non-blocking* supervision is desired which can be specified as:

$$pr(T^m(\mathcal{P}\ {}_A\|_B\ \mathcal{S})) = T(\mathcal{P}\ {}_A\|_B\ \mathcal{S}).$$

Next we extend the notions of controllability and relative-closure to the real-time setting and show that these two conditions are jointly necessary and sufficient for the existence of a supervisor achieving the desired behavior.

Definition 4 Given a plant $\mathcal{P}$ with priority set A, a priority set B of the supervisor to be designed such that $A \cup B = \Sigma$, and a desired behavior $K \subseteq T^m(P^{\Sigma-A})$:

K is said to be *real-time controllable* if

$$pr(K)[(A - B) \times \mathcal{R}_+] \cap T(\mathcal{P}) \subseteq pr(K).$$

K is said to be *real-time relative-closed* if

$$pr(K) \cap T^m(\mathcal{P}) \subseteq K.$$

Conditions similar to these were first given by Brave-Heymann [7]. The difference arises due to the discretized as opposed to the dense model of time used in that reference. The following result states that controllability and relative-closure are necessary and sufficient for the existence of a supervisor.

Theorem 4 Given a plant $\mathcal{P}$ with priority set A, a priority set B of the supervisor such that $A \cup B = \Sigma$, and a desired behavior $K \subseteq T^m(\mathcal{P}^{\Sigma-A})$, there exists a non-blocking supervisor $\mathcal{S}$ such that $T^m(\mathcal{P}\ {}_A\|_B\ \mathcal{S}) = K$ if and only if $(pr(K), pr(K))$ is a timed trace model, K is real-time controllable and real-time relative-closed. In this case $\mathcal{S}$ can be chosen to be any timed automaton with timed trace model $(pr(K), pr(K))$.

Remark 4 The result of Theorem 4 is similar to its untimed counterpart. However, it is easy to show that the real-time controllability (respectively, real-time relative-closure) does not imply the untimed controllability (respectively, untimed relative-closure) and vice-versa. A condition is given in [7] under which the real-time controllability is equivalent to its untimed counterpart.

On the other hand, the similarity between the conditions of Theorem 4 and their untimed counterpart can be used to deduce useful conclusions. For example one can conclude that the real-time controllability as well as the real-time relative-closure are preserved under union. So if K does not satisfy the conditions of Theorem 4, then there exists a unique maximal subset of K satisfying the conditions. So a unique *maximally permissive supervisor* exists. Wong-Toi–Hoffman [25] present a technique for its computation by reducing its computation to the untimed setting [19, 6, 13].

Next to illustrate how the existence of a supervisor can be verified, we provide an algorithmic test for the real-time controllability. Using a result from the untimed case [6], it is easy to show that K is real-time controllable if and only if

$$pr(K)[(A - B) \times \mathcal{R}_+]^* \cap T(\mathcal{P}) \subseteq pr(K),$$

which is equivalent to

$$pr(K)[(A - B) \times \mathcal{R}_+]^* \cap T(\mathcal{P}) \cap (pr(K))^c = \emptyset, \tag{2}$$

where $(pr(K))^c$ denotes the complement of $pr(K)$.

Let $\mathcal{Q}$ be a timed automaton with timed trace model $(pr(K), pr(K))$. We first construct a timed automaton which accepts $(pr(K))^c$. Since $\mathcal{Q}$ is deterministic such a timed automaton is easily obtained by adding a "dump" activity state, and defining a transition from each activity state on each event to the dump activity state with its occurrence time set being the complement of the union of the time sets for the existing transitions on that event. The dump activity state is the only final activity state. Formally, the complement of $\mathcal{Q}$, denoted $\mathcal{Q}^c$, is the timed automaton:

$$\mathcal{Q}^c := (X_\mathcal{Q} \cup \{x^d_\mathcal{Q}\}, \Sigma, \delta_{\mathcal{Q}^c}, \mathcal{T}_{\mathcal{Q}^c}, x^0_\mathcal{Q}, \{x^d_\mathcal{Q}\}),$$

where $x^d_\mathcal{Q} \notin X_\mathcal{Q}$ is the added dump activity state; for each $x \in X_\mathcal{Q} \cup \{x^d_\mathcal{Q}\}$ and $\sigma \in \Sigma$:

$$\delta_{\mathcal{Q}^c}(x, \sigma) := \delta_\mathcal{Q}(x, \sigma) \cup \{x^d_\mathcal{Q}\};$$

and for each transition $(x, \sigma, x^d_\mathcal{Q})$ in $\mathcal{Q}^c$ (but not in $\mathcal{Q}$):

$$\mathcal{T}_{\mathcal{Q}^c}(x, \sigma, x^d_\mathcal{Q}) := \mathcal{R}_+ - \bigcup_{x' \in \delta_\mathcal{Q}(x,\sigma)} \mathcal{T}_\mathcal{Q}(x, \sigma, x'),$$

whereas the occurrence time sets of the existing transitions remain the same.

Next we construct a timed automaton which accepts $pr(K)[(A - B) \times \mathcal{R}_+]^*$. Again this is obtained by adding a dump activity state in $\mathcal{Q}$, and defining a transition from each activity state on each uncontrollable event to the dump activity state with its occurrence time set being the complement of the existing transitions on that event. In this case we make all the activity states (including the dump one) of the resulting timed automaton, say $\mathcal{Q}^u$, to be final. Then from (2) it follows that K is real-time controllable if and only if

$$T^m((\mathcal{Q}^u\ {}_\Sigma\|_\Sigma\ \mathcal{P})\ {}_\Sigma\|_\Sigma\ \mathcal{Q}^c) = \emptyset,$$

which can be verified by constructing the region automaton associated with $(\mathcal{Q}^u\ {}_\Sigma\|_\Sigma\ \mathcal{P})\ {}_\Sigma\|_\Sigma\ \mathcal{Q}^c$ and checking the emptiness of its accepted (untimed) language.

7 Conclusion

We have shown that the timed automata model and the prioritized synchronous composition of timed automata provides a suitable framework for supervisory control of real-time discrete event systems. The verification of existence of a supervisor and also its computation remains algorithmic, so an automated synthesis of supervisor is possible. The associativity property of the prioritized synchronous composition suggests that the framework is suitable for modular and decentralized control as well. Results from the untimed setting for control under partial observation using prioritized synchronization [16] can also be easily generalized to the present setting. Finally, although our results are applicable to the systems modeled using timed automaton, they can be generalized to the systems modeled using decidable hybrid automaton [18].

References

1. R. Alur. *Techniques for automatic verification of real-time systems*. PhD thesis, Department of Computer Science, Stanford University, 1991.
2. R. Alur, C. Courcoubetis, and D. Dill. Model-checking for real-time systems. In *Proceedings of 1990 IEEE Symposium on Logic in Computer Science*, pages 414–425, Philadelphia, PA, 1990.
3. R. Alur and D. Dill. Automata for modeling real-time systems. In *Proceedings of 1990 International Colloquium on Automata, Languages and Programming*, pages 322–335, Warwick, UK, 1990.
4. B. Berthomieu and M. Diaz. Modeling and verification of time dependent systems using timed Petri nets. *IEEE Transactions on Software Engineering*, 17(3):259–273, 1991.
5. B. A. Brandin and W. M. Wonham. Supervisory control of timed discrete event systems. *IEEE Transactions on Automatic Control*, 39(2):329–342, February 1994.
6. R. D. Brandt, V. K. Garg, R. Kumar, F. Lin, S. I. Marcus, and W. M. Wonham. Formulas for calculating supremal controllable and normal sublanguages. *Systems and Control Letters*, 15(8):111–117, 1990.
7. Y. Brave and M. Heymann. Formulation and control of a class of real-time discrete-event processes. Technical Report EE-714, Department of Electrical Engineering, Technion-Israel Institute of Technology, Hafia, Israel, 1989.

8. J. E. Coolahan and N. Roussopoulos. Timing requirements for time-driven systems using augmented petri-nets. *IEEE Transactions on Software Engineering*, 9(9):603–616, 1983.
9. M. Heymann. Concurrency and discrete event control. *IEEE Control Systems Magazine*, 10(4):103–112, 1990.
10. M. Heymann and G. Meyer. Algebra of discrete event processes. Technical Report NASA 102848, NASA Ames Research Center, Moffett Field, CA, June 1991.
11. C. A. R. Hoare. *Communicating Sequential Processes*. Prentice Hall, Inc., Englewood Cliffs, NJ, 1985.
12. F. Jahanian and A. Mok. Safety analysis of timing properties in real-time systems. *IEEE Transactions on Software Engineering*, 12(9):890–904, 1986.
13. R. Kumar and V. K. Garg. Extremal solutions of inequations over lattices with applications to supervisory control. *Theoretical Computer Science*, 148:67–92, November 1995.
14. R. Kumar and V. K. Garg. *Modeling and Control of Logical Discrete Event Systems*. Kluwer Academic Publishers, Boston, MA, 1995.
15. R. Kumar and M. A. Shayman. Non-blocking supervisory control of nondeterministic systems via prioritized synchronization. *IEEE Transactions on Automatic Control*, 1995. Accepted.
16. R. Kumar and M. A. Shayman. Supervisory control of nondeterministic systems under partial observation and decentralization. *SIAM Journal of Control and Optimization*, 1995. Accepted.
17. J. S. Ostroff and W. M. Wonham. A framework for real-time discrete event control. *IEEE Transactions on Automatic Control*, 35(4):386–397, 1990.
18. A. Puri and P. Varaiya. Decidable hybrid automata. *Computer and Mathematical Modeling*, 1995. To appear.
19. P. J. Ramadge and W. M. Wonham. On the supremal controllable sublanguage of a given language. *SIAM Journal of Control and Optimization*, 25(3):637–659, 1987.
20. P. J. Ramadge and W. M. Wonham. Supervisory control of a class of discrete event processes. *SIAM Journal of Control and Optimization*, 25(1):206–230, 1987.
21. P. J. Ramadge and W. M. Wonham. The control of discrete event systems. *Proceedings of IEEE: Special Issue on Discrete Event Systems*, 77:81–98, 1989.
22. G. M. Reed and A. W. Roscoe. A timed model for communicating sequential processes. In L. Kott, editor, *13th ICALP (Lecture Notes in Computer Science, 226)*, pages 314–323. Springer-Verlag, New York, 1986.
23. M. Shayman and R. Kumar. Supervisory control of nondeterministic systems with driven events via prioritized synchronization and trajectory models. *SIAM Journal of Control and Optimization*, 33(2):469–497, March 1995.
24. J. G. Thistle. Logical aspects of control of discrete event systems: a survey of tools and techniques. In Guy Cohen and Jean-Pierre Quadrat, editors, *Lecture Notes in Control and Information Sciences 199*, pages 3–15. Springer-Verlag, New York, 1994.
25. H. Wong-Toi and G. Hoffmann. The control of dense real-time discrete event systems. Technical Report STAN-CS-92-1411, Stanford University, Stanford, CA, 1992.

ϵ-Approximation of Differential Inclusions*

Anuj Puri[1], Vivek Borkar[2] and Pravin Varaiya[1]

[1] Department of Electrical Engineering and Computer Sciences,
University of California, Berkeley, CA 94720.
[2] Department of Electrical Engineering,
Indian Institute of Science, Bangalore 560012, India.

Abstract. For a Lipschitz differential inclusion $\dot{x} \in f(x)$, we give a method to compute an arbitrarily close approimation of $Reach_f(X_0, t)$ — the set of states reached after time t starting from an initial set X_0. For a differential inclusion $\dot{x} \in f(x)$, and any $\epsilon > 0$, we define a finite *sample graph* A^ϵ. Every trajectory ϕ of the differential inclusion $\dot{x} \in f(x)$ is also a "trajectory" in A^ϵ. And every "trajectory" η of A^ϵ has the property that $dist(\dot{\eta}(t), f(\eta(t))) \leq \epsilon$. Using this, we can compute the ϵ-*invariant* sets of the differential inclusion — the sets that remain invariant under ϵ-perturbations in f.

1 Introduction

A dynamical system $\dot{x} \in f(x)$ describes the flow of points in the space. Associated with a dynamical system are several interesting concepts: from an *invariant set*, points cannot escape; and a recurrent set is visited infinitely often. For the controlled system $\dot{x} = f(x, u)$, the question of whether there is a control $u \in U$ to steer the system from an initial state x_0 to a final state x_f is fundamental.

We approach the subject from the viewpoint of applications and an interest in computational methods. For the differential inclusion $\dot{x} \in f(x)$, we want to compute the invariant sets and the recurrent sets. For the controlled differential equation $\dot{x} = f(x, u)$, we want to determine the control $u \in U$ which steers the system from an initial state x_0 to a final state x_f. And we want to determine the reach set $Reach_f(X_0, [0, t])$ — the set of states that can be reached from the initial set of states X_0 within time t.

In this paper, we propose a computational approach to solve some of these problems. For a Lipschitz differential inclusion $\dot{x} \in f(x)$ with initial set X_0, we propose a polyhedral method to obtain an arbitrary close approximation of $Reach_f(X_0, [0, t])$. For a differential inclusion $\dot{x} \in f(x)$, and any $\epsilon > 0$, we construct a *finite sample graph* A^ϵ which has the property that every trajectory ϕ of $\dot{x} \in f(x)$ is also a "trajectory" in the graph A^ϵ. And every "trajectory" η of the finite graph A^ϵ has the property that $dist(\dot{\eta}(t), f(\eta(t))) \leq \epsilon$. Since A^ϵ is

* Research supported by the California PATH program and by the National Science Foundation under grant ECS9417370.

a finite graph, it can be analyzed using graph theoretic techniques. Using the finite graph A^ϵ, we can compute the ϵ-*invariant* sets of $\dot{x} \in f(x)$ — the sets which remain invariant under ϵ-perturbations in f.

In Section 2, we introduce our notation, and define the basic terms. In Section 3, we conservatively approximate the differential inclusion by a piecewise constant inclusion, and obtain an approximation of $Reach_f(X_0, [0,t])$. In Section 4, we obtain a finite graph A^ϵ from the differential inclusion $\dot{x} \in f(x)$, and use it to determine the properties of the differential inclusion. In Section 5, we discuss the application of techniques from Sections 3 and 4 to computing the ϵ-invariant sets of differential inclusions. In Section 6, we apply these methods to compute the invariant sets for two examples: a pendulum moving in the vertical plane, and the Lorenz equations. We also discuss procedures to improve the efficiency of our methods. Section 7 is the conclusion.

2 Preliminaries

Notation

$\mathbb{R}$ is the set of reals and $\mathbb{Z}$ is the set of integers. $B = \{x : |x| \leq 1\}$ is the unit ball. For sets $U, V \subset \mathbb{R}^n$, $U + V = \{u + v | u \in U \text{ and } v \in V\}$ and for $\alpha \in \mathbb{R}$, $\alpha U = \{\alpha u | u \in U\}$. For $\delta > 0$, $B_\delta(x)$ is the δ-ball centered at x, i.e., $B_\delta(x) = \{y : |y - x| \leq \delta\}$. For $X \subset \mathbb{R}^n$, $X_\epsilon = X + \epsilon B$.

For $x \in \mathbb{R}^n$, and $Y \subset \mathbb{R}^n$, the distance $dist(x, Y) = inf\{|x - y| : y \in Y\}$. For two sets $X, Y \subset \mathbb{R}^n$, the *Hausdorff distance* is $dist(X, Y) = inf\{r : X \subset Y + rB \text{ and } Y \subset X + rB\}$. Notice, that if $dist(X, Y) \leq \epsilon$, then for any $x \in X$, $dist(x, Y) \leq \epsilon$. For $X \subset \mathbb{R}^n$, $cl(X)$ is the closure of X, and $\overline{co}(X)$ is the smallest closed convex set containing X. For $X, Z \subset \mathbb{R}^n$, the restriction of X to Z is $X|_Z = X \bigcap Z$. For a set J, the complement of J is J^c. For sets X and Y, the difference $X \backslash Y = \{z | z \in X \text{ and } z \notin Y\}$.

A set-valued (multi-valued) function is $f : \mathbb{R}^n \longrightarrow \mathbb{R}^n$ where $f(x) \subset \mathbb{R}^n$. For a set-valued $f : \mathbb{R}^n \rightarrow \mathbb{R}^n$, the set-valued function $f_\epsilon : \mathbb{R}^n \rightarrow \mathbb{R}^n$ is given by $f_\epsilon(x) = f(x) + \epsilon B$. For $Z \subset \mathbb{R}^n$, $f(Z) = \bigcup_{x \in Z} f(x)$. We assume the infinity norm on $\mathbb{R}^n$ (i.e., $|x| = \max\{|x_1|, \ldots, |x_n|\}$).

Differential Inclusions

A differential inclusion is written as $\dot{x} \in f(x)$ where $f : \mathbb{R}^n \longrightarrow \mathbb{R}^n$ is a set-valued function. Differential inclusions can be used to model disturbances and uncertainties in the system. A differential equation $\dot{x} = f(x, u)$, where $u \in U$ is control or disturbance can be studied as the differential inclusion $\dot{x} \in g(x)$ where $g(x) = \{f(x, u) | u \in U\}$. The differential inclusion $\dot{x} \in g(x)$ captures every possible behaviour of f.

We say a differential inclusion $\dot{x} \in f(x)$ is Lipschitz with Lipschitz constant k provided $dist(f(x_1), f(x_2)) \leq k|x_2 - x_1|$. A trajectory $\phi : \mathbb{R} \longrightarrow \mathbb{R}^n$ is a solution of $\dot{x} \in f(x)$ provided $\dot{\phi}(t) \in f(\phi(t))$ *a.e.* We say f is convex-valued when $f(x)$ is convex for every x.

Definition 2.1 *For a differential inclusion $\dot{x} \in f(x)$ with initial set X_0, the set of states reached at time t is $Reach_f(X_0,t) = \{\phi(t) | \phi(0) \in X_0$ and ϕ is a solution of $\dot{x} \in f(x)\}$; the set of states reached upto time t is $Reach_f(X_0,[0,t]) = \bigcup_{\tau \in [0,t]} Reach_f(X,\tau)$, and the set of all states reached is $Reach_f(X,[0,\infty)) = \bigcup_t Reach_f(X,t)$.*

Example 1. Consider the differential equation $\dot{x} = f(x) = -2x$, and $X_0 = [1,2]$. Then $Reach_f(X_0,t) = [e^{-2t}, 2e^{-2t}]$, $Reach_f(X_0,[0,t]) = [e^{-2t},2]$ and $Reach_f(X_0,[0,\infty)] = (0,2]$.

There is a close relationship between the Lipschitz differential inclusion $\dot{x} \in f(x)$ and the convex-valued differential inclusion $\dot{x} \in \overline{co}(f(x))$. This is made by the following relaxation theorem [4, 15].

Theorem 1. *For a Lipschitz differential inclusion $\dot{x} \in f(x)$, $cl(Reach_f(X_0,t)) = Reach_{\overline{co}(f)}(X_0,t)$.*

Lemma 2. *If $\dot{x} \in f(x)$ is Lipschitz with constant k, then $\dot{x} \in f_\epsilon(x)$ is also Lipschitz with constant k.*

A solution η of the differential inclusion $\dot{x} \in f_\epsilon(x)$ has the property that $dist(\dot{\eta}(t), f(\eta(t))) \leq \epsilon$.

Example 2. For the differential equation $\dot{x} = f(x) = -2x$, the differential inclusion $\dot{x} \in f_\epsilon(x) = [-2x-\epsilon, -2x+\epsilon]$. For $X_0 = [1,2]$, the reach set $Reach_{f_\epsilon}(X_0,t) = [e^{-2t}+\epsilon(e^{-2t}-1), 2e^{-2t}+\epsilon(1-e^{-2t})]$ and for $\epsilon < 2$, $Reach_{f_\epsilon}(X_0,[0,\infty)] = (-\epsilon, 2]$.

For further details on differential inclusions, see [5, 4, 15]. The following two results are obtained by using the Bellman-Gronwall inequality [9].

Lemma 3. *If $\dot{x} = f(x)$ is Lipschitz with constant k, and $y(t)$ and $z(t)$ are solutions of the differential equation, then*

$$|y(t) - z(t)| \leq |y(0) - z(0)| e^{kt}.$$

Lemma 4. *Let f, g be continuous functions such that $|f(x) - g(x)| < \epsilon$. If $\dot{x} = f(x)$ is Lipschitz with constant k, and $y(t)$ and $z(t)$ are solutions with $\dot{y}(t) = f(y(t))$ and $\dot{z}(t) = g(z(t))$, and $y(0) = z(0)$, then*

$$|y(t) - z(t)| \leq \frac{\epsilon}{k}(e^{kt} - 1).$$

Grids and Graphs

For $\beta > 0$, define the β-grid in $\mathbb{R}^n$ to be the set $G = ((\mathbb{Z} + \frac{1}{2})\beta)^n$ where $((\mathbb{Z}+\frac{1}{2})\beta) = \{\cdots, -\frac{3}{2}\beta, -\frac{1}{2}\beta, \frac{1}{2}\beta, \frac{3}{2}\beta, \cdots\}$. For $x \in \mathbb{R}^n$, define the quantization of x as $[x] = g$ where g is the nearest grid point (i.e., $g \in G$ and $|x - g| \leq \frac{\beta}{2}$). For $g \in G$, define $\langle g \rangle = \{x : [x] = g\}$. For the grid in figure 1, $(\frac{1}{2}\beta, \frac{1}{2}\beta) \in G$, and $\langle(\frac{1}{2}\beta, \frac{1}{2}\beta)\rangle = [0,\beta] \times [0,\beta]$. Notice, some points maybe equi-distant from two grid points. For example, $[(0, \frac{1}{2}\beta)] = (\frac{1}{2}\beta, \frac{1}{2}\beta)$ and $[(0, \frac{1}{2}\beta)] = (-\frac{1}{2}\beta, \frac{1}{2}\beta)$.

Definition 2.2 *Given a β-grid, a differential inclusion $\dot{x} \in f(x)$, a sampling time Δ, and an initial set $X_0 \subset \mathbb{R}^n$, define the sampled trajectories $Traj_f(X_0) = \{([\phi(m\Delta)])_{m\in\mathbb{Z}^+} : \phi(0) \in X_0, \text{ and } \dot{\phi}(t) \in f(\phi(t))\}$.*

The trajectories of $\dot{x} \in f(x)$ are sampled every Δ time units and then quantized to obtain the sampled trajectories $Traj_f(X_0)$.

Example 3. For the differential equation $\dot{x} = -2x$ and $X_0 = [1,2]$, $Traj_f(X_0) = \{([x(0)e^{-2m\Delta}])_{m\in\mathbb{Z}^+} : x(0) \in [1,2]\}$.

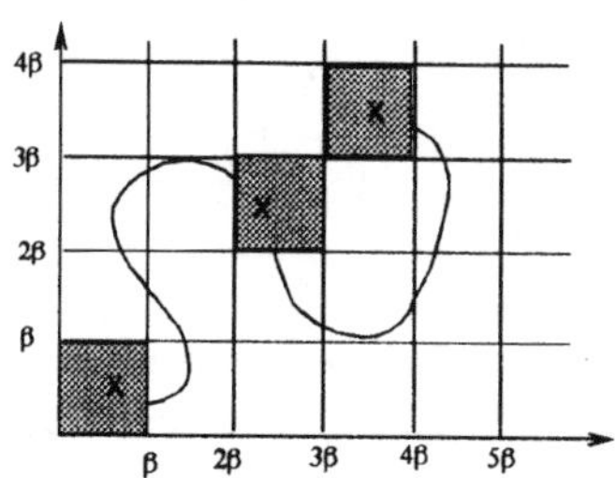

Fig. 1. A β-grid and a sample trajectory

Figure 1 shows a β-grid and a trajectory. The "crosses" on the trajectory mark the points that are sampled every Δ time units. The sequence of grids in which the "crosses" appear is recorded, and forms the sampled trajectory. Notice, it is not the sampled value that is recorded, but the grid in which the sample point appears that is recorded.

Definition 2.3 *A directed graph is $A = (V, E)$ where V is the set of vertices and $E \subset V \times V$ is the set of edges. A path $\pi = v_0 v_1 \ldots v_n$ where $(v_i, v_{i+1}) \in E$. For a set $W \subset V$, $Reach_A(W) = \{v_n | \pi = v_0 \ldots v_n \text{ is a path and } v_0 \in W\}$.*

The set $Reach(W)$ is the set of vertices of the graph that can be reached from the vertices in W. For a graph $A = (V, E)$, $Reach(W)$ can be computed using graph search algorithms such as depth-first search or breadth-first search.

Definition 2.4 *For a graph $A = (V, E)$ and a set $X_0 \subset V$, define $Traj_A(X_0) = \{(q_i)_{i\in\mathbb{Z}^+} : q_0 \in X_0 \text{ and } (q_i, q_{i+1}) \in E\}$.*

3 Computing the Reach Set of Differential Inclusions

In this section, we give a method to compute the reach set of a convex-valued Lipschitz differential inclusion $\dot{x} \in f(x)$. We conservatively abstract the differential inclusion by a piecewise constant inclusion, and then compute the reach set of the piecewise constant inclusion. As a result, we overestimate the reach set of the original differential inclusion. We show the error in the estimate can be made arbitrarily small by abstracting the differential inclusion arbitrarily closely.

Approximating by Piecewise Constant Differential Inclusions

A convex polyhedron is a bounded set defined by a set of linear inequalities. Define $\mathcal{P}$ to be the set of all convex polyhedra. We will approximate a convex valued differential inclusion $\dot{x} \in f(x)$ on a region R where $R \in \mathcal{P}$. Let $C = \{c_1, \ldots, c_k\}$ be a cover of R where each $c_j \in \mathcal{P}$. We say C is a δ-cover provided for every $x \in R$, $B_\delta(x)|_R \subset c_i$ for some i. The δ-cover property states that the δ-ball around each point x, when restricted to R, is completely contained within some c_i.

Let C be a δ-cover of R. Associate with C a collection $D = \{d_1, \ldots, d_k\}$ such that for each $c_i \in C$, $d_i \in \mathcal{P}$, $f(c_i) \subset d_i$ and $dist(f(x), d_i) \leq \epsilon$ for all $x \in c_i$. We say $\langle C, D \rangle$ is an ϵ-approximation of the differential inclusion $\dot{x} \in f(x)$.

Construction to form the cover:
To obtain an ϵ-approximation of the convex-valued Lipschitz differential inclusion $\dot{x} \in f(x)$ with Lipschitz constant k, define a $\frac{\epsilon}{6k}$-grid G. The cover is $C = \{c_g | g \in G \text{ where } c_g = \{x : |x-g| \leq \frac{\epsilon}{4k}\}\}$. First, notice the cover satisfies the δ-cover property for $\delta = \frac{\epsilon}{6k}$ (since for any x, $B_\delta(x) \subset c_g$ where $g = [x]$). With c_g, we associate the constant inclusion $f(g) + \frac{\epsilon}{4}B$. First note that for $x \in c_g$, $f(x) \subset f(g) + k|x-g|B$. Thus $f(x) \subset f(g) + \frac{\epsilon}{4}B$. Similarly $f(g) \subset f(x) + \frac{\epsilon}{4}B$. Therefore $dist(f(x), f(g) + \frac{\epsilon}{4}B) \leq \frac{\epsilon}{2}$. Since $f(g) + \frac{\epsilon}{4}B$ is convex, it can be approximated by a polyhedron d_g such that $f(x) \subset d_g$ and $dist(f(x), d_g) \leq \epsilon$ for all $x \in c_g$. We get a finite cover for R by restricting C to R. Using the above construction, we can approximate any convex valued lipschitz differential inclusion $\dot{x} \in f(x)$ by an ϵ-approximation $\langle C, D \rangle$.

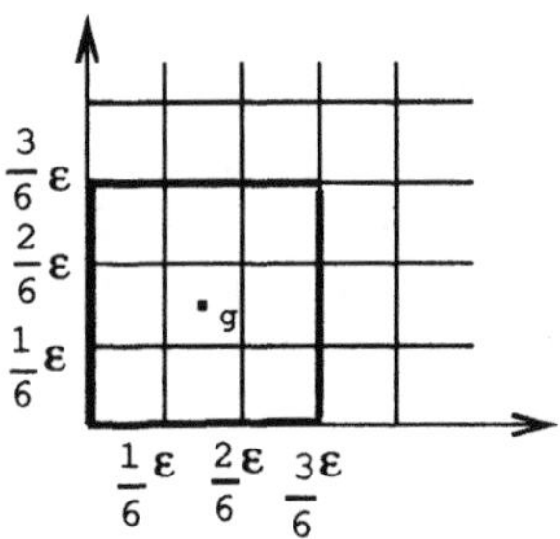

Fig. 2. A $\frac{\epsilon}{6k}$-grid

Figure 2 shows a $\frac{\epsilon}{6k}$ grid. One of the grid point is indicated by the letter "g". The cover c_g is indicated by the bold square. Note, for $x \in \langle g \rangle$, $\mathcal{B}_\delta(x) \subset c_g$ for $\delta \leq \frac{\epsilon}{6k}$.

Reach Set Computation

Suppose C is a δ-cover of R and $\langle C, D\rangle$ is an ϵ-approximation of the differential inclusion $\dot{x} \in f(x)$. In this section we obtain an approximation of $Reach_f(X_0, t)$ using the ϵ-approximation $\langle C, D\rangle$.

Definition 3.1 *For $W \subset R$, define $Next(W) = \bigcup_k \{y \in c_k | y = x + t\alpha$ for $x \in c_k \bigcap W, \alpha \in d_k$, and $t \geq 0$ \}.*

For a set of states W, $Next(W)$ is the set of states that is reached after some time. For each $c_k \in C$, $Next(W)$ comprises states that are reached from $c_k \bigcap W$ by following a direction in d_k and remaining inside c_k. Note that when W is a union of polyhedra, Next(W) is also a union of polyhedra.

Lemma 5. *If V is a closed convex set and $f : [0, T] \longrightarrow V$, then $\frac{1}{T}\int_0^T f(t)dt \in V$.*

Let M be the maximum value of $|f|$ on R. Using Lemma 5 and the δ-cover property, we show that $Reach_f(W, [0, \frac{\delta}{M}]) \subset Next(W)$.

Theorem 6. *If $\dot{x} \in f(x)$ is a differential inclusion, M is the maximum value of $|f|$ on R, and C is a δ-cover of R then $Reach_f(W, [0, \frac{\delta}{M}]) \subset Next(W)$.*

Proof: Suppose $y \in Reach_f(W, [0, \frac{\delta}{M}])$. Then $y = \phi(\lambda)$, where ϕ is a trajectory of the differential inclusion $\dot{x} \in f(x)$ over interval $[0, \lambda]$, $\lambda \leq \frac{\delta}{M}$, starting at $\phi(0) \in W$. For $t \in [0, \lambda]$, $|\phi(t) - \phi(0)| \leq tM \leq \lambda M \leq \frac{\delta}{M}M = \delta$. From the δ-cover property, there is a j such that $\phi(t) \in c_j$ and $\dot{\phi}(t) \in d_j$ *a.e* for $t \in [0, \lambda]$. Thus $\phi(\lambda) - \phi(0) = \int_0^\lambda \dot{\phi}(t)dt = \lambda\alpha_j$ where $\alpha_j \in d_j$ (from Lemma 5). Therefore $y = \phi(\lambda) \in Next(W)$. ∎

Notice, we require C to be a δ-cover to obtain the "time advancing" property in Theorem 6, i.e., the trajectory stays in c_j for time at least $\frac{\delta}{M}$. The reach set can be computed using the following iteration.

Reach Set Computation:

$$R_0 = X_0$$
$$R_{i+1} = Next(R_i) \bigcup R_i$$

Assume X_0 is a union of polyhedra. From the previous discussion each R_i is a union of polyhedra. When R_i is a union of polyhedra, we can compute $Next(R_i)$, and hence R_{i+1}. From Theorem 6, each iteration of the algorithm advances the time by at least $\frac{\delta}{M}$ units. To compute $Reach_f(W, [0, t])$ requires at most $l = \lceil \frac{Mt}{\delta} \rceil$ iterations (i.e., $Reach_f(W, [0, t]) \subset R_l$).

In general, R_i will be a proper subset of R_{i+1}. But if $R_i = R_{i+1}$, then the *Reach Set Computation* terminates. In this case, as the following theorem shows, we get an approximation of the infinite time reachable set $Reach_f(X_0, [0, \infty))$ in a finite number of steps.

Theorem 7. *If $\langle C, D\rangle$ is an ϵ-approximation of the differential inclusion $\dot{x} \in f(x)$, and $R_i = R_{i+1}$ in the* Reach Set Computation, *then $Reach_f(X_0, [0, \infty)) \subset R_i \subset Reach_{f_\epsilon}(X_0, [0, \infty))$. Furthermore R_i is invariant under $\dot{x} \in f(x)$.*

The *Reach Set Computation* procedure can also be used to compute the reach set at a specific time t. This is done by augmenting the state space to $y = (x, \tau)$ where $\dot{y} \in h(y) = (f(x), \{1\})$ (i.e., $\dot{x} \in f(x)$ and $\dot{\tau} = 1$). The variable τ keeps track of the time. The ϵ-approximation $\langle C^h, D^h\rangle$ of $\dot{y} \in h(y)$ is obtained from the ϵ-approximation $\langle C, D\rangle$ of $\dot{x} \in f(x)$ by defining $C^h = \{c_g \times [0, Max] : c_g \in C\}$ where Max is the largest time for which we want to compute the reach set, and $D^h = \{d_g \times \{1\} | d_g \in D\}$. Using the *Reach Set Computation* on the augmented system, we can compute R_l where $l = \lceil \frac{Mt}{\delta} \rceil$, and $Reach_h(W \times \{0\}, [0, t]) \subset R_l$. Define $R_l(\tau = t)$ to be the intersection of R_l with the hyperplane $\tau = t$, and $R_l(\tau \leq t)$ to be the intersection of R_l with the half-space $\tau \leq t$. Clearly $Reach_f(W, t) \subset R_l(\tau = t)$, and $Reach_f(W, [0, t]) \subset R_l(\tau \leq t)$.

Lemma 8. *If $\langle C, D\rangle$ is an ϵ-approximation of the differential inclusion $\dot{x} \in f(x)$, then for $l = \lceil \frac{Mt}{\delta} \rceil$, $Reach_f(X_0, t) \subset R_l(\tau = t) \subset Reach_{f_\epsilon}(X_0, t)$.*

We also want to get a bound on the error in the approximation $dist(Reach_f(X_0, t), R_l(\tau = t))$. The following theorem shows that the error can be made arbitrarily small.

Theorem 9. *Suppose $\dot{x} \in f(x)$ is a Lipschitz differential equation with Lipschitz constant k. Then for any $\gamma > 0$, and any $t \geq 0$, using the Reach Set Computation procedure, we can compute R_l as a union of polyhedra such that $Reach_f(X_0, t) \subset R_l(\tau = t)$ and $dist(Reach_f(X_0, t), R_l(\tau = t)) < \gamma$.*

Proof: Given $t > 0$ and $\gamma > 0$, choose $\epsilon = \frac{\gamma k}{(e^{kt} - 1)}$ where k is the lipschitz constant. In the augmented system, for $l \geq \lceil \frac{4Mtk}{\epsilon} \rceil$, $Reach_f(X_0, t) \subset R_l(\tau = t)$. For $y \in R_l(\tau = t)$, there is a trajectory ϕ with $\phi(0) \in X_0$ and $\phi(t) = y$ such that $\dot{\phi}(\alpha) \in f_\epsilon(\phi(\alpha))$ *a.e* (from construction of $R_l(\tau = t)$). Using Lemma 4, we get $dist(Reach_f(X_0, t), R_l(\tau = t)) \leq \frac{\epsilon(e^{kt} - 1)}{k} = \gamma$. ∎

We can compute $Reach_f(X_0, [0, t])$ with the same error using $R_l(\tau \leq t)$.

In this section we discussed only convex-valued Lipschitz differential inclusions. But from the relaxation theorem (theorem 1), for a Lipschitz differential inclusion $\dot{x} \in f(x)$, it suffices to study the convex-valued differential inclusion $\dot{x} \in \overline{co}(f(x))$.

The *Reach Set Computation* procedure we described can be automated using computer tools available for analysis of hybrid systems [2, 3, 8, 12, 10]. An equivalent hybrid automaton can be constructed by associating location l_g with c_g, differential inclusion d_g with location l_g, and guard $c_g \bigcap c_h$ with the edge from location l_g to l_h. See [2, 3, 8, 12, 11, 10] for more details on hybrid systems and their analysis.

We used polyhedral inclusions to approximate the differential inclusion $\dot{x} \in f(x)$. Instead, a decidable class of hybrid systems such as [11, 8], can be used to approximate a differential inclusion and prove the same result as Theorem 9 [6]. The decidable hybrid systems have the intersting property that the infinite time reachable set for them can be computed in a finite number of steps. In the next section, we provide another method which can be used to compute the infinite time reachable set in a finite number of steps.

4 Sample Graph Approximation

In this section, we prove the following result: given a Lipschitz differential inclusion $\dot{x} \in f(x)$, for any ϵ we can find a finite graph A^{ϵ} such that $Traj_f(X_0) \subset Traj_{A^{\epsilon}}([X_0]) \subset Traj_{f_{\epsilon}}(X_0)$. That is, A^{ϵ} contains the trajectories of $\dot{x} \in f(x)$, and the trajectories of A^{ϵ} are contained within the trajectories of $\dot{x} \in f_{\epsilon}(x)$. As a consequence, we get that for every $\epsilon > 0$, there is a finite graph A^{ϵ} such that for every "trajectory" η of A^{ϵ}, $dist(\dot{\eta}(t), f(\eta(t))) \leq \epsilon$. Using this, we can compute the ϵ-invariant sets of the inclusion $\dot{x} \in f(x)$. These are sets which remain invariant under ϵ-perturbations of f. We also use the sample graph A^{ϵ} to find other properties of the differential inclusion $\dot{x} \in f(x)$.

Definition 4.1 *Given a differential inclusion $\dot{x} \in f(x)$, and a sampling time Δ, define the map $S_f : \mathbb{R}^n \to \mathbb{R}^n$ with $S_f(y) = Reach_f(\{y\}, \Delta)$.*

Note that when f is a differential inclusion, S_f is a set-valued map. The map S_f samples the trajectory every Δ time units. Instead of working with the differential inclusion $\dot{x} \in f(x)$, we will work with the discrete dynamical system $x_{k+1} \in S_f(x_k)$.

Example 4. For the differential equation $\dot{x} = f(x) = -2x$, $S_f(y) = ye^{-2\Delta}$.

Sample Graph Construction:
For a differential inclusion $\dot{x} \in f(x)$ and the β-grid, we construct the sample graph. *The vertices of the sample graph are the grid points $((\mathbb{Z}+\frac{1}{2})\beta)^n$, and there is an edge from $[x]$ to $[y]$ provided $y \in S_f(x)$. That is, there is an edge from vertex g to vertex h provided there is a trajectory which takes some $x \in \langle g \rangle$ to some $y \in \langle h \rangle$. More formally, the sample graph is $A = (V, E)$ where $V = ((\mathbb{Z}+\frac{1}{2})\beta)^n$ are the vertices, and $E \subset V \times V$ are the edges with $(g, h) \in E$ for $g, h \in V$ provided $S_f(\langle g \rangle) \bigcap \langle h \rangle \neq \emptyset$ (i.e, $y \in Reach_f(\langle g \rangle, \Delta)$ for some $y \in \langle h \rangle$). When we are interested in studying the differential inclusion on a bounded region, we restrict the graph A to the bounded region and get a finite graph.*

Example 5. For the differential equation $\dot{x} = -2x$, figure 3 shows the sample graph for interval $[0, 2]$ where the sample time $\Delta = 0.5$ and grid separation is $\beta = 0.25$.

To get an ϵ-approximation of the differential equation $\dot{x} \in f(x)$, we need to construct the sample graph from a sufficiently small grid. The following theorem will enable us to choose an appropriate grid for a given ϵ.

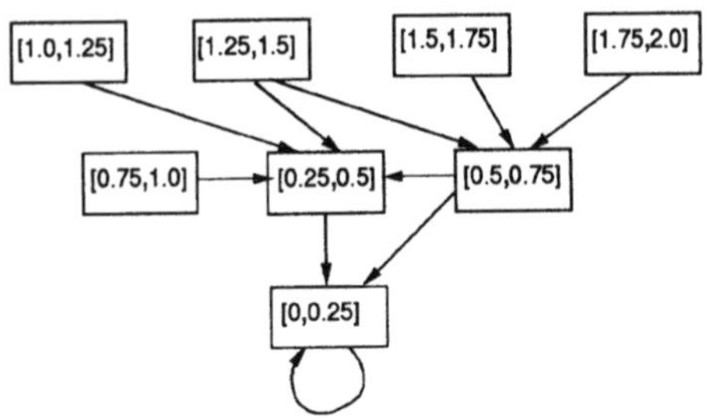

Fig. 3. The Sample Graph of $\dot{x} = -2x$

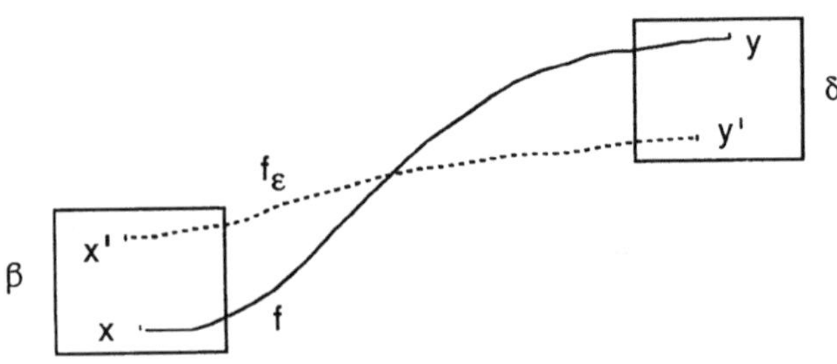

Fig. 4. Trajectories of $\dot{x} \in f(x)$ and $\dot{x} \in f_\epsilon(x)$

Theorem 10. *If f is a Lipschitz differential inclusion with Lipschitz constant k, $|x - x'| \leq \beta$, $|y - y'| \leq \delta$, and $y \in S_f(x)$ with sample time Δ, then for $\epsilon \geq (k + \frac{1}{\Delta})(\delta + \beta)$, $y' \in S_{f_\epsilon}(x')$ (figure 4).*

Proof: Suppose $\alpha : [0, \Delta] \longrightarrow \mathbb{R}^n$ is a trajectory for which $\alpha(0) = x$, $\alpha(\Delta) = y$, and $\dot{\alpha}(t) \in f(\alpha(t))$. We define the trajectory $\eta : [0, \Delta] \longrightarrow \mathbb{R}^n$ by

$$\eta(t) = \alpha(t) + \frac{t}{\Delta}(y' - y) + \frac{(\Delta - t)}{\Delta}(x' - x).$$

Note that $\eta(0) = x'$, $\eta(\Delta) = y'$, and

$$|\dot{\eta}(t) - \dot{\alpha}(t)| \leq \frac{(\delta + \beta)}{\Delta} \tag{1}$$

$$|\eta(t) - \alpha(t)| \leq (\delta + \beta) \tag{2}$$

We will show $\dot{\eta}(t) \in f_\epsilon(\eta(t))$. From equation 1, it follows that

$$\dot{\eta}(t) \in f(\alpha(t)) + \frac{(\delta + \beta)}{\Delta} B$$

Since f is Lipschitz, from equation 2 we get

$$f(\alpha(t)) \subset f(\eta(t)) + k(\delta + \beta)B$$

Therefore

$$\dot{\eta}(t) \in f(\eta(t)) + (k + \frac{1}{\Delta})(\delta + \beta)$$

Thus $\dot{\eta}(t) \in f_\epsilon(\eta(t))$ when $\epsilon \geq (k + \frac{1}{\Delta})(\delta + \beta)$. ■

We can show, using the above theorem, that for any $\epsilon > 0$, we can find a β-grid such that $Traj_f(X_0) \subset Traj_{A^\epsilon}([X_0]) \subset Traj_{f_\epsilon}(X_0)$ where A^ϵ is the finite graph obtained from the *sample graph construction*.

Theorem 11. *If $\dot{x} \in f(x)$ is a Lipschitz differential inclusion with Lipschitz constant k, and $\epsilon > 0$, then for $\beta \leq \frac{\epsilon}{(k+\frac{1}{\Delta})}$, $Traj_f(X_0) \subset Traj_{A^\epsilon}([X_0]) \subset Traj_{f_\epsilon}(X_0)$ where A^ϵ is the sample graph on the β-grid.*

Proof: By construction of graph A^ϵ on the β-grid, $Traj_f(X_0) \subset Traj_{A^\epsilon}([X_0])$. Next suppose $q = (q_0, q_1, \ldots) \in Traj_{A^\epsilon}([X_0])$. Then for each i, there are $x_i \in \langle q_i \rangle$ and $y_i \in \langle q_i \rangle$ such that for $i \geq 1$, $y_i \in S_f(x_{i-1})$ (define $y_0 = x_0$). From theorem 10 $y_i \in S_{f_\epsilon}(y_{i-1})$ (by choosing $\delta = 0$) for a grid with $\beta \leq \frac{\epsilon}{k+\frac{1}{\Delta}}$. We can construct a trajectory y with $\dot{y}(t) \in f_\epsilon(y(t))$ and $y(j\Delta) = y_j \in \langle q_j \rangle$. Therefore $Traj_A([X_0]) \subset Traj_{f_\epsilon}(X_0)$. ■

Modification of Sample Graph Construction: The construction of the graph A^ϵ required us to compute $S_f(\langle g \rangle)$. This is not necessary to prove the approximation result of Theorem 11. Instead, a conservative approximation of $S_f(\langle g \rangle)$ can be made. We do this either with the methods of Section 3 using Theorem 9 or by using Lemma 3. A conservative approximation of $S_f(\langle g \rangle)$ is made by computing $W(\langle g \rangle)$ where $S_f(\langle g \rangle) \subset W(\langle g \rangle)$, and the error $dist(S_f(\langle g \rangle), W(\langle g \rangle)) < \zeta$. We use $W(\langle g \rangle)$ instead of $S_f(\langle g \rangle)$ to form the graph A^ϵ. That is, the sample graph is $A^\epsilon = (V, E)$ where $V = ((\mathbb{Z} + \frac{1}{2})\beta)^n)$ are the vertices, and $(g, h) \in E$ for $g, h \in V$ provided $W_f(\langle g \rangle) \bigcap \langle h \rangle \neq \emptyset$. Using Theorem 10, we obtain the same result as Theorem 11 when the β-grid is chosen so that $\epsilon \geq (k + \frac{1}{\Delta})(\beta + \zeta)$.

Example 6. For a differential equation $\dot{x} = f(x)$ with Lipschitz constant k, we construct a sample graph on a β-grid using the modified Sample Construction method. We note that $S_f(\langle g \rangle) \subset S_f(\{g\}) + \frac{\beta}{2} e^{k\Delta} B$ from Lemma 3. For $\Delta = \frac{ln 2}{k}$, $S_f(\langle g \rangle) \subset S_f(\{g\}) + \beta B$. Hence, for $\epsilon \geq 2(k + \frac{1}{\Delta})\beta$, $Traj_f(X_0) \subset Traj_{A^\epsilon}([X_0]) \subset Traj_{f_\epsilon}(X_0)$.

The trajectories of finite graph A^ϵ contain information about the trajectories of the differential inclusion $\dot{x} \in f(x)$. From any trajectory (q_k) of A^ϵ, we can obtain a continuous trajectory ϕ_q such that $[\phi_q(k\Delta)] = q_k$ and $dist(\dot{\phi}_q(t), f(\phi_q(t))) \leq \epsilon$. Because we can "sandwich" the trajectories of A^ϵ between the trajectories of the differential inclusion $\dot{x} \in f(x)$ and $\dot{x} \in f_\epsilon(x)$, we can obtain useful results about the invariant sets and the recurrent sets of $\dot{x} \in f(x)$ from the graph A^ϵ.

Using the finite sample graph A^ϵ, we can get an approximation of the infinite time reachable set $Reach_f(X_0, [0, \infty))$.

Theorem 12. *For a Lipschitz differential equation, and any* $\epsilon > 0$, $Reach_f(X_0, [0, \infty)) \subset W \subset Reach_{f_\epsilon}(X_0, [0, \infty))$ *where* $W = Reach_f(\langle Reach_{A^\epsilon}([X_0])\rangle, [0, \Delta])$ *is an invariant set of* $\dot{x} \in f(x)$.

Notice the similarity between Theorem 7 and Theorem 12. The difference is that $Reach_{A^\epsilon}([X_0])$ in Theorem 12 is computed in a finite number of steps. We will discuss other advantages and disadvantages of the polyhedral approach vs. the graph approach in Section 6. We discuss a small technicality: the set W satisfying $Reach_f(X_0, [0, \infty)) \subset W \subset Reach_{f_\epsilon}(X_0, [0, \infty))$ in Theorem 12 can be computed in a finite number of steps by using the sample graph $A^{\frac{\epsilon}{2}}$ for inclusion $\dot{x} \in f_{\frac{\epsilon}{2}}(x)$, and then using an $\frac{\epsilon}{2}$-approximation of $\dot{x} \in f(x)$ to compute W using the method of Section 3.

The sample graph for the continuous system was created by looking at the discrete system $x_{m+1} \in S_f(x_m)$. We next state our theorem directly for discrete systems. For the discrete system $x_{m+1} \in g(x_m)$ where g is lipschitz with constant k, define $Traj_g(X_0) = \{([\alpha(m)])_{m \in \mathbb{Z}^+} | \alpha(m) \in g(\alpha(m-1)) \text{ and } \alpha(0) \in X_0\}$. The sample graph A^ϵ is created on the β-grid by putting an edge from vertex j to vertex h provided $g(\langle j\rangle) \bigcap \langle h\rangle \neq \emptyset$.

Theorem 13. *If* $x_{m+1} \in g(x_m)$ *is a discrete system where* g *is lipschitz with constant* k, *then for* $\beta \leq \frac{\epsilon}{k}$, $Traj_g(X_0) \subset Traj_{A^\epsilon}([X_0]) \subset Traj_{g_\epsilon}(X_0)$. *The size of the graph* A^ϵ *is* $O((\frac{k}{\epsilon})^n)$ *where* n *is the dimension of the state space.*

5 Invariant Sets

In this section, we will use the results from Section 3 and 4 to compute the ϵ-invariant sets of differential inclusions. These are sets which remain invariant under the inclusion $\dot{x} \in f_\epsilon(x)$. Intuitively I is an invariant set provided f points "inwards" at the boundary. The idea can be formalized using *contingent cones* [5, 1]. Any trajectory starting from an initial condition inside the invariant set remains inside the invariant set.

Definition 5.1 *A set* I *is invariant for* $\dot{x} \in f(x)$ *when* $Reach_f(I, [0, \infty)) \subset I$.

Definition 5.2 *A set* I *is* ϵ*-invariant for* $\dot{x} \in f(x)$ *when* $Reach_{f_\epsilon}(I, [0, \infty)) \subset I$.

A set I is ϵ-invariant provided it is invariant under ϵ-perturbations of f. Figure 5 shows an example of a ϵ-invariant set for some $\epsilon > 0$. Since f is not "tangential" to the boundary, the set remains invariant under small perturbations in f.

We next make a relationship between the invariant sets of differential inclusions and the infinite time reachability problem. To compute invariant set of $\dot{x} \in f(x)$ in R, we can compute $J = Reach_{-f}(R^c, [0, \infty))$ for $\dot{x} \in -f(x)$. Then J^c is the largest invariant set of $\dot{x} \in f(x)$ in R.

Lemma 14. *For a region* R, *the largest invariant set of* $\dot{x} \in f(x)$ *in* R *is* $I_0 = (Reach_{-f}(R^c, [0, \infty)))^c$.

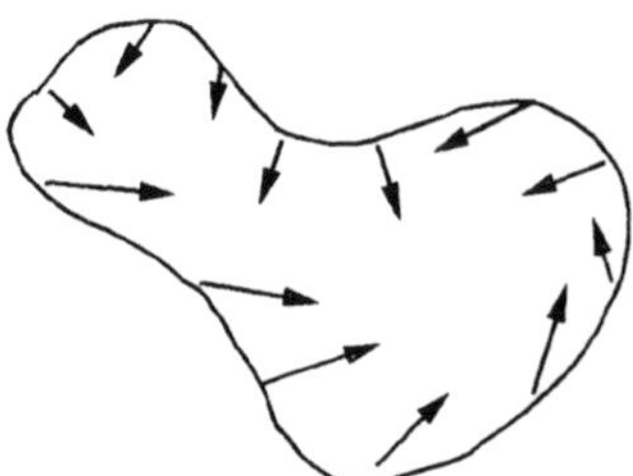

Fig. 5. An ϵ-invariant set

Proof: $(Reach_{-f}(R^c, [0,\infty)))^c$ is the set of states in R which cannot reach R^c by following the inclusion $\dot{x} \in f(x)$. Hence, it is the largest invariant set in R. ∎

Similarly $I_\epsilon = (Reach_{-f_\epsilon}(R^c, [0,\infty)))^c$ is the largest ϵ-invariant set in R.

Theorem 15. *For a Lipschitz differential inclusion $\dot{x} \in f(x)$ on a region R, and $\epsilon > 0$, we can compute an invariant set I such that $I_\epsilon \subset I \subset I_0$.*

Proof: Consider the differential inclusion $\dot{x} \in -f(x)$. From Theorem 7 and Theorem 12, we can compute a set J such that $Reach_{-f}(X_0, [0,\infty)) \subset J \subset Reach_{-f_\epsilon}(X_0, [0,\infty))$ and J is invariant for $\dot{x} \in -f(x)$. Therefore $I = J^c$ is invariant for $\dot{x} \in f(x)$ and $I_\epsilon \subset I \subset I_0$. ∎

As a consequence of Theorem 12, the invariant set I in Theorem 15 can be computed in a finite number of steps.

6 Computational Aspects and Examples

In this section we compute the invariant sets of some differential equations using the methods discussed in the previous sections. We also describe some techniques which can be used to increase the efficiency of these methods.

6.1 Pendulum Example

The differential equation describing a pendulum moving in the vertical plane is

$$\dot{x}_1 = x_2 \tag{3}$$

$$\dot{x}_2 = -g\sin(x_1) - cx_2$$

where $x_1 = \theta$, $x_2 = \dot{\theta}$, $g = 9.8$ is the acceleration of gravity and $c = 1$ is the frictional coefficient. We want to compute the largest invariant set contained in region $R = [-\pi, \pi] \times [-12, 12]$. The invariant set can be calculated exactly. Its boundary is given by $x_1 = -\pi$, $x_1 = \pi$, $U = \{x | x \in R \text{ and } \lim_{t\longrightarrow\infty} \phi(x,t) = (\pi, 0)\}$, and $L = \{x | x \in R \text{ and } \lim_{t\longrightarrow\infty} \phi(x,t) = (-\pi, 0)\}$ where $\phi(x,t)$ is the solution of Equation 3 with initial condition x. The actual invariant set is shown

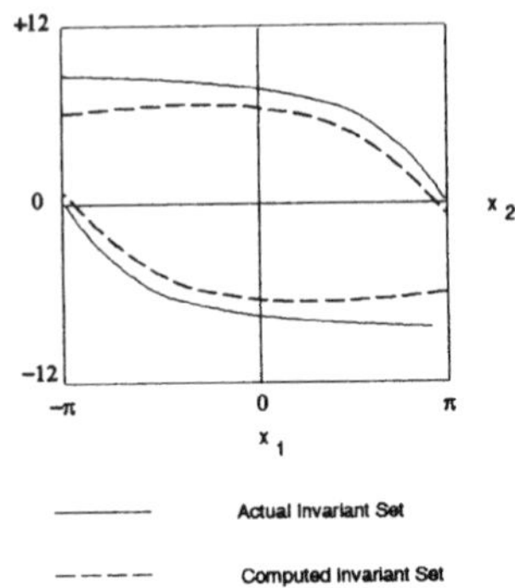

Fig. 6. Invariant Set for the Pendulum

in Figure 6. The invariant set is an attracting set of the equilibrium point (0,0) (see [7]).

We next use the graph method of Theorem 15 and Theorem 12 to compute the invariant set for Equation 3. A straightforward computation shows that $k = 11$ is a Lipschitz constant. We choose $\Delta = \frac{ln2}{k}$ to be the sample time (see Example 6). The graph is constructed on a grid of size 300×300 on R ($\beta = \frac{\pi}{150} = 0.021$) using the *Modified Sample Graph Construction*. We use Lemma 3 to obtain an approximation of $S_f(\langle g \rangle)$ where g is a grid point. The algorithm of Section 2 is then used to compute the reach set of the graph. The computed invariant set is shown in Figure 6. We note that the computed set is an invariant set, and it contains any ϵ-invariant set for $\epsilon \geq 2\beta(k + \frac{1}{\Delta})$ (i.e., $\epsilon \geq 1.12$).

As is to be expected, finer grids (smaller values of β) give better approximation of the actual invariant set, and coarse grids give a worse approximation. In particular, for grids with $\beta \geq 0.045$ we get no invariant set. From discussion in Example 6, it follows that there is no ϵ-invariant set in R for $\epsilon \geq 2.41$.

6.2 The Lorenz Equations

In this section, we study the Lorenz equations [7, 14]. The equations are

$$\dot{x} = \sigma(y - x) \tag{4}$$

$$\dot{y} = \rho x - y - xz$$

$$\dot{z} = -\beta z + xy$$

We study the system for $\sigma = 1$, $\rho = 2$ and $\beta = 1$. The system has three fixed points (see [7, 14] for a detailed description of the dynamics of the system). The fixed point at the origin is a saddle point with one dimensional unstable manifold. The other two fixed points at (1,1,1) and (-1,-1,1) are stable. We compute the largest invariant set contained in the region $R = [-3,3] \times [-3,3] \times [-3,3]$.

It can be shown that $k = 9$ is a Lipschitz constant. The sample time is $\Delta = \frac{ln2}{k}$ (see discussion in Example 6). A graph is constructed on a grid of size

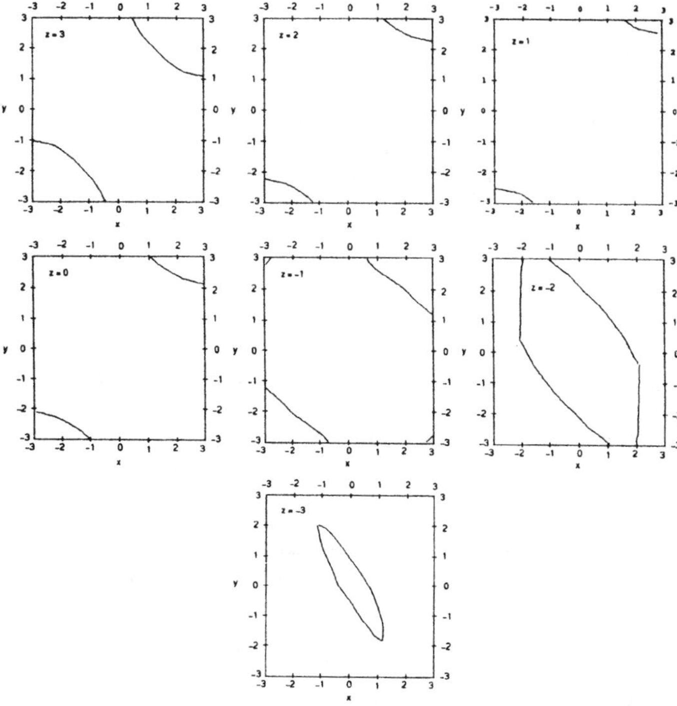

Fig. 7. Computed Invariant Set for the Lorenz Equations

$90 \times 90 \times 90$. The algorithm of Section 2 is then used to compute the invariant set. In Figure 7, we show the cross sections of the invariant set for $z = k$, $k \in \{-3, -2, \ldots, 2, 3\}$.

6.3 Efficient Storage Methods

The main limitation of the grid method is the amount of memory required to store the grid points. The main limitation of the polyhedral method is that the iteration in the *Reach Set Computation* may never terminate. It may be possible to combine the desirable features of the two methods to obtain better efficiency. Rather than storing the grid points explicitly, a set of grid points can be stored as a polyhedron using linear inequalities. Similarly the termination problem in the *Reach Set Computation* for the polyhedral method may be addressed by using some features of the grid method.

7 Conclucion

We presented a method to compute $Reach_f(X_0, t)$ — the reach set of the differential inclusion $\dot{x} \in f(x)$ at time t. We also presented a method to compute the

ϵ-invariant sets of the inclusion $\dot{x} \in f(x)$. We do this by relating the differential inclusion $\dot{x} \in f(x)$ to an ϵ-perturbation $\dot{x} \in f_\epsilon(x)$.

Computing the invariant sets and reach sets is an important problem. It is finding increasing use in the study of hybrid systems (see [12, 13]). An important problem is to find techniques to make the algorithms and methods presented in this paper more efficient in terms of space and time usage.

References

1. R. Abraham, J.E. Marsden, and T. Raitu, *Manifolds, Tensor Analysis, and Applications*, Springer-Verlag, 1988.
2. R. Alur et. al., The Algorithmic Analysis of Hybrid Systems, *Theoretical Computer Science*, Feb. 1995.
3. R.Alur, C.Courcoubetis, T.A. Henzinger and P.-H. Ho, Hybrid automata: an algorithmic approach to the specification and verification of hybrid systems, *Hybrid Systems*, LNCS 736, Springer-Verlag.
4. J.P. Aubin and A. Cellina, *Differential Inclusions*, Springer-Verlag, 1984.
5. J.P. Aubin, *Viability Theory*, Birkhauser, 1991.
6. V. Borkar and P. Varaiya, ϵ-Approximation of Differential Inclusion using Rectangular Differential Inclusion, Notes.
7. J. Guckenheimer and P. Holmes, *Nonlinear Oscillations, Dynamical Systems, and Bifurcations of Vector Fields*, Springer-Verlag, 1983.
8. T. Henzinger, P. Kopke, A. Puri and P. Varaiya, What's Decidable About Hybrid Automata, *STOCS 1995*.
9. M. W. Hirsh and S. Smale *Differential Equations, Dynamical Systems, and Linear Algebra*, Academic Press, Inc., 1974.
10. X.Nicollin, A. Olivero, J. Sifakis, and S.Yovine, An Approach to the Description and Analysis of Hybrid Systems, *Hybrid Systems*, LNCS 736, Springer-Verlag, 1993.
11. A. Puri and P. Varaiya, Decidability of Hybrid System with Rectangular Differential Inclusions, *CAV 94: Computer-Aided Verification*, Lecture Notes in Computer Science 818, pages 95-104. Springer-Verlag, 1994.
12. A. Puri and P. Varaiya, Verification of Hybrid Systems using Abstractions, *Hybrid Systems II*, LNCS 999, Springer-Verlag, 1995.
13. A. Puri and P. Varaiya, Driving Safely in Smart Cars, California PATH Research Report UCB-ITS-PRR-95-24, July 1995.
14. C. Sparrow, *The Lorenz Equations*, Springer-Verlag, 1982.
15. P. P. Varaiya, On the Trajectories of a Differential System, in A.V. Balakrishnan and L.W. Neustadt, editor, *Mathematical Theory of Control*, Academic Press, 1967.

Linear Phase-Portrait Approximations for Nonlinear Hybrid Systems*

Thomas A. Henzinger and Howard Wong-Toi
Department of Computer Science, Cornell University, Ithaca, NY 14853

Abstract. We use linear hybrid automata to define linear approximations of the phase portraits of nonlinear hybrid systems. The approximating automata can be analyzed automatically using the symbolic model checker HyTech. We demonstrate the technique through the study of predator-prey systems, where we compute population bounds for both species. We also identify a class of nonlinear hybrid automata for which linear phase-portrait approximations can be generated automatically.

1 Introduction

Hybrid systems combine discrete and continuous dynamics, and their analysis requires techniques from both computer science and control theory. Computer scientists typically model hybrid systems as discrete programs augmented with continuous environment variables undergoing simple dynamics, whereas control theorists typically study complex behaviors of continuous parameters within a simple discrete structure of control modes. This paper attempts to narrow the gap between the two disciplines by pushing the computer science end of the frontier. Algorithmic program analysis techniques can be extended for analyzing certain properties, such as reachability, of *linear hybrid automata* [ACHH93, ACH+95]. These automata model hybrid systems with linearity restrictions on discrete jumps (linear inequalities between sources and targets of jumps) and continuous flows (differential inequalities of the form $A\dot{\mathbf{x}} \geq \mathbf{b}$). Algorithmic analysis techniques for linear hybrid automata have been implemented in HyTech [AHH93, HHWT95b] and used to check properties of distributed real-time protocols [HH95b, HW95].

The definition of linearity for hybrid automata is different from that for linear systems in systems theory. For instance, linear hybrid automata cannot model directly continuous flows of the form $\dot{x} = x$. Since most control applications cannot be modeled directly using linear hybrid automata, we employ the idea of *abstract interpretation* [CC77] to establich properties of hybrid systems using linear hybrid automata as approximations. Suppose that we are given a complex hybrid system A and a property ϕ. Typically, checking if A satisfies ϕ is difficult. Our goal is to perform the simpler task of checking, automatically, if a linear hybrid automaton B that approximates A satisfies ϕ. We choose B such that if ϕ holds for B, then ϕ holds also for A. If, on the other hand, ϕ is not satisfied by B, then we cannot infer anything about A, and instead must try to find a closer approximation B' of A. Our main thesis is that linear automata approximations are adequate for checking certain interesting properties of complex hybrid systems.

The approximation of hybrid systems using linear hybrid automata has been advocated previously. Two translation techniques from nonlinear to linear hybrid automata are suggested in [HH95a]. The first translation, called *clock translation*, requires that

* This research was supported in part by the ONR YIP award N00014-95-1-0520, by the NSF CAREER award CCR-9501708, by the NSF grants CCR-9200794 and CCR-9504469, by the AFOSR contract F49620-93-1-0056, and by the ARPA grant NAG2-892. Authors' email: (tah|howard)@cs.cornell.edu.

the continuous flows are described by solvable differential equations, and replaces continuous variables by clock variables with constraints that are equivalent to the constraints on the original variables. The second translation, called ***rate translation***, approximates continuous behavior with piecewise-constant bounds on the first derivatives. The rate translation conservatively approximates a set of continuous trajectories using piecewise-linear envelopes over a state space that is partitioned into linear regions. The method is applied in two steps. First, every control mode of a hybrid system is split into several copies, each of which corresponds to a region of the partitioned state space. Second, within every new control mode, the nonlinear dynamics is replaced by a linear dynamics: the first derivative of each variable is bounded by two constants that correspond to the extremal rates (with respect to time) of the variable in the corresponding region of the state space.

In this paper, we improve on the rate translation technique by suggesting ***linear phase-portrait approximations*** that are strictly more accurate. These approximations are motivated by a time-invariant view of hybrid automata [Hen95]. They differ from the rate translation by approximating directly over the vector field of flow tangents, thus taking into account the relative rates of variables. This leads to more accurate approximations that still allow algorithmic analysis using HyTech. (The rate translation, which approximates the rate of each variable independently, was designed for automatic analysis using the restricted version of HyTech available at the time. Recently HyTech has been extended to permit arbitrary linear flow fields [HHWT95a], thereby enabling us to approximate with a more expressive form of linear hybrid automata.) Since rate translations are linear phase-portrait approximations, the linear phase-portrait approximation technique inherits the asymptotic completeness property of rate translations, which states that well-behaved nonlinear hybrid automata can be approximated arbitrarily closely [HH95a].

Outline We first define the model of nonlinear hybrid automata (Section 2) and formalize the approximation of hybrid automata (Section 3). We then define linear hybrid automata, the class that can be analyzed algorithmically, and linear phase-portrait approximations (Section 4). Section 5 applies linear phase-portrait approximation to a simple predator-prey ecology and verifies a control strategy for maintaining population bounds. We do not claim that linear phase-portrait approximation can replace standard analytic techniques for nonlinear behavior. On the contrary, our examples show that some understanding of the solutions of given differential inequalities is often necessary for obtaining useful approximations, and better understanding leads to better approximations. Section 6 presents as simple exception to this rule the class of ***pseudo-linear hybrid automata***, for which linear phase-portrait approximations can be generated automatically.

Related work Phase portraits have been studied extensively in the literature on dynamical systems [HS74, Arn83]. Typically, researchers concentrate on the continuous dynamics of a system and analyze extremely nontrivial properties, such as stability and convergence. Our work differs in two respects. First, we consider products of nondeterministic dynamical systems with discrete transition structures. Second, our goal is to analyze and derive simple properties of such systems ***automatically***. The theory of hybrid automata is presented in [Hen95, HKPV95]. In [HRP94, HH95c], abstract interpretation techniques are used to provide linear approximations of linear hybrid systems, whereas here we approximate nonlinear hybrid systems.

2 Hybrid Automata

We define ***hybrid automata***, which are used to model systems consisting of mixed discrete and continuous components. Informally, a hybrid automaton consists of a finite

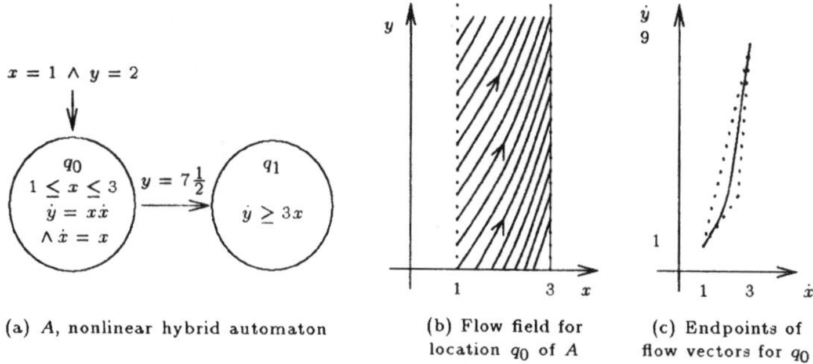

(a) A, nonlinear hybrid automaton

(b) Flow field for location q_0 of A

(c) Endpoints of flow vectors for q_0

Fig. 1. The hybrid automaton A

set X of real-valued variables and a labeled multigraph (V, E). The edges E represent discrete jumps and are labeled with guarded assignments to variables in X. The vertices V represent continuous flows and are labeled with differential inequalities over the first derivatives of the variables in X. The state of the automaton changes either instantaneously when a discrete jump occurs ("transition step") or, while time elapses, through a continuous flow ("time step").

Definition A *hybrid automaton* A consists of the following components:

Variables. A finite ordered set $X = \{x_1, \ldots, x_n\}$ of real-valued *variables*. For example, the automaton A in Figure 1, part (a), has two variables, x and y. A *valuation* is a point $(s_1, \ldots, s_n)$ in the n-dimensional real space $\mathbb{R}^n$, or equivalently, a function that maps each variable x_i to a value a_i. Each predicate ϕ over X defines a set $[\![\phi]\!] \subseteq \mathbb{R}^n$ of valuations, such that $s \in [\![\phi]\!]$ if $\phi[X := s]$ is true.

Locations. A finite set V of vertices called *locations*, used to model control modes. For example, the automaton A has two locations, q_0 and q_1. A *state* (v, s) consists of a location $v \in V$ and a valuation $s \in \mathbb{R}^n$. A *region* is a set of states.

Invariants. A labeling function *inv* that assigns to each location $v \in V$ a predicate $inv(v)$ over X, the *invariant* of v. For example, location q_0 of the automaton A has the invariant $1 \leq x \leq 3$. Invariants of the form *true* are omitted from figures, as in location q_1. A state (v, s) is *admissible* if $s \in [\![inv(v)]\!]$. The automaton control may reside in location v only while the invariant $inv(v)$ is true. Therefore invariants can be used to force transitions.

Initial conditions. A labeling function *init* that assigns to each location $v \in V$ a predicate $init(v)$ over X, the *initial condition* of v. For example, location q_0 of the automaton A has the initial condition $x = 1 \wedge y = 2$. Initial conditions of the form *false* are omitted from figures, as in location q_1. A state (v, s) is *initial* if it is admissible and $s \in [\![init(v)]\!]$. The automaton control may start in location v when the initial condition $init(v)$ and the invariant $inv(v)$ are true.

Flow conditions. A labeling function *fl* that assigns a *flow condition* to each location $v \in V$. The flow condition $fl(v)$ is a predicate over $X \cup \dot{X}$, where $\dot{X} = \{\dot{x}_1, \ldots, \dot{x}_n\}$. The dotted symbol $\dot{x}$ refers to the first derivative of the variable x with respect to time, *i.e.* $\dot{x} = dx/dt$. For example, location q_1 of the automaton A has the flow condition $\dot{y} \geq 3x$. While the automaton control resides in location v, the variable values change along differentiable trajectories whose first derivatives satisfy the flow condition. Formally, for each real $\delta \geq 0$, we define the binary *time-step relation* $\xrightarrow{\delta}$ such that $(v, s)\xrightarrow{\delta}(v', s')$

if $v' = v$, and there is a differentiable function $\rho\colon [0,\delta] \to \mathbb{R}^n$ such that

- the endpoints of the flow match those of ρ, *i.e.* $\rho(0) = s$ and $\rho(\delta) = s'$;
- the invariant is satisfied, *i.e.* for all reals $t \in [0,\delta]$, $\rho(t) \in [\![inv(v)]\!]$; and
- the flow condition is satisfied, *i.e.* for all reals $t \in (0,\delta)$, $fl(v)[X, \dot{X} := \rho(t), \dot{\rho}(t)]$ is true, where $\dot{\rho}(t) = (\rho_1(t)/dt, \ldots, \rho_n(t)/dt)$.

Transitions. A finite multiset E of edges called ***transitions***. Each transition (v, v') identifies a source location $v \in V$ and a target location $v' \in V$. For example, the automaton A has a single transition, (q_0, q_1).

Jump conditions. A labeling function jp that assigns a ***jump condition*** to each transition $e \in E$. The jump condition $jp(e)$ is a predicate over $X \cup X'$, where $X' = \{x'_1, \ldots, x'_n\}$. While the unprimed symbol x refers to the value of the variable x before the jump, the primed symbol x' refers to the value of x after the jump. Formally, for the transition $e = (v, v')$, we define the binary ***transition-step relation*** $\stackrel{e}{\to}$ on the admissible states such that $(v, s)\stackrel{e}{\to}(v', s')$ if $jp(e)[X, X' := s, s']$ is true. When writing jump conditions in the figures of this paper, we omit the conjunct $\bigwedge_{x\in X} x' = x$. For example, the transition (q_0, q_1) of the automaton A has the jump condition $y = 7\frac{1}{2} \wedge x' = x \wedge y' = y$.

Verification Let A be a hybrid automaton with n variables. The *state space* $\Sigma \subseteq V \times \mathbb{R}^n$ of A is the set of admissible states. We define the binary *successor relation* $\to_A$ on the state space Σ as $\bigcup_{\delta\in\mathbb{R}_{\geq 0}} \stackrel{\delta}{\to} \cup \bigcup_{e\in E} \stackrel{e}{\to}$. For a region $R \subseteq \Sigma$, we define the *successor region* $post(R)$ to be the set of states that can be reached from some state in R via a single time step or transition step, *i.e.* $post(R) = \{\sigma' \mid \exists \sigma \in R \text{ such that } \sigma \to_A \sigma'\}$. The region $post^*(R)$ *reachable from* R is the set of states that can be reached from R by a finite number of steps, *i.e.* $post^*(R) = \bigcup_{i\geq 0} post^i(R)$.

In practice, many verification tasks about hybrid systems can be posed in a natural way as reachability problems. Often, the system can be composed with a monitor process that "watches" the system and enters a violation state whenever a system trajectory violates a given safety or timing requirement. For a hybrid automaton A, the *reachable region* $reach(A)$ is the region that is reachable from the set of initial states. The automaton A is *correct* with respect to a set S of violation states if the reachable region contains no violation states, *i.e.* $reach(A) \cap S$ is empty.

Example 1. Consider the hybrid automaton A of Figure 1. Throughout the paper, we consider the task of verifying that location q_1 is not reachable, *i.e.* $reach(A)$ contains no state of the form (q_1, v). The flow condition for location q_0 is $\dot{x} = x \wedge \dot{y} = x\dot{x}$. We may solve these simple equations to see the solutions are of the form $y = \frac{1}{2}x^2 + k$. From the initial valuation $(1, 2)$, the valuation $(3, 6)$ is reached, and we see that location q_1 is not reached. ∎

3 Approximation

A hybrid automaton may be approximated by another automaton by relaxing the invariants, the initial conditions, the flow conditions, or the jump conditions.

Flow fields and jump fields Given a set X of n real-valued variables, a *flow vector* for X is a point in $\mathbb{R}^n$. A (nondeterministic) *flow field* for X is a map $flow\colon \mathbb{R}^n \to 2^{\mathbb{R}^n}$ that assigns to each valuation a set of flow vectors. Intuitively, if the vector $(a_1, \ldots, a_n)$ is in $flow(s)$, then the rate of change with respect to time of each variable x_i at the valuation $s \in \mathbb{R}^n$ can be a_i. We define an order on flow fields such that $flow_1 \preceq flow_2$ if for all valuations $s \in \mathbb{R}^n$, $flow_1(s) \subseteq flow_2(s)$. With each location of a hybrid automaton, we associate a flow field in the natural way: the flow field for location v

assigns to each valuation $s \in [\![inv(v)]\!]$ the set $\{a \mid fl(v)[X, \dot{X} := s, a] \text{ is true}\}$ of flow vectors. For example, for the automaton A of Figure 1, the flow field for location q_0 is given by $flow(x, y) = \{(x, x^2) \mid 1 \leq x \leq 3\}$. The ***automaton flow field*** $flow(A)$ of a hybrid automaton A is the function mapping each location to its flow field.

Given a set X of n real-valued variables, a ***jump vector*** for X is a point in $\mathbb{R}^n$. A (nondeterministic) ***jump field*** for X is a map $jump : \mathbb{R}^n \to 2^{\mathbb{R}^n}$ that assigns to each valuation a set of jump vectors. Intuitively, if the vector b is in $jump(s)$, then the valuation $s \in \mathbb{R}^n$ can be instantaneously incremented by b. We define an order on jump fields such that $jump_1 \preceq jump_2$ if for all valuations $s \in \mathbb{R}^n$, $jump_1(s) \subseteq jump_2(s)$. With each location of a hybrid automaton, we associate a jump field in the natural way: the jump field for transition $e = (v, v')$ assigns to each valuation $s \in [\![inv(v)]\!]$ the set $\{s' - s \mid jp(e)[X, X' := s, s'] \text{ is true and } s' \in [\![inv(v')]\!]\}$ of jump vectors. The ***automaton jump field*** $jump(A)$ of a hybrid automaton A is the function mapping each transition to its jump field.

The automaton flow field and the automaton jump field are collectively referred to as the *phase portrait* of a hybrid automaton [Hen95].

Phase-portrait approximation A hybrid automaton B *approximates* the hybrid automaton A if $reach(A) \subseteq reach(B)$. If the approximating automaton B is correct with respect to a set of violation states, then so is the approximated automaton A. The following lemma states a sufficient condition for B to approximate A.

Let two hybrid automata be *compatible* if they have the same set of variables, locations, and transitions. For compatible hybrid automata A and B, we define $inv(A) \preceq inv(B)$ if for all locations $v \in V$, $inv(A)(v) \subseteq inv(B)(v)$; $init(A) \preceq init(B)$ if for all locations $v \in V$, $init(A)(v) \subseteq init(B)(v)$; $flow(A) \preceq flow(B)$ if for all locations $v \in V$, $flow(A)(v) \preceq flow(B)(v)$; and $jump(A) \preceq jump(B)$ if for all transitions $e \in E$, $jump(A)(e) \preceq jump(B)(e)$. We define $A \preceq B$ if (1) $inv(A) \preceq inv(B)$, (2) $init(A) \preceq init(B)$, (3) $flow(A) \preceq flow(B)$, and (4) $jump(A) \preceq jump(B)$. The following lemma follows from the fact that $\preceq$ is a simulation over compatible hybrid automata [HH95a].

Lemma 1. *Let A and B be compatible hybrid automata. If $A \preceq B$, then $reach(A) \subseteq reach(B)$.* ■

For approximating a hybrid automaton A, it may be beneficial to divide the state space of A into subsets, and then approximate over each subset of the state space. A *partitioning* $\mathcal{P}$ for A is a function that maps each location v of A to a finite set $\{inv_1, \ldots, inv_{k(v)}\}$ of invariants, such that (1) the disjunction of the invariants is equivalent to the invariant of v, and (2) each valuation in the interior of $[\![inv(v)]\!]$ either lies in the interior of $[\![inv_i]\!]$ for some $1 \leq i \leq k(v)$, or lies in the intersection $[\![inv_i \wedge inv_j]\!]$ for some $1 \leq i < j \leq k(v)$. The partitioning $\mathcal{P}$ leads to the *partitioned automaton* $\mathcal{P}(A)$. For each location v of A, $\mathcal{P}(A)$ has the locations $v_1, \ldots, v_{k(v)}$, with $inv(v_i) = \mathcal{P}(v)_i$, $init(v_i) = init(v)$, and $fl(v_i) = fl(v)$ for all $1 \leq i \leq k(v)$. For each transition $e = (v, v')$ of A, $\mathcal{P}(A)$ has the transitions $e_{ij} = (v_i, v'_j)$ for $1 \leq i \leq k(v)$ and $1 \leq j \leq k(v')$, with $jp(e_{ij}) = jp(e)$. In addition, $\mathcal{P}(A)$ has transitions that let control pass freely between locations of $\mathcal{P}(A)$ that correspond to a common location of A, *i.e.* for each location v of A and all $1 \leq i \neq j \leq k(v)$, $\mathcal{P}(A)$ has the transition (v_i, v_j) with the jump condition $\bigwedge_{x \in X_A} x' = x$.

We define the function $\text{hom}_{\mathcal{P}} : V_{\mathcal{P}(A)} \to V_A$ such that for all locations v_i of $\mathcal{P}(A)$, $\text{hom}_{\mathcal{P}}(v_i) = v$. The function extends to states, and sets of states, in the natural way, *e.g.* $\text{hom}_{\mathcal{P}}(v_i, s) = (v, s)$.

Lemma 2. *Let A be a hybrid automaton A, and let $\mathcal{P}$ be a partitioning for A. Then* $\text{hom}_{\mathcal{P}}(reach(\mathcal{P}(A))) = reach(A)$. ■

A hybrid automaton B is a ***phase-portrait approximation*** of the hybrid automaton A with partitioning $\mathcal{P}$ if B is compatible with $\mathcal{P}(A)$ and $\mathcal{P}(A) \preceq B$. It follows from the previous two lemmas that $reach(A) \subseteq \mathrm{hom}_{\mathcal{P}}(reach(B))$. This gives an upper bound on the reachable region $reach(A)$.

Iterating approximations Bounds on the reachable region can be used to obtain tighter approximations of flow fields. Suppose that B is a phase-portrait approximation of A with the trivial partitioning. Reachability analysis using B may show that only some proper subset of each invariant is reachable. A second phase-portrait approximation may then be generated, where, in essence, the approximating flow fields need only include flow vectors for the valuations that are reachable in the first approximation. Iterating this procedure may lead to more and more accurate approximations. Similar reasoning may be used to generate tighter jump fields in the approximating automata.

4 Linear Approximation

Linear hybrid automata Linear hybrid automata are a subclass of hybrid automata whose reachability problem can be analyzed algorithmically. A ***linear expression*** over a set X of real-valued variables is a linear combination of variables with rational coefficients. A ***linear inequality*** is an inequality between linear expressions; a ***convex linear predicate*** is a finite conjunction of linear inequalities; and a ***linear predicate*** is a finite disjunction of convex linear predicates.

A hybrid automaton with the set X of variables is ***linear*** if (1) for all locations v, the invariant $inv(v)$ is a convex linear predicate over X, (2) for all locations v, the initial condition $init(v)$ is a convex linear predicate over X, (3) for all locations v, the flow condition $fl(v)$ is a convex linear predicate over $\dot{X}$, and (4) for all transitions e, the jump condition $jump(e)$ is a convex linear predicate over $X \cup X'$ (the convexity conditions can be relaxed by splitting locations and transitions). In flow conditions, linear dependencies between the rates of variables can be expressed, although the flow field must be independent of the ***values*** of the variables. For example, the automaton A'' in part (b) of Figure 2 is a linear hybrid automaton. Algorithmic analysis techniques for linear hybrid automata are implemented in tools such as HyTech [AHH93, HH95b, HHWT95a]. In particular, HyTech includes a semidecision procedure for solving the reachability problem of linear hybrid automata.

Rate translation The rate translation [HH95a] approximates nonlinear hybrid automata by linear hybrid automata. It consists of two steps: partitioning the state space within each location, and replacing nonlinear dynamics within each region of the partitioned state space by piecewise-constant bounds on derivatives. For simplicity, we assume that all invariants, initial conditions, and jump conditions of the given nonlinear hybrid automaton A are convex linear predicates. A linear hybrid automaton B is a *rate approximation* of A if (1) B is a phase-portrait approximation of A, and (2) for all locations v of B, $fl(v)$ is of the form $\bigwedge_{x_i \in X_B} l_i \leq \dot{x}_i \leq u_i$, where l_i and u_i are rational or infinite. Thus the flow conditions for each location are independent of the valuations, and *rectangular*, *i.e.* they consist of independent upper and lower bounds on the derivatives of all variables. Given a partitioning $\mathcal{P}$, if there exists a minimal rate approximation of A with $\mathcal{P}$ with respect to $\preceq$, it is referred to as the ***rate translation*** $rate_{\mathcal{P}}(A)$ of A with $\mathcal{P}$.

Example 2. Consider automaton A of Figure 1. The invariant at q_0 requires the value of x to remain between 1 and 3. The flow vectors are of the form (x, x^2), for all $1 \leq x \leq 3$. Their endpoints, with respect to the origin, are shown in part (c) of the figure. Figure 2, part (a), shows the rate translation A' for the hybrid automaton A with the partitioning

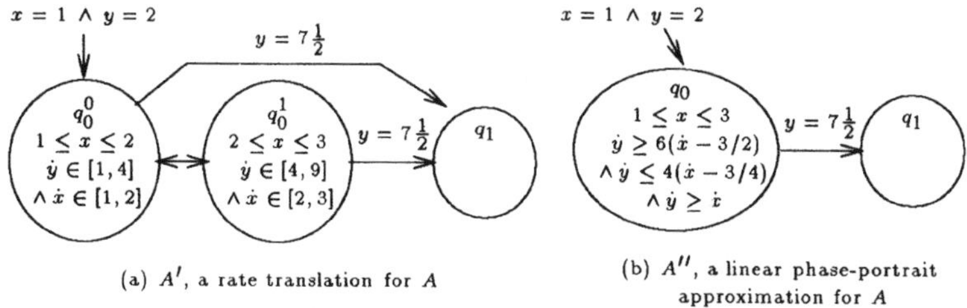

(a) A', a rate translation for A

(b) A'', a linear phase-portrait approximation for A

Fig. 2. Linear phase-portrait approximations for A

that splits the invariant along the line $x = 2$ in location q_0. Since $\dot{x}$ may vary only from 1 to 2 while the automaton control remains in location q_0^0, the flow condition in A' for q_0^0 is $\dot{x} \in [1, 2] \wedge \dot{y} \in [1, 4]$. Computing the time-step successors from the valuation $(1, 2)$ shows that all valuations with $x = 2$ and $2\frac{1}{2} \leq y \leq 6$ are reachable. Similarly, reachability for location q_0^1 shows that all valuations with $x = 3$ and $3\frac{5}{6} \leq y \leq 10\frac{1}{2}$ are reachable, and thus location q_1 is reachable. Indeed, no partitioning that divides q_0 into two locations avoids trajectories to q_1. ■

Linear phase-portrait approximation We generalize rate approximation in two respects. First, rather than individually approximating the rate of each variable, we approximate the phase portrait of the joint evolution of all variables. This extension, which enables approximations with fewer trajectories than rate translation, has been made viable by our recent reimplementation of HyTech [HHWT95a], which now allows the modeling of nonrectangular linear flow fields. Second, rather than partitioning with rectangular grids over $\mathbb{R}^n$ [HH95a], we partition using arbitrary linear regions. This, again, enables approximations with fewer trajectories than rate translation. A hybrid automaton B is a *linear phase-portrait approximation* of A if (1) B is a phase-portrait approximation of A, and (2) B is linear. Given a partitioning $\mathcal{P}$, if there exists a minimal linear phase-portrait approximation of A with $\mathcal{P}$ with respect to $\preceq$, it is referred to as the *linear phase-portrait translation* $phase_{\mathcal{P}}(A)$ of A with $\mathcal{P}$.

In many cases, linear phase-portrait approximations can be obtained by approximating, for each location, the flow field using a convex linear predicate containing the convex hull of the set of flow vectors.

Example 3. The automaton A'' in Figure 2, part (b), is a linear phase-portrait approximation of A (with the trivial partitioning). It has the flow condition $\dot{y} \geq \dot{x} \wedge \dot{y} \geq 6(\dot{x} - 3/2) \wedge \dot{y} \leq 4(\dot{x} - 3/4)$, defining the convex hull of the flow vectors $\{(x, x^2) \mid 1 \leq x \leq 3\}$ at q_0. Reachability analysis reveals that the maximal value of y obtained in location q_0 of A'' at $x = 3$ is 8. The location q_1 is reachable. While this approximation has fewer trajectories than the rate approximation A', it is still insufficient to establish that location q_1 is not reachable.

Both the rate approximation A' and the linear phase-portrait approximation A'' above can be improved through use of a finer partitioning. For linear-phase portrait approximation, using the partitioning of the rate translation A' shows that y never exceeds 7 in location q_0, and hence establishes that q_1 is unreachable. For rate approximation, dividing the invariant into three equal parts — $x \in [1, 5/3]$, $x \in [5/3, 7/3]$, and $x \in [7/3, 3]$ — instead of two is still insufficient to bound y sufficiently, but dividing into four equal parts suffices to show that q_1 is unreachable. ■

Asymptotic completeness A hybrid automaton can be approximated arbitrarily closely by choosing a sufficiently fine partitioning of the invariants. Given a real $\epsilon \geq 0$,

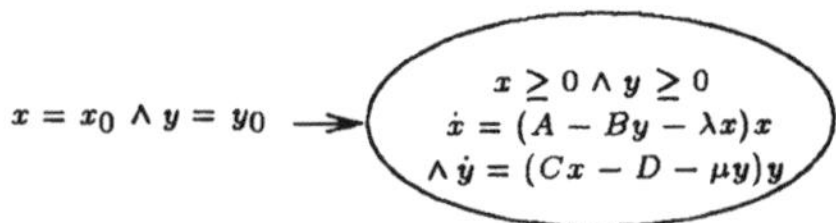

Fig. 3. Predator-prey hybrid automaton

the *ε-extension* of a predicate ϕ over $\mathbb{R}^n$ is the predicate ϕ' such that $[\![\phi']\!] = \{s' \mid \exists s \in [\![\phi]\!]$ such that $dist(s, s') \leq \epsilon\}$, where $dist(s, s')$ is the maximal value of the absolute difference between corresponding coordinates of s and s'. For a hybrid automaton A, let A^ϵ be the hybrid automaton obtained from A where all invariants, initial conditions, flow conditions, and jump conditions are replaced by their ε-extensions. Intuitively, A^ϵ models a system that differs from A by at most ϵ in its measurements of the values for continuous variables. A partitioning $\mathcal{P}$ is of *width* ϵ if, for each invariant ϕ occurring in $\mathcal{P}$ and for all valuations $s_1, s_2 \in [\![\phi]\!]$, $dist(s_1, s_2) \leq \epsilon$. A hybrid automaton is *monotonic* if, in each location, each variable is either nondecreasing or nonincreasing. A hybrid automaton is *bounded* if for all locations v, $inv(v)$ is a bounded set (this requirement can be relaxed without affecting the following two results nor Theorem 5; see [HH95a]). Rate approximations, and therefore linear phase-portrait approximations, are asymptotically complete for monotonic bounded automata.

Theorem 3 [HH95a]. *Let A be a monotonic bounded hybrid automaton. For all reals $\epsilon > 0$, (1) there exists a rate approximation B with some partitioning $\mathcal{P}$ such that $\mathcal{P}(A) \preceq B \preceq \mathcal{P}(A^\epsilon)$, and (2) there exists a real $\delta > 0$ such that for all partitionings $\mathcal{P}$ of width δ, if $rate_{\mathcal{P}}(A)$ exists, then $\mathcal{P}(A) \preceq rate_{\mathcal{P}}(A) \preceq \mathcal{P}(A^\epsilon)$.* ■

Corollary 4. *Let A be a monotonic bounded hybrid automaton. For all reals $\epsilon > 0$, (1) there exists a linear phase-portrait approximation B with some partitioning $\mathcal{P}$ such that $\mathcal{P}(A) \preceq B \preceq \mathcal{P}(A^\epsilon)$, and (2) there exists a real $\delta > 0$ such that for all partitionings $\mathcal{P}$ of width δ, if $phase_{\mathcal{P}}(A)$ exists, then $\mathcal{P}(A) \preceq phase_{\mathcal{P}}(A) \preceq \mathcal{P}(A^\epsilon)$.* ■

While splitting locations and finding rate approximations can be used for arbitrary accuracy, it may be easier to obtain sufficiently accurate linear phase-portrait approximations with fewer locations, as suggested above for the example automaton A.

5 Example: Predator-Prey Systems

We demonstrate the use of linear phase-portrait approximations on nonlinear systems modeling the population growth of two interacting species [Lot20]. We show that some interesting properties of such systems can be discovered automatically through algorithmic analysis.

A predator-prey ecology with limited growth Much of our exposition defining predator-prey systems is derived from Chapter 12 of [HS74]. One species is the *predator*, whose population is modeled by the variable y, and the other species is the *prey*, modeled by x. The prey forms the entire food supply for the predator, and we assume that the per capita food supply for the predator at any instant of time is proportional to the number of prey. The growth of the predator population is proportional to the difference between its actual per capita food supply and a basic per capita food supply required to maintain its population. The population of the prey is subject to two competing forces. First, the population may grow because there is a constant food supply available: the prey's population would increase without bound in the absence of predators. Furthermore, we assume this rate of increase would be proportional to the number

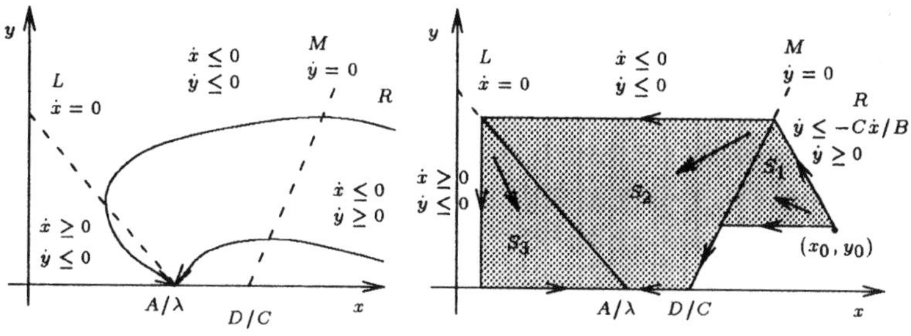

Fig. 4. Predator-prey populations

of prey. Second, the predators consume the prey at a rate that is proportional to the number of predators and to the number of prey. No population has the potential to increase without bound. There are social phenomena, such as overcrowding, spread of disease, and pollution, that imply that populations experience negative growth once they exceed a threshold limiting population. Assuming these negative growth factors are proportional to the species population and its difference from the threshold population leads to the Volterra-Lotka predator-prey equations. $\dot{x} = (A - By - \lambda x)x$ and $\dot{y} = (Cx - D - \mu y)y$, where A, B, C, D, λ, and μ are all positive real-valued constants.

The hybrid automaton for the system appears in Figure 3. By examining the flow field determined by the flow condition above, we partition the state space along the lines where either $\dot{x}$ or $\dot{y}$ have value 0, *i.e.* along the coordinate axes, and along the lines $L: A - By - \lambda x = 0$ and $M: Cx - D - \mu y = 0$. For the case that the lines L and M do not intersect in the northeastern quadrant of $\mathbb{R}^2$, the phase portrait of the system is shown in Figure 4, part (a).

Linear phase-portrait approximation In the region R, to the right of the line M in Figure 4, we infer tighter constraints on $\dot{x}$ and $\dot{y}$ than their signs. The values taken by the function $f(x,y) = \dot{y}/\dot{x}$ in the region R determine the flow vectors in R, because $\dot{x}$ is nonpositive and $\dot{y}$ nonnegative. The absolute value of $f(x,y)$ is bounded above by any Max/Min, where Max is an upper bound on the value of $\dot{y}$ in R, and Min is a lower bound on the absolute value of $\dot{x}$ in R. We can take Cxy for Max, because $D + \mu y$ is always positive. Since the lines L and M do not intersect in the northeastern quadrant, we know that $A/\lambda < D/C$, and hence that $A - \lambda D/C < 0$. Since x is no less than D/C in R, we infer that $A - \lambda x < 0$, and hence that $A - \lambda x - By < -By$. We may therefore take Byx for Min. We conclude that $f(x,y)$ is bounded below by $-Cxy/(Bxy) = -C/B$, and thus that all flow vectors in R have directions between $(-B, C)$ and $(-1, 0)$, *i.e.* they all satisfy the flow condition $\dot{y} \geq 0 \wedge \dot{y} \leq -C\dot{x}/B$.

The automaton for a linear phase-portrait approximation appears in Figure 5. The layout of the locations matches the partitioning of the state space as shown in Figure 4. The implicit invariant constraint $x \geq 0 \wedge y \geq 0$ has been omitted from all invariants. The constraint M refers to all valuations on the line M, *i.e.* all valuations where $Cx - D - \mu y = 0$. The constraint $M^{\geq}$ refers to all valuations at, or to the right of, the line M, *i.e.* $M^{\geq}$ is $Cx \geq D + \mu y$. Similarly $M^{\leq}$ is $Cx \leq D + \mu y$, L is $A - By - \lambda x = 0$, $L^{\leq}$ is $\lambda x \leq A - By$, and $L^{\geq}$ is $\lambda x \geq A - By$.

Computing population bounds The phase-portrait approximation above can be used to compute, for given starting populations, bounds on the populations of both species. For simplicity, we consider only the case where the initial populations x_0 and

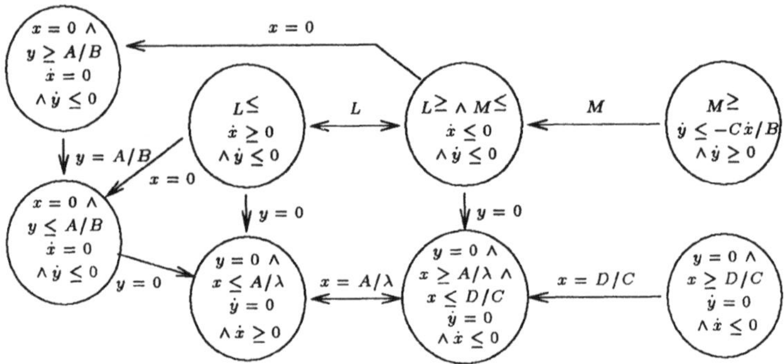

Fig. 5. Linear phase-portrait approximation for the predator-prey system

y_0 lie in the region R of the state space. The set of time-step successors of the state (x_0, y_0) is obtained by following all flow vectors in the cone indicated in Figure 4, part (b). First, the states in region S_1 are reached. Control may then pass to the location corresponding to the central region in the partition, where both $\dot{x}$ and $\dot{y}$ are nonpositive. After adding the states in region S_2, and then S_3, reachability analysis terminates. The maximum value of y among the reachable states is $(By_0 + Cx_0 - D)/(B + \mu)$. For example, using the equations $\dot{x} = (2000 - y - 5x)x$ and $\dot{y} = (4x - 2600 - 4y)y$, and the initial population vector $(900, 150)$, HyTech automatically computes a bound of 230 for y.

The given phase-portrait approximation yields a strictly tighter bound than the rate translation when applied to the same partitioning. The rate translation for each of the quadrants above provides no further information than the sign of the derivatives $\dot{x}$ and $\dot{y}$. Therefore, given initial starting populations x_0 and y_0 in R, the upper bound we obtain for y is $(Cx_0 - D)/\mu$ by following the initial point vertically up to the line M, as opposed to following the diagonal to M for the linear phase-portrait approximation. Naturally, either approximation method can yield tighter bounds at the expense of a finer partitioning. (If the lines L and M do intersect in the northeastern quadrant, reachability analysis on a linear phase-portrait approximation can be used to obtain bounds on both populations in this case, too.)

Iterating approximations As suggested in Section 3, bounds on the reachable region can be used to generate better phase-portrait approximations. For example, it can be shown that in the rightmost region R of Figure 4, the absolute value of $f(x, y)$, the flow tangent at (x, y), is bounded above by $Cy/(\lambda x + By - A)$. Let Z be a bounded subset of R. Let y_{max} be an upper bound for y over all valuations in Z, and x_{min} (resp. y_{min}) be a lower bound for x (resp. y) over Z. It follows that $|f(x, y)| \leq Cy_{max}/(\lambda x_{min} + By_{min} - A)$, provided that $(\lambda x_{min} + By_{min} - A) \geq 0$. Previously, we showed how reachability analysis of the automaton in Figure 5 leads to the region S_1 in R, from which we infer bounds of $y_{max} = 230$, $y_{min} = 150$, and $x_{min} = 800$. We can therefore replace the flow condition $\dot{y} \leq -C\dot{x}/B$ in the region S_1 with $\dot{y} \leq -92\dot{x}/215$. Recomputation now shows that only a subset of the region S_1 is reachable. In particular, we obtain the tighter bound of $y_{max} = 55250/307 \approx 180$ for y_{max}. We can iterate this process, obtaining successively lower values of y_{max}, and more restrictive flow conditions.

Controlling the ecology Standard analysis techniques can be used to show that in our setup, the predator population always tends toward 0, while the prey population tends to A/λ. Suppose, however, that we wish to keep the predator population above a nontrivial minimal value, or more generally, that the populations need to be controlled so that they remain within given lower and upper bounds. Assume that the prey population can be measured accurately, but that the predator population is unobservable. Our control strategy consists of monitoring the prey population, and releasing a fixed number k of additional prey into the system whenever it reaches its minimal allowable value. In general, it is unwise to increase the prey population to its maximal allowable value, because the abundance of prey may cause the predator population to grow too large.

In our example, we require the predator population to lie within the range $[100, 350]$, and the prey population within $[800, 1100]$. HyTech confirms automatically that both population bounds are successfully maintained when $k \leq 200$. For larger values of k, our linear phase-portrait approximation admits trajectories where the predator population exceeds the upper bound of 350. (This does not imply that all values of k greater than 200 lead to excessively large predator populations, because the approximation yields more reachable states than the original system.)

6 Example: Pseudo-linear Hybrid Automata

It is nontrivial to construct useful linear phase-portrait approximations for arbitrary hybrid automata, because this may involve understanding a set of differential inequalities. Here we identify a restricted class of hybrid automata for which linear phase-portrait approximations may be constructed automatically. A hybrid automaton with the set X of variables is *pseudo-linear* if (1) for every flow condition, replacing all occurrences of undotted variables with arbitrary rational constants results in a convex linear predicate over the dotted variables in $\dot{X}$, and (2) for every location v, every operator (function symbol) in the flow condition $fl(v)$ is monotonic in each argument over the domain $inv(v)$. For instance, the automaton A of Figure 1 is pseudo-linear.

Given a pseudo-linear hybrid automaton A, the following transformation yields a linear phase-portrait approximation $\lambda(A)$. For each location v, every occurrence of a variable x in the flow condition $fl(v)$ is replaced by either x_{max} or x_{min}, depending on the force of the occurrence of x in $fl(v)$, where x_{max} is a rational or infinite upper bound on the values that x may take along any trajectory satisfying the invariant $inv(v)$ and the flow condition $fl(v)$, and x_{min} is a rational or infinite lower bound. The replacement of each variable occurrence by a constant is chosen so that the transformed flow condition is implied by the conjunction of the invariant with the original flow condition. For simplicity, we assume that $fl(v)$ is a finite conjunction of inequalities. Then, an occurrence of x at the right-hand (left-hand) side of an inequality has positive force, and is replaced with x_{max}, if the occurrence lies within the scope of an even (resp. odd) number of operators that are monotonically nonincreasing in the occurrence of x over $inv(v)$. Otherwise, the occurrence of x has negative force and is replaced with x_{min}.

Theorem 5. *Given a pseudo-linear hybrid automaton A, the automaton $\lambda(A)$ is a linear phase-portrait approximation of A (with the trivial partitioning).* ■

Example 4. The automaton A of Figure 1 is pseudo-linear. The transformation above leads to the linear hybrid automaton $\lambda(A)$ with the flow condition $\dot{y} \geq \dot{x} \wedge \dot{y} \leq 3\dot{x} \wedge \dot{x} \leq 3 \wedge \dot{x} \geq 1$ for q_0. The first two conjuncts are derived from $\dot{y} = x\dot{x}$, and the latter two from $\dot{x} = x$. In this case, the derived flow conditions exactly match those of the linear phase-portrait translation with the trivial partitioning. ■

Example 5. The predator-prey system of the previous section is also pseudo-linear. However, the phase-portrait approximation we derive by the transformation above is the rate translation. This demonstrates the limitation of automatic methods: often a more careful analysis can provide tighter approximations. ■

Acknowledgement We thank Pei-Hsin Ho for interesting discussions about approximating nonlinear hybrid systems and the cumulative errors involved.

References

[ACH+95] R. Alur, C. Courcoubetis, N. Halbwachs, T.A. Henzinger, P.-H. Ho, X. Nicollin, A. Olivero, J. Sifakis, and S. Yovine. The algorithmic analysis of hybrid systems. *Theoretical Computer Science*, 138:3–34, 1995.

[ACHH93] R. Alur, C. Courcoubetis, T.A. Henzinger, and P.-H. Ho. Hybrid automata: an algorithmic approach to the specification and verification of hybrid systems. *Hybrid Systems I*, LNCS 736, pp. 209–229. Springer-Verlag, 1993.

[AHH93] R. Alur, T.A. Henzinger, and P.-H. Ho. Automatic symbolic verification of embedded systems. *14th Annual Real-time Systems Symposium*, pp. 2–11. IEEE Computer Society Press, 1993.

[Arn83] V. I. Arnol'd. *Geometric Methods in the Theory of Ordinary Differential Equations*. Springer-Verlag, New York, 1983.

[CC77] P. Cousot and R. Cousot. Abstract interpretation: a unified lattice model for the static analysis of programs by construction or approximation of fixpoints. *4th Annual Symposium on Principles of Programming Languages*. ACM Press, 1977.

[Hen95] T.A. Henzinger. Hybrid automata with finite bisimulations. *ICALP 95: Automata, Languages, and Programming*, LNCS 944, pp. 324–335. Springer-Verlag, 1995.

[HH95a] T.A. Henzinger and P.-H. Ho. Algorithmic analysis of nonlinear hybrid systems. *CAV 95: Computer-aided Verification*, LNCS 939, pp. 225–238. Springer-Verlag, 1995.

[HH95b] T.A. Henzinger and P.-H. Ho. HyTech: The Cornell Hybrid Technology Tool. *Hybrid Systems II*, LNCS 999, pp. 265–293. Springer-Verlag, 1995.

[HH95c] T.A. Henzinger and P.-H. Ho. A note on abstract-interpretation strategies for hybrid automata. *Hybrid Systems II*, LNCS 999, pp. 252–264. Springer-Verlag, 1995.

[HHWT95a] T.A. Henzinger, P.-H. Ho, and H. Wong-Toi. HyTech: the next generation. *16th Annual Real-time Systems Symposium*, pp. 56–65. IEEE Computer Society Press, 1995.

[HHWT95b] T.A. Henzinger, P.-H. Ho, and H. Wong-Toi. A user guide to HyTech. *TACAS 95: Tools and Algorithms for the Construction and Analysis of Systems*, LNCS 1019, pp. 41–71. Springer-Verlag, 1995. Full version available as Technical Report CSD-TR-95-1532, Cornell University (write to hytech@cs.cornell.edu, or check http://www.cs.cornell.edu/Info/People/tah/hytech.html).

[HKPV95] T.A. Henzinger, P.W. Kopke, A. Puri, and P. Varaiya. What's decidable about hybrid automata? *27th Annual Symposium on Theory of Computing*, pp. 373–382. ACM Press, 1995.

[HRP94] N. Halbwachs, P. Raymond, and Y.-E. Proy. Verification of linear hybrid systems by means of convex approximation. *SAS 94: Static Analysis Symposium*, LNCS 864, pp. 223–237. Springer-Verlag, 1994.

[HS74] M.W. Hirsch and S. Smale. *Differential Equations, Dynamical Systems, and Linear Algebra*. Academic Press, 1974.

[HW95] P.-H. Ho and H. Wong-Toi. Automated analysis of an audio control protocol. *CAV 95: Computer-aided Verification*, LNCS 939, pp. 381–394. Springer-Verlag, 1995.

[Lot20] A.J. Lotka. Analytical note on certain rhythmic relations in organic systems. *Proceedings of the National Academy of Sciences of the United States of America*, 6:410–415, 1920.

Deciding Reachability for Planar Multi-polynomial Systems *

Kārlis Čerāns and Juris Vīksna

Institute of Mathematics and Computer Science
The University of Latvia
Rainis boulevard 29, Rīga, LV - 1459, Latvia
email: jviksna@cclu.lv

Abstract. In this paper we investigate the decidability of the reachability problem for planar non-linear hybrid systems. A planar hybrid system has the property that its state space corresponds to the standard Euclidean plane, which is partitioned into a finite number of (polyhedral) regions. To each of these regions is assigned some vector field which governs the dynamical behaviour of the system within this region. We prove the decidability of point to point and region to region reachability problems for planar hybrid systems for the case when trajectories within the regions can be described by polynomials of arbitrary degree.

1 Introduction

During recent years intensive research has been devoted to the problem of automated analysis of various classes of hybrid systems (HS). The difficulty of this problem is due to the presence of a continuos projection of the system state space (every system state of a HS typically consists of control location, which is chosen from some finite domain, and the value vector for some continuous variables), this usually makes the system state space (wildly) infinite. However, there has already been much progress in the area, starting from the region graph based methods for Timed Automata [2, 3, 6], and leading to recent more general results and systematic investigations on what is decidable about hybrid systems (see, for instance, [1, 9, 8]).

Still, most of these results are concerned with the analysis automation for *linear* hybrid systems, where the continuous variables are allowed to change the value during the course of time at some fixed rate (or the value change can be non-deterministic, with any rate from a certain fixed interval).

It can be noted, however, that for the full class of linear HS even the simpliest verification problems are undecidable (see, for instance [6, 5, 1]), so any decidability result in this area is bound to indentify a certain subclass of systems to which it does apply.

* This work has been partially supported by Grant No.93-596 from Latvian Council of Science.

On the other hand, the behaviour of practical hybrid systems is most often governed by some non-linear laws. Therefore it is natural to ask, whether there are natural classes of non-linear HS, which do admit automated verification. An important study of this problem is already [7], where the possibility of verification on nonlinear hybrid systems via the reduction to linear clock and rate hybrid automata is discussed, and corresponding at least sound verification methods are presented.

In this paper we investigate the decidability of the reachability problem for planar non-linear hybrid systems. A planar hybrid system has the property that its state space corresponds to the standard Euclid plane, which is partitioned into a finite number of (polyhedral) regions. To each of these regions is assigned some vector field which governs the dynamic behaviour of the system within this region. We prove the decidability of point to point, edge to edge and region to region reachability problems for planar hybrid systems for the case when trajectories within the regions can be described by polynomials of arbitrary degree.

Our results are a generalization of those of [10], where the subcase of our problem with the vector fields within the regions being constant (the so-called multi-linear model) was considered. We are able to reuse also a part of the proof from [10] to show that every infinite trajectory of the system either intersects only with a finite number of the region boundaries, or starting from some point will repeatingly intersect certain fixed sequence of region boundaries (in fact this result holds even for much wider classes of systems, its demonstration relies essentially on the fact that trajectories within the regions do not intersect).

The main problem to be dealt with in our "multi-polynomial" case essentially consists in showing the decidability of the "abandonment" of an edge (region boundary, or some its part): given some repeating sequence of edges intersected by a trajectory, decide, whether this repetition will last forever, or after some finite number of edge-to-edge steps some other edge intersection sequence will appear.

This problem is solved, in essence, by explicating the polynomial dependencies of future region border intersection points from the previous ones on the trajectories, and characterizing the "limit points" of the intersection point sequences in the terms of fixed points and roots of appropriate polynomials.

Our results can be viewed as showing the non-essentiality of the *linearity* requirement for the decidability results in the setting of [10]. However, as it has been shown in [4], the 2-dimensionality requirement is essential for the decidability of the reachability even for the case of multi-linear systems (in [4] a construction modeling Turing machines by 3-dimensional multi-linear systems is presented, thus proving the undecidability of any nontrivial verification problem for that class of systems).

The organization of the rest of the paper is, as follows. In the next section we give main definitions and notation used throughout the paper. Section 3 reminds already known results about general planar hybrid systems. Section 4 contains our results about decidability results for multi-polynomial systems.

Finally, Section 5 contains some conclusions and indicates possible directions for future work.

2 Main definitions

Definitions and notations in this paper are more or less standard and similar to [10].

Symbols $\mathbf{R}$ and $\mathbf{R}_+$ will stand for the sets of real and real positive numbers, $\mathbf{Q}$ and $\mathbf{Q}_+$ for the sets of rational and rational positive numbers. With $\mathbf{N}$ we denote the set of natural numbers, with $\mathbf{N}_+$ – the set of positive natural numbers.

By $\mathbf{A}$ we denote the set of algebraic numbers - i.e. the set of numbers which are roots of polynomials $p(x)$ with rational coefficients. We represent each such number a as a pair $\langle p(x), i\rangle$, where $p(x)$ is some polynomial with coefficients from $\mathbf{Q}$, such that $p(a) = 0$, and $i \in \mathbf{N}_+$ is the index of a in the increasingly ordered sequence of p roots, i.e., $i = card(\{x \in \mathbf{R} \mid p(x) = 0 \;\&\; x < a\}) + 1$. (Of course, such representation is not unique.) We say that an algebraic number a is computable (from some subset A of natural numbers), if there exists an algorithm that on input A computes coefficients of some $p(x)$ and number i, such that $a = \langle p(x), i\rangle$.

We consider the Euclid plane $\mathbf{R}^2$ with standard metric d, i.e. such that for any two points $a = (x_1, y_1), b = (x_2, y_2) \in \mathbf{R}^2$ the distance $d(a, b)$ between a and b is defined by the equality $d(a,b) = \sqrt{((x_1 - x_2)^2 + (y_1 - y_2)^2)}$.

A closed half-plane is defined as a set H in the form $H = \{(x, y) \in \mathbf{R}^2 \mid Ax + By + C \geq 0\}$ for some constants $A, B, C \in \mathbf{R}$.

For an arbitrary set $S \subseteq \mathbf{R}^2$ we define the set of interior points of S as $int(S) = \{a \in S \mid \exists\varepsilon \in \mathbf{R}_+ : U(a,\varepsilon) \subseteq S\}$, where $U(a,\varepsilon) = \{b \in \mathbf{R} \mid d(a,b) < \varepsilon\}$. We define the closure of S as $cl(S) = \{a \in \mathbf{R}^2 \mid \forall\delta \in \mathbf{R}_+ \,\exists b \in S : d(a,b) < \delta\}$, and the boundary of S as $bd(S) = cl(S) - int(S)$.

A (closed) polyhedral set P is an intersection of finitely many closed half-planes, such that $int(P) \neq \emptyset$.

Definition 1. A finite polyhedral partition of $\mathbf{R}^2$ is a family of polyhedral sets $\mathcal{P} = \{P_1, \ldots, P_n\}$ with disjoint sets of interior points, such that $\bigcup_{i=1}^{n} P_i = \mathbf{R}^2$.$\diamond$

By $bd(\mathcal{P})$ we denote the set of all points which belong to $bd(P_i)$ for some $P_i \in \mathcal{P}$.

Let P be some polyhedral set. We say that a vector field is defined in the set P, if a system of following differential equations is assigned to the set P

$$\begin{cases} \dot{x} = f_1(x, y), \\ \dot{y} = f_2(x, y), \end{cases} \tag{1}$$

where $f_1(x, y)$ and $f_2(x, y)$ are continuous functions jointly in x and y.

Such equation allows to split the region P into set of disjoint trajectories, i.e. into set of curves with equations

$$\begin{cases} x(t) = g_x(t), \\ y(t) = g_y(t), \end{cases} \tag{2}$$

which satisfy the given system (1) and are defined for values of $t \in \mathbf{R}$, such that $(x(t), y(t)) \in P$. We assume that these curves are oriented in the direction in which the value of t is increasing.

In this paper we restrict our attention to the case when all trajectories in P are polynomial and without singularities, i.e. such that for some polynomial $p(x, y)$ all trajectories satisfy equation $p(x, y) = C$ for some $C \in \mathbf{R}$, and such that all trajectories that enter the region P also leave it and vice versa. It is known that this case corresponds to the situation given in the next definition.

Definition 2. We say that in a polyhedral region P a vector field is defined by polynomial $p(x, y)$, if it is defined by system

$$\begin{cases} \dot{x} = p'_y(x, y), \\ \dot{y} = -p'_x(x, y), \end{cases} \tag{3}$$

and $p(x, y)$ is a polynomial, such that for all points $a = (x, y) \in int(P)$ either $p'_y(x, y) \neq 0$, or $p'_x(x, y) \neq 0$.◇

All trajectories in P in this case will satisfy equation $p(x, y) = C$ for some $C \in \mathbf{R}$. We shall assume that in parametrical form these trajectories can be described by equation

$$\begin{cases} x(t) = g_{p,x}(t, C), \\ y(t) = g_{p,y}(t, C). \end{cases} \tag{4}$$

It is known that functions $g_{p,x}$ and $g_{p,y}$ can be effectively approximated from $p(x, y)$ (i.e. it is possible to compute $g_{p,x}(t, C)$ and $g_{p,y}(t, C)$ up to an arbitrary degree of approximation). However, in general case they are neither polynomial, nor can be effectively found.

If P is a polyhedral set in which a polynomial vector field satisfying the system (3) is defined, then any point $A \in bd(P)$ belongs to one of three different types with respect to the region P (see Fig. 1).

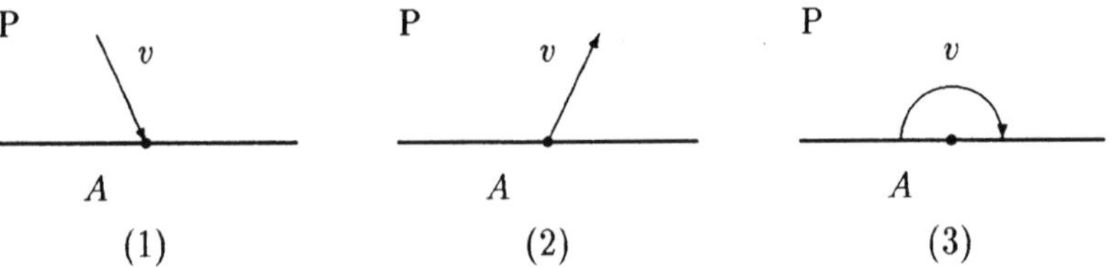

Fig. 1. *Three different types of boundary points for a region with polynomial trajectories. In case 1 point A is an exit from P, in case 2 point A is an entry to P and in case 3 point A is neutral with respect to P.*

Each point on border of P can belong either to one of the types 1–3, or simultaneously to types 1 and 2.

These three types can be described more formally in the following way.

If the vector field in P is given by the system (3), then point $A = (x_0, y_0)$ belongs to some trajectory T which satisfies equation (4) for some functions $g_{p,x}$ and $g_{p,y}$. We assume that $g_{p,x}(t_0, C) = x_0$ and $g_{p,y}(t_0, C) = y_0$ for some $t_0 \in \mathbf{R}$.

We say that point $A \in bd(P)$ is an entry to P, if there exists $t' > t_0$, such that $(x(t), y(t)) \in P$ for all $t \in [t_0, t']$, where $x(t) = g_{p,x}(t, C)$ and $y(t) = g_{p,y}(t, C)$.

We say that point $A \in bd(P)$ is an exit from P, if there exists $t' < t_0$, such that $(x(t), y(t)) \in P$ for all $t' \in [t', t_0]$, where $x(t) = g_{p,x}(t, C)$ and $y(t) = g_{p,y}(t, C)$.

Otherwise we say that point A is neutral with respect to P. In this case the trajectory T consists of a single point A.

The set of all entry points to P we shall denote by $In(P)$, the set of all exit points from P – by $Out(P)$ and the set of all neutral points – by $Neut(P)$.

Definition 3. A multi-polynomial hybrid system on $\mathbf{R}^2$ is $\mathcal{H} = (\mathcal{P}, \varphi)$, where $\mathcal{P}$ is a polyhedral partition of $\mathbf{R}^2$ and φ is a function which assigns to each region of $\mathcal{P}$ a vector field defined by some polynomial $p(x, y)$.◇

Thus, a multi-polynomial hybrid system gives a partition of the Euclid plane into polyhedral sets in each of which some polynomial vector field without singularities is defined.

Since we are interested in the decidability of reachability problems in such systems, we have to ensure that multi-polynomial hybrid system is represented in some effective way. Therefore, throughout this paper we shall further assume (if not explicitly stated otherwise) that for a given hybrid system $\mathcal{H} = (\mathcal{P}, \varphi)$ all regions in $\mathcal{P}$ are defined as intersections of half-planes $Ax + By + C \geq 0$ with algebraic coefficients A, B and C (i.e. such that $A, B, C \in \mathbf{A}$). Similarly, we shall further assume that function φ to each $P \in \mathcal{P}$ will assign a polynomial with algebraic coefficients.

Definition 4. A step of a multi-polynomial hybrid system $\mathcal{H} = (\mathcal{P}, \varphi)$ is a pair (a, a') of boundary points $a = (a_x, a_y), a' = (a'_x, a'_y) \in bd(P)$, for some $P \in \mathcal{P}$, such that for the polynomial $p(x, y) = \varphi(P)$ the equalities $a_x = g_{p,x}(t_0, C)$, $a_y = g_{p,y}(t_0, C)$, $a'_x = g_{p,y}(t', C)$ and $a'_y = g_{p,y}(t', C)$ hold for some $t_0, t', C \in \mathbf{R}$, with $t' > t_0$, and for all $t \in [t_0, t']$ we have inclusion $(g_{p,x}(t, C), g_{p,y}(t, C)) \in P$.◇

In such case we shall also say that the step (a, a') defines trajectory $p(x, y) = C$.

Definition 5. A path of a hybrid system $\mathcal{H} = (\mathcal{P}, \varphi)$ is a sequence (finite or infinite) $s = a_1, a_2, \ldots$ of points $a_1, a_2, \ldots \in bd(\mathcal{P})$, such that either $s = a_1$, or for every $i > 0$, and a_{i+1} from s:

1. the pair (a_i, a_{i+1}) is a step, and
2. there does not exist $a'_{i+1} \in bd(\mathcal{P})$, such that $a_{i+1} \neq a'_{i+1}$, and (a_i, a'_{i+1}) is a step.◇

The second condition in the definition of the path allows to eliminate non determinism in hybrid system – i.e. if in some situation we can proceed by two different trajectories we are not allowed to choose either of them.

A finite path $s = a_1, \ldots, a_k$ is extendable, if there exists a path $s' = a_1, \ldots, a_k, a_{k+1}$.

For a polyhedral set of a given hybrid system $\mathcal{H} = (\mathcal{P}, \varphi)$ we partition the boundary of P into edges in such a way that each edge (if we do not consider its end points)

- intersects with boundaries of exactly two polyhedral sets $P, Q \in \mathcal{P}$, and
- contains only entry, or only exit, or only neutral points with respect to both regions P and Q.

A line segment S in $\mathbf{R}^2$ is a set in the one of the forms $S = \{(x, y) \in \mathbf{R}^2 \mid Ax + By + C = 0,\ u_1 \leq x \leq u_2\}$ or $S = \{(x, y) \in \mathbf{R}^2 \mid Ax + By + C = 0,\ w_1 \leq y \leq w_2\}$ for some constants $A, B, C \in \mathbf{R}$, $u_1, u_2, w_1, w_2 \in \mathbf{R} \cup \{\infty\}$, with $u_1 < u_2$ and $w_1 < w_2$. Point $A(x_0, y_0) \in S$ is an end point of S, if $x_0 \in \{u_1, u_2\} \cap \mathbf{R}$ or $y_0 \in \{w_1, w_2\} \cap \mathbf{R}$. The set of all (i.e. of one or two) end points of S we denote by $B(S)$. By $I(S)$ we denote the set $S - B(S)$.

Definition 6. The line segment e is an edge of $P \in \mathcal{P}$, if

1. $e \subseteq P \cap Q$ for some $Q \in \mathcal{P}$,
2. each point of $I(e)$ belongs to only one type with respect to region P and to only one type with respect to region Q, and
3. if $A \in B(e)$, then either $A \in R$ for some $R \in \mathcal{P}$, $R \neq P$, $R \neq Q$, or A is of different type than points in $I(e)$ with respect to one of the regions P or Q.$\diamond$

Set of all edges of $P \in \mathcal{P}$ we shall denote by $E(P)$. By $E(\mathcal{P})$ we shall denote $\bigcup_{P \in \mathcal{P}} E(P)$.

Definition 7. Let $s = a_1, a_2, \ldots$ be a path in $\mathcal{H}$. We say that $X(s) = S_1, S_2, \ldots$ is a signature of s, if for each $i \geq 1$ we have $S_i = \{e \in E(\mathcal{P}) \mid a_i \in e\}$.$\diamond$

Finally, we define the notion of the reachability from point a to point b. We begin with a more technical notion of 1-reachability which covers the case when b is reachable from a by a trajectory within one region.

Definition 8. Let $\mathcal{H} = (\mathcal{P}, \varphi)$ be a (non singular) hybrid system. Let $a = (a_x, a_y), b = (b_x, b_y) \in \mathbf{R}^2$. We say that b is 1-reachable from a, if $a, b \in P$ for some $P \in \mathcal{P}$ and, if there exist $a_1, a_2 \in bd(P)$, such that (a_1, a_2) is a step and both a and b lie on the trajectory $p(x, y) = C$ defined by the step (a_1, a_2), and, besides that, there exist $t_1, t_2 \in \mathbf{R}$, such that $g_{p,x}(t_1, C) = a_x$, $g_{p,y}(t_1, C) = a_y$, $g_{p,x}(t_2, C) = b_x$, $g_{p,y}(t_2, C) = b_y$ and $t_1 \leq t_2$.$\diamond$

Definition 9. Let $\mathcal{H} = (\mathcal{P}, \varphi)$ be a (non-singular) hybrid system. Let $a, b \in \mathbf{R}^2$. We say that b is reachable from a, if there exists a finite path $s = a_1, \ldots, a_n$, such that a_1 is 1-reachable from a and b is 1-reachable from a_n.$\diamond$

We say that an edge e_2 is reachable from an edge e_1, if there exist $a_1 \in e_1$ and $a_2 \in e_2$, such that point a_2 is reachable from point a_1. Similarly, we say that a region P_2 is reachable from a region P_1, if there exist $a_1 \in P_1$ and $a_2 \in P_2$, such that point a_2 is reachable from point a_1.

3 Some properties of planar deterministic systems

In this section we are going to remind some general properties of planar hybrid systems, which are proved (or can be proved similarly as) in [10] and which in particular hold also for multi-polynomial systems.

Let $\mathcal{H} = (\mathcal{P}, \varphi)$ be some hybrid system. We shall assume that with an arbitrary edge $e \in E(\mathcal{P})$ there is associated an ordering of the points of e, namely, that to some point $a_0 = (a_{0,x}, a_{0,y}) \in e$, such that $a_{0,x}, a_{0,y} \in \mathbf{A}$, there is assigned coordinate 0, and to any other point $a \in e$ there is assigned some coordinate $c(a, e) \in \mathbf{R}$, such that for any two points $a_1, a_2 \in e$ the equality $(c(a_1, e) - c(a_2, e))^2 = d(a_1, a_2)^2$ holds. By $a \preceq b$, where $a, b \in E$, we shall denote the fact that $c(a, e) \leq c(b, e)$. (It is not important, exactly which systems of coordinates for edges we chose, we only assume that such systems of coordinates are fixed for a given hybrid system $\mathcal{H}$ and that the coordinates are effectively computable from $\mathcal{H}$.)

The following result can be proved similarly as in [10].

Theorem 10 (Maler, Pnueli). *Let $s = a_1, a_2, \ldots$ be a path that intersects $e \in E(\mathcal{P})$ in three points $b_1 = a_i, b_2 = a_j, b_3 = a_k$, such that $i < j < k$. Then, $b_1 \preceq b_2$ implies $b_2 \preceq b_3$ and $b_1 \succeq b_2$ implies $b_2 \succeq b_3$.*$\diamond$

Let $e_1, \ldots, e_n \in E(\mathcal{P})$. We say that the sequence $e_1, \ldots, e_n$ forms a cycle, if $e_1 = e_n$ and the edges $e_2, \ldots, e_{n-1}$ are mutually distinct.

An edge e is said to be abandoned by a path $s = a_1, a_2, \ldots$ with signature $X(s) = S_1, S_2, \ldots$ after position i, if $e \in S_i$ and either s is finite and $e \notin S_j$ for $j > i$, or s is infinite and for some j, k, with $i < j < k$, there is a cycle $e_j \in S_j, \ldots, e_k \in S_k$.

Theorem 11 (Maler, Pnueli). *If and edge e is abandoned by a path $s = a_1, a_2, \ldots$ with signature $X(s) = S_1, S_2, \ldots$ after position i, then $e \notin S_j$ for an arbitrary $j > i$.*$\diamond$

As a corollary it is possible to obtain the following result.

Corollary 12 (Maler, Pnueli). *Every infinite path $s = a_1, a_2, \ldots$ has a signature in the form $X(s) = S_1, S_2, \ldots, S_i, (S_{i+1}, \ldots, S_{i+j})^\star$ for some $i, j \in \mathbf{N}_+$. Besides, the number j does not exceed the number of regions in hybrid system $\mathcal{H} = (\mathcal{P}, \varphi)$.*$\diamond$

Thus, for a path $s = a_1, a_2, \ldots$ with $X(s) = S_1, S_2, \ldots$ and for an edge $e \in S_i$ for some $i \in \mathbf{N}_+$ we have $e \in S_j$ for some $j > i$ if and only if edge e will not be abandoned.

4 Reachability results

In this section we shall show that for a given multi-polynomial hybrid system $\mathcal{H}$ the reachability problems between points, edges or regions are decidable. Our results to a large extent are based on the following three theorems about algebraic numbers. For the sake of brevity we are giving them here without proofs. We also do not expect the novelty of these results.

Theorem 13. *Let* $p(x) = p_n x^n + p_{n-1} x^{n-1} + \cdots + p_1 x + p_0$ *be a polynomial with algebraic coefficients* $p_n, \ldots, p_0 \in \mathbf{A}$. *Then all real roots of* $p(x)$ *are algebraic and computable from* $p_n, \ldots, p_0$.◇

Theorem 14. *It is decidable, whether two algebraic numbers* $a, b \in \mathbf{A}$ *are equal or not.*◇

For an arbitrary function $f : \mathbf{R} \to \mathbf{R}$ we iteratively define functions $f^{(1)}(x) = f(x), f^{(2)}(x) = f(f^{(1)}(x)), \ldots, f^{(n)}(x) = f(f^{(n-1)}(x)), \ldots$.

Theorem 15. *Let* $p(x) : \mathbf{R} \to \mathbf{R}$ *be a polynomial that is monotonous in some interval* $[a, b] \subseteq \mathbf{R}$ *(i.e. either, for all* $x, y \in [a, b]$, *with* $x > y$, *we have inequality* $p(x) \leq p(y)$, *or, for all* $x, y \in [a, b]$ *with* $x > y$, *we have inequality* $p(x) \geq p(y)$*). Let* $x_0 \in [a, b]$ *be such that* $l(x_0) = \lim_{n \to \infty} p^{(n)}(x_0) \in [a, b]$. *Then* $l(x_0)$ *is the first root of the polynomial* $p(x) - x$, *larger than* x_0, *if* $p(x_0) > x_0$. *Similarly,* $l(x_0)$ *is the first root of the polynomial* $p(x) - x$, *smaller than* x_0, *if* $p(x_0) < x_0$.◇

We shall also use the following relatively simple propositions. For the sake of brevity their proofs are omitted.

Proposition 16. *Let* $\mathcal{H} = (\mathcal{P}, \varphi)$ *be a hybrid system (with algebraic coefficients) and let* $a \in \mathbf{A}^2$, $P \in \mathcal{P}$. *Then it is decidable, whether or not* $a \in P$.◇

Proposition 17. *Let* $\mathcal{H} = (\mathcal{P}, \varphi)$ *be a multi-polynomial hybrid system (with algebraic coefficients). Then the set of edges* $E(\mathcal{P})$ *is finite and for each* $e \in E(\mathcal{P})$ *the elements of* $B(e)$ *are algebraic and computable from* $\mathcal{H}$.◇

Proposition 18. *Let* $\mathcal{H} = (\mathcal{P}, \varphi)$ *be a multi-polynomial hybrid system and let* $a = (a_x, a_y) \in e \cap \mathbf{A}^2$ *for some* $e \in E(\mathcal{P})$. *Then the maximal (i.e. non-extendable) path* $s = (a_1 = a), a_2, \ldots$ *containing* a *is computable (i.e. all numbers* a_i *are algebraic and computable from* a *and* i, *and if* s *is finite of length* n, *then there is an algorithm which for* $i > n$ *produces the answer that* a_i *is undefined).*◇

Proposition 19. *Let* $\mathcal{H} = (\mathcal{P}, \varphi)$ *be a multi-polynomial hybrid system. Let* $s = a_1, a_2, \ldots$ *be a path, such that* $a_1 \in \mathbf{A}^2$. *Then signature* $X(s)$ *is computable, i.e. for each* $i \in \mathbf{N}_+$ *we can compute points in* $B(e)$ *for all edges* $e \in S_i$.◇

Proposition 20. *Let* $\mathcal{H} = (\mathcal{P}, \varphi)$ *be a multi-polynomial hybrid system. Let* $a = (a_x, a_y) \in int(P) \cap \mathbf{A}^2$ *for some* $P \in \mathcal{P}$ *and let* $p(x, y) = \varphi(P)$. *Then there exists a step* $(a_1 = (a_{1,x}, a_{1,y}), a_2 = (a_{2,x}, a_{2,y}))$, *such that* $p(a_x, a_y) = p(a_{1,x}, a_{1,y}) = p(a_{2,x}, a_{2,y})$, *and the numbers* a_1, a_2 *are computable from* a *(i.e. there exists a trajectory through* a, *end points of which can be computed).*◇

From Proposition 17 it easy follows that for a given hybrid system $\mathcal{H} = (\mathcal{P}, \varphi)$ and for any edge $e \in E(\mathcal{P})$ it is decidable whether signature $X(s)$ for some path $s = a_1, a_2, \ldots$ will contain an edge e in the i-th position. The following principal lemma shows that it is also decidable whether the edge e will be eventually abandoned.

Lemma 21. *Let $\mathcal{H} = (\mathcal{P}, \varphi)$ be a multi-polynomial hybrid system. Let $s = a_1, a_2, \ldots$ be a path in $\mathcal{H}$ with signature $X(s) = S_1, S_2, \ldots$ and with $a_1 \in \mathbf{A}^2$. Let $e \in S_i$ for some $i \in \mathbf{N}_+$. Then it is decidable, whether or not the edge e will be abandoned.*$\diamond$

Proof. From the definition of abandonment and Theorem 12 it follows that e will not be abandoned if and only if $X(s) = S_1, S_2, \ldots, S_i, (S_{i+1}, \ldots, S_{i+j})^\star$ for some $i, j \in \mathbf{N}_+$ and $e \in S_{i+k}$ for some $k \in \mathbf{N}_+$, with $1 \leq k \leq j$.

Thus, the abandonment of e is decidable, if for arbitrary edges $e_1 \in S_{m+1}, \ldots, e_n = e_1 \in S_{m+n}$ it is decidable whether in the cycle $e_1, \ldots, e_n$ some edge will be eventually abandoned. It is not hard to see that it is sufficient to show that it is decidable whether edge e_k, with $1 \leq k \leq n$, will be abandoned, if either e_k is the first edge from the cycle $e_1, \ldots, e_n$, which actually will be abandoned, or there are no edges in $e_1, \ldots, e_n$, which will be abandoned.

Without loss of generality we can assume that e_1 is an edge with such a property. We have to show that it is decidable, whether e_1 will be abandoned or not. Let a_{m+1} be the point in the path s that corresponds to the set S_{m+1} from the signature $X(s)$. We denote $b_1 = a_{m+1}$, $b_2 = a_{m+n}$, $b_3 = a_{m+2n-1}, \ldots$. Clearly the edge e_1 will not be abandoned if and only if for all $i \in \mathbf{N}_+$ we have $b_i \in e_1$.

Let P be the region containing edges e_1 and e_2. Let $p(x, y) = \varphi(P)$. Let $p(x, y) = C_1$ be the trajectory going through points a_{m+1} and a_{m+2}. Since e_1 is a line segment, we have that C_1 is algebraic and can be computed from a_{m+1}. Also a_{m+2} is algebraic and can be computed from C_1, and thus, by Theorem 13, also from $b_1 = a_{m+1}$. Similarly, we can show that a_{m+3} is algebraic and computable from a_{m+2}, and, thus, by Theorem 13, also from b_1, etc., up to $b_2 = a_{m+n}$.

Thus, b_2 is algebraic and computable from b_1. Let $b_2 = \langle p_1(x, b_1), i_1 \rangle$. Similarly, we can show that $b_3 = \langle p_2(x, y), i_1 \rangle$, etc., while $b_i \in e_1$ holds. Since the polynomials p_i depend only on regions defined by the pairs of edges $(e_1, e_2), (e_2, e_3), \ldots, (e_{n_1}, e_n)$, then $p_1 = p_2 = \cdots$. We denote $p_1(x, y)$ by $g(x, y)$.

However, we can not guarantee that $g(x, y)$ as polynomial on x has the same number of roots for all $y \in \mathbf{A}$. Thus, we shall not necessarily have $i_1 = i_2 = \cdots$. Still, it is not hard to see that the number of roots for $g(x, y)$ can change only on values of y, such that $g'_x(x, y) = 0$ and $g(x, y) = 0$ for some $x \in \mathbf{A}$. The number of such values of y is finite, they are algebraic and computable from $g(x, y)$. Thus, we can split the edge e_1 into finite number of (open or closed) subintervals $I_1, \ldots, I_r$, such that for an arbitrary q, with $1 \leq q \leq r$, for all $y \in I_q$ the polynomial $g(x, y)$ has the same number of roots. Since in each region $P \in \mathcal{P}$ trajectories $p(x, y) = C$ change continuously with respect to C, for all $b_u \in I_q$, the values of i_u must be equal.

By Theorem 10 the sequence $b_1, b_2, \ldots$ is monotonous, thus, by one or more applications of Theorem 15, $b = \lim_{i \to \infty} b_i$ is computable from b_1. Clearly, we shall have $b_i \in e_1$ if and only if $b \in e_1$. Therefore, it is decidable whether the edge e_1 will be abandoned, and, thus, also for an arbitrary $e \in S_i$ it is decidable whether or not the edge e will be abandoned.$\diamond$

Theorem 22 Main result. *Let $\mathcal{H} = (\mathcal{P}, \varphi)$ be a multi-polynomial hybrid system. Let $a, b \in \mathbf{A}^2$. Then it is algorithmically decidable whether point b is reachable from point a.* $\diamond$

Proof. **Case 1.** Let $a = (a_x, a_y) \notin e$ for all $e \in E(\mathcal{P})$. Then $a \in int(P)$ for some $P \in \mathcal{P}$ (and such P is uniquely defined), and due to Proposition 16 region P can be found algorithmically. From Proposition 20 it follows that we can compute algebraic numbers a_1, a_2, such that (a_1, a_2) is a step and the point a lies on a trajectory from a_1 to a_2. Similarly, we can compute region Q and points b_1, b_2, such that $b = (b_x, b_y)$ lies on a trajectory defined by step (b_1, b_2).

If $a_1 = b_1$ (and thus also $a_2 = b_2$), then points a and b lie on the same trajectory given by equations

$$\begin{cases} x(t) = g_{p,x}(t, C), \\ y(t) = g_{p,y}(t, C), \end{cases}$$

and $p(x, y) = C$, for $p(x, y) = \varphi(P)$. Since $C = p(a_{1,x}, a_{1,y})$, the number C is algebraic and computable from a. Up to an arbitrary degree of approximation we can compute t_1 and t_2, such that $a_x = g_{p,x}(t_1, C)$, $a_y = g_{p,y}(t_1, C)$ and $b_x = g_{p,x}(t_2, C)$, $b_y = g_{p,y}(t_2, C)$. By definition b is reachable from a if and only if either $t_1 < t_2$, or $a = b$. Decidability whether $a = b$ follows from Theorem 14. If $a \neq b$, we can eventually decide whether $t_1 < t_2$ or $t_1 > t_2$. Therefore, in this subcase, it is decidable, whether b is reachable from a.

If $a_1 \neq b_1$, then by definition b is reachable from a if and only if b_1 is reachable from a_1. This subcase is covered by Case 2.

Case 2. Let $a = (a_x, a_y) \in e$ for some $e \in E(\mathcal{P})$. Let (b_1, b_2) be the step containing trajectory through b, and let $S = \{e \in E(\mathcal{P}) \mid b_1 \in e\}$.

If $a \neq b$ (case $a = b$ is trivial), then by definition b is reachable from a if and only if b_1 is reachable from a. By Proposition 18 all elements in maximal path $s = (a_1 = a), a_2, \ldots$ are computable. We continue computation of a_i for $i \in \mathbf{N}_+$ until one of the following holds.

1. There exists $i \in \mathbf{N}_+$ with $a_i = b_1$. Then, by definition, b is reachable from a.
2. For some i element a_i becomes undefined (i.e. s turns out to be finite) and for all $j < i$ we have $a_j \neq b_1$. Then, by definition, b is not reachable from a.
3. We have computed the path $s = (a_1 = a), a_2, \ldots, a_i, \ldots, a_{i+j}$, such that in the signature $X(s) = S_1, S_2, \ldots, S_i, (S_{i+1}, \ldots, S_{i+j})^\star$, none of the sets $S_{i+1}, \ldots, S_{i+j}$ contains an edge that will be abandoned (by Lemma 21 this problem is decidable).
   If there is no k, with $1 \leq k \leq j$, such that $S = S_{i+k}$, then due to Corollary 12 b is not reachable from a.
   Otherwise, let $S = S_{i+k'}$. If $card(S) > 1$, then clearly $a_{i+k'} = b_1$, thus b is reachable from a.
   If $card(S) = 1$ (we assume in this case that $S = \{e\}$), then by c_m, where $m \in \mathbf{N}_+$, we shall denote the coordinate $c(a_{i+mk'}, e)$. Let $c = c(b_1, e)$. Numbers $c, c_1, c_2, \ldots, c_m, \ldots$ are algebraic and computable from a, b and

m. Similarly as in proof of Lemma 21 we can show that there exists a polynomial with rational coefficients $p(x, y)$ and number $u \in \mathbf{N}_+$, such that $c_{m+1} = \langle p(x, c_m), u \rangle$. Due to Theorem 10 the sequence $c_1, c_2, \ldots$ is monotonous, and due to Theorem 15 it converges to some computable c'. Therefore, by definition b is unreachable from a, if $c > c_1$ and $c > c'$, or $c < c_1$ and $c < c'$. Otherwise we can eventually find $w \in \mathbf{N}_+$, such that either $c_w \leq c \leq c_{w+1}$, or $c_{w+1} \leq c \leq c_w$. In both cases b is reachable from a, if $c = c_w$ or $c = c_{w+1}$, and b is unreachable from a otherwise.

Thus, we have shown that also in Case 2 reachability from a to b is decidable.$\diamond$

Similarly, as it is done in [10], we can modify the proof of Theorem 22 to show that the reachability problem from edge to edge is also decidable.

Theorem 23. *Let $\mathcal{H} = (\mathcal{P}, \varphi)$ be a multi-polynomial hybrid system. Let $e_1, e_2 \in E(\mathcal{P})$. Then it is algorithmically decidable whether edge e_2 is reachable from edge e_1.*$\diamond$

As an easy corollary we obtain decidability result for regions of $\mathcal{P}$.

Corollary 24. *Let $\mathcal{H} = (\mathcal{P}, \varphi)$ be a multi-polynomial hybrid system. Let $P_1, P_2 \in \mathcal{P}$. Then it is algorithmically decidable whether region P_2 is reachable from region P_1.*$\diamond$

5 Some conclusions and open problems

In this paper we have demonstrated that the reachability problem is decidable for planar multi-polynomial hybrid systems. This shows that the fact that HS state space fits on the topology of the plane and has continuous execution trajectories is quite a strong requirement which makes the algorithmic analysis of HS possible even in the case of rather complicated non-linear behaviour rules.

The model of multi-polynomial systems in our paper contains a technical restriction that the vector fields within the regions do not have singularities, however, it is clear that this is not essential, and the decidability results can be proved also for the case when the singularities are allowed. We conjecture that the same results hold also for systems which allow nondeterministic behaviour on the borders between the regions.

It seems that our results can be generalized also for the case, when the borders of the regions of the partition of the plane are polynomial curves, instead of just being straight line segments.

It also would be interesting to study further the classes of HS for which the decidability of the reachability can be proved by exploiting mainly the planar topological properties of the state space (for instance, this method would apply to most of systems where the vector fields inside the regions are defined by some linear autonomous systems, what would amount to having the trajectories of the form $p(x, y, C) = 0$ instead of just $p(x, y) = C$).

We conjecture that it should be possible to generalize our decidability results also for 2-dimensional systems with continuous trajectories (no reset operations), where more general kinds of non-linearity can be admitted. An interesting future study could be looking also at the systems with 2-dimensional state space which is topologically more complicated than the Euclid plane (this is what could be obtained by relaxing the requirement that the values of continuous variables should uniquely determine the control state).

At some point it would be interesting to compare the classes of non-linear HS for which the decidability of the reachability can be shown using primarily the topological arguments with the classes which can be shown decidable by some other means. This largely remains to be a subject of a future work.

Acknowledgements

We thank Silvija Čerāne for explaining us some facts from the theory of differential equations, needed for this paper. We are very grateful also to Oded Maler for presenting our paper at the Workshop.

References

1. R. Alur, C. Courcoubetis, N. Halbwachs, T.A. Henzinger, P.H. Ho, X. Nicollin, A. Olivero, J. Sifakis, and Y. Yovine. The algorithmic analysis of hybrid systems. *Theoretical Computer Science*, 138:3–34, 1995.
2. R. Alur and D. Dill. Automata for modeling real time systems. In *Proceedings of ICALP'90*, volume 443 of *Lecture Notes in Computer Science*, pages 322–335, 1990.
3. R. Alur and D. Dill. A theory of timed automata. *Theoretical Computer Science*, 126:183–235, 1994.
4. E. Asarin and O. Maler. On some relations between dynamical systems and transition systems. In *Proceedings of the 21st International Colloquium ICALP94*, volume 820 of *Lecture Notes in Computer Science*, pages 59–72, 1994.
5. K. Čerāns. *Algorithmic problems in analysis of real time system specifications.* PhD thesis, University of Latvia, 1992.
6. K. Čerāns. Decidability of bisimulation equivalences for parallel timer processes. In *Proceedings of CAV'92*, volume 663 of *Lecture Notes in Computer Science*, pages 302–315, 1992.
7. P.A. Henzinger and P.H. Ho. Algorithmic analysis of nonlinear hybrid systems. In *Proceedings of CAV'95*, Lecture Notes in Computer Science, 1995.
8. T.A. Henzinger. Hybrid automata with finite bisimulations. In *Proceedings of ICALP'95*, volume 944 of *Lecture Notes in Computer Science*, pages 324–335, 1995.
9. T.A. Henzinger, P. Kopke, A. Puri, and P. Varaiya. What's decidable about hybrid automata? In *Proceedings of the 27th ACM Symposium on Theory of Computing*, 1995.
10. O. Maler and A. Pnueli. Reachability analysis of planar multi-linear systems. In *Proceedings of the 5th International Conference of Computer Aided Verification*, volume 697 of *Lecture Notes in Computer Science*, pages 194–209, 1993.
11. R. Zippel. *Effective polynomial computation.* Kluwer Academic Publishers, 1993.

Modeling Hybrid Dynamical Systems

Ingo Hoffmann and Karsten-Ulrich Klatt

Department of Chemical Engineering, University of Dortmund 44221, Germany
e-mail: ingo@astaire.chemietechnik.uni-dortmund.de (corresponding author)

Abstract. We present a modeling scheme for multivariate hybrid dynamical systems. From given time series embedded in appropriate state spaces we predict future outputs by making local linear fits in the neighbourhood of the actual state vectors. In particular, the proposed algorithm can be used online. Thus the quality of the forecast is improved by enclosing new measured data.

Keywords: Hybrid dynamical systems, chaotic behavior, tiled state spaces, local linear fits.

1 Introduction

Systems with a discrete control of continuous variables are called hybrid dynamical systems. The dynamics of such systems can be very complex, i. e. the description of their behavior by mathematical models can be a difficult task. Many studies have been done to build appropriate models for hybrid systems[1, 2, 3]. In this work we propose an algorithm for modeling such dynamical systems where the presented algorithm is not only restricted to time series from hybrid dynamical systems. Moreover, it is a basic approach to the task of modeling time series for short prediction-horizons and is applicable to a wide range of different time series[4, 5, 6].

Time series of hybrid systems often show non-equidistant time steps between successive control switchings. Moreover, in some cases they feature chaotic behavior and the manifold on which their dynamics act consists of a union of distinct subparts (tiled state spaces)[7, 8]. Therefore, they are a challenging test for modeling strategies.

Using local linear fits we predict future events of the system from information belonging to the past. Assume we have measured a certain number T of state vectors $\mathbf{x}_n = \mathbf{x}(t_n) \in \mathbf{R}^N$ which describe the state of the system at times t_n for $n = 1, \ldots, T$. Embedding them in $\mathbf{R}^N$ we get a portrait of the manifold $S \subseteq \mathbf{R}^N$ on which the dynamics $G : S \rightarrow S$ of the system is defined. Suppose that $\mathbf{x}_T$ is

the actually measured state vector. We are searching for neighbours $\mathbf{x}_k$ for $k < T$ in a small ϵ-ball around $\mathbf{x}_T \in S$. Fitting a local linear time discrete dynamics g, we predict future states by applying g on $\mathbf{x}_T$ in the form $\mathbf{x}_{T+1} = g(\mathbf{x}_T)$. With this approach we get excellent precisions for the one time-step prediction of future states. We will show that our forecast-error is lower than 0.1% in the case of a 3-dimensional chaotic hybrid plant and is smaller than 0.02% for a 2-dimensional non-chaotic hybrid system.
This paper is organized as follows. In the following section we develop the prediction algorithm based on local linear fits. The main algorithmic features will be explained. In section 3 we present two examples of hybrid dynamical systems. The first one is a model of a forced hybrid level control plant. In form of a short review we focus on the main features of a chaotic N-Buffer-System[7, 8] which is the second example. The feasibility of the prediction algorithm will be examined in section 4 by applying it to the examples of section 3. Conclusions and topics for further research are presented in section 5.

2 Prediction model

Proceeding form earlier studies[4, 5, 6] we develop and describe a strategy to predict future events of hybrid dynamical systems. In order to control such hybrid dynamical systems one is often interested in predicting future states for a certain number of time steps. First of all, we develop a model based on a local linear fit which is able to predict future states.

Model

Consider a ground set of measured state vectors $\mathbf{x}_n \in \mathbb{R}^N$ for $n = 1, \ldots, T$. Note that by this we are able to consider multivariate time series. Suppose that $\mathbf{x}_T$ is the actually measured state vector. We predict the next state $\mathbf{x}_{T+1}$ by the linear approach:

$$\mathbf{x}_{T+1} = \mathbf{A}^{(T)}\mathbf{x}_T + \mathbf{b}^{(T)}. \tag{1}$$

In order to fit the parameter matrix $\mathbf{A}$ and the parameter vector $\mathbf{b}$ of equation (1) we have to find the adjacent state vectors in the state space. Denoting the neighbourhood of $\mathbf{x}_T$ by $\mathcal{U}_\epsilon(\mathbf{x}_T)$:

$$\mathcal{U}_\epsilon(\mathbf{x}_T) = \left\{\mathbf{x}_k^{(T)} \Big| \parallel \mathbf{x}_T - \mathbf{x}_k^{(T)} \parallel < \epsilon,\, k \in \{1, \ldots, T-1\}\right\}, \tag{2}$$

we determine $\mathbf{A}^{(T)}$ and $\mathbf{b}^{(T)}$ by solving the minimizing problem:

$$\mathcal{L}^2 = \sum_{\mathbf{x}_k^{(T)} \in \mathcal{U}_\epsilon(\mathbf{x}_T)} \left(\mathbf{x}_k^{(T+1)} - \mathbf{A}^{(T)}\mathbf{x}_k^{(T)} - \mathbf{b}^{(T)}\right)^2. \tag{3}$$

Minimization of $\mathcal{L}^2$ leads to

$$W_{ij}^{(T)} = \left\langle x_{k,i}^{(T+1)} x_{k,j}^{(T)} \right\rangle_{\mathcal{U}_\epsilon|k} - \left\langle x_{k,i}^{(T+1)} \right\rangle_{\mathcal{U}_\epsilon|k} \left\langle x_{k,j}^{(T)} \right\rangle_{\mathcal{U}_\epsilon|k} \tag{4}$$

$$V_{ij}^{(T)} = \left\langle x_{k,i}^{(T)} x_{k,j}^{(T)} \right\rangle_{\mathcal{U}_\epsilon|k} - \left\langle x_{k,i}^{(T)} \right\rangle_{\mathcal{U}_\epsilon|k} \left\langle x_{k,j}^{(T)} \right\rangle_{\mathcal{U}_\epsilon|k} \tag{5}$$

and for all $i, j = 1, \ldots, N$ we find

$$\mathbf{A}^{(T)} = \mathbf{W}\mathbf{V}^{-1}. \tag{6}$$

Here $\langle \bullet \rangle_{\mathcal{U}_\epsilon|k}$ denotes the average over the neighbourhood, and $x_{k,i}^{(T)}$ is the i-th component of the vector $\mathbf{x}_k^{(T)} \in \mathcal{U}_\epsilon(\mathbf{x}_T)$. Similarly we find

$$\mathbf{b}^{(T)} = \left\langle \mathbf{x}_k^{(T+1)} \right\rangle_{\mathcal{U}_\epsilon|k} - \mathbf{A}^{(T)} \left\langle \mathbf{x}_k^{(T)} \right\rangle_{\mathcal{U}_\epsilon|k} \tag{7}$$

for the parameter vector.
Now we are able to predict the future state $\mathbf{x}_{T+1}$ by

$$\mathbf{x}_{T+1} = \mathbf{A}^{(T)} \left(\mathbf{x}_T - \left\langle \mathbf{x}_k^{(T)} \right\rangle_{\mathcal{U}_\epsilon|k} \right) + \left\langle \mathbf{x}_k^{(T+1)} \right\rangle_{\mathcal{U}_\epsilon|k}. \tag{8}$$

This equation (8) supplies a linear forecast model. Predicting one time step we get the new state vector $\mathbf{x}_{T+1}$. Searching for new neighbours in a neighbourhood $\mathcal{U}_\epsilon(\mathbf{x}_{T+1})$ and forecasting according to equation (8) we get the two time step prediction $\mathbf{x}_{T+2}$. Repeating this m times we get the m time step prediction. If one is just interested in the m-time forecast (without knowing the results for $\mathbf{x}_{T+1}, \ldots, \mathbf{x}_{T+m-1}$) the algorithm alternatively is able to determine directly

$$\mathbf{x}_{T+m} = \tilde{\mathbf{A}}^{(T)} \mathbf{x}_T + \tilde{\mathbf{b}}^{(T)}. \tag{9}$$

This results in a short computing time for the prediction.

Algorithmic features

To optimize the algorithm we employ some special features. The design of the algorithm is dynamical and not pre-given. I.e. at each time the ϵ-size of the neighbourhood is adjusted to an optimal value.

- **Ground set:** First of all we have to provide some ground set T of measured state vectors. We have to choose a suitable inital ground set which roughly approximates the manifold S in the embbeding space.
- **Initial ϵ-size:** For noiseless time series we are able to determine the initial size as follows. Consider a minimum number J of neighbours required. By using

$$\epsilon = \left(\frac{J}{T} \right)^{\frac{1}{N-C}}, \tag{10}$$

  where C is the codimension of the manifold S in the embedding space, we get a suitable choice for the initial value. For dynamical systems where the state space consists of a fractal subset of the embedding space we choose $(N - C)$ equal to the fractal dimension. In the case of noise contaminated time series we choose $\epsilon > \eta$ where η is the noiselevel[9].

- **Dynamical ϵ-size:** The algorithm should predict the future state vector $\mathbf{x}_{T+1}$ from the neighbourhood of the actual measured state vector $\mathbf{x}_T$. Thus the local linear fit should be based on a certain number J of neighbours. In order to find the required number of neighbours the algorithm varies the ϵ-size. For noise contaminated time series this will be done under the condition that $\epsilon > \eta$.
- **Growing ground set:** The algorithm is able to predict online while the dynamics act. The new measured state vector is enclosed to the ground set. Thus the state space fills densly over time and the forecast improves. Limited by the finite memory, the enclosing has to stop at a certain cardinality T_c of the ground set. An alternative is to "forget" earlier state vectors. However, this is involved with fixing the forecast at a small part of the state space (wind-up-problem).

3 Models of plants

Recently, there is spent much research effort in the field of the so called hybrid dynamical systems. Their characteristic feature is the discrete control of continuous variables where the discrete control often is performed by switching between certain values of the manipulated variable. The switching is described by so called *switching-rules* and causes a tiled state space. The hybrid dynamical systems are described by equations of the form:

$$\dot{\mathbf{x}} = F(\mathbf{x}, \mathbf{k}) \ , \tag{11}$$

where $F : S \subset \mathbb{R}^N \times \mathbb{R}^n \to \mathbb{R}^N$ is a smooth map defined on an open, connected subset of the Euclidean space which possibly depends on a vector of parameters, $\mathbf{k} \in \mathbb{R}^n$. The domain S may be decomposed into the form:

$$S = \bigcup_{\alpha \in I} S_\alpha, \tag{12}$$

where I is a finite index set and S_α is an open, connected subset of $\mathbb{R}^N$ and is called a chart. Each chart itself encloses a patch. It is assumed that a trajectory starts and evolves in a patch. If the trajectory reaches the boundary of the patch a "jump" into another chart (or into the chart itself) occures, for further information cf. [10]. The numerical solution of the ordinary differential equation (11) results in a time discrete map $G : S \to S$ with $\mathbf{x}_{n+1} = G(\mathbf{x}_n, \mathbf{k})$. If $\mathbf{x}_n$ is an element of a switching boundary, i. e. certain target values are reached, we have to adapt our model on the jump. Therefore we have to assure that the neighbourhood of the actual measured vector belongs to the same transition set, i. e. the set which is mapped under the action of G into one next chart. This can be done by checking that the mapped neighbours are also neighboured according to a precision $\delta = \delta(\epsilon, m)$.
To demonstrate the feasibility of the developed prediction algorithm we have choosen two examples of hybrid systems. The first one is a simple theoretical model of a hybrid level control plant and the second one is the standard N-Buffer-System which is well described in several articles[7, 8].

Forced Hybrid Level Control Plant

Our first example of a hybrid dynamical system is a modified theoretical model for a level control plant. Proceeding from earlier studies[11] we develop a hybrid model of the plant.
The plant consist of two communicating tubes. The first tube has a direct inlet flow k_1 whereas the inlet of the second tube depends on the difference of both levels $(x_1 - x_2)$ and the valve position k_2. Furthermore, the inlet in the second tube gets an offset level k_3. The outlet of the second tube is described by k_4. Putting all together w.r.t. Toricelli's law yields our basic model:

$$\begin{pmatrix} \dot{x}_1 \\ \dot{x}_2 \end{pmatrix} = \begin{cases} \begin{pmatrix} k_1 - k_2\sqrt{\delta x} \\ k_2\sqrt{\delta x} - k_4\sqrt{x_2} \end{pmatrix} & \text{if } x_2 > k_3 \\ \begin{pmatrix} k_1 - k_2\sqrt{x_1} \\ k_2\sqrt{x_1} - k_4\sqrt{x_2} \end{pmatrix} & \text{if } x_2 \leq k_3 \end{cases}, \tag{13}$$

where $\delta x = x_1 - x_2 + k_3$. One can easily show that the above defined phase space flow $\dot{\mathbf{x}} = F(\mathbf{x}, \mathbf{k})$ tends to an equilibrium state (fixed point) $\mathbf{x}^*$ for all $k_j > 0$ and $x_i > 0$ for $j = 1, \ldots, 4$ and $i = 1, 2$. We are able to switch between different equilibrium states $\mathbf{x}_j^*$ by changing $k_1 = k_{1j}$ j times between certain predefined values. This results in our hybrid model which is combined with the switching rule:

$$\begin{array}{l} \|\mathbf{x} - \mathbf{x}_1^*\| < \epsilon : k_{11} \rightarrow k_{12} \\ \|\mathbf{x} - \mathbf{x}_2^*\| < \epsilon : k_{12} \rightarrow k_{11} \end{array}. \tag{14}$$

The phase space of the hybrid level control plant consist of a limit cycle which reaches the vicinity of the first fixed point, switches and iterates to the second fixed point. In order to get a somewhat attractiver dynamics we disturbe the inlet flow rate k_{1j} by an additional forcing term $a\sin(\omega t)$. Where ϵ is adjusted to 0.01. Solving numerically the ordinary differential equation (13) leads to the time discrete map G. Iterating G results in the phase space shown in figure 1.

N-Buffer-System

Our next example is a technical plant which consists of N buffers. Each buffer i is able to store a certain amount of substrat x_i. Here Substrat is abstractly defined and represents a continuous measurment variable. It is convenient to accociate substrat with thermal energy, chemical energy or stored electrical energy in a capacitor. The buffers lose substrat over time according to a given ordinary differential equation (11). The i-th buffer will be filled up if it reaches a given threshold x_s. For simplicity, we restrict the example-systems by the assumption that only one buffer can be filled up at the same time. Detecting the state vector $\mathbf{x}(t_n)$ of the hole plant just at times t_n where a filling takes place we get a time series of the system. Embedding this time series in $\mathbb{R}^N$ we get the state space of the system. As an example of the state space see fig. 2 for $N = 3$. Figure 2 shows the evolving neighbourhood for some time steps in the case of the 3-dimensional Buffer-System. The time discrete dynamics G of the system under consideration

Fig. 1 State space of the level control plant

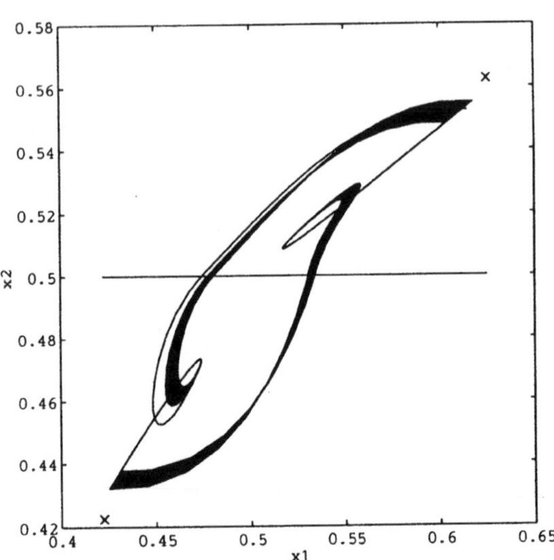

This picture show the state space of the defined forced hybrid level control plant. The constant model parameters are $k_2 = k_4 = 1$, c.f. equation (13). Changing k_1 between the two possible values $k_{1j} = \{0.65, 0.75\}$ we get two fixed points (marked with crosses). While passing $x_2 = k_3 = 0.5$ the dynamics changes its structure. This takes place in a cyclic manner. The plotted cycle consist of 8800 points, whereas one period consist of 92 points. The plant was forced by a periodic variation of the inlet flow with $a = 0.03875$ and $\omega = 0.1$. This causes the loops shown above.

is defined by the equation:

$$x_i(t_n + \Delta t) = x_i(t_n) + (\delta_{ij} - \rho_i)\,\Delta t, \tag{15}$$

where Δt is the time interval needed until the next buffer empties. With δ_{ij} we denote a non-standard kroneckerdelta, i.e. the index j depends on the levels $\mathbf{x}(t_n)$ in the buffers and gives the actuall position of the server. The constant parameter vector $\boldsymbol{\rho} = (\rho_1, \ldots, \rho_N)$ (transition point in fig. 2) represents the outlet rates per time unit in the respective buffers. We choose $\sum_i \rho_i = 1$ to get a closed system where the whole amount of stored substrat per time is constant and we use the 3 dimensional Buffer-System.
Generally, the state space S of a N-dimensional Buffer-System in $\mathbb{R}^N$ consists of a simplex of order N [8] with codimension $C = 2$.

Parameters

The above defined Buffer-System has a positiv Kolmogorov-Sinai-Entropy h_μ [8], therefore its behavior is of chaotic nature. This causes the divergence of

Fig. 2 State space and evolving neighbourhood

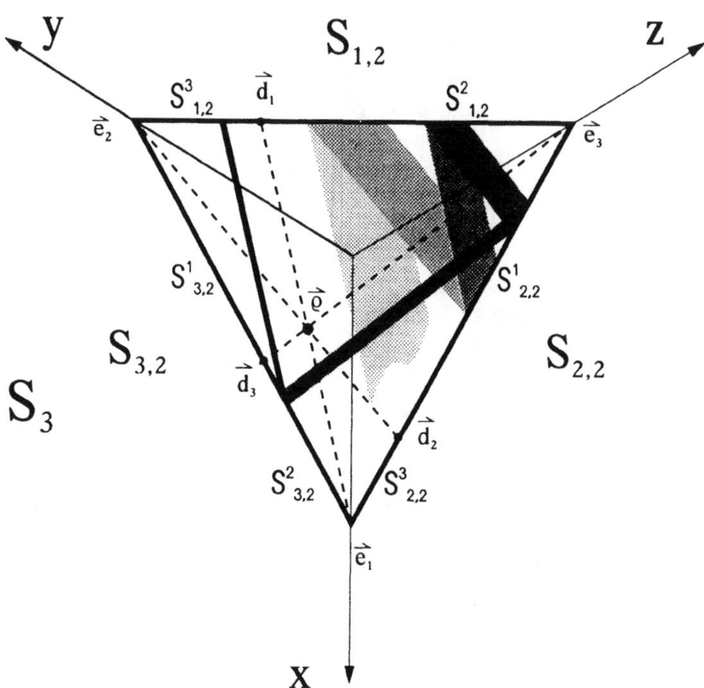

This picture shows the 3-dimensional state space S_3 of the chaotic Buffer-System. The state space consist of three connected subsets $S_{i,2}$. The special points $\mathbf{d}_i$ (intersection points) divide each subset into two subparts $S^j_{i,2}$ ($i, j = 1, 2, 3$ and $j \neq i$). The dynamics is determined by ρ (transition point). The figure illustrates how a neighbourhood of an arbitrary choosen center point is stretched under the action of $G : S^j_{i,2} \rightarrow S_{j,2}$.

adjacent trajectories[12] as shown in fig. 2. In tab. 1 we show the parameters and the resulting entropy for the respective Buffer-System.

4 Applications

Using the forecast model defined by equation (8) we try to predict future states within a certain number of time steps m. Applying the proposed algorithm to a time series (stationary w.r.t. an invariant measure[12, 13]) within a long time horizon L and enclosing the new measured state vectors to the ground set we expect that the forecast improves. In order to get a valuation criterion we define

Table 1 Parameters for the Buffer-System

Parameter		Value
Dimension	$[N]$	3
Codimension	$[C]$	2
Threshold	$[x_s]$	0
Outlet-Rate	$[\rho]$	$(0.2, 0.5, 0.3)$
Entropy	$[h_\mu]$	0.6447

the forecast error σ as follows:

$$\sigma = \sqrt{\frac{1}{M}\sum_{t=T}^{T+M} \|\mathbf{x}_t^{\text{predicted}} - \mathbf{x}_t^{\text{original}}\|^2} . \tag{16}$$

Here M denotes the considered time of applying the algorithm to the original time series and call it the *epochal time*. By T we denote the initial ground set. In the following we use the forecast-error and the ϵ-size normalized by the size

$$\operatorname{diam}(S) = \max_{\mathbf{x}_i, \mathbf{x}_j \in S} \|\mathbf{x}_i - \mathbf{x}_j\| \tag{17}$$

of the manifold S. With this $\epsilon = \sigma = 1$ is equal to the size of the manifold. Tab. 2 shows the parameters for the prediction algorithm in the case of the Buffer-System. In fig. 3 we show the corresponding prediction results by plotting

Table 2 Parameters

Parameter	Symbol	Value
Length of time series	$[L]$	10000
Ground Set	$[T]$	1000
Epochal time	$[M]$	1
Embedding dimension	$[N]$	3
Min. number of neighbours	$[J]$	50

the actual ϵ-size and the resulting forecast-error σ versus the time-step. It is obvious, that the feasibility of the forecast improves by enclosing the new state vectors. For every prediction the size of the ϵ-ball is scanned from low values to high values to get the required number of neighbours J. The quality of the prediction mainly depends on the ϵ-size of the neighbourhood. That means using small ϵ-balls results in small values for σ as well until ϵ is smaller than a critical ϵ_c from there on the neighbourhoods begin to empty. If we enclose new measured

Fig. 3 Results for the noisefree Buffer-System.

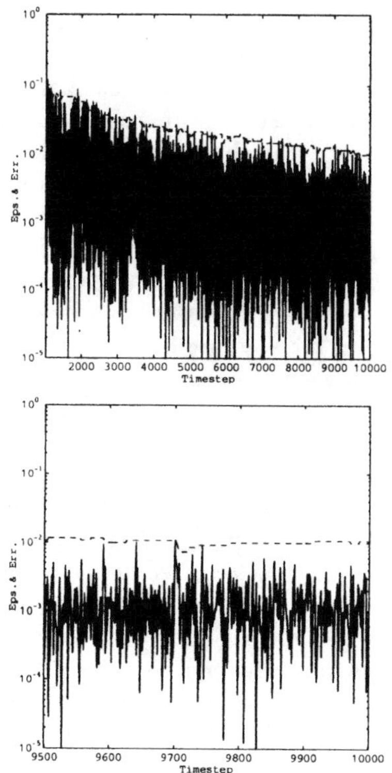

Here we present the results for the Buffer-System. The pictures show the actual ϵ-size of the neighbourhood (dashed) and the error σ of the forecast using the parameters listed in tab. 2. The left picture shows the one-time step forecast. One can easily verify that the forecast improves while enclosing new measured state vectors to the ground set. The right picture is a zoom of the left picture.

data to the ground set, we expect that $\epsilon_c \to 0$ for $T \to \infty$. Hence, for a noiseless and stationary (w.r.t. an invariant measure) time-series we suppose that the decrease of the forecast-error σ will follow the relation

$$\sigma \propto T^{-(N-C)}, \tag{18}$$

deduced from equation (10) under the assumption that $\sigma \propto \epsilon$. Indeed, for the Buffer-System we found numerically an exponent of -1 which is identical to $-(N-C) = -1$.

In the case of chaotic time series the initial ϵ-size of the neighbourhood will grow exponentially under the action of G. This is simply the consequence of the positiv Lyapunov-Exponent[13] which is directly related to the Entropy of the dynamics[12]. Actually, under certain conditions h_μ is equal to the sum of the positiv Lyapunov-Exponents (Pesin-Theorem[14]). We expect that the forecast-error σ will grow exponentialy as well. Plotting the forecast-error versus the considered prediction-time we suppose that up to a certain number of prediction-time steps the curve follows the mentioned exponential grow. In a single log-plot this causes a linear ascend. The slope β of the curve should be of the order of the entropy. While the evolving neighbourhood spreads over different branches, respectively subparts of the manifold for a certain critical prediction-time m_c, we expect a progressive ascend. This will be called the prediction-horizon. A further increase of the prediction-time results in reaching the limits of the manifold, so that we are confronted with foldings of the manifold. As a consequence, we presume a limit value for the forecast-error. A similar course of the plotted curve should be obtained in the presence of noise (considering low noiselevels), whereas for non-chaotic time series the forecast-errors sumarize according to the law of error propagation. We expect a linear increase of the forecast-error which causes a very flat curve in a single log-plot.

In the following we analyses the dependence of the forecast-error from the prediction-time for both models of hybrid plants by using a ground set of $T = 4000$ for each system. The forecast-error is determined within an epochal time of $M = 500$. Here we have fixed the required number of neighbours at $J = 22$. At first we predict future state vectors of the 2-dimensional forced hybrid level control plant. Afterwards we apply the proposed algorithm to the 3-dimensional Buffer-System. We analyse the behavior of the forecast-error while increasing the prediction-time. The results for both applications are shown in fig. 4. One can easily detect the expected behavior. In that case we have fixed the prediction-horizon at $m_c = 4$. The slope of the curve within this range is of the order of the entropy. Analysing the noiseless system for the prediction-horizon $m_c = 4$ we found a forecast-error of roughly 2% whereas for the one-time step prediction we get an excellent precision where the forecast-error is smaller than 0.1%. Considering the results for the non-chaotic example of a forced hybrid level control plant, fig. 4 shows the expected course of the forecast-error curve. The forecast-error remains small for a wide range of the prediction-horizon. We assume that the forecast-error for the noiseless system will reach a limit value of roughly one half of the thickness of the cycle in fig. 1 that correspond to $\sigma = 0.005$. As it can be seen in fig. 4, line (d) tends to the supposed value. In this example we get a very small forecast-error for the one time-step where the error is less than 0.02%.

5 Conclusion

The present work proposes an algorithm to predict future outputs of multivariate time series and especially for hybrid dynamical systems. We show that the forecast quality for a short time prediction m is very satisfying. The main advantage of the presented forecast algorithm is that it may be used online where the new measured state vectors are enclosed to the ground set. Thus, the state space fills

Fig. 4 Prediction-time and Error for the Hybrid Plants

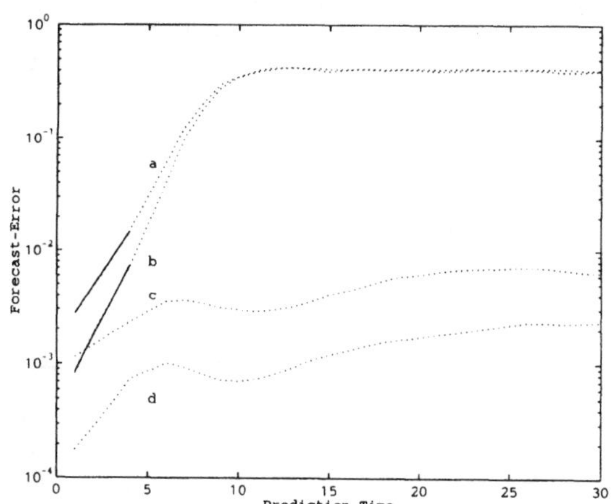

This figure shows the forecast-error σ versus the considered prediction-time m for the hybrid plants. We get the curves (a,b) for the Buffer-System with a noiselevel of 0 % and 0.1 % respective. For the level control plant we get the curves (c,d) with a noiselevel of 0 % and 1 % respective. In the case of the chaotic Buffer-System we get a prediction-horizon of $m_c = 4$. Within this range we found a slope of the curve of $\beta_a = 0.6 \pm 0.1$ and $\beta_b = 0.7 \pm 0.1$ which is of the order of the entropy $h_\mu = 0.6447$.

densly and the forecast improves. Future research has to be done to improve the forecast in the case of noisy time series by pre-filtering the data. After that, we intend to test the proposed algorithm in combination with a predictive controller in order to control a real technical plant. A further interesting aspect for future research is the adaptability of the algorithm to smooth changing parameters of the plant in time. This will result in non-stationary time series.

References

1. A. Göllü and P. Varaiya, "Hybrid dynamical systems," *Proc. 28th Conf. Decision Contr.*, Tampa, FL, pp. 2708-2712, 1989.
2. J. A. Stiver and P. J. Antsaklis, "A novel discrete event system approach to modeling and analysis of hybrid control systems," Control Systems Tech. Rep. #71, Dept. of Elect. Eng., Univ. of Notre Dame, IN, 1991.
3. P. Peleties and R. Decarlo, "A modeling strategy for hybrid systems based on event structures," preprint: School of Elect. Eng., Purdue Univ., West Lafayette, IN.
4. J. D. Farmer and J. J. Sidorowich, "Predicting chaotic time series," *Phys. Rev. Lett.* **59**, 845, 1987.
5. J. D. Farmer and J. J. Sidorowich, "Exploiting chaos to predict the future and reduce noise," *Evolution, Learning and Cognition* ed. Lee, Y. C. (World Scientific), 1988.

6. G. Sugihara and R. May, "Nonlinear forecasting as a way of distinguishing chaos form measurement errors in time series," *Nature* **344**, 744, 1990.
7. C. Chase, J. Serrano and P. J. Ramadge, "Periodicity and Chaos from Switched Flow Systems: Contrasting Examples of Discretely Controlled Continous Systems," *IEEE Trans. Automat. Contr.*, Vol. 38, No. 1, pp. 70-83, 1993.
8. T. Schürmann and I. Hoffmann, "The entropy of "strange" billiards inside n-simplexes," *J. Phys.* **A 28**, pp. 5033-5039, 1995.
9. H. Kantz, T. Schreiber, I. Hoffmann, T. Buzug, G. Pfister, L. G. Flepp, J. Simonet, R. Badii and E. Brun, "Nonlinear noise reduction: a case study on experimental data," *Phys. Rev. E* **48**, 1529, 1993.
10. A. Back, J. Guckenheimer and M. Myers, "A Dynamical Simulation Facility for Hybrid Systems," *Lect. Notes in Comp. Science*, Vol. 736, pp. 255-267, 1993.
11. T. Heckenthaler and S. Engell, "Approximately Time-Optimal Fuzzy Control of a Two-Tank System," *IEEE Control Systems*, Vol. 14, No. 3, pp. 24-30, 1994.
12. P. Grassberger, T. Schreiber and C. Schaffrath, "Nonlinear Times sequence Analysis," *International Journal of Bifurcation and Chaos*, Vol. 1, No. 2, pp. 521-547, 1991.
13. R. W. Leven, B.-P. Koch and B. Pompe, "Chaos In Dissipativen Systemen," *Vieweg & Sohn*, Braunschweig, 1989.
14. Ya. B. Pesin, "Characteristic lyapunov exponents and smooth ergodic theory," *Russ. Math. Surveys* **32**, 55, 1977.

Stability of Hybrid Systems*

Mikhail Kourjanski and Pravin Varaiya

Department of Electrical Engineering and Computer Science
University of California at Berkeley
Berkeley, California 94720
{michaelk, varaiya}@eecs.berkeley.edu

Abstract. Hybrid systems combine discrete and continuous behavior. We study properties of trajectories of a rectangular hybrid system in which the discrete state goes through a loop. This system is viable if there exists an infinite trajectory starting from some state. We show that the system is viable if and only if it has a limit cycle or fixed point. The set of fixed points is a polyhedron. The viability kernel may not be a polyhedron. However, under a "controllability" condition, the viability kernel is a polyhedron.

1 Introduction

Hybrid systems (HS) couple discrete and continuous dynamics. The state of the system is a pair—the discrete state and the continuous state. Within each discrete state, the continuous state obeys a dynamical law until an event occurs. Then the discrete state changes instantaneously; in addition there may be a reset of the continuous state.

The continuous dynamics are represented by constant differential inclusions. Each discrete state can be identified with an "enabling zone," the inclusion, and the reset map. When the continuous state trajectory enters the enabling zone, the condition for a transition of the discrete state is satisfied. (Thus the enabling set is a "guard.") The reset map is given by an affine map.

The control of the system is achieved via the choice of an admissible velocity, a switching point within the enabling zone, and an admissible reset value.

In this paper we study properties of systems with a predefined order of enabling zones. In other words, the discrete states form a finite chain or a loop. The study of a finite chain leads to a problem of convex programming. When the system permits a loop, there arises the question of the existence of a fixed point (limit cycle) and its stability.

Most results presented here use a general assumption of convexity and compactness of the controls; but special attention is paid to "rectangular" systems where the controls belong to the sets described by linear inequalities, especially rectangles ([1], [4], [7], [8]).

* Research supported by NSF Grant ECS9417370. The authors are grateful to Mireille Broucke for posing the questions addressed here, and to Anuj Puri for discussion.

2 Fixed Chain Hybrid System (FCHS)

2.1 FCHS Setting

Discrete states are triples of the form [EZ, RS, DYN]. EZ is a zone which enables an abrupt change in dynamics and reset. RS is a reset map which specifies the change of state. DYN is the new inclusion to be used after the discrete change. The control of the system is implemented via the choice of the switching point within the EZs, admissible velocity, and admissible resets. The order in which the trajectory visits the EZs is given; and the reset is applied at a switching point of our choice followed by the change of the continuous dynamics. Each EZ is a convex compact set of $\mathbb{R}^N$. RS is a linear map applied to the continuous state. The continuous dynamics is described by the differential inclusion

$$\dot{x} \in U_i, \tag{1}$$

where i is the discrete state and U_i is a convex compact set in $\mathbb{R}^N$. We choose a starting point within Z_1—the first EZ of the chain, apply the reset, and immediately start to move with the dynamics given by (1). If we can reach points in Z_2 then we choose a switching point within Z_2; when we are in Z_2 we apply the reset map and follow the next dynamics towards Z_3; and so on. Our main interest is to evaluate the reach set of the system. The *reach sets* are the subsets of the Z_i that can be reached from Z_1 in finite time. We distinguish two situations:

- Finite chain of EZs: the question is whether the final EZ of the chain $Z_1, ..., Z_M$ is reachable?
- Looping phenomenon, $Z_1 \equiv Z_M$: the question is the existence of a "fixed point" (which is a point or a limit cycle as we will see later) of the system, and its stability.

2.2 Reduction to Multistage Discrete Dynamic System

We show that FCHS is a special type of discrete dynamic system. First we describe the one–step evolution of the FCHS. The set reachable from 0 using (1) is the convex cone

$$C_i = \cup_{\tau \geq 0} \, \tau U_i \ . \tag{2}$$

The set of points reachable from $X \subset \mathbb{R}^N$ using (1) is

$$F_i^c(X) = X + C_i. \tag{3}$$

Departing from $x \in Z_i$ we apply the reset which is specified in the form

$$F_i^{rs}(x) = \mathcal{A}_i x + R_i, \tag{4}$$

where $\mathcal{A}_i$ is a linear "diagonal" operator, and R_i are the admissible "resets." The operator $\mathcal{A}_i$ may be not invertible. The set reachable from Z_1 is given by the composition

$$Y_1(Z_1) = F_1^c F_1^{rs}(Z_1). \tag{5}$$

The reach set for the chain $\{Z_1, Z_2\}$ is the set–valued map $T_1^+(Z_1) = Y_1 \cap Z_2$. The backward map $T_1^-(Z_2)$ gives all points in Z_1 from which there starts a feasible trajectory for the chain $\{Z_1, Z_2\}$:

$$T_1^-(Z_2) = A_1^{-1}[Z_2 - C_1 - R_1] \cap Z_1. \tag{6}$$

Following these definitions we note that

$$T_1^+(Z_1) = T_1^+(T_1^-(Z_2)), \quad T_1^-(Z_2) = T_1^-(T_1^+(Z_1)). \tag{7}$$

We extend this approach with the following maps:

$$T_{i,j} = \begin{cases} (i < j) \text{ Reach set in } Z_j \text{ starting from } Z_i \\ (i > j) \text{ Backward mapping from } Z_i \text{ to } Z_j \\ (i = j) \text{ Identity mapping on } Z_i \end{cases} \tag{8}$$

Using these definitions we can represent the FCHS as a discrete dynamic system:

$$x(i+1) = A_i x(i) + u(i)t_i + r(i), \; i = 1, ..., M. \tag{9}$$

Here A_i is a $N \times N$ diagonal matrix. The elements on the diagonal represent the scaling factor and $r(i)$ is a vector of resets. M is the length of the chain. The elements of the system should satisfy the following constraints:

$$x(i) \in Z_i, \; u(i) \in U_i, \; r(i) \in R_i, \; t_i \geq 0, \tag{10}$$

where Z_i, U_i, R_i are specified convex compact sets.
The scalar form of (9) is

$$\begin{aligned} x_j(i+1) &= a_j(i)x_j(i) + u_{N+1}(i)u_j(i) + r_j(i), \; j = 1, ..., N; \\ x_{N+1}(i+1) &= x_{N+1}(i) + u_{N+1}(i). \end{aligned} \tag{11}$$

The coordinate x_{N+1} represents time. A sequence $x(i)$, $i = 1, ...M$, which satisfies (9)–(10) is called a *trajectory* of the FCHS.

2.3 Rectangular Hybrid Systems and Linear Programming

We pay special attention to the case of the rectangular FCHS (RFCHS). In this case the sets in (10) are rectangles. Each finite–length RFCHS is represented by a finite number of linear inequalities. Denote:

t_i – instants of switching
x_{ij} – switching points, $i = 1, ..., M, \; j = 1, ..., N$,
Z^l_{ij}, Z^u_{ij} – enabling zones
U^l_{ij}, U^u_{ij} – velocity limitations
R^l_{ij}, R^u_{ij} – reset additions

Starting from the first EZ of the given chain

$$Z^l_{1j} \leq x_{1j} \leq Z^u_{1j}, \; j = 1, ..., N, \tag{12}$$

we proceed further through the chain of EZs ($m = 2, ..., M$) subject to the following:

$$Z^l_{mj} \le x_{mj} \le Z^u_{mj} \tag{13}$$

$$a_{(m-1)j}x_{(m-1)j} + U^l_{mj}t_m \le x_{mj} - r_{(m-1)j} \le a_{(m-1)j}x_{(m-1)j} + U^u_{mj}t_m \tag{14}$$

$$R^l_{(m-1)j} \le r_{(m-1)j} \le R^u_{(m-1)j} \tag{15}$$

$$j = 1, ..., N$$

The feasibility of the finite–length RFCHS can be checked by Linear Programming techniques. The resulting LP system is a "staircase-structured" problem; the relevant methods can be found in [6].

Remark. For each *fixed* set of $\{t_i\}$, $i = 1, ..., M$, the reachability set within each of the Z_i, $i = 1, ..., M$, is a rectangle.

3 Loops in FCHS

Consider the case $Z_1 \equiv Z_M$.

Definition 1. A *loop* is a trajectory which starts and ends in the same EZ. A *simple loop* is a loop in which each EZ is visited exactly once during the loop. A *fixed loop* is a loop which ends precisely at its own starting point of a given EZ: $x(M) = x(1)$. A *looping trajectory* is a finite or infinite number of trajectories

$$\{x(i)\}|_1, \{x(i)\}|_2, ..., \{x(i)\}|_L,$$

(L may be equal to infinity), with

$$x(M)|_1 = x(1)|_2, ..., x(M)|_{l-1} = x(1)|_l, ..., x(M)|_{L-1} = x(1)|_L.$$

The looping trajectory is *viable* iff it is infinite ($L = \infty$ in the definition of a looping trajectory). A *point is viable* if there exists a viable trajectory starting from that point.

The phase portrait of the FCHS is in the Euclidean space $\mathbb{R}^N$. For each starting point $\bar{x}(1)$ within Z_1, the first EZ of the chain, there is a reach set $F(\bar{x}(1)) \subset Z_1$. Here F is a point-to-set mapping. The reach set for each starting point is a convex compact set since it is an intersection of a closed convex cone with a convex compact EZ. We need the following lemma.

Lemma 2. *The set of viable points is convex and compact.*

Proof. Follows from definition of compactness and convexity.

Definition 3. The set $K \subset Z$ of all viable points is called *the viability kernel* [2], [3].

Theorem 4. *The FCHS has a viable point iff it has a fixed point.*

Proof. Suppose there is a non-empty viability kernel K. Then K is a convex compact set, $K \subset Z_1$. There exists a set-valued function F_K which is closed and maps each point $x \in K$ to the nonempty convex compact subset of K:

$$F_K(x) = F(x) \cap K.$$

This set is not empty since x is viable. By the Kakutani fixed point theorem there is a point x^* such that $x^* \in F_K(x^*)$. But this immediately means that there is a set of velocities, switching points, times and reset additions such that:

$$x^*(2) = A(1)x^*(1) + u^*(1)t^*(1) + r^*(1);$$

$$\vdots$$

$$x^*(1) = A(M-1)x^*(M-1) + u^*(M-1)t^*(M-1) + r^*(M-1)$$

and all these equalities satisfy (10). We can repeat this simple fixed loop infinitely. This is a fixed point of the system. Now suppose that there is a fixed point in the system. It is obvious that this is a viable trajectory.

Definition 5. An *FP-set* is a set of all fixed points of the system within one Z_i.

Corollary 6. *If there is no fixed point in the FCHS then each looping trajectory can be extended through only a finite number of simple loops (L is finite).*

Corollary 7. *The FP-set in the RFCHS can be determined by solving a finite number of LP problems as in subsection 2.3 by adding the condition $x_{1j} = x_{Mj}$, $j = 1, ..., N$ to the conditions (12)-(15).*

Note that an FP-set is always a polyhedron.

4 Stability

4.1 Single–valued FCHS

First we investigate stability properties of a single–valued subclass of FCHS. No control is available in this case, i.e., the U_i are singletons.

Definition 8. The FCHS is *single-valued* iff for each starting point x^0 its image $T_{1,j}(x^0)$ is either a single point or an empty set for every $j > 1$.

We assume the EZs are convex polyhedra contained in $(N-1)$-dimensional hyperplanes; the velocities are constants; the velocity vectors make a non-zero angle with the relevant EZs and the reset additions are constants. This design provides us with a single–valued FCHS: there is a unique single–valued trajectory for each starting point. The fixed points of a single–valued FCHS are then the solutions to a linear system

$$x = Hx + D, \tag{16}$$

where H is a square matrix and D is a vector. This system may have one, many or no solution at all; but for a fixed point to exist, the solution of (16) should also satisfy all state constraints of FCHS. We will now try to investigate and characterize the stability properties of the system.

Theorem 9. *Suppose there is a fixed point in the FCHS. The stability properties of a single–valued FCHS are then characterized by a $(N-1)$–dimensional linear return map.*

Proof. Following the discrete dynamic representation (9) we construct a composition of the linear steps which is also linear. Without loss of generality we may consider one of the EZs to be an oriented hyperplane (parallel to $(N-1)$ coordinate axes). Taking the composition of transformations of a perturbation from a fixed point through the loop we have a system

$$\delta x(i+1) = G\,\delta x(i) \tag{17}$$

where G is a $(N-1)\times(N-1)$ matrix.

Corollary 10. *Consider all EZs to be oriented. The transformation of the perturbation $\delta x(i)$ through one step of single–valued RFCHS is*

$$\delta x(i) = \begin{pmatrix} \delta x_1^i \\ \vdots \\ \delta x_k^i = 0 \\ \vdots \\ \delta x_m^i \\ \vdots \\ \delta x_N^i \end{pmatrix} \rightarrow \begin{pmatrix} a_1^i \delta x_1^i - a_m^i \frac{u_1^i}{u_m^i} \delta x_m^i \\ \vdots \\ -a_k^i \frac{u_k^i}{u_m^i} \delta x_m^i \\ \vdots \\ a_m^i \delta x_k^i = 0 \\ \vdots \\ a_N^i \delta x_N^i - a_m^i \frac{u_N^i}{u_m^i} \delta x_m^i \end{pmatrix} = \delta x(i+1) \tag{18}$$

when $k \neq m$ — that is, when the coordinates of degeneracy of EZs are different. The perturbation $\delta x(i)$ is multiplied by the scaling factor when $k = m$.

The eigenvalues $\lambda_i,\ i = 1, ..., N-1$ of G characterize the stability of the single-valued FCHS. The system is *hyperbolic* if none of the eigenvalues has magnitude 1 [5].

4.2 An Example

Consider the following example. There are six discrete states and the continuous state is in $\mathbb{R}^3$. The EZs are two–dimensional rectangles with sides parallel to the coordinate axis. The reset map is identity.

```
DIMENSION 3
 STATE 1     EZONE (x1: 7..10;  x2: 5.5..9;  x3: 0.0)
             DYNAMICS (u1: -6; u2: 6; u3: 4)
 STATE 2     EZONE (x1: 0; x2: 11..19; x3: 1..9)
             DYNAMICS (u1: 4; u2: 6; u3: 2)
 STATE 3     EZONE (x1: 50..65; x2: 100; x3: 30..39)
             DYNAMICS (u1: -2; u2: -4; u3: 4)
 STATE 4     EZONE (x1: 30..39; x2: 50..59; x3: 80)
             DYNAMICS (u1: 2; u2: 2; u3: 3)
 STATE 5     EZONE (x1: 40; x2: 53..68; x3: 80..99)
             DYNAMICS (u1: -23; u2: -12; u3: -40)
 STATE 6     EZONE (x1: 16..25; x2: 50; x3: 50..63)
             DYNAMICS (u1: -9; u2: -36.1..-36; u3: -46..-45.9)
```

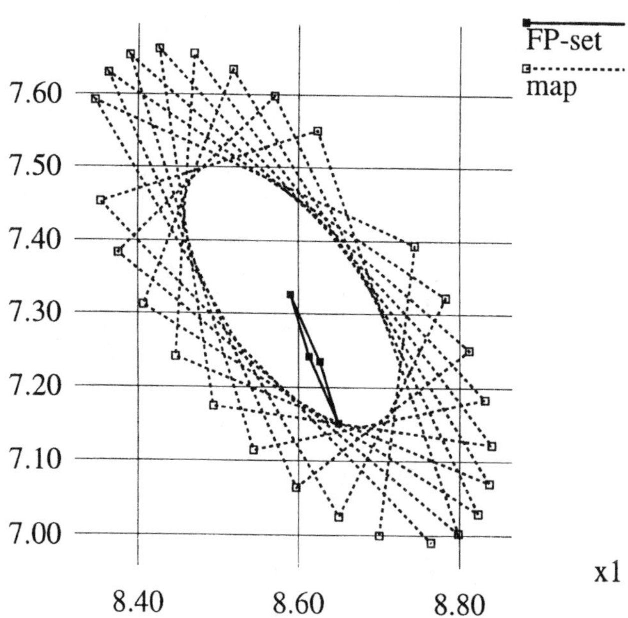

Fig. 1. Example: Poincare map of a stable trajectory; diamond-shaped FP-set

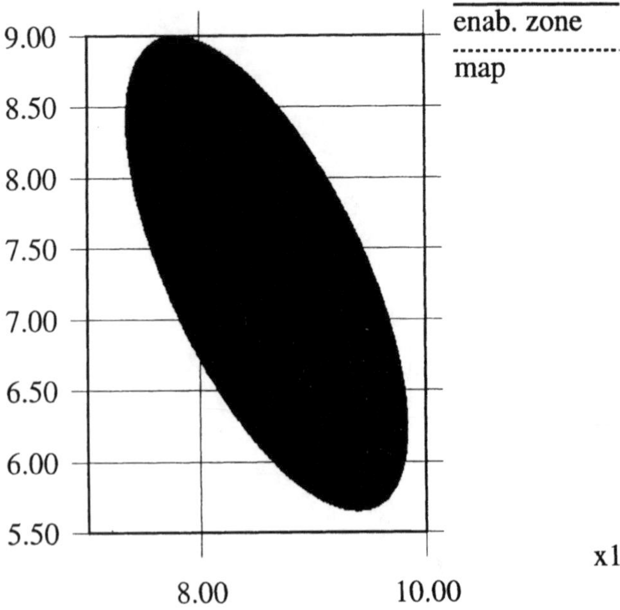

Fig. 2. Example: ellipsoidal viability kernel

There is a choice of admissible velocities only in state 6. There is a unique set of parameters (`u2: -36; u3: -46`), which gives stable (but not asymptotically stable!) eigenvalues. The characteristic matrix for this case is

$$G = \begin{pmatrix} -1.2005 & -0.8768 \\ 1.587 & 0.3261 \end{pmatrix}$$

The eigenvalues are $\lambda_{1,2} = -0.4372 \pm 0.8994i$; their magnitude is 1. The return map from the EZ of state 1 into itself for this case is shown in figure 1. The FP-set for the whole (set-valued) case is also shown in this picture. It is the thin diamond–shaped region. Let us investigate the shape of invariant curves of this example. Note that in fact it is a 2-dimensional linear recurrence:

$$x_{k+1} = ax_k + by_k, \quad y_{k+1} = cx_k + dy_k$$

The linear transformation

$$x = \alpha u + \beta v, \quad y = p_1 \alpha u + p_2 \beta v, \tag{19}$$

converts the initial recurrence into diagonal form

$$u_{k+1} = \lambda_1 u_k, \quad v_{k+1} = \lambda_2 v_k, \tag{20}$$

where α, β are constants, and

$$p_{1,2} = (\lambda_{1,2} - a)/b, \ b \neq 0; \qquad p_{1,2} = c/(\lambda_{1,2} - d), \ b = 0. \tag{21}$$

The eigenvalues are complex: $\lambda_{1,2} = \alpha \pm i\beta = \sigma e^{\pm i\phi}$. Here we apply one more transformation

$$\xi = u + iv, \quad \nu = -i(u - v) \tag{22}$$

which converts the complex–valued recurrence (20) into the real–valued canonical form:

$$\xi_{k+1} = \sigma(\xi_k \cos\phi - \nu_k \sin\phi), \ \nu_{k+1} = \sigma(\xi_k \sin\phi + \nu_k \cos\phi). \tag{23}$$

Consider the case $\sigma = 1$. The general form of the solution of the recurrence is

$$\xi_k = a\cos(n\phi + \phi_0), \ \nu_k = a\sin(n\phi + \phi_0), \ \xi_0 = a\cos\phi_0, \ \nu_0 = a\sin\phi_0. \tag{24}$$

This yields $\xi^2 + \nu^2 = a^2 = \xi_0^2 + \nu_0^2$. The invariant curves of (24) are the concentric circles and of the initial recurrence are the concentric ellipses. When the rotation angle is commensurable with 2π, the trajectories are closed l–periodic orbits (this is an exceptional case, or resonance). Otherwise the subsequent iterations cover the whole ellipse. Returning back to the single–valued FCHS sample system we note that each variation of the velocity parameters yields a variation of the fixed point. However the impact of those perturbations on the stability properties is somewhat different. Each transition in the system is from one oriented hyperplane to another. The variation (not shown in the example) of the velocity component whose coordinate is not degenerated during this transition, for example, `STATE 6; DYNAMICS { u1: 9`$\pm\delta$`}`, changes the rotation angle only[2]. This immediately follows from (18). Indeed the characteristic equation is

$$\lambda^2 + \eta\lambda + 1 + \zeta = 0 \tag{25}$$

— the variation above affects only η; $\zeta = 0$. Variations of $\eta \in (-2, 2)$ influence the rotation angle only. Variations of other velocity components affect ζ as well; this leads to abrupt change to asymptotically stable or unstable behavior.

In our example every fixed set of parameters gives an unstable system except for the unique extremal case `STATE 6;  DYNAMICS (u1: -9; u2: -36; u3: -46)`. Suppose the rotation angle is not commensurable with 2π. The viability kernel for this extremal stable case is an ellipse—which implies that it can not be represented by a finite number of set-valued operations over the initial data—such as union, intersection, sum and difference. The viability kernel is shown in figure 2. We note that there exists a sequence of non-viable points which converges to the viable point located on the boundary of the viability kernel, and the time for which a trajectory starting at each of the elements of the sequence is defined, grows to infinity. The viability kernel for all other fixed sets of parameters is a single (fixed!) point.

---

[2] Note that the viability kernel changes discontinuously with the variation of this parameter.

Returning to the original set-valued case, we note that its viability kernel *can not* be represented as a union of viability kernels of all single–valued cases. For example, the point (7.5, 7.6, 0) is not viable in any of the single–valued cases, but if the whole set of velocities is available then the dynamics

```
STATE 6;    DYNAMICS (u1: -9; u2: -36; u3: -45.9)
```

delivers it after 2 simple loops to the point (8.837483, 8.325626, 0) which is viable under the fixed stable set of velocities. This shows that the viability kernel for the whole set–valued case *is larger* than the union of viability kernels of all possible single–valued cases.

Next we provide sufficient conditions guaranteeing a finite procedure for evaluating of the viability kernel.

4.3 Set-valued Procedure for Viability Kernel

We first specify an iterative set-valued process to find the viability kernel. In fact, the viability kernel is a maximal invariant set—that is, for every point from this set there exists a trajectory which returns to this set. To fix notation, we choose the "first" enabling zone; the choice is irrelevant for the procedure. For each EZ we build a chain of subsets $Z_i = \mathcal{Z}_{i,0} \supset \mathcal{Z}_{i,1} \supset \ldots$ We define the forward and backward maps through one discrete state (see (7)) as

$$\tilde{T}_1^+(\mathcal{Z}_{1,k}) = Y_1(\mathcal{Z}_{1,k}) \cap \mathcal{Z}_{2,k}, \quad \tilde{T}_1^-(\mathcal{Z}_{2,k}) = \mathcal{A}_1^{-1}[\mathcal{Z}_{2,k} - C_1 - R_1] \cap \mathcal{Z}_{1,k}, \qquad (26)$$

and through the chain of states as

$$\tilde{T}_{i,j}^k = \begin{cases} (i < j) \text{ Reach set in } \mathcal{Z}_{j,k} \text{ starting from } \mathcal{Z}_{i,k} \\ (i > j) \text{ Backward mapping from } \mathcal{Z}_{i,k} \text{ to } \mathcal{Z}_{j,k} \\ (i = j) \text{ Identity mapping on } \mathcal{Z}_{i,k} \end{cases} \qquad (27)$$

Taking $E_{i,k} = \tilde{T}_{1,i}^k(\mathcal{Z}_{1,k})$ and $S_{i,k} = \tilde{T}_{M,i}^k(\mathcal{Z}_{M,k})$ we construct the next iteration of the procedure as $\mathcal{Z}_{i,k+1} = S_{i,k} \cap E_{i,k}$. Suppose that the viability kernel is non–empty. Then it is clear that $\mathcal{Z}_{i,\infty} = \cap_k \mathcal{Z}_{i,k}$ is the viability kernel. However $\mathcal{Z}_{i,\infty}$ may not be a polyhedron even though the $\mathcal{Z}_{i,k}$ is a polyhedron. The only situations which may occur over each iteration of the procedure are the following:

a $S_{1,k} = E_{1,k}$
b $E_{1,k} \subset S_{1,k}$
c $S_{1,k} \subset E_{1,k}$
d $S_{1,k} \cap E_{1,k} \neq \emptyset$

Conditions **[a]**,**[b]** mean the viability kernel is found (it is $T_{M,1}(S_{1,k})$); in these cases the procedure stops after a finite numbers of steps. Conditions **[c]**,**[d]** require further iterations.

The procedure builds an exterior approximation of a viability kernel with polyhedra. The example in section 4.2 shows that an infinite number of iterations may occur. Note: if there exist a number K^* such that no nonviable point is feasible after K^* loops then the procedure will stop after a finite number of iterations.

Proposition 11. *Suppose there is a transition* $(Z_{i_*} \to Z_{i_*+1})$ *(that is a discrete state* i_**) such that:*

$$\exists \rho_* \ \forall x \in Z_{i_*+1}, \forall y \in \{\mathcal{A}_{i_*}^{-1}[x - C_{i_*} - R_{i_*}] \cap Z_{i_*}\}$$

$$\left[Y_{i_*}(y) \cap \mathcal{A}_{i_*}^{-1}[x - C_{i_*} - R_{i_*}] \text{ contains a union of } \rho_*\text{-balls}\right].$$

Then the procedure will stop after a finite number of iterations.

The proof of this proposition can be derived from Theorem 5 of [3].

5 Conclusion

The study of rectangular hybrid systems has largely been concerned with the questions of verification. Those questions often are decidable because the hybrid system can be shown to be equivalent (in an appropriate sense) to a finite automaton. In this paper we consider the question of existence of fixed points (limit cycles) and their stability. We have shown that the set of fixed points is given by a finite set of linear inequalities. That set is non-empty if and only if there is a viable state, i.e., a state from which a trajectory can be continued for infinite time. These results bring together the question of hybrid system viability with that of the existence of a fixed point or limit cycle and the latter with stabilizability.

References

1. R. Alur, L. Fix and T.A. Henzinger. A Determinizable Class of Timed Automata. *Proc. 6th Workshop Computer-Aided Verification 1994*, LNCS 818, Springer-Verlag, 1994. pp. 1-13.
2. J.-P. Aubin. *Viability Theory* , Birkhäuser, 1991.
3. A. Deshpande and P. Varaiya. Viable Control of Hybrid Systems. *to appear.*
4. T.A. Henzinger, P. Kopka, A. Puri and P. Varaiya. What's decidable about hybrid automata?. *STOCS*, 1995.
5. A. Katok and B. Hasselblatt. *Introduction to the Modern Theory of Dynamical Systems.* Cambridge University Press, 1995.
6. J.L. Nazareth. *Computer Solution of Linear Programs.* Oxford University Press, 1987.
7. A. Olivero, J. Sifakis and S. Yovine. Using Abstractions for the Verification of Linear Hybrid Systems. *Proc. 6th Workshop Computer-Aided Verification 1994*, LNCS 818, Springer-Verlag, 1994. pp. 81-94.
8. A. Puri and P. Varaiya. Decidability of Hybrid Systems with Rectangular Differential Inclusions. *Proc. 6th Workshop Computer-Aided Verification 1994*, LNCS 818, Springer-Verlag, 1994. pp. 95-104.

Model and Stability of Hybrid Linear System

Hong Seong Park†, Young Sin Kim‡, Wook Hyun Kwon‡, and Sang Jeong Lee§

†: Dept. of Control and Instrumentation Engr.
Kangwon National University, Kangwon-do, 200-701, KOREA
E-mail : hspark@cc.kangwon.ac.kr

‡: Dept. of Control and Instrumentation Engr.
Seoul National University, Seoul 151-741, KOREA
E-mail : kys@isltg.snu.ac.kr

§: Dept. of Electronics Engineering
Chungnam National University, Daejeon 305-764, KOREA
E-mail : eesjl@cslab.chungnam.ac.kr

Abstract. This paper presents a hybrid model suitable for analysis of hybrid systems and for synthesis of hybrid controllers, and the linear hybrid system which combines continuous linear dynamics in each discrete state with discrete dynamics having the Markov property. The stochastic stability of the linear hybrid system is defined and the stability condition and the stabilizability condition is proposed. A simple example is given to illustrate the proposed framework.

1 Introduction

Hybrid systems are those that involve both continuous variable dynamic systems(CVDS) and discrete event dynamic systems(DEDS). Many examples can be found in various chemical plants, manufacturing systems, and intelligent vehicle highway systems. Hybrid systems also arise whenever logical decision making is combined with the generation of continuous control laws, for instance, in boiler control systems using a gain-scheduled controller. The structure and parameters of hybrid systems can change according to events such as switching functions and the change of operation condition. Conventional control theories can tackle the problem of analysis and control synthesis for such systems: for example, the variable structure control [1, 2] and jump linear system [15]. However, in order to control both CVDS and DEDS in hybrid systems simultaneously, it is natural to resort to a hybrid controller consisting of three part: a control part for CVDS, a control part for DEDS and a interface part governing ther interaction between the two.

There has been a considerable effort to develop theoretical frameworks and models for hybrid systems. Benveniste [2] and Brockett [16] presented the model for hybrid systems using the language. Holloway [5] presented a class of models for on-line monitoring of complex system containing both continuous dynamics and discrete dynamics. Kohn [7] discussed a formal model for the control of autonomous dynamic systems, in which multiple decision makers control the plant and provides a framework to represent the interaction between the continuous and discrete subsystems. Lemmon [8] suggested sufficient conditions on DES/CVDS interface which guarantee the existence of a supervisor which control the plant and shows that this interface can control the continuous-time plant using an inductive inference. Peleties [10] presented a hybrid system model in which the discrete dynamics are modeled by Petri-net. Stiver [11] and Lennartson [17] presented a model of the hybrid control system with the DES controller. Stiver [12] suggested the controller design method for hybrid systems, where concepts of the controllability and of the supremal controllable sublanguage developed by Ramadge and Wonham [14, 13] were used and the hybrid controller was similar to the supervisor for DES. Branicky [3] discussed a framework for hybrid control system in which differential equations and finite automaton interacted and the fuzzy controller was used for the analysis of differential equations. Lu [9] considered the dynamics of hybrid system as sets of dynamics of continuous systems switching according to discrete states changed by events and discussed optimal control design for hybrid systems.

This paper considers the linear hybrid sysem composed of the linear CVDS in each discrete state and DEDS having the Markov property in the sojourn time of each state. The paper is organized as follows. Section 2 details the hybrid model for linear hybrid systems. In order to formulate the hybrid model the hybrid state space is defined as the direct sum of the conventional continuous state space and a discrete state space. The discrete state is defined to include not only the purely discrete stae of DEDS but also the partitioned continuous state of CVDS. Also introduced is the notion of stochastic stability for the linear hybrid system, which is a natural expansion of that for jump linear systems [15]. The condition for the linear hybrid system to be stochastically stable is given. In section 3, we propose a framework of the hybrid controller which consists of a supervisor, a conventional continuous controller and an interface between the two. The supervisor controls DEDS and CVDS as well, while the continuous controller governs CVDS only. A sufficient condition for stabilizability is also given. In section 4, a simple example illustrates the application of the proposed framework. Finally, some concluding remarks are given in section 5.

2 Hybrid Model for Linear Hybrid System

The primary purpose of hybrid modeling is to synthesis a hybrid controller. A possible approach is to model the plant as CVDS and the supervisor as DEDS. This framework has been recently suggested and use synthesizing controllers [18]. However, the plant itself may have discrete event features. The structure and parameters of the plant can change accoding to events such as switching functions and different operation conditions. Hence, the plant model need to incorporate both continuous variable dynamics and discrete event dynamics, that is, it should be hybrid one. The hybrid state of the hybrid system consists of the continuous state and the discrete state. The continuous state is defined in the common way and belongs to R^n. The discrete state consists of the purely discrete state and the partitioned continuous state. Transition from one partitioned continuous sate to another can be caused by various events, for example, the change of operating conditions in CVDS.

Definition 2.1 (Continuous state)
Given an initial time t_o, a function $x : [t_o, \infty) \rightarrow R^n$ is a continuous state in R^n if $x(t)$ is right continuous.

Definition 2.2 (Discrete state)
Given a nonempty set Q and an initial time t_0, a function $q : [t_0, \infty) \rightarrow Q$ is a discrete state in Q.

We will denote the purely discrete state and the partitioned continuous state by q_i and q_{ix_j}, respectively. If $q_i \in S_i \subset R^n$ and $q_{ix_j} \in S_{ij} \subset R^n$, then $\bigcup_j S_{ij} = S_i$, $\bigcup_i S_i = R^n$, $S_i \bigcap S_j = \phi$ for $i \neq j$ and $S_{ik} \bigcap S_{il} = \phi$ for $k \neq l$. Fig. 1 shows the relationship between the purely discrete state and the partitioned continuous state.

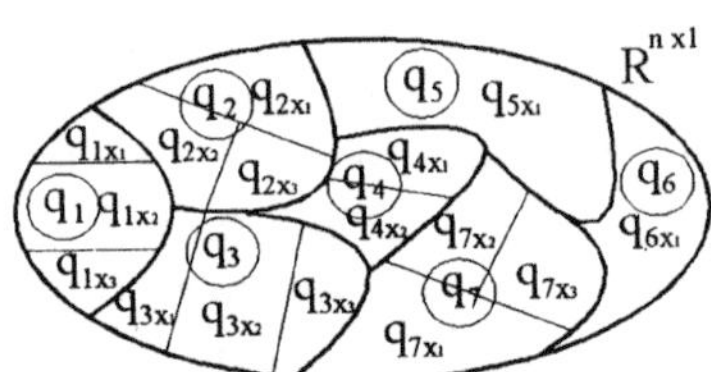

Fig. 1. Relationship between the purely discrete state and the partitioned continuous state

The transition from q_{ix_j} to q_{ix_k} represents the change in the physical mode, for example, the change in continuous dynamics due to different operating conditions. The transition from q_i to q_j is caused by a conventional event defined by [13, 14]. In this paper, the conventional event is called the discrete event while the change in the physcal mode, which will result in the transition between the partitioned state, is called the mode event. We will now define the event including the both.

Definition 2.3 (Event)
Given two nonempty sets Q and Σ_1, a null symbol $\epsilon \notin \Sigma_1$, and an initial time t_0, a function

$$\sigma : [t_0, \infty) \to \Sigma$$

is an event in $\Sigma = \Sigma_1 \bigcup \{\epsilon\}$ and characterized by

$$\begin{cases} \sigma(t) = \epsilon & \text{if } t = t_0 \text{ or } q(t) = q(t^-) \\ \sigma(t) \in \Sigma_1 & \text{otherwise} \end{cases} \tag{1}$$

where $q \in Q$ denotes the discrete state.

The hybrid state is a pair of the continuous state $x(t)$ and the discrete state, that is, $h(t) = (x(t), q(t))$. Then a hybrid model of linear hybrid systems can be expressed by

$$\left.\begin{matrix} \dot{x}(t) = f(x(t), q(t), t) \cdot x(t) \\ (Q, \Sigma, \delta, q_0, Q_m) \end{matrix}\right\} \tag{2}$$

where Q, Σ and Q_m denote the set of discrete states, the set of events and the set of marked discrete states, respectively; f is a continuous function $f : R^n \times Q \times R^+ \to R^n$, δ is the transition function $\delta : \Sigma \times Q \to Q$ so that $q(t^+) = \delta(q(t^-), \sigma(t))$, and the initial state is (x_0, σ_o).

It can be said that the stable state of the hybrid system means one that the discrete event system mainly exist in Q_m and the continuous dynamic system is in the equilibrium state. For the hybrid system in (2), we can naurally expand the concept of the sochastic stability for jump linear system [15].

Definition 2.5 (stochastic stability of hybrid systems)
For system (2), the equilibrium point $(0, q_l)$ $(q_l \in Q_m)$ is stochastically hybrid-stable if for any (x_0, q_0)

$$\begin{aligned} &\text{(i)} \quad \lim_{t \to \infty} P(q(t) \notin Q_m) \to 0 \\ &\text{(ii)} \int_0^\infty E\{\| x(t, x_0, w) \|^2\} dt < +\infty \end{aligned}$$

where w is one sample discrete state sequence in sequences satisfying (i).

In order to simplify the analysis of the hybrid system, we make the following assumptions:

($A1$) x(t) and q(t) are jointly Markovian.

($A2$) q(t) is a finite state homogeneous Markov process.

($A3$) Events do not occur simultaneously.

($A4$) Transition probabilities by discrete events are given.

($A5$) All events must be observed.

Note that the state sequence is equivalent to the event sequence if the initial discrete state is known and all event are observed. Therefore, the hybrid model (2) can be written as

$$\left.\begin{array}{l}\dot{x}(t) = A(q(t),t)\cdot x(t)\\ (Q,\Sigma,\delta,q_0,Q_m)\end{array}\right\} \qquad (3)$$

where $A(q(t),t) : Q \times R^+ \rightarrow R^{n\times n}$.

Note that the hybrid model (3) is linear when $q(t)$ is given. That is, the continuous dynamics can be expressed by

$$\dot{x}(t) = \begin{cases} A_0 x(t) \text{ if } q(t) = q_0 \\ \vdots \\ A_m x(t) \text{ if } q(t) = q_m \end{cases} \qquad (4)$$

where $A_i \in R^{n\times n}$ and $q_i \in Q$.

From the assumption (A1), it can be said that the continuous state sojourns in the discrete state q_i for a specified duration of time exponentially distributed with the parameter μ_i. Suppose that the continuous state jumps to the discrete state q_j with the probability p_{ij}. Then the continuous state sojourns in q_j for a specified duration of time exponentially distributed with μ_j. From now on, the subscript i is assumed to be associated with the discrete state q_i. The sequence of states is denoted by $\{q_i\}$, and the corresponding event sequence is denoted by $\{\sigma_i\}$. The sojourn time of q_i is denoted by τ^i having independent exponential distribution with parameters μ_i.

Let t_k denote the occurrence time of the k-*th* event. Then

$$t_k = \tau^{(0)} + \tau^{(1)} + \cdots + \tau^{(k-1)}$$

and the characteristic function $\Phi(t)$ of (3) may be written as

$$\Phi(t) = e^{A_{q_k}(t-t_k)} \cdot e^{A_{q_{k-1}}\tau^{(k-1)}} \cdots e^{A_{q_0}\tau^{(0)}} . \qquad (5)$$

for $t \in [t_k, t_{k+1})$. From these properties, we can establish the stability condition for linear hybrid system with Markov property.

Proposition 2.1

The hybrid system (3) is stochastically hybrid stable if
(i) all discrete states are coaccessible, the steady state probability $P(q(t) \in Q - Q_m)$ is sufficiently less than the steady state probability $P(q'(t) \in Q_m)$, and
(ii) there exist positive definite matrices M_j s.t.

$$-\mu_i M_i + A_i \sum_{j\neq i} p_{ij}\mu_i M_j + A_i' M_i + M_i A_i = -I$$

where $i, j = 1, 2, \cdots$ and I is the identity matrix.

Proof:

The proof will be explained briefly. To satisfy (i), the hybrid system always exists in the states in Q_m or it should be able to return to the states in Q_m though it enters into the states in $Q - Q_m$. If the steady state probability $P(q \in Q_m)$

is sufficiently larger than the probability $P(q \in Q - Q_m)$, the former holds. And if all states in Q coaccessible, the latter holds. (ii) is the result of the stability condition of jump linear system [15].

Actually, there can be some relation between the condition (i) and the conditon (ii) in Proposition 2.1. Though the continuous dynamics is unstable in some states in Q_m, the hybrid system can be stable if the hybrid system sojourns during the sufficiently small time in those states. This condition may mean that the probabilities being those states are sufficiently small.

Till now, we have considered the dynamics and the stability of hybrid system. It can be thought that hybrid systems presented in this paper is general. In next section, a framework of hybrid control system using the plant model shown in this section will be presented and the stabilizability condition will be discussed.

3 HYBRID CONTROL SYSTEMS

Given an open loop hybrid plant model such as (3), the hybrid controller must be designed to satisfy a specification for the desired closed loop behavior, which can be classified into two parts as follows:

(i) For the continuous dynamics, the continuous state (or output) must follow a given command.

(ii) For the discrete dynamics, the discrete state should belong to the set of the marked states.

From now on, a control law synthesis will be disscussed. Given the hybrid plant model, the hybrid controller guarantees the continuous control signal and the event control signal based on the previous hybrid states and the given specifications. For example, consider a level control system with on/off valves. If the control objective of this hybrid system is to keep the level at a desired level, the continuous control law and the discrete control law interacts to keep the desired level. That is, the hybrid controller controls simulataneously both the continuous variable and the event variable in order to achieve the desired objective. We will now define the event control signal and the continuous control signal. The former and the latter is the same as that used in the supervisory control [13] and that used in the conventional control theories, respectively.

Definition 3.1 (Event Control Signal)

$$u_e : ([t_0, \infty), \sigma) \to \{0, 1\}^{\Sigma}$$

is called the event control signal for the given set of discrete events Σ, the set $\{0,1\}^{\Sigma}$ and an initial time $t_0 \in R$, where $\sigma \in \Sigma$.

Definition 3.2 (Continuous Control Signal)
For the given nonempty R^m and an initial time $t_0 \in R$, a function

$$u_c : [t_0, \infty) - R^m$$

is called the continuous control signal in R^m on $[t_0, \infty)$.

The hybrid control signal is given by a pair of the continuous control signal and the event control signal. The hybrid control signal, the continuous control signal, and the event control signal are denoted by $u(\cdot), u_c(\cdot),$ *and* $u_e(\cdot)$, respectively.

The controlled linear hybrid system is represented by

$$\left.\begin{array}{l}\dot{x}(t) = A(q(t),t)x(t) + B(q(t),t)u_c(t) \\ (Q, \Gamma \times \Sigma, \delta_c, q_0, Q_m)\end{array}\right\} \tag{6}$$

where $B(\cdot) \in R^{n \times m}$, $u_c(\cdot) \in R^m$, $u_e(\cdot) \in \{0,1\}^{\Sigma}$, and $\delta_c : \Gamma \times \Sigma \times Q \to Q$ is the transition function according to

$$\delta_c(u_e(\cdot), \sigma, q) = \begin{cases} \delta(\sigma, q) & \text{if } \delta(\sigma, q)) \text{ is defined and } u_e(\cdot, \sigma) = 1 \\ undefined & \text{otherwise} \end{cases} \tag{7}$$

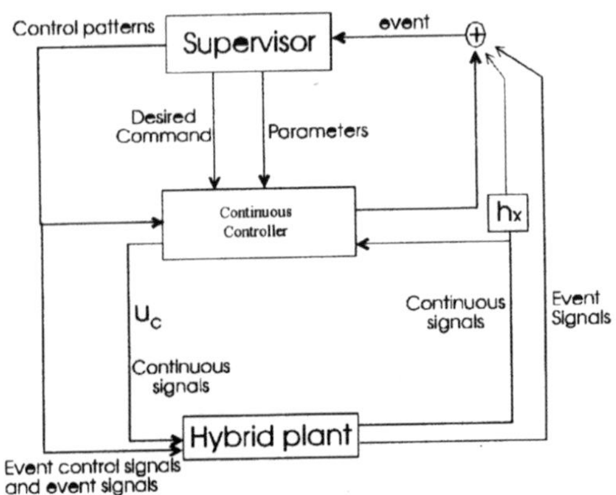

Fig. 2. Architecture for Hybrid Control

Fig. 2 shows the proposed scheme of the hybrid control system. The framework of hybrid controller shown in Fig.2 contains a supervisor, a continuous controller, and the interface part. There exist the desired command and the parameters set for the continuous controller in each discrete state in the supervisor. Especially, the supervisor use the mode events which can be incorporated into the framework by the mapping or the interface:

$$h_x : R^n \times R^n \to \Sigma \tag{8}$$

$$h_x(x(t), x(t^-)) = \begin{cases} \sigma \text{ if } \exists x(t^-) \in q \text{ and } x(t) \notin q \text{ s.t. } q \in Q \\ \epsilon \text{ otherwise} \end{cases} \tag{9}$$

A controller for the hybrid plant must control both the continuous variable and the event variable in order to obtain the desired performance measures. The hybrid system can be stabilizable using hybrid control signals and the stabilizability of hybrid systems is shown in Proposition 3.1.

Proposition 3.1

Let $u_c(q_i(t), t) = -K_i x(q_i(t))$ $(K_i \in R^{m\times n})$. Hybrid system is stabilizable if (i) there exists at least one string sequence S_k which makes the steady state probability $P(q(t) \notin Q_m)$ sufficiently smaller than the steady state probability $P(q(t) \in Q_m)$ or makes it zero.
(ii) For a string $s \in S_k$, there exist positive definite matrices M_j s.t.

$$-\mu_i M_i + \sum_{i\neq j} p_{ij}\mu_i M_j + (A_i - B_i K_i)' M_i + M_i(A_i - B_i K_i) = -I$$

where $p_{ij} = 0$ if the transition or event from q_i to q_j does not involve in S.
Proof:

We will explain the proof of Proposition 3.1 briefly. There exist the controllable events and the uncontrollable events in Proposition 3.1 while there exist only the uncontrollable events in Proposition 2.1 since all events are considered as uncontrollable events in case that the hybrid system has no control. Therefore, if there exists a string to be able to prohibit the hybrid system from entering the discrete states in $Q-Q_m$ or to be able to make the probability $P(q \in Q-Q_m)$ sufficiently small by control of the controllable events, we can design the supervisor to be stabilizable in view of (i) of Proposition 3.1. Finally, we find the continuous control law K_i for hybrid systems to be stabilizable. Using $u_c(\cdot) = -K_i x(q_i(t))$, the continuous part in (6) becomes

$$\dot{x} = (A_i - B_i K_i x(q_i(t)).$$

Using thes equation and the Proposition 2.1, we derive (ii) in Proposition 3.1.

Using the Proposition 3.1 we make the linear hybrid system stable. That is event control signal and the continuous control signal can be designed from the first condition and the second condition in Proposition 3.1, respectively. The former makes the supervisor.

4 An Example of Hybrid System

For an example, a simple model for hybrid system is shown in Fig. 3. λ_{ij} denote the rate that the event σ_{ij} generates. Let Λ denote a vector

$$\Lambda = [\lambda_{12}\ \ \lambda_{21}\ \ \lambda_{23}\ \ \lambda_{25}\ \ \lambda_{32}\ \ \lambda_{34}\ \ \lambda_{43}\ \ \lambda_{45}\ \ \lambda_{52}\ \ \lambda_{54}\ \ \lambda_{56}\ \ \lambda_{64}\ \ \lambda_{67}],$$

and assume that

$$\Lambda = [2\ \ 1\ \ 2\ \ 4\ \ 0.3\ \ 0.3\ \ 1\ \ 3\ \ 1\ \ 2\ \ 1\ \ 1\ \ 1]$$

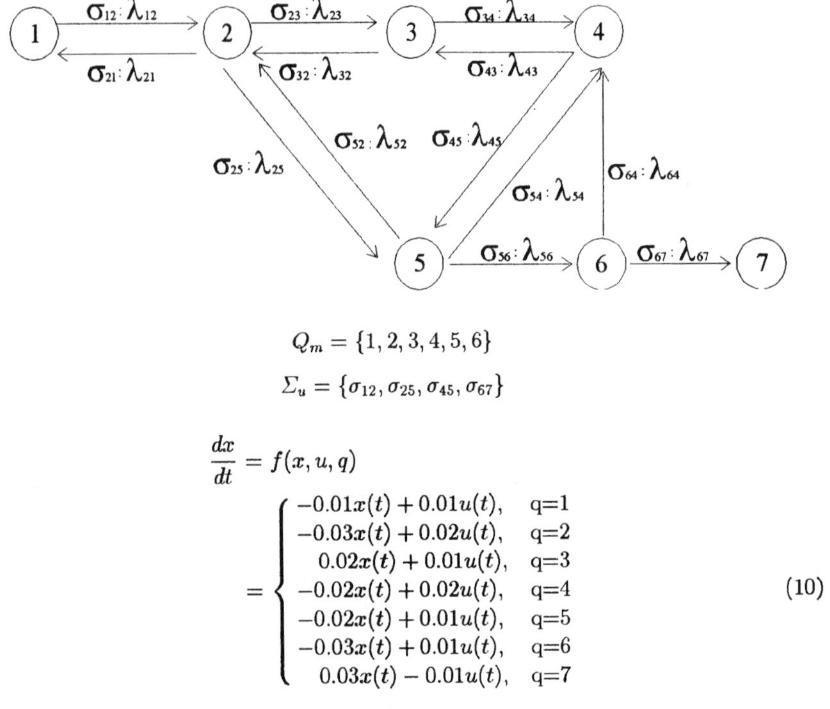

Fig. 3. Model of hybrid system

The continuous dynamics is stable in discrete states $q = 1, 2, 4, 5, 6$, but is unstable in discrete states $q = 3, 7$. And the discrete dynamics is unstable because there is a possibility to enter the discrete state $q = 7$, which is not an element of Q_m and is not coaccessible and then the system stays at the state $q = 7$ permanently. Therefore, the hybrid system shown in Fig.3 is unstable by the first condition of Proposition 2.1. Also, using the second condition of Proposition 2.1 we obtain M_3 and M_7 with negative values. That is, the hybrid system in Fig.3 is unstable by the second condition of Proposition 2.1. But in case that $\lambda_{34} = 0.8$ and $\lambda_{35} = 0.8$, M_3 is positive value while M_7 is negative value.

From now on consider the stabilizability of the hybrid system in Fig.3. First, we should design the supervisor to meet the first condition in Proposition 3.1. To do this, the occurrence of the event σ_{56} must be prohibited so that the discrete dynamics should not enter the state $q = 7$. Fig 4 is one example of such supervisors.

If the event σ_{56} is uncontrollable, the supervisor must be designed not to enter the state $q = 5$.

Finally, using the second condition in Proposition 3.1 we should find the

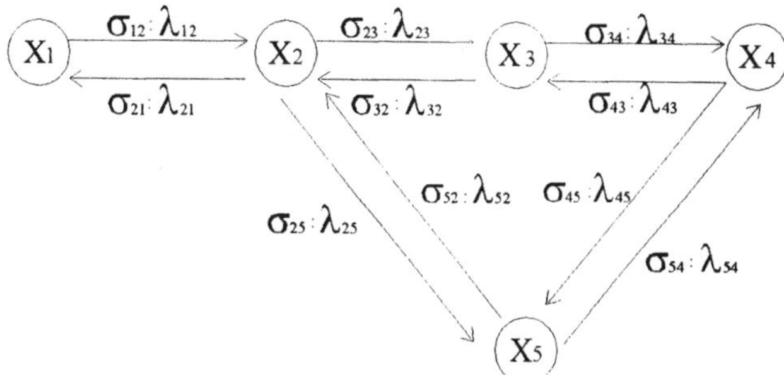

Fig. 4. An automaton of supervisor for the hybrid system in Fig.2

continuous control signal,

$$u_c(q_i(t),t) = -K_i x(q_i(t),t)$$

to be able to stabilize the hybrid system under the given supervisor and, where $i = 1,\cdots,5$ and i associates with the discrete state q_i. We found out the K_i, $(i = 1,\cdots,5)$ easily using MATLAB. If the K_i does not exist to stabilize the hybrid system under the given supervisor, we must redesign the supervisor. For example, consider the following supervisor in Fig.5. If the continuous dynamics is stable

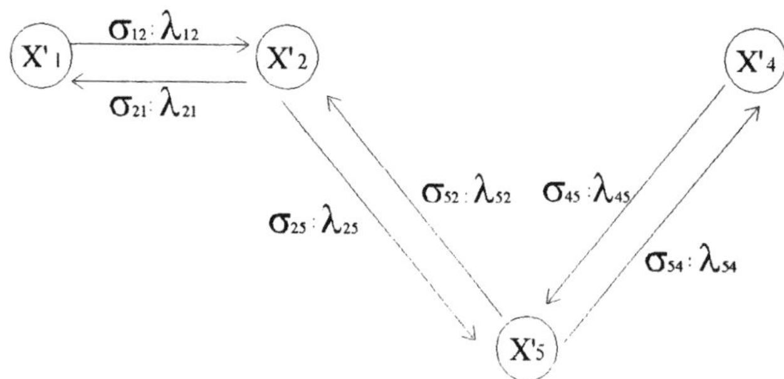

Fig. 5. Another supervisor

in all discrete states, the K_i can be found easily. This exmaple shows that the hybrid control system is stabilizable though the continuous dynamics is unstable in at least one discrete state.

Let the supervisor given in Fig.4 apply to the tracking problem. Fig.6 shows that the hybrid control system has the better performance than the gain scheduling method, where the states used in the gain schduling are $q = 1, 2, 4, 5$. This is due to whether or not the event control is used.

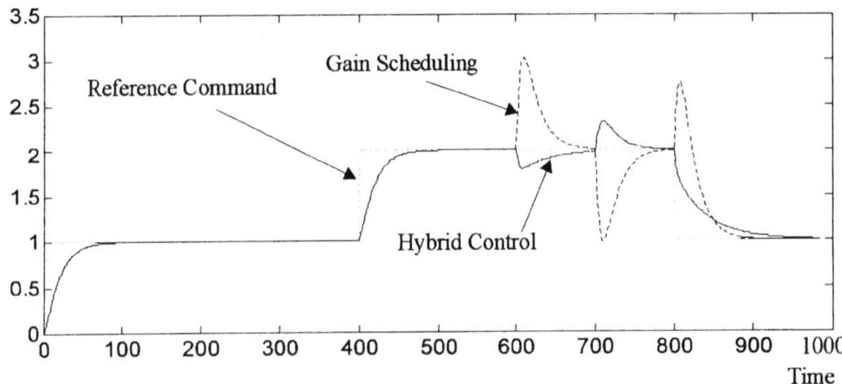

Fig. 6. Simulation result

5 CONCLUSION

This paper presented a hybrid model suitable for analysis of hybrid systems and for synthesis of hybrid controllers, and the linear hybrid system which combine continuous linear dynamics in each discrete state with discrete dynamics having the Markov property. The stochastic stability of the linear hybrid system is defined and the stability condition and the stabilizability condition are proposed. A simple example is given to illustrate the proposed framework. The example shows that the hybrid controller have the better performance than the conventional controller such as gain scheduling. It should be noted that the properties of hybrid system, such as controllability and observability, remains for further investigation.

References

1. K.J. Astrom and B. Wittenmark(1989), *Adaptive Control*, USA: Addison-Wesley Pub. Co.
2. A.Benveniste and P.Le Guernic(1990), *Hybrid Dynamical Systems Theory and the SIGNAL Language*, IEEE Trans. Automat. Contr., Vol. 35, No. 5, pp.535-546.
3. M.S. Branicky(1993), *Topology of Hybrid Systems*, Proc. of the 32th Conf. Decision and Control, pp.2309-2314.
4. C.M. *Özveren* and A.S. Willsky(1991), *Stability and Stabilizability of Discrete Event Dynamic*, J. of ACM, vol. 38, No. 3, pp. 730-752.
5. L.Holloway and B.Krogh(1992), *Properties of Behavioral Models for a Class of Hybrid Dynamical Systems*, Proc. of the 31th Conf. Decision and Control, pp.3752-3757.
6. J.Y. Hung, W. Gao, and J,C, Hung(1993), *Variable Structure Control : A Survey*, IEEE Trans. on Industrial Electronics, Vol. 40, No. 1, pp.2-22.
7. W.Kohn and A.Nerode(1992), *Multiple Agent Autonomous Hybrid Control Systems*, Proc. of the 31th Conf. Decision and Control, pp.2956-2966.

8. M.D. Lemmon, J.A. Stiver, and P.J. Antsaklis(1993), *Learning to Coordinate Control Polices of Hybrid Systems*, Proc. of American Control Conf., pp.31-35.
9. J.Lu, L.Liao, A.Nerode and J.H.Taylor(1993), *Optimal Control of Systems with Continuous and Discrete state*, Proc. of the 32th Conf. Decision and Control, pp.2292-2297.
10. P. Peleties and R. DeCarlo(1989), *A Modeling Strategy with Event Structures for Hybrid Systems*, Proc. of the 28th Conf. Decision and Control, pp.1308-1313.
11. J.A. Stiver and P.J. Antsaklis(1992), *Modeling and analysis of hybrid control Systems*, Proc. of the 31th Conf. Decision and Control, pp.3748-3751.
12. J.A. Stiver and P.J. Antsaklis(1993), *On the Controllability of Hybrid Control Systems*, Proc. of the 32th Conf. Decision and Control, pp.294-299.
13. P.J. Ramadge and W.M. Wonham(1987), *Supervisory Control of A Class of Discrete Event Processes*, SIAM J. Control and Optimization, Vol.25, No.1, pp.206-230.
14. W.M. Wonham and P.J. Ramadge(1987), *On the supremal controllable sublanguage of a given language*, SIAM J. Control and Optimization, Vol.25, No.3, pp.637-659
15. X. Feng, K.A. Loparo, Y. Ji, H.J. Chizeck(1992), *Stochastic Stability Properties of Jump linear Systems*, IEEE Tr. on AC, Vol. 37, No. 1, pp 38-53.
16. R. Brockett(1994), *Language Driven Hybrid Systems*, Proc. of the 33rd Conf. Decision and Control, pp.4210-4214.
17. B. Lennartson, B. Egardt, and M. Tittus(1994), *Hybrid Systems in Process Conrol*, Proc. of the 33rd Conf. Decision and Control, pp.3587-3592.
18. J.A. Stiver, P.J. Antsaklis, and M.D. Lemmon(1994), *Digital Control from a Hybrid Perspective*, Proc. of the 33rd Conf. Decision and Control, pp.4241-4246.

Interconnected Automata and Linear Systems: A Theoretical Framework in Discrete-Time

Eduardo D. Sontag*

Department of Mathematics
Rutgers University
New Brunswick, NJ 08903, USA
sontag@control.rutgers.edu

Abstract. This paper summarizes the definitions and several of the main results of an approach to hybrid systems, which combines finite automata and linear systems, developed by the author in the early 1980s. Some related more recent results are briefly mentioned as well.

1 Introduction - The Need for Hybrid Systems

Linear control theory is well-developed and highly sophisticated, and is widely applied in areas ranging from aerospace to automotive control. Linear systems provide highly accurate models of many physical systems; furthermore, the use of linear systems as "robust" controllers often allows the tolerance of even severe model nonlinearities and uncertainties. However, it remains a fact that many continuous physical processes cannot be satisfactorily modeled linearly, nor can be adequately regulated by means of linear controllers alone.

It has long been recognized that the control of more complex systems than those handled by the linear theory will require *switching mechanisms* (discontinuities) of various types; an early discussion of when such discontinuities are unavoidable can be found in [12]; see also the textbook [10], Section 4.8. Thus it is necessary to study hybrid designs in which the *controller* incorporates switching as well as linear elements.

As a parallel and independent development, the spread of consumer electronics has made relevant the control of devices which themselves include logical elements; in this context, it is essential to understand the *modeling* of mixed linear/switched mechanisms.

Automata theory and related areas of computer science provide a powerful set of tools for studying logical operations. Thus it is natural to attempt to develop a systems theory that combines aspects of automata and linear systems, exploring the capabilities of interconnections of both classes of systems. Given that each subclass in itself is already well-understood, it is interesting to ask how much more powerful such interconnections can be expected to be, and whether a systematic and elegant theoretical unifying framework can be developed.

---

* Supported in part by US Air Force Grant F49620-95-1-0101

There are two dual aspects in which the power of hybrid systems may be exhibited in this context:

- As *models of systems to be controlled*: one may expect that –via piecewise-linear approximations– it will be possible to model fairly arbitrary dynamic behavior with high precision.
- As *candidates for controllers:* the integration of logical and arithmetic capabilities allows performing control operations which neither finite automata nor finite-dimensional linear systems can carry out by themselves: finite automata cannot deal with all the information in continuous variables, while linear systems cannot exhibit switching behavior.

In the early 1980s, the author wrote the paper [7], whose purpose was to propose a theoretical foundation for such hybrid systems. This paper provided several basic theorems on representation and control, based on the use of a certain logic formalism together with elementary tools of "piecewise linear algebra" developed in the companion paper [8].

Given the resurgence of interest in hybrid systems, it seems timely to present an expository summary of a few of the main concepts and results in these papers, as well as to mention briefly some later work by the author and collaborators which dealt with the study of some particular subclasses. The presentation is informal; in particular, no proofs are given, since they are readily available from the cited literature. Since the audience for this conference –and surely for the proceedings– is so heterogeneous, many of the explanations are of necessity totally redundant for computer scientists, while many others are absolutely obvious to control theorists –apologies to the respective audiences are offered in advance.

Time Scales

In the context of systems with discontinuities, several technical difficulties arise when using continuous time models, including fundamental questions such as the lack of existence theorems guaranteeing solvability of evolution equations. These problems dissappear when using instead *discrete* time increments. As a matter of fact, because of the use of digital devices, modern control design is largely already turning to the latter. Through the device of sampling (measure the plant at discrete intervals, apply a constant control during the next period), continuous-time physical processes are seen by the regulator as a discrete-time system. Thus we took in [7] the point of view of defining hybrid systems only in discrete-time. Of course, the subject of interactions among components operating at distinct time scales is a challenging and most important area of research, with great practical consequences; on the other hand, the use of a common time scale allows one to focus on system-theoretic and control issues which are somewhat obscured when having to worry about additional technical problems.

Theory, Verification, Design

As already mentioned, the paper [7], as is the case with most papers in control theory, was by and large concerned with theory, as opposed to algorithm design. In general, research in control theory includes three complementary objectives: *theoretical analysis*, verification, and design. The first aspect deals with issues such as: (1) the analysis of potential capabilities of classes of systems, both as models of systems to be controlled (representational power) and as controllers, (2) the derivation of necessary and sufficient conditions characterizing properties such as controllability, (3) the classification of systems under natural equivalence relations (changes of variables, action of "feedback group"), or (4) theorems guaranteeing existence and uniqueness of "internal" black box representations of given "external" behaviors. One of the main issues is the reduction of what are *a priori* infinite-dimensional questions, posed in spaces of sequences or continuous functions (controls) –e.g.: is a system controllable; is a given trajectory optimal?– to finite-dimensional ones which can be expressed in terms of finitely many unknowns –e.g., is the controllability Lie algebra full rank? does the given trajectory satisfy the Euler-Lagrange equations?. Such theoretical analysis is not in principle focused on effective computational techniques; rather, obtaining "finite" characterizations is the first goal. Of course, computational feasibility is a desirable ultimate goal, but the problems of control theory are hard enough even before such issues are considered. This part of control theory has very much a "pure mathematical" flavor.

Regarding the issue of *verification*, at an abstract level, this includes all necessary-conditions results, such as the "verification theorems in optimal control" (the theory of the Hamilton-Jacobi equation and "regular synthesis"), but in the current context one means the search for *computational tests* for properties such as controllability or optimality. Typically, the types of nonlinear systems for which such algorithms have been developed are those for which theoretical analysis is very simple. In general, there are difficult open computational questions regarding the computational implementation of abstract mathematical characterizations of most systems properties. The topic of *design* includes the development of computer-aided tools. Linear systems theory has been extremely successful in the formulation and solution of nontrivial design problems and their practical implementation, but few computationally-friendly classes of nonlinear systems have been identified.

The class of behaviors that can be represented by the systems encompassed by the approach in [7] is extremely large, so it should come as no surprise that many of the basic verification and design objectives are NP-hard (or worse). Nonetheless, the basic theoretical framework is useful even from the computational point of view, since it affords an umbrella under which one can formulate subclasses of systems, and restricted problems, among which computational issues can be compared.

2 Piecewise Linear Systems as a Unifying Model

Recall that linear systems (discrete-time) are described by evolution equations of the type

$$x(t+1) = Ax(t) + Bu(t)\,, \tag{1}$$

(or, as we summarize by dropping the "t" argument and using "+" to denote a unit time-shift, $x^+ = Ax + Bu$). The state $x(t)$ evolves in some finite-dimensional

Euclidean space $\mathbb{R}^n$, control (or "input") values $u(t)$ are taken in some space $\mathbb{R}^m$, and $A \in \mathbb{R}^{n\times n}$ and $B \in \mathbb{R}^{n\times m}$ are matrices that define the system dynamics. Often, one adds a measurement or read-out map $y(t) = Cx(t)$ to this basic setup. Models of this type constitute the "bread and butter" of modern control design; their theory is well-understood (see e.g. [10]) and computer aided design packages are widely available.

Piecewise linear (or more precisely, piecewise-affine) systems arise if one has *different affine transitions in different parts of the state space and/or the input-value set*, and each of these pieces is described by linear equalities and inequalities. In addition, one may allow different affine measurement maps in different parts. Linear systems are a particular case (just one region). Multiple regions may appear naturally in many ways, as in the examples which we discuss next.

2.1 Some Motivating Examples

As a first illustration, consider the case in which there are logical decisions on input values. For instance, systems with actuators subject to saturation are quite common in applications: valves that cannot open more than a certain limit, control surfaces in aircraft that cannot be deflected more than a certain angle, and so forth. In such cases, a pure linear model (1) is not appropriate; instead one needs to consider a piecewise linear system of the type:

$$x^+ \;=\; Ax + B\,\mathrm{sat}\,(u) \tag{2}$$

where, setting the saturation levels at ± 1, we write $\mathrm{sat}\,(u_1,\ldots,u_m)$ for the vector whose ith component is u_i if $|u_i| \leq 1$ and $\mathrm{sign}\,(u_i)$ otherwise. (See e.g. [13] and references there, for such saturated-input systems, as well as feedback laws for them which combine saturations and linear transformations –for definiteness, the results in [13] are given for continuous-time systems, but analogous theorems hold in discrete-time.) Dually, it often the case that measurement devices may saturate, in which case it is proper to use $y = \mathrm{sat}\,(Cx)$ instead of linear observations $y = Cx$. (See e.g. [3, 4] for some recent results for such models.)

Alternatively, there might be a specified a hyperplane H in $\mathbb{R}^n$, and six matrices $A_0, A_+, A_-, B_0, B_+, B_-$, so that the state at time $t+1$ is $A_-x + B_-u$, $A_0x + B_0u$, or $A_+x + B_+u$ depending on whether the the current state $x(t)$ is on one side of the hyperplane, the hyperplane itself, or the opposite side respectively.

Yet another possibility is to have transitions that take different linear forms on different regions of the *joint* space of states of controls. For example, it may be the case that transitions that would result in a new state which falls in a certain set S are disallowed; in that case a special value, say $x = x_0$, which may indicate a flagged condition, should be produced. We model this situation by the transitions: $x^+ = Ax + Bu$ if $(x, u) \notin S$, and $x^+ = x_0$ if $(x, u) \in S$. A variation is that case in which underflows and overflows of state variables are truncated; this is represented (again taking max and min levels at ± 1 for simplicity) by an equation of the type

$$x^+ \;=\; \mathrm{sat}\,(Ax + Bu)\;. \tag{3}$$

It corresponds in the current context to systems in which $2n$ hyperplanes in $\mathbb{R}^n \times \mathbb{R}^m$ are given (namely, $A_ix + B_iu = \pm 1$, $i = 1, \ldots, n$, where A_i and B_i are the ith rows of A and B respectively) and transitions are expressed by a different affine map in each of the regions that result. These models are sometimes called "recurrent neural networks," treated for instance in [1, 2, 5, 6]; later we mention some results that hold specifically for this class.

Finally, an even further enrichment of the model is obtained if we allow, as part of the specification of the system, the addition of explicit constraints on controls and states. Thus, the state space and control-value sets are taken to be subsets $\mathcal{X}$ and $\mathcal{U}$ of $\mathbb{R}^n$ and $\mathbb{R}^m$ respectively, which indicate *a priori* restrictions on the allowed ranges of variables. To make the theory stay "piecewise linear", we ask that these sets be definable in terms of a finite number of linear equalities and inequalities. These are called *piecewise linear* (from now on, "PL" for short) sets in [7, 8] (a more formal definition is given below). Note that, in particular, all finite subsets of an Euclidean space, and all its linear subspaces, are PL sets. Given a PL set Z, a map $P : Z \to X$ into another PL set is said to be piecewise linear if there is a partition of Z into finitely many PL subsets $Z_1, \ldots, Z_k$ so that the restriction of P to each of the subsets Z_i is an affine map.

2.2 The Formal Setup

Thus a *piecewise linear system* is specified by a triple $(\mathcal{X}, \mathcal{U}, P)$ consisting of two PL sets $\mathcal{X}$ and $\mathcal{U}$ (the state space and control-value set, respectively) and a PL map $P : \mathcal{X} \times \mathcal{U} \to \mathcal{X}$. Dynamically, one interprets such a system as describing a recursion

$$x^+ = P(x, u) \tag{4}$$

for updating states on the basis of previous states and inputs. A PL measurement map $\mathcal{X} \to \mathcal{Y}$ into a set of possible output values is incorporated into the model if restrictions on observations need to be taken into account. We emphasize again that linear systems are a particular example of this concept. Finite automata are, too: we may identify the states of any given automaton with a finite set of integers $\{1, \ldots, k\}$, and the possible input values with a set $\{1, \ldots, \ell\}$; each of these two sets is a PL set (as a subset of $\mathbb{R}$) and the transition map of the automaton can be represented as a PL map. Later we remark why arbitrary interconnections of linear systems and automata also give rise to PL systems.

The definition of PL sets and PL maps in terms of partitions is cumbersome and unnecessarily complicated from a mathematical point of view. A far simpler but equivalent definition is as follows: The *PL subsets* of $\mathbb{R}^n$ are those belonging to the smallest Boolean algebra that contains all the open halfspaces of $\mathbb{R}^n$. A map $f : X \to Y$ between two PL subsets X and Y of $\mathbb{R}^a$ and $\mathbb{R}^b$ respectively, is a *PL map* if its graph is a PL subset of $\mathbb{R}^a \times \mathbb{R}^b$. (It is not hard to show that these definitions are equivalent to the informal definitions given earlier.)

By a *PL set* one means a PL subset of some $\mathbb{R}^n$; it is obvious how to define PL subsets of PL sets, isomorphisms of PL sets, etc; several "category theoretic" aspects of PL algebra are covered in [7].

It is useful at this point to introduce the first order theory of the real numbers with addition and order. That is, we take the first-order language L consisting of constants r and unary functions symbols $r(\cdot)$, for each real number r (the latter corresponding to "multiplication by the constant r"), as well as binary function symbol + and relation symbols $>$ and $=$. A basic fact is that a quantifier elimination theorem holds: *every set defined by a formula in L is a PL set.* That is to say, for any formula $\Phi(x)$ with n free variables $x = x_1, \ldots, x_n$, the set $\{x \mid \Phi(x)\}$ is a PL set. (Of course, we can enlarge the language by adding symbols for sets and maps already known to be PL.) This fact is very simple to establish (see e.g. [7]) and it provides a very convenient tool for establishing the basic theoretical properties of PL systems. Moreover, the proofs of these facts are constructive, in that the actual quantifier algorithm could be in principle used to compute feedback laws and the like.

Another constructively-proved fact is the following "global implicit function theorem" which can also be found in [7]): Assume that $\phi : X \times Y \to \mathbb{R}^n$ is a PL map, and assume that for each x the equation $\phi(x, y) = 0$ can be solved for y. Then there is a PL map $\pi : X \to Y$ so that $\phi(x, \pi(x)) = 0$ for all x. (Equivalently: for any PL subset $R \subseteq X \times Y$ with onto projection into X, there is a PL map $\pi : X \to Y$ (a "section") so that $(x, \phi(x)) \in R$ for all $x \in X$.) This fact is central to the existence of feedback controllers.

The main results in [8] regard the classification of PL sets (from which we may deduce, in turn, classification properties of PL systems); We describe them very briefly in this paragraph, which can be skipped without loss of continuity. Two PL sets X and Y are said to be isomorphic if there is a PL map $\phi : X \to Y$ which is one-to-one and onto (or, equivalently, since the graph of the inverse is the transpose of the original graph, ϕ has a PL inverse). Identifying isomorphic PL sets, the class of all such sets turns out to be endowed with a natural structure of semiring, which is isomorphic to the quotient of $\mathbb{N}[x, y]$ (polynomials in two variables with nonnegative integer coefficients) by the smallest congruence that includes the equations $x = 2x + 1$, $y^2 = 2y^2 + y$, and $y = x + y + 1$. This provides a characterization of the Grothendieck group of the category, as well as a generalization of the Euler characteristic for polyhedra. Moreover, it provides an algorithm for deciding if two PL sets (given in terms of formulas in L) are isomorphic, via results on decidability of word problems and results of Eilenberg and Schützenberger on finitely generated commutative monoids.

2.3 Interconnections

We mentioned above that arbitrary interconnections of linear systems and finite automata can be modeled by PL systems. This is quite obvious, but it is worth sketching a proof simply as an illustration of the use of the formalism afforded by the language L.

Assume given an automaton with finite state space Q and input-value space $T = \{t_1, \ldots, t_{|T|}\}$, also a finite set, and transition function $\delta : Q \times T \to Q$. We consider the case where the state q of the automaton is used to switch among $|Q|$ possible linear dynamics:

$$
\begin{aligned}
x^+ &= A_q x + B_q u + c_q \\
q^+ &= \delta(q, h(x, u))
\end{aligned}
$$

where $A_1, \ldots, A_q$ are matrices of size $n \times n$, $B_1, \ldots, B_q$ are matrices of size $n \times m$, and $c_1, \ldots, c_q$ are n-vectors, and where $h : \mathbb{R}^n \times \mathbb{R}^m \to T$ is a PL map (representing quantized observations of the linear systems). (As before, we are not displaying time arguments; for instance, in the first equation we mean $x(t+1) = A_{q(t)}x(t) + B_{q(t)}u(t) + c_{q(t)}$.) In order to represent this as a PL system, we first identify Q with the set of integers $\{1, \ldots, |Q|\}$. Then the system just described is a PL system with states in the PL subset $\mathbb{R}^n \times \{1, \ldots, |Q|\}$ of $\mathbb{R}^{n+1}$. To show this fact, we need to see that the update equation can be defined using the language L. Indeed, (x, q, u, x^+, q^+) belongs to the graph if and only if it belongs to one of the sets $F_{ij}(x, q, u, x^+, q^+)$, for some $i, j = 1, \ldots, |Q|$, where each such set is described by the sentence:

$$(q = i) \ \& \ \Phi_j(x, u) \ \& \ \left(x^+ - A_i x - B_i u - c_i = 0\right) \ \& \ \Delta_j(i, q^+) \,,$$

where $\Phi_j(x, u)$ is the property "$h(x, u) = t_j$" (described by a PL map), and Δ_j is characteristic function of the set of pairs so that $\delta(i, t_j) = k$.

Conversely, any PL system can be written as an interconnection of the above form, if the state space is $\mathbb{R}^n$ and the input set is $\mathbb{R}^m$. Indeed, assume that the original transitions have the form $x^+ = A_i x + B_i u + c_i$ if $x \in L_i$, for a given partition into k PL sets L_i. Then we may view these equations as those of a switched system, letting $Q := \{1, \ldots, k\}$ and using $h(x, u) := (j_1, \ldots, j_k)$ where for each i, j_i is the index of that set L_{j_i} for which $A_i x + B_i u + c_i \in L_{j_i}$; the update equation for the finite states is then given by $\delta(i, (j_1, \ldots, j_k)) = j_i$.

3 A Summary of Results From [7]

We now briefly summarize, in informal terms, some of the main results of the basic paper [7]. For reasons of space we must omit most precise definitions and statements, which can be found in that reference, and concentrate instead on providing the main intuitive ideas.

3.1 Finite-Time Problems

The first part of the paper covers topics that are extremely simple, at least once that the basic PL setup has been developed. It concerns problems that can be theoretically solved by simple application of the elimination of quantifiers and "implicit function" results mentioned above. These are *finite horizon* problems, in which a fixed time interval is considered.

A typical problem of this type, and its solution, are as follows. For a fixed but arbitrary time interval $[0, T]$, we wish to decide if every initial state at time $t = 0$ can be controlled to a desired target state $x(T) = x^*$ by a suitable application of controls in (4), and, if the answer is positive, whether there is any feedback law $K : \mathcal{X} \to \mathcal{U}$ so that, for any initial state $x(0) = x_0$, the recursive solution of the closed-loop equations

$$x^+ \;=\; P(x, K(x))$$

results in $x(T) = x^*$. Such feedback designs are of central interest in control theory, since they have obvious error-correction (noise tolerance) properties.

In the current context, when the system is a PL system, checking the property of controllability amounts to checking the truth of a sentence in L (namely, "for all x_0 there exist $u_0, \ldots, u_{T-1}$ so that (solving recursively) there results $x(T) = x^*$" where the "solving recursively" statement can obviously be written as a formula in L, using iterated compositions of P. Of course, the complexity of the formula increases exponentially as a function of the time horizon T, but at least in principle this reasoning shows that the problem is decidable and suggests an algorithm.

More interestingly perhaps, the following theorem holds: if the system is controllable to x^*, then there is a feedback controller $K(x)$ as above (the converse is obviously also true). The construction of K is by means of a straightforward dynamic programming argument, using the "implicit function" result at each step. Thus PL systems are a very well-behaved class from a theoretical point of view, much as linear systems are: if the controllability problem can be solved at all, it can also be solved by feedback (definable within the class being considered, namely PL maps). This is a desirable property, which fails for other reasonable general classes of nonlinear systems (e.g. polynomial or analytic transitions).

Many other problems can be posed and analyzed in an analogous fashion. Among the ones treated in [7] are the existence of observers (state estimators or "filters"), stabilization using dynamical controllers, and systems inverses. We omit details, due to lack of space.

3.2 Asymptotic Problems

More interesting than finite-horizon problems are questions involving infinite-time, and in particular asymptotic, behavior. Most of the results in [7] are in connection with such issues. We discuss now a representative result of this type.

Assume that a system to be controlled (the "plant") is described by

$$\frac{dz}{dt} = f(z(t), v(t)), \tag{5}$$

that is, the state $z(t) \in \mathbb{R}^n$ satisfies the set of first order differential equations specified by the coordinates of the vector function f and $v(t) \in \mathbb{R}^m$ is the control applied at time $t \in [0, \infty)$. (Technical assumptions will be made more precise after we describe the intuitive ideas.) In addition, there is given a function h from states to outputs $y(t) \in \mathbb{R}^p$ which indicates which measurements are available to a controller at time t:

$$y(t) = h(z(t)). \tag{6}$$

The question is whether it is possible to stabilize the system (5), to a desired equilibrium state z^* (without loss of generality, we assume that $z^* = 0$, and $f(0,0) = 0$, $h(0) = 0$), while subject to the constraint of using only the information provided by the output measurements (6). More specifically, we wish to know what intrinsic properties of the system guarantee that there is a *PL* system that can stabilize the system in closed loop.

Since PL systems are defined only in discrete-time, it is first necessary to clarify how one uses a PL system (4) in order to control a continuous-time plant. The meaning is the standard one in control theory: one uses *sample and hold*. Assume a sampling period $\delta > 0$ has been picked. At each sampling instant

$k = 0, \delta, 2\delta, \ldots$, the following events take place: (1) the output $y(k)$ is measured, (2) the discrete-time PL system makes a transition into the next state specified by its update equation (4) (where the input "u" at time k is $y(k)$, so $\mathcal{U} = \mathbb{R}^p$), and (3) a constant control signal $v(t) \equiv v_k$ is applied to the plant during the next inter-sampling interval $(k\delta, (k+1)\delta)$, according to a fixed feedback rule $v_k = K(x(k), y(k))$ which is a PL function of the current state $x(k)$ of the controller and the current observation. (See e.g. [10] for a definitions, examples, and elementary properties of sampling.)

Next we explain the meaning of closed-loop stabilization. For the purposes of this short exposition, we will assume that an arbitrary but fixed compact subset $\mathcal{Z}$ of the state space $\mathbb{R}^n$ has been given, and stabilization means that, for some fixed initial state x_0 of the PL controller, every trajectory of the system (5) obtained by the procedure just sketched, starting from any $z(0) \in \mathcal{Z}$, is such that $z(t)$ is well-defined for all $t \geq 0$ and $\lim_{t\to\infty} z(t) = 0$. (A stronger Lyapunov stability-like property can be required –see [7]– namely that if $z(0)$ is small then the obtained trajectory should remain small.)

Observe that for there to exist any type of stabilizing controller, PL or not, it is necessary that the system (5) be *null-asymptotically controllable* (n.a.c.) when starting from the subset $\mathcal{Z}$: for each $z(0) \in \mathcal{Z}$, there is some control function $v(\cdot)$ so that the solution of (5) converges to zero. (Proof: look at the $v(t)$ produced by a controller, if one exists.) Theorem 3.11 in [7] then states that conversely, under assumptions that are quite mild in the context of nonlinear control, a PL controller exists if the plant has the n.a.c. property.

We describe these assumptions now (in a stronger form than needed, so as to make the discussion concise). The first is that the mappings $f : \mathbb{R}^n \times \mathbb{R}^m \to \mathbb{R}^n$ and $h : \mathbb{R}^n \to \mathbb{R}^p$ are real-analytic (admitting locally convergent power series representations around each point in their domains). It is important to note that, while including usual descriptions of mechanical systems (which are obtained by combining trigonometric, polynomial, and other analytic functions), this assumption does rule out switching behavior in the system itself, or even infinitely differentiable but non-analytic nonlinearities. The second assumption is that the Jacobians of the maps f and h at the origin are well-behaved: if A, B, and C are the matrices for which $f(x,u) = Ax + Bu + o(x,u)$ and $h(x) = Cx + o(x)$, then the linearized system $\dot{z} = Az + Bv$, $y = Cz$ is stabilizable and detectable (these constitute generically satisfied rank conditions on the triple of matrices (A, B, C); see [10]). This hypothesis is essential for the proof (it is in fact also necessary for the existence of a controller if exponential convergence is required). Finally, we assume that the plant is *observable*. This means (cf. [10]) that given any two states z_1 and z_2, there is some control function (which depends on the particular pair (z_1, z_2)) so that when applied to the system, different measurement signals $y(t)$ result when starting at z_1 or at z_2. This hypothesis can be relaxed considerably, and can be replaced by a condition which is necessary if a controller exists (a "nonlinear detectability" condition).

The proof of Theorem 3.11 provides a PL controller whose state space consists of a cartesian product of an Euclidean space and a finite set, and whose dynamics are described in terms of "if-then-else" linear equality and inequality decisions and linear operations. Usually a stronger property for the controller is desirable, namely that convergence to zero occur for every initial state of the controller. This means, in a practical sense, that a sudden and unobserved state change in the plant, due to noise or unmodeled inputs, will not affect convergence (since the controller, starting from the state at the given time, still regulates the plant). This stronger property is called "strong regulation" in [7], and the main theorem there, valid under slightly stronger observability assumptions on the system, assures such regulation by PL systems (cf. Theorem 3.15).

4 Computational Complexity

We conclude with some remarks about computational issues. As remarked earlier, finite-horizon problems are decidable for PL systems. Thus it is of interest to study their computational complexity. Unfortunately, there is a rather negative result in that regard. To explain this result, given in [9] and not difficult to establish, we first recall some basic concepts from logic. Given a fixed piecewise-linear system, a fixed time horizon, and a pair of initial and target states x_0 and x^* respectively, asking if there is any control which steers x_0 to x^* is a purely-existential problem, or a "$\exists$" problem, for the language of piecewise linear algebra, because it is possible to write a logical formula of the type "there exists u so that $\Phi(u)$" which is true if and only if the property holds (and Φ does not involve any free variables besides the components of u which represent the control sequence; Φ is simply the sentence that asserts that the composition of the dynamics T times, using this control, lands the state at x^* when starting from x_0). Other (still finite-horizon) problems in control are not formulated originally in $\exists$ form. For instance, to ask if the whole system is controllable to x^* in T steps would require a formula of $\forall\exists$ type, namely a formula that reads "for all x there exists u such that $\Phi(x, u)$" whose truth is equivalent to the desired controllability (and now Φ has the coordinates of the initial state x represented by a set of variables, as well as the control). Another variant appears in design problems. For instance, given a parametric form for a closed-loop controller, say $P(\lambda)$, asking that some value of the parameter result in a feedback law which controls each state to zero in T steps would be given by an $\exists\forall$ formula ("there is some parameter λ so that, for each initial state state x, $\Phi(x, u)$"). Even more alternations of quantifiers might appear. For example, in the context of "control Lyapunov functions" one might ask whether there is a value for a parameter λ so that a scalar "energy" function $V_\lambda(x)$ decreases along suitable trajectories, giving rise to a $\exists\forall\exists$ formula ("there is a λ so that, for each x, there is some u so that either $x = 0$ or $V_\lambda(P(x, u)) < V_\lambda(x)$"). In the same manner, one can define of course $\exists\forall\ldots\exists$ types of problems, for all finite sequences of quantifiers.

Roughly stated, the "polynomial hierarchy" in logic and computer science is obtained in this same way when the basic quantifier-free formulas Φ are propositional formulas, and the variables over which one quantifies are Boolean-valued. Problems are in the class NP (non-deterministic polynomial time) if they can be described by just $\exists$ formulas, and in P (polynomial time) if they can be described with no quantifiers at all. It is widely believed, and one of the most important open problems in theoretical computer science to prove, that the various levels are very different in complexity. Thus, not only should P be different from NP, but problems whose definition requires $\forall\exists$ should be much harder to solve than those in NP, and so forth going "up" along the hierarchy.

The main result in [9] was that problems in any given level, such as for instance $\exists\forall\exists$, for PL systems are of exactly *same complexity* (in a precise sense of reduction of one problem to another) as problems in the corresponding level of the polynomial hierarchy. Thus one has a complete understanding of complexity for such problems modulo the same understanding for the classical hierarchy, including decidability in polynomial space, and a rich theory of complexity when using parallel computing.

The situation is radically different for *infinite* horizon problems, such as asking if a system is controllable (in some finite but not prespecified number of steps). Obviously, such problems will be in general undecidable, as it is easy to encode a Turing machine halting problem into PL behavior. On the other hand, it is perhaps surprising that even for "mildly" PL systems such as those given by an Equation as in (3), undecidability holds, as we discuss next.

4.1 A Special Subclass: Saturated Transitions

A special class of PL systems is that modeled by the saturated-transition systems ("recurrent neural networks") of the type displayed in Equation (3). Models like this are of interest for several different reasons, including their computational universality (discussed below), approximation properties (cf. [11]), and use in experimental "neural network" work; they arise naturally when linear systems have variables subject to amplitude limitations. One might think that control problems for such systems, being so close to linear systems, and appearing so often in the literature, may be simpler to solve than problems for more complicated classes of PL systems. We show next, through a simple controllability question, that this is quite far from being true.

We call a state ξ *null-controllable* if there is some some nonnegative integer k and some input sequence $u(0), \ldots, u(k-1)$ which steers ξ to $x(k) = 0$. This is as considered earlier, except that now we are not assuming that the time $k = T$ has been fixed in advance. Before proceeding further with this class, note for purposes of comparison that if there would be no saturation, we would be studying the standard class of linear systems (1), and for linear systems one can determine null-controllability of a state ξ in a computationally simple manner. Indeed, ξ is null-controllable for (1) if and only if the null-controllability property is verified with $k = n$ (this is a standard elementary fact; see for instance Lemma 3.2.8 in [10]); thus a state ξ is null-controllable if and only if $A^n\xi$ is in the the reachability space of (1), that is, the span of the columns of $B, AB, \ldots, A^{n-1}B$. This property can in turn be checked by Gaussian elimination, so it can be verified in a number of algebraic operations that is polynomial in n and m ("strong polynomial time"). Alternatively, we may ask the question of null-controllability in a bit-computational (Turing-machine) model, assuming that the entries of the matrices A and B, as well as the coordinates of the state ξ, and all rational (as opposed to arbitrary real) numbers, and are each given by specifying pairs of integers in a binary basis. Then the fact is that null-controllability of a state ξ for the system (1) can be checked in a number of elementary Turning-machine steps which is polynomial in the size of the input data, that is, the total number of bits needed to specify A, B, ξ. Thus, the problem is in the class "P" of polynomial-time computable problems. (From now on, we use the Turing machine model, to stay close to classical computational complexity.)

Thus it is natural to ask if adding a saturation can change matters in a fundamental way. The answer is yes. In fact, the change is as big as it could be: *For saturated linear systems (3), the null-controllability question is recursively unsolvable.*

In other words, there is no possible computer program which, when given A, B, ξ with rational entries, can answer after a finite amount of time "yes" if the state ξ is null-controllable for the corresponding system, and "no" otherwise. (In particular, there is no possible characterization in terms of rank conditions, such as was available for linear systems, nor any characterization in terms of checking higher-order algebraic conditions in terms of polynomials constructible from the entries of the matrices and vector in question.) The proof of this fact relies upon the work on simulation of Turing machines by devices such as (3); see [5]. From that work it follows that there exists a certain matrix A (with n approximately equal to 1000 in the construction given in [5], and most entries being 0, 1, or certain small rational numbers) for which there is no possible algorithm that can answer the following question: "Given ξ, is there any integer k so that the first coordinate of the solution of

$$x(t+1) = \text{sat}\,(Ax(t))\,, \quad x(0) = \xi \tag{7}$$

has $x_1(k) = 1$?" (Of course, (7) is a particular case of (3), when $B = 0$.) Moreover, the matrix A is built in such a manner that the above property is impossible to check even if ξ is restricted to be a vector with the property that the solution of (7) has $x_1(t) \in \{0, 1\}$ for all $t = 0, 1, \ldots$. It is easy to convert the problem "is $x_1(k) = 1$ for some k?" to "is $x(k) = 0$ for some k?" simply by changing each coordinate update equation $x_i(t+1) = \text{sat}\,(\ldots)$ to $x_i(t+1) = \text{sat}\,(\ldots - \alpha x_1(t))$, where α is a positive integer bigger than the possible maximum magnitude of the expression "...". While $x_1(t) = 0$ nothing changes, but if x_1 ever attains the value 1 then the next state is $x = 0$. So the null-controllability question is also undecidable, even in the case in which the system is this one particular system of dimension about 1000 (which in the proof corresponds to a simulation of a universal Turing machine, with the initial condition ξ corresponding to the program for such a machine). This negative result shows that adding a saturation has changed the problem dramatically from the linear case.

One may of course ask about related problems such as observability. For instance, given a system (3) and a linear output map $y = Cx$, one may ask for the decidability of the problem, for a given state ξ: "is ξ indistinguishable from 0?" Again this is essentially trivial for linear systems (just check if ξ is in the kernel of the Kalman observability matrix), but the problem becomes undecidable for saturated systems (take $Cx := x_1$ and use the above construction; as $Cx(t) = x_1(t)$ is always zero or one, distinguishability from zero is equivalent to determining if it is ever one).

While on the topic of the systems of type (3), we should point out that when real (as opposed to merely rational) coefficients are allowed for the matrices A and B, and the initial state, it is possible to formulate precisely the question of determining the computational power of such devices. The, perhaps surprising, answer, is that they are computationally no less powerful than essentially arbitrary continuous discrete-time systems (up to polynomial time speedups). This makes such models of PL systems a universal model for "real number" computation. Moreover, their capabilities can be understood in the context of "Turing machines that consult sparse oracles," in the language of computational complexity; the reader is referred to [6] for this topic.

References

1. Albertini, F., and E.D. Sontag, "Identifiability of discrete-time neural networks," *Proc. European Control Conference*, Groningen, June 1993, pp. 460-465.
2. Albertini, F., and E.D. Sontag, "State observability in recurrent neural networks," *Systems & Control Letters* **22**(1994): 235-244.
3. Koplon, R.M., L.J. Hautus, and E.D. Sontag, "Observability of linear systems with saturated outputs," *Lin. Alg. Appl.* **205-206**(1994): 909-936.
4. Koplon, R.M. and E.D. Sontag, "Sign-linear systems as cascades of automata and continuous variable systems," *Proc. IEEE Conf. Decision and Control, San Antonio, Dec. 1993*, IEEE Publications, 1993, pp. 2290-2291.
5. Siegelmann, H.T., and E.D. Sontag, "On the computational power of neural nets," *J. Comp. Syst. Sci.* **50**(1995): 132-150.
6. Siegelmann, H.T., and E.D. Sontag, "Analog computation, neural networks, and circuits," *Theor. Comp. Sci.* **131**(1994): 331-360.
7. Sontag, E.D., "Nonlinear regulation: The piecewise linear approach," *IEEE Trans. Autom. Control* **AC-26**(1981): 346-358.
8. Sontag, E.D., "Remarks on piecewise-linear algebra," *Pacific J.Math.*, **98**(1982): 183-201.
9. Sontag, E.D., "Real addition and the polynomial hierarchy," *Inform. Proc. Letters* **20**(1985): 115-120.
10. Sontag, E.D., *Mathematical Control Theory: Deterministic Finite Dimensional Systems*, Springer, New York, 1990.
11. Sontag, E.D., "Systems combining linearity and saturations, and relations to "neural nets," in *Proc. Nonlinear Control Systems Design Symp., Bordeaux, June 1992* (M. Fliess, Ed.), IFAC Publications, pp. 242-247.
12. Sontag, E.D., and H.J. Sussmann, "Remarks on continuous feedback," *Proc. IEEE Conf. Decision and Control, Albuquerque, Dec.1980*, pp. 916-921.
13. Sussmann, H.J., E. Sontag, and Y. Yang, "A general result on the stabilization of linear systems using bounded controls," *IEEE Trans. Autom. Control* **39**(1994): 2411-2425.

Modelling and Verification of Automated Transit Systems, Using Timed Automata, Invariants and Simulations

Nancy Lynch *

Laboratory for Computer Science, Massachusetts Institute of Technology, Cambridge, MA 02139.

1 Introduction

This paper contains an overview of recent and current work in the M.I.T. Theory of Distributed Systems research group on modelling, verifying and analyzing problems arising in automated transit systems. The problems we consider are inspired by design work in the Personal Rapid Transit (PRT) project at Raytheon (as described to us by Roy Johnson, Steve Spielman and Norm Delisle), and in the California PATH project (as described to us by Shankar Sastry, Datta Godbole and John Lygeros) [7, 6, 13, 3]. Our work is based on the Lynch-Vaandrager timed automaton model [19, 20, 18], extended to include explicit state trajectories and continuous interaction [17]. The formal tools we use include standard techniques for reasoning about concurrent algorithms – invariants, simulations (levels of abstraction) and automaton composition, plus standard methods for reasoning about continuous processes – differential equations.

Our work so far suggests that these methods are capable of providing good results about safety and performance of automated transit systems. The methods support modular system description, verification, analysis and design. They allow a smooth combination of discrete and continuous reasoning in the same framework. They are especially good at handling nondeterminism and approximate information.

2 Background

2.1 Timed Automata and Hybrid I/O Automata

The starting point for our transit project was the Lynch-Vaandrager timed automaton model, which has been used over the past few years to describe and analyze many distributed algorithms and simple real-time systems. The definition of a timed automaton appears in [20, 18]. A variety of proof techniques for timed automata have been developed, including invariant assertions and simulations [20], compositional methods based on shared actions [18, 5, 16], and

* Research supported by ARPA contracts N00014-92-J-4033 and F19628-95-C-0118, NSF grant 922124-CCR, ONR-AFOSR contract F49620-94-1-0199, and U. S. Department of Transportation contract DTRS95G-0001.

temporal logic methods [24]. Applications of the model to asynchronous and timing-based distributed algorithms appear in [22, 15, 12, 11, 16], applications to communication systems appear in [24, 9, 1], and applications to real-time control (trains and gates, steam boiler control) appear in [8, 10].

Briefly, a timed automaton is a labelled transition system having real-valued as well as discrete state components, and allowing continuous state evolution as well as discrete state changes. A timed automaton has a set of states of which a subset are distinguished as start states, a set of actions classified as external (input or output), internal, or time-passage actions, and a set of steps (both discrete and time-passage). As a derived notion, it also has a set of trajectories, which describe evolution of the state over time. A trajectory is obtained by filling in an interval of time solidly with states, so that time-passage steps connect all pairs of states. An execution is an alternating sequence of (possibly trivial) trajectories and discrete steps.

Most of the proofs that have been done using timed automata use invariants (statements that are true about all reachable system states) and simulations (statements of relationships between states of an implementation system and states of a more abstract specification system). Even proofs of timing properties are done in this way; the key idea that makes this work is to build time deadlines (first and last times for certain events to occur) into the automaton state and to involve these deadlines in assertions. Some of the proofs have been automated, using the Larch Prover (LP) [4] and PVS [23]. Other proofs use composition and temporal logic. In these examples, the model works well, yielding clear, unambiguous, and understandable descriptions and proofs.

The work on real-time control suggested to us that some additions to the model would be useful for modelling hybrid systems. In particular, it would be convenient to have trajectories as primitive rather than derived objects; this would allow more direct modelling of physical behavior using physical laws. Also, it would be useful to allow continuous interaction between components via shared continuously-changing variables, in addition to discrete interaction via shared actions; this would allow modelling of systems with continuous controllers or shared clocks, for example. These considerations led us to work on developing a new "hybrid automaton" model.

Some conditions we wanted the new model to satisfy were: (a) We wanted it to be an extension of the timed automaton model, in order to take advantage of earlier results. (b) It should support modular system description, design, verification and analysis (using, for example, composition, abstraction, and system transformation). Modular techniques work very well in reasoning about distributed algorithms, and they should work equally well for hybrid systems. (c) It should be mathematical, not tied to or skewed toward any particular language for programming or specification, nor to any particular proof method or verification system. This would allow us to formulate results quite generally, only introducing restrictions (finite-state, differentiability, integrability, Lipschitz, etc.) where necessary. This generality would make the model flexible enough to be used as the formal basis for many different languages and proof methods. (d) The model should support the effective use of different methods, in particular, those of discrete algorithm analysis and those of control theory, in combination.

Our strategy for obtaining a good hybrid automaton model was to develop the model along with case studies in a particular application. This meant that we needed to choose the "right" application: one that was really hybrid (with lots of interesting continuous and discrete activity), that was simple enough for us to handle yet complicated enough to exercise the theory, and that afforded many opportunities for modular system description. Moreover, in carrying out application case studies, our strategy was to model and analyze many related designs rather than isolated examples; such a coordinated study would permit the formal structure that is useful for the particular application to emerge.

2.2 Automated Transit Systems

The application we chose was Automated Transit Systems (ATS). Among our reasons for this choice were:

1. We originally considered studying air-traffic control. However, air-traffic control is too complex to use in developing basic theory, because it adds the complexities of three-dimensional geometry to those of combining continuous and discrete behavior. Many of the problems arising in the ATS domain seem to be simpler (one-dimensional) versions of problems arising in air-traffic control.
2. The ATS application is important in its own right. There has been a recent surge of interest in ATS, on at least three fronts: Personal Rapid Transit (PRT) systems, in which small public vehicles circulate on tracks under automated control, Intelligent Vehicle Highway Systems (IVHS), in which ordinary cars are augmented with sensor, communication and control devices to allow some automated assistance, and traditional transportation systems, which are now being augmented with some automated control features.
3. ATS is a rich application, appearing to provide the right features to exercise the theory. It contains issues of safety (avoiding crashes, observing maximum speed limits), performance, and comfort. It contains a rich combination of continuous and discrete behavior – a complex real-world system may be controlled by an equally complex distributed computer system. It seems to have a good deal of modularity, for example, system decompositions involving separate vehicles, separate nodes of a distributed computer system, or separate functions. It appears that a system can be described at different levels of abstraction, by considering a derivative-based view versus an explicit function view, or a discrete view versus a continuous view.
4. The ATS area has many similarities with other areas we had studied extensively, in particular, the area of communication systems. Both communication and transit systems involve getting something successfully from a source to a destination, with good throughput and timely arrival.[2] This sim-

[2] There are differences. Messages are not usually thought of as having velocity and acceleration. And it is generally worse to lose a vehicle than it is to lose a message.

ilarity makes it likely that techniques that have been used successfully for communication will carry over to ATS.
5. Engineers working in ATS seem amenable to the use of formal methods, because the area is so safety-critical.

2.3 Our Project

We have begun using timed automata and some extensions to describe and obtain results about typical problems arising in ATS's. The methods we are using include invariants and simulations, composition, and differential equations.

With help from application engineers Johnson, Spielman, Delisle, Sastry, Godbole, and Lygeros, we have been identifying problems arising in ATS's, involving, for example,

1. Attaining and maintaining safe speeds.
2. Attaining and maintaining safe inter-vehicle distances.
3. Implementing typical vehicle *maneuvers*, such as lane changes, merging and diverging at Y-junctions, joining and splitting "platoons" of vehicles, etc.
4. Resolving conflicts among several different planned vehicle maneuvers.
5. Tracking specified vehicle trajectories.
6. Handing off control of vehicles from one computer to a neighboring computer in a distributed computer system.
7. Protecting against catastrophes.
8. Routing.

We are modelling versions of these problems formally and proving various properties (safety, throughput, timely arrival, passenger comfort) of the systems we describe. We consider these problems in the presence of various types of uncertainty, for instance, communication delays and uncertainty in vehicle response. We are trying to identify and use modularity wherever possible. We aim not only for results about the particular problems, but also at a general structured theory for ATS's. Also, as I described above, we are using this work to help us to develop general models for hybrid systems.

The next four sections contain descriptions of some of the particular problems we have modelled. Section 3 contains a study of a simple deceleration maneuver. Section 4 shows two uses of levels of abstraction in reasoning about a simple acceleration maneuver: to relate a derivative view of a system to a function view, and to relate a discrete view to a continuous view. Sections 5 and 6 provide brief summaries of our work on vehicle protection systems and platoon join safety, respectively. The paper closes with a brief conclusion section.

Two other papers in this volume are closely related to this one. In [26], Weinberg, Lynch and Delisle provide a detailed description of our work on vehicle protection systems. And in [17], Lynch, Segala, Vaandrager and Weinberg present the latest version of our general hybrid automaton model, which we call the *hybrid I/O automaton (HIOA) model.*

3 Deceleration

Our first project [21, 25] was the analysis of a simple control maneuver designed to ensure that a vehicle's speed is within a given range $[v_{min}, v_{max}]$ when it reaches a particular track position x_f. The vehicle is assumed to start at position 0 with known velocity $v_s > v_{max}$. A version of this problem was studied earlier by Schneider and co-workers [2].

We considered this problem with uncertain vehicle response and communication delay, and with and without periodic sensor feedback. We proved, using invariants and simulations, that certain example controllers guarantee correct behavior.

3.1 No Feedback

In the simplest version of the problem, there is no feedback from the vehicle to the controller. The controller is allowed to apply a brake at any time, which causes the vehicle to decelerate at some unknown, possibly varying rate in the interval $[a - \epsilon, a]$, where a is a known negative real. The controller can also disengage the brake ("unbrake") at any time. The controller can use only its knowledge of the constants v_s, v_{min}, v_{max} and a to decide when to brake and unbrake. Of course, some restrictions on the constants are needed in order to make such a maneuver possible.

We modelled the vehicle by a single hybrid I/O automaton (HIOA), V, using the model of [17].[3] Its discrete actions are the two inputs, *brake* and *unbrake*. Its state consists of values of the following variables:

$x \in \mathsf{R}$, initially 0
$\dot{x} \in \mathsf{R}$, initially v_s
$\ddot{x} \in \mathsf{R}$, initially 0
$acc \in \mathsf{R}$, initially 0
braking, a Boolean, initially *false*

Here, acc represents the acceleration proposed by the automaton's environment (presumably, a controller) while $\ddot{x}$ represents the actual acceleration. The variables x and $\dot{x}$ represent the position and velocity, respectively. The effects of the discrete inputs are described by the following "code".

brake
  Effect:
    $braking := true$
    $acc := a$
    $\ddot{x} :\in [a - \epsilon, a]$

unbrake
  Effect:
    $braking := false$
    $acc := 0$
    $\ddot{x} := 0$

The trajectories are all the mappings w from left-closed subintervals I of $\mathsf{R}^{\geq 0}$ to states of V such that:

[3] At the time we carried out this project, we actually used a less powerful extension of the timed automaton model, but the newer model works even better.

1. *braking* is unchanged in w.
2. $\ddot{x}$ is an integrable function in w.
3. For all $t \in I$, the following conditions hold in state $w(t)$:
   (a) If $braking = true$ then $\ddot{x} \in [acc - \epsilon, acc]$, otherwise $\ddot{x} = 0$.
   (b) $\dot{x} = w(0).\dot{x} + \int_0^t w(u).\ddot{x} du$.
   (c) $x = w(0).x + \int_0^t w(u).\dot{x} du$.

(The dot after a state is used to indicate state components.) Thus, the *acc* variable is set by the environment (controller), by braking and unbraking. The actual acceleration, velocity and position are determined accordingly: the actual acceleration $\ddot{x}$ is assumed to be in an interval bounded above by *acc* if the brake is on, and otherwise is 0, while the actual velocity and position are determined from $\ddot{x}$ using integration. Our choice of notation for describing V is not important – other notation could be used, as long as it denotes the same HIOA.

Many controllers could be combined with automaton V. We considered a trivial controller that just brakes once, at some time in the interval $[0, t_1]$, then unbrakes once, at some time in the interval $[t_2, t_3]$ after braking. The specific times t_1, t_2 and t_3 were chosen to be as nonrestrictive as possible. We modelled the controller by another HIOA, C. Its discrete actions are the two outputs, *brake* and *unbrake*. It enforces the time bounds t_1, t_2 and t_3 by including deadline variables *last-brake*, *first-unbrake*, and *last-unbrake* in its state, and manipulating them so as to ensure that the *brake* and *unbrake* actions occur at allowed times. That is, initially *last-brake* $= t_1$. When *brake* occurs, *first-unbrake* and *last-unbrake* are set to times t_2 and t_3 in the future, respectively. C does not allow time to pass beyond any *last* deadline currently in force, and does not allow an *unbrake* action to occur if its *first* deadline has not yet been reached. The trajectories are trivial – there is no interesting continuous behavior in the controller, so time just passes without changing anything else.

The entire system is modelled formally as the composition of the two HIOA's, V and C. We proved two properties of this composed system, $V \times C$, both involving the behavior of V:

1. If $x = x_f$ then $\dot{x} \in [v_{min}, v_{max}]$.

2. x eventually reaches position x_f.

For example, consider the velocity upper bound, that is, the claim that the velocity at position x_f is at most v_{max}. This claim can be expressed as an invariant, so we wanted to prove it in the usual way for invariants – by induction on the length of an execution. For executions of an HIOA, we take the "length" to be the total number of discrete steps and trajectories. As usual for invariants, we had to strengthen the property so that it could be proved inductively; this involved saying something about states where $x \neq x_f$. By using laws of motion, we came up with the following stronger assertion:

Assertion 3.1 *In all reachable states, if* $x \leq x_f$ *then* $x_f - x \geq \frac{v_{max}^2 - \dot{x}^2}{2a}$.

This says that there is enough remaining distance to allow the velocity to decrease to v_{max} by position x_f, even if deceleration is the slowest possible.

We proved this strengthened claim using induction. In this inductive proof, the cases involving discrete steps needed only discrete reasoning, while the trajectory cases needed only continuous analysis based on laws of motion. The combined argument implies that the assertion is always true, even with the given combination of continuous and discrete behavior.

For both the velocity lower bound and the "eventuality" property, the key was to show:

Assertion 3.2 *In all reachable states,* $\dot{x} \geq v_{min}$.

Again, this property cannot be proved alone using induction. The key to the proof turned out to be the following claim about the *last-unbrake* deadline while the vehicle is braking:

Assertion 3.3 *In all reachable states, if braking = true then* $\textit{last-unbrake} \leq \textit{now} + \frac{v_{min} - \dot{x}}{a - \epsilon}$.

This says that the brake must be turned off before the velocity has a chance to drop below v_{min}, assuming the maximum deceleration $a-\epsilon$, Here, *now* represents the current time. Again, this statement can be proved using induction.

This simple deceleration example already illustrates several aspects of our model and methods: It shows how vehicles and controllers can be modelled using HIOA's and composition, and in particular, how deadline variables can be used to express timing restrictions. It shows some typical correctness conditions – an invariant and an eventuality property – both expressed in terms of the real-world component of the system. It shows how invariants can provide the keys to proofs. Invariants can involve real-valued quantities representing real-world behavior, thus allowing facts about velocities, etc. to be proved by induction; invariants can also involve deadline variables, thus allowing time bounds to be proved by induction.

This example also shows how continuous and discrete reasoning can be combined in a single proof, with formal criteria to ensure that the combination is correct. It illustrates careful handling of uncertainty. Finally, the arguments are general – they don't handle just the apparent worst cases, but all cases at once.

We extended this example slightly to demonstrate some uses of abstraction and composition. Namely, in place of the very nondeterministic automaton C given above, we described the causes of uncertainty in the braking and unbraking times in detail – we supposed that the uncertainty arose entirely from communication delay from a less uncertain controller C' to V. That is, the composition of C' and a "delay buffer" automaton D, $C' \times D$, exhibits behavior that remains within the bounds allowed by the more abstract controller C. Formally, it "implements" C, in the sense of inclusion of external behavior (here, sets of sequences of *brake* and *unbrake* actions, each with an associated time of occurrence).

We showed this inclusion using a *simulation relation* to relate states of $C' \times D$ to states of C. The most important part of the definition of this simulation relation was a set of inequalities involving the deadlines in the two automata. The proof that the relation is a simulation followed the normal pattern for such proofs – it involved showing a correspondence involving start states, one involving discrete steps, and one involving trajectories. Existence of a simulation implies inclusion of external behavior.

External behavior inclusion wasn't quite enough, however. What we really wanted was an exact correspondence between velocity and position values in V, when it is composed with the controller C and when it is composed with the implementation $C' \times D$. But this correspondence can be obtained from the external behavior inclusion result, using basic *projection* and *pasting* results about composition of HIOA's.

3.2 Feedback

We also considered a version of the problem with periodic feedback from the vehicle to the controller, triggering immediate adjustment by the controller of the proposed acceleration. This time, we allowed the controller to set *acc* to any real value, not just to a fixed value a or 0. As before, the controller's request need not be followed exactly, but only within a tolerance of ϵ.

Our new version of the vehicle automaton V was very similar to the one we used for the no-feedback case. A change is that the new V reports its position x and velocity $\dot{x}$ every time d. In order to express this in terms of an HIOA, we added a *last-sample* deadline component and managed it appropriately. The new V has an *accel*(a) input action, which causes *acc* to be set to a. The actual acceleration $\ddot{x}$ is anything in $[acc - \epsilon, acc]$. C performs an *accel* output immediately after receiving each report.

Now C has more information than before, so it can guarantee more precise velocity bounds. We modelled a controller that initially sets *acc* to aim so that, if the vehicle followed *acc* exactly, it would reach velocity exactly v_{max} when $x = x_f$. Since the vehicle might actually decelerate faster than *acc*, C might observe at any sample point that the vehicle is going slower than expected. In this case, C does not change *acc* until the velocity actually becomes $\leq v_{max}$. Thereafter, at each sample point, C sets *acc* to aim to reach v_{max} at exactly the next sample point.

We proved the same two properties for this case as we did for the no-feedback case, but for tighter bounds on the final velocity. The argument again used invariants. For example, consider the argument that in all reachable states, $\dot{x} \geq v_{min}$. Now to prove this by induction, we needed auxiliary statements about what is true between sample points, for example:

Assertion 3.4 *In all reachable states between sample points,* $\dot{x} + (acc - \epsilon)(\textit{last-sample} - now) \geq v_{min}$.

That is, if the current velocity is modified by allowing the minimum acceleration consistent with the current *acc*, until the next sample point, then the result will still be $\geq v_{min}$. Note the use of the *last-sample* deadline to express the time until the next sample point. This statement is proved using induction.

This example illustrates how our methods can be used to handle more complicated examples, including periodic sampling and control. It shows how to reason about periodic sampling using intermediate invariants involving the *last-sample* deadline: The controller issues control requests to the system at sample times, but can "lose control" of the system's behavior between sample points; the invariants are used to bound how badly the system's performance can degrade between sample points. Again, we handle all cases reliably, not just the apparent worst cases.

4 Levels of Abstraction

Our second project [14] showed how levels of abstraction, one of the most important tools of discrete system analysis, can be used to reason about a simple acceleration maneuver. In this case, the goal is for a vehicle to reach a specified velocity v_f at a specified time t_f in the future. We assumed that the vehicle starts at time 0 with velocity 0. The vehicle reports its velocity to the controller every time d. The controller can send an $accel(a)$ control signal to set $acc := a$ immediately after each sample point. The actual acceleration $\dot{v}$ is anything in the range $[acc - \epsilon, acc]$. The controller we considered aims to reach the goal of v_f at time t_f. That is, it proposes acceleration $\frac{v_f - v}{t_f - now}$, where v is the current velocity.

Using invariants and simulations, we proved bounds on velocity at every point in time. The proofs use levels of abstraction in two ways: relating a derivative view of a system to an explicit function view, and relating a system in which corrections are made at discrete sampling points to a system in which corrections are made continuously. The uncertainty ϵ in the acceleration is integrated throughout the levels.

First, we ignored the discrete sampling and considered a controller that continuously sets acc to the ratio given above, with $\dot{v} \in [acc, acc - \epsilon]$. It was easy to see that the velocity at time t is at most $g(t) = \frac{v_f t}{t_f}$. For the lower bound, by solving the differential equation:

$$\dot{f}(t) = \frac{v_f - f(t)}{t_f - t} - \epsilon,$$

we got a conjectured lower bound of:

$$f(t) = \frac{v_f t}{t_f} + \epsilon(t_f - t)\log(\frac{t_f - t}{t_f})$$

(patched with v_f at t_f). The function f is the result of aiming at (t_f, v_f) and consistently missing low by ϵ.

To prove that f is indeed a lower bound, we used two levels of abstraction. The high level is an HIOA V giving explicit bounds on v. Its state contains only v and now, and the only constraint is that in every reachable state, $v \in [f(now), g(now)]$. The low level is another HIOA D giving bounds on the derivative of v. It keeps acc aiming at (t_f, v_f) and ensures that $\dot{v} \in [acc, acc - \epsilon]$. In a sense, D describes *how* the system is supposed to guarantee the bounds expressed by V.

We showed that D "implements" V, in the sense of inclusion of external behavior (here, the values of v and now). We showed this inclusion using a simulation relation to relate states of D and V. As usual, the proof involved showing a correspondence involving start states, one involving discrete steps, and one involving trajectories. The only interesting case is the one for trajectories. Basically this involved showing that, if the pair (now, v) starts within the region specified by V, the rule used by D does not cause the pair to leave that region. This is in turn proved using standard methods of continuous analysis, expressed formally as invariants involving $\dot{v}$.

Unfortunately, the actual controller does not behave as nicely as D. It only sets acc to aim at (t_f, v_f) at sample points rather than continuously. Between sample points, the value of acc can degrade. In fact, it is not hard to see that v does not necessarily remain above f – the uncertainty introduced by periodic sampling is reflected in a change to the actual behavior produced. Therefore, we had to modify V to reflect the new source of uncertainty. The result was a new V' with a new lower bound f' constructing by aiming not at the "real goal" (t_f, v_f), but at an adjusted goal that depends on d and ϵ, specifically, $(t_f, v_f - \epsilon d)$.

At this point, we could have shown directly (using a simulation relation) that the real system, I, implements V'. However, we found it useful to instead introduce a third level of abstraction, in the form of a modified version D' of D. D' differs from D by having a looser rule for acc: instead of continuously setting acc to aim exactly at (t_f, v_f) it can instead (continuously) set it to point anywhere between (t_f, v_f) and $(t_f, v_f - \epsilon d)$. Thus, D' contains uncertainty in acc, in addition to the ϵ uncertainty in $\dot{v}$. With these simple modifications, we easily modified our proof that D implements V to show that D' implements V'.

Having shown that D' implements V', we were able to forget about V' and just show that I implements D'. Using a transitivity result, this implies that I implements V', as needed.

To show that I implements D', we showed that the identity on all the state components of D' is a simulation relation from I to D'. The key to this proof is the fact that any acc that is set in I is in the range permitted by D'. Note that acc is set to aim at the upper end of its range, (t_f, v_f), at each sample point, but can degrade between sample points. As before, we had to bound the amount of degradation that occurs between sample points. The key claim is that:

Assertion 4.1 *Between sample points,* $acc \geq \frac{v_f - \epsilon(now + d - last\text{-}sample) - v}{t_f - now}$.

This says, roughly speaking, that the value of acc has not degraded too badly if there is still a long time until the next sample point. In particular, at the beginning of a sample interval, $now + d = last\text{-}sample$, so the right-hand side of the inequality simplifies to $\frac{v_f - v}{t_f - now}$, which is exactly the upper end of the range allowed by D'. Also, at the end of a sample interval, $now = last\text{-}sample$, so the right-hand side simplifies to $\frac{v_f - \epsilon d - v}{t_f - now}$, which is exactly the lower end of the range. The complete assertion gives bounds for all the intermediate points as well. This assertion is proved by induction.

This example illustrate more uses of HIOA's and invariants, and the use of *last-sample* deadlines to limit degradation between sample points. Most importantly, it demonstrates two uses of levels of abstraction in reasoning about hybrid control problems: relating a derivative view of a system to a function view, and relating a discrete view to a continuous view. Uncertainties are included throughout, and are handled accurately.

The example also illustrates the useful strategy of specifying the highest-level correctness conditions in terms of an explicitly-specified region of allowed values for the important physical variables. Derivative-based descriptions can be regarded as ways to guarantee that the behavior remains within the high-level regions. For instance, in air-traffic control, the highest-level specification might involve regions in space-time "owned" by particular airplanes. Disjointness of regions then would imply that planes do not collide. The mechanisms for ensuring that individual planes remain within their regions could be reasoned about individually, and separately from consideration of the disjointness of regions.

Note that the bounding functions for the high-level region are obtained using usual methods of continuous analysis – our techniques do not provide any help here. However, our methods do allow systematic checking that the results of the analysis are correct (in particular, that they really capture the worst cases and that they cope correctly with uncertainties).

5 Vehicle Protection Systems

Our third project [26] has been the analysis of automated Vehicle Protection (VP) systems, which are sometimes added to automated Vehicle Operation (VO) systems in order to enforce particular safety constraints. We model both VP and VO systems as HIOA's, and model their combination by composition. Each VP automaton monitors the physical system, using discrete sampling, and checking for "dangerous" conditions. When such conditions occur, the VP triggers an emergency response. For example, a VP might check whether a vehicle's speed is "close" to a specified "overspeed", in order to apply an emergency brake before the overspeed could actually be exceeded. In [26], we analyze both overspeed protection and maintenance of safe separation distance between pairs of vehicles.

This project demonstrates how to model the important interactions between VP and VO systems, using HIOA's and composition. Again, bounding the degradation of physical variables between sample points is a key to the analysis. The project also shows how to compose several VP systems with the same VO system, thereby obtaining the guarantees of all the VP's at once. In this composition, some of the VP's might assume the effects achieved by others. Our work has yielded useful methods for thinking carefully about the design of such systems.

6 Joining Platoons

Finally, our fourth project, just beginning, is the analysis of a "platoon join" maneuver arising in the PATH project [3]. The problem is for cars travelling in a "platoon" to join with another platoon travelling ahead of it in the same lane. The join is accomplished by having the second platoon accelerate to catch up with the first. This introduces the possibility of collisions: We assume that there is some maximum possible deceleration a, the same for all vehicles. If the first platoon suddenly brakes at rate a, and the second platoon is near the first and going faster, then the second platoon will collide with the first, even if the second can react immediately. However, this is considered acceptable by the PATH researchers as long as the relative velocity of the two platoons upon collision is no greater than a small constant v_{allow}.

In [3], a particular controller is described that ensures this relative velocity bound, while allowing the join to be completed as fast as possible and observing passenger comfort limits (expressed by bounds on acceleration and jerk). The controller causes the second platoon to accelerate as fast as possible, subject to safety limits and passenger comfort limits, in order to catch up, and then to decelerate as fast as possible to move into the correct position.

Our goals are to model this system using HIOA's, and to formulate and prove its properties. There are four separate properties to prove: observance of the v_{allow} limit, eventual success in joining platoons, passenger comfort, and optimal join time. Our idea is to use these four separate properties as a basis for decomposing the system and its proof.

So far, we have just considered the safety property – that is, the v_{allow} limit. For this, we are describing a very nondeterministic *safety controller* that just guarantees safety (but not necessarily the other three properties). Our plan is to prove that the safety controller guarantees safety, and then to show that the actual controller implements the safety controller. A bonus is that the safety controller should be reusable for analyzing other maneuvers besides platoon join.

We define a *Platoons* HIOA to model the behavior of the platoons, and allow platoon 1 to be under the control of an arbitrary controller HIOA, C_1. C_1 is unconstrained, subject only to a known maximum deceleration a. The designer's job is to design a safety controller, C_2, for platoon 2 that works with any C_1. That is, the combination of *Platoons*, C_2 and an arbitrary C_1 should guarantee the safety property.

The key to the safety property is an invariant that says that platoon 2's velocity is slow enough, relative to the velocity of platoon 1 and the inter-platoon distance. There are two possibilities, either of which is fine. First:

$$x_1 - x_2 \geq \frac{\dot{x_1}^2 + v_{allow}^2 - \dot{x_2}^2}{2a}$$

This says that enough distance remains to allow platoon 2 to reach v_{allow} by the time a collision occurs, even if platoon 1 decelerates as fast as possible. And second:

$$\dot{x_2} \leq \dot{x_1} + v_{allow}$$

This says that the relative speed is already small enough. The analysis is essentially the same as in [3] (ignoring delays in response), but it is expressed in our invariant style. We can prove that a particular nondeterministic C_2 maintains the disjunction of these two inequalities, and hence guarantees safety.

This example illustrates how our techniques (here, invariants and composition) apply to reasonably complex, realistic systems. It shows how to model a controller that is supposed to work in the presence of unpredictable behavior on the part of some of the real-world entities. Again, we handle all cases reliably, not just the apparent worst cases. Our analysis has given us some insights about the application. For example, we realized that it is important to also model what happens *after* a collision; our techniques appear to be suitable for doing this, but this still remains to be done.

7 Conclusions

We have used hybrid I/O automata to model and verify examples arising in automated transit. We began with very simple deceleration examples, and have progressed to more realistic examples involving vehicle protection systems and platoon join safety. Our methods allow accurate handling of nondeterminism, uncertainties and discrete sampling. All cases are considered, not just the apparent worst cases. The methods support modular system description, verification, analysis and design. They allow a smooth combination of discrete and continuous reasoning, in the same framework.

I have pointed out the key technical features of our approach in various places throughout the paper. The most important of these are: our modelling of all system components (physical world and computer system) as HIOA's; our use of deadline variables to express timing restrictions; our use of composition to describe interactions among components; our statement of correctness conditions in terms of the real world; our extensive use of invariants, including those involving real-valued quantities such as deadlines; our handling of periodic sampling by limiting the degradation of key parameters between sample points; our description of systems at many levels of abstraction; our specification of correctness in terms of regions of allowed values for important physical variables; our use of simulations to show correspondences between different levels of abstraction; and our use of composition to model controllers that work in the presence of unpredictable behavior on the part of some of the system components.

Our preliminary results say that these methods work well to provide useful results about safety and performance of automated transit systems. They have already had some impact on system designers. Our work on ATS modelling has also influenced the development of the basic HIOA model. It remains to use the model and methods to study many more ATS problems, and to integrate the results obtained for all these problems into a coherent theory for automated transit systems.

Acknowledgment: Michael Branicky provided useful information about control theory methods and useful discussions of the platoon join maneuver.

References

1. Doeko Bosscher, Indra Polak, and Frits Vaandrager. Verification of an audio control protocol. In H. Langmaack, W.-P. de Roever, and J. Vytopil, editors, *Proceedings of the Third International School and Symposium on Formal Techniques in Real Time and Fault Tolerant Systems. (FTRTFT'94)*, volume 863 of *Lecture Notes in Computer Science*, pages 170–192, Lübeck, Germany, September 1994. Springer-Verlag. Full version available as Report CS-R9445, CWI, Amsterdam, July 1994.
2. Richard A. Brown, Jacob Aizikowitz, Thomas C. Bressoud, Tony Lekas, and Fred Schneider. The trainset railroad simulation. Technical Report TR 93-1329, Cornell University, Department of Computer Science, February 1993.
3. Jonathan Frankel, Luis Alvarez, Roberto Horowitz, and Perry Li. Robust platoon maneuvers for AVHS. Manuscript, Berkeley, November 10, 1994.
4. Stephen J. Garland and John V. Guttag. A guide to LP, the Larch Prover. Research Report 82, Digital Systems Research Center, 130 Lytton Avenue, Palo Alto, CA 94301, December 1991.
5. Rainer Gawlick, Roberto Segala, Jørgen Søgaard-Andersen, and Nancy Lynch. Liveness in timed and untimed systems. In Serge Abiteboul and Eli Shamir, editors, *Automata, Languages and Programming* (21st International Colloquium, ICALP'94, Jerusalem, Israel, July 1994), volume 820 of *Lecture Notes in Computer Science*, pages 166–177. Springer-Verlag, 1994. Full version in MIT/LCS/TR-587.
6. Datta Godbole and John Lygeros. Longitudinal control of the lead car of a platoon. California PATH Technical Memorandum 93-7, Institute of Transportation Studies, University of California, November 1993.
7. Datta N. Godbole, John Lygeros, and Shankar Sastry. Hierarchical hybrid control: A case study. Preliminary report for the California PATH program, Institute of Transportations Studies, University of California, August 1994.
8. Constance Heitmeyer and Nancy Lynch. The generalized railroad crossing: A case study in formal verification of real-time systems. In *Proceedings of the Real-Time Systems Symposium*, pages 120–131, San Juan, Puerto Rico, December 1994. IEEE. Full version in MIT/LCS/TM-511. Later version to appear in C. Heitmeyer and D. Mandrioli, editors *Formal Methods for Real-time Computing*, chapter 4, *Trends in Software* series, John Wiley & Sons, Ltd.
9. Butler W. Lampson, Nancy A. Lynch, and Jørgen F. Søgaard-Andersen. Correctness of at-most-once message delivery protocols. In Richard L. Tenney, Paul D. Amer, and M. Ümit Uyar, editors, *Formal Description Techniques, VI* (Proceedings of the IFIP TC6/WG6.1 Sixth International Conference on Formal Description Techniques - FORTE'93, Boston, MA, October 1993), pages 385–400. North-Holland, 1994.
10. Gunter Leeb and Nancy Lynch. A steam boiler controller. In *Methods for Semantics and Specification*, Schloss, Dagstuhl, Germany, June 1995.
11. Victor Luchangco. Using simulation techniques to prove timing properties. Master's thesis, Department of Electrical Engineering and Computer Science, Massachusetts Institute of Technology, Cambridge, MA 02139, June 1995.
12. Victor Luchangco, Ekrem Söylemez, Stephen Garland, and Nancy Lynch. Verifying timing properties of concurrent algorithms. In Dieter Hogrefe and Stefan Leue, editors, *Formal Description Techniques VII: Proceedings of the 7th IFIP WG6.1 International Conference on Formal Description Techniques* (FORTE'94, Berne, Switzerland, October 1994), pages 259–273. Chapman and Hall, 1995.

13. John Lygeros and Datta N. Godbole. An interface between continuous and discrete-event controllers for vehicle automation. California PATH Research Report UCB-ITS-PRR-94-12, Institute of Transportations Studies, University of California, April 1994.
14. Nancy Lynch. A three-level analysis of a simple acceleration maneuver, with uncertainties. Manuscript. WWW URL=http://theory.lcs.mit.edu/three-level.html.
15. Nancy Lynch. Simulation techniques for proving properties of real-time systems. In W. P. de Roever, J. W. de Bakker and G. Rozenberg, editors, *A Decade of Concurrency: Reflections and Perspectives* (REX School/Symposium, Noordwijkerhout, The Netherlands, June 1993), volume 803 of *Lecture Notes in Computer Science*, pages 375–424. Springer-Verlag, 1994.
16. Nancy Lynch. *Distributed Algorithms*. Morgan Kaufmann Publishers, Inc., San Mateo, CA, 1996. To appear.
17. Nancy Lynch, Roberto Segala, Frits Vaandrager, and H.B. Weinberg. Hybrid I/O automata. This volume.
18. Nancy Lynch and Frits Vaandrager. Action transducers and timed automata. *Formal Aspects of Computing*. To appear. Available now as MIT/LCS/TM-480.c.
19. Nancy Lynch and Frits Vaandrager. Forward and backward simulations for timing-based systems. In J. W. de Bakker et al., editors, *Real-Time: Theory in Practice* (REX Workshop, Mook, The Netherlands, June 1991), volume 600 of *Lecture Notes in Computer Science*, pages 397–446. Springer-Verlag, 1992.
20. Nancy Lynch and Frits Vaandrager. Forward and backward simulations – Part II: Timing-based systems. *Information and Computation*, 1995. To appear. Available now as MIT/LCS/TM-487.c.
21. Nancy Lynch and H.B. Weinberg. Proving correctness of a vehicle maneuver: Deceleration. In *Second European Workshop on Real-Time and Hybrid Systems*, pages 196–203, Grenoble, France, May/June 1995.
22. Nancy A. Lynch and Hagit Attiya. Using mappings to prove timing properties. *Distributed Computing*, 6(2):121–139, September 1992.
23. Sam Owre, N. Shankar, and John Rushby. User guide for the PVS specification and verification system (draft). Technical report, Computer Science Lab, SRI Intl., Menlo Park, CA, 1993.
24. Jørgen Søgaard-Andersen. *Correctness of Protocols in Distributed Systems*. PhD thesis, Department of Computer Science, Technical University of Denmark, Lyngby, Denmark, December 1993. ID-TR: 1993-131. Full version in MIT/LCS/TR-589, titled "Correctness of Communication Protocols: A Case Study."
25. H. B. Weinberg. Correctness of vehicle control systems: A case study. Master's thesis, Department of Electrical Engineering and Computer Science, Massachusetts Institute of Technology, Cambridge, MA 02139, 1995. In progress.
26. H.B. Weinberg, Nancy Lynch, and Norman Delisle. Verification of automated vehicle protection systems. This volume.

An Invariant Based Approach to the Design of Hybrid Control Systems Containing Clocks

James A. Stiver, Panos J. Antsaklis, and Michael D. Lemmon

Department of Electrical Engineering
University of Notre Dame
Notre Dame, IN 46556

Abstract. The class of hybrid control systems considered here contain a discrete event system controller and a continuous-time plant modeled as an integrator, $\dot{\mathbf{x}} = \mathbf{c}, \mathbf{c} \in \Re^n, \mathbf{c} \neq 0$. A design procedure based on the natural invariants of the plant, which was developed for a more general class of hybrid systems, is applied to this more tractable class. It is shown that the invariant based approach provides a straightforward procedure for designing an interface and controller for this class of hybrid systems.

1 Introduction

Recent attention in the area of hybrid systems has focused on a particular class of hybrid system referred to as *linear hybrid systems* [8] or *timed hybrid systems* [2]. These systems all feature a continuous-time plant governed by

$$\dot{\mathbf{x}}(t) = \mathbf{c} \tag{1}$$

where $\mathbf{c} \in \Re^n$ is a constant vector and $\mathbf{c} \neq 0$. Here they will be referred to as integrators or clocks. In [8], the authors consider a state space partitioned with hyperplanes, and they explore the ability to drive the system between two desired regions by switching $\mathbf{c}$ among a set of values. The authors develop an algorithm to decide whether or not this is possible for a given system. In [2], the authors examine partitions of the plant state space that can be refined to obtain a finite congruence. This enables the system to be modeled with a finite deterministic automaton. Other authors have studied systems of this type (see for example [3]); they are referred to as *timed automata*.

In this paper, a general design procedure for hybrid control systems is first outlined. The procedure is based on the natural invariants of the plant and its purpose is to design an interface and controller for the hybrid control system. For more details see [4, 6]. This approach is applied to the case of hybrid control systems containing integrators.

In Section 2, the general model used in this paper is presented. More details on this model can be found in [1, 5]. Section 3 describes the invariant approach for the general case. Finally, Section 4 presents results for the special case.

2 Hybrid Control System Modeling

A hybrid control system, can be divided into three parts, the plant, interface, and controller as shown in Figure 1.

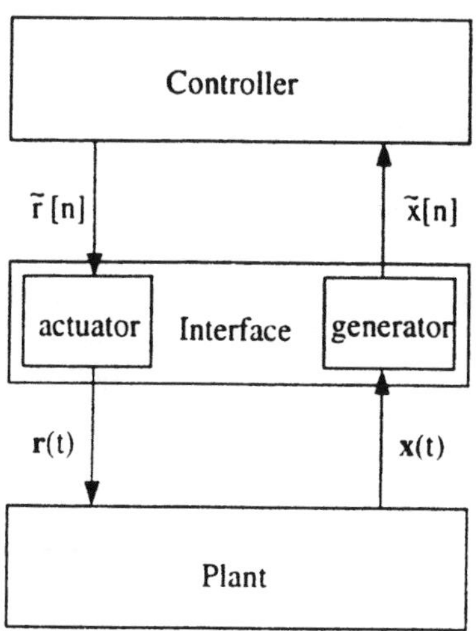

Fig. 1. Hybrid Control System

The plant is a nonlinear, time-invariant system represented by a set of ordinary differential equations,

$$\dot{\mathbf{x}}(t) = f(\mathbf{x}(t), \mathbf{r}(t)), \tag{2}$$

where $\mathbf{x}(t) \in \mathbf{X}$ and $\mathbf{r}(t) \in \mathbf{R}$ are the state and input vectors respectively, and $\mathbf{X} \subset \Re^n, \mathbf{R} \subset \Re^m$, with $t \in (a, b)$ some time interval. For any $\mathbf{r}(t) \in \mathbf{R}$, the function $f : \mathbf{X} \times \mathbf{R} \to \mathbf{X}$ is continuous in $\mathbf{x}$ and meets the conditions for existence and uniqueness of solutions for initial states, $\mathbf{x}_0 \in \mathbf{X}$. Note that the plant input and state are continuous-time vector valued signals. Boldface letters are used here to denote vectors and vector valued signals.

The controller is a discrete event system which is modeled as a deterministic automaton, $(\tilde{S}, \tilde{X}, \tilde{R}, \delta, \phi)$, where $\tilde{S}$ is the set of states, $\tilde{X}$ is the set of *plant symbols*, $\tilde{R}$ is the set of *controller symbols*, $\delta : \tilde{S} \times \tilde{X} \to \tilde{S}$ is the state transition function, and $\phi : \tilde{S} \to \tilde{R}$ is the output function. The symbols in set $\tilde{R}$ are called controller symbols because they are generated by the controller. Likewise, the symbols in set $\tilde{X}$ are called plant symbols and are generated based on events in the plant. The action of the controller is described by the equations

$$\tilde{s}[n] = \delta(\tilde{s}[n-1], \tilde{x}[n])$$
$$\tilde{r}[n] = \phi(\tilde{s}[n])$$

where $\tilde{s}[n] \in \tilde{S}, \tilde{x}[n] \in \tilde{X}$, and $\tilde{r}[n] \in \tilde{R}$. The index n is analogous to a time index in that it specifies the order of the symbols in the sequence. The input and output signals associated with the controller are sequences of symbols.

The interface consists of two simple subsystems, the *generator* and the *actuator*. The generator converts the continuous-time output (state) of the plant, $\mathbf{x}(t)$, to an asynchronous, symbolic input for the controller, $\tilde{x}[n]$. The set of plant events recognized by the generator is determined by a set of smooth functionals, $\{h_i : \Re^n \to \Re, i \in I\}$, whose null spaces form $n-1$ dimensional smooth hypersurfaces in the plant state space. Whenever the plant state crosses one of these hypersurfaces, a plant symbol is generated according to

$$\tilde{x}[n] = \alpha_i(\mathbf{x}(\tau_e[n])) \tag{3}$$

where i identifies the hypersurface which was crossed and $\tau_e[n]$ is the time of the crossing. The plant symbol generating function, $\alpha_i : \mathcal{N}(h_i) \to \tilde{X}$, maps the states in the null space of h_i to the set of plant symbols.

The actuator converts the sequence of controller symbols to a plant input signal, using the function $\gamma : \tilde{R} \to \mathbf{R}$, as follows.

$$\mathbf{r}(t) = \sum_{n=0}^{\infty} \gamma(\tilde{r}[n]) I(t, \tau_c[n], \tau_c[n+1]) \tag{4}$$

where $I(t, \tau_1, \tau_2)$ is a characteristic function taking on the value of unity over the time interval $[\tau_1, \tau_2)$ and zero elsewhere. $\tau_c[n]$ is the time of the nth control symbol which is based on the sequence of plant symbol instants,

$$\tau_c[n] = \tau_e[n] + \tau_d \tag{5}$$

where τ_d is the total delay associated with the interface and controller. The above actuator generates elements of an input set, which is taken to be finite. The elements of this set, which are the distinct inputs to the continuous plant, are referred to as control policies.

3 Invariant Based Approach

Here a methodology is presented to design the controller and the interface together based on the natural invariants of the plant. In particular, this section discusses the design of the generator, which is part of the interface, and also the design of the controller. We assume that the plant is given, the set of available control policies is given, and the control goals are specified as follows. Each control goal for the system is given as a starting set and a target set, each of which is an open subset of the plant state space. To realize the goal, the controller must be able to drive the plant state from anywhere in the starting set to somewhere in the target set using the available control policies. Generally, a system will have multiple control goals.

We propose the following solution to this design problem. For a given target region, identify the states which can be driven to that region by the application of a single control policy. If the starting region is contained within this set of states, the control goal is achievable via a single control policy. If not, then this new set of states can be used as a target region and the process can be repeated. This will result in a set of states which can be driven to the original target region with no more than two control policies applied in sequence. This process can be repeated until the set of states, for which a sequence of control policies exists to drive them to the target region, includes the entire starting region (provided the set of control policies is adequate).

When the regions have been identified, the generator is designed to tell the controller, via plant symbols, which region the plant state is currently in. The controller will then call for the control policy which drives the states in that region to the target region.

A *common flow region* (CFR), for given target region, is a set of states which can be driven to the target region with the same control policy. The following definition is used.

Definition 1. For a plant given by Equation (2) and a target region, **T**, the set **B** is a common flow region for **T** if

$$\forall \mathbf{x}(0) \in \mathbf{B}, \exists \tilde{r} \in \tilde{R}, t_1, t_2, t_1 < t_2$$

such that

$$x(t) \in \mathbf{B}, t \leq t_1$$

and

$$x(t) \in \mathbf{T}, t_1 < t < t_2$$

subject to

$$\dot{\mathbf{x}}(t) = f(\mathbf{x}(t), \gamma(\tilde{r}))$$

To design the generator, it is necessary to select the set of hypersurfaces, $\{h_i : \mathbf{X} \to \Re \mid i \in I\}$ and the associated functions, $\{\alpha_i : \mathcal{N}(h_i) \to \tilde{R} \mid i \in I\}$, described above. These hypersurfaces will form the boundaries of the CFR's and thus permit the interface to alert the controller that the plant state is in a CFR. Hypersurfaces that form invariants of the plant are especially useful for this purpose.

Definition 2. For a plant given by Equation (2) and a control policy, $\gamma(\tilde{r})$, the hypersurface described by the null space of h_i is an invariant hypersurface if

$$\nabla_\xi h_i(\xi) \cdot f(\xi) = 0.$$

We present two propositions which can be used to determine whether a given set of hypersurfaces identifies a common flow region. In different situations, one of the propositions may be easier to apply than the other. The following propositions give sufficient conditions for the hypersurfaces bounding **B** and **T** to ensure that all state trajectories in **B** will reach **T**.

Proposition 3. *Given the following:*

1. *A flow generated by a smooth vector field, f*
2. *A target region, $\mathbf{T} \subset \mathbf{X}$*
3. *A set of smooth hypersurfaces, $h_i, i \in I_B \subset 2^I$*
4. *A smooth hypersurface (exit boundary), h_e*

such that $\mathbf{B} = \{\xi \in \mathbf{X} : h_i(\xi) < 0, h_e(\xi) > 0, \forall i \in I_B\} \neq \emptyset$. For all $\xi \in \mathbf{B}$ there is a finite time, t, such that $\mathbf{x}(0) = \xi, \mathbf{x}(t) \in \mathbf{T}$, if the following conditions are satisfied:

1. $\nabla_\xi h_i(\xi) \cdot f(\xi) = 0, \forall i \in I_B$
2. $\exists \epsilon > 0, \nabla_\xi h_e(\xi) \cdot f(\xi) < -\epsilon, \forall \xi \in \mathbf{B}$
3. $\mathbf{B} \cap \mathcal{N}(h_e) \subset T$

Proof. See [4, 7].

The second proposition uses a slightly different way of specifying a common flow region. In addition to the invariant hypersurfaces and the exit boundary, there is also a cap boundary. The cap boundary is used to obtain a common flow region which is bounded. So for this case

$$\mathbf{B} = \{\xi \in \mathbf{X} : h_i(\xi) < 0, h_e(\xi) > 0, \\ h_c(\xi) < 0, \forall i \in I_B\}. \tag{6}$$

Proposition 4. *Given the following:*

1. *A flow generated by a smooth vector field, f*
2. *A target region, $\mathbf{T} \subset \mathbf{X}$*
3. *A set of smooth hypersurfaces, $h_i, i \in I_B \subset 2^I$*
4. *A smooth hypersurface (exit boundary), h_e*
5. *A smooth hypersurface (cap boundary), h_c*

such that $\mathbf{B} = \{\xi \in \mathbf{X} : h_i(\xi) < 0, h_e(\xi) > 0, h_c(\xi) < 0, \forall i \in I_B\} \neq \emptyset$ and $\overline{\mathbf{B}}$ (closure of $\mathbf{B}$) is compact. For all $\xi \in \mathbf{B}$ there is a finite time, t, such that $\mathbf{x}(0) = \xi, \mathbf{x}(t) \in \mathbf{T}$, if the following conditions are satisfied:

1. $\nabla_\xi h_i(\xi) \cdot f(\xi) = 0, \forall i \in I_B$
2. $\nabla_\xi h_c(\xi) \cdot f(\xi) < 0, \forall \xi \in \mathbf{B} \cap \mathcal{N}(h_c)$
3. $\mathbf{B} \cap \mathcal{N}(h_e) \subset T$
4. *There are no limit sets in $\overline{\mathbf{B}}$*

Proof. See [4, 7].

Remark: Each of the two propositions gives sufficient conditions for a set of hypersurfaces to form a common flow region. They can be used in hybrid control system design as a verification tool.

Two important problems in the invariant based approach to interface design are now described. The first is the existence of the common flow regions. What is required is a set of conditions involving the target region and the control policy, under which a common flow region can be guaranteed to exist. Further conditions may be required to guarantee that a common flow region can be bounded by a set of invariant hypersurfaces. The second open problem is the construction of the hypersurfaces that bound the common flow region. Solutions to these problems for the general case have yet to be derived. The following section shows that these two problems are solved for the special case, described in the introduction, where the plant is given by (1).

4 The Invariant Based Approach for Clocks

The advantage of using the plant characterized by Equation 1 is that under a mild restriction (specified below), the CFR can be guaranteed to exist; furthermore the set of invariant hypersurfaces is readily determined. A systematic process exists to select a subset of these hypersurfaces to bound the common flow region. In the following, a particular approach is presented.

Notice that the following change of coordinates can be performed on the state space of the plant.

$$\hat{\mathbf{x}} = P\mathbf{x} \tag{7}$$

where

$$P^{-1} = \begin{bmatrix} c_1 & 0 & 0 & \cdots & 0 \\ c_2 & 1 & 0 & \cdots & 0 \\ c_3 & 0 & 1 & \ddots & \vdots \\ \vdots & \vdots & \ddots & \ddots & 0 \\ c_n & 0 & \cdots & 0 & 1 \end{bmatrix} \tag{8}$$

In the transformed coordinates, the plant is described by

$$\dot{\hat{\mathbf{x}}} = Pf(P^{-1}\hat{\mathbf{x}}) = \hat{f}(\hat{\mathbf{x}}) = \begin{bmatrix} 1 \\ 0 \\ \vdots \\ 0 \end{bmatrix}. \tag{9}$$

More generally, the inverse of the transformation matrix can be $P^{-1} = [c, M]$, where M is an n by $n-1$ matrix such that $[c, M]$ is a nonsingular matrix.

In the transformed coordinates, the set of invariant hypersurfaces is given by the set of functions

$$\{\hat{h} : \nabla\hat{h}(\hat{\mathbf{x}}) \cdot \hat{f}(\hat{\mathbf{x}}) = 0\}$$

which can be simplified, due to the structure of $\hat{f}$, to

$$\{\hat{h} : \frac{\partial \hat{h}(\hat{\mathbf{x}})}{\partial \hat{x}_1} = 0\}.$$

Therefore any $\hat{h}(\hat{\mathbf{x}})$ that is not a function of $\hat{x}_1$ will describe an invariant hypersurface in the transformed coordinates. The relationship between $\hat{h}$ and h is defined by

$$\hat{h}(\hat{\mathbf{x}}) \equiv h(P^{-1}\hat{\mathbf{x}}).$$

Assumption: Assume the target region is defined by a single invariant hypersurface, $h_T(\mathbf{x})$, in the original coordinates. A straightforward procedure then exists to select a single invariant hypersurface which bounds a common flow region for that target. This imposes only a mild loss of generality, because in most cases any desired region can be approximated in this way.

An outline of the procedure follows.

1. Use the coordinate transformation, P, to get the target region in the new coordinates according to equation 7.
2. Select an exit boundary (hyperplane), normal to the $\hat{x}_1$ axis, which intersects the transformed target region. It will be of the form $\hat{h}_e(\hat{\mathbf{x}}) = -\hat{x}_1 + e$, for some $e \in \Re$.
3. Determine the curve that forms the intersection of the exit boundary and the target boundary. This curve is described by
$$\hat{h}_T(\hat{\mathbf{x}})\Big|_{\hat{x}_1=e} = 0, \hat{x}_1 = e.$$
4. Project the above curve onto the $\hat{x}_1 = 0$ hyperplane, along the $\hat{x}_1$ axis. This simply entails replacing the $\hat{x}_1 = e$ with $\hat{x}_1 = 0$ in the expression for the curve.
5. The above projection, without the $\hat{x}_1 = 0$ condition,
$$\hat{h}_T(\hat{\mathbf{x}})\Big|_{\hat{x}_1=e} = 0,$$
forms an invariant hypersurface bounding a common flow region in the transformed coordinates.
6. Apply the inverse transform of equation 7 to get the above hypersurface, as well as the exit boundary, in the original coordinates.

A modification of the above procedure can be used if the target region boundary consists of several hypersurfaces. In such a case, the target is considered to be the intersection of several regions, each of which is bounded by one of the hypersurfaces. The CFR will then consist of the intersection of the CFR's for each of the several regions. This means the final CFR will have a boundary consisting of several hypersurfaces just as the target region does.

Proposition 5. *The hypersurface obtained in the above procedure identifies a common flow region for the target region, T.*

Proof. First we prove that the first condition of Proposition 3 is satisfied. By construction the following relation holds in the transformed coordinate system.
$$\nabla_{\hat{\mathbf{x}}}\hat{h}(\hat{\mathbf{x}}) \cdot \hat{f}(\hat{\mathbf{x}}) = 0$$
Substituting for $\hat{h}$ and $\hat{f}$ reveals
$$\nabla_{\hat{\mathbf{x}}}h(P^{-1}\hat{\mathbf{x}}) \cdot Pf(P^{-1}\hat{\mathbf{x}}) = 0.$$

Noting that

$$\nabla_{\hat{\mathbf{x}}} h(P^{-1}\hat{\mathbf{x}}) = \nabla_{\mathbf{x}} h(P^{-1}\hat{\mathbf{x}})P^{-1}$$

this implies

$$\nabla_{\mathbf{x}} h(P^{-1}\hat{\mathbf{x}})P^{-1} \cdot Pf(P^{-1}\hat{\mathbf{x}}) = 0.$$

which can be simplified to yield the first condition of Proposition 3

$$\nabla_{\mathbf{x}} h(\mathbf{x}) \cdot f(\mathbf{x}) = 0.$$

Second, we prove that the second condition of Proposition 3 is satisfied. Since we have defined $\hat{f}(\hat{\mathbf{x}})$ according to Equation 9, and chosen $\hat{h}_e(\hat{\mathbf{x}}) = -\hat{x}_1 + e$, we know that

$$\nabla_{\hat{\mathbf{x}}} \hat{h}_e(\hat{\mathbf{x}}) \cdot \hat{f}(\hat{\mathbf{x}}) = -1$$

By the same steps as followed in the first part of this proof, we therefore know that

$$\nabla_{\mathbf{x}} h_e(\mathbf{x}) \cdot f(\mathbf{x}) = -1,$$

which satisfies condition two of Proposition 3 for $\epsilon < 1$. Finally, the third condition of the proposition is satisfied because the invariant hypersurface is chosen, based on the intersection of the target region and the exit boundary, to satisfy it. □

The only portion of the above procedure which requires some heuristic effort is step 2. The selection of the exit boundary will determine the cross section of the common flow region. This is because the CFR boundary will intersect the target region boundary along the same curve that the exit boundary intersects the target region boundary. Next, another procedure is presented, which requires no heuristic effort and is optimal in the sense that is finds the largest possible common flow region that exists. This procedure is more difficult to implement.

1. Use the coordinate transformation, P, to get the target region in the new coordinates according to equation 7.
2. Select an exit boundary (hyperplane), normal to the $\hat{x}_1$ axis, which intersects the transformed target region. It will be of the form $\hat{h}_e(\hat{\mathbf{x}}) = -\hat{x}_1 + e$, where $e \in \Re$.
3. Project the target region boundary onto the $\hat{x}_1 = 0$ hyperplane, along the $\hat{x}_1$ axis.
4. Determine the curve on the $\hat{x}_1 = 0$ hyperplane that forms the boundary of the above projected region.
5. The above curve, without the $\hat{x}_1 = 0$ condition, forms an invariant hypersurface bounding a common flow region in the transformed coordinates.
6. Apply the inverse transform of equation 7 to get the above hypersurface, as well as the exit boundary, in the original coordinates.

5 Example

Given the following plant

$$\dot{\mathbf{x}} = \begin{bmatrix} c_1 \\ c_2 \\ c_3 \end{bmatrix}$$

with $c_1 \neq 0$, let the transformation matrix be

$$T = \begin{bmatrix} \frac{1}{c_1} & 0 & 0 \\ -\frac{c_2}{c_1} & 1 & 0 \\ -\frac{c_3}{c_1} & 0 & 1 \end{bmatrix}$$

Let the target region be defined by the unit sphere centered at the origin. It is bounded by the hypersurface

$$h_T(\mathbf{x}) = x_1^2 + x_2^2 + x_3^2 - 1.$$

In transformed coordinates it becomes

$$\begin{aligned} \hat{h}_T(\hat{\mathbf{x}}) &= (c_1\hat{x}_1)^2 + (c_2\hat{x}_1 + \hat{x}_2)^2 + (c_3\hat{x}_1 + \hat{x}_3)^2 \\ &= (c_1^2 + c_2^2 + c_3^2)\hat{x}_1^2 + \hat{x}_2^2 + \hat{x}_3^2 + 2c_2\hat{x}_1\hat{x}_2 + 2c_3\hat{x}_1\hat{x}_3 - 1 \end{aligned}$$

The exit boundary is a plane normal to the $\hat{x}_1$ axis that intersects the target region. For simplicity, the exit boundary is chosen as the $\hat{x}_1 = 0$ hyperplane, which is convenient because the projection is then trivial. Projection onto the $\hat{x}_1 = 0$ hyperplane yields the following curve

$$\hat{x}_2^2 + \hat{x}_3^2 - 1 = 0, \hat{x}_1 = 0.$$

The common flow region is bounded by

$$\hat{h}_B(\hat{\mathbf{x}}) = \hat{x}_2^2 + \hat{x}_3^2 - 1.$$

Finally, the inverse transform is used to obtain the hypersurfaces in the original coordinates.

$$\begin{aligned} h_B(\mathbf{x}) &= (x_2 - \frac{c_2}{c_1}x_1)^2 + (x_3 - \frac{c_3}{c_1}x_3)^2 - 1 \\ h_e(\mathbf{x}) &= \frac{1}{c_1}x_1 \end{aligned}$$

Figure 2 shows the target regions and CFR's in both the original and transformed coordinates.

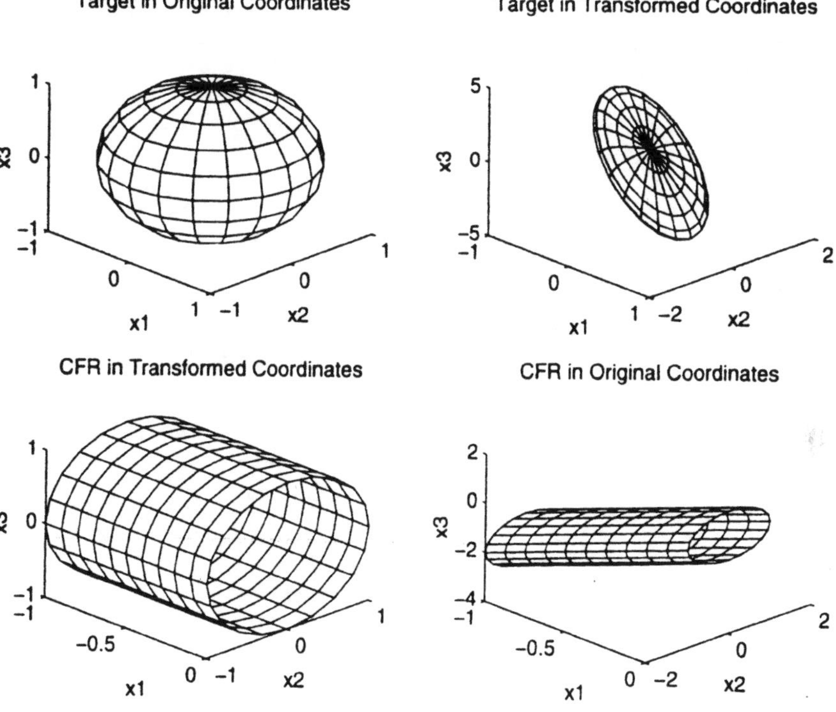

Fig. 2. Regions for the Example

References

1. P. J. Antsaklis, M. D. Lemmon, and J. A. Stiver, "Learning to be autonomous: Intelligent supervisory control", In *Intelligent Control: Theory and Applications*, M. Gupta and N. Sinha, Eds., chapter 2, pp. 28–62. IEEE Press, 1996.
2. S. Di Gennaro, C. Horn, S. Kulkarni, and P. Ramadge, "Reduction of timed hybrid systems", In *Proceedings of the 33rd IEEE Conference on Decision and Control*, pp. 4215–4220, Lake Buena Vista, FL, December 1994.
3. A. Gollu, A. Puri, and P. Varaiya, "Discretization of timed automata", In *Proceedings of the 33rd Conference on Decision and Control*, pp. 957–960, Lake Buena Vista, FL, December 1994.
4. J. A. Stiver, P. J. Antsaklis, and M. D. Lemmon, "Digital control from a hybrid perspective", In *Proceedings of the 33rd Conference on Decision and Control*, pp. 4241–4246, Lake Buena Vista, FL, December 1994.
5. J. A. Stiver, P. J. Antsaklis, and M. D. Lemmon, "A Logical DES Approach to the Design of Hybrid Systems", *Mathematical and Computer Modeling*, 1995, To appear.
6. J. A. Stiver, P. J. Antsaklis, and M. D. Lemmon, "Interface and controller design for hybrid control systems", In *Hybrid Systems II*, P. Antsaklis, W. Kohn, A. Nerode and S. Sastry, Eds., Lecture Notes in Computer Science. Springer-Verlag, 1995, To appear.

7. J. A. Stiver, P. J. Antsaklis, and M. D. Lemmon, "Interface Design for Hybrid Control Systems", Technical Report of the ISIS Group (Interdisciplinary Studies of Intelligent Systems) ISIS-95-001, University of Notre Dame, January 1995.
8. M. Tittus and B. Egardt, "Control-law synthesis for linear hybrid systems", In *Proceedings of the 33rd IEEE Conference on Decision and Control*, pp. 961–966, Lake Buena Vista, FL, December 1994.

Refinements of Approximating Automata for Synthesis of Supervisory Controllers for Hybrid Systems

Toshihiko Niinomi
Mitsubishi Heavy Industries
Hiroshima, Japan
niinomi@hir.mhi.co.jp

Bruce H. Krogh
Carnegie Mellon Univ.
Pittsburgh, PA, USA
krogh@ece.cmu.edu

José E. R. Cury
Univ. Fed. S. Catarina
Florianopolis SC, Brazil
cury@lcmi.ufsc.br

Abstract

The problem of supervisory controller synthesis is considered for a class of continuous-time hybrid systems (plants) in which the continuous-state dynamics are selected by a discrete-valued input signal, and output events are generated when the continuous output signal encounters specified thresholds. A discrete-state supervisor controls the hybrid plant by switching the discrete input when threshold events are observed. The objective is to synthesize a nonblocking supervisor (in the ω-language sense) such that the sequential behavior of the closed-loop system is contained within a specified set of admissible behaviors. This problem can be converted into a supervisor synthesis problem for a controlled discrete event system (DES) and solutions may be obtained by constructing finite-state generators that accept outer approximations to the exact DES model of the hybrid plant. This paper presents the construction procedure for the approximating automata and a demonstration that increasing the order of the construction computations by appropriate amounts leads to refinements of the outer approximations.

1 Introduction

This paper concerns continuous-time hybrid systems of the form illustrated in Fig. 1 [3],[4]. All signals are defined on $[0, \infty)$. The *plant* $\mathcal{H}$ contains the continuous dynamics; the *supervisor* $\mathcal{F}$ contains the discrete dynamics. The input signal u to the system $\mathcal{H}$ is a piecewise constant, right continuous *condition signal* taking on values in a finite set of conditions U. The output signal v from $\mathcal{H}$ is a vector of *event signals* taking on non-zero values in $V = \{0, 1\}^{n_v} - \{0\}^{n_v}$ at isolated points in time. We assume the condition and event signals are *nonexplosive*, that is, signals u and v have a finite number of discontinuities on any finite interval. The sets of all such condition signals and event signals are denoted by $\mathcal{U}$ and $\mathcal{V}$ respectively.

The dynamics in the system $\mathcal{H}$ are defined by a *continuous state trajectory* x in R^{n_x}. At each instant t the state trajectory satisfies a differential inclusion of the form $\dot{x}(t) \in f_{u(t)}(x(t))$, where $f_u: R^{n_x} \rightarrow 2^{R^{n_x}}$ for each $u \in U$. The input condition signal selects the differential inclusion at each instant. The initial value of the state trajectory is in a given set $X_0 \subseteq R^{n_x}$. The set of all possible state trajectories for a given input signal u is denoted by X_u. The function $g: R^{n_x} \rightarrow R^{n_v}$ generates a *continuous output signal* y from the continuous state trajectory. Each component of y is compared to a threshold defined by the components of the *threshold vector* $T \in R^{n_v}$, and the output event signal v is generated by a *zero detector* defined for each component of the input signal by

$$v_i(t) = \begin{cases} 1 \text{ if } y_i(t) - T_i = 0 \text{ and } \exists\ \Delta > 0 \text{ s.t. } y_i(t-\delta) - T_i \neq 0 \text{ for } 0 < \delta < \Delta \\ 0 \text{ otherwise} \end{cases}$$

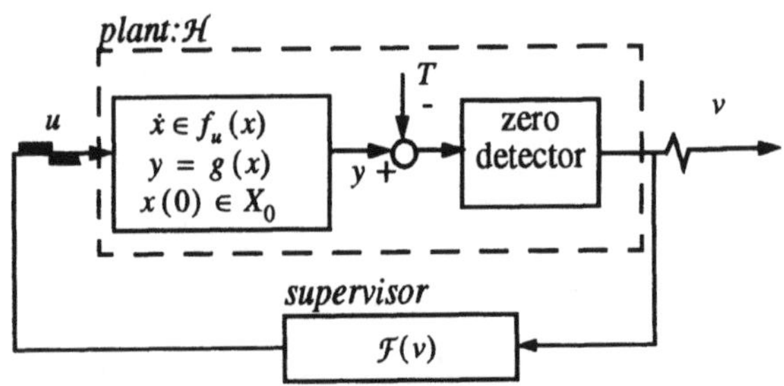

Fig. 1. Hybrid system with switched continuous dynamics, threshold events, and supervisory control.

As illustrated in Fig. 1, the *supervisor* $\mathcal{F}$ observes the threshold event signal v and generates the input condition signal u to control the plant $\mathcal{H}$. Since $\mathcal{F}$ maps an event signal v into a condition signal u, it is a type of condition/event system as defined in [5]. We assume the supervisor can change the input signal u only when threshold events are observed. Thus, discontinuities in the signal u can occur only at instants when the event signal v is nonzero. Furthermore, we assume $\mathcal{F}$ is *deterministic* (only one condition signal u is associated with a given event signal v), *causal* (if two event signals are equal up to some time t_1, the associated condition signals are also equal up to time t_1), and *strictly discrete* (the sequence of values in u depends only on the sequence of events in v, not the inter-event times). We also assume the feedback system does not exhibit "chattering", which corresponds to the assumption that u and v are nonexplosive.

We define the *synchronized cross product* of $\mathcal{U}$ and $\mathcal{V}$, denoted by $\mathcal{U} \underline{x} \mathcal{V}$, as the set of all pairs (u, v) such that discontinuities in u occur only at instants when v is not zero, which is consistent with the behaviors assumed for $\mathcal{F}$. Since we are only interested in the possible behaviors of $\mathcal{H}$ under supervision, $\mathcal{H}$ is defined as a subset of $\mathcal{U} \underline{x} \mathcal{V}$. Similarly, a supervisor $\mathcal{F}$ is defined as a subset of $\mathcal{U} \underline{x} \mathcal{V}$, and the behavior of the closed-loop system, denoted $\mathcal{F}/\mathcal{H}$, is then the intersection of the signal pairs in $\mathcal{H}$ and $\mathcal{F}$, that is, $\mathcal{F}/\mathcal{H} = \mathcal{F} \cap \mathcal{H}$. The objective of the supervisor synthesis problem considered in this paper is to design $\mathcal{F}$ so that the possible sequential behaviors of $\mathcal{F}/\mathcal{H}$, that is, the sequences of control inputs and threshold events in $\mathcal{F}/\mathcal{H}$, are contained within a given set of admissible infinite-length sequences, $E \subseteq (U \times V)^{\omega}$. Note that implicit in this specification is the requirement that the supervisor be *nonblocking* in the sense that threshold events are generated indefinitely.

To represent the sequential behavior of $\mathcal{F}/\mathcal{H}$, we define a projection of pairs of signals in $\mathcal{U} \underline{x} \mathcal{V}$ into sequences of pairs of input values and events in $U \times V$ (a special case of the general condition/event system input-output signal projection defined in [5]). Specifically, we define $Pr: \mathcal{U} \underline{x} \mathcal{V} \rightarrow [(U \times V)^* \circ (U \times \{\perp\})] \cup (U \times V)^{\omega}$ as follows. For $(u, v) \in \mathcal{U} \underline{x} \mathcal{V}$, let $t_{v,k}$ denote the time of the kth event (nonzero value) in v. If v has an infinite number of events,

$$Pr[(u, v)] = (u(t_{v,1}^-), v(t_{v,1})) \circ (u(t_{v,2}^-), v(t_{v,2})) \circ \cdots,$$

were $u(t_{v,k}^-)$ is the input value applied *before* the event $v(t_{v,k})$ occurs. When v has a finite number of events, K_v denotes the total number of events in v and the string of input-event pairs in $Pr[(u,v)]$ is terminated with the pair $(u(t_{v,K_v}), \perp)$ indicating no further events are generated after the application of the input value $u(t_{v,K_v})$. (If there are no events in v, $K_v = 0$ and $t_{v,0} = 0$.) The projection operator is extend to sets of signal pairs in the natural way. In particular, $Pr[\mathcal{F}/\mathcal{H}]$ denotes the sequential behavior of the closed loop system, and the supervisory control problem can be stated as:

Hybrid System Supervisory Control Problem (HSSCP). Given a hybrid plant $\mathcal{H} \subseteq \mathcal{U} \underline{x} \mathcal{V}$ as defined above and sequential specification $E \subseteq (U \times V)^{\omega}$, find a deterministic, causal, strictly discrete supervisor $\mathcal{F} \subseteq \mathcal{U} \underline{x} \mathcal{V}$ such that the closed-loop system $\mathcal{F}/\mathcal{H}$ satisfies $Pr[\mathcal{F}/\mathcal{H}] \subseteq E$.

It is shown in [1] that the HSSCP can be solved by formulating an equivalent supervisory control problem for a controlled discrete event system (DES) and applying standard techniques for synthesis of DES supervisors. A problem arises with this approach because the representation of the plant language for the exact DES model of the hybrid plant dynamics can be extremely large, and it is possible a finite representation does not exist. A solution may be found, however, using a finite state automaton that accepts languages that are outer approximations of the exact DES languages modeling $\mathcal{H}$. A construction procedure (CP) exists to generate approximating automata from the definition of $\mathcal{H}$. The CP generates an approximation of order N, where N is the depth of the forward mappings of the continuous dynamics between threshold manifolds in the continuous state space. These results from [1] are summarized in the following two sections.

If a solution to the HSSCP is not found for a given approximation, it might be possible to find a solution with an automaton that accepts a tighter outer approximation. Section 4 concerns the question of whether a higher-order approximation from the CP produces a better approximation to the exact DES plant. It is shown that this is the case, provided the order of the new approximation is an integer multiple of $(N - 1)$ greater than the previous approximation of order N. Section 5 summarizes the results presented in this paper and discusses current research directions.

2 The Equivalent DES Control Problem

Given a hybrid plant $\mathcal{H}$ as defined in the introduction, the associated DES plant H is defined as a pair of languages (L_H, S_H), $L_H \subseteq [(U \times V)^* \circ (U \times \{\perp\})] \cup (U \times V)^*$ and $S_H \subseteq (U \times V)^{\omega}$, where $L_H = pre(Pr[\mathcal{H}])$ (*pre* denotes the set a prefixes for the given set of sequences) and $S_H = Pr[\mathcal{H}] \cap (U \times V)^{\omega}$. Thus, H represents all possible sequential input-output behaviors of the hybrid plant $\mathcal{H}$ as a DES with both finite-length and infinite-length strings, the type of DES defined in [7]. To capture the fact that the value of the input condition signal determines the set of next possible threshold events in $\mathcal{H}$, the DES control structure for H, denoted Γ_H, is defined as

$$\Gamma_H = \{\gamma \in 2^{U \times (V \cup \{\perp\})} | \gamma = \{u\} \times (V \cup \{\perp\}), u \in U\}.$$

Γ_H is a general DES control structure as defined in [2].

A DES supervisor f for H is a mapping $f: (U \times V)^* \to \Gamma_H$. The closed-loop DES constructed when supervisor f is applied to DES H, denoted f/H, is defined as the pair of languages $(L_{f/H}, S_{f/H})$ which are the sequences in L_H and S_H that subsist under the application of f, as defined in [7]. Given a DES supervisor f for H we define an associated supervisor for $\mathcal{H}$, denoted $\mathcal{F}_f$, as

$$\mathcal{F}_f = \{ (u, v) \in \mathcal{U} \times \mathcal{V} | \forall [\omega \circ \sigma \in pre(Pr[(u, v)]), \sigma \in (U \times V) \cup (U \times \{\perp\})], \sigma \in f(\omega) \}$$

With these definitions the following theorem is proved in [1].

Theorem 1: Given a hybrid system $\mathcal{H}$ and the associated DES $H = (L_H, S_H)$ with control structure Γ_H, if f is a DES supervisor for H, then $pre(Pr[\mathcal{F}_f/\mathcal{H}]) = L_{f/H}$ and $Pr[\mathcal{F}_f/\mathcal{H}] \cap (U \times V)^\omega = S_{f/H}$.

It follows from Theorem 1 that the HSSCP can be solved by solving a DES supervisory control problem for the associated DES H, which is to find a *nonblocking* supervisor f such that $S_{f/H} \subseteq E$. Techniques for computing such a supervisor are developed in [7] and [8], provided the DES plant H can be represented by a finite automaton. Unfortunately, there may not be a finite representation for the DES H. It is shown in [1] that a supervisor for H satisfying the specifications can be computed using a DES $A = (L_A, S_A)$, with $L_A \subseteq [(U \times V)^* \circ (U \times \{\perp\})] \cup (U \times V)^*$ and $S_A \subseteq (U \times V)^\omega$, that is an *outer approximation* for H, that is, $L_A \supseteq L_H$ and $S_A \supseteq S_H$, provided A satisfies the conditions in the following theorem.

Theorem 2: Let $A = (L_A, S_A)$ be an outer approximation for $H = (L_H, S_H)$ with the same control structure Γ_H, and suppose for any $\omega \in (U \times V)^*$

$$\omega \circ (u, \perp) \in L_H \Rightarrow \omega \circ (u, \perp) \in L_A. \tag{1}$$

Given $E \subseteq (U \times V)^\omega$, if f is a nonblocking supervisor for A such that $S_{f/A} \subseteq E$, then f is a nonblocking supervisor for H and $S_{f/H} \subseteq E$.

In words, condition (1) in Theorem 2 states that any terminating strings in H must also be terminating strings in A. By Theorem 2, if a finite automaton (called an *approximating automaton*) can be constructed that represents an outer approximation for H satisfying (1), and if the supervisory control problem can be solved using this automaton, then the DES supervisor provides a solution to the HSSCP. The following section presents a procedure for constructing approximating automata based on the original hybrid plant $\mathcal{H}$.

3 Approximating Automata for Hybrid Systems

In this section we present a procedure to compute outer approximations for H using Muller automata. A deterministic Muller automaton is a 5-tuple $\mathcal{A} = (\Sigma, Q, \delta, q_0, \mathcal{R})$ where Σ is a finite alphabet, Q is a finite set of states, $q_0 \in Q$ is the initial state, $\delta: Q \times \Sigma \to Q$ is a transition (partial) function, and $\mathcal{R} \subseteq 2^Q$ is a recurrence family [6]. We extend the transition function δ to strings by defining a function $\hat{\delta}: Q \times \Sigma^* \to Q$ in the natural way. The pair of languages $(L(\mathcal{A}), S(\mathcal{A}))$ accepted by $\mathcal{A}$ are defined as: $L(\mathcal{A}) = \{\omega \in \Sigma^* | \hat{\delta}(q_0, \omega) \text{ is defined}\}$; and S_A is the set of all strings $s \in \Sigma^\omega$ such that: (i) $pre(s) \subseteq L_A$, and (ii) the set of states visited infinitely often when generating s is an element of $\mathcal{R}$.

The following definitions and notation are used in the construction procedure. Threshold events are generated by $\mathcal{H}$ when the state trajectory encounters one or more of the *threshold manifolds* in R^{n_x} defined as $M_i = \{x \in R^{n_x} | g_i(x) = T_i\}$, for $i = 1, \ldots, n_v$. We denote the set of all threshold manifolds by $M = \bigcup_{i=1,\ldots,n_v} M_i$. Distinct events correspond to each of the possible non-zero values of the event signals. To identify the sets of states corresponding to each distinct event, we define for each $v \in V = \{0,1\}^{n_v} - \{0\}^{n_v}$, $\pi_v = \bigcap_{j:v_j=1} M_j$. In words, π_v is the set of states that could generate the threshold event v.

To characterize the sequences of states that generate threshold events along admissible state trajectories in $\mathcal{H}$, we define for each state $x \in R^{n_x}$ and each $u \in U$ a *forward dynamic mapping* $\mathcal{M}_u(x) \subseteq M$ which maps the state x to the subset of the manifolds first encountered under condition input value u. That is,

$$\mathcal{M}_u(x) = \{x' \in M | \exists (x \in X_{u \equiv u}, t_f > 0) \text{ s.t. } x(0) = x, x(t_f) = x' \text{ and } \forall\, 0 \le t < t_f, x(t) \notin M\}$$

We also define a *backward dynamic mapping* from each state on a threshold manifold onto the states on manifolds from which the first state would be reached. That is, for $x \in M$ and each $u \in U$, we define $\mathcal{B}_u(x) \subseteq M$ as

$$\mathcal{B}_u(x) = \{x' \in M | x \in \mathcal{M}_u(x')\}.$$

Finally, for each $u \in U$ we define $\mathcal{N}_u \subseteq X$ as the set of states from which there is some admissible state trajectory which never reaches a manifold under the condition input u. That is,

$$\mathcal{N}_u = \{x' \in R^{n_x} | \exists (x \in X_{u \equiv u}, t_f > 0) \text{ s.t. } x(0) = x', \text{ and } \forall t > 0, x(t) \notin M\}.$$

Each of these mappings are extended to sets of states in the usual way.

We use the following notation below: for $\omega \in (U \times V)^n$, $\omega = \omega^1 \circ \ldots \circ \omega^n$ and $\omega_{[j,k]} = \omega^j \circ \ldots \circ \omega^k$, where $\omega^l = (u^l, v^l)$.

Construction Procedure (CP) for Approximating Automaton $\mathcal{A}_N$

Given a hybrid plant $\mathcal{H}$ and integer $N>1$.

1. Initial forward mapping. Define $D\colon (U \times V)^* \rightarrow \bigcup_{v \in V} 2^{\pi_v}$ recursively by

(i) $D(\varepsilon) = \varnothing$

(ii) $D((u, v)) = \pi_v$

(iii) For k>0, $\omega \in (U \times V)^k$, and $(u, v) \in U \times V$,

$$D(\omega \circ (u, v)) = \mathcal{M}_u(D(\omega)) \cap \pi_v .$$

Remark 1: D(ω) identifies the set of states reached along admissible trajectories on the manifold corresponding to the last threshold event in the string ω, beginning from any state on the entire manifold corresponding to the first threshold event in ω. For the construction procedure, *D*(ω) is computed only for $|\omega| \le N$. The definition for longer strings is used in the proof of Theorem 4 below.

2. Backward mapping.

a. For $\omega \in (U \times V)^N$, define $\Theta_N^N(\omega) = D(\omega)$, and

$$\Theta_l^N(\omega) = D(\omega_{[1,l]}) \cap \mathcal{B}_{u^{l+1}}(\Theta_{l+1}^N(\omega)) \text{ for } l = N-1,...,1 .$$

b. For $\omega \in (U \times V)^k \circ (U \times \{\perp\})$, $k = N-1,...,1$, define

$$\Theta_j^N(\omega) = \varnothing \text{ for } j = N, ...,k+1 ,$$

$$\Theta_k^N(\omega) = D(\omega_{[1,k]}) \cap \mathcal{N}_{u^{k+1}}, \text{ and}$$

$$\Theta_l^N(\omega) = D(\omega_{[1,l]}) \cap \mathcal{B}_{u^{l+1}}(\Theta_{l+1}^N(\omega)) \text{ for } l = k-1,..,1 .$$

Remark 2: $\Theta_j^N(\omega)$ is the subset of states on the manifold corresponding to the jth threshold event in ω along admissible trajectories that generate the complete sequence of events in ω for $|\omega| \le N$.

3. Second forward mapping. Define $D_N(\omega)$ as

(i) For $k = 1, ...,N-1$, $\omega \in (U \times V)^k$, $D_N(\omega) = D(\omega)$

(ii) For $\omega \in (U \times V)^N$, $D_N(\omega) = \bigcup_{\omega' \in \Omega_N(\omega)} \Theta_1^N(\omega')$, where

$$\Omega_N(\omega) = \{\omega' \in \left[\bigcup_{k=1}^{N-1} (U \times V)^k \circ (U \times \{\perp\})\right] \cup (U \times V)^N \mid$$

$$\omega'^{1} = \omega^N, \Theta_1^N(\omega') \cap D(\omega) \ne \varnothing \}$$

(iii) For $\omega \in (U \times V)^k, k = N, ...,2N-2$, $D_N(\omega) = \mathcal{M}_{u^k}(D_N(\omega_{[1,k-1]})) \cap \pi_{v^k}$

(iv) For $\omega \in (U \times V)^k$, $k = 2N-1, \dots$, with $k = m(N-1)+j$, for $1 \le j \le N-1$,

$$D_N(\omega) = D_N(\omega_{[(m-1)\cdot(N-1)+1,k]})$$

Remark 3: Steps 3(i) and 3(iii) are the same as step 1(iii) in that $D_N(\omega)$ is computed by the forward dynamic mapping. Step 3(iv) is formal to be used in the proof of Theorem 4 below; it merely repeats the definitions of $D_N(\omega)$ periodically using the tail of the string of length $mod_{(N-1)}|\omega| + N$. Step 3(ii) is the key computation: at the Nth stage the forward dynamic mappings are terminated and the set of possible states reached after N events, $D(\omega)$, is replaced by the union of the sets of states on the Nth event manifold, created by the backward mapping in step 2, that have nonempty intersections with $D(\omega)$ (see the definition of $\Omega_N(\omega)$).

4. Construction of Muller automaton. $\mathcal{A}_N = (\Sigma_N, Q_N, \delta_N, q_o, \mathcal{R}_N)$

$\Sigma_N = (U \times V) \cup (U \times \{\perp\})$;

$Q_N = \{q_0, q_\perp\} \cup \{q_\omega | \omega \in pre[(U \times V)^* \circ (U \times \{\perp\})], |\omega| < 2N-1\}$;

δ_N is defined by:

a. $\forall (\mathrm{u}, \mathrm{v}) \in U \times V \ni \mathcal{M}_\mathrm{u}(X_o) \cap \pi_\mathrm{v} \neq \emptyset$, $\delta_N(q_0, (\mathrm{u}, \mathrm{v})) = q_{(\mathrm{u}, \mathrm{v})}$;

b. $\forall (\mathrm{u}, \perp) \in U \times \{\perp\} \ni \mathcal{N}_\mathrm{u} \cap X_o \neq \emptyset$, $\delta_N(q_0, (\mathrm{u}, \perp)) = q_\perp$;

c. $\forall \omega \in (U \times V)^k, k = 1, \ldots, 2N-3$, $(\mathrm{u}, \mathrm{v}) \in U \times V$,
$\delta_N(q_\omega, (\mathrm{u}, \mathrm{v})) = q_{\omega \circ (\mathrm{u}, \mathrm{v})}$ if $D_N(\omega \circ (\mathrm{u}, \mathrm{v})) \neq \emptyset$;

d. for $\omega \in (U \times V)^{2N-2}$, $(\mathrm{u}, \mathrm{v}) \in U \times V$,
$\delta_N(q_\omega, (\mathrm{u}, \mathrm{v})) = q_{\omega_{[N, 2N-2]} \circ (\mathrm{u}, \mathrm{v})}$ if $D_N(\omega_{[N, 2N-2]} \circ (\mathrm{u}, \mathrm{v})) \neq \emptyset$,

e. $\forall \omega \in (U \times V)^k, k = 1, \ldots, 2N-2, \mathrm{u} \in U$
$\delta_N(q_\omega, (\mathrm{u}, \perp)) = q_\perp$ if $\mathrm{u} \in U, D_N(\omega) \cap \mathcal{N}_\mathrm{u} \neq \emptyset$;

$\mathcal{R}_N = 2^{Q_N}$.

Remark 4: The states in the Muller automaton are labeled by the sequences of control-event pairs that lead to the corresponding sets of states on the threshold manifolds. The definition of the recurrence set $\mathcal{R}_N$ gives the trivial ω language, $S(\mathcal{A}_N)=lim[L(\mathcal{A}_N)]$.

The following theorem is proved in [1].

Theorem 3: Given a hybrid plant $\mathcal{H}$ and the associated DES plant H, if $\mathcal{A}_N$ is the Muller automaton from the CP for $N \geq 2$, the DES $A_N = (L_{A_N}, S_{A_N})$ where $L_{A_N} = L(\mathcal{A}_N)$ and $S_{A_N} = S(\mathcal{A}_N)$, is an outer approximation for H satisfying the conditions of Theorem 2.

In the course of proving Theorem 3, the following properties are established as a lemma in [1]. These properties are used in the proof of Theorem 4 next section.

Lemma 1: Given outer approximation $A_N=(L_N,S_N)$ from the CP as defined in Theorem 3, for $\omega \in (U \times V)^*$, $|\omega| > 0$: (i) $\omega \in L_N \Leftrightarrow D_N(\omega_{[1,k]}) \neq \emptyset, k = 1, \ldots, |\omega|$; and (ii) $D_N(\omega) \supseteq D(\omega)$.

From the construction of the Muller automaton $\mathcal{A}_N$ in step 4 of the CP and the definition of $D_N(\omega)$ in step 3, a subset of the threshold manifolds can be identified with each state q_ω in $\mathcal{A}_N$. Property (ii) in Lemma 1 states that this subset contains the subset of states that would be obtained by consecutive applications of the forward dynamic mapping.

4 Refinements of Approximating Automata

Solutions to the HSSCP can be computed using approximating automata generated by the CP, as discussed in section 2. If a solution does not exist for a given approximating automata, one cannot conclude there is no solution to the HSSCP. It may be that the outer approximation is not sufficiently tight, that is, there may be a solution to the HSSCP, but a DES supervisor may not exist to satisfy the specifications for the approximating automaton because there are behaviors admitted by the approximation that are not actually behaviors of the exact DES model H for the hybrid plant $\mathcal{H}$. Therefore, an issue of practical importance is to determine methods for computing a *refinement* of a given approximating automaton. By this we mean that if a given automaton $\mathcal{A}$ does not give a sufficiently tight outer approximation to H, it is desirable to have a method to construct an approximating automaton $\mathcal{A}'$ such that

$$L_H \subseteq L(\mathcal{A}') \subset L(\mathcal{A}) \text{ and } S_H \subseteq S(\mathcal{A}') \subset S(\mathcal{A}) .$$

Since the CP is defined in terms of N, the depth of the forward dynamic mappings, it is natural to assume that increasing the depth of the forward dynamic mappings will naturally lead to better outer approximations of the DES H. The following theorem identifies a condition under which increasing the value of N to $K > N$ guarantees the outer approximation generated by the Muller automaton $\mathcal{A}_K$ is at least as good as the outer approximation generated by $\mathcal{A}_N$.

Theorem 4: Given outer approximations $A_N = (L_N, S_N)$ and $A_K = (L_K, S_K)$ generated by the CP as defined in Theorem 3, for $N, K \geq 2$, if $K = m(N-1)+1$ for some $m>1$, then $L(\mathcal{A}_K) \subseteq L(\mathcal{A}_N)$ and $S(\mathcal{A}_K) \subseteq S(\mathcal{A}_N)$.

Proof: From Lemma 1(i) and the definition of the recurrence set for the Muller automaton defined in step 4 of the CP, it suffices to show that

$$\forall (\omega \in L(\mathcal{A}_K) \cap (U \times V)^*, |\omega| > 0), D_K(\omega) \subseteq D_N(\omega) . \tag{2}$$

We prove (2) based on the length of the string ω:

$1 \leq |\omega| \leq K-1 = m(N-1)$: (2) holds since by step 3(i) $D_K(\omega) = D(\omega)$, and by Lemma 1(ii) $D(\omega) \subseteq D_N(\omega)$.

$|\omega| = K = m(N-1)+1$: From step 3(ii) $D_K(\omega) = \bigcup_{\omega' \in \Omega_K(\omega)} \Theta_1^K(\omega')$, and from step 3(iv) $D_N(\omega) = D_N(\omega_{[K-N+1,K]})$.

Since $|\omega_{[K-N+1,K]}| = N$, step 3(ii) implies

$$D_N(\omega) = \bigcup_{\omega'' \in \Omega_N(\omega_{[K-N+1,K]})} \Theta_1^N(\omega'') .$$

Now, from step 2 (the backward mapping), it can be shown that if $N' > N$ and $|\omega'| = N'$, then $\Theta_1^{N'}(\omega') \subseteq \Theta_1^{N}(\omega'')$ when $\omega'' = \omega'_{[1,N]}$. Therefore, from the definitions in step 3(ii) one can conclude that $\Omega_K(\omega) \subseteq \Omega_N(\omega_{[K-N+1,K]})$. These observations and the expressions for $D_K(\omega)$ and $D_N(\omega)$ imply (2).

$|\omega| > K$: We consider three cases.

$mod_{K-1}\{l\} = 1$: Step 3(iv) implies $D_K(\omega) = D_K(\omega_{[l-K+1,l]})$, and since $|\omega_{[l-K+1,l]}| = K$, step 3(ii) implies

$$D_K(\omega_{[l-K+1,l]}) = \bigcup_{\omega' \in \Omega_K(\omega_{[l-K+1,l]})} \Theta_1^K(\omega').$$

The remainder of the proof for this case is identical to the case $|\omega| = K = m(N-1)+1$ with $D_K(\omega)$ replaced by $D_K(\omega_{[l-K+1,l]})$.

For the remaining cases we apply induction, assuming (2) is true for $|\omega| = l-1$ and proving this implies (2) for $|\omega| = l$.

$mod_{K-1}\{l\} \neq 1$ and $mod_{N-1}\{l\} \neq 1$: From step 3(iii), when $|\omega| = l$, $D_K(\omega)$ and $D_N(\omega)$ are computed by applying the same forward mapping to $D_K(\omega_{[1,l-1]})$ and $D_N(\omega_{[1,l-1]})$, respectively, (after applying 3(iv)) which means (2) for $|\omega| = l-1$ implies (2) for $|\omega| = l$.

$mod_{K-1}\{l\} \neq 1$ and $mod_{N-1}\{l\} = 1$: In this case $D_N(\omega)$ is computed by applying 3(iv) and then 3(ii). But the set obtained from 3(ii) contains the set that would be obtained by applying the forward mapping in 3(iii). Therefore, the result is obtained by the same argument as in the previous case. □

Theorem 4 implies, for example, the following relations among the languages accepted by the Muller automata generated by the CP: $L(\mathcal{A}_2) \supseteq L(\mathcal{A}_3), L(\mathcal{A}_4), L(\mathcal{A}_5), \ldots$; $L(\mathcal{A}_3) \supseteq L(\mathcal{A}_5), L(\mathcal{A}_7), L(\mathcal{A}_9), \ldots$; and, in general,

$$L(\mathcal{A}_N) \supseteq L(\mathcal{A}_{N+l(N-1)}) \quad \text{for } l > 0.$$

5 Discussion

This paper presents a method for computing solutions to the supervisory control problem for a class of hybrid systems using finite automata that approximate the sequential behavior of the actual hybrid plant. It is shown that increasing the order, N, of the computations in the procedure for constructing the approximating automata leads to refinements of the approximations, provided the increase in the order is a multiple of N-1.

Current research is focusing on extensions of the approximation theory to other supervisory control problems, and issues related to the application of this theory to practical problems. The computation of the forward and backward dynamic mappings appears to be the most difficult issue for real hybrid systems. We note that by using differential inclusions rather than exact differential equations, one can use the conservative outer approximations of the actual system dynamics in the computation of these mappings. The forward dynamic mappings can be approximated, and the refinement result in section 4 still holds.

Other important issues being investigated include conditions which guarantee the feedback supervisor will not lead to chattering; extensions to cases including condition outputs from the plant (e.g., state feedback), and event inputs to the plant (which appear as impulses in the continuous dynamics); and the incorporation of dynamic elements such as timers in the supervisor as part of the design problem.

Acknowledgments

The authors gratefully acknowledge the following sources of financial support: the first author was supported by Mitsubishi Heavy Industries, Ltd.; the second author was supported in part by Rockwell International; and the third author was supported in part by CNPq, Brazil.

References

[1] Cury, J.E.R., B.H. Krogh, and T. Niinomi, Synthesis of supervisory controllers for hybrid systems based on approximating automata, submitted to *IEEE Trans. on Automatic Control*; a preliminary version of this paper appeared in *Proc. 34th IEEE Conf. on Decision and Control*, pp. 1461-1466, Dec. 1995.

[2] Golaszewski, C.H. and P.J. Ramadge, Supervisory control of discrete event processes with arbitrary controls, in *Advanced Computing Concepts and Techniques in Control Engineering*, M.J. Denham and A.J. Laub, Eds., Springer, 1988; see also, Control of discrete event systems with forced events, *Proc. 26th Conference on Decision and Control*, pp. 247-257, 1987.

[3] Krogh, B.H., Condition/event signal interfaces for block diagram modeling and analysis of hybrid systems, *Proc. 1993 Symposium on Intelligent Control*, pp. 180-185, Aug 1993.

[4] Niinomi, T., and B. H. Krogh, Modeling and analysis of switched-mode hybrid systems driven by threshold events, in *Advances in Control Systems, Lecture Notes in Control and Information Sciences*, H. Khalil and J. Chow, Eds., Springer, 1995.

[5] Sreenivas, R.S. and B.H. Krogh, On condition/event systems with discrete state realizations, *Discrete Event Dynamic Systems: Theory and Applications*, 1991, pp. 209-236.

[6] Thistle, J.G., *Control of Infinite Behavior of Discrete-Event Systems*, Ph.D. Thesis, University of Toronto, Systems Control Group Report No. 9012, January 1991

[7] Thistle, J.G. and W.M. Wonham, Supervision of infinite behavior of discrete-event systems, *SIAM J. Contr. and Opt.*, Vol. 32, no. 4, July 1994, pp. 1098-1113.

[8] Thistle, J.G., On control of systems modelled as deterministic Rabin automata, *Discrete Event Dynamic Systems: Theory and Applications,* 1995, pp. 357-381.

A Data Intensive Computing Approach to Path Planning and Mode Management for Hybrid Systems*

S. Bailey, R. L. Grossman,** L. Gu, D. Hanley

Laboratory for Advanced Computing, Department of Mathematics, Statistics, & Computer Science (M/C 249), University of Illinois at Chicago, 851 South Morgan Street, Chicago, IL 60607

Abstract

We describe an approach to the design, analysis, and control of hybrid systems which is data intensive in contrast to more traditional approaches which tend to be compute-intensive. A key idea is to use a low overhead, high performance persistent object manager to trade space for time, even when the amount of data is very large. The main advantage is that near real time solutions to problems can be obtained which would be prohibitive with other approaches. To illustrate the effectiveness of this approach, we show how millions of trajectories segments can be stored and retrieved to solve path planning problems and how hundreds of modes can be stored to aid in the study of mode switching strategies.

1 Introduction

This paper describes data intensive algorithms and software tools for the design, analysis and control of hybrid systems. By a hybrid system, we mean an interacting network of control systems and automata, together with interfaces describing how the control systems and automata interact. The basic idea is to exploit a software tool which provides low overhead, high performance access to the data defining a hybrid system, as well as to the intermediate data which arises when computing flows and control laws for hybrid systems, as a basis for developing a new class of algorithms which trade space for time and precompute much of the data that is computed in real time by traditional algorithms. The system we have developed is called HSStore.

In this paper, we restrict attention to hybrid systems defined by a collection of nonlinear control systems, each corresponding to a mode of the hybrid system. In the open loop version, switching between modes is determined by a finite

* This research was supported in part by NASA grant NAG2-513, DOE grant DE-FG02-92ER25133, and NSF grants DMS-9101089, IRI-9224605, CDA-9303433, and CDA-9413948.

** Please send correspondence to Robert Grossman at the address above, 312 413 2176, 312 413 1491 fax, grossman@uic.edu

state automaton which reacts to discrete input events. In addition, there may be discrete output events. This is one of several approaches to hybrid systems. It has been articulated by George Meyer in [20] and [19] and can be formalized in several ways. See, for example, [5], [8], and [14]. Other approaches are described below.

Here are two motivating examples of this philosophy:

Path Planning Problem. In this problem, one is given a path in phase space and asked to find a trajectory of the hybrid system which approximates the desired path. In essence, this means that one must find an allowable sequence of mode changes accepted by the discrete automaton governing the hybrid system and, for each mode, a trajectory of the appropriate control system, with the property that the sequence of control system trajectories approximates the desired path. The approach taken in [4], [6] and [9] is to precompute very large numbers of trajectory segments for each mode of the hybrid system. With the appropriate algorithm, indexing and software [6], it is feasible to provide near-real time retrieval of a sequence of trajectories, with the corresponding mode attached, to approximate the desired path. Our approach to this problem is to precompute *trajectory segments* and provide low overhead, high performance access to this data as a component in the path planning algorithm. This problem is discussed at greater length below.

Mode Management Problem. This problem is motivated by the work of George Meyer [19] which involves the design and analysis of a hybrid system for vertical lift aircraft containing over two hundred modes. To each mode is attached the control system governing the dynamics, control laws for flying the aircraft in that mode, as well as a variety of other data. The additional data may include simulation data, design data, and information about related modes. The management of all this data becomes an important problem as does the high performance access of the appropriate data for particular control algorithms. To better understand this problem, we stored approximately two hundred modes of a hybrid system and retrieved and visualized selected data about each mode in real time as an open loop automaton governed the discrete time evolution of the hybrid system. To summarize, our approach to this problem is to store information about the individual *control systems* corresponding to each mode and to provide low overhead, high performance access to this data as a component of the design, analysis and control of the hybrid system. This problem is discussed at greater length below.

2 Background and Related Work

For the purposes of this paper, a hybrid system is defined by the following data:

Automata. A hybrid system consists of one or more automata. Each automaton accepts discrete input symbols, undergoes a state transition, and emits discrete output symbols. The data and transitions are both discrete.

Input-output systems. A hybrid system consists of one or more input-output systems. Given a continuous input $u(t)$, the state $x(t)$ of an open loop input-output system evolves continuously in time:

$$\dot{x}(t) = F(x, u),$$

and defines a continuous output $y(t) = h(x(t))$, which is a function of the state. Here F is a vector field and the control, state, and output may all be vector valued. The inputs, states, and outputs all evolve continuously in time.

Interfaces. For a hybrid system to exhibit interesting behavior, the automata and input-output systems must interact. A variety of of interfaces for these interactions and mechanisms for triggering transitions have been studied: The trigger can be an exogenous discrete input to an automaton, an output function of the input-output passing a threshold, or an update of a rule. The trigger can select an input-output system, the connections between input-output systems, or an automaton. Here are four concrete examples. It is easy to construct variants of these, and combinations involving several interfaces are very common.

The four examples are named using the scheme E/F/G, where E indicates the trigger, F indicates the transition and update mechanism, and G indicates what is selected. Triggers can be external events "E", including timings, or measurements "M". Transition mechanisms can be automaton "A" or rule based systems "R". The objects selected can be automaton "A", control systems "C" or interfaces "I". For example, mode switched hybrid systems are indicated by E/A/C, representing triggering by discrete inputs to an automaton, update by evolution of the automaton, and selection of control systems.

Case E/A/C. Triggering by external events, Update by automaton evolution, Selection of Input-Output Systems. Whenever an automaton undergoes a state transition, the discrete output of the automaton may be used to choose an appropriate input-output system, to select an appropriate continuous control function for the input-output system, and to fix any free parameters in the input-output system. This can be done asynchronously, whenever a new input event is processed by an automaton, at regular intervals, by letting the input-output system evolve for a fixed period of time, or at irregular intervals, by letting the automaton select both the input-output system and the time to evolve it.

Case M/A/C. Triggering by measurements, Update by automaton evolution, Selection of Input-Output Systems. In a symmetrical fashion, an input-output system can also trigger a hybrid system transition. The trigger event can be caused by an output function of the input-output system passing a certain threshold or taking a value in a certain region. A very common trigger is a so-called guard condition, which is set off by the state passing into a specified region of phase space. The trigger specifies a discrete input event for an automaton, the automaton undergoes a state transition, and the discrete output of the automaton is used to choose an appropriate input-output system, control functions, and free parameters as in the case above.

E/A/I. Triggering by external events, Update by automaton evolution, Selection of Interfaces. State transitions in the automaton can be used to select new interfaces and connections among a collection of automata and input-output systems. For example, specific input events can be used to specify that one or more input-output systems should be brought "on-line" or taken "off-line." As in the cases above, state transitions of the automaton can be triggered asynchronously, whenever a new input event is processed by an automaton, at regular intervals, by letting the input-output system evolve for a fixed period of time, or at irregular intervals, by letting the automaton select both the input-output system and the time to evolve it.

R/R/A. Triggering by Rules, Update by rule based system, Selection of Automaton. A rule based system may be used to select one of several automata and to fix any free parameters in the automaton. As variables in the hybrid system evolve, predicates can be re-evaluated, and rules used to select appropriate automaton.

Example 1. This is a simple example illustrating Case E/A/C and is taken from [14]. It can be thought of as "taxicab-on-the-streets-of-Manhattan." There are two input-output systems in the plane. All flows of System 1 are north-south, while all flows of System 2 are east-west. The hybrid system contains one automaton with two (or more states), accepts discrete input symbols (the back seat driver, indicating to go straight, turn left, or turn right) and outputs discrete symbols indicating which input-output system to use next, and which direction to take ($u \equiv +1$ or $u \equiv -1$). It is important to note that both input-output systems are *planar* systems and not one-dimensional systems, but for simplicity their flows are restricted as indicated. The example can easily be generalized so that the planar systems have more complicated dynamics.

Example 2. This is a simple example illustrating Case M/A/C and is taken from [17]. The goal of this example is to control the motion of a pendulum around an unstable equilibrium point using state feedback. The idea is to introduce two modes with free parameters, appropriate guard conditions to trigger the mode transitions, and an automaton to select the next mode and parameters values.

Example 3. A more complicated example can be found in [11]. In this example, a hybrid system of the form R/R/A, uses a rule based system for triggering and selecting an automaton, which in turn is coupled to a hybrid system of the form Case E/A/C, in which an automaton selects an appropriate control system and control law.

Remark 1. Notice that the for Case M/A/C, triggers map continuous data (the outputs of the input-output system) to discrete symbols (the inputs to the automaton), and therefore some authors speak of analog to digital (A/D) converters. Similarly, one can view the process of converting the discrete output of the automaton to the continuous inputs of the input-output as a digital to analog (D/A) converter. This viewpoint is explored thoroughly in [18]. Note that from this framework the length of time to evolve the input-output system can be specified by the same map that is specifying the input function itself.

Remark 2. As we have seen, there are a variety of approaches to modeling hybrid systems. We have mentioned several with close connections to the control theory tradition. For others arising from the verification and validation tradition, see the collection [7]. The dynamics arising in problems from the control theory tradition are usually too complex to be verified or validated using the current state of the theory. A popular approach is to consider hybrid systems whose dynamics are restricted to piecewise linear systems [1], which has some very nice procedures for verification.

Remark 3. Broadly speaking, any flow on a manifold can be viewed as a hybrid systems. A point on the manifold may be in one of several coordinate patches: as the point moves, the coordinate patches to which it belongs change. A simple automaton is often used to select the next coordinate patch so that this is an example of case C/A/C, but if a rule based system is used to select the next coordinate patch, it can also be viewed as an example of Case C/R/C.

3 Persistent Object Stores

In our approach, the trajectories for the path planning problem and the modes for the mode management problem are viewed and managed as objects, in the broad sense of the term objects as it is used in the field of persistent object stores [3]. A persistent object store is a collection of objects which are persistent. Objects are called persistent if they can be accessed and queried independently of the processes which create them. Otherwise, objects are called transient and are co-terminal with the processes which create them. An object-oriented database provides a variety of functionality that is absent in a persistent object store, such as back-up and recovery, integrity constraints, and a query language [2].

There are several reasons that we use persistent object stores rather than object-oriented databases to manage the underlying data for data intensive computing related to hybrid systems:

Low Overhead and High Performance. Queries in traditional database management systems, including relational and object-oriented databases, have a high overhead. For example, transaction consistency mechanisms, query language parsing, query optimization, table merging, and database administration all add to the complexity of data management. Such overhead is acceptable when trying to manage frequently changing data. However, our persistent trajectories never change once they are produced. Therefore, our persistent object model trades transaction based functionality for a very low overhead data management scheme allowing for extremely fast, real-time access.

Scalability. Our approach involving data intensive computing produces a very large amount of data and a very large number of objects. There are a variety of technical hurdles when managing this much data. Since there is less functionality, it is much easier to scale a persistent object manager than an object-oriented database.

Low Impedance Interface to Programming Languages. The complexity of our algorithms is such that they are most easily expressed using conventional programming languages rather than a standard query language, such as Object Query Language (OQL). The data structures of conventional programming languages can be managed without change by persistent object managers.

Complex Structure. Scientific data often has a complex structure which easily fits into an object data model, while it must be "flattened" to fit into a file. Flattening data to fit into flat files or tables throws away part of the structure of the problem. Adding the structure back later increases the cost of a computation. In other words there is a basic trade off between the complexity of the stored data and the cost of a computation. By storing more complex data, it is sometimes possible to decrease the cost of a later computation.

Application Specific Indexing. By attaching methods to the objects, it is easy to provide application specific indexing and access methods in order to provide higher performance access to the data.

4 Path Planning and Object Stores of Trajectory Segments

In this section, which is based in part upon [9] and [6], we describe how to solve a path planning problem for hybrid systems by an appropriate query on a persistent object store of trajectory segments.

The basic idea is that although it may be computationally expensive to *compute* a sequence of trajectory segments and mode switches satisfying certain prescribed behavior, it may be inexpensive to *search* for the appropriate trajectory segments once they have been precomputed. In other words, persistent object stores can be used to trade space for time, even when the number of objects or amount of data is very large.

There are two distinct phases in the basic algorithm:

> *Phase 1: Precomputation of trajectory segments.* In a precomputation, the persistent object store is populated with short duration trajectory segments, each representing a reference trajectory to be followed using a regulator. Each trajectory segment is also assigned a sequence of indices. Trajectory segments representing all the modes of the hybrid system are used.
>
> *Phase 2. Path planning query.* The input to each query is the desired flight path and a tolerance. The output of a successful query is a sequence of trajectory segments with the property that they approximate the desired flight path to within the tolerance. The controls necessary to generate each trajectory segment are attached to the trajectory segment and can be used as the basis for a robust control algorithm to follow the retrieved reference trajectory. Only those trajectory segments with the appropriate modes are used to build the sequence.

The retrieved trajectory segments are computed as follows [9] and [6]:

Break up the query path. The query path is broken up into a number of smaller query path segments which are placed on a stack and the index of the query path segment and its mode are computed. Notice that breaking up the query path into smaller paths, which is done to obtain greater accuracy, is orthogonal to the process of attaching the appropriate modes to various segments in the query path, which is done to satisfy the mode switching requirements of the hybrid system, as specified by the automaton governing the mode transitions.

Retrieve the trajectory segments. For each query path segment on the stack, the query path is removed from the stack and all trajectory segments in the store with the same index and mode are retrieved and compared to the query path segment. If the one which most closely matches the query path *actually* matches the query path segment within the desired tolerance, the trajectory segment is returned with the query. If not, the query path segment is broken up into smaller segments and the algorithm continues recursively until the query path has been broken up to the smallest segments existing in the object store.

Each trajectory segment and query path segment has a sequence of indices attached to it. If a query path segment has been broken up n times by the algorithm, the nth index is used. When we have broken up some query path segments into the smallest segments existing in the object store , it may happen that the algorithm still cannot find a trajectory segment that matches the corresponding query segment within the tolerance at this indexing level. In this case, it returns the best approximating sequence of trajectory segments in the store. The threshold can then be adjusted or additional trajectory segments added to the store to provide better approximating sequences of trajectory segments.

5 Mode Management and Object Stores of Nonlinear Systems

This problem is motivated by the work of George Meyer [19] which involves the design and analysis of a hybrid system for vertical lift aircraft containing over two hundred modes. Each mode consists of: the control system governing the dynamics, control laws for flying the aircraft in that mode, specific input parameters, and related information. Additional information such as design data is also associated with each mode.

For a open loop E/A/C hybrid system, mode switching is governed by an automaton. As the number of modes increases, management of the data associated with each mode and its associated control system becomes an important problem. It is useful, if the system software can retrieve a given mode in its entirety. In other words, when a desired mode is known, the system must be able to retrieve that mode based on some key identification and access the appropriate flight data for the given input parameters.

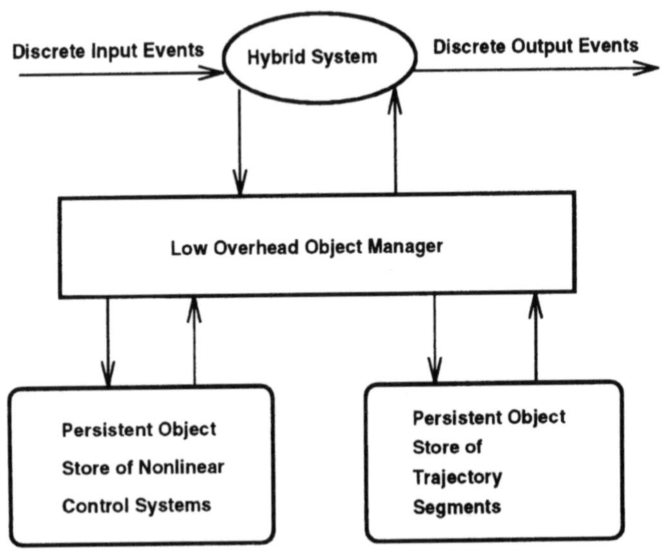

Fig. 1. Architecture and design of the HSStore system.

Figure 2 from [19] illustrates the mode sequence that the hybrid system control automata for a harrier aircraft must step through in order to perform the maneuver: step forward 300 ft. In this example, there are two modes, VTOL, a vertical lift mode, and HELI, a helicopter mode.

mode	VTOL	VTOL	VTOL	HELI	VTOL
time	2 sec	5 sec	8 sec	11 sec	14 sec
position	0 ft	26 ft	150 ft	275 ft	300 ft
speed	0 fps	25 fps	50 fps	25 fps	0 fps
accel	0 fps^2	12 fps^2	0 fps^2	-12 fps^2	0 fps^2
pitch	0 deg	0 deg	0 deg	10 deg	0 deg
nozzle	90 deg	67 deg	87 deg	100 deg	90 deg
input events	hover	accelerate	coast	decelerate	hover

Fig. 2. Modes for aircraft maneuver: step forward 300 feet in 12 seconds, reprinted from [19].

In order to more fully explore this problem, we stored approximately two hundred modes of the harrier-like aircraft system described in [19]. Each mode consisted of a control system on a five dimensional state space, input parameters, and the flight paths which are the result of integration on the differential equations with the given input parameters. We then retrieved and visualized selected data about each mode in real time. This was done as an open loop automaton governed the discrete mode evolution of the hybrid system.

To summarize, the goal of the mode management problem is to store information about the individual *control systems* corresponding to each mode and to provide low overhead, high performance access to this data as a component of the design, analysis and control of the hybrid system.

6 Experimental Results

We have tested these ideas by developing a series of prototypes over several years. Our first prototypes used commercial relational databases and commercial object-oriented databases. But since this technology was not able to achieve the performance we desired nor able to handle the number of trajectory segments or modes we required, we began developing a series of persistent object managers called PTool designed specifically for this problem [10], [12] and [13].

PTool is a light weight software tool which provides persistence for instances of objects defined by C++ classes or through a variant of the OMG's Interface Definition Language. For C++ applications, the application programming interface (API) consists of several classes and an overloaded "new" operator and is broadly compliant with the ODMG 93 standard for object-based data management systems.

More importantly, we designed and implemented specialized access methods and indices for working with trajectory segments and hybrid system modes [15]. With the current implementation of PTool, we are able to manage Gigabytes of data and millions of trajectory segments.

For the current path planning study reported here, we used a small store containing 30 Megabytes of data and 6000 trajectory segments; a medium store containing 629 Megabytes and 200,000 trajectory segments; and a large store containing 5.5 Gigabytes and 1,800,000 trajectory segments. Worst case accuracy increases as the size of the store does—with the largest store, we are able to achieve approximately 5% relative error for path planning queries. Our design also allows us to complete path planning queries using standard Unix workstations in less than 0.5 seconds, even for the large store, as Figure 3 indicates.

For the current mode management study reported here, we created persistent object stores of modes containing up to 200 modes, and were able to access and analyze trajectory segments from the various modes independent of the number of modes for the range tested.

7 Conclusions

In this paper, we have reviewed the path planning algorithm for hybrid systems introduced in [6] and introduced new experimental evidence of its effectiveness, even when working with millions of trajectory segments. We have also introduced the mode management problem when designing, analyzing, and controlling hybrid systems and provided preliminary evidence that the system we have developed called HSStore can efficiently manage hundreds of modes.

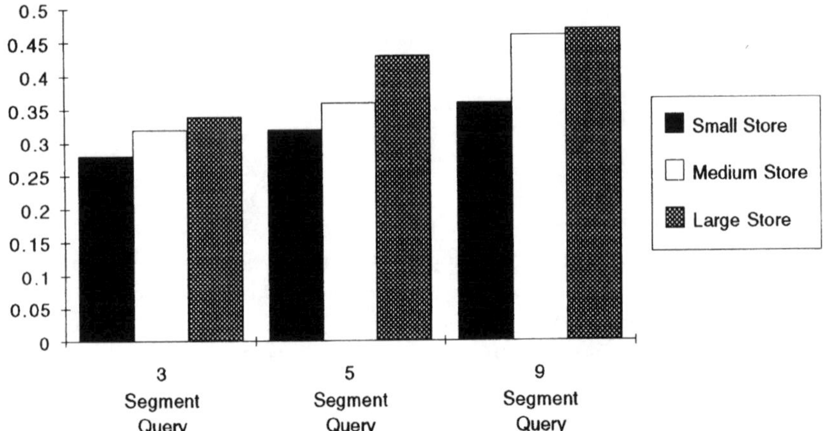

Fig. 3. Performance of path planning query as the size of the store varies. The small store contained 30 Megabytes of data and 6000 trajectory segments; the medium store contained 629 Megabytes and 200,000 trajectory segments; and the large store contained 5.5 Gigabytes and 1,800,000 trajectory segments. We ran three queries: one a short path which returned 3 trajectory segments; one on a medium path which returned 5 trajectory segments; and one on a long path which returned 9 trajectory segments. The time to complete the path planning query was broadly speaking independent of the size of the store, the number of trajectory segments, and the number of segments returned, demonstrating the scalability of this approach.

We have attacked both of these problems by introducing a new class of algorithms, which can broadly characterized as being data intensive. The basic idea is that with current data management technology it is possible to precompute very large amounts of data and to retrieve it in near constant time. This allows algorithms which trade space for time even when working with very large numbers of object or very large data sets.

We developed a specialized data management software tool called PTool for these types of algorithms. PTool is a light weight, low overhead, high performance persistent object manager.

Current work is focusing on implementing more complex examples, using data centered parallelism to obtain higher performance, and developing more sophisticated access methods and corresponding indices.

References

1. R. Alur, C. Courcoubetis, T. A. Henzinger, and P-H. Ho, "Hybrid Automata: An Algorithmic Approach to the Specification and Verification of Hybrid Systems," in R. L. Grossman, A. Nerode, A. P. Ravn, and H. Rischel, editors, *Hybrid Systems*, Lecture Notes in Computer Science, Volume 736, Springer-Verlag, New York, 1993, pp. 209–229.

2. R. G. G. Cattell, *Object Data Management*, Addison-Wesley Publishing Company, Reading, Massachusetts, 1991.
3. A. Dearle, G. M. Shaw, and S. B. Zdonik, *Implementing Persistent Object Bases: Principles and Practice,* Morgan Kaufmann, San Mateo, California, 1991.
4. R. Grossman, "Querying databases of trajectories of differential equations I: data structures for trajectories," *Proceedings of the 23rd Hawaii International Conference on Systems Sciences,* IEEE, 1990, pp. 18–23.
5. R. L. Grossman and R. G. Larson, "Viewing hybrid systems as products of control systems and automata," *Proceedings of the 31st IEEE Conference on Decision and Control,* IEEE Press, 1992, pp. 2953–2955.
6. R. L. Grossman, D. Valsamis and X. Qin, "Persistent stores and hybrid systems," *Proceedings of the 32nd IEEE Conference on Decision and Control,* IEEE Press, 1993, pp. 2298-2302.
7. R. L. Grossman, A. Nerode, A. P. Ravn, and H. Rischel, editors, *Hybrid Systems,* Lecture Notes in Computer Science, Volume 736, Springer-Verlag, New York, 1993.
8. R. L. Grossman and R. L. Larson, "Some Remarks About Flows in Hybrid Systems," in R. L. Grossman, A. Nerode, A. P. Ravn, and H. Rischel, editors, *Hybrid Systems,* Lecture Notes in Computer Science, Volume 736, Springer-Verlag, New York, 1993, pp. 357–365.
9. R. L. Grossman, S. Mehta, and X. Qin, "Path planning by querying persistent stores of trajectory segments," submitted for publication. *Laboratory for Advanced Computing Technical Report,* Number LAC93-R3, University of Illinois at Chicago, submitted for publication.
10. R. L. Grossman and X. Qin, "Ptool: a scalable persistent object manager," *Proceedings of SIGMOD 94,* ACM, 1994, page 510.
11. R. L. Grossman, A. Nerode, and W. Kohn, "Nonlinear Systems, Automata, and Agents: Managing their Symbolic Data Using Light Weight Persistent Object Managers," *International Symposium on Fifth Generation Computer Systems, 1994: Workshop on Heterogeneous Cooperative Knowledge-Bases,* Kazumasa Yokota, editor, ICOT, pp. 65–74.
12. R. L. Grossman, D. Hanley, and X. Qin, "PTool: A Light Weight Persistent Object Manager," *Proceedings of SIGMOD 95,* ACM, 1995.
13. R. L. Grossman, N. Araujo, X. Qin, and W. Xu, "Managing physical folios of objects between nodes," *Persistent Object Systems (Proceedings of the Sixth International Workshop on Persistent Object Systems),* M. P. Atkinson, V. Benzaken and D. Maier, editors, Springer-Verlag and British Computer Society, 1995.
14. R. L. Grossman and R. G. Larson, "An algebraic approach to hybrid systems," *Journal of Theoretical Computer Science,* Volume 138, pp. 101–112, 1995.
15. S. Bailey, R. L. Grossman, L. Gu, and D. Hanley, "Two Data Intensive Algorithms for Hybrid Systems," to appear.
16. J. Guckenheimer and A. Nerode, "Simulation for hybrid systems and nonlinear control," *Proceedings of the 31st IEEE Conference on Decision and Control,* IEEE Press, 1992.
17. J. Guckenheimer, "A Robust Hybrid Stabilization Strategy for Equilibria," *IEEE Transactions on Automatic Control,* Volume 40, pp. 321–326, 1995.
18. W. Kohn and A. Nerode, "Models for hybrid systems: Automata, topologies, controllability and observability," in R. L. Grossman, A. Nerode, A. P. Ravn, and H. Rischel, editors, *Hybrid Systems,* Lecture Notes in Computer Science, Volume 736, Springer-Verlag, New York, 1993, pp. 317–356.
19. G. Meyer, "Design of Flight Vehicle Management Systems," to appear.
20. G. Meyer, personal communication.

Hybrid I/O Automata

(extended abstract)

Nancy Lynch[1*] Roberto Segala[2] Frits Vaandrager[3**] H.B. Weinberg[1***]

[1] MIT Laboratory for Computer Science
Cambridge, MA 02139, USA
{lynch,hbw}@theory.lcs.mit.edu
[2] Dipartimento di Matematica, Universita' di Bologna
Piazza di Porta San Donato 5, 40127 Bologna, Italy
segala@cs.unibo.it
[3] CWI
P.O. Box 94079, 1090 GB Amsterdam, The Netherlands
fritsv@cwi.nl

Abstract. We propose a new *hybrid I/O automaton* model that is capable of describing both continuous and discrete behavior. The model, which extends the timed I/O automaton model of [12, 7] and the phase transition system models of [15, 2], allows communication among components using both shared variables and shared actions. The main contributions of this paper are: (1) the definition of hybrid I/O automata and of an implementation relation based on *hybrid traces*, (2) the definition of a *simulation* between hybrid I/O automata and a proof that existence of a simulation implies the implementation relation, (3) a definition of *composition* of hybrid I/O automata and a proof that it respects the implementation relation, and (4) a definition of *receptiveness* for hybrid I/O automata and a proof that, assuming certain compatibility conditions, receptiveness is preserved by composition.

1 Introduction

In recent years, there has been a fast growing interest in *hybrid systems* [8, 18] — systems that contain both discrete and continuous components, typically computers interacting with the physical world. Because of the rapid development of processor and circuit technology, hybrid systems are becoming common in many application domains, including avionics, process control, robotics and consumer electronics. Motivated by a desire to formally specify and verify real-life applications, we are generalizing existing methods from computer science to the setting

* Supported by NSF Grant 9225124-CCR, U.S. Department of Transportation Contract DTRS95G-0001-YR.8, AFOSR-ONR Contract F49620-94-1-0199, and ARPA Contracts F19628-95-C-0118 and N00014-92-J-4033.

** Current affiliation: Computing Science Institute, University of Nijmegen, P.O. Box 9010, 9500 GL Nijmegen, The Netherlands, Frits.Vaandrager@cs.kun.nl.

*** Research partially supported by a National Science Foundation Graduate Fellowship.

of hybrid systems. We are applying our results in a number of projects in the areas of personal rapid transit [14, 10, 20], intelligent vehicle highway systems, and consumer electronics [5].

Within the theory of *reactive systems*, which has been developed in computer science during the last 20 years, it is common to represent both a system and its properties as abstract machines (see, for instance [11, 4, 9]). A system is then defined to be correct iff the abstract machine for the system *implements* the abstract machine for the specification in the sense that the set of behaviors of the first is included in that of the second. A major reason why this approach has been successful is that it supports *stepwise refinement*: systems can be specified in a uniform way at many levels of abstraction, from a description of their highest-level properties to a description of their implementation in terms of circuitry, and the various specifications can be related formally using the implementation relation. In this paper we generalize this and related ideas from the theory of reactive systems to the setting of hybrid systems. More specifically, we propose answers to the following four questions:

1. What system model do we use?
2. What implementation relation do we use?
3. How do we compose systems?
4. What does it mean for a system to be receptive?

The system model. Our new *hybrid I/O automaton (HIOA)* model is based on infinite state machines. The model allows both discrete state jumps, described by a set of labelled transitions, and continuous state changes, described by a set of trajectories. To describe the external interface of a system, the state variables are partioned into input, output and internal variables, and the transition labels (or actions) are partitioned into input, output and internal actions. Our model is very general and contains no finiteness restrictions. More structure will have to be added in order to deal with applications, but the general model that we propose allows us to answer questions 2–4. HIOA's are inspired by the timed I/O automata of [12, 7] and the phase transition system models of [15, 2]. The main difference between HIOA's and timed I/O automata is that, as in phase transition systems, trajectories are primitive in our model and not a derived notion. In the work on phase transition systems the main emphasis thus far has been on temporal logics and model checking. Questions 2–4 have not been addressed and perhaps for this reason the external interface is not an integral part of a phase transition system.

The implementation relation. The implementation relation that we propose is simply inclusion of the sets of hybrid traces. A *hybrid trace* records occurrences of input and output actions, and the evolution of input and output variables during an execution of a system. Thus HIOA B *implements* HIOA A if every behavior of B is allowed by A. In this case, B is typically more deterministic than A, both at the discrete and the continuous level. For instance, A might produce an output at an arbitrary time before noon, whereas B produces an output sometime between 10 and 11AM. Or A might allow any smooth trajectory for output variable y with $\dot{y} \in [0, 2]$, whereas B only allows trajectories with $\dot{y} = 1$.

Within computer science, *simulation relations* provide a major technical tool to prove inclusion of behaviors between systems (see [13] for an overview). In this paper we propose a definition of a *simulation* between HIOA's and show that existence of a simulation implies the implementation relation.

Composition. Within computer science various notions of composition have been proposed for models based on transition systems. One popular approach is to use the product construction from classical automata theory and to synchronize on common transition labels ("actions") [11]. In other approaches there are no transition labels to synchronize on, and communication between system components is achieved via shared variables [16, 9]. Shared action and shared variable communication are equally expressive, and the relationships between the two mechanisms are well understood: it depends on the application which of the two is more convenient to use. In control theory studies of dynamic feedback, communication between components is typically achieved via a *connection map*, which specifies how outputs and inputs of components are wired [19]. This communication mechanism can be expressed naturally using shared variables. Since we find it convenient to use communication via shared actions in the applications that we work on, our model supports both shared action and shared variable communication. Whereas shared actions always correspond to discrete transitions, shared variables can be used equally well for communication of continuously varying signals and for signals that can only change value upon occurrence of a discrete transition.

We prove that our composition operator respects the implementation relation: if A_1 implements A_2 then A_1 composed with B implements A_2 composed with B. Such a result is essential for compositional design and verification of systems.

Receptiveness. The class of HIOA's is very general and allows for systems with bizarre timing behavior. We can describe systems in which time cannot advance at all or in which time advances in successively smaller increments but never beyond a certain bound, so called Zeno behavior. We do not want to accept such systems as valid implementations of any specification since, clearly, they will have no physical realization. Therefore we only accept *receptive* HIOA's as implementations, i.e., HIOA's in which time can advance to infinity independently of the input provided by the environment. Inspired by earlier work of [6, 1, 7] on (timed) discrete event systems, we define receptivity in terms of a game between system and environment in which the goal of the system is to construct an infinite, nonZeno execution, and the goal of the environment is to prevent this. It is interesting to compare our games with the games of Nerode and Yakhnis [17]. Since the purpose of the latter games is the extraction of digital control to meet performance specifications, the environment player may choose all disturbances. Irrespective of the disturbances the system should realize a given performance specification. The purpose of our games is to show that regardless of the input provided by its environment, a HIOA can exhibit proper behavior. Therefore, in our games the system resolves all nondeterminism due to internal disturbances (which express implementation freedom), even though the environment may choose all the input signals.

The main technical result that we prove about receptivity is that, assuming certain compatibility conditions, receptiveness is preserved by composition.

2 Hybrid I/O Automata and Their Behavior

In this section we introduce HIOA's and define an implementation relation between these automata. Since the notion of a *trajectory* plays an important role in the model, we start out with the definition of trajectories and some operations on them.

2.1 Trajectories

Throughout this paper, we fix a *time axis* T, which is a subgroup of $(\mathsf{R},+)$, the real numbers with addition. Usually, $T = \mathsf{R}$ or Z, but also the degenerated time axis $T = \{0\}$ is allowed. An *interval* I is a convex subset of T. We denote intervals as usual: $[t_1,t_2] = \{t \in T \mid t_1 \leq t \leq t_2\}$, etc. For I an interval and $t \in T$, we define $I + t \triangleq \{t' + t \mid t' \in I\}$.

We assume a universal set $\mathcal{V}$ of *variables*. Variables in $\mathcal{V}$ are typed, where the type of a variable, such as *reals*, *integers*, etc., indicates the domain over which the variable ranges. Let $Z \subseteq \mathcal{V}$. A *valuation* of Z is a mapping that associates to each variable of Z a value in its domain. We write $\mathbf{Z}$ for the set of valuations of Z. Often, valuations will be referred to as *states*.

A *trajectory* over Z is a mapping $w : I \to \mathbf{Z}$, where I is a left-closed interval of T with left endpoint equal to 0. With $dom(w)$ we denote the domain of w and with $trajs(Z)$ the collection of all trajectories over Z. If w is a trajectory then $w.ltime$, the *limit time* of w, is the supremum of $dom(w)$. Similarly, define $w.fstate$, the *first state* of w, to be $w(0)$, and if $dom(w)$ is right-closed, define $w.lstate$, the *last state* of w, to be $w(w.ltime)$. A trajectory with domain $[0,0]$ is called a *point* trajectory. If s is a state then define $\wp(s)$ to be the point trajectory that maps 0 to s.

For w a trajectory and $t \in T^{\geq 0}$, we define $w \trianglelefteq t \triangleq w \lceil [0,t]$ and $w \lhd t \triangleq w \lceil [0,t)$. (Here $\lceil$ denotes the restriction of a function to a subset of its domain.) Note that $w \lhd 0$ is not a trajectory. By convention, $w \trianglelefteq \infty = w \lhd \infty \triangleq w$. Similarly we define, for w a trajectory and I a left-closed interval with minimal element l, the *restriction* $w \dagger I$ to be the function with domain $(I \cap dom(w)) - l$ given by $w \dagger I\ (t) \triangleq w(t + l)$. Note that $w \dagger I$ is a trajectory iff $l \in dom(w)$.

If w is a trajectory over Z and $Z' \subseteq Z$, then the *projection* $w \downarrow Z'$ is the trajectory over Z' with domain $dom(w)$ defined by $w \downarrow Z'\ (t)(z) \triangleq w(t)(z)$. The projection operation is extended to sets of trajectories by pointwise extension.

Also, if w is a trajectory over Z and $z \in Z$, then the *projection* $w \downarrow z$ is the function from $dom(w)$ to the domain of z defined by $w \downarrow z\ (t) \triangleq w(t)(z)$.

If w is a trajectory with a right-closed domain $I = [0, u]$, w' is a trajectory with domain I', and if $w.lstate = w'.fstate$, then we define the *concatenation* $w \frown w'$ to be the trajectory with domain $I \cup (I' + u)$ given by

$$w \frown w'\ (t) \triangleq \begin{cases} w(t) & \text{if } t \in I, \\ w'(t-u) & \text{otherwise.} \end{cases}$$

We extend the concatenation operator to a countable sequence of trajectories: if w_i is a trajectory with domain I_i, $1 \leq i < \infty$, where all I_i are right-closed, and if $w_i.lstate = w_{i+1}.fstate$ for all i, then we define the *infinite concatenation*, written $w_1 \frown w_2 \frown w_3 \ldots$, to be the least function w such that $w(t + \sum_{j<i} w_j.ltime) = w_i(t)$ for all $t \in I_i$.

A trajectory w is *closed* if its domain is a (finite) closed interval and *full* if its domain equals $T^{\geq 0}$. For W a set of trajectories, *Closed*(W) and *Full*(W) denote the subsets of closed and full trajectories in W, respectively. Trajectory w is a *prefix* of trajectory w', notation $w \leq w'$, if either $w = w'$ or $w' = w \frown w''$, for some trajectory w''. With *Pref*(W) we denote the *prefix-closure* of W: $Pref(W) \triangleq \{w \mid \exists w' \in W : w \leq w'\}$. Set W is *prefix closed* if $W = Pref(W)$. A trajectory in W is *maximal* if it is not a prefix of any other trajectory in W. We write *Max*(W) for the subset of maximal trajectories in W.

2.2 Hybrid I/O Automata

A *hybrid I/O automaton (HIOA)* $A = (U, X, Y, \Sigma^{in}, \Sigma^{int}, \Sigma^{out}, \Theta, \mathcal{D}, \mathcal{W})$ consists of the following components:

- Three disjoint sets U, X and Y of variables, called *input*, *internal* and *output* variables, respectively.
  Variables in $E \triangleq U \cup Y$ are called *external*, and variables in $L \triangleq X \cup Y$ are called *locally controlled*. We write $V \triangleq U \cup L$.
- Three disjoint sets Σ^{in}, Σ^{int}, Σ^{out} of *input*, *internal* and *output actions*, respectively.
  We assume that Σ^{in} contains a special element e, the *environment action*, which represents the occurrence of a discrete transition outside the system that is unobservable, except (possibly) through its effect on the input variables. Actions in $\Sigma^{ext} \triangleq \Sigma^{in} \cup \Sigma^{out}$ are called *external*, and actions in $\Sigma^{loc} \triangleq \Sigma^{int} \cup \Sigma^{out}$ are called *locally controlled*. We write $\Sigma \triangleq \Sigma^{in} \cup \Sigma^{loc}$.
- A nonempty set $\Theta \subseteq \mathbf{V}$ of *initial states* satisfying
  Init (start states closed under change of input variables)
  $\forall s, s' \in \mathbf{V} : s \in \Theta \wedge s \lceil L = s' \lceil L \;\Rightarrow\; s' \in \Theta$
- A set $\mathcal{D} \subseteq \mathbf{V} \times \Sigma \times \mathbf{V}$ of *discrete transitions* satisfying
  D1 (input action enabling)
  $\forall s \in \mathbf{V}, a \in \Sigma^{in}\ \exists s' \in \mathbf{V} : s \xrightarrow{a} s'$
  D2 (environment action only affect inputs)
  $\forall s, s' \in \mathbf{V} : s \xrightarrow{e} s' \;\Rightarrow\; s \lceil L = s' \lceil L$

D3 (input variable change enabling)
$\forall s, s', s'' \in \mathbf{V}, a \in \Sigma : s \xrightarrow{a} s' \wedge s' \lceil L = s'' \lceil L \;\Rightarrow\; s \xrightarrow{a} s''$
Here we used $s \xrightarrow{a} s'$ as shorthand for $(s, a, s') \in \mathcal{D}$.

- A set $\mathcal{W}$ of trajectories over V satisfying
  T1 (existence of point trajectories)
  $\forall s \in \mathbf{V} : \wp(s) \in \mathcal{W}$
  T2 (closure under subintervals)
  $\forall w \in \mathcal{W}, I$ left-closed, non-empty subinterval of $dom(w)$: $w \dagger I \in \mathcal{W}$
  T3 (completeness)
  $(\forall t \in T^{\geq 0} : w \dagger [0, t] \in \mathcal{W}) \Rightarrow w \in \mathcal{W}$

Axiom **Init** says that a system has no control over the initial values of its input variables: if one valuation is allowed then any other valuation is allowed also.

Axiom **D1** is a slight generalization of the input enabling condition of the (classical) I/O automaton model: it says that in each state each input action is enabled, including the environment action e. The second axiom **D2** says that e cannot change locally controlled variables. Axiom **D3** expresses that, since input variables are not under control of the system, these variables may be changed in an arbitrary way after any discrete action. The three axioms together imply the converse of **D2**, i.e., if two states only differ in their input variables then there exists an e transition between them. Axioms **D1-3** play a crucial role in our study of parallel composition. In particular **D2** and **D3** are used to avoid cyclic constraints during the interaction of two systems.

Axioms **T1-3** state some natural conditions on the set of trajectories that we need to set up our theory: existence of point trajectories, closure under subintervals, and the fact that a full trajectory is in $\mathcal{W}$ iff all its prefixes are in $\mathcal{W}$.

Notation Let A be a HIOA as described above. If $s \in \mathbf{V}$ and $l \in \mathbf{L}$, then we write $s \xrightarrow{a} l$ iff there exists an $s' \in \mathbf{V}$ such that $s \xrightarrow{a} s'$ and $s' \lceil L = l$. In the sequel, the components of a HIOA A will be denoted by V_A, U_A, Σ_A, Θ_A, etc. Sometimes, the components of a HIOA A_i will also be denoted by V_i, U_i, Σ_i, Θ_i, etc.

2.3 Hybrid Executions

A *hybrid execution fragment* of A is a finite or infinite alternating sequence $\alpha = w_0 a_1 w_1 a_2 w_2 \cdots$, where:

1. Each w_i is a trajectory in $\mathcal{W}_A$ and each a_i is an action in Σ_A.
2. If α is a finite sequence then it ends with a trajectory.
3. If w_i is not the last trajectory in α then its domain is a right-closed interval and $w_i.lstate \xrightarrow{a_{i+1}}_A w_{i+1}.fstate$.

An execution fragment records all the discrete changes that occur in the evolution of a system, plus the "continuous" state changes that take place in between. The third item says that the discrete actions in α span between successive trajectories. We write *h-frag*(A) for the set of all hybrid execution fragments of A.

If $\alpha = w_0 a_1 w_1 a_2 w_2 \cdots$ is a hybrid execution fragment then we define the *limit time* of α, notation $\alpha.ltime$, to be $\sum_i w_i.ltime$. Further, we define the *first state* of α, $\alpha.fstate$, to be $w_0.fstate$.

We distinguish several sorts of hybrid execution fragments. A hybrid execution fragment α is defined to be

- an *execution* if the first state of α is an initial state,
- *finite* if α is a finite sequence and the domain of its final trajectory is a right-closed interval,
- *admissible* if $\alpha.ltime = \infty$,
- *Zeno* if α is neither finite nor admissible, and
- a *sentence* if α is a finite execution that ends with a point trajectory.

If $\alpha = w_0 a_1 w_1 \cdots a_n w_n$ is a finite hybrid execution fragment then we define the *last state* of α, notation $\alpha.lstate$, to be $w_n.lstate$. A state of A is defined to be *reachable* if it is the last state of some finite hybrid execution of A.

A finite hybrid execution fragment $\alpha = w_0 a_1 w_1 a_2 w_2 \cdots a_n w_n$ and a hybrid execution fragment $\alpha' = w'_0 a'_1 w'_1 a'_2 w'_2 \cdots$ of A can be *concatenated* if $w_n \frown w'_0$ is defined and a trajectory of A. In this case, the *concatenation* $\alpha \frown \alpha'$ is the hybrid execution fragment defined by

$$\alpha \frown \alpha' \triangleq w_0 a_1 w_1 a_2 w_2 \cdots a_n (w_n \frown w'_0) a'_1 w'_1 a'_2 w'_2 \cdots$$

2.4 Hybrid Traces

Suppose $\alpha = w_0 a_1 w_1 a_2 w_2 \cdots$ is a hybrid execution fragment of A. In order to define the *hybrid trace* of α, let

$$\gamma = (w_0 \downarrow E_A) vis(a_1)(w_1 \downarrow E_A) vis(a_2)(w_2 \downarrow E_A) \cdots,$$

where, for a an action, $vis(a)$ is defined equal to τ if a is an internal action or e, and equal to a otherwise. Here τ is a special symbol which, as in the theory of process algebra, plays the role of the 'generic' invisible action. An occurrence of τ in γ is called *inert* if the final state of the trajectory that precedes the τ equals the first state of the trajectory that follows it (after hiding of the internal variables). The *hybrid trace* of α, written $htrace(\alpha)$, is defined to be the sequence obtained from γ by removing all inert τ's and concatenating the surrounding trajectories.

The *hybrid traces* of A are the hybrid traces that arise from all the finite and admissible hybrid executions of A. We write *h-traces*(A) for the set of hybrid traces of A.

HIOA's A_1 and A_2 are *comparable* if they have the same external interface, i.e., $U_1 = U_2$, $Y_1 = Y_2$, $\Sigma_1^{in} = \Sigma_2^{in}$ and $\Sigma_1^{out} = \Sigma_2^{out}$. If A_1 and A_2 are comparable then $A_1 \leq A_2$ is defined to mean that the hybrid traces of A_1 are included in those of A_2: $A_1 \leq A_2 \triangleq h\text{-}traces(A_1) \subseteq h\text{-}traces(A_2)$.

3 Simulation Relations

Let A and B be comparable HIOA's. A *simulation* from A to B is a relation $R \subseteq \mathbf{V}_A \times \mathbf{V}_B$ satisfying the following conditions, for all states r and s of A and B, respectively:

1. If $r \in \Theta_A$ then there exists $s \in \Theta_B$ such that $r \; R \; s$.
2. If $r \xrightarrow{a}_A r'$ and $r \; R \; s$ then B has a finite execution fragment α with $s = \alpha.fstate$, $htrace(\wp(r) \; a \; \wp(r')) = htrace(\alpha)$ and $r' \; R \; \alpha.lstate$.
3. If $r \; R \; s$ and w is a closed trajectory of A with $r = w.fstate$ then B has a finite execution fragment α with $s = \alpha.fstate$, $htrace(w) = htrace(\alpha)$ and $w.lstate \; R \; \alpha.lstate$.

Note that by Condition 3 and the existence of point trajectories (axiom **T1**), $r \; R \; s$ implies that $r \lceil E_A = s \lceil E_B$.

Theorem 1. *If A and B are comparable HIOA's and there is a simulation from A to B, then $A \leq B$.*

4 Parallel Composition and Hiding

We say that HIOA's A_1 and A_2 are *compatible* if, for $i \neq j$,

$$X_i \cap V_j = Y_i \cap Y_j = \Sigma_i^{int} \cap \Sigma_j = \Sigma_i^{out} \cap \Sigma_j^{out} = \emptyset.$$

If A_1 and A_2 are compatible then their *composition* $A_1 \| A_2$ is defined to be the tuple $A = (U, X, Y, \Sigma^{in}, \Sigma^{int}, \Sigma^{out}, \Theta, \mathcal{D}, \mathcal{W})$ given by

- $U = (U_1 \cup U_2) - (Y_1 \cup Y_2)$, $X = X_1 \cup X_2$, $Y = Y_1 \cup Y_2$
- $\Sigma^{in} = (\Sigma_1^{in} \cup \Sigma_2^{in}) - (\Sigma_1^{out} \cup \Sigma_2^{out})$, $\Sigma^{int} = \Sigma_1^{int} \cup \Sigma_2^{int}$, $\Sigma^{out} = \Sigma_1^{out} \cup \Sigma_2^{out}$
- $\Theta = \{s \in \mathbf{V} \mid s \lceil V_1 \in \Theta_1 \wedge s \lceil V_2 \in \Theta_2\}$
- Define, for $i \in \{1,2\}$, projection function $\pi_i : \Sigma \rightarrow \Sigma_i$ by $\pi_i(a) \triangleq a$ if $a \in \Sigma_i$ and $\pi_i(a) \triangleq e$ otherwise. Then $\mathcal{D}$ is the subset of $\mathbf{V} \times \Sigma \times \mathbf{V}$ given by

  $$(s, a, s') \in \mathcal{D} \Leftrightarrow s \lceil V_1 \xrightarrow{\pi_1(a)}_1 s' \lceil V_1 \; \wedge \; s \lceil V_2 \xrightarrow{\pi_2(a)}_2 s' \lceil V_2$$

- $\mathcal{W}$ is the set of trajectories over V given by

  $$w \in \mathcal{W} \Leftrightarrow w \downarrow V_1 \in \mathcal{W}_1 \wedge w \downarrow V_2 \in \mathcal{W}_2$$

Proposition 2. *$A_1 \| A_2$ is a HIOA.*

Theorem 3. *Suppose A_1, A_2 and B are HIOA's with $A_1 \leq A_2$, and each of A_1 and A_2 is compatible with B. Then $A_1 \| B \leq A_2 \| B$.*

Two natural hiding operations can be defined on any HIOA A:
(1) If $S \subseteq \Sigma_A^{out}$, then $\mathsf{ActHide}(S, A)$ is the HIOA B that is equal to A except that $\Sigma_B^{out} = \Sigma_A^{out} - S$ and $\Sigma_B^{int} = \Sigma_A^{int} \cup S$.
(2) If $Z \subseteq Y_A$, then $\mathsf{VarHide}(Z, A)$ is the HIOA B that is the equal to A except that $Y_B = Y_A - Z$ and $X_B = X_A \cup Z$.

Theorem 4. *Suppose A and B are HIOA's with $A \leq B$, and let $S \subseteq \Sigma_A^{out}$ and $Z \subseteq Y_A$.*
Then $\mathsf{ActHide}(S, A) \leq \mathsf{ActHide}(S, B)$ *and* $\mathsf{VarHide}(Z, A) \leq \mathsf{VarHide}(Z, B)$.

5 Receptiveness

We call a HIOA *feasible* if any finite execution can be extended to an admissible execution. The main significance of feasibility is to guarantee that a HIOA is meaningful in the sense that it cannot block time. Unfortunately feasibility is not preserved by parallel composition, and thus we need to impose additional restrictions on a HIOA so that the feasibility property is guaranteed to be preserved by parallel composition. Our ideal objective would be to find the weakest restrictions that need to be imposed; here we just propose some restrictions, although we have not proved that they are the weakest. Below we define a notion of *receptiveness* and prove that it is preserved by composition under some reasonable assumptions.

5.1 I/O Behaviors

The concept of an *I/O behavior* plays an important role in the definition of receptiveness. Intuitively, an I/O behavior is a set of trajectories that arise from an HIOA after choosing initial values for the local variables and resolving all internal nondeterminism.

We assume, for each variable $v \in \mathcal{V}$, a *dynamic type* $\mathcal{F}_v$, which is a nonempty collection of functions from T to the domain of v. We require the sets $\mathcal{F}_v$ to be *time-invariant*: for each $f \in \mathcal{F}_v$ and each $t \in T$, also $f^t \in \mathcal{F}_v$, where f^t is the function from T to the domain of v given by $f^t(t') \triangleq f(t' + t)$. Intuitively, the dynamic type $\mathcal{F}_v$ gives the collection of allowed trajectories for v. For instance, if $T = \mathsf{R}$ and v has domain R, then $\mathcal{F}_v$ will be the set of all continuous or smooth functions, or the set of all measurable locally essentially bounded functions [19]. If v is a "discrete" variable (in the sense of [15]), then $\mathcal{F}_v$ is the set of all the constant functions. If $Z \subseteq \mathcal{V}$ then we write $\mathcal{F}$-*trajs*(Z) for the set of trajectories w over Z with the property that for all $z \in Z$, $w \downarrow z \in \mathcal{F}_z \lceil dom(w)$.

An *I/O behavior* is a triple $P = (U, Y, \mathcal{B})$, where

- U is a set of typed *input* variables;
- Y is a set of typed *output* variables with $U \cap Y = \emptyset$; we write $V \triangleq U \cup Y$;
- $\mathcal{B} \subseteq \mathcal{F}$-*trajs*$(V)$ is a prefix closed set of trajectories satisfying
  B1 (functional dependence of outputs from inputs)
  For all $w, w' \in \mathcal{B}$ and for all $t \in dom(w) \cap dom(w')$,
  $$(w \lhd t) \downarrow U = (w' \lhd t) \downarrow U \Rightarrow w(t) \lceil Y = w'(t) \lceil Y$$
  B2 (freedom of inputs)
  $\forall w \in Full(\mathcal{F}\text{-}trajs(U))\ \exists w' \in Max(\mathcal{B}) : w' \downarrow U \leq w$
  B3 (nonZenoness)
  $Max(\mathcal{B}) \subseteq Closed(\mathcal{B}) \cup Full(\mathcal{B})$

Axiom **B1** says that the output at time t is fully determined by the inputs at times up to, but not including, t. Roughly speaking, axiom **B2** expresses that the input is a signal that is imposed by the environment and over which the system has no control. However, in a hybrid world a continuous phase of a system can be interrupted at any time by the occurrence of a discrete transition. A system may, for instance, perform a locally controlled discrete action as soon as the input reaches a threshold value. Therefore, axiom **B2** only requires that for each full input signal there exists a maximal trajectory that, when projected on its input, forms a prefix of this input signal. Axiom **B3** states that each maximal trajectory is either closed or full. Together, **B2** and **B3** imply that in an I/O behavior each input signal is accepted up to and including some finite time t or up to ∞. Note that for any I/O behavior P there is an output state $s \in \mathbf{Y}$ such that all trajectories w in $\mathcal{B}$ begin with s, i.e., $w(0)\lceil Y = s$.

Our I/O behaviors can be viewed as a special case of the I/O behaviors of Sontag [19]. Sontag defines I/O behaviors in terms of a *response map* from input signals up to time t to the output at time t, but this presentation is equivalent to our definition in terms of trajectories over both inputs and outputs. Technically, we found it a bit easier to use trajectories in this paper. In [19], no assumptions are made about possible input signals and the length of maximal trajectories (our axioms **B2** and **B3**). However, [19] singles out the so-called $\mathcal{V}$-*complete* I/O behaviors, which are I/O behaviors that accept any input of type $\mathcal{V}$.

In the sequel, the components of an I/O behavior P will be denoted by V_P, U_P, Y_P and $\mathcal{B}_P$. Also, if no confusion can arise, the components of an I/O behavior P_i will be denoted by V_i, U_i, Y_i and $\mathcal{B}_i$, etc.

Two I/O behaviors P_1 and P_2 are *compatible* if $Y_1 \cap Y_2 = \emptyset$. In this case, we define the *composition* $P_1 \| P_2$ to be the structure $P = (U, Y, \mathcal{B})$ where

- $U = (U_1 \cup U_2) - (Y_1 \cup Y_2)$,
- $Y = Y_1 \cup Y_2$, and
- $\mathcal{B} \subseteq \mathcal{F}\text{-}trajs(U \cup Y)$ is given by $w \in \mathcal{B} \Leftrightarrow w \downarrow V_1 \in \mathcal{B}_1 \wedge w \downarrow V_2 \in \mathcal{B}_2$.

In general, the composition of two compatible I/O behaviors need not be an I/O behavior since there may be "too many solutions":

Example 1. Suppose $T = \mathsf{R}$. For u, y variables whose dynamic type is the set of functions from R to R that have left-hand limits, define $\mathsf{Copy}(u, y)$ to be the I/O behavior that, for $t > 0$, copies input u to output y, and with the initial value of y set to 0. Then the composition of $\mathsf{Copy}(u, y)$ and $\mathsf{Copy}(y, u)$ has no input variables and therefore just one full input trajectory is allowed. However, there is more than one output trajectory and thus the composition does not satisfy axiom **B1**.

It may also occur that the composition of two compatible I/O behaviors yields an I/O behavior, even though there exists no "solution" in the sense that maximal trajectories can be merged. This motivates the following definition.

Two compatible I/O behaviors P_1 and P_2 are *strongly compatible* if $P = P_1 \| P_2$ is an I/O behavior and, for each trajectory w of P,

$$w \in Max(\mathcal{B}_P) \Leftrightarrow (w \downarrow V_1 \in Max(\mathcal{B}_1) \vee w \downarrow V_2 \in Max(\mathcal{B}_2)).$$

Example 2. Suppose $T = \mathsf{R}$. For u, y variables whose dynamic type is the set of functions from R to R that have left-hand limits, define $\mathsf{Add1}(u, y)$ to be the I/O behavior whose output y is, for $t > 0$, equal to the input u incremented by 1, and with the initial value of y set to 0. Then the I/O behaviors $\mathsf{Add1}(u, y)$ and $\mathsf{Add1}(y, u)$ are compatible but not strongly compatible, even though their composition is an I/O behavior.

Let A be a HIOA and let $l \in \mathbf{L}_A$ be a valuation of the local variables of A. A nonempty set W of trajectories of A is called an *l-process* (or *process*) of A if (U_A, L_A, W) is an I/O behavior and, for all $w \in W$, $w(0)\lceil L_A = l$, i.e., the initial states of all trajectories in W agree with l.

Two compatible HIOA's A_1 and A_2 are *strongly compatible* if for each reachable state s of $A_1 \| A_2$, for each $(s\lceil L_1)$-process W_1 of A_1, and for each $(s\lceil L_2)$-process W_2 of A_2, the I/O behaviors (U_1, L_1, W_1) and (U_2, L_2, W_2) are strongly compatible.

5.2 Games and Strategies

Intuitively, a system is receptive if time can advance to infinity independently of the input provided by its environment, or equivalently, if it does not constrain its environment. In [6, 1, 7] various notions of receptivity have been defined in terms of games. Below, we extend these ideas to the setting of HIOA's. The interaction between a system and its environment is represented as a two person game in which the goal of the system is to construct an admissible execution, and the goal of the environment is to prevent this. The system is receptive if it has a strategy by which it can always win the game, irrespective of the behavior of the environment.

Formally, a *strategy* ρ for A is a function that specifies, for each sentence α of A with $l = \alpha.lstate\lceil L_A$,

1. an l-process W^α of A,
2. a function $g^\alpha : Closed(W^\alpha) \times \Sigma_A^{in} \to \mathbf{L}_A$ satisfying
$$g^\alpha(w, a) = l \Rightarrow w.lstate \xrightarrow{a}_A l.$$
3. a function $f^\alpha : Closed(Max(W^\alpha)) \to (\Sigma_A^{loc} \times \mathbf{L}_A)$ satisfying
$$f^\alpha(w) = (a, l) \Rightarrow w.lstate \xrightarrow{a}_A l,$$

At the beginning and immediately after each discrete transition, a strategy produces a process W that starts in the current local state. By doing this, a strategy resolves all nondeterminism for the next continuous phase. Typically, choosing a process amounts to fixing the trajectories for certain internal variables that represent disturbances, and deciding at which time the next locally controlled action will be performed. Once a process has been selected, the input signal fully determines the next trajectory in the execution of the system. Since at any point the environment may produce a discrete input action, a strategy also specifies, through the function g, what will be the next local state after such an action.

The values of the input variables after a discrete step are determined by the environment. Through the function f, a strategy specifies, for each maximal and closed trajectory of the selected process, which locally controlled step will be performed at the end of this trajectory.

In the game between the environment and the system the behavior of the environment is represented by an *environment sequence*. This is an infinite alternating sequence

$$\mathcal{I} = w_1\ a_1\ b_1\ w_2\ a_2\ b_2\ \cdots$$

of closed or full trajectories $w_i \in \mathcal{F}\text{-}trajs(U_A)$, actions $a_i \in \Sigma_A^{in}$, and booleans $b_i \in \{\mathsf{T}, \mathsf{F}\}$

In the i-th move of the game, the environment produces input signal w_i. If w_i is finite then the environment produces discrete action a_i right after signal w_i. The boolean b_i serves to break ties in case the environment and the system both want to perform a discrete action at the same time: if $b_i = \mathsf{T}$ then the environment is allowed to make a move and otherwise the system may perform an action. As in [7], our game starts after a finite execution α. The outcome of the game is described formally in the following definition.

Let A be a HIOA, ρ a strategy for A, $\mathcal{I}$ an environment sequence for A (with ρ and $\mathcal{I}$ as defined above), and let α be a finite hybrid execution of A. We define the *outcome* $\mathcal{O}_{\rho,\mathcal{I}}(\alpha)$ as the limit of the sequence $(\alpha_i)_{i\geq 0}$ of hybrid executions that is constructed inductively below. Each α_i is either a sentence or admissible.

Let $l = \alpha.lstate\lceil L_A$. Then $\alpha_0 \triangleq \alpha\ e\ \wp(w_1(0) \cup l)$.

Here we extend α in a trivial way to a sentence in order to get into a situation where strategy ρ can be applied in combination with environment sequence $\mathcal{I}$. In the definition, $\cup$ is the operation that takes the union of two functions, each viewed as a set of pairs. The first argument of $\cup$ yields the values for the input variables and the second argument the values for the locally controlled variables.

For $i > 0$, define α_i in terms of α_{i-1} as follows.

If α_{i-1} is admissible then $\alpha_i \triangleq \alpha_{i-1}$.

Otherwise, α_{i-1} is a sentence. Pick any full trajectory $w_i^+ \in \mathcal{F}\text{-}trajs(U_A)$ with $w_i \leq w_i^+$. Then by axiom **B2** there is a maximal execution $w_i' \in W^\alpha$ with $w_i' \downarrow U_A \leq w_i^+$. By axiom **B1**, w_i' is uniquely determined by the choice of w_i^+. Let $t = w_i.ltime$ and $t' = w_i'.ltime$. We distinguish between three cases:

1. If $t = t' = \infty$ then

$$\alpha_i \triangleq \alpha_{i-1} \frown w_i'.$$

This is the case where both the system and the environment have decided not to perform any discrete action.

2. If $t < t'$ or $t = t' < \infty \wedge b_i = \mathsf{T}$, then

$$\alpha_i \triangleq \alpha_{i-1} \frown ((w_i' \trianglelefteq t)\ a_i\ \wp(w_{i+1}(0) \cup g^{\alpha_i}(w_i' \trianglelefteq t, a_i))).$$

This is the case where, after an initial fragment of w_i', the environment produces an input action a_i. The resulting state after this action is obtained by taking the union of the first state of the next input trajectory and the local state that is specified by the g-part of the strategy.

3. If $t' < t$ or $t = t' < \infty \wedge b_i = \mathsf{F}$ and if we let $f^{\alpha_i}(w_i') = (a_i', l_i)$, then

$$\alpha_i \triangleq \alpha_{i-1} \frown (w_i' \; a_i' \; \wp(w_{i+1}(0) \cup l_i)).$$

This is the case where, after w_i' has been completed, the system performs a locally controlled step as specified by the f-part of the strategy.

Note that the definition of α_i does not depend on the choice of w_i^+ since by axiom **B1** the prefix $w_i' \trianglelefteq t$ of w_i' that is used in the construction is determined uniquely by the fixed prefix w_i of w_i^+.

Proposition 5. *$\mathcal{O}_{\rho,\mathcal{I}}(\alpha)$ is a Zeno or admissible hybrid execution of A.*

A hybrid execution α of a HIOA A is *Zeno-tolerant* iff it is Zeno, contains infinitely many input actions and only finitely many locally controlled actions. A strategy ρ for A is *Zeno-tolerant* if for each environment sequence $\mathcal{I}$ and for each finite execution α, $\mathcal{O}_{\rho,\mathcal{I}}(\alpha)$ is either admissible or Zeno-tolerant. We call A *receptive* iff there exists a Zeno-tolerant strategy for A. Note that each receptive HIOA is trivially feasible.

We now come to the main result of this paper.

Theorem 6. *Suppose A_1 and A_2 are strongly compatible, receptive HIOA's. Then $A_1 \| A_2$ is receptive.*

The corresponding result for the hiding operations is much easier to prove:

Theorem 7. *Suppose A is a receptive HIOA, and let $S \subseteq \Sigma_A^{out}$ and $Z \subseteq Y_A$. Then $\mathsf{ActHide}(S, A)$ and $\mathsf{VarHide}(Z, A)$ are receptive.*

5.3 Strong Compatibility vs. Compatibility

In order to apply Theorem 6, one has to establish that the HIOA's A_1 and A_2 are strongly compatible. From control theory it is well-known that this is a difficult problem in general. However, it is possible to identify certain classes of I/O behaviors for which strong compatibility reduces to compatibility. This means that for all processes of A_1 and A_2 in such a class, the condition of strong compatibility in Theorem 6, which in general is hard to check, reduces to the syntactic condition of compatibility.

A first example can be obtained by considering what we call *autistic* I/O behaviors. These are I/O behaviors that accept any input but produce an output that is totally unrelated to this input. Formally, an I/O behavior is called *autistic* if it satisfies the axiom

B4 $\forall w, w' \in \mathcal{B} : dom(w) = dom(w') \Rightarrow w \downarrow Y = w' \downarrow Y$

It is easy to verify that two autistic processes are strongly compatible iff they are compatible. From the perspective of classical control theory autistic processes are definitely of no interest: why have an input if it is not used at all? In a hybrid setting, however, an automaton that does not process its input in a continuous manner can still monitor this input and perform a discrete transition when some threshold is reached. In *linear hybrid automata* [3, 2], for instance, there is no continuous processing of inputs and all underlying processes are autistic.

Less trivial examples of classes of I/O behaviors for which strong compatibility reduces to compatibility can be found in the literature on control theory [19]. In control theory it is common to express the continuous behavior of a system by means of differential equations; thus, to be sure that a system is well described, the differential equations need to admit a unique solution for each possible starting condition of the system. A typical approach is to describe a system through differential equations of the form

$$E \triangleq \begin{cases} \dot{x} = f(x,u) \\ y = g(x) \end{cases}$$

where u, y, and x are the input, output, and internal vectors of variables, respectively. It is known from calculus that if f is globally Lipschitz and u is C^1, then for each fixed starting condition $x(0) = x_0$ there is a unique solution to the equations of E, defined on a maximal neighborhood of 0, such that $x(0) = x_0$. Suppose that the dynamic type of each input variable is the set of all C^1 functions. Consider the set W of all the solutions to E for each possible choice of x_0 and of $u(t)$, and let $(U, X \cup Y, W')$ be any I/O behavior whose trajectories are prefixes of trajectories in W. We say that $(U, X \cup Y, W')$ is an I/O behavior of E.

Consider now two systems, described by equations E_1 and E_2 with the same form as E, and suppose there are no common locally controlled variables in E_1 and E_2. The interaction between E_1 and E_2 can be described by a new set of equations E_3 obtained by considering together the equations of E_1 and E_2. If also the g functions of E_1 and E_2 are globally Lipschitz, then it is easy to show that E_3 can be represented in the same form as E where f and g are globally Lipschitz. Furthermore, let P_1 and P_2 be any two I/O behaviors of E_1 and E_2, respectively. Then it is the case that P_1 and P_2 are strongly compatible and that P_3 is an I/O behavior of E_3.

Therefore, if we choose the dynamic type of each variable to be the set of all C^1 functions, then strong compatibility reduces to compatibility for I/O behaviors of systems of equations E, where f and g are globally Lipschitz. In general, any choice of conditions on f and u that guarantee local existence of unique solutions and that are preserved by interaction between systems can be used as a basis to define a class of processes for which strong compatibility reduces to compatibility.

Acknowledgment We thank Jan van Schuppen for constructive criticism.

References

1. M. Abadi and L. Lamport. Composing specifications. *ACM Transactions on Programming Languages and Systems*, 1(15):73–132, 1993.
2. R. Alur, C. Courcoubetis, N. Halbwachs, T.A. Henzinger, P.-H. Ho, X. Nicollin, A. Olivero, J.Sifakis, and S. Yovine. The algorithmic analysis of hybrid systems. *Theoretical Computer Science*, 138:3–34, 1995.
3. R. Alur, C. Courcoubetis, T.A. Henzinger, and P.-H. Ho. Hybrid automata: an algorithmic approach to the specification and verification of hybrid systems. In Grossman et al. [8], pages 209–229.
4. J.C.M. Baeten and W.P. Weijland. *Process Algebra*. Cambridge Tracts in Theoretical Computer Science 18. Cambridge University Press, 1990.
5. D.J.B. Bosscher, I. Polak, and F.W. Vaandrager. Verification of an audio control protocol. In *Proc. FTRTFT'94*, LNCS 863, pages 170–192. Springer-Verlag, 1994.
6. D. Dill. *Trace Theory for Automatic Hierarchical Verification of Speed-Independent Circuits*. ACM Distinguished Dissertations. MIT Press, 1988.
7. R. Gawlick, R. Segala, J.F. Søgaard-Andersen, and N. Lynch. Liveness in timed and untimed systems. In *Proceedings* 21th *ICALP*, LNCS 820. Springer-Verlag, 1994. A full version appears as MIT Technical Report number MIT/LCS/TR-587.
8. R.L. Grossman, A. Nerode, A.P. Ravn, and H. Rischel, editors. *Hybrid Systems*, LNCS 736. Springer-Verlag, 1993.
9. L. Lamport. The temporal logic of actions. *ACM Transactions on Programming Languages and Systems*, 16(3):872–923, March 1994.
10. N.A. Lynch. Modelling and verification of automated transit systems, using timed automata, invariants and simulations, 1996. This volume.
11. N.A. Lynch and M.R. Tuttle. Hierarchical correctness proofs for distributed algorithms. In *Proceedings* 6th *PODC*, pages 137–151, August 1987. A full version is available as MIT Technical Report MIT/LCS/TR-387.
12. N.A. Lynch and F.W. Vaandrager. Forward and backward simulations – part II: Timing-based systems. Report CS-R9314, CWI, Amsterdam, March 1993. To appear in *Information and Computation*.
13. N.A. Lynch and F.W. Vaandrager. Forward and backward simulations. part I: Untimed systems. *Information and Computation*, 121(2):214–233, September 1995.
14. N.A. Lynch and H.B. Weinberg. Proving correctness of a vehicle maneuver: Deceleration. In *Proceedings Second European Workshop on Real-Time and Hybrid Systems*, Grenoble, France, June 1995.
15. O. Maler, Z. Manna, and A. Pnueli. From timed to hybrid systems. In *Proceedings REX Workshop*, LNCS 600, pages 447–484. Springer-Verlag, 1992.
16. Z. Manna and A. Pnueli. *The Temporal Logic of Reactive and Concurrent Systems: Specification*. Springer-Verlag, 1992.
17. A. Nerode and A. Yakhnis. Concurrent programs as strategies in games. In Y. Moschovakis, editor, *Logic from Computer Science*. Springer-Verlag, 1992.
18. A. Pnueli and J. Sifakis, editors. *Special Issue on Hybrid Systems of Theoretical Computer Science*, 138(1). Elsevier Science Publishers, February 1995.
19. E.D. Sontag. *Mathematical Control Theory — Deterministic Finite Dimensional Systems*, TAM 6. Springer-Verlag, 1990.
20. H.B. Weinberg, N.A. Lynch, and N. Delisle. Verification of automated vehicle protection systems, 1996. This volume.

A Formal Description of Hybrid Systems*

Zhou Chaochen,** Wang Ji*** and Anders P. Ravn†

Abstract. Inspired by [He94], a language to describe hybrid systems, i.e. networks of communicating discrete and continuous processes, is proposed. A semantics of the language is given in Extended Duration Calculus [ZRH93], a real-time interval logic with a proof system that allows reasoning in mathematical analysis about continuous processes to be embedded into the logic. The semantics thus provides a secure link to hybrid system models based on a general theory of dynamical systems.

1 Introduction

Hybrid systems occur when developers model complex control applications with a mixture of continuous and discrete states. The complexity can arise from a large state space; or it may come from complex phenomena in a physical system in an attempt to make untractable non-linear systems piecewise linear. Whatever cause, it seems that description of such systems calls for a language with compositional features, such that the complex can be described as a parallel composition of sequential components. Parallel composition models components that evolve concurrently, while sequential composition models successive phases of operations in a (sub)system.

A language with such features may be developed from existing programming languages for reactive, real-time computing systems, because great effort in computing science has been given to finding suitable component interactions that preserve compositionality, and this work has led to frameworks like process algebras, e.g. CCS [Milner89] and CSP [Hoare85]. Real-time has posed new problems, but compositionality has been handled successfully by e.g. [Wang91, RR87].

A further aspect that has arisen as part of the investigation of programming languages is the benefits of non-determinism in specification of components, i.e. the ability of a component to evolve differently either through external influence when receiving signals from partners or through internal choices. These features seem to correspond to *controlled/autonomous jumps* [BBM94] or *important events* [MP93] in hybrid systems.

* This work has been partially supported by DeTfoRS project, a joint research of Chinese 863 Hi-tech Programme and UNU/IIST.

** Department of Computer Science, Technical University of Denmark. On leave of absence from UNU/IIST, Macau, and Institute of Software, Beijing.

** Department of Computer Science, Changsha Institute of Technology, Changsha.

† Department of Computer Science, Technical University of Denmark.

In order to develop a hybrid system language from a programming language, one must introduce continuous variables into programming, and at the same time preserve the compositionalities. [He94] has taken a significant step towards a hybrid system language by introducing ***continuous statements*** into CSP in the form of differential equations, such as $\mathcal{F}(\dot{s}, s) = 0$, where s is a vector of continuous variables. With the extended notation it describes the ***Cat and Mouse*** system and ***Water Tank Controller***. Communication of continuous variables is, however, not included, so analog/digital conversions cannot be described. Without communications of continuous variables, shared variables are unavoidable in a distributed network. Shared variables governed by different differential equations can easily make systems inconsistent, and require extra restrictions in order to preserve compositionality.

In this paper, we iterate [He94] to develop a hybrid system language, called Hybrid CSP ($\mathcal{HCSP}$), with the below features and mechanisms.

- Differential equation groups can be written in $\mathcal{HCSP}$ directly as continuous statements.
- Interactions among processes will be described solely as communications; shared variables are forbidden.
- Six kind of events are included. They are timeout and Boolean conditions, A/D, D/A, A/A and D/D communications, where A stands for analog (continuous), and D for digital.
- A process evolution can be preempted by any kind of event.

The following Section 2 takes a closer look at the interactions between evolutions of continuous variables and discrete events of hybrid systems. Section 3 introduces primitive statements and composition combinators, and stipulate suitable context conditions that allow compositionality to be preserved during construction. Section 4 illustrates the language through examples. Section 5 maps the language to piecewise continuous functions as mathematical models by giving a semantics in Extended Duration Calculus ($\mathcal{EDC}$). Section 6 concludes with some further work in this respect.

2 Interactions

The behavior of a hybrid system is determined by not only its differential equations which govern the time evolution of its continuous variables, but also events which drive transitions among evolutions. The causalities in hybrid systems are that evolution causes (explicitly or implicitly) events to occur, while events promote switching of evolutions. So, in order to capture behavior of hybrid systems, a hybrid system language must be capable of describing such interactions between evolutions and events.

This section briefly recapitulates the interaction mechanism of CSP and its timing extensions. Then corresponding mechanisms for interactions among evolutions and events are introduced.

2.1 Communication Events

The means of interaction in CSP and other process algebras is *communication*. Each component (called *process*) has an alphabet listing the communications in which it participates. Given a particular communication belonging to the alphabet, the communication occurs just when all processes engaged in the communication are ready for it. A communication is thus a marker for a common synchronisation point among processes.

Often, a communication is structured as a pair of channel name and message. Furthermore, interaction with communication of messages is best understood when a channel is uni-directional, and occurs in at most two process alphabets. An output of message m on channel ch is then denoted in CSP as

$$ch!m$$

It is matched by a choice among all possible messages that can be received in another process by an input statement

$$ch?x$$

where x is a variable to denote the matching message. A communication is thus a synchronisation of these two statements, and the effect is essentially a distributed assignment of value m in the sender to the variable x in the receiver.

In CSP, communications can only pass discrete messages, such as signals and values of programming variables. With CSP communications, one can model external events of hybrid system.

Example: Controlled Switch.
A decision maker or planner process can use

$$switch!n$$

to send its desire to switch a controller process to a particular control mode n, and the controller can use

$$switch?x$$

to model when it is ready to switch modes.

In $\mathcal{HCSP}$, communications can carry values of continuous variables, and also assign values to continuous variables. Therefore A/D and D/A converters can be modelled as communications.

Example: A/D and D/A Converters.

1. A D/A converter can be modelled as the pair of

$$ch_{d2a}!d, \qquad\qquad ch_{d2a}?u$$

   where d is a discrete value, and u is a continuous variable. It means that a process (e.g. a digital controller) sends discrete value d via channel ch_{d2a} to its partner (e.g. an actuator), and the partner will receive and assign the value to its continuous variable u.

2. An A/D converter transforms a continuous variable value to a discrete message, and can be modelled as

$$ch_{a2d}!s, \qquad\qquad ch_{a2d}?v$$

   It means that a process (e.g. a sensor) sends the current value of continuous variable s to another process (e.g. a digital controller), which receives and assign the value to a discrete (programming) variable v.

[He94] includes a notation to describe *Interrupt by Communication*. For example,

$$P \trianglerighteq (ch?x \rightarrow Q)$$

It initially proceeds like P, and is interrupted on occurrence of communication along channel ch, and then proceeds like Q. *Interrupt by Communication* provides a mechanism to describe a change of system evolution driven by an external event, such as *Controlled Jump* in [BL84].

Example: Inventory Management System.
Let P be an initial evolution governing ***stock*** x:

$$\dot{x} = -\alpha + \beta_0$$

where α represents ***utilization dynamics***, and β_0 is an initial order amount. Let Q be the evolution after receiving an order amount β:

$$\dot{x} = -\alpha + \beta$$

Thus, $P \trianglerighteq (ch?\beta \rightarrow Q)$ describes a controlled jump of the system evolution upon receiving a new ***order amount*** via channel ch.

2.2 Timeout Events

Timed CSP [RR87] extends CSP with a (`Wait` t) statement which means that a process extends unchanged for t time units. [NOSY93] has proposed a convenient binary timeout combinator. Given P, Q and a timeout period t, the statement

$$P \trianglerighteq_t Q$$

behaves as P for up to t time units. If no communication has taken place in P by t, it continues with Q.

This binary combinator provides CSP with another mechanism to define changes of system evolutions triggered by timeout events, such as Autonomous Switching in [BBM94].

Example: Hysteresis.
Let P be an evolution

$$\dot{x} = u + 1$$

and Q be another evolution

$$\dot{x} = u - 1$$

Therefore, $P \trianglerighteq_t Q$ models an autonomous switching of P to Q in t time units, as there is no communication occurring in P.

2.3 Boolean Events

[He94] introduces Boolean expressions over continuous variables. A notation,[5]

$$(P \to B); Q,$$

means that the process behaves like P until B becomes true, and then behaves like Q, where B is a Boolean expression of continuous variables.

When B defines the boundary of a region in a system state space, and P and Q are descriptions of system evolutions, $((P \to B); Q)$ specifies a part of trajectory of system behavior, which evolves according to P until it reaches the boundary, and then evolves like Q. It is called Autonomous Jump in [BGM93].

Example: Ball Motion in a Room.
Let P be equations

$$\begin{aligned} \dot{x} &= v_x \\ \dot{y} &= v_y \\ \dot{v}_x &= 0 \\ \dot{v}_y &= -g \end{aligned}$$

where (x, y) represents horizontal and vertical coordinates of the ball, v_x and v_y are its horizontal and vertical velocities, and g is the constant acceleration of gravity. Let Q_1 be an evolution obtained from P by replacing $\dot{y} = v_y$ with

$$\dot{y} = -\rho v_y$$

where ρ $(0 < \rho < 1)$ is the coefficient of *restitution*. That is,

$$Q_1 = P[-\rho v_y / v_y]$$

[5] In [He94], the notation is $(P[B]Q)$ instead.

Let the room of size $([0,a] \times [0,b])$, and B_1 be $(y = 0 \ \vee \ y = b)$ which specifies the vertical boundaries of the room. Therefore

$$(P \rightarrow B_1); Q_1$$

describes an autonomous jump of the ball when it hits the vertical boundaries. Likewise, one can describe the autonomous jump when the ball hits the horizontal boundaries by

$$(P \rightarrow B_2); Q_2$$

where B_2 is

$$(x = 0 \ \vee \ x = a)$$

and Q_2 is $P[-\rho v_x/v_x]$.

3 Hybrid CSP ($\mathcal{HCSP}$)

In this section we present the full $\mathcal{HCSP}$ language. It is based on the following design criteria:

1. A hybrid system in $\mathcal{HCSP}$ is a network composed of sequential processes (continuous or discrete). It combines not only digital devices and analog devices but also event dependent choices of dynamic evolutions.
2. Shared variables governed by different differential equations are a sure way to make a system inconsistent. Therefore communication is the only interaction among processes of a hybrid system.
3. Connections among the processes are synchronous communication channels as in CSP while the messages can be exchanged between either continuous or discrete processes.
4. Time is over a continuous domain (non-negative real numbers), and the behavior of a system will relate to a conceptual global clock.

Alphabets

Alphabets describe the objects manipulated by a process. For a given process these are variables and communications. Henceforth, the alphabet sets of a process P are State, Var and Chan, and they are disjoint.

- State is the finite set of continuous variables.
- Var is the finite set of discrete variables.
- Chan is the finite set of channels, which can be divided into two exclusive parts, the set of input channels InChan and the set of output channels OutChan.

Sequential Processes

Sequential processes (SP) in $\mathcal{HCSP}$ can be defined as

$$SP \mathrel{\hat{=}} Primitive \mid Composite$$

and

$$\begin{aligned} Primitive \mathrel{\hat{=}}\ & \texttt{Stop} \mid \texttt{Skip} \mid v := e \mid ch?x \mid ch!e \\ & \mid \ < \mathcal{F}(\dot{s}, s) = 0 > \ \mid \ < \mathcal{F}(\dot{s}, s) = 0 >_e \end{aligned}$$

$$\begin{aligned} Composite \mathrel{\hat{=}}\ & P; Q \mid P \rightarrow B \mid B \rightarrow P \mid P \trianglerighteq_d Q \\ & \mid P \trianglerighteq [\!]_{i \in I}(io_i \rightarrow Q_i) \mid \mu X.F(X) \end{aligned}$$

In the syntax v is a discrete variable ($v \in \mathsf{Var}$), s is a continuous variable ($s \in \mathsf{State}$), x is a variable either discrete or continuous ($x \in (\mathsf{State} \cup \mathsf{Var})$), B and e are Boolean and arithmetical expressions over ($\mathsf{Var} \cup \mathsf{State}$), ch is a channel name ($ch \in \mathsf{Chan}$), d is a non-negative real number, and P and Q denote sequential processes ($\in SP$).

Primitive Statements

Stop is a non-terminating idle process.

Skip terminates immediately with no effect on the process.

$v := e$ assigns the value of expression e to v and then terminates.

$ch?x$ is an ***input statement***. It is willing to accept a message from the channel ch ($\in \mathsf{InChan}$), and assigns it to a variable x, which could be discrete or continuous.

$ch!e$ is an ***output statement***. It is willing to send the value of the expression e to the output channel ch ($\in \mathsf{OutChan}$).

$< \mathcal{F}(\dot{s}, s) = 0 >$ is called a ***continuous statement***. It defines an evolution by a differential equation over s. In fact s could be a vector of continuous variables, and $\mathcal{F}$ be a group of equations. Continuous statements are in general system equations governing the continuous variables.

$< \mathcal{F}(\dot{s}, s) = 0 >_e$ is a continuous statement, which behaves like $< \mathcal{F}(\dot{s}, s) = 0 >$, but resets the initial value of s to value of e.

Composite Statements

$P; Q$ behaves like P first and if P terminates then behaves like Q.

$P \rightarrow B$ behaves like P until B becomes true and then terminates.

$B \rightarrow P$ behaves like P if B is true. Otherwise it terminates.

$P \trianglerighteq_d Q$ will behave like P at first and will behave like Q if there does not occur any communication of P within d time units. Hence, we can define a *wait* statement, which can postpone process behavior for d time units:

$$\texttt{Wait}\ d \mathrel{\widehat{=}} \texttt{Stop} \trianglerighteq_d \texttt{Skip}.$$

$P \trianglerighteq [\!]_{i\in I}(io_i \to Q_i)$ behaves like P initially and like Q_i immediately after a communication (io_i) occurs, where I is a non-empty finite set of indices, and $\{io_i | i \in I\}$ are input and output statements which do not appear in P. The $\to$ in the notation can be replaced by ;. For examples, $io_i \to Q_i$ can be replaced by $io_i; Q_i$, and $io_i \to \texttt{Skip}$ by $io_i; \texttt{Skip}$, i.e. io_i. When I is a singleton, we will delete $[\!]$ from the notation to write down $P \trianglerighteq (io_1 \to Q_1)$ instead. Furthermore the conventional *external choice* statement of CSP can be defined

$$[\!]_{i\in I}(io_i \to Q_i) \mathrel{\widehat{=}} \texttt{Stop} \trianglerighteq [\!]_{i\in I}(io_i \to Q_i).$$

$\mu X.F(X)$ gives a recursive process. Here, we neither consider nested recursion nor other complicated patterns, but just *tail* recursion such as $F(X)$ is in form of $(P; X)$ or $(P \trianglerighteq_d X)$.

We define the following recursions.

$$\begin{array}{ll} P \rhd io & \mathrel{\widehat{=}} \mu X.((P \trianglerighteq io);\ X) \\ P \rhd_d io & \mathrel{\widehat{=}} \mu X.((P \trianglerighteq_d io); X) \\ \rhd_d P & \mathrel{\widehat{=}} \mu X.(P \trianglerighteq_d X) \end{array}$$

where io stands for a non-empty sequence of input/output statements.

Parallel Processes

A hybrid system is composed of a set of sequential processes connected with channels, and is called a *parallel process.*

$$HS \mathrel{\widehat{=}} SP \mid (HS \parallel HS)$$

Here we assume that SP_1 and SP_2 in $(SP_1 \parallel SP_2)$ have no shared continuous or discrete variables, and neither share input nor output channels. That is

$$\begin{array}{ll} ((\mathsf{State}(SP_1) \cup \mathsf{Var}(SP_1)) \cap (\mathsf{State}(SP_2) \cup \mathsf{Var}(SP_2))) & = \emptyset \\ (\mathsf{InChan}(SP_1) \cap \mathsf{InChan}(SP_2)) & = \emptyset \\ (\mathsf{OutChan}(SP_1) \cap \mathsf{OutChan}(SP_2)) & = \emptyset \end{array}$$

However they can interact via communications along their common channels

$$(\mathsf{InChan}(SP_1) \cap \mathsf{OutChan}(SP_2)) \cup (\mathsf{OutChan}(SP_1) \cap \mathsf{InChan}(SP_2))$$

Therefore $(SP_1 \parallel SP_2)$ behaves as if two processes are working independently except that all communications along the common channels between SP_1 and

SP_2 are to be synchronised. The above assumptions generalises to a parallel process with multiple sequential processes, so that any channel is uni-directional, and owned by at most two sequential processes, one at an end of the channel.

The following table gives an overview of processes which compose a hybrid system in $\mathcal{HCSP}$.

		Discrete Sequential Process	Continuous Sequential Process
Primitive	Assignment	$v := e$	$< \mathcal{F}(\dot{s}, s) = 0 >_e$
	Skip	`Skip`	
	Idle	`Stop`	
	Input	$ch?v$	$ch?s$
	Output	$ch!e$	$ch!e$
Composite	Condition	$B \rightarrow P \quad P \rightarrow B$	
	Sequential	$P; Q$	
	Timeout	$P \trianglerighteq_d Q$	
	Preemption	$P \trianglerighteq \|_{i \in I}(io_i; Q_i)$	
	Recursion	$\mu X.F(X)$	
Parallel Processes			
$P \parallel Q$			

4 Examples

In this section, we illustrate the language by four examples. The first two are the examples of the inventory management system and the ball motion in a room introduced in Section 2. The third one is a Closed Control Loop, which includes elementary components of a controlled system. The last one is a generalised Cat & Mouse System.

4.1 Inventory Management System

Whenever the inventory system receives an order of amount β, it switches its behavior to

$$\dot{x} = -\alpha + \beta$$

where x represents ***stock***, and α represents ***utilization dynamics***. Thus a description of the inventory system will be

$$ch?\beta; (< \dot{x} = -\alpha + \beta >) \triangleright ch?\beta)$$

where the initial communication provides the initial value of β, and $\triangleright$ is an abbreviation of a recursion defined in Section 3.

4.2 Ball Motion in a Room

Let P be

$$\left\langle \begin{aligned} \dot{x} &= v_x \\ \dot{y} &= v_y \\ \dot{v}_x &= 0 \\ \dot{v}_y &= -g \end{aligned} \right\rangle$$

where (x, y) represents horizontal and vertical coordinates of the ball, v_x and v_y are its corresponding velocities, and g is the constant acceleration of gravity. P specifies the horizontal and vertical motion of the ball in a room.

Let the room of size $([0, a] \times [0, b])$. Thus $P[-\rho v_y/v_y]$ defines the motion of the ball after hitting the boundary $(y = 0 \vee y = b)$ (denoted B_1), and $P[-\rho v_x/v_x]$ defines the motion of the ball after hitting the boundary $(x = 0 \vee x = a)$ (denoted B_2), where ρ $(0 < \rho < 1)$ is the coefficient of restitution.

A description of the ball motion will be

$$\begin{aligned} \mu X.\, (P \rightarrow (B_1 \vee B_2)); (B_1 \wedge B_2) \rightarrow X[-\rho v_y/v_y][-\rho v_x/v_x]; \\ (B_1 \rightarrow X[-\rho v_y/v_y]); X[-\rho v_x/v_x] \end{aligned}$$

4.3 Closed Control Loop

Given a plant $\dot{x} = f(x, u)$, one can design a control law $\dot{u} = g(x, u)$ to control the plant in order to satisfy some performance specification, such as stability. This mathematical design can be described as a single continuous statement in $\mathcal{HCSP}$.

$$\left\langle \begin{aligned} \dot{x} &= f(x, u) \\ \dot{u} &= g(x, u) \end{aligned} \right\rangle$$

Embedding a computer as controller, we need a digital implementation whose architecture can be depicted in Figure 1.

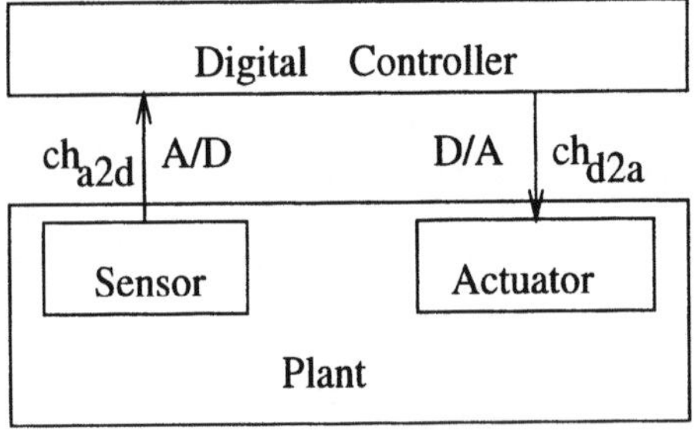

Figure 1. Closed Control Loop

Sensor, Plant and Actuator

A sensor is a device which sends to the controller the measured state x of the plant. In general, before sending, it will transform the plant state value x by an appropriate function h. For example,

$$Sensor ::< y = h(x) >$$

An actuator is a device acting as an expansion of a pulse. The most ordinary one is *zero order hold* as below.

$$Actuator ::< \dot{u} = 0 >$$

Then, a process describing the continuous component (the plant and its sensor and actuator) can be obtained by a continuous statement consisting of the three equations.

$$Plant :: \left\langle \begin{array}{c} y = h(x) \\ \dot{x} = f(x, u) \\ \dot{u} = 0 \end{array} \right\rangle$$

However, they can not interact with the controller without the attachment of A/D and D/A converters.

Attaching A/D and D/A

As we explained in Section 2, the A/D and D/A converters can be described as pairs of communications which assign value of continuous variable to discrete variable and vice versa. That is, the continuous component outputs y to the digital controller via an A/D channel ch_{a2d}, and inputs u from the digital controller via a D/A channel ch_{d2a}:

$$A/D :: ch_{a2d}!y$$

and

$$D/A :: ch_{d2a}?u.$$

By attachment, we finally give a formal description of the continuous component

$$InterfacedPlant :: (Plant \rhd (ch_{a2d}!y \ ; \ ch_{d2a}?u))$$

Here, we take no care of the clock (*sample period*) which will be embedded in the controller.

Digital Controller

A control program often does the following things.
(1) Sample the output of the plant $\hat{y}$.
(2) Compute the next control, according a control law that depends on the current sampled value $\hat{y}$ and previous control $\hat{u}$.
(3) Send the new control $\hat{u}$ to the plant.
So, we have,

$$Program :: (\hat{u} := u_0; \rhd_T \ (ch_{a2d}?\hat{y}; \hat{u} := ALG(\hat{y}, \hat{u}); ch_{d2a}!\hat{u}))$$

where T is the sample period, and ALG is the numerical form of the control law. In general, $\hat{y}$ and $\hat{u}$ are sequences of former values, but we elide this detail.

Closed Control Loop

The entire system can be described as the parallel process:

$$InterfacedPlant \parallel Program$$

4.4 Cat & Mouse

The informal description of the problem is a mechanical cat to be controlled to chase a mouse. If we assume that the cat, the controller and the mouse are one continuous system, we can easily group their system equations into one continuous statement.

$$\left\langle \begin{array}{l} \dot{m} = f(m) \\ \dot{a} = g(a, m) \end{array} \right\rangle$$

where the first equation defines the motion (m) of the mouse, and the second one defines the motion (a) of the controlled cat. Of course, it is unrealistic to let the controller share the state variables of the mouse. So, an A/A communication between two continuous components can be assumed as an initial specification, with a channel c that models obsercation of the mouse by the cat.

$$\begin{array}{l} \dot{m} = f(m) \rhd c!m \\ \parallel \\ \left\langle \begin{array}{l} \dot{a} = g(a, s) \\ \dot{s} = 0 \end{array} \right\rangle \rhd_t c?s \end{array}$$

where a zero hold (i.e. $\dot{s} = 0$) of receiving the mouse motion observation is assumed in the controller. The cat and the mouse have been modelled as two processes in parallel. They have no shared variables but synchronized communications. For every t time units, the controller of the cat will sample the position of the mouse. If one likes to refine the controlled cat into separate components – Cat and Controller, one may follow the idea presented in the example of the closed control loop, and end up with a description of a parallel process with three sequential processes.

5 A Duration Semantics of $\mathcal{HCSP}$

5.1 Extended Duration Calculus ($\mathcal{EDC}$)

Syntax

We give a brief introduction of $\mathcal{EDC}$. For more details, please refer to [ZRH93].

Duration Terms

Duration terms, dt, are real valued terms, which are built from the special symbol ℓ, global variables z, and *beginning* values (**b.**) and *previous* values (**p.**) for temporal variables x.

$$dt ::= \ell \mid z \mid \mathbf{b}.x \mid \mathbf{p}.x \mid \oplus(dt_1, \ldots, dt_n)$$

where $\oplus$ stands for the conventional arithmetical operators, such as $+$, $-$ and $*$.

Duration Formulas

$$D ::= \lhd(dt_1, \ldots, dt_n) \mid \lceil S \rceil \mid \neg D \mid D_1 \wedge D_2 \mid D_1 \frown D_2 \mid \forall z.D$$

where $\lhd$ stands for the conventional arithmetical relations, such as $=$ and $>$, and S for pointwise properties of temporal variables x and y, such as $x \geq y$.

Usual Abbreviations

$$\begin{array}{ll} true & \widehat{=}\ \ell \geq 0 \\ \lceil\,\rceil & \widehat{=}\ \ell = 0 \\ \Diamond D & \widehat{=}\ true \frown D \frown true \\ \Box D & \widehat{=}\ \neg\Diamond\neg D \end{array}$$

Semantics

Let R be real numbers, and R^+ be non-negative reals. We now define the semantics of duration terms and formulas over an interpretation $\mathcal{I}$, evaluation $\mathcal{V}$ and interval $[c,d]$, where $\mathcal{I}$ assigns each temporal variable x a function $x_{\mathcal{I}}$ $(\in (R^+ \rightarrow R))$, and $\mathcal{V}$ assigns each global variable z a value $\mathcal{V}(z)$ $(\in R)$. Let $\mathcal{V}al$ be the set of all evaluations and $\mathcal{I}ntv$ be the set of all closed intervals of R^+.

Semantics of Duration Terms

$\mathcal{I}(dt) : \mathcal{V}al \times \mathcal{I}ntv \rightarrow R.$

$$\begin{array}{ll} \mathcal{I}(\ell)(\mathcal{V},[c,d]) & \widehat{=}\ d-c \\ \mathcal{I}(z)(\mathcal{V},[c,d]) & \widehat{=}\ \mathcal{V}(z) \\ \mathcal{I}(\mathbf{b}.x)(\mathcal{V},[c,d]) & \widehat{=} \begin{cases} x_{\mathcal{I}}(c^+) & \text{if } c<d \\ x_{\mathcal{I}}(c) & \text{if } c=d \end{cases} \\ \mathcal{I}(\mathbf{p}.x)(\mathcal{V},[c,d]) & \widehat{=} \begin{cases} x_{\mathcal{I}}(c^-) & \text{if } c>0 \\ x_{\mathcal{I}}(c) & \text{if } c=0 \end{cases} \\ \mathcal{I}(\oplus(dt_1,\ldots,dt_n))(\mathcal{V},[c,d]) & \widehat{=}\ \oplus(\mathcal{I}(dt_1)(\mathcal{V},[c,d]),\ldots,\mathcal{I}(dt_n)(\mathcal{V},[c,d])) \end{array}$$

where $x_{\mathcal{I}}(c^+)$ and $x_{\mathcal{I}}(c^-)$ are *right* and *left* limits of function $x_{\mathcal{I}}$ at point c.

Semantics of Duration Formulas

$\mathcal{I}\ (D) : \mathcal{V}al \times \mathcal{I}ntv \ \rightarrow \ \{tt, ff\}$.

$$
\begin{array}{ll}
\mathcal{I}\ , \mathcal{V}, [c,d] \models \triangleleft(dt_1,\ldots,dt_n) & \text{iff } \triangleleft(\mathcal{I}\ (dt_1)(\mathcal{V},[c,d]),\ldots,\mathcal{I}\ (dt_n)(\mathcal{V},[c,d])) = tt \\
\mathcal{I}\ , \mathcal{V}, [c,d] \models \lceil S \rceil & \text{iff } S_{\mathcal{I}}\ (t) = 1 \ for\ every\ t \in (c,d)\ and\ c < d \\
\mathcal{I}\ , \mathcal{V}, [c,d] \models \neg D & \text{iff } \mathcal{I}\ , \mathcal{V}, [c,d] \not\models D \\
\mathcal{I}\ , \mathcal{V}, [c,d] \models D_1 \wedge D_2 & \text{iff } \mathcal{I}\ , \mathcal{V}, [c,d] \models D_1\ and\ \mathcal{I}\ , \mathcal{V}, [c,d] \models D_2 \\
\mathcal{I}\ , \mathcal{V}, [c,d] \models D_1 \frown D_2 & \text{iff } \mathcal{I}\ , \mathcal{V}, [c,e] \models D_1\ and\ \mathcal{I}\ , \mathcal{V}, [e,d] \models D_2 \\
 & \quad for\ some\ e \in [c,d] \\
\mathcal{I}\ , \mathcal{V}, [c,d] \models \forall\ z_i.D & \text{iff } \mathcal{I}\ , \mathcal{V}', [c,d] \models D\ for\ all\ valuations\ \mathcal{V}' \\
 & \quad for\ which\ \mathcal{V}'(z_k) = \mathcal{V}(z_k)\ for\ all\ k \neq i
\end{array}
$$

5.2 Observations

Alphabets describe the objects manipulated by a process. Based on the alphabets, we can define the *observations* as the semantic domain lifting the alphabets over the dense time domain R^+, i.e. observations of a hybrid system are composed of a family of functions as below.

- Variable observations.
  - For each continuous variable s in **State**, the observation of s is

    $$s : R^+ \rightarrow R$$

  - For each program variable v in **Var**, the observation of v is

    $$v : R^+ \rightarrow R$$

    and it is a step function.
- For each channel c, we assign three channel observations.

  $$c? : R^+ \rightarrow \{0,1\}$$

  $c?$ is 1 if a process is willing to receive some message along the channel c, otherwise 0.

  $$c! : R^+ \rightarrow \{0,1\}$$

  $c!$ is 1 if a process is willing to send some message along the channel c, otherwise 0.

  $$c : R^+ \rightarrow R$$

  c is a step function giving the message value carried on the channel during the communication.

Based on the observations of a process, we define some shorthands.

- $inactive^P$ represents that a process P refuses to engage in any communication in a time interval.

$$inactive^P \mathrel{\widehat{=}} \lceil\,\rceil \vee \lceil \neg chan^P \rceil$$

where

$$chan^P \mathrel{\widehat{=}} \bigvee_{ch \in \mathsf{InChan}(P)} ch? \quad \bigvee_{ch \in \mathsf{OutChan}(P)} ch!$$

- $comm^P$ represents that one of the channels of a process P succeeds in communication synchcronisation. Therefore a communication can take place over the channel.

$$comm^P \mathrel{\widehat{=}} \bigvee_{ch \in \mathsf{Chan}(P)} ch? \wedge ch!$$

- $keep^P$ means all variables in process P maintain their previous value for a time period.

$$keep^P \mathrel{\widehat{=}} \lceil\,\rceil \vee \bigwedge_{x \in (\mathsf{State}(P) \cup \mathsf{Var}(P))} \exists r \in R.(r = \mathbf{p}.x \ \wedge \ \lceil x = r \rceil)$$

Similarly, $keep^{P \backslash x}$ holds the value of variables except variable x.

$$keep^{P \backslash x} \mathrel{\widehat{=}} \lceil\,\rceil \vee \bigwedge_{y \in (\mathsf{State}(P) \cup \mathsf{Var}(P) - \{x\})} \exists r \in R.(r = \mathbf{p}.y \wedge \lceil y = r \rceil)$$

We often write *inactive* and *keep* with no superscript wherever the process P can be identified from the context.

- $wait(\alpha, ch\odot)$ means channel ch is willing to communicate with its partner and is waiting for synchronization. At the same time, no communication in α is required. Here $\odot \in \{?, \ !\}$.

$$wait(\alpha, ch\odot) \mathrel{\widehat{=}} \lceil\,\rceil \vee \lceil ch \odot \wedge \neg ch\bar{\odot} \bigwedge_{c\odot \in \alpha, c \neq ch} \neg c\odot \rceil$$

where $\bar{?}$ is !, and $\bar{!}$ is ?.

- $syn(\alpha, ch?, x)$ and $syn(\alpha, ch!, m)$ give the synchronization and message passing along channel ch corresponding to $ch?x$ and $ch!m$.

$$syn(\alpha, ch?, x) \mathrel{\widehat{=}} keep^{\backslash x} \wedge (\lceil ch! \wedge ch? \wedge x = ch \bigwedge_{c\odot \in \alpha, c \neq ch} \neg c\odot \rceil$$

$$syn(\alpha, ch!, e) \mathrel{\widehat{=}} \exists r \in R.r = \mathbf{p}.e \wedge keep \wedge (\lceil ch! \wedge ch? \wedge r = ch \bigwedge_{c\odot \in \alpha, c \neq ch} \neg c\odot \rceil$$

where $\mathbf{p}.e$ stands for the value of expression e, when any variable x of e takes its previous value $\mathbf{p}.x$.

5.3 Duration Semantics

The semantics of a $\mathcal{HCSP}$ process is captured by interval formulas defining observations of its alphabet. Recall that the observations are the variables and communications lifted to piecewise continuous functions. A process generates its behavior by defining these function piece by piece. A discrete variable is a step function which can be defined by assignment and communication. A continuous variable is governed by a continuous statement, and its initial value can be reset by either the continuous statement or a communication. A channel is defined by the three channel observations as mentioned before. Therefore, it is possible to use $\mathcal{EDC}$ to give a duration semantics for $\mathcal{HCSP}$, similar to the approaches in [ZHRR92, HOS+93].

Continuation Semantics

We define the semantics in a continuation style, and the semantic function is

$$[\![\,]\!] \in \mathcal{D} \rightarrow \mathcal{D},$$

where $\mathcal{D}$ is the set of $\mathcal{EDC}$ formulas. So, $[\![P]\!]C$ gives a formula describing the interpretation of P when it proceeds with C after termination of P.

Primitive Statements

Stop

Stop is a non-terminating idle process.

$$[\![\texttt{Stop}]\!]C \mathrel{\widehat{=}} (\mathit{inactive} \wedge \mathit{keep})$$

Skip

Skip does nothing but terminates immediately.

$$[\![\texttt{Skip}]\!]C \mathrel{\widehat{=}} C$$

Next, we consider changes of program variables and continuous variables. They are assignment and continuous statements.

Assignment

$$[\![v := e]\!]C \mathrel{\widehat{=}} \lceil\,\rceil \vee (\exists r \in R . r = \mathbf{p}.e \ \wedge \ \lceil v = r \rceil \wedge \mathit{keep}^{\backslash v})^\frown C$$

Continuous

$$[\![< \mathcal{F}(\dot{s}, s) = 0 >]\!]C \ \mathrel{\widehat{=}} \lceil\,\rceil \vee (\mathbf{b}.s = \mathbf{p}.s \wedge \lceil \mathcal{F}(\dot{s}, s) = 0 \rceil \wedge \mathit{inactive} \wedge \mathit{keep}^{\backslash s})$$

$$[\![< \mathcal{F}(\dot{s}, s) = 0 >_e]\!]C \mathrel{\widehat{=}} \lceil\,\rceil \vee (\mathbf{b}.s = \mathbf{p}.e \wedge \lceil \mathcal{F}(\dot{s}, s) = 0 \rceil \wedge \mathit{inactive} \wedge \mathit{keep}^{\backslash s})$$

Input

$$[\![ch?x]\!]C \mathrel{\hat=} wait(\alpha, ch?) \wedge keep \\ \vee \\ (wait(\alpha, ch?) \wedge keep) \frown syn(\alpha, ch?, x) \frown C$$

where $(\alpha \mathrel{\hat=} \bigcup_{c\in \mathsf{InChan}} \{c?\} \cup \bigcup_{c\in \mathsf{OutChan}} \{c!\})$.

Output

$$[\![ch!e]\!]C \mathrel{\hat=} wait(\alpha, ch!) \wedge keep \\ \vee \\ (wait(\alpha, ch!) \wedge keep) \frown syn(\alpha, ch!, e) \frown C$$

where α is defined as above.

Composite Statements

Condition

$$[\![B \to P]\!]C \mathrel{\hat=} \lceil\,\rceil \\ \vee \\ (\lceil B \rceil \wedge inactive \wedge keep) \frown [\![P]\!]C \\ \vee \\ (\lceil \neg B \rceil \wedge inactive \wedge keep) \frown C$$

$$[\![P \to B]\!]C \mathrel{\hat=} \lceil\,\rceil \\ \vee \\ (\lceil B \rceil \wedge inactive \wedge keep) \frown C \\ \vee \\ (\lceil \neg B \rceil \wedge inactive \wedge keep) \frown (\lceil \neg B \rceil \wedge [\![P]\!]\mathtt{stop}) \\ \vee \\ (\lceil \neg B \rceil \wedge inactive \wedge keep) \\ \frown (\lceil \neg B \rceil \wedge [\![P]\!]\mathtt{stop}) \frown (\lceil B \rceil \wedge inactive \wedge keep) \frown C$$

where $\mathtt{stop}^P \mathrel{\hat=} (inactive^P \wedge keep^P)$.

Sequential

$$[\![P;Q]\!]C \mathrel{\hat=} [\![P]\!]([\![Q]\!]C)$$

Timeout

$$[\![P \trianglerighteq_d Q]\!]C \mathrel{\hat=} \lceil\,\rceil \\ \vee \\ \ell < d \wedge [\![P]\!]C \\ \vee \\ ((\ell = d \wedge \Diamond\lceil comm^P \rceil) \frown true) \wedge [\![P]\!]C \\ \vee \\ ((\ell = d \wedge \lceil \neg comm^P \rceil \wedge [\![P]\!]\mathtt{stop}) \frown [\![Q]\!]C$$

Preemption

We only present the semantics for a simple case. One can easily generalise it for other cases.

$$\begin{aligned}[\![P \trianglerighteq (ch?x \to Q)]\!]C \mathrel{\widehat{=}}\ & \lceil\,\rceil \\ & \vee \\ & (inactive^{P} \wedge syn(\beta, ch?, x))^\frown [\![Q]\!]C \\ & \vee \\ & [\![P]\!]\mathtt{stop} \wedge wait(\beta, ch?) \\ & \vee \\ & [\![P]\!]\mathtt{stop} \wedge wait(\beta, ch?)^\frown syn(\beta, ch?, x)^\frown [\![Q]\!]C\end{aligned}$$

where

$$\beta \mathrel{\widehat{=}} (\{ch?\} \cup \bigcup_{c \in \mathsf{InChan}(Q)} \{c?\} \cup \bigcup_{c \in \mathsf{OutChan}(Q)} \{c!\})$$

Recursion

First we lift the semantic function as

$$[\![\;]\!] \in (\mathcal{D} \to \mathcal{D}) \to (\mathcal{D} \to \mathcal{D})$$

because X is a place holder for a sequential process. Thus $[\![X]\!]QC \mathrel{\widehat{=}} QC$. We assign the semantics of a recursive process as the limit of its finite approximations,[6] and standardly as in [HOS+93] let

$$[\![F(X)]\!]^{i} \in (D \to D) \to (D \to D)$$

be defined by

$$\begin{aligned}[\![F(X)]\!]^{0}QC &\mathrel{\widehat{=}} QC \\ [\![F(X)]\!]^{i+1}QC &\mathrel{\widehat{=}} [\![F(X)]\!]([\![F(X)]\!]^{i}Q)C\end{aligned}$$

Therefore

$$[\![\mu X.F(X)]\!]C \mathrel{\widehat{=}} \bigwedge_{i \in N} [\![F(X)]\!]^{i} CHAOS\ C$$

where N is the set of natural numbers, and $(CHAOS(C) = true)$ for any $C \in \mathcal{D}$.

Parallel Statements

Parallel

$$\begin{aligned}[\![P \parallel Q]\!] \mathrel{\widehat{=}}\ & [\![P]\!]\mathtt{skip} \wedge [\![Q]\!]\mathtt{skip} \\ & \vee \\ & [\![P]\!]\mathtt{skip} \wedge [\![Q]\!]\mathtt{stop}^{Q} \\ & \vee \\ & [\![P]\!]\mathtt{stop}^{P} \wedge [\![Q]\!]\mathtt{skip}\end{aligned}$$

where skip is $\lceil\,\rceil$.

[6] The continuity of a *tail* recursion has been proved in [KM95].

6 Conclusion

The $\mathcal{HCSP}$ language has replaced the shared continuous state paradigm with communications corresponding to transducers (A/D and D/A converters). The main benefit of the added structure is that descriptions of hybrid systems can become more faithful, and compositionality of the descriptions becomes easier. The semantics is based on a mathematical universe consisting of piecewise continuous functions of real time, and thus fits smoothly into the hybrid system frameworks developed by [NK93, ASL93, BGM93] and others in the control theory community, as generalised by [BBM94].

We intend $\mathcal{HCSP}$ to serve as a notation, which has a well formed foundation, and can describe hybrid systems and their refinements. Based on the semantics, we can define a refinement relation among processes.

Equivalence. $\mathcal{S}_1$ is an equivalence of $\mathcal{S}_2$

$$\mathcal{S}_1 \equiv \mathcal{S}_2$$

iff for any context $\mathcal{C}$,

$$[\![\mathcal{S}_1]\!] * \mathcal{C} \Leftrightarrow [\![\mathcal{S}_2]\!] * \mathcal{C}$$

where $*$ stands for continuation or parallel combinator.

Relative Refinement with respect to $\mathcal{P}$. $\mathcal{S}_2$ is a relative refinement of $\mathcal{S}_1$ with respect to $\mathcal{P}$,

$$\mathcal{S}_1 \prec_{\mathcal{P}} \mathcal{S}_2$$

iff $\mathcal{S}_2$ is *more* executable than $\mathcal{S}_1$ and for any context $\mathcal{C}$,

$$[\![\mathcal{S}_1]\!] * \mathcal{C} \vdash \mathcal{P} \Rightarrow [\![\mathcal{S}_2]\!] * \mathcal{C} \vdash \mathcal{P}$$

Here in some sense "more executable " means that, given a specification which is a process with a mix of continuous variables and discrete variables, it is desired to implement it by parallelism among processes each of which only encapsulates one kind of variables. On the other side, the events expressed in Boolean expressions over continuous variables should also be refined into a supervisor process for event detection.

However, criteria and laws for refining hybrid systems are research, not an established theory. In such a theory, a kind of *fixed point* inference rule seems essential. But it is not clear how to adapt the fixed point theory to include continuous variables. Real-time aspects of hybrid system refinement are also crucial. The duration semantics proposed here assumes that discrete transitions take time. One may prefer to use a model where discrete transitions take no time and can take place 'simultaneously' in a specified order (e.g. in [MP93]). Such a semantics can be given by adding a variable environment to the semantic function and removing discrete variables from the observations (as in [He94]). A more direct encoding of a super dense computation in Duration Calculus [ZHR91] is subject for ongoing research.

References

[ASL93] P.J. Antsaklis, J.A. Stiver and M.D. Lemmon. Hybrid System Modeling and Autonomous Control Systems. In *Hybrid Systems, LNCS 736, R. Grossman, A. Nerode, A.P. Ravn and H. Rischel eds.*, pp 366-392, Springer Verlag, 1993.

[BBM94] M.S. Branicky, V.S. Brokar and S.K. Mitter. A Unified Framework for Hybrid Control. In *Proceedings of the 33rd Conference on the Decision and Control*, pp 4228-4234, IEEE Press, 1994

[BGM93] A. Back, J. Guckenheimer and M. Myers. A Dynamical Similation Facility for Hybrid Systems, In *Hybrid Systems, LNCS 736, R. Grossman, A. Nerode, A.P. Ravn and H. Rischel eds.*, pp 255-267, Springer Verlag, 1993.

[BL84] A. Bensoussan and J.-L. Lions. *Impulse Control and Quasi-Variational Inequalities.* Gauthier-Villars, Paris, 1984.

[He94] Jifeng He. From CSP to Hybrid Systems, In *A Classical Mind, Essays in Honour of C.A.R. Hoare, A.W. Roscoe ed.*, pp 171-189, Prentice-Hall International, 1994.

[Hoare85] C.A.R. Hoare. *Communicating Sequential Processes*, Prentice-Hall International, 1985.

[HOS+93] M.R. Hansen, E.-R. Olderog, M. Schenke, M. Fränzle, M. Müller-Olm, B. von Karger and H. Rischel. A Duration Semantics for Real-Time Reactive Systems. *Technical Report, No. OLD MRH 1/1, ProCoS ESPRIT BRA 7071*, Oldenburg University, Germany, 1993.

[KM95] N.F. Karstensen and S. Mørk. *Duration Calculus Semantics for SDL*, Master's Thesis, Department of Computer Science, Technical University of Denmark, 1995.

[Milner89] R. Milner. *Communication and Concurrency*, Prentice-Hall International, 1989.

[MP93] Z. Manna and A. Pnueli. Verifying Hybrid Systems. In *Hybrid Systems, LNCS 736, R. Grossman, A. Nerode, A.P. Ravn and H. Rischel eds.*, pp 4-35, Springer Verlag, 1993.

[NK93] A. Nerode and W. Kohn. Models for Hybrid Systems: Automata, Topologies, Controllability Observability. In *Hybrid Systems, LNCS 736, R. Grossman, A. Nerode, A.P. Ravn and H. Rischel eds.*, pp 317-356, Springer Verlag, 1993.

[NOSY93] X. Nicollin, A. Olivero, J. Sifakis and S. Yovine. An Approach to the Description and Analysis of Hybrid Systems. In *Hybrid Systems, LNCS 736, R. Grossman, A. Nerode, A.P. Ravn and H. Rischel eds.*, pp 149-178, Springer Verlag, 1993.

[RR87] G.M. Reed and A.W. Roscoe. Metric Spaces as Models for Real-Time Concurrency. In *Mathematical Foundations of Programming, LNCS 298*, pp 331-343, Springer Verlag, 1987.

[Wang91] Wang Yi. CCS + Time = an Interleaving Model for Real Time Systems. In *Proc. of ICALP'91, LNCS 510*, Springer Verlag, 1991.

[ZHR91] Zhou Chaochen, C.A.R. Hoare and A.P. Ravn. A Calculus for Durations. In *Information Processing Letters, 40(5)*, pp 269-276, 1991.

[ZMAH92] Zhou Chaochen, M.R. Hansen, A.P. Ravn and H. Rischel. Duration Specifications for Shared Processors. In *Proc. of Symposium on Formal Techniques in Real-Time and Fault-Tolerant Systems, LNCS 571*, pp 21-32, Springer Verlag, 1992.

[ZRH93] Zhou Chaochen, A.P. Ravn and M.R. Hansen. An Extended Duration Calculus for Hybrid Systems. In *Hybrid Systems, LNCS 736, R. Grossman, A. Nerode, A.P. Ravn and H. Rischel eds.*, pp 36-59, Springer Verlag, 1993.

Logics vs. Automata: The Hybrid Case (Extended Abstract)

Ahmed Bouajjani[1] Yassine Lakhnech[2*]

[1] VERIMAG, Miniparc-Zirst, Rue Lavoisier, 38330 Montbonnot St-Martin, France.
email: Ahmed.Bouajjani@imag.fr

[2] Institut für Informatik und Praktische Mathematik Christian-Albrechts-Universität zu Kiel, Preußerstr. 1-9, D-24105 Kiel, Germany.
email: yl@informatik.uni-kiel.d400.de

1 Introduction

Hybrid systems can be seen as extensions of reactive and timed systems [13, 14]. Hence, their specification formalisms are obtained naturally by extending those of reactive systems in such a way to be able to reason about the notions of (real) time, duration (time relatively to some state property), etc. There are mainly two families of such formalisms: timed/hybrid automata that are finite-state automata supplied with continuous variables like clocks (to measure time) or integrators (to measure durations) [13, 14, 3], and timed/hybrid logics that are temporal logics allowing time or duration constraints, as for instance the timed temporal logics TPTL [6] and MITL [5], the duration temporal logic DTL [7], or the calculus of durations CoD [10].

The verification problem of hybrid systems is whether some given *control design* of a system *satisfies* (implements) some given *requirements* on its behaviours. There are three approaches to tackle this problem depending on the formalisms used to describe the control design and the requirements. The first one is the *logic-based* approach where the design and the requirements are described by formulas φ_1 and φ_2 of a same logical language, and the verification problem is stated as the implication $\varphi_1 \Rightarrow \varphi_2$. The second approach is the *automata-based* approach where the design and the requirements are described using hybrid automata and the implementation relation is inclusion of languages (sets of trajectories). The third approach, the *automata-logic-based* approach, is a mixed approach where the design is described by an automaton $\mathcal{A}$ whereas the requirements are expressed by a formula φ, and the implementation relation is the inclusion of the language of $\mathcal{A}$ in the set of trajectories satisfying φ. Methods for solving the verification problem are either *deductive*, i.e., based on the use of proof systems, or *algorithmic*, i.e., based on applying decision procedures or approximate analysis techniques to solve reachability problems in the (sub)classes of hybrid automata under consideration.

Logic-based formalisms provide high-level, concise, and expressive description languages; they are naturally associated with deductive verification techniques. On the other hand, automata-based formalisms are more concrete and suitable for modeling the dynamics of a system, and they allow automatic verification techniques. Hence, it is interesting to combine the different approaches of specification and

* This work has been performed while this author was visiting VERIMAG.

verification to benefit from their respective advantages. The kernel of such a combination is the link between logics and automata. Indeed, it is possible to translate a verification problem from one approach to another one if it is possible to characterize formulas by automata and conversely. In particular, constructing for any given formula φ an automaton $\mathcal{A}_\varphi$ that recognizes exactly the set of trajectories satisfying φ (in the spirit of [17]), allows to apply the existing algorithmic analysis techniques of hybrid automata, e.g. see [1], for verification problems stated in the logic or the automata-logic based approaches. Moreover, this allows to identify decidable logical specification languages, namely those corresponding to automata with decidable emptiness problem. The problem we address in this work is to identify expressive logical languages that can be translated to hybrid automata, in particular, to subclasses of hybrid automata with decidable emptiness problem.

We introduce a logic called HATL which is an extension of the linear-time temporal logic with (hybrid) automata constraints. These constraints allow to say that the segment of a trajectory since some designated point in the past is accepted by a given linear hybrid automaton. The reference points are introduced using the *position quantification* "$u.$" which gives the current point the name u. For instance, the formula $\Box(P \Rightarrow u.\Diamond A^u)$ means that whenever P holds at some point, let us call it u, then there exists some future point such that the trajectory since u until that point is accepted by the automaton A. The logic HATL generalizes the timed logic TATL [8] where only timed automata [4] are used, as well as dense-time TPTL [6] and MITL [5].

Then, we define two fragments of HATL, called HATL$^+$ and HATL$^-$, such that the negation of each formula in HATL$^+$ is equivalent to a formula in HATL$^-$ and conversely, and show that for every formula φ in HATL$^-$, we can construct a linear hybrid (Büchi) automaton $\mathcal{A}_\varphi$ which recognizes the set of trajectories satisfying φ. This allows to reduce the verification problem of hybrid automata w.r.t. HATL$^+$ formulas to the emptiness problem of hybrid automata. The specialization of our reduction to timed automata and the timed logics TATL and TPTL allows to show that the verification problem of timed automata w.r.t. the fragments TATL$^+$ and TPTL$^+$ is decidable [8].

Finally, we consider the logic-based approach using the CoD. Fragments of this logic have been identified in [11] for the description of control systems and their requirements. We show that a verification problem stated in CoD using these fragments is decidable. To obtain this result, we define first two fragments of HATL called CDF (Control Design Formulas) and RF (Requirement Formulas), and prove that we can translate CDF formulas and negations of RF formulas to hybrid automata, reducing by that the verification problem of CDF formulas w.r.t. RF formulas to the emptiness problem of hybrid automata. Then, we define subclasses of CDF and RF subsuming their corresponding fragments of CoD, such that the obtained emptiness problem by our reduction consists of solving a decidable reachability problem (using [2]). These results generalize those in [9].

2 Preliminaries

2.1 Simple constraints

Let $\mathcal{V}$ be a set of variables ranging over reals ($\mathbb{R}$). A *simple constraint* over $\mathcal{V}$ is a boolean combination of constraints of the form $x \prec c$ where $x \in \mathcal{V}$, $\prec \in \{<, \leq\}$, and

c is an integer constant ($c \in \mathbb{Z}$). The symbols $<$ and $\leq$ represent the usual (strict and non-strict) ordering relations over $\mathbb{R}$. Let $\mathcal{C}_\mathcal{V}$ be the set of simple constraints over $\mathcal{V}$.

A *valuation* over $\mathcal{V}$ is a function in $[\mathcal{V} \rightarrow \mathbb{R}]$. A satisfaction relation is defined as usual between valuations and constraints. Given a valuation ν and $f \in \mathcal{C}_\mathcal{V}$, we denote by $\nu \models f$ the fact that ν satisfies f.

We denote by $\mathbf{0}$ the valuation that associates with each clock the value 0. Given a valuation ν and a set of variables $X \subseteq \mathcal{V}$, we denote by $\nu[X \mapsto 0]$ the valuation which associates with each variable in X the value 0, and coincides with ν on all the other variables.

2.2 States, interval sequences, and trajectories

Let $\mathcal{P}$ be a finite set of *atomic propositions*. A *state* is a subset of $\mathcal{P}$. Let Σ be the set of all possible states, i.e., $\Sigma = 2^\mathcal{P}$.

Let I be a nonempty subinterval of $\mathbb{R}_{\geq 0}$. Then, we denote respectively by $lb(I)$ and $ub(I)$ the lower and upper bounds of I. We denote also by $\ell(I)$ the length of the interval I, i.e., $\ell(I) = ub(I) - lb(I)$. Given two nonempty intervals I_1 and I_2, I_1 is called *adjacent to* I_2, if $I_1 \cap I_2 = \emptyset$ and $lb(I_2) = ub(I_1)$.

Let I be a left-closed nonempty subinterval of $\mathbb{R}_{\geq 0}$ such that $lb(I) = 0$. An *interval sequence* over I is a finite or infinite sequence of nonempty intervals $\vec{I} = I_0 I_1 \cdots I_i \cdots$ such that

- $\forall i < |\vec{I}|$, I_i is adjacent to I_{i+1},
- $\forall t \in I$, $\exists i < |\vec{I}|$, $t \in I_i$,
- If I is bounded (resp. unbounded), the sequence $\vec{I}$ is finite (resp. infinite).

A mapping $\tau : I \rightarrow \Sigma$ is called *finite-variable* if in every finite subinterval of I, τ changes its value a finite number of times (τ has a finite number of discontinuity points). We call *trajectory* over I any mapping $\tau : I \rightarrow \Sigma$ which is finite-variable. We say that a trajectory $\tau : I \rightarrow \Sigma$ is *bounded* (resp. *unbounded*) if the interval I is bounded (resp. unbounded).

Let $\tau : I \rightarrow \Sigma$ be a trajectory, and I' a bounded closed nonempty subinterval of I. Then, we denote by $\tau(I')$ the bounded trajectory $\tau' : [0, \ell(I')] \rightarrow \Sigma$ such that $\forall t \in [0, \ell(I')]$, $\tau'(t) = \tau(t + lb(I'))$.

3 Linear Hybrid Automata

We define in this section linear hybrid automata on bounded or unbounded trajectories.

3.1 Linear hybrid transition tables

Recall that $\Sigma = 2^\mathcal{P}$ where $\mathcal{P}$ is a finite set of atomic propositions. A *linear hybrid transition table* $\mathcal{T}$ over Σ consists of the following components:

- $\mathcal{X}$, a finite set of variables,
- $\mathcal{Q}$, a finite set of control locations,
- $\mathcal{I}nit$, a set of initial control locations ($\mathcal{I}nit \subseteq \mathcal{Q}$),
- $\mathcal{E}$, a set of edges. Each edge is a triplet $E = (q, X, q')$ where $q, q' \in \mathcal{Q}$ are the source and target locations, and $X \subseteq \mathcal{X}$ is the set of reset variables,

- Π, a function in $[Q \to \Sigma]$, associating a state with each control location.
- Γ, a function in $[Q \to C_{\mathcal{X}}]$, associating with each control location q a simple constraint under which the computation is allowed to stay in q.
- ∂, a function in $[Q \times \mathcal{X} \to \mathbb{Z}]$, associating with each $q \in Q$ and $x \in \mathcal{X}$, an integer rate at which x changes continuously while the control is at q.

A *clock* (resp. *integrator*) is a variable $x \in \mathcal{X}$ such that $\forall q \in Q.\ \partial(q,x) = 1$ (resp. $\partial(q,x) \in \{0,1\}$). A *timed transition table* is a linear hybrid transition table such that all the variables in $\mathcal{X}$ are clocks.

Given a valuation ν, a control location q, and $t \in \mathbb{R}_{\geq 0}$, we denote by $[\nu+t]_q$ the valuation ν' such that $\forall x \in \mathcal{X}.\ \nu'(x) = \nu(x) + \partial(q,x) \cdot t$, i.e., the valuation obtained from ν by staying at q for an amount of time equal to t.

Let I be a left-closed subinterval of $\mathbb{R}_{\geq 0}$ such that $lb(I) = 0$. Then, a *run* of $\mathcal{T}$ over the interval I is a finite or infinite sequence $\rho = \langle q_0, \nu_0, I_0\rangle \cdots \langle q_i, \nu_i, I_i\rangle \cdots$ such that

- $q_0 \in \mathcal{I}nit$, $\nu_0 = \mathbf{0}$, and
- $I_0 I_1 \cdots I_i \cdots$ is an interval sequence over I, and
- $\forall i < |\rho|.\ \forall t \in I_i.\ [\nu_i + (t - lb(I_i))]_{q_i} \models \Gamma(q_i)$, and
- $\forall i < |\rho|.\ q_i = q_{i+1}$ and $\nu_{i+1} = [\nu_i + \ell(I_i)]_{q_i}$, or $\exists (q_i, X, q_{i+1}) \in \mathcal{E}.\ \nu_{i+1} = [\nu_i + \ell(I_i)]_{q_i}[X \leftarrow 0]$.

With every run $\rho = \langle q_0, \nu_0, I_0\rangle \cdots \langle q_i, \nu_i, I_i\rangle \cdots$ defined as above, we associate a *path* of $\mathcal{T}$ over I which is a mapping $\theta : I \to Q$ such that $\forall i < |\rho|.\ \forall t \in I_i.\ \theta(t) = q_i$. Then, the *trajectory* generated by ρ is defined as the mapping $\tau = \Pi \circ \theta$.

Deterministic linear hybrid transition tables can be defined straightforwardly (see the definition given in [8] for timed transition tables).

3.2 Linear Hybrid Automata on bounded trajectories

A bounded trajectories *linear hybrid automaton* (LHA) over Σ is a pair $\mathcal{A} = (\mathcal{T}, \mathcal{F})$, where $\mathcal{T} = (\mathcal{X}, Q, \mathcal{I}nit, \mathcal{E}, \Pi, \Gamma)$ is a linear hybrid transition table over Σ, and $\mathcal{F} \subseteq Q$ is a set of *final* control locations.

Let $\rho = \langle q_0, \nu_0, I_0\rangle \cdots \langle q_n, \nu_n, I_n\rangle$ be a finite run of $\mathcal{T}$. Then, we say that ρ is an *accepting run* of $\mathcal{A}$ if $q_n \in \mathcal{F}$. We denote by $L(\mathcal{A})$ the set of bounded trajectories generated by accepting runs of $\mathcal{A}$.

When $\mathcal{T}$ is a timed transition table, $\mathcal{A}$ is called *timed automaton* (TA). The automaton $\mathcal{A}$ is *deterministic* if its table $\mathcal{T}$ is deterministic. A *simple linear hybrid automaton* is a deterministic LHA such that all its variables are clocks except at most one which may be an integrator, and if it has an integrator, say y, then only control locations with no outgoing edges can have constraints on y, and every constraint on y appearing on any final location must be of the form $(y \sim c) \vee f$ where $\sim \in \{>, \geq\}$.

3.3 Linear Hybrid Automata on unbounded trajectories

A linear hybrid automaton on unbounded trajectories is defined, as in the case of bounded trajectories, by a transition table and an accepting condition. We consider here the 1, 2, and 3 acceptance conditions of the ω-automata theory [16]. For $i \in \{1,2,3\}$, an *i-linear hybrid automaton* over Σ (*i*-LHA) is a pair $\mathcal{A} = (\mathcal{T}, \mathcal{F})$ where

$\mathcal{T}$ is a linear hybrid transition table over Σ, $\mathcal{F} \subseteq Q$ when $i \in \{1, 2\}$, and $\mathcal{F} \subseteq 2^Q$ when $i = 3$.

Given an infinite run $\rho = \langle q_0, \nu_0, I_0 \rangle \cdots \langle q_i, \nu_i, I_i \rangle \cdots$, we denote by $Loc(\rho)$ the set of all control locations q such that $q = q_i$ for some $i \geq 0$, and by $Inf(\rho)$ the set of all contol locations q such that $q = q_i$ for infinitely many i's. Then, we say that ρ is i-accepting if $Loc(\rho) \cap \mathcal{F} \neq \emptyset$ when $i = 1$, $Inf(\rho) \cap \mathcal{F} \neq \emptyset$ when $i = 2$, or $Inf(\rho) \in \mathcal{F}$ when $i = 3$. Notice that the 2-acceptance (resp. 3-acceptance) condition is the Büchi's (resp. Muller's) acceptance condition, whereas the 1-acceptance condition consists of a reachability condition.

As in the case of bounded trajectories, when $\mathcal{T}$ is a timed transition table, $\mathcal{A}$ is called *i-timed automaton* (i-TA), and an i-LHA is *deterministic* if its table $\mathcal{T}$ is deterministic. We call *linear hybrid graph* (resp. *timed graph*) a (1-)linear hybrid automaton (resp. (1-)timed automaton) with a trivial acceptance condition (i.e., $\mathcal{F} = Q$). A 1-LHA is called *restricted* if all its variables are clocks except at most one which may be an integrator, and if it has an integrator, say y, then only control locations with no outgoing edges can have constraints on y, and every constraint on y appearing on any location in $\mathcal{F}$ must be of the form $(c_1 \sim y \sim c_2) \wedge f$ where $\sim \in \{\leq, <\}$.

4 Hybrid Automata Temporal Logic

We introduce the logic HATL which is an extension of the propositional temporal logic PTL [15] with bounded trajectories linear hybrid automata.

4.1 The logic HATL

Recall that $\mathcal{P}$ is a finite set of atomic propositions, and that $\Sigma = 2^{\mathcal{P}}$. We use letters $P, Q, \ldots$ to range over atomic propositions, and greek letters $\pi, \delta, \ldots$ to range over their boolean combinations. We introduce a set $\mathcal{W}$ of *position variables*, and use letters $u, v, \ldots$ to range over $\mathcal{W}$. Finally, we use $A, B, \ldots$ to range over bounded trajectories LHA's over Σ. The set of formulas of HATL is defined by:

$$\varphi ::= P \mid \uparrow\pi \mid u.\varphi \mid A^u \mid \neg\varphi \mid \varphi \vee \varphi \mid \varphi\,\mathcal{U}\,\varphi$$

We consider as abbreviations the usual boolean connectives as conjunction ($\wedge$) and implication ($\Rightarrow$), as well as $\Diamond\varphi$ for $true\,\mathcal{U}\,\varphi$, and $\Box\varphi$ for $\neg\Diamond\neg\varphi$.

HATL formulas are interpreted on unbounded trajectories. The operators $\mathcal{U}$, $\Diamond$, and $\Box$, are the classical *until*, *eventually*, and *always* operators of PTL. The formula $\uparrow\pi$ is true at some point of a trajectory if π changes its value from false to true exactly at that point. Such a formula allow to refer to the starting point of some new phase. In the formula $u.\varphi$, the current time is associated with the position variable u. Then, subformulas of φ of the form A^u are used to express the fact that the bounded trajectory since the time associated with u is accepted by the automaton A. Formulas of the form A^u, which we call *automata constraints*, allow to express constraints on delays, i.e., time distances since some designated points in the past, or, more generally, on *durations* of state properties, i.e., accumulated times that some properties hold. For example, let B be the (deterministic) automaton represented by the following picture:

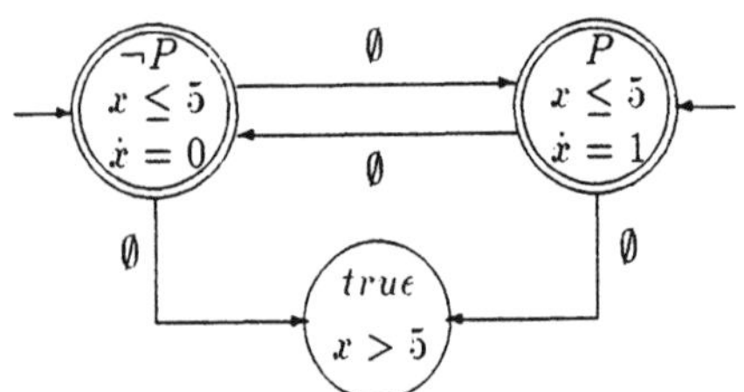

Then, the formula $u.\Diamond(Q \wedge B^u)$ expresses the fact that "*Q will be eventually true while the duration of P is less than* 5 *time units*".

In the formula $u.\varphi$ (e.g., $u.\Diamond(Q \wedge B^u)$), the construction "$u.$", called *position quantification*, binds the position variable u in the subformula φ. We suppose without loss of generality that in every formula, each position variable is bound at most once. Then, every variable appearing in some formula is either *bound* or *free*. A formula is *open* if it contains free variables, otherwise it is *closed*.

The formal semantics of HATL is defined using a satisfaction relation $\models$ between unbounded trajectories, time values, and formulas. Since formulas may be open, the satisfaction relation between a trajectory τ, a time value t, and a formula φ, is defined w.r.t. a *position association* E that associates with each position variable u appearing in φ the time (which is less or equal than t) where u has been introduced. Then, the position association E is updated along the trajectory τ due to the introduction of new position variables. We denote by $E[u \leftarrow t]$ the position association whose domain is the extension of the domain of E by u, and which associates with u the time value t and coincides with E on all the other position variables.

Let τ be an unbounded trajectory. For every $t \in \mathbb{R}_{\geq 0}$, every position association E (such that for every u in the domain of E, $0 \leq E(u) \leq t$), and every HATL formula φ, we define the meaning of $\langle \tau, t\rangle \models_E \varphi$ inductively on the structure of φ.

$$
\begin{array}{ll}
\langle \tau, t\rangle \models_E P & \text{iff } P \in \tau(t) \\
\langle \tau, t\rangle \models_E \lceil\pi & \text{iff } \exists\epsilon > 0.\ \forall t' \in (t, t+\epsilon).\ \langle \tau, t'\rangle \models_E \pi, \text{ and} \\
 & \quad \forall t' \in \mathbb{R}_{\geq 0} \cap (t-\epsilon, t).\ \langle \tau, t'\rangle \models_E \neg\pi \\
\langle \tau, t\rangle \models_E u.\varphi & \text{iff } \langle \tau, t\rangle \models_{E[u \leftarrow t]} \varphi \\
\langle \tau, t\rangle \models_E \mathcal{A}^u & \text{iff } \tau([E(u), t]) \in L(\mathcal{A}) \\
\langle \tau, t\rangle \models_E \neg\varphi & \text{iff } \langle \tau, t\rangle \not\models_E \varphi \\
\langle \tau, t\rangle \models_E \varphi_1 \vee \varphi_2 & \text{iff } \langle \tau, t\rangle \models_E \varphi_1 \text{ or } \langle \tau, t\rangle \models_E \varphi_2 \\
\langle \tau, t\rangle \models_E \varphi_1 \mathcal{U} \varphi_2 & \text{iff } \exists t' \geq t.\ \langle \tau, t'\rangle \models_E \varphi_2, \text{ and } \forall t'' \in [t, t').\ \langle \tau, t''\rangle \models_E \varphi_1
\end{array}
$$

When φ is a closed formula, we omit the position association E, and write simply $\langle \tau, t\rangle \models \varphi$. Given a closed formula φ, we denote by $[\![\varphi]\!]$ the set of unbounded trajectories τ such that $\langle \tau, 0\rangle \models \varphi$. The formula φ is *satisfiable* iff $[\![\varphi]\!] \neq \emptyset$; it is *valid* iff $[\![\varphi]\!]$ is the set of all possible unbounded trajectories.

4.2 Sublogics

The logic TATL introduced in [8] is obtained by imposing the restriction that only timed automata can be used to express automata constraints.

Moreover, the (dense-time) TPTL [6] corresponds to the fragment of TATL where automata constraints involve only the timed automata $T_{<c}$ and $T_{\leq c}$, where c is some natural constant, that are represented respectively by the following pictures:

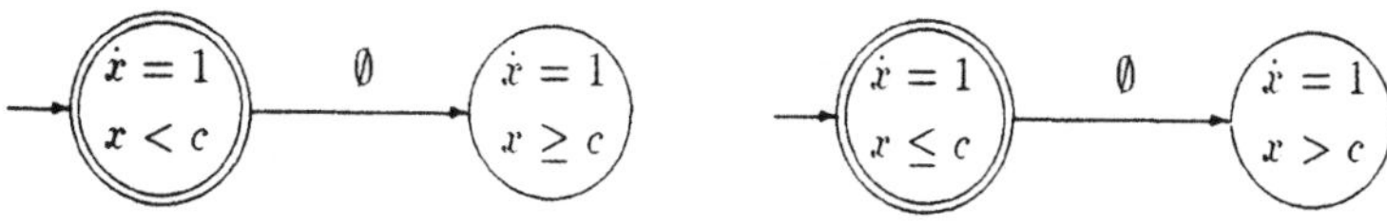

Notice that $T_{<c}$ and $T_{\leq c}$ are deterministic and that the automata $T_{\geq c}$ and $T_{>c}$ can be respectively obtained from them by inversing final and nonfinal locations.

Finally, the logic MITL [5] is a sublogic of TPTL obtained by restraining the use of position quantification (called reset quantification in TPTL) and constraints: time constraints can only be expressed using the constrained until operator $\mathcal{U}_I$ where I is a *nonponctual* interval with integer bounds.

4.3 The fragments HATL$^+$ and HATL$^-$

We introduce hereafter syntactical fragments of the logic HATL. In these fragments, we use two new operators $\widetilde{\mathcal{U}}$ and $\overline{\mathcal{U}}$ defined by:

$$\varphi_1 \widetilde{\mathcal{U}} \varphi_2 = (\varphi_1 \vee \varphi_2) \mathcal{U} \varphi_2 \qquad \varphi_1 \overline{\mathcal{U}} \varphi_2 = \varphi_1 \mathcal{U} (\varphi_1 \wedge \varphi_2)$$

A motivation for introducing these operators can be found in [8]. Notice that $\Diamond \varphi$ is equivalent to $true \widetilde{\mathcal{U}} \varphi$ as well as to $true \overline{\mathcal{U}} \varphi$. Then, the fragment HATL$^+$ consists of the set of formulas φ defined by:

$$\varphi ::= \upsilon \mid u.\varphi \mid \neg A^u \mid \varphi \vee \varphi \mid \varphi \wedge \varphi \mid \Box \varphi \mid \varphi \widetilde{\mathcal{U}} \upsilon \mid \varphi \overline{\mathcal{U}} \upsilon$$

and the fragment HATL$^-$ corresponds to the set of formulas φ defined by:

$$\varphi ::= \upsilon \mid u.\varphi \mid A^u \mid \varphi \vee \varphi \mid \varphi \wedge \varphi \mid \Box \upsilon \mid \upsilon \widetilde{\mathcal{U}} \varphi \mid \upsilon \overline{\mathcal{U}} \varphi$$

where the formulas υ are defined by:

$$\upsilon ::= P \mid \uparrow \pi \mid A^u, A \text{ is deterministic } \mid \neg \upsilon \mid \upsilon \vee \upsilon \mid \upsilon \widetilde{\mathcal{U}} \upsilon \mid \upsilon \overline{\mathcal{U}} \upsilon \tag{1}$$

We consider also the fragments TATL$^+$, TPTL$^+$, TATL$^-$, and TPTL$^-$ defined in the obvious way.

We can prove that HATL$^-$ characterizes exactly the complements of the HATL$^+$ definable sets of trajectories, and conversely. It is easy to see that this fact holds also when we consider the corresponding fragments of TATL and TPTL.

Proposition 4.1 *For every HATL$^+$ (resp. TATL$^+$, TPTL$^+$) closed formula φ, we can construct an HATL$^-$ (resp. TATL$^-$, TPTL$^-$) closed formula φ' such that $[\![\neg\varphi]\!] = [\![\varphi']\!]$, and conversely.*

4.4 Expressiveness

The fragments TPTL$^+$, TATL$^+$, and HATL$^+$ allow to express the important classes of timed and duration properties that are the *constrained invariance properties* corresponding to formulas of the form

$$u_0.\Box(A^{u_0}_{(0,0)} \Rightarrow \cdots u_n.\Box(\bigwedge_{i=0}^{n} A^{u_i}_{(i,n)} \Rightarrow v.\Box(\bigwedge_{i=0}^{n} B^{u_i}_i \wedge C^v))\cdots)$$

and the *constrained response properties* corresponding to formulas of the form:

$$u.\Box(A^u \Rightarrow v.\Diamond(B_0^u \wedge C_0^v \wedge \Diamond(B_1^u \wedge C_1^v \wedge \cdots \Diamond(B_n^u \wedge C_n^v))\cdots))$$

As for the fragments TPTL$^+$, TATL$^+$, and HATL$^+$, they allow to express the dual properties that are *constrained eventuality* and *constrained persistence properties*.

The fragment TATL$^+$ (resp. TATL$^-$) is more expressive than TPTL$^+$ (resp. TPTL$^-$) since the latter cannot express all the properties that are definable by means of automata constraints. Moreover, HATL$^+$ (resp. HATL$^-$) is more expressive than TATL$^+$ (resp. TATL$^-$) since, for instance, it allows to reason about duration properties, in the style of DTL [7].

We can show also that the logic MITL, which is less expressive than 2-TA's [5], is comparable with none of the fragments TPTL$^+$, TATL$^+$, TPTL$^+$, and TATL$^-$. Indeed, these fragments allow ponctual time constraints as well as overlaping of time constraints using position (reset) quantification. On the other hand, MITL allows to express properties with nested constrained until operators that are expressible in TPTL$^-$ but not in TPTL$^+$, whereas their negations are expressible in TPTL$^+$ but not in TPTL$^-$. The same reasons make the logic EMITL [18] not comparable with the four fragments mentioned above.

5 Logics vs. Automata

We show the links between HATL$^+$, HATL$^-$, and linear hybrid automata. First of all, we prove that deterministic 3-LHA's can be characterized by HATL$^+$ as well as by HATL$^-$ closed formulas.

Theorem 5.1 *For every deterministic 3-LHA (resp. 3-TA) $\mathcal{A}$, there exists a closed formula φ in HATL$^+$ and HATL$^-$ (resp. TATL$^+$ and TATL$^-$) with $L(\mathcal{A}) = [\![\varphi]\!]$.*

Indeed, let $\mathcal{A} = (\mathcal{T}, \mathcal{F})$ be a deterministic linear hybrid (resp. timed) Muller automaton over $\Sigma = 2^P$, with $\mathcal{F} = \{\Delta_1, \cdots, \Delta_n\}$. For every control location q in $\mathcal{A}$, we denote by A_q the deterministic timed automaton $(\mathcal{T}, \{q\})$ which accepts the set of bounded trajectories reaching q. Then, it can easily be seen that the set of trajectories recognized by the automaton $\mathcal{A}$ is characterized by the formula

$$u.\bigvee_{i=1}^{n}((\bigwedge_{q\in\Delta_i}\Box\Diamond A_q^u)\wedge(\bigwedge_{q\notin\Delta_i}\neg\Box\Diamond A_q^u)) \qquad (2)$$

which is in both fragments HATL$^+$ and HATL$^-$ (resp. TATL$^+$ and TATL$^-$).

Let us address now the problem of characterizing formulas by automata. It can be shown that HATL$^+$ cannot in general be characterized by linear hybrid automata (with finitely many variables). On the other hand, we show that every HATL$^-$ closed formula can be characterized by a 2-LHA (linear hybrid Büchi automaton). This allows to reduce the verification problem of 2-LHA's w.r.t. HATL$^+$ closed formulas to the emptiness problem of 2-LHA's.

Theorem 5.2 *For every HATL$^-$ closed formula φ, we can construct a 2-LHA $\mathcal{A}_\varphi$ such that $L(\mathcal{A}_\varphi) = [\![\varphi]\!]$.*

This construction is possible because HATL$^-$ formulas allow to consider on trajectories only a finite number of points (positions) where automata constraints can be initialized. Indeed, we can show that each HATL$^-$ formula can be transformed into an equivalent formula in *normal form*, i.e., a disjunction of formulas of the form

$$u_0.(\psi_0 \wedge (\psi'_0 \widetilde{\mathcal{U}}_{>0}\, u_1.(\psi_1 \wedge (\psi'_1 \widetilde{\mathcal{U}}_{>0} \cdots u_n.(\psi_n \wedge (\psi'_n \widetilde{\mathcal{U}}_{>0}\, u_{n+1}.\psi_{n+1}))\cdots))))$$

where the ψ_i's and the ψ'_i's are of the form given by (1).

Then, given a closed formula φ in normal form, we proceed as follows: In a first step, we abstract from each automata constraint A^u by replacing it by a new atomic proposition $[A^u]$. The obtained formula φ^* is in the propositional temporal logic. Therefore, using the construction of [17], we get a Büchi automaton $\mathcal{B}_{\varphi^*}$ which characterizes φ^*. Interpreted as a Büchi LHA (by adding trivial timing constraints), this automaton accepts the trajectories that are propositionally consistent with φ. In a second step, we constrain $\mathcal{B}_{\varphi^*}$ by an LHA $\mathcal{B}_{const}$ which is constructed from the automata constraints appearing in φ. This automaton ensures that whenever the proposition $[A^u]$ appears at some point of a trajectory, then the automaton A accepts indeed the bounded trajectory since the point associated with u.

The translation from HATL$^-$ formulas to 2-LHA's outlined above yields a 2-TA when applied to TATL$^-$ formulas. Therefore, we obtain the following result.

Theorem 5.3 *For every TATL$^-$ closed formula φ, we can construct a 2-TA $\mathcal{A}_\varphi$ such that $L(\mathcal{A}_\varphi) = [\![\varphi]\!]$.*

6 Verification problem: the automata-logic-based approach

Let $\mathcal{A}_S$ be a 2-LHA that models the behaviours of some hybrid system, and let φ be an HATL$^+$ closed formula expressing its specifications. Then, the problem whether $\mathcal{A}_S$ satisfies φ, i.e., whether $L(\mathcal{A}_S) \subseteq [\![\varphi]\!]$, can be reduced using Proposition 4.1 and Theorem 5.2 to the emptiness problem $L(\mathcal{A}_S \times \mathcal{A}_{\neg\varphi}) = \emptyset$. Since 2-LHA are closed under product, we have the following fact.

Theorem 6.1 *The verification problem of 2-LHA's w.r.t. HATL$^+$ closed formulas is reducible to the emptiness problem of 2-LHA's.*

Using Theorem 5.3 and the same arguments as for Theorem 6.1, we can reduce the verification problem of 2-TA's w.r.t. TATL$^+$ closed formulas to the emptiness problem of 2-TA's. Since this latter is decidable [4], we obtain the following result.

Theorem 6.2 *The verification problem of 2-TA's w.r.t. TATL$^+$ closed formulas is decidable.*

7 Control Design and Requirement Formulas

We consider now the logic-based approach where the system as well as its specifications are expressed using formulas.

We introduce hereafter two subsets of HATL called CDF (Control Design Formulas) and RF (Requirement Formulas). Formulas in CDF and RF are positive boolean combinations of invariance formulas of the general form

$$\Box(\psi \Rightarrow u.\Box(A^u \Rightarrow \bigvee_{j=1}^{m} B_j^u)) \tag{3}$$

where ψ stands for a formula of the form π or $\uparrow\pi$, and such that the formula ψ, the automaton A, and the automata B_j's satisfy some conditions we define below.

Control Design Formulas: Given an automaton A, the *prolongation* of A is an automaton $\vec{A}$ which accepts all the bounded trajectories having a prefix accepted by A. The construction of this automaton is straightforward. Now, we say that the automaton A is π-alternation-free if, when we consider the control transition graph associated with its transition table, all the paths relating an initial location with a final one do not contain any occurrence of a transition from π to $\neg\pi$ which is followed by an occurrence of a transition from $\neg\pi$ to π. This constraint ensures that for every trajectory τ, $\forall t_1, t_2 \in I\!R^+$ such that $t_1 \leq t_2$ and $\tau[t_1, t_2] \in L(A)$, and $\forall t \in [t_1, t_2)$, if $\langle \tau, t\rangle \models \uparrow\neg\pi$ then $\forall t' \in (t, t_2)\langle \tau, t'\rangle \not\models \uparrow\pi$. Then, CDF formulas are defined as positive boolean combinations of formulas of the form (3) where

- ψ is of the form $\uparrow\pi$,
- A is timed automaton $T_{>c}$ for some natural constant c,
- the B_j's are prolongations of deterministic π-alternation-free automata.

A *pure-time* CDF formula is a CDF formula which is a TATL formula, i.e., where only timed automata are used in automata constraints.

Requirement Formulas: RF formulas are defined as positive boolean combinations of formulas of the form (3) where the automata B_j's are deterministic. Notice that every RF formula is in HATL$^+$. A *simple* RF formula is a conjunction of formulas of the form (3) where A is a timed automaton, and all the B_j's are timed automata except at most one which may be a simple LHA.

8 From CDF and RF to Linear Hybrid Automata

We show hereafter translations from the fragments CDF and RF to linear hybrid automata. We start by showing that for every CDF formula φ, we can construct an automaton $\mathcal{A}_\varphi$ which recognizes $[\![\varphi]\!]$. Consider a formula φ of the general form $\Box(\uparrow\pi \Rightarrow u.\Box(T^u_{>c} \Rightarrow \bigvee_{j=1}^m B_j^u))$. Intuitively, an automaton that recognizes $[\![\varphi]\!]$ does the following. Given a trajectory τ, it checks for each time t where $\uparrow\pi$ holds and each $t' > t+c$, whether the trajectory $\tau[t,t']$ is accepted by some B_j. We can show that in general (without any restriction on the B_j's and π), this automaton would need infinitely many variables because the number of points where $\uparrow\pi$ may hold in a bounded interval (of 1 time unit, say) is unbounded, and since for each point t where $\uparrow\pi$ holds, the automaton has to check that for every $t' > t+c$, some B_j accepts $\tau[t,t']$. However, if φ is a CDF formula, then we can prove that there are deterministic π-alternation-free automata C_j's contructed from the B_j's such that, "*for every $t' > t+c$, there exists B_j accepting $\tau[t,t']$*" if and only if "*there exists some length d and some automaton C_j which accepts $\tau[t, t+d]$*". Hence, we can construct an automaton characterizing φ which repetitively looks for the next point where $\uparrow\pi$ holds and then guesses d and C_j.

Theorem 8.1 *For every CDF formula φ, we can construct a linear hybrid graph $\mathcal{A}_\varphi$ such that $L(\mathcal{A}_\varphi) = [\![\varphi]\!]$. Moreover, if φ is a pure-time CDF formula, then $\mathcal{A}_\varphi$ is a timed graph.*

Now, since RF is a subset of HATL$^+$, by Proposition 4.1 and Theorem 5.2 we deduce that for every RF formula φ we can construct a linear hybrid Büchi automaton $\mathcal{A}_{\neg\varphi}$ which recognizes $[\![\neg\varphi]\!]$. It can be seen that the specialization of the construction used in Theorem 5.2 to the cases of RF formulas and simple RF formulas leads to the following fact.

Theorem 8.2 *For every RF formula φ, we can construct a 1-LHA $\mathcal{A}_{\neg\varphi}$ such that $L(\mathcal{A}_{\neg\varphi}) = [\![\neg\varphi]\!]$. Moreover, if φ is a simple RF formula, then $\mathcal{A}_{\neg\varphi}$ is a restricted 1-LHA.*

9 Verification problem: the logic-based approach

Let φ_1 be a CDF formula, and φ_2 be an RF formula. Deciding whether $\varphi_1 \Rightarrow \varphi_2$ is valid consists in checking whether $[\![\varphi_1]\!] \subseteq [\![\varphi_2]\!]$, or equivalently, whether $[\![\varphi_1]\!] \cap [\![\neg\varphi_2]\!] = \emptyset$. Then, by Theorems 8.1 and 8.2, and since 1-LHA's (resp. restricted 1-LHA's) are closed under product with linear hybrid graphs (resp. timed graphs), we deduce the following fact.

Theorem 9.1 *The verification problem of CDF (resp. pure-time CDF) formulas w.r.t. RF (resp. simple RF) formulas is reducible to the emptiness problem of 1-LHA's (resp. restricted 1-LHA's).*

The emptiness problem of 1-LHA is undecidable [12], however, it is decidable for restricted 1-LHA's (using [2]). Hence, we obtain the following result.

Theorem 9.2 *The verification problem of pure-time CDF formulas w.r.t. simple RF formulas is decidable.*

Consider now the fragments of CoD defined in [11] to describe control designs and their requirements. We show that the verification problem stated as implication between two formulas in these fragments is decidable. For that, we show that the CoD formulas we are interested in can be translated to pure-time CDF and simple RF formulas.

Proposition 9.1 *For every CoD control design (resp. CoD requirement) formula, there exists an equivalent pure-time CDF (resp. simple RF) formula.*

Using Proposition 9.1 and Theorem 9.2, we obtain the following result.

Theorem 9.3 *The verification problem for CoD control design formulas w.r.t. CoD requirement formulas is decidable.*

10 Conclusion

We provided a framework for the specification and the verification of hybrid systems. We introduced a general specification logic HATL which is an extension of the temporal logic allowing constraints on bounded trajectories expressed by means of hybrid automata. We have shown how to translate verification problems stated in the automata-logic-based or in the logic-based approaches into the automata-based approach in order to apply algorithmic analysis techniques on automata. These translations are based on effective constructions of timed or hybrid automata from formulas in some fragments of HATL. Using these translations, we proved the decidability of the verification problems of timed Büchi automata w.r.t. TATL$^+$ formulas, and of pure-time CDF formulas w.r.t. simple RF formulas.

The fragment TATL$^+$ is a fairly powerful specification language since it subsumes deterministic timed Muller automata, and allows the expression of response as well as invariance timed properties. Its sublanguage TPTL$^+$ constitues a fragment of TPTL whose verification problem is decidable. Moreover, TATL$^+$ (as well as TPTL$^+$) is not comparable with the known logics whose verification problem is decidable, as MITL and EMITL.

Pure-time CDF and simple RF are more expressive than the fragments of CoD that have been suggested to specify control systems and requirements. Thus, our results show, in particular, that the verification of CoD control designs w.r.t. CoD requirement formulas is decidable. This is the first decidability result concerning fragments of (dense time) CoD that are not purely propositional.

References

1. R. Alur, C. Courcoubetis, N. Halbwachs, T. Henzinger, P. Ho, X. Nicollin, A. Olivero, J. Sifakis, and S. Yovine. The Algorithmic Analysis of Hybrid Systems. *TCS*, 138, 1995.
2. R. Alur, C. Courcoubetis, and T. Henzinger. Computing Accumulated Delays in Real-time Systems. In *CAV'93*. LNCS 697, 1993.
3. R. Alur, C. Courcoubetis, T. Henzinger, and P-H. Ho. Hybrid Automata: An Algorithmic Approach to the Specification and Verification of Hybrid Systems. In *Hybrid Systems*. LNCS 736, 1993.
4. R. Alur and D. Dill. A Theory of Timed Automata. *TCS*, 126, 1994.
5. R. Alur, T. Feder, and T. Henzinger. The Benefits of Relaxing Punctuality. In *PODC'91*. 1991.
6. R. Alur and T. Henzinger. A Really Temporal Logic. In *FOCS'89*. IEEE, 1989.
7. A. Bouajjani, R. Echahed, and J. Sifakis. On Model Checking for Real-Time Properties with Durations. In *LICS'93*. IEEE, 1993.
8. A. Bouajjani and Y. Lakhnech. Temporal Logic + Timed Automata : Expressiveness and Decidability. In *CONCUR'95*. LNCS 962, 1995.
9. A. Bouajjani, Y. Lakhnech, and R. Robbana. From Duration Calculus to Linear Hybrid Automata. In *CAV'95*. LNCS 939, 1995.
10. Z. Chaochen, C.A.R. Hoare, and A.P. Ravn. A Calculus of Durations. *IPL*, 40, 1991.
11. J. He, C.A.R. Hoare, M. Fränzle, M. Müller-Olm, E.R. Olderog, M. Schenke, M.R. Hansen, A.P. Ravn, and H. Rishel. Provably Correct Systems. In *FTRTFT'94*. LNCS 863, 1994.
12. Y. Kesten, A. Pnueli, J. Sifakis, and S. Yovine. Integration Graphs: A Class of Decidable Hybrid Systems. In *Hybrid Systems*. LNCS 736, 1993.
13. O. Maler, Z. Manna, and A. Pnueli. From Timed to Hybrid Systems. In *REX workshop on Real-Time: Theory and Practice*. LNCS 600, 1992.
14. X. Nicollin, J. Sifakis, and S. Yovine. From ATP to Timed Graphs and Hybrid Systems. In *REX workshop on Real-Time: Theory and Practice*. LNCS 600, 1992.
15. A. Pnueli. The Temporal Logic of Programs. In *FOCS'77*. IEEE, 1977.
16. W. Thomas. Automata on Infinite Objects. In *Handbook of Theo. Comp. Sci.* Elsevier Sci. Pub., 1990.
17. M.Y. Vardi and P. Wolper. An Automata-Theoretic Approach to Automatic Program Verification. In *LICS'86*. IEEE, 1986.
18. Th. Wilke. Specifying Timed State Sequences in Powerful Decidable Logics and Timed Automata. In *FTRTFT'94*. LNCS 863, 1994.

H_∞ Gain Schedule Synthesis of Supervisory Hybrid Control Systems

Christopher J. Bett and Michael Lemmon *

Department of Electrical Eng.
University of Notre Dame
Notre Dame, IN 46556

Abstract. Hybrid control systems (HCS) arise when the plant, a continuous state system (CSS), is controlled by a discrete event system (DES) controller. As with any complex engineering system, the synthesis of a supervisory HCS is done as part of an iterative process. Here, we consider a synthesis procedure where an initial hybrid system is formulated and then refined until a set of symbolic and nonsymbolic specifications is satisfied. The refinements take the form of logically stable extensions of a previously given symbolic specification on the plant behaviour. This paper shows how such an extension can be constructed using multiple H_∞ control agents exhibiting robust stability. The problem formulation leads to a design problem which can be solved using existing H_∞ control techniques.

1 Introduction

This paper investigates synthesis methods for a specific class of hybrid systems which was introduced in [4]. These hybrid systems use discrete event system (DES) controllers to supervise the coordination of a smooth (continuous-state) plant's behaviour. Due to the supervisory nature of the DES controller, these systems can be referred to as supervisory hybrid control systems (SHCS) [2]. There has been recent interest in the development of automated synthesis procedures for such systems [5]. This paper presents a specific synthesis method which uses H_∞ gain scheduling techniques to ensure that the controlled plant satisfies formal symbolic specifications and constraints on continuous-state system norms.

In recent years, a variety of methods have been proposed for the systematic synthesis of supervisory hybrid systems. The early methods of Kohn-Nerode [5] rely on relaxed optimization techniques. Another approach proposed in [12] uses gain-scheduled H_∞ controllers to synthesize supervisory hybrid systems. The objective of this paper is to formally present this synthesis procedure and provide an example of its use.

The remainder of this paper is organized as follows: A brief description of the assumed HCS modeling framework [4] establishes some of the notational conventions used in this paper (section 2). The HCS design problem examined by our group is

* The authors gratefully acknowledge the partial financial support of the National Science Foundation (MSS92-16559), the Electric Power Research Institute (RP8030-06) and the Army Research Office (DAAH04-95-0600).

formally stated in section 3. This section also provides a formal definition for the stability of specified behavioural transitions. Section 4 describes the design method proposed in this paper and a numerical example is provided in section 5.

2 Supervisory Hybrid Control Systems

The class of hybrid systems considered in this paper uses a discrete event supervisor to control the behaviour of a continuous state system plant. We remark that this is by no means the most general hybrid system formulation. Many complex engineering systems, however, do fit into this framework. This class of hybrid systems can be referred to as *supervisory hybrid control systems* (SHCS) and has been previously discussed in [4].

For notational purposes, we briefly summarize the SHCS modeling framework. The plant is usually modeled by a system of ordinary differential equations

$$\frac{d\bar{x}}{dt} = f_0(\bar{x}) + \sum_{i=1}^{M} r_i f_i(\bar{x}), \tag{1}$$

where $\bar{r}' = (r_1, r_2, \ldots, r_M) \in \bar{R}$ is called the reference vector and $\bar{x}$ is the state vector. Functions $f_i : \Re^n \to \Re^n$ $(i = 1, \ldots, M)$ are assumed to form a nonsingular involutive distribution $\Delta = \{f_1, f_2, \ldots, f_m\}$ of vector fields mapping the state space back onto itself. The various vector fields are referred to as *control policies*. The controller is a discrete event system (DES) accepting a sequence $\tilde{x}[n]$ of symbolic inputs marking the occurrence of special events within the plant. The controller's output is a sequence $\tilde{r}[n]$ of symbolic directives marking *control directives* which have been selected by the controller. The controller is generally represented as a discrete event system. This can be a finite automaton, Petri net, or other structure. The specific form is not important in this paper and we simply denote the controller as a DES, $\mathcal{K}$.

An *interface* connects the plant and controller. The interface consists of two subsystems: the generator and the actuator. The *generator* transforms plant state trajectories, $\bar{x}(t)$ into a sequence of plant symbols $\tilde{x}[n]$ generated with respect to a collection of compact *goal sets*, $\mathrm{G} = \{\mathrm{g}_1, \mathrm{g}_2, \ldots, \mathrm{g}_N\}$. The generator issues a symbol $\tilde{x}_i \in \tilde{X}$ whenever the plant state trajectory crosses the boundary, $\partial \mathrm{g}_i$, of the ith goal set in a transverse manner. The sequence, $\tilde{x}[n]$, issued by the generator marks the entrance of the plant's state into different goal sets in G. The DES controller accepts $\tilde{x}[n]$ and outputs a sequence of control dirctives $\tilde{r}[n]$. The control directives are symbolic inputs drawn from a finite alphabet $\tilde{R}$. The interface *actuator*, $\alpha : \tilde{R} \to \bar{R}$ maps the ith control directive, $\tilde{r}_i$, onto a vector $\bar{r}_i$. The action of the actuator is therefore used to switch between the control policies in Δ.

With the preceding notational conventions, a supervisory hybrid control system can be denoted by the 4-tuple, $\mathcal{H} = (\mathcal{K}, \mathrm{G}, \Delta, \alpha)$. The problem of interest is the synthesis of an HCS which realizes a specified set of symbolic and nonsymbolic constraints. The control objectives are often referred to as *specifications*. These specifications constitute formal symbolic and non-symbolic (continuous-state) constraints on the plant behaviour. From the controller's side of the interface, the plant can be treated as an equivalent DES plant and formal specifications can be placed on the DES behaviour of this DES plant. ¿From the plant's side of the interface, there are traditional control theoretic constraints bounding the operator norms. Any HCS synthesis procedure will need to address both types of constraints.

3 SHCS Synthesis Procedure

The synthesis of any complex engineering system is done as part of an iterative process. System engineers devise an initial system (prototype) and then incrementally refine and modify that prototype until the desired performance specifications are met. The process provides incremental refinements to both the system and the specification in such a way that the resulting system provides a realistic compromise between desired behaviour and innate system limitations. The supervisory HCS synthesis method used in this paper will also be formulated as an iterative process. In this procedure, an initial hybrid system $\mathcal{H}_0$ is formulated and then refined until a set of symbolic and nonsymbolic specifications are satisfied. This section describes the HCS synthesis procedure in more detail.

As noted above, the "initial" hybrid control system

$$\mathcal{H}_0 = (\mathcal{K}_0, \mathbf{G}_0, \Delta_0, \alpha_0), \tag{2}$$

represents an initial assumption about the behaviour and structure of the system. Assumptions on $\mathbf{G}_0$, Δ_0, and α_0 fix the hybrid system interface. The goal sets in $\mathbf{G}_0$ will be determined by the set of sensors available to monitor the plant. The control policy distribution, Δ_0, and the actuator mapping, α_0, represent the initial set of actuators (controllers) which the system can use. The DES controller, $\mathcal{K}_0$, represents a formal specification on the plant's desired symbolic behaviour. The specification is also assumed to be known by the system engineer.

The initial hybrid system is therefore a preliminary prototype for the desired system. For complex systems, however, this prototype may not be entirely satisfactory. For example, the original formal specification, $\mathcal{K}_0$, may lack certain desirable properties such as liveness and controllability. Note, however, that from the controller's side of the interface, the plant appears to be an equivalent DES plant. We could then treat the determination of $\mathcal{K}_0$ as a pure DES synthesis problem with respect to the DES plant. The value of this insight is that there are already a variety of DES controller synthesis methods. This is, essentially, the approach taken in [4]. This approach fails, however, to address constraints on the continuous-state portion of the hybrid system. In particular, it is quite possible that while a DES controller satisfies all of the required symbolic specifications, the performance of the controlled plant can exhibit significant sensitivity to perturbed initial conditions, plant perturbations, or unmodeled disturbances generated in the CSS state-space. Therefore, satisfaction of symbolic behaviour does not guarantee that the system's implementation will be desirable from a traditional control theoretic standpoint.

These traditional control theoretic requirements are often stated as bounds on appropriately defined operator norms. In particular, these bounds are used to ensure that the resulting plant exhibits performance and stability properties which are robust with respect to unmodeled (but bounded) perturbations of the plant. To address these control theoretic objectives, we need to focus our attention on the interface. In particular, this means that we need to refine the interface goal sets and control policies so that the continuous state plant realizes the commanded symbolic transitions in an acceptable manner. With the revised controller and interface, we now obtain a new hybrid system

$$\mathcal{H}^e = (\mathcal{K}^e, \mathbf{G}^e, \Delta_c^e, \alpha^e). \tag{3}$$

which then serves as our next prototype. This process is then repeated until a satisfactory design is obtained.

In the preceding discussion, it is seen that one crucial step in the systematic synthesis of supervisory hybrid control systems involves the extension of the interface. The refinement of the DES controller can be done using a variety of existing synthesis methods. In the context of finite automatons, such work will be found in [11] and [7]. Interface refinement has also been examined by researchers. The well-known Kohn-Nerode method provides one approach to interface refinement. In this method, the goal sets, G are extended to yield a chattering control approximating "optimal" trajectories [8]. This method relies heavily on traditional optimal control formalisms and does not explicitly account for plant uncertainty. An alternative method for interface refinement synthesizes a gain-scheduled collection of H_∞ controllers. There have recently appeared a variety of methods formalizing the use of gain scheduled controllers for linear parameter varying plants. In [12], it was suggested that such techniques might provide a mode robust method for interface refinement than the existing Kohn-Nerode method. The following section summarizes the gain scheduled synthesis method.

4 H_∞ Gain Schedule Interface Extensions

We now present a method for constructing safe extensions of a given behavioural specification. Safe transitions have sometimes been referred to as T-stable transitions [3]. T-stability means that the symbol sequence generated during the transition is invariant to small perturbations in initial condition. The method determines those additional goal sets and control policies that must be added to $\mathbf{G}$ and Δ, respectively, to ensure that a commanded transition occurs in a safe manner. The following discussion introduces a gain-scheduling method for constructing this extension.

The method may be outlined as follows. We assume that there exists an ideal reference trajectory, $\bar{x}_r(t)$, between an initial goal set $\mathbf{g}_i$ and the terminal goal set $\mathbf{g}_j$. We then construct a sequence of goal sets $\mathbf{g}_m$ $(m = 1, \ldots, N_g)$ which are all bounded subsets of the state space chosen to cover the reference trajectory. These goal set extensions are identified by constructing an aggregated linear plant model which approximates the CSS plant dynamics near the reference trajectory. The mth aggregated plant model is used to synthesize the mth robust linear control agent by solving a linear H_∞ synthesis problem [9]. The controllers will be selected to ensure T-stable transitions between intermediate goal sets. These new control policies are then added to Δ_0 and the new "intermediate" goal sets are added to $\mathbf{G}_0$.

Linear control agents can only be used if the plant's perturbation over the reference trajectory is relatively smooth [6]. This notion of smoothness can be formalized as follows. Rewrite the plant's state equations in a linear state variable form,

$$\dot{\bar{x}} = A(\bar{x})\bar{x} + B(\bar{x})\bar{r} \tag{4}$$

$$\bar{y} = C(\bar{x})\bar{x}. \tag{5}$$

in which the system matrices are functions of the plant state, $\bar{x}$. At a point $\bar{x}_0$ within the plant's state space, the plant's nominal transfer function matrix is defined as

$$P(s|\bar{x}_0) = C(\bar{x}_0)\left(sI - A(\bar{x}_0)\right)^{-1} B(\bar{x}_0) \tag{6}$$

Now, consider points $\bar{x}$ near $\bar{x}_0$. We will assume that any local plant, $P(s|\bar{x})$, associated with a point $\bar{x}$ is related to $P(s|\bar{x}_0)$ through a bounded multiplicative perturbation yielding

$$P(s|\bar{x}) = (I + \Delta(s|\bar{x}, \bar{x}_0))P(s|\bar{x}_0) \tag{7}$$

with

$$\bar{\sigma}(\Delta(j\omega|\bar{x}, \bar{x}_0)) \leq \delta(\omega)\|\bar{x} - \bar{x}_0\|_2 \tag{8}$$

for all real ω. Here, $\|\bar{x}\|_2$ is a Euclidean 2-norm, $\Delta(s|\bar{x}, \bar{x}_0)$ is a stable, rational transfer function matrix, $\bar{\sigma}$ represents the maximum singular value, and $\delta(\omega)$ is a non-negative real function of ω. To model the plant in this fashion, we will assume that the multiplicative uncertainty does not change the number of closed right half plane (CRHP) poles of $P(s|\bar{x}_0)$. It will be further assumed that the plant state changes in a continuous manner with the output; i.e. $\|\bar{x} - \bar{x}_0\| < K\|\bar{y} - \bar{y}_0\|$ and $K < \infty$. In the remainder of this paper we will assume that $K = 1$. The preceding bounds indicate that the local linear plant changes in a bounded manner as we move about within some neighborhood of $\bar{x}_0$.

The control agent architecture to be used is shown in figure 1. The controller is a model following state feedback control system. It uses an internal reference model which is represented by a stable minimum phase transfer function, $\tilde{P}(s)$. This reference represents an "ideal" trajectory, denoted $\bar{x}_r(t)$, between the two goal sets corresponding to a T-stable transition. As the reference model state moves along $\bar{x}_r(t)$, the controller that is used switches sequentially between N_g control agents. The index $m(= 1, \ldots, N_g)$ will be used to specify which control agent is "active". The mth control agent uses output feedback through the linear system $F_m(s)$.

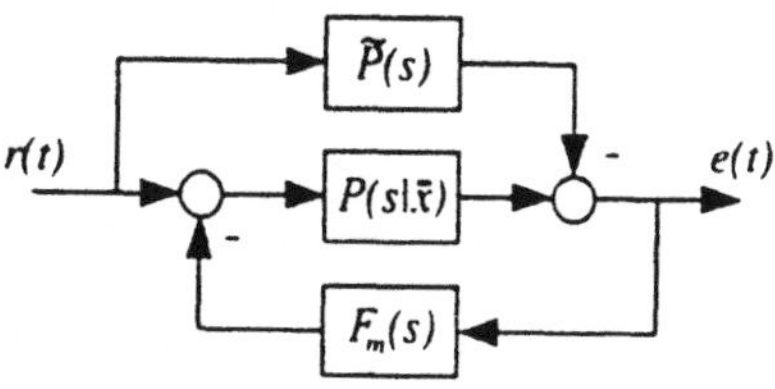

Fig. 1. HCS Control Agent

Care must be taken in the design of the reference model so that the reference trajectory does not pass too close to regions in the state space associated with events other than initial event $\mathbf{g}_i$ and terminal event $\mathbf{g}_j$. For the remainder of the paper, we will assume that the reference trajectory remains at least a distance ϵ from goal sets other than $\mathbf{g}_i$ and $\mathbf{g}_j$. This condition is expressed as follows: *if* $\bar{x}_q \in \mathbf{g}_q$ *for* $q \neq i, j$ *then* $\|\bar{x}_q - \bar{x}_r(t)\|_2 > \epsilon$ *for all* $t \in (t_0, t_f)$. The conditions for T-stability mentioned in [3] indicate one way in which this condition might be satisfied.

The objective of HCS design is to find intermediate goal sets and associated controllers that ensure T-stable transitions between intermediate goal sets. To accomplish this objective, we first generate the reference trajectory, $\bar{x}_r(t)$, according to the guidelines discussed above. Denote $\bar{x}_r^i = \bar{x}_r(t_i)$ for $t_0 \leq t_i < t_{i+1} \leq t_f$. The reference trajectory is sampled, yielding a sequence of *setpoints*, $\mathcal{S} = \{\bar{x}_r^j\}_{j=1,\ldots,M}$. We will assume that the sample points are spaced closely enough so that the reference trajectory between consecutive setpoints will be interior to the union of two open spheres of radius γ centered at the setpoints. With the mth control agent, we will associate a subsequence of N_m contiguous setpoints denoted

$$\mathcal{S}_m = \{\ \bar{x}_r^{m_i} | \bar{x}_r^{m_i} \in \mathcal{S},\ \ m_{i+1} = m_i + 1 \text{ for } i = 1, \ldots, N_m - 1\ \} \tag{9}$$

For each m, there will be a unique m_1 and N_m which identifies the subsequence. The corresponding subset of the reference trajectory will be denoted

$$\mathcal{X}_m = \{\bar{x}_r(t) | t \in [t_{m_1}, t_{m_{N_m}}]\} \tag{10}$$

For each subsequence $\mathcal{S}_m$, a linear *aggregated plant*, $\hat{P}_m(s)$ will be constructed to satisfy

$$P(s|\bar{x}_r^{m_i}) = (I + \hat{\Delta}_m(s|\bar{x}_r^{m_i}))\hat{P}_m(s) \quad \text{with} \quad \bar{\sigma}(\hat{\Delta}_m(j\omega|\bar{x}_r^{m_i})) \leq \delta_m(\omega) \tag{11}$$

for all $\bar{x}_r^j \in \mathcal{S}_m$. $\hat{\Delta}_m(j\omega|\bar{x}_r^{m_i})$ is assumed to be a stable rational transfer function representing a multiplicative perturbation such that $P(s|\bar{x}_r^{m_i})$ and $\hat{P}_m(s)$ have the same number of CRHP poles for all $\bar{x}_r^j \in \mathcal{S}_m$. $\delta_m(\omega)$ is an upper bound on the perturbation allowed between the aggregated plant and local linear plants; it is specified by the design engineer. For each $\mathcal{S}_m$, the quantity N_m will be defined as the maximum length of $\mathcal{S}_m$ beginning at $\bar{x}_r^{m_1}$ such that an aggregated plant as defined in 11 may be constructed.

With the mth control agent, the mth intermediate goal set will be defined as

$$\mathbf{g}_m = \bigcup_{\bar{x}_r \in \mathcal{X}_m} \mathbf{n}(\bar{x}_r, \gamma) \tag{12}$$

where $\mathbf{n}(\bar{x}_r, \gamma)$ is the special neighborhood set

$$\mathbf{n}(\bar{x}_r, \gamma) = \{\bar{x} : \|\bar{x} - \bar{x}_r\|_2 < \gamma\}. \tag{13}$$

The goal set $\mathbf{g}_m$ is the set of all points within a distance γ of some point in $\mathcal{X}_m$.

We now discuss the derivation of the aggregated plant model. Derivation of an aggregated plant for a subsequence $\mathcal{S}_m$ is an important part of the design methodology presented here. One way of approaching the problem is to find a $\hat{P}_m(s)$ of the same order as the local plants which simultaneously solves a set of model-matching problems derived from a formulation of the relative error model reduction problem (see [10]). Let $\mathcal{RL}_\infty^{p\times q}$ represents the set of all rational transfer function matrices having finite infinity norm. For ease of exposition, assume that $q \leq p$ and that all linear plant approximations satisfy this assumption; the results presented in this section will easily generalize. The following proposition, proven in [12], relates one way we might find an aggregated plant $\hat{P}_m(s)$ which satisfies equation 11.

Proposition 1. *Let S be a sequence of setpoints drawn from the reference trajectory generated by $\tilde{P}(s)$. Let S_m be the mth local subsequence of S. Let $P_i(s) = P(s|\bar{x}_r^{m_i}) \in \mathcal{RL}_\infty^{p\times q}$ for each $\bar{x}_r^{m_i} \in S_m$. Assume $q \leq p$. Let*

$$W_4(\omega) = \frac{1-\delta_m(\omega)}{\delta_m(\omega)}$$

where $\delta_m(\omega)$ was defined in 11. Let $V_i(s)$ represent a square spectral factor of $P_i(s)$ so that $P_i^*(s)P_i(s) = V_i(s)V_i^*(s)$ (where $V_i^*(s) = V_i^T(-s)$). Suppose $\hat{P}_m(s) \in \mathcal{RL}_\infty^{p\times q}$. If

$$\left\| Z_{11} + Z_{12}\hat{P}_m Z_{21} \right\|_\infty < 1. \tag{14}$$

where

$$Z_{11} = \left[-W_4 P_1 V_1^{*-1} \cdots -W_4 P_{N_m} V_{N_m}^{*-1} \right], Z_{12} = W_4 I_{p\times p}$$

and

$$Z_{21} = \left[V_1^{*-1} \cdots V_{N_m}^{*-1} \right].$$

then for all $i = 1, \ldots, N_m$,

$$P(s|\bar{x}_r^{m_i}) = (I + \hat{\Delta}_m(s|\bar{x}_r^{m_i}))\hat{P}_m(s) \qquad \text{with} \qquad \bar{\sigma}(\hat{\Delta}_m(j\omega|\bar{x}_r^{m_i})) \leq \delta_m(\omega)$$

Furthermore, if $\mathbf{g}_m$ is the goal set associated with S_m as defined in equation 12, then for any $\bar{x} \in \mathbf{g}_m$,

$$P(s|\bar{x}) = (I + \Delta_m(s|\bar{x}))\hat{P}_m(s) \qquad \text{with} \qquad \bar{\sigma}(\Delta_m(j\omega|\bar{x})) \leq \delta_1(\omega) \tag{15}$$

where $\delta_1(\omega) = (1+\gamma\delta(\omega))^2(1+\delta_m(\omega)) - 1$

The implication of the above results is that by designing a controller for a single uncertain linear plant $\hat{P}_m(s)$ that meets robust stability and peformance requirements, we simultaneously satisfy the criteria for all local plants $\{P(s|\bar{x})|\bar{x} \in \mathbf{g}_m\}$. In this case, the performance objective is to keep the plant state confined to the goal set $\mathbf{g}_m$ whenever $\bar{x}_r \in \mathcal{X}_m$. We now state the following proposition which provides a sufficient condition for the plant state to be confined to the goal set defined in equation 12. The result implies that we may synthesize robust linear control agents by solving an appropriately weighted mixed performance sensitivity problem. The proof is contained in [12].

Proposition 2. *Let S be a sequence of setpoints drawn from the reference trajectory generated by $\tilde{P}(s)$ with associated sets S_m, $\mathcal{X}_m$, and $\mathbf{g}_m$ as defined in equations 9, 10, and 12. Let $\hat{P}_m(s)$ be the aggregated plant for S_m satisfying the conditions of proposition 1 so that*

$$P(s|\bar{x}) = (I + \Delta_m(s|\bar{x}))\hat{P}_m(s) \tag{16}$$

with $\bar{\sigma}(\Delta_m(j\omega|\bar{x})) \leq \delta_1(\omega)$ for all $\bar{x} \in \mathbf{g}_m$ where $\delta_1(\omega)$ is defined in proposition 1. If the plant state $\bar{x}(t_{m_1}) \in \mathbf{g}_m$, then the linear control agent $F_m(s)$ robustly stabilizes *the local linear error dynamics and $\bar{x}(t) \in \mathbf{g}_m$ for all $t \in [t_{m_1}, t_{m_{N_m}}]$ provided the nominal closed loop characteristic function, $I + \hat{P}_m(s)F_m(s)$, has no zeros in the closed right half plane and*

$$\|W_1(\omega)S_m(j\omega)\|_\infty + \|W_2(\omega)T_m(j\omega)\|_\infty < 1 \tag{17}$$

where

$$S_m(s) = (I + \hat{P}_m(s)F_m(s))^{-1} = I - T_m(s) \tag{18}$$

and $W_1(\omega)$ and $W_2(\omega)$ satisfy

$$W_1(\omega) = \frac{1}{\gamma}[\bar{\sigma}(\hat{P}_m(j\omega) - \tilde{P}(j\omega)) + \delta_1(\omega)\bar{\sigma}(\hat{P}_m(j\omega))] \quad \text{and} \quad W_2(\omega) = \delta_1(\omega). \tag{19}$$

A collection of goal sets $\mathbf{g}_m$ will be said to be connected if their associated subsequences have non-null intersections. For connected collections of goal sets, $\mathbf{g}_m$, the following corollary results from the preceding proposition. The result shows that the control agents and goal sets generated above form a T-stable extension to the interface. The proof is located in [12].

Corollary 3. *Consider a sequence of connected intermediate goal sets $\{\mathbf{g}_m\}$ ($m = 1, \ldots, N_g$) between initial goal set $\mathbf{g}_I$ and terminal goal set $\mathbf{g}_F$ with the non-null intersection $(\mathbf{g}_1 \cap \mathbf{g}_I) \subset \mathbf{n}(\bar{x}_1^0, \gamma)$ and $\mathbf{n}(\bar{x}_m^M, \gamma) \subset \mathbf{g}_F$. Let the symbol $\tilde{x}_m$ denote the entry of the reference model state into $\mathcal{X}_m$ and let $\tilde{x}_{N_g+1}$ indicate that the reference model state has reached $\bar{x}_r^M \in S$. If the connected intermediate goal sets and their associated controllers satisfy the hypotheses of proposition 2, then the the sequence of transitions $\tilde{x}_m \to \tilde{x}_{m+1}$ for $m = 1, \ldots, N_g$ represents a T-stable transition $\tilde{x}_I \to \tilde{x}_F$.*

The preceding results provide a very simple method for generating T-stable extensions of a given specification. This procedure is outlined below.

- **Step 1:** Generate a reference trajectory, $\bar{x}_r(t)$, and obtain a sequence of M setpoints $S = \{\bar{x}_r^j\}$ ($j = 1, \ldots, M$).
- **Step 2:** For each setpoint in S determine the local linear transfer function $P(s|\bar{x}_r^j)$.
- **Step 3:** Initialize the iteration with i=1, N=0, and $m = 1$.
- **Step 4:** Compute an aggregated plant, $\hat{P}_m(s)$ for all $j \in [i, i + N]$.
- **Step 5:** Determine the H_∞ norm controller, $F_m(s)$. If no such controller exists then set $i = i + N - 1$, N=0, and $m = m + 1$. Otherwise set $N = N + 1$.
- **Step 6:** Go to step 4 if $i + N < M$.
- **Step 7:** If no controller was found in the last iteration of Step 5, then declare a failure. The procedure was unable to T-stablize the transition. Otherwise declare success.

5 Example

A specific example of the preceding design procedure is provided below. Consider a plant of the following form

$$\dot{x}_1 = -5x_1 - 4x_2 - 5(x_1^2 + x_2^2) - 25x_1x_2(1 + x_2); \quad \dot{x}_2 = x_1; \quad y = 4x_2$$

where r is a step input signal. The control objective is to move the plant's state along a desired reference trajectory from an initial output of $\bar{y}_0 = 0$ to a final output of $\bar{y} = 1$. The reference trajectory is generated by the following linear system,

$$\dot{x}_{r1} = -5x_{r1} - 6x_{r2}; \quad \dot{x}_{r2} = x_{r1}; \quad y_r = 6x_{r2}$$

The preceding procedure was applied to this problem assuming $\delta(\omega) = |0.45/(j\omega+1)|$ and varying γ between .005 and .05. The aggregation bound was set to $\delta_m(\omega) = 0.1$. For the candidate goal sets, the H_∞ controller was computed via the 2-Riccati solution discussed in [9].

As expected, the procedure generated a collection of goal sets and controllers which allowed the plant output to track the reference model's output. The number of individual control agents that were required remained constant, however the synthesized control agents achieved better performance with decreased γ. Figure 2a

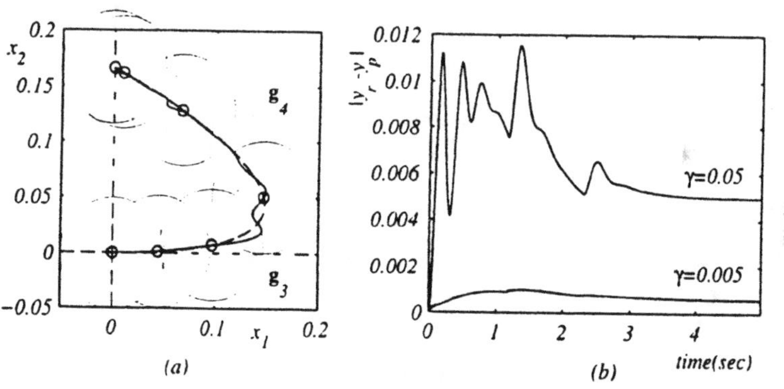

Fig. 2. (a) State trajectories (plant:solid) with goal sets; (b) Output error;

shows the controlled plant state-trajectory and the goal sets generated in the CSS plant state space along the reference trajectory for $\gamma = 0.05$. The number of models required was 6. In figure 2b, the output error is shown for $\gamma = 0.005$ and $\gamma = 0.05$. The number of models required in both cases was 6. In both cases, the maximum output error is well-bounded below the desired bound of 0.005.

6 Conclusions

Synthesis procedures for supervisory hybrid systems are iterative processes in which a system prototype is incrementally refined to produce the desired system. The objects of this refinement are both the system interface and the DES specification.

While there has been significant effort in the refinement of DES objects, relatively few computationally tractable methods have been proposed for interface refinement. Of these methods, the best known approach [5] relies on optimal control theoretic methods which do not explicitly consider the role of modeling uncertainty in the design process. The objective of this paper was to present a more modern framework for hybrid system synthesis in which the interface is refined using H_∞ synthesis methods. The approach is essentially a discretized form of gain scheduling and therefore allows us to explicitly address robustness issues while providing a computationally tractable framework. The specific method that we have explored is closely related to gain scheduling methods for linear parameter varying plants [1] [6]. While the method presented here was formulated specifically with the hybrid synthesis problem in mind, it is still unclear whether more elegant LFT formulations [1] might also be recast in this manner.

References

1. A. Packard, "Gain scheduling via linear fractional transformations". *Systems and Control Letters*, 22 (1994) 79-92.
2. R.L. Grossman, A. Nerode, A.P. Ravn, and H. Rischel (eds.), *Hybrid Systems*, Lecture Notes in Computer Science 736, Springer Verlag, 1993.
3. M.D. Lemmon and P.J. Antsaklis, "Inductively Inferring Valid Logical Models of Continuous-State Dynamical Systems", *Theoretical Computer Science*, 138 (1995) 201-210.
4. P. Antsaklis, J. Stiver, and M. Lemmon, "Hybrid system modeling and autonomous control systems", in [1] , pp. 366-392. Springer-Verlag, 1993.
5. A. Nerode and W. Kohn, "Multiple agent hybrid control architecture", in [2], pp. 297-316, Springer-Verlag, 1993.
6. J.S. Shamma, and M. Athans, "Analysis of gain scheduled control for nonlinear plants", *IEEE Trans. on Automatic Control*, Vol. AC-35, No. 8, pp. 898-907, August 1990.
7. X. Yang, M.D. Lemmon, and P.J. Antsaklis, "On the supremal controllable sublanguage in the discrete event model of nondeterministic hybrid control systems", accepted for publication *IEEE Transactions in Automatic Control*, 1995.
8. X. Ge, W.Kohn, and A. Nerode, "Algorithms for chattering approximations to relaxed optimal controls", Technical Report 94-23, Mathematical Sciences Institute, Cornell University, April 1994.
9. M.G. Safonov, D.J.N.Limebeer, and R.Y. Chiang, "simplifying the H^∞ theory via loop shifting, matrix pencils, and descriptor concepts", *International Journal of Control*, vol 50, no. 6, pp. 2467-2488, 1989.
10. K. Glover, "Multiplicative approximation of linear multivariable systems with L^∞ error bounds", in *Proceedings of the American Control Conference*, pp. 1705-1709, 1986.
11. Stiver, J.A., Antasaklis, P.J., and Lemmon, M.D., "A logical DES approach to the design of hybrid control systems," technical report of the ISIS group ISIS-94-011, University of Notre Dame, Oct. 94 (revised:May 1995). to appear *Mathematical and Computer Modeling* special issue on discrete event systems.
12. M. Lemmon, C. Bett, P. Szymanski, and P. Antsaklis, "Constructing hybrid control systems from robust linear control agents", in *Hybrid Systems II*. Lecture Notes in Computer Science, Springer-Verlag, 1995.

A New Approach to Robust Control of Hybrid Systems

Andrey V. Savkin * Robin J. Evans* Ian R. Petersen **

Abstract. The paper presents a new approach to robust control synthesis problems for hybrid dynamical systems. The hybrid system under consideration is a composite of a continuous plant and a discrete event controller. State and output feedback problems are considered. The main results are given in terms of the existence of suitable solutions to a dynamic programming equation and a Riccati differential equation of the H^∞ filtering type. These results show a connection between the theories of hybrid dynamical systems and robust and nonlinear control.

1 Introduction

Hybrid dynamical systems (HDS) have attracted considerable attention in recent years (see e.g. [1, 2, 3, 4]). In general, HDS are those that consist of a logical discrete event decision-making system interacting with a continuous time process. A simple example is a climate control system in a typical home. The on-off nature of the thermostat is modelled as a discrete event system, whereas the furnace or air-conditioner are modelled as continuous time systems. Other examples include vehicle transmission systems and stepper motors, computer disk drives, robotic and high-level flexible manufacturing systems and intelligent vehicle/highway systems (see e.g. [1, 3, 2, 5]).

In this paper, we consider robust control problems for a class of HDS consisting of a continuous time plant with control and disturbance inputs and a discrete event controller. The controller is defined by a collection of given controllers which are called basic controllers. Then, our control strategy is a rule for switching from one basic controller to another. The control goal is to achieve a level of performance defined by an integral performance index similar to the requirement in standard H^∞ control theory (see e.g. [6, 7, 8]). The switching rule is computed by solving a Riccati differential equation of the game type and a discrete-time dynamic programming equation. Riccati differential equations of the type considered in this paper have been widely studied in the theory of H^∞ control and there exist reliable methods for obtaining solutions. The solution to discrete-time dynamic programming equations has been the subject of much research in the field of optimal control theory. Furthermore, many methods of obtaining numerical solutions have been proposed for specific optimal control problems.

* Department of Electrical and Electronic Engineering, University of Melbourne, Australia

* Department of Electrical Engineering, Australian Defence Force Academy

Section 2 provides a necessary and sufficient condition for a state feedback problem. This condition is given in terms of the existence of a solution to a dynamic programming equation. In section 3, we obtain a solution for an output feedback problem with a linear plant. The main result of this section is given in terms of the existence of suitable solutions to a Riccati differential equation of the H^∞ filtering type and a dynamic programming equation. If such solutions exist, then it is shown that they can be used to construct a corresponding controller. Also, we consider a special case when the basic controllers are linear. Since dynamic programming equations and H^∞ type Riccati equations are well known in modern robust and nonlinear control theories (see e.g. [6, 7, 8]), this paper shows that these theories when suitably modified, provide a framework for studying HDS.

2 State Feedback Problem

Let N be a given number and $t_0 < t_1 < \ldots < t_{N-1} < t_N$ be given times. Consider the time-varying nonlinear system defined on the finite time interval $[t_0, t_N]$:

$$\dot{x}(t) = f(t, x(t), u(t), w(t)) \tag{1}$$

where $x(t) \in \mathbf{R}^n$ is the *state*, $w(t) \in \mathbf{R}^p$ is the *disturbance input*, $u(t) \in \mathbf{R}^h$ is the *control input*, $f(\cdot,\cdot,\cdot,\cdot)$ is a continuous vector function.

Controlled Switching Suppose we have a collection of given controllers

$$u_1(t) = U_1(t, x(t)), \quad u_2(t) = U_2(t, x(t)), \quad \ldots, \quad u_k(t) = U_k(t, x(t)) \tag{2}$$

where $U_1(\cdot,\cdot), U_2(\cdot,\cdot), \ldots, U_k(\cdot,\cdot)$ are given continuous matrix functions. The controllers (2) are called *basic controllers*. We will consider the following class of state feedback controllers. Let $I_j(\cdot)$ be a function which maps from the set of the state measurements $\{x(\cdot)\mid_{t_0}^{t_j}\}$ to the set of symbols $\{1, 2, \ldots, k\}$. Then, for any sequence of such functions $\{I_j\}_{j=0}^{N-1}$, we will consider the following dynamic nonlinear state feedback controller:

$$\begin{aligned} \forall j \in \{0, 1, \ldots, N-1\} \;\; u(t) = U_{i_j}(t, x(t)) \;\; \forall t \in [t_j, t_{j+1}) \\ \textit{where} \;\; i_j = I_j(x(\cdot)\mid_{t_0}^{t_j}). \end{aligned} \tag{3}$$

Hence, our control strategy is a rule for switching from one basic controller to another. Such a rule constructs a sequence of symbols $\{i_j\}_{j=0}^{N-1}$ from the state measurement $x(\cdot)$. The sequence $\{i_j\}_{j=0}^{N-1}$ is called a *switching sequence*. Also, $\mathcal{L}$ denotes the class of all controllers of the form (2), (3).

Definition 1. Let $S_0(x(t_0)) \geq 0, S_f(x(t_N)) \geq 0$ and $W(t, x(t), u(t), w(t))$ be given continuous functions. If there exists a controller of the form (2), (3) such that

$$S_f(x(t_N)) + \int_{t_0}^{t_N} W(t, x(t), u(t), w(t))dt \leq S_0(x(t_0)) \tag{4}$$

for all solutions to the closed loop system (1), (3) with any disturbance input $w(\cdot) \in \mathbf{L}_2[t_0, t_N]$, then the robust control problem (4) is said to have a solution via *controlled switching* with the basic controllers (2).

Remark If $W(t,x,u,w) \equiv \|z(t,x,u)\|^2 - \|w\|^2$, where $z(t,x,u)$ is the controlled output of the system (1), condition (4) is the finite interval H^∞ control requirement (see e.g. [6, 7, 8]).

Notation Let $M(\cdot)$ be a given function from $\mathbf{R}^n$ to $\mathbf{R}$ and let $x_0 \in \mathbf{R}^n$ be a given vector. Then,

$$F_j^i(x_0, M(\cdot)) \triangleq \sup_{w(\cdot)\in \mathbf{L}_2[t_j, t_{j+1})} [M(x(t_{j+1})) + \int_{t_j}^{t_{j+1}} W(t, x(t), U_i(t, x(t)), w(t))dt] \quad (5)$$

where the supremum is taken over all solutions to the system (1) with $w(\cdot) \in \mathbf{L}_2[t_j, t_{j+1})$, $u(t) \equiv U_i(t, x(t))$ and initial condition $x(t_j) = x_0$.

Now we are in a position to present the main result of this section.

Theorem 1. *Consider the system (1) and the basic controllers (2). Let $S_0(x(t_0)) \geq 0, S_f(x(t_N)) \geq 0$ and $W(t,x,u,w)$ be given continuous functions. Suppose, that $F_j^i(\cdot,\cdot)$ is defined by (5). Then, the following statements are equivalent:*

(i) The robust control problem (4) has a solution via controlled switching with the basic controllers (2).

(ii) The dynamic programming equation

$$V_N(x_0) = S_f(x_0); \quad V_j(x_0) = \min_{i=1,\ldots,k} F_j^i(x_0, V_{j+1}(\cdot)) \quad (6)$$

has a solution for $j = 0, 1, \ldots, N-1$ such that $V_0(x_0) \leq S_0(x_0)$ for all $x_0 \in \mathbf{R}^n$.

Furthermore, if condition (ii) holds and $i_j(x_0)$ is an index such that the minimum in (6) is achieved for $i = i_j(x_0)$, then the controller (2), (3) associated with the switching sequence $\{i_j\}_{j=0}^{N-1}$ where $i_j \triangleq i_j(x(t_j))$ solves the robust control problem (4).

Proof ($(i) \Rightarrow (ii)$) Introduce for any $j = 0, 1, \ldots, N$ the following function

$$V_j(x_0) \triangleq \inf_{u(\cdot)\in\mathcal{L}} \sup_{w(\cdot)\in\mathbf{L}_2[t_j,t_N]} \left[S_f(x(t_N)) + \int_{t_j}^{t_N} W(t, x(t), u(t), w(t))dt \right] \quad (7)$$

where the supremum is taken over all solutions to the system (1) with initial condition $x(t_j) = x_0$. According to the theory of dynamic programming (see e.g. [6, 8]) $V_j(\cdot)$ satisfies the equations (6). Also, it follows from (7), that if condition (i) holds, then $V_0(x_0) \leq S_0(x_0)$.

($(ii) \Rightarrow (i)$) The equations (6) imply that for the controller associated with the switching sequence $\{i_j\}_{j=0}^{N-1}$ we have

$$\sup_{w(\cdot)\in\mathbf{L}_2[t_0,t_N]} \left[S_f(x(t_N)) + \int_{t_0}^{t_N} W(t, x(t), u(t), w(t))dt \right] \leq V_0(x(t_0)).$$

Since $V_0(x(t_0)) \leq S_0(x(t_0))$, the controller associated with the switching sequence $\{i_j\}_{j=0}^{N-1}$ solves the problem (4). □

3 Output Feedback Problem

In this section, we consider the time-varying linear system defined on the time interval $[t_0, t_N]$:

$$\begin{aligned} \dot{x}(t) &= A(t)x(t) + B_1(t)\xi(t) + B_2(t)u(t); \\ z(t) &= K(t)x(t) + G(t)u(t); \\ y(t) &= C(t)x(t) + v(t) \end{aligned} \tag{8}$$

where $x(t) \in \mathbf{R}^n$ is the *state*, $\xi(t) \in \mathbf{R}^p$ and $v(t) \in \mathbf{R}^l$ are the *disturbance inputs*, $u(t) \in \mathbf{R}^h$ is the *control input*, $z(t) \in \mathbf{R}^q$ is the *controlled output* and $y(t) \in \mathbf{R}^l$ is the *measured output*, $A(\cdot), B_1(\cdot), B_2(\cdot), K(\cdot), G(\cdot)$ and $C(\cdot)$ are bounded piecewise continuous matrix functions.

Output Feedback Controlled Switching Suppose we have a collection of given controllers

$$u_1(t) = U_1(t, y(t)), \quad u_2(t) = U_2(t, y(t)), \quad \ldots, \quad u_k(t) = U_k(t, y(t)) \tag{9}$$

where $U_1(\cdot,\cdot), U_2(\cdot,\cdot), \ldots, U_k(\cdot,\cdot)$ are given continuous matrix functions such that $U_1(\cdot, 0) \equiv 0, U_2(\cdot, 0) \equiv 0, \ldots, U_k(\cdot, 0) \equiv 0$. The controllers (9) are called *output feedback basic controllers*. We will consider the following class of output feedback controllers. Let $I_j(\cdot)$ be a function which maps from the set of the output measurements $\{y(\cdot)\mid_{t_0}^{t_j}\}$ to the set of symbols $\{1, 2, \ldots, k\}$. Then, for any sequence of such functions $\{I_j\}_{j=0}^{N-1}$, we will consider the following dynamic nonlinear output feedback controller:

$$\begin{aligned} \forall j \in \{0, 1, \ldots, N-1\} \;\; u(t) = U_{i_j}(t, y(t)) \;\; \forall t \in [t_j, t_{j+1}) \\ \textit{where} \;\; i_j = I_j(y(\cdot)\mid_{t_0}^{t_j}). \end{aligned} \tag{10}$$

As above, our control strategy is a rule for switching from one basic controller to another. Such a rule constructs a symbolic sequence $\{i_j\}_{j=0}^{N-1}$ from the output measurement $y(\cdot)$. The sequence $\{i_j\}_{j=0}^{N-1}$ is called a switching sequence.

Definition 2. Let $X_0 = X_0' > 0$ and $X_f = X_f' > 0$ be given matrices. If there exists a function $\tilde{V}(x_0) \geq 0$ such that $\tilde{V}(0) = 0$ and for any vector $x_0 \in \mathbf{R}^n$, there exists a controller of the form (9), (10) such that

$$\begin{aligned} x(t_N)'X_f x(t_N) + \int_{t_0}^{t_N} (\|z(t)\|^2 - \|\xi(t)\|^2 - \|v(t)\|^2)dt \\ \leq (x(t_0) - x_0)'X_0(x(t_0) - x_0) + \tilde{V}(x_0) \end{aligned} \tag{11}$$

for all solutions to the closed loop system (8), (10) with any disturbance inputs $[\xi(\cdot), v(\cdot)] \in \mathbf{L}_2[t_0, t_N]$, then the output feedback robust control problem (8), (11) is said to have a solution via controlled switching with the output feedback basic controllers (9).

Remark The problem (11) is a H^∞ control problem with transients (see e.g. [7]) with a special class of output feedback controllers.

Our solution to the above problem involves the following Riccati differential equation

$$\begin{aligned}\dot{P}(t) = B_1(t)B_1(t)' + A(t)P(t) + P(t)A(t)' \\ +P(t)[K(t)'K(t) - C(t)'C(t)]P(t)\end{aligned} \tag{12}$$

Also, we consider a set of state equations of the form

$$\begin{aligned}\dot{\hat{x}}(t) = [A(t) + P(t)[K(t)'K(t) - C(t)'C(t)]]\,\hat{x}(t) \\ +P(t)C(t)'y(t) + B_2(t)u(t).\end{aligned} \tag{13}$$

Notation Let $M(\cdot)$ be a given function from $\mathbf{R}^n$ to $\mathbf{R}$ and let $x_0 \in \mathbf{R}^n$ be a given vector. Introduce the following cost function

$$W(t, \hat{x}(t), u(t), y(t)) \triangleq \|(K(t)\hat{x}(t) + G(t)u(t))\|^2 - \|(C(t)\hat{x}(t) - y(t))\|^2. \tag{14}$$

Then,

$$\begin{aligned}F_j^i(\hat{x}_0, M(\cdot)) \triangleq \sup_{y(\cdot)\in\mathbf{L}_2[t_j,t_{j+1})} [M(\hat{x}(t_{j+1})) + \\ \int_{t_j}^{t_{j+1}} W(t, \hat{x}(t), U_i(t, y(t)), y(t))dt]\end{aligned} \tag{15}$$

where the supremum is taken over all solutions to the system (13) with $y(\cdot) \in \mathbf{L}_2[t_j, t_{j+1})$, $u(t) \equiv U_i(t, y(t))$ and initial condition $\hat{x}(t_j) = \hat{x}_0$.

Now we are in a position to present the main result of this section.

Theorem 2. *Consider the system (8) and the output feedback basic controllers (9). Let $X_0 = X_0' > 0$ and $X_f = X_f' > 0$ be given matrices. Suppose, that $K(\cdot)'G(\cdot) \equiv 0$ and $F_j^i(\cdot,\cdot)$ is defined by (15). Then, the following statements are equivalent:*

(i) The output feedback robust control problem (11) has a solution via controlled switching with output feedback basic controllers (9).

(ii) The solution $P(\cdot)$ to the Riccati equation (12) with initial condition $P(t_0) = X_0^{-1}$ is defined and positive definite on the interval $[t_0, t_N]$, $P(t_N)^{-1} > X_f$ and the dynamic programming equation

$$\begin{aligned}V_N(\hat{x}_0) = \hat{x}_0'[X_f + X_f(P(t_N)^{-1} - X_f)^{-1}X_f]\hat{x}_0; \\ V_j(\hat{x}_0) = \min_{i=1,\dots,k} F_j^i(\hat{x}_0, V_{j+1}(\cdot))\end{aligned} \tag{16}$$

has a solution for $j = 0, 1, \dots, N-1$ such that $V_0(\hat{x}_0) \geq 0$ for all $\hat{x}_0 \in \mathbf{R}^n$ and $V_0(0) = 0$.

Furthermore, suppose that condition (ii) holds and let $i_j(\hat{x}_0)$ be an index such that the minimum in (16) is achieved for $i = i_j(\hat{x}_0)$ and $\hat{x}(\cdot)$ be the solution to the equation (13) with initial condition $\hat{x}(t_0) = x_0$. Then the controller (9), (10) associated with the switching sequence $\{i_j\}_{j=0}^{N-1}$ where $i_j \triangleq i_j(\hat{x}(t_j))$ solves the output feedback robust control problem (11) with $\tilde{V}(\cdot) \equiv V_0(\cdot)$.

In order to prove this theorem, we will use the following lemma.

Lemma. Let $X_0 = X_0' > 0$ and $X_f = X_f' > 0$ be given matrices, $x_0 \in \mathbf{R}^n$ be a given vector, $\tilde{V}(x_0)$ be a given constant and $y_0(\cdot)$ and $u_0(\cdot)$ be given vector functions. Suppose that the solution $P(\cdot)$ to the Riccati equation (12) with initial condition $P(t_0) = X_0^{-1}$ is defined and positive definite on the interval $[t_0, t_N]$. Then, condition

$$x(t_N)'X_f x(t_N) + \int_{t_0}^{t_N} (\|z(t)\|^2 - \|\xi(t)\|^2 - \|v(t)\|^2)dt \leq (x(t_0) - x_0)'X_0(x(t_0) - x_0) + \tilde{V}(x_0) \tag{17}$$

holds for all solutions to the system (8) with $y(\cdot) = y_0(\cdot)$ and $u(\cdot) = u_0(\cdot)$ if and only if

$$\int_{t_0}^{t_N} W(t, \hat{x}(t), u_0(t), y_0(t))dt \leq \tilde{V}(x_0) + (x_f - \hat{x}(t_N))'P(t_N)^{-1}(x_f - \hat{x}(t_N)) - x_f'X_f x_f \tag{18}$$

for the cost function (14) and the solution to the equation (13) with $u(\cdot) = u_0(\cdot)$, $y(\cdot) = y_0(\cdot)$ and initial condition $\hat{x}(t_0) = x_0$.

Proof Given an input-output pair $[u_0(\cdot), y_0(\cdot)]$, if condition (11) holds for all vector functions $x(\cdot), \xi(\cdot)$ and $v(\cdot)$ satisfying equation (8) with $u() = u_0(\cdot)$ and such that

$$y_0(t) = C(t)x(t) + v(t) \quad \forall t \in [t_0, t_N], \tag{19}$$

then, substitution of (19) into (11) implies that (11) holds if and only if

$$J[x_f, \xi(\cdot)] \geq 0 \tag{20}$$

for all $\xi(\cdot) \in \mathbf{L}_2[t_0, t_N]$, $x_f \in \mathbf{R}^n$ where $J[x_f, \xi(\cdot)]$ is defined by

$$J[x_f, \xi(\cdot)] \triangleq (x(t_0) - x_0)'X_0(x(t_0) - x_0) + \int_{t_0}^{t_N} (\|\xi(t)\|^2 - \|(K(t)x(t) + G(t)u_0(t))\|^2 + \|(y_0(t) - C(t)x(t))\|^2)dt \tag{21}$$

and $x(\cdot)$ is the solution to (8) with disturbance input $\xi(\cdot)$ and boundary condition $x(t_N) = x_f$.

Now consider the following minimization problem

$$\min_{\xi(\cdot) \in \mathbf{L}_2[t_0, t_N]} J[x_f, \xi(\cdot)] \tag{22}$$

where the minimum is taken over all $x(\cdot)$ and $\xi(\cdot)$ connected by (8) with the boundary condition $x(t_N) = x_f$. This problem is a linear quadratic optimal tracking problem in which the system operates in reverse time.

We wish to convert the above tracking problem into a tracking problem of the form considered in [9] and [10]. In order to achieve this, first define $x_1(t)$ to be the solution to the state equations

$$\dot{x}_1(t) = A(t)x_1(t) + B_2(t)u_0(t); \quad x_1(t_0) = 0. \tag{23}$$

Now let $\tilde{x}(t) \stackrel{\Delta}{=} x(t) - x_1(t)$. Then, it follows from (8) and (23) that $\tilde{x}(t)$ satisfies the state equations

$$\dot{\tilde{x}}(t) = A(t)\tilde{x}(t) + B_1(t)\xi(t) \tag{24}$$

where $\tilde{x}(t_0) = x(t_0)$. Furthermore, the cost function (21) can be re-written as

$$\begin{aligned} J[x_f, \xi(\cdot)] = \tilde{J}[\tilde{x}_f, \xi(\cdot)] = (\tilde{x}(t_0) - x_0)'X_0(\tilde{x}(t_0) - x_0) + \\ \int_{t_0}^{t_N} (\|\xi(t)\|^2 - \|(K(t)[\tilde{x}(t) + x_1(t)] + G(t)u_0(t))\|^2 \\ + \|(y_0(t) - C(t)[\tilde{x}(t) + x_1(t)])\|^2)dt \end{aligned} \tag{25}$$

where $\tilde{x}(t_N) = \tilde{x}_f = x_f - x_1(t_N)$. Equations (24) and (25) now define a tracking problem of the form considered in [9] where $y_0(\cdot)$, $u_0(\cdot)$ and $x_1(\cdot)$ are all treated as reference inputs. In fact, the only difference between this tracking problem and the tracking problem considered in the proof of the result of [10] is that in this paper, we have a *sign indefinite* quadratic cost function.

The solution to this tracking problem is well known (e.g. see [9]). Indeed, if the Riccati equation (12) has a positive-definite solution defined in $[t_0, t_N]$ with initial condition $P(t_0) = X_0^{-1}$, then the minimum in $\min \tilde{J}[\tilde{x}_f, \xi(\cdot)]$ will be achieved for any x_0, $u_0(\cdot)$ and $y_0(\cdot)$. Furthermore as in [10], we can write

$$\begin{aligned} \min_{\xi(\cdot)\in \mathbf{L}_2[t_0,t_N]} \tilde{J}[\tilde{x}_f, \xi(\cdot)] = (\tilde{x}_f - \hat{x}_1(t_N))'P(t_N)^{-1}(\tilde{x}_f - \hat{x}_1(t_N)) \\ - \int_{t_0}^{t_N} W(t, x_1(t) + \hat{x}_1(t), u_0(t), y_0(t))dt \end{aligned} \tag{26}$$

where $\hat{x}_1(\cdot)$ is the solution to state equations

$$\begin{aligned} \dot{\hat{x}}_1(t) = [A(t) + P(t)[K(t)'K(t) - C(t)'C(t)]]\,[x_1(t) + \hat{x}_1(t)] \\ -A(t)x_1(t) + P(t)C(t)'y_0(t) \end{aligned}$$

with initial condition $\hat{x}_1(t_0) = x_0$. Now let $\hat{x}(\cdot) \stackrel{\Delta}{=} x_1(\cdot) + \hat{x}_1(\cdot)$. Using the fact that $\tilde{x}_f = x_f - x_1(t_N)$, it follows that (26) can be re-written as

$$\begin{aligned} \min_{\xi(\cdot)\in \mathbf{L}_2[t_0,t_N]} J[x_f, \xi(\cdot)] = (x_f - \hat{x}(t_N))'P(t_N)^{-1}(x_f - \hat{x}(t_N)) \\ - \int_{t_0}^{t_N} W(t, \hat{x}(t), u_0(t), y_0(t))dt \end{aligned}$$

where $\hat{x}(\cdot)$ is the solution to state equations (13) with initial condition $\hat{x}(t_0) = x_0$. From this we can conclude that condition (17) with a given input-output pair $[u_0(\cdot), y_0(\cdot)]$ is equivalent to the inequality (18). □

Proof of Theorem 2 If condition (i) holds, then there exists a solution to the output feedback finite interval H^∞ control problem. Hence, it follows from the standard H^∞ control theory (see e.g. [7, 6]), that the solution $P(\cdot)$ to the Riccati equation (12) with initial condition $P(t_0) = X_0^{-1}$ is defined and positive definite on $[t_0, t_N]$. Now Lemma implies that condition (i) is equivalent to the existence of a controller (9), (10) such that the inequality (18) holds for all solutions to the system (13) with any initial condition $\hat{x}(t_0) = x_0$ and any input-output pair $[y(\cdot), u(\cdot)]$ connected by (10). The inequality (18) is equivalent to the following two conditions: $P(t_N)^{-1} > X_f$ and

$$\hat{x}(t_N)'[X_f + X_f(P(t_N)^{-1} - X_f)^{-1}X_f]\hat{x}(t_N) + \int_{t_0}^{t_N} W(t, \hat{x}(t), u(t), y(t))dt \leq \tilde{V}(\hat{x}(t_0)).$$

Finally, consider the system (13) with $y(\cdot)$ treated as the disturbance input apply Theorem 1 with the functional (14), $S_0(\cdot) \equiv \tilde{V}(\cdot)$ and

$$S_f(x(t_N)) = \hat{x}(t_N)'[X_f + X_f(P(t_N)^{-1} - X_f)^{-1}X_f]\hat{x}(t_N).$$

The statement of the theorem follows immediately. □

Now consider the case of linear basic controllers

$$u_1(t) = L_1(t)y(t),\ u_2(t) = L_2(t)y(t),\ \ldots,\ u_k(t) = L_k(t)y(t). \tag{27}$$

Suppose that the solution $P(\cdot)$ to (12) with initial condition $P(t_0) = X_0^{-1}$ is defined and positive definite on $[t_0, t_N]$. Introduce for all $i = 1, 2, \ldots, k$ and all $j = 0, 1, \ldots, N-1$ the following Hamiltonian system:

$$\begin{pmatrix} \dot{p}(t) \\ \dot{\hat{x}}(t) \end{pmatrix} = H_{ij}(t) \begin{pmatrix} p(t) \\ \hat{x}(t) \end{pmatrix} \quad \forall t \in [t_j, t_{j+1})$$

$$H_{ij}(t) \triangleq \begin{pmatrix} -(A + PK'K + B_2L_iC)' & -2K'K \\ \frac{1}{2}(PC' + B_2L_i)(PC' + B_2L_i)' & A + PK'K + B_2L_iC \end{pmatrix}. \tag{28}$$

Let $\Psi_{ij}(t_j, t)$ be the transition matrix function of this system. That is, $\Psi_{ij}(t_j, t_j) = I$ and $\dot{\Psi}_{ij}(t_j, t) = H_{ij}(t)\Psi_{ij}(t_j, t)$ for $t \in [t_j, t_{j+1})$. Also, introduce $n \times n$ matrices Y_{ij}, Z_{ij}, R_{ij} and M_{ij} by partitioning $\Psi_{ij}(t_j, t_{j+1})$ as follows:

$$\Psi_{ij}(t_j, t_{j+1}) \triangleq \begin{pmatrix} Y_{ij} & Z_{ij} \\ R_{ij} & M_{ij} \end{pmatrix}. \tag{29}$$

Now suppose that

$$det R_{ij} \neq 0 \quad \forall i = 1, \ldots, k \ and \ j = 0, 1, \ldots, N-1 \tag{30}$$

and introduce quadratic forms

$$\hat{F}_j^i(\hat{x}_j, \hat{x}_{j+1}) \stackrel{\Delta}{=} \hat{x}_j' R_{ij}^{-1} \hat{x}_{j+1} - \hat{x}_j' R_{ij}^{-1} M_{ij} \hat{x}_j$$
$$-\hat{x}_{j+1}' Y_{ij} R_{ij}^{-1} \hat{x}_{j+1} + \hat{x}_{j+1}' (Y_{ij} R_{ij}^{-1} M_{ij} - Z_{ij}) \hat{x}_j \quad (31)$$

where $\hat{x}_j, \hat{x}_{j+1} \in \mathbf{R}^n$. We are now in a position to present the following result.

Theorem 3. *Consider the system (8) and the output feedback basic controllers (27). Let $X_0 = X_0' > 0$ and $X_f = X_f' > 0$ be given matrices. Suppose, that $G(\cdot) \equiv 0$, the solution $P(\cdot)$ to the equation (12) with initial condition $P(t_0) = X_0^{-1}$ is defined and positive definite on $[t_0, t_N]$, assumption (30) holds and $\hat{F}_j^i(\cdot,\cdot)$ is defined by (31), Then, the following statements are equivalent:*

(i) The output feedback robust control problem (11) has a solution via controlled switching with linear output feedback basic controllers (27).

(ii) The inequality $P(t_N)^{-1} > X_f$ holds and the dynamic programming equation

$$V_N(\hat{x}_N) = \hat{x}_N'[X_f + X_f(P(t_N)^{-1} - X_f)^{-1} X_f]\hat{x}_N;$$
$$V_j(\hat{x}_j) = \min_{i=1,\dots,k} \sup_{\hat{x}_{j+1} \in \mathbf{R}^n} \left[\hat{F}_j^i(\hat{x}_j, \hat{x}_{j+1}) + V_{j+1}(\hat{x}_{j+1})\right] \quad (32)$$

has a solution for $j = 0, 1, \dots, N-1$ such that $V_0(\hat{x}_0) \geq 0$ for all $\hat{x}_0 \in \mathbf{R}^n$ and $V_0(0) = 0$.

Furthermore, suppose that condition (ii) holds and let $i_j(\hat{x}_j)$ be an index such that the minimum in (32) is achieved for $i = i_j(\hat{x}_j)$ and $\hat{x}(\cdot)$ be the solution to the equation (13) with initial condition $\hat{x}(t_0) = x_0$. Then the controller (27), (10) associated with the switching sequence $\{i_j\}_{j=0}^{N-1}$ where $i_j \stackrel{\Delta}{=} i_j(\hat{x}(t_j))$ solves the output feedback robust control problem (11) with $\tilde{V}(\cdot) \equiv V_0(\cdot)$.

Proof Let $M(\cdot)$ be a function and $W(\cdot,\cdot,\cdot,\cdot)$ is defined by (14). Consider the problem

$$\tilde{F}_j^i(\hat{x}_j, \hat{x}_{j+1}, M(\cdot)) \stackrel{\Delta}{=} \sup_{y(\cdot) \in \mathbf{L}_2[t_j, t_{j+1})} M(\hat{x}(t_{j+1})) +$$
$$\int_{t_j}^{t_{j+1}} W(t, \hat{x}(t), L_i(t)y(t), y(t))dt] \quad (33)$$

where the supremum is taken over all solutions to the system (13) with $y(\cdot) \in \mathbf{L}_2[t_j, t_{j+1})$ and boundary conditions $\hat{x}(t_j) = \hat{x}_j$ and $\hat{x}(t_{j+1}) = \hat{x}_{j+1}$. The standard optimal control theory (see e.g. [9]) implies that if condition (30) holds for Hamiltonian system (28), then the supremum in (33) is achieved and $\tilde{F}_j^i(\hat{x}_j, \hat{x}_{j+1}, M(\cdot)) = \hat{x}(t_j)'p(t_j) - \hat{x}(t_{j+1})'p(t_{j+1}) + M(\hat{x}_{j+1})$ where $[\hat{x}(\cdot), p(\cdot)]$ is the solution to the system (28) with boundary conditions $\hat{x}(t_j) = \hat{x}_j$ and $\hat{x}(t_{j+1}) = \hat{x}_{j+1}$. From (29) and (30) we obtain that $\hat{x}(t_j)'p(t_j) - \hat{x}(t_{j+1})'p(t_{j+1}) = \hat{F}_j^i(\hat{x}_j, \hat{x}_{j+1})$. Hence,

$$F_j^i(\hat{x}_j, M(\cdot)) = \sup_{\hat{x}_{j+1} \in \mathbf{R}^n} \left[M(\hat{x}_{j+1}) + \hat{F}_j^i(\hat{x}_j, \hat{x}_{j+1})\right]$$

where F_j^i is defined by (15). Now the statement follows from Theorem 2. □

References

1. A. Gollu and P.P. Varaiya. Hybrid dynamical systems. In *Proceedings of the 28rd IEEE Conference on Decision and Control*, Tampa, 1989.
2. P.J. Antsaklis, J.A. Stiver, and M. Lemmon. Hybrid systems modeling and autonomous control systems. In R.L. Grossman, A. Nerode, A.P. Ravn, and H. Rishel, editors, *Hybrid Systems*. Springer-Verlag, New York, 1993.
3. R.W. Brockett. Hybrid models for motion control systems. In H.L. Trentelman and J.C. Willems, editors, *Essays in Control*. Birkhauser, Boston, 1993.
4. M.S. Branicky, V.S. Borkar, and S.K. Mitter. A unified framework for hybrid control. In *Proceedings of the 33rd IEEE Conference on Decision and Control*, Lake Buena Vista, Fl, 1994.
5. P.P. Varaiya. Smart cars on smart roads: Problems of control. *IEEE Transactions on Automatic Control*, 38(2):195–207, 1993.
6. T. Basar and P. Bernhard. *H^∞-Optimal Control and Related Minimax Design Problems: A Dynamic Game Approach*. Birkhäuser, Boston, 1991.
7. P. P. Khargonekar, K. M. Nagpal, and K. R. Poolla. H_∞ control with transients. *SIAM Journal on Control and Optimization*, 29(6):1373–1393, 1991.
8. M.R. James and J.S. Baras. Robust H infinity output feedback control for nonlinear systems. *IEEE Transactions on Automatic Control*, 40(6):1007–1017, 1995.
9. F. L. Lewis. *Optimal Control*. Wiley, New York, 1986.
10. D. P. Bertsekas and I. B. Rhodes. Recursive state estimation for a set-membership description of uncertainty. *IEEE Transactions on Automatic Control*, 16(2):117–128, 1971.

A DES Approach to Control of Hybrid Dynamical Systems

Jörg Raisch[1] * and Siu O'Young[2] **

[1] Institut für Systemdynamik und Regelungstechnik
Universität Stuttgart
Pfaffenwaldring 9
D-70550 Stuttgart, FR Germany
email: raisch@isr.uni-stuttgart.de
[2] Systems Control Group
Department of Electrical and Computer Engineering
University of Toronto
Toronto, Ontario, Canada, M5S 1A4
email: oyoung@control.utoronto.ca

Abstract. We consider a special discrete-time hybrid problem: the plant state "lives" in $\mathbb{R}^n$ and is affected by real-valued norm-bounded disturbances; the control input and measurement signals are sequences of symbols. The control problem is to find a feedback strategy which maps the sequence of measurement symbols into an appropriate sequence of plant input symbols. It is converted into, and solved as, a supervisory control problem for discrete-event systems (DES).

1 Introduction

We consider a special class of hybrid dynamical systems: the plant state evolves in $\mathbb{R}^n$ and is affected by real-valued unknown but bounded disturbances, whereas control input and measurement signals are discrete-valued, or symbolic. The problem will be discussed in a discrete-time framework, i.e. the domain of all signals will be $\{t_0, t_1, \ldots\}$. This understood, the adjectives "discrete" and "continuous" will in the sequel only be used to refer to the *codomain* of signals: the codomain of a discrete, or discrete-valued, signal is a set of symbols, which, for our purposes, will be assumed to be finite (e.g. { "valve open", "valve closed" } or { "liquid level too low", "ok", "too high" }). The codomain of a continuous, or continuous-valued, signal are the real numbers.

In this setting, the control problem is to find a feedback strategy which maps the sequence of measurement symbols into an appropriate sequence of control symbols. Such problems frequently arise in process control (and other areas of application): process models typically have a continuous state space, but

* Research supported by Deutsche Forschungsgemeinschaft under Grant Ra 516/2-1
** Research supported by the Information Technology Research Centre and Condata Technologies Ltd., both of Ontario, Canada

continuous *and* discrete control inputs and measurement signals. Often, there is also a clearly defined hierarchical structure where feedback loops from continuous measurement to continuous control variables are interpreted to be "low level" (dealing, for example, with set-point regulation), and discrete signals are used for "high level", or supervisory, control. Examples for the latter are start-up/shut-down procedures and handling of "irregularities" (represented by discrete alarm signals). In this paper, we will take plant model and continuous control loops as an entity P ("the plant"), for which a discrete controller K has to be designed.

Our solution is as follows: in a first step, we convert the hybrid problem to a nondeterministic discrete one by "lumping" all states which are compatible with finite-length strings of measurement and control symbols and the dynamical plant model. Conceptually similar approaches have been suggested by *Antsaklis* and co-workers (e.g. [1, 11]) and *Lunze* (e.g. [4, 5]); our approach, however, is "finer" as it is based not only on *present* measurement information but also on strings of *past* control and measurement symbols. The resulting problem is then formulated in a discrete-event control framework and is solved by applying "limited lookahead policies" in the style of *Chung et al.* [3]. In the spirit of much of the work in DES (discrete event systems) theory (e.g. [9, 10]), we consider it desirable that the supervisory control level is minimally restrictive. Remaining degrees of freedom can then be exploited by lower levels in the control hierarchy. This contribution extends earlier work by the authors [7, 8]: it discusses a broader class of models and includes the effects of signal and model uncertainty; another difference is the restriction to *fixed-length* strings of symbols, which facilitates both computation and interpretation of the resulting discrete model. In [6], which appeared in the "Hybrid Systems II" volume [2], a complementary approach was suggested: there, hybrid control problems were solved within the "conventional" framework of continuous systems theory.

Our notation is as follows: variables (both discrete and continuous) at time t_k are represented by lower case letters; discrete variables have a subscript "d": $y_d[k]$, for example, stands for the discrete measurement at time t_k. Sets of symbols or real values are represented by capital letters, e.g. $y_d[k] \in Y_d$.

In section 2, we describe the class of models which can be handled within our framework. In section 3, we show how to transform the hybrid problem into a discrete one. In section 4, limited lookahead control policies are applied to the resulting discrete problem. Computational details are given in section 5.

2 The Plant Model

The plant is modeled as a discrete-time dynamic system:

$$x[k+1] = \underbrace{f(u_d[k])x[k] + g(u_d[k]) + h(u_d[k])w[k]}_{:=\delta(x[k],\, u_d[k],\, w[k])} + \delta_\Delta(x[k],\, u_d[k],\, w[k]) \quad (1)$$

$$z_d[k] = Q_z(C_z x[k]) := q_z(x[k]), \quad (2)$$

$$y_d[k] = Q_y(C_y x[k]) := q_y(x[k]). \quad (3)$$

$k \in \{0,1,2,\ldots\}$ is the time index, $x[k] \in \mathbb{R}^n$ the state at time t_k, and $w[k] \in \mathbb{R}^r$ an unknown but bounded disturbance:

$$w[k] \in W := \{w \mid w \in \mathbb{R}^r, \|w\|_\infty \leq 1\} \ ,$$

where $\|w\|_\infty = \max_i |w_i|$. $u_d[k] \in U_d$, $z_d[k] \in Z_d$ and $y_d[k] \in Y_d$ are control, output and measurement symbols, respectively, at time t_k. The sets U_d, Z_d and Y_d are finite:

$$U_d = \{u_d^{(1)}, \ldots, u_d^{(\alpha)}\}, \quad Z_d = \{z_d^{(1)}, \ldots, z_d^{(\beta)}\}, \quad Y_d = \{y_d^{(1)}, \ldots, y_d^{(\gamma)}\}.$$

Output symbols are used to specify desired performance[3]; the sequence of measurement symbols is fed back into a controller, which, in response, generates a sequence of control symbols. $\delta : \mathbb{R}^n \times U_d \times \mathbb{R}^r \to \mathbb{R}^n$ is the nominal one-step transition function. δ_Δ in (1) represents model uncertainty. For any given control symbol $u_d \in U_d$, $\delta_\Delta(x, u_d, w) := \delta_{u\Delta}(x, w)$ is an unknown but norm-bounded map from $\mathbb{R}^n \times \mathbb{R}^r$ into $\mathbb{R}^n$. Hence, model errors belong to the class

$$\Delta := \{\delta_{u\Delta}(x,w) \mid \delta_{u\Delta}(0,0) = 0; \ \|\delta_{u\Delta}\| \leq b(u_d)\} \ ,$$

where

$$\|\delta_{u\Delta}\| := \sup_{(x,w)\in \mathbb{R}^n \times W, (x,w)\neq 0} \frac{\|\delta_{u\Delta}(x,w)\|_\infty}{\max(\|x\|_\infty, \|w\|_\infty)} \ .$$

The only assumption regarding the functions $f : U_d \to \mathbb{R}^{n\times n}$, $h : U_d \to \mathbb{R}^{n\times r}$, and $g : U_d \to \mathbb{R}^n$ is that the "combined" function $(f, g, h) : U_d \to \mathbb{R}^{n\times n} \times \mathbb{R}^n \times \mathbb{R}^{n\times r}$ is injective.

The output and measurement maps $q_z : \mathbb{R}^n \to Z_d$ and $q_y : \mathbb{R}^n \to Y_d$ are onto. They induce equivalence relations on $\mathbb{R}^n$, their cosets (or equivalence classes) are referred to as z-cells and y-cells. C_z and C_y in (2) and (3) are real $l \times n$- and $p \times n$-matrices. The "quantizers" Q_z and Q_y partition $\mathbb{R}^l$ and $\mathbb{R}^p$ into finitely many rectangular boxes with edges parallel to the coordinate axes.

Example 1. This example is based on the three-tank system discussed in [6]. To facilitate graphical representation of results, we consider the simplified version shown in Fig. 1.

The states x_1 and x_2 describe the deviation of the water levels in tank A and B from a common reference value. The valve between the two tanks is either "open" or "closed". The pump can perform three different actions: it can pump water *into* or *from* tank A (at a constant rate r), or it can be switched off. Hence, in this example, U_d consists of $2 \cdot 3$ symbols:

[3] Clearly, the choice of the outputs is part of the design process. In principle, Z_d can be a discrete *or* a continuous set. In this contribution, we address the case where design specifications are "naturally" formulated in discrete terms; this emphasizes the discrete part of the hybrid control problem, and discrete-event control theory provides the tools for its solution. If specifications need to be formulated exclusively in terms of continuous variables, the balance would be tipped the other way. For an approach to the latter problem, see [6] and the references therein.

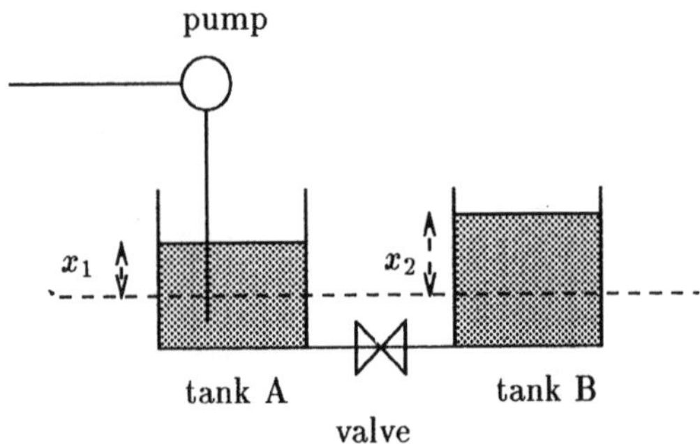

Fig. 1. Example 1

$u_d^{(1)}$:= "valve open" & "pumping water into tank A"
$u_d^{(2)}$:= "valve open" & "pumping water from tank A"
$u_d^{(3)}$:= "valve open" & "pump switched off"
$u_d^{(4)}$:= "valve closed" & "pumping water into tank A"
$u_d^{(5)}$:= "valve closed" & "pumping water from tank A"
$u_d^{(6)}$:= "valve closed" & "pump switched off"

We assume that the flow rate between the two tanks is $a(x_2 - x_1)$, and denote the cross section of each tank by F. Δt is the (constant) sampling interval. Then, we get:

$$f(u_d^{(i)}) = e^{\tilde{f}(u_d^{(i)})\Delta t}, \quad i = 1, \ldots, 6,$$

$$\tilde{f}(u_d^{(i)}) = \frac{1}{F}\begin{bmatrix} -a & a \\ a & -a \end{bmatrix}, \quad i = 1, 2, 3,$$

$$\tilde{f}(u_d^{(i)}) = \begin{bmatrix} 0 & 0 \\ 0 & 0 \end{bmatrix}, \quad i = 4, 5, 6,$$

$$g(u_d^{(i)}) = \int_0^{\Delta t} e^{\tilde{f}(u_d^{(i)})(\Delta t - \tau)}\tilde{g}(u_d^{(i)})\,\mathrm{d}\,\tau, \quad i = 1, \ldots 6,$$

$$\tilde{g}(u_d^{(1)}) = \tilde{g}(u_d^{(4)}) = \frac{1}{F}\begin{bmatrix} r \\ 0 \end{bmatrix},$$

$$\tilde{g}(u_d^{(2)}) = \tilde{g}(u_d^{(5)}) = \frac{1}{F}\begin{bmatrix} -r \\ 0 \end{bmatrix},$$

$$\tilde{g}(u_d^{(3)}) = \tilde{g}(u_d^{(6)}) = \begin{bmatrix} 0 \\ 0 \end{bmatrix}.$$

The parameters in this example are chosen as $F = 1m^2$, $a = 10^{-3}m^2\,sec^{-1}$, and $r = 10^{-3}m^3\,sec^{-1}$.

Suppose, control specifications are in terms of both state variables, and quantized measurements of x_1 and x_2 are available. Then, the output equations (2), (3) become $z_d[k] = Q_z(x[k])$ and $y_d[k] = Q_y(x[k])$.

3 Plant State Estimates

At time t_k, the information on the state x which is available to the outside world consists of a string of observed measurement symbols, $y_d[k]$, ..., $y_d[0]$, and a string of previously applied control symbols, $u_d[k-1]$, ..., $u_d[0]$. Clearly, this information increases as time progresses and, with the exception of very few special cases, cannot be represented in a finite way. Hence, we discard "old" data and work with finite strings of symbols not exceeding a given maximum length.

$$s^*[k] := \begin{cases} ([y_d[k], \ldots, y_d[0]], [u_d[k-1], \ldots, u_d[0]]), & if\ k = 0, 1, \ldots, v-1 \\ ([y_d[k], \ldots, y_d[k-v]], [u_d[k-1], \ldots, u_d[k-v]]), & if\ k \geq v \end{cases} \tag{4}$$

is called the *current history* of the process, if t_k represents the present sampling instant. If t_k is *any* (not necessarily the present) sampling instant, $s^*[k]$ is simply referred to as a *history* of the process at time t_k. It is important to note that, in our terminology, the *current history* consists of observed data, whereas a *history* is just a postulated (and therefore nonunique) collection of symbols from U_d and Y_d of the form (4). $y_d^*[k]$ and $u_d^*[k-1]$ are the strings of measurement and control symbols in $s^*[k]$. The "forgetting operator" $\mathcal{F}$ deletes the "oldest" symbol from strings $y_d^*[k]$ and $u_d^*[k-1]$, if $k \geq v$:

$$\mathcal{F}(y_d^*[k]) := \begin{cases} [y_d[k], \ldots, y_d[0]], & if\ k = 0, 1, \ldots, v-1 \\ [y_d[k], \ldots, y_d[k-v+1]], & if\ k \geq v. \end{cases}$$

Definition 1. The history $s^*[k+1]$ is a *successor* of $s^*[k]$ if there exists a symbol $y_d^{(i)} \in Y_d$ and an input $u_d^{(j)} \in U_d$ such that $y_d^*[k+1] = [y_d^{(i)}, \mathcal{F}(y_d^*[k])]$ and $u_d^*[k] = [u_d^{(j)}, \mathcal{F}(u_d^*[k-1])]$. Similarly, $s^*[k]$ is referred to as a *predecessor* of $s^*[k+1]$.

Definition 2. A history $s^*[k]$ is called *feasible* if its strings of input and measurement symbols are compatible with the plant model (1), (3), i.e. if there exists an $x[\max(k-v, 0)] \in \mathbb{R}^n$, disturbances $w[i] \in W$, $i = \max(k-v, 0), \ldots, k-1$, and a perturbation $\delta_\Delta \in \Delta$ such that applying the input string $u_d^*[k-1]$ actually produces $y_d^*[k]$ as string of measurements.

Remark. If the model set covers the real system, the current history is feasible by definition – all its symbols have actually been observed.

To determine an appropriate sequence of control inputs, an intuitively appealing first step is to find the subsets of $\mathbb{R}^n$ which are compatible with the current history and its successors.

Definition 3. The *plant state estimate* $\hat{X}[k]$ is the set of all plant states $x[k] \in \mathbb{R}^n$ which are compatible with a given history $s^*[k] = (y_d^*[k], u_d^*[k-1])$. With $\rho := \max(k - v, 0)$, it can be defined recursively by:

$$\begin{aligned} \Xi[\rho] &:= \{x \mid y_d[\rho] = q_y(x)\} & (5)\\ \Xi[i] &:= \{x \mid y_d[i] = q_y(x)\} \cap \{x \mid x = \delta(\xi, u_d[i-1], w) + \delta_{u\Delta}(\xi, w) & (6)\\ &\quad \& \ \xi \in \Xi[i-1] \ \& \ w \in W \ \& \ \delta_{u\Delta} \in \Delta\}, \quad i = \rho+1, \ldots, k, \\ \hat{X}[k] &:= \Xi[k] & (7)\end{aligned}$$

Thus, the "initial condition" $\Xi(\rho)$ is just the y–cell corresponding to the measurement symbol $y_d[\rho]$. The set $\Xi[i]$ is obtained by a "worst-case" propagation of the set $\Xi[i-1]$ via the plant state equation (1) and a subsequent intersection with the y-cell corresponding to the next measurement symbol $y_d[i]$.

The (one-step) *plant state prediction* $\hat{X}_{k-1}[k]$ is the set of all plant states $x[k] \in \mathbb{R}^n$ which are compatible with $(\mathcal{F}(y_d^*[k-1]), \mathcal{F}(u_d^*[k-2]))$ and a control symbol $u_d[k-1]$. It can be determined by

$$\begin{aligned} \Xi[\rho] &:= \{x \mid y_d[\rho] = q_y(x)\} & (8)\\ \Xi[i] &:= \{x \mid y_d[i] = q_y(x)\} \cap \{x \mid x = \delta(\xi, u_d[i-1], w) + \delta_{u\Delta}(\xi, w) & (9)\\ &\quad \& \ \xi \in \Xi[i-1] \ \& \ w \in W \ \& \ \delta_{u\Delta} \in \Delta\}, \quad i = \rho+1, \ldots, k-1, \\ \hat{X}_{k-1}[k] &:= \{x \mid x = \delta(\xi, u_d[k-1], w) + \delta_{u\Delta}(\xi, w) \ \& \ \xi \in \Xi[k-1] & (10)\\ &\quad \& \ w \in W \ \& \ \delta_{u\Delta} \in \Delta\}.\end{aligned}$$

Remark. It is trivial to note that $\hat{X}[k] \subseteq \{x \mid y_d[k] = q_y(x)\}$, and in most cases the inclusion will be proper – by considering *strings* instead of only using one measurement symbol we cannot lose and will in general gain accuracy. Obviously, the plant state estimate $\hat{X}[k]$ is nonempty if and only if the corresponding history $s^*[k]$ is feasible.

Remark. The plant state estimates corresponding to all (feasible) histories form a cover for $\mathbb{R}^n$. It is obvious that the set of all feasible histories can be interpreted as the states of a nondeterministic automaton, the latter constituting a discrete dynamical model for the underlying continuous system (1), (3).

The following definition formalizes the problem of whether the plant state can be forced to stay within a given z-cell:

Definition 4. The system (1) – (3) with feasible history $s^*[k]$, or, equivalently, with nonempty plant state estimate $\hat{X}[k]$, is said to be *confinable* to cell $z_d^{(j)}$ if (i) $\hat{X}[k] \subseteq \{x|z_d^{(j)} = q_z(x)\}$ and (ii) there exists a sequence of control symbols $u_d[k+i]$, $i = 0, 1, 2, \ldots$, such that all plant state estimates $\hat{X}[k+i] \subseteq \{x|z_d^{(j)} = q_z(x)\}$, $i = 1, 2, \ldots$

Theorem 5. *The system (1) – (3) with history $s^*[k]$ is confinable to cell $z_d^{(j)}$ if (i) $\hat{X}[k] \subseteq \{x|z_d^{(j)} = q_z(x)\}$ and (ii) for every history for which (i) holds there exists at least one value for $u_d[k]$ such that the plant state prediction $\hat{X}_k[k+1]$ satisfies $\hat{X}_k[k+1] \subseteq \{x|z_d^{(j)} = q_z(x)\}$.*

Proof. Omitted because of space restrictions.

Example 1 (revisited): The system in example 1 is simulated for one hour with valve open and water being pumped into tank A. The initial conditions are $x_1(t_0) = 0.6\text{m}$ and $x_2(t_0) = 0.5\text{m}$. Threshold values for measurement quantization in both states are {0m, 1m, 2m, 3m}. Hence, we have 25 measurement symbols $y_d^{(1)}, \ldots, y_d^{(25)}$. Figure 2 shows the (set-valued) plant state estimates[4], when the sampling interval is 4 minutes and v, the maximum length of histories, is 8. The evolution of the estimates in time is very intuitive: the first three measurement symbols all indicate that the current state is in the quantization box [0m, 1m] × [0m, 1m]. Nevertheless, the estimates get "finer" as knowledge of plant dynamics and past control inputs imply that the state must have "moved" in a certain direction inside the box. Once the state crosses a quantization threshold (i.e. the measurement symbol changes), the quality of the estimate improves drastically.

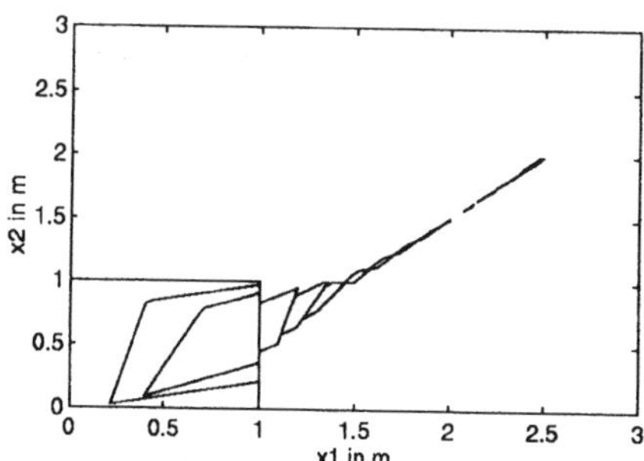

Fig. 2. Evolution of state estimate for a sampling interval of 4 minutes.

4 Control For Safety

Suppose the control objective is to avoid, via disablement of control symbols in U_d, the entrance into a subset of forbidden, or "bad", z-cells: $Z_B \subseteq Z_d$. We will present an on-line strategy for generating least restrictive disablement patterns based on plant state estimates corresponding to feasible successors of the current history.

An *m-step tree* is a pictorial representation of the current history $s^*[k]$ and the set of all feasible j-step successors ($0 < j \leq m$; m a given positive integer). $s^*[k]$ is referred to as the *root node*, its feasible j-step successors as *nodes* of the tree; feasible m-step successors are called *exit nodes* and all non-exit nodes are referred to as *interior nodes*. Branches between nodes are labelled by control symbols $u_d^{(j)} \in U_d$ as shown in Fig. 3. Note that the tree is in general nondeterministic: a

[4] How to do the computations is discussed in section 5.

node may have more than one feasible successor when a certain control symbol $u_d^{(j)}$ is applied. Branches originating from the same node and carrying the same label are called *partners*.

The root node corresponds to the set $\hat{X}[k] \subset \mathbb{R}^n$ (the current plant state estimate), all other nodes to plant state estimates of feasible j-step successors of the current history, $j = 1, \ldots, m$. A node is called ***forbidden*** if the intersection of the corresponding plant state estimate and any of the forbidden z-cells is non-empty. Forbidden nodes are shown as black dots (Fig. 3), nodes which are confinable to a non-forbidden z-cell as squares. All other nodes are represented by circles. If a node is forbidden or confinable to a non-forbidden z-cell, none of its successors is shown in the tree: successors of a forbidden node are irrelevant by definition; on the other hand, once a confinable (and non-forbidden) node is entered, control decision can always be deferred since safety is guaranteed by simply staying within the present z-cell.

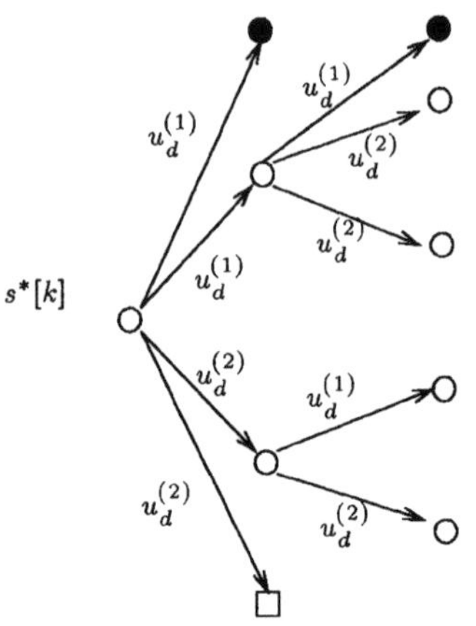

Fig. 3. Example of a tree for $m = 2$, $U_d = \{u_d^{(1)}, u_d^{(2)}\}$, $Y_d = \{y_d^{(1)}, y_d^{(2)}\}$.

A *subtree* is any part of an m-step tree that one gets by disabling, at any time j, $k \leq j < k + m$, any combination of up to α control symbols. A subtree shares the same root node as its parent tree and all nodes of a subtree are connected to the root node via some non-disabled branches. Subtrees of a parent tree can be partially ordered in the sense that if T_1 and T_2 are two subtrees of the same parent tree, then $T_1 \subseteq T_2$ if all branches of T_1 are also in T_2. In this case, we say that T_2 is *larger* than T_1. It is obvious that the smallest subtree consists only of one root node which has no exiting branch. Disabling control symbols can be represented graphically as "pruning" of branches of the tree, but not all subtrees are physically realizable via disablement of control symbols: obviously, a branch can only be pruned when all its partners are being pruned.

Definition 6. A subtree of an m-step tree T is *admissible* if it has no branch with a pruned partner, and every interior node which is neither confinable nor forbidden has at least one exiting branch. It is *legal* if its root is not forbidden and all branches entering into a forbidden node have been pruned. It is *safe* if it is legal and all its branches terminate in confinable nodes.

Note that in an admissible subtree, at any time k, at most $\alpha - 1$ control symbols can be disabled (α is the number of symbols in U_d) – we can't stop time.

Let T_1 and T_2 be two subtrees of a given tree T. Then, the *union* of T_1 and T_2, denoted by the symbol $T_1 \cup T_2$, represents the usual merging of subtrees, and it is clear that $T_1 \cup T_2$ is also a subtree of T. The properties of the $\cup$ operation imply the following:

Theorem 7. *The admissibility, legality and safety properties are preserved by the union operation on subtrees.*

Proof. (Admissibility) Let T_1 and T_2 be admissible subtrees of T. Define $T_3 := T_1 \cup T_2$. Let N_1, N_2, and N_3 be the sets of nodes of T_1, T_2 and T_3, respectively. $\forall n \in N_3$, $\exists i, i = 1, 2$, $n \in N_i$; hence, by admissibility of T_i, no branch exiting from n has a pruned partner. Suppose $n \in N_3$ is an interior node of T_3 which is neither confinable nor forbidden. Then, n has at least one exiting branch in T_1 or T_2 and hence in T_3. (Legality) Let T_1 and T_2 be admissible subtrees of T; let $T_3 := T_1 \cup T_2$. By the legality of T_1 and T_2, the tree T_3 does not contain any forbidden node. (Safety) Similarly, if T_1 and T_2 are safe, all branches of T_1 and T_2 terminate in confinable nodes. Therefore do the branches of T_3.

Example 2. Consider the 2-step tree in Figure 4 which is obtained by pruning the dotted branches. It is legal but not safe because it can exit via Nodes 4 or

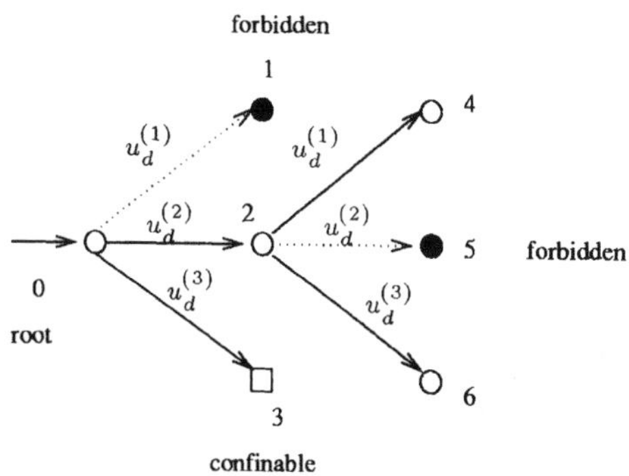

Fig. 4. Safety Tree

6 which are not confinable. Transitions from Node 0 to 1 and from Node 2 to 5

are pruned because Nodes 1 and 5 are forbidden. Control $u_d^{(1)}$ must therefore be disabled at the root node. Entrance into Node 3 via control $u_d^{(3)}$ is safe because there always exists a control sequence to keep the state estimate within the z-cell associated with Node 3. Control $u_d^{(3)}$ is therefore allowed without the need to examine the properties of the successors to Node 3. The disablement of $u_d^{(2)}$ at the root depends on the choice of a pessimistic or optimistic control strategy.

4.1 A Pessimistic Strategy

From the closure property in Theorem 7, we have the following result.

Theorem 8. *Assume at least one subtree of a given tree is admissible and safe. Then, there exists a (unique) largest subtree which is admissible and safe.*

Proof. By Theorem 7, admissibility and safety are preserved by the union operation $\cup$ on subtrees; hence, the set of admissible and safe subtrees of a given tree forms an upper semi-lattice with $\subseteq$ and $\cup$ as the partial ordering and the join operator. Therefore, a unique top (largest) element in that set exists.

Let $\tilde{T}$ be the largest subtree of an m-step decision tree T which is admissible and safe. A pessimistic strategy is to issue a disablement pattern based on $\tilde{T}$; in other words, control symbols associated with branches in T which do not appear in $\tilde{T}$ are to be disabled. For example, in Figure 4, $\tilde{T}$ consists of only Nodes 0 and 3, and the control inputs $u_d^{(1)}$ and $u_d^{(2)}$ at the root are disabled. A pessimistic strategy can be interpreted as deeming Nodes 4 and 6, the exit nodes, to be forbidden because their successors are not known.

4.2 An Optimistic Strategy

From the closure property in Theorem 7, we have the following result.

Theorem 9. *Assume at least one subtree of a given tree T is admissible and legal. Then, there exists a (unique) largest subtree which is admissible and legal.*

Proof. By Theorem 7, admissibility and legality are preserved by the union operation $\cup$ on subtrees; hence, the set of admissible and legal subtrees of a given tree forms an upper semi-lattice with $\subseteq$ and $\cup$ as the partial ordering and the join operator. Therefore, a unique top (largest) element in that set exists.

Let $\bar{T}$ be the largest subtree of an m-step tree T which is admissible and legal. An optimistic strategy is to issue a disablement pattern based on $\bar{T}$; in other words, control symbols associated with branches in T which do not appear in $\bar{T}$ are to be disabled. For example, in Figure 4, $\bar{T}$ consists of all nodes in T except the forbidden Nodes 1 and 5, and only control symbol $u_d^{(1)}$ is disabled at the root. An optimistic strategy can be interpreted as deeming Nodes 4 and 6, the exit nodes, to be acceptable. The potential danger of this optimism is that all successors to Nodes 4 and 6 might turn out to be forbidden nodes. In this case, all available control will eventually be illegal if control $u_d^{(2)}$ has been actuated at the root.

5 Computation

The decision tree in section 4 can be constructed off-line by computing the plant state estimates corresponding to the finite number of histories (hence determining feasibility of histories), and by establishing whether these sets (if nonempty) intersect any forbidden z-cell.

In the *nominal* case ($\delta_\Delta = 0$), this can be done without any approximations: consider the quantization box corresponding to a certain measurement symbol $y_d[k]$. Denote the vectors of its upper and lower bounds by $\hat{y}[k]$ and $\check{y}[k]$, respectively: $\check{y}[k] < \{\zeta | Q_y(\zeta) = y_d[k]\} \leq \hat{y}[k]$, where the "<" and "≤"-signs are understood to be elementwise. $\rho := \max(k - v, 0)$. The case $k = 0$ is trivial. For $k \geq 1$, define

$$\hat{y}_P := \begin{bmatrix} \hat{y}[k-1] \\ \vdots \\ \hat{y}[\rho] \end{bmatrix}, \quad \check{y}_P := \begin{bmatrix} \check{y}[k-1] \\ \vdots \\ \check{y}[\rho] \end{bmatrix}, \quad g_P := \begin{bmatrix} g(u_d[k-1]) \\ \vdots \\ g(u_d[\rho]) \end{bmatrix}, \quad w_P := \begin{bmatrix} w[k-1] \\ \vdots \\ w[\rho] \end{bmatrix},$$

i.e. collect the "forcing terms" $g(u_d[k-1]), \ldots, g(u_d[\rho])$ in g_P and the (unknown) disturbance inputs $w[k-1], \ldots, w[\rho]$ in w_P. 1_{vr} and I_{vr} denote a column vector with $(\min(k,v)r)$ "ones" and the $(\min(k,v)r)$-dimensional identity matrix. f_i and h_i are short for (the matrices) $f(u_d[i])$ and $h(u_d[i])$. Then, the history $s^*[k]$ is feasible if and only if the set of solutions $[x^T[k]\ w_P^T]^T$ for the following linear inequalities is nonempty:

$$\begin{bmatrix} \check{y}[k] \\ \check{y}_P \\ -1_{vr} \end{bmatrix} + \begin{bmatrix} 0 \\ \Phi_{PU} \\ 0 \end{bmatrix} g_P < \begin{bmatrix} C_y & 0 \\ \begin{bmatrix} C_y f_{k-1}^{-1} \\ \vdots \\ C_y \prod_{i=\rho}^{k-1} f_i^{-1} \end{bmatrix} & \Phi_{PW} \\ 0 & I_{vr} \end{bmatrix} \begin{bmatrix} x[k] \\ w_P \end{bmatrix} \leq \begin{bmatrix} \hat{y}[k] \\ \hat{y}_P \\ 1_{vr} \end{bmatrix} + \begin{bmatrix} 0 \\ \Phi_{PU} \\ 0 \end{bmatrix} g_P$$

where

$$\Phi_{PU} := \begin{bmatrix} C_y f_{k-1}^{-1} & 0 & \cdots & 0 \\ C_y f_{k-2}^{-1} f_{k-1}^{-1} & C_y f_{k-2}^{-1} & \cdots & 0 \\ \vdots & & \ddots & \vdots \\ C_y \prod_{i=\rho}^{k-1} f_i^{-1} & \cdots & \cdots & C_y f_\rho^{-1} \end{bmatrix},$$

$$\Phi_{PW} := -\begin{bmatrix} C_y f_{k-1}^{-1} h_{k-1} & 0 & \cdots & 0 \\ C_y f_{k-2}^{-1} f_{k-1}^{-1} h_{k-1} & C_y f_{k-2}^{-1} h_{k-2} & \cdots & 0 \\ \vdots & & \ddots & \vdots \\ C_y \prod_{i=\rho}^{k-1} f_i^{-1} h_{k-1} & \cdots & \cdots & C_y f_\rho^{-1} h_\rho \end{bmatrix},$$

and $\prod$ means "right product" (i.e.:$\prod_{i=\rho}^{k-1} f_i^{-1} = f_\rho^{-1} \cdots f_{k-1}^{-1}$). Existence of a solution for this set of inequalities can be checked using the "feasibility part" of any linear programming algorithm. By adding another set of inequalities, it can then easily be determined whether the corresponding plant state estimate intersects any forbidden z-cell.

In the perturbed case ($\delta_\Delta \neq 0$), a similar set of inequalities can be used to construct the decision tree. A possible procedure is to introduce an additional (fictitious) variable which accounts for the effects of model uncertainty. As the norm of this additional term depends on the norm of the state, one ends up with an *approximate* solution. It is *conservative* in the sense that it generates a decision tree with too many nodes, and too many nodes declared to be forbidden. A safe (legal) subtree of such a conservative decision tree will of course correspond to implementation of a safe (legal) supervisory control policy for the underlying system.

6 Conclusions

We have considered a discrete-event framework for a particular hybrid control problem: by taking into account present *and* past measurement information, we have improved the accuracy of the non-deterministic discrete substitute for the underlying continuous model.

References

1. P. J. Antsaklis, J. A. Stiver, and M. Lemmon. Hybrid system modelling and autonomous control systems. In R. L. Grossman, A. Nerode, A. P. Ravn, and H. Rischel, editors, *Hybrid Systems*, pages 366–392. Springer-Verlag, Berlin, 1993.
2. P. J. Antsaklis, W. Kohn, A. Nerode, and S. Sastry, editors, *Hybrid Systems II*, *Lecture Notes in Computer Science 999*, 1995. Springer-Verlag.
3. S. Chung, S. Lafortune, and F. Lin. Limited lookahead policies in supervisory control of discrete event systems. *IEEE Trans. Aut. Contr.*, 23:1921–1935, 1992.
4. J. Lunze. Qualitative modelling of linear dynamical systems with quantized state measurements. *Automatica*, 30:417–431, 1994.
5. J. Lunze. Stabilization of nonlinear systems by qualitative feedback controllers. *Int. J. Control*, 62: 109–128, 1995.
6. J. Raisch. Control of Continuous Plants by Symbolic Output Feedback. In [2], pages 370–390.
7. J. Raisch and S. D. O'Young. A discrete-time framework for control of hybrid systems. In *Proc. 1994 Hong Kong International Workshop on New Directions of Control and Manufacturing*, pages 34–40, 1994.
8. J. Raisch and S. D. O'Young. Symbolic control of uncertain hybrid systems. In *European Control Conference ECC95*, pages 2041–2046, Roma, 1995.
9. P. J. Ramadge. *Control and Supervision of Discrete Event Processes.* PhD thesis, University of Toronto, 1983.
10. P. J. Ramadge and W. M. Wonham. The control of discrete event systems. *Proceedings of the IEEE*, 77:81–98, 1989.
11. J. A. Stiver and P. J. Antsaklis. Modeling and analysis of hybrid control systems. In *Proc. 31st CDC*, pages 3748–3751, Tucson, 1992. IEEE.

Diagnostic Model-Checking for Real-Time Systems*

Kim G. Larsen[1] *Paul Pettersson*[2] *Wang Yi*[2**]

[1] BRICS*** , Aalborg University, DENMARK. E-mail: kgl@iesd.auc.dk
[2] Department of Computer Systems, Box 325, Uppsala University, S751 05, Uppsala, Sweden. E-mail: {paupet,yi}@docs.uu.se.

Abstract. UPPAAL is a new tool suit for automatic verification of networks of timed automata. In this paper we describe the diagnostic model-checking feature of UPPAAL and illustrates its usefulness through the debugging of (a version of) the Philips Audio-Control Protocol. Together with a graphical interface of UPPAAL this diagnostic feature allows for a number of errors to be more easily detected and corrected.

1 Introduction

UPPAAL is a new tool for automatic verification of safety and bounded liveness properties of real-time systems modeled as networks of timed automata [10]. The current version of UPPAAL deals with the traditionally encountered state-explosion problem by combining on-the-fly verification with a symbolic technique based on constraint-solving. UPPAAL contains a suit of tools and features including:

- a graphical interface allowing networks of timed automata to be defined by drawing,
- an automatic compilation of the graphical definition into a textual format used by the model-checker, thus supporting the important principle "what you see is what you verify" (WYSIWYV),
- compilation of certain types of hybrid automata into ordinary timed automata (again supporting WYSIWYV), and
- in case verification of a particular real-time system fails (which happens more often than not), a *diagnostic* trace is automatically reported by UPPAAL in order to facilitate debugging. Here the principle supported could be called "What You Don't Verify You Are Explained"(WYDVYAE).

This paper concentrates on describing the diagnostic model-checking feature of UPPAAL, and on demonstrating its usefulness through the debugging of an early version of the Philips Audio-Control Protocol [6].

The paper is organized as follows: In the next section we give a short review of the notions of timed automata and networks; in section 3 the logic for safety and

* This work has been supported by the European Communieties (under CONCUR2 and REACT), NUTEK (Swedish Board for Technical Development) and TFR (Swedish Technical Research Council)

** This author would also like to thank the Chinese NSF and the Hong Kong Wang's Foundation for supporting a visit to the Institute of Software, Chinese Academy of Sciences, in 1995.

*** Basic Research in Computer Science, Centre of the Danish National Research Foundation.

bounded liveness properties is presented. Section 4 describes the diagnostic model-checking procedure; in section 5 we show how these results have been applied in a case study where Philips Audio-Control Protocol was analyzed.

2 Real-Time Systems

We shall use *timed transition systems* as a basic semantical model for real-time systems. The type of systems we are studying will be a particular class of timed transition systems that are syntactically described by *networks of timed automata* [12, 8].

2.1 Timed Transition Systems

A timed transition system is a labeled transition system with two types of labels: atomic actions and delay actions (i.e. positive reals), representing discrete and continuous changes of real-time systems.

Let *Act* be a finite set of actions and $\mathcal{P}$ be a set of atomic propositions. We use $\mathbf{R}$ to stand for the set of non-negative real numbers, Δ for the set of delay actions $\{\epsilon(d) \mid d \in \mathbf{R}\}$, and L for the union $Act \cup \Delta$.

Definition 1. *A timed transition system over Act and $\mathcal{P}$ is a tuple $\mathcal{S} = \langle S, s_0, \longrightarrow, V\rangle$, where S is a set of states, s_0 is the initial state, $\longrightarrow \subseteq S \times L \times S$ is a transition relation, and $V : S \rightarrow 2^{\mathcal{P}}$ is a proposition assignment function.* □

We will need for $\longrightarrow$ to satisfy the following well known properties:

- *(Time Determinism)* $s \xrightarrow{\epsilon(d)} s_1$ and $s \xrightarrow{\epsilon(d)} s_2 \Rightarrow s_1 = s_2$.
- *(Time Continuity)* $s \xrightarrow{\epsilon(d+e)} s' \Leftrightarrow \exists s''. s \xrightarrow{\epsilon(d)} s'' \xrightarrow{\epsilon(e)} s'$.

Whenever defined, we will use the notation s^d for the state satisfying $s \xrightarrow{\epsilon(d)} s^d$. Note that the state s^d is unique due to time determinism.

In order to study compositionality problems we introduce a parallel composition between timed transition systems. Following [7] we use synchronization functions that generalize a large range of existing notions of parallel compositions. A *synchronization function* f is a partial function $(Act \cup \{0\}) \times (Act \cup \{0\}) \hookrightarrow Act$, where 0 denotes a distinguished no-action symbol[4]. Now, let $\mathcal{S}_i = \langle S_i, s_{i,0}, \longrightarrow_i, V_i\rangle$, $i = 1, 2$, be two timed transition systems and let f be a synchronization function. Then the *parallel composition* $\mathcal{S}_1 \mid_f \mathcal{S}_2$ is the timed transition system $\langle S, s_0, \longrightarrow, V\rangle$, where $s_1 \mid_f s_2 \in S$ whenever $s_1 \in S_1$ and $s_2 \in S_2$, $s_0 = s_{1,0} \mid_f s_{2,0}$, $\longrightarrow$ is inductively defined as follows:

- $s_1 \mid_f s_2 \xrightarrow{c} s_1' \mid_f s_2'$ if $s_1 \xrightarrow{a}_1 s_1'$, $s_2 \xrightarrow{b}_2 s_2'$ and $f(a, b) = c$
- $s_1 \mid_f s_2 \xrightarrow{\epsilon(d)} s_1' \mid_f s_2'$ if $s_1 \xrightarrow{\epsilon(d)}_1 s_1'$ and $s_2 \xrightarrow{\epsilon(d)}_2 s_2'$

[4] We extend the transition relation of a timed transition system such that $s \xrightarrow{0} s'$ iff $s = s'$.

and finally, the proposition assignment function V is defined by $V(s_1 \mid_f s_2) = V_1(s_1) \cup V_2(s_2)$.

We now introduce the notion of a *trace*. A trace σ of a timed transition system is a finite alternating sequence of the form:

$$\sigma = s_0 \xrightarrow{\epsilon(d_0)} s_0' \xrightarrow{a_1} s_1 \xrightarrow{\epsilon(d_1)} s_1' \xrightarrow{a_2} s_2 \xrightarrow{\epsilon(d_2)} \dots \xrightarrow{a_n} s_n \xrightarrow{\epsilon(d_n)} s_n'$$

where $d_i \in \mathbf{R}$. A position π of a trace σ is a pair $\pi = (i, d)$ where $i \in 0 \dots n$ and $0 \leq d \leq d_i$. We use $\Delta(\sigma, \pi)$ to stand for the accumulated delay of the trace σ before the position π, i.e. $\Delta(\sigma, \pi) = \sum_{j<i} d_j + d$ and $\sigma(\pi)$ for the suffix of σ starting from π, i.e.

$$\sigma(\pi) = s_i^d \xrightarrow{\epsilon(d_i-d)} s_i' \xrightarrow{a_{i+1}} s_{i+1} \xrightarrow{\epsilon(d_{i+1})} \dots \xrightarrow{a_n} s_n \xrightarrow{\epsilon(d_n)} s_n'$$

Whenever $s \xrightarrow{l} s_0$ ($l \in L$) we shall denote by $s \xrightarrow{l} \sigma$ the trace obtained by extending σ[5]. We order positions lexicographically, denoted $\pi < \pi'$. Finally, we write $V(\sigma)$ for the set $V(s_0)$.

2.2 Networks of Timed Automata

A timed automaton [1] is a standard finite-state automaton extended with a finite collection of real-valued clocks. The clocks are assumed to proceed at the same rate and their values may be tested (compared with natural numbers) and reset (assigned to 0).

Definition Clock Constraints *Let C be a set of real-valued clocks. We use $\mathcal{B}(C)$ to stand for the set of formulas ranged over by g, generated by the following syntax: $g ::= c \mid g \wedge g$, where c is an atomic constraint of the form: $x \sim n$ or $x - y \sim n$ for $x, y \in C$, $\sim \in \{\leq, \geq, =, <, >\}$ and n being a natural number. We shall call $\mathcal{B}(C)$ clock constraints or clock constraint systems over C.* □

We shall use $\mathtt{tt}$ to stand for a constraint like $x \geq 0$ which is always true, and $\mathtt{f}$ for a constraint $x < 0$ which is always false as clocks can only have non-negative values.

Definition 2. *A timed automaton A over actions Act, atomic propositions $\mathcal{P}$ and clocks C is a tuple $\langle N, l_0, E, I, V\rangle$, where N is a finite set of nodes (control-nodes), l_0 is the initial node, and $E \subseteq N \times \mathcal{B}(C) \times Act \times 2^C \times N$ corresponds to the set of edges. In the case, $\langle l, g, a, r, l'\rangle \in E$ we shall write, $l \xrightarrow{g,a,r} l'$. $I : N \to \mathcal{B}(C)$ is a function which for each node assigns an invariant condition, and $V : N \to 2^{\mathcal{P}}$ is a proposition assignment function which for each node gives a set of atomic propositions true in the node.* □

A *state* of an automaton A is a pair (l, u) where l is a node of A and u a *clock assignment* for C, mapping each clock in C to a value in $\mathbf{R}$. The initial state of A is (l_0, u_0) where u_0 is the initial clock assignment mapping all clocks in C to 0. The semantics of A is given by the timed transition system $S_A = \langle S, s_0, \longrightarrow, V\rangle$, where S is the set of states of A, s_0 is the initial state (l_0, u_0), $\longrightarrow$ is the transition relation defined as follows:

[5] In order to keep the extended trace alternating we might have to apply the time continuity property to avoid two neighboring delay-transitions and we might have to insert 0-delay transition in order to avoid neighboring action-transitions.

- $(l,u)\xrightarrow{a}(l',u')$ if there exist r, g such that $l \xrightarrow{g,a,r} l'$, g is satisfied by u and $u' = r(u)$[6],
- $(l,u)\xrightarrow{\epsilon(d)}(l',u')$ if $(l = l')$, $u' = u + d$[7] and $I(l')$ is satisfied by u',

and V is extended to S simply by $V(l,u) = V(l)$. We denote by $Tr(A)$ all traces of $\mathcal{S}_A$ starting from the initial state (l_0, u_0).

Parallel composition may now be extended to timed automata in the obvious way: for two timed automata A and B and a synchronization function f, the parallel composition $A\,|_f\,B$ denotes the timed transition system $\mathcal{S}_A\,|_f\,\mathcal{S}_B$.

3 A Logic for Safety and Bounded Liveness Properties

It has been pointed out [4, 12], that the practical goal of verification of real-time systems, is to verify simple safety properties such as deadlock-freeness and mutual exclusion. Our previous work [12, 10] shows that such properties can be verified on-the-fly by simple reachability analysis which avoids to construct the whole reachable state-space of systems.

We consider a timed modal logic to specify safety and bounded liveness properties (sometimes called bounded response time properties). The logic may be seen as a fragment of the timed μ-calculus presented in [5], and also studied in [9][8].

Definition 3. *(Syntax) Assume K is a finite set of clocks. Then formulas over K is defined by the following abstract syntax:*

$$\varphi ::= a \mid \varphi_1 \wedge \varphi_2 \mid a \vee \varphi \mid Inv(\varphi) \mid \varphi \; Until_r \; a$$

where $r \subseteq K$ and $a ::= c \mid p$ where c is an atomic clock constraint over K and $p \in \mathcal{P}$ □

Intuitively, for $Inv(\varphi)$ to be satisfied all reachable states must satisfy φ. $\varphi \; Until_r \; a$ is a weak until-property expressing that φ must either hold invariantly or until a. The use of the clock set r allows for *bounded* liveness properties to be expressed, e.g. $(x < 5) \; Until_{\{x\}} \; a$ insists that a must hold within 5 time units. We interpret a formula φ with respect to a trace σ relative to a time assignment v over formula clocks K. We use $\sigma \models_v \varphi$ to mean that σ satisfies φ under u. The interpretation is defined on the structure of φ in Table 1. Naturally, if all the traces of an automaton satisfy a formula, we say that the automaton satisfies the formula.

Definition 4. *Let $Tr(\varphi) = \{\sigma \mid \sigma \models_{v_0} \varphi\}$ where v_0 is the initial time assignment. For a timed automaton A and a formula φ we write $A \models \varphi$ when $Tr(A) \subseteq Tr(\varphi)$. If there exists a trace σ s.t. $\sigma \in Tr(A) \setminus Tr(\varphi)$, we write $A \not\models \varphi$ and in this case, σ is called a diagnostic trace of A w.r.t. φ.* □

[6] $r(u)$ is the assignment s.t. $r(u)(x) = 0$ if $x \in r$ and $r(u)(x) = u(x)$ otherwise.

[7] $(u + d)$ is the assignment s.t. $(u + d)(x) = u(x) + d$.

[8] The connectives of our logic are expressible as derived operators w.r.t. those of [9].

$$
\begin{array}{rl}
\sigma \models_v c & \text{iff } c(v) \\
\sigma \models_v p & \text{iff } p \in V(\sigma) \\
\sigma \models_v \varphi_1 \wedge \varphi_2 & \text{iff } \sigma \models_v \varphi_1 \text{ and } \sigma \models_v \varphi_2 \\
\sigma \models_v a \vee \varphi & \text{iff } \sigma \models_v a \text{ or } \sigma \models_v \varphi \\
\sigma \models_v Inv(\varphi) & \text{iff } \forall \pi : \sigma(\pi) \models_{v+\Delta(\sigma,\pi)} \varphi \\
\sigma \models_v \varphi\ Until_r\ a & \text{iff } \begin{cases} \forall \pi : \sigma(\pi) \models_{r(v)+\Delta(\sigma,\pi)} \varphi, \\ \text{or} \\ \exists \pi : \Big(\sigma(\pi) \models_{r(v)+\Delta(\sigma,\pi)} a \ \wedge\ \forall \pi' < \pi : \sigma(\pi') \models_{r(v)+\Delta(\sigma,\pi')} \varphi\Big) \end{cases}
\end{array}
$$

Table 1. Definition of satisfiability.

4 Diagnostic Model-Checking

Given a network of timed automata A and a formula φ in the logic specifying a property, the so-called model-checking problem is to check if the formula is satisfied by the system. We will take an opposite point of view and check for $A \not\models \varphi$ instead of $A \models \varphi$. From a proof of $A \not\models \varphi$ we will then be able to synthesize a diagnostic trace which may prove useful in subsequent debugging. However, if we fail to prove $A \not\models \varphi$ we can assert that $A \models \varphi$.

4.1 Operations on Clock Constraints

To develop the diagnostic model-checking algorithm, we need a few operations to manipulate clock constraints. Given a clock constraint D, we shall call the set of clock assignments satisfying D, the *solution set* of D.

Definition 5. *Let A and A' be the solution sets of clock constraints $D, D' \in \mathcal{B}(C \cup K)$. We define*

$$
\begin{aligned}
A^{\dagger} &= \{w + d \mid w \in A \text{ and } d \in \mathbf{R}\} \\
\{x\}A &= \{\{x\}w \mid w \in A\} \\
A \wedge A' &= \{w \mid w \in A \text{ and } w \in A'\} \\
A{\downarrow}C &= \{w{\downarrow}C \mid w \in A\}
\end{aligned}
$$

where $w{\downarrow}C$ denotes the restriction of w to the clock set C. □

First, note that $A \wedge A'$ is simply the intersection of the two sets. Intuitively, $A^{\dagger}$ is the set of time assignments that may be reached from A by some delay. We extend the projection operator $\{x\}A$ to sets of clocks. Let $r = \{x_1 ... x_n\}$ be a set of clocks. We define $r(A)$ recursively by $\{\}(A) = A$ and $\{x_1 ... x_n\}(A) = \{x_1\}(\{x_2 ... x_n\}A)$. The following Proposition establishes that the class of clock constraints $\mathcal{B}(C \cup K)$ is closed under the four operations defined above.

Proposition 6. *Let $D, D' \in \mathcal{B}(C \cup K)$ with solution sets A and A', and $x \in C \cup K$. Then there exist $D_1, D_2, D_3, D_4 \in \mathcal{B}(C \cup K)$ with solution sets $A^{\dagger}$, $\{x\}A$, $A \wedge A'$ and $A{\downarrow}C$ respectively.* □

In fact, the resulted constraints D_i's can be effectively constructed from D and D' [11, 10]. In order to save notation, from now on, we shall simply use $D^{\uparrow}$, $\{x\}D$ $D \wedge D'$ and $D{\downarrow}C$ to denote the clock constraints which are guaranteed to exist due to the above proposition. We will use $D^{\uparrow l}$ to denote $(D \wedge I(l))^{\uparrow} \wedge I(l)$ where $I(l)$ is the invariant condition of node l.

We will also need a few *predicates* over clock constraints for the diagnostic model-checking procedure. We write $D \subseteq D'$ to mean that the solution set of D is included in the solution set of D', $D = \emptyset$ to mean that the solution set of D is empty and $u \in D$ to denote that the time assignment u belongs to the solution set of D[9].

4.2 Model-Checking with Diagnostic Synthesis

Note that the definition $A \not\models \varphi$ means that there exists a trace σ of A s.t. $\sigma \notin Tr(\varphi)$. Intuitively, σ is a possible execution of A that does not meet the requirement φ, and therefore it may be used as diagnostic information for subsequent debugging. In order to effectively construct diagnostic traces, we define a relation $\not\Vdash$ of the following type: $\sigma \not\Vdash [l, D] : \varphi$, where σ is a trace of automaton A over the automata clocks C, l is a node of A, D is a constraint system over $C \cup K$ and φ is a formula over K. Now $\not\Vdash$ is the smallest relation satisfying the rules of Table 2.

We use the third invariant rule to exemplify the intuitive explanation of the inference rules. The assertion $(l, u) \xrightarrow{a} (l', u') \longrightarrow \cdots \not\Vdash [l, D] : Inv(\varphi)$ can be justified if any of the symbolic states, reachable using an edge $l \xrightarrow{g,a,r} l'$ from the symbolic state $[l, D]$, does not satisfy the invariant property $Inv(\varphi)$. The clock assignments in this resulting symbolic state is restricted to the (non-empty) constraint system $r(g \wedge D)$. The premise of the rule assumes the existence of a diagnostic trace for $[l', r(g \wedge D)] : Inv(\varphi)$ and the side-condition of the rule provides information as to how one may extend this trace (obviously with an a-transition) in order to obtain a diagnostic trace for $[l, D] : Inv(\varphi)$.

The rules in Table 2 are sound and complete in the following sense:

Theorem 7. *Let A be a timed transition system with initial node l_0. Then*

1. *Whenever $\sigma \not\Vdash [l_0, D_0] : \varphi$ then $\sigma \in Tr(A)$ and $\sigma \notin Tr(\varphi)$.*
2. *Whenever $A \not\models \varphi$ then $\sigma \not\Vdash [l_0, D_0] : \varphi$ for some $\sigma \in Tr(A)$.* □

4.3 Obtaining an Algorithm

Given a symbolic state $[l, D]$ of the automata A and a property φ it is decidable whether there exists a diagnostic trace σ such that $\sigma \not\Vdash [l, D] : \varphi$. We obtain an algorithm by using the rules in Table 2 in two phases, In Phase 1 a goal directed search, starting in the symbolic state $[l, D]$, searching for a violating symbolic state, is performed by using the inference rules in Table 2. We have the following two termination criteria for the symbolic state $[l_n, D_n]$ and the property φ_n:

- (Success) c or p axiom can be applied,
- (Fail) for some i, $l_n = l_i$, $D_n \subseteq D_i$ and $\varphi_n = \varphi_i$.

[9] We will also write $u \in D$ to mean the operation of computing a time assignment u given a constraint system D.

c	$\dfrac{}{(l,u) \not\vdash [l,D] : c}$ $\quad w \in D \wedge \neg c, u = w{\downarrow}C$
p	$\dfrac{}{(l,u) \not\vdash [l,D] : p}$ $\quad w \in D, u = w{\downarrow}C, p \notin V(l)$
$\varphi_1 \wedge \varphi_2$	$\dfrac{\sigma \not\vdash [l,D] : \varphi_i}{\sigma \not\vdash [l,D] : \varphi_1 \wedge \varphi_2}$ $\quad i = 1$ or $i = 2$
$a \vee \varphi$	$\dfrac{\sigma \not\vdash [l, D \wedge \neg c] : \varphi}{\sigma \not\vdash [l,D] : c \vee \varphi}$ $\quad \dfrac{\sigma \not\vdash [l,D] : \varphi}{\sigma \not\vdash [l,D] : p \vee \varphi}$ $\; p \notin V(\sigma)$
$Inv(\varphi)$	$\dfrac{\sigma \not\vdash [l,D] : \varphi}{\sigma \not\vdash [l,D] : Inv(\varphi)}$ $\quad \dfrac{(l,u') \longrightarrow \cdots \not\vdash [l, D^{\uparrow l}] : Inv(\varphi)}{(l,u) \xrightarrow{\epsilon(d)} (l,u') \cdots \not\vdash [l,D] : Inv(\varphi)}$ $\; u \in D{\downarrow}C, u' = u + d$ $\dfrac{(l',u') \longrightarrow \cdots \not\vdash [l', r(g \wedge D)] : Inv(\varphi)}{(l,u) \xrightarrow{a} (l',u') \longrightarrow \cdots \not\vdash [l,D] : Inv(\varphi)}$ $\; l \xrightarrow{g,a,r} l',\ u' = r(u), u \in (g \wedge D){\downarrow}C$
$\varphi\ Until_r\ a$	$\dfrac{\sigma \not\vdash [l, r(D)] : \varphi Until_\emptyset\ a}{\sigma \not\vdash [l,D] : \varphi Until_r\ a}$
$\varphi\ Until_\emptyset\ c$	$\dfrac{\sigma \not\vdash [l, D \wedge \neg c] : \varphi}{\sigma \not\vdash [l,D] : \varphi\ Until_\emptyset\ c}$ $\quad \dfrac{(l,u') \longrightarrow \cdots \not\vdash [l, (D \wedge \neg c)^{\uparrow l}] : (\varphi\ Until_\emptyset\ c)}{(l,u) \xrightarrow{\epsilon(d)} (l,u') \longrightarrow \cdots \not\vdash [l,D] : (\varphi\ Until_\emptyset\ c)}$ $\dfrac{(l',u') \longrightarrow \cdots \not\vdash [l, r(g \wedge D \wedge \neg c)] : (\varphi\ Until_\emptyset\ c)}{(l,u) \xrightarrow{a} (l',u') \longrightarrow \cdots \not\vdash [l,D] : (\varphi\ Until_\emptyset\ c)}$ $\; l \xrightarrow{g,a,r} l',\ u' = r(u), u \in (D \wedge g \wedge \neg c){\downarrow}C$
$\varphi\ Until_\emptyset\ p$	$\dfrac{\sigma \not\vdash [l,D] : \varphi}{\sigma \not\vdash [l,D] : \varphi\ Until_\emptyset\ p}$ $\quad \dfrac{(l,u') \longrightarrow \cdots \not\vdash [l, D^{\uparrow l}] : (\varphi\ Until_\emptyset\ p)}{(l,u) \xrightarrow{\epsilon(d)} (l,u') \longrightarrow \cdots \not\vdash [l,D] : (\varphi\ Until_\emptyset\ p)}$ $\dfrac{(l',u') \longrightarrow \cdots \not\vdash [l, r(g \wedge D)] : (\varphi\ Until_\emptyset\ p)}{(l,u) \xrightarrow{a} (l',u') \longrightarrow \cdots \not\vdash [l,D] : (\varphi\ Until_\emptyset\ p)}$ $\; l \xrightarrow{g,a,r} l',\ u' = r(u), u \in (D \wedge g){\downarrow}C$

Table 2. Inference rules for $\not\vdash$.

The search will be terminated on the Fail criterion if all the possibilities of backtracking have been exhausted. It can then be asserted that the automaton A in any state complying with $[l, D]$ satisfies φ. However, if Phase 1 terminates on the Success criterion it follows that $\sigma \not\vdash [l, D] : \varphi$. The rules in Table 2 provide a way to synthesize the diagnostic trace of the conclusion from a diagnostic trace of the premise, constituting Phase 2. If the search in Phase 1 is performed using a breadth-first strategy, a resulting trace will be a shortest diagnostic trace.

The implementation of both phases relies on efficient implementation of the operations and predicates on clock constraint systems discussed in Section 4.1. In fact, they can be efficiently implemented by representing constraint systems as weighted directed graphs [11, 10].

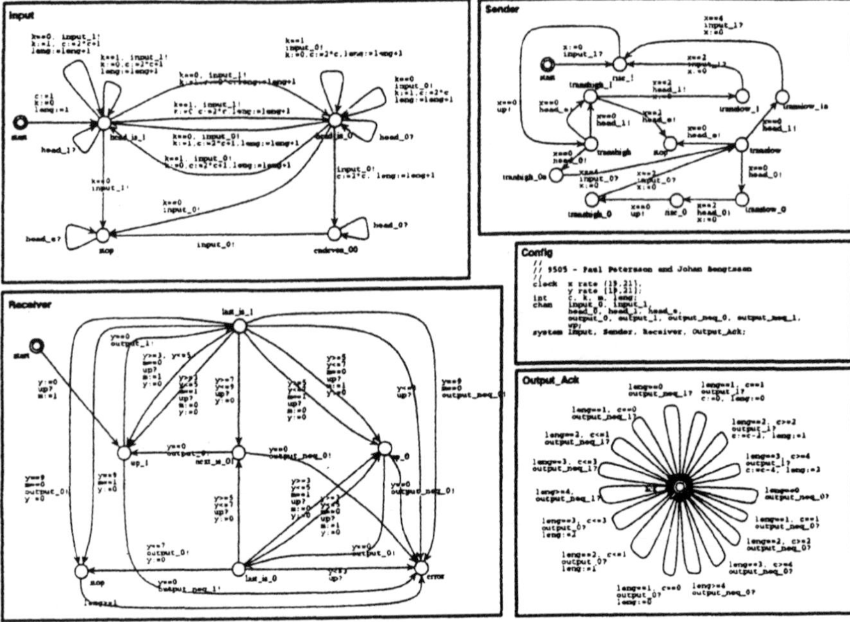

Fig. 1. Philips's Audio-Control Protocol — Final Version.

5 Applications

The techniques presented in previous sections have been implemented in the verification tool UPPAAL. The tool has been used in a case study, where Philips Audio-Control Protocol was verified. We demonstrate the usefulness of the diagnostic model-checking feature of UPPAAL by debugging an early description of the protocol. For detailed information about the tool UPPAAL, see [2] in this volume.

5.1 Philips Audio-Control Protocol

This protocol by Philips was first verified by Bosscher et al [3] and recently using verification tools [6]. The protocol is used for exchanging control information in tiny local area networks between components in modern audio equipment. Bit streams are encoded using the well-known Manchester encoding that relies on timing delay between signals. The protocol uses bit slots of four time units, a 1 bit is encoded by raising the voltage from low to high in the middle of the bit slot. A 0 bit is encoded in the opposite way. The goal of the protocol is to guarantee reliable communication with a tolerance of $\pm 5\%$ on all the timing. The communication is further complicated since the voltage changing from high to low can not be reliably detected. The decoding has to be done using only the changing from low to high. A linear hybrid automaton network description of the protocol is shown in Figure 1.

To perform experiments on the protocol we used an early draft version of a description by Wong–Toi and Ho [6][10]. In their work they automatically verifies the audio-control protocol using the tool HyTech (The Cornell Hybrid Technology Tool is a symbolic model checker for linear hybrid systems). By reusing their description we avoid the difficult and time-consuming work of modelling the protocol. The protocol is modeled as a parallel composition of four processes described below. Several integer variables are used for recording information: `leng` for recording the number of bits generated by the input automaton but not yet acknowledged as being received; `c` for representing the binary encoding of these bits; `k` for recording the parity of the number of bits generated; and `m` for recording the parity of the number of bits received. The four parallel processes are:

- Input. The Input automaton nondeterministically generates valid bit sequences for the Sender automaton. Valid bit sequences are restricted to either odd length or ending in two 0 bits. The values of the integer variables `k`, `c` and `leng` are also updated appropriately. The Input automaton is also used by the Sender automaton to decide the next input bit.
- Sender. This automaton encodes the bit sequences by reading the value of the next bit from the Input automaton and determine the time delay for the next high voltage, modeled as an `up!`-action.
- Receiver. The Receiver automaton decodes the bit stream by measuring the time delay between two subsequent up?-actions received from the Sender. The decoded bits are then acknowledged by synchronizing on the `output_1` or `output_0` port with the output-acknowledgment automaton. The Receiver also records the parity of the received number of bits by updating `m`.
- Output_Ack. The output-acknowledgment automaton checks the current number of unacknowledges bits (`leng`) together with their binary encoding (`c`) and acknowledges the bits decoded by the receiver. It also updates the values of the variables `leng` and `c`.

The way the protocol has been modeled enables correctness of the received bits to be verified by reachability analysis. By introducing the edge stop $\xrightarrow{\texttt{leng}\geq 1}$ error in the receiver automaton, the received bit stream is guaranteed to be identical to the sent bit stream precisely when the system satisfies the property $Inv(\neg \mathsf{at}(\mathsf{error}))$.

First Version. The first version was an adjusted version of the description in [6]. The adjustments were necessary due to differences in HyTech and Uppaal. This step comprised: transforming the invariant conditions of the original description into enabling conditions of the model in Uppaal; introducing complementary synchronization actions; adding the edge stop $\xrightarrow{\texttt{leng}\geq 1}$ error in the receiver automaton; and model the modulo-2 counters `m` and `k` as integer variables. Modulo-2 addition $\oplus$ was modeled as a conditional value assignment on integers (e.g. `m==0, m:=1` or `m==1, m:=0`)[11]. This first version was also free from some obvious typing errors found in the original description of the system.

---

[10] Available, at that time, from the Web server at Cornell University (`http://www.cs.cornell.edu/`).

[11] Alternatively, modulo-2 addition $\oplus$ can be modeled using the integer assignment `m:=-m+1`.

((start,start,start,ack), (0, 0), (0, 0, 0, 0)) $\xrightarrow{0}$
((head_is_1,start,start,ack), (0, 0), (1, 0, 0, 1)) $\xrightarrow{\texttt{input\_1}}$
((head_is_0,rise_1,start,ack), (0, 0), (2, 1, 0, 2)) $\xrightarrow{\texttt{up}}$
((head_is_0,transhigh,up_1,ack), (0, 0), (2, 1, 1, 2)) $\xrightarrow{\texttt{head\_0}}$
((head_is_0,tranhigh_0a,up_1,ack), (0, 0), (2, 1, 1, 2)) $\xrightarrow{\texttt{output\_1}}$
((head_is_0,tranhigh_0a,last_is_1,ack), (0, 0), (0, 1, 1, 1)) $\xrightarrow{\epsilon(76)}$
((head_is_0,tranhigh_0a,last_is_1,ack), (76, 76), (0, 1, 1, 1)) $\xrightarrow{\texttt{input\_0}}$
((head_is_1,translow,last_is_1,ack), (0, 76), (1, 0, 1, 2)) $\xrightarrow{\texttt{head\_1}}$
((head_is_1,translow_1a,last_is_1,ack), (0, 76), 1, 0, 1, 2)) $\xrightarrow{\epsilon(76)}$
((head_is_1,translow_1a,last_is_1,ack), (76, 152), (1, 0, 1, 2)) $\xrightarrow{0}$
((head_is_1,rise_1,last_is_1,ack), (0, 152), (1, 0, 1, 2)) $\xrightarrow{\texttt{up}}$
((head_is_1,transhigh,up_0,ack), (0, 0), (1, 0, 0, 2)) $\xrightarrow{\texttt{output\_neq\_0}}$
((head_is_1,transhigh,error,ack), (0, 0), (1, 0, 0, 2))

Fig. 2. Diagnostic Trace from the First Version of the Protocol.

The protocol was then attempted verified but found erroneous[12]. Using the diagnostic trace shown in Figure 2[13][14], automatically synthesized by UPPAAL, the system was further improved. The trace indicates errors in several ways. First recall that the existence of a trace implies that the correctness property is not satisfied. This particular trace is wrong since a `head_1`-action is followed by a subsequent up-action without an interjacent `input_1`-action. Also, from the diagnostic trace in Figure 2, it was revealed that the action labels `output_neq_1?` and `output_neq_0?` was swapped in the Output_Ack automaton. This must be the case since c = 1 and `leng` = 2 implies that the next output should be 0 while `output_neq_0?` is signaled to acknowledge that the next output can *not* be 0.

Improved Version no.1. In the first improved version, missing actions `input_1?` on the edges translow_1 $\longrightarrow$ rise_1 and translow_1a $\longrightarrow$ rise_1 in the Sender automaton was added. Furthermore, the action labels `output_neq_0?` and `output_neq_1?` was swapped in the Output_Ack automaton.

Once again, we attempted to verify the system; the systems was found erroneous. From the diagnostic trace shown in Figure 3, a timing error was discovered. In the control-state (endeven_00,transhigh_0,up_1,ack) the Receiver automaton has decoded a 1 bit, but this is not the bit sent by the sender. The disagreement is monitored by the Output_Ack automaton that makes the system violating the correctness property by offering an `output_neq_1?`-action. The reason for this error was found on the edges last_is_1 $\longrightarrow$ next_is_01 and last_is_1 $\longrightarrow$ up_0 where the enabling conditions on clock y was swapped.

---

12 UPPAAL, installed on a SparcStation 10, performs the attempted verification and reports a diagnostic trace in 2.2 seconds.

13 The states are shown in this trace as triples, where the first component is the control-node, the second component is the clock assignment for the clocks `x` and `y`, and the third component is the value assignment for the auxiliary variables `c`, `k`, `m` and `leng`.

14 This is a trace of the transformed version of the description, where the non-zero linear hybrid automata have been compiled into timed automata.

((start,start,start,ack), (0, 0), (0, 0, 0, 0)) $\xrightarrow{0}$
((head_is_1,start,start,ack), (0, 0), (1, 0, 0, 1)) $\xrightarrow{\texttt{input\_1}}$
((head_is_0,rise_1,start,ack), (0, 0), (2, 1, 0, 2)) $\xrightarrow{\texttt{up}}$
((head_is_0,transhigh,up_1,ack), (0, 0), (2, 1, 1, 2)) $\xrightarrow{\texttt{head\_0}}$
((head_is_0,tranhigh_0a,up_1,ack), (0, 0), (2, 1, 1, 2)) $\xrightarrow{\texttt{output\_1}}$
((head_is_0,tranhigh_0a,last_is_1,ack), (0, 0), (0, 1, 1, 1)) $\xrightarrow{\epsilon(76)}$
((head_is_0,tranhigh_0a,last_is_1,ack), (76, 76), (0, 1, 1, 1)) $\xrightarrow{\texttt{input\_0}}$
((endeven_00,translow,last_is_1,ack), (0, 76), (0, 1, 1, 2)) $\xrightarrow{\texttt{head\_0}}$
((endeven_00,translow_0,last_is_1,ack), (0, 76), (0, 1, 1, 2)) $\xrightarrow{\epsilon(38)}$
((endeven_00,translow_0,last_is_1,ack), (38, 114), (0, 1, 1, 2)) $\xrightarrow{\texttt{head\_0}}$
((endeven_00,rise_0,last_is_1,ack), (0, 114), (0, 1, 1, 2)) $\xrightarrow{\texttt{up}}$
((endeven_00,transhigh_0,next_is_01,ack), (0, 0), (0, 1, 1, 2)) $\xrightarrow{\texttt{output\_0}}$
((endeven_00,transhigh_0,up_1,ack), (0, 0), (0, 1, 1, 1)) $\xrightarrow{\texttt{output\_neq\_1}}$
((endeven_00,transhigh_0,error,ack), (0, 0), (0, 1, 1, 1))

Fig. 3. Diagnostic Trace from the First Improved Version of the Protocol.

Improved Version no.2. An even further improved version was made by swapping the enabling conditions on clock y between the edges last_is_1 $\longrightarrow$ next_is_01 and last_is_1 $\longrightarrow$ up_0 in the receiver automaton.

Once again a diagnostic trace was produced. The error was found by inspection of the action sequence. In the control-node (head_is_0,tranhigh_0a,last_is_1,ack) three output_1-actions and one output_0 has been performed but the value of m indicates an odd parity of the accumulated output bit stream. We concluded that some update operation of m was wrong or missing.

Final Version. When the modulo-2 addition on the variable m was removed from the edges last_is_1 $\longrightarrow$ next_is_01 and last_is_0 $\longrightarrow$ next_is_01 in the receiver automaton we got the final version of the protocol (Figure 1). By adjusting the rate of the senders and the receivers clocks (i.e. x and y) it can be confirmed that the correctness property is not satisfied if the tolerance is equal to $\pm\frac{1}{17}$.

6 Conclusion and Future Work

In this paper we have presented a diagnostic model-check procedure for real-time systems, capable of, not only deciding if a property is satisfied by a model, but also providing a violating trace whenever the property is not satisfied. Such a trace may be considered as diagnostic information of the error, useful during the subsequent debugging of the model. This principle could be called WYDVYAE.

The presented techniques have been implemented in the new verification tool UPPAAL. Besides a diagnostic model-checker for networks of timed automata, the UPPAAL tool kit have a graphical interface (Autograph), allowing system descriptions to be defined by drawing and thereby allowing the user to see what is verified, i.e. WYSIWYV. In this way, a number of errors can be avoided. In a case study where UPPAAL was used to verify (a version of) Philips Audio-Control Protocol, both the graphical interface and the automatically generated diagnostic traces proved useful for detecting and correcting several errors in the description of the protocol.

A diagnostic trace, generated by the current version of UPPAAL, is sometimes unnecessarily long. Thus, future work includes implementing synthesis of a *shortest* diagnostic trace. Another future extensions will follow the principle of WYSIWYV. Whenever needed, clock assignments of a diagnostic trace will be transformed back into values in accordance with the original description. This is sometimes needed since UPPAAL is able to compile descriptions of certain types of hybrid systems into timed automata.

Acknowledgment

The UPPAAL tool has been implemented in large parts by Johan Bengtsson and Fredrik Larsson. The authors would like to thank them for their excellent work and also for several discussions concerning the verification of the Audio Control Protocol.

References

1. R. Alur and D. Dill. Automata for Modelling Real-Time Systems. *Theoretical Computer Science*, 126(2):183–236, April 1994.
2. Johan Bengtsson, Kim G. Larsen, Fredrik Larsson, Paul Pettersson, and Wang Yi. UPPAAL— a Tool Suite for Automatic Verification of Real–Time Systems. In *Proc. of the 4th DIMACS Workshop on Verification and Control of Hybrid Systems*, Lecture Notes in Computer Science, October 1995.
3. D. Bosscher, I. Polak, and F. Vaandrager. Verification of an Audio-Control Protocol. In *Proc. of FTRTFT'94*, volume 863 of *Lecture Notes in Computer Science*, 1993.
4. Nicolas Halbwachs. Delay Analysis in Synchronous Programs. *Lecture Notes in Computer Science*, 697, 1993. In Proc. of CAV'93.
5. T. A. Henzinger, Z. Nicollin, J. Sifakis, and S. Yovine. Symbolic Model Checking for Real-Time Systems. In *Logic in Computer Science*, 1992.
6. Pei-Hsin Ho and Howard Wong-Toi. Automated Analysis of an Audio Control Protocol. In *Proc. of CAV'95*, volume 939 of *Lecture Notes in Computer Science*. Springer Verlag, 1995.
7. H. Hüttel and K. G. Larsen. The use of static constructs in a modal process logic. *Lecture Notes in Computer Science, Springer Verlag*, 363, 1989.
8. F. Laroussinie and K.G. Larsen. Compositional Model Checking of Real Time Systems. In *Proc. of CONCUR'95*, Lecture Notes in Computer Science. Springer Verlag, 1995.
9. F. Laroussinie and K.G. Larsen. From Timed Automata to Logic — and Back. In *Proc. of MFCS'95*, Lecture Notes in Computer Sciencie, 1995. Also BRICS report series RS–95–2.
10. K.G. Larsen, P. Pettersson, and W. Yi. Compositional and Symbolic Model-Checking of Real-Time Systems. To appear in *Proc. of the 16th IEEE Real-Time Systems Symposium*, December 1995.
11. Mihalis Yannakakis and David Lee. An efficient algorithm for minimizing real–time transition systems. In *Proceedings of CAV'93*, volume 697 of *Lecture Notes in Computer Science*, pages 210–224, 1993.
12. Wang Yi, Paul Pettersson, and Mats Daniels. Autfomatic Verification of Real-Time Communicating Systems By Constraint-Solving. In *Proc. of the 7th International Conference on Formal Description Techniques*, 1994.

Specification and Verification of Hybrid Dynamic Systems with Timed ∀-automata

Ying Zhang[1] and Alan K. Mackworth[*2]

[1] Wilson Center for Research, Xerox Corporation, M/S 128-51E, Webster, N.Y., USA 14580, zhang@wrc.xerox.com
[2] Department of Computer Science, University of British Columbia, Vancouver, B.C., Canada V6T 1Z4, mack@cs.ubc.ca

Abstract. The advent of computer-controlled embedded systems coupled to physical environments requires the development of new theories of dynamic system modeling, specification and verification. We present Timed ∀-automata, a generalization of ∀-automata [10], for the specification and verification of dynamic systems that can be discrete, continuous or hybrid. Timed ∀-automata are finite state and serve as a formal requirements specification language for dynamic systems so that (1) timed as well as temporal properties can be specified or recognized, and (2) global properties of either discrete or continuous behaviors can be characterized. In addition, we propose a formal model-checking method for behavior verification of dynamic systems. This method generalizes stability analysis of dynamic systems and can be completely automated for discrete-time finite-domain systems.

1 Motivation and Introduction

A robot is, typically, a real-time embedded system, consisting of a controller coupled to its plant. In general, all the computer-controlled systems in our daily lives, such as cars, elevators and copiers, can be considered to be robots. With the growing demand for robots, we face a major challenge: the development of intelligent robots that are reliable, robust and safe in their working environments [7]. Computer-controlled systems are discrete and physical plants or environments are, in general, continuous. Therefore, the coupling of a controller, a plant and its environment constitutes a complex dynamic system that is, in general, hybrid.

A robotic system is the symmetrical coupling of a robot to its environment. We have decomposed the development of a robotic system into three phases: system modeling, requirements specification and behavior verification [17, 20]. System modeling represents a complex dynamic system in terms of its compositions and interconnections, so that the overall behavior of the system is precisely defined. Requirements specification expresses global properties such as safety, reachability, liveness and real-time response. Behavior verification ensures

* Fellow, Canadian Institute for Advanced Research

that the behavior of the modeled system satisfies the specified requirements. We replace the vague question "Is the robot intelligent?" with the question "Will the robot do the right thing?" [18]. The answer to that question follows if we can:

1. model the coupled robotic system at a suitable level of abstraction,
2. specify the required global properties of the system, and
3. verify that the model satisfies the specification.

Most robot design methodologies use hybrid models of hybrid systems, awkwardly combining off-line computational models of high-level perception, reasoning and planning with on-line models of low-level sensing and control. We have developed Constraint Nets (CN) as a semantic model for hybrid dynamic systems [16, 19]. CN introduces an abstraction and a unitary framework to model discrete/continuous hybrid systems; therefore, the robot and its environment can be modeled symmetrically in a uniform model.

In this paper, we present Timed $\forall$-automata for the specification and verification of dynamic systems that can be discrete, continuous or hybrid. Timed $\forall$-automata are a generalization of $\forall$-automata [10] that have been developed for the specification and verification of concurrent programs. $\forall$-automata are powerful enough to specify global properties such as safety, reachability and liveness, and simple enough to have a formal verification procedure. Timed $\forall$-automata are finite state and serve as a formal requirements specification language for dynamic systems so that (1) timed as well as temporal properties can be specified, and (2) global properties of either discrete or continuous behaviors can be characterized. The link between a constraint net model and a timed $\forall$-automata specification is the behavior of the system, which can be represented as a generalized Kripke structure. We propose a formal model-checking method for behavior verification of hybrid dynamic systems. This method generalizes stability analysis of dynamic systems and can be completely automated for discrete-time finite-domain systems.

The rest of this paper is organized as follows. Section 2 defines the basic concepts of dynamic systems: time, traces, transductions, behaviors, and generalized Kripke structures. Section 3 develops Timed $\forall$-automata, giving the syntax and semantics. Section 4 proposes a formal method for behavior verification. Section 5 concludes this paper and points out future research directions. Theorems and lemmas are proved in Appendix A. A typical cat-mouse [4] example is used throughout the paper to illustrate the ideas. However, the method is applied to various robot testbeds in our Laboratory for Computational Intelligence at UBC, including robot soccer players [13, 21].

2 Dynamic Systems and Behaviors

In this section, we define the basic concepts of dynamic systems: time, traces, transductions, behaviors and generalized Kripke structures.

2.1 Time, Traces and Transductions

The key to understanding dynamic systems is understanding time. For our purpose, time is a linearly ordered set with a least element, the start time point. A measure is defined on some subsets of time points so that the duration of an interval of time can be captured. Formally, a time structure is defined as follows.

Definition 2.1 (Time structure) *A* time structure *is a pair* $\langle \mathcal{T}, \mu \rangle$ *where*

- $\mathcal{T}$ *is a linearly ordered set* $\langle \mathcal{T}, \leq \rangle$ *with* $\mathbf{0}$ *as the least element;*
- *let* σ *be a family of subsets of* $\mathcal{T}$ *including* $[\mathbf{0}, t)$[3] *for all* $t \in \mathcal{T}$, $\langle \mathcal{T}, \sigma \rangle$ *be a measurable space, and* $\mathcal{R}^+$ *be the set of non-negative real numbers; then,* $\mu : \sigma \to \mathcal{R}^+ \cup \{\infty\}$ *is a measure and* $\langle \mathcal{T}, \sigma, \mu \rangle$ *forms a measure space*[4].

In this paper, we assume that (1) time is *complete*, i.e., for any subset of time points, if there is an upper (lower) bound, there is a least upper (greatest lower) bound, and (2) time is *infinite*, i.e., $\mu(\mathcal{T}) = \infty$. Condition (1) is important for our purpose; it guarantees that the time structure is well-defined: both Zeno sequence and rational time are excluded. Any time structure can be augmented to satisfy condition (2) by adding infinite number of time points. A time structure is *discrete* iff $\forall t > \mathbf{0}, [\mathbf{0}, t)$ is finite; it is *continuous* iff $\forall t_1, t_2, t_1 < t_2 \Rightarrow \exists t, t_1 < t < t_2$. For example, the set of natural numbers $\mathcal{N}$ and the set of non-negative real numbers $\mathcal{R}^+$, with $\mu([0, t)) = t$, are both time structures; $\mathcal{N}$ is discrete and $\mathcal{R}^+$ is continuous. If $\mathcal{T}$ is discrete, for any $t > \mathbf{0}$, let $pre(t)$ denote the least upper bound of $[\mathbf{0}, t)$. Furthermore, let $\mu([t_1, t_2)) = \mu([\mathbf{0}, t_2)) - \mu([\mathbf{0}, t_1))$.

The study of dynamic systems is the study of changes over time. Changes over time can be captured by traces. Formally, let $\mathcal{T}$ be a time structure and A be a domain of values. A *trace* v is a mapping from time to a domain, i.e., $v : \mathcal{T} \to A$. For example, $v = \lambda t.e^{-t}$ is a trace. The set of all traces from time $\mathcal{T}$ to domain A forms a *trace space*, denoted $A^{\mathcal{T}}$.

A dynamic system is composed of a set of interconnected transformational processes. Transformational processes can be captured by transductions. A transduction is a causal mapping from an input trace space to an output trace space. Formally, let $\mathcal{T}$ be a time structure, A and A' be domains, which can also be products of domains. Let $A^{\mathcal{T}}$ and $A'^{\mathcal{T}}$ be trace spaces. Two traces v_1, v_2 in the same trace space are *coincident up to t*, written $v_1 \simeq_{\leq t} v_2$, iff $\forall t' \leq t, v_1(t') = v_2(t')$. A mapping $F : A^{\mathcal{T}} \to A'^{\mathcal{T}}$ is a *transduction* iff $\forall v_1, v_2, t, v_1 \simeq_{\leq t} v_2 \Rightarrow F(v_1) \simeq_{\leq t} F(v_2)$. For example, a state automaton with an initial state defines a transduction on discrete time; a temporal integration with a given initial value is a typical transduction on continuous time. A *transliteration* is a primitive transduction where the output at any time is a function of the input at that time. Just as nullary functions represent constants, nullary transductions represent traces.

---

[3] $[t_1, t_2) = \{t | t_1 \leq t < t_2\}$.

[4] The concepts of measurable space, measure and measure space follow [12].

2.2 Behaviors of Dynamic Systems

A dynamic system can be represented as a set of equations, each of which corresponds to a transduction: $v_i = F_i(v_1, ..., v_n), i = 1, ..., m, m \leq n$. A *trace of the dynamic system* is a tuple $\langle v_1, ..., v_n \rangle$ that satisfies the set of equations [16]. The *behavior of the dynamic system* is the set of traces of the dynamic system.

Consider an example of *Cat and Mouse* modified from [4]. Suppose a cat and a mouse start running from initial positions X_c and X_m, respectively, with $X_c > X_m > 0$ and with constant velocities $V_c < V_m < 0$. Both of them will stop running when the cat catches the mouse, or the mouse runs into the hole in the wall at 0. Let x_c and x_m be the position traces of the cat and the mouse, respectively. This system can be modeled by the following set of equations:

$$x_c = \int(X_c)(V_c \cdot r), \quad x_m = \int(X_m)(V_m \cdot r), \quad r = (x_c > x_m) \wedge (x_m > 0) \qquad (1)$$

where $\int(X)$ is a temporal integration with initial state X. At any time t, $r(t)$ is 1 if the running condition $(x_c(t) > x_m(t)) \wedge (x_m(t) > 0)$ is satisfied and 0 otherwise. The behavior of this system is the set of tuples $\langle x_c, x_m \rangle$, each of which satisfies the set of equations.

A useful and important type of behavior is state-based and time-invariant. Intuitively, a state-based and time-invariant behavior is a behavior whose traces after any time are totally dependent on the current snapshot. State-based and time-invariant behaviors can be defined using generalized Kripke structures. We define a *generalized Kripke structure* $\mathcal{K}$ as a triple $\langle \mathcal{S}, \leadsto, \Theta \rangle$ where $\mathcal{S}$ is a set of states, $\leadsto \subset \mathcal{S} \times \mathcal{R}^+ \times \mathcal{S}$ is a state transition relation, and $\Theta \subseteq \mathcal{S}$ is a set of initial states. We denote $\langle s_1, t, s_2 \rangle \in \leadsto$ as $s_1 \overset{t}{\leadsto} s_2$. The state transition relation $\leadsto$ satisfies the following conditions:

- *initiality*: $s \overset{0}{\leadsto} s$;
- *transitivity*: if $s_1 \overset{t_1}{\leadsto} s_2$ and $s_2 \overset{t_2}{\leadsto} s_3$, then $s_1 \overset{t_1+t_2}{\leadsto} s_3$;
- *infinity*: $\forall s \in \mathcal{S}, \exists t > 0, s' \in \mathcal{S}, s \overset{t}{\leadsto} s'$.

For example, $\langle \mathcal{R}, \leadsto, \Theta \rangle$ with $s_1 \overset{t}{\leadsto} s_2$ iff $s_2 = s_1 e^{-t}$ is a generalized Kripke structure.

A time structure $\mathcal{T}$ is a time structure of $\mathcal{K}$ iff (1) for any time point t_1 in $\mathcal{T}$ and any transition $s_1 \overset{t}{\leadsto} s_2$ in $\mathcal{K}$, there is $t_2 > t_1$ in $\mathcal{T}$ such that $t = \mu([t_1, t_2))$, and (2) for any time points t_1 and t_2 with $t_1 < t_2$ and any state s_1 in $\mathcal{S}$, there is s_2 in $\mathcal{S}$ such that $s_1 \overset{\mu([t_1,t_2))}{\leadsto} s_2$.

Lemma 2.1 *If $\mathcal{T}$ is a discrete time structure of $\mathcal{K}$, then there is $\delta > 0$, for any $t > 0, \mu([pre(t), t)) = \delta$. And $\mathcal{K}$ can be represented as the transitive closure of transitions of next relation $s_1 \overset{\delta}{\leadsto} s_2$.*

For example, $\langle \mathcal{R}, \leadsto, \Theta \rangle$ with $s_1 \overset{n\delta}{\leadsto} s_2$ iff $s_2 = f^n(s_1)$[5] is a generalized Kripke structure with discrete time.

[5] apply function f n times

Not all generalized Kripke structures have time structures. For example, the transitive closure of a two-state transition system $s_1 \overset{1}{\leadsto} s_2, s_2 \overset{2}{\leadsto} s_1$ has no time structure. However, by adding an intermediary state s_2', the transitive closure of $s_1 \overset{1}{\leadsto} s_2, s_2 \overset{1}{\leadsto} s_2', s_2' \overset{1}{\leadsto} s_1$ has a time structure. A generalized Kripke structure is *well-defined* iff it has a time structure.

A *trace of a well-defined generalized Kripke* $\mathcal{K}$ on its time structure $\mathcal{T}$ is a mapping $v : \mathcal{T} \to S$ such that (1) $v(0) \in \Theta$ and (2) $\forall t_1, t_2, t_1 < t_2 \Rightarrow v(t_1) \overset{\mu([t_1,t_2))}{\leadsto} v(t_2)$. The *behavior of* $\mathcal{K}$ on $\mathcal{T}$ is the set of traces of $\mathcal{K}$ on $\mathcal{T}$. The behavior of a dynamic system is *state-based and time-invariant* iff it is equal to the behavior of some generalized Kripke structure. In the rest of this paper, we focus on state-based and time-invariant behaviors represented as generalized Kripke structures.

3 Timed ∀-automata for Requirements Specification

In this section, we define Timed ∀-automata, giving the syntax and semantics. First, we introduce Discrete Timed ∀-automata where time is discrete. Then, we generalize Discrete Timed ∀-automata to Timed ∀-automata where time can be either discrete or continuous.

3.1 Discrete Timed ∀-automata

Discrete ∀-automata are non-deterministic finite state automata over infinite sequences. These automata were originally proposed as a formalism for the specification and verification of temporal properties of concurrent programs [10]. Formally, a ∀-automaton is defined as follows.

Definition 3.1 (Syntax of ∀-automata) *A* ∀-automaton $\mathcal{A}$ *is a quintuple* $\langle Q, R, S, e, c\rangle$ *where* Q *is a finite set of* automaton-states, $R \subseteq Q$ *is a set of* recurrent states *and* $S \subseteq Q$ *is a set of* stable states. *With each* $q \in Q$, *we associate an assertion* $e(q)$, *which characterizes the* entry condition *under which the automaton may start its activity in* q. *With each pair* $q, q' \in Q$, *we associate an assertion* $c(q, q')$, *which characterizes the* transition condition *under which the automaton may move from* q *to* q'.

R and S are generalizations of *accepting* states to the case of infinite inputs. We denote by $B = Q - (R \cup S)$ the set of *non-accepting (bad)* states.

A ∀-automaton is called *complete* iff the following requirements are met:

- $\bigvee_{q \in Q} e(q)$ is valid.
- For every $q \in Q$, $\bigvee_{q' \in Q} c(q, q')$ is valid.

Any automaton can be transformed to a complete automaton by introducing an additional bad (error) state q_E, with the entry condition: $e(q_E) = \neg(\bigvee_{q \in Q} e(q))$, and the transition conditions:

$$\begin{aligned} c(q_E, q_E) &= true \\ c(q_E, q) &= false \quad \text{for each } q \in Q \\ c(q, q_E) &= \neg(\bigvee_{q' \in Q} c(q, q')) \quad \text{for each } q \in Q. \end{aligned}$$

One of the advantages of using automata as a specification language is its graphical representation. It is useful and illuminating to represent ∀-automata by diagrams. A ∀-automaton can be depicted by a labeled directed graph where automaton-states are depicted by nodes and transition relations by arcs. The basic conventions for such representations are the following:

- The automaton-states are depicted by nodes in a directed graph.
- Each initial automaton-state ($e(q) \neq false$) is marked by a small arrow, an *entry arc*, pointing to it.
- Arcs, drawn as arrows, connect some pairs of automaton-states.
- Each recurrent state is depicted by a diamond inscribed within a circle.
- Each stable state is depicted by a square inscribed within a circle.

Nodes and arcs are labeled by assertions. The labels define the entry conditions and the transition conditions of the associated automaton as follows.

- Let $q \in Q$ be a node in the diagram corresponding to an initial automaton-state. If q is labeled by ψ and the entry arc is labeled by φ, the entry condition $e(q)$ is given by $e(q) = \varphi \wedge \psi$. If there is no entry arc, $e(q) = false$.
- Let q, q' be two nodes in the diagram corresponding to automaton-states. If q' is labeled by ψ, and arcs from q to q' are labeled by $\varphi_i, i = 1 \cdots n$, the transition condition $c(q, q')$ is given by $c(q, q') = (\varphi_1 \vee \cdots \vee \varphi_n) \wedge \psi$. If there is no arc from q to q', $c(q, q') = false$.

A diagram representing an incomplete automaton can be interpreted as a complete automaton by introducing an error state and associated entry and transition conditions. Some examples of ∀-automata are shown in Fig. 1.

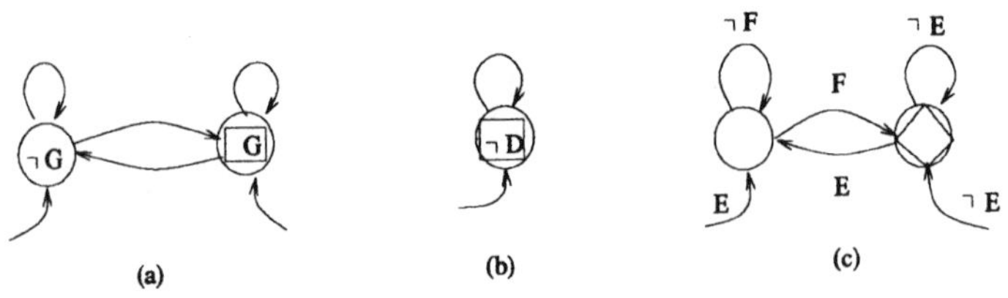

Fig. 1. ∀-automata: (a) reachability (b) safety (c) bounded response

The formal semantics of discrete ∀-automata is defined as follows. Let A be a domain of values. An assertion α on A corresponds to a subset $V(\alpha)$ of A. A value $a \in A$ satisfies an assertion α on A, written $a \models \alpha$ or $\alpha(a)$, iff $a \in V(\alpha)$. Let $\mathcal{T}$ be a discrete time structure and $v : \mathcal{T} \to A$ be a trace. A *run* of $\mathcal{A}$ over v is a mapping $r : \mathcal{T} \to Q$ such that (1) $v(0) \models e(r(0))$; and (2) for all $t > 0$, $v(t) \models c(r(pre(t)), r(t))$. A complete automaton guarantees that any discrete trace has a run over it.

If r is a run, let $Inf(r)$ be the set of automaton-states appearing infinitely many times in r, i.e., $Inf(r) = \{q | \forall t \exists t_0 \geq t, r(t_0) = q\}$. Notice that the same definition can be used for continuous as well as discrete time traces. A run r is defined to be *accepting* iff:

1. $Inf(r) \cap R \neq \emptyset$, i.e., *some* of the states appearing infinitely many times in r belong to R, or
2. $Inf(r) \subseteq S$, i.e., *all* the states appearing infinitely many times in r belong to S.

Definition 3.2 (Semantics of ∀-automata) *A ∀-automaton $\mathcal{A}$* accepts *a trace v, written $v \models \mathcal{A}$, iff* all *possible runs of $\mathcal{A}$ over v are accepting.*

For example, Fig. 1(a) accepts any trace that satisfies $\neg G$ only finitely many times, Fig. 1(b) accepts any trace that never satisfies D, and Fig. 1(c) accepts any trace that will satisfy F in the finite future whenever it satisfies E.

In order to represent timeliness, we extend ∀-automata with time. Timed ∀-automata are ∀-automata augmented with timed automaton-states and time bounds. Formally, a timed ∀-automaton is defined as follows.

Definition 3.3 (Syntax of Timed ∀-automata) *A* timed ∀-automaton $\mathcal{TA}$ *is a triple $\langle \mathcal{A}, T, \tau \rangle$ where $\mathcal{A} = \langle Q, R, S, e, c \rangle$ is a ∀-automaton, $T \subseteq Q$ is a set of* timed *automaton-states and $\tau : T \cup \{bad\} \to \mathcal{R}^+ \cup \{\infty\}$ is a* time function.

A ∀-automaton is a special timed ∀-automaton with $T = \emptyset$ and $\tau(bad) = \infty$. Graphically, a T-state is denoted by a nonnegative real number indicating its time bound. The conventions for complete ∀-automata are adopted for timed ∀-automata. Fig. 2 shows an example of a timed ∀-automaton.

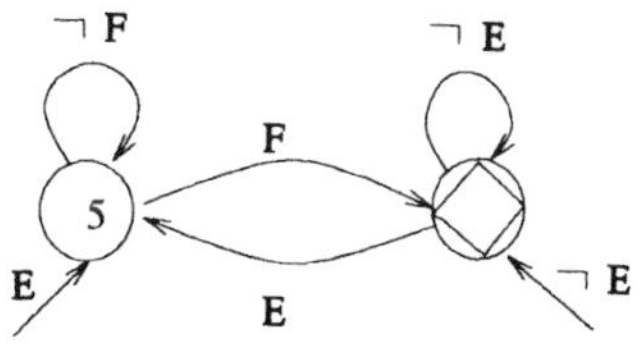

Fig. 2. Real-time response

The formal semantics of Discrete Timed $\forall$-automata is defined as follows. Let $r : \mathcal{T} \to Q$ be a run and $I \subseteq \mathcal{T}$ be a time interval. For any $P \subset Q$, let $Sg(P)$ be the set of consecutive P-state segments of r, i.e., $r_{|I} \in Sg(P)$ for some interval I iff $\forall t \in I$, $r(t) \in P$. A run r *satisfies the time constraints* iff

1. (local time constraint) for any $q \in T$ and any interval I of $\mathcal{T}$, if $r_{|I} \in Sg(\{q\})$ then $\mu(I) \leq \tau(q)$ and
2. (global time constraint) let $B = Q - (R \cup S)$ and $\chi_B : Q \to \{0,1\}$ be the characteristic function for set B; for any interval I of $\mathcal{T}$, if $r_{|I} \in Sg(B \cup S)$ then $\int_I \chi_B(r(t))dt \leq \tau(bad)$.

Let $v : \mathcal{T} \to A$ be a trace. A *run* r of $\mathcal{TA}$ over v is a run of $\mathcal{A}$ over v; r is *accepting* for $\mathcal{TA}$ iff

1. r is accepting for $\mathcal{A}$ and
2. r satisfies the time constraints.

Definition 3.4 (Semantics of Timed $\forall$-automaton) *A timed $\forall$-automaton $\mathcal{TA}$* accepts *a trace v, written $v \models \mathcal{TA}$, iff* all *possible runs of $\mathcal{TA}$ over v are accepting.*

For example, Fig. 2 specifies a real-time response property meaning that any event (E) will be responded to (F) within 5 time units.

3.2 Timed $\forall$-automata

Now we generalize Discrete Timed $\forall$-automata to Timed $\forall$-automata that can accept general traces, with discrete time traces as special cases. The syntax and semantics of Timed $\forall$-automata are the same as those of Discrete Timed $\forall$-automata, except for the definitions of runs.

The important concept of general runs is the generalization of the consecution condition. Let $\mathcal{A} = \langle Q, R, S, e, c \rangle$ be a $\forall$-automaton and $v : \mathcal{T} \to A$ be a trace. A *run* of $\mathcal{A}$ over v is a mapping $r : \mathcal{T} \to Q$ satisfying

1. *Initiality*: $v(0) \models e(r(0))$;
2. *Consecution*:
   - *Inductivity*: $\forall t > 0, \exists q \in Q, t' < t, \forall t'', t' \leq t'' < t, r(t'') = q$ and $v(t) \models c(r(t''), r(t))$ and
   - *Continuity*: $\forall t, \exists q \in Q, t' > t, \forall t'', t < t'' < t', r(t'') = q$ and $v(t'') \models c(r(t), r(t''))$.

When $\mathcal{T}$ is discrete, the two conditions in *Consecution* reduce to one, i.e., $\forall t > 0, v(t) \models c(r(pre(t)), r(t))$ and if, in addition, $\mathcal{A}$ is complete, every trace has a run. However, if $\mathcal{T}$ is not discrete, even if $\mathcal{A}$ is complete, not every trace has a run. For example, a trace with infinite transitions among automaton-states within a finite interval has no run. A trace v is *specifiable* by $\mathcal{A}$ iff there is a run of $\mathcal{A}$ over v. Any discrete trace is specifiable by a complete automaton.

The definitions of accepting runs for ∀-automata and for Timed ∀-automata are the same as those in discrete cases. For example, Fig. 1(a) accepts the traces $x = \lambda t.Ce^{-t}$ for $G \equiv |x| < \epsilon$. Fig. 1(b) accepts the traces $x = \lambda t.\sin(t)$ for $D \equiv |x| > 1$. Fig. 1(c) and Fig. 2 accept the traces $x = \lambda t.\sin(t)$ for $E \equiv x \geq 0$ and $F \equiv x < 0$.

For the *Cat and Mouse* example, a formal requirements specification is shown in Fig 3: indicating that the cat should win.

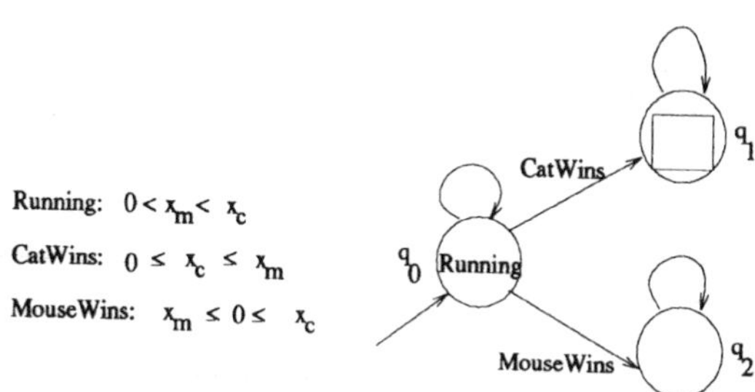

Fig. 3. Requirements specification: the cat should win

The distinguished features of timed ∀-automata are the following:

- Unlike other timed and/or hybrid automata, they are language recognizers rather than language generators. For example, they cannot generate traces like $\lambda t.Ce^{-t}$ and $\lambda t.sin(t)$, but can recognize some qualitative properties of these traces.
- They are finite state but can accept continuous-time hybrid-domain traces. Pre-sampling of the behavior of dynamic systems is not required.

Using timed ∀-automata, qualitative properties such as liveness, reachability and safety of hybrid systems can be formally specified and verified.

3.3 The Power of Timed ∀-automata

It has been shown [10] that Discrete ∀-automata have the same expressive power as Buchi Automata [14] and the Extended Temporal Logic (ETL) [15], which are strictly more powerful than (discrete) Propositional Linear Temporal Logic (PLTL) [14, 15]. Discrete Timed ∀-automata is a non-trivial generalization of Discrete ∀-automata; therefore, Discrete Timed ∀-automata is strictly more powerful than Discrete ∀-automata. However, when time is continuous, ∀-automata is no longer more powerful than PLTL, since the ability of counting in automata [11] is lost when time is dense. We have also developed Timed Linear Temporal Logics (TLTL) [21]. The relationship among Timed ∀-automata, TLTL and other automata and logics is discussed in [16].

4 A Formal Method for Behavior Verification

Let v be a trace and $\mathcal{A}$ be a $\forall$-automaton; we have defined that v is specifiable by $\mathcal{A}$ iff there is a run of $\mathcal{A}$ over v. Let $\mathcal{B}$ be the behavior of a dynamic system; $\mathcal{B}$ is *specifiable* by $\mathcal{A}$ iff $\forall v \in \mathcal{B}$, v is specifiable by $\mathcal{A}$. Let $\mathcal{B}$ be a behavior specifiable by $\mathcal{A}$ and $\mathcal{TA} = \langle \mathcal{A}, T, \tau \rangle$ be a timed $\forall$-automaton; $\mathcal{B}$ satisfies $\mathcal{TA}$, written $\mathcal{B} \models \mathcal{TA}$, iff $\forall v \in \mathcal{B}, v \models \mathcal{TA}$.

In this section, we propose a formal method for behavior verification, given a state-based and time-invariant behavior represented by a generalized Kripke structure and a requirements specification represented by a timed $\forall$-automaton.

Let φ and ψ be assertions on states and time durations. For a generalized Kripke structure $\mathcal{K} = \langle S, \rightsquigarrow, \Theta \rangle$, let $\{\varphi\}\mathcal{K}\{\psi\}$ denote the validity of the following two consecution conditions:

- *Inductivity* $\{\varphi\}\mathcal{K}^-\{\psi\}$: $\exists \delta > 0, \forall 0 < t \leq \delta, \forall s, (\varphi(s) \wedge (s \overset{t}{\rightsquigarrow} s') \Rightarrow \psi(s', t))$.
- *Continuity* $\{\varphi\}\mathcal{K}^+\{\psi\}$: $\varphi(s) \Rightarrow \exists \delta > 0, \forall 0 < t < \delta, \forall s', ((s \overset{t}{\rightsquigarrow} s') \Rightarrow \psi(s', t))$.

If $\mathcal{T}$ is discrete, these two conditions reduce to one, i.e., $\varphi(s) \wedge (s \overset{\delta}{\rightsquigarrow} s') \Rightarrow \psi(s', \delta)$ where δ is the minimum time duration between two states.

The formal method for behavior verification consists of a set of model-checking rules, which is a generalization of the model-checking rules developed for concurrent programs [10].

There are three types of rules: invariance rules (I), stability or eventuality rules (L) and timeliness rules (T). Let $\mathcal{A}$ be a $\forall$-automaton $\langle Q, R, S, e, c \rangle$ and $\mathcal{K}$ be a generalized Kripke structure $\langle S, \rightsquigarrow, \Theta \rangle$. The invariance rules check to see if a set of assertions $\{\alpha\}_{q \in Q}$ is a set of invariants for $\mathcal{A}$ and $\mathcal{K}$, i.e., for any trace v of $\mathcal{K}$ and any run r of $\mathcal{A}$ over v, $\forall t \in \mathcal{T}, v(t) \models \alpha_{r(t)}$. Given $B = Q - (R \cup S)$, the stability or eventuality rules check if the B-states in any run of $\mathcal{A}$ over any trace of $\mathcal{K}$ will be terminated eventually. Given $\mathcal{TA}$ as a timed $\forall$-automaton $\langle \mathcal{A}, T, \tau \rangle$, the timeliness rules check if the T-states and the B-states in any run of $\mathcal{A}$ over any trace of $\mathcal{K}$ are bounded by the time function τ. The set of model-checking rules can be represented in first-order logic, some of which are in the form of $\{\varphi\}\mathcal{K}\{\psi\}$.

Here are the model-checking rules for a behavior represented by $\mathcal{K} = \langle S, \rightsquigarrow, \Theta \rangle$ and a specification represented by $\mathcal{TA} = \langle \mathcal{A}, T, \tau \rangle$ where $\mathcal{A} = \langle Q, R, S, e, c \rangle$:

Invariance Rules (I): A set of assertions $\{\alpha_q\}_{q \in Q}$ is called a set of *invariants* for $\mathcal{K}$ and $\mathcal{A}$ iff

(I1) *Initiality*: $\forall q \in Q, \Theta \wedge e(q) \Rightarrow \alpha_q$.
(I2) *Consecution*: $\forall q, q' \in Q, \{\alpha_q\}\mathcal{K}\{c(q, q') \Rightarrow \alpha_{q'}\}$.

The Invariance Rules are the same as those in [10] except that the condition for consecution is generalized.

Stability or Eventuality Rules (L): Given that $\{\alpha_q\}_{q \in Q}$ is a set of invariants for $\mathcal{K}$ and $\mathcal{A}$, a set of partial functions $\{\rho_q\}_{q \in Q} : \mathcal{S} \rightarrow \mathcal{R}^+$ is called a set of *Liapunov functions* for $\mathcal{K}$ and $\mathcal{A}$ iff the following conditions are satisfied:

(L1) *Definedness*: $\forall q \in Q,\ \alpha_q \Rightarrow \exists w, \rho_q = w$.
(L2) *Non-increase*: $\forall q \in S, q' \in Q$, $\{\alpha_q \wedge \rho_q = w\}\mathcal{K}^-\{c(q,q') \Rightarrow \rho_{q'} \leq w\}$ and $\forall q \in Q, q' \in S$, $\{\alpha_q \wedge \rho_q = w\}\mathcal{K}^+\{c(q,q') \Rightarrow \rho_{q'} \leq w\}$.
(L3) *Decrease*: $\exists \epsilon > 0$, $\forall q \in B, q' \in Q$, $\{\alpha_q \wedge \rho_q = w\}\mathcal{K}^-\{c(q,q') \Rightarrow \frac{\rho_{q'}-w}{t} \leq -\epsilon\}$ and $\forall q \in Q, q' \in B$, $\{\alpha_q \wedge \rho_q = w\}\mathcal{K}^+\{c(q,q') \Rightarrow \frac{\rho_{q'}-w}{t} \leq -\epsilon\}$.

The Stability or Eventuality Rules generalize both stability analysis of discrete or continuous dynamic systems [8] and well-foundedness for finite termination in concurrent systems [10].

Timeliness Rules (T): Corresponding to two types of time bound, we define two timing functions. Let $\{\alpha_q\}_{q\in Q}$ be invariants for $\mathcal{K}$ and $\mathcal{A}$. A set of partial functions $\{\gamma_q\}_{q\in T}$ is called a set of *local timing functions* for $\mathcal{K}$ and $\mathcal{TA}$ iff $\gamma_q : \mathcal{S} \rightarrow \mathcal{R}^+$ satisfies the following conditions:

(T1) *Boundedness*: $\forall q \in T$, $\alpha_q \Rightarrow \gamma_q \leq \tau(q)$ and $\forall q \in T, q' \in Q$, $\{\alpha_q \wedge \gamma_q = w\}\mathcal{K}^-\{c(q,q') \Rightarrow w \geq t\}$.
(T2) *Decrease*: $\forall q \in T, \{\alpha_q \wedge \gamma_q = w\}\mathcal{K}\{c(q,q) \Rightarrow \frac{\gamma_q - w}{t} \leq -1\}$.

A set of partial functions $\{\eta_q\}_{q\in Q}$ is called a set of *global timing functions* for $\mathcal{K}$ and $\mathcal{TA}$ iff $\eta_q : \mathcal{S} \rightarrow \mathcal{R}^+$ satisfies the following conditions:

(T3) *Definedness*: $\forall q \in Q, \alpha_q \Rightarrow \exists w, \eta_q = w$.
(T4) *Boundedness*: $\forall q \in B, \alpha_q \Rightarrow \eta_q \leq \tau(bad)$.
(T5) *Non-increase*: $\forall q \in S, q' \in Q$, $\{\alpha_q \wedge \eta_q = w\}\mathcal{K}^-\{c(q,q') \Rightarrow \eta_{q'} \leq w\}$ and $\forall q \in Q, q' \in S$, $\{\alpha_q \wedge \eta_q = w\}\mathcal{K}^+\{c(q,q') \Rightarrow \eta_{q'} \leq w\}$.
(T6) *Decrease*: $\forall q \in B, q' \in Q$, $\{\alpha_q \wedge \eta_q = w\}\mathcal{K}^-\{c(q,q') \Rightarrow \frac{\eta_{q'}-w}{t} \leq -1\}$ and $\forall q \in Q, q' \in B$, $\{\alpha_q \wedge \eta_q = w\}\mathcal{K}^+\{c(q,q') \Rightarrow \frac{\eta_{q'}-w}{t} \leq -1\}$.

The Timeliness Rules are modifications of the Eventuality Rules; they enforce real-time boundedness, in addition to termination.

A set of model-checking rules is *sound* if verification by the rules guarantees the correctness of the behavior against the specification; it is *complete* if the correctness of the behavior against the specification guarantees verification by the rules.

Theorem 4.1 *The set of model-checking rules (I), (L) and (T) is sound given that the behavior of $\mathcal{K}$ is specifiable by $\mathcal{A}$.*

Theorem 4.2 *The set of model-checking rules (I), (L) and (T) is complete given that time is discrete.*

These theorems are proved in Appendix A. The general condition for the completeness of the rules has been described elsewhere [16].

We illustrate this verification method with the *Cat and Mouse* example. We show that the behavior of the cat and mouse in Section 2 satisfies the requirements specification in Fig. 3, given that the constant $\Delta = \frac{X_c}{V_c} - \frac{X_m}{V_m}$ satisfies $\Delta > 0$. The generalized Kripke structure $\mathcal{K}$ for the system can be derived from the constraint net equations Eq. 1: i.e., $\langle \mathcal{R}\times\mathcal{R}, \leadsto, \Theta\rangle$ where $\langle x_c, x_m\rangle \overset{t}{\leadsto} \langle x'_c, x'_m\rangle$ if

- $x_c > x_m > 0$, $x_c' > x_m' > 0$, $x_c' = x_c + V_c t$, $x_c' = x_c + V_c t$; or
- $x_c > x_m > 0$, $x_c' = x_m' = \frac{x_c V_m - x_m V_c}{V_m - V_c} \geq 0$, $t = \frac{x_c - x_m}{V_m - V_c}$; or
- $x_c > x_m > 0$, $x_m' = 0$, $x_c' = \frac{x_c V_m - x_m V_c}{V_m} \geq 0$, $t = -\frac{x_m}{V_m}$; or
- $\neg(x_c > x_m > 0)$, $x_c' = x_c$, $x_m' = x_m$.

and $\langle X_c, X_m \rangle \in \Theta$ with $\frac{X_c}{V_c} > \frac{X_m}{V_m}$.

Let Inv denote the invariant assertion $\frac{x_c}{V_c} - \frac{x_m}{V_m} = \Delta$. Associate with automaton-states q_0, q_1 and q_2 (Fig. 3) the assertions $Running \wedge Inv$, $CatWins$ and $false$, respectively. Note that

$$\{Running \wedge Inv\}\mathcal{K}\{Running \Rightarrow Running \wedge Inv\}$$

since the derivative of $\frac{x_c}{V_c} - \frac{x_m}{V_m}$ is 0 given that $Running$ is satisfied, and

$$\{Running \wedge Inv\}\mathcal{K}\{MouseWins \Rightarrow false\}$$

since $MouseWins$ implies $\frac{x_c}{V_c} - \frac{x_m}{V_m} \leq 0$. Therefore, the set of assertions is a set of invariants.

Associate with q_0, q_1 and q_2 the same function $\rho : \mathcal{R} \times \mathcal{R} \rightarrow \mathcal{R}^+$, such that $\rho(x_c, x_m) = 0$ if not $Running$ and $\rho(x_c, x_m) = -(\frac{x_m}{V_m} + \frac{x_c}{V_c})$ if $Running$. Function ρ is decreasing at q_0 with rate 2. Therefore, it is a Liapunov function.

Furthermore, the behavior of the cat and mouse is specifiable by the automaton in Fig. 3. According to the soundness of the rules, the behavior satisfies the required property.

A model-checking algorithm can be deduced from the set of rules (I), (L) and (T) for discrete-time finite-domain systems. The algorithm has polynomial time complexity with respect to both the size of the system and the size of the specification [16].

5 Conclusion and Further Research

We have presented in this paper Timed ∀-automata for the specification and verification of dynamic systems. To our knowledge, Timed ∀-automata are the first proposal for recognizing or representing timed dynamic behaviors, such as safety, reachability, liveness and real-time response, of continuous as well as discrete time dynamic systems using a finite number of states. In addition, we have proposed a formal model-checking method for behavior verification of dynamic systems. This method generalizes stability analysis of dynamic systems and can be completely automated for discrete-time finite-domain systems.

Much related work has been done in the last few years. The Timed Buchi Automata (TBA) model has been proposed [2] to express constant bounds on timing delays between system events. Other developments along this line include Timed Transition Systems [5] and Time Petri Nets [3]. Hybrid Automata [1] can be viewed as a generalization of TBA, in which the behavior of variables is governed in each state by a set of differential equations. Similar work includes Hybrid Statecharts and Phase Transition Systems [9].

The major difference between our work and others is that we use Constraint Nets as language generators and Timed ∀-automata as language recognizers. Timed ∀-automata can capture qualitative properties of traces, but they are not "fine" enough to distinguish all the different continuous traces. In the near future, we intend to explore semi-automatic and automatic verification procedures for various classes of hybrid dynamic systems.

Acknowledgements

This research is supported by Wilson Center for Research and Technology of Xerox Corporation, Natural Sciences and Engineering Research Council in Canada and the Institute for Robotics and Intelligent Systems.

References

1. R. Alur, C. Courcoubetis, T. A. Henzinger, and P. Ho. Hybrid automata: An algorithmic approach to the specification and verification of hybrid systems. In R. L. Grossman, A. Nerode, A. P. Ravn, and H. Rischel, editors, *Hybrid Systems*, number 736 in Lecture Notes on Computer Science, pages 209 – 229. Springer-Verlag, 1993.
2. R. Alur and D. Dill. Automata for modeling real-time systems. In M. S. Paterson, editor, *ICALP90: Automata, Languages and Programming*, number 443 in Lecture Notes on Computer Science, pages 322 – 335. Springer-Verlag, 1990.
3. B. Berthomieu and M. Diaz. Modeling and verification of time dependent systems using Time Petri Nets. *IEEE Transactions on Software Engineering*, 17(3):259 – 273, March 1991.
4. R. L. Grossman, A. Nerode, A. P. Ravn, and H. Rischel, editors. *Hybrid Systems*. Number 736 in Lecture Notes on Computer Science. Springer-Verlag, 1993.
5. T. A. Henzinger, Z. Manna, and A. Pnueli. Timed transition systems. In J.W. de-Bakker, C. Huizing, W.P. dePoever, and G. Rozenberg, editors, *Real-Time: Theory in Practice*, number 600 in Lecture Notes on Computer Science, pages 226–251. Springer-Verlag, 1991.
6. G. F. Khilmi. *Qualitative Methods in the Many Body Problem*. Science Publishers Inc. New York, 1961.
7. N. G. Leveson and P. G. Neumann, editors. *IEEE Transactions on Software Engineering*. IEEE Computer Society, January 1993. Special Issue on Software for Critical Systems.
8. D. G. Luenberger. *Introduction to Dynamic Systems: Theory, Models and Applications*. John Wiley & Sons, 1979.
9. O. Maler, Z. Manna, and A. Pnueli. From timed to hybrid systems. In J.W. de-Bakker, C. Huizing, W.P. dePoever, and G. Rozenberg, editors, *Real-Time: Theory in Practice*, number 600 in Lecture Notes on Computer Science, pages 448 – 484. Springer-Verlag, 1991.
10. Z. Manna and A. Pnueli. Specification and verification of concurrent programs by ∀-automata. In *Proc. 14th Ann. ACM Symp. on Principles of Programming Languages*, pages 1–12, 1987.
11. R. McNaughton and S. Papert. *Counter-Free Automata*. MIT Press, 1971.
12. H. L. Royden. *Real Analysis, 3rd edition*. Macmillan Publishing Company, 1988.

13. M. Sahota and A. K. Mackworth. Can situated robots play soccer? In *Proc. Artificial Intelligence 94*, pages 249 – 254, Banff, Alberta, May 1994.
14. W. Thomas. Automata on infinite objects. In Jan Van Leeuwen, editor, *Handbook of Theoretical Computer Science*. MIT Press, 1990.
15. P. Wolper. Temporal logic can be more expressive. *Information and Control*, 56:72 – 99, 1983.
16. Y. Zhang. A foundation for the design and analysis of robotic systems and behaviors. Technical Report 94-26, Department of Computer Science, University of British Columbia, 1994. Ph.D. thesis.
17. Y. Zhang and A. K. Mackworth. Specification and verification of constraint-based dynamic systems. In A. Borning, editor, *Principles and Practice of Constraint Programming*, Lecture Notes in Computer Science 874, pages 229 – 242. Springer Verlag, 1994.
18. Y. Zhang and A. K. Mackworth. Will the robot do the right thing? In *Proc. Artificial Intelligence 94*, pages 255 – 262, Banff, Alberta, May 1994.
19. Y. Zhang and A. K. Mackworth. Constraint Nets: A semantic model for hybrid dynamic systems. *Theoretical Computer Science*, 138(1):211 – 239, 1995. Special Issue on Hybrid Systems.
20. Y. Zhang and A. K. Mackworth. Constraint programming in constraint nets. In V. Saraswat and P. Van Hentenryck, editors, *Principles and Practice of Constraint Programming*, pages 49 – 68. MIT Press, 1995.
21. Y. Zhang and A. K. Mackworth. Synthesis of hybrid constraint-based controllers. In P. Antsaklis, W. Kohn, A. Nerode, and S. Sastry, editors, *Hybrid Systems II*, Lecture Notes in Computer Science 999, pages 552 – 567. Springer Verlag, 1995.

A Proofs of Theorems and Lemmas

Lemma 2.1 *If $\mathcal{T}$ is a discrete time structure of $\mathcal{K}$, then there is $\delta > 0$, for any $t > 0, \mu([pre(t), t)) = \delta$. And $\mathcal{K}$ can be represented as the transitive closure of transitions of next relation $s_1 \overset{\delta}{\leadsto} s_2$.*
Proof: Assume $\mu([pre(t), t)) = \delta$ and $\mu([pre(t'), t')) = \delta'$, such that $\delta < \delta'$. For time point $pre(t')$ and $s_1 \overset{\delta}{\leadsto} s_2$, there is no time t'' such that $\mu([pre(t'), t''))) = \delta$. Therefore, $\delta = \delta'$. □

Theorem 4.1 *The set of model-checking rules (I), (L) and (T) is sound given that the behavior of $\mathcal{K}$ is specifiable by $\mathcal{A}$.*

In order to prove this theorem, we shall introduce a method of continuous induction modified from [6]. A property Γ is *inductive* on a time structure $\mathcal{T}$ iff Γ is satisfied at all $t < t_0 \in \mathcal{T}$ implies that Γ is satisfied at t_0, for all $t_0 \in \mathcal{T}$. Γ is *continuous* iff Γ is satisfied at $t_0 \in \mathcal{T}$ implies that $\exists t_1 > t, \forall t, t_0 < t < t_1$, Γ is satisfied at t. We should notice that when $\mathcal{T}$ is discrete, any property is trivially continuous. The theorem of continuous induction says:

Theorem A.1 *If a property Γ is inductive and continuous on a time structure $\mathcal{T}$ and Γ is satisfied at 0, Γ is satisfied at all $t \in \mathcal{T}$.*

Proof: We call a time point $t \in \mathcal{T}$ *regular* iff Γ is satisfied at all t', $\mathbf{0} \leq t' \leq t$. Let T denote the set of all regular time points. T is not empty since Γ is satisfied at $\mathbf{0}$. We prove the theorem by contradiction, i.e., assume that Γ is not satisfied at all $t \in \mathcal{T}$. Therefore, $T \subset \mathcal{T}$ is bounded above; let $t_0 = \bigvee T \in \mathcal{T}$ be the least upper bound of T ($\mathcal{T}$ is complete). Since t_0 is the least upper bound, it follows that Γ is satisfied at all t, $\mathbf{0} \leq t < t_0$. Since Γ is inductive, it is satisfied at time t_0. Therefore, $t_0 \in T$.

Since $T \subset \mathcal{T}$, t_0 is not the greatest element in $\mathcal{T}$. Let $T' = \{t | t > t_0\}$. There are two cases: (1) if T' has a least element t', since Γ is inductive, $t' \in T$ is a regular time point. (2) otherwise, for any $t' \in T'$, $\{t | t_0 < t < t'\} \neq \emptyset$. Since Γ is also continuous, we can find a $t' \in T'$ such that Γ is satisfied at all $T'' = \{t | t_0 < t < t'\}$. Therefore, t is a regular time point $\forall t \in T''$. Both cases contradict the fact that t_0 is the least upper bound of the set T. □

Using the method of continuous induction, we obtain the following three lemmas.

Lemma A.1 *Let $\{\alpha_q\}_{q \in Q}$ be invariants for $\mathcal{K}$ and $\mathcal{A}$. If r is a run of $\mathcal{A}$ over a trace v of $\mathcal{K}$, $\forall t \in \mathcal{T}, v(t) \models \alpha_{r(t)}$.*

Proof: We prove that the property $v(t) \models \alpha_{r(t)}$ is satisfied at $\mathbf{0}$ and is both inductive and continuous on any time structure $\mathcal{T}$.

- Initiality: Since $v(\mathbf{0}) \models \Theta$ and $v(\mathbf{0}) \models e(r(\mathbf{0}))$, we have $v(\mathbf{0}) \models \Theta \wedge e(r(\mathbf{0}))$. According to the *Initiality* condition of invariants, we have $v(\mathbf{0}) \models \alpha_{r(\mathbf{0})}$.
- Inductivity: Suppose $v(t) \models \alpha_{r(t)}$ is saisfied at $\mathbf{0} \leq t < t_0$. Since r is a run over v, according to the *Inductivity* of runs, $\exists q \in Q$ and $\exists t_1' < t_0, \forall t_1' \leq t < t_0, r(t) = q$ and $v(t_0) \models c(q, r(t_0))$. According to the *Inductivity* condition of the invariants, $\exists t_2' < t_0, \forall t_2' \leq t < t_0$, $v(t) \models \alpha_q$ implies $v(t_0) \models c(q, r(t_0)) \Rightarrow \alpha_{r(t_0)}$. Therefore, let $t' = \max(t_1', t_2'), \forall t' \leq t < t_0$, $r(t) = q$, $v(t) \models \alpha_q$ (assumption), $v(t_0) \models c(q, r(t_0)) \Rightarrow \alpha_{r(t_0)}$ and $v(t_0) \models c(q, r(t_0))$. Thus, $v(t_0) \models \alpha_{r(t_0)}$.
- Continuity: Suppose $v(t_0) \models \alpha_{r(t_0)}$. Since r is a run over v, according to the *Continuity* of runs, $\exists q \in Q$ and $\exists t_1' > t_0, \forall t_0 < t < t_1'$, $r(t) = q$ and $v(t) \models c(r(t_0), q)$. According to the *Continuity* condition of the invariants, $\exists t_2' > t_0, \forall t_0 < t < t_2'$, $v(t) \models c(r(t_0), q) \Rightarrow \alpha_q$. Therefore, let $t' = \min(t_1', t_2')$, $\forall t_0 < t < t'$, $r(t) = q$, $v(t_0) \models \alpha_{r(t_0)}$ (assumption), $v(t) \models c(r(t_0), q) \Rightarrow \alpha_q$ and $v(t) \models c(r(t_0), q)$. Thus, $\forall t_0 < t < t'$, $v(t) \models \alpha_{r(t)}$.

□

Lemma A.2 *Let $\{\alpha_q\}_{q \in Q}$ be invariants for $\mathcal{K}$ and $\mathcal{A}$ and r be a run of $\mathcal{A}$ over a trace v of $\mathcal{K}$. If $\{\rho_q\}_{q \in Q}$ is a set of Liapunov functions for $\mathcal{K}$ and $\mathcal{A}$, then*

- *$\rho_{r(t_2)}(v(t_2)) \leq \rho_{r(t_1)}(v(t_1))$ when $\forall t_1 \leq t \leq t_2, r(t) \in B \cup S$,*
- *$\frac{\rho_{r(t_2)}(v(t_2)) - \rho_{r(t_1)}(v(t_1))}{\mu([t_1, t_2))} \leq -\epsilon$ when $t_1 < t_2$ and $\forall t_1 \leq t \leq t_2, r(t) \in B$, and*
- *for any run r and any interval I of $\mathcal{T}$, if $r_{|I} \in Sg(B \cup S)$, $\int_I \chi_B(r(t))dt < \infty$.*

Proof: For any run r over v and for any interval I of $\mathcal{T}$, if $r_{|I} \in Sg(B \cup S)$, ρ on I is nonincreasing, i.e., for any $t_1 < t_2 \in I$, $\rho_{r(t_1)}(v(t_1)) \geq \rho_{r(t_2)}(v(t_2))$, and the decreasing speed at intervals of the bad states is no less than ϵ. Let m be the upper bound of $\{\rho_{r(t)}(v(t)) | t \in I\}$. Since $\rho_q \geq 0$, $\int_I \chi_B(r(t))dt \leq m/\epsilon < \infty$. □

Lemma A.3 *Let $\{\alpha_q\}_{q \in Q}$ be invariants for $\mathcal{K}$ and $\mathcal{A}$ and r be a run of $\mathcal{A}$ over a trace v of $\mathcal{K}$. If there exist local and global timing functions for $\mathcal{K}$ and $\mathcal{TA}$, then*

- *for any $q \in T$, any run r and any interval I of $\mathcal{T}$, if $r_{|I} \in Sg(\{q\})$, $\mu(I) \leq \tau(q)$ and*
- *for any run r and any interval I of $\mathcal{T}$, if $r_{|I} \in Sg(B \cup S)$, $\int_I \chi_B(r(t))dt \leq \tau(bad)$.*

Proof: Similar to the proof of Lemma A.2. □

Proof of Theorem 4.1: For any trace v of $\mathcal{K}$, there is a run since v is specifiable by $\mathcal{A}$. For any run r of $\mathcal{A}$ over v, if any automaton-state in R appears infinitely many times in r, r is accepting for $\mathcal{A}$. Otherwise there is a time point t_0, such that the sub-sequence r on $I = \{t \in \mathcal{T} | t \geq t_0\}$ has only bad and stable automaton-states. If there exist a set of invariants and a set of Liapunov functions, $\int_I \chi_B(r(t))dt$ is finite. Therefore, all the automaton-states appearing infinitely many times in r belong to S; r is accepting for $\mathcal{A}$ too. If there exists a set of local and global timing functions, r satisfies the time constraints; r is accepting for $\mathcal{TA}$. Therefore, the behavior of $\mathcal{K}$ satisfies the specification $\mathcal{TA}$. □

Theorem 4.2 *The set of model-checking rules (I), (L) and (T) is complete given that time is discrete.*
Proof: If $\mathcal{TA}$ is valid over $\mathcal{K}$, then there exist a set of invariants, a set of Liapunov functions, and a set of local and global timing functions that satisfy the requirements.

Let $n(s, s')$ denote $s \overset{\delta}{\leadsto} s'$ where δ is the minimum time duration between two states. The invariants can be constructed as the fixpoint of the set of equations:

$$\alpha_{q'}(s') = (\exists q, s, \alpha_q(s) \wedge n(s, s') \wedge c(q, q')(s')) \bigvee (\Theta(s') \wedge e(q')(s')).$$

We can verify that $\{\alpha_q\}_{q \in Q}$ is a set of assertions on the states of $\mathcal{K}$ and satisfies the requirements of initiality and consecution. Furthermore, $s \models \alpha_q$ iff $\langle q, s \rangle$ is a reachable pair for $\mathcal{A}$ and $\mathcal{K}$.

Given the constructed invariants $\{\alpha_q\}_{q \in Q}$, a set of Liapunov functions $\{\rho_q\}_{q \in Q}$ and a set of global timing functions $\{\eta_q\}_{q \in Q}$ can be constructed as follows:

- $\forall q \in R, s \models \alpha_q$, let $\rho_q(s) = 0$ and $\eta_q(s) = 0$.

- $\forall q \notin R, s \models \alpha_q$, $\rho_q(s)$ and $\eta_q(s)$ are defined as follows. Construct a directed graph $G = \langle V, E \rangle$, such that $\langle q, s \rangle \in V$ iff $q \notin R, s \models \alpha_q$, and $\langle q, s \rangle \mapsto \langle q', s' \rangle$ in E iff $n(s, s') \wedge c(q, q')(s')$. For any path p starting at $\langle q, s \rangle$, let $|p|_B$ be the number of B-states in p. Let $\rho_q(s) = \sup\{|p|_B\}$ and $\eta_q(s) = \delta \rho_q(s)$.

We can verify that $\{\rho_q\}_{q \in Q}$ is a set of Liapunov functions, and that $\{\eta_q\}_{q \in Q}$ is a set of global timing functions.

Similar construction can be carried out for local timing functions. A set of local timing functions $\{\gamma_q\}_{q \in T}$ can be constructed as follows. For all $q \in T$, construct a directed graph $G = \langle V, E \rangle$, such that $s \in V$ iff $s \models \alpha_q$, and $s \mapsto s'$ in E iff $n(s, s') \wedge c(q, q)(s')$. For any path p starting at s, let $|p|$ be the number of states in the path. Let $\gamma_q(s) = \delta \sup\{|p|\}$. We can verify that $\{\gamma_q\}_{q \in T}$ is a set of local timing functions. □

This proof is the basis of the verification algorithm for discrete systems [16].

Fischer's Protocol Revisited: A Simple Proof Using Modal Constraints

Kim G. Larsen*[1], Bernhard Steffen[2], Carsten Weise[3]

[1] BRICS[†], Aalborg Univ., Denmark, kgl@iesd.auc.dk
[2] FB Math. u. Informatik, Univ. of Passau, Germany, steffen@fmi.uni-passau.de
[3] Lehrstuhl fuer Informatik I, Univ. of Tech. Aachen, Germany, carsten@informatik.rwth-aachen.de

Abstract. As a case study, we apply a constraint-oriented state-based proof methodology to Fischer's protocol. The method exploits compositionality and abstraction to reduce the investigated verification problem. This reduction avoids state space explosion. Key concepts of the reduction process are *modal constraints*, *separation of proof obligations*, *Skolemization* and *abstraction*. Formal basis for the method are Timed Modal Specifications (TMS) allowing loose state-based specifications, which can be refined by successively adding constraints. TMS's can be easily translated into *Modal* Timed Automata, thus enabling automatic verification. A central issue of the method is the use of *Parametrized* TMS's.

1 Introduction

The use of state-based formal methods – in particular formal verification of concurrent systems – is still limited to very specific problem classes, mainly due to the state explosion problem: the state graph of the system grows exponentially with the number of its parallel components – and clocks in the real-time case –, leading to an unmanageable size for most practically relevant systems. Consequently, several techniques have been developed to tackle this problem. Among these four main streams can be identified: *compositional* methods (e.g. [ASW94, CLM89, GS90][5]), which due to the nature of parallel compositions are unfortunately rarely applicable, *partial order* methods ([GW91, Val93, GP93]), which try to avoid the state explosion problem by suppressing unnecessary interleavings of actions, *Binary Decision Diagram*-based codings of the state graph (e.g. [Br86, BCMDH90, EFT91]) and *abstraction*([CC77, CGL92, GL93]): depending on the particular property under investigation, systems may be dramatically reduced by suppressing details that are irrelevant for verification. All

* This author has been partially supported by the European Communities under CONCUR2, BRA 7166.

† Basic Research in Computer Science, Centre of the Danish National Research Foundation.

[5] In contrast to the first reference, the subsequent two papers address compositional reduction of systems rather than compositional verification.

these methods cover very specific cases without hope for a uniform approach. Thus more application specific approaches are required, extending the practicality of formal methods.

As a case study, we will prove that mutual exclusion is guaranteed by Fischer's protocol [AL93]. Although quite simple, Fischer's protocol is an ideal benchmark for real time analysis systems – used e.g. in [AC+95] or [LPY95] –, as its correctness depends on certain timing criteria. While the above publications verified Fischer's protocol (automatically) for a fixed number of processes the result presented here gives a proof for an arbitrary number of processes.

Our methodolgy is constraint-oriented, state-based and suitable for concurrent software systems. It exploits compositionality and abstraction for the reduction of the investigated verification problem. As formal basis we use Modal Transition Systems (MTS) [LT88] permitting loose state-based specifications, which can be refined by successively adding constraints. This allows extremely fine-granular specifications characteristic for our approach: each aspect of a system component is specified by a number of independent *modal constraints*, one for each parameter configuration. Our approach leads to a usually infinite number of extremely simple constraints which must all be satisfied by a corresponding component implementation. This extreme component decomposition supports the exploitation of compositionality in the standard (vertical) fashion as well as in a horizontal way, leading to separate proof obligations for subcomponents or subproperties but also for the various parameter instantiations. This is the key to the success of the following three step reduction, which may reduce a problem of infinite size to a small number of automatically verifiable problems of finite size:

- *Separating the Proof Obligations.* Section 4.1 presents a proof principle justifying the separation and specialization of the various proof obligations, which prepare the ground for the subsequent reduction steps.
- *Skolemization.* The separation of the first step leaves us with problems smaller in size but larger in number. Due to the nature of their origin, these problems often fall into a small number of equivalence classes requiring only one prototypical proof each.
- *Abstraction.* After the first two reduction steps there may still be problems with infinite state graphs. However, the extreme specialization of the problem supports the power of abstract interpretation, which finally may reduce all the proof obligations to finite ones.

Our proof methodology is not complete, i.e., there is neither a guarantee for the existence of a finite state reduction nor a straightforward method for finding the right amount of separation for the success of the subsequent steps or the adequate abstraction for the final verification. Still, as should be clear from the example in the paper, there is a large class of problems and systems, where the method can be applied straightforwardly. Of course, the more complex the system structure the more involved will be the required search of appropriate granularity and abstraction.

Whereas complex data dependencies may exclude any possibility of 'horizontal' decomposition, our approach elegantly includes real time systems, even over dense time. Using real time does not affect the reduction steps. To model real time systems, we use Timed Modal Specifications [CGL93], for which (weak) refinement is decidable and the EPSILON tool can be used to verify refinements.

To model the general case of Fischer's protocol, we use *parametrized* timed modal specifications. Parameters may appear either in actions (*parametrized actions*) or in timing constraints. While parametrized actions do not interfere with decidability here, the decision procedures used in the EPSILON tool cannot be directly applied to transition systems with parameters in timing constraints. Therefore we will discuss how to extend EPSILON by combining techniques of [AC+95, Čer92, AHV93] for Timed Automaton[AD94].

The next section recalls the basic theory of (Timed) Modal Transition Systems, which we use for system specification. Thereafter we describe Fischer's protocol. The following sections explain our method in detail. Section 4.1 discusses the first reduction step and presents our notion of modal constraints. The subsequent two sections are devoted to the second and third reduction step, while Section 5 discusses how to check the reduced problem automatically. Finally, Section 6 summarizes our conclusion and directions to future work.

2 Modal and Timed Modal Specifications

This section gives a brief introduction to the existing theory of modal transition systems (MTS) and timed modal specifications (TMS). More elaborate introductions are found in [LT88, HL89, Lar90] for MTS and in [CGL93, God94] for TMS.

The following assumes familiarity with CCS [Mil89]. In contrast with traditional Process Algebras, MTS's distinguish between actions *required* of the implementation and actions *admissible* in the implementation, thus allowing a more flexible specification and a much more generous notion of implementation, improving the practicality of the operational approach:

Definition 1. *A modal transition system is a structure* $\mathcal{S} = (\Sigma, A, \rightarrow_\Box, \rightarrow_\Diamond)$, *where* Σ *is a set of states,* A *is a set of actions and* $\rightarrow_\Box, \rightarrow_\Diamond \subseteq \Sigma \times A \times \Sigma$ *are transition relations, satisfying the consistency condition* $\rightarrow_\Box \subseteq \rightarrow_\Diamond$. □

The requirement $\rightarrow_\Box \subseteq \rightarrow_\Diamond$ expresses consistency (anything required should be allowed). In the case $\rightarrow_\Box = \rightarrow_\Diamond$, the above reduces to the traditional notion of labelled transition systems.

The syntax of CCS is slightly extended by prefix constructs $a_\Box.P$ and $a_\Diamond.P$ (yielding *modal CCS*) with the following semantics: $a_\Diamond.P \xrightarrow{a}_\Diamond P$, $a_\Box.P \xrightarrow{a}_\Box P$ and $a_\Box.P \xrightarrow{a}_\Diamond P$. The other constructs of CCS have rules for $\rightarrow_\Box$ and $\rightarrow_\Diamond$ respectively.

A *refinement relation* $\triangleleft$ allows to perform the design process as a sequence of refinement steps. A specification (implementation) S is stronger than T, if anything allowed by S is allowed by T, while everything required by T must be required by S:

Definition 2. *A refinement $\mathcal{R}$ is a binary relation on Σ such that whenever $S\,\mathcal{R}\,T$ and $a \in A$ then the following holds:*

1. *Whenever $S \xrightarrow{a}_\diamond S'$, then $T \xrightarrow{a}_\diamond T'$ for some T' with $S'\,\mathcal{R}\,T'$,*
2. *Whenever $T \xrightarrow{a}_\Box T'$, then $S \xrightarrow{a}_\Box S'$ for some S' with $S'\,\mathcal{R}\,T'$.*

S is said to be a refinement of T in case (S,T) is contained in some refinement $\mathcal{R}$. We write $S \lhd T$ in this case. □

If $\rightarrow_\Box = \rightarrow_\diamond$, we obtain the well–known notion of bisimulation [Par81, Mil89]. The relation $\lhd$ is a preorder preserved by all modal CCS operators, which allows *loose* specifications.

Intuitively, S and T are *independent* if they are not contradictory, i.e. any action required by one is not constraint by the other. The following formal definition is due to the fact that for S and T to be *independent* all 'simultaneously' reachable processes S' and T' must be indenpendent too:

Definition 3. *An independence relation $\mathcal{R}$ is a binary relation on Σ such that whenever $S\,\mathcal{R}\,T$ and $a \in A$ then the following holds:*

1. *Whenever $S \xrightarrow{a}_\Box S'$, there is a unique T' such that $T \xrightarrow{a}_\diamond T'$ and $S'\,\mathcal{R}\,T'$,*
2. *Whenever $T \xrightarrow{a}_\Box T'$, there is a unique S' such that $S \xrightarrow{a}_\diamond S'$ and $S'\,\mathcal{R}\,T'$,*
3. *Whenever $S \xrightarrow{a}_\diamond S'$ and $T \xrightarrow{a}_\diamond T'$ then $S'\,\mathcal{R}\,T'$.*

S and T are said to be independent *in case (S,T) is contained in some independence relation $\mathcal{R}$.* □

Note in particular that two specifications are independent if none of them requires any actions. Conjunction $\wedge$ can be defined for independent processes by:

$$\frac{S \xrightarrow{a}_\Box S' \quad T \xrightarrow{a}_\diamond T'}{S \wedge T \xrightarrow{a}_\Box S' \wedge T'} \qquad \frac{S \xrightarrow{a}_\diamond S' \quad T \xrightarrow{a}_\Box T'}{S \wedge T \xrightarrow{a}_\Box S' \wedge T'} \qquad \frac{S \xrightarrow{a}_\diamond S' \quad T \xrightarrow{a}_\diamond T'}{S \wedge T \xrightarrow{a}_\diamond S' \wedge T'}$$

In fact, $S \wedge T$ is again a modal specifications defining *logical* conjunction if S and T are independent:

Theorem 4. Let S and T be independent modal specifications. Then $S \wedge T \lhd S$ and $S \wedge T \lhd T$. Moreover, if $R \lhd S$ and $R \lhd T$ then $R \lhd S \wedge T$.

In order to compare specifications at different levels of abstraction, it is important to abstract from internal communication (modelled by τ-actions). This is done in the traditional way by substituting the relations $\rightarrow_\Box, \rightarrow_\diamond$ by their τ-closures $\Rightarrow_\Box, \Rightarrow_\diamond$. The notion of *weak refinement* $\unlhd$ is introduced as the relation $\lhd$ on the resulting transition system. Weak refinement essentially enjoys the same pleasant properties as $\lhd$: it is a preorder preserved by all modal CCS operators except $+$ [HL89] (including restriction, relabelling and hiding). For $\rightarrow_\Box = \rightarrow_\diamond$ weak refinement reduces to the usual notion of weak bisimulation ($\approx$).

To model real time behaviour, modal transition systems can be extended to *Timed Modal Specifications* (TMS) by means of delay-transitions. Delay-transitions are labelled by actions $\varepsilon(d)$, where d is a positive real number (or from any other suitable time domain) Syntactically, delays are written as prefixes $\varepsilon(d)$, with rules $\varepsilon(c+d).P \xrightarrow{c}_{\Box} \varepsilon(d).P$ and $\varepsilon(d).P \xrightarrow{d}_{\Box} P$(analogously for $\rightarrow_{\diamond}$). The process $\varepsilon(d).P$ will delay for time d, and then behave as P. For $a_{\Box}.P$, action a is ready immediately, but may be taken after any delay. This is reflected by additional rules $a_{\Box}.P \xrightarrow{\varepsilon(d)}_{\Box} a_{\Box}.P$ (analogously for $a_{\diamond}.P$).

Timed Modal Specifications come equipped with operators such as restriction, non-deterministic choice and parallel composition, which are defined as conservative extension of Wang's TCCS[Yi91]. TCCS relies on *maximal progress*: internal communication takes place as soon as it becomes available. Therefore, in TMS parallel composition satisfies:

1. a TMS will not allow time-steps if it requires an internal action
2. a TMS will not require time-steps if it allows an internal action

Intuitively by (1) a state requiring a τ may not delay for any amount of time, thus forcing either the communication or another discrete change to happen, while by (2) if a delay is required, no internal communication may be enabled.

Lower time bounds are easily specified in TMS, but for upper time bounds maximal progress is required. We will use a macro operator to specify intervals. The process $a[\ell, u].P$ ($\ell, u \in \mathbb{R}^{\geq 0}, \ell \leq u$) allows a to happen within time ℓ and requires a to be enabled after time u. The macro is defined as $(\varepsilon(l).a_{\diamond} + \varepsilon(u).a_{\Box}).P$. The upper bound u will only be fulfilled due to maximal progress.

The notions of refinement, weak refinement, independence and conjunction carry over from Modal Specifications to TMS without problem.

3 Fischer's Protocol

In this section we explain Fischer's protocol[AL93] and specify the verification problem using TMS.

The investigated system consists of n processes $P(1)$ to $P(n)$ all ready to enter their critical section. To ensure mutual exclusion a shared variable V is used. All processes start with testing V against 0. After the test is met, every process $P(i)$ tries to set V to its process identifier i. If successful, process $P(i)$ enters its critical section. On leaving the critical section, the variable is reset.

There is an upper bound b_i on the time process $P(i)$ needs to set the variable V, and a lower bound c_i on the time between setting and testing the variable. The claim is that if $b_i < c_j$ for all pairs $i \neq j$, then mutual exclusion is guaranteed.

3.1 Specification

We need to model the processes $P(1)$ to $P(n)$, the shared variable V and our notion of mutual exclusion in TMS. For this the following actions are used:

$\mathtt{rd}(i)/\mathtt{wr}(i)$: read/write value $i \in \mathbb{N}$ from/to shared variable

$\mathtt{enter}(i)/\mathtt{leave}(i)$: process $P(i)$ enters/leaves its critical section

These kind of actions are called *paramterized* actions: there are four essential actions, all with a parameter i. These actions and their inverses $\overline{\mathtt{rd}(i)}$ etc. are sufficient to model the problem.

First we give the specification of mutual exclusion, called $MUTEX$. Informally it can be expressed by: *After $P(i)$ has entered its critical section, $P(j)$ may not enter its critical section before $P(i)$ leaves it, for all pairs $i \neq j$.*

Let $\texttt{Act}_{cs}$ be the set of all actions for entering and leaving criticial sections:

$$\texttt{Act}_{cs} := \{\texttt{enter}(i), \texttt{leave}(i) \mid i \in \{1, \ldots, n\}\}$$

and let $A(i) := \texttt{Act}_{cs} \setminus \{\texttt{enter}(i)\}$ and $B(i,j) := \texttt{Act}_{cs} \setminus \{\texttt{enter}(j), \texttt{leave}(i)\}$. Then mutual exclusion for $P(i)$ and $P(j)$ can be defined as the following TMS:

$$\begin{aligned} EX(i,j) &:= EX_0(i,j) \\ EX_0(i,j) &:= \sum_{a \in A(i)} a_\diamond.EX_0(i,j) + \texttt{enter}(i)_\diamond.EX_1(i,j) \\ EX_1(i,j) &:= \sum_{a \in B(i,j)} a_\diamond.EX_1(i,j) + \texttt{leave}(i)_\diamond.EX_0(i,j) \end{aligned}$$

This can be depicted as the following transition system (where dotted lines indicate may-transitions):

EX(i,j): Act \ {enter i} (0) —enter(i)→ (1) Act \ {leave i, enter j}; (1) —leave(i)→ (0)

Using $EX(i,j)$, mutual exclusion of all processes is defined by

$$MUTEX_n = \bigwedge_{i,j \in \{1,\ldots,n\}, i \neq j} EX(i,j)$$

This approach is typical of our method: a specification is a conjunction of a number of *modal constraints* (or *projective views*). Each projective view constrains the behaviour of the system focusing on a certain aspect.

Next we model the shared variable V with initial value 0:

$$\begin{aligned} V &:= V(0) \\ \forall i \in \mathbb{N} : V(i) &:= \sum_{j \in \mathbb{N}} \texttt{wr}(j)_\diamond.V(j) + \overline{\texttt{rd}(i)}_\diamond.V(i) \end{aligned}$$

In state $V(i)$ the variable has the value i. In this state the variable accepts any write $\texttt{wr}(j) (j \in \mathbb{N})$, leading to state $V(j)$, while it can only issue $\overline{\texttt{rd}(i)}$. Note that V has infinitely many states $V(i)$.

Finally, we give a specification of a process $P(i)$ as a TMS:

$$P(i) := P_0(i) \qquad P_0(i) := \texttt{rd}(0)_\diamond.P_1(i) \qquad P_1(i) := \overline{\texttt{wr}(i)}[0, b_i].P_2(i)$$
$$P_2(i) := \varepsilon(c_i).\texttt{rd}(i)_\diamond.P_3(i) \qquad P_3(i) := \texttt{enter}(i)_\diamond.\texttt{leave}(i)_\diamond.\texttt{wr}(0)_\diamond.P_0(i)$$

which can be depicted as:

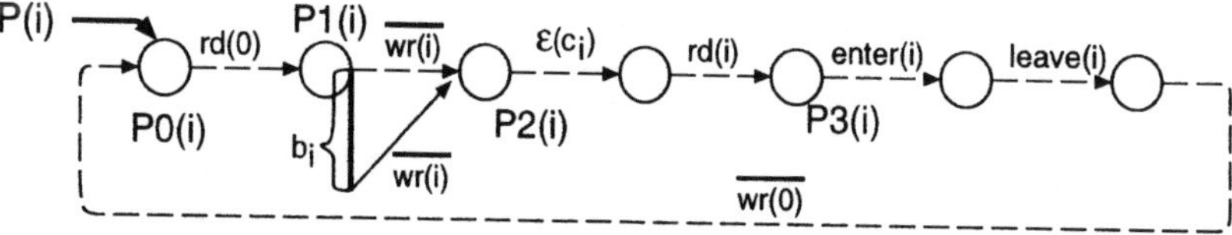

With these definitions, Fischers's protocol for n processes becomes

$$F(n) := \big(P(1) \mid \ldots \mid P(n)\big) \mid V$$

i.e. the parallel execution of the processes $P(i)$ and the shared variable V.

To specify that the protocol guarantees mutual exclusion, we must internalise the access of the process to the shared variable. As restriction set we use $L := \{\mathtt{rd}(i), \mathtt{wr}(i) \mid i \in \{1, \ldots, n\}\}$. We need to verify the following claim:

$$\forall n \in \mathbb{N}.\ (\forall i \neq j.\, b_i < c_j) \ \Rightarrow\ F(n) \setminus L \ \trianglelefteq\ MUTEX_n \tag{1}$$

This claim cannot be directly solved using automatic methods as

- this is a family of problems, one for each $n \in \mathbb{N}$,
- for fixed n, the transition systems are infinitely large,
- the timing information is not explicit, i.e. there are parameters b_i, c_i within the timing constraints.

In the following section we will show how to reduce the problem so that the diminished problem can be solved by automated methods.

4 Reducing the Problem

The reduction process follows the three steps mentioned in the introduction:

4.1 Reduction Step 1: Separation

The first step is *separation* of proof goals. For a fixed n, using the definition of $MUTEX_n$, claim (1) can be rewritten as

$$(\forall i \neq j.\, b_i < c_j) \ \Rightarrow\ F(n) \setminus L \ \trianglelefteq \bigwedge_{i,j \in \{1,\ldots,n\}, i \neq j} EX(i,j)$$

It is easy to see that a sufficient condition is

$$\forall i \neq j.\ \big(b_i < c_j \ \Rightarrow\ F(n) \setminus L \ \trianglelefteq\ EX(i,j)\big) \tag{2}$$

From intuition it should be clear that verifying mutual exclusion of two processes $P(i)$ and $P(j)$ should rely on these two processes only. We will make this claim precise in the following, using a general principle for the separation.

To apply this principle, we need some more notation. The set of actions of process $P(i)$ is $\mathtt{Act}(i) := \{\overline{\mathtt{wr}(0)}, \mathtt{rd}(0), \overline{\mathtt{wr}(i)}, \mathtt{rd}(i), \mathtt{enter}(i), \mathtt{leave}(i)\}$. Let $\mathcal{U}_A$ be the universal process relative to a given set A of actions, i.e. the process

$$\mathcal{U}_a := \sum_{a \in A} a_\diamond . \mathcal{U}_a$$

Let $\mathcal{U}_i$ be the universal process relative to $P(i)$, i.e. $\mathcal{U}_i := \mathcal{U}_{\mathtt{Act}(i)}$. Then for all $i \in \{1, \ldots, n\}$ we have $P(i) \trianglelefteq \mathcal{U}_i$, implying $P(i) \trianglelefteq P(i) \wedge \mathcal{U}_i$. Trivially,

$P(i) \wedge \mathcal{U}_i \trianglelefteq P(i)$ and $P(i) \wedge \mathcal{U}_i \trianglelefteq \mathcal{U}_i$ hold as well. Substituting a process of a parallel composition by a finer one yields a finer process, thus

$$\forall i \neq j.\, F(n) \trianglelefteq (P(1) \wedge \mathcal{U}_1 \mid \ldots \mid P(n) \wedge \mathcal{U}_n) \mid V \tag{3}$$

and

$$\begin{aligned}\forall i \neq j.\, (P(1) \wedge \mathcal{U}_1 \mid \ldots \mid P(n) \wedge \mathcal{U}_n) \mid V \trianglelefteq \\ (\mathcal{U}_1 \ldots \mathcal{U}_{i-1} \mid P(i) \mid \mathcal{U}_{i+1} \ldots \mathcal{U}_{j-1} \mid P(j) \mid \mathcal{U}_{j+1} \ldots \mathcal{U}_n) \mid V\end{aligned} \tag{4}$$

By observing that for two sets A and B of actions we have $\mathcal{U}_A \,|\, \mathcal{U}_B \trianglelefteq \mathcal{U}_{A \cup B}$, and by letting $\texttt{Act}(\neq i, j) := \bigcup_{k \neq i,j} \texttt{Act}(k)$ and $\mathcal{U}_{\neq i,j} := \mathcal{U}_{\texttt{Act}(\neq i,j)}$, we find

$$(\mathcal{U}_1 \ldots \mathcal{U}_{i-1} \mid \mathcal{U}_{i+1} \ldots \mathcal{U}_{j-1} \mid \mathcal{U}_{j+1} \ldots \mathcal{U}_n) \trianglelefteq \mathcal{U}_{\neq i,j} \tag{5}$$

From (3), (4) and (5) we find that in order to prove (2) it suffices to show

$$\forall i \neq j.\, (b_i < c_j \Rightarrow (P(i) \mid P(j) \mid \mathcal{U}_{\neq i,j} \mid V) \setminus L \trianglelefteq EX(i,j)) \tag{6}$$

There is a general proof principle behind this reduction: in order to conclude:

$$\Big(\bigwedge_{i \in I_1} A_i^1 \mid \ldots \mid \bigwedge_{i \in I_k} A_i^k\Big) \backslash L \trianglelefteq \bigwedge_{j \in I} C_j$$

it suffices for each $j \in I$ to establish:

$$\Big(\bigwedge_{i \in I_{1,j}} A_i^1 \mid \ldots \mid \bigwedge_{i \in I_{k,j}} A_i^k\Big) \backslash L \trianglelefteq C_j$$

where $I_{\ell,j} \subseteq I_\ell$ for each $\ell = 1 \ldots k$. Of course, the power of this proof principle strongly depends on a good choice of the $I_{\ell,j}$, which was trivial in our example.

Note once more that the separation step yields a sufficient proof condition, not a neccessary one.

4.2 Reduction Step 2: Skolemization

Obviously (6) does not depend on the choice of i and j. Therefore i and j can be replaced by arbitrary Skolem constants r and s. It then suffices to show

$$(b_r < c_s \Rightarrow (P(r) \mid P(s) \mid \mathcal{U}_{\neq r,s} \mid V) \setminus L \trianglelefteq EX(r,s)) \tag{7}$$

It should be emphasized once more that establishing (7) for r and s implies the validity for any pair $i \neq j$, thus proving (6).

4.3 Reduction Step 3: Abstraction

But even the reduced problem (7) consists of an infinite number of actions and states. A close investigation reveals that we can find an equivalence relation on the actions and states of the components which is of finite index, but fine enough to establish the proof goal. This abstraction is constructed in two consecutive steps: first we collapse the state space, then the transition state. In the following, $[s]^{\equiv}$ is the equivalence class of s under $\equiv$. If $\equiv$ is understood we write $[s]$.

Given an equivalence relation on the state space, the collapsed transition system is defined as follows:

Definition 5. Let P be a TMS with reachable states S and transition relations $\rightarrow_\Box, \rightarrow_\Diamond$. Each equivalence relation $\equiv$ on S induces a *collapsed TMS* $P_\equiv$ with reachable states $S_\equiv := \{[p] \mid p \in S\}$ and transition relations $\rightarrow'_\Box, \rightarrow'_\Diamond$ defined by

$$\frac{p \xrightarrow{a}_\Box p'}{[p] \xrightarrow{a}{}'_\Box [p']} \qquad \frac{p \xrightarrow{a}_\Diamond p'}{[p] \xrightarrow{a}{}'_\Diamond [p']}$$

Note that the collapsed system is once again a TMS. For a certain kind of equivalence relations, the collapsed system is coarser than the original one:

Proposition 6. *Let P be a TMS, and $\equiv$ an equivalence relation on the reachable states of P satisfying $p \xrightarrow{a}_\Box q$ iff $p' \xrightarrow{a}_\Box q'$ for all $p' \in [p], q' \in [q]$ and $a \in$ `Act`. Then $P \trianglelefteq P_\equiv$.*

All components but the shared variable V have a finite number of states. By identifying all states $V(q)$ where $q \notin \{0, r, s\}$, while the left states are equivalence classes by themselves, we find a TMS $V_{red} := V_\equiv$ which has only four states. This equivalence relation satisfies the condition of Prop. 6, as there are no must-transitions in V, so $V \trianglelefteq V_{red}$ holds. To prove (7) it is then sufficient to show

$$(b_r < c_s \Rightarrow (P(r) \mid P(s) \mid \mathcal{U}_{\neq r,s} \mid V_{red}) \setminus L \;\trianglelefteq\; EX(r,s)) \tag{8}$$

Next we use a collapse of the transitions to turn these systems into finite ones.

Definition 7. Let P be a TMS over `Act` with transition relations $\rightarrow_\Box, \rightarrow_\Diamond$. Each equivalence relation $\equiv$ on `Act` induces a *collapsed TMS* $P^\equiv$ over the alphabet $\mathtt{Act}_\equiv := \{[a] \mid a \in \mathtt{Act}\}$ and transition relations $\rightarrow'_\Box, \rightarrow'_\Diamond$ defined by

$$\frac{p \xrightarrow{a}_\Box p'}{p \xrightarrow{[a]}{}'_\Box p'} \qquad \frac{p \xrightarrow{a}_\Diamond p'}{p \xrightarrow{[a]}{}'_\Diamond p'}$$

An equivalence relation $\equiv$ on `Act` is *compatible* with P iff for all $a' \in [a]$ and all reachable states p, p' of P:

$$p \xrightarrow{a}_\Box p' \text{ iff } p \xrightarrow{a'}_\Box p' \qquad \text{and} \qquad p \xrightarrow{a}_\Diamond p' \text{ iff } p \xrightarrow{a'}_\Diamond p'$$

For compatible equivalence relations, we have the following reduction lemma:

Lemma 8. *Let P and Q be two TMS's and $\equiv$ an equivalance relation on their common alphabet compatible with P and Q. Then the following holds:*

- $P^{\equiv} \trianglelefteq Q^{\equiv}$ *implies* $P \trianglelefteq Q$,
- *if* $[\tau] = \{\tau\}$ *then* $\equiv$ *is compatible with* $P \mid Q$,
- *if* $[\tau] = \{\tau\}$ *and for* $L \subseteq \mathtt{Act}$ *and every* $a \in \mathtt{Act}$ *either* $[a] \cap L = [a]$ *or* $[a] \cap L = \emptyset$, *then* $\equiv$ *is compatible with* $P \setminus L$.

This Lemma allows us to replace infinite systems by finite ones in our verification problem, as soon as an appropriate equivalence relation can be found.

For the specification of Fischer's protocol, the appropriate equivalence relation is obvious. Any actions $a(i), a(i')$ where i, i' are different from r, s and 0 are equivalent. Chose $a(q)$ as the representative of this class, and let $a(r), a(s), a(0)$ and τ be classes for themselves, then the set of actions after factorization is $\tau, \mathtt{rd}(i), \mathtt{wr}(i), \mathtt{enter}(i'), \mathtt{leave}(i')$ $(i \in \{0, q, r, s\}, i' \in \{q, r, s\})$ and their inverses. This equivalence relation satisfies all the conditions in Lemma 8, so the components of (8) can be substituted by their collapsed counterparts.

This leads to a representation of (8) where the processes $P(r), P(s)$ have five states each, V_{red} has four states, $\mathcal{U}_{\neq r,s}$ has one state and $EX(r, s)$ has two states. The product automaton of these processes has at most two hundred states, but in fact a lot less due to restriction. This size should be manageable by tools for automatic verification. While at the moment no tool to check refinement in the presence of parametric timing constraints exists, the next section discusses how to obtain a refinement relation. Here it should be noted that the choice of the equivalence relations strongly depends on the previous reduction steps.

5 Automatic Verification of the Reduced Problem

This section assumes familiarity with Timed Automaton [AD94, AC+95]. A *Modal* Timed Automaton (MTA) is one with may- and must-transitions and the usual consistency condition of MTS. TMS's can easily be translated into MTA's. and the operator for TMS's can be directly defined for MTA's.

As an example, we give the MTA for process $P(r)$:

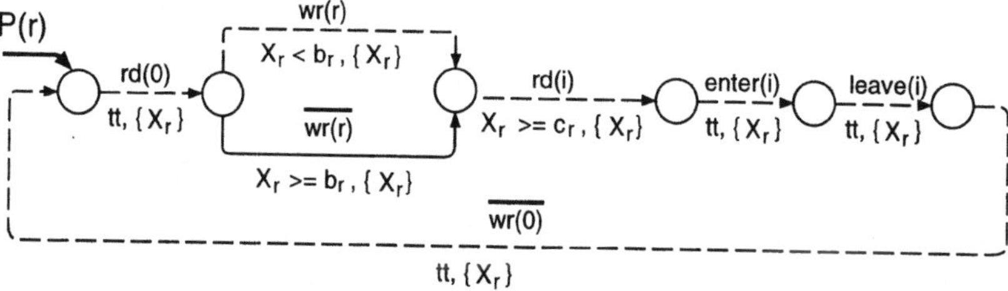

Here two clocks X_r, X_s control the timing constraints over b_r, b_s, c_r, c_s. Actions are written above the arcs, regions and reset-sets are indicated below the arcs. May-transitions are indicated by dotted lines as before. The region $\mathtt{tt}$ is the set of all valuations, while $X_r \geq b_r$ are the valuations where clock X_r has a value larger than or equal to $b(r)$. Due to maximal progress, parallel composition will restrict the region $X_r \geq b_r$ to $X_r = b_r$.

Checking the existence of the weak refinement needs the construction of the product of the MTA's for $P(r), P(s), \mathcal{U}_{\neq r,s}, V$ and $EX(i,j)$. Due to the close relation between refinement and bisimulation, the weak refinement can be found by methods described in [Čer92] and [CGL93]. These methods are already implemented in the verification tool EPSILON. However, EPSILON cannot handle parametrized timing constraints. While the tools HYTECH and KRONOS can handle the parameters, they are intended for model-checking and therefore cannot deal with refinement.

Refinement can be verified in the presence of parametric timing constraints by a combination of the methods found in [Čer92],[AC+95] and [AHV93]. This was done by hand for Fischer's protocol, and a weak refinement could easily be established. Due to space limitations we cannot give details here. We are currently looking at the problem of implementing this method in general.

6 Conclusion and Future Work

We have demonstrated a new constraint-oriented method for the (automated) verification of concurrent systems. Key concepts of our 'divide and conquer' method are *modal constraints*, *separation of proof obligations*, *Skolemization* and *abstraction*, which together support a drastic reduction of the complexity of the relevant subproblems. Of course, our proof methodology does neither guarantee the existence of a finite state reduction nor a straightforward method for finding the right amount of separation or the adequate abstraction. Still, there is a large class of problems and systems, where the method can be applied straightforwardly. Typical examples are systems with limited data dependence. Whereas involved data dependencies may exclude any possibility of 'horizontal' decomposition, the approach elegantly includes real time systems over a dense time domain. In fact, the resulting finite state problems can be automatically verified using extensions of verification tools like EPSILON, HYTECH and KRONOS. All this was illustrated by application to Fischer's protocol. Our experience indicates that our method scales up to practically relevant problems, and we have already presented a more complicated problem of a transparent RPC in [LSW95].

Beside further case studies and the search for good heuristics for proof obligation separation and abstraction, we are investigating the limits of tool support during the construction of constraint based specifications and the application of the three reduction steps. Whereas support by graphical interfaces and interactive editors is obvious and partly implemented in the META-Framework, a management system for synthesis, analysis and verification currently developed at the university of Passau, the limits of consistency checking and tool supported search for adequate separation and abstraction are still an interesting open research topic.

As pointed out, a remaining problem are parameters in the timing constraints. We are currently investigating methods along the lines of [AHV93, AC+95] for checking refinement for *parametrized timed modal specifications*.

References

[AL93] M. Abadi, L. Lamport. An Old-Fashioned Recipe for Real Time. LNCS 600.

[AC+95] R. Alur,C. Coucoubetis, N. Halbwachs, T.A. Henzinger, et al. The algorithmic analysis of hybrid systems. Theoretical Computer Science, February 1995

[ASW94] H. Andersen, C. Stirling, G. Winskel. A Compositional Proof System for the Modal Mu-Calculus. in: Proceedings LICS, 1994.

[AD94] R. Alur, D.L. Dill. A Theory of Timed Automata. TCS 126(2):183–236, 94.

[AHV93] R. Alur, T.A. Henzinger, M.Y. Vardi. Parametric real-time reasoning. Proc. 25th STOC, ACM Press 1993, pp. 592–601.

[Br86] R. Bryant. Graph-Based Algorithms for Boolean Function Manipulation. in: IEEE Transactions on Computation, 35 (8). 1986.

[BCMDH90] J. Burch, E. Clarke, K. McMillan, D. Dill, L. Hwang. Symbolic Model Checking: 10^{20} States and Beyond. in: Proceedings LICS'90.

[Čer92] K. Čerāns. Decidability of Bisimulation Equivalences for Parallel Timer Processes. Proceedings CAV '92, pp. 289 – 300.

[CGL93] K. Čerāns, J.C. Godesken, K.G. Larsen. Timed Modal Specification - Theory and Tools. in: C. Courcoubetis (Ed.), Proc. 5th CAV, 1993, LNCS 697, pp. 253–267.

[CGL92] E. Clarke, O. Grumber, D. Long. Model Checking and Abstraction. in: Proceedings XIX POPL'92.

[CLM89] E. Clarke, D. Long, K. McMillan. Compositional Model Checking. in: Proceedings LICS'89.

[CC77] P. Cousot, R. Cousot. Abstract Interpretation: A Unified Lattice Model for Static Analysis of Programs. in: Proc. POPL'77.

[EFT91] R. Enders, T. Filkorn, D. Taubner. Generating BDDs for Symbolic Model Checking in CCS. in: Proc. CAV'91, LNCS 575, pp. 203–213

[GW91] P. Godefroid, P. Wolper. Using Partial Orders for the Efficient Verification of Deadlock Freedom and Safety Properties. in: Proc. CAV'91, LNCS 575, pp. 332–342.

[GP93] P. Godefroid, D. Pirottin. Refining Dependencies Improves Partial-Order Verification Methods. in: Proc. CAV'93, LNCS 697, pp. 438–449.

[God94] J. C. Godskesen. Timed Modal Specifications – A Theory for Verification of Real–Time Concurrent Systems. Ph.D.Thesis, Aalborg Univ., R–94–2039, Oct. '94.

[GL93] S. Graf, C. Loiseaux. Program Verification using Compositional Abstraction. in: Proceedings FASE/TAPSOFT'93.

[GS90] S. Graf, B. Steffen. Using Interface Specifications for Compositional Minimization of Finite State Systems. in: Proceedings CAV'90.

[HL89] H. Hüttel and K. Larsen. The use of static constructs in a modal process logic. Proceedings of Logic at Botik'89. LNCS 363, 1989.

[Lar90] K.G. Larsen. Modal specifications. in: LNCS 407, 1990.

[LPY95] K.G. Larsen, P. Pettersson, W. Yi. Compositional and Symbolic Model-Checking for Real-Time Systems. Proc. CONCUR'95.

[LSW95] K.G. Larsen, B. Steffen, C. Weise. A Constraint-oriented Proof Methodology using Modal Transition Systems. Proc. TACAS'95, to appear as LNCS 1019.

[LT88] K. Larsen and B. Thomsen. A modal process logic. In: Proc. LICS, 1988.

[Mil89] R. Milner. Communication and Concurrency. Prentice-Hall, 1989.

[Par81] D. Park. Concurrency and automata on infinite sequences. In P. Deussen (ed.), 5th GI Conference, LNCS 104, pp. 167–183, 1981.

[Val93] A. Valmari. On-The-Fly Verification with Stubborn Sets. in: C. Courcoubetis (Ed.), Proc. 5th CAV, 1993, LNCS 697, pp. 397–408.

[Yi91] W. Yi. CCS + Time = an Interleaving Model for Real-Time Systems, Proc. 18th ICALP, 1991, LNCS 510, pp. 217-228.

List of Authors

Lecture Notes in Computer Science

For information about Vols. 1–1001

please contact your bookseller or Springer-Verlag

Vol. 1002: J.J. Kistler, Disconnected Operation in a Distributed File System. XIX, 249 pages. 1995.

VOL. 1003: P. Pandurang Nayak, Automated Modeling of Physical Systems. XXI, 232 pages. 1995. (Subseries LNAI).

Vol. 1004: J. Staples, P. Eades, N. Katoh, A. Moffat (Eds.), Algorithms and Computation. Proceedings, 1995. XV, 440 pages. 1995.

Vol. 1005: J. Estublier (Ed.), Software Configuration Management. Proceedings, 1995. IX, 311 pages. 1995.

Vol. 1006: S. Bhalla (Ed.), Information Systems and Data Management. Proceedings, 1995. IX, 321 pages. 1995.

Vol. 1007: A. Bosselaers, B. Preneel (Eds.), Integrity Primitives for Secure Information Systems. VII, 239 pages. 1995.

Vol. 1008: B. Preneel (Ed.), Fast Software Encryption. Proceedings, 1994. VIII, 367 pages. 1995.

Vol. 1009: M. Broy, S. Jähnichen (Eds.), KORSO: Methods, Languages, and Tools for the Construction of Correct Software. X, 449 pages. 1995. Vol.

Vol. 1010: M. Veloso, A. Aamodt (Eds.), Case-Based Reasoning Research and Development. Proceedings, 1995. X, 576 pages. 1995. (Subseries LNAI).

Vol. 1011: T. Furuhashi (Ed.), Advances in Fuzzy Logic, Neural Networks and Genetic Algorithms. Proceedings, 1994. (Subseries LNAI).

Vol. 1012: M. Bartošek, J. Staudek, J. Wiedermann (Eds.), SOFSEM '95: Theory and Practice of Informatics. Proceedings, 1995. XI, 499 pages. 1995.

Vol. 1013: T.W. Ling, A.O. Mendelzon, L. Vieille (Eds.), Deductive and Object-Oriented Databases. Proceedings, 1995. XIV, 557 pages. 1995.

Vol. 1014: A.P. del Pobil, M.A. Serna, Spatial Representation and Motion Planning. XII, 242 pages. 1995.

Vol. 1015: B. Blumenthal, J. Gornostaev, C. Unger (Eds.), Human-Computer Interaction. Proceedings, 1995. VIII, 203 pages. 1995.

VOL. 1016: R. Cipolla, Active Visual Inference of Surface Shape. XII, 194 pages. 1995.

Vol. 1017: M. Nagl (Ed.), Graph-Theoretic Concepts in Computer Science. Proceedings, 1995. XI, 406 pages. 1995.

Vol. 1018: T.D.C. Little, R. Gusella (Eds.), Network and Operating Systems Support for Digital Audio and Video. Proceedings, 1995. XI, 357 pages. 1995.

Vol. 1019: E. Brinksma, W.R. Cleaveland, K.G. Larsen, T. Margaria, B. Steffen (Eds.), Tools and Algorithms for the Construction and Analysis of Systems. Selected Papers, 1995. VII, 291 pages. 1995.

Vol. 1020: I.D. Watson (Ed.), Progress in Case-Based Reasoning. Proceedings, 1995. VIII, 209 pages. 1995. (Subseries LNAI).

Vol. 1021: M.P. Papazoglou (Ed.), OOER '95: Object-Oriented and Entity-Relationship Modeling. Proceedings, 1995. XVII, 451 pages. 1995.

Vol. 1022: P.H. Hartel, R. Plasmeijer (Eds.), Functional Programming Languages in Education. Proceedings, 1995. X, 309 pages. 1995.

Vol. 1023: K. Kanchanasut, J.-J. Lévy (Eds.), Algorithms, Concurrency and Knowlwdge. Proceedings, 1995. X, 410 pages. 1995.

Vol. 1024: R.T. Chin, H.H.S. Ip, A.C. Naiman, T.-C. Pong (Eds.), Image Analysis Applications and Computer Graphics. Proceedings, 1995. XVI, 533 pages. 1995.

Vol. 1025: C. Boyd (Ed.), Cryptography and Coding. Proceedings, 1995. IX, 291 pages. 1995.

Vol. 1026: P.S. Thiagarajan (Ed.), Foundations of Software Technology and Theoretical Computer Science. Proceedings, 1995. XII, 515 pages. 1995.

Vol. 1027: F.J. Brandenburg (Ed.), Graph Drawing. Proceedings, 1995. XII, 526 pages. 1996.

Vol. 1028: N.R. Adam, Y. Yesha (Eds.), Electronic Commerce. X, 155 pages. 1996.

Vol. 1029: E. Dawson, J. Golić (Eds.), Cryptography: Policy and Algorithms. Proceedings, 1995. XI, 327 pages. 1996.

Vol. 1030: F. Pichler, R. Moreno-Díaz, R. Albrecht (Eds.), Computer Aided Systems Theory - EUROCAST '95. Proceedings, 1995. XII, 539 pages. 1996.

Vol.1031: M. Toussaint (Ed.), Ada in Europe. Proceedings, 1995. XI, 455 pages. 1996.

Vol. 1032: P. Godefroid, Partial-Order Methods for the Verification of Concurrent Systems. IV, 143 pages. 1996.

Vol. 1033: C.-H. Huang, P. Sadayappan, U. Banerjee, D. Gelernter, A. Nicolau, D. Padua (Eds.), Languages and Compilers for Parallel Computing. Proceedings, 1995. XIII, 597 pages. 1996.

Vol. 1034: G. Kuper, M. Wallace (Eds.), Constraint Databases and Applications. Proceedings, 1995. VII, 185 pages. 1996.

Vol. 1035: S.Z. Li, D.P. Mital, E.K. Teoh, H. Wang (Eds.), Recent Developments in Computer Vision. Proceedings, 1995. XI, 604 pages. 1996.

Vol. 1036: G. Adorni, M. Zock (Eds.), Trends in Natural Language Generation - An Artificial Intelligence Perspective. Proceedings, 1993. IX, 382 pages. 1996. (Subseries LNAI).

Vol. 1037: M. Wooldridge, J.P. Müller, M. Tambe (Eds.), Intelligent Agents II. Proceedings, 1995. XVI, 437 pages. 1996. (Subseries LNAI).

Vol. 1038: W: Van de Velde, J.W. Perram (Eds.), Agents Breaking Away. Proceedings, 1996. XIV, 232 pages. 1996. (Subseries LNAI).

Vol. 1039: D. Gollmann (Ed.), Fast Software Encryption. Proceedings, 1996. X, 219 pages. 1996.

Vol. 1040: S. Wermter, E. Riloff, G. Scheler (Eds.), Connectionist, Statistical, and Symbolic Approaches to Learning for Natural Language Processing. IX, 468 pages. 1996. (Subseries LNAI).

Vol. 1041: J. Dongarra, K. Madsen, J. Waśniewski (Eds.), Applied Parallel Computing. Proceedings, 1995. XII, 562 pages. 1996.

Vol. 1042: G. Weiß, S. Sen (Eds.), Adaption and Learning in Multi-Agent Systems. Proceedings, 1995. X, 238 pages. 1996. (Subseries LNAI).

Vol. 1043: F. Moller, G. Birtwistle (Eds.), Logics for Concurrency. XI, 266 pages. 1996.

Vol. 1044: B. Plattner (Ed.), Broadband Communications. Proceedings, 1996. XIV, 359 pages. 1996.

Vol. 1045: B. Butscher, E. Moeller, H. Pusch (Eds.), Interactive Distributed Multimedia Systems and Services. Proceedings, 1996. XI, 333 pages. 1996.

Vol. 1046: C. Puech, R. Reischuk (Eds.), STACS 96. Proceedings, 1996. XII, 690 pages. 1996.

Vol. 1047: E. Hajnicz, Time Structures. IX, 244 pages. 1996. (Subseries LNAI).

Vol. 1048: M. Proietti (Ed.), Logic Program Syynthesis and Transformation. Proceedings, 1995. X, 267 pages. 1996.

Vol. 1049: K. Futatsugi, S. Matsuoka (Eds.), Object Technologies for Advanced Software. Proceedings, 1996. X, 309 pages. 1996.

Vol. 1050: R. Dyckhoff, H. Herre, P. Schroeder-Heister (Eds.), Extensions of Logic Programming. Proceedings, 1996. VII, 318 pages. 1996. (Subseries LNAI).

Vol. 1051: M.-C. Gaudel, J. Woodcock (Eds.), FME'96: Industrial Benefit and Advances in Formal Methods. Proceedings, 1996. XII, 704 pages. 1996.

Vol. 1052: D. Hutchison, H. Christiansen, G. Coulson, A. Danthine (Eds.), Teleservices and Multimedia Communications. Proceedings, 1995. XII, 277 pages. 1996.

Vol. 1053: P. Graf, Term Indexing. XVI, 284 pages. 1996. (Subseries LNAI).

Vol. 1054: A. Ferreira, P. Pardalos (Eds.), Solving Combinatorial Optimization Problems in Parallel. VII, 274 pages. 1996.

Vol. 1055: T. Margaria, B. Steffen (Eds.), Tools and Algorithms for the Construction and Analysis of Systems. Proceedings, 1996. XI, 435 pages. 1996.

Vol. 1056: A. Haddadi, Communication and Cooperation in Agent Systems. XIII, 148 pages. 1996. (Subseries LNAI).

Vol. 1057: P. Apers, M. Bouzeghoub, G. Gardarin (Eds.), Advances in Database Technology — EDBT '96. Proceedings, 1996. XII, 636 pages. 1996.

Vol. 1058: H. R. Nielson (Ed.), Programming Languages and Systems – ESOP '96. Proceedings, 1996. X, 405 pages. 1996.

Vol. 1059: H. Kirchner (Ed.), Trees in Algebra and Programming – CAAP '96. Proceedings, 1996. VIII, 331 pages. 1996.

Vol. 1060: T. Gyimóthy (Ed.), Compiler Construction. Proceedings, 1996. X, 355 pages. 1996.

Vol. 1061: P. Ciancarini, C. Hankin (Eds.), Coordination Languages and Models. Proceedings, 1996. XI, 443 pages. 1996.

Vol. 1062: E. Sanchez, M. Tomassini (Eds.), Towards Evolvable Hardware. IX, 265 pages. 1996.

Vol. 1063: J.-M. Alliot, E. Lutton, E. Ronald, M. Schoenauer, D. Snyers (Eds.), Artificial Evolution. Proceedings, 1995. XIII, 396 pages. 1996.

Vol. 1064: B. Buxton, R. Cipolla (Eds.), Computer Vision – ECCV '96. Volume I. Proceedings, 1996. XXI, 725 pages. 1996.

Vol. 1065: B. Buxton, R. Cipolla (Eds.), Computer Vision – ECCV '96. Volume II. Proceedings, 1996. XXI, 723 pages. 1996.

Vol. 1066: R. Alur, T.A. Henzinger, E.D. Sontag (Eds.), Hybrid Systems III. IX, 618 pages. 1996.

Vol. 1067: H. Liddell, A. Colbrook, B. Hertzberger, P. Sloot (Eds.), High-Performance Computing and Networking. Proceedings, 1996. XXV, 1040 pages. 1996.

Vol. 1068: T. Ito, R.H. Halstead, Jr., C. Queinnec (Eds.), Parallel Symbolic Languages and Systems. Proceedings 1995. X, 363 pages. 1996.

Vol. 1069: J.W. Perram, J.-P. Müller (Eds.), Distributec Software Agents and Applications. Proceedings, 1994 VIII, 219 pages. 1996. (Subseries LNAI).

Vol. 1070: U. Maurer (Ed.), Advances in Cryptology - EUROCRYPT '96. Proceedings, 1996. XII, 417 pages 1996.

Vol. 1071: P. Miglioli, U. Moscato, D. Mundici, M Ornaghi (Eds.), Theorem Proving with Analytic Tableau: and Related Methods. Proceedings, 1996. X, 330 pages 1996. (Subseries LNAI).

Vol. 1072: R. Kasturi, K. Tombre (Eds.), Graphic Recognition. Proceedings, 1995. X, 308 pages. 1996.

Vol. 1073: J. Cuny, H. Ehrig, G. Engels, G. Rozenber (Eds.), Graph Grammars and Their Application t Computer Science. Proceedings, 1995. X, 565 pages 1996.

Vol. 1074: G. Dowek, J. Heering, K. Meinke, B. Mölle (Eds.), Higher-Order Algebra, Logic, and Term Rewriting Proceedings, 1995. VII, 287 pages. 1996.

Vol. 1075: D. Hirschberg, G. Myers (Eds.), Combinatoria Pattern Matching. Proceedings, 1996. VIII, 392 pages 1996.

Vol. 1076: K. O'Hara, G. Schreiber, N. Shadbolt (Eds. Advances in Knowledge Acquisition. Proceedings, 199(XII, 371 pages. 1996. (Subseries LNAI).